GAZETTEER
OF
BURMA

(GAZETTEER
OF
BURMA)

(IN TWO VOLUMES)

Compiled by Authority

VOLUME II

ISBN : 978-81-212-0017-2(Set)

ISBN : 978-81-212-0166-7

Published, 2018

Published by

Gyan Publishing House
5, Ansari Road
Daryaganj, New Delhi-110002
Phone: 011-47034999, 9811692060
www.gyanbooks.com
E-mail: books@gyanbooks.com

Printed at: G. Print Process, Delhi.

Contents

AGWON.—A revenue circle on the sea-coast of the Thanlyeng (*Syriam*) township, Rangoon district, north-east of the mouth of the Rangoon river. The southern part of the coast-line is formed by a sandy beach fringed by a belt of tree and grass jungle whilst further to the north-east the sand gives place to mud ; the rest of the country is an open plain undulating slightly towards the north with, here and there, depressed and marshy spots which form the principal inland fisheries. The inhabitants are engaged in agricultrue, in fishing, and in salt-making. The population in 1876 numbered 11,568 and the gross Revenue amounted to Rs. 1,04,178 of which Rs. 87,020 were derived from the land.*

A-HLAT.—A village of about 600 inhabitants, in the extreme south-western portion of the Martaban township, Amherst district.

A-HPYOUK.—A village, or rather group of three villages, in the Henzada district, on the left bank of the Irrawaddy, some miles south of the latitude of Zalwon. In 1875 the group contained a population of 2,150 souls.

A-HPYOUK.—A revenue circle in the south-eastern portion of the Zalwon township of the Henzada district, with much rice cultivation in its southern part and along the bank of the Irrawaddy. This circle contains numerous lakes and fisheries of which the largest are the Gnyee-re-gyee nearly three miles long and half a mile broad and from fifteen to twenty feet deep in the dry weather and, further east, the Biendaw from two to two and a half miles long but narrow and about ten feet deep.

In 1876 the circle had a population of 6,605 souls and produced a gross Revenue of Rs. 16,245 of which Rs. 9,623 were from the land, Rs. 5,133 from the capitation tax, Rs. 959 from fishery and net tax, and Rs. 530 from other sources.

AING-GYEE.—A large village in the Henzada district a little to the north of the great Doora lake and on the edge of an extensive rice plain the cultivation of which forms the principal occupation of the inhabitants.

AING-KA-LOUNG.—A revenue circle in the Hlaing township, Rangoon district, on the right bank of the Hlaing river and adjoining the Henzada dis-

---

*NOTE.—This circle has since been divided into two, distinguished as North Agwon and South Agwon ; the statistics given above are for the two.

trict. The surface of the country is flat and parts of the circle are subject to inundation during the rains. The principal products are rice, cotton and tobacco. The inhabitants of some of the villages are largely employed in the fisheries. Population in 1876, 3,623 land Revenue Rs. 6,916 and gross Revenue ; Rs. 20,598.

AING-THA-BYOO.—A village in the Myenoo township, Bassein district, on the Bassein river, a short distance below Le-myct-hua, containing a population of over 600 souls.

AING-TOON.—A small river in the Shwe-gyeen district, which rises in a spur of the Pegu Yomas and after a generally easterly course through the Anan-baw circle falls into the Tsittoung near the village of Doungmo.

AKOUK-TOUNG.—The name given to the eastern extremity of a spur running down from the Arakan Yoma mountains which abuts on the Irrawaddy, less than a mile south of the boundary between the Henzada and Prome districts, in an abruptly scarped cliff some 300 feet high, artificially honeycombed with caves containing images of Gaudama Boodha and of Rahans : here the Irrawaddy enters the delta and gradually spreads out into numerous anastomosing creeks and rivers. This hill was the scene of two or three engagements between the English and the Burmese during the second Burmese war and it was here that Major Gardner was surprised and killed (vide Henzada district :—History). The spur which terminates at Akouktoung formed the northern limit of the ancient Talaing kingdom of Pegu, west of the Irrewaddy, and before the formation of the delta was a Customs station, whence the name "Customs Revenue Hill."

AKYAB.—A town on the coast of Arakan, in 20° 8′ N. and 92° 57′ E., at the mouth of the Kooladan river, the head-quarters of the Arakan division and of the Akyab district. Originally a Mug fishing village it was chosen as the chief station of the province of Arakan soon after the close of the first Anglo-Burmese war when the extreme unhealthiness of Mrohoung or old Arakan, the last capital of the ancient Arakanese kingdom and subsequently the seat of the Burmese governor of Rakhaing, rendered the removal of the troops and civil establishments a matter of necessity. The site, only fifteen feet above the level of the sea at half tide and with places below high-water mark, was laid out with broad raised roads, forming causeways, with deep ditches on either side. Owing principally to its situation, easily accessible by boats from the rich rice land in the interior and with a fine harbour formed by the mouth of the river, it soon became an emporium of trade and was resorted to by numerous ships seeking rice cargoes. A large influx of population took place from Chittagong, Ramoo and Cox's Bazaar in the Chittagong division of Bengal, and from Mrohoung, and the town rapidly increased in wealth and in importance. Though well laid out at starting and at first rapidly and then more gradually increasing in population and in size the want of labourers was a bar to any very great improvement, and the raising and metalling of the roads, digging ditches and tanks, filling up swamps, and planting trees had to be carried on almost entirely by convict labour. In 1836 the shops were found "well supplied with the different varieties of grain which are in use amongst the inhabitants of Bengal, from whence they are imported; and British cloths, consisting of piece-goods, muslins and broad-cloths, cutlery, crockery, glass-ware and native manufactures" were exposed for sale. A few years later the troops were withdrawn and the cantonment abandoned except by the European civil officers. As years rolled on and commerce increased the town progressed and substantial houses were constructed. The population which in 1868 numbered 15,536 souls had increased in 1872 to 19,230, who at the census taken that year were found to consist of :—

HINDOOS.		MAHOMEDANS.		BOODHISTS.		CHRISTIANS.		OTHERS.		TOTAL.	
Male.	Female.	Male.	Female.	Male.	Female.	Male.	Female.	Male.	Female.	Male.	Female.
1,884	27	3,516	1,502	5,892	5,627	216	109	387	70	11,895	7,335

These figures include the floating population, the *bonâ fide* residents numbered 15,775 who in 1876 had increased to 18,306.

To a great extent the disproportion in the sexes amongst the Mahomedans and Hindoos is caused by the number of men who come for the rice season to work either in conveying the unhusked rice from the interior (in the boats they bring with them from Chittagong and Cox's Bazaar), or as coolies in the rice godowns.

The principal public buildings are the Court-house, Gaol, Custom-house, Hospital and Markets. The Court-house, containing the Courts and offices of the Commissioner of the division, of the Deputy Commissioner of the district, of the Assistant Commissioner, of the Town Magistrate and of the Superintendent of Police, is of masonry and was completed in 1872 at a cost of Rs. 1,30,680. The custom-house, a fine building on the bank of the river at the shore end of the main wooden wharf, was finished in 1869. The gaol has been in existence for a considerable period and is now being improved, a wall being raised round the work yard within which new buildings will be constructed the site of the existing prison being utilized for work sheds. The hospital and dispensary consist of two buildings joined by a covered way, one for Europeans and one for Asiatics ; a new hospital is now in course of construction : the income in 1874 was Rs. 9,763 of which Rs. 2,040 was given by the State and Rs. 1,640 by the Port Fund, and the expenditure was Rs. 5,360 : the number of persons treated was 2,450 of whom 1,890 were out-patients and 560 in-patients. The town contains three markets one of which was till lately private property ; of the other two one has been in existence for many years, and the other, in the Shwe-bya quarter, was completed in 1870 at a cost of Rs. 6,500. There are two churches, one of masonry and one (the Roman Catholic) of wood and a new school-house besides a travellers' bungalow and a circuit-house. The school, which is now of the higher class, was established by the State in 1846, and in 1875 the average daily attendance of pupils was 224 of whom nearly all were Arakanese. The other public offices are the post office, telegraph office and Master Attendant's office. There are also several merchants offices and five steam rice-husking mills. At the mouth of the harbour is Savage Island light-house.

The gross municipal revenue derived from port dues, market rents and other municipal sources, the rent and sale of town lands, the dispensary fund, and a five per cent. cess on certain imperial taxes was in 1871-72 Rs. 47,650 and in 1872-73, Rs. 70,290. In 1874 Akyab was constituted a Municipal town and a Municipal Committee, with the Town Magistrate as President, was appointed. The revenue administered by this body in 1876-77 was Rs. 90,662.

There are no returns available shewing the value of the trade during the first year or two but, according to Pemberton, the value of the exports carried by square-rigged vessels during seven months of 1833 was Rs. 93,800.

The value of the trade in 1863-64, 1873-74, 1875-76 and 1876-77 was—

	Imports.	Exports.	Total.
	Rs.	Rs.	Rs.
1863-64	57,72,140	64,13,310	1,21,85,450
1873-74	91,14,210	91,03,470	1,82,17,680
1875-76	40,48,000	59,83,860	1,00,31,860
1876-77	66,71,325	71,62,137	1,38,33,462

The exports consist almost entirely of rice, of which large quantities are sent to Europe, and the imports of machines and machinery—for which however there will not be a steady demand—coal, vegetable oils, canes and tobacco from foreign ; and tobacco, vegetable oils, cotton piece-goods and twist with silk and wool goods from Indian ports, some of which are of Indian but the larger quantity of foreign manufacture. A comparatively large amount of specie is imported annually for the rice trade the unexpended balance being returned at the end of the season. In 1873 the imports and exports of specie were Rs. 54,73,710 and Rs. 8,89,750 respectively.

The name of the town is supposed to be a corruption of *Akhyatdaw*, the title of a pagoda in the neighbourhood which was, probably, a good land-mark for ships in former times. By the Burmese-speaking inhabitants it is called *Tsit-twe*, because the British army encamped there in 1825.

AKYAB.—A district in the Arakan division, lying on the sea-coast in the north of the province, 5,337 square miles in extent,* separated on the west from Chittagong by the Naaf estuary and the Thooloo hills and on the south from the Kyouk-hpyoo district by a spur of the Arakan Yoma mountains and towards the sea-coast by straits and tidal creeks : on the east are the Arakan Yomas, inhabited by wild tribes, with Upper Burma lying beyond and on the north a country of tangled forest and mountains taken from the district in 1868 and formed into the " Hill Tracts of Northern Arakan" (q. v.). Working their way out from the sea of mountains in the north are three main ranges forming the water partings of the Naaf and the three principal rivers, the Mayoo, the Kooladan and the Lemro, and gradually sinking into broad and fertile plains which even at some distance from the coast are intersected by anastomosing streams whilst the lower portion is a network of tidal creeks in many places dry at low water but all navigable by boats at the flood.

---

* Note.—In 1871 several square miles of the Mengbra township were transferred to the Kyouk-hpyoo district, reducing Akyab to the area given above.

The principal range of mountains is the Arakan Yoma (the eastern

Mountains. boundary of the district) which here has a general south-easterly direction and throws out innumerable spurs completely filling the country east of the Lemro river. A pass leads up the valley of the Tseng and across this range to Upper Burma. In the west, forming the water parting between the Naaf and the Mayoo, are the Mayoo hills which terminate at Agnoo-hmaw near the mouth of the latter river the southern part of their length being nearly parallel to, and not far from, the sea-coast. This range is steep and can be crossed only by regular passes; the most northern is now but little used but is the easiest and in the Burmese time was protected by a fort of which traces still remain. The next two are the Gnet-khyeng-douk and the Alai-khyoung; in both the ascents are steep and practicable only for foot passengers: the latter was the one crossed by the Burmese force which retreated before General Morrison's division during the first Burmese war. South of these are others used only by the inhabitants of the neighbouring country.

The principal rivers are the Mayoo, the Kooladan and the Lemro. The

Rivers. Mayoo rises in the mountains which form the northern boundary of this part of the district and has a generally south-south-easterly course to the sea which it reaches a few miles north-west of Akyab. The Kooladan rises in the main range in the neighbourhood of the Blue mountain and falls into the sea at Akyab its mouth forming a spacious harbour but with a bar running across it rendering the entry difficult. In the rainy season it is navigable by boats of 400 tons burden for 70 miles above Akyab and for boats of 40 tons 50 miles beyond to Dalekmai in the Hill Tracts. The Lemro rises far in the north and falls into the sea in Hunters' Bay. All these streams, traversing as they do in the upper portion of their course a highly mountainous country, are formed by the junction of numerous torrents but as soon as they escape from the hills their character changes and they expand into broad creeks and vast estuaries communicating with each other and the sea and spreading over the country at high water like the threads of an enormous net to form the main—and indeed almost the only—channels of communication.

The forests of this district have never been completely explored but

Forests. in 1869-70 Dr. Schlich was especially deputed by the Local Government to report on the Pyengkado forests of Arakan and was able to make a partial examination of the tracts east of the Kooladan river. On the low ground near the coast subject to tidal influence mangrove jungle covers the face of the country; above this are the rice tracts, the forests here consisting of low jungle with a few trees; the most important are Tsit (*Albizzia procera*), Pyengma (*Lagerstrœmia Reginæ*), Ka-gnyeng (*Dipterocarpus alata*), Khaboung (*Strychnos Nux Vomica*) and Lekpan (*Bombax Malabaricum*). On slightly hilly ground still further inland are the dry forests forming a belt along the lower slopes of the Arakan Yoma and its spurs; where Pyengkado (*Xylia dolabriformis*) furnishes the most valuable timber; it occurs in patches of which many were discovered in that part of the country which was examined; wherever it is found it forms on an average about one-third of all the trees. A considerable quantity of the wood has been exported for sleepers: from 1864 to 1868 inclusive the East Indian Railway Company received 70,377 sleepers, costing Rs. 3,87,660, the greater portion cut in this district in the neighbourhood of the bamboo forest. No definite experience has been gained as to how long Pyengkado sleepers will endure but an opinion exists that they will last over fifteen years. Locally the timber is used for house-posts, bridges and for many other purposes. With Pyengkado are found Pyengma (*Lagerstrœmia Reginæ*), which furnishes a wood used for boats and house-posts and which might possibly answer for railway sleepers, Tsengbwon (*Dillenia pentagyna*) and, in the south only, Myouk-khyaw (*Homalium tomentosum*), not of much value as it is not very durable. Thit-pouk (*Dalbergia sp.*), which yields a wood used for canoes and boats said to last two or three years in fresh and seven years in salt water, and several other kinds which belong to the green forests such as Ka-gnyeng (*Dipterocarpus alata*) are met with. These green forests extend further inland still into the Arakan Yomas and contain several useful trees, as Dipterocarpus *turbinatus* and Thenggan (*Hopea odorata*), the best of all for boats. Up the Mrothit khyoung, in the Naaf township, oil trees of vast size are used for building the larger kind of boats but the timber is becoming scarce. Bamboo forests cover by far the greater area, in many places containing no trees and in others with both green forest and dry forest timber intermixed. Teak plantations have been made in the upper portions of the tracts drained by the Kooladan and the Lemro rivers and though too young yet to warrant any positive opinion as to the success of the experiment they promise well.

The early history of the country is involved in mist; the existing records,

History.

compiled by Arakanese, are filled with impossible stories invented in many cases in others based upon tradition but so embellished as almost to conceal their foundation and all made to shew forth the glories of the race and of the Booddhist religion. Rama-waddee, near the present Sandoway in the south of the Arakan division, was, the chroniclers relate, the capital of a kingdom over which reigned Thamooddee-dewa who was tributary to the king of Baranathee (*Benares*). Many ages later Tsekkyawaddee, who in a future life was to become the Boodh Gaudama, reigned in Baranathee and to his fourth son, Kanmyeng, he allotted "all the countries inhabited by the Burman, Shan and Malay races" from Manipur to the borders of China. "Kanmyeng came to Rama-waddee and, dispossessing the descendants of Tha- " mooddee-dewa, married a princess of that race named Thoo-won-na-ga-blya, " while Maha-radza-gnya, a male descendant of Thamoodde-dewa, was sent to " govern the city of Wethalee, in Arakan Proper.* King Kanmyeng peopled " his dominions with various tribes and amongst the rest appear the progeni- " tors of the Arakanese as being now brought to the country for the first time." The names of these tribes are Thek, Khyeng (a tribe living amongst the Yoma mountains), Myo (the Mroos, now nearly extinct, inhabiting the hills), Kyip (a small tribe near Manipur), Shandoo (a tribe in the northern hills), Moodoo, Proo (a name by which a portion of the Burmese nation was formerly distinguished), Mekhalee (a Shan tribe), Dzengme, Leng, Tautengthaye (a tribe said to live on the borders of China), Atsim (the Malays), Lengkhe (a tribe in the hills north-west of Arakan Proper), Pyanloung (a Shan tribe),

* NOTE.—Sir Arthur Phayre calls the country known to Burmans as *Rakhaing-pyee*, which comprised the Akyab district and part of Khyouk-hpyoo, "Arakan Proper." The existing Arakan division, together with that portion of Bassein which lies west of the Arakan Yomas, was known as *Rakhaing-pyee-gyee*, or "the great Arakan country," that is the Arakanese dominions.

Kathe (Manipuris), Kanran (said to be the present Rakhaing race or a portion of them called Khyoungthas), Thodoon, Talaing, Kanteekamyoon, Lawaik and Lagwon* (said to be the ancestors of the Siamese.) The dynasty thus established reigned for an indefinite period, which the chroniclers describe as lasting a term indicated by a unit followed by one hundred and forty cyphers : even up to a comparatively late period the palm leaf histories are filled with equally incredible statements, continual wars and rebellions in which one side or the other was miraculously aided fill up the accounts and it is not till the end of the eighth century that any approach to accuracy seems to be made. About 788 A. D. Maha-taing Tsandaya ascended the throne, founded a new city on the site of the old Rama-waddee and died after a reign of 22 years. In his reign several ships were wrecked on Ramree Island and the crews, said to have been Mahomedans, were sent to Arakan Proper and settled in villages. The ninth king, who lived during the tenth century, made an expedition into Bengal and set up a pillar at Chittagong which according to the Arakanese is a corruption of the Burmese " Tsit-ta-goung," and was so named from the king abandoning his conquest saying, somewhat late, that to make war was improper. Towards the end of the tenth century the Proo king of Prome invaded the kingdom but was unable to bring his army across the Yoma mountains and a few years later the capital was removed to Arakan (or Mrohoung). In 976 A. D. a Shan prince conquered the country and took the capital, withdrawing with much spoil after eighteen years' occupation. Just about this time the king of Pagan invaded Arakan but was forced to retreat. In 994 a son of the king who had advanced into Bengal ascended the throne and removed the capital to Tsambhawet on the Lemro river but was killed during a second invasion by the king of Pagan after reigning for twenty-four years : he was succeeded in 1018 A. D. by Khetta-theng, of the same family, who established his capital at Pengtsa.

The further history of the country up to 1404 A. D. may be related in the words of Sir Arthur Phayre. Khettatheng reigned for ten years and was succeeded in 1028 by his brother Tsandatheng. "Four of his descend-" ants reigned in succession. In the reign of the fifth, named Mengphyugyi, " a noble usurped the throne; another noble deposed him, but in the year 423 ".(1061 A. D.), the son of Mengphyugyi, named Mengnanthu, ascended the " throne and reigned five years. The third in descent from him, named " Mengbhilu, was slain by a rebellious noble named Thengkhaya, who " usurped the throne in the year 440 (1078 A. D.) The heir apparent, " Meng-re-bhaya, escaped to the court of Kyan-tsit-tha king of Puggan " (Pagan). The usurper reigned 14 years; his son Mengthan succeeded him " in 454 (1092 A. D.) and reigned eight years ; on his death his son Meng " Padi ascended the throne. During this period the rightful heir to the " throne, Meng-re-bhaya, was residing unnoticed at Puggan (Pagan) ; he had " married his own sister Tsu-pouk-ngyo, and there was born to them a son " named Letya-meng-nan. The exiled king died without being able to pro-" cure assistance from the Puggan (Pagan) Court for the recovery of his " throne. At length the king of that country Alaung-tsi-thu, the grand-" son of Kyan-tsit-tha, sent an army of 100,000 Pyus and 100,000 Talaings " to place Letya-meng-nan upon the throne. This army marched in the

---

*NOTE.—There is a tract of this name in Zengmai east of the Salween.

" year 464 (1102 A. D.), and after one repulse the usurper Meng Padi was
" slain and Letya-meng-nan restored to the throne of his ancestors in 465.
" A Burmese inscription on a stone discovered at Buddhagaya serves to con-
" firm the account given in this history of the restoration of Letya-meng-
" nan, or, as he is called in the stone inscription Pyu-ta-thin-meng, i. e.,
" Lord of a hundred thousand Pyus. It is evident, from the tenor both of
" the history and of the inscription, that the Arakan prince was regarded as
" a dependant of the Puggan (*Pagan*) king, to whom he had from his birth
" been a supplicant for aid : in return for the assistance granted him for the
" recovery of his grandfather's throne he was to aid in rebuilding the temple
" at Buddhagaya, in the name of the Puggan (*Pagan*) sovereign. The
" royal capital was established at Loung-kyet, but that site proving un-
" healthy, the city of Marim was built in the year 468 (1106 A. D.) Four
" kings followed in quick succession, after whom Gan-laya ascended the
" throne in 495 (1133 A. D.) He is described as a prince of great power,
" to whom the kings of Bengal, Pegu, Puggan (*Pagan*), and Siam did hom-
" age, but his chief claim to distinction lies in his having built the temple
" of Mahati, a few miles south of the present town of Arakan, the idol in
" which was, in sanctity, inferior only to that of Mahamuni. This temple
" and image were destroyed during the late war (*the first Burmese war*), the
" height on which they stood being occupied as a post by the Burmese forces.
" This king died after a reign of twenty years, in 515 (1153 A. D.) He was
" succeeded by his son Datha Radza, who upheld his father's fame, and
" repaired Mahamuni temple, which, since its partial destruction by the Pyu
" army in Letya-meng-nan's time, had remained neglected ; the idol which
" had been mutilated was also restored, the tributary kings being employed
" upon the work. This king died after a reign of twelve years in 527 (1165
" A. D.) He was succeeded by his son Anan-thi-ri, a prince who grievously
" oppressed his people, and, neglecting the affairs of government, passed his
" days in riot and debauchery. He lost the extensive empire possessed by
" his father and grandfather, neglected religious duties, and extorted large
" sums of money from the people, till the whole country, says the historian,
" cursing him in their hearts, a general rising occurred : he was deposed and
" killed, and his younger brother, Mengphuntsa, reigned in his stead. In
" the year 529 (1167 A. D.), this prince established his capital at Khyit, on
" the river Lemyo. A Shan army attempting to invade the kingdom was
" defeated in the Yoma mountains, and a number were taken prisoners and
" settled in two villages in the tract of country in Arakan Proper now
" known as Toungbhek. This king died after a prosperous reign of seven years."

" In the reign of his grandson, Gana-yu-bau, a noble named Tsa-leng-
kabo usurped the throne, but, proving oppressive, was murdered in the first
" year of his usurpation."

" Midzu-theng, the younger brother of Gana-yu-bau, was now raised
" to the throne ; he removed the capital to Pingtsa, close to the present
" town of Arakan. The oldest Arakanese coins extant, having the emblems
" of royalty engraved upon them, but without any date or inscription, are
" traditionally said to have been struck during this reign. This prince was
" surnamed Taingkhyit, or ' country beloved.' With characteristic extrava-
" gance he is said to have reigned over the present Burmese dominions, and a
" great part of India as far as the river Narindgana, and to the borders of

" Nipal. The succeeding ten kings pass like shadows, without anything
" worthy of notice except their short reigns. The five last of them reigned
" only for one year each, and by their oppression and neglect of religious
" duties the people were dissatisfied, while sickness and famine desolated the
" country. The *nats* or spirits of the seasons withheld their aid : the earth
" no longer yielded her fruits, and general misery prevailed. The last of
" these wicked kings was deposed, and his son, Letya-gyi, ascended the throne
" in 572 (1210 A. D.), and by his mild government restored the prosperity
" of the country. In the year 599 (1237 A. D.), Alau-ma-phyu succeeded
" to the throne, and removed the capital to Loungkyet in 601. This king
" made war upon the Puggan (*Pagan*) sovereign, and received tribute from
" the king of Bengal. He died after a reign of six years. His son, Radza-
" thugyi succeeded. In this reign the Talaings invaded the southern portion
" of the kingdom, but were repulsed by the Arakanese general, Ananthugyi.
" Nothing worthy of notice occurs until the reign of Nan-kyagyi, who
" ascended the throne in the year 630 (1268 A. D.) This king oppressed
" the people with heavy taxes, and levied contributions of goods which he
" stored up in his palace. By various acts of tyranny he incurred the hatred
" of many influential men ; and even the priests, whose religion forbids them
" to notice worldly affairs, are represented as inimical to him. Eventually
" he was killed in the fourth year of his reign, and was succeeded by his son,
" Mengbhilu, who married the daughter of the Tsi-tha-beng, or commander
" of the body-guard, the conspirator against the former sovereign. This
" prince is described as being, if possible, more hateful than his father.
" Being jealous of the supposed high destinies of his infant son, Mengdi, he
" ordered him to be cast into the river, but the child was miraculously pre-
" served, rescued by some fishermen, and was sent to a remote part of the
" kingdom. These and other similar acts inflaming the mind of the people
" against the king, he was slain in a conspiracy headed by the ·Tsi-tha-beng
" after a reign of four years. Tsi-tha-beng, the king-maker, now usurped
" the throne, but was himself killed in the third year of his reign. The son
" of Mengbhilu, named Mengdi, was then raised to the throne, but he was
" only seven years of age. This king gave general satisfaction, and enjoyed
" a long and prosperous reign. In the year 656 (1294 A.D.), the Shans
" invaded the kingdom, but were repulsed. The king of Thooratan,* or
" (*Eastern*) Bengal, named Nga-pu-kheng (*Bahadar Khan ?*), courted his
" alliance and sent presents of elephants and horses. After this his dominions
" again being attacked in various quarters by the Shans, the Burmese, the
" Talaings and the Thek tribe in the north, the king went to the Mahamuni
" temple, and, depositing his rosary before the idol, vowed to rid the country
" of its enemies. In pursuance of this vow, he marched in person in the
" year 674 (1312 A. D.) to repel the Talaings, who had possessed themselves
" of the country south of the town of Thandwai (*Sandoway*). His uncle,
" Udzdza-na-gyee, was sent with an army to attack Puggan (*Pagan*). Tsa-
" lenggathu, his brother-in-law, advanced into Pegu, and the general, Radza-
" theng-kyan was sent against the Thek tribe. The city of Puggan (*Pagan*)
" was taken, the Talaings were overawed, and the expedition against the Thek,

---

* NOTE.—Sonargaon, now called Painam, the capital of the eastern district of Bengal when
it first revolted from the Dehli empire, A. D. 1279.

" after being once repulsed, was eventually crowned with success. After this,
" the general Radza-theng-kyan subdued the country along the sea-coast as
" far as the Brahmaputra river. In the year 689 (1327 A.D.), the Puggan
" (*Pagan*) sovereign made an attack upon the island of Ranbyi (*Ramree*), and
" carried away a number of the inhabitants who were planted upon the
" Manipur frontier. After this, the Thandwai (*Sandoway*) viceroy having
" gained possession of a relic of Gaudama brought from Ceylon, by virtue
" of which he expected to obtain sovereignty, rose in rebellion, but was finally
" reduced to obedience. Soon after this, Mengdi died, after a reign of 106
" years, at the age of 113. Nothing worthy of notice occurred until 756
" (1394 A.D.), when the reigning sovereign marched to attack the Puggan
" (*Pagan*) empire, the capital of which was established at Engwa, or Ava.
" During his absence the governor of Thandwai (*Sandoway*) revolted, and
" seizing the boats which had conveyed the king's army along the seacoast,
" and were now left on the shore for his return, made the best of his way to
" Loungkyet, the capital, where he set up the king's infant son, Radza-thu.
" The king returned without delay, but his army deserting him he was slain
" and his son proclaimed. The Tsi-tha-beng, as the rebellious governor was
" called, not long after sent the young king to the southern extremity of the
" kingdom, and governed in his name ; but, becoming unpopular, he was,
" after two years, deposed and killed by a noble named Mying-tsaing-gyi,
" who in his turn, became disliked and had to fly to the Burmese dominions,
" when the lawful king Radza-thu was restored. He was succeeded by his
" younger brother, Thing-gathu. This prince, after a reign of three years, was
" murdered by the chief priest of the country in a monastery, with the con-
" nivance of his nephew, Meng-tsaw-mwon, who then succeeded to the
" throne in the year 766 (1404 A.D)."

Worn-out by his cruelties the people rose against him and called in
the aid of Meng-tshwai, king of Ava, who despatched a force of 30,000 men
under his son. Meng-tsaw-mwon fled to Bengal and found refuge with the
ruler of Thooratan who, being himself engaged in war, could render no assistance. At this period the empire of Dehli was torn to pieces by an ambitious
aristocracy and many of the subordinate governors had declared themselves
independent. The Arakanese histories state that when Meng-tsaw-mwon was
in Bengal the king of Dehli came to attack the chief or king of Thooratan who
was greatly assisted by the fugitive; this most probably refers to the invasion
of Bengal by Sultan Ibrahim of Joanpur.

The King of Ava had no intention of resigning his grasp on Arakan
whilst the Arakanese had no intention of allowing him to retain possession of
the country ; aided by the Talaings they made constant endeavours to drive
out the Burmese and in 1426 A.D. they were completely successful. In the
meanwhile Meng-tsaw-mwon by his crafty devices had, as noticed above,
greatly assisted the ruler of Thooratan and in gratitude an army was sent to
restore him to his kingdom. After some reverses it was successful and in
1430 A.D., Meng-tsaw-mwon re-ascended the throne of his fathers amidst
the acclamations of his subjects who, with the usual fickleness of eastern
nations, rejoiced that a descendant of their ancient line of kings, whom they
themselves had expelled for his cruelty, was restored to them.

After his return Meng-tsaw-mwon determined on changing the site of
his capital and was, the native histories state, miraculously guided to Myoukoo,

now called old Arakan or Mrohoung : the real cause of the selection of the situation may more reasonably be found in the strength of the position and the facility with which its natural advantages for defence could be added to. " When Meng-tsaw-mwon found his end approaching, as his sons were infants, he appointed his brother, Meng Khari, heir to the throne, and closed his chequered career in the fourth year of his restoration, aged fifty-three years." From this time the Arakan kingdom, undisturbed by its eastern neighbours who were at continual war with each other, continued to flourish. In 1531 A.D. the twelfth king, Mengba, worried by the aggressiveness of the Burmese and fearing the Portuguese adventurers who had settled on the coast, surrounded his capital with a stone wall eighteen feet high with six gates, and a devout Booddhist erected therein a pagoda, the remains of which still exist, called Shit-Thoung Bhoora, from the 80,000 images (cut out of soft stone) which he is supposed to have placed in and around it : very many, but all more or less injured, are still in existence and vary in height from an inch to six feet. During the next few years the kings of Arakan extended their conquests westward and between 1560 and 1570 made themselves masters of Chittagong. In 1571 Meng Thaloung excavated lakes round old Arakan, building raised causeways across them, to protect his capital from surprise by the Burmese and by the hill tribes who made incursions into the country plundering villages and carrying off their inhabitants as slaves. His son, Mengnala, was governor of Chittagong. The turbulent conduct of the Portuguese adventurers, who were independent of the Portuguese viceroy at Goa, led Meng Radza-gyee, the son and successor of Meng Thaloung, to drive them from his dominions and in 1609 he resumed the land which had been granted to them and attacked them in force. Many were killed but some succeeded in escaping and took possession of the islands in the mouth of the Ganges, living by piracy. Sebastian Gonzales was elected as their chief and in a short time he collected a formidable force and established a regular government on Sundeep Island. In the same year a brother of the king, having been guilty of some offence, escaped to Gonzales and persuaded him to attempt an attack on Arakan which failed. The following year the Arakanese, who were now aided by the Portuguese, took possession of the country in the neighbourhood of Luckim-poor but were eventually driven off with great slaughter the king effecting his escape with considerable difficulty. Gonzales immediately turned upon him, seized his boats and, proceeding down the coast, took and plundered the towns and villages and even advanced on the capital but was defeated and forced to retire. He then sent to the Portuguese viceroy of Goa, Don Hierome de Azvedo, suggesting an attack on Arakan and promising an annual tribute. An expedition was fitted out and the command given to Don Francis de Meneses who proceeded to the month of the Kooladan. Here he was unsuccessfully attacked by the king aided by the Dutch and held his own for a month, till November, when he was joined by Gonzales who bitterly reproached him for not waiting for him. The two commanders proceeded up the river and were signally defeated ; Don Meneses was killed in the action which took place and Gonzales, retiring to Sundeep, was abandoned by a large number of his followers. In the following year the King of Arakan took possession of Sundeep and for some years the Arakanese regularly invaded and plundered the lower parts of Bengal, carrying off numerous captives.

In the meanwhile the country was in great disorder. Meng Radza-gyee was succeeded by his son Meng Kanoung who, after a reign of thirteen years, was poisoned by his queen and her paramour, Moung Koot-tha, the governor of Loungkyet. Moung Koot-tha was imprisoned and Meng-tsa-gnay, the son of the murdered sovereign, proclaimed king but only to be poisoned within seven days by his mother who by her intrigues succeeded in effecting the release of Moung Koot-tha, whom she married, and who ascended the throne and reigned for seven years.

In 1661, Shah Shuja having been utterly defeated by his brother Aurungzeb was driven to seek refuge in Arakan. On the frontier he was received by an envoy who assured him of welcome and on nearing the capital he and his family and followers were met by an escort which conducted them to quarters set apart for them. At first he was well treated but in a short time the king, either instigated by Aurungzeb's Lieutenant in Bengal or excited by reports of the beauty of Shah Shuja's daughter, demanded her in marriage. That a Mussulmani, a descendant of kings, should be asked for by a Kafir was intolerable and Shah Shuja sent back a haughty refusal. His destruction was then determined on, his party was attacked, he himself made captive and drowned and the ladies of his household carried prisoners to the palace. The princess, the cause of her father's death, stabbed herself sooner than submit to the embraces of the king ; her brothers, one a lad of sixteen and the other an infant, were killed ; two of her sisters poisoned themselves ; and a third, forced to wed the Arakanese monarch, died of grief; not one of Shah Shuja's family remained and when the news was brought to his father, the dethroned Shah Jehan, he exclaimed "Could not the cursed infidel have left one son alive to avenge the wrongs of his grand-father?"

From the death of the usurper Koot-tha twelve kings reigned till circa 1701 A.D. For some years before this the kingdom had been in a very disturbed state and Kyet-tseng near the mouth of the Lemro, Lemro and other places were seized by robber chiefs whose gangs devastated the country. Twon-gnyo, a man of low origin but of strong will, having, more by good luck than by anything else, defeated one of those gangs and gained over the inhabitants of the capital, declared himself king and justified his authority by clearing the country of the dacoits who infested it. He repaired Mahamoonee, Maha-htee and the walls of the city, built himself a new palace, and avaged the lower part of Bengal with his armies, taking advantage of the disturbances which arose on the accession of Jehandar Shah. He died in 1731 and was succeeded by ten kings all of whom except Narapaya had short reigns. The country was gradually falling into anarchy. In 1775 A.D. one Eng-tswon, a native of Ramree, dethroned the reigning Sovereign Waimala Radza and proclaimed himself king, and, having put down a rebellion which shortly broke out, was succeeded, in 1783 A.D , by his son-in-law Thamada Radza, the last independent Sovereign of Arakan.

The following year, when Bhodaw Bhoora was king of Burma, the discontented Arakanese who hated their Ramree ruler invited the Burmans to aid them in dethroning him. A large Burman Force assembled at Prome under three royal Princes and invaded Arakan by three different routes. After some severe fighting the Arakanese army was defeated near Kyouk-hpyoo and the Burmans advanced on the capital and took possession, meeting with hardly any resistance; the country was annexed and Thamada Radza was carried prisoner to Ava where he shortly afterwards died.

This acquisition brought the Burmese into contact with the British and disputes soon arose. Large numbers of the inhabitants escaped from the cruelties of the Burmese and settled in Chittagong and other parts of Lower Bengal. Khyeng-byan—who is usually styled King Berring in the official accounts of this period—the son of the man who had invited the Burmese into Arakan, twice raised a revolt and his standard was joined by most of the respectable Arakanese families ; but the rising was finally suppressed and those who could do so escaped to Chittagong. Here Khyeng-byan continued his intrigues till he died in 1815 and the differences which arose in consequence between the two Governments and the retaliatory irruptions of the Burmese, who attacked and carried off the East India Company's elephant-hunters, together with the attitude assumed and the demands made by the Burmese Court not only regarding this part of the country but also in connection with the northern frontier in Manipur, led eventually to an open rupture. In 1824 war was declared and the Burmese dominions were invaded ; a force under General Morrison moved on Arakan and another under Sir Archibald Campbell operated by way of the valley of the Irrawaddy. On the 2nd February 1825 the first detachment of British troops crossed the Naaf from Chittagong and after a tedious but unopposed march arrived in front of Arakan town on the 28th of the same month, supported by the Flotilla under Commodore Hayes which, not altogether without resistance on the part of the Burmese, had proceeded up the Kooladan and through the creeks. The town was found to be strongly fortified, the Burman Commander having taken advantage of and added to the old Arakanese entrenchments and erected along the hills a line of stockades.

The only pass through the hills to the town was at the northern extremity of the line of defence and this was protected by several guns and four thousand muskets: the total garrison was nine thousand men. The ground in front was clear and open and the only cover was a belt of jungle which ran along the base of the hills whilst beyond this again the ground was fully exposed to the enemy's fire. On the morning of the 29th March the storming party, under Brigadier-General McBean, advanced to attack the pass. It consisted of the light company of the 54th Regiment, four companies of the 2nd Regiment L. I., the light companies of the 10th and 16th M. N. I., and the rifle company of the Mug levy, and was supported by six companies of the 16th Regiment, M. N. I. Under the well-directed and steady fire of the Burmese and the avalanche of stones which they poured down upon the heads of the troops the British were repulsed, and at last, when Captain French of the 16th Regiment, M. N. I., had been killed and all the remaining officers wounded, the storming party retreated. The plan of attack was then changed and it was determined to attempt to turn the right flank of the Burmese whilst their attention was occupied by an attack on their front. On the 30th March a battery was erected to play upon the works commanding the pass and on the 31st it opened fire. At about eight in the evening a force under Brigadier Richards left the camp: it consisted of six companies of the 44th Regiment, three of the 26th and three of the 49th Native Infantry, thirty seamen under Lieutenant Armstrong of the *Research* and thirty dismounted troopers of Gardener's Horse. The hill was nearly five hundred feet high and the ascent steep and winding. All remained quiet till shortly after eleven when a shot from the hill shewed that the enemy had discovered the approach of Brigadier Richards' party. This single shot was followed by a short but sharp fire when the Burmans turned and the hill was in the possession of the British. The next day a six-pounder was dragged up the hill and fire was opened on the heights commanding the pass whilst at the same time Brigadier Richards moved against it from the position which he had taken the night before and Brigadier McBean along his original line of advance; the Burmese, after a feeble defence, abandoned all the works and the town. The capture of Arakan ended the war as far as the Arakan Province was concerned; the Burmese troops at once abandoned Ramree and Sandoway and retreated across the mountains into Pegu; and the steady advance of Sir Archibald Campbell up the valley of the Irrawaddy, driving the Burmese forces before him, prevented any attempt on their part to disturb our possession. This advance ended at Yandaboo where a treaty was signed on the 24th February 1826 by which Arakan and Tenasserim became British territory.

When, shortly afterwards, the main body of the British troops was withdrawn one regiment was left in Arakan and a local battalion was raised, partly to keep order and partly to repel the incursions of the wild tribes occupying the hills. For several years the country was more or less in a disturbed state and within two years the establishment of a native dynasty was plotted for. The leaders were three men named Oung Gyaw-rhee a brother-in-law of Khyeng-byan, Oung Gyaw-tsan, his nephew, both of whom had rendered assistance to the British army and had received appointments under the British Government and Shwe-pan, also a British official, who had escaped or been allowed to return from Ava whither his father had been carried captive. In 1827 attempts were made to tamper with the men of the local battalion; the flame was smothered for a time, Oung Gyaw-rhee and Oung Gyaw-tsan were dismissed for cruelty and malpractices and the latter was sentenced to seven years' rigorous imprisonment for seriously wounding a Police daroga. In 1836 the rebellion broke out but was suppressed before it had developed into anything further than a series of dacoities: the instigators believed that the British Government would retire and accept a yearly tribute in lieu of full occupation. Since then the country has remained undisturbed.

The only town is Akyab, built on low ground at the mouth of the Kooladan river, which in 1826 was an insignificant village, and in 1876 contained a population of 18,306 souls. It is the head-quarters of the Arakan division as well as of the district and contains numerous public buildings. The streets are raised, well drained, and except in the native portion of the town, lined with trees.

Towns.

Arakan town, now called Mrohoung or "old town," the head-quarters of the township of the same name, with about 3,000 inhabitants, is worthy of note as having been at one time the capital of the Arakanese kingdom and strongly fortified.

Besides these two, Akyab and Mrohoung, the district contains, according to the census of 1872, only one town with 1,000 inhabitants, 70 villages with 500 to 1,000, 840 with 200 to 500, and 890 with less than 200 making in all 1,803 towns and villages.

In 1831, when the district included the present Hill Tracts and a
part of what is now the Myaiboon township of Kyouk-
Population. hpyoo, the inhabitants numbered 95,098 souls; the follow-
ng year the number had risen to 109,645, and thenceforward till 1854 the
ncrease was rapid.

Years.	Population.	
1832	109,645	The special census taken in 1872 shows a population of 276,671, but this includes the floating labouring population,
1842	130,034	sailors in the port of Akyab, travellers, &c. The figures given for that year are those of the annual population re-
1852	201,677	turns which include only *bonâ fide* inhabitants.
1862	227,231	
1872	271,099	
1875	283,160	
1876	284,119	

When Arakan was first ceded it was found to be almost depopulated
but immigrants soon flocked in, composed mainly of persons who had been
driven out by the Burmese or who had escaped during the war and who came
back to their homes from Chittagong and other neighbouring districts, and
as the country became more settled the immigration increased. About 1838
rumours prevailed of an impending attack by the Burmese which somewhat
checked the flow, but these soon subsided and in 1840 Lieutenant (now Sir
Arthur) Phayre was able to write :—" Numbers of the descendants of those
who fled in troublous times from their country and settled in the southern
part of Chittagong, the islands off the coast, and even the Sunderbuns of Bengal are gradually returning; and during the north-east monsoon boats filled
with men, women, and children, with all their worldly goods, may be seen
steering south along the eastern coast of the Bay of Bengal to return to the
land their fathers abandoned thirty or forty years before. They have told me
that in their exile the old men used to speak with regret for its loss of
the beauty of their country, the fertility of the land, which returned a hun-
dredfold, the heavy ears of rice, the glory of their kings, the former splendour
of the capital, the pagodas, and the famous image of Gaudama,* now carried
away, with which the fortunes of the country were indissolubly united."
After the second Burmese war, when Pegu fell into our hands, the
stream was again slightly checked but since 1862, when Arakan, Pegu and
Tenasserim were formed into one Government, the population has considerably increased. It is clear that those who came were not to any great extent
Burmans for the whole number of that people in 1872 was only 4,632, whilst
there is not a single Talaing, and that, therefore, there was no drain on the
indigenous population of the delta of the Irrawaddy or of Upper Burma.

---

* NOTE.—A gigantic image of brass carried off by the Burmese to Ava, where it now is, from
the sacred Mahamuni temple near old Arakan, the former capital.

The races represented in the district and their numbers in 1872 were, according to the census :—

1.	Europeans and Americans	..	..	..	150
2.	Eurasians and Indo-Portuguese	..	..	..	184
3.	Chinese	..	..	..	264
4.	Afghans	..	..	..	8
5.	Hindoos	..	..	..	2,655
6.	Mahomedans of pure and mixed blood		..	..	58,255
7.	Burmese	..	..	..	4,632
8.	Shans	..	..	..	334
9.	Arakanese	..	..	..	171,612
10.	Hill Tribes—Khyoungtha, Khwemee, Mro, &c.,			..	38,577

Total .. 276,671

The Arakanese, who form the major part of the inhabitants, are " a section of the Burman nation separated from the parent stock by mountains, which, except towards the southern extremity of the Yoma range, admit of little intercourse from one side to the other ; hence those living in this district, which adjoins Bengal, have some peculiarities in dialect and manners." Subjects of an independent monarch conquered by the Burmese towards the close of the last century, they have remained distinct from their conquerors, who are represented by only 4,632 souls. They appear to have gradually imbibed " some of the physical as well as the moral and social characteristics of the natives of India, with whom they have been for at least centuries much intermixed. They are darker than the Talaings, and perhaps rather darker than Burmans, and the type of countenance is as much Aryan as Mongolian. Morally, too, they are I think (writes Colonel Stevenson), more like natives of India than Burmans are, and they appear to be sliding into Indian habits and social usages. They are a coarser, more violent-tempered people than the Burmans, and have more of the pride of race and concomitant indolence." To some extent, more especially among the higher classes, the Indian custom of secluding the females has been adopted and early marriages of girls are now by no means uncommon.

Of the 58,255 Mahomedans many are men who come down for the working season only from Chittagong and were included in the census returns, but are not, properly speaking, inhabitants of the country. Those who are *bonâ fide* residents, though recruited by immigrants from Bengal, are for the most part descendants of slaves captured by the Arakanese and Burmese in their wars with their neighbours. The Arakan kings in former times had possessions all along the coast as far as Chittagong and Dacca and many Mahomedans were sent to Arakan as slaves. Large numbers are said to have been brought by Meng Radza-gyee after his first expedition to Sundeep and the local histories relate that in the ninth century several ships were wrecked on Ramree Island and the Mussulman crews sent to Arakan and placed in villages there. They differ but little from the Arakanese except in their religion and in the social customs which their religion directs ; in writing they use Burmese but amongst themselves employ colloquially the language of their ancestors.

The Hindoos, that is those who are permanent residents, whose numbers are to some very slight extent increased yearly by immigration, have been in the country for many generations ; some of them are Manipuri Brahmans brought by the Burmese as astrologers and others, also Brahmans, are descendhnts of colonists from Bengal brought by the Arakan kings. Amongst them are a few '*Doms*'* whose history is thus related by Sir Arthur Phayre " The Doms it would appear, were brought from Bengal to act as *Phra Kywon* (Bhoora Kywon) or pagoda slaves. It is a strange anomaly in the Booddhist religion (as it prevails in Burma) that the servitors of the temples are invariably outcasts, with whom the rest of the community will hold no intercourse. In Burma Proper pagoda slaves are pardoned convicts or persons condemned to the employment on account of crimes. The kings of Arakan, finding in Bengal a number of degraded castes ready made to their hands, imported them and their families as perpetual and hereditary pagoda slaves. These people, of course, are now released from their compulsory servitude, and have become cultivators, but in consequence of their former condition, they are regarded by the people with as much disgust as they would be from their low caste by Hindoos."

One noticeable difference between Hindoo and Mussulman immigrants is that the latter intermarry freely with the women of the country who, nominally at least, become Mussulmanis, whilst the former rarely do, as they could not associate and eat with their wives and children without losing caste one of the results is shown in the paucity of Hindoo children.

The hill tribes are fully described in the account of the Hill Tracts and under their tribal names. The Khyoungtha are of the same race as the Arakanese, the name being given to those who inhabit the banks of mountain streams. How they came to be separated so markedly from their country-men does not appear and it is curious that they should remain so and should so steadily prefer the hills where it is so difficult to procure a livelihood to the plains where, comparatively speaking. it is so easy.

There is a greater disproportion between the sexes in this district than in any other, the males being 53·56 and the females 46·44 per cent. of the population. The difference is greatest amongst the Hindoos, who form 0·96 of the whole population, 0·07 only being females and 0·89 males.

According to ages, there were found to be at the census in 1872—

	Males.	Females.
Not exceeding 1 year	6,817	6,473
Above 1 year and under 6 years	19,504	19,302
,, 6 ,, ,, ,, 12 ,,	22,068	20,813
,, 12 ,, ,, ,, 20 ,,	23,116	22,775
,, 20 ,, ,, ,, 30 ,,	27,411	21,203
,, 30 ,, ,, ,, 40 ,,	22,707	16,316
,, 40 ,, ,, ,, 50 ,,	14,103	10,542
,, 50 ,, ,, ,, 60 ,,	7,115	6,417
,, 60 ,, ,, ,, ,,	5,309	4,650
Total	148,180	128,491

* NOTE.—The Doms are a very low caste of Hindoos, utterly despised, and supposed to have sprung from a Tior father and Baiti mother in India they are basket-makers.

At every age, therefore, from birth to death the males predominate but it is between the ages of 20 and 50 that the difference in the number of males and of females is greatest and it is accounted for partly by immigration but mainly by the influx of workers for the rice season who bring few or no women with them. To confirm this view it is only necessary to look at the figures shewing the proportion between the sexes of Booddhists, Hindoos and Mahomedans at different ages :—

	Males.	Females.	Total.
Indigenous population other than Mahomedan, as Booddhist, &c.	113,114	102,305	215,419
Mahomedans	32,387	25,876	58,263
Hindoos	2,457	198	2,655

Taken by races, however, the males do not always exceed the females :—

Natives of India—Mahomedans ..	Males from 1 to 6, there are	3,691
	Females „ „ „ „ „ „	3,746
Arakanese—Booddhists ..	Males „ „ „ „ „ „	13,119
	Females „ „ „ „ „ „	13,250
Europeans—Christians ..	Males „ „ „ „ „ „	8
	Females „ „ „ „ „ „	12
Others	Males „ 6 to 20 „ „	29
	Females „ „ „ „ „	33

The following table gives the distribution of infirmities as affecting the population by sexes; the percentages are calculated on the total number of each sex :—

Sex.	Insanes.		Deaf and dumb.		Blind.		Lepers.	
	No.	Per cent.	No.	Per cent.	No.	Per cent.	No.	Per cent.
Males	220	0·15	296	0·19	232	0·16	44	0·03
Females ..	98	0·85	145	0·11	121	0·09	35	0·03

The number of persons employed in service or performing personal offices was found to be 97,295 (a far larger number than in any other district in the province), in agriculture and cattle-dealing 44,830, and in mechanical arts, manufactures, &c. 10,111. Of the agriculturists, who form 16·20 per cent. of the whole population, 39,573 were over 20 years old.

Of manufactures the district has none of any importance. A little salt is made near the Naaf by a mixed process of solar evaporation and boiling but year by year the outturn is decreasing owing to the cheaper rate at which foreign salt can be sold. Earthen pots are made in Akyab, Kyailet, Mengbra and Rathai-doung and the process is everywhere exceedingly simple : the clay is exposed to the weather for one season and in the dry weather pulverized and mixed with water, a small

Manufactures.

proportion of sand being added ; the pots are moulded by hand, exposed to the sun till dry and then burned, the whole process lasting about twelve days. The manufacture gives employment during the working season to some 700 persons all told.

The staple product of the district is rice and for this the rich and extensive plains (the average produce per acre is lbs. 1,300)

Agriculture.

stretching from the foot of the northern hills towards the sea-coast are admirably adapted whilst the facilities for reaching Akyab through the numerous anastomosing creeks and the demand for export have greatly encouraged its growth by the ever-increasing population. During the nine years ending with 1875 the acreage under cultivation, excluding toungyas, has been :—

	Rice.	Oil-seed.	Sugar.	Indigo.	Tobacco.	Tea.	Cocoanuts.	Betel-nuts.	Dhanee.	Plantains.	Pauvine.	Vegetables.	Hemp.	Mixed fruit-trees.	Mixed products.
1867	268,014	35	20	3	4	100	403	769	7,443	1,858	423	*10,297	99	...	...
1868	238,438	34	44	2	1	100	376	746	7,468	1,701	416	2,447	148	7,014	827
1869	244,190	30	77	2	6	Not given.	367	759	7,581	1,623	443	2,068	113	9,046	1,125
1870	248,975	27	153	...	1	do.	335	771	7,471	1,528	392	2,195	101	7,311	1,183
1871	258,114	143	130	42	38	50	283	816	7,398	1,410	362	2,051	109	7,306	1,356
1872	263,375	53	113	73	17	50	310	816	7,170	1,275	395	2,130	100	7,422	1,352
1873	260,486	78	82	2	18	110	321	822	7,431	1,385	477	3,695	84	3,201	328
1874	270,342	14	87	1	1	110	285	335	7,500	1,367	...	3,814	...	7,729	...
1875	272,902	13	30	...	...	110	283	824	7,625	1,355	463	2,259	74	9,238	8,918

* Includes Mixed products.

The most noticeable feature in this statement is the sudden decrease in 1868 in the area of rice land, a decrease so great that even in 1871 the recovery was not complete. The causes may be stated in the words of the Commissioner :—" Loss of cattle from widely spread and persistent cattle disease during the two previous years has doubtless impoverished a number of people who now cannot afford to cultivate much ; the cyclone of the 13th November last (1867) injured much good rice land and added not a little to other losses of the community ; and the cholera finally, which prevailed throughout the town and district, has not only carried off many who could and would work, but has put it out of the power of those who can but will not work to obtain the labour necessary to till their lands. This has hitherto been drawn from Chittagong, but its annual swarms of labourers have not arrived this year for the cultivating season. Large numbers of them fled the country during the prevalence of the epidemic." Thus to cattle disease on the one hand and to the sudden loss of hired labour on the other supplemented by the serious damage done by the cyclone may be attributed a check to cultivation which it took six years to overcome. The high price realized for rice in 1873-74 on account of the scarcity in Bengal so stimulated cultivation that the total area under rice during the following year, including rent-free grants and hill clearings, was 286,588 acres whilst the whole cultivated area was 308,814 acres. The holding of each cultivator averages 8·42 acres.

The *toungya* or hill system of cultivation was formerly followed to a considerable extent even in the plains but is giving place to the better plan of ploughing and harrowing. The *toungyas* are not, as a rule, measured but the area is estimated at two acres for each cutter. In 1855 the number of workers was 5,355, in 1864, 4,414, and during the nine years ending with 1875 :—

1867	..	..	..	..	..	.. 3,428
1868	..	..	..	..	..	.. 3,293
1869	..	..	..	..	..	.. 3,124
1870	..	..	..	..	..	.. 3,718
1871	..	..	..	..	..	.. 3,919
1872	..	..	..	..	..	.. 3,341
1873	..	..	..	..	..	.. 3,051
1874	..	..	..	..	..	.. 3,122
1875	..	..	..	..	..	.. 2,983

The district is rich in agricultural stock which, notwithstanding the murrain that carried off so many head of cattle in 1865, 1866 and 1867, has increased very considerably. In 1867 and 1875 the published official returns give the numbers as follows :—

Year.	Buffaloes.	Cows, bulls, and bullocks.	Ponies.	Sheep and goats.	Pigs.	Ploughs.	Boats.	Carts.	Remarks.
				*	*				* Not given. In 1869-70, the numbers were—sheep and goats 1,981, pigs 5,928.
1867 ..	82,710	82,470	158	..	..	36,391	14,159	3,327	
1875 ..	121,073	167,431	271	8,748	8,783	55,353	14,370	4,712	

The large proportion of boats in comparison with carts is due to the nature of the country the tidal creeks which traverse it forming the principal channels of communication. The increase in ploughs and in plough-cattle is remarkable and notably so when compared with the small increase in the number of boats and carts. The carriage of the grain from the interior to Akyab for export is largely in the hands of Chittagonians who bring down their boats after the rains and take them back when the season is over and before the enumeration is made. The rate of wages is on the whole higher than anywhere else unskilled labourers receiving about Rs. 5 a week and skilled labourers Rs. 14.

With the increasing population the agriculture and the revenue have
Revenues. more than kept pace. In 1828 Mr. Paton, the Civil Officer in charge, calculated that for the ensuing five years the revenue which would be derived from the whole of Arakan would not exceed Rs. 2,20,000 per annum whereas in 1831 the assessment in this district alone yielded Rs. 2,40,190 : this was at the rate of two rupees twelve annas per head of population. During the following nine years the amounts realized were :— ·

		Rs.				Rs.
1832	..	2,48,570	1837	..	..	3,35,730
1833	..	2,80,300	1838	..	..	3,80,290
1834	..	3,10,170	1839	..	..	3,79,810
1835	..	2,87,020	1840	..	..	3,79,700
1836	..	3,26,290				

In 1837 the taxes on forest produce, huts, boats, houses, sugar-presses, handicraftsmen &c. which prevailed as part of the ancient revenue system in force when we took the country were abolished and Rs. 97,350 thus lost; the figures given above show how little the revenue suffered. In 1856 the amount derived from this district was Rs. 10,06,570, in 1862 Rs. 14,20,430, in 1872 Rs. 19,24,627 and in 1875 Rs. 20,83,693.

	Land.	Capitation.	Excise.	Fisheries.	Customs, including fines, confiscations, &c.	All other items.	Total.
	Rs.	Rs.	Rs.	Rs.	Rs.	Rs.	Rs.
1862	5,73,350	2,73,260	95,920	..	4,04,490	73,410	14,20,430
1875	5,94,656	2,83,594	1,57,734	5,822	7,00,062	1,63,669	10,05,537
Increase	21,306	10,334	61,814	5,822	4,04,490	73,410	4,85,107

The amount received by the State as land revenue and the area worked, divided into their main heads, were :—

	Rice.		Garden.		Miscellaneous.		Special grants.		Total.		Toungyas.	Total.
	Acres.	Rev.	Acres.	Rev.	Acres.	Rev.	Acres.	Rev.	Acres.	Revenue.	Revenue.	
		Rs.		Rs.		Rs.		Rs.		Rs.	Rs.	
1862 ...	2,43,037	5,19,080	15,259	40,450	3,800	9,540	...	...	2,62,096	4,280	5,73,350	
1875 ...	2,72,902	5,34,837	17,984	36,994	4,493	9,140	8,389	10,362	3,03,768	3,313	5,91,646	

the decrease in *toungyas* being due to the Hill Tracts having been separated from the district and to a gradual cessation of that system of cultivation the cultivators taking up land in the plains instead.

The capitation tax, which is paid by all males between 18 and 60 years of age except those living in Akyab town who pay an assessment on their houses in lieu and persons specially exempted such as immigrants or persons engaged in education or devoted to the performance of religious duties, &c., was in 1875 assessed on 70,040 souls and yielded Rs. 2,83,594 or a little over four rupees a head of those assessed.

The excise revenue, which is derived from licenses to sell intoxicating liquor and drugs, is to some extent fluctuating, depending necessarily upon the consumption of these articles and upon the method in which it is raised not only here but in the neighbouring Chittagong district of Bengal.

The tax on fisheries and fishing nets was first imposed in 1864-65 and in that year yielded Rs. 6,820.

The increase in receipts from Customs is entirely due to increased trade. In the following table are shewn, year by year, the receipts for the last 21 years :—

Year.	Amount.	Year.	Amount.	Year.	Amount.
	Rs.		Rs.		Rs.
1855-56 ..	1,81,590	1862-63 ..	4,04,490	1869-70 ..	2,97,860
1856-57 ..	86,470	1863-64 ..	4,92,080	1870-71 ..	6,78,030
1857-58 ..	1,46,850	1864-65 ..	4,09,220	1871-72 ..	5,26,530
1858-59 ..	1,25,090	1865-66 ..	3,77,850	1872-73 ..	8,81,610
1859-60 ..	2,30,830	1866-67 ..	2,93,370	1873-74 ..	7,05,940
1860-61 ..	4,31,650	1867-68 ..	4,42,720	1874-75 ..	6,34,946
1861-62 ..	3,60,120	1868-69 ..	5,49,560	1875-76 ..	7,00,062

The fluctuations are considerable and are due partly to changes in the rates of duty and partly to the state of trade and not unfrequently to the shipments falling mainly before or after the close of the financial year. The rapid falling-off from 1863 to 1866, when the tide turned, was due to the state of the rice trade. In 1863-64 there was a sudden inflation owing to an increased demand for rice in the ports to the eastward of the province the result of scarcity in China; in the following year the exports fell, in 1865 they fell still lower, and in 1866 fell very considerably but rose again with great rapidity in 1867. During this period there had not only been great stagnation in the home markets but the Siamese ports had been thrown open and in 1866 the returns were made up for 11 months only owing to a change in the financial year—a change which took place during the rice shipping season. The next great fluctuation was in 1869 and this was caused by shippers holding back in expectation of a reduction in, if not the total abolition of, the export duty on rice (which was eventually lowered by about 33 per cent.) ; the result of this holding back is seen in the increased duty realized in the following year notwithstanding the great reduction in the duty.

The gross revenue collected in the district, exclusive of municipal and local funds, during each of the last nine years was :—

1867	.. Rs. 14,89,312	1872	.. Rs. 19,24,647
1868	.. „ 15,70,464	1873	.. „ 18,18,769
1869	.. „ 13,10,233	1874	.. „ 17,87,858
1870	.. „ 17,00,770	1875	.. „ 20,83,698
1871	.. „ 15,36,717		

Deducting from these figures the Customs dues which have been shewn to fluctuate greatly the revenues were—

1867	.. Rs.	10,46,592	1872	.. Rs.	10,43,037
1868	.. ,,	10,20,904	1873	.. ,,	11,12,829
1869	.. ,,	10,12,373	1874	.. ,,	11,42,922
1870	.. ,,	10,22,740	1875	.. ,,	13,83,631
1871	.. ,,	10,10,187			

Deducting from the gross revenues the expenditure on administration— that is the cost of civil offices of all kinds (and the establishment for the control of the whole of the Arakan Division is included)—the balances available for the general purposes of the State were :—

Year.	Gross revenue.	Cost of Administration.	Balance.	
	Rs.	Rs.	Rs.	
1867	14,89,312	4,28,817	10,60,495	
1868	15,70,464	3,00,869	12,69,595	
1869	13,10,283	2,82,393	11,27,841	
1870	17,00,770	3,01,355	13,99,415	
1871	15,35,717	2,47,697	12,88,020	
1872	19,24,647	2,09,356	17,15,291	
1873	18,18,769	3,21,828	14,96,941	
1874	17,87,358	3,20,813	14,67,045	
1875	20,83,693	3,21,459	17,62,134	Average per annum, Rs. 13,73,732.

The local revenues increased with the Imperial. In 1857 the Ferry Fund alone had a balance of Rs. 157,860 ; this was amalgamated with the general Bengal Ferry Fund allotments being made to the district according to its stated requirements but on the formation of the province in 1862 Bengal no longer received any contributions from Arakan and did not return the balance, if there was any. In 1873-74, 1874-75 and 1875-76, the revenues derived from local sources were—

			1873-74.	1874-75.	1875-76.
Port Fund ..	..	.. Rs.	46,313	43,212	47,013
Municipal Fund	..	.. ,,	22,849	..	..
Bazaar Fund	..	.. ,,	3,480	1,235	2,007
Dispensary Fund ..	..	.. ,,	1,287	1,640	1,899
Land Sale and Rent Fund	..	.. ,,	194	159	176
Five per Cent. Cess Fund	..	.. ,,	43,314	33,974	54,639
District Fund	..	.. ,,	7,391	7,859	10,097
Total	.. Rs.		1,24,828	88,079	1,15,931
Add Revenue collected by the Municipality	.. ,,		..	26,172	44,480
GRAND TOTAL	.. ,,		1,24,828	1,14,251	1,60,411

The trade of the district is mainly confined to Akyab. Before the British

Trade. occupation large sea-going boats from Mrohoung visited the ports of Bengal and brought away numerous articles of British manufacture such as muslins, woollens, cutlery, piece-goods, glass and crockery with which every town and village was fairly supplied, whilst a small trade was carried on with the other Burman ports to the eastward. The establishment of the British Government, resulting in the removal of the vexatious restrictions on trade imposed by the Burmese, was the signal for English ships to visit Akyab for the rice which the surrounding country produced in larger quantities year by year, bringing in return piece-goods, tobacco and other articles. To rice was subsequently added timber for sleepers for the Indian railways (but for a short period only) hides, horns and but little else, the rice trade occupying by far the larger number of ships frequenting the port.

From October 1830 to April 1831—that is during the shipping season— 140 square-rigged vessels cleared out carrying cargoes valued at Rs. 73,780. In 1833 the number of such vessels had increased to 178 and the value of their cargoes to Rs. 93,810. The trade from 1855-56 to 1875-76 is shewn in the following table, that of each of the first ten and of the last three years being given separately :—

Year.	Value of grain exports.	Value of timber exports.	Value of all other exports, including treasure.	Imports including treasure.	Tonnage of vessels cleared out.
	Rs.	Rs.	Rs.	Rs.	Tons.
1855-56	1,06,76,040	2,910	8,00,010	77,88,450	1,93,512
1856-57	29,88,580	6,210	13,07,770	47,55,470	91,472
1857-58	61,08,930	2,000	21,34,340	51,39,580	1,7,0635
1858-59	28,19,710	470	11,24,800	84,76,650	1,17,528
1859-60	27,93,570	3,220	12,60,110	48,33,670	69,878
1860-61	45,54,350	150	4,46,650	29,16,670	1,21,719
1861-62	35,12,850	4,900	10,83,780	56,27,490	1,14,696
1862-63	39,51,660	2,790	10,64,180	51,72,340	1,15,975
1863-64	48,37,240	19,820	15,56,260	57,72,140	1,55,973
1873-74	72,76,010	6,920	28,31,280	91,04,970	1,93,444
1874-75	59,46,850	20,430	23,05,970	64,20,090	1,79,260
1875-76	45,53,920	16,120	17,43,200	41,01,810	1,94,470

The rice is exported to India and to foreign countries. In the calendar year 1871 the exports to Europe were 113,047 tons; in 1872 they were 141,634 tons; in 1873, when there was a great demand for Bengal and the Madras coast 123,452; in 1874 141,280 tons; and in 1875 136,247 tons. The timber, which consists of ironwood, goes to Chittagong for house posts and to Bengal for railway sleepers. Cutch goes mainly to Chittagong and is brought into the country across the Arakan Romas from Upper Burma and the hill districts. Gunnybags come in from Calcutta empty to be re-exported filled with rice when their numbers and value are not entered in the returns. The trade in piecegoods is with the Indian and provincial ports and is carried on almost exclusively by native merchants. Tobacco was and indeed still is imported in quantities but the trade is falling off and little found in the market outside Akyab. It is a branch of trade which may very possibly become largely developed as the tobacco grown in the Hill Tracts has been favourably reported on and is found to contain important constituents in amount closely resembling those in the most favourite tobaccos of European smokers—the Havanna and Manilla tobaccos of the English market. A small quantity of very fair cotton, the produce of the Hill Tracts, is exported to Chittagong but the native looms are chiefly supplied with Manchester thread.

The number and gross tonnage of the ships which cleared out during each of the last three years were:—

Class.	1873-74.		1874-75.		1875-76.	
	Number.	Tonnage.	Number.	Tonnage.	Number.	Tonnage.
British	158	110,998	166	112,819	173	108,731
Foreign	95	61,024	62	43,317	94	63,362
Asiatic	316	21,422	347	23,127	318	22,376
Total ..	569	193,444	575	179,263	585	194,469

When Arakan was ceded to the British in 1826 by the treaty of Yandaboo it was found that the Burmese Government had divided the country into governorships of which Akyab formed one with its head-quarters at Arakan town, the capital of the former Arakan kingdom which had been conquered and annexed to the Burmese dominions towards the end of the eighteenth century. The system adopted by the English Government for the management of the country is thus described by Lieutenant (now Sir Arthur) Phayre, who was for many years in civil employ in Arakan and subsequently Chief Commissioner of the province:—" Arakan (that is the Akyab district to which this name is, properly speaking, restricted) is divided into 160 circles, of which 148 are denominated kywn [kywvn] or islands, being situated in the lowlands, and 12 are called khyoung or streams being in the hill districts. They contain a total of 960 villages. Each of these circles is

Administration.

placed under an officer designated *Kywn-aop* [*Kywon-oop*] (this is pronounced as one syllable, *Kyok*); or *Khyoung-aop*, according to the locality of his charge. The duties of a *Kywn-aop* [*Kywon-oop*] are to collect the revenue, to preserve order in his circle, and to assist the police in the apprehension of criminals ; through him are made all statistical inquiries, and to him are referred many disputes concerning land ; he is paid 15 per cent. upon his collections. In each circle there are from three or four to 15 or 20 villages ; the revenue collected by the different *Kywn-aops* [*Kywon-oop*] varies from Rs. 200 to Rs. 10,000. This great difference results from the rapid increase within a few years of some circles compared with others, consequent on superiority or fertility of soil, more convenient locality for exporting grain, and other causes. The office of *Kywn-aop* [*Kywon-oop*] is not hereditary, but the son of any man who has rendered essential services generally succeeds on his father's demise. Next to the *Kywn-aop* [*Kywon-oop*] is the *Rawa-goung* [*Rwa-goung*], or village head. This officer is elected by the villagers themselves ; if there are two or more candidates for the appointment, the villagers meet and sign their names to a document containing the name of him whom they vote for; these lists are then forwarded by the *Kywn-aop* [*Kywon-oop*] to the officer in charge of the district (called *Myo-won*), who appoints him that has a majority of votes, unless, indeed, there be some good reason for rejecting him. . . The *Rawa-goung* [*Rwa-goung*] collects the revenue of his village and delivers it to the *Kywn-aop* [*Kywon-oop*], who carries it to the Government treasury. He is paid four per cent. on his collections. A village of 30 houses is entitled to a *Rawa-goung* [*Rwa-goung*], that is, to a stipendiary one. If a village has less than that number of houses they pay their tax to a neighbouring *Goung*; but if the villagers, as frequently happens, dislike this arrangement and elect a *Goung* of their own, the proceeding is confirmed, but they must pay him themselves. Their object then is to induce settlers to come among them, whereby their village may be raised to the privileged standard of 30 houses. Under the orders of the *Rawa-goung* [*Rwa-goung*] is the *Rawa-tsare* [*Rwa-tsare*], or village scribe. He is paid two per cent. on the village collections. The appointment is usually held by the son or by some relation of the *Rawa-goung* [*Rwa-goung*]. His duties are to prepare, under the orders of the *Goung*, the village *Sarang* (*T'sareng*), or register, containing the name of each householder in the village, with the amount of tax demandable from him upon each item.

"There are no agents of police in the village, the village officers being held responsible for the preservation of order and the seizure of criminals.

" Throughout the district there are six police stations, at which the police ordinarily remain until information being given by a village officer or other person of any occurrence requiring their presence, they proceed to the spot: nearly all communication in the district is carried on by water.

" The European functionary in charge is styled a Senior Assistant to the Commissioner of Arakan (by the people, *Myowon*). To conduct all revenue affairs there is an officer styled *Myo-thoo-jyce*, whose office under the Arakan and Burman Governments was considered the most important in the country. He then apportioned to each the amount of revenue demanded by the Government ; his duty now is, under the orders of the Senior Assistant, to superintend all the *Kywn-aops* [*Kywon-oop*], and to inspect and report upon the annual registers of their circles : the office still carries with it a great deal of importance in the minds of the people. This officer is paid a fixed salary, and resides at the chief town of the district."

The existing system of administration is but a development of that first adopted. The office of *Kywon-oop* (now called Thoogyees) still exists but the incumbents have no longer regular police duties and are paid by a much smaller percentage on their collections, the *Goungs* are village police officers appointed by the Government who receive a fixed salary and have little or nothing to do with the Revenue, and a regular police force has been established. The district has been divided into townships over each of which, except Akyab which is under a European Magistrate, is placed a Native Extra Assistant Commissioner with revenue, civil and criminal powers. Of these townships there are eight. The Kooladan in the valley of the river of the same name is the most northern and adjoins the Hill Tracts. It is divided into eight revenue circles and contains no large towns and but little cultivation : the Extra Assistant Commissioner in charge holds his Court at a village on the right bank of the river not far from the celebrated Mahamoonee temple. South and east of the Kooladan township is the Old Arakan or Mrohoung township which is divided into 21 revenue circles with the head-quarters at Arakan : in this township is situated the temple of Maha-htee. On the other or western side of the Kooladan is the Ooreetoung West township extending down nearly to Akyab, divided into 19 revenue circles. The Raithaidoung township adjoins Chittagong on the north and Ooreetoung West on the east whilst on the south it touches the coast and occupies the country on both banks of the Mayoo ; it is divided into 21 circles and the head-quarters are at Rathaidoung on the Mayoo river. The Naaf, known to the Arakanese as Anouk-gnay, occupies the country between the Mayoo hills and the Naaf from the sea-coast northwards and is divided into 11 circles. The Ooreetoung East township is south of Mrohoung and extends along the sea-coast below Akyab : it is divided into 17 circles and includes the Borongo islands. Mengbra extends from the Ooreetoung East township to Kyouk-hpyoo and the Arakan Roma mountains and is bounded on the south by the sea ; it is divided into 19 circles. Lastly Kyailet, containing 18 circles, occupies the small tract of country round the town of Akyab.

The officers now entrusted with the administration of the country in all its branches, exclusive of Thoogyees or *Kywon-oop* and the *Goungs* and *Kyedangyees* (who hold much the same position that the *Goungs* formerly held but in lieu of salary are excused the payment of capitation-tax) are a Deputy Commissioner, an Assistant Commissioner, a Magistrate for the island and town of Akyab, eight Extra Assistant Commissioners, an Akhwonwon who holds the place of the Myo-thoogyee alluded to above, a Superintendent of Police, a Civil Surgeon who is in charge of the Gaol, an Executive Engineer, a Collector of Customs, a Master Attendant, a Deputy Inspector of Schools, a Superintendent of the Telegraph Department and a Post Master. The Deputy Commissioner and the Assistant and Extra Assistant Commissioners are the Judges, Magistrates and Revenue officials for the whole of the district each within his own territorial limits, the jurisdiction of the Magistrate extending over Akyab Island within which the other officers have no criminal judicial authority. The " Tarama-thoo-gyee," now called an Extra Assistant Commissioner and stationed in Akyab, has civil jurisdiction over Akyab Island and is Judge of the Court of Small

Causes with final jurisdiction up to Rs. 100. The town of Akyab was formed into a Municipality in 1874, and a Municipal Committee was appointed which deals with the local revenues and expenditure.

The police force, which was raised in 1861, is a portion of the general police force of the province under the Inspector-General in Rangoon and, as far as this district is concerned, replaces the old local police and the local battalion. The strength has varied at different times: in 1875 it consisted of a District Superintendent, 32 subordinate officers and 419 men, who cost Rs. 93,799. For several years the Police were to a large extent engaged in repelling attacks of, and in following up, marauding parties from amongst the hill tribes in the north but since the Hill Tracts have been separated from this district their duties have lain more entirely in preventing and detecting local crime, amongst which murders and gang robberies at one time filled an important place.

The Gaol in Akyab is under the charge of the Civil Surgeon and consists of wooden buildings raised from the ground and surrounded by a wall. A new wall is being built round what has hitherto been the work-yard, and new Gaol buildings will be constructed within it, the site of the existing prison being used for work-sheds. The difficulty in obtaining and the expense of employing hired labour, together with the absolute necessity for making roads and drains, filling up swamps, and, generally, laying out and keeping in order the town of Akyab led to the prisoners confined in this Gaol being to a very great extent employed in out-door labour, but gradually in-door labour has been introduced with, as regards the prison, very satisfactory results. In 1855 the average cost of each prisoner was Rs. 111-12; in 1857 it had fallen to Rs. 79-12 and in 1859 to Rs. 60-8. In 1875 the gross cost was Rs. 52-14 and owing to the value of the Gaol labour the nett cost was only Rs. 24-9, excluding the cost of the new buildings. The works on which the prisoners are employed are stone-breaking, coir-pounding, spinning jute and weaving the twist into bags, cotton-spinning and hand-weaving, pounding bricks, making coir-mats, rugs and ropes, and carpentry and smiths' work ; timber-sawing was introduced in 1875. The gross earnings during 1875 were Rs. 14,298 and the cost of materials having been Rs. 5,630 the nett amount paid into the Government treasury was Rs. 8,668. The whole cost of the Gaol was Rs. 16,770 so that more than a third was defrayed from profits. In 1873 Carolina rice-seed was sown in the garden and produced lbs. 115 for every pound of seed sown. The average number of prisoners in confinement—some of whom were transferred from Kyouk-hpyoo and Sandoway, as this prison is a divisional one, during each of the last nine years was :—

1867	..	295	1872	..	332
1868	..	367	1873	..	369
1869	..	471	1874	..	334
1870	..	490	1875	..	330
1871	..	361			

The hospital and charitable dispensary in Akyab consist of two large blocks of buildings raised from the ground on piles, with a covered way running between them, one for Europeans and the other for natives, the latter built many years ago. An entirely new building is in course of erection. The number of patients treated during the last seven years was :—

Years.			PATIENTS.		
			In.	Out.	Total.
1869	..	..	..	..	2,012
1870	..	..	579	1,564	2,143
1871	..	..	298	1,389	1,687
1872	..	..	398	1,893	2,291
1873	..	..	461	2,280	2,741
1874	..	..	560	1,890	2,450
1875	..	..	374	1,993	2,367

In 1871 a lock hospital was completed.

For many years education in this district was left very much to itself, as it had been left in the Burman time ; in 1846 a Government school was established in Akyab and placed under the Director of Public Instruction in Bengal ; but in 1857 it was withdrawn from him and placed under the control of the local authorities. Of late years, since the formation of an Education Department in the province, this school has had more attention paid to it : a new school-house has been built for it, and in 1875 it was raised to the position of a High School : the average number of pupils who attended daily in that year was 224. In 1873 a cess school, that is one the cost of which is defrayed from the five per cent. local cess fund, was opened at Moungdoo, in the Naaf township, which at the end of the year had 20 pupils on its rolls, and at the end of 1875, 43. This school affords a good example of the craving of parents for the instruction of their children in English to enable them to obtain employment as clerks in the Government service and in merchants' offices and of their disregard of education for its own sake. The Director of Public Instruction in his report for 1875 quotes the following extract from the remarks of the Deputy Inspector of Schools :—" This school under Moung Tha Doon Oung, the vernacular teacher, made a very good commencement but afterwards dwindled away—parents wanted education in English, they did not care much for the vernacular. At last there were only four or five boys in the school when Moung Shwe Oo, a teacher from the Akyab High School, was sent to Moungdoo on the 20th July 1875. Then it was that the boys re-entered, and now the school . . . . . has 43 boys on the rolls. The parents of the boys have expressed a wish for another teacher of English, and they would like the present Vernacular to be removed. They do not wish for any vernacular education. . . . . " In 1874 another cess school was opened at Mrohoung.

The endeavours to make use of the existing indigenous lay and monastic schools for the purposes of general education and to bring them to some extent under control have not been extraordinarily successful. In 1875 120 lay and monastic schools submitted to the examination of their pupils; the lay schools alone did not come up to the standards—necessarily low—fixed by the Education Department: pupils passed the examination in 43 monastic but in only three lay schools; in these latter out of the 15 prize winners seven were girls. The census of 1872 showed that, as regards mere reading and writing, the Mahomedans and Booddhists—that is by far the larger proportion of the inhabitants—were farther advanced than almost anywhere else in the province. Of those of these religions of 20 years of age and upwards 11,589 Mahomedan males out of 22,979, 31,938 Booddhist males out of 64,549, 1,543 Mahomedan females and 3,275 Booddhist females could read and write.

Outside the island of Akyab the numerous inosculating creeks which traverse the low country in every direction and unite the streams flowing down from the hills to the sea form the principal highways. An unmetalled fair-weather road, extending for 20 miles from Mrohoung to Mengbra, has lately been made and a road from Moung-daw in the Naaf township to Akyab, a distance of 65 miles, which will unite this town with the Chittagong division, is under construction, and the first section, ten and half miles out of Akyab, has been completed.

Communications.

AKYAW.—A revenue circle in the Donabyoo township of the Thoon khwa district, on the right bank of the Irrawaddy and some distance inland, more cultivated in the north than towards the south where there is a good deal of tree-forest of which a large portion is suitable only for firewood. The inhabitants are principally traders, fishermen and rice-cultivators. The land revenue in 1874-75 amounted to Rs. 2,990 and the capitation-tax in 1875-76 to Rs. 1,800. This circle has lately been placed under the Kyoon-tanee Thoogyee.

AKYAW.—A village in the Thoon-khwa district about four miles to the west of the Irrawaddy with a brick-laid road running through it, containing a population of some 600 souls. The inhabitants are principally Talaings.

A-LA-BHWOT.—A lake in the northern portion of the Rangoon district, on the right bank of the Hlaing river with which it communicates. In the dry weather it has a depth of about 10 feet.

ALAY-BOUK.—A creek in the Alay-kywon, at the entrance to the Bassein river, about 100 feet wide and admitting boats of 200 baskets burden at all times.

ALAY-KHYOUNG.—A village of about 50 houses in 18° 57' 50" N. and 95° 1' 20" E., in the Htangouk revenue circle, Kama township, Thayet district on the Pyagyee a little mountain torrent which flows down from the Tswotpoung spur to the Made river.

ALAY-KHYOUNG.—A revenue circle with an area of 25 square miles occupying the extreme north of the Ramree township of the Kyouk-hpyoo district with about 1,600 inhabitants. Salt is made here to some extent. The land revenue in 1874-75 was Rs. 1,130 and the capitation-tax in 1875 Rs. 2,010.

ALAY-KYWON.—A revenue circle in the Ngapootaw township, Bassein district, with an estimated area of 65 square miles, occupying the central portion of the island, or rather mass of islands, which lie in the Bassein river between the Bassein and the Thek-kay-thoung mouths, the northern and southern boundaries being formed by the Lwongan and the Hnget-kywno creeks which flow between them. The country is flat and covered with jungle but low sand-hillocks appear to the south-west of Thek-kay-thoung village. Intersected by numerous anastomosing channels communication is usually carried on by water and the roads are little else than footpaths. The principal villages are Thek-kay-thoung and Oon-khyoung, close together on the bank of the Thek-kay-thoung, which together contain a population of some 1,000 souls. The inhabitants, who are principally Talaings, are mainly employed in salt making and in fishing. The land revenue in 1875-76 amounted to Rs. 2,563, the capitation-tax in 1876 to Rs. 2,517, the local funds revenue to Rs. 260, the gross revenue to Rs. 8,159, and the population to 1,893 souls.

ALAY-KYWON.—The north-western revenue circle of the Mye-boon township of the Kyouk-hpyoo district, covering an area of about 27 square miles and lying on the northern coast of Hunter's Bay and west of the Kyattseng, one of the numerous mouths of the Lemro river. In 1875 the population numbered 1,084 souls, the land revenue was Rs. 4,660 and the capitation-tax Rs. 1,380.

ALEE-RWA.—A village in the Gnyoung-le-beng circle of the Shwegyeng township, Shwe-gyeng district, to the west of the Tsittoung river, with about 650 inhabitants.

ALGUADA.*—A dangerous reef of rocks in the Bay of Bengal, bearing from Diamond Island, S.S.W. 3¼ leagues, level with the surface of the sea and extending north and south about 1¼ miles with outlying and detached rocks at a considerable distance from it. The reef now carries a light-house, standing in 15° 42′ N. lat. and 94° 11′10″ E. long., 144 feet high and built of granite masonry in alternate black and white bands which was commenced in February 1861 and finished in April 1865 and thus took nearly five years to build, besides two years of preparation. Considering the difficulty of procuring proper labour and the distance it was necessary to go to obtain suitable materials (the stone was brought from an island on the coast of Tenasserim) this light-house does not compare unfavourably with others of a similar type such as the Skerry Vohr and the Bell Rock. It bears a first order catadioptric light revolving once in a minute and visible 20 miles.

ALLAN-MYO.—A town in the Thayet district, situated in 19° 22′ 50″ N. latitude and 95° 17′ 20″ E. longitude on the left bank of the Irrawaddy close to the old Burman town of Myedai. During the second Burmese war when the fort at Myedai was occupied by British troops a native village sprang up close to it on the opposite or south bank of the Kye-nee stream which here enters the Irrawaddy. The situation being a favourable one as the outlet of the produce of a large tract of country on the east of the river the village rapidly rose into a town which has of late years been much improved and extended. A market has been built and an Assistant Commissioner who is also ex-officio Assistant Collector of Customs has been stationed here. The population in 1872 amounted to 9,697 souls. The town was named after Major Allan of the Madras Quartermaster-General's Department who demarcated the

* The reef is known to the Burmans as *Nagarit Kyouk* but to all others by its Portuguese name *Alguada*.

frontier line. The name was readily adopted by the Burmese, whose word for flag ("Alan") has much the same sound except that the emphasis is placed on the last syllable, as it was the most advanced post at which the British flag was hoisted.

ALO-DAW-RA.—A revenue circle in the Prome district on the North Naweng river which now contains four of the old village tracts. In 1876-77 the land revenue amounted to Rs. 2,759, the capitation-tax to Rs. 3,573, and the gross revenue to Rs. 6,924. In 1876 the inhabitants numbered 5,476.

ALO-DAW-RA.—A village in the Prome district on the North Naweng river seven miles in a direct line from its junction with the South Naweng and 19 miles north-east of Prome. A small body of Police is quartered in this village.

ALOON.—A little river in the Henzada district which rises in the Arakan Roma mountains and flowing through a narrow valley, of which the Tagoung-gyee spur, the northern boundary of the district in that direction, forms the northern watershed, falls into the Tshanda near Bhet-rai after a course of about 25 miles, at first to the north-east then east and for the last few miles south. The lower part of its course is rocky and boats cannot ascend even in the rains above Tatkoon, a distance of nine or ten miles. The banks are steep towards its source and flat near its mouth: on the banks are found teak, cutch, ironwood and bamboos.

ALOON.—A revenue circle in the Kyankheng township, lying in the north-western corner of the Henzada district and extending eastwards from the Arakan Roma mountains. The whole area is hilly and covered with forest containing, amongst other trees, Teak (*Tectona grandis*), Pyengma (*Lagerstrœmia Reginæ*) and Pyenggado (*Inga xylocarpa*). The cultivation is carried on almost entirely in *toungyas* where rice, cotton and other hill produce are grown. In 1876 it had a population of 1,634 souls and in 1876-77 the land revenue was Rs. 2,629, the capitation-tax Rs. 1,820, and the gross revenue demand Rs. 4,413.

AMAT.—A creek in the Kwengbouk circle, Myoungmya township, Bassein district, connecting the Rwe and the Pyamalaw, rather over 20 miles from the sea and navigable by the largest native boats.

AMHERST.*—A district in the Tenasserim division, occupying the country north, south and east of the mouths of the Salween, the Gyaing and the Attaran rivers, which unite near the town of Maulmain, the head-quarter station of the district and of the division, and including Bheeloogywon a large island west of and not a mile from Maulmain. From where the Thoung-yeng pours its waters into the Salween, in the extreme north, the north-western boundary of the district follows the latter river for some 40 miles, as far as the mouth of the Rwonzaleng, another of its tributaries. Here it turns northwest, and five or six miles up the latter river inclines west, then north, and then west again to the Doonthamee river, which it descends for some distance when inclining westward again it strikes the Kyouk-tsarit which it follows southwards to the eastern mouth of the Kyoon-iek. Turning west it follows the course of this natural canal to its western mouth in the Bheeleng river. Here it turns south and follows the Bheeleng to its mouth and thence the

---

* The district takes its name from the town of Amherst q. v.

coast line southward, outside Bheeloogywon and past Amherst, to a spot a few miles below the Re or Ye river where the Ma-hlwai spur comes down towards the sea. In the south the Ma-hlwai spur separates this district from Tavoy, and to the eastward the main range as far north as the source of the Thoung-yeng and thence that stream to its mouth form the boundaries between British and Siamese territory. The area comprised within these limits is 15,205 square miles. The major portion of the district, that part lying to the east of the Salween and of the sea-coast, was, with Tavoy and Mergui ceded to the British by the treaty of Yandaboo, which terminated the first Burmese war. The Tha-htoon sub-division, that is the country between the Salween and the Bheeleng, was annexed with Pegu by Lord Dalhousie after the second Burmese war and for some years formed a portion of the Shwe-gyeng district. The inconvenience of this arrangement led to its being adjoined to Amherst in 1864-65. Looked at on the map the district is seen to consist of five distinct tracts :—To the north, north-east, east and south-east of Maulmain are alluvial plains intersected by the Salween, the Gyaing and the Attaran and shut in on the east by the Dawna and on the west, south of Maulmain, by the comparatively low Toung-gnyo chain running parallel to the sea-coast; beyond these plains, in the extreme east, is the narrow and densely wooded mountainous region formed by the Dawna chain and its spurs ; from Maulmain southwards to the Ma-hlwai spur is a narrow strip of country between the Toung-gnyo chain and the sea, gradually widening out in the south into the valley of the Re and drained by numerous small streams with a general east and west direction ; west of the Salween is Tha-htoon with one main chain running up north and numerous other high grounds ; and lastly Bheeloogywon with as it were a backbone and ribs of hills forming the skeleton which supports and holds together rich rice lands.

To the eastward is the Dawna chain which starts from the

Mountains.

Moolai-yit hill (5,500 feet high) in the main range in 16° 5′ 45″ N. and 98° 42′ 3″ E., and extending N.N.W. for a distance of 200 miles divides the waters of the Houng-tharaw and of the Hlaing-bhwai from those of the Thoung-yeng. The general appearance of the chain is that of an-elevated wooded tableland of laterite worked by drainage into a mountainous form rather than that which would be produced by sudden upheaval. At intervals, however, are outcrops which, in uplifted crests of the underlying rocks extending into the bed of the Thoung-yeng and forming dangerous obstructions to navigation, look like indications of powerful volcanic disturbance.

Starting from Moolai-yit, an immense mass of rock throwing out innumerable spurs, the mountains in the south-east and south are formed by the main dividing range and its offshoots, the central axis of the mountainous system which drains itself into the Gulf of Siam and the Bay of Bengal. At the head waters of the Thoung-yeng, which has its source amongst these mountains, is a high tableland of laterite, 1,100 feet above the sea, covered with Eng forest and dotted with alluvial spots clothed with evergreen forest or cultivated by Karengs. Westward is the valley of the Houng-tharaw, bounded on the west by a low range of hills of soft wavy outline emanating from the high tableland of Pantoonaw and the sandstone formations round Thoungboon (3,472 feet above the sea level). Here and there the peaked and jagged summits of isolated limestone rocks may be seen rising out of the plain, some half hidden by struggling vegetation others bare and white. For some distance southward the country west of the main range preserves its character of softly-undulating hills but this is soon lost in barren limestone ridges.

There are several passes across the main range from this district to Siamese territory. The first, which can in strictness hardly be called a pass from Burma to Siam as it lies wholly in the latter, requires notice as it is on one of the highways from British territory to Bangkok. Myawadee, an old and once fortified town on the left bank of the Thoung-yeng in 16° 42′ 15″ N. and 98° 32′ 30″ E., can be reached in seven days. Rahaing in Siam lies 45 miles almost due east of Myawadee. The route between them, being much frequented, is clear and open and the journey can thus be performed in two days. In the south-west monsoon boats go down the Meinam from Rahaing to Bangkok in eight days. During the hot weather it takes 15, owing to the diminished velocity of the current and the winding of the channel which leads through innumerable sand-banks and shoals. Another pass leads from the Houng-tharaw river in 15°41′ 19″ N. and 98° 35′ E. to the Siamese village of Phra May-klaung the capital of the district of that name, where the Governor resides. There is a track called the Menanda road up a river of that name, a tributary of the Houng-tharaw, and thence near the main watershed northwards to the sources of the Thoung-yeng. The next pass is by the Three Pagodas. The journey up the Attaran is made by boat as far as Kannee, a police station, and thence by elephants across the watershed. The average time occupied in the journey from Maulmain to Bangkok by this route is 25 days—eight days to the Three Pagodas and 17 from the pass to Bangkok. The view from the summit of this pass is thus described by Assistant Surgeon Helfer who visited it in 1838 or 1839 :—" One of the most beautiful sights " I ever enjoyed was visiting that famous pass. It is a high tableland, upon " which, again, a number of mountain ridges is planted. I ascended one solitary " limestone rock, lying to the north of the three heaps of stones indicating " the former site of the Three Pagodas. The view from thence, though exhi- " biting no snowy peaks or glaciers, was in many respects grander than the " scenery in Switzerland, on the Appenines, or the Jura Alps. It was an " unbounded view, ridges after ridges in succeeding lines running in the " same direction emerged one above the other: in the Siamese territories " I counted eight different chains."

From the Tsadaik hill of the main range, in 15° 17′ 25″ N. and 98° 15′ E., the Toung-gnyo chain extends N.N.W. to Maulmain forming the western water-shed of the Attaran. These hills, nowhere of any very great elevation, finally disappear north of Maulmain in a small island in the Salween called Goung-tse-kywon.

North of Maulmain and east of the Salween is a short range of lime-stone rocks called Zwai-ka-beng some 16 miles in length.

To the west of the Salween a range of hills runs northward from Martaban of which one peak, the Koolama-toung, east of the Poung circle, is over 3,000 feet high. At the Zeng-gyaik peak a spur is thrown off to the N.N.W. which extends to Kawthan close to Tha-htoon and forms the western limit of the Dheba-rien valley: at Reng-gnyiem the Reng-gnyiem, which rises in this valley, flows through a gorge westward to the sea. The main chain continues northward and terminates at Kama-thaing a little to the south of the Kyoon-iek, the northern boundary of the district. There are two passes across these hills; the northern by a cart track from Kyouk-tsarit, a little village on the stream of the same name at the eastern mouth of the Kyoon-iek, to Thien-tshiep, a rising village on the, as yet unfinished, main road from Martaban to Toung-nyoo, 13 miles north of Tha-htoon; and the southern by a metalled road from Zemathway, a village on a small and partially artificially made stream, 4½ miles to Tha-htoon, through the Gaw gap where the Gaw stream flows westward through the pass and under the road. By this route large quantities of unhusked rice are annually exported from the neighbourhood of Tha-htoon to Maulmain vid the Bhenglaing and Salween rivers. As many as 200 carts a day are said to traverse this road in the height of the season.

Running from north to south and extending from one end of Bheeloo-gywon to the other is a low range with short spurs which would seem to have been at one time connected with the Martaban hills before the Salween forced its way or was forced between them. Near the centre of the island the hills suddenly dip and form a narrow pass but a few feet, comparatively, above the sea-level where nestled amongst trees, lies Khyoung-tshoon the principal village of the township.

Owing to the mountainous nature of a great portion of the country the rivers are very numerous but except the Salween, the Gyaing, with its tributaries the Houng-tharaw and the Hlaing-bhwai, the Attaran and the Thoung-yeng there are none of any great size. The Salween, the sources of which, far away to the north somewhere in unexplored China, have never been seen by European eye, falls into the sea at Maulmain. Notwithstanding the distance of its source it cannot rank for commercial value with any of the great rivers of Asia. Its channel is broad, shallow and obstructed by numerous island shoals and though navigable by country boats as far as the passless rapids just below the mouth of the Thoung-yeng and in reaches above that point is, except in its southern mouth, unfit for the accommodation of sea-going vessels which cannot ascend much above Maulmain. Immediately below the town of Martaban, which lies on its right bank opposite Maulmain, it is divided into two branches by Bheeloo island. The southern, the entrance for ships, is at its mouth, between Amherst and Bheeloo-gywon or Bheeloo island, not less than seven miles wide, and its northern mouth, dangerous and altogether impracticable for shipping, is still broader. Below the mouth of the Thoung-yeng it receives from the north-west the waters of the Rwonzaleng, a river of the Salween Hill Tracts district and still lower, from the same direction, the Bhenglaing brings to it the waters collected by the Doonthamee, the Kyouk-tsarit and other small rivers and during the rains a considerable share of the spill of the Bheeleng which formerly flooded the Thien-tshiep and Tha-htoon plains but has been forced round the Martaban hills and into the Kyouk-tsarit by an embankment extending from Doonwoon to Kama-thaing. At Maulmain it is joined from the eastward by the Gyaing and the Attaran.

The Gyaing, formed by the junction of the Hlaing-bhwai and the Houng-tharaw, flows almost due west. It is a stream of considerable breadth but of no great depth and its channel is obstructed by islands and sandbanks. It is navigable for ordinary boats during all seasons throughout its course.

The Hlaing-bhwai rises in the north of the district and flows southwards to Gyaing village where it is joined by the Houng-tharaw from the south, the united waters flowing westward. Its principal tributary is the Dagyaing which joins it from the east about 30 miles above Gyaing. In the rains it is navigable by boats to above Hlaing-bhwai, 45 miles up and 85 miles from Maulmain, but in the dry season the sand bar below that village can be crossed only at high water springs.

The Houng-tharaw rises in Siamese territory to the south-south-east of Maulmain and crossing the frontier in 15° 41′ 19′ N. and 98° 35′ E., flows in a N.N.W. direction at first amongst the spurs of the main range, uniting with the Hlaing-bhwai in about 16° 34′ N., and 98° 3′ E. A peculiar feature of the Houng-tharaw valley is that it consists of several table lands separated by abrupt descents. The soil is a sandy loam which would seem to have been well cultivated in former years. The current is exceedingly rapid in the rains and boats then ascend with difficulty. It is navigable beyond Meetan which is 40 miles from the mouth and 80 miles from Maulmain. One of the main feeders is the Kawkariet which joins it from the east, and in the rains forms the route to Kawkariet village and thence viá Myawadee to Siam. In the dry season this little streamlet is not navigable and the whole journey from the Houng-tharaw is made by land.

The Attaran, which drains the tract of country between the Toung-gnyo chain and the low undulating hills west of the Houng-tharaw is, like the Gyaing, formed by the junction of two main streams and fed by numerous rivulets. The Zamee, navigable by boats for 40 miles from its mouth but difficult of ascent by reason of the rapidity of the current, and the Wengraw unite a few miles above the site of ancient Attaran to form this narrow deep and sluggish river from which, 60 miles above Maulmain, the light of day is almost shut out by high banks and dense masses of overhanging foliage. In 1827 Mr. Crawfurd, the Civil Commissioner, ascended as far as Attaran in the Diana, a small river steamer.

The Thoung-yeng, which from its source in 16° 27′ 47″ N., and 98° 50′ 50″ E. to its mouth in 17°50′ 40″ N. and 97° 45′ 35″ E., forms the north-eastern boundary of the district, rises in the main range of mountains and has a general N.N W course of about 197 miles to the Salween. Its breadth varies considerably, in some places narrowing to 100 feet and in others widening out to 1,000 Its course is filled with rapids and falls rendering navigation impossible. Near its mouth it receives from the north the waters of the Hmaing-lwon-gyee a large affluent the whole length of which is in foreign territory.

The remaining streams are small and of but little present importance. The Rwonzaleng, a river of the Salween Hill Tracts, joins the Salween from the north-north-west below the Thoung-yeng and still lower down the Bhenglaing brings the collected waters of numerous small rivers and torrents. The Bheeleng, which rises in the mass of mountains forming the Salween Hill Tracts, falls into the sea considerably to the north and a little to the west of the northern mouth of the Salween and is, in the lower portion of its course, the western boundary of the district. The Wakharoo rises in the Toung-gnyo chain and passing through a hilly country flows due westward to the sea near Amherst; its mouth affords an excellent harbour. The Re, in the extreme south, rises in the main range and falls into the sea in 15° 5′ N.: it is an inconsiderable stream and is not accessible except during the fine season a group of reefs and breakers about four miles out to sea rendering approach difficult, if not impossible, at other periods of the year.

Off the coast between the mouths of the Wakharoo and the Re, a little south of the 16th parallel, is Double Island on which, at a cost of Rs. 90,340, has been erected a light-house showing a first order dioptric fixed light with a cata-dioptric mirror visible 19 miles and first lighted in December 1866.

Geology.

Of the geology of the district but little is known as it has never been regularly and completely examined by a professed geologist. Mr. Theobald of the Geological Survey of India had several opportunities of examining portions of it and a brief notice by him was published in the *Memoirs of the Geological Survey of India*, Vol. X., Part 2.

Dr. Oldham divides the rocks which cover so large a portion of Tenasserim into a lower division, which he terms the " Mergui," series well developed in the south, and an upper, or " Moulmein," series largely developed to the north and the most conspicuous member of which is the massive limestone which forms so picturesque a feature in the country round Maulmain and in the Salween valley. The entire thickness of these two divisions is placed at about 9,000, and the age of the whole fixed as Palæozoic, the Maulmain beds being provisionally placed in the " lower carboniferous group of European geologists." Since Dr. Oldham's account of these beds was written nothing has been added to our knowledge of them save that from the evidence of a few fossils procured from Zwai-ka-beng, a limestone hill forming a prominent landmark above Maulmain popularly known as the " Duke of York's nose ;" the limestone in question may certainly be pronounced to be of the age of the carboniferous limestone of Europe. Dr. Oldham remarks that this limestone is more sparingly developed to the south than in Martaban but it is probable that the limestone met with in the Mergui Archipelago belongs to the same formation. The most marked feature of this limestone is its mode of occurrence in steeply-scarped hills the sides of which overhang, as may be seen in the case of the hills near Maulmain which rise abruptly from the low inundated plains between the Gyaing and the Attaran rivers and exhibit the precise appearance of what they undoubtedly were at no remote geological period, sea-girt rocks such as still stud the Mergui Archipelago and which from their position in low-lying alluvial plains even now, during the rains, are approachable only by boats through a mimic freshwater sea. The exploration of the caves in these hills—of which there are no less than 23 groups in the district, each distinguished by its proper name, scattered over the country and all more or less ornamented by pious Booddhists and filled with images of Gaudama and of Rahans—has been suggested in the hope of enlarging our knowledge of an extinct local fauna such as, in Europe, has so often rewarded cave research ; but as regards all caves similarly situated to those near Maulmain the chances are much against finding anything to repay the labour expended, as, form their former position as rocky islands in the sea, it is improbable that they ever afforded retreat to any vertebrata save the edible nest-building swallow or a few bats. In the case, however, of caves situated in limestone rocks at a greater elevation and consequently not like the others guarded from approach, by the surrounding sea the case is different and such caves hold out promise of a rich harvest to future explorers.

It is probable that this group may prove to be metalliferous, as it is traversed by the same series of granite and elvan dykes as the older crystalline rocks of the district ; and these may not improbably be connected with the development of the ores of tin, lead, iron and copper occurring in the Salween Hill Tracts. The lead ore at Toung-nyoo occurs in the next group, but possibly both this group and the next will equally be found to be the repositories of the metallic deposits of the Salween Hill Tracts whether these should ultimately prove of economic value or not.

To the next group the term " Martaban " is applied, for convenience merely, from its large development in Martaban. Of its age we know nothing, but, petrologically considered, it is a group of true crystalline rocks undistinguishable in character from the ordinary gneissose rocks of Bengal. Near Martaban specimens of schorl rock and fragments of schorl crystals of not less than three inches in diameter have been found which the natives who picked them up evidently supposed might have some connection with coal. Micaceous schists are common but in Martaban hornblendic rock would seem less abundant than in the same group of rocks in India. To this group Mr. Theobald refers much of the so-termed granite of the country lying to the east of the Salween.

From the little he saw of the relation of the Martaban and Maulmain groups he judged that, in places at least, the former constituted the higher hills whilst the lower country was occupied by the latter ; but his opportunities were, he considers, too limited to allow of safely generalizing from such data or in authorizing him to say if the last group rests immediately on the present one in Martaban or if any representatives of the " Mergui " group of the southern provinces intervene, as is probably the case. The denudation, however, to which these Palæozoic beds have been subjected has been enormous and to this is due the curiously isolated appearance of so many of the hills and ranges in the vicinity of Maulmain and elsewhere.

Hot springs exist in eleven spots in various parts of this district but always in more or less close proximity to the limestone outcrops. The largest and most important are those at " Attaran Reboo* " (reboo signifies hot water), on the Attaran which can be reached in two tides by boat from Maulmain and, according to Dr. Helfer's description, belong to the carbonated class. They are situated about two miles inland from the old town of Attaran and of them Dr. Helfer writes.—"There are 10 hot springs, or rather hot-water ponds, of which I could only examine the nearest as the access to the others was through deep water at 130° Fahrenheit. This one was a semi-circular pond, about 50 feet in circumference; in one place it was 35 feet deep. The quantity of carbonic acid which the springs evolve seems to render the neighbourhood peculiarly adapted to support vegetable life. The ground around the spring is strongly impregnated with iron, and the water which runs over the ochre mud has a strong styptic taste. The springs on the Attaran approach in their composition nearest to the celebrated spring of Töplitz. Their medical properties would render them excellent remedies in a number of diseases; liver-complaints would find a powerful remedy in them." The Burmese are aware of the medicinal properties of the water in these springs and employ it in fever and in some forms of cutaneous affections. They use it externally in the form of a bath when cooled and as a vapour bath when hot; in the latter case the patient sits on a bamboo platform erected over the spring and under a large inverted basket covered with cloths to retain the steam. Dr. Morton

---

* The other hot springs are at Ka-hgnyaw, Pa-nga, Thoon-tshay Thoon-tshoo, Mai-kala, Oon-kharien, Myawadee, Dham-matha, Doonreng and Poung.

found on analysis that the water contains a considerable quantity of calcareous matter and that the tufa which it deposits on the margin is a carbonate of lime. The springs appear to rise from the mountain limestone and thus to hold a geological position similar to that of the hot springs of Great Britain most of which rise from strata below the coal and hence from or through the limestone.

Large areas on all the hills are occupied by evergreen forest abounding in many valuable species. This is particularly the case with the Dawna chain, the watershed between the valleys of the Thoung-yeng and of the Hlaing-bhwai and Houng-tharaw rivers, where the timber attains stupendous proportions and where *Hopea odorata, Dipterocarpus alata* and other valuable trees are abundant.

Forests.

The teak localities are some of the most important in the province. For forest conservancy purposes they have been divided into the Doonthamee, the Hlaing-bhwai, the Lower Salween, the Thoung-yeng, the Houng-tharaw and the Attaran. The Doonthamee forests, between the Salween and the Doonthamee rivers stretching down as far south as Hpagat about 32 miles from Maulmain, are estimated to cover an area of 60 square miles and in 1859 to have contained 14,340 1st-class trees. They are on dry and even or undulating ground. The stems are branched and frequently crooked and the timber is generally small but hard. The great value of these tracts is that they produce excellent "crooks" for ship-building. The Salween and the Doonthamee rivers afford the means of transit but in many instances the timber must be dragged or carted overland for considerable distances before reaching a waterway.

The Hlaing-bhwai and Lower Salween forests, situated east of the Salween on the Hlaing-bhwai river and its feeders, are valuable mainly from the supply of crooked timber which they have yielded almost since the occupation of the country. Teak here grows on even ground; no trace of it can be found on the hills which skirt the valley of the Hlaing-bhwai river although these hills are covered with similar trees and bamboos to those which are usually found associated with teak. The teak-producing forests are dry and open and much exposed to jungle fires. Pyengma is frequently associated with teak. The growth of the tree is very inferior. Almost all large trees are forked with short stems that are crooked or of irregular shape. Much of this may be ascribed to the remains of old *toungya* cultivation, but it is principally owing to the fact that the best trees of good size have been removed and that in a locality like this the teak does not naturally attain a fine regular stature.

The Thoung-yeng forests, on the hills forming the western watershed of the Thoung-yeng river cover a considerable proportion of the tract and contain trees of gigantic size and of most regular growth. Dr. Brandis, who visited the forests, states that the first 40 miles from the river's mouth are without any teak forests of importance. Here the mountains approach close to the Thoung-yeng or dense evergreen forest covers the level ground between them and the river's bank. On the Shan side there are teak forests of great value in this part of the river but only a few scattered trees on the British. The south-western tributary streams drain some valuable teak localities of some importance, hedged in almost on all sides by dense evergreen forest which covers the flanks of the mountains and higher hills and which here and there stretches down to the banks of the Thoung-yeng. Teak is found in bamboo forest or in the mixed dry forest in which Pyenggado forms a prominent feature but there are also extensive tracts covered with bamboo forest or with the mixed dry forest in which not a single teak tree is to be met with.

Higher up the hills are covered with impenetrable forests never touched by the hand of man where the trees attain a height which, though not equal to that of the gigantic fir of California, would scarcely be believed had it not been ascertained by careful measurement. A specimen of a species of the *Dipterocarpus* family had a girth of 20 feet and a height to the first branch of 160 feet. The forest is so dense that the height of the trees can only be measured on the banks of a stream or on the sides of a hill and in such localities the forest appears like a green unbroken wall standing up nearly 200 feet from the ground. Teak is not found in forests of this kind but it is abundant on the northern hills not only in the Thoung-yeng valley but also in that of the Mai-hpa-lai river, a tributary of the former, running nearly parallel to it but in an opposite direction, and on the sandstone of the hills between the two are found some of the finest teak localities in British Burma in one of which 550 1st class trees were observed on an area of one-third of a square mile. The stature of the trees is tall and regular : they stand up in the forest like so many wax tapers. The size may be gathered from the following measurements taken at random from among the larger trees of the Mai-hpa-lai forest :—

Girth,	6 ft.	Length of stem to first branch,	72 ft. 6 in.
,,	10 ft.	,, ,,	77 ft. 9 in.
,,	10 ft. 4 in.	,, ,,	70 ft.
,,	16 ft. 4 in.	,, ,,	84 ft.
,,	12 ft.	,, ,,	66 ft.

But the teak localities are not spread over the whole of this part of the Thoung-yeng valley. Large tracts, especially on the undulating hills near the main river, are covered with dry and open *Dipterocarpus* forest interspersed occasionally with the Thoung-yeng fir (*Pinus Massoniana*, Lamb.) but without a trace of teak except on the margin towards the lower ground along the smaller streams.

The Houng-tharaw forests were visited by Captain Tremenhere in 1841. He particularly mentions teak localities with trees having straight stems of great dimensions but of very slow growth. Captain Guthrie (1845) estimated the number of the teak trees on the Houng-tharaw at 1,600, of which 473 belonged to the 1st class or in girth above six feet. Captain Guthrie mentions that in the forests on some of the tributaries there were trees abandoned that had been girdled 10 years previously. Mr. E. O'Riley, in a paper entitled " Observations in connection with the route across to the head of the Houng-tharaw river," states that " a few patches of teak, of small extent and widely separated, are found on the banks of the streams falling into the Houng-tharaw the whole, however, rifled of the best trees ; and at one locality situated above the falls of the 99 islands, where, owing to the favourable nature of the soil (composed of the detritus of granite and schistose rocks mixed with the alluvium), the trees were of magnificent growth and dimensions the teak had been completely annihilated and, after conversion into short logs, had been abandoned in consequence, it was said, of some obstruction which prevented their conveyance through the channels of the islands. Unlike the large teak of the forests on the Weng-raw and Zimmo (*Zamee*), this patch appears to have been composed of the most valuable timber for mast pieces : the logs, after an exposure on the bank of the river for the last ten years, with the exception of being weather-worn outside are sound throughout some of them measuring 10 cubits in girth, and from the original spar converted into four lengths of 10 to 12 cubits each." Blasting operations have within the last few years been carried on to clear the channel of the Houng-tharaw and afford an exit to the timber of these forests. In 1873-74, 545 tons of stone were thus removed near the " Ninety-nine islands."

The Attaran group of forests is situated on both banks of the Zamee and Wengraw streams, which by their junction in the hilly country to the south of the great plains round Maulmain form the Attaran river, and covers an estimated area of 100 square miles. For some years after the cession of the Martaban and Tenasserim provinces the timber in most of these forests was so recklessly and indiscriminately felled, the grantees working for speedy returns, that Dr. Falconer in 1850 reported that " but for the timber in two small " reserved forests it would now be a matter of record only that teak of large " size has ever been produced on the Attaran," and even these two " instead of " being intact forests have been partially worked by trespass by the adjoining " forest holders." In 1860 Dr. Brandis examined the forests and found that in those on the Wengraw the growth of teak was good " almost the whole of the " large trees having tall straight stems free from branches to a considerable " height but the greater number were hollow or attacked with epiphytic " ficus or injured in their growth by a load of creepers" whilst " with few " exceptions all good trees above five cubits in girth and most of those " above four cubits have been removed, numerous stumps indicating their " former existence and the numerous logs, once good but half destroyed by a " fire, remaining as a proof of the wasteful mode of working." Similarly the result of an examination of the forests further east on the Zamee shewed vast numbers of stumps remaining in what had been one of the finest teak local-ities. Higher up the stream the forests were poorer and from one tract very little timber had been removed but the trees " had been killed in a " wholesale manner, many had since fallen or been destroyed by fire, and the " traveller finds himself in a forest of dead fallen trees." For some years after 1824 hardly any restrictions were placed on the grantees ; subse-quently, on Dr. Wallich's recommendation, the forests were worked on account of Government but in 1829 they were again thrown open to private indivi-duals. In 1841 the Commissioner, Mr. Blundell, proposed the resumption of all permits and the leasing or farming out of the tracts under new rules, which were sanctioned by the Government in the same year. In 1842, when the forests were visited by Captain Tremenheere, it was found that the rules had been disregarded and new rules were framed and sanctioned. These three sets of rules under which licenses or leases for cutting timber in these forests were granted may be thus summarized :—

1. Rules of 1829, without any penalties.

2. Rules of 1841, imposing the penalty of immediate resumption on the breach of any of the rules.

3. Rules of 1842, substituting fines and other penalties for immediate resumption.

In 1845, the utter neglect of all rules continuing, the Commissioner summarily resumed several forests under the penalty clause of 1841 ; but this measure was disapproved of by the Government of India and his orders were cancelled. From this time the supply of timber gradually diminished and the northern forests on the Thoung-yeng and Upper Salween took the place of those on the Attaran and its affluents. In 1853 Sir A. Bogle cancelled a number of permits which were in the hands of native foresters who entirely neglected their forests not even bringing timber down. In 1860 Dr. Brandis, having carefully examined these forests, proposed that they should be left in the hands of private parties, hoping that this measure would, considering the objections at that time felt to the administration of forests by Government, " prove the safety valve for the administration of forests in India." Subsequently, however, they were declared reserved Government forests and brought under the general forest rules of the province. Such tracts as lapsed to the Government were worked under one year permits for the removal of seasoned timber only while in the tracts the tenure of which was recognized and for which 30 year permits had been given the prohibition of the removal of timber under 7 ft. 6 ins. in girth was rigidly enforced.

Teak, however, is not the only valuable timber tree. The Padouk furnishes a beautiful hard heavy wood ; the Anan (*Fragroea fragrans*) a timber which hardens under water ; Pyengma possesses strength, pliability and durability ; and Thenggan (*Hopea odorata*) is much used for boats ; besides these numerous other kinds exist in abundance the wood of which could well be used for furniture and for building and other purposes.*

The history of the country now comprised within the limits of the Amherst district is little else than an account of petty wars and marauding incursions. Claimed by the Siamese on the east and by the Peguans on the west, until the one was driven out and the other conquered by the Burmans, the country had no rest for many centuries. Martaban, on the right bank of the Salween, was founded in 1269 A. D. by a Burman monarch who reigned in Pagan—Narapadeetseethoo—" on a rocky promontory with the country of the Shans (Siamese) on the east and the sea on the west;" and this sovereign, whose great ambition it was to spread the doctrines of Booddha, planted on the point a colony of thirty families to take care of the Pagoda which he had erected and appointed Aliengma as Governor. At this period the major portion of the district, that lying to the east of the Salween was Siamese territory. Aliengma, summoned to Court by Narapadeetseethoo's son and successor, escaped into the Shan country and Talapya was appointed Governor in his stead. Aliengma soon returned and, aided by the Shans, drove out and killed Talapya and resumed the governorship, probably as tributary to the King of Siam. For many years the Burman kingdom was harassed by the Chinese from the north and its sovereigns were unable to exert any authority in the south. Magadoo, a native of Martaban and a trader by profession, having travelled into Siam had risen in favour at Court and been appointed Governor of the capital during one of the absences of the King. He eloped with the King's daughter and, returning to Martaban, treacherously

History.

---

* The felling without permission of Padouk, Anan, Pyengma and Thenggan, and of some other kinds is prohibited in certain tracts throughout the Province. See Introduction : *sub tit.* FORESTS.

killed Aliengma, seized the reins of Government in 1281 and was recognized by the King of Siam who bestowed on him a title, and from this time he is known in history as King Wareeyoo. The ambition of Wareeyoo was not satisfied. North of Martaban was a country called Kanpalanee and on one occasion of the King of that country going into the forests on a hunting excursion Wareeyoo sallied forth, pillaged the capital and carried away captive the King's daughter, eventually making himself master of the country. About this time the King of Pegu also had succeeded in effecting his independence and the two monarchs entered into friendly relations. The Chinese army from the north having overcome the King of Pagan advanced south and attacked Pegu upon which the King of Martaban joined his forces with those of Pegu and defeated the invaders. Quarrels soon arose and eventually Wareeyoo annexed Pegu. Wareeyoo was succeeded by his brother who was killed in a rebellion and was succeeded by his nephew Zaw-aw-bheng-hmaing. In his reign the boundaries of the kingdom were widely extended, Labong, Tavoy and Tenasserim being added to dominions which already stretched nearly to Prome on the north and to Bassein on the west. From this time the history of Martaban merges in that of Pegu. Between 1563 and 1581 A. D. Cæsar Frederic the Venetian visited Martaban : he found there " ninety Portugal merchants and other base men which had fallen at difference with the Governor of the city." The King of Pegu " had gone with a million and four hundred thousand men to conquer the kingdom of Siam," and in his absence some of the Portuguese had killed four or five of the inhabitants in a street quarrel ; " the captain of the Portugals would not deliver these men, but rather set himself up with all the rest in arms." From this time forward for many years the country was continually the theatre of wars and rebellions. The Kings of Burma gradually recovered some of their lost territory but only to lose it again, whilst the Kings of Siam took advantage of the disturbances to re-annex the site of the present Maulmain and the country to the south and to carry their arms across the Salween. In the latter half of the eighteenth century Aloungbhoora and his successors conquered the country and retained possession till after the first Anglo-Burmese war, when the Burmese were forced to cede to the British the whole tract lying to the east of the Salween : the remaining portion was annexed after the second war by Lord Dalhousie.

Of architectural remains worthy of notice there are not a few in this district. The Kalaw Pagoda, towards the northern end of Bheeloo island, is supposed to have been erected over a relic of Gaudama during the reign of Asoka, King of Kapilavastu, the great protector of Booddhism—a period to which the Burmans are fond of attributing the erection of very many of their sacred buildings. On this island alone are some sixty of these structures, held to be of great antiquity, of which no written histories are in existence.

Architectural remains.

On the hill just above the town of Martaban is a Pagoda the foundation of which, in 1282 A.D., is attributed to King Wareeyoo. Its Burman name *Myathiendhan*, which is by some supposed to be a corruption of Myathiendeng, is, according to the Burman records, derived from the fact of a large emerald having been placed in it. The Burmese account of its erection is that the King of Ceylon sent an Embassy to obtain certain relics of Gaudama buried here under eight pillars ; the relics could not be found but the pillars were carried to Ceylon and the Pagoda raised on the site. Its Talaing name is Kyaik Moothamien. Here also are the Shwe Dagon, so called from having been founded at the same time as the great Shwe-Dagon Pagoda in Rangoon, the Kyaik-hpyeng-koo or Doo-an, founded in 1288 A.D. and the Kyaik-kha-lwon-bhwon, the erection of which is placed in the sixth century B.C., during Gaudama's apocryphal visit to this country. The Kyaik-kha-pan Pagoda was founded in 1199 A.D. by Aliengma to commemorate the conversion of the inhabitants by Gaudama who had been invited to the spot to be eaten but whose preaching changed the evil intention of his hosts. The Shwe-koo is of a much later date, having been built by the Governor of Martaban in 1785 A.D. by order of Bhodaw-Bhoora, the then reigning sovereign of Burma. The Khyan-tha-gyee Pagoda at Zetawon close to Martaban was built in 1299 A.D. by King Tsaw-theng-hmaing, and was restored in 1785 A.D., by order of King Bhodaw-Bhoora. The Talaing name, which has the same meaning as the Burmese, viz. " cool, comfortable," is *Kyaik-khaba* and was given to the structure from a tradition that Gaudama had pronounced the waters of a neighbouring tank to be cool and pleasant. At Zeng-kyaik in about 16° 42′ N., about 18 miles north-west of Martaban on the range of hills which extends towards Tha-htoon, is one of the numerous Pagodas supposed to have been built in the reign of Asoka and to contain one of Gaudama's hairs. The most ancient and the most celebrated of all is the Tha-htoon Pagoda which bears in its construction evidences of its great age though it is certain that it cannot claim the origin given to it by the Burmese chroniclers according to whom it was founded in 594 B.C. by Theeharaga King of Thoowonnabhoome, of which country Tha-htoon was the capital, to commemorate the visit of Gaudama. During the reign of Tsawta-koomma it was rebuilt by Thawna and Ootara, the two Booddhist apostles who had been commissioned by the great Booddhist council held at Pataliputra in 241 B.C. to teach and preach in Pegu.

South of the town of Maulmain there are a large number of Pagodas of which little or nothing is known but that all except two have no claim to any great antiquity; some have been built since the occupation of the country by the English. The Nattoung and the Toung-gnyo are said to have been built in the time of Ramapoora, the original founder of Maulmain.

In Maulmain, on the ridge of hills which runs through the town, are several Pagodas of which the Kyaik-than-lan, occupying a commanding position on the Northern spur of the hill over against Martaban, is the principal. According to the received traditions the spot was first selected by the Siamese during an abortive attempt to invade Pegu and the present structure was afterwards built by the hermit Thee-gnya or Theela who enshrined therein a hair of Gaudama. Many years later it was repaired by the King of Martaban. When the British occupied Tenasserim it was almost a ruin but was repaired in 1831 by Moung Tawlai, a native Extra Assistant Commissioner, at a cost of Rs. 1,000 raised by private subscription. The name is supposed to be a corruption of Kyaik-Shan-lan, or " the Pagoda of the overthrow of the Siamese." On the same hills, farther south, is the Oozeena Pagoda so called from the name of its last restorer who in 1838 expended Rs. 600 on it; its original name was Kyaik-padhan, derived from the white hill on which it stands; the Burmese believe it to have been founded during the reign of Asoka and to contain a hair of Gaudama. On the same hills are three small and undoubtedly very ancient Pagodas, also supposed to contain Gaudama's hairs : the Pathada, not far from the Kyaik-than-lan, the Dhatke and the Kyaik-matan. The Kyaik-hpanee, supposed to have been built about 1,000 years ago by the Peguan King Bhanai-tsiet-tsaw to commemorate a victory over the Siamese (Bhanai in Talaing means victory) is situated close to the water's edge on the north point of the land on which the town stands. In 1863 it was enlarged by one Moung Shwe Bhoo. In the plain west of the hills is another small Pagoda, also said to contain a hair of Gaudama, built very many years ago but enlarged and restored about 1838 at a cost of Rs. 1,000, raised by public subscription, by a Booddhist priest of considerable note whose name "in religion" was no less formidable than "Tshaya-daw-gyee-aniet Wonthakalayana Tietkhalengkara Teereetedzha Mahadhammaraza Tierazagooroo." To the south of the town are two very old Pagodas supposed to contain relics of Gaudama.

Besides Pagodas the ruins of ancient towns remain as signs of the former glory of the kingdom. Tha-htoon and Martaban, once the capital of a powerful monarchy, still exist but Myawaddee in the valley of the Thoungyeng a little south of the 17th degree of north latitude and Attaran on the river of the same name, once great cities, are now almost entirely deserted ; the former contained some 50,000 inhabitants and was enclosed by a regularly built high and thick wall, of which the remains are still traceable, with a deep double ditch, which formed a parallelogram, the longer sides two miles in length and the shorter one mile. Traders in large numbers from Siam and from the neighbouring States resorted to it and annually caravans arrived from Muangla and from China whilst from the west came European goods, imported into Martaban, and salt from the coast.

The parts of the district which are most cultivated are the Tha-htoon subdivision, principally in its south-western portion,
Agriculture and products.
Bheeloo island, the lower part of the country between the Salween and the Hlaingbhwai, the plain land east of Maulmain, the north-western borders of the lower portion of the Houng-tharaw and the tract between the Toung-gnyo range and the sea from Maulmain southwards towards Amherst and in the extreme south near Re. The Tha-htoon sub-division furnishes about five-sixteenths of the cultivated area of the whole district and of this four-fifths are in the Martaban township of which the western portion is the richer. Bheeloogywon and the large township of Zaya, between Maulmain and Amherst, have about the same area under cultivation and together include about three-eighths of that of the whole district.

In the mountainous country forming the Houngtharaw and southern portion of the Gyaing Attaran townships there is but little cultivation whilst almost the whole of the plains between the Salween and the undulating ground bordering the Hlaingbhwai and those between the Houngtharaw and the Attaran are inundated during the rains and at some periods are several feet under water. In parts of the Gyaing Than-lweng township, especially near Htoon-aing on the Salween about twenty miles above Maulmain, inhabited by Talaings who or whose fathers emigrated from Pegu in a body after the first Burmese war, and along the banks of the Gyaing rice is extensively grown.

The cultivated area is increasing markedly; in 1869-70 there were 318 square miles under tillage ; five years later, in 1873-74, 401 and in 1875-76 461. Rice is the main produce: in 1875-76 2,46,022 acres or 390 square miles, that is more than the whole cultivated area in 1869-70, were planted with this grain, and the average rate of produce per acre being 1,635 lbs. the gross produce of unhusked rice in this district was about 179,574 tons, of which about 117,421 were exported in the shape of husked rice. Dhanee palms and betel palms are largely cultivated; Akyab alone has a more extensive area of the former and Shwe-gyeng of the latter. Of tobacco a small quantity is raised both by Burmans and by Karengs, by the former principally on the sand banks in the Hpagat circle at the junction of the Salween and the Bhenglaing, by the latter in small patches for their own use; sessamum is grown by the latter and sold to the former who express the oil. Of sugar-cane plantations there were 1,189 acres in 1875-76: some of the cane is exported to Rangoon and from some sugar is made for local consumption and for export. Though but little cane is grown in Tha-htoon this sub-division has the largest number of mills. The cane is cultivated in the neighbouring Shwe-gyeng district on the banks of the Bheeleng, where in the season a brisk trade is carried on, purchasers going up from Tha-htoon. Excellent cotton might be grown but at present other crops offer a better return ; for some years small quantities have been exported to India, Arakan, Tavoy and Mergui but it is principally cultivated by the Karengs on the hill sides for home consumption. Considering the very large extent of the district and the proportion of that extent which is mountainous and unsuited for regular cultivation the number of Toungyas or Hill gardens is not large, even Thayetmyo and Prome in the northern portion of the valley of the Irrawaddy having more; this is mainly due to the sparseness of the population which is congregated in the lower parts leaving the hills and mountains comparatively speaking uninhabited. The land is almost entirely in the hands of small proprietors who hold it direct from the State and cultivate it themselves aided by the members of their families and occasionally by hired labourers, who are paid in kind to the value of from six to eight rupees a month according as they live and board with their employers or not. Of large proprietors there are none and the average holding is from 10 to 15 acres, which is shewing a tendency to increase, but at a very slow rate. As a rule the proprietors reside near their lands and have not yet reached that stage of advancement in which they take up their abode in towns and live on the rent of their landed property nor can they do so until the average holdings increase in size and the rent increases from the present average rate of two or three rupees per acre a year. The area under cultivation according to crops was, in acres, in :—

Year.	Rice.	Sugar.	Cotton.	Vege-tables.	Betel Nut.	Cocoa-nut.	Dhanee.	Fruits.	All other kinds.	Total.
1855-56	77,459	..	..	Unknown		..	..		13,329	90,788
1868-69	1,61,345	133	1,313	7,180	3,430	110	3,083	12,930	3,009	1,92,533
1869-70	1,70,400	948	569	7,702	3,375	1,023	4,262	12,470	3,262	2,04,011
1870-71	1,76,998	875	599	7,660	3,386	1,062	4,312	13,754	2,955	2,11,601
1871-72	1,87,353	834	1,610	..	3,375	1,062	4,307	12,601	2,439	2,13,581
1872-73	1,97,082	993	1,016	..	3,472	1,066	4,644	12,585	2,520	2,23,378
1873-74	2,20497	955	877	..	3,468	1,060	4,585	12,731	2,249	2,46,422
1874-75	2,42,848	1,107	778	..	3,500	1,060	4,643	14,027	2,530	2,70,493

There still remain (in 1875-76) 4,813 square miles of culturable land waiting only for cultivators.

Keeping pace with the increase in the area cultivated has been the increase in agricultural stock :—

Year.			Buffaloes.	Cows, Bulls, Bullocks.	Carts.	Ploughs.	Boats.
1855-56	..	..	...	36,501	5,297	2,356	1,029	4,320
1867-68	..	..	..	43,169	18,442	3,837	10406	4,452
1868-69	..	..	..	40,984	20,820	4,088	10,533	4,754
1869-70	..	..	..	44,561	28,897	4,096	10,181	5,250
1870-71	..	..	..	49,988	28,473	4,109	13,872	5,771
1871-72	..	..	..	52,893	31,471	6 20	19,163	5,873
1872-73	..	..	..	55,286	28,988	5,450	20,615	5,883
1873-74	..	..	..	65,672	34,611	5,359	22,472	6,086
1874-75	..	..	..	77,886	39,254	6,400	23,020	6,187

This district has suffered terribly from cattle-disease which is imported almost annually from the Shan States *viâ* Myawaddee and the Three Pagodas. In 1876 between the 1st January and the 30th August 12,562 head of cattle (11,290 buffaloes and 1,272 cows, bulls and bullocks) died. The most important natural product is, undoubtedly, teak. Ever since the country came under the British Government this article of trade has attracted the attention of almost every class ; an immense amount of capital has been sunk and lost and whilst the forests have been the grave of many a few fortunes have been made but ruin has overtaken the majority of the Foresters. To the attractions of the timber-trade and its ramifications is mainly due the growth of Maulmain and at first the prosperity of the district. The more considerable portion of the timber is of foreign growth and is brought down the rivers from Siam and Zeng-mai for shipment at Maulmain. The mode of bringing timber to market is as follows :—the selected trees are girdled (almost everywhere in British territory by responsible Government officers) by a rim of bark being cleared off right round the stem about five feet from the ground. Three years later the trees are felled, marked, and dragged by elephants to the bed of the river or stream which taps the forest and left there till the waters rise during the height of the rains when the logs float down—in some cases untouched and unseen in others, as in the Thoungyeng, followed and guided by men and elephants—till they reach the Kyodan where their further progress in artificially arrested. Here are stationed parties of Foresters who recognize their own timber by the marks put on in the forest, draw each log to the bank and form them into rafts which are taken down by raftsmen to the Government timber-station where they must be deposited, entered on the forest revenue books and duty, if any is due, paid before they can be taken further down to the ships waiting to receive them for export, or to the saw-pit in Maulmain. At the Kyodan or rope station on the Salween, some distance below the great rapids, where the river is narrowed to a third of its natural breadth between two perpendicular cliffs, a deep blue clear swift stream running between them, an immense cable is stretched from one side to the other which intercepts the floating logs as they collect during the night. At dawn a number of foresters may be seen scrambling over them, diving under them, and swimming amongst them shouting with laughter as a rolling log precipitates a novice into the water. Each one is trying to select a log and paddle it ashore clear of the assembled mass. Sometimes the weight of the timber snaps the cable and the whole accumulated body of wood, logs, drift and rubbish from the forest tears down the river till it is stranded by the current or with great difficulty landed by practised men who make this their profession and receive salvage at a fixed scale. Some of it is often lost by being carried out to sea or stranded on unfrequented islands. The salvors are also busily employed in collecting logs which accidentally pass the rope : these they form into rafts from which the owners select their particular logs.

A product having all the same properties as camphor is extracted by distillation from a syngeneseous plant belonging to the sub-division of *Verbenaceæ Eupatoriæ*, which is very common throughout the country. The quantity which is obtained from this plant in the dry season is not inconsiderable and might probably be increased by a more perfect process of distillation. A kind of gamboge is obtained from the juice of two trees in the district which, though not fitted for use as a colour, promises to afford an excellent varnish and, like gamboge, is a powerfully drastic purgative. The Ka-guyeng which grows abundantly in the forests yields an oil used as a varnish, which is extracted by making a large hole in the trunk in which a fire is kindled the heat drawing out the oil which is collected in earthen pots. Sticklac occurs in the north produced by the *Coccus Laccæ* on several species of ficus.

When the Tenasserim provinces were ceded by the King of Burma under the treaty of Yandaboo they were considered so unproductive that their surrender was at one time seriously contemplated. The rapid tide of immigration, the discovery of valuable teak forests and the careful and fostering measures of the officers placed in charge soon bore fruit and in 1855-56 the revenues of this district, exclusive of those of the Tha-htoon sub-division which then formed a part of what is now called the Shwe-gyeng district, amounted to Rs. 449,360, and up to 1862-63 increased rapidly :—

						Rs.
1856-57	..	..	..	..	..	.. 522,150
1857-58	..	..	..	..	..	.. 552,480
1858-59	..	..	..	..	..	.. 671,500
1859-60	..	..	..	..	..	.. 720,050
1860-61	..	..	..	..	..	.. 916,930
1861-62	..	..	..	..	..	.. 962,530
1862-63	..	..	..	..	..	.. 934,860

In 1863-64 there was a considerable diminution from customs and in 1864-65 from land, in the latter case due mainly to a lowering of the rates.

In the next decennial period, or from 1862-63 to 1872-73, the revenues continued to rise :—

YEAR.	Land.	Capitation.	Fisheries and Net.	Customs.	Excise.	All other items.	Total.
	Rs.	Rs.	Rs.	Rs.	Rs.	Rs.	Rs.
1862-63 ..	204,600	72,240	1,350	111,390	266,330	278,950	934,860
1872-73 ..	403,190	187,470	14,310	354,750	255,150	162,500	1,377,370

The principal increases were under the heads of customs and fisheries but the land revenue had very nearly doubled and the proceeds of the capitation tax had more than doubled. Three years later the total revenue amounted to Rs. 1,687,413.

In 1873 there was a remarkable increase in the land revenue owing to the largely increased area which became taxable. This was partly due to an increase in actual cultivation, caused by the improvement in the rice-trade which up to a year or two before was insignificant timber being the principal and almost only important export from Maulmain, partly to land in the Tha-htoon and Zaya townships having been reclaimed and rendered fit for rice cultivation and partly to numerous leases having fallen in and the area which the lease-holders had added to their fields during the exist-nce of the lease now for the first time becoming liable to Revenue demand.

The land revenue, gross revenue and cost of officials of all kinds in this district, including those employed in the town of Maulmain and the divisional staff, during the last ten years were :—

YEAR.	Land Revenue.	Gross Revenue.	Cost of officials.
	Rs.	Rs.	Rs.
1867	336,080	1,492,400	239,180
1868	338,790	1,085,930	158,240
1869	358,990	1,097,080	172,210
1870	369,080	1,158,260	167,950
1871	382,570	1,245,970	332,270
1872	403,194	1,377,370	171,090
1873	453,130	1,361,080	174,220
1874	492,877	1,434,416	155,035
1875	462,520	1,687,413	189,681

For some years after the cession of the Tenasserim provinces the land revenue was represented by a levy of 25 per cent. upon the value of the crop, calculated at an average *ad valorem* rate which was arranged periodically to suit the mutations in the market price of grain. In 1834 this system was changed and payment on the area substituted, the English acre being the measure employed and two rupees eight annas fixed as the maximum per acre for the best lands. This plan has been continued ever since, though the rates have often been varied.

In addition to the imperial revenue a local revenue is raised from (a) town funds, levied in towns and derived from bazaar-stall rents and other sources, (b) a district fund including all other local receipts except those from the five per cent. cess, and (c) the cess levied on the land Revenue and fisheries. In 1873 the produce of these local rates was Rs. 40,200, an increase of Rs. 11,830 over the receipts in 1872 and of Rs. 12,510 over those of 1871: the increase was especially in the five per cent. cess. In 1875-76 the amount realized was Rs. 54,449.

The scene of continual conflicts between the Siamese and the Peguan kingdoms and subsequently ravaged by the Burman armies of Aloungbhoora and his successors on the one hand and by the troops of the King of Siam on the other the country to the east of the Salween was found in 1826 to be almost uninhabited. In 1829 the country stretching from the Thoung-yeng to the Pakchan (which includes the present districts of Tavoy and Mergui) contained a population estimated at a little over 70,000 souls. From this time until the annexation of Pegu the increase was extraordinarily and increasingly rapid. In 1835 the number had risen to 85,000, or by 21 per cent. ; in 1845 to 127,455, or by 50 per cent. in the decade ; and in 1855 to 213,629, or by 69 per cent. in the decade. It is impossible now to tell how much of the increase was due to births but it is certain that only an infinitesimal proportion was and that it was immigration which swelled the numbers : immigration from India to Maulmain, which rapidly rose into a flourishing town, and immigration into Maulmain and the district generally from Pegu where Burman Governors still ruled and whence in this period, from 1826 to 1855, 257,000 souls, it is calculated, emigrated to the neighbouring British provinces, Arakan on the west and Tenasserim on the south-east. In February 1827 Moung Tsat, a Talaing chief known in the histories of the first Burmese war as the Syriam Raja, who had rebelled against the Burmans and endeavoured to re-establish the Talaing kingdom, escaped to Maulmain with 10,000 followers, half of whom settled at a place now known as Htoon-aing about 20 miles north of Maulmain, and the other half, under Moung Gan, at Wakharoo, to the south ; this party was soon followed by others and at a moderate computation some 20,000 souls arrived from Burmese territory in the first few years. So rapid was the influx that the Commissioner had some difficulty in obtaining a sufficient supply of rice and had to send to Tavoy and to Re for grain. In 1855 the population of the district, which then comprised only the country east of the Salween from the Thoung-yeng to the Tavoy district, numbered 83,146 souls, in 1860 it had increased to 130,953, or by 56 per cent. in the five years, and in 1870 to 235,747 ; but during this decade the whole of the Tha-htoon sub-division was transferred from what up to that time was called the Martaban, and since then the Shwe-gyeng, district. Two years later, when the first regular census was taken, the number had risen to

Population.

239,940, of whom 46,472 were residents of Maulmain—a fishing-village in 1825—the remaining 193,468 being spread throughout the district and, being to a considerable extent agriculturists, found most numerous where the soil is most fertile and culturable; Martaban, Bheeloo-gywon and the plain country east and north of Maulmain shewing the largest numbers, whilst the hilly Houngtharaw and Hlaingbhwai townships had only a small population almost entirely composed of Karengs and Siamese. The population in 1872, exclusive of that of Maulmain, was :—

Talaings	..	.. 94,476	Natives of India.—		
Karengs	..	.. 53,751	Hindoos	..	.. 4,236
Toungthoos	..	.. 19,636	Mahomedans		.. 826
Arakanese	..	.. 8,215	Chinese	..	.. 1,848
Shans	..	.. 5,891	Malays	..	.. 72
Burmans	..	.. 4,241	All others	..	.. 646

During the Burman occupation of the country the coast-tracts of Tenasserim were peopled for the most part by Talaings, called by themselves Moon, and subsequently to the cession of these provinces to the British, after the English had abandoned the valley of the Irrawaddy, their numbers were largely reinforced by immigration from Pegu. The lower portion of the Tha-htoon sub-division round about Martaban, the country extending northward along the left bank of the Salween, and more especially the tract of country from Maulmain southward to Re between the sea and the Toung-gnyo hills are inhabited mainly by this race. A people of the same stock as the Kols and other aboriginal tribes of India, who may have occupied that country even before the Dravidians entered it, seem to have arrived in Burma both from the north and by the coast, though, as stated by Sir Arthur Phayre, " we " have now no means of tracing whether the Muns (*Moon*) of Pegu came direct " down the Erawati (*Irrawaddy*) or parting from their kinsmen the Kolarian " tribes, in the lower course of the Ganges or the Brahmaputra, came through " Arakan to their present seat. There appear now to be no indications of " their presence either in Arakan or in the country of the upper Erawati." Later, about a thousand years before Christ, the Dravidians from Talingana arrived by sea and established trading colonies on the coast of " Ramayana," that is the country between the mouths of the Bassein and of the Salween. They found the Moon wild and uncivilized, " yet the Dravidian colonists have been merged into the mass of that wild race" losing, except for foreigners, even their name but leaving, as it were, in the word " Talaing" by which this mixed people is known to all but themselves, a mark to shew their connection with the Talingana from which they came.

Their use of their own language, which is harsh and guttural, differing from Burmese in almost every word and totally different in combination of words and sentences and in idiom, was more than strongly discouraged by the Burman conqueror Aloungbhoora and by his successors, and after the first Anglo-Burmese war was " furiously proscribed " and no longer permitted in the monasteries or elsewhere within the Burman dominions : in Pegu it has almost died out but in this district, in places coastward remote from the principal towns, the enforcement of the orders prohibiting its use was a work of much difficulty and was checked by the British occupation, whilst the immigrants from Pegu brought it with them and reinforced largely the number of those who adhered to their mother tongue. In 1772 a Talaing chief named Bec-gnya Theng rebelled against the Burmans, in 1791 Myat Poo followed his example in Tavoy, in 1814 Thoot Paw rose against them, and in 1824 Meng Kyaik raised an insurrection, also in Tavoy. These rebellions were unsuccessful and were put down with great cruelty, the Talaings escaping in vast numbers to Siam : the enforced emigration reached an estimated number of over 200,000 souls and the descendants of the emigrants are now living in the country to which they escaped.

The Karengs occupy, generally, the hilly country, the whole extent of the valley of the Thoung-yeng and the western slopes of the Dawna spur, the banks of the Houngtharaw, of the Wengraw and of the Zamee and the mountains amongst which these rivers flow, and the upper portion of the valley of the Re ; both Sgaws and Pwos, or Pgho, are fully represented. Of pure Burmese there are but few. The Toungthoos are " an isolated race, whose origin has not been very accurately fixed," of whom by far the larger number are, in this district, in and around Tha-htoon with a few villages on the Salween though some are found in the valley of the Tsittoung as far north as the Toung-ngoo district and a few to the eastward as far as the Houngtharaw. " They are a swarthy race, sturdily built and differing in language, dress, " customs and physique from the surrounding races. They have no written " character and their traditions are preserved to them by professional story- " tellers." Their language is said by competent authorities " to approach nearer to that of " the Pwo Karengs than to that of any of the other surrounding races," and in dress they resemble the Shans, wearing loose trousers and jackets, white or blue. The Arakanese and the Shans who have immigrated from the west and from Siam may be considered as permanent residents who have settled definitely in the country as, doubtless, have most of the Chinese and some of the Hindoos and Mahomedans—amongst whom are included Burmese women converted before marriage with Mussulmans, a process to which they have little or no aversion, and the mixed descendants of these marriages—but of these many have come only to make money and look forward to a return to India. On the banks of the Attaran in the Theetharo circle, some distance below Maulmain, is a colony of Mahomedans, and others scattered by twos and threes are found in most of the trading towns and villages. The Hindoos, rarely penetrating far into the interior, are clustered in the town and larger villages near Maulmain.

As almost everywhere else in the province the males are more numerous than the females (the numbers being 52·07 of the former to 47·93 of the latter) and as might be expected this is most so amongst the Hindoos and Mahomedans and least so amongst the indigenous population : of the Hindoo population 69·33 per cent. are males and of the Mahomedans 64·03, whilst of the Booddhists—Talaings, Burmans, Toungthoos, Arakanese, &c. — 51 66 per cent. are males. Though not entirely yet in a great measure this disproportion is due to the constant tide of immigration which is to a great extent confined to males. In 1872 the immigrants numbered 19,906 and in 1873 12,631, the emigrants numbering 9,796 and 5,395.

The population of the district in 1875-76 was 2,75,432, of whom 57,719 were in Maulmain.

The number of towns and villages spread over the face of the country is
Towns and villages. 759, of which 420 have less than 200 inhabitants, 257 from 200 to 500, 61 from 500 to 1,000, 18 between 1,000 and 2,000, 1 from 2,000 to 3,000, 1 from 3,000 to 5,000 and 1 over 20,000.

The only town having a population exceeding 5,000 is Maulmain which, lying in 16° 38' N. and 97° 38' E., is situated on a bend of the Salween at the junction of that river with the Gyaing and the Attaran opposite to the small town of Martaban on the north and Bheeloo island on the west. When the British occupied Tenasserim in 1826 Maulmain was little else than a fishing-village. It was selected as the site for the cantonment of the main body of the troops in that province by the Commander-in-Chief, Sir Archibald Campbell, as the best position from which to overawe the Burmese who still retained Pegu and had a force at Martaban on the opposite bank of the Salween, and as having a better supply of water than Amherst, at the mouth of the river. The large areas fitted for cultivation, the cruelties of the Burmese in Pegu and the discovery and working of the valuable teak-forests in the interior led to a stream of immigration and the town rapidly rose in size and in importance. In 1855 it had a population of 23,683 inclusive of 2,211 troops, which ten years later had increased to 70,347 ; but after that year the number of its inhabitants fell year by year till in 1872-73 it had only 46,742 ; this falling off was largely caused by the losses in the timber-trade on which the town depended for its prosperity. In 1873-74 the number rose again to 53,873, owing partly to an influx of Hindoos from the famine stricken districts in Bengal ; and in 1875-76 the population was 57,719 souls.

Amherst is a small station in 16° 15' N. and 97° 34' E. on the sea coast, about 30 miles south of Maulmain by river and 54 by road. On the cession of Tenasserim to the British Mr. Crawford the Commissioner selected it as the seat of the local Government and called it Amherst after Lord Amherst the Governor-General, its native name being *Kyaik Khamee.* Mr. Crawford appears to have been guided in his selection by its position, easily accessible from the sea, well elevated and open to the sea breeze and on the Wakharoo a river navigable for some distance by large ships the mouth of which affords a good harbour. The General Commanding, however, preferred Maulmain which eventually, in 1827, became the head-quarter station. A bold range of wooded hills rises within a short distance on the inland side of the town, leaving a limited space of level ground partially cleared of jungle between it and the sea on one side and the river on the other. As a sanatarium for invalids it is highly recommended and the residents of Maulmain visit it as a seaside retreat during the hot season. For some years it was garrisoned by a small detachment which was eventually replaced by a Police guard

Martaban opposite Maulmain on the right bank of the Salween came into the possession of the British on the annexation of Pegu by Lord Dalhousie in 1854 and for some years was included in the then formed Martaban (now called Shwe-gyeng) district but, with the Tha-htoon sub-division, was transferred to stmherst in 1864-65. In 1544, when it was the capital of a kingdom, it was besieged by the Burmese aided by some Portuguese, taken and sacked, the King cast into the sea and the kingdom annexed to Burma. During the wars which lasted with hardly any intermission from this period till the subjugation of the whole country from Arakan to Mergui by Aloungbhoora and his successors Martaban was sometimes the capital of an independent State, at others ruled by a governor appointed by the Burman, Peguan or Siamese Government to each of which it belonged at different periods. Ralph Fitch who visited Pegu at the end of the sixteenth century described Martaban as a flourishing city with a large trade with China and Malacca. In the eighteenth century the Peguans rose against the Burmese and succeeded in re-establishing the Pegu Monarchy which a few years later was overthrown by Aloungbhoora and from that time till 1852 Martaban remained in the possession of the Burmans. During both Burmese wars it was attacked by the English and, on both occasions, taken after a short and feeble resistance.

The demand for rice and teak timber in the Home and Indian markets, the rapid influx of population, which followed on the British occupation, who settled on the fertile but uncultivated waste land which abounded, the discovery of vast and valuable teak tracts, and the site of the town on the Salween, which taps a foreign country rich in teak forests for the produce of which this river is the only outlet, led to a rapid increase of trade. In January 1855 the Customs Department was established and from that year onwards the values of the imports and exports have been :—

Trade.

YEAR.				Imports.	Exports.	Total.
				Rs.	Rs.	Rs.
1855-56	..	..	..	..	3,583,020	4,390,920	7,973,940
1856-57	..	..	..	..	5,036,750	5,320,760	10,357,510
1857-58	..	..	..	..	5,396,880	5,786,210	11,183,190
1858-59	..	..	..	..	5,505,710	5,773,860	11,279,570
1859-60	..	..	..	..	5,930,590	4,966,430	10,897,020
1860-61	..	..	..	..	5,302,340	4,463,710	9,766,050
1861-62	..	..	..	..	8,236,480	7,812,980	16,049,460
1862-63	..	..	..	..	5,536,240	6,141;250	11,677,490
1863-64	..	..	..	..	4,884,430	5,419,240	10,303,670
1864-65	..	..	..	..	6,930,210	8,748,340	15,678,560
1865-66	..	..	..	..	7,95,2490	9,537,370	17,489,860
1866-67	..	..	..	..	5,971,940	5,631,940	11,603,880
1867-68	..	..	..	..	6,352,173	6,043,726	12,395,899
1868-69	..	..	..	..	6,760,680	8,398,130	15,158,810
1869-70	..	..	..	..	6,079,555	6,407,004	12,486,559
1870-71	..	..	..	..	6,167,590	6,220,360	12,387,950
1871-72	..	..	..	..	6,439,480	7,207,440	13,646,920
1872-73	..	..	..	..	7,909,040	8,494,650	16,403,690
1873-74	..	..	..	..	10,686,380	12,441,130	23,127,510
1874-75	..	..	..	..	9,098,135	9,276,384	18,374,519
1875-76	..	..	..	..	5,987,377	11,844,357	17,831,734

The principal articles of export are timber and rice and the fluctuations in these were the main causes of the fluctuations of trade. Teak is sent to the United Kingdom and to India largely, increasingly to Foreign Europe and in small quantities to the Straits : the first shipment to England was in 1839. The increase in the value of this trade is shewn by the Forest revenue till the Custom House was established and since then by the value of the exports :—

Timber revenue.

						Rs.
1836	..	..	..	..	..	.. 20,800
1839-40	..	..	..	..	..	.. 21,730
1840-41	..	..	..	..	..	.. 29,240
1841-42	..	..	..	..	..	.. 55,110
1842-43	..	..	..	..	..	.. 58,920
1843-44	..	..	..	..	..	.. 54,180
1844-45	..	..	..	..	..	.. 23,710
1845-46	..	..	..	..	..	.. 61,870
1846-47	..	..	..	..	..	.. 88,870
1847-48	..	..	..	..	..	.. 96,480
1848-49	..	..	..	..	..	.. 90,650
1849-50	..	..	..	..	..	.. 63,440
1850-51	..	..	..	..	..	.. 79,460
1851-52	..	..	..	..	..	.. 71,630
1852-53	..	..	..	..	..	.. 84,790
1853-54	..	..	..	..	..	.. 102,370
1854-55	..	..	..	..	..	.. 188,350

Value of timber exported.

1855-56	..	..	..	..	.. 1,438,960
1856-57	..	..	..	..	.. 2,070,570
1857-58	..	..	..	..	.. 2,949,250
1858-59	..	..	..	..	.. 3,744,850
1859-60	..	..	..	..	.. 3,189,520
1860-61	..	..	..	..	.. 2,964,970
1861-62	..	..	..	..	.. 6,062,900
1862-63	..	..	..	..	.. 4,302,020
1863-64	..	..	..	..	.. 3,728,440
1873-74	..	..	..	..	.. 5,824,830

The rice trade had formerly been mainly with the Straits, for which in ordinary seasons the bulk of the crop was purchased, but the grain has now acquired a more favourable standing in the European markets and year by year larger shipments are made to Europe besides shipments to India. In 1863-64 only 4,033 tons were sent to the United Kingdom and in 1866-67 only 1102 : in 1868-69 the quantity increased to 8,552 tons, in 1871-72 it was 14,280 and in 1873-74, notwithstanding the large demand in India on account of the scarcity in Bengal it was 21,341 tons. In the same years the exports to the Straits were—6,476 ; 3,477 ; 3,942 ; 29,765 and 15,712 tons. The increase in this branch of the trade of the district, depending as it did on the rice having obtained a better footing in the European markets, led to the erection of steam-cleaning mills, of which there were twelve in 1875-76. The following statement of the total exports shews the fluctuations of the trade :—

1864-65	..	.. tons 21,567	1873-74	..	..	tons 71,949
1870-71	..	.. „ 37,572	1874-75	..	..	„ 44,791
1871-72	..	.. „ 56,257	1875-76	..	..	„ 77,987
1872-73	..	.. „ 51,718	1876-77	..	..	„ 56,383

Cotton is produced in the district and exported as are hides, but the trade in these is very small.

The principal imports are cotton and woollen piece-goods, tea, sugar and sugarcandy, spirits, vegetable oils, silk piece-goods, twist and tobacco : the quantities of these in 1873-74 were :—

		From Foreign ports.	From India.		Total.
			Foreign manufacture.	Indian manufacture.	
Cotton piece-goods	.. Yds. ..	155,508	280,683	222,028	658,119
Twist ..	.. ,, ..	..	180,100	..	180,100
Spirits ..	.. Galls. ..	21,953	..	..	21,953
Spices ..	.. Cwts. ..	9,785	..	5,572	15,357
Sugar and sugarcandy ..	.. ,, ..	5,045	..	1,191	6,236
Tea ..	.. lbs. ..	38,031	..	..	38,031
Woollen piece-goods	.. Yds. ..	23,499	..	..	23,499
Vegetable oils..	.. Galls. ..	..	..	32,719	32,719
Silk piece-goods	.. Yds. ..	..	174,884	26,698	201,582
Tobacco ..	.. Cwts. ..	..	19,068	17.474	36,542

For administrative purposes the district is divided into eleven townships, *viz:* Tha-htoon, Hpagat and Martaban, on the west side of the Salween, joined to it in 1865, now forming the Tha-htoon, until very lately called the Martaban, Sub-division under an Assistant Commissioner whose head-quarters are at Tha-htoon. Bheeloogywon an island off Maulmain dividing the northern from the southern mouth of the Salween; the Than-lweng Hlaingbhwai occupying the northern portion between the Salween and its tributary the Thoung-yeng; the Gyaing Than-lweng between those two rivers but further south and reaching down to the Gyaing and, near Maulmain, a short way beyond it; the Gyaing Attaran stretching southwards behind Maulmain to the extreme southern limit of the district, shut in on the west by the Toung-gnyo spur and on the east by the Houngtharaw river; the Zaya, the Wakharoo and the Re Lamaing occupying the stretch of sea-coast from Maulmain southwards to the Ma-hlwai spur, the southern watershed of the Re, and bounded on the east by the Toung-gnyo spur; and the Houngtharaw occupying the hilly country between the Thoung-yeng and the Houngtharaw southwards from the Pata stream, an eastern tributary of the Hlaingbhwai which joins it a little north of the junction of that river with the Houngtharaw. These townships again are sub-divided into revenue circles. The Judicial tribunals of the district are precisely similar to those elsewhere in the province, except that the Recorder of Rangoon is here replaced by a Judge of Maulmain with less extensive powers. Of the eighteen presiding officers fourteen exercise criminal, civil and revenue powers; one, the Judge of Maulmain, civil and criminal; one, the Magistrate of Maulmain, criminal only; and two, Forest Officers, deal only with breaches of the Forest Rules. The maximum distance of villages from the nearest Court is forty miles, the average distance nine. For guarding this territory and for the prevention of crime and detection and arrest of offenders 581 Police Constables and 36 River Policemen were entertained in 1876 under three superior and sixty-five subordinate officers at a total cost of Rs. 1,55,974. It is with the Toungthoo and Kareng population that the Police have most to do for these are the people who are most concerned in crimes of violence of which there were annually not a few, many however committed by Shans who rush across the eastern and south-eastern frontier and back again before it is possible for the Police to do anything, indeed in some cases before the Police are made aware that any crime has been committed. Sometimes a band of robbers sprang up in the district and, perfectly at home on the hills and in the wild jungles, it was only with great difficulty that it could be dispersed and then only after some months. In 1870 a leader of one of these gangs offered a reward of Rs. 600 for the head of an Inspector of Police who was energetically hunting him down and who eventually came up with him and shot him after a sharp fight. A great difficulty under which the Police laboured was the unwillingness of the inhabitants to give information which would lead to the capture of a band until the atrocities become too great even for *them* to bear. Latterly there have been fewer crimes of violence such as robberies and dacoities and no organized gang has been known for some years. The town of Maulmain is protected by a body of Police, under the same Superintendent and forming a portion of the same force, numbering 149 men, of whom 99 are for the Military cantonment. The salaries of the men employed in the town are partly defrayed by the Municipality.

The large Gaol in Maulmain, one of the great Central Prisons of the province, has been in existence for some years but has been much improved of late and rendered more fitted for the reception of the large numbers of prisoners who used formerly to be retained in the districts where they had been tried and convicted. Before the establishment of the Penal Settlement on the Andaman Islands Maulmain was one of the places of transportation of prisoners from India. As originally constructed this Gaol was simply a collection of large barracks within four high walls but work-yards, work-sheds and store-rooms have been added. The Gaol now consists of double-storied brick-work buildings with wooden floors and tiled roofs. The prisoners sentenced to hard labour are employed as gardeners in the Gaol garden, as wicker-workers, coir-workers, tailors, blacksmiths, cotton-spinners, stone breakers, and especially in upholstery and as carpenters and the nett value of their labour credited to the Government in 1875 was Rs. 26,513. The expenditure in 1875 was :—

					Rs.
Rations	...	...	...	...	24,462
Establishment	...	...	...	...	19,750
Police Guard	...	...	...	...	5,229
Hospital charges	...	...	...	...	605
Clothing*	...	...	...	...	127
Contingencies	...	...	...	...	2,128
			Total	...	52,371

The cost of clothing in 1871 was Rs. 3,550.

The prison population in the same year was :—

Criminal prisoners sentenced to rigorous imprisonment		...	1,456
„ „ simple „		...	206
Civil „ (debtors)		„	...	284

Total	...	1,946

Deducting from the charges the profits of the Gaol labour, the nett cost for each prisoner was Rs. 31-7-6.

Including Maulmain the district possesses 195 schools, *viz.*, two Government and 195 private of which 11 are Missionary and a considerable number Monastic. Until of late these monastic schools, spread over the whole

Education.

face of the country and found in almost every village, in which the Booddhist Hpoongyees live and teach the village lads, received little or no active attention from the Government but they are now being gradually and cautiously taken in hand so that, if possible, they may be improved and strengthened and made the means of spreading a sounder and better education among the people. In 1835 a Government school was established in Maulmain which is now classed as a High School, has about 100 pupils, Europeans and Eurasians, and has absorbed a neighbouring English school which was receiving State aid.

St. Patrick's School was established in 1842 by the Roman Catholic Mission. In 1871 the Moung-gan Anglo-Vernacular School was opened under a master of pure Burmese origin: this was found not to be sufficiently well supported and has been amalgamated with the Government school. Of schools for girls only the town of Maulmain has several: the Morton Lane Girls' School for Burmese girls, an excellent institution, attached to which are five ancillary girls' schools in different parts of the town ; St. Joseph's School established by the Roman Catholic Mission and consisting of two distinct seminaries, *viz.*, a convent school and an orphanage for destitute girls of mixed European origin ; and the Church of England orphanage which holds a deservedly respectable place amongst the girls' schools of the province. In 1843 the American Baptist Mission set up a normal school in Maulmain for Karengs in which Burmese is taught as a subject and English will probably follow. At Tha-htoon the Government has lately established a town school for boys and girls. The extent to which the improvement of the monastic schools has been carried in this district is brought out in the Report of the Director of Public Instruction for 1873. Eighty-nine of such schools were visited with the consent of the Hpoongyees, and the pupils examined and prizes given. In Maulmain the result was not successful ; no less than 50 Hpoongyees refused to admit the Examiner. Into these schools boys alone are received and for the education of girls other agencies have to be depended on. Though, speaking generally, the women of Burma are content to leave education to their fathers, husbands, brothers and sons yet in many places laymen have started village schools in which girls are taught to read and write. In this district in 1873 twelve lay village schools were visited and the pupils examined and among those so examined were 71 girls.

Communication is carried on principally in boats. A metalled road extends

Communications.

southwards as far as Kwan-hla, a distance of 38 miles, and is in course of construction as far as Re, 73 miles further whence it will eventually be prolonged to Tavoy and Mergui. At

Kwan-hla a branch road leaves this main road westwards to Amherst, a distance of 16 miles. A road has been carried from Maulmain eastward, past the "Farm Cave" Rocks, to the Gyaing ; this was intended as the first section of a road to Hlaingbhwai. A road is now being made from Martaban northwards to Tha-htoon whence it will be extended to Shwe-gyeng. Besides these there is a short metalled road about 4½ miles long from Zemathway on the stream of that name to Tha-htoon.

A telegraph line extends from Maulmain past Tha-htoon to Shwe-gyeng (with a branch thence to Rangoon) and on to Toung-ngoo, and another from Maulmain to Amherst. The only Telegraph Stations are at Maulmain and Amherst.

AMHERST.—A small town in the Amherst district at the southern mouth of the Salween River in latitude 16° 15' north and longitude 97° 34' east about 30 miles south of Maulmain by river and 54 miles by road. A bold range of wooded hills rises within a short distance on the inland side of the town leaving a limited space of level ground partially cleared of jungle between it and the sea on one side, and the Wakharoo river on the other. As a sanatorium for invalids Amherst is highly recommended by most medical men. The town displays a goodly collection of planked houses belonging to residents of Maulmain, who go down occasionally to benefit by the sea breezes. It is also resorted to by invalids from Maulmain and Rangoon during the hot and dry months of February, March and April as well for the benefit of change of air as for the enjoyment of the cool sea-breeze and salt-water bathing. The chief importance of Amherst is its convenience as a pilot-station. The site was selected, on the cession of Tenasserim, by the Civil Commissioner, Mr. Crawford, as the capital of the Province and named after the Governor-General, Lord Amherst. The head-quarters were subsequently removed to Maulmain. The town gives its name to the district.

AMHERST.—An island in the Kyouk-hpyoo district.—*See Tsagoo.*

AMHERST.—A circle in the Amhert district.—*See Kyaik-Khamee.*

AMHERST.—A township in the district of the same name.—*See Kyaik-Khamee.*

AN.—A village in the Kyouk-hpyoo district on the An river, the head-quarter station of the An township. It contains a Court-house for the Extra Assistant Commissioner and a police station and in 1875 had a population of 1,528 souls, largely engaged in trade. Ponies and cattle, dried tea, cutch and other goods are brought over the mountains from Upper Burma and passed down to the coast for distribution throughout the country and piece-goods, tobacco and other articles are brought hither for export to Upper Burma in return.

AN.—A river in the Kyouk-hpyoo district, more generally known as the *Aeng*, which rises in the Arakan Romas and falls into Combermere Bay. During spring tides large boats can ascend as far as An village, 45 miles from the mouth, but at all other periods they are obliged to stop some five miles lower down.

AN.—An extensive township occupying the whole of the eastern portion of the Kyouk-hpyoo district from the Mace river northwards, bounded on the east by the Arakan Roma mountains and traversed by the An river. It has never been surveyed but the estimated area is 2,883 square miles or more than half that of the whole district. The inhabitants, who number 20,631 souls, are mainly Arakanese on the coast and Burmans inland in the villages on the Maee and the An whilst Khyengs occupy the northern part of the township. In the north and east the country is hilly and densely wooded but in the valleys of the rivers and towards the sea-coast there is a good deal of cultivation. The principal products, besides rice, are sessamum and tobacco both of which are exported, whilst from Upper Burma across the An pass come ponies, tea, coarse sugar, lacquered ware, cutch and other articles. The head-quarters of the township are at An a village on the river of the same name some 45 miles from its mouth. In 1876 the land revenue amounted to Rs. 10,519, and the capitation-tax to Rs. 15,736: in the same year the gross Revenue was Rs. 25,649.

Before the conquest of Arakan by the British this township formed a Burman Governorship, and after the conquest it was joined to Sandoway. In 1833 it was formed into a separate district with portions of the present Kyouk-hpyoo and Akyab districts added to it. In 1838 the head-quarters were transferred from An to Kyouk-hpyoo and eleven circles joined to it from Ramree then a separate district. In 1852 Ramree and An were united into the Kyouk-hpyoo district and the township re-formed. In 1871 two circles, Ro and Tsitkan, were taken from it and added to others from the Kyouk-hpyoo township and the Akyab district to form the Myeboon township.

ANAN-BAW.—An extensive revenue circle covering an area of more than 270 square miles in the Kyouk-kyee township, Shwe-gyeng district, west of the Tsittoung river and adjoining Toung-ngoo on the north. It has a population of 4,418 inhabitants who are principally Karengs. Silk-worms are bred to some extent in this circle and the silk exported, principally across the Roma mountains to Prome and Shwe-doung in the Prome district. In 1876 the capitation tax was Rs. 3,967 the land Revenue Rs. 2,148 and the gross Revenue Rs. 6,652. (*The name is derived from the Anan tree*).

AN-DAW. (*Sacred double tooth*).—A small Pagoda in the Sandoway district on a hill on the right bank of the Sandoway river opposite the town of that name, said to have been erected in 761 A.D. by King Tsek-khyoop to contain a tooth of Gaudama Booddha. In 1865 the outer shell gave way and was repaired. Feasts are held thrice yearly during the months of March, June and October, which each last one day ; those who attend—chiefly from Sandoway town—pass on for another day to the Nandaw and for a third to the Tshandaw Pagoda, both of which are in the neighbourhood.

AN-GYEE.—A township in the Rangoon district rather over 600 square miles in extent extending from the sea-coast northward as far as the Pan-hlaing creek and stretching westwards from the Rangoon river, which forms its eastern boundary, to the To or China Bakir, the lower portion of which bounds it on the south towards the east. The Tha-khwot-peng, more commonly known as the Bassein creek, the ordinary route for river steamers from Rangoon to the Irrawaddy during the dry season, traverses it from N.N.W. to S.S.E. The principal villages are Htan-ma-naing where salt is made, Pyaw-bhway inhabited chiefly by rice cultivators, Lek-khaik, Kwon-khyan-goon and Thoon-khwa where pots for salt-boiling are manufactured. The soil is exceedingly fertile and a considerable quantity of rice is produced for the Rangoon market. In 1876 the population numbered 75,147 souls, the land revenue amounted to Rs. 319,535 and the capitation-tax to Rs. 93,386 ; the gross Revenue was Rs 444,888. It contains 14 Revenue circles. The head-quarters are at Twante. The old name of this tract was Dala. It was changed to An-khyee (" wonderful" " admirable"), of which An-gyee is a corruption, about fifty years ago when Moung Shwe Tha the Myo' Thoogyee or headman had sent to the annual boat races on the Royal lake at Rangoon a boat so named, manned by men from Dala, which won all the races in which it competed.

AN-KHYOUNG. *(An stream)*.—A revenue circle in the An township of the Kyouk-hpyoo district stretching westward from the Arakan mountains beyond the An river. It has an area of 481 square miles and a population (in 1876) of 3,036 souls. Its principal produce is sessamum. The land revenue in 1876-77 was Rs. 2,000 the capitation-tax Rs. 2,510 and the gross Revenue Rs. 4,653.

AN-LET-WAI. *(Left An)*.—A revenue circle in the Kyouk-hpyoo district 1,200 square miles in extent, stretching southwards from the extreme north of the district on the right bank of the An river. Exceedingly mountainous and almost entirely covered by forest : the area under cultivation is very small ; sessamum is its main produce : the population numbers 2,105. The land revenue in 1876-77 was Rs. 6,646 and the capitation-tax Rs. 2,000. The gross Revenue was Rs. 2,680.

AN-LET-YA. *(Right An)*.—A revenue circle in the An township, Kyouk-hpyoo district, with little cultivation and a population of 4,997 souls including those of the village of An. It lies in the hilly country towards the north-east of the district in the valley of the An. The land revenue in 1876-77 was Rs. 4,922 and the capitation-tax Rs. 3,234.

ANOO.—A small tribe living in the Arakan Hill Tracts of whom little or nothing is known except that the few villages which they occupy in this province are difficult of access, that they dress like the Kbamies but speak a distinct dialect, and bury their dead in the Forest. They are the only tribe who live at any distance from a navigable stream.

ANOUK-BHET.—A township of Tavoy occupying, as its name (*Western Side*) denotes, the western portion of the district. It extends southwards in a narrow strip between the coast and the Tavoy river from the northern boundary of the district to Tavoy point. Throughout its entire length it is traversed by a low range of wooded hills nowhere exceeding 500 feet in height which form the western watershed of the Tavoy river. In the north and separated from the coast by a still lower range is the Hien-tsai basin, a large sweet-water lake 15 miles long and from 6 to 8 miles broad which is fed by numerous streams and empties itself into the sea by a narrow mouth closed by a sand-bar. The principal products of the township are rice and the Nipa palm ; salt is made in several places.

It is divided into 12 Revenue circles and contains no towns or villages of any size or importance. The population in 1876 numbered 26,732 souls : the land revenue amounted to Rs. 37,489 the capitation-tax to Rs. 19,932 and the gross Revenue to Rs. 63,086 including Rs. 1,962 local cess.

APENG-HNIT-TSHAY. *(Twenty tree creek)*.—A creek in the Bassein district flowing between the Daga and Shwe-gnyoung-beng rivers. It is about 200 feet wide and has a depth of 15 feet increased to 19 at the flood. In the rains it is navigable from the Shwe-gnyoung-beng as far as Kangoon, but in the dry weather small boats cannot ascend above Koon-tsabay-oon.

ARAKAN.—The most northern of the three divisions of British Burma extending in a long narrow strip along the coast of the Bay of Bengal from the Naaf estuary in the north to the Khwa river in the south and shut in on the east by the Arakan Roma mountains. The name is a corruption of "Rakhaing" the native name for the Arakanese. It covers an area of 12,525 square miles and is divided into four districts :—The Arakan Hill Tracts, Akyab, Kyouk-hpyoo and Sandoway. After the first Burmese war " Rakhaing-pyee-gyee," or the Arakan kingdom, was ceded to the British by the King of Burma and formed into a Province which was placed under the Bengal Government. It then extended as far south as Cape Negrais and was divided into four districts ;—Akyab, An, Ramree and Sandoway. Various changes took place in the boundaries of the districts and after the second Burmese war, when Pegu was annexed, the lower strip, between the Khwa and Cape Negrais, was joined to the Bassein district of Pegu. In 1875 it contained a population of 497,632 souls and produced a gross revenue of Rs. 2,528,828. It is administered by a Commissioner whose head-quarters are at Akyab and by three Deputy Commissioners of districts and a Superintendant of Hill Tracts. Of the total area 12,668 square miles are reputed to be unculturable and only 785 square miles as actually under cultivation.

ARAKAN.—The ancient capital of Arakan.—*See Mrohoung.*

ARAKAN HILL TRACTS.*—This district, lying amongst the wilderness, of mountains in the north of Arakan, for many years formed a portion of the Akyab district. Inhabited by wild tribes continually at feud with each other and occupied largely in committing forays not only in the hills but even occasionally in the lower and more civilised country to the south it was found impossible for the local officers to do more than occasionally to copy the habits of these almost savages and to make occasional raids for the punishment of the marauders. In 1865 in order to bring the country more under control and, as far as possible, to civilize the inhabitants and reduce them gradually to more peaceful habits it was separated from Akyab and an officer placed in independent charge subject directly to the Commissioner of Arakan. In 1868 with a view of encouraging trade and traffic with the Hill Tribes and the gradual winning of them over to a more frequent peaceable communication with the people of the plains a market was established towards the south at Myouk-toung, far enough in the hills to attract the hill people whilst not too far from Akyab to attract traders, where the sessamum, cotton, tobacco and other hill produce could be disposed of instead of being, as formerly, exchanged for other goods with petty travelling hucksters who were an inducement to the hillmen to commit dacoity and who could not be prevented from carrying about for sale or barter arms, sulphur, saltpetre and gunpowder. The market has proved a success and is now the common resort of hill men from the Kooladan and the Mee. The Superintendent can personally super-intend their dealings with the traders from the plains and many cases of violence and murder have thus been prevented. In the same year, 1868, the establishment was increased and an Assistant Superintendent appointed.

---

* [With the exception of a few unimportant verbal alterations, some additions from subsequent reports by Captain Hughes and a change in the method of spelling so as to bring it, as far as possible, into accordance with Colonel Horace Browne's system, approved by the Chief Commissioner, the account of these tracts is taken almost entirely word for word from a report dated in 1872 by Mr. R. F. St. A. St. John of the Uncovenanted Service formerly of the 60th Royal Rifles who was for some time Superintendent.—EDITOR.]

The jurisdiction of the Superintendent comprises the whole of the country drained by the Pay or Pee and the Kooladan with their tributaries north of the latitude of the Kooladan police-station (which is situated about a mile south of the junction of the Mee with the Kooladan) together with the whole of the country drained by the Le-mro and its tributaries north of the police post situated at the junction of the Roo with that stream and by streams joining the Le-mro, above that river also the whole of the country north of a line drawn westward from the mouth of the Roo to a point on the east bank of the Kooladan about fifteen miles below the Kooladan post. Until a regular boundary is laid down the actual limits of the district cannot be fixed. On the Kooladan river the utmost limit of the real practical power of control of the Superintendent is twenty miles north of Dalekmai; beyond this there are only one or two villages and then comes an uninhabited tract of country reaching far north. On the Mee his control is not felt further north than a mile or two beyond the police post at the junction of the Thamie and Mee or Walien. Above this post there are a few villages on the Thamie, but the Mee or Walien is uninhabited until the Bookie Shandoo villages are reached after seven or eight days' journey. On the Le-mro owing to the police post being on the boundary between this district and that of Akyab it is impossible to say how far actual control extends. Roughly the Hill Tracts may be said to be bounded on the south by the district of Akyab and on the west by Chittagong, whilst on the north and east are no defined boundaries but unknown tracts of mountainous jungle, stretching away towards Burma on the east and Manipur on the north.

The Kooladan or Yam-pang is the principal river. It is called Kooladan by the Arakanese from "dan" a place or location and "koola" a foreigner, as it was on this river that the Kings of Arakan located their Bengali slaves: Yam-pang is the Khamie name. The source is unknown; its general course, which is said to be for some miles underground, is nearly north and south and even in the dry weather it is navigable for large boats for about 120 miles from Akyab. The tide is felt as far north as Koon-daw, 15 miles higher up. Above this the river is a succession of rapids and shallows, and above the Tsala stream the bed is excessively rocky. Its principal tributaries are the Tsala which joins it about 25 miles above Dalekmai; the Rala, the Kola, the Palak, the Kan, the Mee which also receives the Thamie, and the Pay or Pee. The valleys of the Palak and Kan are fertile and open and it is said that the tobacco formerly grown there was especially good; owing to frequent raids these two valleys are now uninhabited. The banks of the Mee are inhabited chiefly by Mro as far north as the river's junction with the Thamie, the small breadth of its valley, however, affords but little space for tobacco cultivation, as is the case also with the Thamie; far north on the head waters of the Mee are Shandoo tribes whilst to the south-west is the small tribe of Khoungtso who generally join in their raids. With the exception of a few miles above its junction with the Kooladan the Mee is a very shallow and impracticable stream. The Pee, which runs parallel to the Kooladan on the west, is navigable for large boats up to the latitude of the Kooladan police post, and thence is a shallow mountain torrent flowing through a country inhabited by Mro and Khamie.

The Le-mro has its sources in the eastern Roma, the watershed between Arakan and Upper Burma, some distance to the north of the latitude of

Dalekmai and after a course due south for about 60 miles is joined by the Pee from the east and turning westwards receives the waters of the O from the north and then, after running south and west for about eight miles, it takes an abrupt turn to the north and receives the waters of the Peng or Wakrien. On the head waters of these streams reside tribes of Khyeng and Shandoo of whom little is known but below their junction are tributary Khyeng whose villages are found from this point south to within a few miles of Old Arakan (*Mrohoung*). On the Roo are three or four villages of Mro who settled there by permission of the Khyeng clan who claim that part. The Le-mro at its mouth is much silted up and the tide ascends only a few miles so that in the dry weather small canoes alone can pass up, whilst in the rains the current is very rapid. Above the mouth of the Roo the Le-mro is joined from the east by two large streams, the Wet and the Tseng, which receive the greater part of the drainage from the south-east; the valleys through which they flow are sparsely inhabited by Khyeng.

The total area of the district is generally calculated at between 4,000 and 5,000 square miles but a large part is almost inaccessible and generally speaking the population is confined to the large streams. This area is composed of broken parallel ridges of sandstone hills covered with dense forest drained by innumerable streamlets. The general run of the ranges is north and south and wherever the rivers have been forced to take an eastilly or westerly course may still be seen the broken barriers which formerly dammed up the waters and raised the alluvial deposits on their banks far above the level of the highest rise in modern times. The scenery is sometimes very wild and beautiful but still there is, necessarily, a great sameness.

Natural products. Amongst the wild animals may be mentioned the elephant, rhinoceros, bison, deer, goat, antelope, pig, tiger, bear and monkey. The domestic animals are the gayal, buffalo, ox, goat, pig and dog. The timber trees are ironwood, kamoung, thit-ka-do, ye-ma-nay (*gmelina*), theng-gan-net (*hopea*), mee-gyoung-ye (*pentaptera glabra*), ka-gnyeng (*dipterocarpus lævis*) and in one spot north of Dalekmai there is a little teak. Bamboos are plentiful and are taken down in large quantities to Akyab.

Inhabitants. The great tribes inhabiting the hills are* :—

1. Rakhaing or Khyoungtha		..	1,219
2. Shandoo	..	..	2
3. Khamie or Khwe-myee	..	..	7,172
4. Anoo or Khoungtso	..	..	29
5. Khyeng	..	..	1,634
6. Khyaw or Kookie	..	..	84
7. Mro	..	..	2,162
Total (exclusive of the Police)		..	12,302

The Rakhaing, commonly called Khyoung-tha, are of Burmese stock and speak a dialect differing but little from Arakanese. They are divided into seven clans, viz : I. Loon-hie (Arakanese),—II. Dala (Talaing),—III. Tansiet (Arakanese),—IV. Moon-htouk (Talaing),— V. Koon-tsway (Arakanese),—VI. Shwe-ba-dzwai (Arakanese), and—VII. Rook (Talaing); all live on the Kooladan river, their most northern village being about eight miles above Dalekmai.

---

* The figures given are for 1875-76.

Some clans, however, are said to be descended from Talaings or Moon who came over to Arakan with a princess of Pegu who was married to an Arakanese King in the sixteenth century ; a story borne out by the fact that one clan is still called the " Moon" clan whilst Dalekmai is said to be named from Dala opposite Rangoon. In manners and customs they differ but little from the Arakanese and Burmese and belong to the great Myamma or Mramma (Burman) family : "Khyoung-tha" simply means "the sons-of-the-river." Their numbers in this district are 1,219, but there are many in Akyab. They are a quiet, pleasant people, more like the Burmese than the Arakanese in disposition. Their dress consists of the Arakanese waist cloth of dark home-spun cotton and a white turban, the hair being tied in a knot on the top of the head : the women wear the Arakanese petticoat which is the same as the Burmese save that it comes further round so as not to expose the leg in walking ; the colours however are sad and throughout the whole of the Arakanese family there seems to be a want of appreciation of the harmonious blending of gorgeous colours so dear to the eastern Burman's eye. Tattooing is practised but not as in Burma, the utmost being a few charms on the back or shoulders. Though professedly Booddhists the spirit worship of their fathers finds a much larger place in their hearts and many customs common to primitive tribes are strictly observed. The written character used by the Khyoung-tha was originally the same as the Burmese but in repeating the alphabet they call some of the letters by different names : the books which they use are written on rough home-made paper cut to look like palm leaves and the characters used in these books differ greatly from the usual Burmese form ; this arises from the originals having been copied by Bengali writers who were ignorant of the true form.

The next tribe in order is the Shandoo but of them we know so little that no trustworthy information can be given ; it appears, however, that the customs of the tribes differ. Major Tickell in 1852 had an interview with a Chief of the Bookie clan, which is nearest to us on the river Mee, and those seen by Mr. Davis and Mr. St. John were from southern tribes. In appearance they resemble the Khamie but their language is very different though a few words are found common to both. In comparing the languages of these tribes, who use monosyllabic words and are always in a state of feud with one another, little result can be obtained from vocabularies as compared with the consonantal sounds and the construction of the sentences. The tract inhabited by them for the most part lies to the east and north-east of the mountain which is commonly called the "Blue Mountain," and which is situated at the north-west point of the Akyab district as laid down by the Survey officers previous to the formation of the Hill Tracts District. There are, however, outlying tribes on the Mee and head waters of the Le-mro and it is impossible to say how far they extend north and east. The only points which the accounts given by Captain Lewin the Superintendant of Hill Tribes in Chittagong, by Major Tickell, and by Mr. St. John have in common are :—that they frequently use timber in building their houses and that they raise them from the ground ; that they are polygamous (though all the tribes are polygamous yet as in Burma monogamy is the rule more than the exception); that they have a dread of water above knee deep ; and that they bury their dead in graves dug in the village and lined with stones instead of burning them. In this latter custom they seem to differ from the Burmese and every other tribe. Captain Lewin states that their features do not bear any signs of Mongolian physiognomy and Major Tickell remarks this of one specimen but not of the other. Those, however, seen by Mr. St. John were decidedly Mongolian and in no way differed in stature or appearance from the Khamie. Strictly speaking a description of this tribe is out of place as they can hardly be called one of the district tribes though some of their clans are within the limits of the survey map.

The Khamie, or as they are more commonly called the Khwe-myee, are the principal tribe of the district. Three or four generations ago they dwelt on the mountain ranges to the north-east but having quarrelled with their neighbours the Shandoo they were driven down towards the Kooladan, gradually pushing before them the Mro and the Khyoung-tha who formerly dwelt there. They are divided, like all the hill people, into clans and doubtless in their former *habitat* had their own lands and obeyed influential heads of clans ; but their forced immigration has destroyed all this and now they are scattered and confused though keeping together in villages composed for the most part of members of the same clan under a headman or *toung-meng* whose office is generally hereditary. "Toung-meng" is a Burmese word derived from "toung" a hill and "meng" a chief : their own word for chief is "a-raing." The name "Khamie" is the one by which they call themselves and means "man" (*homo*) ; the Burmese, however, as is their wont, have seized upon the peculiarity of their dress which hangs down behind like a tail and adapting the word "Khamie" to their own language make it into "Khyoung-myee" from "khwe" a dog, and "myee" a tail. In features, language and manners they are of the same family as the Mram-ma. The dress of the male Khamie is a long home-spun cotton cloth about one foot in width which is passed several times round the waist and once between the legs, the coloured ends hanging down in front and behind ; the hair is knotted over the front part of the head and a long twisted white cloth is bound round the head so as to make a turban standing well up over the forehead ; this adds to the height and sets them off to great advantage. They are generally well set up and muscular but vary greatly in stature ; they are wary and occasionally deceitful ; "their distrust is the result of their dealings with people who they know deceive them and if once convinced that you will keep your word they will always trust you." Generally speaking they are more open to improvement than any of the other tribes not even excepting the Khyoung-tha and there can be no doubt but they are now fully able to understand the benefits of peace and trade and are desirous of changing their former predatory habits.

The Mro (whom Mr. St. John is inclined to consider as a sept of the Khamie) wear but a small blue waist cloth about four inches wide and are not particular as to their head dress or personal appearance ; their houses, too, are small and the desire for improvement is not so great. The women of both tribes dress almost exactly alike. A short dark blue cloth reaching to the knee and open at the side is fastened round the waist with a belt of cords covered either with large beads or copper rings; over the breast is worn a small strip of cloth. Unlike the men they are very squarely built but the habit of carrying very heavy weights on their backs in baskets with a band passing over their forehead up the precipitous hill paths makes them walk with a constrained and waddling gait. Some when young are good looking but constant labour soon destroys their personal appearance. This tribe lives on the Mee, a tributary of the Kooladan, and on some streams to the south, and appears to be looked upon by the others as inferior to themselves. It was their custom to form a nest, as nearly musketproof as they could make it, in some high tree connected with the ground by a bamboo ladder, in which men women and children took refuge in case of attack, cutting the ladder after they had gone up. The practice has died out owing to the freedom from danger which they now enjoy.

The Anoo, Koon or Khoungtso are a small tribe of whom there is one village east of Dalekmai, very difficult to get at, and three or four on the Tsala and near the head waters of the Thamie, also difficult of access : little, therefore, is known of them save that they dress like Khamie but speak a distinct dialect which contains many words and expressions intelligible to the Manipuri. They also bury their dead, but in the forest.

The Khyeng are the most widely spread of all the tribes and inhabit the Arakan Roma mountain range, east of the Le-mro river, that divides Arakan from Burma, and extends from far south down into the Sandoway district and across the Romas into the Pegu division. Though all acknowledge that they are of the same family and universally tattoo the faces of their women, a practice peculiar to their tribe, yet there is a great difference between the dialects of those who are brought captives from the east side and of those who inhabit these hills : generally speaking they are shy and averse to improvement, cultivating neither cotton nor tobacco for sale. They are divided into numerous clans each of which is located on certain tracts sufficiently large to supply them with cultivation the boundaries of which they never exceed.

It has been said that they adopted the custom of tattooing the womens' faces to prevent their being taken by the Burmese rulers and this is the explanation almost universally accepted in the plains and in the Pegu division; but the reason may have been as suggested by Mr. St. John, that they mark them thus so as to know them when carried away by other tribes and also to enable them to conceal the women of other tribes carried off by them. Their language though not understood by either Khamie or Mro has many words in common with theirs. The men knot their hair over the forehead and the waist cloth is, in these hill tracts, reduced to the smallest possible dimensions; in fact it can hardly be said to have the slightest pretensions to decency. Those of the tribe who live east of the Roma mountain dress somewhat differently (*See Khyeng*).

The women wear a short waist cloth but open on both sides and a smock frock like that worn by the Kareng but very short; the clans further south wear it long.

The Khyaw inhabit a village of about 30 houses near the junction of the Tsala with the Kooladan : they are undoubtedly of the Kookie family but how they became separated from the main body is not known. The men knot their hair at the back and shave over the forehead ; the women plait it into two tails which are brought up over the forehead : their features are different to the other tribes and their complexion far darker.

Though there may be a few minor differences in the manners and customs of these tribes yet on the whole there is great similarity. The religion of all is spirit worship of the most primitive kind and consists in paying a sacrifice of blood to the spirits of the hills and rivers as a means of averting evil; the smallest act cannot be performed without shedding the blood of some kind of animal or bird.

In the year there are two important ceremonies for the propitiation of the " Ka-nie," or spirit, *viz.*, at the time of sowing seed and before harvest. At the first a fowl or pig is taken alive to the place to be sown, a small heap of rice seed is placed on the ground and the blood from the animal is poured on it; the flesh is taken home and eaten. The second is performed when the rice plant is well grown but before the ear has come up; a fowl, pig or dog is killed at home and the blood is smeared on long bamboos decorated by shaving round the joints so as to leave tassels and tufts hanging from them; these bamboos are then taken to the field and stuck up in various parts of it.

There is also another annual feast, in honour of departed spirits who are called " hpalaw." This custom is followed by the Khamie and Khyoung-tha but not by the Mro. The ceremony is performed by the Khamie after harvest and is called " ta-proungpa-oung or the opening of the dead-house. When a person dies and has been burnt the ashes are collected and placed in a small house in the forest, together with his spear or gun which has first been broken in pieces. These small houses are generally placed in groups near a village, for which they are sometimes numerous enough to be mistaken. After harvest the whole of the deceased's relatives cook various kinds of dishes and rice and take them with pots of "a-moo" (liquor made from rice) to the small houses where the ashes repose; the doors of the house are opened and food having been placed for the departed are re-closed: the relatives then weep, eat and drink and return home in the evening. Khyoung-tha perform this ceremony thrice a year but with them it consists simply of setting aside food and drink for the departed for a short time and then throwing it away into the river.

During the dry weather numerous feasts are given at which large numbers of cattle are killed and eaten and rice-beer and spirits consumed. It is a mark of distinction amongst them to have it said that they have killed so many head at a feast; the largest number Mr. St. John heard of was 150 killed at one feast by a headman (A-raing) and his sons. The gayals, buffaloes and oxen are tied up to a post and speared behind the right shoulder but other animals have their throats cut. Dogs are castrated when young for use at feasts. The post used by the Mro is Y shaped; and just below the fork carved so as to represent two or more beasts. There is some peculiar but at present unknown significance attached to this symbol both by Mro and Khamie and it is often carved on the posts of headmen's houses and on the house ladder. The Khamie and Khyeng do not carve their posts but set them up rough; in the Khyeng villages some rough stones are set up.

At the feasts there is always a drinking of "khoung" or rice-beer which is made by soaking rice with certain ferment-causing roots in a large pot: this pot is then put away till required and then filled to the brim with water; a reed with two little holes cut at the side above the bottom joint having been thrust down into the liquor it is sucked up and when the first man has drank his quantum he marks it with a slip of bamboo and fills up with water for the next comer. One pot is sufficient for a large number of men. When five or six pots are put in a row the drinkers are supposed to commence at one and move on up the line until they come to the other. This liquor is not disagreeable and is moderately intoxicating.

Dancing must be seen to be clearly understood : it is more of a side

Dances.

closing step than a dance the line being headed by drummers, small gong players, wind instrument blowers and men armed with spears, "Wa-raik" (a peculiar brass handled sword said to be made by the Shandoos and much prized), muskets and shields. The step consists of closing two steps to the right and one to the left in time to the music and at the same time bending the body so as to throw the posteriors outwards : the young men commence it and then drag in the girls between them to whom they make love and whom they stimulate with ardent spirits. "I have seen" writes Mr. St. John "a young man thus dancing away and murmuring a love song into the ears of two girls at the same time, one on each side, with his arms round their necks." Before commencing the faces of all are often smeared with a mixture of saffron and rice flour which is supposed to ward off the bad effects of drinking. Occasionally they dance a wild sort of war dance with "dhas" and shields and there is also a very clever dance something resembling the sword dance of Scotland but between two heavy rice pounders which are clapped together by two other men to the sound of a drum : if the dancer is not very agile or exact he is liable to get his leg broken between the pounders.

Till marriage, intercourse between the sexes is perfectly free and unres-

Marriage.

trained ; and it is considered highly proper to marry a girl great with child though it be that of another man ; if however a girl bring forth before marriage the child is, it is said, exposed. Marriage is a simple contract consequent on making valuable presents to the parents. It is an insult to tell a girl that the young men will not sleep in her house.

Tabooing.

The ceremony of "Ya" for tabooing is strictly observed on the following occasions :—

1st.—When any person belonging to the village is killed by a tiger or crocodile ; when the body of any person so killed is brought into a village ; or when any woman of the village dies in childbirth all intercourse with other villages is cut off until the appearance of the next new moon.

2nd.—When a village or house is burnt ; or when a new village is erected intercourse is forbidden for the period of three days.

3rd.—When any epidemic breaks out intercourse is forbidden with that village until the disease has disappeared.

4th.—When the rice plants are well up and require weeding intercourse is forbidden for seven days.

5th.—When a villager dies by accident intercourse is forbidden for one day.

Any person breaking this custom is fined by the headmen of the neighbouring villages. To show that a village is tabooed strings or canes are suspended across the road.

At harvest time the people are forbidden to eat flesh or fish ; and any person who has killed another or been wounded by a tiger or crocodile is obliged to abstain from flesh for a period extending from three months to one year. It is also considered wrong to take money for a tiger's skin.

When the inhabitants of a village have been successful in a raid or in
Customs. repelling an attack a sacrifice is offered to the "Kanie"
or guardian spirit; all the men dancing a war dance
with spears and shields round the village post.
When a person dies the body is laid out in the house and a feast made;
food is set apart for the ghost which is supposed to remain over the house
as long as the body is there. Seven bundles of rice for a man and six for a
woman are left at the place of cremation for the ghost to feed on, and neglect
of this custom is a bar to inheritance.

According to the Hill custom all offences or injuries are remedial by fine
only, and this fine is called in the Burmese "*goung-hpo*," or head money;
by the Mro it is called "*aloo-wang*"; and by the Khamie "*loo-wang.*"
If the fine or debt be not paid means are first taken to try and recover
the money by restraining the person and if this be ineffectual the judgment-
debtor becomes the slave of the injured party who either keeps him in his
house to work or sells him. In cases where it is impossible to apprehend
the party or recover the amount due the creditor will bide his time and,
when least expected, a raid will be committed on the village of the debtor.
As this "goung-hpo" is constantly demanded for purely imaginary reasons,
and in a very arbitrary manner, raids are sometimes committed and feuds
established on very frivolous pretences; for instance the feud between the
Shandoo and the Karay clan of Khamie, who formerly lived in the Palook
valley, is said to have originated in a dispute concerning a bamboo pipe head, an
article of but small value, and has resulted in the expulsion of the whole
of the Khamie from that valley. In another case a young Mro found the
body of a small deer that had been killed by a tiger and threw it into the forest
near another man's field at a great distance from the village; this came to
the knowledge of the owner of the "joom," or patch of cultivation and one of
his children dying shortly afterwards he attributed it to the act and
demanded "goung-hpo" from the young man. The village elders admitted
the claim and a small forfeit was paid and it was thought that the matter
was fully settled but about a year afterwards another child died and its
death, was by some curious process of reasoning, attributed to the same act
and another demand of larger value was made; this was too much and the
person of whom the demand was made fled to the Superintendent for succour.

Laws. The following is an abstract of the Hill laws as
given by Mr. Davis and quoted by Mr. St. John, two
successive Superintendents.

Criminal.

i.—If a person commit murder he should be fined the value of two
Murder or Homicide. slaves and several spears, swords and gongs, say in all
about Rs. 600. If death be caused accidentally the
fine should be half the above.

ii.—When a village is plundered by a body of raiders the leader alone
Raid. is to be held responsible and if apprehended is
bound to return the value of all property taken (including the head money of persons killed) and also to pay a fine.

iii.—If a village be burnt down in committing a raid the leader is
Raid and arson. bound to make good the damage done and to pay a fine
in addition.

iv.—A person who commits theft is bound to return the pro-
Theft. perty, or its value, and to pay a fine not exceeding
Rs. 30.

Grievous hurt. v.—A person who causes grievous hurt may be
fined Rs. 100.

Assault. vi.—If a person assault another he is to pay a fine not
exceeding Rs. 30.

vii.—If rape be committed on a married woman the husband is entitled
Rape. to demand a sum not exceeding Rs. 60. Rape of
an unmarried woman is to be punished by a fine not
exceeding Rs. 30.

Besides the fine the offender has to pay for the animal (pig) slain to make
the agreement binding.

When murder is committed in a raid any raiders caught red-handed are
at once beheaded and the heads stuck up in the village.

A woman may not receive a fine but a male relative or husband may
receive it for her.

Civil.

i.—If two persons dispute about a debt or other matter and neither
Ordeal. can produce evidence they are obliged to go through
the ordeal of ducking the head in water, and the decision
is given in favour of him who keeps under longest.

ii.—If a debt be not paid and the debtor is not apprehended the
Execution. creditor's party, if strong enough, attacks the debtor's
village and carries off as many captives as it can.

iii.—The interest on a debt is double the principal if one year
Interest. be allowed to expire from the date on which it was
contracted.

Sons liable for father. iv.—The debts of the father must be paid by the
sons.

v.—If a man die without male issue his property is claimed by his near-
No male issue. est male relative ; he, therefore, is responsible for the
debts of the deceased whether there be property or not.

vi.—Should a man die leaving a son who is a minor the nearest male
Minority. relative acts as guardian until minority ceases on
marriage when he is bound to give account of his
stewardship.

Women. vii.—A woman cannot inherit and is, therefore, not
responsible for a debt.

Division of inherit- viii.— If a man die leaving two or more sons the
ance. property is divided as follows :—

If there are only two they divide equally : if there be more than two
the eldest and the youngest take two shares each and the others one share
each.

ix.—On the death of the father the eldest son must give his maternal
Customs to be ob- uncle a full-grown buffalo or the value. On the death of
served. the mother the youngest son must give a paternal uncle
a full-grown buffalo or the value. If this cannot be done a son should be
given.

Bequeathing sons. x.—If a man be on the point of death and cannot pay his debts he must leave a son to the creditor to work it off.

xi.—Slaves do not inherit unless adopted according to rule ; if inheriting **Slaves.** as having been adopted they will be held responsible for debts. If a slave, however, be adopted by a master who has sons he cannot inherit.

xii.—There is no fixed age for marriage, nor any constraint used to **Marriage.** influence choice. Marriage is contracted on consent of the woman's parents after payment of the fixed dowry by the suitor.

xiii. *a.*—If a husband wish to divorce his wife he may do so and take **Divorce.** all the children ; but in so doing he will forfeit claim to dowry.

b.—If a woman have children by a former husband she is entitled to them on divorce.

c.—A divorced woman must, until re-married, be supported by the male relative who received her dowry or by his heir.

Dowry. xiv. *a.*—No female can receive dowry : it must be received by the nearest male relative.

b.—If a husband chastise or ill-treat his wife and she absconds in consequence he is nevertheless entitled to receive back the dowry.

c.—If a wife abuse or ill-treat her husband he may chastise her ; but if on that account he divorce her he forfeits claim to dowry.

xv. *a.*—If the husband divorce the wife for proved adultery he is entitled **Adultery.** to receive the dowry paid by him and may also demand a sum equal to the dowry from the adulterer in addition to fine and costs.

b.—If a man commit adultery the wife has no redress.

xvi.—Should a woman die in giving birth to a child before marriage the reputed father must pay her value to her father or nearest male relative.

Oath is usually taken by swearing to speak the truth on a musket, spear, **Oaths.** sword, tiger's tusk, crocodile's tooth and stone hatchet (supposed to be a meteoric stone, they are occasionally found when cutting the jungle); these are all held together in the hands whilst repeating the oath. This is not much feared and it is said that the Khamie consider an oath taken on the skull of a cat or tiger more binding. Some Mro say that an oath taken on the praying *mantis* is binding whilst this is denied by others.

Cultivation is of the simplest character, *viz.*, that commonly called **Cultivation.** *toungya* in Burma and *joom* in India : it consists in selecting a suitable spot of forest on the side of a hill and clearing it by cutting down the underwood; early in April this is set fire to and immediately afterwards the seed is sown broadcast. The only implements used are a chopper about twelve inches long and about three inches broad at the end, in fact an isosceles triangle of iron with a base of three inches, the apex being fitted into a bamboo handle, and a small axe or triangular "celt" of iron with the small end run through a hole in a bamboo to form the handle. Unlike Burmese choppers however the wash is only on one side. During the rains cotton and sessamum are planted on the same piece of ground. In August the rice ripens and the family on some fine day repair to the field with a basket four or five feet in diameter; the women and children reap the ears with a rough jagged sickle and carry them to a man who tramples out the grain which when taken home is dried in the sun or, if the weather will not allow of this, over fires.

The cotton is much sought after by the Arakanese and of late years the cultivation has considerably increased as the Khamie on the Kooladan are quite alive to the advantage of a good market. It is inferior to Egyptian in staple, fibre and texture but it yields a much larger crop and it has been reported by the Secretary to the Chamber of Commerce, Bombay, to be somewhat superior to ordinary Bengal cotton.

Tobacco is cultivated by all the villagers on the Kooladan and is remarkably good, almost equal to Manilla. It is sown broadcast on the alluvial deposits along the banks after the fall of the river in November, the long elephant grass having first been cut and burnt. The plants are not transplanted but well weeded and thinned out; a good deal, however, depends upon the season as the plants require a little rain though the heavy fogs no doubt do a great deal for them. When the plants are about two feet high the shoots and lower leaves are broken off to make the good leaves grow larger. In April and May the leaves are picked and strung through the stalk on a thin bamboo skewer about one cubit in length, from 20 to 30 leaves on a skewer, and hung up in the house roof to dry ; after five or six days they are taken down and shaken about to prevent the leaves from adhering to one another : they are then re-hung and after six or seven days, when quite dry, thrown into a large basket in which they undergo heavy pressure; after about a month and a half, when the rain has well set in, they are taken out and sorted into bundles. The tobacco is never exposed to the sun and is kept till the rains for sorting so that the leaves may be pliant. The Mro have a tradition that the seed was brought from Cheduba Island where also good tobacco is produced. The Khamie call it " tsa-rak," the Mro " tsa-rook," and the Khyeng " tsee-met." These words are evidently corruptions of the Burmese " tshe-rwek" tobacco leaf. The Shandoo call it " oma," or " koma-kouk."

The women do most of the cultivation with the exception of cutting the jungle for *toungya.*

Of the climate Mr. St. John writes:—" I think that the deadliness of the
Health and climate. " climate has been overstated; but it affects people " differently. I do not consider, however, that the Hill " fever is to be attributed to malaria but to constant severe changes of " temperature. From my own experience I have found that the only dangerous " months are April, May and June ; April is excessively hot and May and " June are the beginning of the rains, the end of the rains I have found " pleasant. The time for moving about is from the 1st of November to the 31st " March. The people are generally speaking healthy but subject to skin " diseases. What tells most on the European is want of proper food. It is " evident from the custom of the people that a very strong diet is necessary, " and chickens, therefore, and tin-meats are not sufficient for the European ; " occasionally he may obtain a little venison but beef and mutton are out of " the question." Arakanese do not stand the climate well and it is deadly to most Burmese who seldom get over the fever and almost always suffer from

enlargement of the spleen. From December to March the prevailing wind is north and during the monsoon south or south-west.

The dispensary at head-quarters is a well raised building with a planked floor and bamboo mat walls, and consists of two rooms for indoor patients and another which is used as an office and dispensary. The total number of persons treated in 1875 was 1,441 of whom 277 were in-patients. Included in these figures are 225 Policemen of whom 102 were in-patients.

The number of cases of each class of disease treated was—

Fever	...	...	292	Disease of the respiratory system			93
Measles	...	...	69	Ditto	digestive	do.	229
Dysentery	...	...	57	Ditto	urinary	do.	10
Diarrhœa	...	...	61	Ditto	skin		208
Disease of the eye		...	77	Others			845

The weapons used by the Shandoo, Khamie and Mro are muskets, spears, short swords or bills, knives and shields. The *Weapons.* muskets are old English ones obtained from Arakan, Chittagong and Upper Burma: the spears are of two or three different shapes but all short (about four feet long) with a long iron spike; "sanroteer" as the Greeks called it. The Khamie and Mro chopper is about one foot long in the blade and is carried in a basket-work sheath; the end is not pointed but is about two inches broad. The Shandoo have a very curious bill about the same length but with a brass handle four or five inches long with a guard for the fingers and a tuft of stained hair. This guard is, however, too small for a European's hand and even for that of many Khamie : this is carried in a curiously-cut wooden scabbard. The shields used by the Shandoo and Khamie are similar in shape and are made of buffalo-skin; they are about two feet long one cubit wide at the top and fourteen inches at the bottom, and the centre is slightly raised ; inside there is a double handle by which to hold them. Those of the Shandoo Chiefs are ornamented with rows of small brass saucer-shaped plates which are fastened on in rows of eight and occupy the upper half; from the lower row hang pendants of coloured horse or goats hair. The second in command of a war-party and a chief's son carry the same shaped shield with one large brass plate, about ten inches in diameter, in the centre. The knives or daggers are sharp-pointed and carried by a leather belt over the shoulder in a bone sheath usually ornamented with cowries.

The spear of the Khyeng is very long and heavy and their shield is long and rounded like the Roman " scutum": it has only one handle and has no ornamentation. They also use a large cross-bow like the Kareng and some tribes use a small long-bow with short iron-tipped arrows, but these are now scarce.

From the Arakanese histories, which, like all Burmese records, are, as far *Origin of tribes.* as the accounts of the more early times are concerned, a mixture of tradition and romance worked up with a view to fabricating for the first kings a fabulous descent from the solar race of India and to introducing the imaginary visit of Gaudama to Indo-China, very little of value is to be gleaned. The first Booddhist monks seem to have pursued much the same course as the Brahmins did in Manipur when, after converting a portion of these same tribes, they made out a fabulous connection between them and the heroes of the Maha Bharata. From the facts, however, that the Burmese do admit that all the tribes are related to them and to one

another and that frequent reference is made to immigrations *viâ* the Kooladan
river and from the stories of "bhee-loos" or monsters it would seem that in very
remote ages a great Mongolian horde consisting of several tribes passed southward from Thibet and dividing into two streams either in or near the valley of
Manipur the one proceeded down the Kyeng-dweng and peopled Upper Burma
whilst the other followed the valley of the Kooladan driving before it an
aboriginal race similar to the Yak-ko of Ceylon, or the present Andamanese,
who either were or were believed to be cannibals and whom the new arrivals
termed " Yek-kha."* As soon as the heads of these columns reached the sea
a reaction would set in naturally resulting in the improvement of those who
held the plains and in the isolation of the smaller families in the hills : this by
the process of natural selection and isolation and their want of a written
language would soon result in the various tribes talking very different
dialects. The different dialects, however, are more alike and have more affinity
with the Burmese than is at first apparent. All have a few words in common
as "ien" or "iem" a house, and "lan" or "lam" a road ; the Burman is the
only tribe that pronounces the final as *n*.

The houses of all the tribes are built of bamboos with either wooden or
Architecture. bamboo posts; those of the Khamie being decidedly
the best and largest. The Khamie house is raised five
or six feet from the ground and is usually three fathoms broad by five or six
in length (the fathom is an ordinary man's stretch from the tips of the fingers
of the right hand to those of the left), some however are larger. The interior
of the house is one large hall; at one end the mat walls are double and at
both are fireplaces. There is a door leading to a raised platform and at the
usual entrance there is a sort of vestibule where the water-bottles are kept.
Inside on the centre post are fixed the skulls of animals killed at feasts and
also spears, gongs, drums &c.; outside on the wall at the entrance end are the
skulls of animals killed in the chase. The floor is of woven bamboos and
the roof, which is round and brought down at the corners, is thatched with
grass or bamboo leaves placed over a rough bamboo mat and kept down on
the outside with another ; at the end of the house between the double walls is
a place for fowls; below are the piggeries. Generally each married couple
have a house to themselves. The Khyoung-tha house—never very large—is
built in the usual Arakanese fashion, raised five or six feet from the ground
with a door at one end and a fowl-house on one side : the roof is brought up
to a ridge. The Mro house is very similar but the side where the fireplace
is put instead of being of mat is made of unsplit bamboos so that the smoke
may escape. The Khyeng vary in their style but all build well off the
ground ; some build their houses so that they are pentagon-shaped with a

* The name Arakan, " Rakhaing, " now given to the whole tract south of the Naaf and west of
"the Roma mountains as far south as the Khwa stream "appears to be a corruption of
"*Rekkhaik*, derived from the Pali word *Yek-kha* which in its popular signification means a
"monster, half-man half-beast which, like the Cretan Minotaur, devoured human flesh. The
"country was named Rek-kha-pu-ra by the Booddhist Missionaries from India, either because
"they found the tradition existing of a race of monsters which committed devastation in a
"remote period or because they found the Mramma people worshippers of spirits and demons.
" It is possible that these traditions of human-flesh-devouring monsters arose from exaggerated
"stories concerning the savage tribes who inhabited the country when first the Mramma race
"entered it. The names given to some of these monsters bear a close resemblance to the names
"common among the Khyeng and Khamie tribes to this day". Phayre's History of Arakan.
" Journal Beng : As : Soc : Vol. XII. pp. 24, 25.

door at the end and three large openings at the side. The Khyaw houses are much the same but they do not weave the bamboo floor, simply laying down the split bamboos loose so that dust may easily be swept away.

Villages are, wherever the ground admits, built in a rough circle in the centre of which are the slaughter-posts and a shed for travellers, which is also used as a forge. The chief men, too, generally have a detached building for strangers to sleep in. The hill-people always weave the mats of the walls in the place where they are to remain and do not follow the Burmese custom of first weaving on the ground and fixing up afterwards.

The only arts practised are those of weaving cotton cloths and baskets. The blankets made by the Khamie are, generally speaking, white and have thick ribs of cotton run in to make them warm ; some are like large Turkish towels. The Mro usually weave blankets with a black and white pattern, shewing only on one side. The Khyeng weave them in broad stripes of bright colours like those worn by the Toungthoo. There are also long earthenware pots which are said to be made by the Khyeng high up the Le-mro : they are covered with a cane network with a wide ring at the bottom to make them stand.

Manufactures.

The population returns for this district are very inaccurate as the hill people object to telling the number of children they have. The statistics are collected by the " Khyoung-ook" who corresponds to the " Thoogyee" of other parts of the Province.

Population.

The total population in 1875-76 was supposed to be 12,442.

The proportion of males to females by races is shewn below :—

Races.	Males.	Females.
European	4	..
Burmese	28	19
Arakanese and Khyoung-tha	710	650
Khamie	3,769	3,403
Mro	1,026	1,136
Khyeng	811	823
Anoo	15	14
Shandoo	2	..
Other	21	11
Total ..	6,386	6,056

Nearly the whole population are agriculturists.

The prevailing languages are Arakanese and Khamie.

The estimated area under cultivation is nine square miles and of this 2,500 acres are under cotton and 4,000 under tobacco. There are only 15 acres of rice-land under cultivation and these are in the plain near Myouk-toung at the foot of the hills ; the rate of assessment per acre is twelve annas : rice is grown in the " joom " or " ya," but no measurements are made or rate per acre fixed, each family being charged one Rupee a year ; the number of ya in 1875-76 was 5,196. An experimental tobacco farm has been opened by the State at Myouk-toung. A capitation tax was formerly charged on all Mro and Khyeng living near the borders of the Akyab district and on Khyoungtha generally : the rates were two rupees for married men and one rupee for widowers ; bachelors were not charged at all. This tax has since been abolished and tribute has been levied at the rate of one rupee per family. The only other sources of revenue are timber-duty and fines. A tax of one rupee is levied as in other parts of Arakan on all iron wood trees felled.

Fiscal.

Total receipts. 1869-70 :—

The following table shews the amount realized during 1875-76 as compared with the receipts for

Items of Revenue realized.	Amount realized for 1875-76.	Amount realized for 1869-70.	Increase.	Decrease.
	Rs.	Rs.	Rs.	Rs.
1. Land Revenue	2,720	690	2,030	..
2. Capitation-tax	..	1,420	..	1,420
3. Excise (Tari Sale License)	..	60	..	60
4. Tribute	2,479	1,190	1,289	..
5. Miscellaneous	1,610	340	1,270	..
Total	6,800	3,700	4,589	1,480
Nett Increase	..	..	8,109	

Mr. Davis's estimate for 1868 shewed that Rs. 80,000 worth of produce found its way yearly down to Akyab and nearly the whole of this from the Kooladan Khamie.

Trade.

The exports from the Kooladan in 1875-76 were :—

				Value.
				Rs. A. P.
Tobacco leaves, 126,428 bundles	...	...	...	28,462 8 0
Ditto roots, 185,000 do.	...	...	...	62 8 0
Ditto ditto, 18 sers	...	...	...	7 0 0
Cotton, 1,603 baskets	...	...	...	3,325 8 0
Sessamum, 3,291	...	...	...	3,004 0 0
Bamboos, 513,442	...	...	...	3,222 4 0
Plantains, 108,335	...	...	...	1,121 7 0
Miscellaneous	...	...	...	5,539 1 6
Cash*	...	...	...	139,541 2 0
Goods unsold...	...	...	...	32,327 5 0
			Total ...	216,612 11 6

* On account of the State.

The trade on the Le-mro river amounts to about Rs. 12,000 and the principal exports are bamboos and sessamum whilst miscellaneous goods form the bulk of the imports.

On the Pee river there is a trade of the value about Rs. 8,000, consisting of tobacco, cotton, sessamum and miscellaneous goods.

The whole of the salt used in the district is brought from Ramree in large boats, which begin to arrive in November. The price is four to five baskets (12 sers) for one rupee. The Shandoo obtain their salt by barter from the villagers near the frontier, who make very large profits from the trade, and, as the salt has afterwards to be carried on men's backs for several days' journey, it must be a highly-prized article by the time it reaches the Shandoo villages. All the trans-frontier tribes are dependent on our administration for their supplies of salt, which might, if necessary, be cut off without any trouble or expense.

Cotton.

Cotton is grown in the *toungya* and the crop is gathered soon after the rains. The export season is from December to March. The late rains of 1875 were very destructive to the cotton crop which amounted to about 2,000 baskets only, some of this was not purchased until after the close of the year. The cotton is sold by the basket of 30 sers (so called), but this has been found to contain little more than 40lbs. The usual price is two rupees a basket, which would make the price of a maund of 80lbs about Rs. 4.

Tribunals and Police.

There are two Judicial Officers in the district both exercising Criminal and Civil jurisdiction *viz.* :—the Superintendent and the Assistant Superintendent. The Superintendent exercises all the powers of a District Magistrate and on the 27th July 1870 was invested with special powers under the Criminal Procedure Code. He also exercises all the Civil powers of a District Judge as defined in Act XVI. of 1875 and elsewhere. The Assistant Superintendent exercises in Criminal matters the powers of a subordinate Magistrate of the 2nd class with power of committal, and in Civil matters the power of a Court of the 1st grade as defined in Section 6 of Act XVI of 1875. The Superintendent of Hill Tribes is also *ex-officio* Superintendent of Police. The men are divided among ten guards, eight of which are stockaded. The stockades are built with upright posts, six feet apart, and *chevaux-de-frise* of split bamboos, sharpened, between. One hundred of the men are armed with muzzle-loading cavalry carbines while the remainder have the old Brown Bess.

The whole length of the north-eastern frontier, from Dalekmai to Prengwa, is regularly patrolled once a week during the raiding months by strong parties of men of the frontier guards, who meet and exchange reports. Weekly communication by patrol is also kept up by the guards which are within the line of frontier. It requires strong and hardy men to stand the climate and the work incidental to the Police of these hills and the admissions to hospital stand as high as 84 per cent.

In 1875 the stockade at Dalekmai was removed from its former position on the bank of the river to the top of a small hill ; this besides increasing the strength of the place has proved beneficial to the health of the men. The guard-house at this station has been built sufficiently strong to bear two-inch planking being fixed all round below the flooring, as well as for three feet above the floor, which will convert it into a block-house that can be held by a handful of men leaving nearly the whole guard available to follow up raiders.

A new guard-house has been built on the same plan at Tsamee and new guard-houses have also been put up on the Kan and Pee rivers.

The composition of the Police force on the 1st January 1876 is shewn in the table below :—

Europeans	...	...	...	...	... 8
Khyoungtha	...	...	...	...	... 9
Khamie	...	...	...	...	... 50
Khyeng	...	...	...	...	... 5
Mro	...	...	...	...	... 12
Manipuri	...	...	...	...	... 82
Rajbansi*	...	...	...	...	... 25
Burmese	...	...	...	...	... 4
Arakanese	...	...	...	...	... 22
Goorkhas and Tipperah men	...	...	...	... 81
Madrassis	...	...	...	...	... 8
Bengalis	...	...	...	...	... 4
	Vacancies	...	...	...	... 6

Total sanctioned strength ... 256

The European element consists of one Assistant Superintendent of Police who is stationed on the northern frontier at Dalekmai, and two Chief Inspectors of Police, one of whom is stationed on the Le-mro and the other at Tsamee. The Inspectors of Police in this district are styled, Chief Inspectors and draw a local allowance of Rs. 75 a month in addition to their pay of Rs. 175.

The above table shows that 76 inhabitants of the country are drawing Government pay as policemen. That there are not more is due to the large number of Goorkhas who find their way up here seeking employment and it is not thought advisable to discourage the practice by turning them back. That the work has not become distasteful is shewn by the number of hill-men who apply for enlistment and have to be told to wait for vacancies. The time has not yet arrived when it would be safe to trust to a police force composed chiefly of hill-men although mixed up as they now are with men from the Indian hills they do their work well.

The Police of the Hill Tracts have little of the work common to other districts and they really constitute. a *quasi* military force whose duty is to repel raids from outside and to keep order amongst the tribes within our administrative boundary.

ASHE-KHYOUNG.—A village in the Mobya circle, Theekweng township, Bassein district, on the Kyoon-la-ngoo stream, in the middle of a large extent of rice fields, inhabited principally by Kareng.

ASHE-MYOUK.—A township in Tavoy occupying the whole of the eastern portion of the district from Amherst on the north to Mergui on the

---

* The Rajbansi in Lower Bengal are fishermen and cultivators and are said to be a branch of the Tiors who are divided into two classes, the Rajbansi Tiors and the ordinary Tiors. In Eastern and North-Eastern Bengal on the other hand the Koch or ancient ruling class as they embrace Hinduism are called Rajbansi, literally " of the royal kindred." The Rajbansi in the Hill Tracts are from Eastern Bengal.

south, and from the high range of hills forming the boundary between British territory on the east to the Tavoy river as far south as about the latitude of Tavoy town, and below that to the range of hills forming the eastern watershed of that river in the lower portion of its course. The whole face of the country is mountainous and forest-clad, producing valuable timber of various kinds but containing little cultivation and that only in clearings on the hill sides. The principal river is the Tenasserim which has its source in the southern boundary of the district amongst the spurs of the Myeng-mo-let-khat hill, the summit of which is supposed to attain an elevation of 7,000 feet, and flowing N. by W. for a considerable distance is joined at Myetta by the Khamoung-thwai and turning west and south rounds the northern end of a range of hills and runs southward, almost parallel to its original course, into the Mergui district. The Tenasserim before receiving the waters of the Khamoung-thwai, a shallow river in the dry season but much swollen during the rains, is about 55 yards broad at low water. It, like its northern tributary, flows through a narrow valley fed by numerous mountain torrents over a rocky bed which forms a succession of rapids rendering it unnavigable by boats.

There are no towns or villages of any importance in the township Myetta at the junction of the Tenasserim and the Khamoung-thwai was once a large town, traditionally the capital of an independent Siamese principality, but is now only a small Kareng village at which, soon after the British occupation, the American Baptist Missionaries formed a settlement.

The population of the township, which is divided into twelve Revenue circles, was 18,061 souls in 1876, the land revenue Rs. 28,261, the capitation tax Rs. 13,210 and the gross Revenue Rs. 42,933. The name literally means " North-east."

ASHE-TOUNG (*South-east*).—A township in Tavoy, divided into ten Revenue circles, lying on the left bank of the Tavoy river and extending southwards along the seacoast to the Mergui district : a range of hills which send their spurs down nearly to the river and the coast separates it from the North-Eastern Township. It is drained by numerous streams which have generally an E. and W. direction, with broad mouths fringed with mangrove ; the most important is the Toung-byouk in the south which, rising in the north-western slopes of the Myeng-mo-let-khat hill and flowing through a fertile valley towards the N.W. turns west and falls into the mouth of the Tavoy river through an outlet about half a mile wide. The principal products are rice, sessamum, cardamoms, betel-nuts, fruit, and nipa palms from which is extracted tari and sugar the leaves being extensively used for thatch.

The population in 1876 was 17,943 souls, the land revenue Rs.28,720, the amount realized from the capitation tax Rs. 12,593 and the gross Revenue Rs. 43,332.

ATHAY-GYEE.—A revenue circle in the Bassein township of the Bassein district with an area of about 15 square miles, between the Bassein and Paibeng rivers on the east and west and the Let-khoot on the north. Towards the Bassein river it is undulating and the soil gravelly. The inhabitants, Burmans and Kareng, are employed in rice and garden cultivation. A broad belt of forest skirts the rivers and creeks and there is a good deal of low land in the south. To the north is the large town of Bassein, a portion of which is within the limits of this circle. There are no made roads but dry weather footpaths from village to village. The land Revenue in 1876 was Rs. 5,119, the capitation tax Rs. 1,520, and the gross revenue Rs. 6,898 ; the population numbered 1,542 souls. The Zhe-khyoung circle is under the same Thoogyee.

ATHAY-GYEE.—A quarter of the town of Bassein. The quarter received its name, Athay, from being occupied in the Burmese time by a class of people who were exempt from regular service under the Government, paying a tax in lieu thereof.

A-THOOT.—A stream in the Tsambay-roon township of the Bassein district, which rises in the Kyoonlaha lake or swamp and trending gradually towards the south-west meanders through large waste plains sparsely covered with forest and falls into the Kyoon-khabo a short distance above Bhoora-thoon-tshoo. It is tidal and for about fifteen miles from its mouth, as far as Kywon-ta-leng-goon, is, in the rains, open for laden boats of all sizes. In the dry season it is divided off into fisheries.

A-THOOT.—A revenue circle in the Tsambay-roon township—to which is now joined Kyoung-goon—in the Bassein district about 84 square miles in extent. The northern portion consists of undulating ground covered with good timber ; the remainder of low waste plains subject to inundation. The inhabitants, who in 1876 numbered 4,528, are largely engaged in the lake and pond fisheries which are numerous. The land Revenue in 1876 was Rs. 9,260, the capitation tax Rs. 4,350, and the gross Revenue Rs. 18,060.

A-THOOT.—A village or rather a cluster of villages in the Bassein district on the stream of the same name between seven and eight miles from its mouth. The name is Talaing and means " after-birth" (*placenta*) and is said to have been given to the village as being the birth place of one of the early kings of Bassein*.

A-TSAI.—A village in the Thanlyeng township, Rangoon district, in 16° 35′ N. and 96° 32′ E. near the source of an insignificant branch of the Hmawwon and 31 miles west of Khanoung. The inhabitants, who are principally Shan and are engaged mainly in rice cultivation, numbered, in 1877, 672 souls. The name is Talaing and means a glazed earthenware pot, of which there was once a large manufactory here.

A-TSEE.—A revenue circle in the Re Lamaing township, Amherst district, sometimes called A-tsen. It is situated on the sea coast at and south of the mouth of the Re river. The inhabitants are chiefly Talaing. A-tsee is the Talaing name for the *Eria odoratissima* a sweet smelling orchid, a favourite with Burmans and Talaing, which is common on the trees in this circle. In 1876 the population numbered 1,185 souls, the land revenue was Rs. 2,710, and the capitation tax Rs. 1,270.

A-TSEN.—A revenue circle in the Amherst district. (*See Atsee.*)

ATTARAN.—A river in the Amherst district, formed by the junction of the Zamie and the Wengraw, which falls into the Salween at Maulmain. It is a narrow, deep and somewhat sluggish stream with a N.N.W. course and is navigable for a considerable distance. Mr. Crawford, the first British Commissioner of the Tenasserim Provinces, ascended in a small steamer

---

* " Akhyeng (*in Talaing Athoot*) bhay-ma hmyoop-thee-le" literally " where was your after-"birth buried?" is an idiomatic way of asking a Burman where he was born.

very nearly to the junction of the Zamie and the Wengraw. Two tides or one day's journey from the mouth are some hot springs (*vide Amherst district*). In former years a considerable quantity of teak was brought down from the forests—now almost exhausted—which clothe the hills on the banks of the Zamie and the Wengraw.

BASSEIN.—A creek in the Rangoon district—*See Tha-khwot-peng.*

BASSEIN.—A river, or perhaps more correctly a creek, in the Pegu division ; the most westerly of the main channels through which the waters of the Irrawaddy reach the sea. Its northern entrance, about nine miles above the town of Henzada, is 300 yards wide but is choked by a bank of sand uncovered in the dry season through which at this period a little water finds its way to form a small rivulet in the bed. Flowing in a south-westerly direction the Daga leaves it three miles from the main stream of the Irrawaddy to rejoin it again a few miles further on ; beyond this it is joined by the Panmawaddee, and lower down other large tidal creeks connect it by a thousand smaller channels with the other mouths of the great river till after a tortuous course of two hundred miles it falls into the sea at Hmawdeng or Pagoda Point. In the rains it is navigable throughout by river steamers but in the dry season it is fordable as far down as Nga-thaing-khyoung beyond which point steamers cannot then ascend. From Le-myet-hna, where it is about 100 yards wide, it gradually broadens to 900 yards, a width which it retains for some distance in its winding course above Ngapootaw. From this point downwards its course is generally S.S.W. and many rocks and islands occur but navigation is by no means difficult. The right bank from Ngapootaw down to Long Island is low, muddy and covered with jungle; thence to the site of Dalhousie it is low and from Dalhousie to Hmawdeng somewhat hilly. The left bank is hilly and low alternately to Huget-pouk ; from thence to the mouth of the Pyeng-kha-raing it is low and very muddy ; a fine sandy beach stretches to Yeethoung and from here to Poorian point, which marks the eastern shore of the mouth, the margin is rocky. From a little above the Sesostris rock off Long Island the river contracts but directly Long Island is passed it opens out and gradually widens to its mouth. Just at the mouth and close to the right bank is Haing-gyee or Negrais Island celebrated in Anglo-Burmese history. " There are two channels leading into this river one " on each side of Negrais Island and the western channel forms a good harbour. " The eastern channel is not so safe for an extensive reef projects from the " land about Poorian nearly to Diamond Island—which faces the mouth of the " river—and a reef also projects from Negrais Island about five miles to the " south-west which with other detached shoal banks nearly join the extremity " of the former reef and Diamond Island." Seventy-five miles up is the large and important town of Bassein, the head-quarters of the district of the same name, which does a large export trade in rice and is one of the principal ports of the province, annually visited by numerous ships of considerable tonnage.

BASSEIN.—A Municipal town in the delta of the Irrawaddy on both banks of the Bassein river 75 miles from the sea, in 16° 45' N. and 94° 40' E. the head-quarters of the Bassein district, with 22,417 inhabitants in 1876. On the left bank of the river on a slight eminence in the Zhe-khyoung quarter stands the Shwe Moo-htaw Pagoda now in the centre of a fort constructed by the English within the walls of which are the Court-houses and the Treasury and in the neighbourhood a newly laid out public garden. To the east, beyond an open space which served as a parade-ground for the troops, is the Myothit quarter with two principal streets running through it east and west about a mile in length terminating in a plain covered with pagodas, zayats or rest-houses, monasteries and massive images in all stages of decay where the inhabitants assemble for their feasts and religious festivals. North of the Fort and the open space round it is the Talaing-khyoung quarter extending along the bank of the river and pierced by a large street running north and south and others at right angles thereto, whilst to the southward lies the Athaygyee quarter traversed by two good streets running north and south and by cross streets at right angles, the richest and most populous of the Municipal divisions. Here are the Chief Market, the Custom-house, the Roman Catholic Church and institute of St. Peter, and the principal shops. Across the river is the small Theng-bhaw-gyeng suburb containing the rice-mills and store-yards of the principal merchants. Outside the Fort is the Gaol, completed in 1868-69 at a cost of Rs. 172,600, consisting of shingled wooden buildings well raised from the ground, radiating from the centre and surrounded by a wall. There are two markets ; the principal built in the Athay-gyee quarter in 1860-61 and the second completed in 1873-74 in the Talaing khyoung quarter ; a circuit-house, two hospitals, one a wooden building for Europeans and the other of masonry for natives, Customs office, and a Master Attendant's Office. There are also an Anglican Catholic Church, a Roman Catholic Church, a Roman Catholic School, and a Chapel and two Kareng Normal Schools belonging to the American Baptist Missionaries, one for Pwo and one for Sgaw Kareng.

The town having been utterly depopulated in the time of the Burman conqueror Aloung-bhoora no trustworthy records are obtainable. It is by one account said to have been founded in 1249 A.D. by Oom-ma-dan-dee a Talaing Princess, whilst according to another it was in existence many years earlier. Situated in a fertile rice country intersected by numerous navigable creeks which afford means of communication with Rangoon and with the Irrawaddy and the country to the north and accessible by the largest ships from the sea Bassein has always been a port of considerable importance and is alluded to as " Cosmin " by Ralph Fitch and other travellers who found Rangoon, or as it was then called Dagon, a small village. Endeavours were continually made by the English to obtain a permanent footing and factories were formed on Negrais and in Bassein itself but they never succeeded and the establishments were eventually withdrawn. During the first Burmese war the occupation of the town by the British under Major Sale was unopposed the Burman Governor having set fire to and deserted it and retreated up the Bassein river to Le-myet-hna. The population gradually returned and the place was not abandoned till the conclusion of the war when all troops were withdrawn. During the second Burmese war it was taken by assault by detachments of the 51st K. O. L. I. and of the M. N. I.

In 1855-56 the value of grain exports by sea and land was Rs. 435,050, and of all other exports including treasure Rs. 90,396 ; the value of the imports was Rs. 243,000 : the tonnage of the vessels which cleared out in the same year was 2,847. In 1864-65, when the English had been for ten years in undisputed possession of the whole country from which Bassein could draw its export supplies, the values had varied to Rs. 2,672,822, Rs. 67,702 and Rs. 166,519. In 1876-77 the value of grain exported (104,516 tons) was Rs. 5,000,427, of all other exports Rs. 34,268, of imports Rs. 369,519, and the tonnage of vessels which cleared out, excluding those in ballast, was 79,176.

The main article of export is rice and the principal imports by sea are coal, salt and gunny-bags, the last brought down from Calcutta to be filled with the rice to be exported ; whilst the piece-goods and other articles of foreign manufacture with which the markets and shops are supplied are brought principally from Rangoon.

Within the last few years the town has been connected with Rangoon by a telegraph line which it is proposed to extend to the mouth of the river where ships call for orders.

In 1876-77 the town had a gross Municipal revenue of Rs. 97,784.

BASSEIN.—A district in the Pegu division occupying the extreme western portion of the delta of the Irrawaddy and a small strip of country on the sea coast on the other side of the Arakan mountains north of Hmawdeng. To the north lie Henzada on the east and Sandoway on the west of the Arakan hills, to the east Thoon-khwa and to the south and west the Bay of Bengal.

From the mouth of the Khwa river in about 17° 34′ N. and 94° 37′ E. the coast line stretches for 110 miles, measured in a straight line, in a generally south-south-west direction to Cape Negrais, thence it inclines south by east for nine miles to Hmawdeng or Pagoda Point the southern extremity of the Arakan mountains. The first few miles consist of a gently shelving sandy beach backed by undulating ground covered with forest, below this rocky headlands alternate with stretches of narrow sandy beach the forest here and there coming down to the water's edge : beyond Cape Negrais, where the hills enter the sea abruptly forming a bold and rugged escarpment, the coast is generally rocky. From Hmawdeng westwards the whole aspect and character as well as the direction of the coast line changes. The rocky shore with forest-clad hills behind it gives place to a flat and sandy beach with narrow grass-covered plains running along its margin soon passing into mangrove swamps intersected in every direction by tidal creeks.

The eastern boundary is formed almost throughout its entire length by creeks. From the Pyengthaloo or eastern mouth of the Pyamalaw it runs northward along the course of that stream to the Zalai-htaw Oukpouk thence it is marked by the Zalai-htaw, the Thaigoon, the Tawbadaik, the Regoo, the Wawmee, the Khaya-gan, the Roon-ngoo, the Kawthaleng (as far as Danaw), the Bawzat-gale, the Mezalee, the Pouk-padan to its junction with the Taw-da-loo below Kyoon-tanee, thence by the Taw-da-loo as far as Natmaw Koola-tshiep from which by a line drawn to the southernmost point of the Ngabyema Lake, thence along the western bank of that lake to its northern and and then by a line drawn to the Ieng-khyoung near Myo-goon-rwa at the head of the Shakhaigyee lake ; from this point it inclines north-west till it strikes the Daga river. From the Daga the boundary runs in a north-westerly direction for 26 miles to the Bassein river which it crosses in about 17° 3′ 5″ N, a few miles above Le-myet-hna, only eight or nine miles as the crow flies from the Daga. From the Bassein river westwards it follows the crest of the Mo-htee spur for 28 miles to its root in the Arakan mountains : there it turns south for 10 miles following the crest of the main range to near the source of the Khwa which it follows to the sea coast, 16 miles off due west but more than 36 miles measured along the bed of the river.

The appearance of the district on the map is that of an irregular parallelogram extending northwards from the Bay of Bengal divided into two very unequal parts by the Arakan mountains, that to the west forming a narrow strip of mountainous country that to the east a stretch of alluvial land traversed by three large rivers, branches of the Irrawaddy, which flow nearly parallel to one another from their parent source to the sea. Of this the northern and largest portion as far south as the latitude of Ngapootaw is well watered and exceedingly fertile, the southern, with cultivated plains scattered here and there and with large tracts of forest, gradually passes into low marshy ground cut into innumerable islands by the network of tidal creeks which unite the mouths of the Irrawaddy. The area contained within the limits given above is about 6,517 square miles of which, in 1876-77, 431 were cultivated and 4,986 culturable waste leaving 1,100 unculturable.

The principal rivers are the Pyamalaw—with its two mouths the Pyamalaw and the Pyengthaloo—the boundary of the district, the Rwe with the small Daye-bhyoo mouth and the Bassein with the Thekkay-thoung mouth. With the exception of the Bassein these names are those by which the mouths only are known. The Pyamalaw leaves the Kyoenpat at Shwe-loung and flows for some distance north-west and west before it turns south to the sea. The Rwe is formed by the junction a little to the south-east of Myoungmya of several inosculating creeks. All these streams appear to be almost entirely dependent upon the Irrawaddy and the tide for their water. The Bassein river though itself leaving the Irrawaddy some miles above Henzada and connected with that river by numerous creeks and smaller streams, of which the Daga is the most important, receives much of its water from the eastern slopes of the Arakan hills and is the only mouth used by large sea-going vessels, which ascend to Bassein the head-quarters of the district and one of the principal ports of the Province. The whole country south of the 17th degree, except to the west of the Arakan Romas and in their immediate neighbourhood on the east, consists of numerous islands formed by vast numbers of anastomosing tidal creeks some navigable by large boats and even by steamers, others only by canoes.

Rivers.

The only hills of any size are the Arakan mountains across which are several passes used by travellers but they are all more or less difficult and impracticable except during the driest portion of the year. The most northern pass which is entirely in this district is the Bhawmee, the highest point of which is 270 feet only above the sea level, from the junction of the Tsa-loo and Bhawmee streams to the village of Thit-nan-koo on the Thien. Further south there are two passes by the Kyoung-tha and Tsheng-ma streams ; the crest of the first is 381 and of the second 284 feet above the sea. By the Nga-root river a pass leads over the mountains to the Pien stream ; the principal obstructions are the rocks and boulders the elevation of the hills being insignificant. Lastly from Rwotpa to Letpan in the extreme south, a little north of the latitude of Cape Negrais, a rarely used track crosses the hills at an elevation of 270 feet.*

Hills.

---

* For the passes north of Bhawmee see *Sandoway District.*

Nothing definite is known of the character and resources of the forests
in this district beyond the fact that they comprise large
tracts of mangrove forest and of evergreen forest, the dry
or upper mixed forest being, it would seem, somewhat limited in area. These
forests are resorted to yearly for considerable quantities of Pyeng-gado (*Xylia
dolabriformis*), Sha (*Acacia catechu*), Toungpien (*Artocarpus sp.*), Thit-kha
(*Quercus semiserrata*) and other woods for use at Bassein and at the large
villages in the delta and along the Bassein river. Teak is not met with in
any great abundance on any part of the hills.

Along the coast, especially between Cape Negrais and Hmawdeng
occur beds of blown sand, somewhat more earthy than
sandy, which from their reddish colour when viewed
from a distance are named *Kannee* or "red bank." A deposit of a somewhat
similar origin only coarser and distinctly accumulated under water is met
with along the course of some of the less sheltered tidal creeks; it is a
calcareous sand composed of comminuted shells and corals of living species
consolidated into a more or less calcareous sandstone or ragstone and displaying the same local variations as are seen in the deposits now forming along
the Indian shores. When this littoral concrete does not form on the banks of
the tidal streams its place is taken by the fœtid mud or sand and mud of
the mangrove swamps. East of Ngapootaw on the Bassein river a considerable
area is covered with sandy deposits, as is also a tract of country stretching
northward from Bassein which Mr. Blanford of the Geological Survey of
India thus describes :—"In the northern portion of the district and as far south
" as the neighbourhood of Bassein a considerable tract of low hills skirting the
" higher range is composed of gravel and sand of considerable thickness. This
" formation includes a bed of laterite covered to some depth by a sandy deposit
" and cropping out at the small escarpment which in most places rises from
" the flat alluvium of the delta. A similar laterite and gravelly deposit
" covers a considerable area east of the Bassein river in the neighbourhood of
" the town of Bassein." In the northern part of this district these sandy
beds attain a greater importance than elsewhere and it is not unlikely that
these vast accumulations are mainly derived from the denudation of the
incoherent beds of the fossil wood group, which at present occupies a very
restricted area in Pegu in comparison with its former limits. A remarkable
patch of beds, somewhat recalling in appearance the Porebunder beds of
Kattiawar, occurs on the western coast of the district. These beds embrace
Kaw-ran-gyee Island in Lat. 18° 30′ 50″ N. together with a small portion of
the mainland. The most characteristic bed is a calcareous sandstone or soft
rather earthy limestone of a very pale brown or cream colour, containing
four species of as many genera of echinoderms the most common being a
species of *lobophora* very close to that now inhabiting the adjoining coast and a
species of *Echinolampas* (near *E. Affinis*) and one pelecypod, a rather small
species of *Amussium*. Kaw-ran-gyee Island consists of beds of thin calcareous
sandstone having a high dip W. by N. nearly. Denudation has, save at this
spot, removed every trace of this deposit. On the mainland the rocks are
entirely isolated by a low swampy channel running into the Nga-root creek.
Just opposite the northern extremity of Kaw-ran-gyee Island some beds of
earthy bluish sandstone come in vertically along the shore. At the mouth
of the Nga-root creek small sharks teeth are not rare and from the same

earthy beds two conical fish teeth, some fragmentary crustacean claws and the ossicles (palatal or dermal) of some species of Ray were found by Mr. Theobald of the Geological Survey of India. On Kaw-ran-gyee Island he also procured a small reptilian tooth with cultrate edges, smooth and mottled yellow longitudinally. On this island and on the adjoining mainland a soft calcareous sandstone or earthy limestone occurs, easy to work and unusually well situated for shipment into lighters or small coasting craft. The island is composed of these beds and under its leeside a channel exists having a depth of two or three fathoms at low water with a good bottom of sand or mud. The channel shoals gradually towards the mainland and is protected by the island on the west or seaward and by a bar almost dry at low water to the north but enjoying a safe and easy entrance from the south save during the prevalence of the southwest monsoon.

The Nummulitic or Eocene group of rocks is well developed, extending throughout this district as far as Pooriam point, a rocky spit running into the sea on the eastern side of the mouth of the Bassein river, but its precise extent towards the west is uncertain from its joining, if not blending with, the altered rocks of the southern portion of the Arakan hills which are almost devoid of organic remains or present so few as to be useless for any purpose of subdivision of the group or even for estimating its geological age. The difficulty of separating the groups is increased by the similar capricious sort of submetamorphism which prevails in both. For these altered rocks of the southern region a provisional classification and name has been accepted by Mr. Theobald who has named them the Negrais beds, from their being very characteristically displayed about Cape Negrais, a term which includes all the rocks met with in the country stretching northward from Cape Negrais along the Arakan range and western coast older than the Nummulitic and younger than the Triassic. The difference in mineral character in the Negrais rocks is very great. In some places flaggy and massive sandstones occur quite unaltered and dipping at moderate angles whilst in places sections are exposed of highly altered shales and sandstones and in some spots the sandstone is seen converted into a cherty rock seamed with silica and evidently subjected to an alteration of an intense kind. The following sketch of the beds seen in crossing the Arakan range from east to west between Gnyoung-beng-tha and Re-poot will illustrate the character of the present group. " When well within the hills, proceeding in a " westerly direction; the first rocks passed over in descending order are blue " slaty shales of great thickness with a dip to the east. These shales are soft " and silky and contain numerous beds of blue limestone varying from a few " inches to a few feet in thickness. The limestone is fine-grained and sub- " crystalline, breaking with a conchoidal fracture, blue on its freshly broken " surface but weathering to a pale yellow or nankeen colour. It is rather " silicious and hardened and although a very probable looking rock for fossils " a close search failed to discover any traces whatever of organic remains " in it. After passing these shales, but still on the east side of the range, " a group of coarse thick bedded silicious sandstones is met with, with harsh " silicious or jaspery shales and thin-bedded silicious sandstones intermixed. " The whole of these beds are internally hardened and silicified. One very " thick bed has a hardened appearance from containing irregularly shaped " earthy portions which decay and leave great angular hollows three or four

88

"inches across. Some dark blue thin-bedded slaty shale also occurs associated
"subordinately with the silicious beds as though here foreshadowing the
"approaching deposition of similar shales in much greater force which are seen
"as above mentioned to overlie these silicious beds. After leaving these silicious
"beds no very clear section is seen. The dip appears however to remain easterly
"till the axis of the main range is crossed.

"The axis of the range here consists of a great thickness of beds of a very
"homogeneous clay, of a reddish or pinky yellow colour, and obscurely bedded.
"It is much broken up and comminuted as though through severe pressure, but
"little altered, and neither to the eastward nor westward are its relations with
"the other rocks well seen. After crossing the axis of the range the succession
"of beds was not well seen ; and though I did not remark the silicious beds to
"be so prominent as on the east of the range I am inclined to believe that the
"same beds as are met with in the east are again crossed on the west, in a
"reverse order, that is to say that the range forms a great anticlinal, the pre-
"vailing dips on its Eastern side being Easterly, and on its Western side Wes-
"terly. On the west, however, there is (locally at all events) greater irregu-
"larity in dip and strike than on the east ; and I have there noticed beds with
"an east and west strike, or nearly at right angles to the prevailing one of
"the range. Much allowance must be made for imperfect observation, as all
"one sees of the rock is such glimpses as can be obtained along the narrow
"path threading these forest-clad ranges. When well past the main range
"the road descends and runs over a thick succession of the but little altered
"sandstones of the Kyouk-gyee (*big stone*) stream. Part of this rocky stream
"is quite impassable for elephants, and the nature of the country may be
"imagined from it requiring four hard days marches to accomplish the distance
"from Nyoung-ben-tha (*Gnyoung-beng-tha*) to Yaypot (*Re-poot*), though these
"villages are in a direct line only fifteen miles apart.

"A little south of Phon-sa-khyoung(*Hpoon-tsa-khyoung*), near Matha on
"the coast, a good section of beds of this group is seen ; but their proper place
"in the series can hardly be determined, owing to the want of any sort of
"geological horizon in the group, either lithological or otherwise. I am
"inclined, however, to place them high in the series, above the vast series of
"sandstones seen above Yaypot.(*Re-poot*), in the bed of the Kyouk-gyee
"stream.

"Section near Matha (ascending). The beds veer round from 15° to
"south-by-west, to 45° to west-by-south.

1.	Dark arenaceous shales, with faint carbonaceous markings and stringy beds of sandstone much contorted and squeezed about	300
2.	Harsh thin-bedded sandstones in one and two-inch beds, with shaly partings and a few beds five and seven inches thick	85
3.	Beds similar to the above, but one and two feet beds predominating	23
4.	Very thin-bedded sandstones not averaging half an inch, with a few one and two-inch beds interspersed	69
5.	Thicker bedded sandstones in from nine to twenty-inch beds	52
6.	Similar to the last, but thinner bedded	49
7.	Thin-bedded shaly sandstones	99
8.	Thicker bedded sandstones in from nine to twelve-inch beds	46
9.	Thin shaly beds	30

753

" The section here becomes confused, but thick beds of sandstone come in,
" which seem identical with the sandstones commonly seen along the coast, and
" which I will now describe. Along most parts of the coast, from Negrais
" upwards, a group of sandstones occurs, thin-bedded and massive, but present-
" ing no very prominent mineral character, or affording any fossil. The sand-
" stones are very little altered, generally not at all, and usually dip at moderate
" angles and with much less show of disturbance than other and older beds
" along the coast. . . . .
          " The massive beds at the base of this group are everywhere most con-
" spicuous and of a peculiar greenish hue very characteristic of this rock,
" which hue, however, in some places towards the north is changed into a
" bluish tinge. The rock is a very fine-grained argillaceous sandstone, rather
" compact, but where exposed to the action of the sea, its surface usually pre-
" sents a honeycombed or cancellated appearance, the result of a peculiar mode
" of weathering, the *modus operandi* and proximate cause of which is somewhat
" obscure. Subordinate to the thick-bedded greenish or cancellated sandstone,
" as it may conveniently be termed, occurs an irregular, and in places almost
" stringy bed of conglomerate, a prominent feature connected with which is its
" great irregularity and capricious mode of occurrence. It nowhere forms a
" marked bed, save perhaps near Ywot-pa (*Rwot-pa*), but dies out and re-ap-
" pears along a certain horizon as an integral constituent of the cancellated sand-
" stone, in places forming a stringy course in it, reduced in places to little more
" than a sprinkling of small pebbles in a sandstone matrix, whilst in other
" places it would seem to expand into a thick mass of conglomerate, though
" such instances are very local and circumscribed in extent.
          " This is the conglomerate, I think, which is so largely developed in the
" hill behind Phoung-do (*Hpoung-do*) ; if so, it nowhere else attains the same
" importance. To this bed may also be referred the masses of conglomerate
" seen on the shore opposite Ywot-pa (*Rwot-pa*), where they stand quite
" isolated between tidemarks, and are so compact as to have resisted the full
" force of the waves on an exposed coast.
          " This conglomerate is in places almost a pseudo-breccia. the fragments
" composing it being but imperfectly rounded. The included fragments are all
" small, rarely half an inch across, and usually much smaller, and mainly consist
" of a comminuted dark blue or cream-colored shale highly indurated, the latter
" variety only effervescing very feebly with acid. Quartz fragments are here
" very subordinate and small. This conglomerate is very soon lost sight of,
" going north, and may be said to cease almost at once as an independent bed,
" though re-appearing here and there at intervals. It may be recognised, for
" instance, a little north of the Yaytho (*Re-tho*) stream on the coast between
" Broken Point and Kyoungthah (*Khyoung-tha*). The rocks along the shore
" here are thick-bedded massive sandstones, mingled with which a thin string
" of conglomerate occurs, rather irregularly, composed mainly of small white
" quartz pebbles with a little shaly detritus as elsewhere. Some few miles
" south of Matha, strings of fine conglomerate are noticed in the sandstone,
" and still further north, between Kyouk-kyon (*Khyouk-kywon*) and Gwah
" (*Khwa*), considerable bands of a coarse conglomerate, made up of shaly and
" cherty fragments, are dispersed through the sandstone, all which represent,
" probably within narrow limits, what may be called a common horizon

" These thick-bedded sandstones are often tilted up at high angles but are
" more usually seen either horizontal or dipping at low angles. In addi-
" tion to the cancellated form of weathering, the rock is sometimes seen
" with a tendency to divide into polygonal fragments, the fissures separating
" which seem to originate spontaneously, the nucleus of each fragment retaining
" the original green or bluish hue of the undecayed rock, while the fissures are
" represented by yellow bands, as though the result of chemical rather than
" mechanical causes.

" Nowhere is the variable character of the beds of this group better dis-
" played than along the coast immediately north of Cape Negrais. Below the
" point where the Ywot-pa (*Rwot-pa*,) stream falls into the sea, beds are expos-
" ed very similar in general character to those already given in the section near
" Matha, higher up the coast. These beds contain crushed carbonaceous trunks
" and branches, and dip at angles varying from 10° to 40° east-by-north.
" South of these beds, thin shaly sandstone, quite unaltered, come in, dipping
" 15° west-by-north. Nearer Negrais, a thick series of dark shales, with
" subordinate beds of cherty limestone, comes in, displaying signs of having
" been subjected to great mechanical strain as well as to chemical alteration.
" This latter is displayed in the numerous veins of fibrous calcite and fibrous
" quartz which traverse the rock, the former attaining a thickness of a
" couple of inches, the latter rarely attaining half an inch. Some of the
" shale where the veins are most numerous is of a deep black color and very
" hard and glossy, and I can convey no better idea of the lumps of this rock
" scattered along the shore than by comparing them to lumps of black putty,
" which they precisely resemble. A little nodular soapstone is also found
" scattered here and there, and the occurence of this mineral, together with
" its invariable associate, the fibrous vein-quartz, points to this being a focus
" for that peculiar metamorphism which has so generally affected this group.
" These shales constitute the low ridge, which here forms the axis of the range,
" where crossed by the pass leading to Ywot-pa (*Rwot-pa*), but on which, from
" its forest-clad nature, little is seen of the rocks passed over. It is here
" that the "mud volcano" of the charts of this coast is situated, a complete
" misnomer, as it has no connection with volcanic action properly so called,
" and neither lava, ashes, nor other volcanic rocks are seen about it.

" This " mud volcano" is situated on the hill side, where it rapidly slopes
" down to the shore, and within a stone's throw of the sea. A narrow footpath
" exists along the coast here, on the east of which at one spot a small mound of
" loose pulverulent shale rises a few feet in height, and about thirty feet at most
" in diameter, over which any one might walk without having his attention
" arrested by any peculiarity. This mound is the " mud volcano." A very
" similar instance is seen near the shore near Ngan-khyoung, and my remarks
" on one will be equally applicable to both. This mound consists of a
" greenish shale, very much comminuted and mixed with fragments of veins of
" calcite, from the thickness of cardboard to one or two inches. These fragments
" have evidently resulted from the spontaneous dehiscence of the compact shale
" they originally traversed; and this is seen in the constitution of the thicker
" veins, which are formed by the union and anastomosis of numerous smaller
" veins, wherein portions of the shaly matrix are seen enveloped and preserved.
" A very little hydrated peroxide of iron in small lumps is seen lying about,

"but nothing else to indicate any peculiarity, still less volcanic action. The
"form of the low mound suggests a certain amount of intumescence or
"upheaving of the clay having taken place, but in the case of the Ngan-
"khyoung "volcano" this is less seen, and I am inclined to pronounce the
"'mud volcano' in either case as *the vent for a very feeble discharge of*
"*marsh-gas*. In the rains, when the surface was plastic, a feeble ebullition of
"gas would be quite adequate to produce the low mound in question, which
"on drying would present the incoherent heap of shale fragments described;
"the combustion of the marsh-gas at some period or other from burning
"grass, probably attracting notice during the night to the locality. . . .
    "Most of the outcrops of limestone through the southern portion of the
"Arakan Range, both those along the coast and those met with occasionally in
"the hills, present the appearance of subordinate beds among the shales and
"sandstones of this group; but there are some cases where limestone occurs in
"such extensive masses as to favor the idea of their being continuations of the
"thick bed of Nummulitic limestone which occurs on the east side of the
"range, and such may be their character, though not yet established on fossil
"evidence. First of these in importance is the limestone a couple of miles or so
"east-north-east from Baumi (*Bhaw-mee*), on the Arakan coast, about Lat. 17°
"18', forming a low ridge striking north-north-east from the margin of the
"mangrove swamp, where it terminates towards the river, and soon disappear-
"ing in the forest-clad ground in the interior. It is only approachable by a small
"boat up a tidal creek traversing the mangrove swamp, after three-quarter flood.
"The rock is massive and subcrystalline, with an apparent dip of 20° to 50° to
"east-south-east, as far as the cyclopean masses in which the rock lies enables
"us to judge. It is of a blue or gray color, and generally devoid of fossils; in
"some 'of the blocks corals are seen, but none have hitherto been obtained,
"capable of being determined. Its thickness is probably not much under one
"hundred feet. Above the limestone (as well as the ground enabled
"me to judge) occurs an intensely hard ferruginous conglomerate, charac-
"terised by numerous quartz pebbles. Below the limestone comes in a very
"hard silicious sandstone like a quartzite, of a gray color on its freshly-
"fractured surface, but weathering red, and then displaying the original
"thin layers of sand, which in the aggregate form the thick-bedded rock before
"us. Near Sat-wa, (*Tsat-wa*) a little boss of limestone which may belong to this
"bed is exposed in the jungles, and is used for lime by the villagers in the neigh-
"bourhood. This rock is a white and somewhat argillaceous rock, not well
"seen, but with an apparent dip to the east. Strewed about the vicinity are a
"few pieces of conglomerate, like that associated with the Baumi (*Bhaw-mee*)
"limestone; and a little to the south, in a line indicating a lower position
"strategraphically, stands a huge fang of harsh sandstone very similar to the
"Baumi (*Bhaw-mee*) rock. The distance of this spot from Baumi (*Bhaw-mee*)
"is about thirty miles, and though I know of no other outcrop in the interval,
"I am inclined to regard both outcrops as belonging to one bed. Great as
"the thickness of the limestone is at Baumi(*Bhaw-mee*) it is much isolated, most
"probably by denudation; and I failed after a careful search to detect any
"traces of it on the opposite side of the Baumi (*Bhaw-mee*) river, nor were my
"enquiries among the Burmese more successful. Another enormous isolated
"mass of limestone of very similar character occurs on the On-ben (*Oon-beng*)

" stream, a tributary of the Gwah (*Khwa*) river. It is situated in dense tree
" forest away from any village. . . . . . . There is small question that the
" Baumi (*Bhaw-mee*) and Oʻ -ben (*Oon-beng*) limestones are the same bed."*
Soapstone which is used by the Burmese for writing on parabaik or
blackened fibre-paper is largely imported from Upper Burma, but occurs at
a variety of spots in the Arakan range, chiefly, though not exclusively, on its
eastern side. Among the altered rock towards Cape Negrais it is found in
the form of veins, among altered shale along the shore, and a few miles east
of Kweng-boo, thirty miles north of Cape Negrais among sandstones, which
are indurated and disturbed; but at neither of these spots are any intruded rocks
visible. At Kweng-boo, the steatite occurs in veins traversing sandstone
lenticularly intermixed with the peculiar fibrous quartz, but not averaging
an inch in thickness. In these veins the steatite is a little in excess of the
fibrous quartz, but the two minerals are very intimately united, the lenticular
masses of the former being often enveloped with a layer of the latter, and
portions are sometimes seen presenting almost the appearance of a conglomerate
of steatite kernels, some no larger than hemp-seeds, enveloped in a paste of
fibrous quartz. These steatite kernels have, however, nothing to do with a
mechanical origin, but are bounded by lustrous burnished surfaces, much resembling the silken sides produced in shales by pressure, but in this case of quite
another character, and the result of the peculiar chemical composition and mode
of origin of the mineral—the smaller and purer portions of which being those
with most lustrous surface.
Most of the lime used in the district is procured near Thamandewa and
Kyouk-thaing-baw on the Bassein river a few miles below Ngapootaw on
which Mr. Blanford, of the Geological Survey of India, remarked :—
" This is by far the most important locality in the province, and perhaps
" in the whole of Pegu. At Kyouk-theingbaw (*Kyouk-thaing-baw*) several
" very large masses of limestone crop out from the alluvium on the river
" bank. The quantity here, though considerable, would, however, soon be
" exhausted if there were a large demand for lime. South of the village,
" Thamandewa, a tidal creek stretches for some miles into the country, and
" on the south of this creek the outcrop of a bed at least thirty or forty
" feet thick stretches across the country in a direction nearly south 20°
" west, for a distance of about a mile, re-appearing at intervals for about
" a mile further, the most southerly point where it is seen being near the
" bank of the river bed not far from the village of Toung-gale. The quan-
" tity is inexhaustible, the quality good, and the access easy, Thamandewa
" creek being navigable for Burmese boats of the largest size, and probably
" at high tide for sea-going vessels."†
Of the early history of the district but little is known. The Bassein
History. river has been claimed as the Besynga of the Geographer Ptolemy but its right to this distinction
has never been universally admitted, though the weight of evidence is in
favor of this view. " In his sketch of the hydrography of India beyond the
" Ganges" observes that learned and cautious officer Colonel Yule " the

---

* *Report on the Geology of Pegu :* By W. Theobald, Geological Survey of India.
† *Apud* Theobald : " Report on the Geology of Pegu.

' Geographer (*Ptolemy*) says distinctly, ' From the range of Mœndrus flow' " ' down all the rivers beyond Ganges, *until you come to the river Besynga.*' " This remark seems infallibly to identify Mons Mœandrus with Yoma-doung, " the great spinal range of Arakan, and the river Besynga with the Bassein " branch of the Irawadi."* In the old Talaing histories the " 32 cities of Bassein" are mentioned under the date 625 A.D. as forming a portion of the kingdom of Pegu. *Circa* 1250 A.D. a princess named Oommadandee ascended the throne but a few years later Bassein was conquered by the Burmans. In 1272 the Chinese invaded Burma and the reigning king Narathee-ha-pade, subsequently nicknamed Taroop-pye-meng or "the king who ran away from the Tartars", escaped southward to Bassein. Very few years later on, in 1289 A.D., Bassein, according to Talaing histories, again passed over to Pegu; this occurred probably when the Talaing kingdom increased in power owing to the gradual sinking of the Burman authority in the north. About 1383 A.D., when Razadhierit, the greatest monarch of the Talaing, ascended the throne, one Louk-bya, Governor of Myoungnya, proposed to the Burmans to assist them in conquering Pegu and the acceptance· of his offer led to long and almost incessant wars between the two kingdoms.

In 1686 the Governor of Madras determined on establishing a settlement on Negrais, which was then considered as a portion of the Arakan dominions, and despatched a sloop to make a survey of the island but she lost her passage and was obliged to return. The following year Captain Weldon, on his return from Mergui, landed on Negrais and hoisting the British flag took possession of the island in the name of the East India Company. No further steps were taken till 1753 when Mr. Hunter was sent in charge of an expedition which landed on the island and formed the first British settlement. The settlement did not thrive and Mr. Hunter soon died and was succeeded by Mr. Burke. At this time the war between the kingdoms of Pegu and Burma, which ended in the complete subjugation of the former, was raging in all its fierceness. Both Peguans and Burmans sought the assistance of the British which was refused by Mr. Burke. In 1755 the English had a settlement at Bassein itself and Captain Baker who was then in charge of the factory wrote that the Talaing having quitted Bassein the Burmans had attacked and destroyed the place respecting however the East India Company's factory and property. In his report to the Madras Government Mr. Burke strongly urged the advisability of our siding with the Burmans whose cause was flourishing and whose enemies the Talaing had · succeeded in obtaining the assistance of our rivals the French who then had a settlement at Syriam below Rangoon. The King of Burma sent ambassadors to Negrais who were escorted from Bassein by Captain Baker. A mission was sent to the Burman King with the object of obtaining, amongst other advantages, a formal grant of Negrais and a grant of the land at Bassein occupied by the Company's factory as the whole country had now, in the opinion of the English officers, passed to the Burman monarchy. Unfortunately the British ships near Rangoon had been forced to assist the Talaing and the Burman King could not forgive this treachery as he considered it. The English authorities insisted on absolute neutrality and

---

* Yule's *Mission to Ava*, page 205. Colonel Yule does not adopt this view as *absolutely* correct, but his opinion appears to lean very strongly to it.

their local agents were in consequence suspected by both sovereigns. In 1757 Ensign Lister obtained what was considered as a cession in perpetuity of Negrais and of ground at Bassein. In 1759 the establishment was withdrawn from Negrais and a few persons only left to take charge of the Company's property there as well as to hold possession of the island and for the superintendance of these Captain Southey was sent from Madras. He landed on the 5th October 1759 and on the 7th, when all the Europeans were collected to meet the Burmese authorities, they were treacherously attacked and, with the exception of a midshipman who escaped to his ship the *Victoria*, Captain Alves, murdered. After the Europeans, 10 in number, had been despatched a general massacre took place. In 1760 a mission was sent to obtain redress but without effect, the Burman King absolutely forbidding our return to Negrais. but granting a site for the factory at Bassein of which the English Government did not avail itself. From this time until the first Burmese war the inglish Government took no further steps for forming a settlement in this district. During that war a detachment under Major Sale attacked and occupied Bassein which was retained until the evacuation of Pegu, in accordance with the terms of the treaty of Yandaboo. During the second Burmese war the town was again captured, after a feeble resistance, by a force under Commodore Lambert and since then has remained in possession of the British. On the annexation of Pegu the district, which in the Burmese times had been divided into 14 districts, eleven under Paineng or steersmen of royal war-boats and three under Myothoogyee who were hereditary office holders, was placed under a Deputy Commissioner. At this time the whole of the district was a prey to anarchy: the British troops were kept within the limits of the seaport towns and frontier stations and in the interior numerous bandit chiefs set up a pseudo-independent authority, in more than one case claiming to be officers of the Burman Court deputed to regain the country, and there can be no doubt that had they been successful they would have been rewarded by the King provided that they handed over their conquests and settled down into peaceable offices about the Court. A kind of civil war was now carried on; on the one side were those who were averse to us or who looked to plunder for profit, on the other were those who had in any way sided with the English. So far was animosity carried that villages on the banks of the Irrawaddy were destroyed because fuel had been supplied to the steamers. To clear the country of these gangs, to afford protection to the people and restore their confidence in us was now the great object of all civil officers and in this district as well as in Henzada and Tharrawaddy this was the more necessary as no one dared to accept even small appointments and the country was without local officials owning obedience to the British. In January 1853 Captain Fytche, the Deputy Commissioner, succeeded in dispersing a force which kept the whole country in the south and south-east in a state of terror, attacking it first on Negrais Island, whither it had gone to plunder the village of Haingyee, and following it up northwards into the Shwelonng township, eventually destroying the three large villages in which it had made its head-quarters.

No sooner was this effected than Captain Fytche with a party of seamen from the *Zenobia* and *Nemesis*, one or two guns, and his Kareng levies proceeded northward up the Daga river and encountering a party under three

Burman leaders routed them with considerable loss and drove the remainder northward to join another chief, Mengyee Moung Gnyoon the former Governor of Bassein, whom he attacked a few days later and utterly defeated capturing his two sons. Two days after the engagement the Mengyee's dead body was found in the jungles. In the words of the official report:—"The Bassein "district was cleared of the remnant of Burmese troops and of numerous "marauders by the gallant exertions of Major A. Fytche. He received a "brevet-majority as a reward for his services." The nucleus and heart of this force was a party of seamen of the steam frigate *Zenobia* under Commander Rennie of the Indian Navy. By the beginning of March 1853 the lower tracts were freed from the large marauding parties which hitherto had occupied them and nothing but straggling bands of robbers remained. The northern part of the district was still disturbed by a man named Nga Myat Htoon who held out in the south of Henzada (*q.v.*) and was finally defeated and his party broken up by Sir John Cheape operating from the north and Major Fytche and Captain Rennie from the south. In January 1854 fresh disturbances broke out. Two men named Shwe Too and Kyaw Zan Hla came down from Ava and issued a proclamation to the effect that they had been commissioned by the heir apparent to drive out the English and had been appointed the one Governor of Bassein and the other Commander-in-chief. They were aided and abetted by a Booddhist priest, a resident of the district, in whose monastery the plan of the outbreak was settled. They gradually assembled a number of desperate characters from the borders of this district and from Henzada and suddenly seized the three large adjoining towns of Doungyee, Ngathaing-khyoung and Regyee and this success induced numbers to join them, amongst others Nga Tha Oo formerly Royal Steersman of Regyee who had fled to Ava on our taking possession of the country but had returned some six months previously and was on parole. The upper part of the district, unprotected by any British troops, fell at once into the hands of the rebels who exercised no oppression of any kind except against those who had accepted office under the English. On the receipt of the information Major Fytche moved up the river with a small military force of Europeans and Madras Native Infantry and 400 of the inhabitants of the country and found the enemy advancing on Bassein on either bank of the river ; some three hundred on the right bank and eleven hundred in two parties on the left : on the approach of the British force the Burmans on the right bank retreated to Ngathaing-khyoung but those on the left were attacked and driven into Pandaw which was evacuated on the arrival of the British in pursuit. During the night Shwe Too moved out from Ngathaing-khyoung and surrounded Pandaw but was kept off by the Burmese pickets till daybreak when the main body moved out against him. He had taken up a position at the head of the village and his force was drawn up in a plain with the flanks resting in groves of mango trees and low bushes filled with skirmishers. After a sharp struggle the Burmese broke and fled and the British force moved on to Ngathaing-khyoung where it joined Major Baker's detachment and a force of Burmese who had been sent to attack another leader, a duty which it performed with success bringing him in captive. In the meanwhile a party under the Goung-gyoop of Le-myet-hna had attacked the rebels at Doungyee but had been defeated with great loss and was pursued by the rebel chief. Major Fytche followed, conveying his men in carts, and came up with the Burmans the following day surprising them whilst eating and totally defeating them. The Chief escaped but was captured crossing the Bassein river. On the first news of the outbreak information had been despatched to Rangoon and assistance asked for; a detachment was sent under Lieutenant Shuldham 26th M.N.I. which encountered and defeated a rebel party at Myoungmya the Chief being killed during the pursuit. The outbreak was thus speedily crushed by rapid and decisive action and Nga Kyaw Zan Hla, the priest, and most of the inferior leaders killed or captured.

The difficulties encountered were not confined to inspiriting a down trodden people and getting them to resist their old oppressors, to out-manœuvring leaders who knew every footpath and creek, and to obtaining information of their strength and movements from a timid population who were in greater fear of the marauders than of the constituted authority, but the very nature of the country greatly impeded any combined and successful movements, any surprises and sudden attacks. Only one who has traversed the delta of the Irrawaddy can adequately appreciate the difficulty of accomplishing this work. The country is a net-work of creeks which though they afford a ready means of access to any given point yet present serious impediments as soon as a force lands and commences to march.

From this time forward no serious endeavour was made to drive out the English and though there have been several disturbances they were speedily suppressed. In January 1857 there was an outbreak amongst the Kareng but judicious measures were immediately taken by the Deputy Commissioner and within a week they were twice routed and utterly dispersed by the Bassein Talaing Corps raised some time previously by that officer. No time had been given for the disease to spread and the district immediately resumed its usual quiet. This outbreak was an offshoot from the Kareng rebellion then going on in the hills of the Shwe-gyeug district one of the leaders of which was connected with Bassein and his emissaries worked upon the feelings of the Kareng who had settled here and who were induced to rise in order to afford aid to one who, they were led to believe, was destined to be ruler of Pegu.

Population.

The inhabitants of the Bassein district as it then existed, according to the census of 1872, were :—

Burmese	..	..	..	..	..	2,08,551
Kareng	..	..	..	..	..	92,061
Talaing	..	..	..	..	..	14,540
Shan	..	..	..	..	..	1,601
Arakanese	..	..	..	..	..	1,056
Khyeng	..	..	..	..	..	780
Hindoos, including those of mixed parentage..		..	..	..	..	711
Mahomedans	..	..	..	..	..	2,649
Chinese	..	..	..	..	..	454
Other races, Europeans, Indo-Europeans, Malays, &c.	..		..	..	..	288
				Total	..	322,689

In 1875, the Shwe-loung and Pantanaw townships were taken from Bassein. The population in 1874 and in 1876, according to the Thoogyee's rolls, was:—

| | 1874. | | | 1876. |
	Total.	Shwe-loung and Pantanaw.	District as it now exists.	
Burmese and Arakanese ..	221,331	29,251	192,080	198,247
Kareng	108,393	22,635	85,758	87,093
Talaing	11,024	1,591	9,433	9,435
Shan	1,602	..	1,602	1,785
Khyeng	953	..	953	925
Hindoos	1,267	..	1,267	1,264
Mahomedans	2,609	161	2,448	2,638
Chinese	1,160	229	931	1,033
Other races	319	11	308	438
Total ..	348,658	53,878	294,780	302,858

In former years the Talaing mustered strongly but the Burmese conquest by Aloungbhoora and still more the measures adopted by the Burmese when they returned to the delta of the Irrawaddy on the evacuation of Pegu by the British after the first Burmese war drove many into exile and more than decimated the number of those who could not or did not escape from the anger of their rulers whom they had irritated by siding with the English. The Kareng in this district differ from their brethren in the hills in Tenasserim from having adopted the Burmese custom of cultivation but still retain their dress, language, customs and religion except where converted to Christianity, yet many are, at least nominally, Booddhists. The Shan are settlers from the north, whilst many of the Mahomedans and most of the Hindoos are sojourners who come to make money to be spent in their own country. The Khyeng live mostly in the hills to the north-west, the tribe or race stretching far away north and west into Upper Burma and Arakan (vide sub tit : Khyeng). Here, as everywhere else in the Province except in Mergui, the males exceed the females. In 1876 there were 157,142 of the former to 144,715 of the latter. The ratio is materially affected by the town of Bassein and is largely due to immigration. The Madrassees, Chittagonians and others from India bring no women with them but, like the Chinese, take to themselves wives from the women of the country whom they can and do leave behind if they return, whilst large numbers of Burmans come down from Upper Burma for the season only, to work in the rice mills in Bassein and even those who come to settle in the rural tracts do not, to any considerable extent, bring women with them.

The principal occupation of the inhabitants is agriculture and fishing, the large plains affording occupation to the one class and the seacoast and numerous ponds, rivers and tidal creeks in the south to the other.

The number of towns and villages in 1876 was 1,455. The most important are :—

Bassein in about 16° 14′ N. and 94° 46′ E. on the banks of the Nga-woon river some 75 miles from the sea ; the head-quarter station. The three largest quarters of the town are on the left bank of the river surrounding the fort built since the annexation of Pegu and enclosing the conspicuous Shwe-moo-htaw

98

Pagoda, *viz.*, the Athaygyee quarter to the south, the Talaing-khyoung quarter to the north and the Myothit to the east. The small Theng-bhaw-gyeng suburb is on the right bank. Within the walls of the fort are the principal public buildings—the Courts, Treasury and Police Office. The population has rapidly increased since its occupation by the British and in 1876 numbered 22,417 souls. In the year 1860-61 the value of the exports and imports was Rs. 941,710; in 1861-62 it rose suddenly to Rs. 1,623,250 (imports Rs. 550,280, exports Rs. 1,072,970) ; in 1872-73 it amounted to Rs. 3,499,710, of which Rs. 2,823,630 was on account of exports (Rs. 2,763,120 on account of exports to foreign countries other than India) and in 1876-77 reached Rs. 5,582,458, that is :—imports Rs. 447,641 exports to India including other ports in Burma Rs. 65,510, to the Straits and ports to the eastward Rs. 12,961 and to Europe and ports west of India Rs. 4,956,224. The principal trade is in rice, grown in the district and imported from higher up the valley of the Irrawaddy, and husked for export in the mills erected by European merchants. This trade gives employment to a large number of men from Upper Burma who come down for work, leaving their families behind them, and return at the end of the season. Small quantities of timber, cotton, tobacco and oil-seed also are exported : the principal imports are piece-goods, cotton stuffs and crockery. Chinese junks bring small consignments of tea and silk but mainly for the use of the Chinese community. Native craft from the coast of Madras bring cocoanuts and other articles used chiefly by the natives of that country who are employed largely in loading and unloading ships.

Lemyet-hna in 17° 35′ N. and 95° 13′ 30′ E. on the bank of the Bassein river had a population of 5,635 souls in 1867 and of 4,986 in 1876.

Myoung-mya in 16° 35′ N. and 95° E. is on the river of the same name partly on one bank and partly on the other : in 1876 it had a population of of 1,717 souls.

Ngapootaw in 16° 32′ N. and 94° 46′ E. is on the island of the same name in the Bassein river, built on the side of a low range of hills and reaching down to the water's edge : the population in 1876 was 1,010.

Regyee Pandaw in 17° 19′ 30″ N. and 15° 10′ E. is on the creek of the same name, which flows between the Bassein and Daga rivers, and is composed of the once separate towns or villages of Regyee and Pandaw : it had a population in 1867 of 4,695 and in 1876 of 3,506 : it is a place of some importance in the rice trade. It was here that the Talaing army in its retreat before Aloungbhoora made its last stand before its complete and final defeat.

Ngathaing-khyoung in 17° 22′ 30″ N. and 95° 8′ 30′ E. on the Bassein river at the northern entrance of the Regyee creek had a population of 3,512 in 1867 and of 2,737 in 1876; the inhabitants do a considerable trade in rice which is sent to Bassein. For some years a detachment of Native Infantry from Bassein garrisoned the town, a duty now performed by the Police.

Kyoonpyaw in 17° 17′ N. and 95° 16′ E. on the Daga river at the southern entrance of the Regyee creek had a population in 1876 of 2,551 employed in agriculture, in fishing and in trading.

The area of the district under cultivation has rapidly increased. In
Agriculture.   1855-56 it was 134,520 acres; in 1859-60 162,983 acres ; in 1864-65 186,129 acres; in 1869-70 220,160 acres ; and in 1874-75 305,920 acres. In 1876-77, when a considerable tract

on the east had been cut off, the cultivated area was 275,840 acres, or the fifteenth part of the whole area, leaving 3,191,040 acres culturable but uncultivated waste.

The crops cultivated in acres during the last ten years were :—

Year.	Rice.	Oil-seeds.	Sugar.	Cotton.	Tobacco.	Betel vine.	Mixed products, vegetables, fruit trees, &c.
1867-68	193,713	42	412	132	26	..	6,759
1868-69	202,391	..	46	110	20	507	7,650
1869-70	201,610	..	51	83	2	529	29,057
1870-71	206,370	64	224	85	33	..	17,607
1871-72	222,423	10	160	183	67	..	10,399
1872-73	212,884	5	93	206	39	528	6,816
1873-74	239,362	29	100	235	100	471	7,933
1874-75	289,395	41	67	303	40	500	13,649
1875-76	253,597	1	40	96	34	396	23,013
1876-77	262,060	16	201	209	66	781	31,279

The staple product is rice and the average crop 1,600 lbs. an acre : the gross produce of this cereal in 1876-77 may be taken at 187,183 tons which at the then current rates would be worth Rs. 10,295,065. Sessamum and tobacco are cultivated to a small extent. The produce of cotton per acre is small, averaging 83 lbs.

The agricultural stock has, like the area under cultivation, increased largely year by year.

Year.	Cows, bulls and bullocks.	Buffaloes.	Sheep and goats.	Pigs.	Carts.	Ploughs.	Boats.
1869-70	33,746	78,108	1,281	23,464	14,074	23,253	12,623
1874-75	57,327	1,00,339	1,609	30,086	53,635	26,433	16,184
1875-76	55,600	91,772	1,421	26,973	24,728	23,347	12,274
1876-77	65,475	93,753	2,015	26,098	26,480	21,174	12,857

Thus, notwithstanding the loss of two extensive townships, the district has now a larger agricultural stock than it had eight years ago. The average size of individual holdings is about fifteen acres, a larger area considerably than is held further north, as in Thayet for example where about four acres is the average size of a cultivator's land. Hired labourers are rarely employed; their wages vary from about eight rupees and board to ten rupees without board. In almost all cases the owners cultivate their own land and renting out is not common.

Nature has provided the district with lines of communication by which the produce can readily be transported to the most favourable market : intersected by a net-work of creeks, easily navigable for some months after the rains till the hot weather sets in, the country requires but few roads : in the dry season a cart track leads from village to village ; in the rains a boat can pass almost anywhere. Whilst, however, these creeks afford excellent means of communication and fertilise the country they are not without their inconveniences. Annually on the rise of the Irrawaddy large areas of country are flooded and the crops too often destroyed. To remedy this and afford protection to tracts of valuable rice land small embankments were erected by the inhabitants, but these were too weak and too much localized to be of any great or permanent benefit. Since 1865 large embankments have been and are still being made by the State along the banks of the Irrawaddy in the Henzada district to confine that river to its natural channel whilst a similar line is being carried along the left bank of the Bassein from its northern mouth and is complete as far as Ngathaing-khyoung.

The principal manufactures of the district are Salt, Ngapee and Pottery ; Manufactures. the first two mainly on the seacoast in the Ngapootaw and Myoung-mya townships and the last in the Bassein, Myoung-mya and Regyee townships. Within a distance of eight or ten miles of the seacoast and in the alluvial delta several plains occur the soil of which is more or less saline and where these are in the vicinity of creeks salt is prepared. The salt is made by solar evaporation and boiling. About the month of January a salt tract measuring about 5,000 square yards is dammed in and divided into eight or more beds, carefully constructed drains running between them. These beds are then ploughed up to a depth of from 12 to 18 inches, all lumps broken up and the top soil reduced to powder, a work which takes about 25 days. By this time the water in the neighbouring creeks has, owing to the cessation of the rains and the gradual running off of the fresh water, become brackish and is pumped into the salt-beds by means of a wheel worked by buffaloes. This is left for some days until, partly by subsidence partly by evaporation, the beds are dry and a thin layer of salt is left on the surface. More water is then pumped in ; not into all the beds simultaneously but passed from one to the other in regular order till all are filled ; the water in the last having thus passed through all the preceding ones. In the meanwhile tanks have been dug, generally about $40' \times 60' \times 5'$ deep, and the water after remaining 24 hours on the salt-beds is turned into them. The same process is repeated until these tanks are full or the workers think that they have a sufficient quantity for their purpose. From the tanks the water is carried to the boiling place and poured into pots underneath which a fire is kept continually burning ; as soon as all the water in a pot has evaporated it is cleared of the salt and re-filled from the tanks the salt being thrown into a general heap and exposed to the sun on shelving boards to allow the bittern to drain off, a process which is complete in from two to four days. The pots are all of a uniform size and contain about 4½ gallons of brine each and at each evaporation yield about 7lbs. of salt. Each pot is replenished twice in 24 hours and as the boiling continues for some four months (the fire being put out and the pots examined and cracked ones replaced three times in that period) the average produce of one pot during the season is about 1,350 lbs. The boiling places as a rule contain from 100 to 230 pots each, but some are smaller. The salt is sold on the spot for the preparation on the coast of salt-fish and ngapee. The expenditure during a season of from four to five months for a boiling place of 200 pots is about as follows :—

					Rs.
Hire of buffaloes ..	..	..	..	..	80
Six hundred pots (allowing for breakage &c.)		..	..	180
Fuel ..	..	..	..	..	..	600
Cocoanut fibre ..	..	..	..	..	150
Wages of six men for five months	..	..	..	450
Provisons for ditto	..	..	..	..	200
Earth-oil for feeding fires	..	..	..	..	75
Cost of sheds ..	..	..	..	..	50
Tax ..	..	..	..	..	..	100
					1,885
The value of the salt made (about)	..	..	..	2,500
			Nett profit	..	615

Several kinds of ngapee are made of which "Dhameng" is the most important. It is manufactured on the seacoast on the spot where the fish are caught and consists of a mixture of all kinds of fish and prawns which, as they are caught in the traps, are thrown *en masse* on to a raised platform made of bamboos and left there for about eight hours until all the water has drained off. By this time decomposition has generally set in. The mass is then sprinkled thickly with salt and the whole thoroughly crushed and mixed together by hand. It is then ready for the market and if not sold at once is stored in large wicker baskets and more salt occasionllay added as putridity advances. About 4,700 lbs. of salt are required for 100 baskets of ngapee.

Large pots and other kinds of heavy glazed pottery are manufactured principally in the Myoung-mya township at a village near the town of Bassein called Thit-gnyo-goon. The earth used is a kind of red clay with a slight admixture of sand in it which is collected and brought to the site before the season's work commences. The clay is dried and pounded in wooden mortars and mixed with water till it has attained the necessary consistency. A lump is taken up by hand and moulded into the form of a cylinder which is set upon the centre of a wooden wheel revolving horizontally and the clay is fashioned by the hand by one man or woman as the wheel is worked by another. Two persons can turn out from 15 to 20 large or 40 to 60 small pots in a day. When turned the pots are left for a day to dry and the glaze is then applied and the pots at once put into the kiln where they are burned for three days. The glaze is made from the slag obtained in smelting silver ore and is brought from Upper Burma : it is pounded in a mortar, sifted, mixed with thick rice water and applied with a brush. In one season, that is from January to April, two men can turn out about 1,000 pots of sizes which are generally sold to traders on the spot for from Rs. 120 to Rs. 130. The ordinary water and cooking-pots—unglazed—are somewhat differently made. The clay is thoroughly mixed with fine sand and water in a pit and is then placed on hides and kneaded by being trampled with naked feet. The pot is not at once formed on the wheel as in the case of the glazed jars but as soon as a globe has been formed by turning it is enlarged by hammering with a flat piece of wood with a rough surface. It is, when in this stage, exceedingly moist and is dried in a shed for three days and again beaten out. The salt pots are made in the same way but are much thicker. About 100 small or 20 large pots of this description can be made in one day by two men.

The actual revenue raised prior to the annexation—when the district did not include the tract west of the Arakan Romas but extended further eastward into what is now the Thoon-khwa district—cannot be accurately ascertained. The amount remitted to the capital or to the officer about the Court to whom the revenues had been granted—the *Myo-tsa* or "Eater of the Revenues of the Myo"—is known but the amount exacted by the local officials for their own share is no where recorded. A certain sum they were justly entitled to by way of salary, as fees &c., but no record even of this can be found much less of the sums which they extorted from the people whom they ruled. The amount which they received in various forms as fees on the administration of justice, fines in criminal cases &c., may safely be put down at a sum equal to two-thirds of the remittances to the King's Government or to the Myo-tsa. The amounts due were always calculated by viss and tickals and were in "Rwetnee" silver, supposed to contain five per cent. only of alloy. For all practical purposes of comparison with the existing revenue a viss or 100 ticals may be taken as worth Rs. 130. From the local records found in the various offices it appears that the annual revenue furnished by this district, as it existed in the Burmese times, was :—

					Rs.
1.	House and Family Tax—Burmans and Kareng	..	..	..	122,730
2.	Yoke of oxen or rice land tax	..	..	..	35,980
3.	Fisheries	..	..	..	92,030
4.	Salt	..	..	..	13,380
5.	Transit duties	..	..	..	18,380
			Total	..	282,500

Adding two-thirds for the share of the local officers the amount paid by the inhabitants was at least Rs. 470,800.

For the first year or two after the annexation the revenues were necessarily irregular, and 1855-56 is the first year which it is safe to take as shewing the taxation at first imposed on the people who had passed under our rule. In that year the revenue was :—

					Rs.
1.	Capitation	..	..	..	194,650
2.	Land	..	..	..	215,170
3.	Fisheries	..	..	..	81,570
4.	Salt	..	..	..	17,040
5.	Forest Produce	..	..	..	1,650
6.	Excise	..	..	..	55,390
7.	Sea Customs	..	..	..	13,560
8.	Port dues and Marine receipts	..	..	..	10,270
9.	Fees and Fines	..	..	..	16,250
10.	Sale of unclaimed property	..	..	..	1,020
11.	Postage Stamps	..	..	..	650
12.	Miscellaneous	..	..	..	10,700
			Total	..	617,910

The increase was very largely due to indirect taxation, which was felt but slightly, whilst the inhabitants were relieved from the numerous exactions which were all the more burdensome from being indefinite and dependant upon the wants and caprice of the local officials. The result was soon shewn in an increase of the population by immigration, and by the extended area brought under cultivation. Without any extraordinary and sudden increase in the rate of taxation, and indeed the general tendency has been to keep it as low as possible, the amount of revenue derived from the land has year by year increased. Excluding *toungya* or hill gardens the area under cultivation, the revenue derived therefrom and the rate of taxation per acre in 1875-76 as compared with 1855-56 was :—

Year.	Land under cultivation.	Land Revenue.	Average. rate per acre.
	Acres.	Rs	Rs. A. P.
1855-56	134,520	212,220	1 9 0
1875-76	264,320	437,320	1 10 5

The capitation tax represents the House and Family tax of the former rulers, with this great difference, that under the Burmese the total demand was ordered annually by the Governor of the district, the assessment per circle being left to the Akhwonwon and the assessment per house to the Thoogyee, the latter fixing it according to his estimate of the riches of the head of the house, in some cases counting several families as one "Revenue house," whilst under the English rule each married man and each bachelor between 18 and 60, except priests, cripples and some others, pays a fixed amount, fixed not with reference to his circumstances but the same for all *viz.* five rupees and two rupees eight annas respectively. In 1855-56 the yield of this tax was Rs. 194,650, in 1876-77 Rs. 305,300. The Fishery Tax is imposed upon nets and traps used in the sea and in the rivers, and the ponds are leased out for a term of years to the highest bidder, care being taken that, as far as possible, the bidders are *bonâ fide* fishermen residing near the ponds which they wish to rent, a system lately introduced in supersession of one by which no bidding was allowed but the fisheries were given from year to year to inhabitants of neighbouring villages, the Deputy Commissioner exercising his discretion in selecting the worker from amongst the always numerous applicants, a system which itself was successor to one of open auction. In 1855-56 the Revenue derived from both classes, fishermen and fisheries, was Rs. 81,570, in 1876-77 Rs.108,985.*

The salt tax, levied on the pots in which the brine is boiled after being subjected to solar evaporation, is an exceedingly fluctuating source of revenue, but is, on the whole, decreasing owing to the importation of foreign salt which undersells that made in the country except for fish-curing. The system of taxation has been to a certain extent copied from the Burmese who taxed each pot but they, in addition, raised a revenue from shipping dues, about eight

* In this district and in Henzada the receipts varied periodically on account of certain border fisheries which, situated partly in one district and partly in the other, were leased alternately by one Deputy Commissioner and by the other, the revenue derived therefrom being credited in the district the Deputy Commissioner of which held the auction.

annas being paid in this way for every 365 pounds of salt placed on board a boat. In 1855-56 the proceeds of the tax amounted to Rs. 7,040; in 1856-57 it fell to Rs. 8,170; in 1859-60 it rose to Rs. 15,170 and in the following year fell to Rs. 14,420; in 1871-72 it was Rs. 12,290; in 1872-73 only Rs. 7,800; in 1875-76 Rs. 8,783 and in 1876-77 Rs. 7,037. In 1855 the selling price of salt in the Bassein market was about thirteen annas, in 1873 rather over one rupee two annas and in 1876-77 one rupee six annas per maund of 80 lbs.

The excise revenue, derived from licenses to sell intoxicating liquors and drugs, has increased considerably. Under the Burmese rule the use of these stimulants was prohibited but after the annexation it was recognized that as intoxicating liquors and drugs were undoubtedly used their use should be turned to the benefit of the State. The excise revenue in 1855-56 amounted to Rs. 55,390; in 1860-61 to Rs. 61,040; in 1870-71 to Rs. 49,490; in 1872-73 to Rs. 57,600 and in 1876-77 to Rs. 127,895. Sea customs have afforded a continually increasing, but naturally to some extent a fluctuating, revenue, the amount depending not only on the fluctuation of trade but upon the rates of import and export duty levied. In 1855-56 the amount realized, including fines and confiscations, was Rs. 13,560; by 1872-73 it had risen to Rs. 392,270; in 1874-75 to Rs. 385,763 and in 1876-77 to Rs. 546,542 an increase due largely to increased exports of grain. The other items of revenue vary considerably year by year, but the receipts from the sale of postage stamps increase steadily but not rapidly for hitherto the post office has not been extensively used by the indigenous population.

The gross Imperial and Provincial Revenue of the district and the expenditure for officials of all kinds during the ten years ending with 1876-77 has been :—

Year.			Revenue.	Expenditure.
			Rs.	Rs.
1867-68	...	...	...	1,071,890	139,260
1868-69	...	...	...	1,255,660	148,340
1869-70	...	...	...	1,184,640	151,370
1870-71	...	...	...	1,186,730	133,850
1871-72	...	...	...	1,278,720	166,190
1872-73	...	...	...	1,383,962	104,310
1873-74	...	...	...	1,571,850	145,580
1874-75	...	...	...	1,724,486	154,871
1875-76	...	...	...	1,706,062	129,513
1876-77	...	...	...	1,666,466	196,729

The local revenues raised in the district in 1876-77, over and above the Imperial and Provincial revenue and excluding the Port (Rs. 26,614) and

Dispensary funds (Rs. 8,059) and the local revenue of the town of Bassein (Rs. 97,784) which is a Municipal Town with a Committee administering its Revenues, was Rs. 60,051.

Trade. The trade of the Bassein district, like that of every other part of the province, has largely increased since the British occupation. The values of the imports and exports, together with the tonnage of the vessels which cleared out, for each year from 1855-56 to 1876-77 are given in the following table :—

Year.	Value of grain exported.	Value of timber exported.	Value of all other exports including treasure.	Value of all imports including treasure.	Tonnage of vessels cleared out.
	Rs.	Rs.	Rs	Rs.	tons.
1855-56	435,053	2,505	87,891	243,007	2,847
1856-57	363,987	1,861	61,073	363,912	13,295
1857-58	1,165,542	2,359	61,755	974,404	37,403
1858-59	1,437,025	5,017	99,362	932,879	33,008
1859-60	258,731	2,645	98,143	247,838	12,987
1860-61	584,589	...	49,155	307,969	16,615
1861-62	1,010,568	...	62,402	550,282	29,571
1862-63	1,087,116	797	52,412	500,808	29,986
1863-64	1,133,351	...	79,530	289,763	35,126
1864-65	2,672,822	7,956	59,746	166,519	51,635
1865-66	2,852,464	3,520	43,670	328,761	42,163
1866-67	1,306,960	1,160	25,811	163,671	24,737
1867-68	1,542,646	2,516	29,519	205,886	33,749
1868-69	2,619,524	7,455	317,048	242,331	47,077
1869-70	2,160,514	1,055	119,010	247,135	41,515
1870-71	1,798,648	210	331,174	438,538	33,633
1871-72	2,135,371	...	11,452	220,735	41,376
1872-73	2,802,770	...	20,863	676,076	57,088
1873-74	3,765,540	3,03	522,242	2,093,623*	63,202
1874-75	4,057,845	3,327	67,079	449,035	71,020
1875-76	4,820,864	...	22,006	499,023	88,450
1876-77	5,000,426	11,447	22,822	447,641	81,297

* The increase was in treasure on account of the State and was due to the demand for rice for the famine-stricken tracts in Bengal.

The most important article of export is rice, of which by far the larger
quantity goes to Europe. The local price of the unhusked grain depends
very much upon that at Rangoon for both draw their supplies to a great
extent from the large rice-producing country between and north of them. The
great demand for this cereal for export stimulates its production and the
embankments along the Irrawaddy and the Bassein rivers protect, and will
as they are carried on still further protect very extensive areas of excellent
rice land.

The quantities of this grain shipped in each year since 1861-62 was
in tons :—

1862-63	..	.. 38,689	1870-71	..	.. 44,291
1863-64	..	.. 39,366	1871-72	..	.. 55,274
1864-65	..	.. 64,225	1872-73	..	.. 74,927
1865-66	..	.. 62,649	1873-74	..	.. 88,495
1866-67	..	.. 26,690	1874-75	..	.. 89,743
1867-68	..	.. 37,160	1875-76	..	.. 113,957
1868-69	..	.. 60,549	1876-77	..	.. 104,516
1869-70	..	.. 51,063			

Lying in the delta of the Irrawaddy with the surface of the country
intersected by a vast number of creeks the muddy banks
Climate. of which are left exposed for the greater part of the
24 hours and with a heavy rain-fall during the monsoon the climate is relax-
ing and favourable to animal and vegetable decomposition. Cholera and
fever are reported to be endemic, whilst bowel-complaints, dropsy and
rheumatism are common. Small-pox is much spread by inoculation.
The rain-fall and average temperature during the last ten years were :—

	PREVAILING WINDS.			AVERAGE TEMPERATURE IN THE SHADE.									RAIN-FALL IN INCHES.				
YEAR.	January to May.	June to September.	October to December.	May			July.			December.			Total.	October to December.	June to September.	January to May.	
				Sunrise.	2 P.M.	Sunset.	Sunrise.	2 P.M.	Sunset.	Sunrise.	2 P.M.	Sunset.					
1857-...	N. E.	Not given.	N. E.	...	82·75	81·00	...	78·50	79·00	...	79·00	77·30	4·85	10·68	72·52	4·85	
1858-59	N. E.	S. W.	N. E.	80·00	88·00	81·00	79·00	80·00	79·00	63·50	81·00	77·30	12·92	18·11	107·50	12·92	
1859-60	N. W. W	S. W.	E.; N. E.	82·00	88·00	84·00	78·00	82·00	80·00	76·00	85·00	81·00	8·18	8·91	72·11	8·18	
1860-...	N. E.	S. W.	S.W.; N.F.	80·00	85·00	85·00	77·00	83·00	80·00	75·00	82·00	79·00	16·19	7·28	64·08	16·19	
1861-...	N. E.; S. W	S. W.	N. E.	...	85·30	82·00	76·00	No record	...	74·00	85·00	72·00	1·09	11·04	72·93	1·09	
1862-...	N. E.	S. W	N. E.	78·00	90·00	75·00	78·00	79·00	75·00	65·00	85·00	67·00	11·56	11·93	61·98	11·56	
1863-64	N. N. E.; N. W.	S.E.;S.S.W.N.E.;S.E.	N. E.; S.E.	75·00	83·30	...	...	79·50	...	...	77·80	...	2·68	10·79	105·93	2·68	
1864-65	N. N. E.	S. E.	N. E.	...	88·18	...	Not given.	84·57	...	...	84·25	...	21·10	7·50	82·08	21·10	
1865-66	...	Not given.											4·98	13·72	95·80	4·98	
1866-77													11·30	10·10	82·40	11·30	
Mean	...			66·00	74·00	68·00	64·00	72·00	65·00	60·00	72·06	64·00	102·55	9·58	84·56	10·77	

On the annexation of Pegu the Bassein district was formed out of what
had been the Bassein Governorship during the Bur-
Administration. mese time but there was added to it a strip of country,
up till that time a portion of Sandoway, extending along the seacoast west of
the Arakan mountains as far north as the Kyientalee stream which falls into
the Bay of Bengal in about 18° N., divided into two townships. In 1864
it was found that the northern of these two could better be supervised from
Sandoway and westward of the mountains the boundary was brought south to
the Khwa where it has since remained. To the west of the Arakan Romas the
district remained for several years unaltered but in 1875 the Shweloung
and Pantanaw townships in the extreme east were taken from it and in
1876 further slight changes were made in its limits, the existing boundaries
being those given at pages 84 and 85. In the first year of the British occupation
a Deputy Commissioner was placed in charge with one Assistant and
eleven Goung-gyoop who replaced the Paineng and Myothoogyee of the
Burmese time but with considerably less authority and with two peons each
by way of Police for the whole district. Up to the middle of 1853 the country
was in a very disturbed state and the civil officers, aided only by the few troops
that could occasionally be spared from the weak garrison in Bassein and by
seamen from the *Zenobia* and the *Nemesis,* were continually engaged in hunting down and dispersing large gangs of armed marauders. The necessity
for strengthening the civil administration was soon felt ; the Deputy Commissioner was empowered to punish with death all persons convicted of parti-
cipation in open and armed insurrection (an authority subsequently withdrawn
when quiet was restored) and a Police force was raised of a total strength of
546 men (with two European Non-commissioned Officers) the large-majority of
whom were recruited from those who had been employed in a somewhat
similar capacity under the Burmese rule and had in many cases acted with the
gangs only just dispersed and were thus turned to good use and given an
occupation suited to their habits, whilst the discipline enforced eventually rendered them of great service. Amongst others who volunteered and were accepted was a man who had acted as a petty chief under the rebel Myat Htoon up
to the final dispersion of his band, who brought eighty men with him.
In 1857 an outbreak took place amongst the Kareng led by a man who,
though a Kareng, spoke a different dialect from those settled in the district,
and who was connected with the leader of the Kareng rebellion then going
on in the hill country of the Shwe-gyeng district. They occupied Myoungmya
but escaped on the approach of the Deputy Commissioner and were followed
in the direction of Labwotkoola and overtaken and dispersed. They assembled
again in Wakamay where they were attacked and finally defeated, 40 of their
number being taken prisoners ; the leader escaped but was captured somewhat
later. With occasional changes in the civil establishments the administration
remained the same until 1861, when the Police Battalion was disbanded and
a regular Police force for the whole Province under an Inspector-General and
District Superintendents was organized. The main evil with which this force
has had to contend has been dacoity, confined mainly, especially of late years,
to the Shweloung township, now a portion of Thoon-khwa (*q.v.*). In 1868 there
was a serious disturbance in the town of Bassein which was immediately suppressed. Nga Kyaw Tha, a native of Upper Burma who had been residing for
some four years in Bassein, combined with a new arrival, a soothsayer named

Nga Shwe Wa, and with a petty local official and succeeded in enlisting secretly some fifteen or twenty men (persuading them that he was of royal descent) and by forged documents induced them to believe that he had been appointed Prince of Bassein by the King of Upper Burma. On the night of the 27th April he collected his fifteen followers and about a hundred up-country men who had come down for the season to work in the rice-mills and who up to this moment seem to have known nothing of the plot. The whole party went before daylight in the morning to the Pagoda within the fort and, after worshipping, suddenly rushed on the Treasury guard. The Deputy Commissioner speedily arrived on the spot with about fifteen policemen and on their firing the robbers broke and escaped in all directions, having been in possession of the treasury for about twenty minutes only and without even opening the doors. Nearly the whole of the attacking party was captured that day including the leaders except Nga Kyaw Tha who was seized in Rangoon in June following.

Very soon after the occupation of Pegu it was deemed advisable to remove the head-quarters of the district southward from Bassein to " a position " unrivalled as a port in the Bay of Bengal " near the mouth of the river on the right bank, which was named ' Dalhousie' after the Governor-General to whom was due the annexation of Pegu. The site thus selected had " for " many years attracted the attention of naval officers as supplying all that is " required for a harbour of refuge. From its natural position it was admir- " ably adapted as a port of call ; and placed at the natural outlet of a vast tract " of fertile country it was hoped that it would become a mart of importance." In 1855 all preliminary arrangements had been completed, the main roads of the city had been traced out, a strand road had been made, the site of public buildings determined on and a pier was in course of construction. The crest of a rock was levelled to admit of the erection of a battery which should command the passage of the river, and the blocks and allotments in the town were marked out. Beyond a few fishermen's huts the site had been found entirely vacant. In 1856-57, however, the whole site was submerged by a sudden rise of the sea consequent on a cyclone. Almost every building was swept away and several lives were lost but the idea was not abandoned and the Courts and the Gaol were transferred hither from Bassein ; but the same year they were retransferred to Bassein where they have ever since remained and " Dalhousie" has sunk into its former state of waste and jungle. No attempt has since been made to build the city for it was found by practical experience that Bassein was by far the better site.

The district is now divided into eight townships. Adjoining the Henzada district is Le-myet-hna, divided into eight Revenue circles, with the head-quarters at the town of the same name on the Bassein or Nga-won river ; to the south-east of this is Regyee with the head-quarters at Regyee Pandaw, containing twelve Revenue circles ; and still further to the south Tsam-bay-roon, with the head-quarters at Kyoon-pyaw on the Daga river, containing eight Revenue circles. These three townships form the Nga-thaing-khyoung sub-division, under an Assistant Commissioner whose head-quarters are at the town of the same name. South of Le-myet-hna and extending across the hills to the seacoast is the Thaboung township, with the head-quarters at a town of the same name on the Bassein, divided into fourteen Revenue circles ; and below this Bassein, the head-quarter township, with eight Revenue circles, and including the town of Bassein : extending southward to the coast and including the lower portion of the tract west of the Arakan Romas is Ngapoo-taw, divided into eleven Revenue circles, with the head-quarters at Ngapootaw on the Bassein river on an island of the same name. Immediately south of Tsam-bay-roon and east of Bassein is Thee-kweng with the head-quarters at Kan-gyee-doung, containing ten Revenue circles : to the south of Thee-kweng the country, which is generally flat and highly intersected with creeks but with a low range of rising ground running through it on the west, forms the Myoungmya township, with nine Revenue circles and the head-quarters at Myoungmya. To the eastward is the Thoon-khwa district. The actual administrative staff consists of a Deputy Commissioner with two Assistant Commissioners, one stationed in Bassein and one in Ngathaing-khyoung, eight Extra Assistant Commissioners, a Superintendent of Police, a Civil Surgeon, a Collector of Customs, a Master-Attendant, and a Deputy Inspector of Schools.

Ever since the occupation of Pegu this district has enjoyed considerable educational advantages. Almost immediately after the annexation the American Baptist Missionaries, who had for many years devoted much attention to the education of the Kareng in Tenasserim and who found large numbers of this race here, established village schools and at Bassein a Normal School to which both boys and girls were admitted, and in 1858-59 they started a school for Burmese and put up a printing press at Myoungmya to supply their Kareng converts with books.

In 1860 a Kareng Normal and Industrial Institute was opened, also by the Baptist Missionaries, to which both boys and girls were admitted : in 1875-76 the average daily attendance was 160. Of late years a handsome new building has been added for the accommodation of the increasing numbers. In 1861 the Roman Catholic Mission established St. Peter's Institution in two departments, English and Vernacular, which have since been amalgamated and, with a few special exceptions, English is taught throughout the School. In 1875-76 the average daily attendance was 75 ; of the pupils about one-half were Kareng, 16 Burmese, and the rest Eurasians Chinese, &c. In 1868 a Pwo Kareng Normal School was opened by the Baptist Missionaries and in 1875-76 the daily average attendance was 46. All these receive grants-in-aid from the State. In 1874 the Government established a Middle Class School and, with a view of attracting pupils from the interior, a boarding establishment was subsequently attached to it. The number of pupils on the rolls on the 31st March 1876 was 144 of whom 99 were Burmese, one Kareng and the rest principally Natives of India. The average daily attendance in 1875-76 was 117, and the total charges Rs. 6,050 : the cost to the State for each pupil was Rs. 35-10-5 : the school fee is Re. 1 a month. In 1873 the Government established a Cess School at Nga-thaing-khyoung, that is a school the cost of which is defrayed from the Education portion of the Five per Cent. Cess levied on the land and fishery revenue, which is for both boys and girls. At the Examination in 1876, when the school was favourably reported on, 20 boys and 15 girls attended. The monthly fees are eight annas for boys and four annas for girls. The cost to the Government in 1876 for the education of each pupil was Rs. 47-12-0.

Here as in every part of Burma primary education is in the hands of the Booddhist monks and of a few laymen who start a school to gain a livelihood and teach both boys and girls. The schools, monastic and lay, of these masters who will allow it are examined yearly, and prizes given. In 1875-76 133 schools had successful pupils : of these schools 34 were lay and 99 monastic.

The Gaol of this district was at first a mat building ; in 1858 a wall round it was commenced which was not completed until 1861 ; in 1863-64 a new ward and a new hospital were constructed and during the following year a new Gaol was commenced. It was in this year that an Inspector-General was first appointed and a commencement made in a more effective and more regular system of prison management. The new Gaol, which cost Rs. 172,600, was not completed until 1868, up to which period the buildings used were temporary structures raised on piles with wooden floors. Four wards radiate from the main guard in the centre, the necessary offices being between them, and the whole is surrounded with a high wall ; the buildings are brickwork structures with iron roofs and earthwork floors, the prisoners sleeping on benches two feet off the ground. There is accommodation, at 36 superficial feet per head, for 405 males and 16 females. In 1855 the average number in confinement was 317 of all classes. The daily average number of prisoners confined in 1876 was :—

	Males.	Females.	Total.
Convicted prisoners	343	3	346
Under-trial ,,	5	1	6
Debtors, excise prisoners, and revenue defaulters ..	17	..	17
Total of all classes ..	365	4	369

The cost to the State was :—

	Rs.	A.	P.
Rations	9,436	15	1
Establishment	6,961	15	2
Police Guard	4,858	13	4
Hospital charges	530	13	6
Clothing	690	11	7
Contingencies	806	10	5
Total ..	23,285	15	1

Adding the amount expended on the Gaol buildings and deducting the profits from Gaol labour (Rs. 12,313-15-11), on which an average of 209 prisoners were regularly employed, the cost of each convict to the State in 1876 was Rs. 67-8-9. On the 5th July 1876 a small Lock-up was opened at Ngathaing-khyoung in which prisoners who are sentenced in that sub-division to one month's imprisonment and under work out their sentences. The average number of prisoners of all classes confined was 16 and the nett cost to the State Rs. 64-1-6 for each.

The Police force numbered, in 1876, 355 men (of whom 37 were boatmen and river police and 72 employed in the town of Bassein) under a Superintendent and 36 subordinate officers (of whom 11 were employed in Bassein town). The total cost was Rs. 85,776 of which Rs. 70,131 was chargeable to the Provincial Revenues, the rest being chargeable to the Bassein Municipality. The strength gives one policeman to every twenty-three square miles and to every 898 of the population.

In the town of Bassein there is a charitable dispensary and two hospitals one for Europeans and the other for natives, all three being under the Civil Surgeon. A new Hospital, which is to cost about Rs. 8,000—of which

Rs. 4,000 are provided from the Dispensary Fund, Rs. 2,000 by the Municipality, Rs. 1,500 from the Port Fund, and the remainder collected from private individuals—is now being built. It is to be of teak with a shingled roof, and is to contain two large roomy wards, each to hold 10 beds and each having a bath-room. In the centre will be a dispensary, an operation-room and an office : a fine portico will provide a waiting-room for out-patients. In 1866-67 the private contributions, including fees from patients, amounted to Rs. 1,380 and 1,086 persons were treated. In 1876 the gross receipts amounted to Rs. 7,022, of which Rs. 981 were from private contributions, and the expenditure to Rs. 2,520. The total balance at credit of the fund at the close of the year was Rs.7,785. The total number who received aid that year was 3,461, of whom 264, including 10 Europeans, were in-patients. Most of the Europeans are sailors whose cases it is difficult to manage on board ship.

The postal communications are :—

(1.) A four-weekly service by the steamers of the British India Steam Navigation Company between Chittagong and Penang, and *vice versâ*, the steamers calling at Akyab, Kyouk-hpyoo, Sandoway (during the N. E. monsoon), Bassein, Rangoon, Maulmain, Tavoy River, Mergui and Malewon in British, and Renoung, Kopah, and Junk Ceylon in foreign, territory.

(2.) A service twice a week by the steamers of the Irrawaddy Flotilla Company between Rangoon and Bassein and *vice versâ*, calling at Maoobeng, Shwe-loung, Myoungmya and, when practicable, at Pantanaw.

(3.) A service, maintained out of the District Dâk portion of the Five Per Cent Cess Fund, three times a month between Bassein and Ngathaing-khyoung and *vice versâ*, viâ the Daga river ; three times a month between Bassein and Ngathaing-khyoung and *vice versâ*, viâ the Ngawon or Bassein river and three times a month by land from Ngathaing-khyoung to Lemyethna and Henzada, and *vice versâ*.

BASSEIN.—A township in the district of the same name on the left bank of the Nga-won or Bassein river extending southwards from the Daga to the mouth of the Tabeng which for some distance forms its south-eastern boundary. Towards the north the ground is undulating but the country to the south is flat and highly cultivated with rice. The town of Bassein lies in the west centre. In 1876 the population numbered 17,695 souls and the gross revenue was Rs. 58,795 of which Rs. 38,865 were derived from the land and Rs. 17,974 from the capitation-tax.

BAWBENG.—A small stream in the Henzada district which has its source in the western slopes of the Pegu mountains in the south of the Ta-pwon township and, fed by numerous mountain torrents, unites with the Thayet to form the Wet. The banks are for the most part steep and rocky.

BAWDEE.—A revenue circle in the north-eastern portion of the Pantanaw township of the Thoon-khwa district the greater portion of which is low ground. The inhabitants who number 6,756 are mainly fishermen, petty traders and cultivators. The land revenue in 1876 was Rs. 3,395 and the capitation-tax Rs. 7,458 : the gross revenue (very largely derived from the fisheries) being Rs. 56,864. This circle now includes Kaloung.

BEELING.—See *Bheeleng.*

BENG-KOOP.—A village in the Thamboola circle, Myedai township, Thayet district, containing about ninety houses.

BENTINCK.—An island in the Mergui Archipelago between 11° 30′ and 12° N. and a little to the east of 98° E. To the eastward is Domel Island and between the two is a good harbour where ships can lie land-locked and secure from all swell, in good holding-ground, mud and sand.

BGHAI.—One of the three great Kareng families, occupying the whole country between the Tsittoung and Salween, north of the latitude of the Thouk-re-khat stream as far as the Shan State, of Mobye beyond British territory. The family comprises the following sub-divisions : Red Kareng Tunic Bghai or Bghai-ka-teu, Pant Bghai or Bghai-ka-hta, Lay-may or Brek or Pray, Tshawko and Manoo-manaw ; some wearing tunics and some trowsers ; the women all wearing the ordinary Kareng female dress. In this family marriages are always contracted between relations, third cousins being considered as too remote and first cousins as too near : beyond third cousins marriages are prohibited.

The dead are invariably buried and their funeral ceremonies are, therefore, peculiar to themselves ; they have been so fully described by Dr. Mason that the following account is taken verbatim from one published by him in the *Journal of the Bengal Asiatic Society* :—

"When an elder among the Bghais with a large number of descendants " dies the people build a place in the hall for the deposit of the corpse and they " hew a coffin out of the body of a tree and hew a cover for it, like the Chinese " coffins.

"The body lies in state three or four days and during the time men blow " pipes and the young men and maidens march round the corpse to the music. " At night the piping is discontinued and singing is substituted.

"When the piping and marching is not going forward the exercises are " diversified by weeping and mourning; or by the men knocking pestles " together and others showing their dexterity by putting their hands or heads " in between and withdrawing them quickly before the missiles come together " again.*

"Before the burial an elder opens the hand of the dead man and puts " into it a bangle or some other bit of metal and then cuts off a few particles " with a sword saying : ' May we live to be as old as thou art.' Each one in the " company goes through the same ceremonial and the fragments gathered are " looked upon as charms to prolong life.

"When about to bury the corpse two candles made of bees-wax are lighted " and two swords are brought. A sword and a candle are taken by the eldest " son and a sword and a candle by the youngest ; and they march round the " bier in opposite directions three times, each time they meet exchanging swords " and candles. After completing the circuits one candle is placed at the foot " of the coffin and the other at the head.†

"A fowl or a hog is led three times round the building in which the body " is placed and on completing the first round it is struck with a strip of bam- " boo once ; on completing the second round twice ; and at the third round " it is killed. If a fowl it is killed by twisting its head off. The meat is set " before the body as food.

"Young people are buried in a similar manner but with some abridgement
" of the forms.

" When the day of burial arrives and the body is carried to the grave four
" bamboo splints are taken and one is thrown towards the west saying : ' that is
" the east ;' another is thrown to the east saying: ' that is the west ;' a third
" is thrown upwards towards the top of a tree saying : ' that is the foot of the
" tree ;' and a fourth is thrown downwards saying: ' that is top of the tree.'
" The sources of the stream are then pointed to saying: ' that is the mouth
" of the stream ;' and the mouth of the stream is pointed to saying : ' that is
" the head of the stream.' This is done because in Hades everything is upside
" down in relation to the things of this world.

" The body is then buried and the grave filled in without further ceremony
" and when the top of the grave has been neatly smoothed off a little fence
" of trellis-work is built around it. Within this fence boiled rice and other
" food are placed for the dead.

" On returning from the grave each person provides himself with three
" little hooks made of branches of trees and calling his spirit to follow him at
" short intervals as he returns he makes a motion as if hooking it and then
" thrusts the hook into the ground. This is done to prevent the spirit of the
" living from staying behind with the spirit of the dead.*

" After the funeral the grave-digger washes his clothes or the neglect to do
" so renders him unfortunate. Married children may dig the grave for a parent
" but young ones are prohibited. They must hire some one to do the work
" and give him five rupees.

" Like the Chinese the Bghais make annual feasts for the dead for three
" years after a person's death. The feast is made at the new moon near the
" close of August or the beginning of September ; and all the villagers that
" have lost relatives partake in it.

" Before the new moon they prepare food, plantains, sugarcane, tobacco,
" betel-nuts, betel leaves and other articles of consumption. A bamboo is laid
" across one angle of the roof of the room and on it are hung up new tunics, new
" turbans, new petticoats, beads and bangles ; and at the appropriate time when
" the spirits of the dead are supposed to be present, having returned to visit
" them, they say : ' You have come to me, you have returned to me. It has '
" ' been raining hard and you must be wet. Dress yourselves, clothe yourselves '
" ' with these new garments and all the companions that are with you. Eat '
" ' betel together with all that accompany you, all your friends and associates '
" ' and the long dead. Call them all to eat and drink.'

" After dark all the people eat bread made of boiled rice beaten in a
" mortar. The bread is spread out and the people are invited : ' all who are '
" ' hungry eat bread here.'

" Next morning, the first day of the moon, which is deemed the proper
" feast day the previous last day of the month being regarded as the day of
" preparation, all who have kyee-zee† hang them up and beat them. Then
" they kill a hog and make thirty bottles of bamboos. Into one bottle they put
" honey, into another water, in a third native spirit, in a fourth salt, in a fifth oil,
" in a sixth chillies and into the seventh turmeric. The other twenty-three are

---

* Cf. " La" sub. tit. " Kareng."
† A kind of gong peculiar to the Kareng and very highly valued.

" laid aside. Loopholes are made to each bottle through which a string, dyed
" yellow, is tied.

" After setting apart the seven bottles that have been filled the remaining
" twenty-three are filled with food indiscriminately, some with pork, some
" with boiled rice, some with rice bread, some with native spirit and some with
" betel. When these are filled rice bread is rolled up in leaves and the rolls
" piled up together ; and then a large basket of open work is woven, into which
" all these bamboo bottles and the rolls of bread are put.

" When the rice and meat are cooked for the feast, after the above arrange-
" ments have been made, the food is placed on kyee-zee or on little bamboo stools
" if they have no kyee-zee ; and they have to be very particular to spread out
" all the food at the same instant lest some of the spirits of the dead, being
" delayed in eating, should be left behind by their companions.

" So soon as the food is arranged on the tables the people beat the kyee-
" zee and begin to cry, which they say is calling the spirits to come to eat.
" Each one calls on the particular relative for whom he has prepared the feast
" as father, mother, sister, or brother. If a mother he says ; weeping : 'O prince- '
" ' bird mother it is the close of August Oh ! It is the new moon in September '
" ' Oh ! You have come to visit me Oh ! You have returned to see me Oh ! '
" ' I give you eatables Oh ! I give you drinkables Oh ! Eat with a glad heart '
" ' Oh ! Eat with a happy mind Oh ! Don't be afraid mother Oh ! Do not '
" ' be apprehensive Oh ! '

" After the weeping exercises are over the spirits are supposed to have
" finished their repast and the people sit down to eat what is left.

" More food is then prepared and put into the basket with the bamboo
" bottles that the spirits may have food to carry away with them ; and at cock-
" crowing next morning all the contents of the basket including the bamboo
" bottles are thrown out of the house on the ground; when the same scene of
" crying and calling on the spirits of the dead is repeated as detailed above."

Once a year in February or March every Bghai family holds a festival
in which every person's wrist is tied with a thread and prayers are
addressed both to the fowl offered and to Thie-keu, Mo-khie or Indra. The
rite is called " The good to do" but of its origin and object the natives can
give no account beyond what is found in the forms themselves.

" When the time approaches the people prepare beforehand ardent spirits
" and buy hogs and fowls and get everything ready. When the time actually
" comes the villagers perform the ceremony, two or three or four families a
" day till it has gone through the whole village.

" The first thing done is to bring up two jars of arrack and secure
" them by tying them to a bamboo and the next is to bring up a hog and
" fowls. Then an eating dish is washed and filled with water and set by the
" side of the jars with spirits.

" An elder is now called or any one skilled in interpreting fowl's bones
" and a fowl is put into his hands. He cuts off the bill of the fowl dips its
" head and feet in the water and then drops the blood from the bleeding head
" on the forehead of the oldest man of the family that is performing the
" ceremony.

" The master of the ceremonies then addresses the elder and says : ' The
" ' hand-tier devours thee ; thou hast the jaundice ; thou art shrivelled up ; thou'
" ' art not strong ; thou art weakly. Now we give food and drink to the hand-'

" 'tier. Mayest thou be strong; mayest thou be vigorous; mayest thou be'
" 'established as the rock, indestructible as the hearth stones; mayest thou'
" 'have long life; mayest thou have a protracted existence.'
" After besmearing the elder's forehead with the fowl's blood the master
" of the ceremonies pinches a few feathers and a little down from the fowl's neck
" and sticks them on the blood, where they adhere perhaps for the whole day.
" He next addresses the fowl and says : ' Arouse, arouse, Thie-keu's fowl,'
" ' Mo-khie's fowl, we give thee food, we afford thee sustenance. Thou drinkest'
" ' in a knowledge of the future, thou eatest superhuman power. In the morning'
" ' thou seest the hawk, in the evening thou seest man. The seven heavens thou'
" ' ascendest to the top, the seven earths thou descendest to the bottom. Thou'
" ' arrivest at Khu-the, thou goest unto Tha-ma, [i. e. Yu-ma the judge of the
" dead]. ' Thou goest through the crevices of rocks thou goest through the'
" ' crevices of precipices. At the opening and shutting of the western gates'
" ' of rock thou goest in between, thou goest below the earth where the sun'
" ' travels. I implore thee, I exhort thee. I make thee a messenger, I make'
" ' thee an angel. Good thou revealest ; evil thou revealest. Arouse thee'
" ' fowl arouse; reveal what is in thee. Now I exhort thee, I entreat thee.'
" ' If this man is to live to an old age, if his head is not to be bent down,'
" ' if he is not to come down crash like a falling tree, let the right hand bone'
" ' come uneven, let the bones be short and long. Thou art skilled in the words'
" ' of the elders; thou knowest the language of old men. The good thou fully'
" ' knowest; with the evil thou art perfectly acquainted. Fowl I exhort thee,'
" ' I entreat thee; reveal whatever is in thee. And now if this man's head is'
" ' to bend down, if he is to come down crash like a falling tree, if he is unable'
" ' to rest himself from incessant trouble, if unable to overcome obstacles which'
" ' shall meet him on every hand, if unable to rise up or lie down, if his life'
" ' is not to be prolonged, if he cannot live; then fowl come up unpropitious, come'
" ' up with the tendon short on the right side, come wrong end foremost. If he'
" ' be able to obtain sufficient to support life, if he be not overcome by feuds,'
" ' fowl come up even. Thie-keu's fowl, Mo-khie's fowl I pull out thy feathers,'
" ' I pull at thy skin, I dip thy head, I dip thy feet. Arouse fowl, reveal what'
" ' is in thee.'
" Every one in succession is then besmeared on the forehead with the
" blood of a separate fowl; and then every one marks his own fowl by tying
" a string to it that he may recognise it after being cooked. Some tie a string
" on the neck, others on the leg, others on the wing and others elsewhere.
" They next scorch off the feathers and boil the fowls.
" The hog is taken if the gall bladder be deemed a good one otherwise
" it is rejected. When the rice and meat is cooked they bring the rice and
" the pork and the fowls and the threads and the bamboo tubes to suck up
" the drink and the spirits and all are placed together.
" The master of the ceremonies then goes and puts two bamboo tubes into
" the left hand of one and the gall bladder of the hog and the head of the
" fowl into his right hand ; and then the elder of the family takes the thread
" and ties his wrist. Each one in succession takes the articles mentioned above
" in his or her hands and the elder ties every one's wrist, at the same time
" praying with each : ' Mo-khie the hand-tier, the good-to-do, we offer thee food'
" ' and drink, spirits well prepared, a great hog. Defend us ; when we go to and'
" ' fro look after us. If we fall raise us up. When we go or return, when we'

" ' walk on a branch or a beam, when the branches or creepers break down, when'
" ' we go among the Burmese or other tribes, when we climb trees or descend'
" ' into the waters, when we go up into the house or return to the paddy field,'
" ' may no accident befal us, stretch forth thy hand and help us ; put forth thy'
" ' foot and assist us. Go before us, follow behind us. Deliver us from demons,'
" ' deliver us from ghosts.'

"After this the person whose wrist is tied changes the things in his
"hands from right to left and left to right. Then each one tastes the spirits ;
"after which each one tastes the fowl ; and when this is done an elder is called
"upon to pray who prays thus :

" ' Mo-khie of mountain Kie-ku Mo-khie of the seven heavens Mo-khie'
" ' of the seven earths assemble together even the blind the deaf and the'
" ' lame ; and eat and drink the food.'

"A libation of spirits is then poured out ; and after this the drama closes
"with spirits being served out for all to drink".*

In sickness the Bghais like other Kareng (resembling in this respect the
Kakhyen of the north) trust to divination and propitiation of the spirits
but the ceremony of invocation is somewhat different. The whole family
assembles and an elder leads a dog round them, praying as he goes. The
dog is then killed and the elder sits opposite to the family with a green
bamboo held horizontally three or four feet from the ground between him
and them ; over this the dead body of the dog is thrown by the legs towards
the family who catch it and throw it back. After this has been done three
times the animal is cooked and eaten.

Their villages consist of a single house with a passage down the centre and
rooms on each side for each family, some houses containing as many as seventy-
five of such rooms : below are the pigs ; above in the rafters the fowls. The
village is surrounded by a fence and round many are planted pointed bamboos
at an angle of 45°. When a stranger visits them a spot for him is pointed
out and if he moves from it he is speared. In many villages the men sleep
on the ground to be ready to resist an attack. A new village is built every
year when the inhabitants move to a new spot, on which occasion there is a
feast and an ox or a buffalo is sacrificed to the spirits guarding the country.

When about to make a foray, to which the "head of the war" i. e. the
person on whose account the foray is made never goes, volunteers are called for
either from the head of the war's village only or from surrounding ones also and
each individual has his duty allotted to him, some as guides and some as members of the storming party, whilst others are appointed to form the rear guard.

Another peculiarity of this family is their love of dog's flesh which the
other Kareng will not touch. One sept is remarkable for its want of family
affection : a sickly child a grumbling widowed mother or in times of scarcity
an orphan nephew or niece is remorselessly sold into slavery. If an uncle
dies they often sell the widow and if a married brother dies his widow has to
pay ten rupees to her brothers-in-law or be sold. If a married woman dies her
relatives demand a large price from the widower which he must pay or be sold
or fight ; the majority of those who cannot pay adopting the last alternative.

Except amongst the Red Kareng the animal sacrificed to the spirits of their
ancestors is a hog, the hierophant being the oldest woman of the family and no
men taking part in the ceremony which has been described as follows :—

* Dr. Mason in the Bengal Asiatic Society's Journal.

"The first thing is to brew or distil spirits for three days. Then a "little table is made with four bamboo posts. Leaves of a plant of the ginger "tribe are next rolled up in a sugar loaf form, and three joints of bamboos are "cut off even. Spirits are then poured into these three bamboos, and the "conical rolls of leaves with bamboo bottles of drink are all set upright on "the table. Then a living hog is put on a fanning basket.

"The head of the offering or priest is a woman and she takes one of "the conically rolled leaves and turning to the table she prays to Yau as if "he were present there. She prays thus.*

" ' O Yau-peu thou dost now devour the whole family. We feed thee' " ' with old spirits and a great hog. Heal us, watch over us, defend us. When' " ' we fall raise us up, when we slip down set us up again. Make us strong,' " ' make us vigorous, all of us. When we fall on the wood hew it through,' " ' when we fall into a coffin split it open' [*i. e.* raise us up from the point of "death]. 'Establish us, make us immoveable. Let not plots let not devices' " ' against us succeed. Let us have large crops, let us have good paddy. Let' " ' us have little grass, let us have few weeds. Let our labour be light, let' " ' us eat whatever we want. Let us succeed in our works, let us eat with little' " ' work. Let the effects of our labours increase, let our produce swell up' " ' like rice in boiling. Let us ascend to the tops of the mountains, let us " ' descend to the depths of the valleys. Let us spear hogs, let us seize' " ' captives. Let us purchase kyee-zee, let us dig out the pangolin' [*i. e.* let "us accomplish difficult things]. 'In the water let us be great rocks, on land' " ' let us be large wood-oil trees. Let not the tiger seize us, let not the tiger' " ' kill us. When the tiger would leap on us may he growl, when man would' " ' seize us may he cough. When tigers would leap on us may they wait for' " ' each other, when men would seize us may they feel abashed. Let us devour' " ' a stream to its source, let us eat a creek to its mouth' [*i. e.* get possession "of the whole valley]. 'Let us eat up the rock to atoms, let us eat the sand' " ' to dust' [*i. e.* overcome every difficulty].

"The priestess next lays her left hand on the neck of the hog and with "her right she grasps the hand of the oldest person in the company and shak-"ing it slowly up and down she repeats the above prayer. In this way she "goes round the whole company from the oldest to the youngest, repeating "the prayer with each.

"The hog is killed next but it is not killed with a knife or spear; a "sharpened bamboo is forced into it on the right side, under the fore leg. "When the bristles have been singed off a part of the flesh is cooked with "rice flour in a chatty and a part in joints of bamboo; but the head is hung "up whole on the posts of the table.

"When the rice and meat is spread out the priestess shakes hands again "with each one and prays as before. She then tastes the food and after her "the others taste it in succession from the oldest to the younges.

"This done, they rise up and the priestess tastes the spirits; and as before "all the rest follow her example according to seniority. After this they all "return to the food again.

"At evening the stomach of the hog is roasted and all taste of it in the "manner described above.

---

* Alluding to the " supposed duties" of these spirits as servants of the Lord of the Castle, an account of whom is given sub tit. "Karen" Q. V.

" Next morning at dawn, they take the posts of the table and throwing them
" away endwise, as they would throw a javelin, into the earth without the village
" they say : ' now it is done, it is finished. Go thy way, return to thy place.'
" After it is light, they cook the head of the hog and eat it with any meat
" that may be left. On that day the people do not go away from the house."*

In addition to this offering to the manes of their ancestors they have a
custom of making a sacrifice to the " lord of the earth" in July, usually once
in three years, but in calamitous times once in two and in prosperous times
once in four or five only.

" The first thing done is to take a hog to a central position in the village
" lands and placing it under an Eugenia tree, there erect a booth. The Eugenia
" is chosen because regarded as a more holy tree than any other. The booth
" is for the four ' heads of the sacrifice' or priests, and elders to occupy.

" When the booth is built every man cuts three bamboos, one long one
" to represent a post in his barn, and two short ones, which he ties to the long
" one, to represent the height to which he wishes his crop of paddy to reach
" when it is gathered into his barn. Then he makes, in miniature, a paddy-bin
" a long pen, a hen-coop, a trap, and a snare.

" When these preparatory measures have been taken one of the heads of
" the sacrifice calls the people together and all the men assemble about the
" booth. The most wealthy elders sit together with the heads of the sacrifice
" in the booth, but the young people and the poor stay without. No women
" are allowed to be present.

" The ceremonies are introduced by the head of the sacrifice taking a
" small branch of the Eugenia tree in his hand, when all present imitate him
" and take a leafy sprig of the tree. The leader lifts his clasped hands to
" heaven with the sprig between them and prays ; when all follow his example,
" each asking in his prayers for whatever he most desires.

" After the prayers, the head of the sacrifice rises up and, taking a spear,
" spears the hog to death. So soon as the blood begins to flow all the people
" jump up and each one seizes his bamboo which had been set against the tree
" and calls out with a loud voice : ' may my barn be filled with paddy as high'
" ' as my bamboo.' Some cry out : ' I have caught many rats in my trap ;' and
" others : ' I have snared many wild fowls in my snare.' Some dance with
" shields that they have prepared for the purpose, and others beat drums and
" blow pipes.

" They next take the hog to the village and every man, young and old
" who is able, kills a fowl ; and, after they have cooked the hog and fowls and
" prepared the food and drink properly, they carry the whole to the booth.
" There they place the food on a raised platform prepared for the purpose, and
" taking again sprigs of the Eugenia tree between their clasped hands, they
" all pray, saying : ' Lord of the seven heavens and seven earths, lord of the'
" ' water, lord of the land, Thie-kho-mu-kha, all of you, eat our property, eat'
" ' our pork, eat our fowls, make our paddy good, our rice good ; make our'
" ' daughters handsome, our sons skilful ; give us food, give us drink, give us'
" ' to become governors, give us to become elders ; enable us to buy kyee-zee,'
" ' to spear with fatal effect ; make our names famous, heard above and below ;'
" ' make us joyous and happy with our wives and children.'

---

* Dr. Mason in the Bengal Asiatic Society's Journal.

" After praying, they rise up and dance again. When the dancing is
" done they set the food in order in the booth, to remain there all night as
" not a bit of it is to be eaten before the next day, and then return to their
" houses, dancing all the way home. The remainder of the day is spent in
" their houses, drinking, dancing, and beating kyee-zee and gongs.

"The next morning they all repair again to the foot of the Eugenia tree,
" when the heads of the sacrifice and the elders commence eating the food and
" drinking the spirits that have been prepared and placed in the booth. All
" are allowed to partake that choose, but the food is considered holy, and none
" but the holy, clean, and upright persons are considered as proper persons to
" partake of it. The question of fitness is left, however, for every one to
" decide for himself. If a man feels persuaded in his own mind that he is
" guilty of no transgression but is upright and holy he goes forward and
" partakes of the food ; but if his conscience reproves him for some wrong
" deed or word he joins the throng outside the booth and occupies the time
" with others in dancing. Nor is unfitness to partake of this holy food confin-
" ed to immoral acts there are certain ceremonial uncleannesses which are
" regarded as unfitting a man to partake. For instance, if a man's wife is preg-
" nant he is deemed unclean and unfitted to eat of this holy food.

" After the feast is finished the company returns to the village, dancing
" all the way as before ; and on arriving at the houses one or two of the heads
" of the sacrifice, go to the brook and draw two bamboos of water for every
" family in the village. After the water has been drawn the heads of the
" sacrifice call all the members of each family to the hall or verandah—men,
" women, and children—and then he sprinkles or throws the water from one
" bamboo upon them. Those who get wet are said to be free from evil, be-
" cause the water is ' holy water.' One bamboo-full remains in the house till
" next morning when the owners go to the fields and sprinkle it on their
" growing paddy ; and they say because it is ' holy water,' the paddy that
" is wet by it will be good and abundant.

"In all these ceremonies women are carefully excluded, except in partici-
" pating of ' the holy water.'

"The four elders that are called the ' heads of the sacrifice' or priests have
" special names or titles given them to distinguish their office.

" The first   is called Deu-sai, i. e. Lord of the village.
    ,,   second ,,   ,,   Pghai-sen ,, The Messenger.
    ,,   third   ,,   ,,   Ywa-san   ,, Keeper of the village.
    ,,   fourth ,,   ,,   Sa-kai   ,, Signification uncertain.

" These offices are strictly hereditary. The fathers of the present occu-
" pants held them, and their places, when they die, will be held by their sons.

" When the priests officiate they have embroidered tunics given them by
" the people. Sometimes these are embroidered with silk and often with red
" silk, and are made longer than ordinary garments. The people give them
" also ear knobs and beads, and think that it is very meritorious to do so."*

BGHAI-KA-HTA.—A subdivision of the Bghai Kareng tribe, called by
the English Pant Bghai from their wearing trowsers and not tunics. The
Burmese name for them is " Kareng Ayaing" or " Wild Kareng" Their
distinguishing dress is a pair of a short white trowsers with red radiating

* Dr. Mason in Bengal Asiatic Society's Journal.

lines worked in them near the bottom, "as the rays of the rising sun are sometimes represented".*

They inhabit the western slopes of the hills between the Salween and Tsittoung rivers from the frontier down to about five miles north of the latitude of the town of Toung-ngoo. Those whose villages are near the Burmese are comparatively civilized and rear silkworms but those living in the interior are rude and their women, like those of the Wewas, do not know how to weave; they have, therefore, to get their cloths from their neighbours, and generally by begging or stealing. They are fond of dogs' flesh which they eat without salt.

BGHAI-KA-TEU.—A subdivision of the Bghai family of Kareng called by the Burmese *Lieppyagyee* or " big butterflies " and by the English *Tunic Bghai* to distinguish them from another clan of the same division who wear trowsers. Their distinguishing dress is a white tunic or smock frock with red *perpendicular* stripes. They have but few villages all situated in the Toung-ngoo district of the Tenasserim division on the right bank of the Thouk-re-khat stream.

BGHAI-MOO-HTE.—A sept of the Bghai tribe of Kareng, so called by the other Bghai.—*See Kareng-nee.*

BHA-LA.—A small river in the Hpoung-leng township, Rangoon district, which has its source in the Pegu Romas and flowing southwards falls into the Poozwondoung through a mouth 150 feet broad; the banks are steep in some places and sloping at others, except in the hills the bed is muddy and sandy. At low water it is fordable just above its junction with the little Ataroo a few miles from its mouth. The name is Talaing and means *Arrow River.*

BHA-LA-TADA-GYEE.—A village in the Retho circle, Hpoung-leng township, Rangoon district, on the Prome road between eleven and twelve miles from Rangoon. The inhabitants, who are mostly agriculturists, numbered 788 in 1877. The name is partly Talaing and partly Burmese and means literally " the great bridge over the river *Arrow*." The village was so called from the existence at this spot of a large bridge across the Bhala.

BHA-LE.—A village in the Gnyoung-beng circle in the south of the Pegu township, Rangoon district, on the east bank of the Pegu river, a little south of the mouth of the Paing-kyoon stream. The inhabitants are almost entirely agriculturists and in 1877 numbered 789 souls. The name is Talaing and means *Gourd River.*

BHAN.—A revenue circle in the Shwe-gygeng district extending south-east from Shwe-gyeng to the hills and bounded on the south by the Mootta-ma or, as it is more commonly pronounced, Madama river. Over 235 square miles in extent it is sparsely cultivated and inhabited by a small population of 3,846 souls mostly Kareng. The gross revenue in 1876-77 was Rs. 4,951 of which Rs. 3,205 was derived from the land.

BHAN-BHWAI-GOON.—A small revenue circle in the Poungday township, Prome district. In 1876 it had a population of 246 souls and a gross

* *Burma* : by Dr. Mason, second Edition, page 88.

revenue of Rs. 781 of which Rs. 876 were derived from the land and Rs. 835 from the capitation-tax.

BHAN-BHWAI-GOON.—A rising village in the Hmaw-bhee circle of the township of the same name in the Rangoon district. In 1868 it had rather over 100 inhabitants and in 1877 502.

BHAN-BOUNG.—A small river in the Prome district, not navigable by boats, which rises in the Neepa-tshe spur and flowing in a north-westerly direction joins the Teng-gyee a little to the west of the village of Myodoung. The bed of the stream is sandy and muddy and the banks are moderately steep. In the country which it traverses are found several kinds of valuable timber as Pyeng-gado (*Xylia dolabriformis*), Reng-daik (*Dalbergia cultrata*), Htouk-kyan (*Terminalia crenata*), Thabye (*Eugenia sp.*) and Cutch (*Acacia catechu*).

BHANBYENG.—A little village of only thirty houses in the circle of the same name, Thayet township, Thayet district, on the Pwon stream about sixteen miles north-west, by the present road, from Thayetmyo. It does not appear amongst the villages registered in the Burmese " Domesday Book" of 1838 A. D. It is important only in that near it several earth-oil wells have been sunk whence a clear oil is obtained unlike the thick and viscid product found at Padoukbeng and at Renankhyoung the site of the prolific earth-oil wells in Upper Burma.

BHANBYENG.—A revenue circle in the Kama township, Thayet district, stretching up westward to the Arakan hills and occupying the valley of the Nga-wet river and the country on the left bank of the Toung-goung-doon. To the east, beyond the end of the Kyouk spur, the country is fairly level but the whole of the western portion of the circle is forest-covered mountain, the unculturable area being no less than 110 square miles out of the 114 of the whole circle. The regular cultivation measures about 500 acres the remainder being hillside clearings. The population in 1876 numbered 8,873 souls and the gross revenue, derived mainly from capitation tax, amounted to Rs. 5,405. The only village is Thayet-kyoung containing rather under 100 houses and situated at the south-eastern foot of the hills. In 1872 Kyoukpyoot and subsequently Tsee were placed under the Bhanbyeng Thoogyee.

BHANBYENG.—A revenue circle in the valley of the Pouk-khoung in the Prome district eastward of Prome, on the lower slopes of the spurs of the Pegu Roma mountains and south of the Naweng. The neighbouring Tsheng-gaw circle has been joined to it and in 1876-77 the united tracts had a population of 1,261 souls and produced a gross revenue of Rs. 1,996 of which Rs. 755 were derived from the land and Rs. 836 from the capitation tax.

BHAN-GOON.—A revenue circle in the Thayet township, Thayet district, which formerly belonged to the Kama township but was transferred in 1859 as being near Thayetmyo and inconveniently distant from Kama. It has an area of 24 square miles of which about 10 are unculturable waste and about two under cultivation, the remainder being culturable waste. The population in 1876 numbered 2,710 souls, all Burmans. The products are rice, sessamum, cotton, maize, plantains, chillies, cutch and silk.

In 1876-77 the land revenue was Rs. 1,763, the capitation-tax Rs. 2,867 and the gross revenue Rs. 4,744.

BHAN-LAW.—A revenue circle in the Mergui district occupying the valley of the Tenasserim river above its junction with the little Tenasserim. In 1876-77 it had a population of 1,997 souls, a land revenue of Rs. 1,525 and produced Rs. 1,347 as capitation-tax.

BHAN OUNG.—A revenue circle in the Toung-ngoo district north of Toung-ngoo and on the right bank of the Tsittoung river. Regular rice cultivation is carried on to a small extent only, the inhabitants being mainly Toungya cultivators or gardeners. Towards the north of the circle is the Tseeloung lake, five feet deep in the dry weather and eight feet in the rains; at the latter season it can be entered by moderately sized boats. In 1876-77 the land revenue was Rs. 2,253, the capitation-tax Rs. 3,150, the gross revenue Rs. 7,632 and the population 4,135.

BHAW.—A stream in the Rangoon district. Leaving the network of streams and creeks which occupies the central portion of the Than-lyeng township it flows westward and falls into the Pegu river about a mile above Syriam. Throughout its course it forms the boundary between the Poo-gan-doung and the Thanlyeng circles. At its mouth it is about 100 feet wide and about 16 feet deep and, with the tide, is navigable throughout by the largest boats, which bring to the Rangoon market the rice produced in the fertile tract which it drains.

BHAWDEE.—A stream in the Thoonkhwa district which collects, through numerous creeks, a good deal of the drainage of the Donabyoo township west of the Irrawaddy and falls into that river through a mouth 180 feet broad and 13 deep. It is navigable by the largest class of boats for 14 miles, to Shwe-hle.

BHAWKATA.—A stream in the Shwe-gyeng district, which has its source in the western slopes of the Poungloung mountains and falls into the Kyouk-gyee a few miles above its mouth.

BHAW-LAY.—A revenue circle in the Hlaing township, Rangoon district, on the north of the Pan hlaing creek. Rice is cultivated in the north and east but the centre of the circle is covered with tree forest and the western portion consists of low plains liable to inundation. In 1876 the land revenue was Rs. 9,602, the capitation-tax Rs. 5,880 and the gross revenue Rs. 24,994: in the same year the population numbered 4,822.

BHAW-LAY.—A village in the circle of the same name in the Hlaing township, Rangoon district, on the Bhaw-lay creek a little south of its junction with the Pa-khwon. The inhabitants, who in 1877 numbered 527, are mostly rice cultivators. Bhaw-lay is a corruption of the Talaing "Bhoung-lee" which signifies a "progress." The place was so named from having been specially visited by king Narapadee-tseethoo during one of his "royal progresses" *circa* 1190 A.D. A fine kind of matting is made here which finds a ready sale in Rangoon.

BHAW-LAY.—A creek in the northern portion of the Rangoon district which leaves the Hlaing a little above Hle-tshiep and after flowing west and then south rejoins it a little above Htan-ta-beng. Boats of from 400 to 500 bushels burden can traverse it from end to end. The banks are somewhat steep and are sandy and covered with grass and tree forest During the dry weather the tide, at springs, is felt as far as its northern mouth : during the rains it is navigable by river steamers.

BHAWMEE.—A river in the Khyoung-tha township, Bassein district, which has its source in the western slopes of the Arakan mountains and falls into the Bay of Bengal near the village of the same name. It is tidal as far as Thoonkhwa, a distance of some 20 miles : its bed is sandy and gravelly and at the mouth are several rocks which make the entry difficult for large boats. At Shwe-tsheng-kho, twelve miles from the mouth, there is a depth of five feet of water and at Toung-tsakhan, nearly four miles further up, of four feet. The banks are covered with Bamboo and Neepatshe.

BHAWMEE.—A revenue circle, 250 square miles in extent in the Thaboung township, Bassein district, immediately to the south of Khwa-letya (now under the same Thoogyee) between the Bay of Bengal on the west and the Arakan mountains on the east. The whole circle with the exception of a little plain cultivated land near the villages of Kyoodaw and Thaigoon consists of a mountain tract covered with dense forest. From the mouth of the Magyee river, the southern boundary of the circle, for five miles northward a sandy beach is found with the hills and forest coming close down to the water's edge : above the mouth of the *Oon* a rocky headland projects, thence sand and rock alternate to about 1½ miles south of Matha whence, up to the Bhawmee in the north, the coast is rocky and abrupt. The villages are small and the population is sparse. The land revenue in 1876-77 was Rs. 525, the capitation-tax Rs. 1,152, the gross revenue Rs. 2,011 and the population 1,406.

BHAWNEE.—A revenue circle in the Shwe-gyeng district lying on the eastern slopes of the Pegu Romas and extending from the Toung-ngoo district in the north to the Rangoon district in the south. The whole area of 800 square miles, except in the east where there are a few patches of rice cultivation, may be said to consist of a mass of hills covered with dense forest. In 1876 the population numbered 4,738, the land revenue was Rs.. 2,039, the capitation-tax Rs. 8,082 and the gross revenue Rs. 5,432. After the annexation of Pegu this tract was divided into two circles and attached to Rangoon; subsequently the two were amalgamated and the tract attached to the Toung-ngoo district from which, in 1866, it was transferred to Shwe-gyeng. None of the streams are of any importance ; the principal are the Re-nwe and the Bhien-da. A considerable quantity of silk is spun from silkworms reared on the spot and exported mainly to Prome and Shwedoung.

BHAWNEE.—A small village of about 400 inhabitants on the Bhawnee river in the southern part of the circle of the same name in the Shwe-gyeng district.

BHAW-THA-BYE-GAN.—A village in the Poo-gan-doung circle, Than-lyeng township, Rangoon district, on the Bhaw creek, a few miles from its mouth in the Pegu river, easily reached by boats which bring away the un-husked rice largely produced in the surrounding country. The inhabitants are almost all agriculturists and in 1877 numbered 767 souls. The village is generally known as *Bhaw* Thabyegan to distinguish it from the numerous other Thabyegan in the same circle. The name is derived from a tank (*kan* or *gan*) in the neighbourhood near some Tha-bye trees (*Eugenia sp.*)

BHAWTHAIK.—A revenue circle in the Amherst district. *See Thambhaya.*

BHAYAI.—A petty and decreasing village in the Shwebandaw circle, Myedai township, Thayet district. About ten years ago it contained 30 houses which have now decreased to about 16. Moung Kyouk-kai, a follower of the Tsekya Meng, set up his gold umbrella here in the rebellion of 1209 B. E. (1847 A.D.).

BHEELENG.—A revenue circle in the Tsan-rwe township, Henzada district, now joined to the Tsan-rwe Myoma circle.

BHEELENG.—A small stream in the Henzada district which rises in the western slopes of the Pegu Romas and after a south and west course of about 24 miles falls into the Hlaing or Myitmakha at Bheeleng. During the rains boats of 100 bushels burden can ascend for about six miles as far as Kyeedaw : in the dry weather it is not navigable. The banks are steep and the bed muddy.

BHEELENG.—A village on the right bank of the Hlaing at the mouth of the Bheeleng river. In 1876 the inhabitants numbered 1,057. They are principally petty traders and fishermen.

BHEELENG.—A revenue circle in the Tsittoung sub-division of the Shwe-gyeng district on the right bank of the Bheeleng river and including the town of Bheeleng. It has an area of about 220 square miles. In 1875 5,047 acres were under cultivation and in 1876-77 the gross revenue, including the local revenue of the town of Bheeleng, was Rs. 19,009 of which the capitation-tax furnished Rs. 6,460 and the land revenue Rs. 5,878. The population in that year was 8,716.

BHEELENG.—A river in the Shwe-gyeng district. It has its source in about the latitude of Kyouk-gyee, west of the head waters of the Rwonzaleng, in the mass of mountains which lie between the Tsittoung and the Salween and flows southward for about 282 miles, falling into the sea at the head of the Bay of Bengal a few miles to the east of the mouth of the Tsittoung. For many miles it is a shallow rocky stream with a rapid current ; as it enters the plain country it deepens but does not materially widen and after flowing past Yeng-oon and Bheeleng and receiving the waters of numerous creeks it becomes very tortuous and finally spreads out into a bell mouth two miles broad up which a bore rushes with great velocity, in the dry season felt as far as Shwe-le a few miles below Bheeleng, the tide ascending considerably higher : during the rains the current increases and except near the mouth of the river the bore makes no way. At this season the waters spread over the banks and inundate the bordering plains, but the Thein-tshiep and Tha-htoon plains in the south-east which formerly suffered most are now to a great extent protected by the Doonwon and Kamathaing embankment which has been raised a few miles south of the Kyoon-iep, the southern boundary of the Shwe-gyeng district east of this river. From May to September a short portion of its course, from the mouth of the Shwe-le creek to the mouth of the Kyoon-iek, forms part of the main route from the Tsittoung to Maulmain.

BHEELENG.—A town on the right bank of the Bheeleng river, the headquarter station of the Bheeleng Kyaik-hto township, Tsittoung sub-division, ~yeng district, containing a Court-house, Circuit-house, Police station and market. It is well laid out in straight steets crossing each other at right angles. In 1824 Oozana, Governor of Martaban, when he retired before the British settled here with a number of Burman followers and built a stockade and was confirmed as Governor by the King of Burma. Six years later he was murdered by one of his officials and the extent of territory under the Governor's control was then reduced. During the second Burmese war the town was surrendered without resistance to the commander of the British column which advanced from Martaban to Toung-ngoo. After the annexation of the country in 1853 an insurrection broke out headed by a Shan of Keng-rwa, a village to the westward, who had been made a Thoogyee. Troops were sent from Kyaik-hto and the insurgents, after some sharp fighting, driven out of Bheeleng and dispersed. Since then it has more than once been attacked and plundered by dacoits, the last occasion being in 1863, and has twice been burned down and rebuilt. In 1877 it had a population of 2,074 souls, principally Burmans traders with a small admixture of Talaing. In 1876-77 the local revenue realized was Rs. 1,709.

BHEELENG KYAIK-HTO.—A township in the Tsittoung sub-division of the Shwe-gyeng district bounded on the north by the lower range of the mass of mountains which form the Salween Hill Tracts, on the south by the sea, on the east for the most part by the Bheeleng river which separates it from the Tha-htoon township of the Amherst district but in the north-east by the Doonthamie several miles to the eastward of the Bheeleng, and on the west by the Kadat stream which separates it from the Tsittoung township of the same sub-division. The general aspect of the country is that of a wide alluvial plain stretching southwards from the base of the hills to the seacoast and traversed by streams or rather drainage-ways which carry off the rain-fall of the southern slopes of the hills and the plain and, from the formation of the country and of the coastline, admit the full rush of the tide which rapidly covers the coast for miles and rising into a bore in every channel sweeps up almost to the foot of the hills. The fact that at no very remote period the sea covered the whole plain is attested by the geological formation and by the occasional discovery of cables of large size at Kyouk-loon-gyee, Taik-koola and other places : to these local traditions add their testimony. The only river is the Bheeleng. On its banks, near the town of the same name, porcelain clay is found and is used by Shans, who come down for the season only bringing another kind of clay and other minerals from the Shan States, which they use with the local mineral in making pottery. The vessels made are variously ornamented but the designs are rude and inartistic. The principal towns and villages are Bheeleng with a population of 2,074 in 1876, the head-quarters of the township, Kyaik-hto the head-quarters of the sub-division with 3,011 inhabitants, Keng-rwa, Taing-kaw and Kaw-ka-dwot. The inhabitants who in 1876 numbered 40,625 souls are principally Talaing except in the town of Bheeleng where the Burman element largely predominates. There is a Toungthoo settlement at Kyouk-ta-loon and Shan villages are found along the bank of the Bheeleng. During Burman rule members of this race, of which great numbers are now immigrating, were, on account of their predatory habits, forbidden to enter Burman territory. The Bheeleng river annually over-flows its banks and the rich alluvial mud deposited favours the growth of a variety of vegetable products and especially sugarcane which is extens-cultivated round about Bheeleng. The land revenue in 1876 was Rs. the capitation-tax Rs. 31,142 and the gross revenue Rs. 86,638.

BHEELOO.—A sub-tribe of Pwo Kareng so called by the Burmese. —*See Taroo.*

BHEELOO-GYWON.—An extensive island lying in the mouth of the Salween 107 square miles in extent and about 30 miles long and stretching from Martaban to Amherst. It forms a township of the Amherst district. The western portion of the island was formerly cut off from the rest by a large creek called the Tsaibala ; of this the northern end has entirely silted up. This western portion, in the Burmese time, formed a separate ' Myo' or township called Daray. The middle of the island from north to south is occupied by a range of wooded and pagoda topped hills which sends out spurs eastward to the river and westward to the sea ; these traverse rich nice land and their sides and lower slopes are covered with orchards of mango, mangosteen and other fruit trees. The alluvial plains to the west of these hills, between them and the sea, are extensive and fertile ; those to the east are narrow and less productive. The head-quarters are at Khyoung-tshoon lying in about the centre of the island in a dip of the hills. Here there is an artificial reservoir, an embankment, lined with flowering trees, having been thrown across the lower end of a small valley. The villages, which with few exceptions are all situated at the foot of the hills, are generally large and straggling. This is chiefly owing to the Talaing prejudice against living in a house which does not face the north. The houses are large and well raised.

The island is intersected with creeks which enable the produce to be exported with but little expense. There are two short roads both made by Major Broadfoot about thirty years ago : one about three miles long from Kalwee at the northern extremity of the island across a plain to the central range of hills which has been allowed to fall out of repair : the other about three miles long from Natmaw on the Salween to Khyoung-tshoon ; this has been kept in repair and is much used.

In the Burman time this township, exclusive of Daray, was divided into twelve different "Rwa" which in this instance meant tracts of country divided off for fiscal purposes and each placed under one Thoogyee. The boundaries of each Rwa, however, do not appear to have been laid down with any great degree of exactitude. When the township came to be re-peopled, after the cession of Tenasserim to the British, immigrants arrived in parties each under its own leader ; these leaders continued to exercise authority irrespective of the old boundaries and were naturally acknowledged as the Thoogyee of the villages they established and as the collectors of the taxes due by their followers, but it frequently happened that some of the followers cultivated land at a distance from the village in which they lived and amongst the lands of inhabitants of another village yet they still payed the land revenue through their own leader and the revenue divisions of the country then became tribal instead of territorial. Such an arrangement was no doubt politic and convenient in the early years of our occupation but its inconvenience when a closer check upon the Thoogyee became advisable was great.

In 1848 Captain (now Sir Arthur) Phayre, then the Deputy Commissioner, carefully examined the township and fixed the boundaries of the circles ; he retained as much as possible the ancient limits of the old divisions but when it was found that two or more Thoogyee had exercised authority within the limits of one of these divisions for twenty years, when new interests had sprung up or where the reduction of a Thoogyee's office was likely to be felt as hardship by the people he divided the old Rwa. The thirteen Rwa of the Burmese time were thus made into eighteen circles. Since then some of the smaller circles have been joined to others but the boundaries laid down by Captain Phayre have been adhered to except in one instance. In 1868 the number of circles had thus been reduced to fifteen and in 1876 to twelve. The cultivation has very considerably increased :—

In	1848	it was	..	..	15,225 acres.
„	1853	„	..	..	21,049 do.
„	1858	„	..	..	27,606 do.
„	1863	„	..	..	28,002 do.
„	1868	„	..	..	32,545 do.
„	1873	„	..	..	42,318 do.
„	1876	„	..	..	†41,274 do.

Between Khyoung-tshoon and the northern end of the island, amongst the hills at Ka-hgnyaw, there is a hot saline spring the water of which is used on the spot in cases of rheumatism and skin diseases. The township in 1876, when the population numbered 24,141 souls or a little over 225 to the square mile, produced a gross revenue of Rs. 78,866. The name, which means "Cacodemon island," is derived from traditions of its having formerly been inhabited by anthropophagous monsters.*

BHENG-BYAI.—A river in the Toung-ngoo district which rises in the Poungloung range and after a south-westerly course falls into the Tsittoung about 30 miles north of Toung-ngoo. It is not navigable by boats at any season of the year; during the rains a considerable quantity of teak is floated down it.

BHENGLAING.—A river in the Amherst district, formed by the junction of the Doonthamie and the Kyouk-tsarit, which falls into the Salween in about 16° 45′ N. It is navigable throughout and flows between high and wooded banks. During the rains it forms a portion of the ordinary route between Maulmain and the Tsittoung river. Across the mouth is a sand-bar which in the dry season is impassable at low water except by small boats.

BHENGLAING.—A revenue circle in the Hpagat township in the Amherst district, lying in the angle formed by the junction of the Bhenglaing with the Salween. This is the only circle in the district in which tobacco is grown except for home consumption. In 1876, the land revenue was Rs. 2,497, the capitation-tax Rs. 3,325, and the population 3,265.

BHETRAI.—A large village in the Henzada district on the bank of the Pala river about 12 miles in a direct line inland from the Irrawaddy, containing some 700 inhabitants who are principally cultivators, petty traders and foresters ; taree-drawers are numerous as the circle in which the village is situated produces a considerable number of taree-trees.

BHETRAI.—A revenue circle in the Kyan-kheng township, Henzada district, extending southwards down a valley between two subsidiary spurs of the Tazoung-gyee and drained by a small tributary of the Kwon. Near the village of Bhetrai there is some rice cultivation but elsewhere the country is

---

* See page 44, lines 8 and 9, and note on page 75.

† There were 2,340 more acres of rice land left fallow in 1876 than in 1873.

hilly and covered with dense tree forest in which are found Pyengma (*Lagerstrœmia Reginœ*), Pyeng-gado (*Xylia dolabriformis*) and Eng (*Dipterocarpus tuberculatus*). The land revenue in 1876-77 was Rs. 6,750, the capitation-tax Rs. 4,700, the gross revenue Rs. 11,484 and the population 4,622.

BHET-RAI.—A creek in the Bassein district forming the western boundary of the Takaing circle. It extends northwards from the Thandwai to the Thoodan, parallel to the Bassein river. The largest boats can ascend as far as the Thoodan.

BHIEN-DA.—A small stream which rises in the eastern slopes of the Pegu Roma mountains in the Bhaw-nee circle of the Shwe-gyeng district and after an easterly course of about 45 miles falls into the Re-nwe. Towards the source the banks are steep but towards the mouth flat; the bed is rocky and sandy. In the rains small boats can ascend as far as the village of Bhien-da. The principal trees found on the banks are Teak, Sha (*Acacia catechu*), Pyeng-gado (*Xylia dolabriformis*) and Pyeng-ma (*Lagerstrœmia Reginœ*).

BHIEN-DAW-TSHIEP.—A lake in the Donabyoo township, Thoonkhwa district, connected by watercourses with the Hlaing river : it is from 2 to 2½ miles long and 10 feet deep in the hot weather.

BHODAW.—A township in the Bassein district which now forms a portion of Regyee.

BHODAW.—A small river in the Bassein district which rises in the Arakan mountains. After a course of about 14 miles, nearly due east, it falls into the Bassein a mile or so south of Gnyoung-maw village, where it is about 70 feet wide and 10 feet deep. The bed is sandy and muddy ; the banks are covered with fine timber and teak is found near its source. With the flood boats of 100 bushels burden can ascend for about two miles.

BHODAW KANNEE.—A revenue circle in the Kyouk-khyoung-gale township (now joined to Le-myet-hna) Bassein district, about 126 square miles in extent, stretching eastwards from the Arakan mountains to the Bassein river and lying to the north of the Bhodaw stream. Formerly Bhodaw and Kannee were separate circles, both in the Bhodaw township; some years ago they were united and subsequently were transferred to Kyouk-khyoung-gale. The western part is hilly and covered with tree forest including teak but between the lower slopes of the hills and the Bassein river there is some level land where rice is cultivated. At the village of Tsha-daw, at the mouth of the Kwon, pottery for various purposes is manufactured. The felling and sale of the timber and bamboos found to the westward afford a means of livelihood to the inhabitants of the villages in the interior ; fishing, cultivation and trading to those of villages farther east. The land revenue in 1876-77 was Rs. 3,552, the capitation-tax Rs. 4,860, the gross revenue Rs. 9,036 and the population 3,963.

BHODOOP.—A tidal creek in the Thoon-khwa district uniting the To with the Pantabwot and forming the head of the Pyapoon river. Its northern mouth is shallow and it is only at high water that large boats can pass through. The banks are steep and covered with dense tree forest.

BHO-HTIET-RWA.—A large village of some 700 souls or more in the Myoung-mya township, Bassein district, in 16° 33' N. and 95° 7' E.

BHOMBADEE.—*See Bhoommawadee.*

BHOOMMAWADEE.—A township of the Toung-ngoo district on the left bank of the Tsittoung extending north from the Shwe-gyeng district to the Thit-nan-tha river and divided into three revenue circles. The whole of the eastern portion is mountainous and covered with thick forest, in which is found teak and other valuable timber, the only regular cultivation being in the more level country along the bank of the Tsittoung. It contains several lakes the largest of which are the Engwon and the Zengdoon, both in the south-west corner. The inhabitants are Burmese, Kareng and Shan with a few Talaing and in 1876 numbered 18,481 : in that year the land revenue was Rs. 4,491, the capitation-tax Rs. 8,062 and the gross revenue Rs. 19,327.

BHOOMMAWADEE.—A revenue circle in the township of the same name in the Toung-ngoo district on the left bank of the Tsittoung river and adjoining the Shwe-gyeng district on the south ; it is now joined to the Maipalau circle.

BHOOMMAWADEE REGYAW.—A natural channel joining the Rouk-thwa-wa, which it leaves at the village of the same name, to the Tsittoung at Regyaw. During the hot season its bed is in some places dry but during the rains it is navigable throughout for boats of from 25 to 30 feet in length. The banks are here and there high and the bed is muddy and sandy.

BHOON-MAW.—A highly-venerated Pagoda in Talaing Thoung-goon village, about three miles north-east of Tavoy, on a bluff called Kyet-tsha-maw, built in 1341 A.D. by an exiled Peguan Prince. It is 41 feet high, octangular in shape and 117 feet in circumference at the base and still carries a Talaing htee.

BHOORA-GYEE.—A village in the Angyee township of the Rangoon district, south of Khabeng, which takes its name from one of the 37 great Pagodas of Angyee, now a ruin. *See Htaw-koo.*

BHOORA-HLA.—A revenue circle in the Ngapootaw township, Bassein district, with an estimated area of 95 square miles, occupying the southern angle between the Arakan hills on the west and the Bassein river on the east as far north as the Bhoora-hla stream. The general aspect of the country is hilly, the hills being spurs from the Arakan Romas. In this circle is included Haing-gyee or Negrais island, lying in the mouth of the Bassein river and separated from the mainland by a channel 1,500 yards broad at its widest and 800 yards at its narrowest part. The island is about 11 miles in circumference, much intersected by creeks, flat and shelving towards its southern end but abruptly hilly towards the northern, where is the site of the old factory.

The Alguada is a long and dangerous reef 15 miles from the mainland on which now stands a light-house.

Diamond Island or Thamee-hla Kywon, the station of the light-house keepers not on duty at Alguada, is low and covered with brushwood and lies outside the mouth of the Bassein river. It abounds with turtle and is leased out as a turtle bank, the revenue derived therefrom being large.

The inhabitants of the circle are mainly Burmese and Kareng with a few Talaing, and in 1876 numbered 2,004 souls who are chiefly engaged in fishing and in making gnapee. In 1876-77 the land revenue was Rs. 2,647, the capitation-tax Rs. 2,142 and the gross revenue Rs. 18,520.

BHOORA-HLA.—A small river which rises in the eastern slopes of the Arakan Romas about 15 miles from their southern extremity and after a course of some 12 miles E.S.E. falls into the Bassein river at Bhoora-hla village. Boats of 500 bushels burden can ascend for three miles ; beyond this the tide is not felt.

BHOORA-TSHIEP.—A village with a population of about 750 souls on the right bank of the Bheeleng river a few miles above Bheeleng.

BHOO-RO.—A stream in the Prome district with a rocky bed and steep banks which rises in the Arakan mountains and after an E.S.E. course of about 35 miles, almost immediately on its leaving the hills, joins the Thanee near the village of Gnyoung-beng-tha ; shortly after the latter rounds to the southward the spur which forms the water parting between the two. In the rains small boats can ascend a short distance. The hills amongst which it flows are richly timbered ; the most important trees are Teak, Pyeng-gado and Htouk-kyau.

BHOOT-KHYOUNG.—A revenue circle in the Myenoo township—now united to Regyee—in the Bassein district on the left bank of the Bassein river with an area of 45 square miles. There is some rice cultivation towards the east and in patches elsewhere but the major portion of the circle consists of low swampy ground covered with grass and tree forest. The inhabitants are largely engaged in fishing. There are no proper cart roads but merely footpaths from village to village used only during the dry season and tracks to the rice-fields. In 1876-77 the land revenue was Rs. 1,881, the capitation-tax Rs. 6,825, the gross revenue Rs. 10,367 and the population 5,466.

BHOOT-PYENG.—A village in the Mergui district of the Tenasserim division on the right bank of the Bhoot-pyeng, a narrow muddy stream, situated in 11° 12′ N. lat. and 98° 42′ E. long. It was a somewhat important place in the Siamese time but it has dwindled to a village of about 500 inhabitants of Malays, Siamese and Chinese. The two former cultivate rice and employ themselves in fishing, the latter in sugar-planting.

BHOOT-PYENG.—A mountainous revenue circle in the Mergui district occupying the whole of the southern portion of the Le-gnya township. In 1876-77 it had a population of 1,848 souls and produced a gross revenue Rs. 2,524 of which Rs. 137 were derived from the land.

BHOOT-PYENG.—A small stream in the Le-gnya township, Mergui district, traversing a generally mountainous country from south to north till it suddenly turns westward and falls into the sea. Boats can ascend as far as Bhoot-pyeng village.

BHWAI-BENG-GAN.—The northern portion of the town of Poungday.

BHWAI-BENG-GAN.—A revenue circle of the Prome district north of Poungday of which the village of Bhwai-beng-gan forms a portion. The Kyadaw and Hmaw-daw circles are now joined to it. In 1876-77 the land revenue was Rs. 2,597, the capitation-tax Rs. 2,572, the gross revenue Rs. 5,259 and the population 2,738.

BHWOT-GYEE.—A lake in the Henzada district north-east of the great Htoo lake three miles west of the Irrawaddy. It is about two miles long and quarter of a mile wide. In the rains it is 7½ feet deep and in the dry weather from 3 to 4; the banks are flat and the water always clear and fresh. According to local tradition this lake was formerly the bed of the Irrawaddy.

BHWOT-LAY.—A river in the Thayet district flowing into the Irrawaddy from the eastwards. It is formed by the junction of many streams, the largest of which are the Pade and Khyoung-goung-gyee. The volume of water which enters the Irrawaddy by this channel is, during the rains, considerable but the creek is useless for navigation on account of the force of the current and the rapidity with which the water rises and falls. Near its mouth it is spanned by a substantial wooden bridge crossed by the main road between Rangoon and Myedai. During the rains a large quantity of teak is floated down to the mouth of the river where it is rafted for the Rangoon market.

BHWOT-LAY.—A revenue circle in the Myedai township, Thayet district, partially cultivated, principally with rice, and with a population of 2,975 souls. The more important products are rice, sessamum and maize. Within the limits of the circle are, amongst others, the villages and village tracts of Bhwot-lay and Toung-na-tha, over each of which was a Thoogyee in the Burmese time, and Htouk-kyan-daing and Pouk-aing joined to it since the annexation of Pegu. In 1876-77 the united circles produced a revenue of Rs. 5,534 of which Rs. 2,251 was derived from the land.

BODA-MAW.—A revenue circle in the Kyailet township, Akyab district, forming a portion of the town of Akyab.

BO-KHYOOP.—Two villages, distinguished as North and South, in the Syriam circle, Syriam township, Rangoon district, lying in the plain and well cultivated country between the Pegu and Rangoon rivers and the laterite ridge on which stands the Syriam Pagoda. South Bo-khyoop is a mere hamlet with 250 inhabitants; North Bo-khyoop had a population of 1,208 souls in 1877, almost all agriculturists. The name, which literally translated means Commander-in-Chief, was given to the village because it sprang up on the site on which the army of the Burman Commander-in-Chief encamped during the last siege and capture of Syriam by the Burmans.

BOODOUNG.—A revenue circle in the Ooreetoung east township, Akyab district. In 1876 the population numbered 973 souls, the land revenue was Rs. 3,468, the capitation-tax Rs. 1,095 and the gross revenue Rs. 4,772.

BO-TA-HTOUNG.—A small Pagoda in the town of Rangoon on the bank of the river below the principal wharves, which, according to local history, was built in 359 B. E. (997 A.D.) by one thousand (ta-htoung) officers (Bo) by the order of Okkalaba King of Twante on the spot where was burned the body of his son Minhanda who had been drowned in the Pegu river. It gives its name to a quarter of Rangoon.

BREK.—A small sub-tribe of Bghai Kareng called by the Burmese Laymay: q. v.

BUFFALO ROCKS (Liep Kywon or Turtle Island).—A group of detached rugged rocks extending nearly N. and S. for about three miles, situated

29 miles from the shore and bearing N. from the western extremity of Cape Negrais. The North Buffalo is a little more than half a mile to the S. W. of the other island, Perforated Rock and Pillar Rock lying between them. On the west side of the Rocks the soundings are regular, 20 fathoms about a mile from them and 50 or 60 fathoms at 5 leagues distance. Lat. 16° 19' to 16° 22' N. Long 94° 12' E. bearing nearly S. ½ W. from Calventura Rock and distant 10 or 11 leagues.

BYEE.—A small and unimportant stream in the Sandoway district which has a generally southerly course and falls into the Sandoway river a few miles below Sandoway.

BYEE-WA.—A village at the mouth of the Byee stream with from 500 to 600 inhabitants, mainly Arakanese, on the right bank of the Sandoway river about two miles below that town.

BYOO-GAN.—A village of about 60 houses in the Kyan circle, Mengdoon township, Thayet district, on a small affluent of the Ma-htoon. In the Burmese time it was one of the registered villages of an hereditary Thoogyeeship.

BYOO-GOON.—A revenue circle in the Prome district about ten miles east of Prome: the larger part is under rice cultivation. In 1876-77 the land revenue was Rs. 242, the capitation-tax Rs. 87 and the population 95.

BYOO-GOON.—A village in the Prome district in the middle of a large rice tract in 18° 48' 50" N. and 95° 28' E. about eleven miles east of the town of Prome.

CALVENTURA (*Hnget-toung* or *Bird's feather*).—A group of rocks off the coast of Arakan forming two divisions bearing from each other north west and south-east, distant five or six miles, the body of them being in lat. 16° 53 N. The north-west group consists of seven black rocks in lat. 16° 55' N., long. 94° 15' 30" E. of different magnitudes and forms ; one of them resembles an old church with a mutilated spire, another is much larger near the top than it is near the small base on which it stands. The south-east division consists of two high rocky islands, covered with trees and bushes and connected by a reef of rocks with five to seven fathoms water upon it ; about half-way between the islands there is a single rock, dry at low water.

CAP ISLAND.—A small round bushy island off Tavoy Point called *Hnget-thaik* (Bird's nest) by the Burmese.

CAVENDISH ISLAND.—An islet one third of a mile long surrounded by a reef, a little to the south of Kalegouk.

CHEDUBA.—*See Manoung.*

CHINA-BAKIR.—*See To.*

CRAB ISLAND.—*See Pyeng-gyee.*

DAGA.—A creek in the Pegu division which leaves the Bassein or Ngawon river three or four miles from its northern mouth in the Irrawaddy in the Henzada district and flowing in a generally south-westerly direction, but with many windings, it rejoins the Bassein seven or eight miles above the town of Bassein bringing with it the drainage of the country through which it flows and much of the rainfall and spill in the delta poured into its channel by the numerous anastomosing creeks which reticulate over the country. The northern entrance has in a great measure silted up and is now completely closed by the reclamation embankment thrown up along the bank of the Bassein : the bed for about eight miles down, as far as Rwathit, is dry during the hot season. In the rains there is a strong current downwards but in the dry season the tide is felt as far as Thabye-hla at neaps and fifteen miles further at springs. It is navigable by river steamers during the rains for thirty-six miles from its southern outlet as far as the mouth of 'the Meng-ma-hnaing creek but during the dry season those vessels cannot ascend more than ten or twelve miles. Large native boats can go up as high as Kyoon-pyaw at all seasons of the year and small boats still higher : here the river is from 200 to 300 feet wide and 10 to 15 feet deep. A few miles below Kyoonpyaw on the right or western bank is the Eng-rai-gyee lake which it has been supposed was formerly a portion of the Daga and now communicates with it by a small channel.

DAGA.—A revenue circle in the Bassein district to which is now joined Shwe-gnyoung-beng. In 1876 the population of the united circles was 2,227, the land revenue Rs. 4,153, the capitation-tax Rs. 2,045 and the gross revenue Rs. 6,418.

DA-GYAING.—A river in the Amherst district having its source in the Dawna spur and flowing westward to the Hlaingbhwai which it joins about half way between Khazaing and Hlaingbhwai. Au impetuous torrent, the course is obstructed by numerous rocks and it is not navigable even near its mouth except by small canoes. In the rains it brings down a considerable body of water.

DAI-DA-RAI.—A village in the Thoonkhwa district on the right bank of the To river about fifteen miles from its mouth. The inhabitants are Talaing and Burmans and are principally engaged in rice cultivation, fishing and wood-cutting. Lat. 16° 26' 30" N. long. 95° 4' E.

DAI-DA-RAI.—A revenue circle in the north-western portion of the Pyapoon township, Thoonkhwa district, on the right or southern bank of the To river. In 1876, when it had a population of 5,319 souls, the land revenue was Rs. 21,976, the capitation-tax Rs. 6,525 and the gross revenue Rs. 31,062. It was formerly included in the Wakamay circle of the same township.

DAING-BOON.—A revenue circle on the Le-mro river on the northern borders of the Mye-boon township of the Kyouk-hpyoo district, with an area of 117 miles and a population in 1876 of 4,111 souls. Its southern portion is divided into numerous islands by inter-communicating tidal creeks. The land revenue in 1876 was Rs. 5,083, the capitation-tax Rs. 3,900 and the gross revenue Rs. 31,087.

DAI-PAI.—A lake in the Matoungda circle of the Kanoung township in the Henzada district, near the foot of the eastern slopes of the Pegu Roma mountains, covering an area of nearly a square mile in the rains it has a depth of nine and in the dry season of four or five feet. It is supplied principally by the drainage from the neighbouring hills but before the embankments were constructed it received some of the spill of the Irrawaddy during the rains.

DALA.—A creek in the Rangoon district which empties itself into the Rangoon river opposite Rangoon. On the west side of its mouth are dockyards and the Dala suburb of Rangoon and to the east timber yards and steam saw mills. In the dry season it is not navigable for more than two or three miles but during the rains boats can traverse its whole length.

DALA.—A creek in the Thoonkhwa district forming one of the mouths of the Irrawaddy ; so named in the charts but more properly called *Kyoon-toon*.

DALA.—A suburb of Rangoon on the right or western bank of the Rangoon river. In ancient times the Dala district included the present Angyee township of the Rangoon district and the Pyapoon township of Thoonkhwa and was sometimes annexed to Burma, sometimes to Thanlyeng and sometimes to Pegu, at others it was under an independent Governor. In 1650 A.D., according to an inscription on a stone at the Koung-hmoo-daw Pagoda near Ava which was completed in that year, Dala formed a portion of Ramanya, a province subject to the King of Burma. At the end of the last century or the beginning of this Pyapoon was separated from it and subsequently Angyee.

DALA-NWON.—A river in the Shwe-gyeng district which rises in the eastern spurs of the Pegu Roma mountains and, flowing towards the south-east, falls into the Tsittoung a few miles below Thooyaithamee (commonly called Thayet-thamien). It is navigable for large boats as far as Thoonkhwa.

DAN-DOUNG.—A village on the Kyoung-goung-gyee stream some four miles above its junction with the Pade, in the Thamboola circle, Myedai township, Thayet district, containing about sixty houses.

DA-NWON.—A tidal creek in the Shweloung township, Thoonkhwa district, forming, with the Irrawaddy, an island on which stands the village of Kywonpyathat in 16° 25′ N. and 95° 12′ 30″ E. It is navigable by river steamers.

DA-PYOO-KHYAING.—A revenue circle 220 square miles in extent in the south-western portion of the An township, Kyouk-hpyoo district, cut up into numerous islands by inosculating tidal creeks. In 1876 it had a population, principally of Arakanese, of 3,617 souls. The land revenue was Rs. 2,418, the capitation-tax Rs. 2,814 and the gross revenue Rs. 5,490. It now includes the formerly separate Ma-ee circle.

DARAY.—A revenue circle in the Amherst district in the extreme north-west corner of Bheeloo island, having the sea on the west, the Daray-bouk on the north, the Kalwee circle on the east and the Kwonraik circle on the south, with a small Talaing population and a good deal of cultivation. In 1876 the population was 544, the land revenue Rs. 4,024 and the capitation-tax Rs. 595. In the Burmese time Daray was a separate " Myo" or township and included the present circles of Daray, Kwonraik and Tawkama, that is the whole of the western portion of Bheeloogywon which was cut off from the east by a large creek called the Tsaibala of which the northern portion has now silted up. It could not, however, have been a very populous or productive township as in 1808 A.D., the Governor had only twelve families under him and was dismissed on account of his inability to raise any revenue. It was divided into circles in 1848 by the Deputy Commissioner Captain (now Sir Arthur) Phayre.

DARAY-BHYOO.—A creek in the Kweng-bouk-gyee circle of the Bassein district forming one of the entrances from the sea to the Rwe. The mouth, in 15° 51' 20" N. and 90° 41' 20" E., is so filled by sandbanks as scarcely to afford a passage for the smallest sea-going craft but the remaining portion of the river affords easy navigation to river steamers.

DARAY-BOUK.—The name given to the northern mouth of the Salween from Martaban to the sea. Several centuries ago it was the ordinary entrance for ships coming to Martaban, then a great trading port, but for many years it has been so filled with sandbanks as to be impassable for sea-going boats.

DARAY-BOUK.—A village in the Labwotkoola circle, Myoungmya township, Bassein district, on the Tha-ran-boon which reaches the sea by numerous channels the principal of which are the Rwe and the Daray-bhyoo. To the north-west and south are rich rice-fields and the inhabitants, over 600 in number, are principally engaged in cultivation and in trade.

DARIEN.—A revenue circle in the extreme south-western corner of the Martaban township, Amherst district, bounded on the west by the sea and on the south by the Daray-bouk. The circle consists of low highly cultivated plains liable to inundation on the west during high tides, the sea water penetrating into the low land inside the protecting drift-covered beach through a drainage way cut by a villager some years ago. In 1876 the population numbered 8,181, the capitation-tax was Rs. 3,277 and the land revenue Rs. 24,784.

DATTAW.—A small stream which rises in the Khyee-ba spur on the west of the Irrawaddy and falls into that river near Pienthalien. Its banks are moderately steep and its bed sandy and muddy. In the rains and then only boats can ascend for a short distance. On its banks are found Teak, Cutch (*Acacia catechu*) Eng-gyeng (*Pentacme siamensis*) much used in house building, Thenggan (*Hopea odorata*) which is scarce, and Pyengma (*Lagerstroemia Reginæ*).

DAWLAN.—A revenue circle lying between the Dawna hills and the Hlaingbhwai river in the southern portion of the Thanlweng Hlaingbhwai township, Amherst district, opposite Gyaing. Its inhabitants are principally Kareng. In 1876 it produced a land revenue of Rs. 1,925, the capitation-tax amounted to Rs. 2,912, the gross revenue to Rs. 4,837 and the population numbered 2,836 souls.

DETANAW.—A small but once a large and flourishing Talaing village in the Lawadee circle, Angyee township, Rangoon district. At the close of the first Anglo-Burmese war numbers of the inhabitants who had sided with the British escaped to Tenasserim and the rest were seized and massacred by the local Burmese authorities for their adherence to the English. In the neighbourhood are the ruins of a large and ancient Pagoda, one of the 37 great Pagodas of Angyee.

DHABIEN.—A tidal creek in the Rangoon district running between the Poozwondoung and Pegu rivers, past the village of Dhabien where it is fifteen feet deep at high tide : the largest boats can ascend to this village, a distance of a little over a mile, at all times : in the rains its water is sweet and it is navigable throughout its course.

DHABIEN NORTH.—A revenue circle in the Hpoung-eng township of the Rangoon district on the right bank of the Pegu river. In 1876 it had a population of 8,076 souls and 11,831 acres under rice cultivation. The land revenue in the same year was Rs. 23,938, the capitation-tax Rs. 3,573 and the gross revenue Rs. 27,511.

DHABIEN SOUTH.—A revenue circle in the Hpoung-leng township, Rangoon district, between the Pegu and Poozwondoung rivers immediately to the south of Dhabien north of which until a year or two ago it formed a portion. In 1876 the land revenue was Rs. 25,684, the capitation-tax Rs. 3,050, the gross revenue Rs. 28,769, the area of rice land under cultivation 12,688 acres and the population 2,604 souls.

DHA-GNYA-WADEE.—A revenue circle in the Toung-ngoo district, extending eastward from the Pegu Romas along both banks of the Khaboung and occupying the whole of the country drained by that stream and its tributaries. With the exception of a small tract of rice cultivation the whole of this circle is a mass of hills and undulating ground where are found Eng (*Dipterocarpus tuberculatus*), Sha (*Acacia catechu*), Thenggan (*Hopea odorata*), Pyengma (*Lagerstrœmia Reginœ*), Pyenggado (*Xylia dolabriformis*) and Teak (*Tectona grandis*). On the banks of the Khaboung and on the hills there is excellent teak but the forests in the plains are, as regards this tree, limited. In 1876 the inhabitants numbered 3,787, the land revenue was Rs. 717, the capitation-tax Rs. 1,721 and the gross revenue Rs. 2,474.

DHALET.—A revenue circle 420 square miles in extent on the upper course of the Dhalet river in the extreme north of the An township of the Kyouk-hpyoo district. The inhabitants, who are chiefly Khyeng, numbered 4,629 in 1876 and in that year the land revenue was Rs. 2,176, the capitation-tax Rs. 3,083 and the gross revenue Rs. 5,425.

DHALET.—A river in the Kyouk-hpyoo district which rises in the main range and falls into Combermere Bay. It can be ascended by boats of considerable burden as far as the village of the same name (in many reports and works on the country called *Talak*) about 25 miles from the mouth; higher up the stream is a mountain torrent navigable only by small canoes. From Dhalet there is a pass across the hills to Upper Burma which was partially explored during the first Burmese war and was found to be almost impracticable for troops.

DHALET.—A village in the Kyouk-hpyoo district on the river of the same name; a small Police force is stationed here.

DHAM-BHEE.—A revenue circle in the north-east of the Henzada township, Henzada district, on the left bank of the Ngawon or Bassein river. The neighbouring circle of Myo-gweng has of late years been joined to it. The villages are small the largest having in 1875 a little over 500 inhabitants. The united circles had in 1876 a population of 7,471 souls principally engaged in rice cultivation. In that year the land revenue amounted to Rs. 8,275, the capitation-tax to Rs. 7,547 and the gross revenue to Rs. 16,991. The country was formerly subject to inundation from the spill of the Irrawaddy but is now protected by an embankment along that river.

DHAM-MA-THA.—A small village in the Amherst district on the left bank of the Gyaing, opposite a large grass and tree-covered island lying about sixty yards off, seventeen miles above Maulmain. To the south of the village

is an extensive outcrop of limestone rocks covered with dense tree forest
and pierced by a large cave with the walls and roof highly ornamented with figures
in red and gold of Gaudama Booddha and of Rahan and the floor covered
with images. All are in va' ious stages of decay but a few bear marks of wanton destruction, as do so many in the other caves in this district more accessible
to strangers who have no respect for Booddhism or the religious edifices and
shrines of the inhabitants of the country. These rocks terminate immediately
below the village in a cliff overhanging the river and crowned with a small
white Pagoda, reached by a long flight of steps built from the south up
the western side. From the top there is a fine view of the surrounding
country, shut in on the east by the distant blue mountains which bound the
valley of the Thoungyeng and on the west by Bheeloogywon and the Martaban hills, whilst to the north appear the massive and rugged Zwai-ka-beng
limestone rocks popularly known as the "Duke of York's nose." In the distance to the westward Maulmain is conspicuous by the gilded Pagodas and
monasteries on the low hills which traverse the town. Between the cliff and the
village is the Government rest-house with a flight of steps down to the river.

DHANOO.—An extensive but rambling revenue circle in the north-east
of the Tha-htoon township on the right bank of the Kyouk-tsarit and
Bheng-laing rivers and bounded on the south by the Ze-ma-thway, à tributary
of the latter. The name is derived from "Dhanoo" the appellation of a people
who are supposed at one time to have inhabited the tract and who were one
of the one hundred and one races into which all the people of the world are,
according to the Burmese belief, divided : at present the population is mainly
Toungthoo. The surface of the country is hilly and undulating, covered with
tree forest and annually to a considerable extent inundated, partly from the
rain-fall and the spill of the Bhenglaing which is banked up by the Salwéen
and of late years partly by the overflow from the Bheeleng which is excluded
from the Thien-tshiep and Tha-htoon plains and forced round the northern end of
the Martaban hills at Kamathaing by the Doonwon embankment. In 1876
the land revenue was Rs. 1,454, the capitation-tax Rs. 5,891 and the population 7,661. It now includes the Meng-lweng circle. Many of the inhabitants
cultivate land in the neighbouring circles.

DHANOOT BHOORA-GYEE.—A very large Pagoda, now in ruins, in
the Kodoung circle, Angyee township, Rangoon district, about one mile
from the entrance of the Tha-khwot-peng creek. This was formerly the
site of a flourishing village but no habitation has existed within the memory
of any one now living nor are any records traceable which throw light upon
the history of the Pagoda.

DHATHWAI-KYOUK.—A river in the Prome district which rises in
the southern slopes of the Tshenglan subspur, to the north of which is the
valley of the Shwelay, and flowing for some distance southward and then turning west falls into the Zay just above the entrance of this stream into the
Engma lake. It is not open for boats at any time ; its banks are moderately steep and its bed is sandy and gravelly. The lower portion of its course
is through rice-fields but higher up, amongst the hills, it flows through forests
producing valuable timber : Pyenggado (*Xylia dolabriformis*), Eng-gyeng

(*Pentacme Siamensis*), Bhaubhwai (*Careya arborea*) and Eng (*Dipterocarpus tuberculatus*).

DHATHWAI-KYOUK.—A village in the Prome district in 18° 41 N. and 95° 34′ 35″ E. on the river of the same name, at the mouth of the Kyathoung-myoung one of its affluents, twenty miles in a direct line S.E. from Prome. It lies about four or five miles east of the edge of the great rice tract occupying the centre of the valley between the Pegu mountains and the Prome hills and at the western foot of the spurs of the former. It is inhabited mainly by agriculturists engaged in garden and miscellaneous cultivation.

DHATKE.—A small pagoda, now in ruins, on the hills in the town of Maulmain. Of its early history nothing is known. It is supposed to contain one of Gaudama's hairs.

DIAMOND ISLAND.—A low tree covered island about one square mile in extent and visible at five leagues distance lying off the mouth of the Bassein or Ngawon river, in lat. 15° 51′ 30″ N. and long. 94° 18′ 45″ E., distant 50 miles from Pagoda Point and about 8 miles from Negrais Island or Haing-gyee. In shape it is quadrilateral having the angles facing the points of the compass. During strong southerly gales landing is difficult. It does not appear ever to have been inhabited by the Burmese but was and is visited by those engaged in collecting the eggs of the turtles which frequent it in large numbers. For some years it has been occupied by the Light-house establishment as the home station of the detachment in charge of the Alguada reef Light-house. It is connected with Bassein by a telegraph line for the use principally of the masters of ships calling for orders. By the Burmese it is known as *Miemma-hla-kywon.*

DOMEL.—An island in the Mergui Archipelago between 11° 26′ and 11° 28′ N. and 98° 2′ and 98° 11′ E., forming a portion of the Mergui district of the Tenasserim division and lying due west of Kissering island from which it is three or four miles distant, the navigable channel between the two, however, being very narrow. Its extreme length, from north to south, is about twenty-eight miles and its breadth, from east to west, about four miles.

DONABYOO MYOMA.—A revenue circle in the Donabyoo township Thoonkhwa district on the right bank of the Irrawaddy. The upper portion has long been under cultivation ; the southern part was formerly forest waste subject to inundation but is now protected by embankments along the Irrawaddy. In 1876 the land revenue was Rs. 5,550, the capitation-tax Rs. 6,860, the gross revenue Rs. 15,133 and the population 7,328 including the inhabitants of Donabyoo town who numbered 4,331. This circle now includes Thaboung.

DONABYOO.—A township in the Thoonkhwa district lying principally on the right bank of the Irrawaddy with a small portion on the left bank and adjoining Henzada on the north and Rangoon on the east. It was formerly in the Henzada district and included the A-hpyouk circle on the left bank of the river : some three years ago the Thoon-tshay circle, also in the left bank, was added to it from Rangoon. In 1875, on the formation of the Thoonkhwa district, A-hpyouk was cut off and joined to the Za-lwon township of Henzada. Almost the whole township was subject to inundation on the rise of the Irrawaddy but is now protected by extensive embankments along the west bank of that river. The principal town is Donabyoo where the Extra Assistant Commissioner in charge is stationed. In 1876 it produced a land revenue of Rs. 55,431, the capitation-tax amounted to Rs. 34,448, the gross revenue was Rs. 1,08,564 and the population 36,122.

DONABYOO.—A town in the Thoonkhwa district on the right bank of the Irrawaddy about 35 miles south of Henzada, containing a Court house, a Police station and a bazaar or market-place. The population in 1876-77 was 5,800 and the local revenue during each of the nine years ending with 1875-76 were:—

Year.	Population.	Revenue.	Year.	Population.	Revenue.
		Rs.			Rs.
1867-68	3,186	1,296	1872-73	3,950	2,537
1868-69	3,136	1,468	1873-74	3,950	4,412
1869-70	3,950	2,096	1874-75	4,155	4,289
1870-71	3,758	2,817	1875-76	4,331	4,252
1871-72	3,921	2,028	....	....	....

In the first Anglo-Burmese war after the capture of Rangoon the Burmese Commander-in-chief, Bandoola, entrenched himself in this town with a force of fifteen thousand men. The main work was a stockaded paralellogram of one thousand yards by seven hundred which was on the bank well above the level of the river. On the river face were fifty cannon of various calibres whilst the approach on the land side was defended by two outworks. General Cotton's force carried the first stockade at the point of the bayonet but was repulsed from the main work, Captains Cannon and Rose being killed and the greater number of the men killed or wounded. General Cotton then retreated down the river waiting for reinforcements. Sir Archibald Campbell the Commander-in-Chief, who was advancing north up the valley of the Hlaing fell back, established his head-quarters at Henzada and proceeded down the river. On arrival before Donabyoo he constructed batteries of heavy artillery the enemy making numerous sorties with a view of interrupting the work; when the batteries were completed they opened a fire of shot, shell and rockets and next day the Burmans were discovered to be in full retreat: this was subsequently found to be due to the death of Bandoola who had been killed by the bursting of a shell.

During the second war the Burman general made no endeavour to hold the town but evacuated it before the arrival of the British force and retreated on Prome. Shortly after this numerous armed bands spread over the country and, amongst other places, occupied Donabyoo the leader being one Moung Myat Htoon. He was attacked by a force under Captain Hewett I.N. defeated and forced to retreat, but on the British retiring reappeared with his band. Captain Loch R.N. in the early part of January 1853 moved up the river with a small detachment and finally drove him southwards where he was a short time later, after forcing Captain Loch's party to fall back, overtaken by Sir John Cheape and killed. From this time Donabyoo remained in the undisputed possession of the British. The name which is correctly spelt Danoo-hpyoo, means "White peacock" and is partly Pali—Danoo "a peacock"—and partly Burmese—hpyoo "white."

DOONRAN.—A tidal creek in the Thoonkhwa district which runs from the To or China Bakir in an almost southerly direction to the sea, having a total length of about thirteen miles. The depth of the water varies from $\frac{1}{2}$ a fathom to 8 or 9, the northern end being shallow and the southern deep; the water is sweet throughout except at the springs when a high bore is formed which reaches far up. It is navigable by boats of 300 baskets burden but not by very large boats on account of the numerous shoals. On the right bank, in the interior, are extensive plains abounding in game and on the left bank wild elephants are found.

DOONRENG.—The name of a peak in the Zwaikabeng limestone hills north of Maulmain. The ascent is made with considerable difficulty owing to the precipitous nature of the rocks. Almost at the summit a gap is reached " then descending a few yards the spectator is astonished to find himself on " the edge of a large basin like the crater of an extinct volcano; round and " beyond, on the opposite side of the gulph, for miles in extent dark precipitous " crags of every imaginable and unimaginable form fling down their tall " shadows a thousand feet about the place of entrance enclosing an area of " several square miles."

" Down a steep descent of one or two hundred feet an uneven plain " is reached covered with a luxuriant forest. This impregnable natural fortress " has been a place of refuge for the Karens during many generations. While " the Burmans, the Shans and the Talaings were contending in the plains below, " the Karens in this eyrie home peeped out on the belligerents from behind " their battlements in perfect security. The great defect is the want of water " which is obtainable, but not in abundance, from a small stream called Tee- " reng or the 'brook of weeping.' In the days of the Burman conqueror " Alompra (*Aloung-bhoora*) before his successes" in Tenasserim " a large num- " ber of Karens were besieged here by Siamese and tradition says that nearly " the whole perished for want of food and water. From the sufferings of that " period, or a previous one, the place has acquired the name of " Doonreng" or " City of weeping." *

DOONRENG.—A revenue circle in the Gyaing Than-lweng township, Amherst district, on the western slopes of the Zwai-ka-beng hills inhabited mainly by Kareng. In 1876 the land revenue was Rs. 2,861, the capitation-tax Rs. 2,565 and the population 1,881. Included in this circle is the Toung-myouk circle.

DOONTHAMIE.—A river in the Tenasserim division which has never been carefully explored or examined. It has its source somewhat below the latitude of Shwe-gyeng, between the Bheeleng and the Salween rivers, and after a very tortuous course southward unites with the Kyouk-tsarit, in about 16° 59' 30" N. a few miles south of Dhanoo village, to form the Bhenglaing a tributary of the Salween. It is navigable by Burman boats for some distance. The upper part of its course is through hills on which

---

* Mason's *Burma* : Introduction, page 11, editn. of 1860.

are found a considerable number of teak trees of excellent quality. The forests are some distance from the river but several tributary streams facilitate the removal of the timber in the rains.

DOONWON.—Another name of the Bheeleng river. *q. v.*

DOONWON.—A village in the Tha-htoon township of the Amherst district, on the left bank of the Bheeleng river, on slightly rising ground immediately south of the mouth of the Kyoon-iek creek. An embankment now extends eastward from the rising ground for half a mile to Kama-thaing on the western slopes of the northern extremity of the Martaban hills, which keeps out the spill of the Bheeleng river and thus affords protection to the Tha-htoon plain. In 1876 the village had a small population of 281 souls. In former years it was an important walled city, the principal town of the surrounding country though far inferior to Tha-htoon its south-eastern neighbour. In 1306, when it formed a portion of the kingdom of Martaban, it was attacked and plundered by the King of Zeng-mai, east of the Salween, and in 1851 it was again attacked and taken. Shortly afterwards Byat-ta-ba, the half-brother or cousin of Ba-gnya-oo the reigning sovereign, having risen in rebellion and seized the capital the King retired to Doonwon : the rebellion was successful but owing to the intervention of the King of Zeng-mai Ba-gnya-oo remained undisturbed for six years in the retreat he had chosen. Byat-ta-ba then obtained possession of the town by stratagem and Ba-gnya-oo fled to Pegu which formed a portion of his dominions. By a tacit understanding there was peace between them and Byat-ta-ba retained the country east of the Bheeleng. Ba-gnya-oo was succeeded by Radzadierit who, after successfully resisting a Burmese invasion, attacked and took Doonwon. After this the name drops out of history.

Close to the present village, and within the walls and moat of the old town of which the ruins still exist, are two wooden images, evidently from the dress, of foreigners one of which has a hole through both cheeks. These were until lately considered by all the inhabitants of the surrounding country, and still are by some looked upon, as the images of powerful *nat* and it was thought to be dangerous to pass them without making some offering of a little rice or a bunch of leaves or a flower. According to local traditions they represent two natives of India—Ee-bra-hoon and Oo-le (*Ibrahim* and *Ali* or *Wali*)—who were in command and were killed during the assault by the troops of Radzadierit and the hole through the cheeks is intended to represent the bullet-wound which caused the death of the elder of the two. Sir Arthur Phayre, however, in his History of Pegu (*Journal of the Asiatic Society of Bengal, 1873, No. 1, pt. 1, page 48*) states that two officers having these names defended Martaban after the fall of Doonwon and escaped to "the Koola country" and in a foot-note adds : "There is no mention made "of firearms in these operations, but immediately afterwards there is in "the account of the attack on Bassein."

DOORA.—A village in the Atsen circle, Re-Lamaing township, Amherst district to the north of Atsen. In 1876 it had 588 inhabitants.

DOORA.—A revenue circle in the south of the Henzada township of the Henzada district. It is well cultivated on low ground, preserved from inundation by the embankment along the Irrawaddy. In 1876 it had a population of 7,216 souls and produced a land revenue of Rs. 21,374, Rs. 7,450 as capitation-tax and a gross revenue of Rs. 31,536. The two largest villages are Htantabeng and Aing-gyee each containing a population of over 1,000 souls. On the eastern border of the circle is the great Doora lake.

DOORA.—An extensive lake or group of intercommunicating lakes in the Henzada township of the Henzada district. In the most westerly of these is an island which divides it into two called the Doora and the Moshoon : half a mile east of this latter and communicating with it in the rains is the Engtha-nwot and between this and the Irrawaddy and joined to both during the wet season is the Mobalai. The Doora proper is about two square miles in extent and united at its northern extremity to the Irrawaddy by the Atba-rwot stream through which, during the rains and before the Irrawaddy embankments were constructed, boats of from 300 to 400 baskets burden could pass. The Moshoon lake, or more properly the Moshoon portion of the Doora, is 2½ miles in length and from 300 to 400 yards broad with a depth of from 6 to 9 feet in the dry weather. The Engtha-nwot has a length of 1,400 feet and a maximum breadth of 700 with a depth of from 4 to 6 feet in the dry weather. The Mobalai has about 5 feet of water in the dry season. These lakes are fed by the drainage of the surrounding country but have been to some extent affected by the embankments carried along the Irrawaddy which have closed the mouths of the streams by means of which they communicated with this river during the rains.

DOORENGABHO.—A village in the Prome district stretching along the bank of the Irrawaddy to the south-west of Shwedoung and forming a suburb of that town.

DOOTIEYA KHARENG.—A revenue circle in the Gyaing Attaran township, Amherst district, occupying a tract of country extending southward from the junction of the Hlaingbhwai and the Houngtharaw. The area under cultivation is small and the inhabitants, who are mainly Kareng, are few. In 1876 the land revenue was Rs. 464, the capitation-tax Rs. 605 and the population 477.

DOUBLE ISLAND.—A small island about twelve miles south of Amherst point, well raised above the sea and lying in 15° 52' 30" N. and 97° 36' 30" E. On it stands a stone light-house with an iron tower, containing a dioptric fixed light of the first order with a catadioptric mirror visible nineteen miles and first exhibited on the 4th December 1865. The original cost of the work was Rs. 9,03,400. The principal object in building a light-house here was to guide ships making for Maulmain and to prevent their running up the Tsittoung river to certain destruction.

DOUNGBOON.—A village in the Prome district in 15° 33' 55" N. and 95° 30' 15" E. on the bank of the Thitneedaw stream, about five miles above its junction with the Zay, seventeen miles S.E. of Prome as the crow flies. The inhabitants are chiefly agriculturists.

DOUNGBOON.—A revenue circle in the Prome district to the N. E. of the Engma lake, extensively cultivated with rice and including four of the old revenue circles. In 1876 the land revenue was Rs. 8,785, the capitation-tax Rs. 10,372, the gross revenue Rs. 20,787 and the population 9,296.

DOUNG-GYEE.—A village in the Henzada district on the right bank of the Irrawaddy in 17° 32′ N. and 95° 37′ E., about a mile south of the old village of Toungbotara.

DOUNG-GYEE.—A town in the Le-myet-hna township, Bassein district, on the Bassein river in 17° 22′ 30″ N. and 95° 8′ E. The surrounding country is open waste covered with grass and tree forest and liable to inundation. In the hot and dry seasons many of the residents are employed in fishing and in manufacturing large pots for boiling salt and for other purposes ; these are made from the excellent pottery-clay found in the neighbourhood.

DOUNGMANA.—A revenue circle in the Mahathaman township of the Prome district, which in 1876 produced a land revenue of Rs. 1,030; the capitation-tax in the same year was Rs. 543, the gross revenue Rs. 1,573 and the population 544. Included in this circle is Tha-ma-wadee, once independent.

ENG-BAW-NGAY.—A village in the Prome district on the edge of the Eng-Daing (a long stretch of Eng-forest land between the Prome hills and the Myit-makha) thirteen miles in a direct line S. S. E. of Prome but much further by road. To the westward the country is hilly and covered with Eng (*Dipterocarpus tuberculatus*) forest but to the east, north and south it is more open and to some extent under rice cultivation.

ENG-BHET-TAW.—A village in the Kama township, Thayet district, situated in a small tract of rice land about two miles north-east of the Mahtoon river.

ENG-DAING.—A village in the Toung-ngoo district on the Bhengbyai stream, seven miles east of Tsittoung river and five south of the frontier line.

ENG-GA-BHO.—A village of about 1,000 inhabitants in the Kabaing circle, Henzada township, Henzada district, containing several Pagodas and good public rest-houses. The inhabitants are mainly engaged in cultivation and fishing. Lat. 17° 36′ N. Long. 95° 24′ E.

ENG-GA-BOO.—A revenue circle in the Gnyoungdoon township of the Thoonkhwa district extending along the Panhlaing creek from its junction with the Irrawaddy. The land to the east is low and subject to inundation ; the principal rice-fields are towards the west where the land is higher. Many of the inhabitants are engaged in fishing, from the tax on which a considerable revenue is derived. The land revenue in 1876-77 was Rs. 5,518, the capitation-tax Rs. 6,018, the gross revenue Rs. 26,008 and the population 4,736.

ENG-GA-LOON.—(A Talaing name;—from 'Ank' a lake and 'Kaloon' a kind of reed [*Maranta*]). A village in the Angyee township, Rangoon district, on the edge of the Twante Tawgyee a little to the south-west of Tshapoogan, inhabited chiefly by Talaing. In the neighbourhood are the ruins of one of the thirty-seven great Pagodas of the township (*vide Htawkoo* and *Htawkharan*). There is a tradition in the village that not much more than a hundred years ago the sea rolled at the foot of the Tawgyee and the former line of sea coast is still pointed out. Some years ago when a well was being sunk a large ship's cable was found a few feet below the surface and pieces of wreck are still occasionally met with.

ENG-GOON.—A small stream in the north of the Prome district which rises in the southern slopes of the Padouk spur of the Pegu Roma mountains, a few miles east of the source of the Gwe-khyo. Flowing in a south-westerly direction it falls into the south Naweng at the same spot as the Gwe-khyo and the Khyoung-tsaik. In the lower portion of its course the bed is sandy and muddy and higher up rocky ; the banks are steep and clothed with elephant grass, bamboos and forest trees.

ENG-GOON.—A large agricultural village in the Myedai township, Thayet district, situated in an extensive rice plain and on the high road from Rangoon to the north. Lat. 19° 16' 10" N., Long. 95° 18' 20" E.

ENG-GYEE.—A village in the Prome district in 18° 31' 45" N. and 95° 40' 15" E. in a small patch of rice country, about four miles east of the northern end of Poungday. It formerly gave its name to an independent circle now joined to Zee-beng-hla.

ENG-GYEE-RWA-BWA.—A village in the Myedai township, Thayet district, on the Pade stream, five or six miles from its junction with the Khyoung-goung-gyee.

ENG-GYENG.—A revenue circle in the An township of the Kyouk-hpyoo district on the right bank of the An river, about six square miles in extent with a population of 791 souls. In 1876-77 it produced Rs. 425 as land revenue, Rs. 733 as capitation-tax and Rs. 1,125 gross revenue.

ENG-LAY.—A village in the Myedai township, Thayet district, on a stream of the same name, a tributary of the Pade.

ENGMA-MYOMA.—A revenue circle in the Prome district on the Myit-ma-kha river just below the Engma lake. The west and centre of the circle consists of low hills and undulating ground, the source, in the rains, of numerous small streams which flow into the Myit-ma-kha; the eastern portion is fairly level. A narrow belt of rice-cultivation runs nearly throughout the whole length of the circle. The main road from Rangoon to the frontier traverses this circle in a westerly direction.

ENG-RAI.—A town in the circle of the same name, in the Tsam-bay-roon township, Bassein district, on the right bank of the Daga river, about seven miles below Kyoonpyaw, in 17° 10' 30" N. and 95° 18' 30" E. with a population of some 1,500 souls, who are largely engaged in rice-cultivation and in fishing. In former years, before the Kyoung-goon and Tsam-bay-roon townships were united, this town was the head-quarters of the Extra Assistant Commissioner.

ENG-RAI.—A large revenue circle in the Tsam-bay-roon township of the Bassein district on the right bank of the Daga a few miles below the town of Kyoon-pyaw. The upper or northern part of the circle consists of rice-fields and the southern part presents an open plain, interspersed with patches of forest, which affords excellent pasture for cattle. The ground here undulates slightly. A considerable portion of the revenue is derived from the fisheries. In the north (where the great Eng-rai-gyee lake, q. v. is) there are good fair weather cart-roads but in the south footpaths only. The land revenue in 1876-77 was Rs. 11,783, the capitation-tax Rs. 8,018, the gross revenue Rs. 36,425 and the population 6,248.

ENG-RAI-GYEE.—A lake in the Bassein district about five miles in circumference with a pretty uniform breadth of 280 to 300 yards and a depth of from 20 to 45 feet in the centre; it is connected with the Daga, a large branch of the Gnawon or Bassein river, by a small outlet which at the period of the freshes during the S. W. monsoon and on the subsidence of that river serves to replenish the water of the lake from the Irrawaddy and to carry off the surplus water. Both in the small stream and in the river the water is shallower than in the lake whilst the general breadth of the last is greater than that of either of the two first. By some it has been supposed that it was formerly a portion of the bed of the Daga, by others that it was formed by causes totally independent of stream action by a gradual subsidence of the substratum or by a slip of the lower lying beds. It is certainly a fact that the water of the lake when relieved of the surcharge from the river has a different colour (dark opaque olive) from that of the river when uninfluenced by the efflux from the Irrawaddy and its properties are such as to cause the fish in it to attain a large size and a greater degree of fatness than those of either river or lakes in the vicinity.

Under the Burman Government this lake had a far-famed celebrity from the abundance and excellence of the fish caught on the occasion of the annual drawing of its bed during the full moon of June; on which occasion traders from Ava, from Prome and from the large towns on the Irrawaddy assembled to make their investments in smoke-dried fish cured on the spot, whilst, as at present obtains, the fish-dealers from Bassein and other towns on the lower streams purchased the fish alive, and transported them in bamboo cages immersed in water from which they were sold still in a live state; owing to the profits realized in this trade the competition for the purchase of the fish at the lake became so great that it was not unusual to make advances several seasons previous to the completion of the contract.

As a "preserve" for fish to which their natural instincts would direct them for purposes of spawning and breeding the lake is eminently adapted and after the rains of the monsoon have filled the water-courses and the Daga has become swollen and rapid the fish seek the still waters of the lake in vast numbers, making their entrance through the small channel and shallow water at its southern entrance where the land is low and swampy : this entrance is left open until the fish have passed through, it is then closed during the height of the waters and on the subsidence, when the channel has become too shallow to admit of the fish escaping, it is again opened.

So valuable a source of revenue to the Burmese Government as this fishery afforded was not allowed to escape easily ; accordingly the sum of 60 viss of silver or about Rs. 7,800 annually was exacted as a Royal tax from the "Païneng" or hereditary chief of the lake, who exercised sole authority over the villagers employed in the fishery and, with his subordinate officers, formed a distinct and independent establishment. The conditions of the payment of this amount of tax were, however, favourable to the villager, as he was exempt from all other process of taxation and in proportion to his means had a right of investing his capital in the general working of the fishery, the purchase of material for weirs, traps, nets, &c., in proportion with which amount so invested he received a share in the outturn at the end of the season.

On the cessation of the rains of the S. W. monsoon, when the waters have fallen to their lowest level, a fixed weir is placed across the lake at its shallowest part and another some distance from it shutting off between them a small space in which is the mouth of the channel connecting the lake with the Daga river: this small space, made as small as possible, is left unworked. A drag-net of reed and grass, strongly constructed with the toughest forest creepers forming from its great length of about 900 yards a deep concavity and sweeping the bed of the lake, is then placed across inside one weir and gradually moved right round the lake towards the other. The process of dragging is performed by floating capstans worked by hawsers of jungle rope attached to the end of the frame which by this tedious process is carried forward during three months at about 45 fathoms each day until it is opposite to the village at the further end of the lake ; a new weir is now constructed to form one side of the enclosure into which the fish have thus been driven. The ponderous mass of framework is taken to pieces and reconstructed across the water at the second of the two weirs first made whence it is dragged up in the same way as before to the village driving the fish before it and the ends are gradually contracted till an oblong space is included within which the fish are enclosed.

The taking of the fish from the enclosure into which they are ultimately driven is deferred until the full moon of June, by which time the first showers of the monsoon have reduced the temperature of the water, and the fish are then less subject to die than would be the case with the full blaze of the sun, unmitigated by the rain, striking upon the crowded mass ; even with this precaution, however, a large number of fish die before the whole has been cleared and the stench of their corruption taints the air for miles around.

On the near approach of the drag-net to the space forming the enclosure the fish are observed to be in great commotion, rushing in all directions and attempting to force their way through; finding the net too strong many of the larger kind attempt to leap over the barrier which they effect only to fall into nets spread to catch them ere they reach the water; as the space becomes more confined the disturbance of the mass of fish becomes so great that the noise of the splashing, and especially the deep hollow "grunting" of the larger kinds, is heard at several miles distance and although this may appear tinctured with a little exaggeration it will be intelligible when it is stated that the number of fish caught is never below 70,000 to 80,000 of all kinds, some of which weigh upwards of 15 viss or about lbs. 56 each ; mixed up with the mass it is not unusual to find crocodiles of all sizes, from the infant of a month to a grown parent whose skull measures three feet in length. Strange to relate no accident or casualty has been known to occur from the presence of crocodiles in this lake although the men employed in working the drag-net are constantly compelled to dive to the bottom in the deeper parts to clear the lower portion of obstructions in the bed.

During the taking and disposal of the fish some 8,000 to 10,000 persons are collected at the small village in front of the preserve, a market is formed, and temporary sheds for smoking the fish are built where the principal amount of business is transacted ; the scene altogether is exciting and, notwithstanding the fishy odour, fresh and corrupt, which pervades the atmosphere, is well worth the visit of the curious observer.

The principal fish belong to the following genera,—*Cerca, Cyprinus, Gobio, Labeo, Cimelodus, Cirrhinus, Cyprinodon* and *Silurus,* some of which attain the large size previously noted. In addition to these, however, there is a multitude of smaller fry which are converted into the coarser kinds of "Ngapee," and are only interesting to the Ichthyologist, who would here find a large field for observation. Of those named above some 25,000 viss, upwards of 40 tons, are annually disposed of on the spot.*

ENG-ROON.—A river in the northern portion of the Prome district which rises in the Myit-myeng-doung spur and flowing southward falls into the Kouk-khwe, itself a tributary of the north Naweng, near Htangoon a little below Wet-htee-gan. It is navigable during the rains for a short distance by small boats ; the bed is sandy and the banks, on which the Eng tree (*Dipterocarpus tuberculatus*) is found in great abundance, are moderately high.

ENG-THA-NWOT.—A lake in the Henzada district lying a little to the east of the Doora lake with which it communicates by a small channel. It is 1,400 yards long and has a maximum breadth of 700 yards : the depth in the dry weather is from 4 to 6 feet and in the rains from 12 to 14.

ENG-TSOUK.—A revenue circle in the Anouk-bhet township, Tavoy district, about sixteen square miles in extent of which some three are cultivated, mainly with rice. In 1876-77 the land revenue was Rs. 4,338, the capitation-tax Rs. 1,964, the gross revenue Rs. 6,537 and the population 2,656.

ENG-WON.—A lake in the Bhoommawaddee township of the Toung-ngoo district rather more than a mile inland from the left bank of the Tsit-toung river, with a depth of 15 feet of water in the rains and 6 or 7 in the dry weather.

ENG-WON.—A revenue circle in the Anouk-bhet township, Tavoy district, about nine square miles in extent of which a quarter is under cultivation, principally with rice. In 1876-77 the land revenue was Rs. 3,993, the capitation-tax Rs. 2,092, the gross revenue Rs. 6,285 and the population 2,730.

ENG-WON-GYEE.—A lake in the Meng-gyee township of the Henzada district on the right bank of the Myit-ma-kha or Hlaing river north-west of Meng-gyee. In the rains it is 25 feet deep and can then be entered by boats of 100 baskets burden ; in the dry season it is 6 feet deep : the bed is muddy and the banks flat.

ENG-ZAYA.—A large revenue circle in the north-west of the Thoon-khwa township, Thoon-khwa district. The principal products are tobacco, betel vine leaves and vegetables. The eastern part of the circle consists of extensive plains and swamps which in some cases constitute fisheries, yielding a large revenue to the State. In 1876-77 the land revenue was Rs. 9,624, the capitation-tax Rs. 7,130, the gross revenue Rs. 22,900 and the population 3,739.

FOUL ISLAND.—An uninhabited island off the coast of the Sandoway district—called by the Burmese Nan-tha-kywon of which the English

* Taken almost verbatim from a paper by the late Mr. O'Riley, F.R.G.S. [Editor.]

name is a translation—lying in about 18° 3′ N. six leagues from the mainland and seven from Bluff point and visible from a distance of eight leagues. It is about two miles long of conical form sloping from the centre towards the sea and the north end terminating in a low point. To the north-east there are islets and rocks near the shore and a reef partly above water extending southward. The name is derived from a so-called " mud volcano " which gives the island its conical appearance and from which, at times, pours forth a torrent of hot mud bubbling with marsh gas.

GAI-KHO.—A fierce and savage subtribe of Pwo Kareng living north and east of the Shoung and like them wearing trowsers which, however, probably owing to their habit of rearing silkworms, are often made of silk handsomely ornamented. Though a portion of the Pwo branch they wear the same trowsers as the Bghai-ka-hta *viz.*: white with red radiating lines like the rising sun embroidered at the bottom. By the Bghai family they are called *Kai*, a word that is never used alone but with an affix denoting one of the three portions into which they divide the clan :— *Kai-khew* or " Upper Kai " *Kai-la* or " Lower Kai " and *Kai-pie-ya*, or " Kai's people" : the term *Gai-kho* is the Burmanised form of *Kai-khew*. Formerly they were the determined foes of the British but owing to the exertions of the district officers they are now our firm friends. They consider themselves as superior to all the other Kareng clans: the men are stout tall and muscular, daring in adventure and war-like in disposition ; the women large, fair and often with ruddy complexions. Burmese schools have been established by the Baptist missionaries and many amongst them can speak Burmese. Within British territory there are about twenty villages containing an estimated population of 3,000 souls. They have two distinguishing peculiarities, their horror of ponies and elephants which are not allowed to enter their villages and for which they will neither provide nor sell fodder and the barbarous custom, now happily aying out, of burying a slave with the dead body of every slave holder and elder.

GAMOON-AING.—A revenue circle in the valley of the Kyoukgyee stream, an eastern tributary of the Tsittoung, in the Kyoukgyee township of the Shwe-gyeng district, which includes the formerly separate circle of Kyouk-hmaw. It extends over an estimated area of 120 square miles and has a population—towards the east composed principally of Kareng—of 6,538 souls. A large revenue is derived from fishery and net tax mainly in the old Kyouk-hmaw circle : the land revenue in 1876-77 was Rs. 4,983, the capita-tion-tax Rs. 5,712 and the gross revenue Rs. 17,749.

GAW.—A revenue circle in the Tha-htoon sub-division, Amherst district, lying partly in the valley formed by the Martaban hills on the east and the Debharien spur on the west and partly in the plain country between the hills and the seacoast. A few years ago it extended across the Martaban hills eastward to the Bhenglaing but it was found to be too large for supervision by one Thoogyee and was, therefore, reduced to its present limits. In 1876 it had a population of 4,668 souls, mainly Toungthoo, and 6,567 acres under cultivation ; the capitation-tax was Rs. 4,827 and the land revenue Rs. 12,167.

GAW.—A small stream in the Tha-htoon township which rises in the Martaban hills and flowing westward crosses the head of the Debharien valley a few miles south of Tha-htoon and falls into the Tsha or Tha-htoon river not far from Kawthan.

GAWTAMAW.—A small revenue circle in the Mahathaman township, Prome district, about ten miles east of Prome; the major portion is under rice cultivation. The land revenue in 1876-77 was Rs. 505, the capitation-tax Rs. 365, the gross revenue Rs. 890 and the population 855. United with it is the formerly separate Koon-tseng circle.

GNYOUNG-BENG.—A village in the Thanlyeng township of the Rangoon district on the Poogandoung stream and about seven miles from its mouth inhabited chiefly by Talaing who are traders and carriers. In 1877 it had 999 inhabitants. Lat. 16° 59' N. Long. 96° 28' 30" E.

GNYOUNG-BENG.—A revenue circle in the extreme south of the Pegu township, Rangoon district, between the Pegu and the Tsittoung rivers. The principal rice cultivation is in the western part of the circle where the country is undulating. In 1876 it had a population of 8,339 souls. The land revenue in the same year was Rs. 57,514, the capitation-tax Rs. 10,083 and the gross revenue Rs. 88,482.

GNYOUNG-BENG.—A village in the Prome district in a small patch of rice cultivation on the bank of the South Naweng river some eight miles above the mouth of the North Naweng.

GNYOUNG-BENG-GYEE.—A village in the Prome district in 18° 25' 50" N. and 95° 23' 30" E. a short distance to the N. W. of Poungday and about a mile and a half north of the Kyat river, inhabited mainly by rice cultivators.

GNYOUNG-BENG-HLA.—A revenue circle in the Kyouk-hpyoo township, Kyouk-hpyoo district, eight square miles in extent, with a population in 1876 of 1,650 souls. The principal manufacture is salt. The land revenue in 1876-77 was Rs. 2,007, the capitation-tax Rs. 1,770 and the gross revenue Rs. 4,421. United with it is the formerly separate Madai-kywon circle.

GNYOUNG-BENG-RWA.—A village in the Henzada township on the north of the town of Henzada of which it forms a suburb.

GNYOUNG-BENG-RWA.—A small revenue circle in the Henzada township, Henzada district, lying to the north of Henzada on the right bank of the Irrawaddy, the southern and western portions of which are extensively cultivated with rice. It is now joined to the Henzada Myoma circle.

GNYOUNG-BENG-THA.—A village in the Toungngoo district on the left bank of the Tsittoung in 19° 0' 40" N. and 96° 32' 40" E. inhabited principally by gardeners and Kareng cultivators.

GNYOUNG-BENG-THA.—A revenue circle in the Prome district in the extreme north-eastern corner of the Padoung township, separated from the Thayet district by the little Yathaya streamlet and occupying the whole of the river bank opposite Prome. The surface of the country is generally hilly with fruit and vegetable gardens on the hill sides. The villages are all on the bank of the Irrawaddy and are inhabited by cultivators and fishermen. The land revenue in 1876-77 was Rs. 911 and the capitation-tax Rs. 1,147.

GNYOUNG-BENG-THA.—A revenue circle in the Za-lwon township of the Henzada district on the right bank of the Irrawaddy south of and adjoining the Za-lwon Myoma circle. The land is well cultivated with rice an embankment on the river protecting it from inundation. The land revenue in 1876-77 was Rs. 8,417, the capitation-tax Rs. 3,627 and the gross revenue Rs. 12,923. In the same year the population was 4,467 souls.

GNYOUNG-BENG-TSHIEP.—A large village on the left bank of the Irrawaddy in the Myedai township, Thayet district: in the Burmese time it was the head-quarters of a Myothoogyee. It is said to have been founded by the Shan King of Ava Mo-hgnyeng-meng-tara, a usurper who was Tsawbwa of Mo-hgnyeng, when he came down in 1438 A.D. to make peace with the king of Pegu who was besieging Prome. It was originally called Mekhawadee. North of it was founded a small town called Ramawadee and south another called Zeya-wadee. Symes who visited it at the end of the last century describes it as a " fine village situated in a romantic country."

During the first Burmese war General Campbell had an interview in this village with the Burmese Commissioners but the terms of the treaty into which they entered were not ratified at the capital and the British advance continued.

GNYOUNG-BENG-TSHIEP.—A large village in the Gyaing Thanlweng township Amherst district on the right bank of the Attaran river at its mouth. In 1876 it had a population of 1,794 souls.

GNYOUNG-BENG-TSHIEP.—A revenue circle in the Myedai township, Thayet district, six square miles in extent on the left bank of the Irrawaddy : included within its limits are six of the old village tracts each of which in the Burmese time had a Thoogyee of its own. The population in 1876 numbered 4,115 souls almost all Burmans. The land revenue realized in 1876-77 was Rs. 4,437, the capitation-tax Rs. 4,135 and the gross revenue Rs. 10,247. Before the annexation of Pegu Gnyoung-beng-tshiep was an independent jurisdiction and under the Myothoogyee were the Thoogyee of Myo-hla, Tshengdoon, Bwotlay, Pyalo and Pyenbouk which with the exception of the last are still Thoogyeeships but are no longer under the head official in Gnyoungbeng-tshiep who has charge of his own circle only. The last Myothoogyee but one succeeded when four years old in 1798 A.D. and was killed fighting against the British near Rangoon in 1852. His son Moung Tet-hpyo fled with the defeated Burman army and before the annexation succeeded his father in the Myothoogyeeship. On the advance of the British force he abandoned his appointment and retired into private life. Subsequently he took office under the English as an Extra Assistant Commissioner and was placed in charge of the Myedai township. His is the oldest family in the district tracing its descent to Myothoogyee in the time of the great Aloungbhoora (Alompra) A.D. 1756, whilst few of the others can go further back than the days of his son Mengtaragyee A.D. 1780.

GNYOUNG-BENG-TSHIEP.—A revenue circle in the Gyaing Thanlweng township, Amherst district, east of Maulmain at the junction of the Attaran and the Gyaing and on the right bank of the former. The circle is noted for the manufacture of earthen pots from the earth brought down the Attaran from Kyaikparau : these pots are used on the coast for salt boiling and other purposes. The land revenue in 1876-77 was Rs. 4,246, the capitation-tax Rs. 3,237 and the population 2,999 souls.

GNYOUNG-DAN.—A village in the Prome district on the Gnyoung-dan Ro, or wet weather watercourse, which falls into the Waigyee river about four miles east of the Engma swamp and twenty-three E. S. E. of Prome in a direct line.

GNYOUNG-DAN.—A village in the Prome district in 11° 29' 40" N. and 95° 34' 10" E. on the left bank of the Thien stream, one of the small tributaries of the Waigyee, about two miles N. W. of Poungday and one mile north of the main road from Rangoon to the northern frontier of the Province.

GNYOUNG-DAN.—A revenue circle in the Prome district about a mile and a half west of Poungday. Gnyoungdan is its largest village. In 1876-77 the land revenue was Rs. 703, the capitation-tax Rs. 890, the gross revenue Rs. 1,590 and the population 883 souls. Adjoined to it is the formerly separate circle of Thayet-khyeng.

GNYOUNG-DOON.—Sometimes called Yandoon. A town in the Thoon-khwa district with a population of 6,900 souls, 60 miles north-west from Rangoon at the junction of the Pan-hlaing creek, here called the Gnyoungdoon, with the Irrawaddy. The town, which extends for about three miles along both banks of the creek, has sprung up almost entirely since 1852 ; in the Burmese time it was a small village of some 100 houses. It is the rendezvous of all the trading boats which run between the upper part of the valley of the Irrawaddy and Rangoon and during the rains as many as 1,000 boats collect here and dispose of their cargoes, those from up-country to those from Rangoon and *vice versâ.* The principal imports from up-country are wheat, gram, beans, pickled tea, oil, onions, garlic and silk, and the principal exports upwards, rice husked and unhusked, piece-goods, crockery, earthen-ware, tobacco and betel-nuts : small steamers occasionally run between Rangoon and Gnyoungdoon, making the trip with a favourable tide in one day.

GNYOUNG-DOON.—A revenue circle in the township of the same name in the Thoon-khwa district at the northern mouth of the Pan-hlaing creek. In 1876-77 the land revenue was Rs. 16,172 the capitation-tax Rs. 12,708 and the gross revenue Rs. 29,666 ; in the same year the population, including the inhabitants of the town of Gnyoungdoon, was 12,354.

GNYOUNG-GOON.—A revenue circle in the Re Lamaing township, Amherst district, on the spurs of the forest-clad hills which border the valley of the Re. Its inhabitants are chiefly Kareng and the cultivated area is very small and almost entirely on the hill sides. The land revenue in 1876 was only Rs. 307, the capitation-tax Rs. 1,092 and the number of the inhabitants 834.

GNYOUNG-KHARA.—The name of an ancient town two miles north of Tavoy built in 715 A.D. after the destruction of Thagara and At-ka-lien-oung by the Shans. A few mounds only now remain to mark the site.

GNYOUNG-KHYOUNG.—A village in the Henzada district on the right bank of the Irrawaddy. The principal occupation of the inhabitants is the cultivation of the neighbouring extensive tract of rice land. Long. 95° 41' 20" E. : Lat. 17° 21' 40" N.

GNYOUNG-KHYOUNG.—A revenue circle in the Donabyoo township, Thoon-khwa district, on the right bank of the Irrawaddy south of

Donabyoo Myoma. Until the embankment along the river was made the southern portions of the circle were unculturable owing to periodical inundations. In 1876-77 the land revenue was Rs. 15,401, the capitation-tax Rs. 9,345, the gross revenue Rs. 27,611 and the population 10,212. United to it is the Thabyoo circle.

GNYOUNG-LE-BENG.—A revenue circle in the Shwe-gyeng district to the W.N.W. of Shwe-gyeng with an area of about 70 square miles and a population of 5,284 souls, principally Talaing. In 1876-77 the land revenue was Rs. 8,994, the capitation-tax Rs. 5,037 and the gross revenue Rs. 14,480.

GNYOUNG-LE-BENG.—A large village of 1,082 inhabitants in the Shwe-gyeng district a few miles west of Kweng-da-la and about 14 W.N.W. from Shwe-gyeng.

GNYOUNG-RWA-GYEE.—A revenue circle on the southern border of the Kanoung township of the Henzada district with some rising ground towards the west and extensive rice plains in the centre. The land revenue in 1876-77 was Rs. 6,730, the capitation-tax Rs. 4,370, the gross revenue Rs. 11,849 and the population 4,981.

GNYOUNG-RWA-NGAY.—A revenue circle in the south of the Kanoung township of the Henzada district extending eastwards from the Arakan Roma mountains with extensive rice-fields towards the east, the west being mountainous and covered with tree forest. It is now joined to five other circles, viz., Reng-taw, Gnyoung-khyeng, Htien-the, Kywai-tsheng and Thanat-khoon. In 1876-77 the land revenue of the united circles was Rs. 1,412, the capitation-tax Rs. 2,460, the gross revenue Rs. 3,949, and the population 2,556 souls.

GNYOUNG-TSA-RE.—A village in the Shwedoung township, Prome district, in 18° 30′ 6″ N. and 95° 13′ 41″ E. on the left bank of the Irrawaddy about four and a half miles above the southern boundary of the district.

GNYOUNG-TSA-RE.—A revenue circle in the Prome district occupying the south-western corner of the Shwe-doung township between the Irrawaddy on the west, the Henzada district on the south and the Shwe-nat-toung or Kholan hills on the east. Included in this area are the formerly separate circles of Tsheng-rwa, Hmek-khara, Gnyoung-tsa-re, Sha-tsoo-khyoung, Magyee-htoon, Sha-daing, Bai-hla and Kyouk-taga. During the rains a tract of country in the south is completely separated from the rest by the Doon-koola water-course which leaves the Irrawaddy at Shwe-kywon village and joins it again just below Gnyoung-tsa-re : in the dry season when the waters of the river fall this channel is closed up just above Gnyoung-tsa-re and what was an island is converted into a long narrow peninsula connected with the rest of the circle by a neck of sand. The surface of the country in general is level except in the east where the ground undulates considerably. In the centre and towards the south-west rice is extensively cultivated. Gnyoung-tsa-re is the only large village. The land revenue in 1876-77 was Rs. 5,729, the capitation-tax Rs. 6,115, the gross revenue Rs. 12,465 and the population 5,961.

GNYOUNG-TSENG.—A revenue circle in the northern portion of the south-eastern township of the Tavoy district, of which about one-third is under cultivation, principally with rice. In 1876-77 the land revenue was Rs. 3,249, the capitation-tax Rs. 1,432, the gross revenue Rs. 5,457 and the population 1,789.

GNYOUNG-TSENG-GYEE.—A small revenue circle in the Poungday township, Prome district, which in 1876-77 furnished Rs. 281 as land revenue and Rs. 250 as capitation-tax and had a population of 255 souls.

GNYOUNG-TSENG NGAY.—A revenue circle in the Prome district close to and to the west of Poungday. Being one of the old circles it is of very small extent and in 1876 the population was only 281 souls. The land revenue in 1876-77 was Rs. 213, the capitation-tax Rs. 270 and the gross revenue Rs. 483.

GNYOUNG-WAING.—A village of about 500 inhabitants in the Ananbaw circle, Kyouk-gyee township, Shwe-gyeng district, on the Kwon river a few miles above its mouth.

GNYOUNG-WON.—A village in the Prome district in 18° 33' 40" N. and 95° 33' 40" E. about six miles N.N.W. of Poungday and a mile N. of the Waigyee river a small feeder of which runs past the village. Its inhabitants are mainly agriculturists.

GNYOUNG-WON.—A revenue circle in the Prome district a short distance to the north-north-east of Poungday on the right bank of the Waigyee just below Rwa-thit-gyee. It is well cultivated with rice in the central and western portions. The largest village is Gnyoung-goon. In 1876-77 the land revenue was Rs. 1,396, the capitation-tax Rs. 1,683, the gross revenue Rs. 3,115 and the population 1,750.

GNYOUNG-WON.—A revenue circle in the Kama township, Thayet district, containing but little cultivation. In 1860 the Thoogyee of Tharapee and Kyouk-padoung resigned and their circles were joined to the old Gnyoung-won circle to form the present one. The Thoogyee is also in charge of the Myo-hla circle. The land revenue in 1876-77 was Rs. 991, the capitation-tax Rs. 1,037, the gross revenue Rs. 2,098 and the population 993.

GOUNG-TSE-KYWON.—A small rocky island in the Salween, at its junction with the Gyaing close to Maulmain, on which stand a monastery and a few pagodas shaded by trees.

GWE-KHYO.—A river in the northern portion of the Prome district a tributary of the South Naweng. It rises in the southern slopes of the Padouk spur some twenty miles west of the main range of the Pegu Roma mountains and has a south-westerly course to the Naweng which it joins near the village of Khyoung-khwa by the same mouth as the Eng-goon and the Khyoung-tsouk; near its source the bed is rocky but lower down sandy and muddy: it is not navigable by boats. The trees most common on its banks are Eng (*Dipterocarpus tuberculatus*) and Htien (*Nauclea sp.*)

GYAING.—A river in the Amherst district formed by the junction in 16° 34' N. and 98° 8' E. near the village of Gyaing of the Hlaingbhwai and the Houngtharaw. The united waters flow west for 45 miles and fall into the Salween at Maulmain. A broad but shallow river with numerous sandbanks it is navigable only by boats; these can ascend at all seasons. The most important places on the banks are Kado at the mouth, the Government Timber-revenue station; Zatha-byeng, on the same (right) bank a few miles higher up, the head-quarters of the Gyaing Than-lweng township; Tarana on the left bank about four miles higher; Dhammatha a small village remarkable on account of a single scarped and pagoda crowned rock and an amphitheatre of limestone hills in which are large caves filled with images of Gaudama Booddha and of Rahan ; and lastly Gyaing.

GYAING.—A village in the Amherst district at the junction of the Hlaing-bwai and Houngtharaw rivers where a small Police force is stationed.

GYAING.—A revenue circle in the Gyaing Than-lweng township, Amherst district, at the junction of the Hlaing-bhwai and the Houngtharaw. In 1876-77 the land revenue was Rs. 8,506, the capitation-tax Rs. 2,155 and the population 2,983.

GYAING ATTARAN.—A township in the Amherst district occupying the valley of the Attaran river from the hills forming the southern boundary of the district northwards to the Gyaing. A tract on the left bank of that river eastwards from the mouth of the Attaran has of late years, for administrative convenience, been added to the Gyaing Than-lweng township the larger portion of which lies north of the Gyaing.

The township is sparsely populated especially towards the south where the inhabitants are principally Kareng. Above the junction of the Zamee and the Weng-raw, which unite to form the Attaran, are large tracts of forest-land containing much valuable timber which, except *bonâ fide* for purposes of cultivation, cannot be cut without a license. Teak was formerly very plentiful but considerable damage was done in the first years after the British occupation by indiscriminate felling.

The head-quarters are at a small village called Nga-bye-ma with 233 inhabitants in 1876 on the right bank of the Attaran. A few miles above this is Re-boo, a hamlet so called from the neighbouring hot spring which is described by Dr. Helfer—and his description is accurate—as a " semi-cir-" cular pond 50 feet in circumference perfectly calm except in one or two " places where a slight ebullition occasionally takes place. * * * The air " above the spring was 97° 50′ and the water itself 147° F.; notwithstanding this " high temperature the borders are deeply covered with vegetation and a species " of ficus " has " actually its roots in the water. The ground round the springs " is strongly impregnated with iron." In 1874-75 a partially successful experiment in potato cultivation was made in the neighbourhood but beyond the reach of the heat of this spring. Between Nga-bye-ma and Re-boo is the site of the ancient town of Attaran of which traces of the surrounding mound only exist. The Attaran is a deep rapid river flowing in places under cliffs of tree-clad limestone rocks and navigable by vessels of large draught for a considerable distance—Mr. Crawford in 1826 ascended in a steamer as far as old Attaran—but used only by boats as the country it taps has but a small population and no extensive areas of land under cultivation.

For administrative purposes the township is divided into 15 circles and in 1876-77 produced a gross revenue of Rs. 43,184 of which Rs. 20,094 were derived from the capitation-tax and Rs. 23,810 from the land. The population in that year numbered 20,496 souls.

In the dry season parties of Shan cross the frontier at the Three Pagodas and come down the valley of the Attaran bringing ponies and cattle for sale.

GYAING THAN-LWENG.—A township in the Amherst district forming a rectangular tract extending eastwards from the Salween to the Hlaing-bhwai and southwards from the Hpa-an a tributary of the Salween and the Kha-zaing a tributary of the Hlaing-bhwai, the sources of which are close together and in the rains are connected by a small stream navigable by canoes, to the Gyaing and including a small patch of country south of that river round about Gnyoung-beng-tshiep at the mouth of the Attaran on its right bank just behind Maulmain. It contains 16 revenue circles. The headquarters are at Za-tha-byeng on the right bank of the Gyaing twelve miles above Maulmain. The principal villages are Gnyoung-beng-tshiep, Kado at the junction of the Gyaing and the Salween, the Government Timber-revenue station a busy town where many rich foresters and timber traders reside, Hpa-an in the N.W. corner at the mouth of the Hpa-an stream the headquarters of the Assistant Superintendent of Police in charge of the northern range where there is a Police station and a new market, Noung-loon inhabited largely by Toungthoo on the main line of traffic between the Shan States and Tha-htoon, and Kha-rai just above the junction of the Hlaing-bhwai and the Houng-tha-raw which, united, form the Gyaing. With the exception of the three main rivers which bound the township on three sides the streams are of little or no importance; the largest are the Kado with a bar at its mouth impassable at low water, the Hpai-ka-ta and the Hpa-an tributaries of the Salween and the Kha-zaing which falls into the Hlaing-bhwai. During the dry season numerous parties of Shan bringing cattle come in *viâ* Mya-waddy and Kaw-ka-riet in the Houng-tha-raw township and crossing the Hlaing-bhwai at Kha-rai just above Gyaing pass westwards to Tha-htoon and on northwards into the Shwe-gyeng district and at the end of the season return by the same route. The halting-places and distances are Kha-rai to Moot-ka-do 8 miles, Moot-ka-do to Kaw-ka-da 24 miles, Kaw-ka-da to Noung-loon 15 miles, and Noung-loon to Hpa-an 12 miles. Here they cross the Salween and pass into the Hpa-gat township. More commonly the distance between Moot-ka-do and Noung-loon is divided into three and the halting-places and distances then are Kha-rai to Moot-ka-do 8 miles, Moot-ka-do to Noung-goon 10 miles, Noung-goon through Kaw-ka-da to Rwon-gnya 16 miles, Rwon-gnya to Noung-loon 18 miles, and Noung-loon to Hpa-an 12 miles.

In the west and south-west the country consists of an extensive plain traversed by parallel lines of limestone rocks having a general north and south direction with intervening narrow and cultivated valleys. Portions are heavily inundated during the rains partly by the slow escape of the rain-fall and partly by the spill of the Salween which pours in at and above Hpa-an and flows southward through the Noung-loon valley and over the plain country between the Salween and the Zwai-ka-beng hills passing out into the Salween again at and below Hpai-ka-ta. The eastern and north-eastern parts of the township are filled by low laterite hills, covered by open tree and bamboo forest, intersecting small grass plains with little patches of rice near the numerous Kareng villages scattered over this part of the country. These plains are so low that water remains in them in pools throughout the year. The southern tract is a long narrow rice-producing plain between the undulating ground on the north and the Gyaing on the south which on the west unites with the Noung-loon and Doon-reng valleys. The villages on the bank of the Salween and Gyaing are inhabited chiefly by Talaing with a few Burmans, those in the E. and N.E. by Kareng and those in the centre by Toungthoo. In the plain country rice is grown and exported, principally *viâ* Hpa-an whence it comes down the Salween, and from the villages on the banks of the Gyaing. In the more hilly parts where water and fodder are obtainable all the year round cattle are extensively bred and are sold to purchasers who come from Tha-htoon and from Pegu and other places west of the Tsittoung and move about from village to village collecting herds which they drive home by the ordinary trade route. In the dry weather the cattle wander over the low grass plains and in the rains through the forest on the higher ground. In 1876-77 the township had a population of 39,524 souls and produced a revenue of Rs. 103,273 of which Rs. 62,156 were derived from the land revenue and Rs. 41,117 from the capitation-tax.

GYO-BENG.—A village in the Prome district in 18° 26′ 50″ N. and 95° 34′ 25″ E. on the Myolay creek and on the road from Ta-pwon in the Henzada district to Poungday about three miles south of its junction with the main road from Rangoon to the northern frontier.

GYO-BENG-THA.—A village in the Prome district close to and to the north of the Wet-poot stream and about a quarter of a mile from the village of that name on the main road from Rangoon to the northern frontier.

GYO-GOON.—In 19° 17′ 45″ N. Lat. and 94° 52′ 50″ E. Long.; a village in the Ma-oo-daing circle, Mengdoon township, Thayet district, on the bank of the Ma-htoon river.

GYO-WA —A village in 19° 14′ 25″ N. Lat. and 94° 48′ 55″ E. Long. in the Pai-myouk circle, Mengdoon township, Thayet district, on the Hlo-wa stream a little above the villages of Myouk-pyeng and Kan-ma-naing.

GYO-YA-THA.—A village in the Prome district six miles east of Prome town in the middle of large rice fields.

GYWON-DOUNG.—A suburb of Kama in the Thayet district lying on the south bank of the Made.

HAING-GYEE.—An island, better known as Negrais, in the Bassein or Ngawon river near the western bank three and a half miles up from Pagoda Point and rendered conspicuous by a hill at its northern end which slopes away to the centre : a narrow belt of level ground skirts the shore almost all round. The channel between the island and the western bank of the river is one mile broad on the south and four and a half on the north opposite the abandoned station of Dalhousie. In 1686 A.D. the Governor of Madras, who was anxious to push his factories eastward and to open out trade with Burma, actuated by the reports of early travellers and by the knowledge that Negrais possessed the great advantage of being accessible both by sea and land at all seasons of the year, despatched an expedition to survey the island which was believed to be a portion of the Arakan dominions, but the vessel in which it sailed had to put back. In 1687 Captain Weldon, on his return from Mergui whither he had been sent to declare war with the Government of Siam, entered the river, landed and surveyed the island and took possession of it in the name of the British. The report states that he "destroyed some Siamese huts that were on the island." There is no trace in Talaing or Burman history of the Siamese ever having penetrated so far westward and unless the report is altogether wrong the huts were probably those of some Shan immigrants who were also called Siamese by old travellers and writers. Captain Weldon may possibly have confounded Shan with Siamese and have considered that as he had just declared war on the part of the British he was justified in seizing a portion of the enemy's territory, yet it would be an extreme stretch of imagination to suppose that an island three miles up a river belonged to a kingdom many miles to the eastward because a few subjects of that kingdom were found on it. Nothing further was done until 1753 when the Governor of Madras sent a party under Mr. Hunter to form a trading settlement. The following year Mr. Burke reported that the fort which had been erected was built in a swamp influenced by the tides and that the inhabitants were suffering severely from sickness and want of food and attributed it to Mr. Hunter's incapacity. Mr. Hunter was retained in charge and dying shortly afterwards was succeeded by Mr. Burke. The factory had remained undisturbed mainly on account of the war between the Peguans and the Burmans both of whom endeavoured without effect to enlist the English on their side. Bassein some seventy miles up the river, where an English out factory had been established, was attacked and captured by the Burmans who, anxious to obtain British aid, carefully avoided injuring the English inhabitants and after the capture sent envoys to Negrais to press for assistance : this was refused as the agent desired to avoid mixing himself up in the quarrel of the two kingdoms, hoping, doubtless, to be well thought of by the eventually successful Government by reason of his not having aided the unsuccessful. During the absence of the Burman envoys the Peguans retook the town and the envoys therefore returned to Negrais. The Burmans having succeeded in annexing Pegu a mission was sent in 1755 A.D. to the capital to endeavour to obtain amongst other things a formal grant of Negrais : this the King refused. In 1757 another mission was sent for the same purpose under Ensign Lister with no better result as regards the island. In 1759 the establishment was withdrawn and three or four persons only were left in charge of some property and timber as well as to hold possession of the island and Captain Southbey was sent to assume command. The day after his arrival—5th October 1759—Antony, the man who had attended Ensign Lister on his mission to Ava, delivered to him a letter purporting to be from the King of Burma. Antony dined with Captain Southbey that day and was asked to meet all the European gentlemen in the station on the following. The guests assembled at the appointed hour and were on the point of sitting down to dinner when at a given signal a large number of armed Burmese rushed into the house and murdered all except a midshipman who succeeded in escaping to his ship and giving the alarm. After the Europeans, ten in number, had been killed a general massacre of the natives of India took place. In 1760 Captain Alves was despatched to demand satisfaction for these murders; but far from obtaining any redress the King prohibited our returning to the island, though he granted a spot of ground for a factory at Bassein and released the few who escaped death and were taken prisoners at Negrais. In 1802 Captain Symes was sent to claim the island but without avail and it never came into the possession of the British till Pegu was annexed in 1852 by Lord Dalhousie.

HAN-GAN.—A revenue circle in the Re Lamaing township, Amherst district, on the left bank of the Re river reaching from the hills to the sea coast. It is inhabited chiefly by Talaing and is well cultivated. It now includes Khaw-tsa and in 1876 had 2,066 inhabitants; in that year the land revenue was Rs. 8,209 and the capitation-tax Rs. 2,187.

HAN-GAN.—A village in the Amherst district about ten miles up the Han-gan river which falls into the Re at its mouth. In 1876 it had 1,114 inhabitants. Long. 97° 54′ 30″ E. Lat. 15° 11′ N.

HASHWIE.—A clan of the Pwo Kareng family of about 2,000 souls living in some twenty-five to thirty villages on the hills between the Tsittoung and Thouk-re-khat streams in the latitude of the northern boundary of the Province. They are a tall, slender, active and warlike race but their women are ugly, ignorant and degraded. The caves in their country furnish the saltpetre from which they make their gunpowder : to the saltpetre, charcoal and sulphur they add, under the impression that it increases the strength, alcoholic spirits and, since the advent of the Missionaries, Perry Davis' " painkiller" when they can get it.

HENG-THA-GAN.—A village in the Prome district in 18° 27′ N. and 95° 34′ 30″ E. There are two villages of this name distinguished as North Heng-tha-gan and South Heng-tha-gan both so close to Poungday that they form almost the southern end of that town though they are in a different revenue circle. Both, like Poungday, are on the Myolay channel.

HENG-THA-GAN.—A revenue circle in the Prome district immediately south of Poungday. Its largest village is Heng-tha-gan which forms the southern portion of Poungday itself. Kanoo further south on the Myolay and Thabhangoon, also on the Myolay close to its junction with the Kyat or Kan-tha, are populous places. This circle is traversed by the main road from Poungday to Ta-pwon in the Henzada district. It has of late years been placed under the Thoogyee of Kook-ko-beng.

HENZADA.—The head-quarters of the Henzada district, supposed to have been founded in the earlier part of the sixteenth century, on the right bank of the Irrawaddy which opposite to the town is split into several channels by large sandbanks. In 1876 the inhabitants numbered 15,307 souls of whom about two-thirds are Burmese, the remainder being chiefly Talaing though Shan, Chinamen, Madrassees, Mahomedans, Indo-Europeans and Chin-Indo-Europeans are represented. It contains Court-houses, a Treasury, a Police Station, a Public Works Department Inspection Bungalow, a Telegraph Office, a Post Office, a small masonry Gaol or Lock-up with wooden barracks in which an average of 72 prisoners were confined in 1876, a Charitable Dispensary in which during that year 202 in and 2,041 out patients were treated, a fine market place or bazaar and three schools, a Kareng normal, a State town school and one for Burmese established by the Society for the Propagation of the Gospel. In 1876-77 it had a gross Municipal revenue of Rs. 45,648. Lat. 77° 58 Long. 95° 32′ E.

HENZADA.—A township in the district of the same name on the right bank of the Irrawaddy extending westwards to the Arakan Romas. The whole country, which is exceedingly fertile and produces much rice, was formerly liable to annual inundations on the rising of the Irrawaddy but has been very greatly protected by embankments thrown up along that river and the Bassein. The principal town is Henzada with a population of 15,307 souls, the head-quarters of the district. In 1876-77 the land revenue was Rs. 1,16,585, the capitation-tax Rs. 54,830 and the gross revenue Rs. 1,93,698 ; this includes Rs. 6,518 local fund receipts credited to the district and cess funds and expended solely in the district in which raised. The population in the same year was 73,664. The township is divided into twelve circles.

HENZADA.—A district in the Pegu division, covering an area of 4,047 square miles, in the valley of the Irrawaddy at the head of the delta and lying on both banks of that river. The northern boundary which separates it from the Prome district, leaves the Pegu Roma mountains in about 18° 48′ N. and following generally natural features runs about E. by S. down the Poondoung spur and the Kyat river to the Myitmakha or Hlaing and then on past the Irrawaddy and up the Kyouk-piet-tha stream towards the south to the Ta-zoung-gyee spur, thence westward along that spur to the Arakan Roma mountains which it strikes in about 18° 23′ N. The southern boundary which separates the district from Rangoon on the east and Bassein and Thoon-khwa on the west is more irregular in its course ; starting from the Pegu Romas it follows the Mee-neng to its mouth in the Hlaing, then turning south it follows the Hlaing for about a mile and a half to the Ke-nek-khyoung where it inclines west and strikes the Irrawaddy at a spot about eight or nine miles below Henzada ; following the Irrawaddy southwards for a few miles it turns west again along the Pantanaw creek to leave it almost immediately and trend north-west, almost parallel to and not far from the Irrawaddy, to the Bassein river which it crosses and then inclines more to the west to the Arakan mountains. From the north to about the latitude of Henzada the district stretches right across the valley but below this the Bassein district running up north along the Arakan Romas and the Rangoon district along the Pegu Romas give the lower portion the form of a truncated cone lying partly on one bank of the Irrawaddy and partly on the other, with the newly-formed Thoon-khwa district closing it in on the south. The eastern and western boundaries are formed by the two ranges of mountains which enclose the valley of the Irrawaddy : here the face of the country has a rugged character which subsides into undulations and finally into a dead flat in the more central parts near the river. In 1861 Henzada on the west of the Irrawaddy and Tharrawaddy on the east, which shortly after the occupation of Pegu had been separated and had since then formed two independent jurisdictions, were re-united and the head-quarters were moved from Henzada to Myanoung further north. In 1870 the head-quarters were re-transferred to Henzada where they now are. In 1872-73 the Thoon-tshay circle of Rangoon was added to it from Rangoon, and in 1875 the greater part of the Donabyoo township was taken from it and added to others to form the Thoon-khwa district.

The Arakan Romas forming the western boundary and stretching from

Mountains.

far beyond the frontier of Pegu to the Bay of Bengal have nowhere in this district a greater elevation than in the latitude of Myanoung where one of the peaks rises to 4,003 feet above the sea-level : from this point southwards the height rapidly diminishes. Towards the north the spurs stretch down to the Irrawaddy and one, just within the district, ends at Akouk-toung in a precipitous cliff 300 feet high, its feet bathed by the river and its face caverned artificially to contain statues of Gaudama, the only instance in this district in which a hill abuts on the river. Towards the south the course of the Irrawaddy trends away from these mountains and leaves room for vast plains. The ascents of the range are steep though not generally rocky and the entire surface of the tract covered by the main range and its spurs is clothed with dense forest the summits of the highest peaks being the only points destitute of tree jungle.

The Pegu Romas on the east are further removed from the river and their spurs do not extend down so far into the valley. The highest point

(2,000 feet above the sea) in the whole chain is in this district in 17° 55' N., where it branches out southward into several radiating spurs which form the valleys of the Pegu and the Poo-zwon-doung rivers and their tributaries. The slopes are extremely steep and the valleys sharply excavated, the result of the soft character of the shales and earthy sandstone constituting the range and partly also of the heavy rain-fall of Pegu. The country here as in the west is densely wooded and in the hot season is dry and parched.

Plains. The plains are extensive and to some extent cultivated and are almost everywhere suited for the production of rice but were, till a few years ago, annually inundated over a considerable area. To the east of the Irrawaddy these plains stretch from north to south throughout the whole length of the district reaching on the one hand from the Hlaing to the Pegu Romas and on the other to the Irrawaddy. It is these latter which are most subject to inundation. The plains on the western bank of the Irrawaddy extend from Akouktoung in the north to the southern limit of the district and widening out in their lower portion stretch inland from the Irrawaddy towards the Arakan Romas. A great part of this country was subject to extensive inundation but has been greatly protected by embankments constructed along the right bank of the river so that almost the whole area is suitable for rice cultivation except where, here and there, patches of sandy and gravelly soil or lakes and marshes occur.

Rivers. From the two bounding mountain ranges numerous torrents pour down and on reaching the plain country unite to form large streams which fall into the Hlaing, the Irrawaddy and the Bassein rivers, whilst towards the south the Hlaing and the Irrawaddy are connected by several creeks, the waters of whichever of the two may be temporarily the fullest finding its way thus during the rains into the other. The Irrawaddy traverses the district from north to south dividing it into two pretty equal parts but having a general S.S.E. course, and is here navigable by river steamers at all seasons. The Hlaing rises in Prome as the Zay and enters this district as the Myit-makha a few miles east of the Irrawaddy, a low range of hills covered with Eng forest (*Dipterocarpus tuberculatus*) and generally known as the Engdaing lying between them. Its course is about parallel to that of the Irrawaddy and from the east it receives through numerous channels the drainage of the Pegu Roma mountains which fertilises the plain on its eastern bank. A little below the southern extremity of the Engdaing the Tsheng-khoung creek, navigable throughout during the rains only, unites it with the Irrawaddy, and from this point downwards numerous channels exist by which during the rains the waters of the two rivers mingle. Its principal affluents from the east are the Toung-guyo in the north, the Meng-bhou, the Toung, the Meng-hla, the Tsheng-aing, the Toung-bho-hla, the Bheeleng, which has different names in different parts of its course, and in the south the Thoon-tshay, all tapping a country rich in teak and other valuable timber and in the lower portion of their lengths flowing through culturable and partly cultivated land. On the west innumerable small streams form by their union several principal channels along which the accumulated drainage of the western half of the district is carried to the Irrawaddy and Bassein rivers. Many of these streams are either entirely dry or they contain water to the depth of a few inches only during the hot season, and nearly all have high precipitous banks and extremely tortuous courses : after heavy rains they fill with great rapidity and flow with a very strong current. During the continuance of the south-west monsoon they become navigable to a distance of some miles above their mouths and by taking advantage of the freshets which prevail at that season boats of considerable burden can ascend with ease until the stream becomes a mountain torrent. The Pouk-taing rises in the Akonk-toung spur and has an easterly course of only ten miles, but receives many small tributaries in its course. The Tsanda, the Aloon and the Padaw rise in the Arakan mountains and unite to form the Pata-sheng which falls into the Irrawaddy a little below Kyan-kheng : the first has a south-easterly course of about 25 miles, and the others a north-easterly course of about 30 and 40 miles respectively. The Ka-gnyeng rises in the Arakan mountains and runs in a south-easterly direction for about 60 miles and after receiving the waters of the Shwe-naing and the Tsheng-boon falls into the Bassein river about 13 miles from its northern mouth. It communicates with the Irrawaddy by the Thambhaya-daing creek which leaves it at the elbow formed by the sudden bend which it makes S.S.W. when only a mile from the Irrawaddy. It traverses a highly-cultivated country. The Mamya rises in the Arakan mountains and for 30 miles flows south-east when, turning north, it falls into the Htoo lake five miles further on, the surplus waters of which used to find their way to the Irrawaddy. The Nan-ga-thoo is formed by two streams of this name which have their sources in the Arakan mountains and unite a little above Kweng-gouk, and falls into the Bassein river about two miles west of the mouth of the Ka-gnyeng. The Bassein river is in reality a branch of the Irrawaddy recruited by the drainage of the country through which it flows. It leaves the Irrawaddy about nine miles above Henzada and flows south-west to the sea through the Bassein district. At its entrance it is about 300 yards wide but is choked by a sandbank rising above the level of the water of the Irrawaddy during the dry season. In the rains the largest boats can enter it and river steamers have passed through it.

"Recent alluvium, that is the deposit thrown down by the waters of

Geology.

the existing Irrawadi (*Irrawaddy*) occupies a very small area," and from the northern limit of the district "to a"
"little above Pantanaw follows very closely the bed of"
"the river nowhere attaining a greater breadth than six miles. The older"
"alluvium * * * may be divided into an upper and a lower portion ;"
"the latter of irregular development and consisting of coarse gravels"
"transported from a distance, with large included masses of silicified wood"
"derived from the neighbourhood, whilst the former consists of a very homo-"
"geneous clay. This clay deposit comprises the entire level plains of Pegu."
"In constitution it is very homogeneous, somewhat arenaceous * * *"
"and of a uniform yellowish colour, in places assuming a more reddish"
"colour than usual and under certain conditions of exposure and weathering"
"assuming an imperfect lateritic appearance superficially. The last appear-"
"ance is usually seen in the sides of wells and is indicated by the peculiar"
"mottled appearance the rock presents from the irregular manner in which"
"the peroxide of iron arranges itself. The whole deposit is very homogeneous,"
"a little more sandy in some spots than in others, and with occasional thin"
"layers of sand irregularly and sparingly interspersed through it ; the only"

" recognizable band possessing a distinctive character is a dark layer of only "
" a few inches in thickness but of wide distribution. Judging from this "
" band the whole deposit would seem to have a gentle slope to the south at "
" a somewhat greater rate than the present surface of the country; for "
" whilst above Myanoung this dark band is clearly seen high up in the bank "
" and but little below the high flood level of the river, in the tidal parts of the "
" delta it is found about the level of midwater mark or lower * * * The "
" older alluvial clay just described rests in Pegu on a considerable deposit, or "
" bottom bed as it may be considered, of sand or gravel, varying much with "
" locality, and made up partly of the detritus from the nearest rocks, and "
" partly of gravel derived from more distant sources. At Nioungdon, "
" (*Gnyoung-doon*) at the top of the tideway, this bottom bed consists of "
" clean sand with a few small quartz pebbles sparingly dispersed here and "
" there through it; and it is the presence of this underbed of sand which so "
" greatly favours the abrasion of the channel of the Nioungdon (*Gnyoung-*"
" *doon* vel *Panhlaing*) stream, and is the indirect cause of the broad shallow, "
" just below the junction of the stream with the Irrawadi (*Irrawaddy*), "
" which forms so great an obstacle to navigation. Higher up the river a "
" few miles above Monyo (*Mo-gnyo*), on the opposite bank, a large stretch "
" of gravel and boulders is exposed, which is about the lowest point to "
" which these very coarse gravels reach. Above this spot coarse gravels, "
" as a rule, underlie the clay wherever it is cut through.........In many "
" places along the western slopes of the Pegu Yoma (*Roma*) laterite is found of "
" fair quality underlying the sandy soil of the Engdaing forest (*Dipterocarpus*"
" *tuberculatus*) where its position is that of a basal member of the older alluvium."
The fossil wood group which formerly extended as far south as Rangoon is
now but slightly represented in this district. The Nummulitic or Eocene
group of rocks which extends on the west bank of the Irrawaddy from the
frontier to the sea along the Arakan range traverses this district; at Akonk-
toung it is four miles broad. South of Myanoung the extent of the group
becomes somewhat irregular and uncertain, being covered and masked on the
east by a thick deposit of sand and gravel; while on the west its extent cannot satisfactorily be defined. " Opposite Myanoung the width is only ten "
" miles, and at Henzada not more than two. South of Henzada the Nummu- "
" litic beds are much covered up by surface detritus, and their width is incon- "
" siderable. " In about 17° 45′ in the bed of a stream falling into the Nauga-
thoo is an exposed outcrop of a peculiar whitish argillaceous sandstone,
locally used for the construction of images of Gaudama. The beds of this
rock, the position of which in regard to the limestone of the group is doubtful
but, probably, above it, extend still further north but do not seem to
occur in the Prome district. The " Negrais " rocks which include those
here met with older than the Nummulitic and newer than the Triassic extend
throughout the district, as do the latter. The intrusive rocks are in this
district, as far as it has been geologically examined, mainly represented by
serpentine, and with this may be considered the steatite veins of the Arakan
range. There are twenty-one distinct patches of this rock ranged within a
strip of country twenty-one miles in length, which extends south into the
neighbouring Bassein district. " The first and largest display is a broad belt "
" of it crossing the Nungathu (*Nan-ga-thoo*) stream......In all localities in this "
" district the serpentine presents the same appearance, and this great unifor- "

" mity of mineral character would seem to indicate community of origin. In "
" colour it varies somewhat from a pale to a rather dark but not dull green ; "
" and it would yield an ornamental stone, but for the fatal defect of being "
" everywhere seamed by cracks which traverse the rock irregularly in every "
" direction, the largest and soundest-looking blocks falling into numerous "
" polygonal or slabby fragments under a few smart taps from a hammer."
Soapstone which is used by the Burmese for writing on parabaik, a material
still used in many places instead of paper, is largely imported from Upper
Burma but is found almost everywhere where serpentine occurs, though not
in such a form as to furnish the ordinary pencils in use, some six inches long.
It is in all localities " essentially the same though it varies in colour from a
pale grey to nearly black."

Petroleum was discovered some years ago about twelve miles from Myan-
gung, but the well that was sunk was almost immediately abandoned. Gold
occurs in the bed of the Irrawaddy but in too small a quantity to render its
extraction worth the labour. At a village called Shwe-gyeng just above
Mo-gnyo a little is occasionally obtained in a coarse gravel bank left dry on
the subsidence of the river ; but the outturn is insignificant and the metal is
obtained in the finest possible state of division.

The forests in this district comprise every variety except the mangrove.
West of the Irrawaddy in the north, in the tract drain-
ed by the Aloon, the Tsanda and the Padaw which
unite to form the Patasheng, the hills are steep but the
top of the ridges is frequently level and here teak of fine and regular
growth occurs, whilst in the plains it is widely dispersed often alternating with Eng (*Dipterocarpus tuberculatus*), but mature teak of large
girth does not now abound. The forests hereabouts were extensively
worked in the Burmese time and the most valuable timber brought away.
In addition to Eng which grows on the lower slopes of the spurs of the
Arakan range stretching for miles southward from the northern boundary
parallel to the bank of the Irrawaddy, Pyengkado (*Xylia dolabriformis*) used
for house-posts and bridge-piles, ploughs and boat anchors, and with a heart
wood as durable as teak and equally safe from the attacks of white ants,
Htouk-kyan (*Terminalia macrocarpa*), Pyengma (*Lagerstrœmia Reginæ*),
Rendaik (*Dalbergia sp.*) furnishing a heavy wood with a red heart used for
plough and cart poles, Ka-gnyeng, furnishing an excellent oil used as a
varnish in situations unexposed to the weather, Bhan-bhwe (*Careya arborea*)
and other valuable trees are numerous ; the Sha (*Acacia catechu*) from
which is extracted cutch is by no means uncommon. To the east of
the Irrawaddy are large areas of lower mixed forest stretching from the
upper limit of the land subject to inundation from the annual overflow
of the main river and the Hlaing to the Eng forest. This latter extends
throughout the district from north to south and here are patches of
mixed forest with a considerable proportion of teak, especially near the
margin. East of this extending to the foot of the range is a region of low
undulating hills, varying in breadth from one to ten miles, rich in teak,
whilst the forests on the spurs and ridges still further east are the finest and
by far the most extensive. In the north the Toung-gnyo and the Meng-boo
streams, and further south the Toung, Meng-hla, Mok-kha and Bheeleng
traverse a rich forest country. The principal timber trees are :—

Forests.

Name.	Description of wood.	Uses.
Xylia dolabriformis	Dark-coloured, hard and dense, strong and durable.	Too hard to be easily worked. Used for house-posts, bridge-piles, boat anchors, railway sleepers.
Dipterocarpus tuberculatus ..	Light brown	Excellent for every purpose of house-building, especially f o r posts.
Terminalia macrocarpa	Dark brown	Used in house-building: strong but not very durable.
Lagerstrœmia reginæ	Red	Strong and adapted for house-building, but more especially for piles and in situations under water.
Dalbergia sp.	Sapwood readily decays but the heartwood is durable. Heavy; will not float. Black, sometimes with red and white streaks.	Used for plough and cart poles.
Acacia catechu	....	Furnishing cutch. Found growing in abundance in places easy of access and considerably worked.
Dipterocarpus alatus	Light brown	Timber of great size and strength; much used in boat-building; plentiful, furnishing a useful oil.
Careya arborea	Red-coloured	Plentiful. Timber large, used for carts, &c.
Barringtonia	Red	Plentiful east of the Irrawaddy; wood hard and of fine grain. Used for carts.

Besides these trees which are valuable for their timber there are others which are of some worth on account of their products. A species of Bignonia is plentiful, from the inner bark of which is obtained a material much used locally for ropes. *Æschynomene paludosa* springs up sponta-neously in the rice-fields and affords an excellent fibre. *Bombax pentandra* and *B. heterophylla* yield an astringent gum resin. *Sterculia*, of which there are several species, yields a gum probably analogous to *Tragacanth*. From the bark of the *Odina wodier*, which forms a larger proportion of the forests than any other tree, is obtained a gum which may be galbanum, the plant afford-ing which is not well known. *Dipterocarpus turbinatus* already noticed, which in the south takes the place of *Acacia catechu* the two never being found together, furnishes an oil which answers excellently as a varnish in unexposed situations. These and other trees of considerable value are spread over the face of the country but with the exception of *Acacia catechu* have never been extensively used teak having absorbed the attention both of traders and of the Government. This was far from being the case in the time of the Burmese rule when, here as elsewhere, no tree which furnished a wood or an extract of general use could be felled or tapped without payment. The object then, however, was not forest conservancy but the realization of the largest possible revenue for the grantee of the *Myo*, that is the official at Mandalay or the member of the Royal family to whom the tract had been allotted as a strictly personal source of income, or for the officials who were in executive charge.

The unauthorized felling of teak has always been strictly prohibited and in 1873 Thitkha (*Pentace Burmanica*) and Thit-kado (*Schizochiton grandiflorum*) were reserved and in 1877 Padouk (*Pterocarpus macrocarpus*). In the early part of 1876 the State set apart a large area as Government forests in which unauthorized felling of several other kinds of trees was prohibited* and the whole of this district west of the Irrawaddy is included, whilst the country east of that river has formed a portion of the Government forest tracts for many years.

Population.

The changes in the area of the district render it impossible to give any accurate statistics shewing the increase in the number of inhabitants in the tracts now included in Henzada. The figures below shew the population in Henzada and Tharrawaddy from 1855 to 1874-75, and in Henzada as it now exists from that date onwards. There are no statistics available which shew the population of the Donabyoo township in 1855: in 1876-77, when it formed a portion of Thoon-khwa, it had 36,122 inhabitants. In 1872-73 the Thoon-tshay circle was transferred from Rangoon to Henzada and in 1876-77 it had a population of 11,263 :—

1855	..	..	..	171,601	1866	..	..	363,817
1856	..	..	..	204,747	1867	..	..	380,505
1857	..	..	..	219,620	1868	..	..	393,627
1858	..	..	..	239,432	1869	..	..	423,998
1859	..	..	..	239,348	1870	..	..	435,323
1860	..	..	..	246,862	1871	..	..	444,750
1861	..	..	..	302,819	1872	..	..	460,026
1862	..	..	..	300,831	1873	..	..	475,839
1863	..	..	..	307,260	1874	..	..	504,321
1864	..	..	..	313,999	1875†	..	..	490,234
1865	..	..	..	347,615	1876	..	..	501,213

The rapidity of the increase in the early years was undoubtedly due to immigration consequent on the gradual settlement of the country, whilst the fertility of the soil with its proximity to a ready market and the construction of protecting bunds along the Irrawaddy, have kept up the flow. These embankments were commenced not many years ago and the balance of immigration over emigration during the last 10 years has been :—

* See Introductory Chapter on Forests.

† In this year Donabyoo was transferred to Thoon-khwa.

				Emigrants.	Immigrants.	Difference in favour of the district.
1867 ..	..	..	..	13,274	20,179	6,905
1868 ..	..	..	..	14,572	24,327	9,755
1869 ..	..	..	..	17,843	31,510	13,667
1870 ..	..	..	..	18,712	25,868	7,156
1871 ..	..	..	..	19,043	26,215	7,172
1872 ..	..	..	..	22,968	30,596	7,628
1873 ..	..	..	..	19,948	30,969	11,021
1874 ..	..	..	..	18,285	31,989	13,704
1875 ..	..	..	..	19,871	31,162	11,291
1876 ..	..	..	..	5,420	7,718	2,498
		Total	..	....	....	90,797

Still the inhabitants are only 127 to the square mile whilst there are 1,730,399 acres of culturable waste.

Comparing 1856 with 1876, the former year being selected as the first for which statistics of this kind even moderately accurate are available, the races composing the population of the district were :—

						1856.	1876.
Burmans	..	..	..	..	..	80,567	412,800
Talaing ..	..	..	..	..	..	91,101	17,707
Kareng ..	..	..	..	..	..	26,132	53,926
Shan ..	..	..	..	..	..	2,927	1,827
Arakanese	..	..	..	..	..	11	.. *
Khyeng ..	..	..	..	..	..	1,705	5,100
Yabaing ..	..	..	..	..	..	702	2,113
Chinese ..	..	..	..	..	..	156	472
Hindoos ..	..	..	..	..	.. }	1,308 {	1,042
Mahomedans	..	..	..	..	..		1,129
Other races	..	..	..	..	..	138	5,097
				Total	..	204,747	501,213

According to the latest official returns now available (1876) females slightly exceed the males, the former numbering 250,883 the latter 250,330, whereas in the province as a whole exclusive of the two Hill Tract districts, the males exceed the females, and this was the condition of this district when the special census was taken in 1872. The change cannot reasonably be ascribed to the transfer of Donabyoo to Thoon-khwa or to the addition of the Thoon-tshay circle from Rangoon and it is impossible with the information now obtainable to account for it satisfactorily.

The register of births and deaths for 1876 shew the former at 5,607 or 10·98 per mille, and of the latter 3,980 or 7·94 per mille, which would give a rate of increase from natural causes of 3·04 per mille. The registration of vital statistics is of late introduction, and amongst a widely scattered people with no regular local registrars whose duty it is to attend to this alone the

* Included among Burmans, *supra*.

returns cannot be taken as accurate. It is not at all probable, however, that any greater difficulty occurs in the registration of the births of boys than of girls or of girls than of boys and the proportion of one to the other which the returns give may be accepted as fairly accurate and these shew that whilst the births of boys numbered 2,936 those of girls were 2,671. Similarly the proportion of deaths of males to deaths of females may be taken as fairly given in the returns and these shew that in 1876 2,121 males died and 1,859 females, so that the proportion of births of females to that of males is considerably greater than the proportion of deaths : an examination of the figures giving the number of males and females at various ages shews that the boys and old men are but slightly more numerous than the girls and old women whilst the adult males, comparatively, greatly outnumber the adult females.

No returns of diseases later than those of the census of 1872 are available and according to these there were, except possibly in the Salween and in Northern Arakan where the returns cannot from the nature of the country and the wildness of the inhabitants be made out with any approach even to accuracy, fewer insane persons than in any part of the province, 0·09 per cent, whilst the number of deaf and dumb, 0·17 per cent., is large, and the number of blind, 0·32, only exceeded in the upper portion of the valley of the Tsittoung ; of lepers there were 0·12 per cent., principally males.

Although situated south of the limits of the ancient Burmese kingdom the Burmese here as everywhere else in Pegu largely outnumber the Talaing. After the conquest of the lower country by Aloungbhoora a steady endeavour was made to destroy the Talaing nationality ; the use of the language was forbidden and Burmans were encouraged to immigrate, large bodies coming down and settling, as at Kyankheng.

After the first Burmese war when the British troops retired the Burmans by their cruelties still further reduced the numbers, already dwindling, of the Talaing people who had generally assisted us against their former masters and who fled in numbers to Tenasserim to escape the fury of their oppressors under which many succumbed. This diminution has continued but undoubtedly both before and since the annexation it is not due to emigration solely but also to absorption amongst the Burmans. The few in this district are an exemplification of Sir Arthur Phayre's remark that—" scarcely any one of " Talaing descent calls himself anything but a Burman, so completely has the " national spirit been extinguished."

A noticeable feature is the large number of Kareng, Bassein alone having more, who as a race are hill-men shy and fearful of strangers and in their dealings with others ; but long before the occupation of Pegu large numbers had shaken off their timidity and settled in the plains, retaining their own language and customs but adopting the Burmese dress and method of cultivation. The increase in their numbers is not readily to be accounted for. The census returns shew that it has extended through every district of the province, except Rangoon, and cannot therefore be due to intra-provincial emigration and immigration whilst no great influx of their people into the province has taken place of late years. Though undoubtedly partly due to the natural increase it is most probably mainly caused by a more correct enumeration now that all troubles and rebellions amongst them are over and that they have become less timid and frightened of their rulers than they were during and immediately after the Burmese rule. The increase in the number of Khyeng is partly due to the same cause and partly to immigration from Arakan and the north. The number of Yabaing also has lately increased : this is the only district in the Pegu division in which they are found. Sir Arthur Phayre states that the term Yabaing or Zabaing is rather " the description of an occupation than the distinctive name of a race. The " people so called are breeders of silkworms in the hill districts. The term is " probably a Shan word, applied to those who first introduced the worm from " the eastward, and the meaning of it is not now understood."

Agriculture.

Situated at the head of the delta of the Irrawaddy and containing much fertile land the district has always been extensively cultivated with rice which has found a ready sale in the Rangoon and Bassein markets communication with both being easy by the numerous creeks which intersect the country. In former years large tracts were subject to inundation from the periodical overflowing of the Irrawaddy and this is still case with the country to the east. On the west for many years endeavours were made to afford a remedy but there was no systematic effort till about ten years after we had occupied Pegu. The Civil Officers had constructed petty embankments in various places to protect towns or existing cultivation : in 1862-63 these were at

1. Kyan-kheng.	5. Anouk-bhet.
2. Myan-oung.	6. Tham-bo-ta-ra.
3. Kan-oung.	7. Doo-ra.
4. Henzada.	8. Za-lwon.

In 1862 the country was carefully and scientifically examined and it was proposed to take over these embankments from the Civil Officers and run a line along the right bank of the Irrawaddy from Akouktoung to Pantanaw closing up the mouths of nearly all the rivers and leaving only sluices for the necessary exit of the drainage of the country. There was considerable doubt as to the extent to which erosion of the river bank was taking place and it was determined that the line should run some distance inland and not near the river bank so as to avoid all risk of its being gradually cut away. The first fourteen miles from Akouktoung were to be and are really are only a road, and do not reclaim any land. The question of closing the Tham-bha-ya-daing creek and the Bassein river was finally settled in the negative and in consequence extensive embankments along the left bank of the latter have become necessary. In 1868-69 an embankment along the eastern bank of the river was recommended so as to protect the valley of the Hlaing and the intervening country which almost every year is turned into a vast sheet of water.

The Kyan-kheng embankment, excluding the northern fourteen miles which, as has been said, is a road and protects no land, is nine miles long, the last five running westward along the left bank of the Pa-ta-sheng and protecting the country to the north of it from the overflow of that river which extended up behind the first four miles running parallel to the Irrawaddy. The whole country protected does not exceed five square miles, and it is the opinion of very competent authorities that north of the Pa-ta-sheng the construction of expensive protecting works was at least hardly necessary, as the profits from extended cultivation do not nearly cover the cost. The next section proceeding southward is the Myanoung, four miles of which run east and west along the right bank of the Pa-ta-sheng and the remainder southward along the Irrawaddy so far inland as to exclude the large town of Myanoung, (in front of which the exi;ting embankment was improved) to the mouth of the Tham-bha-ya-daing ; another length runs along the Irrawaddy between the Tham-bha-ya-daing and the Bassein river. But as the mouths of these two streams remain open and as the embankment north of the Tham-bha-ya-daing stops at the 45th mile with an abrupt ending large masses of water find their way into the country behind them. The remedy proposed for this will be alluded to further on. South of the Bassein river another embankment was carried on which now reaches as far as Re-lai village below Henzada and is to be carried on considerably farther. From the northern end of this section and joined to it an embankment has been carried along the left bank of the Bassein river past Le-myet-hna as far as Shwe-gnyoung-beng in the Bassein district below Nga-thaing-khyoung and is to be carried farther. Some miles inland an embankment has been constructed running about N. W. and S. E. along the bank of the Ka-gnyeng or Oot-hpo stream from Myeng-goon to Ma-gyee-goon nearly to the Tham-bha-ya-daing creek. It is now proposed to unite the southern end of this with the southern end of the Myanoung section near Loo-daw-tsoo village, and thus afford that protection to the country rendered necessary by the spaces which exist for the passage of the Tham-bha-ya-daing and Bassein rivers. When the works are completed as at present proposed, they will thus consist of : 1. An embankment extending from above Kyan-kheng and turning round west-ward along the Pa-ta-sheng. 2. Another stretching along the right bank of the Pa-ta-sheng to the Irrawaddy then down that river to Loo-daw-tsoo, thence about W. S. W. to Magyee-goon and from that point N.W. along the Oot-hpo or Ka-gnyeng. 3. One more flanking the Bassein river from Shwe-myeng-deng to its northern mouth in the Irrawaddy and down that river to below Zalwon. Before giving an account of the general cultivation of the district it may be as well to notice the results of the protective works already constructed on the increase in cultivation behind them. The area of land cultivated behind the Kyan-kheng section has increased since 1867-68 the year before this work became protective from 1,590 to 2,850 and no more culturable uncultivated land remains. The Myanoung embankment was made in sections : before the Kanoung section was thrown up the acreage of cultivation in the land which it protects was 1,761 which in two years rose to 1,898 : in 1864-65 the Myanoung section became protective and the cultivation which, including that behind the Kanoung, was the previous year 13,044 acres had increased in 1868-69 to 14,543. The following year the 3rd and last section became protective; the cultivation in the area protected by the two upper sections and about to be protected by this one was in 1868-69 16,897, acres which in 1873-74 had increased to 32,504. The large increase (in 1872-73 the area was 17,888 acres) was due to the ten years settlement expiring, during which a cultivator was allowed to extend his cultivation to the utmost of his power paying revenue only on the area he had when the settlement was made his lands being then measured once for the whole ten years. The increase up to 1872-73 represented therefore increased cultivation by new comers or by the few who had refused the settlement ; whereas the figures for 1873-74 shew the real increase the whole cultivated land being measured. The

Bassein river embankment now protects 519 acres in this district, where before only 427 were cultivated; and the Henzada embankment which unites with this protects 65,750 acres where only 22,468 exclusive of those added to their lands by settlement holders existed before. In the Burmese time the export of rice was prohibited and the inhabitants had but little inducement to extend the area under cultivation : after the annexation a brisk demand arose and prices went up from four to six times the rate before the war.

The progressive increase in the price of rice together with a better government under which the cultivator has greater security against arbitrary demands and enhancement of rates, the increase in the population and the extensive protective works described above have borne fruit in the increased area brought under the plough and planted with fruit trees, vegetables and other crops. An excellent rice country producing a rice which is better suited for long sea voyages than that grown further north and possessing in the Irrawaddy and the creeks and rivers which join it an easy means of communicating with the two seaports of Rangoon and Bassein, the crops find a ready sale and the area under cultivation with this cereal has largely increased whilst miscellaneous cultivation—as vegetables, cotton, tobacco &c.—has not by any means remained stationary. The following table shews the increase up to 1863 :—

| Year. | Acreage. | | | Total. |
	Rice land.	Garden and orchard land.	Miscellaneous cultivation.	
1855 ｡｡ ｡｡	104,790	2,921	7,718	115,429
1856 ｡｡ ｡｡	126,156	3,854	12,007	142,017
1857 ｡｡ ｡｡	133,574	4,351	13,189	151,114
1858 ｡｡ ｡｡	143,565	4,939	17,529	166,033
1859 ｡｡ ｡｡	144,552	5,382	13,804	163,738
1860 ｡｡ ｡｡	140,391	5,212	18,893	164,496
1861 ｡｡ ｡｡	141,108	5,886	15,241	162,235
1862 ｡｡ ｡｡	165,371	6,611	23,042	195,024
1863 ｡｡ ｡｡	172,928	6.837	19,713	199,478

· 1860 and 1861 were bad years and 1860 especially so as regards ricelands : this was due to the breaking of the Henzada embankment whereby a large extent of country was seriously damaged from the overflow of the Irrawaddy. This disaster was not without good for it led to the construction of those extensive protective works already alluded to.

The area under cultivation from 1868 to 1876 was :—

	Rice land.	Garden land.	Miscellaneous.	Total.	Remarks.
1868 ..	204,495	8,822	18,729	232,046	
1869 ..	209,725	9,240	24,486	243,451	
1870 ..	215,406	9,424	29,040	253,870	
1871 ..	220,163	9,486	30,212	259,861	
1872 ..	224,331	9,722	28,337	262,390	
1873 ..	278,661	14,617	30,108	323,386	
1874 ..	333,841	16,068	25,859	375,768	
1875 ..	314,673	13,916	14,716	343,305	
1876 ..	320,300	14,230	28,518	363,048	

Since Pegu was annexed there has, therefore, been an increase in the total cultivated area, excluding *Toungya*, of no less than 247,619 acres and this notwithstanding that a whole township has been taken from the district ; an increase greater than the most sanguine could have hoped for.

The crops under cultivation in 1875-76 were :—

	Rice.	Oil-seeds.	Cotton.	Indigo.	Tobacco.	Peas and Pulse.	Vegetables.	Cocoanuts.	Betel-nut.	Plantains.	Pan vine.	Mixed fruit-trees.
1875-76	314,673	4,065	513	7	1,673	2,666	9,140	17	89	1,757	103	4,947

The cotton is inferior to that grown in the north and the produce is locally consumed. The soil of the country has been reported on as in many places well suited for this crop, and several endeavours have been made to improve the growth but with little or no success. In 1873 a further experiment was tried and some Egyptian seed was given to the cultivators but with no better success than formerly ; the soil rapidly cakes round the stems in the dry season and the plants are dwarfed and bear but little seed. Tobacco is carefully planted and well taken care of but the cheapness of Indian tobacco and the extensive areas of good and unoccupied waste rice land have tended to prevent any extensive cultivation of this plant which is grown principally on sand banks left dry by the falling of the Irrawaddy. Sessamum is, next after rice, the most important agricultural product.

The average rent of land has not materially varied during the last ten years as the vast culturable waste and the favourable terms upon which grants are made tend to keep it at about one Rupee eight annas an acre. Its fertility is remarkable, exceeding that in any other part of the province, an acre producing on an average 2,500lbs. of rice or 400lbs. of indigo : the ground sown with cotton and sessamum however yields a comparatively much smaller return 230lbs. of the former per acre and 560lbs. of the latter. The price of rice is mainly regulated by the price in the Rangoon and Bassein markets the latter of which again is greatly dependent upon the former. The rates at which the principal products were selling in the local market during the ten years was, per maund of 80lbs. :—

	Rice.			Cotton.			Tobacco.			Sessamum.		
	Rs.	A.	P.	Rs.	A.	P.	Rs.	A.	P.	Rs.	A.	P.
1867	2	8	0	5	14	0	9	12	0	3	2	0
1868	2	4	0	5	14	0	9	12	0	3	2	6
1869	2	4	0	5	14	0	9	12	0	3	2	0
1870	2	4	0	5	14	0	9	12	0	3	2	0
1871	2	4	0	5	14	0	9	0	0	3	0	1
1872	2	4	0	5	14	0	9	0	0	3	8	0
1873	3	2	0	4	14	0	7	5	0	3	12	0
1874	3	2	0	4	14	0	7	5	0	3	12	0
1875	2	0	0	4	14	0	7	5	0	3	12	0
1876	2	0	0	6	0	0	11	7	0	5	12	0

Up to 1872 inclusive the rates remained stationary, but during the next year there was a sudden rise in rice and sessamum and a fall in cotton and tobacco The cause of these changes is to be found in the state of trade at the ports : in that year there was a very large falling off in the export of cotton, the import of tobacco increased, whilst rice was in great demand not only for Europe but for Bengal, large stocks being purchased by the State. Owing to the large exports in 1876-77 and the high prices given by the merchants the stocks usually kept for home consumption were nearly exhausted and during the rains of 1877 unhusked rice was selling in the local market at from Rs. 40 to Rs. 160 per hundred baskets.

As might be expected in a district having such an extensive culturable area the agriculturists are exceedingly numerous, numbering at the last regular census 160,943 souls; and amongst these are included only those actively engaged in agriculture and with animals, as labourers and dealers in ponies, cattle, pigs, &c., of whom there are very few; but of these only 67,980 are males over 20 years of age and though doubtless many younger males are so employed yet a great proportion of the agriculturists are women who do much of the planting in the rice-fields and generally, as in Italy and some other European countries, do a great deal of what is generally supposed to be almost exclusively man's work. The proportion of agriculturists to those otherwise employed was 33·75 per cent; of persons having no ostensible means of livelihood, women not having special occupations, children, male and female, &c., 41·58, and of persons engaged in mechanical arts, manufactures, and in the sale of articles prepared for consumption about 2·00 per cent., the remainder being principally Government servants, merchants and traders, of whom there were some 5,000, and professional persons.

Nearly all the large towns are on the right bank of the Irrawaddy though many important places are in Tharrawaddy, that is the country east of the river: here, however, the great extent of the annual inundations and the smaller extent of country fitted for the cultivation of rice, the great staple produce of the province, though perhaps favourable to the existence of numerous small villages retard the formation of the large trading towns and nearly all large towns in this district owe their magnitude if not their very existence to trade in the products of the surrounding country.

Kyan-kheng which is not far south of the frontier of the district in 18° 19′ N. and 95° 1′ 50″ E. is a long straggling town stretching for a considerable distance along the bank of the Irrawaddy just above the mouth of the Pa-ta-sheng river. It is the head-quarter town of a township under an Extra Assistant Commissioner and contains a Court-house, Police station and a good market place. Of but small importance prior to the first Burmese war it rapidly increased after the annexation of Pegu and now exports a considerable quantity of rice grown in the neighbourhood. In 1863 it had less than 5,000 inhabitants and in 1876 8,761 a result principally due to its increasing trade which again, depending almost entirely as it does upon rice export, is the result of the increased cultivation of the country in the interior. The inhabitants are almost entirely Burmans with a small sprinkling of Hindoos and Mahomedans.

Myan-oung, once the head-quarters of the Pegu Light Infantry, a local corps disbanded on the formation of the existing Police force, and subsequently the head-quarters of the district till 1870, is some distance below Kyan-kheng and stretches along the bank of the river for two miles whilst its breadth inland is not much over 200 yards. It is now the head-quarter station of a sub-division and contains a Court-house and Treasury, a Police station, Lock-up, Telegraph Office, Post Office, Hospital and Dispensary, Circuit-house and Public Works Department Inspection Bungalow. Though an old Talaing town its inhabitants are mainly Burmans with a very few Hindoos, Mahomedans, Europeans, Indo-Europeans and Chin-Indo-Europeans. Of some importance in the Burmese time its progress of late years has not been great and it has been eclipsed by its northern neighbour Kyan-kheng notwithstanding advantages which it long had as a military and civil station. In 1864 it had a population of 5,125 and in 1876 of 5,859 only.

Kan-oung, seven miles below Myanoung, founded by Aloungbhoora, the Burman conqueror, *circa* 1753 A.D., is the head-quarter station of a township. It possesses a Court-house, a market-place or bazaar, a Police station and a Public Works Department Inspection Bungalow. Its small population of 3,191 souls is composed mainly of Burmans, with a few Hindoos and about 100 Mahomedans.

Henzada is considerably to the south in 17°58' N. and 95°32' E. now the head-quarters of the district, with a gross municipal revenue in 1876-77 of Rs. 45,648 larger than that of any town except the three principal seaports of the province, the military station of Thayetmyo and Prome which has double the population. It contains Court-houses, a Gaol, fine market-places, a Telegraph Office, Post Office, Circuit-house and a Public Works Department Inspection Bungalow. Always of some importance it has increased considerably of late years and during the last ten its population has risen from 14,551 souls to 15,307. The streets have been raised and the town generally much improved out of its large revenue. The inhabitants are principally Burmans, with a few Hindoos, Mahomedans, Europeans (mainly officials), Indo-Europeans, and Chin-Indo-Europeans.

Za-lwon is a rising town farther to the south, which has a population of 4,784 souls, a large increase since 1868 when its inhabitants numbered 2,989 only. It has a Court-house used by the Extra Assistant Commissioner in charge of the township, and a Police station.

Meng-gyee on the left bank of the Irrawaddy in 18° 6' 35" N. and 95° 30' E., which includes Re-kheng, was at one time, after the second Burmese war, of considerable importance and the head-quarter station of Tharrawaddy or the country east of the Irrawaddy now included in Henzada, in which was quartered a detachment of Native Infantry. The Assistant Commissioner was withdrawn some years after the occupation, but it has of late years been found necessary to reconstitute the town into the head-quarter station of a sub-division. It contains a Court-house, bazaar or market-place and a Police station, and has a population of 15,770 souls, largely engaged in trade.

In addition to these towns there are others in different parts of the country which are gradually and steadily rising in importance as Mo-gnyo, Ta-pwon and Tsan-rwe, where Extra Assistant Commissioners hold their Courts, and a large number of villages of various sizes. In villages and in small hamlets of less than 200 inhabitants Henzada may be said to be particularly rich no other district in the province having so many. The larger number of these are along the banks of the Irrawaddy and on the banks of the tributary streams to the west of that river. It may safely be asserted that the embankments along the Irrawaddy which protect such an extensive tract of fertile rice country from the inundations to which it was annually subject will not only produce a steady increase in the size of villages now existing and occupied by cultivators of the neighbouring plains but will cause the establishment of many new ones in spots hitherto waste and waiting only for relief from the superabundant waters of the river and for labour to become valuable and fruitful fields.

Once a portion of the Talaing kingdom of Pegu and annexed to the Burman Empire in 1753 A.D. by Aloungbhoora, the district has no special history : it never seems to have been the scene of much fighting nor to have had at any period an independent existence. Its towns were occasionally attacked and defended but the inhabitants would appear to have taken no special part in any of the wars. Kyan-kheng, Myan-oung, Oot-hpo and Henzada claim to have been founded by Talaing princes in the early days of Talaing history, whilst Kan-oung does not go further back than the days of Aloungbhoora. It possesses no extensive ruins like Thare-khet-tara near Prome or Twan-te in Rangoon. When Colonel Symes visited Ava at the end of the last century he found at Henzada evident signs of wealth but little cultivation, whilst the neighbourhood of Myan-oung he described as exceedingly fruitful, exporting a considerable quantity of rice upcountry. Tharrawaddy or the country on the east of the Irrawaddy was given as an appanage to a prince of royal blood who became famous, or perhaps rather infamous, under the name of " Prince Tharrawaddy" : clever, open hearted and liberal but ambitious, cruel and vindictive, he turned his grant into a nest of robbers who were thoroughly devoted to him and of whom he made use in 1837 to dethrone his brother in his own favour. During the first Burmese war no resistance was offered to the British Army in this district as it now exists. After the fall of Donabyoo Sir Archibald Campbell continued his advance up the valley of the Irrawaddy and was met at Taroop-hmaw by Burman Envoys who wished him to halt and enter into negotiations, a suggestion which, warned by experience, he declined to entertain but offered to treat for peace when in Prome. Soon after the taking of Rangoon and Bassein during the second Burmese war, the *Phlegethon* was sent up the river to reconnoitre and found that the Governor of Dalla had evacuated Donabyoo and had crossed the river to Tsaga, a few miles higher up. On the *Phlegethon* opening fire the force, which consisted of some 5,000 men, retired to Thara-waw (Sarawa), some of them recrossing to Henzada.

In the beginning of July 1852 Commodore Tarleton moved up towards Prome and found a large body of men at Kan-oung who replied to a shell from the flotilla of which he was in command by a vigorous fire from guns and musketry from their defences to which they retreated : as the expedition had been specially despatched to reconnoitre the river it proceeded after shelling the works for an hour and on its return sometime later the place was found to have been abandoned. At Myan-oung all was found quiet but at Akouktoung extensive fortifications were observed crowning the bluff and completely commanding the western channel leaving the eastern undefended ; through this the vessels passed onwards to Prome.

The Burmese, on receiving information of the capture of Prome by the flotilla, abandoned the works at Akouk-toung and were discovered crossing the river ; they were immediately attacked and five brass field pieces captured, and a few days later the works and some of the 28 guns which they were found to contain were destroyed, the remainder being brought away. The Burmese general in command, a grandson of the great Bandoola who had been killed at Donabyoo during the first war, subsequently surrendered. The whole of the delta was, however, not entirely cleared of Burmese troops and many marauders remained who were only waiting for a favourable opportunity to collect together and to carry on a guerilla war with the British and with all who had in any way helped them. After Bandoola had retired to Prome on the advance of Commander Tarleton just related no attempts were made by the British to occupy Akouk-toung as General Godwin passed it and captured and occupied Prome. A force of Burmans took advantage of this and rebuilt the stockades; in these they mounted five guns and seriously threatened our communications: the stockades were stormed by Captain Loch R.N. with a small force of 82 marines and seamen on the 4th November and captured without the loss of a single man. The Burmese rapidly reassembled and on the 9th of November Captain Loch again attacked and captured the heights with less difficulty than before. To prevent any recurrence of this danger a small force under Major Gardner was stationed off Akouk-toung, in the *Enterprize*, and directed to patrol the hills regularly. Early on the morning of the 19th, whilst thus employed, he was surprized and he himself and a Havildar killed and six sepoys wounded. A force was at once despatched from Prome under Colonel Handscomb and Captain Loch R.N. who attacked and drove off the enemy from the two positions which they occupied, one north and one south of Akouk-toung, the latter a few miles from Kyan-kheng, after which Akouk-toung was occupied and no further serious disturbances occurred on the right bank of the Irrawaddy in this neighbourhood. In the meanwhile Bassein and the southern part of Henzada had been, if possible, in a still more disturbed state. In Bassein there had been several risings, not of the people generally but of the disbanded Burman Police, of which each Thoogyee even had several hundreds. The conquest of the country by the English deprived them of all occupation and, encouraged and led by men holding commissions from the Court at Ava, they kept the whole country below the Akouk-toung hills in a continual ferment. The principal leader in this district was one Myathtoon the hereditary Thoogyee of a small circle, a man of daring who had more than once been treated as a rebel by the Burmese Government, who collected a large body of marauders. He was attacked south of Donabyoo by a force under Sir John Cheape with which a Kareng levy under Captain Fytche in civil charge of Bassein co-operated and his force dispersed. He himself escaped but gave no more trouble. In Tharrawaddy a man named Goung-gyee caused much disorder. He was the hereditary Thoogyee of a circle and before the outbreak of the war had refused to furnish his quota of tax or to supply the produce which was due from him to the Burmese Government; he was therefore deposed and a relation of his own appointed to succeed him; this relative he forcibly expelled and when the war broke out, siding with neither army, he established a sort of petty government of his own. The Burmese Governor of the district had marched with a contingent from his province to join the Burmese army before Rangoon and after its defeat he retired to his government. Here, in the rainy season of 1852, Goung-gyee attacked him, upon which a force from the Burman army then at Prome was detached against him but the rapid advance of the British enabled Goung-gyee to elude his opponents. In 1853 he refused to obey a summons from Captain Smith who had been placed in charge and the Burmese Government now secretly supported him, and for a considerable period he was enabled to keep the country in a very disturbed state. " By dint of terror inspired by ruthless cruelties " to those of his countrymen who accepted service from the British Govern-

" ment he deterred many from submitting and from supplying information
" regarding his movements.   Their villages were attacked, plundered and
" burnt; their wives and children driven off into the mountains, and the men
" forced to decide between joining him and death." Not only had Goung-
gyee no intention of acknowledging any master but he was determined
that during his life no one should occupy the post which he had so long
held.   No sooner was a Myooke appointed by the British Government than
Goung-gyee killed him.   It was not until the early part of 1855 that he
was got rid of when, owing to the energetic measures taken by Captain
d'Oyley in Prome and Captain (now Colonel) David Brown in Tharrawaddy,
he was so closely pursued and harassed that at last, almost deserted by his
followers, he acknowledged himself beaten and escaped into Burmese territory.

The defeat of these two leaders and the dispersion of their gangs
together with the energetic and firm but conciliatory policy pursued by the
Civil Officers in charge relieved the whole country and no serious disturbances
have occurred since.

On the annexation of Pegu the present Henzada district was called Sarawa

Revenue.

(*Tha-ra-waw*) and very shortly afterwards was divided
into two called Henzada and Tharrawaddy to be subsequently united and called Myanoung, a name which a few
years ago was changed to Henzada on the removal of the head-quarters from
Myanoung back to Henzada : since then the Thoon-tshay circle has been added
from Rangoon and Donabyoo has been taken from it.   The revenue derived
from Tharrawadddy was comparatively small.   Under the Burmese rule
the two tracts east and west of the Irrawaddy including Donabyoo
remitted annually to the central Government at Ava, or to the Myo-tsa to
whom they had been allotted, the revenue shewn in the following table :—

		Henzada.	Tharrawaddy.	Total.
		Rs.	Rs.	Rs.
1.	House family tax, Burmans and Kareng	96,120	80,110	1,76,230
2.	Yoke of oxen or rice land ..	76,440	970	77,410
3.	Fisheries	25,150	9,910	35,060
4.	Transit duties	....	6,690	6,690
5.	Betel-nut and palm plantations ..	680	....	680
6.	Licensed brokers and miscel-laneous	3,820	1,380	5,200
7.	One township ten per cent. in kind after the rice crop had been threshed	Unknown	....	....
8.	365lbs. honey, 365lbs. wax and 100 mats	....	Unknown	....
	Total ..	2,02,210	99,060	3,01,270

The small revenue derived from rice land and the comparatively large amount derived from transit duties was due to the small area of rice and the comparatively large area of garden and vegetable cultivation; the two latter were not taxed but duties were levied on the produce when carried into another township.

On the British occupation the transit duties and duties on licensed brokers were abolished but the other imposts were retained slightly altered, whilst some other indirect taxes, notably excise, were imposed. In 1855-56 the demand was :—

		Henzada.	Tharrawaddy.	Total.
		Rs.	Rs.	Rs.
1.	Land	148,590	61,770	210,360
2.	Capitation	127,960	75,030	202,990
3.	Fisheries	33,500	7,500	41,000
4.	Salt	120	....	120
5.	Excise	16,980	2,000	18,980
6.	Timber revenue	50	100	150
7.	Sale of unclaimed property	550	....	550
8.	Bazaar rent	1,460	90	1,550
9.	Fines and fees	10,470	5,640	16,110
10.	Ferries	....	40	40
11.	Postage stamps	....	170	170
12.	Miscellaneous	4,850	3,080	7,930
	Total	344,530	155,420	499,950

At the end of the decade the total revenue had increased to Rs. 829,510 or had nearly doubled, exclusive of bazaar rent and other items which were now credited to local revenue. The increase was under every head except excise which had greatly fallen off.

		1855-56.	1864-65.
		Rs.	Rs.
1.	Land	210,360	338,280
2.	Capitation	202,990	355,030
3.	Fisheries	41,000	69,910
4.	Excise	18,480	7,980
5.	Other items	26,620	58,310
	Total	499,950	829,510

Ten years later, in 1874-75, the gross revenue was Rs. 1,356,193, but owing to the rapid growth in the population the rate per head had fallen from about Rs. 2-14 to about Rs. 2-9.

The gross revenue for the year 1876-77 divided into its main heads was :—

1.	Land Revenue	..	..	..	.. Rs.	575,893
2.	Capitation tax	..	..	..	,,	460,061
3.	Fisheries, leases & net licenses	..	..	..	,,	79,498
4.	Salt tax ..	..	..	..	.. ,,	48
5.	Forest Produce	..	..	..	.. ,,	177
6.	Other items—					
	a. Excise on spirits and drugs	..	..	Rs.	89,727	
	b. Fines and forfeitures	..	..	,,	24,843	
	c. Unclaimed property sold	..	..	,,	634	
	d. Miscellaneous ..	..	..	,,	12,739	
	e. Postage and Telegraph stamps ..	..	..	,,	7,695	
	f. Law stamps	..	..	.. ,,	45,332	
						180,970
				Total	..	1,296,642
7.	Local taxes	..	..	..		130,692
			GRAND TOTAL	..		1,327,334

The local revenues are derived from Municipal and Town taxes, Market stall rents, contributions to the dispensaries, fines and the five per cent cess, which are credited either to the town in which they are levied or where levied out of any town to the district generally. The amounts thus received in 1876-77 were :—

Municipal Fund	..	..	..	Rs.	45,648
District Fund	..	..	..	,,	40,875
Five per cent. cess	..	..	..	,,	41,662
Dispensary ..	..	..	..	,,	2,507
		Total	..	,,	130,692

Before the annexation of Pegu the country now forming the Henzada Administration. district was divided into numerous small tracts ruled by officials who, though not of high rank, communicated direct with the Government at Ava. Those in the country south of Akouktoung on the right bank and south of Taroop-hmaw on the left, as far as the Rangoon and Bassein districts, were incorporated into one district and called Sarawa (*Thara-waw*). Very shortly, however, it was found necessary to divide Tha-ra-waw into two and the Irrawaddy was taken as the dividing line ; Henzada to the west with its head-quarters at the town of that name was made one district and Tharrawaddy on the east, the old historical name of that part of the Province, with its head-quarters at Meng-gyee, the other ; at the same time the small township of Taroop-hmaw in the north was taken from Prome and added to the latter.

Each township was placed under a Burmese officer under the designation of Myo-ook and he was entrusted with moderate judicial, fiscal and police power. Immediately under the Myo-ook were the Thoogyee, or revenue and police officers placed over circles, each circle containing several village tracts. These officers held the same general position which they held under the Burmese rule. The area of their jurisdiction varied from three or four to twenty square miles. Each Thoogyee had two peons.

Subordinate to the Thooygee were appointed goung (literally 'heads'). These officers existed under the Burmese Government by no fixed rule but were placed at the caprice of each Thoogyee or other officer wherever a new hamlet sprung up or a few families congregated. They were now appointed over, on the average, every hundred families throughout the several circles and placed under the immediate orders of the Thoogyee, whom they assisted in the revenue and police duties. They received a salary of ten rupees a month each. They constituted the village constabulary and, with the Thoogyee, the detective police. At the same time the goung and ook (or "rulers") over traders, over fishermen, over ploughmen of the royal lands, over brokers, over silver assayers &c. were reduced and these classes, which had hitherto formed distinct bodies each under its own head, were brought under the general laws of the country and any crimes and offences of which their members might be accused made primarily cognizable by the Thoogyee and goung, who at first seemed hardly able to understand that all persons within the limits of the tracts of which they had been placed in charge were within their jurisdiction. It was soon found that the Thoogyee and goung with their two peons each were not able to maintain order in a country lately the seat of war and overrun with men who had hitherto lived upon the land. The Burmese system was to exact a definite and fixed revenue from the various divisions and to allow the officials in charge thereof no defined salary but the criminal fines and the fees on the administration of justice and such other sums as they could squeeze from the inhabitants without causing so much discontent that appeals were made to Ava: at the same time the local officials were held strictly and personally responsible for their quota of revenue in money or in kind as the case might be and the supply of fighting men and war boats in case of necessity. Each official kept as many followers as he could support or as could support themselves without driving the long-suffering inhabitants, who had and have a great awe for constituted authority, into venturing into rebellion or flight. The result of the war was to throw these men loose upon the country and it required vigorous efforts and strong measures to restore confidence.

A local regiment was raised and called the Pegu Light Infantry: it was composed of a commandant, second in command, adjutant, four subalterns, one assistant surgeon, seven native commissioned and seventy-eight non-commissioned officers and 495 rank and file, with their head-quarters at Myanoung; whilst in Tharrawaddy a local police corps of 546 strong, officers and men, was formed by Captain Brown, to which two European non-commissioned officers were attached. At the same time the Deputy Commissioners were authorized to carry out at once any sentence of death which they might pass on persons taken in open and armed insurrection, an authority subsequently withdrawn as the country settled down. The general result of the measures adopted was that in two years the district, except in Tharrawaddy where Goung-gyee caused considerable trouble, was quiet but murders and gang-robberies still continued; of the former there were no less than ten in Henzada in 1855 and six in Tharrawaddy during the same year. Gradually the state of the country improved and more especially was this the case in the once turbulent district east of the Irrawaddy owing to " the indefatigable energy and well directed " exertions of Captain (now Colonel) Brown " who had been in charge since 1853. The inhabitants returned to their homes and, as far as it is possible to judge from their conduct and their general statements, gladly accepted the change of rulers, population increased and the revenue rose in amount whilst its incidence per head fell. The raising of the Pegu Light Infantry was attended with some difficulty as it was found at first that Burmese and Talaing would not enlist; an endeavour was made, with but little success, to get Malay recruits from the Straits but in a few years the corps was raised to its full sanctioned strength, mainly by an accession of Burmans from Tharrawaddy, and in 1858 it furnished detachments which relieved the troops of the line on the detached frontier posts in the Prome district. In 1861 on the formation of the existing provincial police the corps was disbanded, most of the officers and many of the men joining the new body and at the same time the police battalion raised by Captain Brown was similarly reduced.

In 1861 Tharrawaddy and Henzada were united and formed into one district, the head-quarters being removed north to Myanoung which thenceforward for several years gave its name to the district. In 1870 the head-quarters were transferred to Henzada and the district was re-named. In 1873 the Thoon-tshay circle of the Rangoon district was added, and in April 1875 the Donabyoo township was taken away and added to others from Bassein and Rangoon to form the new Thoon-khwa district. Henzada is now divided into three sub-divisions, Henzada, Myanoung and Tharrawaddy and these again into nine townships in charge of each of which is an Extra Assistant Commissioner, and into eighty-one revenue circles.

In 1876 the police force consisted of one Superintendent, one Assistant superintendent, 44 subordinate officers and 354 men, of whom 45 were employed for municipal purposes and nine as river police ; the total cost was Rs. 93,473, Rs. 8,994 being defrayed from local sources.

Almost the last buildings constructed were the gaols and lock-ups. For the first few years the prisoners were confined in temporary mat buildings, except at Meng-gyee in Tharrawaddy where Captain Brown turned an old and abandoned brick building into an efficient place of confinement for his prisoners. In 1856 two outbreaks occurred : twenty-four prisoners endeavoured to escape, fourteen succeeded, six were killed and four re-captured. In 1859 an enclosure wall of masonry was constructed by convict labour round the Menggyee gaol under the superintendence of Lieutenant Lloyd. In 1861 the gaols at Meng-gyee and at Henzada were abolished, though retained as lock-ups in which prisoners were confined pending trial and when sentenced to short terms of imprisonment. The plan then under consideration was to have a gaol in each district in which prisoners sentenced to not more than three years imprisonment should be confined but this was subsequently altered and it was determined that all prisoners undergoing a longer term than six months should be sent to Rangoon. In 1864 the lock-up at Myanoung was a wooden building standing in open country on the banks of the Irrawaddy without enclosure of any sort in which were confined only under-trial prisoners and those sentenced to not more than a month's imprisonment, the remainder being sent to Rangoon. In 1868-69 masonry lock-ups were constructed at Henzada and at Myanoung and some years later it was proposed to build a district gaol at the former station but the plan was abandoned.

The gaol at Henzada though classed as a district gaol is in reality but a lock-up and is inadequate for the wants of the district. It and the lock-up at Myanoung are of similar construction, both consisting of masonry buildings with wooden barracks raised 10 feet off the ground in which, during 1875 and 1876, an average number of 83 and 67 prisoners, respectively, were confined.

At Henzada the average daily number of convicts employed on labour outside the gaol walls was ten, eight were employed on the gaol garden, twenty on manufactures, seven on the gaol buildings, six as gaol servants and four as prison officers. Rs. 992 were realized by the sale of gaol manufactures and Rs. 980 for the extramural labour. The expenditure during the year was—

	Rs.	A.	P.	Rs.	A.	P.
On gaol buildings by Gaol Department	43	0	0			
Ditto by Public Works Department	5,888	0	0	5,931	0	0
Maintaining and guarding prisoners				5,792	0	0
				11,723	0	0
Cash receipts from manufactures	2,223	0	0			
Expenditure for sand, mortar, &c.	1,090	0	0	1,133	0	0
Nett cost				10,590	0	0
Nett cost per head				102	13	0

Excluding the cost of new buildings and repairs, the total cost of each prisoner during the four years ending with 1876 was Rs. 56-13-6, Rs. 69-12-7, Rs. 75-2-1, and Rs. 56-3-6.

In Myanoung where eighteen convicts were employed on manufactures the cash receipts were larger and the nett cost proportionally reduced. In 1876 the gross expenditure on the lock-up was Rs. 6,653 and deducting Rs. 2,785, the profit from the sale of manufactured articles, &c., the nett outlay was Rs. 3,868 or Rs. 47-2-9 per head. The total cost (exclusive of that for buildings) per head of average strength during each of the four years ending with 1876 was Rs. 63-8-6, Rs. 76-1-4, Rs. 53-8-0 and Rs. 62-9-9.

This district has from the first received considerable attention as regards the education of its inhabitants but beyond making grants-in-aid to the missionary societies the State did not interfere for some years. As early as 1855 schools had been established by the American Baptist missionaries and in 1856 a Kareng Normal school was opened in Henzada, in 1867 the Society for the Propagation of the Gospel started a school in the same town, and in 1873 and 1874 the Government formed cess schools in Henzada and Myanoung and in 1875 in Kyan-kheng. In the meanwhile the Baptist missionaries had started numerous village schools amongst the Kareng to which the State for some time afforded aid.

The average daily attendance in the cess schools in 1876 was :—in Henzada 52, Myanoung 36, and Kyan-kheng 20. In Henzada almost all the pupils are Booddhists whereas in Myanoung there were 13 Christians, Mahomedans and Hindoos out of a total of 34 on the rolls on the 31st March 1876, and in Kyan-kheng three out of a total of 31 on the rolls. The total number on the rolls of the S. P. G. Mission School, to which the State made a grant of Rs. 960, was 58 and the average daily attendance 47. In Henzada there are two schools for Burmese girls to each of which the State makes a small grant. The total number of pupils on the rolls in 1876 was 67 and the average daily attendance was 51.

All these are more or less under the supervision of Europeans or Americans. At Henzada and at Meng-gyee there are lay schools, one at each, in which both boys and girls are taught, kept by Burmans who receive small grants and are also assisted by a master paid by the State, whilst at Re-keng the Government employs a master who teaches in a large monastery with the consent and on the application of the head hpoongyee. Numerous monasteries and lay schools are annually inspected and prizes distributed and in 1875-76 the Director of Public Instruction reported that in this district indigenous lay education was founded on a permanently sound and steadily broadening basis.

HENZADA ANOUK-BHET.—A revenue circle in the Henzada township, Henzada district, on the right bank of the Irrawaddy south of Henzada town, partially cultivated in fields which would be a swamp were it not for the protecting embankment on the Irrawaddy. In 1876 the land revenue was Rs. 5,431, the capitation tax Rs. 3,900, the gross revenue Rs. 10,420 and the population 4,725.

HENZADA MYOMA.—A revenue circle in the Henzada township of the Henzada district round and including a portion of Henzada the headquarters of the district. In 1876 including the inhabitants of the town the population was 16,886, and in the same year the land revenue was Rs. 4,035, the capitation tax Rs. 977 and the gross revenue, excluding that of the municipality, Rs. 14,030.

HEUMA.—A tribe inhabiting the hill country of Arakan.—*See Shandoo.*

HIEN-TSAI.—The native name for the north Mosco island. *q.v.*

HIEN-TSAI.—A fresh water basin in the Tavoy district lying on the coast about half way between Re in Amherst and Tavoy. The country slopes from all sides towards a central point, forming the semi-circle of a great cone, in the lower part of which the basin about fifteen miles long by six to eight broad formed by the confluence of all the streams between Re and Tavoy (except the Hangan and the Za-dee) descending from the westernmost ranges, and surrounded by land on all sides except an opening of about half a mile in width through which it communicates with the sea. The entrance is closed by a sand bar. Within the basin and towards its northern end is an extensive island containing land suited for rice cultivation. Wood-oil trees grow in abundance in the neighbourhood.

HLAI-GA-TOUNG.—A small unnavigable river in the Prome district that rises in the hills on the north-east of the Irrawaddy and flows southward in a narrow ravine for some five miles when it receives the waters of the Bho-ra, which has emerged from a still narrower ravine immediately to the west, and three miles further on it joins the North Naweng a mile below the village of Tham-ba-ya-goon.

HLAING.—A township occupying the extreme north-west of the Rangoon district and lying on both banks of the Hlaing river.

The boundary leaves the Pegu Romas near the source of the Mee-neng and following that river to its mouth in the Hlaing, turns southward to the mouth of the Re-nat-eng Khyoung; here turning west it follows that creek to the Re-nat-eng and the northern border of the swamp and then continues west along an imaginary line to the A-lap-tshen-eng; here it inclines south-east to a Ma-oo tree (*Sarcocephalus cadamba*) in about the latitude of Bhiet-naw on the Hlaing : inclining again south-south-east it strikes the Pa-khwon stream and, following this in a generally southerly direction to its mouth in the Bhaw-lay, it runs with that creek at first south and gradually round east to its southern mouth in the Hlaing. Turning abruptly north along that river it bends round west again and follows a spur in an east-north-easterly direction to the Pegu Romas; these form the eastern boundary of the township. The area within these limits is 678 square miles. To the north and west lie Henzada; south and east the Hmaw-bhee and the Hpoung-leng townships of Rangoon. The head-quarters are at Taw-la-tai on the southern bank of the Bhaw-lay creek at its northern junction with the Hlaing. In 1873 the northern circle, Thoon-tshay, was joined to the Henzada district and in 1875-76 other circles on the west were taken from the township when the Thoon-khwa district was formed. The township is divided into four revenue circles, *viz.*, Ook-kan in the north-east, Myoung-ta-nga in the south-east, Aing-ka-loung in the north-west and Bhaw-lay in the south-west. The two first are fully described under their own names but it is desirable to add to the account already given of the two last.

Aing-ka-loung occupies the whole of that portion of the township which lies west of the Hlaing and north of the Bhaw-lay. There are but few spots high enough to escape, during the rains, from the spill of the Hlaing, the Pa-khwon and the Bhaw-lay, supplemented as these are by the waters of the Irrawaddy which find their way over the country by numerous creeks, whilst the rush of the Irrawaddy through the Pan-hlaing banks up the Hlaing, and consequently the Bhaw-lay, and thus adds to the over-flow. The somewhat raised spots, which are found principally along the Hlaing and in the north-western corner at and below the village of Eng-ta-ra, are themselves occasionally submerged on a heavy rise, as in 1877. Except this higher ground the whole circle, more especially in the west, is covered with tree and grass forest, called the Eng-ta-ra Taw-gyee or the " Great Eng-ta-ra forest", in which the principal trees are Htien and Roon (*Anogeissus acuminata*) and is highly intersected with creeks mostly dry even as early as the end of January. There are five principal fens, for they cannot be called lakes : in the centre of the circle is the A-la-bhwot, the largest, and north of it are the Taw-kha-ra and the Ka-law-koon, whilst towards the south is the Ma-tha and in the extreme south-east the Meng-hla. In 1877 the inhabitants were—

Burmans	...	...	...	... 1,736
Talaing	...	...	...	... 642
Kareng	...	...	...	... 991
Chinese	...	...	...	... 4
				3,373

In that year there were only 25 villages, all either on the Hlaing or grouped near Eng-ta-ra. The principal are :—Aing-ka-loung, a long straggling village in the north-eastern corner on the bank of the Hlaing, consisting of two rows of houses one on each side of a road with a much damaged brick path running along its centre leading to a monastery and one or two zayats in an open grove of trees at the lower end. Between the monastery and the river is a good bricked well. The inhabitants, who in 1877 numbered 368, are principally employed in working as fishermen and as coolies on the timber rafts. Hpo-khoung, a similar village about a mile further down and opposite Hlaing with 214 inhabitants; and Taw-ta-ree, still further south and about half a mile inland from the river bank, with 201 inhabitants. In 1876 there were 4,152 acres of rice land under cultivation and none fallow, 79 acres of garden and 292 acres of miscellaneous cultivation; 1,259 buffaloes, 188 cows, bulls and bullocks, 189 carts, 240 ploughs and 18 boats. The inhabitants of all the villages on the Hlaing eke out their means by cutting and selling grass for thatch and in buying bamboos from the forest workers at the head waters of the Ook-kan which they stack on the river bank till an opportunity offers of sending or taking them to Rangoon for sale in the market there.

The Bhaw-lay circle occupies the whole of the township west of the Hlaing below Aing-ka-loung. Like its northern neighbour it is highly intersected by small creeks which form an irregular network with each other and with the Bhaw-lay and the Hlaing. The greater portion of its area is flooded twice during the year on the high rises of the Irrawaddy and of the Hlaing and is thereby rendered unculturable and is covered with open tree forest and elephant grass. The places most free from flooding, though not exempt in high rises, are (a) along the bank of the northern portion of the Bhaw-lay ; here there is an annual spill from the creek but not sufficient in ordinary years to damage cultivation : (b) in the extreme south-eastern corner : and (c) a stretch of slightly higher ground extending, with intervals, southwards from Gnyoung-waing at the junction of the Hlaing with the northern mouth of the Bhaw-lay along the east central tract to rather more than half way down the circle. In 1876 there were 5,706 acres under rice, 112 acres left fallow, 187 acres of garden land and 30 acres of miscellaneous cultivation. In the same year there were 1,263 buffaloes, 107 cows, bulls and bullocks distributed amongst three villages, viz., Tha-bhaw-khyoung, Hlay-tshiep and Taw-la-tai, 108 pigs, 13 goats, 118 carts, 244 ploughs and 16 boats.

The villages, of which in that year there were 25, are almost entirely on the banks of the main streams. The most important are Bhaw-lay on the stream of the same name a little to the south of the mouth of the Kha-noung-pe creek with 472 inhabitants who are principally workers of lake and stream fisheries ; Hlay-tshiep at the junction of Hlaing and the northern mouth of the Bhaw-lay where a small Police force is stationed, with 420 inhabitants, agriculturists and raftsmen ; A-lien-a-lay on the bank of the Hlaing at the mouth of the stream of the same name with 541 inhabitants, agriculturists and raftsmen ; and Taw-la-tai, with its north-eastern and semi-detached quarter Gnyoung-waing, with 626 inhabitants, those living in the former agriculturists and raftsmen and those in the latter traders and rice brokers.

The total number of the inhabitants of the circle in 1877 was :—

Burmans	...	...	...	...	2,002
Talaing	...	...	...	...	1,689
Kareng	...	...	...	...	1,111
Chinese	...	...	...	...	7
Musulmans	...	...	...	...	2
					4,811

To the east of the township the country is hilly and here is found much valuable timber, as teak (*Tectona grandis*), Pyeng-ma (*Lagerstrœmia Reginœ*),

Eng (*Dipterocarpus tuberculatus*), Ka-gnyeng (*D. alatus*), Theng-gan (*Hopea odorata*) and Pyeng-ga-do (*Xylia dolabriformis*). A considerable portion of this tract has been demarcated as a State forest reserve. Below this the country gradually subsides into a plain, the eastern borders of which in the north are lower than the banks of the Hlaing. In consequence, as that river annually overflows the country in its immediate neighbourhood, it is not culturable except, perhaps, in the extreme south. West of the Hlaing the country is one vast flat with a few places high enough to escape the annual floods where rice is grown ; elsewhere it is covered with grass and with tree forest of little or no value.

The principal rivers are the Hlaing, the Bhaw-lay creek and the Ook-kan and the Ma-ga-ree, tributaries of the Hlaing from the eastward : much timber is brought down the two last, and down the Ook-kan bamboos also, and conveyed to Rangoon down the Hlaing.

The principal villages are Taw-la-tai, the head-quarters, on the Bhaw-lay with a population of 626 souls in 1877. Pouk-koon where is the Ook-kan station of the Irrawaddy Valley (State) Railway which traverses the township from south to north, with 494 inhabitants ; and Myoung-ta-nga in the north of the circle of the same name with 802 inhabitants. A little to the south of Hlaing, on the left bank of the river of that name, are the remains of an old city said to have been founded in the time of Rahzadhierit, the great king of the Talaing. The ruins of three pagodas and of the walls are standing ; these latter form a square each side facing one of the cardinal points of the compass and with a gateway in the centre. North of the Dhat, a small mountain tributary of the Ook-kan which it joins from the south-east, are the ruins of another town called Htan-bhoo the crumbling walls only remaining : it is said to have been founded by Meng-ran-ga a son of Rahzadhierit, who, rebelling against his father, was killed in his own camp at a spot now called La-ha-ma-ngay close to Htan-bhoo.

In 1876 the area actually under rice was 28,469 acres, the land revenue was Rs. 48,621, the capitation-tax Rs. 26,123, the gross revenue Rs. 96,205 and the population 19,996 souls.

HLAING.—A river in the valley of the Irrawaddy which flows past the town of Rangoon whence to its mouth it is universally known as the Rangoon river. It rises in the marshy grounds east of Prome and, flowing south over a sandy and muddy bed between low banks in a channel which is only just defined and no more even in the dry season, falls into the Eng-ma lake, after having received the waters of numerous small streams, all like itself in this por-tion of its course unnavigable by boats. It has been supposed that it acts as a sort of escape channel for the flood waters of the Naweng when ponded back by an unusual rise of the Irrawaddy and even that it is an old channel of the Irrawaddy itself but now cut off by an alluvial bar, but there is a sufficient rise in the intervening country to form a watershed between this sluggish river and the eddying volume of the Naweng in flood which sweeps past it a few miles to the north. On leaving the Engma lake, which it enters as the ' Zay', it continues its southward course as the ' Myit-ma-kha', traverses the Henzada district east of and almost parallel to the Irrawaddy and enters the Rangoon district at Myit-kyo. In the north it is separated from the Irrawaddy by a line of low hills covered with Eng forest (*Dipterocarpus tuberculatus*) which ends a little above the latitude of Myanoung. Below this it is connected with the Irrawaddy by numerous creeks which increase in size and importance towards the south. From Tsan-rwe, where it receives the Thoon-tshay from the east, it is navigable upwards at all seasons as far as Ta-pwon, the water being never less than three feet deep, but the channel is in many plac as choked with jungle. Small boats ascend even as far as Eng-ma with cargoes of salt, ngapee and other goods. Owing to the numerous shoals it is impracticable for steamers even of light draught above Tsan-rwe where its width is 180 yards, its depth four feet, the bed sandy and the tidal rise 2½ feet. Below Tsan-rwe it continues between high sandy banks to about 17° 15′ N., where the Bhaw-lay, with a mouth about 120 yards broad, leaves it to the west. A little lower its banks gradually sink and assume the appearance characteristic of those of a tidal stream in the delta, abrupt and steep for a few feet from the top and below high water mark shelving and muddy, the crest either bare or hidden by overhanging shrubs with their lower branches and branchlets washed by the tide and covered with brown slime which, as the water falls, dries into a dirty grey. Large trees such as the Mango and Htien disappear and are succeeded by Lamoo and other timber which thrives in brackish water. The waters have no longer a semblance even of transparency but are thick and muddy every stroke of the oar sending the earthy particles swirling in distinct eddies. A very little north of the 17th parallel the Bhaw-lay, here called the Kook-ko, joins it again and it then widens considerably. Three miles lower it suddenly spreads out to a breadth of several miles and its course is divided by two main islands into three channels ; of these the eastern is the deepest and the one most generally used by boats and always by the river steamers which reach the Irrawaddy during the rains through the Kook-ko. Up to 1874 the route was through the Pan-hlaing, further south, but this is gradually silting up. The western channel is shallow and considerably larger whilst the central is still shallower and so filled with sand banks that, except at high water, it is barely navigable even by a canoe. The two main islands, one on each side of this central channel, are gradually enlarging by accretion : that on the east now contains about sixty acres and that on the west about eighty. Above there is a small round island formerly containing from fifteen to twenty acres, but the banks are steep and fall in every year and its area is now only about five. Below the two main islands is another, larger than either, which has increased and is still increasing in the same way as they are. Just above Rangoon the river is joined by the Pan-hlaing from the westward and sweeping round the town towards the east it is joined by the Pegu and the Poo-zwon-doung when, turning south again, it flows on for 21 miles through an ever-widening channel and falls into the Gulf of Martaban in Lat. 16° 28′ N. Long. 96° 20′ E. through a mouth three miles broad. The land at the entrance is low and for the most part covered with jungle to the water's edge forming dense mangrove and tidal forests. Owing to the great rise and fall of the tide and to the velocity of the tidal stream the water, even far out to seaward, is charged with a large quantity of deposit, causing the river to present a deep yellow hue. At the mouth it is high water, at full and change of the moon, at 3 hrs. 15 mins. : the springs rise 21 feet and neaps 13 feet. It is navigable to Rangoon by large ships, which, however, have to wait for flood tide to cross the Hastings, a shoal formed just above the united mouths of the Pegu and Poo-zwon-doung rivers. In the rains it is navigable for 30 miles above Rangoon by ships of 500 tons burden. The channel up to Rangoon is winding and difficult.

HLAING.—A village in the Rangoon district at a re-entering angle on the left bank of the Hlaing river about 11 miles above the mouth of the Bhaw-lay. The village, the seat of the Governor of the Hlaing province in the Burmese time, was occupied without resistance by the British troops under Sir Archibald Campbell on the 23rd February 1825. In 1877 it had a population of 293 souls. It occupies the site of the river face suburb of the ancient town of Hlaing, which is mentioned in Talaing and Burman histories as early as the latter half of the fourteenth century. The walls and three pagodas only, now all in ruins, remain and the land within, once the scene of busy life, is almost entirely under the plough : the walls are of brick and of earth, the bricks broad, long and flat and exceedingly well burned but without a trace of vitreous glaze, and are about 15 feet high and 30 feet broad at the base ; they form a square, each side facing one of the cardinal points of the compass and about one thousand yards long with a gateway in the centre. The northern wall is now about three hundred yards from the river, but judging from the erosion taking place must originally have been considerably farther. Near the village are the ruins of a pagoda called Hpoung-daw-kau and on the opposite bank of the Hlaing, just above Hpo-khoung village, another, in better repair with its htee still in place but with the gilding worn off, called Hpoung-daw-oo both said to have been built by the Prince of Tharawaddy, who afterwards came to the throne as Koon-boung-meng, on a visit he paid to Pegu in 1820 when he followed the route generally taken by the Burman armies in the wars with Pegu and leaving the Irrawaddy a little below the latitude of Myanoung entered the Hlaing and thus escaped the the waves of lower portion of the former river.

HLAING-BHOON.—A tidal creek in the Bassein district running nearly due north and south from the Bassein river to the Shwe-doung which it joins a short distance from its mouth. It has an average depth of from two to four fathoms at low water and is navigated by large country boats.

HLAING-BHOON-GALE.—A creek in the Bassein district. *See Oot-hpo.*

HLAING-BHWAI.—A village on the left bank of the river of the same name, 108 miles from Maulmain, the head-quarters of the Than-lweng Hlaing-bhwai township of the Amherst district, containing, in 1876, a population of 680 souls. To the south of the village are the Court-house and Police station and between these and the village a very fine monastery, remarkable for the large size of the posts on which it stands. During the dry season a stream of trade passes through this village between the Shan States on the east and the plain country on the west and south. Parties of Shan come in, bringing principally silk piece-goods, men's plaids and women's petticoats which they carry down for sale to Maulmain and towards Tha-htoon returning in a few months with cotton piece-goods and twist. At the same season parties of Shan and Toungthoo from Tha-htoon and the neighbourhood go to the Shan States, carrying principally coin, and purchase large numbers of cattle which they sell in the plain country to the westward. The local trade consists in piece-goods and twist brought up by natives of India, and oil, salt, dried vegetables, salt fish, &c. brought up by Burmans and Talaing, and in fowls, ducks and pigs bred by the Kareng who occupy the surrounding country, especially towards and on the Dawna range to the eastward, and carried down to the Maulmain market, principally by natives of India and Chinamen.

In the rains the current of the river is so rapid that the ascent is tedious and long, but in the dry season the spring tides extend for some two miles above the village and boats can come up rapidly and can then get over the rocky ledge which is about two hundred yards below the village.

HLAING-BHWAI.—A river in the Amherst district which has its sources in the northern portion of the Dawna range and flowing southwards for about 120 miles unites with the Houng-tha-raw at Gyaing to flow almost due west, as the Gyaing, and to fall into the Salween at Maulmain. At its junction with the Da-gyaing, a stream which joins it from the eastward about 24 miles south of Hlaing-bhwai and by the river 42 above Gyaing and is of equal size, it is in the rains about 70 yards wide ; below this it rapidly broadens and and at Gyaing cannot be much less than 400 yards broad. In the rains the water is muddy and the current strong and rapid and boats ascend with difficulty but in the dry season, when the spring tides extend up for 70 miles, boats of five hundred baskets burden go up to Hlaing-bhwai : except at springs, however, they cannot get over the reef of rocks which stretches across the river about two hundred yards below that village. As far as the mouth of the Da-gyaing the banks are high and well defined, lower down they are, in places, low and the bordering scrub forest comes down to the water's edge even in the dry season, the larger tree forest lying more inland and marking the limit of the river at its highest. The usual halting-places on the way up are Khazaing where there is a Police station 26 miles from Gyaing, and, in the wet weather, Khyoung-wa, a small village on the right bank a little above the mouth of the Da-gyaing 16 miles higher up.

HLAY-GOO.—A village on the Rangoon and Pegu road where it crosses the Poo-zwon-doung—whence the name which means a ford for carts—with 557 inhabitants in 1877. It is the head-quarters of the Hpoung-leng township and contains a Court-house and a Police station.

HLAY-THAY.—A revenue circle in the Prome district about seven miles E. N. E. of Prome near the Naweng river, containing six of the old village tracts. In 1876 it had a population of 1,505 souls ; the land revenue was Rs. 1,916, the capitation-tax Rs. 1,713 and the gross revenue Rs. 3,652.

HLAY-TSHIEP.—A revenue circle on the right bank of the Irrawaddy in the north-east corner of the Henzada township, Henzada district, the cultivated part of which lies principally to the south-east. In 1876 the population was 2,269, the land revenue Rs. 3,596, the capitation tax Rs. 2,275 and the gross revenue Rs. 7,799.

HLAY-TSHIEP.—A village in the Bhaw-lay circle of the Hlaing township, Rangoon district, on the right bank of the Hlaing just below the northern mouth of the Bhaw-lay creek and close to Taw-la-tai the head-quarters of the township. The houses are in two rows along the banks of the river with a road between them. The Police station, the only public building, is behind the centre of the village. In 1877 it had 470 inhabitants. The village was founded about twenty years ago by Moung Shwe Tha, the Extra Assistant Commissioner of the township, who was afterwards burned to death near Zee-goon, on the opposite bank of the Hlaing, in a patch of elephant grass which he had caused to be set on fire to drive out the deer which he had gone to shoot.

HLWA.—A river in the Thayet district which rises in the eastern slopes of the Arakan hills near the strange and lofty Shwe-doung peak and after an easterly course of about thirty miles falls into the Ma-htoon river in the Meng-doon township. In the dry season this stream is a trickling brooklet but during the rains small boats can ascend for some miles as far as the village of Gwa-thit : towards the source the bed is very rocky. It has numerous tributaries none of which are of any importance.

HLWA-TSENG.—A village in the Prome district in 19° 0' 25" N. and 95° 30' 55" E. on the left bank of the north Naweng nine miles from its mouth, measured in a direct line, and at the junction of the Hlwa-tseng streamlet with that river. On the opposite side of the North Naweng is a small patch of rice cultivation. The inhabitants are mainly gardeners and rice cultivators.

HLAW-GA-TA.—A creek in the Bassein district. *See Mai-za-lee.*

HMAN-DENG.—A village in the Re-byoo circle, Thayet township, Thayet district, some three miles west of the river bank, and about six north-west of Thayet town, containing from eighty to ninety houses : the inhabitants are mostly employed in cultivating hill gardens and the narrow strip of rice land about half a mile broad which stretches in a north-western direction towards Oot shit-goon.

HMAW-BHEE.—A revenue circle in the north of the township of the same name in the Rangoon district, extending from the Pegu Romas on the east to the Hlaing on the west and separated from Myoung-ta-nga on the north by the little Myo Khyoung and other insignificant streams and towards the east by a cart track, and from Lien-goon on the south by the Hmaw-bhee stream. On the east the country is hilly and covered with tree forest but in the centre of the circle there is a good deal of rice cultivation though the soil is poor; towards the west shrub and brush forest appear and the face of the country is broken here and there by marshy ground. The area under cultivation and the agricultural stock and population during each of the last five years were :—

Year.	Population.	Area under cultivation.				Agricultural stock.					
		Rice.	Garden.	Miscellaneous.	Total.	Buffaloes.	Cows, Bulls and Bullocks.	Pigs.	Carts.	Ploughs.	Boats.
1872..	3,802	6,251	220	..	6,471	1,292	406	65	256	622	17
1873..	4,926	7,665	235	..	7,900	1,416	455	143	260	551	11
1874..	3,587	8,554	254	..	8,808	1,217	520	209	197	659	37
1875..	4,411	9,925	354	..	10,279	1,214	397	181	261	573	82
1876..	4,644	9,704	371	156	10,231	1,385	508	161	303	684	194

The principal village is Hmaw-bhee, the head-quarters of the sub-division, with 803 inhabitants.

HMAW-BHEE.—A village of 803 inhabitants in the Rangoon district a short distance east of the Hmaw-bhee stream in 17° 4' 20" N. and 96° 7' E. to which, during the rains, boats of 250 bushels burden can ascend *viâ* the Lien-goon, the entrance to the Hmaw-bhee having to a great extent silted up. At this village, on the bank of the stream, are the remains of an old Peguan fort forming a parallelogram with an east and west entrance and a deep ditch round it. Almost all the bricks in the old walls have been taken for metal for the Irrawaddy Valley Railway. During the first Burmese war the Burman general occupied this fort in his retreat northward before the main British column under Sir Archibald Campbell, but after firing a few shots evacuated it without waiting for the attack of the English troops. The inhabitants are mainly employed in rice cultivation.

HMAW-BHEE.—A sub-division of the Rangoon district occupying the country north of the town of Rangoon and of the Angyee township of the Syriam division and lying to the westward of the Pegu Romas. The Rangoon and Irrawaddy Valley (State) Railway traverses the sub-division from south to north, and from Hmaw-bhee station—a few miles north-east of Hmaw-bhee village—occupies the great northern military road. The principal river is the Hlaing which flows from north to south and, joined by the Pan-hlaing in the south, forms the Rangoon river. In the rains steamers can ascend for some distance and boats of 400 bushels burden can at all seasons go up as high as the mouth of the Re-nek. In the rains large boats can traverse the whole extent of the river in this sub-division. The sub-division is divided into two townships, Hlaing containing four revenue circles in the north and Hmaw-bhee containing eleven revenue circles in the south : the head-quarters are at Hmaw-bhee. In 1876 the population numbered 70,433 souls, the land revenue was Rs. 228,503, the capitation-tax Rs. 80,730 and the gross revenue Rs. 337,421.

HMAW-BHEE.—A township in the sub-division of the same name in the Rangoon district with the Hlaing township on the north, the Thoon-khwa district on the west, the An-gyee and the Than-lyeng townships on the south and the Hpoung-leng township on the east. It extends from the town of Rangoon northwards along the western slopes of the Pegu Romas and north-west beyond the Hlaing river to the Pan-hlaing, and east and south-east across the Poo-zwon-doung into the valley of the Pegu and along the bank of that river as far as the Ma-tso stream, and consists of three portions each differing considerably from the others. (*a*) West of the Hlaing are the Htan-ta-beng, Ka-tseng, Pa-dan and Kyoon-oo circles : here the country on the west is traversed by a large number of intercommunicating tidal creeks through which the tide and the waters of the Irrawaddy find their way over the land and every second or third year, since the construction of the embankments along the west bank of the Irrawaddy, flood the fields and destroy the crops. There is but little cultivation and the country is to a great extent covered with open tree forest and elephant grass. (*b*) In the tract north of Rangoon the country loses the flat appearance which it has near the sea coast and gradually passes into undulating ground which, towards the north-east, rises into hills covered with tree forest. The soil is poor but, everywhere below the high ground, is cultivated with rice which is exported through the creeks which communicate with the Hlaing and up which the tide extends almost to the foot of the hills. Towards the south the country has been denuded of wood for fuel for Rangoon and the streams are no longer fringed with brushwood which afforded shade for the spawning fish and the fry. (c) East of Rangoon the country is open, level and highly cultivated, and the soil is rich and productive, but is beginning to suffer from the exhaustion caused by continued cultivation with no rest and no rotation of crops.

The area under cultivation, the agricultural stock and the population during the last five years were :—

Year.	Population.	AREA IN ACRES.				AGRICULTURAL STOCK.					
		Rice.	Garden.	Miscellaneous.	Total.	Buffaloes.	Cows, Bulls and Bullocks.	Pigs.	Carts.	Ploughs.	Boats.
1872..	46,062	65,747	5,876	505	72,128	12,757	5,589	949	2,357	5,223	1,033
1873..	52,810	73,922	6,273	515	80,710	11,928	6,111	1,052	2,596	5,342	1,326
1874..	50,612	82,573	6,957	635	90,165	11,725	5,802	1,461	2,261	5,227	944
1875..	51,620	95,990	6,840	665	103,495	9,602	5,400	1,265	2,059	4,410	963
1876..	50,487	90,840	6,260	819	97,919	11,726	5,772	1,232	2,264	5,124	1,051

The revenue during the same period was :—

Year.	IMPERIAL AND PROVINCIAL.					LOCAL.	Grand total.	Remarks.
	Land.	Capitation tax.	Fisheries.	All others.	Total.	Cess.		
1872 ..	67,982	26,977	1,135	..	96,905	3,455	99,550	In 1874 Tsit-peng and Kyouk khyoung were added from Than-lyeng, and Htan-ta-beng Katseng, Padan and Kyoon-oo from Eng-ga-bhoo.
1873 ..	74,404	31,460	1,135	..	106,999	3,776	110,776	
1874 ..	184,909	57,392	6,679	500	249,480	9,604	159,085	
1875 ..	210,555	56,355	6,679	462	274,051	10,884	284,935	
1876 ..	200,882	54,605	6,679	48	262,214	10,380	272,594	

The head-quarters are at present at Lien-goon but it is proposed to move them to Eng-tsien on the Irrawaddy Valley (State) Railway which traverses the township from south to north. The stations, in this township, are at Thamaing (about to be moved to Eng-tsien), Hlaw-ga and Hmaw-bhee (about to be moved some two miles south from Shan-tsoo where it now is too near Hmaw-bhee.)

During the Burmese rule the Hmaw-bhee "Myo" included only the Hmaw-bhee, Lien-goon and Kyoung-goon circles and was bounded on the west by the Hlaing, on the north by the Myo, on the south by the Tagoo-kyaw, whilst towards the west the official boundary is given as the Kyaik-ka-loot pagoda. The Myo-thoo-gyee resided at Wa-hta-ya where there were then 500 to 600 houses. The total revenue was :—

			Ticals of silver equal to about		Rs.
Fisheries	..	..	250	ditto	.. 325
Toungya	..	..	250	ditto	.. 325
Land	..	..	250	ditto	.. 325
Charges for taking the revenue to the Myo-tsa at Amarapoora		..	250	ditto	.. 325
Capitation and other taxes		..	300	ditto	.. 390
	Total	..	1,300		.. 1,690

In addition a tax equalling Rs. 1-8-0 was levied on each plough and sent to the Governor at Rangoon, and 25 baskets of unhusked rice for each plough were paid to the local Government and stored in the public granary in Rangoon. The Myo-thoo-gyee got 15 baskets of unhusked rice for each plough. The taxes paid in kind were carried at the expense of the cultivators.

HMAW-BHEE.—A small river in the township of the same name in the Rangoon district which rises in the lower slopes of the Pegu Romas and flowing southwards past Hmaw-bhee turns west and falls into the Hlaing at Hmaw-bhee-wa-rwa, a few miles below A-lien-a-lay on the opposite bank. In the rains boats of considerable burden can go up to Hmaw-bhee. Where it turns west, near Kyee-beng-tshiep and Mo-gyo-pyit villages, the Lien-goon leaves it and falls into the Hlaing at Wa-hta-ya. Of late years the Lien-goon has become the main outlet, the lower portion of the Hmaw-bhee having silted up.

HMAW-DAW.—A village of 536 inhabitants in 1877 in the Ien-da-poo-ra circle, Anygee township, Rangoon district, on the edge of the Twan-te Taw-gyee.

HMAW-KAN.—A village in the Prome district eleven miles in a direct line south-east of Prome, in 18° 43' 50" N. and 95° 25' 40" E. on the bank of the Zay stream, six miles north of the Eugma lake, on the western portion of the large rice tract which extends from the Naweng river southwards to the limit of the district.

HMAW-THE.—A stream in the Bassein district which rises in the Kyoon-la-ha lake and after flowing for some distance eastwards turns north and joins the Re-gyee. It is about one hundred feet wide near its mouth and four or five feet deep. In the rains it is navigable by boats about 30 feet long but in the dry season it consists of a series of lakes fringed with scrub forest. The banks are in some parts high and there is much rice cultivation in the country on both sides.

HMAW-WON.—A stream in the Than-lyeng or Syriam township of the Rangoon district formed by the junction of numerous rivulets which rise in the plains-towards the north and, fed by several creeks which communicate with the Pegu river and with each other, it falls into the Hlaing or Rangoon river not far from its mouth. It is tidal beyond Re-bhaw-gan where it is joined by the Bhaw from the west ; through this channel communication can be kept up with the Pegu river which that creek joins just above Syriam or Than-lyeng. The banks are steep and muddy and free of tree forest. At flood tides large boats can ascend for a considerable distance but at and below Kyouktan, the head-quarters of the Syriam sub-division of the district, about seven miles from the mouth, rocks render the passage difficult and dangerous at other seasons. Traversing a rich rice-producing country the stream flows past numerous villages of some size and importance.

HMAW-WON.—A revenue circle in the Than-lyeng township of the Rangoon district at the mouth of the Rangoon river. The aspect of the southern portion of the country is that of an extensive plain richly cultivated, the uncultivated parts being low and subject to inundation : the northern portion has a good deal of tree forest. In the extreme south is a masonry pillar which marks the entrance to the Rangoon river. The inhabitants, who are principally agriculturists, numbered 7,740 in 1876 when the land revenue was Rs. 58,606, the capitation-tax Rs. 8,415 and the gross revenue Rs. 67,167.

HMAW-ZA.—A village about five and a half miles E. S. E. of the town of Prome on the edge of a large tract of rice country. There is here a station of the Irrawaddy Valley (State) Railway.

HNAI-GYO.—A revenue circle in the north-western portion of the Donabyoo township of the Thoon-khwa district, forming a level tract at one time covered with tree and grass forest but now coming under cultivation owing to the construction of protecting embankments. The inhabitants are principally traders, gardeners and rice cultivators. It now includes the once independent circle of Kan-goo. In 1876 it had 5,828 inhabitants, a land revenue of Rs. 11,267 and a gross revenue of Rs. 19,382 of which Rs. 5,765 were derived from the capitation-tax.

HNA-MOUNG-GYA.—A small revenue circle in the Mye-boon township, Kyouk-hpyoo district, half a square mile in extent and with a population of 159 souls in 1876. It is a tract of country given as a grant under the waste land rules and being by the effect of these rules independent of any Thoogyee, the grantee dealing directly with the State, it is shewn in the returns as a circle.

HNGET-KHOUNG.—A conspicuous pagoda-crowned rock at the mouth of Kyouk-hpyoo harbour, called Pagoda rock in the charts.

HNGET-KYOON.—A creek in the Nga-poo-taw township, Bassein district. See Thoung-gale.

HNGET-PYAW.—A tidal creek in the Shwe-loung township, Thoon-khwa district, about 14 miles in length connecting the Re-zoo-daing and the Tharwot creeks. It is navigable throughout by river steamers.

HNGET-THAIK.—A small island off Tavoy Point, at the mouth of the Tavoy river, called Cap Island in the charts.

HNIT-KAING.—A revenue circle in the Wa-kha-roo township, Amherst district, stretching east and west 12 miles along the whole length of the Wa-kha-roo river from its source in the Toung-gnyo range to its junction with the Salween, with an area of 25,715 acres. It has the Pa-gna circle and the sea on the south. As seen from an eminence the whole surface of the circle appears to consist of an almost unbroken extent of uplands covered with tree forest, with several lofty hills in the south-west portion. The only rice land is in a narrow plain along the Wa-kha-roo river. The soil of the upland is generally poor and in the dry weather waterless, there being no wells or other artificial means of obtaining water, but as the soil rests on a laterite formation it is to some extent used for garden cultivation. The hills near the sea shore contain ores which are extracted in very minute quantities by some of the residents in the vicinity. The majority of the inhabitants of the village of Wa-kha-roo cultivate land on the other side of the Wa-kha-roo river in the Zaya township. The inhabitants of the other villages are mostly Burmanised Talaing who settled here when there was a sugar manufactory at Amherst. In 1868 the inhabitants numbered 1,523, the land revenue was Rs. 937, the capitation-tax Rs. 1,610 and the gross revenue Rs. 2,748. In 1876 the numbers and amounts were 2,357, Rs. 4,022, Rs. 2,595, and Rs. 6,617 respectively.

HOON.—A river in Ramree (Ranbyai) which falls into the sea on the eastern shore of that island near the southern extremity.

HOON-MYOUK-BHET.—A revenue circle in the Kyouk-hpyoo district, in the southern portion of Ramree island, about 24 square miles in extent, in which rice, sugar-cane and indigo are cultivated. The population in 1876 numbered 2,668 souls, the land revenue was Rs. 2,770, the capitation-tax Rs. 2,920 and the gross revenue Rs. 5,885.

HOON-TOUNG-BHET.—A revenue circle in the Kyouk-hpyoo district in the south of Ramree island and on its western coast, with an area of some 29 square miles, in which sugar-cane is largely cultivated. It had, in 1876, an Arakanese population of 1,802 souls. In that year the land revenue was Rs. 2,327, the capitation-tax Rs. 1,950 and the gross revenue Rs. 4,413.

HOUNG-THA-RAW.—A river in the Amherst district which rises in Siamese territory east of the province and flows through the mountains which mark the boundary between the two countries. Crossing the frontier in 15° 41' 19" N. and 98° 35' E., where the demarcating line traverses a broad glen, it rushes with great velocity amongst a mass of mountains densely clothed with thick and heavy tree forest, here passing between high and scarped banks, there washing the feet of the spurs sent down by the dark walls which shut in its valley on the east and on the west, now silent and still, now white and foaming as it dashes over rocky steeps from one table-land to another. Gradually the hills recede, feathery bamboos waving over the reflecting waters are seen mixed with the dense forest; these gives place to elephant grass and at last near Gyaing, where it joins the Hlaing-bhwai from the north, patches of cultivation appear on the gradually sinking banks. It is navigable by boats for some distance beyond Meetan, 80 miles from Maulmain.

HOUNG-THA-RAW.—A township in the extreme south-eastern corner of the Amherst district, bounded on the east by Thoung-yeng and on the west by the Houng-tha-raw. Highly mountainous and densely wooded it produces much valuable timber but is sparsely inhabited, chiefly by Kareng, and contains but little cultivation and that principally in hill-gardens or toungya. It is divided into five revenue circles and in 1876 had a population of 11,625 souls and produced only Rs. 6,902 as land revenue and Rs. 9,576 as capitation-tax. One of the most important trade routes traverses the township. Siamese cattle-dealers annually bring in large numbers of beasts *via* Mya-waddee—an ancient town of some celebrity now a small village on the Thoung-yeng—to Kaw-ka-riet, the head-quarters of the township, where there is a cattle market, and thence to Gyaing and on through the Gyaing Than-lweng township towards Tha-htoon, Shwe-gyeng and Pegu.

HPA-AN.—A revenue circle in the Gyaing Than-lweng township, Amherst district, on the left bank of the Salween but lying south of the Hpa-an stream and inhabited mainly by Toungthoo. In 1876 it had a population of 2,746 souls, a land revenue of Rs. 2,245 and a gross revenue of Rs. 5,056, of which Rs. 2,810 were from the capitation-tax.

HPA-AN.—A village in the Amherst district on the left bank of the Salween at the mouth of the Hpa-an stream, which separates the Gyaing Than-lweng from the Than-lweng Hlaing-bhwai township, where is stationed a detachment of regular police. A bazaar has lately been built. The village is divided into two portions; in the north on the bank of the Hpa-an the inhabitants are principally Burmans and numbered 573 souls in 1876; to the south are Toungthoo gardeners who in the same year numbered 718. This village is on the main trade route with Siam and immediately below is a public ferry by which large numbers of Shan and home-bred cattle are annually taken to Tha-htoon and thence to Shwe-gyeng and Pegu and the Rangoon district generally.

HPA-AN.—A small tidal stream in the Amherst district which falls into the Salween at the village of the same name about 34 miles above Maulmain. It rises in the plain between the Salween and the Hlaing-bhwai near the source of the Kha-zaing, a tributary of the latter, the two intercommunicating during the rains. It is navigable only by canoes or small boats.

HPA-BYOUK.—A revenue circle in the Gyaing Attaran township, Amherst district, lying in the centre of the country between the Houng-tha-raw and the Attaran rivers on the east and west respectively, and the hilly country and the Gyaing on the north and south. It was inhabited in 1876 by 360 persons mostly Talaing, but contains hardly any cultivated spots. The land revenue that year was Rs. 188 and the capitation-tax Rs. 330.

HPA-GAT.—A village in the Amherst district, the head-quarters of the township of the same name, on the right bank of the Salween, 30 miles from Maulmain. Immediately to the north of the village is an outcrop of limestone rocks containing a large cave highly ornamented with images of all sizes of Gaudama Booddha and of Rahan. Most of these have been much damaged by the natives of India and others who resort to the cave to collect the bats' dung for manure.

HPA-GAT.—A township in the Amherst district occupying the country between the Salween on the east and the Doon-tha-mee and Bheng-laing on the west. It is divided into three revenue circles, Myaing-gyee, Myaing-gale and

Bheng-laing, the last in the south and the most cultivated. In the north the country is hilly and densely wooded and in the south it is undulating with low marshy tracts here and there. In the southern circle tobacco is extensively grown on the sand banks left dry after the waters of the Bheng-laing and Salween fall. The head-quarters are at Hpa-gat, a small village on the Salween 30 miles from Maulmain. In 1876 the inhabitants numbered 9,192 souls, the land revenue was Rs. 5,376 and the capitation-tax Rs. 8,114. This township together with Tha-htoon and Martaban were transferred from Martaban (now Shwe-gyeng) to Amherst in 1864-65.

HPA-GOO.—A large village in the Hpa-goo west circle, Rangoon district, on the left bank of the Pegu river in 16° 54′ N. and 96° 26′ E., inhabited by Talaing and Burmans who are mainly engaged in rice cultivation. In 1876 the inhabitants numbered 1,956 souls.

HPA-GOO ANOUK.—A revenue circle in the Than-lyeng township, Rangoon district, extending eastwards from the left bank of the Pegu river north of and adjoining the Poo-gan-doung circle. In 1876 the population was 4,830, the land revenue Rs. 26,050, the capitation-tax Rs. 5,648 and the gross revenue Rs. 31,698.

HPA-GOO ASHE.—A revenue circle in the Than-lyeng township, Rangoon district, at the mouth of the Tsit-toung river, lying on the north of the A-dwon creek. In 1876 the population was 3,020, the land revenue Rs. 20,464, the capitation-tax Rs. 3,743, and the gross revenue Rs. 30,907. Until 1874 Hpa-goo Ashe and Hpa-goo Anouk formed one circle.

HPAI-KHA-TA.—A revenue circle in the Gyaing Than-lweng township, Amherst district, on the left bank of the Salween river, extending for some distance northward from the Hpa-won stream. It has a large population of Talaing and is well cultivated. In 1876 the population was 2,253, the land revenue Rs. 3,110 and the capitation-tax Rs. 2,372.

HPAI-KHA-TA.—A small stream in the Amherst district which falls into the Salween river and helps to carry off from the Doon-reng plain the natural rainfall and the spill of the Salween which comes in at and above Hpa-an.

HPAI-KHA-TA.—A small village, of 551 inhabitants in 1876, in the circle of the same name in the Amherst district, lying on both banks of the Hpai-kha-ta at its mouth in the Salween.

HPA-LAT.—A village in the Martaban township, Amherst district, at the foot of the Koo-la-ma peak of the Martaban hills, a little north of Martaban. In 1876 it had 1,086 inhabitants.

HPA-TENG.—A village of 661 inhabitants in 1876 on the east bank of the Salween north of Htoon-aing, in the Htoon-aing circle of the Gyaing Than-lweng township, Amherst district.

HPAN-HPA.—A village with 818 inhabitants in 1876 on Bheeloo island, Amherst district. In 1868 it had 616 inhabitants.

HPAN-KHA-BENG.—A revenue circle in the Taroop-hmaw township, Henzada district, on the left bank of the Irrawaddy, south of Taroop-hmaw Myoma, containing but little cultivation. In the centre of the circle is a narrow stretch of water called the Hpan-kha-beng lake, valuable as a fishery. In 1876 the population numbered 7,049, the land revenue was Rs. 2,855, the capitation-tax Rs. 6,588 and the gross revenue Rs. 18,473.

HPA-NOON.—A revenue circle in the Gyaing Attaran township, Amherst district, on the lower slopes of the hills which cover the face of the southern part of the district, and lying between the Houng-tha-raw on the east and the Attaran on the west, immediately above the junction of the Zamee and the Weng-raw which form the latter river. It is inhabited by Kareng and contains but little cultivation. In 1876 the land revenue was Rs. 865, the capitation-tax Rs. 1,442 and the population 1,510.

HPA-OUK.—A revenue circle in the Zaya township, Amherst district, between the Toung-gnyo hills and the Salween below the town of Maulmain, lying between the Kaw-kha-nee and Kyouk-tan circles. It is divided into five distinct longitudinal belts of country : (a) the slopes of the range, unadapted for cultivation ; (b) the upland tract at the foot of the range, suitable for gardens ; (c) undulating ground, fitted for gardens and in some places for rice but with poor soil ; (d) the alluvial plain ; (e) swampy land, where the dhanee palm is grown. The population, composed mainly of Talaing, in 1868 numbered 2,144, and in 1876, 2,847 souls. The land revenue in these years was Rs. 7,360 and Rs. 8,018 and the capitation-tax Rs. 2,247 and Rs. 2,585 respectively.

HPA-OUK.—A village of 1,583 inhabitants in the circle of the same name, Zaya township, Amherst district.

HPARO-TSIEN.—A revenue circle in the Than-lweng Hlaing-bhwai township, Amherst district, on the left bank of the Thoung-yeng, stretching from its mouth south-eastwards. It is inhabited by a few Kareng, who in 1876 numbered 340 souls, and may be said to be without any cultivation. The land revenue in 1876 was Rs. 92 and the capitation-tax Rs. 126.

HPA-THIEN.—A revenue circle in the Gyaing Attaran township, Amherst district, on the Zamee a little above the junction of that river with the Weng-raw. It is a hilly and forest-covered tract, thinly cultivated and inhabited by Kareng. In 1876 the population numbered 1,319 souls, the land revenue was Rs. 860 and the capitation-tax Rs. 1,497.

HPA-THIEN.—A village in the circle of the same name in the Amherst district, with 743 inhabitants in 1876.

HPE-TRAI.—See Bhe-trai.

HPOUNG-GYEE.—A thinly inhabited revenue circle in the northern portion of the Hpoung-leng township of the Rangoon district, on the upper part of the course of the Poo-zwon-doung river. The country consists of numerous low laterite hills covered with bamboo and tree forest with a few patches of rice cultivation on the banks of the streams. The principal timber trees are Ka-gnyeng (Dipterocarpus alatus), Bhan-bhwai (Careya arborea), Htouk-sha (Vitex leucoxylon), Nabai (Odina Wodier) and Gyo (Schleichera trijuga.) In 1876 the population numbered 3,881 souls, the land revenue was Rs. 8,279, the capitation-tax Rs. 6,197 and the gross revenue Rs. 14,476.

HPOUNG-LENG.—The most northern township of the Rangoon district, now including A-kha-reng and Daw-boon and extending from the bank of the Pegu river northward along the valley of the Poo-zwon-doung into the hills which form the lower slopes of the Pegu Romas. It has an area of about 880 square miles and is divided into seven revenue circles. Towards the south the country is well cultivated with rice which is brought down the Poo-zwon-doung and Pegu rivers to Rangoon. In the north the hills are covered with dense forest amongst which teak, Pyeng-gado, Pyeng-ma, Eng, and other valuable timber are found. The most important and largest villages are in the rice plains to the south where the country is intersected by numerous creeks which fall into the Poo-zwon-doung and Pegu rivers and afford the inhabitants a ready means of conveying their crops to Rangoon. The township is also traversed by the road to Pegu, constructed and kept in repair by the Public Works Department. The Poo-zwon-doung is navigable by large boats as far as Bhoora-gyee and the Pegu river throughout its length in this township. In 1876 the population was 34,477, the land revenue Rs. 169,546, the capitation-tax Rs. 41,842 and the gross revenue Rs. 212,510. The head-quarters are at Hlay-goo on the Poo-zwon-doung river and the Rangoon and Pegu road 28 miles from Rangoon.

HPYOO.—A river in the Toung-ngoo district which rises in the eastern slopes of the Pegu Romas and after a south-easterly course of about seventy miles falls into the Tsit-toung 28 miles south of Toung-ngoo. The first 56 miles are through a narrow valley, almost a ravine, intersected by subsidiary spurs and with numerous mountain torrents bringing down the drainage. The last five or six miles before it enters the plains are blocked by rapids and in some places the water rushes through narrow channels dug out between high walls of rock that once opposed themselves to the torrent. The northern slopes of the hills amongst which the river winds are covered with dry open forest of Pyeng-gado (*Xylia dolabriformis*), Myouk-khyaw (*Homalium tomentosum*) and Teak (*Tectona grandis*), whilst the southern are seen covered with large heavy climbing bamboos, Theng-gan (*Hopea odorata*), Ka-gnyeng (*Dipterocarpus alatus*) and other species (as *D. turbinatus, &c.*), Oak (*Quercus Brandisiana*) and other "green forest" trees. During the rains boats can ascend for some 15 miles as far as Meng-lan village where the plain country ceases and the hills commence, and at this season a considerable quantity of timber and of raw silk (the worm is extensively bred by the inhabitants) are brought down to the Tsit-toung for conveyance to the local markets. According to Mason it derives its name from a colony of Pyoo having settled on its banks. *See Prome.*

HPYOUK-TSHIEP.—The southern portion of the large town of Shwe-doung in the Prome district seven miles below Prome on the left bank of the Irrawaddy at the mouth of the little Koo-la stream, forming a separate revenue circle. In 1876 the population numbered 8,356.

HPYOUK-TSHIEP-GOON.—A tiny village in the Meng-dai circle, Thayet township, Thayet district, about six miles south-west from Thayet-myo ; in the neighbourhood are two salt wells which were worked in the Burmese time and yielded a small quantity of brine.

HTAN-BENG-GYO.—A revenue circle in the Re-gyee township, Bassein district, on the left bank of the Bassein river which forms its northern boundary. It has an area of about eleven square miles and is fairly well populated and cultivated, the villages being more numerous than further south in the township. The inhabitants are engaged in agriculture and in fishing. In the west of the circle is the Myit-kyo lake, which was once a portion of the Bassein river and has been formed by the current cutting a channel through the narrow neck of a bend. There are good fair-weather cart roads throughout the circle. In 1876 the population numbered 1,315 souls, the land revenue was Rs. 3,505, the capitation-tax Rs. 4,220 and the gross revenue Rs. 8,636.

HTAN-BOUK.—A revenue circle in the Ma-ha-tha-man township of the Prome district just to the east of Prome and on the left bank of the Na-weng river, containing five village tracts. In 1876 the population numbered 1,784, the land revenue was Rs. 2,092, the capitation-tax Rs. 1,780 and the gross revenue Rs. 3,997.

HTAN-DAW-GYEE.—A revenue circle in the Pegu township of the Rangoon district, lying in the hilly country at the source of the Pegu river along which it extends south-south-east, and but very little cultivated. The principal trees are Teak (*Tectona grandis*), Pyeng-gado (*Xylia dolabriformis*), Pyeng-ma (*Lagerstroemia reginae*), Ka-gnyeng (*Dipterocarpus alatus*), the two last in abundance, and bamboos. Wild elephants, deer, tiger and hog are met with. It contains no large villages. In 1876 the population was 3,844, the land revenue Rs. 3,530 and the capitation-tax Rs. 4,248.

HTAN-GOUK.—A revenue circle in the Kama township, Thayet district, lying between the Made stream on the north and the boundary of the district on the south. It has an area of 25,600 acres of which 21,879 are unculturable waste and about 1,750 only cultivated. In 1872 the revenue was Rs. 3,240, about two-thirds of which were derived from the capitation-tax, and the population was found by the census to number 1,827 souls. This circle now contains Kyouk-mai and Pyen-doung, the first of which was added in 1862 when its Thoogyee resigned, and the second in 1864 when its Thoogyee was dismissed for harbouring dacoits. In 1876 the population numbered 1,387 souls, the land revenue was Rs. 1,497, the capitation-tax Rs. 1,708 and the gross revenue Rs. 3,301.

HTAN-LE-BENG.—A revenue circle in the Za-lwon township, Henzada district, with a large area under rice cultivation. In 1876 the population numbered 2,791 souls, the land revenue was Rs. 4,902, the capitation-tax Rs. 2,377 and the gross revenue Rs. 7,589.

HTAN-LE-BENG.—A revenue circle in the Thee-kweng township, Bassein district, enclosed between the Pan-ma-wad-dee and the Myoung-mya rivers on the east, west and south and joining the Thee-kweng circle of the same township on the north. It has an estimated area of 109 square miles. The country generally is low and much intersected by creeks none of which are of much importance: the Kyoon-toon, a tributary of the Myoung-mya which it joins near Kwe-le, is perhaps the most worthy of notice but it is navigable by boats 40 feet in length for ten miles only from its mouth. The largest village is Kan-gyee in 16° 44′ N. and 95° 5′ E. in the centre of a patch of rice cultivation, inhabited mainly by Burmese. In 1876 the population was 6,662, the land revenue Rs. 22,602, the capitation-tax Rs. 6,900 and the gross revenue Rs. 31,970.

HTAN-MA-NAING.—A tidal creek in the Laugoon district which has its source in the marshy ground in the centre of the Angyee township and falls into the Bassein or Tha-khwot-beng creek. It is fed by the tide and at all seasons during the flood boats of 400 baskets burden can ascend as far as the village of Htan-ma-naing, situated in a rice-producing tract : at the ebb it is almost dry.

HTAN-MA-NAING.—A village in the Rangoon district in 16° 32' N. and 96° 12' E. about four miles from the mouth of the Htan-ma-naing creek, which at the village is still a considerable stream. In 1859 it was the residence of the Extra Assistant Commissioner of the Angyee township and contained about 1,250 inhabitants, almost all Talaing, who in 1877 had decreased to 1,162. They are nearly all engaged in the manufacture of salt or in trade although the village is surrounded by fertile land well adapted for the cultivation of rice. This village is noted for its unhealthiness for all who are not natives of the place.

HTAN-MA-NAING.—A revenue circle in the Angyee township of the Rangoon district, bounded on the north by the A-hpa-roon stream which separates it from the Ko-doung circle ; on the south by the Tha-khwot-peng ; and on the south-east by the To. On the west it is separated from La-wa-dee, by the Taw-kha-ran and Taw-dwon streams, and from Kaw-hmoo by the Taw-koo stream. Its greatest length from north to south is about 14 miles, its greatest breadth about eight miles and the area 92 miles. In 1859 it had 4,286 inhabitants, and in 1876, 2,678. In the former year but little cultivation was carried on, the energies of the people being entirely thrown into the manufacture of salt, the pans occupying 1,580 acres of ground. Some parts of the circle are very fertile and in 1876 the land revenue had risen to Rs. 13,515, whilst the amount realized on account of the capitation-tax was Rs. 3,473 and the gross revenue Rs. 23,703.

HTAN-PA-DAING.—A revenue circle in the Gyaing Than-lweng township, Amherst district, which in 1876 had 4,178 inhabitants. In that year the land revenue was Rs. 4,250 and the capitation-tax Rs. 4,157. It now includes the Iendoo circle.

HTAN-TA-BENG.—A long straggling and poor village built in three rows of houses, in the circle of the same name in the Rangoon district on the right bank of the Hlaing river a few miles south of the Kook-ko, or southern mouth of the Bhaw-lay stream. Annually under water there are no roads, but here and there are patches of bricked footpaths and elsewhere logs of trees to keep the pedestrian's feet from getting wet. At high rises of the Hlaing this is not sufficient and the logs themselves are sometimes, as in 1877, one or two feet under water. At the lower end of the village there is a monastery, a zayat or public rest-house and a good well. In the centre of the village there is an old tank, the water green and muddy, and behind the village a larger one, dug a few years ago. Stretching away westward are rice fields but the soil is poor and they are liable to be submerged on any high rise of the river. The inhabitants, who are rice cultivators, fishermen and raftsmen, numbered 1,012 in 1877. In the first Burmese war a body of some 8,000 Burmese being strongly stockaded near this village a force under Colonel Godwin was sent to disperse it. The British were received by a brisk fire from 36 pieces of artillery of various calibres but the stockade was carried by storm with little difficulty or loss whilst the Burmese suffered severely.

HTAN-TA-BENG.—A revenue circle in the Hmaw-bhee township of the Rangoon district south of the junction of the Bhaw-lay creek and the Hlaing river. A part of the circle is under rice cultivation and the rest of the country is covered with tree and grass forest subject to inundation during the rains. The inhabitants of some of the villages are largely engaged in fishing. In 1876 the land revenue was Rs. 11,707, the capitation-tax Rs. 4,180 and the gross revenue Rs. 17,027. The only villages of any importance are Htan-ta-beng and Htien-nhit-peng. In 1876 there were 5,442 acres under rice and 714 acres fallow. The agricultural stock consisted of 1,111 buffaloes, 61 cows bulls and bullocks, 280 pigs, 131 carts, 338 ploughs and 54 boats. The population in 1877 was—

Burmans	..	..	..	1,760
Talaing	..	..	..	657
Kareng	..	..	..	1,491
Chinese	..	..	..	4
Natives of India	..	..	..	1
			Total ..	3,913

HTAN-THOON-BENG.—A large village in the Henzada district, nine or ten miles inland, west of Kanoung, in an extensive rice tract.

HTAN-THOON-BENG.—A revenue circle in the Myanoung township of the Henzada district south of the town of Hyanoung, very largely cultivated with rice. In 1876 it had 6,080 inhabitants, the land revenue was Rs. 12,735, the capitation-tax Rs. 5,565 and the gross revenue Rs. 18,968.

HTAN-THOON-KHWA.—A revenue circle in the Prome district well cultivated with rice, lying to the westward of Poungday and about a mile south of the high road to the north. Its largest village, Htan-thoon-khwa, is in the north. It now includes three village tracts. In 1876 it had 849 inhabitants, the land revenue was Rs. 884 and the capitation-tax Rs. 813.

HTAN-THOON-KHWA.—A village in the Prome district in 18° 28′ N. and 95° 32′ 10″ E. about two and a half miles west of Poungday and a mile south of the military road from Rangoon to the northern frontier. It is inhabited principally by rice growers.

HTAN-ZENG-HLA.—A revenue circle in the Re-gyee township, Bassein district, occupying a long narrow strip of country on the left bank of the Htan-zeng-hla from the Kyaik-pee to the Tshat-poo on the north. Its area is about 27 square miles. The country is, generally, flat and open, but on the north there is a ridge of elevated land. This circle is fairly well cultivated but the inhabitants are largely employed in fishing. In 1876 it had 2,856 inhabitants, the land revenue was Rs. 5,528, the capitation-tax Rs. 2,950 and the gross revenue Rs. 14,342.

HTAW-KA-NO.—A village in the Shwe-loung township, Thoon-khwa district, about 13 miles W. S. W. from Shwe-loung, as the crow flies. It has a population of about 600 souls.

HTEE-LOON.—A revenue circle in the Than-lweng Hlaing-bhwai township, Amherst district, with a small population of Toungthoo engaged in agriculture. In 1876 the inhabitants numbered 1,197, the land revenue was Rs. 1,628 and the capitation-tax Rs. 1,355.

HTEE-LOON.—A village in the circle of the same name in the Amherst district on the road between, and about equidistant from, Hpa-an and Hlaing-bhwai inhabited by Toung-thoo. The low forest-covered hills south of this village were up to 1870 the resort of gangs of robbers who harried the inhabitants far and wide.

HTEE-TSHWAI.—A revenue circle in the Ra-thai-doung township, Akyab district. In 1876 the land revenue was Rs. 4,801, the capitation-tax Rs. 3,537, the gross revenue Rs. 8,698 and the number of inhabitants 3,294.

HTIEN-DAW.—A large village of some 2,000 inhabitants in the Henzada district in 17° 51′ 40″ N. and 95° 34′ E. on a backwater of the Irrawaddy and about two miles east of the main channel. The inhabitants are principally traders and cultivators of miscellaneous products. It contains a Police station.

HTIEN-DAW.—A revenue circle in the Henzada district on the east bank of the Irrawaddy and south of Mo-gnyo; the centre is under rice cultivation. In 1876 the land revenue was Rs. 5,642, the capitation-tax Rs. 6,715, the gross revenue Rs. 14,258 and the population 8,191.

HTIEN-HNIT-PENG.—A village in the Htan-ta-beng circle of the Hmaw-bhee township, Rangoon district, which in 1876 had 681 inhabitants.

HTIEN-POUK-GYO-GOON.—A village in the Prome district in 31° 10′ N. and 95° 28′ 40″ E. in the Engma township, to the east of the Myit-ma-kha river and inhabited mainly by agriculturists.

HTOO.—A small stream in the Henzada district which has its source in the Pegu mountains and after a south-westerly course of about 35 miles falls into the Myit-ma-kha near Bhoora-ngoo, having received numerous additions in its course from mountain torrents and streams of the same character as its own. In the rains small boats can ascend for a considerable distance. The higher part of its course is rocky and the banks are steep. It traverses a valuable teak tract in which other important forest trees are found, as Pyeng-gado (*Xylia dolabriformis*), Eng (*Dipterocarpus tuberculatus*) and Htouk-kyan (*Terminalia macrocarpa*) which are floated down during the rains.

HTOO.—A lake in the Henzada district, a little north of the 18th parallel of latitude and, in a direct line, about ten miles west of the Irrawaddy. It is bounded on the north and west by low hills and trickling down from these numerous small springs keep up the supply of water which is augmented during the rains by the Ma-mya stream with the drainage from the Arakan hills. The banks are low and marshy and shew that at one time this lake was much larger than it is now. The average depth in the dry weather is not more than three or four feet and at this season the water is clear. In the centre of the lake is a small island.

HTOON-AING.—A village on the left bank of the Salween river opposite the mouth of the Bheng-laing with 1,174 inhabitants in 1876. In 1827 a large body of Talaing emigrants from Pegu settled here and in the surrounding country which is now well cultivated.

HTOON-AING.—A revenue circle in the Gyaing Than-lweng township, Amherst district, on the left bank of the Salween river opposite the mouth of the Bheng-laing ; it is well cultivated and inhabited mainly by Talaing of whom some 6,000 settled hereabouts in 1827 under the "Syriam Raja," who had escaped from Pegu after attempting to drive out the Burmese and re-establish the Peguan kingdom. In 1876 it had 3,806 inhabitants, the land revenue was Rs. 4,919 and the capitation-tax Rs. 3,940. It now includes the Kawgaik and the Kaw-hlaik circles.

HTOON-BHO.—A large village in the Padoung township, Prome district, also called Toung-ngoo, in 18° 30′ 15″ N. and 95° 10′ 15″ E. on the right bank of the Irrawaddy at the mouth of the Kha-wa stream a mile and a half above the southern boundary of the district. It has acquired the name of Htoon-bho from the fact that limestone is brought hither from the Kyouk-htoon hill some six miles off and burned on the banks of the river. The inhabitants are cultivators, lime burners and petty merchants who carry on trade with the inland villages.

HTOON-BHO.—A revenue circle in the south of the Padoung township of the Prome district lying on the bank of the Irrawaddy between the Kha-wa stream on the east and the Henzada district on the west. A little rice cultivation is carried on near the river. Htoon-bho at the mouth of the Kha-wa is the largest village. In 1876 the population numbered 4,185, the land revenue was Rs. 3,611, the capitation-tax Rs. 4,705 and the gross revenue Rs. 8,992. It now includes the Tha-bye-hla and the Kweng-hla circles.

HTOON-BHO.—A small hamlet in the centre of the Kya-gan circle, Myoung-mya township, Bassein district; the few inhabitants are employed in burning the lime quarried in the neighbourhood.

HTOON-MAN.—A revenue circle in the Zaya township, Amherst district, which extends westwards from the Toung-gnyo range towards the Salween, from which it is cut off by a portion of the Kwon-hla circle. It has the Wa-kha-roo river and the Kwon-hla circle on the south and the Ka-law-thaw circle on the north, and contains a total area of about 14,000 acres most of which is fertile plain land. It was originally called the Kwon-ka-moo circle (*pronounced Kwan-ka-moo*). Htoon-man was separated from Kwon-ka-moo as a police measure but the Thoogyee having been relieved of police duties the two circles were again united as Htoon-man where the Kwon-ka-moo Thoogyee died. In 1868 the population, all Talaing, numbered 754 souls, the land revenue was Rs. 5,107 and the capitation-tax Rs. 777. In 1876 these were 1,043, Rs. 8,315 and Rs. 1,077 respectively.

HTOON-TA-LOOT.—A revenue circle, now including A-byeng, in the south-east of that portion of the Za-lwon township lying on the right bank of the Irrawaddy. In 1876 the land revenue was Rs. 7,946, the capitation-tax Rs. 3,742, the gross revenue Rs. 15,161 and the population 4,458.

HTOUK-MA.—A revenue circle in the Kama township, Thayet district, on the bank of the Irrawaddy, shut in on the north and west by the Kyouk-poon hill and on the south by the Toung-mouk-theng-gan spur, the boundary of the district. In 1872 it furnished as revenue Rs. 1,880 from a population of 1,225 souls. Its largest village is Tsit-ta-ran on the bank of the Irrawaddy containing some 120 houses. It now includes the Tsit-ta-ran circle which was united with it in 1868. Subsequently Mya-wad-dee, Myoma and Toung-tsa-gaing were joined to it. In 1876 the population numbered 3,812 souls, the land revenue was Rs. 2,245, the capitation-tax Rs. 4,057 and the gross revenue Rs. 6,889.

IEM-MAI.—A revenue circle in the Bassein district, adjoining the Thoon-khwa district. In 1876, the population was Rs. 4,222, the land revenue Rs. 8,276, the capitation-tax Rs. 5,290 and the gross revenue Rs. 13,982.

IEM-MAI.—A large village in the extreme north of the circle of the same name and of the Bassein district, at the junction of the Meng-ma-hnaing and the Iem-mai Re-gyaw. In 1877 it had a population of 1,230 souls.

IEM-MAI RE-GYAW.—A creek, partly in the Bassein and partly in the Thoon-khwa district, joining the Meng-ma-hnaing and the Keng-bhet streams. Boats of 50 or 60 feet in length can pass through with the flood tide in the dry weather and in the rains at all times.

IEN-DA-POO-RA.—A revenue circle on the western borders of the Angyee township of the Rangoon district. It is separated from the La-wa-dee circle on the north by the Kyoon-ka-lway creek, on the west it is bounded by the To, on the north by the Kha-doon creek which divides it from the Twan-te circle and on the east by an imaginary line drawn through the Twan-te Taw-gyee : the area comprised within these limits is 73 square miles. The greater portion consists of high undulating ground. In 1876 the population numbered 5,741 souls, the land revenue was Rs. 14,782, the capitation-tax Rs. 6,683 and the gross revenue Rs. 21,775.

IRRAWADDY.—The principal river in the province ; traversing the Pegu division from north to south. Its sources have never been explored. d'Anville, in the middle of the eighteenth century, considered it as identical with the Tsanpoo which flows through Thibet from west to east, and in Dalrymple's map which accompanies Symes' " Embassy to Ava" the Tsanpoo is shewn as one of its sources, but the junction of the two is indicated by a dotted line to mark that the connection between them is uncertain . In 1825 Klaproth adopted another idea, viz., that the Irrawaddy was a continuation of the Pinlaing-kiang which, after flowing through Western Yunan, entered the valley of the Irrawaddy at Ba-mhaw. Even as late as 1854 Dr. McClelland, in a note on the discharge of water by this river, wrote that "making all allowance for the extravagance of Burmese historians there is enough "in the authenticated history of the country to shew that great armies have "passed and repassed to and from China. Besides which the Chinese "characters of the boats and houses of Burma, together with some of the "ceremonies of the people, suggest a more immediate and direct intercourse "with China on the part of the Burmese than any other nation on the "western side of the Himalayas, so much so that I have often heard it "surmised by our officers at Prome, as one way of accounting for the "resemblances, that the Irrawaddy probably flows from China, not that "it was supposed to be navigable to that extent, but that its valleys may "afford comparatively easy passes between the two countries." After noticing the discoveries of Lieutenant Wilcox and that geographer's opinion that the source of the Irrawaddy is in the Khamtee country, three hundred and sixty miles above Ava, he adds " there can scarcely be a doubt that it "must necessarily have a more extended course, more especially as it has been "traced two hundred miles above Ava without observing any perceptible "difference or diminution of size." In 1827, Lieutenants Wilcox and Burlton made a determined attempt to reach the sources of the Irrawaddy and they satisfactorily proved that the Tsanpoo was the upper portion of the Dihong and was not connected with the Irrawaddy at all. The result of the explorations of these officers and of others has been to shew, as conclusively as can be shewn until the river is traced to its source, that it rises in the southern slopes of the Patkoi mountains, one branch in 28° N. Lat. and 97° 30' E. Long. and another in the same mountains a few days' journey further eastward, the two, that to the west called by the Burmese Myit-gyee or "Large river" and that to the east Myit-nge or " Small river", uniting to form the Irrawaddy in about 26° N. Lat.* Drs. Griffith and Bayfield and Captain Hannay shewed that Klaproth's idea was erroneous, for they personally visited Ba-mhaw and found that the Ta-peng, the stream which enters the Irrawaddy at that town, was navigable only for small boats and was but an insignificant tributary of the great river which flows here, 250 miles above Ava, in a broad stream intersected by islands (one channel alone between Ba-mhaw and the island lying opposite to it being 800 yards across) and navigable for steamers of light draught. If anything further was necessary it was furnished by the party under Major Sladen which visited Yunan in 1868 and followed the Ta-peng through a great portion of its course.

Dr. Griffith found that the Irrawaddy where it receives the waters of the Mogoung stream above the first defile was about 600 yards broad. If Lieutenant Wilcox is right this point is 200 miles from the source and the area of country drained by the river here about five and a half square degrees ; at Ava 13½ square degrees ; at Prome 81 square degrees ; and at the head of the delta 32½ square degrees.

The principal affluents are the Mogoung from the westward, which throws its waters into the main stream in 24° 50', the Shwe-lee which joins it from the east in 23° 40', and the Kyeng-dweng which unites with it from the west in 21° 30'.

The general course of the river is north and south. Shortly after leaving the mouth of the Mogoung where, as has already been stated, it is 600 yards broad, it enters the first or upper defile. " Here the greatest " breadth of the river does not exceed 250 yards and in all the bad places is " contracted to within 100 and even 50. In the places above referred to the " river rushes by with great velocity, while the return waters, caused on " either side by the surrounding rocks, occasion violent eddies and whirlpools " so as to render " a " boat unmanageable and if upset the best swimmer could not live in these places." When the river is at its lowest no bottom is found in many places even at 40 fathoms.

At Ba-mhaw, a short distance below the defile, it receives the waters of the Ta-peng from the east and then, after a long bend to the westward, turns south again and enters the second defile. This though not so grand as the first is exceedingly picturesque ; the stream, greatly contracted, winding in deathlike stillness under high bare rocks rising sheer out of the water. Still lower down, and not far from Mandalay, is the third or lowest defile. In this there are none of the dangers of the first and none of the rugged beauty of the

---

* Wilcox himself placed the junction in about 25° but Captain Hannay fixed it, and probably more correctly, in 26°.

second, but the banks are covered with dense vegetation sloping down to the stream and with occasional almost perpendicular but wooded heights, afford a pleasing picture, its softness contrasting with the grand and striking scenery of the first and second defiles. Except when the river is at its highest and the current consequently rapid and strong the navigation of the two lower defiles is easy and safe for all but very long steamers. " Below " this third defile the valley of Ava may be said to commence. It lies "entirely on the east side of the Irrawaddy, the range of hills which " terminates at Sagain opposite Ava hemming the river closely in on the " west. At the lower end of the valley comes in the fine stream of the Myit- " nge. Just above this the great river contracts from a mile and more in " width to about 800 yards, in passing between the rocky roots of the Sagain " hills, and an isolated temple-crowned eminence on the left bank."* At a very short distance below Tsa-gaing the river takes a sharp turn to the westward and, after flowing in this direction for about 40 miles, to Tseng-dat, it gradually comes round to the south again, receiving the waters of the Kyeng-dweng from the westward near the southern extremity of the sweep. From this point its course is due south for a considerable distance when, deflecting, it runs about south-west to Tsa-lay-myo. From this point its course is, roughly, east-south-east to the British frontier which it crosses in 19° 29′ 3″ N. and 95° 15′ E., having then a breadth of three quarters of a mile. Continuing east-south-east it rapidly widens and opposite Thayetmyo, about eleven miles lower down, is nearly three miles broad. Below this it contracts and flowing between bold and densely wooded banks it passes Prome 48 miles further south and takes a great bend round to the west and then east-south-east again, the hills receding on both banks and the stream broadening considerably till, at Akouk-toung, a few miles above Myan-oung, a spur of the Arakan hills juts down to the river and ends abruptly in a precipice some three hundred feet high. Here the river enters the delta the hills finally receding and giving place to low alluvial plains formerly inundated for miles on both banks every year on the rise of the river but now protected on the west by extensive embankments. In about 17° 19′ N. it takes another and sharper bend to the west, almost immediately returning to its former course and as it does so throwing off to the westward its first branch, the Bassein river. Gradually trending round westward, it a little north of 17° sends off a branch eastward, the Panhlaing creek, which joins the Hlaing just above Rangoon, the two forming the Rangoon river. In 17° the Pan-ta-naw leaves it to the west, and from this point the main river runs due south till, a few miles further on, it throws off a stream, which eventually reaches the sea as the To or China Bakir, and inclining westward breaks into numerous creeks. From 17° N. it divides and sub-divides, recommunicating on each side with the streams which have already left it, and converts the whole of the lower portion of its valley into a network of anastomosing tidal creeks till it reaches the sea by nine principal mouths including on the west the Bassein river and its eastern entrance the Thek-ngay-thoung and on the east the Rangoon, the others and intervening ones being, from east to west, the To or China Bakir, the Pya-poon, the Kyoon-toon, the Irrawaddy, the Pya-ma-law and its western branch the Pyeng-tha-loo, and the Rwe, all of which, as already stated,

---

* Yule's " Mission to Ava."

intercommunicate by numerous channels. The eastern and western are the only ones used by seagoing ships, but a portion of the To or China Bakir is used by river steamers and large boats going from Rangoon to the Irrawaddy during the dry season when the route used during the rains, *via* the Pan-hlaing or *via* the Kook-ko, is closed for want of water, and others are traversed in places by boats and river steamers passing inland between Rangoon and Bassein. This maritime delta, the protuberance of which has been caused by the deposition of the immense quantity of silt brought down by the river and which in this manner is still encroaching on the sea, is, especially in its lower part, cut up into an infinity of islands by a vast labyrinth of tidal creeks and channels. Within the full tidal influence these are lined with mangrove thicket and forest of Htien and other brackish-water loving trees, or a fringe of gigantic grasses, and for a considerable distance inland bear the peculiar and unmistakeable appearance of all tidal creeks : the banks steep for a few feet from the top, then shelving and muddy, the top either bare or covered with grass or tall black-stemmed trees with no undergrowth, or with low shrubs, the lower branches bearing, in their mud-covered leaves, evidence of the rise and fall of the tide. Scattered along the channels and sheets of water in the extreme south, are, during the dry season, temporary villages occupied by salt boilers and makers of nga-pee or fish paste. A little more inland, patches of cultivation appear gradually passing into extensive tracts.

The total length of the Irrawaddy from its sources to the sea is about 900 miles, the last 240 of which are in British territory, and considering its few windings its development in this latter distance may be about 50 miles. As far down as Akouk-toung in the Henzada district its bed is rocky but below this sandy and muddy. It is full of islands and sandbanks, many of the former and all the latter submerged during the rains. New sandbanks are continually forming and old ones being removed, and the deep channel changes in many places every season and in some places even oftener but the course of the river, flowing as it does everywhere except in the delta between high banks, alters inappreciably. Its waters are extremely muddy and the mud is carried far out to sea. It commences to rise in March, some months before the rains set in, but whether owing to the melting of the snows in the mountains in which it takes its rise or to heavy rains at that season in the extreme northern portion of the country which it drains, or to both causes, is not yet known. Certain it is that as high as Ba-mhaw it rises before any rain has fallen there. It rises and falls several times till about June and then rising pretty steadily it attains its maximum height about September at which time it is, at Prome, from 33 to 34 feet above its dry season level, and at this period, below the latitude of Myan-oung inundates a vast tract of country on the east and unprotected bank. Several and differing calculations have been made of its discharge : those by Lieutenant Heathcote from data obtained near Tsa-gaing in October gave 316,580 cubic feet per second ; those by Dr. McClelland from data obtained at Prome in April 1853 when the river was about five inches above its lowest gave 105,794 per second ; Mr. Login calculated it at 75,000 cubic feet per second at the head of the delta ; whilst from careful observations and calculations made at Myan-oung by Mr. Gordon the flood maximum discharge in August 1872 was 1,442,007 feet and the mean velocity 6,451 feet.

The following table gives the result, in metre-tons, of 37 cubic feet, of Mr. Gordon's observations :—

Discharge of the Irrawaddy River at Myan-oung in metre-tons.

Years.	January.	February.	March.	April.	May.	June.	July.
1869	....	....	....	....	....	34,765,499,860	76,105,405,900
1870	*7,784,560,960	5,352,928,040	4,723,168,500	5,708,339,980	7,489,872,280	23,889,172,240	83,128,778,160
1871	7,931,747,860	5,248,863,960	6,768,772,420	9,339,342,640	11,555,532,840	44,536,287,840	88,977,030,860
1872	9,852,990,780	6,798,773,620	6,212,467,160	6,517,161,600	14,014,777,860	21,036,761,600	85,529,495,380
1873	9,640,860,600	6,663,855,280	6,466,004,340	6,594,821,880	8,663,618,900	37,160,697,280	68,222,287,000
1874	6,706,940,840	4,812,304,380	6,491,819,550	10,672,768,480	18,234,967,180	23,806,045,980	73,196,606,040
1875	7,819,046,720	5,538,467,980	6,087,990,460	10,983,351,300	21,047,452,920	45,354,289,660	94,027,283,760
1876	6,662,423,840	4,665,610,940	6,171,721,380	9,003,367,300	10,555,613,960	27,887,805,580	88,970,275,980
1877	5,978,016,080	4,463,610,440	4,166,609,100	8,055,460,540	7,140,188,860	31,489,887,520	66,882,182,700
Total	54,591,926,720	48,544,404,640	47,088,552,920	66,869,613,720	99,301,524,860	289,927,287,560	725,030,345,780
Average	7,784,560,960	5,449,050,580	5,886,069,115	8,358,701,715	12,412,690,607	32,214,148,062	80,558,927,309

* The discharge for January 1870 is assumed to be the same as the average of the other years, and has been interpolated.

Discharge of the Irrawaddy River at Myan-oung in metre-tons.—(Concluded).

Years.	August.	September.	October.	November.	December.	Total Discharge for each year.
1869 ..	83,129,560,800	71,926,954,600	67,585,097,800	14,548,196,480	....	348,060,715,440
1870 ..	93,661,181,220	87,377,500,500	53,624,269,540	19,922,747,040	12,639,276,440	405,495,994,900
1871 ..	102,173,847,920	94,451,981,760	58,366,151,900	36,701,425,700	15,588,073,600	481,639,049,300
1872 ..	94,557,343,680	77,758,373,400	81,917,359,980	32,915,434,980	14,445,287,360	451,556,227,400
1873 ..	85,100,009,680	63,013,555,700	52,263,959,240	26,986,522,480	10,812,722,460	381,658,894,900
1874 ..	66,859,213,000	75,221,939,260	64,483,588,320	20,662,689,780	11,787,789,580	388,937,467,400
1875 ..	109,506,569,980	84,249,129,570	49,989,140,050	19,734,842,580	10,575,437,040	465,442,502,020
1876 ..	98,754,468,200	53,141,862,860	46,041,450,880	19,536,670,080	10,277,036,180	381,667,297,180
1877 ..	122,604,179,620	86,515,369,560	84,336,110,520	30,300,861,080	14,187,872,920	466,120,288,940
Total ..	866,346,364,100	693,656,867,210	558,557,123,280	227,307,890,200	100,513,495,589	3,770,508,437,480
Average ..	95,149,596,011	77,072,929,690	62,061,902,581	25,256,432,244	12,564,186,947	418,945,881,942

The greatest discharge took place on the 20th August 1877, when 4,900,985,480 metre tons passed down in one day ; or at the rate of 2,040,123 cubic feet per second. In the flood of 1875 the greatest discharge was on the 17th August and was 4,608,024,970 tons, on the 7th August 1871 : the discharge reached 4,091,620,500 tons. The lowest measured discharge was on the 3rd March 1878 and was 103,183,000 tons or 78,966 cubic feet per second ; while the smallest discharge ascertained from computation occurred on the 5th March 1877, when it was 112,892,940 tons in one day, or 46,146 cubic feet per second.

The river is navigable at all seasons by steamers of light draught as high as, and probably beyond, Ba-mhaw, and during the dry season for steamers drawing six feet as far at least as the frontier. In the rains steamers and large boats enter the main river from Rangoon by the Pan-hlaing or the Bhaw-lay creeks, but during the dry season they have to descend the Rangoon river for some distance and, passing through the Bassein creek (not to be confounded with the Bassein river), enter the Irrawaddy through the To or China Bakir. At this season the entrance of the Bassein river from the Irrawaddy is entirely closed by a large sandbank but in the rains steamers can pass up and down by this channel. The tide is felt as far up as Henzada and at Poo-zwon-doung it rises 18½ feet at springs.

Its principal affluents in British territory are the Ma-htoon (or Meng-doon), the Ma-de and the Tha-lai-dan from the west, and the Kye-nee, the Bhwot-lay and the Na-weng from the east. Below Akouk-toung on the west and Prome on the east it has no tributaries of any importance.

KA-BAING.—A revenue circle in the Henzada township, Henzada district, on the left bank of the Nga-won river. The land revenue in 1876 was Rs. 4,055, the capitation-tax Rs. 4,647, the gross revenue Rs. 9,462, and the population 5,340 souls.

KA-BENG.—A revenue circle in the Mergui district north of the northern mouth of the Tenasserim river. In 1876 the land revenue was Rs. 5,258, the capitation-tax Rs. 2,011 and the population 3,277.

KA-DAING-TEE.—A revenue circle on the Rwon-za-leng river below Pa-pwon in the Salween Hill Tracts. In 1876 it had a population of 5,576 souls and produced as land revenue—principally from hill gardens—Rs. 2,490 and as capitation-tax Rs. 2,211.

KA-DAN-GYEE.—A tidal creek in the Myoung-mya township, Bassein district, joining the Rwe and Pya-ma-law rivers, its western entrance being about four miles below La-bwot-ta. It is navigable by river steamers.

KA-DAT.—A stream which has its source in the hills north of Kyaik-hto and flowing through that town, where it is spanned by a wooden bridge, it enters the plains and during the rains unites with the numerous creeks then intersecting that part of the country, which is to a great extent under water at that season. It falls into the Tsit-toung near its mouth and is navigable for large boats as far as Kyaik-hto during the monsoon.

KA-DA-WA.—A revenue circle in the Mro-houng township, Akyab district, to which is now joined Loo-leng-byo. The population of the united circles in 1876 was 1,672, the land revenue Rs. 5,561, the capitation-tax Rs. 1,993 and the gross revenue Rs. 7,832.

KA-DO.—A small creek in the Amherst district which at both ends communicates with the Salween north of Maulmain. Its southern mouth like that of all similar streams affected by the tide is large and forms the Ka-do timber station, where the Forest Office is located and where all timber coming down the Salween, the Gyaing and the Attaran is collected and registered. A sand bar stretches across the southern entrance impassable except at flood tides.

KA-DO.—A revenue circle in the Gyaing Than-lweng township, Amherst district, opposite Maulmain at the junction of the Gyaing, the Attaran and the

Salween. It has a large population of Talaing, and is pretty well cultivated. In 1876 the land revenue was Rs. 4,372, the capitation-tax Rs. 3,692 and the population 3,672. It now includes Kaw-hla.

KA-DO.—A village on the bank of the Gyaing at the mouth of the creek of the same name and close to the junction of the Gyaing and the Salween. It is well laid out with brick-laid streets shaded by trees. The inhabitants are principally timber traders and their followers. It is the Government timber station at which all logs brought down the Salween are collected and taken by the owners after payment of duty. The whole of the village lies within the jurisdiction of the Judge and of the Magistrate of Maulmain. The number of inhabitants in 1877 was 2,232.

KA-DWAI.—A sparsely cultivated, hilly revenue circle in the southeastern township, Tavoy district, to which is now joined its southern neighbour Pa-aw. The united circles occupy the extreme southern portion of the district on the coast and adjoin Mergui. In 1876 the population numbered 1,561, the land revenue was Rs. 473, the capitation-tax Rs. 614 and the gross revenue Rs. 1,118. The principal products are sessamum and cardamoms.

KA-GNYENG.—A river in the Bassein district, which rises in the Arakan Romas and after a south-easterly course of some twelve miles falls into the Bassein river about two and a half miles above the mouth of the Shwe-gnyoungbeng. The breadth at the mouth is about 100 feet and the depth about 12. The bed is sandy and muddy. Large boats can ascend for a little over a mile only. The banks are covered with fine and valuable timber, Ka-gnyeng (*Dipterocarpus alatus*), Pyengma (*Lagerstrœmia Reginæ*), Pyeng-gado (*Xylia Dolabriformis*), Rengdaik (*Dalbergia cultrata*) and Shaw (*Sterculia sp*).

KA-GNYENG-DAING.—A revenue circle in the Le-myet-hna township, Bassein district, on the eastern slopes of the Arakan Romas. The country is mountainous, except towards the east where the ground is level and the soil suitable for rice. Pyengma (*Lagerstrœmia Reginæ*), Pyeng-ga-do (*Xylia Dolabriformis*), Reng-daik (*Dalbergia cultrata*) and Ka-gnyeng (*Dipterocarpus alatus*) are abundant, and a little teak is found on the banks of the Mai-za-lee river. The inhabitants in 1876 numbered 3,238, and in that year the land revenue was Rs. 3,330, the capitation-tax Rs. 3,530 and the gross revenue Rs. 7,027.

KA-GNYENG-GOON.—A village in the Zhe-pa-thway circle, Angyee township, Rangoon district, about a mile from the seacoast, a few miles east of the mouth of the To river, at the head of the Meng-ga-loon, a small tributary of the former. The inhabitants, who are chiefly Burman and Talaing agriculturists, numbered 1,121 in 1877. In the Burman time the population was very small; the village has increased principally owing to an influx of the inhabitants of To at the mouth of the river of the same name. The culturable land in the neighbourhood is extensive and fertile. Near the village is the old ruined pagoda of Meng-galoon, known as the Kyouk-tshoo Bhoora. It is built upon the spot where the vessel carrying the holy relic, now enshrined under the Shwe-tshan-daw at Twan-te, first cast anchor, hence the name ('Kyouk-tshoo,' an anchor). It is, therefore, one of the most famous of the 37 Pagodas of Angyee.

KA-GNYENG-KWA.—A small village of 503 inhabitants in 1877 in the Bhoot-khyoung circle, Re-gyee township, on the western bank of the Re-nouk, towards the north-east of the Bassein district.

KA-GNYOON-KYWON.—An island forming a revenue circle in the south-eastern township of the Tavoy district, thinly populated but very largely culti-vated. Its principal products are rice, dhanee leaves and dhanee sugar. The fishery and net tax is large. In 1876 the land revenue was Rs. 5,934, the capitation-tax Rs. 292, the gross revenue Rs. 7,150, and the population 421.

KA-HGNYAW.—A revenue circle in the north-east corner of Bhee-loo-gywon in the Amherst district, having the Salween river on the north and east, the circle of Ka-lwee on the west and that of Thek-kaw on the south. Its total area is 4,766 acres, all plain land, and almost all under cultivation. Its eastern portion consists of some extensive islands in the Salween, immediately opposite to Maulmain, the soil of which is well adapted both for gardens and for rice cultivation. It comprises the two old circles of Kahgnyaw and Douk-yat, which were united in 1865. A small area is to some extent damaged by the overflow from hot salt springs at a spot known as the Nga-raikywon or "Hell Island." There is a large and constant flow of very hot saline water and the whole of the land near them is more or less impregnated with salt. The crystalized produce has a distinct bitter taste. The "garden" cultivation consists principally of the dhanee and cocoanut palms. In 1860 the land revenue was Rs. 8,663, the capitation-tax Rs. 1,547 and the gross revenue Rs. 10,220. In 1876 the land revenue was Rs. 10,057, the capita-tion-tax Rs. 1,827 and the population 1,757.

KA-HGNYAW.—A village in the circle of the same name on the west of Bhee-loo-gywon in the Amherst district near the Ka-gnyoung stream. The inhabitants are principally Talaing and in 1867 numbered 928 souls and 966 in 1877.

KAI.—A sub-tribe of the Pwo division of Kareng so called by the Bghai. *See Gaikho.*

KAI-LENG.—A revenue circle in the south-eastern corner of the Tha-ga-ra township, Toung-ngoo district, on the right bank of the Tsit-toung river. In this circle is the Pouk-aing lake nine feet deep during the rains and five only in the dry season. In 1876 the population numbered 2,683, the land revenue was Rs. 1,003, the capitation-tax Rs. 2,006 and the gross revenue Rs. 3,300.

KAING-GYEE.—A village in the Padoung township, Prome district, on the bank of the Bhoo-ro stream, just above its mouth. The inhabitants are chiefly rice cultivators, gardeners and coolies.

KAING-KHYOUNG.—A revenue circle in the Kyouk-hpyoo district, or the north-eastern coast of Ramree island, north of and adjoining the Ramree township, having an area of 11 square miles which are not much cultivated. The inhabitants, who are mainly Arakanese, numbered 1,994 in 1876 and are extensively engaged in fishing and in manufacturing salt. The land revenue in 1876 was Rs. 1,116, the capitation-tax Rs. 2,237 and the gross revenue Rs. 5,074.

KA-KA-RAN.—A tidal creek in the lower portion of the Shwe-loung town-ship, Thoon-khwa district, connecting the Irrawaddy with the Pya-ma-law.

having a general N. N. E. and S. S. W. direction : its northern entrance is about eight miles below Kywon-pya-that village. It is navigable at all times by the largest boats.

KA-LA-BE.—A revenue circle on Bhee-loo-gywon in the Amherst district, which extends from the Salween westwards across the central range of hills to the Tsai-ba-la khyoung. It has Kharaik-thit on the north and Kwon-taw and Ka-ma-ke on the south. In the Burmese time Ka-la-be comprised only that portion of the present circle which lies between the Salween and the hills; the other portion, to the west of the hills, was called Pan-hpa and was under a Kareng Tsaw-kai. When Captain Phayre (then Deputy Commissioner) visited the locality he found that the Talaing Thoogyee of Ka-la-be collected tax from the Talaing both in Ka-la-be and in Pan-hpa and the Kareng Tsaw-kai in the same way had charge of the Kareng in both circles. He made arrangements for the amalgamation of the two circles which were shortly afterwards carried out. The united circles comprise an area of 4,674 acres, of which almost the whole is under cultivation. In 1868 the population numbered 2,091 souls (congregated principally in the villages of Ka-la-be Moo-rit-gale, Rwa-thit, Pan-hpa and Kaw-ka-dai), the land revenue was Rs. 7,016, the capitation-tax Rs. 2,585 and the gross revenue Rs. 9,627. In 1876 there were 2,890 inhabitants, the land revenue was Rs. 7,136 and the capitation-tax Rs. 3,057.

KA-LAING-OUNG.—A revenue circle in the north-eastern township, Tavoy district, with a small population of 719 souls in 1876. The face of the country is mountainous and forest-clad and but little cultivation is carried on. In 1876 the land revenue was Rs. 257, the capitation-tax Rs. 321 and the gross revenue Rs. 590.

KA-LAI-TO.—A village in the Kha-raik-thit circle of the Bhee-loo-gywon township, Amherst district, south of Khyoung-tshoon and west of Kha-raik-thit. The population in 1867 numbered 576 souls and 854 in 1877.

KA-LAW.—A village in the Rwa-lwot circle of the Bhee-loo-gywon township of the Amherst district, on the south bank of the A-byaing stream. In 1867, when the surrounding country formed the Ka-law circle, the inhabitants, who are principally Talaing, numbered 588 and 614 in 1877.

KA-LAW.—A pagoda on Bheeloo island supposed to have been founded during the reign of Asoka in the third century B. C., to enshrine a relic of Gaudama.

KA-LAW-THWOT.—A village in the centre of the circle of the same name in the Zaya township of the Amherst district south of Ka-ma-wek and near the Ka-law-thwot stream. The name in Talaing means "Betel-nut tree." In 1868 it had 691 inhabitants and 1,076 in 1877.

KA-LAW-THWOT.—A narrow and irregularly shaped revenue circle in the Zaya township, Amherst district, reaching from the Toung-gnyo range nearly to the Salween, having Ka-ma-wek on the north and Htoon-man on the south, with an area of 8,914 acres, the greater part of which is plain land. The present limits of the circle comprise three old Thoogyeeships, viz., Ka-law-thwot, Ka-ma-ta-ke and Mai-bouk. In 1868 the inhabitants, who are principally Talaing, numbered 1,074 and the gross revenue was Rs. 4,150, of which Rs. 3,000 was derived from the land. In 1876 the population was 1,600, the land revenue Rs. 3,302 and the capitation-tax Rs. 1,592.

KA-LEE-TAW.—A village in the Ma-hoo-ra circle, Hpoung-leng township, Rangoon district, on the Poo-zwon-doung river about fifteen miles below Hpoung-gyee. In 1877 it had 516 inhabitants.

KA-LE-GOUK.—An island off the coast of the Amherst district, 50 miles long and running north by west and south by east with its northern extremity thirty miles from Cape Amherst. Its woodiest part which is at the north end is about a mile in extent, whilst towards the south the island runs to a point. According to Dr. Macpherson the "northern half, on the western side, is compos-" ed of a long granite ridge with an average perpendicular drop to the sea. The " eastern side descends to the shore in gentle or abrupt slopes, while the west is " broken into abrupt hills with level, well-raised, intervening spaces forming three bays." From one of these, Quarry Bay, the stones were dug for the Alguada Reef light-house. The entire island is clothed with fine trees and water of a good quality is found at a depth of fifteen feet from the surface, whilst " a peren-" nial spring of sweet water flows through the centre of the island." The centre of the island is in 15° 33' North.

KA-LIET-PAT.—A small stream which rises in the Arakan mountains and falls into the Thee-da or Kyouk-khyoung-gale river in the Bassein district. The banks are composed of sandy loam and are fringed with tree forest. After leaving the hills its banks spread out forming in various places, in the hot season when this river is dry, separate lakes leased out as fisheries.

KA-LOUNG-TOUNG.—A village in the Pan-ta-naw township, Thoon-khwa district, in 16° 58' North and 95° East at the mouth of the Bhaw-dee stream a short distance above Pan-ta-naw. It has a population of about 600 souls.

KA-LWEE.—A revenue circle in the Amherst district at the northern end of Bheeloo island having the northern entrance of the Salween, known as the Daray-bouk, on the north and bordering on the circles of Ka-hgnyaw, Ka-ma-mo and Daray on the other side. The total area is 2,675 acres, nearly the whole of which is culturable plain land. At the northern extremity of the circle is a detached hill, round which Ka-lwee and other villages are built. It includes the formerly distinct circle of Moon-aing. It is inhabited chiefly by Talaing and is well cultivated. In 1868 the inhabitants numbered 1,758 and the gross revenue was Rs. 6,899. In 1876 the population was 3,255, the land revenue Rs. 7,118 and the capitation-tax Rs. 3,525.

KA-LWEE.—A village in the circle of the same name in the Amherst district in the extreme north of Bhee-loo-gywon on the bank of the Daray-bouk or northern mouth of the Salween, lying on the side of a detached hill connect-ed with the main Bhee-loo-gywon range by a road across the rice plain. In 1860 it had 931 inhabitants and 1,138 in 1876. The neighbouring pic-turesquely situated pagodas and zayat, embosomed amongst trees and over-looking the Salween river, are a favourite resort of the European inhabitants of Maulmain.

KA-LWEN.—A revenue circle in the Mergui district north of Mergui, to the south of the northern mouth of the Tenasserim river. In 1876 the land revenue was Rs. 2,883, the capitation tax Rs. 1,074 and the population 1,839.

KA-MA.—A village of about 600 inhabitants on the western coast of Cheduba.

KA-MA.—The head-quarters of the township of the same name in the Thayet district on the right bank of the Irrawaddy river, prettily situated on low hills, most of them crowned by a pagoda or a monastery. According to the census taken in 1872, it had a population of 2,943 souls and according to the Thoogyee's rolls of 2,829 in 1877. The Ma-de stream flows through the town, that portion lying to the south being known as Gywon-doung. A short distance above the village is the mouth of the Ma-htoon river and all the surplus produce of the valley of that stream, consisting of tobacco, chillies, onions, cutch and cotton, that does not go down straight to Prome is disposed of here.

Two legends are current as to the manner in which the place obtained its name. According to one it was an important and flourishing town in the days of Rek-kan, king of Prome (250 B.C.,) paying much revenue to the king who, therefore, named it Ma-ha-ga-ma, Ma-ha meaning 'great' and 'ga-ma' being the designation in Pali of a second class city, that is one with a market but without walls. This name it bore until the time of the great Burman king Aloungbhoora. This conqueror of Pegu, finding it compare unfavourably with the other cities of that country such as Prome and Rangoon, considered it unworthy of the name of Ma-ha-ga-ma, and with prurient pleasantry suggested that henceforth it should be called Kama (*sensual desire*). The second legend derives the name from a more reverend source. King Na-ra-pa-dee-tsee-thoo (A.D. 1167) when rebuilding the Bhoora-baw pagoda on the ruins of an old one wished to make an offering of a piece of fine cotton cloth. As the finest kind of cloth was not always obtainable, the king was in doubt as to whether he would be able to fulfil his pious wish when a man from Tha-byeng-tshoung presented himself with a piece, on which the king exclaimed : "I desired cloth ; through my former merits my wish has been gratified ; let this town be called ' Hpyeng-ta-kan-ma ' (assisted by fortune the cloth has been obtained)." This name was shortened into Kan-ma (assisted by fortune) which subsequently was corrupted to Kamma and Kama.

KA-MA.—A township of the Thayet district between Lat. 19° 5' and 18° 49' N. and Long. 94° 45' and 95° 14' 20" E. It contains an area of 575 square miles and is bounded on the north by the townships of Thayet and Meng-doon ; on the west by the Arakan mountains ; on the east by the Irrawaddy river ; and on the south by the Padoung township of the Prome district.

The present township of Ka-ma contains the whole of what was the Myo-thoogyeeship of Ka-ma, less the circles of Ban-goon and Nga-tshaw which have been transferred to Thayet, and the whole of the Myo-thoogyeeship of Mya-wadee.

Mya-wadee (the emerald country) derives its name from the expiatory offerings of a royal parricide. In 1278 A.D. Nara-thee-ha-pa-de, after escaping from the Tartars, became the victim of his son Thee-ha-thoo whom he had appointed Governor of Prome. He was poisoned at Shwe-boon-tha opposite Prome and his son afterwards raised nine pagodas to his memory on the right bank of the river above the Hpo-oo hill, enshrining within each pagoda one of the emerald-adorned regalia. Hence the land where these pagodas are situated came to be known as Mya-wadee—" the emerald land."

At the great settlement of 1145 B.E. (1783), five Taik Thoogyee and fifty-nine village Thoogyee were appointed under the Myo-thoogyee of Kama, with hereditary succession to all the appointments. The hereditary system, however, was not of long duration, except in the case of the officials of the lowest rank, the village Thoogyee. Forty-five years later the hereditary Taik Thoogyee had all disappeared and the family of the first Myo-thoogyee having kept the office for three generations, during a period of 50 years, was ousted in 1837 A.D.

To the small division of Mya-wadee one Myo-thoogyee and fourteen village Thoogyee were appointed in 1145 B.E. The Myo-thoogyee of Mya-wadee did not rank high amongst his class. He was not entitled to carry a gold umbrella as most of them were. Neither the Myo-thoogyee of Ka-ma nor of Mya-wa-dee had the power of life and death, but there is in the river just off the town of Ka-ma a whirlpool of a dangerous character into which criminals, or others whom it was desirable to get rid of, were not unfrequently dropped.

At the time when the Doomsday Book was prepared, 1783 A.D., the Myo-thoogyeeship of Ka-ma is said to have contained 142 villages. These were divided into five circles and 59 village Thoogyeeships. Any village, however small, which contained an inhabitant of means sufficient to enable him to purchase the headship was registered. The five circles, named generally after the streams on which they were situated, were Mah-toon, Myit-gyoung, Pa-nee, Poon-na and Ma-de. The registered villages contained in each of these five circles were as follows :—

Name of circle 1783 A.D.	Village.	Name of Circle 1783 A.D.	Village.
Mah-toon	Toung-dee. Pa-yeng-niem. Meng-dai. Pa-yeng-myeng. Oot-shit-goon. Thit-ngoop. Re-nan-tha. Tham-ba-ya. Taw-ma. Kyouk-tsoung. Kyee-myee. Myo-hla. Ouk-ma-niem. Ouk-ma-myeng. Kat-tswon-myoung	Pa-nee	Alat-lay. Tha-byeng-tshoung. Tshan-doon. Nga-hlaing. Nat-mee. Poon. Pouk-oo-ga. Oot-hpo. Tweng-lay. Ran-goon. Kyap. Pa-bwot. Tha-man-byong.
Myit-gyoung	Tshoon-goon. Oot-hpo. Htoon-gyee. Won-lo-gaing. Toung-rwa. Kyouk-o. Tha-ret-taw. Gnyan-lay. Khyeng-tsouk. Alay-rwa. Pya-ro. Pietha-lien. Ka-nee. Poo-hto.	Poon-na	Kan-gyee, now Poon-na. Shaw-doung. Rwa-ma. Gnyoung-won. Tha-ra-pee. Kyouk-pa-doung.
		Ma-de	Tha-guya. Zee-daw. Tsheng-tsway-myoung. Tsa-bay-khyoon. Ka-htoo-byeng. Kywai-goung. Peng-ga-daing. Kyouk-pyoot. Pya-oung. Bhan-beng. Tha-tsee.

Mya-wadee does not appear to have been divided into circles in the Burmese time : the Myo being a small one was managed by the Myo-thoogyee without the intervention of the Thoogyee of Taik as in other Myo.

The annual tribute which Ka-ma had to remit to the capital was fixed at 60 viss of silver or Rs. 8,571 and Mya-wa-dee had to send 30 viss or Rs. 4,285. The Myo-thoogyee decided annually how much should be paid by each circle. The heads of the circles decided in like manner what amount should be borne by each village and the heads of villages then proceeded to collect the amount, and as much more as they could get, in whatever manner they chose.

The incomes of the Myo-thoogyee seem to have depended mainly upon the fees derived from suitors. Justice was dispensed in the verandahs of the Myo-thoogyees' houses by deputies appointed by them for that purpose. The heads of fiscal circles (Taik Thoogyee) had, also, the power of disposing of petty civil cases, accounting for a portion of the fees received to the Myo-thoogyee. The heads of villages (Rwa Thoogyee), likewise, were permitted to dispose of such petty cases as were voluntarily brought before them. Neither Ka-ma nor Mya-wadee were required to furnish any soldiers for the service of the State.

The township is now divided into seventeen revenue circles. In 1876 the population was 30,363, the land revenue Rs. 29,116, the capitation-tax Rs. 33,029 and the gross revenue Rs. 69,848. The head-quarters are at Ka-ma.

KA-MA.—A revenue circle in the Ka-ma township, Thayet district, lying on the right bank of the Irrawaddy to the immediate north of the Gaw-beng hills and roundabout the town of Ka-ma, with an area of three square miles and a population of 3,319 souls in 1876, nestling amongst the hills which stretch down to the bank of the Irrawaddy ; the area under cultivation is small. The once independent circle of Htoon-gyee has of late years been placed under the same Thoogyee. The land revenue in 1876 was Rs. 2,711, the capitation-tax Rs. 3,270 and the gross revenue, including the local revenue raised in the town, Rs. 10,875.

KA-MA.— A revenue circle of the Kyouk-hpyoo district on the western coast of Cheduba, about 36 square miles in extent and with a population of 2581 souls in 1876. Rice and tobacco are the principal crops raised. At the north-western point is a round hill 200 feet in height from which are evolutions of marsh gas which have led to its being considered a volcano. The land revenue in 1876 was Rs. 1,979, the capitation-tax Rs. 2,515 and the gross revenue Rs. 4,615.

KA-MA-GA-LE.—A village of about sixty houses in the Gnyoung-beng-tshiep circle, Myedai township, Thayet district, on the left bank of the river opposite to the town of Ka-ma, of which it is an off-shoot.

KA-MA-KA-ROOT.—A village in the Hmaw-won circle, Than-lyeng township, Rangoon district, on a stream of the same name about nine miles from its junction with the Hmaw-won river, a little below Kyouk-tan and about three miles from the seacoast. The majority of the inhabitants, who in 1876 numbered 1,373, are Talaing agriculturists who cultivate the extensive plains on both sides of the stream. The name is Talaing, and is derived from " kam " a tank and " karoot " a mango tree, a tank with mango trees near it having formerly existed in the neighbourhood.

KA-MA-KE.—A revenue circle occupying the extreme southern point of Bheeloo island in the Amherst district, opposite to the town of Amherst; having the sea on the south and east, the Kwon-taw (*pronounced Kwantaw*) circle on the west and Ka-la-be on the north. To the south and east are detached hills on which are situated the villages. The rest of the circle consists of extensive alluvial plains, but much is damaged by salt water.

In the Burmese time this circle extended over what now forms the two circles of Ka-ma-ke (exclusive of Abyit) and Kwon-taw. When the circle was re-peopled, after the cession of Tenasserim, three Thoogyee settled down in this tract at Ka-ma-ke, Kwon-hla and Kwon-taw respectively, and collected tax each from his own followers. When Captain Phayre re-arranged the boundaries in 1848 he placed Ka-ma-ke and Kwon-hla under one Thoogyee and gave him also superintendence over Abyit which joined Ka-ma-ke, Kwon-taw being made a separate Thoogyeeship. In 1876 the land revenue amounted to Rs. 7,136 and the capitation-tax to Rs. 2,113 ; the population in the same year was 2,112. In 1868 the population was 1,684, and the gross revenue Rs. 7,754.

KA-MA-KE.—A village in the circle of the same name in the south of Bheeloo-gywon in the Amherst district. The population in 1868 numbered 794 souls including the inhabitants of the adjoining village of Toung-tsoung and 812 in 1877.

KA-MA-MO.—A village in the Ka-lwee circle on the western slopes of the main Bhee-loo-gywon range, a short distance south of Ka-lwee. The inhabitants, who are principally Talaing with a few Chinese, numbered 693 souls in 1867 and 796 in 1877.

KA-MA-NAT.—A village in the Pegu circle, Pegu township, Rangoon district, about two miles east of Pegu. In 1877 the inhabitants numbered 1,163 souls.

KA-MA-WEK.—A village in the circle of the same name in the Zaya township of the Amherst district, 14 miles from Maulmain on the great southern road which now extends to Kwon-hla, and is being constructed as far as Re, a little to the south of Moo-doon, the head-quarters of the township. There is a government rest house in this village. In 1877 it had 989 inhabitants.

KA-MA-WEK.—A small and unimportant river in the Amherst district which rises in the Toung-gnyo range, and after a westerly course of 16 or 18 miles falls into the sea a few miles above Amherst.

KA-MAW-KA-NENG.—A village in the Ke-la-tha circle, Re La-maing township, Amherst district, east of Ke-la-tha and near the source of the La-maing river. In 1877 it had 580 inhabitants. The name is Talaing and means "Rock" village.

KAM-BAI.—A village in the Rangoon district to the north-east of Rangoon about one and a half miles east of Ko-kaing (*q. v.*) close to a small lake. The inhabitants are engaged in rice cultivation and in fisheries. There is a Police station in the village. In 1877 it had 877 inhabitants.

KAM-BAI.—A revenue circle in the Tha-boung township, Bassein district, on the left bank of the Bassein river, bounded on the east by the Ta-zeng-hla stream and immediately north of the Tay-goon circle. It has an area of about 29 square miles which are but partially cultivated and are for the most part covered with forest. The inhabitants, who are mainly Burmese, are largely engaged in fishing, and some of them in cultivating. There is a fair-weather cart-road through almost every village. In 1876 the population was 2,353, the land revenue Rs. 2,366, the capitation-tax Rs. 2,397 and the gross revenue Rs. 9,434.

KAM-BAI.—A village of 841 inhabitants in 1877, principally Kareng and Shan, in the Kaw-hmoo circle, Angyee township, Rangoon district, on the Moo-la-man creek about half a mile west of Kha-beng. In some of the old village registers it is called *Kambhet*.

KAM-BHEE-LA.—A river in the Prome district. *See Kouk-gway*.

KAM-BHEE-LA.—A revenue circle in the Prome district on the right bank of the Na-weng, traversed by the Kouk-gway, here called the Kam-bhee-la, a tributary of the Na-weng; in the rains small boats can go up as high as the village which gives its name to the circle, that is for rather over a mile. In 1876 the population was 430, the land revenue Rs. 812, the capitation-tax Rs. 458 and the gross revenue Rs. 1,425.

KAM-BHET.—A village in the Angyee township, Rangoon district. *See Kam-bai.*

KA-MEE-GYWAI.—A revenue circle in the Meng-bra township, Akyab district. In 1876 the land revenue was Rs. 1,987, the capitation tax Rs. 662, the gross revenue Rs. 2,748 and the number of the inhabitants 503.

KAMIE.—A hill tribe in Arakan. A branch of the Khamie (*q. v.*), but having some differences in their language (see appendix); *e. g.*—

English	Khamie.	Kamie.
Air	Ga-lee	A-lee
Ant	Ba-leng	Pa-leng
Boat	Mloung	Ploung
Mother	Na-oo-ee	Am-noo
He	Ha-na-ee	Hoo

In manners, customs, religion and dress they are the same as the Khamie and are of the same stock, living with and amongst them.

KA-NAING-TA.—A large village in the Moo-htee circle of the Tavoy district on the eastern bank of the Tavoy river. In 1877 it had 685 inhabitants.

KA-MYAW-KENG.—A revenue circle in the western township of the Tavoy district, close to Tavoy, with an area of twelve square miles of which about one-sixth is cultivated, mostly with rice. In 1876 the population was 2,280, the land revenue Rs. 1,902, the capitation-tax Rs. 1,872 and the gross revenue Rs. 3,869.

KA-MYIT.—A large, but to a great extent unculturable, revenue circle extending eastwards from the seacoast in the southern part of the central township of the Sandoway district. Its inhabitants, who are mainly Burmese, numbered 3,488 souls in 1876. The principal products are rice, sessamum and tobacco. The land revenue in 1876 was Rs. 3,762, the capitation-tax Rs. 2,944 and the gross revenue Rs. 6,802. This circle was formerly in the southern or Kyien-ta-lee township and, with Toung-ma-gyee, was transferred to the central township in 1876 as it was too far from Khwa, the head-quarter , for effective supervision and as it was easier for suitors to come to Sandoway than to go south to Khwa.

KAN-BAING.—A revenue circle in the Oo-ree-toung East township, Akyab district, to which is now joined Toung-khyoung. The land revenue of the united circles in 1876 was Rs. 8,921, the capitation-tax Rs. 3,095, the gross revenue Rs. 12,595 and the population 2,433 souls.

KAN-BYENG.—A revenue circle in the Oo-ree-toung East township, Akyab district, which in 1876 had a population of 734 souls, a land revenue of Rs. 3,951 and a gross revenue of Rs. 5,267 of which Rs. 997 were derived from the capitation-tax.

KAN-AING.—A revenue circle in the Ramree township of the Kyouk-hpyoo district on the left bank of the Ran-bouk stream, rather over 18 square miles in extent. Coarse sugar and indigo are the main products. The neighbouring circle of Kyouk-twe has of late years been joined to it. In 1876 the population of the two was 4,068, the land revenue Rs. 3,339 and the gross revenue Rs. 7,811 of which Rs. 4,062 were derived from the capitation-tax.

KAN-GAW.—A revenue circle in the Kyouk-hpyoo district, north of the Ra-ba-teng river in the Ramree township, 11 square miles in extent, with a population of 2,728 souls in 1876. In that year the land revenue was Rs. 2,770, the capitation-tax Rs. 2,837 and the gross revenue Rs. 5,792. The Ra-ba-teng circle is now joined to it.

KAN-GYEE.—A village in the Htan-le-beng circle of the Thee-kweng township, Bassein district, on the western bank of the Kyon-toon creek opposite to Goon-gnyeng-dan. In 1877 it had 775 inhabitants.

KAN-GYEE-DOUNG.—The head-quarter town of the Thee-kweng township, Bassein district, in 16° 54′ 30″ N. and 64° 58′ E. with a population of 2,351 souls, situated on the right bank of the Daga river about 15 miles from its junction with the Nga-won. The inhabitants are principally engaged in agriculture. The town contains a court-house and a police station.

KAN-HLA.—A revenue circle in the Shwe-doung township, Prome district, which now includes the Ma-oo-daing, Rwa-thit-gyee, Mai-daw, Sha-daing, Rwa-bai-hla, Hmek-ka-ra, Tsheng-ra and Kyouk-taw-ga circles and extends from the Shwe-nat-toung hills on the west to the Prome hills or Engdaing on the east across the valley of the Kyoon stream just north of Poung-khyoot. The centre of the circle is well cultivated with rice but the extreme eastern and western portions consist of undulating ground and low hills covered with forest and drained by numerous small streams—affluents of the Kyoon. The main road from Rangoon to the north traverses this circle which it enters at Kan-goon and leaves in the Engdaing or great belt of Eng forest which extends away far south into the Henzada district, a little to the south of the source of the Lek-pan-khoon rivulet. In 1876 the population of the united circles was 1,891, the land revenue Rs. 2,285, and the gross revenue Rs. 4,439 of which Rs. 2,027 were derived from the capitation-tax.

KAN-KOO.—A village in the Padoung township, Prome district, in 18° 37′ 40″ N. and 95° 4′ 35″ E. on the Kan-koo stream just above its junction with the Kyouk-bhoo. The name is derived from the soapstone (Kan-koo-kyouk) found on the banks of the Kan-koo.

KAN-KOO.—A small and unnavigable mountain stream which rises in)ne of the spurs of the Arakan Roma mountains and after a short easterly course falls into the Kyouk-bhoo. Its name is derived from Kan-koo (Burmese for soapstone) which is found at various places on its banks.

KAN-LAY.—A village in the Ma-oo-daing circle, Meng-doon township, Thayet district, on the bank of the Ma-htoon river a short distance above the mouth of the Det-Shwe one of its affluents from the north. This village whic⌐   -five houses, is in 19° 18′ 50″ North Lat. and 94° 47′ E. Loug. It formerly gave its name to a separate circle, which, in 1860 on the death of the hereditary Thoogyee, was joined to Ma-oo-daing.

KAN-LET.—A small revenue circle, rather more than one square mile in extent, on the northern coast of Cheduba to the west of Kyet-ro. Rice and tobacco are the principal products. In 1876 the land revenue was Rs. 642, the capitation-tax Rs. 513, the gross revenue Rs. 1,187 and the population 481 souls.

KAN-NEE.—A revenue circle in the Nga-poo-taw township, Bassein district, having an approximate area of 237 square miles, extending northwards between the Arakan hills and the Bassein river from the Tha-man-de-wa circle to the Than-dwai river, which divides it from the former Kyouk-khyoung-gyee township. The north-eastern corner of the circle, above Oot-hpo, is flat but the rest is hilly and covered with forest. An outcrop of sandstone appears to the north of the Shwe-doung stream and another a few miles inland to the west. Bamboos and iron-wood are found in abundance on the western side of the circle at the foot of the Arakan mountains. The inhabitants, who are chiefly Kareng, and who are occupied in cultivation, numbered 2,620 in 1876 when the land revenue was Rs. 4,550, the capitation-tax Rs. 3,030 and the gross revenue Rs. 7,709.

KAN-NEE.—A revenue circle in the Bhoom-ma-wad-dee township, Toung-ngoo district, on the left bank of the Tsit-toung river, extending from the Thit-nan-tha stream on the north to the Pa-thee on the south. To the eastward the country is hilly and covered with tree, brush wood and grass forest. Within the limits of this circle is the Eng-won lake with fifteen feet of water in the rains and from six to eight in the dry season, and one or two other smaller ones. The principal timber is teak, Pyeng-gado (*Xylia Dolabriformis*) and Pyeng-ma (*Lagerstrœmia Reginæ*) ; bamboos are plentiful. In 1876 the population numbered 4,684, the land revenue was Rs. 1,560, the capitation-tax Rs. 2,258 and the gross revenue Rs. 5,753.

KAN-NEE.—A river in the Toung-ngoo district which rises in the Poung-loung range and after a westerly course of about 20 miles falls into the Tsit-toung five miles north of Toung-ngoo. During the rains it is navigable for boats of about 30 feet in length for some distance. From its mouth to the village of Kwon-beng, a distance about four or five miles, its bed is sandy, above that very rocky. A moderate quantity of teak, bamboos and sessamum are brought down this stream to the Toung-ngoo market.

KAN-NEE.—A village in the circle of the same name in the Nga-poo-taw township of the Bassein district on the right bank of the Than-dwai about four miles above its mouth in the Bassein, a little above Ta-man-khyoung ; it is the residence of the Thoogyee of the circle. In 1877 it had 526 inhabitants. The trade is mainly in salt, rice and nga-pee. Lat. 16° 37′ N. Long. 94° 43′ E.

KAN-NGAY.—A revenue circle in the Prome district north-east ᴜ Poung-day and on the left bank of the Wai-gyee; its largest village is Toung-bo-hla on the Wai-gyee river. It now includes the Tha-hla-peng-zee, Reng-ma-hla, and Rat-tha circles. In 1876 the inhabitants numbered 1,832, the land revenue was Rs. 1,718, the capitation-tax Rs. 1,828 and the gross revenue Rs. 3,806.

KAN-OO.—A village in the Prome district in 18°25'20" N. and 95° 34' 15" E. on the Myo-lay channel and about a mile and a h⸱¹ᶜ ᶜ The road from Ta-hpoon in the Henzada district passes this ᵥ.. ᵤᵥ, ...ᵤᵤₕ is about four and a half miles south of Poung-day, measuring from the main road from Rangoon to the northern frontier which runs through that town.

KAN-OUNG.—A town in the Henzada district on the right bank of the Irrawaddy about seven miles below Myanoung, with a population in 1875 of 3,171 souls and in 1877 of 3,315, principally merchants and petty traders. It was founded in 1754 A. D. by the Burman conqueror Aloungbhoora. It contains a Police station, a Public Works Department Inspection Bungalow and several good public resthouses. The name is Talaing and means a "whirlpool" and was given to the town because there was then a whirlpool in the river opposite the spot where it was founded. In the neighbourhood are the remains of an old fort. The local revenue in 1877 was Rs. 1,617. Long. 18° 10' 50" E. Lat. 95° 28' N.

KAN-OUNG.—A well cultivated revenue circle on the bank of the Irrawaddy in the Kan-oung township of the Henzada district. To it have been added the Koon-ta-loon and Kyet-tshoo-daw circles farther north. In 1876 the population numbered 10,542, the land revenue was Rs. 9,259, the capitation-tax Rs. 9,390 and the gross revenue Rs. 21,208. These figures are exclusive of the population and revenue of the town of Kan-oung.

KAN-OUNG.—A township in the Henzada district divided into eight revenue circles, extending westwards from the Irrawaddy to the Arakan Roma mountains, with Myanoung on the north and Oot-hpo on the south. To the westward the country is mountainous and forest-clad but towards the west, low and at one time subject to annual inundations from the overflow of the Irrawaddy; extensive embankments along that river have of late years afforded almost complete protection and rice cultivation is rapidly extending in the fertile country thus rendered fit for the production of this cereal. In the low land between the hills and the Irrawaddy are several lakes of which the largest and most important is the Htoo, fed during the rains by the Ma-mya which comes down from the Arakan mountains. Owing to the Irrawaddy embankments and the want of scape-way the lake is gradually being silted up by the sand brought down by the Ma-mya. The hilly country contains some valuable timber such as teak, htouk-kyan and pyeng-gado, whilst further eastward eng is found in some quantity.

The principal town is Kan-oung, on the bank of the Irrawaddy in the north-eastern part of the township, where the Extra Assistant Commissioner in charge resides and holds his court and where there is a good market and a police station. In 1876 the land revenue was Rs. 27,881, the capitation-tax Rs. 34,000 and the gross revenue Rs. 71,802. In the same year the population and agricultural stock was :—

Population.	Animals.									
	Ponies.	Buffaloes.	Cows, Bulls and Bullocks.	Goats and Sheep.	Pigs.	Carts.	Ploughs.	Sugar mills.	Oil mills.	Boats.
36,336	145	8,790	6,950	185	2,264	6,277	4,018	1	73	109

and the land under cultivation :—

AREA IN ACRES UNDER

Rice.					
Cultivated.	Fallow.	Total.	Garden.	Miscellaneous.	Total.
17,080	476	17,556	1,304	1,228	2,532

KAN-RWA.—A revenue circle with an area of about 41 square miles in the Thee-kweng township, Bassein district, lying between the Pe-beng and the Pan-ma-wad-dee rivers. The country consists of level and well cultivated plains, more especially between the Pe-beng and the Moung-dee rivers. East of the Moung-dee the country is low and portions are occasionally inundated. The plains on either side of the Moung-dee are relieved by patches of forest and the creeks and streams are fringed with trees, none, however, of any value. In 1876 the inhabitants numbered 3,657, the land revenue was Rs. 14,427, the capitation-tax Rs. 3,762 and the gross revenue Rs. 18,935.

KAN-THA.—See Toung-gnyo river.

KAN-THOON-TSENG.—A village in the Prome district between the Irrawaddy and the Shwe-nat-toung hills, a mile and a half west of the latter, eight miles south, as the crow flies, from Shwe-doung and rather more than seven E. S. E. from Kyee-thay, with which, as with most of the neighbouring villages it is connected by a good dry-weather cart road.

KAN-TSHIEP.—A tidal creek near the sea in the Bassein district running from the Daray-bhyoo creek, about five miles from its southern mouth, in a north-easterly direction to the Pya-ma-law. River steamers have passed through it.

KA-RENG.—A small stream in the Toung-ngoo district, which rises in the Poung-loung range and, after a westerly course of about 20 miles, falls into the Tsit-toung nearly opposite Toung-ngoo. It is navigable for boats for about two miles only from its mouth.

KA-RENG.—A race scattered throughout the province from Mergui in the south to beyond Toung-ngoo in the extreme north and from the Salween Hill Tracts in the east as far west as Arakan, but found principally in the Toung-ngoo, Shwe-gyeng, Amherst, Tavoy, Mergui, Bassein and Rangoon districts. *Kareng* is the name by which they are designated by the Burmese and which has been adopted by the English (by Symes they are called *Cariainers* and by later writers *Carians* and *Karyens*); to the Kareng themselves it is unknown and its derivation is uncertain but is, most probably, *Ka-ra* by which the Kareng-nee in the north call themselves, or *Ka-roon*, the designation of the Gai-kho amongst themselves. Those in the north and east, preferring to live far from the bustle of cities and towns, from choice ensconce themselves in the dense forest or perch on the heights of almost inaccessible mountains or hide in the high and nearly impenetrable elephant grass on the margins of streams, whilst those in the south and west have settled in the plains amongst their Talaing and Burmese neighbours. Living hitherto with the dominant race but not of them, timid and suspicious, the natural result of long continued oppression under the Burmese, and with manners coarse and repulsive, they have, in the opinion of the casual observer, the appearance of stolid stupidity. Owing partly to distrust and partly, perhaps, to the supercilious way in which they are often treated they affect an ignorance which, far from being real, is by no means impracticable for, wild and uncultivated to a degree as they naturally are, they are highly susceptible of social, moral and religious influences when once their confidence has been won and their sympathies awakened. The results of the labours amongst them of the members of the American Baptist Mission have the appearance of being almost miraculous and it is not going too far to state that the cessation of blood feuds and the peaceable way in which the various tribes are living together, and have lived together since they came under British rule, is far more due to the influence exercised over them by the Missionaries than to the measures adopted by the English Government, beneficial as these have, doubtless, been.

The Kareng people, who have no one distinctive name for themselves, are composed of three tribes differing somewhat in their customs and traditions and considerably in their language :— the Sgaw, Pwo and Bghai. Each tribe is sub-divided into septs or clans which also differ from each other in some of their customs and idioms and particularly in their dress. Considerable confusion has been caused by the numerous names given to each clan some having no less than four or five ; speaking of themselves each sept calls itself by its own name for man, and were these terms for man adopted in English the clans would be much more accurately distinguished than they are at present.

Tribal and sub-tribal divisions.

The three tribes are thus sub-divided :—

I.—Sgaw. So called by themselves.
    (a) called Myit-tho by the Burmese.
    (b)   ,,   Shan   ,,   Pwo.
    (c)   ,,   Pa-koo   ,,   Kareng-nee.
    (d)   ,,   Burmese Kareng by some English writers and by Burmans in Rangoon and Bassein.
    (e)   ,,   White Kareng by some English writers.
1. Ma-nie-pgha clan.
2. Pa-koo   ,,
3. We-wa   ,,

II.—Pwo. So called by the Sgaw, the name by which they are generally known sometimes written *Pgho*.
- (a) called Sho by themselves.
- (b) „ Myit Khyeng by some Burmese.
- (c) „ Talaing Kareng „ „ and by some English writers.

1. Mo-pgha clan. So called by the Missionaries, the name by which they are generally known.
   - (a) called Taw-pya by Burmese.
   - (b) „ Pie-do by some of themselves.
   - (c) „ Pie-zaw „ „
   - (d) „ Plaw „ „

2. Ta-roo clan. So called by the Kareng-nee, the name by which they are generally known.
   - (a) called Koo hta by themselves.
   - (b) „ Padoung by the Gai-kho.
   - (c) „ Bhee-loo by the Burmese.

3. Shoung clan.

4. Hashwie clan. So called by the Bghai, the name by which they are generally known.
   - (a) called Ha-shoo by themselves.

5. Gai-kho clan. So called by the Bghai, the name by which they are generally known.
   - (a) called Ka-roon by themselves.
   - (b) „ Pra-ka-young by themselves.
   - (c) „ Padoung by the Kareng-nee.

III. Bghai. So called by the Sgaw, the name by which they are generally known.
   - (a) called Pye-ya by themselves.

1. Kareng-nee clan. So called by the Burmese.
   - (a) called Red Kareng by the English.
   - (b) „ Yang-aing „ Shan.
   - (c) „ Ka-ra by themselves.
   - (d) „ Pra-ka-ra „
   - (e) „ Bghai-moo-hte by the other Bghai.
   - (f) „ The-pya „ Gai-kho.

2. Bghai-ka-tew clan.
   - (a) called Tunic Bghai by the English.
   - (b) „ Liep-pya-gyee „ Burmese.

3. Bghai-ka-hta clan.
   - (a) called Pant Bghai by the English
   - (b) „ Kareng-a-yning „ Burmese.
   - (c) „ Liep-pya-ngay „ „

4. Lay-may.
   - (a) called Brec by the Kareng-nee.
   - (b) „ Pray „ „

5. Man-oo-man-aw.

6. Tshaw-kho.

There are thus three clans of Sgaw, five clans of Pwo and six clans of Bghai, but these only include those tribes and sub-tribes representatives of which are found in the province : in the Shan districts beyond our frontier are the Ran-lang, Reng-ban, Reng-tsaik, Reng, Ta-lya *vel* Reng-ka-la *vel* Reng-da-laing (of Mr. O'Riley) and others.

The Kareng are undoubtedly of a different family from the Burmese and Talaing and as certainly they are not the aboriginal inhabitants of the country. Their own tradition is that they came from the north across a " river of running sand," a name given by Fa Hian to the desert between China and Thibet, and the account of it given by this Chinese pilgrim agrees with the traditionary account of the Kareng. He says, " There are evil spirits in this river of sand and such scorching winds " that whoso encountereth them dies and none escape. Neither birds are " seen in the air nor quadrupeds on the ground. On every side as far as the

" eye can reach, if you seek for the proper place to cross, there is no other mark
" to distinguish it than the skeletons of those who have perished there ; these
" alone seem to indicate the route." The Kareng account as given by
Dr. Mason is :—" That was a fearful trackless region, where the sands
" rolled before the winds like the waves of the sea." The first historical
notice of the Kareng was that of Marco Polo, following whom Malte Brun
says, " Thus the country of Caride is the south-eastern point of Thibet, and
" perhaps the country of the nation of the Cariaines, which is spread over
" Ava " : Bghai traditions allude to a town called Bha-maw whither they
went to purchase axes. The Sgaw account is that they came from a country
north of the Shan, whilst the Kareng-nee say that they were driven from a
place north of Ava sixteen or seventeen generations ago and are a portion of
a Chinese army : this would carry us back to about 1400 A. D., and about
that time the Chinese three times invaded Burma and were twice defeated.
It may be taken, therefore, until more materials for the formation of a sound
conclusion are obtained, that the Kareng emigrated some centuries after the
commencement of the Christian era from the north of China and were followed
much later by the Kareng-nee who had formed a portion of an invading
Chinese army.

Those who live in the plains are a muscular people with large limbs
Physical character. whilst the mountaineers are a weaker people with smaller
muscles and with small limbs. The average height is
low ; of the men about five feet four or five feet five and of the women not
more than four feet nine. The unexposed portions of the body are as fair as
those of the Chinese and on many is to be seen the yellow tinge of that race ;
the hair is straight, coarse and, usually, like the eyes, jet black, but in the
north brownish hair and hazel eyes are sometimes found. " The head is
" pyramidal, wider across the cheek bones than across the temples and the
" bridge of the nose rises only slightly above the face."

The houses vary in shape, size and construction ; some living in comparatively permanent houses, some in temporary sheds,
Dwellings, domes- some having separate structures for each family, others one
tic animals and food. for the whole village. (See Bghai and Pwo.) The only
domestic animals which they have are fowls, dogs and pigs of the small
Chinese breed ; the dogs are eaten by the Bghai only. They keep no
cats because they do not eat them, whilst the cats would eat the rats
which the Kareng want for themselves. With this exception they are
omnivorous ; every animal from a rat to an elephant, every reptile from a
sand-lizard to a serpent, ants, grubs, every bird, every fish and the whole
vegetable kingdom adorn their tables. But, curiously, they will eat none
of the monkey tribe except the " White Eyelid Monkey."

Dress. The dress varies with each clan, those in the north
wearing trowsers, those towards the south tunics :

I.—Sgaw.
  1. Ma-nie-pgha clan.
  2. Pa-koo clan.—Tunics, white without stripes and with a narrow border of embroidery
     at the bottom, the patterns of which differ for every village.
  3. We-wa clan.—Dress of all kinds.

II.—Pwo.
  1. Mo-pgha clan.—Same as the Bghai-kn-tew, i.e., tunics white with red perpendicular
     lines : reason of similarity unknown.

2. Ta-roo clan.—Trowsers,
3. Shoung clan.—Trowsers, white with radiating red lines at the bottom, like the Gai-kho but not so handsomely embroidered.
4. Ha-shwie clan.—Trowsers.
5. Gai-kho clan.—Trowsers, often of silk and handsomely embroidered ; red lines at the bottom radiating like the beams of the rising sun.

III.—Bghai.
1. Kareng-nee clan.—Trowsers, red with perpendicular, very narrow black or white stripes, sometimes black with red or white stripes : bright red turban.
2. Bghai-ka-tew clan.—Tunics, white with perpendicular red stripes : same as Mo-pgha.
3. Bghai-ka-hta clan.—Trowsers, white with red radiating lines worked in them at the bottom ; same as Gai-kho but not of silk nor so handsomely embroidered.
4. Lay-may clan.—Go almost naked.
5. Ma-noo-ma-naw clan.
6. Tshaw-kho clan.—Trowsers, white ornamented with red and black vertical stripes.

Like all races they have customs peculiar to themselves. The ceremonies

Ceremonies at births.

performed at the birth of a child are the same amongst all the clans except the Kareng-nee (q. v.)

The navel string having been cut (the knife is carefully kept as the child's life is supposed to be connected with its preservation) the placenta are placed in a bamboo and hung on a tree by the father, who deals in a similar way with an abortion, in this case, however, selecting the Eugenia. On his return to the house he pounds rice and goes through other woman's labour if the child is a girl or spears a hog if a boy. When the navel string sloughs away the father goes out hunting and fishing and his success or want of success is held to be indicative of the child's future prosperity. On his return a feast is given and the child is purified and named. "An elder takes a "thin splint of bamboo and, tying a fowl's feathers at one end, he fans it down "the child's arm, saying—

'Fan away ill luck, fan away ill success :
Fan away inability, fan away unskilfulness :
Fan away slow growth, fan away difficulty of growth :
Fan away stuntedness, fan away puniness :
Fan away drowsiness, fan away stupidity :
Fan away debasedness, fan away wretchedness :
Fan away the whole completely.'

"The elder now changes his motion and fans up the child's arm, saying—

'Fan on power, fan on influence :
Fan on the paddy bin, fan on the paddy barn :
Fan on flowers, fan on dependants :
Fan on good things, fan on appropriate things. '

"He next takes a bit of thread, that has been prepared for the purpose, "and tying it round the child's wrist, says, 'I name thee A. B.' using the "name that the parents had previously determined upon."

The names are sometimes those of ancestors, sometimes descriptive of

Names.

the parent's feelings, as "Joy," "Hope ;" often those of the seasons during which the child was born as "Harvest ;" in many cases the child is named from some circumstance that occurred about the time of its birth as "Father returned," * or from some peculiarity in its appearance as "White" or "Black." On other occasions it is named after some

---

* Khyeng-byan (Khyeng-bran according to Arakanese pronunciation) the Arakanese, commonly called King-berring who rebelled against the Burmans in the beginning of this century and was one of the causes of the first Burmese war (vide sub-tit. AKYAB :—HISTORY) was so named because he was born when his father Moung Khyeng came back from Ava. Pyan-thee is "to return" and the p is softened into b for euphony.

bird, beast, mineral or tree as "Heron," "Tiger," "Tin," "Cotton." Those who, on growing up, develop some peculiarity receive a kind of nick-name to which "Father" or "Mother" is attached as "Father of swiftness," "Mother of contrivance." Probably the greatest peculiarity about names, however, is the custom of changing the parents' names when a child is born to them : thenceforward they are no longer "Tiger" or "Joy" or "Elephant" or "Harvest" but "Father of A." and "Mother of A" : as "Father of Kwa-la" and "Mother of Kwa-la." This practice, however, is not universal.

Frequently, but never amongst the Kareng-nee, infants are betrothed by

Infanticide is rarely practised but sometimes if a mother dies her infant

Infanticide.

is buried with her. The Ka-khyeng east of Ba-mhaw have a similar custom ; with them, if a mother dies within seven days of the birth of her child, the house, dead body, living infant and every article in the house are burnt, but should a stranger be present in the village he may save the child's life by adopting it and carrying it away : no Ka-khyeng will on any account have anything to say to it, nor may it remain in the village.

Frequently, but never amongst the Kareng-nee, infants are betrothed by

Betrothals.

their parents, owing to a prevalent idea that the two children are by this means physically connected so that the good health of the one neutralises the ill-health of the other ; special resort is had to this custom when the child is weak and sickly : a tribe of northern Bghai seem to prefer selling a sickly child into slavery. When an infant's betrothal is desired matters are first arranged by the parents and the inevitable fowl's bones are consulted and only if they give a favourable response is the ceremony proceeded with. A feast is given by the parents of the boy at which the betrothal is completed by an elder praying : " Lord of the " land and water, Mokhie of the land and water, these two are now engaged to " be united together in marriage. May they have long life, may they " produce seed, may their shoots sprout forth, may they grow old together." If, on arriving at a marriageable age, they decline to carry out the contract made for them, the parents of the girl pay half the expenses of the betrothal feast, and the bond is broken.

When a young man chooses his own wife he commences by obtaining the sanction of the girl's parents to his paying his addresses, not to the girl herself but through them. He then selects a go-between who first consults a chicken's bones ; if they give an unfavourable reply the matter is allowed to drop, if on the other hand the answer is favourable the go-between arranges the match, and when this is done a feast is given by the young man's friends to those of the girl, when the gall of the animal killed is examined ; if it is flaccid it is a bad omen and sometimes leads to the breaking off the match, but if plump it is favourable. The marriage sometimes takes place in a few days but is often delayed. If a girl breaks her engagement she has to pay the expenses of the feast, but she is at liberty to receive the addresses of another suitor if her betrothed declares publicly that he desires to forfeit all that has been spent, which is the recognized way of breaking off the match.

The marriage ceremony is simple : the bride is conducted to the house

Marriage.

of the bridegroom's parents in a procession with music, and as she ascends the ladder she is drenched to the skin with water. Before the company leave two elders, one on behalf of the bride and one on behalf of the bridegroom, take, each, a cup of spirits, the first repeats the duties of the husband in case of his wife's death and the latter replies acknowleging that such are his duties (one of which is that should she be killed in a foray or carried into captivity, he must purchase her freedom or obtain the price of her blood). Each elder then gives to the other to drink and says: " Be faithful to your covenant." This concludes the ceremon. The Kareng-nee (*q.v.*) forms are very different.

Chastity and divorce. The southern Kareng, differing in this respect from the Kareng-nee, are chaste, but lapses among the married are not uncommon, although adultery is considered as particularly offensive to God. Polygamy is not permitted, but is practised by some of those who live near the Burmese. Divorces are not infrequent; if the man leaves the woman he forfeits all property which he does not take with him; if the woman leaves the man she receives only what her husband chooses to allow her. Widows retain their husband's houses and endeavour to gain their own livelihood; if they are young they often marry again, but if old are dependent on their relations for support and are not infrequently much neglected.

Widows.

Sickness. Without vigour of constitution the Kareng often succumb to diseases which the stronger European can resist, such as measles which are nearly as fatal in their villages as small-pox is amongst western nations. They suffer from small-pox, cholera, dysentery, dropsy, consumption and fevers and in some places in the hills goitre is common. In ordinary illnesses they treat the sick with a fair amount of kindness, but decline to afford any assistance to an individual attacked by one considered infectious. An outbreak of cholera or small-pox will temporarily depopulate the villages in large tracts of country, the inhabitants flying from the disease with terror and living in the forests till they think that they can return to their homes without danger of contagion. The individual who has, or is supposed to have, imported the disease is held responsible for all the deaths and must pay the price of the lives lost; if he dies himself or is unable to pay the debt remains for his children and descendants to wipe off. Every illness is looked upon as inflicted by the spirits and though the Kareng have some knowledge of medicine resort is not had to it till incantations have been tried and the spirits have declined to be propitious, thus reversing the usual order amongst uncivilized nations.

Disposal of the dead. Some of the tribes bury and some burn their dead, but all those who resort to cremation state that it is, comparatively, a new practice and that formerly they buried.

Bonds of friendship. Individuals often form covenants of friendship of which there are three kinds, *viz:*—*Mghe, Tho* and *Do*, the last being the strongest, one *Do* helping the other in seasons of scarcity and defending his character against attacks. The ceremony connected with the formation of this tie is as follows. The host cuts off the snout of a hog or the bill of a fowl and rubs the blood on the shins of his guest, fowl bones are then consulted and if they are propitious the guest repeats the ceremony and again turns to fowl bones; if the answer is unfavourable all that has preceded goes for nothing and the affair drops, but if it is satisfactory the two are thenceforth *Do* and so call each other dropping, as regards themselves, their proper names.

"Ungoverned and ungovernable.........the Pakoo are the hereditary
Government and laws. "enemies of the Pwo, the Bghai of the Pakoo, the Gaikho "of the Bghai and the Kareng-nee of all"; such was the description given of the northern and eastern Kareng by one who had known them for over a quarter of a century. This state of affairs, however, is rapidly dying out and except, perhaps, on the north-east frontier, and in the recesses of the hills in parts of Toung-ngoo and Shwe-gyeng the Kareng of the Tenasserim division have settled down into nearly if not quite as peaceable cultivators as their brethren in Bassein and Rangoon, with tax collectors, village police and other petty officials selected from amongst themselves. The policy of the British Government, directly the reverse of that of its predecessors, the Burmese and Talaing, has been to deal gently with the Kareng and inspire them with confidence, wherever possible selecting from amongst them and not from Burmese the minor officials who live with them and are in continual and daily contact with them. Shy and retiring and utterly unaccustomed to the delays and forms of our laws, they prefer settling their disputes amongst themselves, but do occasionally resort to the courts. The influence exercised over them by the Missionaries and the schools which these earnest men have built and support amongst them have immensely facilitated the conciliatory measures of such men as the late Sir Henry Durand and Sir Arthur Phayre, and we have only to turn to the still savage hill tribes of Arakan to see how little can be done by Government officers burdened with multifarious duties without the assistance of these indefatigable men who penetrate everywhere, sometimes, perhaps, with more zeal than discretion.

In the north and north-east, amongst the Ha-shwie, the Lay-may, the Tshaw-kho and the Kareng-nee, feuds and forays are, probably, nearly as common now as they were all over the Tenasserim division before its cession to the British, and as they are amongst the Arakan hill tribes and the Ka-khyeng near Bha-maw; the stronger prey on the weaker, seizing their property, burning their villages, slaying those who resist and selling their wretched prisoners into a state of endless slavery. These attacks goaded the most timid to retaliate whence followed most bitter blood feuds, and at the same time treaties offensive and defensive between the weaker villages: an ox or buffaloe is killed and the inhabitants of the two villages feast together, after which the elders arrange the terms of the alliance.

The weapons used are crossbows with poisoned arrows, spears, and javelins for throwing at an enemy, swords, matchlocks and old muskets: round their houses and villages they plant pointed bamboos at an angle of 45°, rising a few inches above the ground: for defence they use shields and breastplates made of hide.

The Kareng never declare war. The great principle of Kareng warfare is
Mode of Warfare. to take their enemy by surprise. Nor is war waged ostensibly between one village and another. There is always an individual at the head of every war, on whose account the war is made and who acts as general but never goes to the fight himself. When he deems it a favourable time for his purpose he kills a hog or a fowl, and taking a bit of the heart, a bit of the liver and a bit of the entrails he mixes them up with salt and rolls the mixture up in a leaf: this he calls tying the heads of his enemies. After finishing his preparations, he prays: "Lord

"of the heavens, Lord of the earth, Lord of the mountains, Lord of the
"hills, mayest thou put down the inhabitants of the village. Make them
"forgetful, make them to forget themselves, help us, we beseech thee."
He then gives the roll to two men, who have been engaged for the
"service, and says to them : " I send you to spy out the road; go look. Is
"the village easy or difficult to attack? Has it caltrops planted around it or
"not? Look accurately. Go up into the village and sleep with the people ;
"and if any one invites you to sit with him, take out this roll and mix up
"its contents privately with their rice and curry. It will tie their heads. I
"will tie their heads with it; when they eat, they will forget themselves ;
"and then we will go and attack them. And because they have eaten
"that which ties their heads they will forget to seize their swords and spears
"and before they can recover themselves we will grasp their arms and over-
"come them and kill them."
When the spies return, they probably say: "These people have not
"planted a single caltrop. There is no difficulty about the village whatever.
"If we go and attack it, we shall take it, and kill all the people."
Then the head of the war sends out his people to collect volunteers
for his foray. The matter having been arranged beforehand 40 or 50
come from one village and 40 or 50 from another, and if when all the
fighting men assemble together they amount to a couple of hundred, it
is quite satisfactory, and they are feasted at the village to which they have
been called.
Before handing round the whiskey, the head of the war pours out some
slowly on the ground and prays : " Lord of the seven heavens and the seven
"earths, Lord of the rivers and streams, of the mountains and hills, we
"give thee whiskey to drink and rice to eat. Help us, we entreat thee.
"We will now go and attack that village. We have tied the heads of
"the inhabitants. Help us. Make their minds forgetful; make them to
"forget themselves. That they may sleep heavily, that their sleep may be
"unbroken, let not a dog bark at us, let not a hog grunt at us. Let them
"not seize a bow, a sword or a spear. And may the Lord help my children
"and grandchildren that are going to attack this village and deliver them
"from all harm. May they overcome their enemies and not be lost. May
"they be delivered from the bow, the sword and the spear." After the
prayer, the elders drink part of the whiskey and it is then circulated freely
among the company.
The head of the war next takes a fowl and after killing it consults its
bones as to the success of the war if commenced then. Before the examination he says: " Fowl, possessor of superhuman powers, fore-endued with
"divine intelligence, thou scratchest with thy feet, thou peckest with thy bill,
"thou goest unto Khoo-hte (king of death), thou goest unto Tha-ma (monarch
"of death), thou goest to Shie-woo, (the brother of God), thou goest into the
"presence of God ; thou seest unto the verge of heaven, thou seest unto the
"edge of the horizon. I now purpose to go and attack that village. Shall
"we be hit, shall we be obstructed? If we go shall we suffer shall we die by
"the bow, shall we be pierced by the spear, shall we weary ourselves, shall
"we exhaust ourselves? If so, reveal thyself unfavourable."
If the omens are unfavourable he dismisses the troops and each one
returns to his home to wait for a more auspicious opportunity. When he

234

calls them again he proceeds as before and on consulting the fowl's bones, prays : " We will go and attack that house. Shall we overcome, shall we " utterly destroy? Shall we escape being hit by the bow, and speared by the " spear? Shall we not stumble on anything? If they will not resist us, but " their lives be destroyed, their village come to utter destruction, then, fowl, " reveal thyself favourable."

If the bones give the desired response, the elder who reads it, says : " The bones are good. If we go, we shall meet with no disaster. We shall " seize and kill the whole, and if any should remain, they will not be able " to resist us."

Then the head of the war leaps up and calls out exultingly to his troops that they will certainly be victorious. He says : " Soldiers, fear " not nor be anxious. Go fight and be strong. If two or three of you are " killed, I am your Lord. If in the battle a spear is broken bring me the " handle ; if the barrel of your musket drops out bring me the stock. I will " replace everything. If one or two are killed bring their bodies to me, I will " clothe them, I will give them shrouds and pay their value."

He calls for two to volunteer to be first to go up the ladder into the first house and these he addresses : " You are a hunting dog, you are a wild " boar. If you succeed, you are worthy of a buffalo, and you shall have it. " If you cannot succeed, if you are killed let not those you leave behind ask " a buffalo of me, let them ask a fowl. Let them not ask of me a silk " garment on account of your death. You say you are bold, you say you are " fearless. You go the first, you return the last. Therefore, if our enemies " follow and you run away and become terrified and anything happens to " the people you are responsible." He closes with the declaration that he will prosecute the war till he overcomes whatever may be the resistance they meet.

The troops then go off singing war songs, of which the following is a specimen :

I go to war, I am sent.
I go to fight, I am sent.
Clothe me with the iron breastplate,
Give me the iron shield.
I am not strong, may I make myself strong ?
I am weak, may I make myself powerful ?

I go with a multitude, many persons.
We will go to the house, the foot of steps.
We will fire musket and holloa.
The people come with wives and children.
Unsheath the spear, draw the sword,
Smite the neck, spear the side
Till blood flows purple.

I go to war, I am employed.
I go to fight, I am employed.
Employer gave me whiskey to drink ;
I drink till I am dizzy.

We march in order, like white ants ;
We cross a stream, and trample it dry :
We arrive at the foot of the house,
We reach the foot of the ladder :
We go up into the bed-rooms.
Blood flows like a stream of water,
The blood flows down under the house.

> The mother cries herself to death.
> The great hawk flies over the house,
> Pounces down on the Chief's red cock.
> The great hawk sweeps around the house,
> Carries off its prey at the foot of the steps,
> Seizes the Chief's white cock.
> The great hawk flies away
> Leaving the Chief behind weeping.

When the expedition reaches the house to be attacked a party rushes into the house killing all the men they meet, while the rest surround the house from below. These intercept all that endeavour to escape and receive in charge such women and children as they wish to bring away alive and bind them. If the inmates resist the house is fired and the people who leap out to escape the flames are killed or taken prisoners. They kill without regard to age or sex. Infants are always killed as they say they would die if carried away. Children are often massacred with the utmost barbarity. Their hands and feet are cut off and their bodies hacked into small pieces. Adults are often embowelled, split in two, their ears cut off and put in their mouths and it is not uncommon to bring away the jaws of their victims as trophies, as the North American Indians bring away scalps. Sometimes, after the house has been burnt up, they sow the seeds of vegetables on the ashes to indicate the utter destruction they have wrought.

On the return of the expedition with their captives, when they come within hearing of the village from which they were sent, they blow their war trumpets and the villagers know by the peculiar call that they are returning victors. On their arrival they place all the captives in the hands of the head of the war, who feasts his troops and then dismisses them to their several homes.

The head of the war keeps the captives a considerable time when, if none of their friends come to redeem them, he sells them off to other districts, for oxen or buffaloes if practicable, that he may have an ox or a buffalo to give to each village that came to his aid.

Captives, except those taken in satisfaction of a debt, are often illtreated, beaten, wounded and occasionally killed. When they are brought in bound and fettered to the head of the war, he sometimes addresses them thus : " I did not begin this war. " You killed my father, you killed my mother ; you have cut off my head, made " my tongue to protrude. You have made the blood to flow to the handle of " the cleaver, to the sheath of the spear ; you snapped the bow string, you " have broken the spear. You have made my father come to corruption, my " mother to rottenness. You have exasperated me, you have made my anger " to rise. I have not attacked you without reason ; there was a righteous " cause. You have dried up the waters, you have made the land barren, the " grain unproductive, the barns empty. You have angered the God of heaven, " you have provoked the Lord of the earth. You have stopped the rains and " made the dry season irregular. You must now redeem yourselves, you must " pay money, you must give kyee-zee. If you do not furnish your price you " must become slaves and die slaves."

Treatment of prisoners.

When part of a village attacked escapes they usually endeavour to redeem the prisoners that have been taken before they are sold away to strangers. For this purpose an elder belonging to a neutral village is hired to go and buy off the captives.

Redeeming captives.

When the messenger comes to the head of the war and explains his object the latter, if favourable, takes a hog and cuts off its snout and with the blood that flows from it he besmears the legs of the messenger, which is the sign that he makes him his friend, and he says he will receive him as an ambassador of peace and he shall make peace between the belligerent parties and they will become brethren again.

After being well entertained that day he is dismissed the next morning with the legs and head of the hog that had been killed, and the sight of these, when he returns, is regarded as legal proof that his mission has been accepted in good faith and that definite arrangements may be made for the redemption of each captive, if they do not quarrel about the price, which they sometimes do. When everything has been arranged satisfactorily filings are made from a sword, a spear, a musket barrel and a stone, and a dog is killed, these filings are then mixed with a part of its blood and with the blood of a hog and a fowl and the whole is put into a cup of water. This is called the " peace-making water." Then the skull of the dog is chopped in two and one takes the lower jaw and suspends it with a string around his neck, the other party takes the part of the skull containing the upper jaw and hangs it around his neck in like manner. They next take in hand the cup of " peace-making water." and say : " We will now make an " end of the feud. Hereafter, we will not attack each other ; we will not " devour each other's property any more, we will become brethren, we will " marry into each other's families. We will entertain no hatred, no malice ; " we will not backbite each other, but we will be happy in each other down to " the generations of our children and grandchildren ; and our children " shall not quarrel, but live in harmony. If you agree to this," says each party addressing the other, " and will agree to live in accordance with this " agreement for ever, into the generations of our children and grandchildren, " then drink of the peace-making water."

After drinking they say : " Now that we have made peace, if any one " breaks the engagement, if he does not act truly, but goes to war again and " stirs up the feud again, may the spear eat his breast, the musket his bowels, " the sword his head ; may the dog devour him, may the hog devour him, may " the stone devour him ! When he drinks whiskey, may it become in him the " water that oozes from a dead body. When he eats the flesh of a hog may " that hog become the hog of his funeral rites."

After these imprecations they drink again and the captives are dismissed.

As they go away a salute of muskets is fired and a shower of arrows is sent after them, typical of the power of the dismissing party.

Sometimes when there have been feuds between different villages and the inhabitants have settled their difficulties both villages Treaty of peace. assemble together and enter into a treaty of peace. Having selected a large and durable tree for a witness, they assemble around it and each party cuts a deep notch in the tree. When the " peace-making water" is prepared and drunk and the imprecation spoken, two elders rise up, spear in hand, and address the people saying : " The cause of action is finished this day. Hereafter act in harmony, associate " with each other as brethren. Hereafter if any one brings up a cause of " contention, this tree is witness against him. If the elders die, the notches "in this tree will remain as evidence against him ; and let this spear spear him. " He shall be fined a chatty (*pot-full*) of silver and a cup of gold." Beyond this notch in a tree no monuments of peace or war are known to exist.

Slavery is common amongst all the tribes and a clan of the Bghai often sell their relations. Defaulting debtors, captives in forays, confirmed thieves, widows and widowers who cannot pay the price of the deceased, those who introduce or are supposed to have introduced contagious diseases and possessors of poison, are all sold into slavery. The prices vary, elderly people find no buyer, men and women from 30 to 40 sometimes fetch as much as Rs. 200 or Rs. 300, but girls and boys between 12 and 15 Rs. 400, whilst children of three or four sell for Rs. 300 or Rs. 400 each.

Slavery.

The Kareng having no written language, or rather having a language the various dialects of which were first reduced into writing by the American Missionaries, have no written laws nor have they any tradition of a lawgiver, their rules having gradually grown up and being passed down from elder to elder and believed to be so perfect as to require no change. Indolence, covetousness, partiality, backbiting, hatred, falsehood, quarrelling, oppression, theft (the punishment for which is being sold into slavery), adultery and fornication are forbidden ; peace, love, charity to the poor and to widows and orphans, industry and respect and obedience to parents inculcated. Suicide is not prohibited but is looked upon, as indeed it is, a cowardly mode of escaping from difficulties or dangers, and yet it is very common and almost invariably by hanging : a taunt or a headache are sufficient inducements to self-destruction. The precepts of the the elders are excellent but little attention is in reality paid to them ; forays are forbidden and yet were of weekly occurrence, lying is spoken against strongly yet Dr. Mason states " I have never yet met with a Kareng in the " church or out of it, that, when he had committed a wrong, would not tell " a falsehood to cover it ;" notwithstanding their command of " do not steal " they will abstract any small article which they think will not be missed, but as theft amongst themselves is severely punished, they are in other respects honest. The general principle of their criminal law is the *lex talionis* and they are implacable and vindictive. For a first theft a man is forgiven on making restoration, an habitual thief is sold into slavery. A suspected thief is tried by ordeal, the accuser and the accused trying which can keep his head longest under water, and the one who fails must pay a fine or is put to death ; another, but rarely used, method is to strip the bark from a *sterculia* tree which is then exceedingly slippery and which the suspected man must attempt to ascend. In cases of adultery or fornication, the transgressor buys a hog, and the man and woman take hold each one of a foot with which they scrape furrows in the ground to receive the blood. If they are unmarried no other fine is paid, but if one or both parties are married, they must pay a fine to the injured husband or wife, or both, who is then *ipso facto* divorced and can marry again, the adulterers being allowed to live together if they choose. Reputed witches and wizards are killed, as are poisoners, whilst the punishment for the mere possession of poison is slavery.

Laws.

The father's property passes by will to his children and it is the custom to share it nearly equally among them, but always giving the eldest son the largest share and sometimes giving a

Law of Inheritance.

little more to the youngest than to those between. Nothing is given to the widow, but she is entitled to the use of the property till her death.

When a Kareng of property made his will, before letters were introduced, he killed an ox or a buffalo and made a feast at which every inhabitant of the village was invited to attend. At the feast he declared his wishes as to the disposal of his property and prayed that the disposition he had made might be carried out after his death.

The mother has no property of her own. If she brought property at her marriage it became her husband's; but at her husband's death she takes his place, the Kareng say, and the property is hers to use till her death after which it goes to the children, according to the will of the father. She has no power to make any other disposition of it.

In the event of a second marriage the children of a mature age take possession of the property their father left them : the second husband is not allowed to appropriate to himself any part of the property of the first husband, nor can the children of the second marriage share in it, though in the case of minors it may remain in the mother's hands.

Formerly, and occasionally even in the present day, when a Kareng, has
Civil Suit. been repeatedly to one that owes him money, without obtaining it, and has perhaps been treated uncivilly, he calls out the *posse comitatus*, so far as his friends constitute it, and when a favourite opportunity occurs, they go and seize the debtor in his house or field and bring him off; sometimes taking also one or two of his family or friends. When the debtor is set down bound before his creditor the latter will say to him :—" I have no feud with thee. On the contrary I compas-" sionate thee. But thou borrowedst money of me, thou borrowedst kyee-zee " of me. The money was in my wallet, and I took it out and gave it to thee; " my kyee-zee was in my room, and I tied a string to it, and slung it on thy " head, and caused thee to bear it away. Therefore I went and asked thee for " the return of my money ; I went and requested thee the price of the kyee-zee. " But thou wouldst not pay me ; thou wert abusive to me ; thou stirredst up " strife. Thy language was contentious ; thy words were not peaceable. Thou " didst not give me food to eat ; thou didst not give me water to drink. Thou " wast angry with me, thou didst hate me. I went after thee ; and returned " hungry and thirsty. I ascended mountains and descended into valleys ; I " suffered from heat, and I suffered from cold. Thou didst not repay me my " money ; thou didst not pay me for my kyee-zee. Many years have elapsed ; " many months have passed over. So now I have commenced an action against " thee ; now I have made an attack on thee. Thou didst borrow one kyee-zee " of me ; now thou must pay me two. Thou didst borrow one share of me ; " now thou must pay me two. Thou didst borrow one hundred rupees of me ; " now thou must repay me two hundred. If thou dost not pay me I will sell " thee to repay me for my money to pay me for my kyee-zee. And when I " sell thee, I shall do that which is right and proper." Cases have been tried in our Courts in which the debtor prosecuted the creditor for his forcible seizure and exaction of the kyee-zee.

The Kareng are remarkable for believing in one Eternal GOD, Creator
Religion. of all things, called by the Sgaw and Pwo *Ywa* and by the Bghai *Ta-ywa*, "who is like the air and lives in the " sky as does the wind and like the wind goes everywhere," but who has no

place in their paradise, and who originally dwelt amongst them and only left them after fruitless endeavours to draw them to himself. Though detesting idolatry and having the greatest contempt for Booddhism they yet credit the most childish myths regarding this Supreme Being, as that he had a brother called *Shie-woo*, who, according to one tribe had three eyes, with whom he fought and, proving the strongest, threw under the earth. The name *Shie-woo* and the tradition of his having had three eyes would seem to point to Shiva, and, consequently, to a Hindu origin for this belief.

It has been asserted that there is a considerable difference between the religion of the Kareng-nee and that of the rest of the race, the former "having arrived at the monotheistic idea," whilst the latter " are still "struggling with the crude religious ideas connected with the primitive belief "in ghosts or spirits." This is an error ; the Kareng-nee, a clan of the Sgaw family, do not differ at all from their brethren in religion, and but little in ceremonies. Excluding those who have been converted to Christianity, the whole race invokes the aid and deprecates the wrath of innumerable unseen spirits but never sacrifice or pray to the Supreme Being, whose existence is equally acknowledged by all. To a non-christian Kareng, be he Sgaw, Pwo or Bghai ; Pakoo, Kareng-nee or Hashwie, the world is filled with invisible spirits: every living being be it man or beast or creeping thing, has its La ; every mountain peak, tree, cataract and river has its lord, and every lord a number of attendants, agents to carry out his will, who are the La of those who have died violent deaths. These lords reside near the physical object which they protect, seated on the mossy crag, under the forest tree, or in the foaming torrent. Their attendants, the ghosts, smoking pipes with gold and silver stems and armed with swords and spears, lurk in every nook and cranny, and should a luckless Kareng ignorantly touch one of these powerful guardians or step upon their attendants' unseen weapons they rise in anger and afflict him with sore diseases and must be propitiated with bloodless sacrifices.

The principal lords are he of the earth and she of the rice crops, and to both appropriate offerings are made at the proper times. Among the southern Sgaw the sacrifices to the first are offered annually in January, whilst amongst the Bghai the ceremony occurs once in three years in July : though ostensibly to the Lord of the earth the prayers and ceremonies shew that all the lords, and their attendants as well, are included. (*See Bghai and Sgaw*).

Lord of the earth.

The goddess of the harvest, called Bie-yaw, is invoked annually when the crops are sown. Two different accounts are given of the origin of the custom ; according to one a poor man surrounded by rich neighbours was much oppressed by them, and they would give him only three grains of rice from which to raise a crop. An old woman named Bie-yaw, who had been inhospitably treated by the opulent, was kindly received by the poor man ; she proved to be a goddess and in return for the treatment which she had received she caused a fall of rain to destroy the wealthy and their possessions, but the three grains of rice of her benefactor to produce a plentiful crop, and before leaving him, then the only man on earth from whom all are descended, she instructed him in the ceremonies to be performed to insure her favour. The second is, that Bie-yaw and her husband assuming the form of pythons wound themselves round

Goddess of the Harvest.

the pile of unhusked rice which thereupon increased enormously, but the owner ignorantly killed the male snake on which the female escaped cursing him and eventually, owing to the curse, he was sold as a slave. When the rice plants are a few inches high a small hut is built in the field, and in it are placed two ropes, whilst the following prayer is offered. " Grand-mother " thou guardest my field, thou watchest over my plantation. Look out for " men entering ; look sharp for people coming in. If they come, bind them " with this string, tie them with this rope, do not let them go. If they will " pay fines of money, do not let them go ; if they will pay fines of silver, do " not let them go ; but if they will pay fines in barns of rice, dismiss them. " Eat, grand-mother, guard my field, watch over my plantation. Pour down " thy children's rice, grand-mother, or thy children's fields will come to " nought, sweep it off with thy hand, bring it down continually." From the time of sowing until the completion of this ceremony Bie-yaw has been sitting on the chained stumps, so that unlike the other deities, she is supposed to be ubiquitous. When the crop is gathered and being threshed Bie-yaw is again prayed to to give a good out-turn.

The ghosts and their masters, the lords, are not the only enemies whom the Kareng dreads : in former times they say that God made a mixture of the flesh of every animal and directed them to eat the whole, for if they omitted to eat any that animal would hereafter become invisible and eat them ; accidentally they neglected to eat of the flesh of the Na since which time it preys upon them causing sickness and death and is incarnate in tigers, serpents and other wild animals and reptiles, and must be driven away from their fields and their houses. But, perhaps, the most formidable danger to which he is exposed is that of the attacks of seven spirits who are always on the watch to kill him and who are pledged to destroy him : one by the mouth of a tiger, one by old age, one by sickness, one by drowning, one by the hand of man, one by a fall and the last by every other means.

Na.

Adverse La.

Though in continual fear of assaults which he can neither foresee nor resist, he is not left unprotected, his guardian spirit, his La, accompanies him seated on his neck or head, and as long as he so remains the Kareng is safe from all attacks ; but the La, may be enticed away by others, or may jump down, or wander away during the body's sleep, and then follows sickness and death. If a man pines away his La is supposed to be wandering and must be called back with an offering of food.

Protecting La.

The Kareng ideas of a future state are confused and indefinite. Some believe that the next world will be precisely like this, but reversed. Day here will be night there, north here south there, and that its inhabitants will be employed precisely as now. Another belief is that at death when the La leaves the body, it is judged by a Minos ; those who have done good go to paradise, whence they exercise a watchful care over their descendants, presiding especially over births and marriages, and are worshipped by their descendants ; those who have done evil go to the place of punishment ; whilst those who have done neither good nor evil are sent to Hades ; those only being excluded from entering any of these three (a) whose bodies are unburied or unburned, these become ghosts ; (b) who have died violent deaths, these become the invisible servants of the numerous earthly gods and (c) those who have been unjust rulers or who have been put to death

Future state.

for their crimes who take the forms of birds and beasts and are propitiated with prayers and sacrifices.

The belief in witchcraft is strong. Witches and wizards, unlike those of European countries, have made no compact with the devil, but are those who have obtained possession of a *Na*, already alluded to : they have the power of producing mortal diseases by introducing foreign substances into the bodies of others, however distant. Dr. Mason records a case which came under his own notice in Tavoy in which a Kareng died from water in the cavity of the viscera and having been supposed to be bewitched his friends were called in to witness the *post mortem* in order to convince them that he had died from natural causes. Very different was the effect produced, for the Kareng exclaimed ; " Before we only suspected it, " but now we know that he died from witchcraft, for there is the water that " was put into him by enchantment." In another case which, however, occurred more than 25 years ago, two Kareng appeared before a petty official, also a Kareng, accusing an individual of having a *Na*. The reply which they received was such that they, in open day, killed the unfortunate man whom they suspected.

Witchcraft.

Almost all Kareng of the Bghai family and of the Pa-koo clan of the Sgaw have in their houses stones to which they make offerings of blood, because " if they do not give it blood to eat, it " will eat them." Some of these stones are supposed to give good crops of rice, others to be the embodiment of beneficent spirits, which, however, sometimes turn out malevolent, and others to kill those whom their owners dislike. These stones have nothing peculiar in their appearance ; they are mere bits of rock crystal, chalcedony, or sometimes even bits of sandstone or stratified rock.

Stone worship.

The year is divided into twelve lunar months commencing with January and ending with December, whereas the Burmese, Shan, and Talaing years commence about March. As the English ninth month is called 'September,' the tenth 'October,' the eleventh 'November,' and the twelfth 'December', shewing that the months must have been named when the year began in March, so the Kareng eighth month is called " seventh month," and the ninth the " eighth month," and must have been so called when the year commenced in December as it does at Asadakh in Thibet. February is the " searching month" ' when the Kareng go out to hunt for sites for their fields; August, the " month of gladness," because the rice is in the ear ; April, the " seed month," when the rice is sown, and December the " month of shades," because then the annual offerings to the *manes* of their ancestors are made. There are some slight differences amongst the Kareng-nee ; June with them is the " seventh month," whilst August is not the " month of gladness" but *Ai-doo* on account of a feast which is described *sub-tit. Kareng-nee.*

Divisions of the the year.

Those Kareng who have settled in the plains have adopted the same method of cultivation as that followed by the Burmese and Talaing but those living in the hills sow their crops in what are called toungya or hill gardens. In January or February the house-owner goes out to search for a site, and having found one which suits him he picks up a clod of earth and puts it under his pillow, if his dreams are favourable well and good, if unfavourable he must renew his search over and over again till he finds a spot the earth of which brings good

System of cultivation.

omens to him in his sleep. He then goes out with his family and cuts down the trees on the patch. The operation is commenced by cutting a slight note hin the largest trees at the bottom and proceeding upwards, leaving the smaller trees untouched but increasing the depth of the incision in the larger trees as the top of the patch, always on the side of a hill, is reached; here the largest trees are cut quite through and thus fall on those below; " an impetus is created which increases as it moves steadily "down the hill side, and with one lengthened crash prostrates the whole " forest vegetation."* All is then left till April when the accumulated mass is dry enough to burn, a new house of bamboos being built in the meanwhile in some secluded spot close by : then the dry timber is lighted and the ashes serve as manure whilst the heat of the fire breaks up the ground to the depth of a few inches. In May, after the first rains, the rice is sown, holes being dibbled into the ground and the grains dropped in. When the rice is well up, cotton, capsicums and Indian-corn are planted between the ridges. Near the house are sugar-cane, yams (near dry logs over which their tendrils creep), and piper betel near some tall trees up which the plant can wind. A small hut is built in the patch in which a boy or a girl is placed to frighten away the birds and wild hogs, and, after two or three weedings, the crop is reaped in October and threshed by the men beating the ears against a beam or treading the grains out with their toes, for they have no buffaloes like their lowland neighbours. Whilst the plants are in the ground the men are employed in fishing and are aided by the women who go to the banks of streams with small hand nets. Animals are trapped, or shot with bows and arrows and food thus provided. In some places they have permanent gardens of the Areca palm, the nuts of which are chewed with the leaf of the piper betel, lime and tobacco, by all races, Burman, Talaing and Kareng. These gardens are generally on the margins of mountain streams and are irrigated by water conducted in artificial channels from the parent streams at spots above the level of the plantation. When the rice crops have been gathered the Kareng visit the villages in the plains bringing in betel-nuts, rice, fowls, wild honey, bees-wax, and in some places cardamoms (found growing wild), and thus obtain funds wherewith to support themselves and to pay their taxes. Often, however, they dispose of their produce to Burmans and others who at this season visit the hills taking with them cotton goods and other articles to exchange.

Population.   The Kareng population according to the census in 1872 numbered 331,255 souls.

KARENG-AYAING.—The Burmese name of a clan of Bghai Kareng. *See Bghai-ka-hta.*

KARENG-NEE.—Called by themselves *Ka-ra*, by Shans *Yang-aing*, by the Gaikho *The-pya*, and *Bghai-moo-hte* or eastern Bghai by the rest of the family. They occupy the country north of the province but some have emigrated into British territory. They are divided into Eastern and Western Kareng-nee, of whom the former are by far the more numerous. They are the most civilized and at the same time the most ferocious of all the Kareng tribes, preying without mercy on their weaker southern neighbours, a practice which the western branch has, however, to a great extent given up. They belong to the

---

*Report by Mr. O'Riley, Assistant Commissioner in the Toung-ngoo district, 1855.

Bghai tribe and, like the majority of that clan, wear trowsers. " The men " wear short red pants with perpendicular, very narrow, black or white stripes. " Sometimes the pants have a black ground and the stripes are red or white. " Below the knee are black bands formed of twisted thread and varnished " with the black varnish that abounds in this country obtained from the *Melan-* " *norrhœa usitatissima.* A wrapper of white with a few red or black stripes is " wrapped around the body, and many wear Shan jackets which seem to be an " addition to the Kareng dress. A bright red turban is worn on the head and an " ornamented bag is hung across the shoulder..................The female dress is " peculiarly picturesque, though every garment is only a rectangular piece of " cloth. The head dress is a large red or black turban, wound up to form a " small tower on the top of the head. There is no gown but a cloth like the " Roman toga, tied by two corners on the right shoulder, and the left arm " is sometimes kept covered, but more often it is drawn out above the garment. " A second piece of cloth, like the first, is kept on the hand like a loose shawl " or tied around the waist. One of these garments is usually red and the " other black, though occasionally both are red. For a petticoat another " rectangular piece of cloth is wrapped two or three times around the person, " and is kept in its place by a wampum belt, some half a dozen inches in " diameter. Another enormous band of beads is worn below the knee and on " the ankles large silver bangles. Both sexes wear bangles on the wrists, and " the women a profusion of silver necklaces formed of ingots of silver, or coins, " to which are added a dozen or more strings of beads. Ear-drops are worn by " both men and women, and the latter add silver ear-plugs an inch or more in " diameter."* The men have the rising sun tattooed in red across the small of the back.

The majority of their customs are the same as those of the rest of the Bghai family but in some points they differ. At the birth of a child, when the mother is able to move about, which is generally in about three days, a feast is given by the father to all who choose to come, and the mother, taking the child on her back, goes down out of the house and, digging the ground a little, pulls up a few weeds, thus symbolizing her undertaking to support her infant (for she is supposed to have gone to the rice field and worked therein) and then returns; after this presents are made to the child (of silver or of iron if a boy and of beads or of a fowl or of a pig if a girl) and it is named after some relation or after some one who has given large presents.

They never betroth their children in infancy and their marriage ceremony is peculiar. The two young people having made up their minds to marry and the parents having given their consent (which they rarely refuse) the bridegroom makes a feast in his house to which the bride and some female companions come. During the feast the bridegroom presents a cup of spirits to the bride asking " Is it agreeable ?" This she takes, replying " It is" "agreeable." She and her companions remain all night and returning home next morning prepare a feast to which the bridegroom and his friends come and the ceremony of presenting the cup of spirits is again gone through, this time the bride being the questioner ; occasionally the reply, given playfully, is " Not agreeable," when the spirits must be offered and the question

---

* Burma, by Dr. Mason ; pp. 89,90.

asked till a favourable answer is received. The feast in the bride's house completes the whole ceremony.

The names of their months are slightly different from those employed by other Kareng. Though their year commences in January, June is the " seventh month," but July is not called the " eighth," and August instead of being called the " month of gladness " is named " Ai-doo," after a feast peculiar to themselves, the origin of which is unknown ; hogs, fowls and oxen are killed and all the villagers feast together and send food and spirits to their friends elsewhere. Drums are beaten, muskets loaded only with powder fired off, and the whole is a three days saturnalia during which accidents often happen and houses are set on fire. In another point are their customs different from those of the rest of the Bghai : they never offer a hog to the spirits of their ancestors.

KA-REE-THENG.—A small village, of 390 inhabitants in 1877, on the eastern bank of the Ka-rwa-dai river, the head-quarters of the Mek-ka-la-gya circle, Oo-rit-toung west township, Akyab district.

KARENG-LE-KHYENG.—A small village in the Toung-ngoo district on the bank of the Re-nwe stream, at the foot of the western slopes of the Rek-kan-tseng spur, about seven miles due west of the Tsit-toung and five south of Upper Burma : there is here one of the frontier police posts.

KA-ROOP-PEE.—A small river in the Amherst district, formed by the junction of numerous mountain streams which rise in the western slopes of the Toung-gnyo range. It falls into the sea nearly opposite Double Island.

KA-ROOP-PEE.—A revenue circle in the Wa-kha-roo township, Amherst district, situated between the Toung-gnyo hills on the east, the sea on the west, the Pa-nga circle on the north, and the Tsam-ba-ra circle on the south. The eastern portion is hilly, producing valuable timber such as Ka-gnyeng and Pyeng-gado. The remainder consists of sandy hillocks with intervening plains of considerable extent and the whole is intersected by tidal creeks of large size. Communication with other places is difficult except in the fine season, when boats can venture out of the creeks into the open sea. Salt is made near the sea coast. The population, who are principally Talaing, numbered 1,219 in 1868 and 1,844 in 1876, when the land revenue was Rs. 2,692 and the capitation tax Rs. 1,732.

KA-ROOP-PEE.—A large village in the Wa-kha-roo township of the Amherst district, in the circle of the same name, on the left bank of the Ka-roop-pee stream near its mouth. In 1869, when an Assistant Commissioner was placed in charge of the sub-division, the Extra Assistant Commissioner in charge of the township was transferred hither from Amherst. A few years later, when the Assistant Commissioner was removed, Amherst again became the head-quarters of the township. In 1868 it had 865 and in 1877 1,297 inhabitants. The name is Talaing and is derived from a tradition of its having been originally founded by three Chinamen.

KA-TA-WA.—A revenue circle in the Mro-houng township of the Akyab district on the Koo-la-dan river. In 1876 the population was 2,020, the land revenue Rs. 7,080, the capitation tax Rs. 2,464 and the gross revenue Rs. 9,898. The Thoogyee resides in a small village of the same name situated on the eastern bank of the Koo-la-dan, which had 252 inhabitants in 1877.

KA-THA-HPA-KARENG.—A village in the Kyaik-kaw circle, Tha-htoon township, Amherst district, at the foot of the western slopes of the Martaban hills. In 1877 the inhabitants numbered 529 souls.

KATOO-BYENG.—A revenue circle in the Ka-ma township, Thayet district, to which have been added Tha-gnyan, Tsheng-tshway-myoung, Zee-daw, Kywai-goung, Goon-meng-myoung and Tsam-bay-khyoon. The Tha-gnyan Thoogyee resigned in 1863, when his circle was joined to Zee-daw, and the Zee-daw Thoo-gyee in 1872, and the united circles were added to Tsam-bay-khyoon. In 1870 the Goon-myeng-myoung Thoogyee resigned and the circle was added to Kywai-goung. Subsequently Tsam-bay-khyoon (with Tha-gnyan and Zee-daw) and Kywai-goung (with Goon-myeng-myoung) were joined to Katoo-byeng. In 1872 these circles had a population of 1,608 souls and in 1876 of 1,626 : in 1872 the land revenue was Rs. 1,758 and in 1876 Rs. 2,425 ; in the latter year the capitation tax was Rs. 1,812 and the gross revenue Rs. 4,379. The Thoogyeeship of Katoo-byeng was held heredi-tarily, but in 1826, before the annexation of Pegu, the then Thoogyee, Moung Oung Tsee, sold his birthright to one Moung Khat. The principal products are rice, sessamum, plantains, maize, thatch-grass and cutch, the last principally in the old Kywai-goung circle. In the Zee-daw circle was an irrigation reservoir known as the "Zee-daw-kan" or Zee-daw tank, but the embankment gave way several years ago.

KATOO-BYENG.—A village in the circle of the same name in the Ka-ma township, Thayet district, on the left bank of the Ma-de stream, con-taining rather over fifty houses.

KA-TSENG.—A circle in the Hmaw-bhee township, Rangoon district, added to it, with Htan-ta-beng, Pa-dan and Kyoon-oo, in 1874, from the Eng-ga-bhoo township which was then broken up. In shape it is an irregular triangle with the apex towards the west and the base formed by the Hlaing river. On the north it is separated from the Htan-ta-beng circle by the Hta-ka-loung creek, on the west from Kyoon-oo by the Eng-ka-laing, and on the south from Pa-dan by the Tsoo-la-gan. The area comprised within these limits is about 20 square miles. The country is a vast flat plain, treeless, except near the villages which are thinly shrouded in bamboos of inferior growth and cocoanut trees, and highly intersected by tidal creeks, most of them navigable by large boats at the flood and in many cases spanned at the villages by high wooden foot bridges. The whole area is subject to inunda-tion during the rains and the soil is poor, producing only from 30 to 40 baskets of unhusked rice per acre.

In 1876 there were 17,788 acres of rice (excluding 1,579 acres left fallow), two acres of dhanee, five acres of garden and seven acres of miscellaneous cultivation.

In 1877 the agricultural stock was :—

Buffaloes	..	..	..	..	1,006
Cows, bulls and bullocks	..	..	..	178
Pigs	..	..	..	..	..	106
Ploughs	..	..	..	..	..	502
Carts	..	..	..	..	..	129
Boats	..	..	:	..	..	186

The buffaloes are owned principally by the Talaing and Kareng inhabitants, the cows, bulls and bullocks by the Talaing and Burmans, and the pigs by the Burmans and Chinese.

In the same year the inhabitants were :—

Talaing	..	..	..	..	1,436
Burmans	..	..	..	..	1,043
Shan	..	..	..	..	872
Kareng	..	..	..	..	44
Chinese	..	..	..	..	4
Natives of India	..	..	..	..	11
					3,410

living in ten villages, of which the largest was Pouktan on the stream of the same name rather more than a mile from its mouth, with 604 inhabitants, and Rakhaing-yo, where the Thoogyee lives, on the Rakhaing-yo creek about a mile and a half south of Pouktan, with 611 inabitants. By far the larger portion of the population are agriculturists and coolies.

In 1876 the land revenue was Rs. 19,408, the capitation tax Rs 3,858 and the gross revenue Rs. 23,371.

KA-WA.—A large village in the Rangoon district, with 1,053 inhabitants in 1877, on the right bank of the Pegu river in 17° 4' 30" N. and 96° 31' 10" E., inhabited principally by Talaing agriculturists and petty traders. In 1878 a considerable portion of the village was burned down, the result of the spreading of a jungle fire.

KA-WA.—A tidal creek in the Shwe-loung township, Bassein district, joining the Irrawaddy on the east to the Kyoon-pa-doot on the west, which at the floods can be traversed by boats fifty feet in length. In the rains it unites with the Moung-dee, another tidal creek running north and south.

KA-WAI.—A small river which rises amongst the eastern slopes of the Arakan mountains and, flowing eastwards, falls into the Irrawaddy just above the town of Thayet. It is of no importance, is not navigable, and in the hot weather is almost dry.

KAW-BHIEN.—A revenue circle in the Gyaing Attaran township, Amherst district, extending southwards from the left bank of the Gyaing east of Maulmain from which it is separated by the Kyaik-paran circle. In 1876 the land revenue was Rs. 5,642, the capitation tax Rs. 1,878, the gross revenue Rs. 7,520 and the population 2,883.

KAW-BHIEN.—A village in the circle of the same name in the Gyaing Attaran township of the Amherst district, on the east or right bank of the Attaran and south of the Kaw-bhien, one of its tributaries, a stream of little or no importance. In 1877 it had 1,400 inhabitants.

KAW-BOUK.—A village in the Kaw-bhien circle, Gyaing Attaran township, Amherst district, to the north of and near Kaw-bhien. In 1877 it had a population of 570 souls.

KAW-DWON.—A revenue circle in the Gyaing Than-lweng township, Amherst district, formed of the islands opposite Maulmain on the south and Kado on the east, at the junction of the Salween, the Gyaing and the Attaran rivers. These islands are fertile and are well cultivated by their Talaing inhabitants who in 1876 numbered 777 ; that year the land revenue was Rs. 4,428 and the capitation tax Rs. 972.

KAW-DWOT.—A village in the Rwa-lwot circle of the Bhee-loo-gywon township, Amherst district, east of Ka-law. In 1867, this village had a population of 343 souls, principally Talaing, and in 1877 of 682.

KAW-DWOT.—A village in the circle of the same name in the Re La-maing township of the Amherst district, on the left bank of the La-maing river, near its mouth. In 1877 it had 975 inhabitants. The name is Talaing and means " island " village.

KAW-DWOT.—A revenue circle on the sea coast in the Re La-maing township of the Amherst district, well cultivated by the inhabitants who are mostly Talaing and who in 1876 numbered 1,600 souls. The land revenue in that year was Rs. 4,820 and the capitation tax Rs. 1,653.

KA-WEK.—A revenue circle, about 15 square miles in extent, in the Myoung-mya township, Bassein district, in the delta of the Irrawaddy, between the Poo-loo and the Tha-yaw-boon channels on the south, east and west, and bounded on the north by the small Ka-wek creek which flows between these two. The north-western and western portion of the circle only are cultivated. It has no roads. The only stream of any importance is the Poo-loo which is navigable by river steamers at all times ; the banks are densely wooded, but the timber is of no value. In 1876 the population was 2,211, the land revenue Rs. 4,778, the capitation tax Rs. 2,210 and the gross revenue Rs. 7,292.

KA-WEK.—A tidal creek in the Than-lyeng township, Rangoon district, which falls into the Pegu five or six miles above Hpa-goo village. The banks are sandy and shelving and fringed in places with tree forest; with the flood tide boats of 500 bushels burden can ascend for a considerable distance, as far as A-htoon village. In the rains, when the plains are flooded, boats can pass through from the Pegu river to the sea.

KAW-HLA.—A village in the Kado circle, Gyaing Than-lweng township, Amherst district, on the right bank of the Gyaing a little to the north of Kado from which it is separated by a rice plain. In 1877 the inhabitants numbered 620 souls.

KAW-HMOO.—A village in the Rangoon district, in 16° 31′ 30″ N. and 96° 8′ E. near the source of the Lek-khaik, divided into two or three parts. The inhabitants who are mainly Burmese and Kareng numbered 476 in 1877 and are engaged principally in agriculture, but some are fishermen working the neighbouring A-twot lake and some are salt workers.

KAW-HMOO.—A revenue circle in the centre of the lower half of the Angyee township, Rangoon district, lying between Pyaw-bhway, Ko-doung and Htan-ma-naing on the east, La-wa-dee on the south, Twan-te and Ien-da-poora on the west and Ma-hlaing and Pan-hlaing on the north. Its extreme length is about fifteen miles and its extreme breadth about nine. The western portion of the circle consists of high undulating ground covered with forest, whilst the eastern consists of low swampy ground or extensive sheets of water—the Bhoora-gyee, A-hpyouk and A-twot Eng. In the centre is a strip of rice land where most of the villages are found. During the last five years the population, area under cultivation and the revenue realized have been :—

Year.	Popula-tion.	AREA, IN ACRES, UNDER			REVENUE, IN RUPEES, FROM			
		Rice.	Garden	Total.	Land.	Capita-tion.	All other sources.	Total.
1872-73	..	5,216	3,334	44	3,378	13,375	5,107	1,990	20,552
1873-74	..	4,554	5,426	51	5,477	15,521	5,242	2,000	22,763
1874-75	..	5,660	4,426	52	4,478	12,021	6,022	2,500	20,543
1875-76	..	6,045	3,560	53	3,613	13,040	5,525	2,520	21,115
1876-77	..	7,012	4,526	61	4,587	11,420	4,522	2,600	18,543

and the agricultural stock during the same period was :—

Year.			Buffaloes.	Cows, bulls and bullocks.	Goats.	Pigs.	Carts.	Ploughs.	Boats.
1872-73	..	..	723	980	20	282	375	159	135
1873-74	..	..	802	990	13	300	425	149	124
1874-75	..	...	904	804	29	425	352	156	130
1875-76	..	..	742	664	35	423	424	200	160
1876-77	..	..	824	724	45	282	355	190	170

In former years the fisheries constituted the riches of the circle, but in 1876 the land revenue was Rs. 16,550, the capitation tax Rs. 7,928 and the gross revenue Rs. 26,543.

KAW-HNAT.—A village in the Kado circle of the Gyaing Than-lweng township, Amherst district, north of and close to Kado. In 1877 it had 523 inhabitants.

KAW-KA-DWOT.—A village in the Zoot-thoot circle, Bheeleng Kyaik-hto township, Shwe-gyeng district, on the high road from Bheeleng to Kyaik-hto where it crosses the Thai-hpyoo river at the elbow formed by its sudden bend westward. In 1877 it had 1,333 inhabitants; agriculturists and fisher-men who work the numerous fisheries in the neighbourhood. There is a police station in this village and a cattle market is held twice a week in the dry season.

KAW-KA-LEE.—A small, but high and remarkable, island inside the mouth of the Tavoy river, called "Reef Island" in the charts.

KAW-KA-MAY.—A village in the circle of the same name in the Tsit-toung sub-division of the Shwe-gyeng district, in the southern portion of the plains stretching southward to the sea from Kyaik-hto, and on the bank of the Thai-hpyoo, a tributary of the Tsit-toung. In 1877 it had 955 inhabitants.

KAW-KA-MAY.—A revenue circle in the Tsit-toung sub-division of the Shwe-gyeng district, about 112 square miles in area, which extends from Kyaik-hto southwards to the coast along both banks of the Thai-hpyoo creek. In 1876 it had a population of 4,723 souls, of whom the majority are Talaing and a few Kareng. The river and sea fisheries furnish a small proportion of the revenue. The land revenue in 1876 was Rs. 12,480, the capitation tax Rs. 4,455 and the gross revenue Rs. 19,787.

KAW-KA-RIET.—A small stream in the Amherst district, which has its source in the western slopes of the Dawna spur and after a W.S.W. course of a few miles flows past the village of Kaw-ka-riet and a mile or two lower down, where it receives from the eastward the waters of the Hlaing, another mountain torrent, it turns westward and with a winding but generally westerly course between high banks dotted here with long grass, there with open tree forest, with occasional clumps of feathery bamboos hanging over the dark waters, it falls into the Houng-tha-raw a few miles above Kya-eng village. In the rains it is navigable by boats as far as Kaw-ka-riet village, but in the dry season it is impracticable above the mouth of the Hlaing: even in September it is little else than a shallow mountain torrent, depositing pebbles, coarse sand and gravel at the salient angles of the banks. At Kaw-ka-riet it is spanned by a wooden bridge connecting the two quarters of the village.

KAW-KA-RIET.—The head-quarters of the Houng-tha-raw township, Amherst district. It is a straggling village on both banks of the Kaw-ka-riet stream, which is here spanned by a wooden bridge. Kareng live on the left and Burmans and Toungthoo on the right bank where are the Court-house of the Extra Assistant Commissioner in charge of the township, the police station and the Government market. In 1876 the population numbered 2,135 souls and the land revenue was Rs. 2,318. There is here a cattle market held once a week.

KAW-KA-RIET.—A revenue circle in the Houng-tha-raw township, Amherst district, between the crest of the Dawna spur and the Houng-tha-raw river. It is inhabited mainly by Kareng and is not extensively cultivated. In 1876 the population was 3,240, the land revenue Rs. 2,803 and the capitation tax Rs. 3,700.

KAW-KA-RIT.—A revenue circle in the extreme south of the Salween Hill Tracts on the Rwon-za-leng river, near its mouth in the Salween, and adjoining the Amherst district. In 1876 the number of inhabitants was 3,601, the land revenue Rs. 1,483 and the capitation tax Rs. 1,539.

KAW-KHA-NEE.—A revenue circle in the Zaya township, Amherst district, south of and adjoining Kyouk-tan, which separates it from Maulmain, cut off from the Salween by a narrow strip of land which separates it from the Kyouk-tan and Hpa-ouk circles. Its total area is about 4,260 acres of which about two-thirds are upland adapted for garden cultivation. The tracts just below the high land are very poor, some yielding not more than from 15 to 20 baskets an acre; the lands nearer the Salween are good. Its inhabitants are principally Talaing and in 1876 numbered 1,406 souls; in that year the land revenue was Rs. 3,154 and the capitation tax Rs. 1,415.

KAW-LEE-YA.—A revenue circle lately added to the Shwe-gyeng

township of the Shwe-gyeng district from Rangoon, 192 square miles, about, in extent, lying west of Thoo-yai-tha-mee, with a population, in 1876, of 3,312 souls, mainly Talaing. At the end of the rains the inhabitants are largely engaged in working the numerous lake and pond fisheries in the circle, from which the State derives a large revenue. In 1876 the land revenue was Rs. 1,933, the capitation tax Rs. 3,510 and the gross revenue Rs. 17,562.

KAW-LOO-DO.—A block-house and Police post in the Salween Hill Tracts, four marches north of Pa-pwon, constructed in 1861 for the protection of the surrounding wild and mountainous country. In 1878 it was attacked and burned down by a marauding party of Kareng-nee.

KAW-LOO-DO.—A mountainous and forest-clad revenue circle in the north of the Salween hill-tracts. In 1876 the population, Kareng, numbered 4,074 souls, the land revenue was Rs. 905 and the capitation tax Rs. 1,378.

KAW-LOON.—A revenue circle in the Than-lweng Hlaing-bhwai township, Amherst district. In 1876 the land revenue was Rs. 834, the capitation tax Rs. 1,784 and the population 2,215 souls.

KAW-PA-RAN.—A revenue circle in the Zaya township of the Amherst district, which now includes Paing-ka-ma and extends from the Toung-gnyo spur westwards to the sea coast immediately south of the Moo-doon and north of the Kwon-te circles. The old Paing-ka-ma circle consisted of two portions, one at the foot of the Toung-gnyo hills and the other on the bank of the Salween, Kaw-pa-ran lying between them. Included within the limits of old Kaw-pa-ran is Bha-louk, once an independent circle, added to Kaw-pa-ran about 25 years ago. The inhabitants are chiefly Talaing agriculturists, who numbered 2,844 in 1876, when the land revenue was Rs. 6,095 and the capitation tax Rs. 2,462.

KAW-RAN-GYEE.—A small island off the western coast of the Bassein district, near the mouth of the Nga-root-khoung river; the "Coringee" of the old charts. Limestone is found on the island and is brought to the mainland and burned.

KAW-THAT.—A village in the Ta-ra-na circle of the Gyaing Than-lweng township, Amherst district, on the left bank of the Gyaing, west of Ta-ra-na. In 1877 the inhabitants numbered 756 souls.

KA-ZEE.—A revenue circle in the south-eastern township of the Tavoy district inhabited by a few Kareng and with very little cultivation, principally of sessamum and cardamoms. It now includes Tha-hpyoo-khyoung and Tsaw-bhoora. In 1876 there were only 845 inhabitants, the land revenue was Rs. 365, the capitation tax Rs. 732 and the gross revenue Rs. 1,115.

KE-LA-THA.—The highest peak in the hills immediately north of Keng-rwa, the end of the mass of mountains between the Tsit-toung and the Bhee-leng rivers. A large and conspicuous pagoda caps the hill and was formerly much resorted to by pilgrims. The site is traditionally said to have been selected by Gaudama as the place in which to deposit one of his hairs which he had given to the hermit living on Ke-la-tha. At the foot of the pagoda is a large slab of stone, unfortunately broken, with an inscription in Talaing the meaning of which is not known. Near the summit of the hill there is a noted well containing excellent water.

KE-LA-THA.—A revenue circle in the Re La-maing township, Amherst district, on the western slopes of the Toung-gnyo chain. It is inhabited principally by Talaing and is to some extent under cultivation. In 1876 the population numbered 1,358 souls, the land revenue was Rs. 2,011 and the capitation tax Rs. 1,620.

KE-LA-THA.—A village in the circle of the same name in the Re Lamaing township of the Amherst district on the left bank of the La-maing river where a small Police force is stationed. In 1877 it had 826 inhabitants.

KENG.—A revenue circle in the Kyouk-hpyoo district, lying in the southwest corner of the township of that name on the west coast of Ramree island, to the north of the mouth of the Ran-bouk stream. It has an area of seven square miles and in 1876 had a population of 3,668 souls. In that year the land revenue was Rs. 3,503, the capitation tax Rs. 3,979 and the gross revenue Rs. 7,767. This circle now includes Moo-reng. In addition to rice the principal products are coarse sugar and indigo.

KENG-DAT.—A revenue circle in the Tha-boung township of the Bassein district, about 30 square miles in extent, occupying the corner formed by the junction of the Nga-won and Daga rivers. The country on the west is undulating but on the east it is flat and cultivated with rice. In 1876 the land revenue was Rs. 8,579, the capitation tax Rs. 4,477, the gross revenue Rs. 13,488 and the number of inhabitants 4,602.

KENG-KHYOUNG.—A revenue circle in the Zaya township, Amherst district, extending from the Toung-gnyo hills on the east to the Salween on the west. It now includes Kwon-ta and a portion of Ka-ma-pa-tai. Towards the east is high forest-land, in the centre poor land and towards the west fertile soil with a fringe of dhanee plantations on the bank of the river. In 1868 the population, who are principally Talaing agriculturists, numbered 979, the the land revenue was Rs. 3,212 and the capitation tax Rs. 985. In 1876 these were 3,267, Rs. 7,215 and Rs. 3,177 respectively.

KENG-RWA.—A large village in the Henzada district, with a population of about 800 souls in 1878, on the right bank of the Irrawaddy in 18° 25′ 30″ N. and 95° 16′ 40″ E. near the northern frontier of the district. The inhabitants, who are mainly Burmese, are principally engaged in trading.

KENG-RWA.—A revenue circle in the Tsit-toung sub-division of the Shwe-gyeng district between the town of Kyaik-hto and the upper course of the Thai-hpyoo. It has an area of about 220 square miles, and in 1876 had a population of 4,865 souls. It is but slightly cultivated and the revenue derived from leasing out the pond and lake fisheries is larger than that derived from the land which, in 1876, was Rs. 1,576; the capitation tax that year was Rs. 3,870 and the gross revenue Rs. 10,031.

KENG-RWA.—A village in the circle of the same name, containing 1,349 inhabitants in 1877, six miles to the south of Kyaik-hto, between that town and Kaw-ka-dwot, at the foot of the hills which bound to the north the plain country of the Tsit-toung sub-division and on the high road from Tsit-toung to Maulmain. There is here a Government rest-house and a small Police force. The inhabitants, many of whom are Toungthoo, are largely engaged in orchard cultivation, growing mangoes, oranges and doorians of notedly pure flavour.

During the Burmese time a small military force was stationed in this village, whence the name—*Keng* " a military post" and *rwa* " a village."

KENG-THAN.—A village in the Prome district in 18° 26′ 50″ N. and 25° 27′ 0″ E. on the right ank of the Myit-ma-kha, seven miles from its source in the Engma lake : from this village a narrow tract of rice country extends southwards along the bank of the Myit-ma-kha into the Henzada district.

KENG-WA.—A tidal creek which traverses the united Zayat-hla and Kyoon-ta-nai circles of the Pan-ta-naw township, Thoon-khwa district, from north to south, nearly parallel to, and a few miles to the west of, the Irrawaddy into which it falls at Keng-wa; after this the river has taken a bend eastwards : at its northern end it communicates with numerous creeks, of which the principal is the Nga-ran ; its total length is from 18 to 20 miles. It is open for large boats with masts at all times and seasons. The banks are fringed with valuable timber.

KHA-BENG.—A village in the An-gyee township of the Rangoon district on the Moo-la-man creek with 125 inhabitants only in 1877, chiefly Talaing and Shan gardeners. It is the site of an ancient city where reigned the King Tha-mien-htaw-byeen-ran and his queen Mien-da-de-wee, the founders of the Shwe Tshan-daw pagoda at Twan-te. The ruins of both the interior and exterior cities are still visible. On the opposite bank of the Moo-la-man is the Kyaik-keng pagoda ; to the south is a large ruined pagoda known as the Moung Tee. Moung Tee is said to have been the husband of a celebrated princess of Kha-beng.

KHA-BOUNG.—A river in the Toung-gnoo district which rises in the Pegu Roma range and after a south-westerly course of 68 miles falls into the Tsit-toung about two miles south of Toung-gnoo. It is navigable for some 25 miles. Rather more than twelve miles from its mouth it flows past the ancient site of Toung-ngoo. Towards its source the banks are steep and its bed rocky. Teak, Theng-gan for boat-building, sessamum and a considerable quantity of betel-nut are brought down this stream for the Toung-ngoo market.

KHA-BOUNG-GAN.—A village in the Prome district E. S. E. of the town of Prome from which it is about eight miles distant.

KHA-DA.—A village in the Poung circle of the Martaban township, Amherst district, south of Poung the head-quarters of the township. In 1876 it had 823 inhabitants.

KHA-LA.— A village in the Mergui district of the Tenasserim division, in 12° 0′ 53″ N. Lat. and 98° 33′ E. Long. with a small population of about 150 souls. Before the conquest by Aloungbhoora it was a flourishing village. The American Baptist and a Roman Catholic Mission formerly had stations here but the former has been abandoned and a native catechist left in charge of the latter. The population is mixed Kareng and Burman.

KHA-DAIK.—A village in the Kyaik-kaw circle, Tha-htoon township, Amherst district, on the bank of the Bhee-leng river not far from its mouth. In 1877 it had 589 inhabitants.

KHA-DAING.—A highly-cultivated revenue circle in the southern portion of the Martaban township, Amherst district, on the west of the Martaban hills. In 1876 the land revenue, derived almost entirely from the rice land, was

Rs. 13,907, the capitation tax Rs. 690 and the population 683. Some of the lands are owned and worked by inhabitants of the neighbouring circles.

KHA-DAT-GYEE.—A revenue circle in the western township of the Tavoy district about 16 square miles in extent which in 1876 had a population of 1,175 souls, and a land revenue of Rs. 2,895 ; in that year the capitation tax was Rs. 902 and the gross revenue Rs. 4,049. The principal products are rice and salt.

KHA-DAT-NGAY.—A revenue circle in the western township, Tavoy district, about 14 square miles in extent. In 1876 the land revenue was Rs. 2,179, the capitation tax Rs. 1,604, the gross revenue Rs. 4,388 and the number of inhabitants 2,045. The principal products are rice, dhanee palms and salt.

KHA-DWON.—A village in the Gaw circle, Martaban township, Amherst district. In 1867 the population of this village numbered 762 souls, and 646 in 1877.

KHA-LOUK-THAIK.—A village, of 659 inhabitants in 1877, in the Kyoon-ka-nee circle of the Myoung-mya township, Bassein district, on the eastern bank of the Kha-louk-thaik stream, about fifteen miles north-east of Myoung-mya.

KHAMIE.—Sometimes written Khoomi, Koomi or Kummi. A hill-tribe in Arakan, of the Toungtha class, inhabiting the hills bordering the Koo-la-dan and numbering about 7,000 souls. Of this race of people there are two divisions, called by themselves Khumie and Khamie but generally known under the common appellation of Khamie. They are the most warlike tribe living within the tribute-paying limits. It is probable that they have not been settled in their present seat for more than five or six generations but have been driven down from the distant hills by the more warlike and stronger Shandoo, and have in their turn driven the Mro to the foot of the hills and even to the plains. When questioned about the country occupied by their ancestors they point to the highest range of the Roma mountains and say that formerly their tribe was very numerous and had strongly stockaded villages in those hills, which are now occupied by Khyeng and Shandoo : indeed portions of the tribe have been driven out by the former within the memory of man. To this enforced immigration is probably due the gradual increase in their numbers. The language of the Khamie portion was reduced to writing by Mr. Stilson of the American Baptist Mission. They are divided into seventeen clans, each having a distinctive name viz., Rek-kha, Hteng-too-dza, Kray, Loon-loo, Tshit-too, Kan-lwe, Lien-kran, A-boung, Hpa-broo, Lien-khoop, Nhan-lay, Bha-leng, Kho-be, Loung-ta, Toung-too, Tsam-bale and Lee-loo. Each clan is under a separate Toung-meng, or " Hill Chief." Their religious system is very vague and consists in Nat, or spirit, worship. They adore the earth, the sun and every object that strikes their fancy, to each of which they accord a separate spirit. "Each peak in their native hills " they hold to be the mountain watchtower of a god. Nothing could better " illustrate this than the accompanying translation of part of a Khamie's prayer. " Previous to an undertaking or an expedition, he lets loose a fowl, as an " offering to the spirits, and utters the following :—'Oh spirit of the day-sun ; " 'oh spirit of the rock-ledged gate ; oh spirit of the streams of the Hoo-tsa-loon ;

"' oh spirit of the surges of the Kalak ; oh lords of the mountain peaks;
"' one, two, three, four, five, six, seven, eight times; take ye this my
" ' offering.' "

Every object which is in motion they conceive to be so in virtue of a
spirit. They have no religious superiors, but pay a certain amount of respect
to those who pretend to be in communication with the spirits and the inter-
preters of their will. Their only visible objects of worship are the trunks of
three or four trees, which have been cut down in clearing a space for the
village, and a similar number of pillar-like stones. These are fixed in the
earth together, in the middle of a large shed, which is also used as the place
of re-union and festivity of the village.

They have no marriage ceremony: the bridegroom gives as much as he can
to the father of the bride and takes her home. The women wear a short
petticoat kept on by numerous brass rings round the waist ; the men are
almost naked, but have a small cloth round the loins the ends hanging in
front and behind, whence the Burmese corruption of the name into Khwe-
myee or "dog's tail."

They have no regular cultivation but clear and plant toungya or hill-
gardens with a species of indigenous rice called hill or red rice. As soon as
the available soil near a village is exhausted, which on an average takes place
in about three years, the whole village migrates to another spot and new
houses are built. Wandering thus every three years and in continual dread
of being massacred by their relentless foes, the Khamie do not know what
comfort or security is and all their valuables are secreted in some hidden
cave ; yet they are a merry and laughter-loving race and fond to a degree of
beads with which they ornament everything they possess.

They pay a tribute to the British Government and, since the appointment
of a Superintendent of Hill Tracts, are gradually learning what peace and
protection are.

KHA-MOUNG-KHYOUNG.—A revenue circle in the Kyouk-hpyoo
district, about 14 square miles in extent in the southern portion of Ramree
island and on its eastern coast, in which sugarcane is largely cultivated. The
population, who are mainly Arakanese, numbered 1,224 in 1876. In that
year the land revenue was Rs. 1,741, the capitation tax Rs. 1,156 and the gross
revenue Rs. 3,000.

KHA-MOUNG-THWAY.—A revenue circle in the north-eastern township of the Tavoy district, sparsely cultivated and inhabited by a few Kareng.
Sessamum and cardamoms are the principal products, but the area under
cultivation, entirely hill gardens, is very small. In 1876 the population was
only 833 and the gross revenue Rs. 226, of which Rs. 48 was derived from the
land and Rs. 176 from the capitation tax.

KHA-NOUNG-TO.—A village in the Kha-noung-to circle, Angyee
township, Rangoon district, on the stream of the same name which flows
between the Rangoon river and the Ka-ma-oung. It is divided into two portions
distinguished as "north" and "south." In 1876 it had 1,382 inhabitants.

KHA-NOUNG-TO.—A revenue circle in the Angyee township, Rangoon
district, west of and adjoining Dalla and north of the Ka-ma-oung stream.
In 1876 the population numbered 5,844, the land revenue was Rs. 24,035,

the capitation tax Rs. 6,715 and the gross revenue Rs. 30,750. It was separated from Ma-hlaing in 1875. Since then the population has been :—

Year.	Talaing.	Burmans.	Kareng.	Shan.	Chinese.	Natives of India.	Total.
1875 ..	4,032	792	131	106	11	53	5,125
1876 ..	1,633	3,690	103	123	16	109	5,674
1877 ..	1,633	3,710	110	129	10	136	5,728

and the area under cultivation and the stock were :—

Year.	Rice, including fallow.	Garden.	Miscellaneous.	Total.	Buffaloes.	Cows, bulls and bullocks.	Pigs.	Carts.	Ploughs,	Boats.
1875 ..	11,641	..	..	11,644	529	937	70	228	571	226
1876 ..	12,554	..	..	12,555	641	821	115	262	640	254
1877 ..	12,501	..	..	12,502	799	799	63	258	596	195

KHA-NWAI-KHA-BHO.—A revenue circle in the south-west of the Pan-ta-uaw township, Thoon-khwa district, now including Myeng-ga-doung and extending along the left bank of the Irrawaddy southwards from the Pan-ta-naw river. The Re-baw-hlee, a shallow winding creek, traverses it in a general north and south direction. The face of the country is flat and covered, except where under cultivation, with grass and tree forest. In 1876 the land revenue was Rs. 6,592, the capitation tax Rs. 5,923, the gross revenue, to a considerable extent derived from fisheries, Rs. 18,321 and the population 5,554. The principal village is Kha-nwai-kha-hbo.

KHA-NWAI-KHA-HBO.—A village in the Pan-ta-naw township, Thoon-khwa district, in 16° 51′ N. and 95° 25′ E., on the left bank of the Irrawaddy. The inhabitants are principally fishermen.

KHA-RAI.—A village on the right bank of the Hlaing at its junction with the Houng-tha-raw, in the Gyaing circle, Gyaing Than-lweng township, Amherst district, divided into two portions distinguished as North Kha-rai and South Kha-rai. In 1877 the two had 1,057 inhabitants. It lies on the edge of a small rice plain and is connected with the undulating ground behind it by a raised road constructed a few years ago by the inhabitants. It is one of the halting places for the Shan caravans which bring in cattle every year, and close by a cattle-market is regularly held.

KHA-RAIK-THIT.—A highly populated and well cultivated revenue circle in the Amherst district, extending from the Salween on the east to the

Tsai-ba-la on the west across almost the whole of Bhee-loo-gywon. It has the Moo-rit-gyee and Weng-tsien circles on the north and Ka-la-be on the south. Though one of the largest circles in Bhee-loo-gywon it was still larger in the Burmese time then comprising the present circle of Weng-tsien, which was cut off from it and divided into two called Weng-tsien and Moo-rit-gyee (since united by Captain Phayre, in 1848). The Heng-tha-kywon or Heng-tha Island in the Salween, which formerly belonged to the small circle of Nat-maw since abolished, has been added to it. In this circle there is a gap in the central line of hills where lies nestled amongst trees the village of Khyoung-tshoon, the head-quarters of the township. The lands on the west of the range are far more fertile than those on the east. A considerable area, between high and low water mark, is planted with Dhanee palms (*Nipa fruticans*). In 1876 the inhabitants of the united circles, who are principally Talaing, numbered 3,980, the land revenue was Rs. 11,170 and the capitation tax Rs. 3,690.

KHA-RAIK-THIT.—A village in the circle of the same name on Bhee-loo-gywon on a range of the hills which traverse the island, near the source of the Kha-raik-thit stream. It is the eastern suburb of Khyoung-tshoon and in 1876 contained 815 and in 1877 1,127 inhabitants.

KHA-RAING.—A small village in the Sandoway district on an island of the same name in the Khoo circle of the Northern or Toung-goop township : in 1877 the inhabitants numbered 437 souls.

KHA-RA-KYWON.—A very largely cultivated revenue circle in the Hpoung-leng township of the Rangoon district, extending from the Poo-zwon-doung to the Pegu river north of the Dha-bien creek, inhabited mainly by Talaing. The whole area consists almost entirely of rice land with but very little grass or tree forest. In 1876 the land revenue was Rs. 36,241, the capitation tax Rs. 5,303, the gross revenue Rs. 42,558 and the population 8,968. The largest village is Dha-bien in the south-east corner of the circle ; the inhabitants in 1877 numbered 1,321.

KHA-RA-TSOO.—A small village in the Shwe-gyeng district, on the right bank of the Tsit-toung river at the mouth of the Kha-ra-tsoo creek which runs between the Tsit-toung and the Pegu rivers and was the old water route from Rangoon to Toung-ngoo and Shwe-gyeng. A small body of police is stationed here.

KHA-RENG.—Two circles in the Amherst district. *See Doo-tie-ya Kha-reng and Pa-ta-ma Kha-reng.*

KHA-RENG.—A village in the Doo-tie-ya Kha-reng circle, Gyaing Attaran township, Amherst district, about four miles from the mouth of the little Kha-reng streamlet. In 1877 it had 541 inhabitants.

KHA-RWAI.—A village in the Shwe-gyeng district, on the left bank of the Tsit-toung river a few miles above Tsit-toung, at the foot of some low pagoda-crowned laterite hills which give it an exceedingly picturesque appearance. It is noted for its knives, choppers and swords.

KHA-TENG-MA-THA.—A small village in the Tham-boo-la circle, Mye-dai township, Thayet district, amongst the western spurs of the Pegu Roma range. For some years after the close of the second Burmese war a small military force was stationed here ; this was subsequently replaced by a detachment of the local Pegu Light Infantry, and since 1861 it has been occupied by a small police force.

KHAT-TEE-YA.—A village of 882 inhabitants in 1877 in the Thee-kweng circle of the Thee-kweng township, Bassein district, on the southern bank of the Pan-ma-wa-dee near its source.

KHAT-TEE-YA.—A creek in the Bassein district, which rises on the eastern slopes of the Arakan mountains and falls into the Bassein river near Oo-tshit-kweng village. Boats 60 feet long can ascend at all seasons as far as Ka-dek-khyoung, a distance of about six miles. In the rains advantage is taken of the strong current downwards to float down rafts of bamboos cut in the hills amongst which the river has its source.

KHAT-TOO.—A small river in the Bassein district which rises in the lower eastern slopes of the Arakan mountains and falls into the Bassein river at Le-myet-hna ; near its mouth it is about 30 feet wide and 12 feet deep, but higher up during the hot season there is little or no water in it; the bed is sandy and gravelly : on its banks are found Pyengma (*Lagerstrœmia reginæ*) and Myouk-khyaw (*Homalium tomentosum*) in abundance and some teak.

KHA-YA.—A revenue circle in the Gyaing Than-lweng township, Amherst district, on the right or northern bank of the Gyaing. In 1876 the land revenue was Rs. 3,035, the capitation tax Rs. 1,637 and the population 1,584.

KHA-YA.—A village in the circle of the same name in the Gyaing Than-lweng township, Amherst district, on the right bank of the Gyaing at the mouth of the Kha-ya streamlet. In 1877 it had 717 inhabitants.

KHA-ZAING.—A revenue circle in the Than-lweng Hlaing-bhwai town-ship, Amherst district, in the angle formed by the junction of the Kha-zaing stream with the Hlaing-bhwai and extending northward to beyond the latitude of Hlaing village. The inhabitants, who are principally Kareng, numbered 1,373 in 1876, when the land revenue was Rs. 860 and the capitation tax Rs. 1,365.

KHA-ZAING.—A small river in the Amherst district which rises in the lowlands between the Salween and the Hlaing-bhwai and flowing eastwards falls into the latter about half a mile below Kha-zaing village. It forms the boundary between the Than-lweng Hlaing-bhwai and the Gyaing Attaran townships towards the east, as the Hpa-an does towards the west, and in the rains the two communicate, when a small canoe can pass between the Hlaing-bhwai and the Salween.

KHA-ZAING.—A village in the circle of the same name in the Than-lweng Hlaing-bhwai township, on the east bank of the Hlaing-bhwai river about half a mile north of the mouth of the Kha-zaing a western tributary of the Hlaing-bhwai. It contains a Police station and is the first halting place after leaving Gyaing on the route by water from Maulmain to Hlaing-bhwai. In 1877 it had 578 inhabitants.

KHE-BOUNG.—A small village, of 551 inhabitants in 1877, in the Thoon-daik circle, in the Kyoon-pyaw township, Bassein district, on the western bank of the Daga river, opposite the town of Kyoon-pyaw. It was formerly known by its Talaing name of Kyaik-kha-nan.

It is several times mentioned in Burmese and Talaing history during the reign of Badza-dhie-rit, king of Pegu. In A.D. 1406 (1410 according to Burmese history) the Burmans under Prince Meng-re-kyaw-tswa invaded Pegu but failed to take several towns in the south amongst which was Khe-boung. At the next invasion in A.D. 1413, however, Khe-boung was captured and remained in the possession of the Burmans until they were driven out in 1414.

KHE-MAN.—A small revenue circle in the Poungday township, Prome district, east of the northern end of Poungday, well cultivated with rice but containing no large villages. Included in it are the formerly separate village tracts of Shwe-ban-daw and Kyoon-daing. In 1876 the land revenue was Rs. 992, the capitation tax Rs. 698 and the population 699.

KHWA.—A small river forming a portion of the boundary between the Arakan and Pegu divisions. It takes its rise in the western slopes of the Arakan Roma range and after a S.S.W. course of about 20 miles it turns to the west for about 10 miles and then N.N.W. for 10 more when it disembogues in the Bay of Bengal in 17° 43' 54" N. Lat. and 94° 38' 9" E. Long., a short distance below the village of the same name. Its mouth forms a good harbour but the entrance is rendered intricate and difficult by a bar of sand which stretches across its mouth and on which during the ebb there are not more than $2\frac{1}{4}$ fathoms of water. It is affected by the tide as far as Than-ga-ta-rwa during neap and Pien-ne-goon-rwa during spring tides, and small boats can ascend as far as the former with the flood. Larger boats cannot go further up than Oon-mheng-rwa which can be reached in one tide.

KHWA.—The head-quarters of the southern township of the Sandoway district, on the right bank of the Khwa river about a mile from its mouth. It has been much improved of late years and is well laid out with good broad, straight roads, crossing at right angles, one of which has been extended to the neighbouring village of Ta-man-goon. The one or two tidal creeks which run up into the village are crossed by wooden foot bridges, built principally by the people who, also, made the roads. The village is buried in a grove of fruit trees; mango, tamarind, jack, cocoanut, &c. The houses are generally large and good, with timber posts, mat walls and thatched roofs. A little trade during the favourable seasons of the year is carried on by sea with parts of the Bassein district further south and Chinese junks are occasionally seen at anchor off the village. The only public buildings are a Court-house and a police station. The population including that of the adjoining villages of Ta-man-goon, Alay-rwa and Khyeng-tsoo was 1,088 in 1875, of whom nearly all were Burmans, with a few Khyeng (52) and natives of India and only six Arakanese, and 1,303 in 1877.

KHWA-LEK-YA.—A revenue circle in the Bassein district, on the left bank of the Khwa river, adjoining Sandoway on the north and lying between the Arakan Romas on the east and the Bay of Bengal on the west. It now includes Bhaw-mee and has, therefore, the Tsheng-ma circle on the south. The northern portion of the seacoast consists for the most part of a gently shelving sandy beach, backed by undulating ground covered with forest, with rocks appearing here and there; below this the coast is rocky and abrupt for some distance; this is succeeded by alternating sand and rock to the Oon stream where a rocky headland projects; further south a sandy beach is again found, with forest-clad hills coming close down to the water's edge. The whole of the circle is a mountain tract covered with dense forest, with patches of rice cultivation, in fields towards the seacoast and elsewhere on the hill slopes. The principal tree is the Ka-gnyeng. In 1867 the population was 1,769 and the land revenue Rs. 715. In 1876 the population was 2,460, the land revenue Rs. 1,010, the capitation tax Rs. 2,012 and the gross revenue Rs. 3,496. The name is derived from its position on the left (*Burmanice* right) bank of the Khwa. See *Khwa-lek-wai*.

KHWA-LEK-WAI.—A revenue circle in the extreme south of the southern township of the Sandoway district, with an area of 194 square miles, extending along the right bank of the Khwa river to the seacoast and including the once independent circle of Rahaing. To the south is the Bassein district and on the north the Loung-gyo circle. In 1875 the population numbered 2,319 souls, of whom 1,698 were in the old Khwa-lek-wai circle, almost entirely Burmans with 65 Khyengs, and 621, almost entirely Arakanese, in Rahaing : in the same year the capitation tax amounted to Rs. 2,160. In 1876 the population was 2,339, the land revenue Rs. 1,135, the capitation tax Rs. 2,214 and the gross revenue, largely derived from the net and fishery tax, Rs. 8,681. From Khwa, the principal village, a road leads *viâ* Rahaing-bya across the Romas to Henzada, used to some extent by Burmese traders. The meaning of the name is literally, " Left hand Khwa," that is the Khwa circle on the left bank of the Khwa, as Burmans call " left " bank what the English call the " right " bank of a river.

KHWA-TSHOON.—A village in the Kyoon-taw circle, Ra-thai-doung township, Akyab district, on the northern bank of the Ra-moung-doon stream at its junction with the Lek-ya-dek and the Lek-wai streams. In 1877 it had 682 inhabitants.

KHWA-TSHOON.—A village in the Thai-gan circle, Ra-thai-doung township, Akyab district, on the western bank of the Ma-yoo river at the mouths of the Tsheng-deng-bwa and Koo-la-pan-zan. It is the residence of the Thoogyee of the circle and in 1877 had 748 inhabitants.

KHYAN-THA-GYEE.—A pagoda at Ze-ta-won in Martaban founded in 1299 A. D. by King Tsaw-theng-hmaing, and restored in 1785 by Moung Pathee, Governor of Martaban, with funds sent to him for this purpose from Ava by King Bhodaw Bhoora. The Talaing name " Kha-ba " means the same as the Burmese, *viz.*, " cool, comfortable " and is supposed to be derived from the coolness of the waters of a neighbouring tank.

KHYA-RA-GOON.—A revenue circle in the Prome district, now including Tha-boung, a short distance south-east of Engma. The inhabitants, who in 1877 numbered 1,661 souls, are mainly agriculturists. In that year the land revenue was Rs. 2,586, the capitation tax Rs. 1,880 and the gross revenue Rs. 4,522.

KHYAW.—A very small tribe of about 100 souls living in one village in the Arakan hills on the banks of the Koo-la-dan. They are a fine strong race said to be braver than any of the others. Though living amongst the Kha-mie there is a marked dissimilarity in feature and dress : they can hardly be distinguised from the lower class of Bengali peasantry of Chittagong: they are dark with large features and the men wear their hair in a knot at the back of the head, like the Khyoung-tha, but shave a few inches from the forehead and wear no head dress: they most probably belong to the Kookie family but they have no traditions regarding their origin nor of how they came amongst the Kha-mie in Arakan. They worship upright stones which they erect in different parts of their villages and consecrate to the Nat. Their language is unwritten: it is monosyllabic and presents marked similarities with the other dialects of Chin-India.

KHYENG*.—A race of mountaineers scattered over all the hilly country between Eastern Bengal, the western provinces of China and the borders of Annam and Cambodia but inhabiting more especially the chain of hills which stretches southwards from the Himalayas to Cape Negrais. In the north they are said to be wild and fierce, and those on the western slopes of the Arakan mountains are described as the least civilised of the wild tribes living in the Hill Tracts. In British territory they are quiet and harmless. They have developed no form of government higher than the patriarchal and have no written language. Almost their only occupation is agriculture of the kind called toungya, the cultivation of patches on the mountain slopes abandoned after the crop is gathered, but under British rule they are gradually taking to ordinary rice cultivation and, with the acquisition of fields in the plains, lose much of their propensity for roving. The number of this tribe in British Burma according to the census of 1872 was 51,117 souls, spread generally all over the Pegu division, but most numerous in the northern portion of the valley of the Irrawaddy; a few inhabit the southern and western slopes of the Arakan mountains and the eastern slopes of the Pegu Romas. Symes, who visited Ava at the end of the last century, describes them as " children " of nature, delighting in their wild and native freedom, for the most part " insuperably averse to hold any communication with the people of the plains."

Colonel Yule describes them as of Indo-Chinese race and related to the
Kookies, Nagas, &c.; Sir Arthur Phayre appears to con-
Origin.   sider that their own tradition of their origin—that they are
of the same lineage as the Arakanese and Burmese the stragglers from armies or moving hordes left in the mountains—is correct, whilst Dr. Mason would class them with the Kareng. They call themselves *Shyoo*. The Burmese name for the Pwo Kareng is *Myit-khyeng* or river Khyeng, which would seem to support Dr. Mason's view, more especially as the Pwo Kareng call themselves *Sho* and as the alphabet made by the Baptist Missionaries for the Pwo Kareng language can, with very slight modifications, be employed to express most of the Khyeng sounds. By this means a version of the Gospel, according to S. John, has been prepared which, though not without defects, can be understood by Khyeng who have been taught to read. A few hymns also have been translated and printed.

The Khyeng tradition as to the origin of the various races of man is that in the beginning of the world, after the sun and moon had been created, the earth by its own powers of productiveness brought forth a woman who was

---

* Extracted mainly from Lieutenant-Colonel Horace Browne's account of the Thayet-myo district, published at Rangoon in 1874.

called Hlee-neu. Hlee-neu laid one hundred eggs* which she hatched in cotton-wool and from which sprang one hundred human beings, the progenitors of the different races of man. She then laid another egg which was beautifully coloured as if by the hand of some skilful artist. In her affection for this egg she placed it in a metal vessel instead of in cotton wool. As it failed to hatch she thought that it was addled and throwing it on to the roof of her house she exclaimed "if it is destined to be hatched let it go and take its chance of " finding a protector." The egg fell from the roof on to some rubbish in the gutter and with it was carried away by the waters of a stream down which it floated till lodged in a Yan-laik tree. Here it was seen by a bird called Asha-eum (*Cuculus paradisæicus, Linn.*), who sat upon it and hatched it. It produced a male and a female, who from the moment of their birth were separated. When the girl had grown up she was carried off by a bear who kept her confined in a tree. From this captivity she was delivered by a bee who directed her to tie a piece of cotton to his tail and by this means guided her to the male who, the bee informed her, was her brother, then living in the valley of the Khyeng-dweng, a tributary of the Irrawaddy. In commemoration of this a piece of cotton is tied to the hand of new-born infants. The male had taken to himself a dog as wife, but he now wished to marry his sister, to which she objected on the ground of their affinity. Hlee-neu was appealed to and she decided that the dog-wife should be sacrificed and the young man and maiden should marry; that their sons and daughters should intermarry, but that after that the brother's daughters should marry the sister's sons. From this marriage sprang the Khyeng race, who still offer up a dog as a sacrifice to the household spirits and give the daughters of brothers in marriage to the sister's sons. Hlee-neu loved her youngest born son, but before she found him she had already partitioned off the world among her other children and had nothing left but inhospitable mountain ranges; these she gave him and added elephants, horses, cattle, goats, pigs and fowls, and directed his Burman brother to look after his education. The Burman turned out to be a very wicked and unscrupulous guardian, he pretended to educate the Khyeng but he shewed him only the blank side of his slate, so that he never learnt a single letter. Before he put him on an elephant he rubbed the animal's back with cowhage, which so sorely tickled the poor Khyeng's bare skin that he refused to have anything more to do with such animals and gave them all to the Burmans. The buffalo too the Burman managed to deprive him of : when he tried to ride it the Burman's wife got in the way and was knocked down; the Burman complained to Hlee-neu who decided that the buffalo should be given to the Burman in compensation for the injury done. Ultimately of all the animals which had been given to him, goats, pigs and fowls alone remained in his possession. The grasping Burman did not even allow the Khyeng to remain in undisturbed occupation of his mountains ; when the boundaries of the different countries were marked out the Burman took care to mark his with permanent objects but the Khyeng set up no marks save tufts of twisted grass which were burned up by the jungle fires, on which the Khyeng had to live wherever the Burman told him. Thus his

---

* The tradition of Hlee-neu having laid 101 eggs from which all human races have sprung corresponds with the Burman idea of the existence of 101 races of men in the world, amongst whom the Khyeng and Koo-la are included ; under the latter designation are grouped all Europeans and natives of India.

race has never had a country of its own but wanders over the mountain ranges of Burma. These traditions point clearly to long-continued and systematic oppression on the part of the Burmese.

The origin of every law and custom is religiously assigned to Hlee-neu, who is said to have laid down a complete code of laws for the guidance of her Khyeng descendants before she died and departed to the happy land where she still lives in eternal happiness.

Religion.

If a Khyeng is able to speak a little Burmese and is asked as to his religion, he will probably answer that, following the custom of his ancestors, he worships the most excellent lord Gaudama, but in saying this he is only repeating the formula that he has often heard from his Burmese neighbours. All he means is that he chiefly venerates the pagodas, and on certain occasions, such as the annual pagoda festivals, follows the multitude and conforms somewhat to the Burmese customs. They acknowledge one God, a spirit, the Creator and Ruler of the universe, who is so good that they have nothing to fear from him and so need not worship him, but they worship, with propitiatory offerings of khoung and sacrificial meats, the demons or nat who are looked upon as the authors of all evil, and of whom there is an innumerable body—of the trees, of the streams, of the hills, of the houses—and the worship of two of these, the Oo-yoo-khoon and Mo-goung nat (nat of the heavens) was specially ordered by Hlee-neu. The offerings to the latter of these two consist of cotton tassels, stones and the flowers of the Tha-bye tree (*Eugenia sp.*), in obedience to the precept of Hlee-neu who said " Earth is the " flesh and stones are the bones of the world. Let the nat of heaven be " worshipped with the flowers of the Tha-bye tree and with a stone." These sacrifices and offerings are made not only to ensure safety in this world but to ensure admission into heaven after death ; to the happy land called Ngathien, where the spirits of good Khyeng join those of their ancestors and live in perpetual enjoyment of the khoung and baked meats which they have offered during life.

Khoung.

This " Khoung"* is a fermented drink, an essential in Khyeng nat oblation and indeed of Khyeng life generally, the excessive drinking of which converts their feasts into scenes of disgusting drunkenness. For their knowledge of khoung they consider themselves indebted to their great mother Hlee-neu. During the infancy of her numerous progeny Hlee-neu made a tank of milk for their sustenance, near which lived a porcupine who drank some of the milk and, as a result, became covered with quills instead of hairs. When the contents of the tank were exhausted there sprang up the rice plant, pepper, brinjal (*Solanum melongena*), garlic, the paitek-nee (a gigantic bean with red seeds) and the thit-khyo plant. The Khyeng, fearing that the strength which they had derived from the milk would now decrease, applied to Hlee-neu who directed them to prepare from the plants growing in the tank a decoction to resemble the milk it had contained. " Take " the bark of the thit-khyo, the root of the brinjal, the bean of the pai-tek-nee, " pepper corns, garlic and the entrails of a porcupine, mix them up in rice flour

---

* Khoung is also made by the Ka-khyeng north and east of Bha-maw in Upper Burma and of a better quality. It has been described as like creaming champagne and was drunk by the Europeans of the Mission to Yunan under Colonel Horace Browne in 1874-75. Probably it was not prepared in precisely the same way as that supposed to resemble Hlee-neu's milk.

"and make balls. Cover these up for three days and then expose them to the
"sun until they become wort; mix the wort with parboiled rice, put it into a
"pot and bury it for several days in a heap of unhusked rice; then add water
"according to taste and the divine khoung is ready to be sucked up through
"tubes. In taste it resembles Hlee-neu's milk and by it is man's strength
"increased. On account of its excellence it must always be offered to the nat."

Khyeng girls are given in marriage by their brothers not by their
Marriage. parents. When a girl is born she is especially assigned to
one of her brothers or, if she has none, to one of her
father's sister's sons whose consent has to be obtained by any one who aspires
to her hand and who, after her marriage, must be treated with the greatest
respect by her husband. If the husband visits the brother he must take with
him a present of khoung, and should the brother visit him he must present to
him khoung and pork, or, if his circumstances are such that he cannot do
this, he must make profound apologies. As a rule girls are affianced early to
one of their cousins, but the match is not seldom broken off and in such a case
the defaulter, if the man, has to give to the girl five pots of khoung, a bullock
worth Rs. 30, a pig three feet in girth, a spear, a fork, a bag and
a piece of ornamented cloth; if the girl, she has to give to the man a brass
dish worth about Rs. 15, a silk cloth and a silk belt each worth about Rs. 5
and a silk turban worth about eight annas.

When a marriage is contemplated, whether the parties have been previously affianced or not, their friends are invited to drink khoung at the man's
house. A pig is slaughtered and the liver placed on a brass dish for inspection
by the wise men.* If there are any marks upon the liver the marriage is post-
poned and the ceremony has to be repeated on a subsequent occasion; if the
signs are unpropitious on three successive occasions the match is finally broken
off and the intended bridegroom receives from the girl's parents a present
of a turban, a dress and a girdle "to wipe away tears." Marriages are celebrated in the bride's house: the bridegroom provides the pot of khoung over
which the ceremony takes place and his friends bring pork, the bride's friends
producing fowls. A bamboo is neatly peeled and slit at the top, a cross
stick is inserted and the whole fastened into the pot of khoung, on each side
of which sit, and must remain, the party, the bridegroom and his friends on
one side and the bride and her friends on the other. Should any one cross
from one side to the other he has to provide a pot of khoung. An elder on
the bridegroom's side rises and proposes that the marriage ceremony be performed according to the commands of Hlee-neu. An elder on the bride's side
then recites Hlee-neu's decision on the application made to her by the first
parents of the tribe. The bridegroom makes presents to the bride's brother
and receives his consent to the marriage (if the brother is not satisfied the
points in dispute are then and there decided by the elders) and the brother
signifies his assent by eating of the bridegroom's pork; the celebration
of the marriage is then complete and the bride belongs to the bridegroom.
The marriage presents are then given. None of the bride's party are allowed
to touch the pork, nor of the bridegroom's to touch the fowls; if this rule is
broken more khoung has to be given and pork if the offender is of the bridegroom's party and fowls if of the bride's.

---

* Cf. Kareng customs, page 280, line 40 *et seq.*

264

Some days later the newly married pair give security that they will behave properly to each other and in evidence of the compact a notch is cut in a tree*. The man's agreement is that he will not beat his wife immoderately or so severely as to break a bamboo over her, to draw blood or to maim her, nor will he cut off her hair; the woman's, that she will behave to her husband as a wife should do. If she misbehaves the husband can chastize her moderately, but should he do so immoderately he has to make peace with her brother, who can take her away if he is not satisfied. If the wife deserts her husband her sureties have to find him another wife. If she commits adultery she forfeits the whole of her property to her husband and has also to give two gongs, a bullock, a brass dish, a dha-lway or sword and a piece of blue cloth. If a man wishes to take a second wife he must obtain the consent of his first wife's brother who, if not satisfied, can deprive him of his first wife. When a man dies his widow belongs to his brother†; she can marry no one else unless they refuse to marry her in which case her brother can give her to anyone else; she can refuse to remarry only on taking a vow to remain unmarried and to worship her husband's household nat. If after this vow she marries she has to pay Rs. 30 and her husband forfeits three bullocks and a cow. Divorces are obtainable and the sentence is pronounced by the elders, but they are rarely sought.

A death is made an occasion for much feasting. Bullocks, buffaloes, pigs
Death.
and fowls are slaughtered, according to the means of the family, to entertain the guests and to propitiate the nat so that the deceased may safely reach the happy land, Nga-thien. The corpse, with a fowl tied to one of its big toes, is carried on a stretcher to the burning place and, together with the fowl, is burned. The bones of the deceased, plucked from the embers, are washed in khoung, rubbed with turmeric and placed in a pot, where they remain for a year or more till they can be taken to the family burying ground where they are finally deposited. These burial places are few in number and considerable reserve is shewn by the Khyeng with regard to their position: there is a very extensive one in Upper Burma to which are carried the relics of many Khyeng who die in British Burma. The ceremony of depositing the bones in the family place of burial is somewhat similar to an Irish wake; there is much eating and drinking and boisterous behaviour. One custom on such occasions is peculiar and would seem to shew that there is amongst the Khyeng some sense of a god as a present disposer of events, whether prosperous or untoward. A man, standing at the grave, brandishes a sword and raises the insolent cry "Art thou "satisfied now with the accomplishment of thy purpose in the death of this "one of thy creatures?"

The chief peculiarities of the Khyeng law of inheritance are that as soon
Inheritance.
as a woman is married she loses all claim to inherit her parents' property, provided that her parents have other children, and that when parents have several children the last married or the one who remains single cannot leave his or her parents' house, but is bound to remain with, work for, and feed them: on the parents' death this child is entitled to three-fifths of the property.

---

* Cf. Kareng custom, page 236, line 7 from bottom.

† Cf. Deuteronomy, chapter XXV.

In obedience to the commands of Hlee-neu Khyeng swear on the flower
Oaths. of the Tha-bye tree and on a stone : "when disputes"
"arise and oaths have to be taken let the swearer hold a"
"Tha-bye flower and let him take up a stone. Let him who ventures to"
"swear in this way gain his cause. "

It has hitherto been the custom with Khyeng young women, soon after
Tattooing. they trive at years of puberty, to tattoo the whole of
their faces with vertical and closely adjoining narrow black
lines which, as Symes very correctly observes, "gives a most extraordinary
appearance." The origin of the custom is not known ; according to some it
was prescribed by Hlee-neu with the object of preventing the young men of
other tribes from falling in love with Khyeng maidens; according to others
it was adopted with a view of preventing the Burmans from depriving them,
as they once did, of their most comely females ; and according to others the
object was that they might be able to trace their women when carried away
by other tribes. The custom was lately universal but in British territory it
is slowly dying out.

The Khyeng in appearance resemble the Burmans much more than any
Dress. of their cognate tribes, the Kareng for instance. A
Khyeng man, when he abandons his natural dress which
is nothing but a narrow strip of cloth and adopts the Burman kilt or waist-
cloth, is indistinguishable from a Burman save by the absence of tattooing
on the legs and now that the custom of so marking the limbs is by no means
universally followed amongst the Burmese this distinguishing mark is not a
safe one : the women are naturally pretty and seem far less willing than the
men to adopt the Burmese costume, generally wearing a dark blouse ornamented with red and with white thread.

Many centuries of oppression have made the Khyeng a timid and a retir-
Character. ing race though, perhaps, less so than the Kareng: they
are seldom genial and communicative unless visited in
their villages or under the influence of khoung. A Khyeng rarely takes to
violent crime but when he does he becomes and remains a most dangerous
character, vindictive, wantonly and brutally cruel and merciless, exhibiting
great boldness in attack and great skill in evading capture.

KHYENG-GOON.—A village in 19° 7′ 10″ N. Lat. and 95° 25′ 15″ E.
Long., containing about eighty houses, in the Tsheng-doop circle, Myedai township, Thayet district. It is close to Tsheng-doop, which gives its name to the
circle, in a rice plain on one of the affluents of the Bhwot-lay. The inhabitants
are chiefly engaged in agriculture.

KHYIET-TOUNG.—A village of 473 inhabitants in 1877, in the Kyien
circle, Meng-bra township, Akyab district, on the western bank of the Thai-dan.

KHYOUK-RWA.—A revenue circle in the Oot-hpo township of the
Henzada district, west of the Irrawaddy and bordering on the Le-myet-hna
township of the Bassein district, on the right bank of the Bassein river.
Towards the west the country is hilly but elsewhere it is well suited for rice
cultivation of which there is a good deal. In 1876 the land revenue was
Rs. 7,615, the capitation tax Rs. 6,657, the gross revenue Rs. 15,525 and the
population 7,776 souls.

KHYOUK-TSHAY.—A revenue circle in the Le-myet-hna township, Bassein district, 80 square miles in extent, occupying the south-eastern corner of the township, between the Bassein river on the east and the Hlaw-ga-ta, its affluent, on the south-east. It is only partially cultivated the ground being generally low and subject to inundation. The inhabitants are employed mainly in cultivation, fishing and forestry. In 1876 the land revenue was Rs. 1,051, the capitation tax Rs. 2,720, the gross revenue Rs. 5,362 and the population 2,485 souls.

KHYOUNG-BYA.—A small village in the Tha-loo circle, Khyouk-hpyoo township, Khyouk-hpyoo district, the head-quarters of the thoo-gyee, locally noted for its pottery manufacture.

KHYOUNG-BYA.—A large revenue circle in the north of the Kyouk-gyee township of the Shwe-gyeng district, lying along the western slopes of the low range running parallel to the Tsit-toung river, about 265 square miles in extent. In 1876 the population, composed mainly of Kareng, numbered 2,062, the capitation tax was Rs. 837, the land revenue Rs. 1,083 and the gross revenue Rs. 2,155.

KHYOUNG-DOUNG-GYEE.—A village in the Shwe-doung township, Prome district, in 18° 38′ 0″ N. and 95° 16′ 40″ E., on the left bank of the Irrawaddy, immediately to the north of Kyee-thay and at the lower end of the Theng-byoo fen.

KHYOUNG-DOUNG-SHAN.—A village in the Shwe-doung township, Prome district, on the left bank of the Irrawaddy above and adjoining Kyee-thay.

KHYOUNG-GOUNG-GYEE.—A river which rises in the western slopes of the Pegu mountains and, flowing through the Thayet district in a westerly direction, unites with the Pa-de and other streams to form the Bhwot-lay.

KHYOUNG-GYEE.—A revenue circle in the Central township of the Sandoway district, east of Sandoway, on the upper course of the Sandoway river, with the Kyien-ta-lee-bya circle on the east, the Lek-wai-a-she circle on the north and the Tsa-wa and Ka-myit circles on the south, separated from the last by the Pa-hoon spur of the main range. The principal villages, all on the banks of the Sandoway river, are Shan-toung, A-gnyit, Daing-baing and Kyoung-toung. The greater portion of the circle is hilly and a great deal of it is unculturable. The most important product is tobacco. In 1876 the land revenue was Rs. 1,087, the capitation tax Rs. 898, the gross revenue Rs. 1,985 and the population 1,072 souls.

KHYOUNG-KHWA.—A revenue circle in the Kyan-kheng township of the Henzada district, having the Rwa-thit circle on the west and north and the Eng-lat circle of the Kyan-kheng and the Pa-daw circle of the Myanoung township on the south and east, containing a good deal of land under rice. In 1876 the land revenue was Rs. 2,590, the capitation tax Rs. 1,352, the gross revenue Rs. 3,962 and the population 1,326.

KHYOUNG-THA.—Literally "children of the stream"; a tribe of which in the hill tracts of Arakan there were 1,261 souls in 1876; they are found only on the banks of the Koo-la-dan river. They are the least uncivilized of all the hill tribes and dress better; some of them are able to read and write the old Burmese or Arakanese character. The men wear a cotton, or sometimes silk, cloth reaching from the hips to below the knee, a short jacket with sleeves, fastening at the throat, and a turban : the hair hangs coiled into a knot towards the back of the head. The women wear the Burmese hta-mien or petticoat, open in front but covering the breast and leaving the arms and shoulders exposed. The men tattoo themselves, but not so much as the Burmans, and the name of God is usually tattooed on the shoulder. They carry on most of the traffic amongst the hill tribes, which is usually done by barter, and are the only tribe which understands the use of medicines. They appear to be a portion of the original inhabitants of Arakan driven up the river at the time of the occupation of the country by the Burmese. They are nominally Booddhists but their religion is mixed up with spirit worship. " Their parent stream is looked upon with a holy love, not only as affording " them sustenance but likewise a ready passage by which to flee from the " attacks of their foes. At the northern outskirts of each village, from which " quarter alone they dread the advent of any danger (all to the south being " in possession of the English), in the direction of the forest, and under " the shade of the comeliest tree, may be seen the shrine of their two Nâts, " the one male the other female. They are represented by two pebbles " picked from the banks of the river.* The female is considered the most " powerful, and is meant to represent the Mayoo Nât, or spirit which pre- " sides over the mouth of the Myoo river ; she is believed to be a most " powerful spirit, the guardian of Arracan from all the dangers of the " sea.........The other, or male spirit, is called Rwatsoung Nât or ' the village ' " ' guardian ' to whom, as his name implies, is entrusted the care of the village. " They believe, to use their identical words, that ' should he withdraw his " ' favour the evil eye would glare upon their children ; sickness would " ' devastate their healths ; the floods would sweep away the foundations of " ' their homes ; and their most favourite haunts would become the prowl of " ' the tiger and wild cat o'mount.' Whenever a new shrine is to be erected " fresh stones are chosen, the village is tabooed for seven days, sentinels are " placed on all the surrounding heights to prevent the ingress or egress of " any person, and sacrifices of fowls and pigs are made. Around each stone " is wound some cotton thread coloured yellow with turmeric.† Before marriage intercourse between the sexes is unrestricted but after marriage chastity is insisted on : girls marry when about fifteen or sixteen, and the boys as young as nineteen. As might be expected from their greater civilization and Burmanised manners the marriage ceremony is not so simple as amongst the other hill tribes. If the man has not selected his wife his parents choose one for him. A relation is sent to the parents of the girl and if they consent a day is fixed on which they meet in the house of the bride's father and arrange the preliminaries ; that night the bridegroom's father and mother remain in the house of the woman's parents. A favourable day is then fixed on and on that day the bridegroom and his relations go to the bride's village and stay in a temporary shed built for them, receiving the visits of the villagers, the bride doing the same in her father's house. At sunset the bridegroom goes to his future father-in-law's house and the religious ceremony is performed. Rice, mango leaves and pots of water are placed on the floor

---

* They are placed lying down in a flat position each having a sort of baby house erected to receive it.
† A note on some hill tribes on the Koo-la-dan river by Lieut. T. Latter, Journal of the Bengal Asiatic Society ; Vol. XV. (1846) pp. 61, 62.

between the bride and bridegroom, who face each other, and a newly-spun cotton thread is wound round the whole. A Booddhist priest then reads some sentences in Pali and taking cooked rice in each hand he feeds the couple seven times, alternately, crossing and recrossing his arms. Finally he hooks the little finger of the bridegroom's right hand into that of the bride's left hand, repeats some more Pali sentences and the ceremony is complete.*

Their funerals, also, are conducted more like those of the Burmese. The body is carried to the burning ground and, if of a man, laid on a pile of three layers, if of a woman of four ; a priest repeats some Pali phrases and the pile is fired by the nearest relative, male or female : the ashes are afterwards collected and buried on the spot.

Three times a year they feast the dead, but simply by putting aside food and drink for them which after a few days are thrown away.

KHYOUNG-THA.—A small river in the Bassein district, which rises in the western slopes of the Arakan mountains and falls into the Bay of Bengal near the village of Khyoung-tha : at the springs the tide reaches nearly to the source of the river. About five miles from the mouth there are five feet of water and boats of 500 baskets burden can ascend thus far.

KHYOUNG-TSHOON.—A long village on Bhee-loo-gywon in the Amherst district, stretching in two lines of houses, one on each side of the road, to and beyond a pass through the low hills which form the backbone, as it were, of the island. The western portion is called Weng-tsien and the eastern Kha-raik-thit. The village lies on the edge of the low hills and in the pass, partly in the plains and partly on the slightly and almost imperceptibly rising ground. On the west a valley extends up northwards between Weng-tsien and the rest of the village and advantage has been taken of this to form an artificial reservoir of water by throwing an embankment across the valley. This embankment is traversed by a road and is lined on the north or reservoir side by a line of trees, the handsome purple-flowering *Lagerstrœmia reginæ* predominating, with the Khyee-beng, with its insignificant bottle-brush-looking, brick-red flowers, and other kinds interspersed. This embankment, on the south of the eastern approach to which is a handsome Thien newly repaired and ornamented with scarlet and gold, retains a large volume of water ; in the hot season the area is about one square mile and the depth ten feet and in the rains very nearly double this both in area and in depth. This most useful work was constructed entirely by the people, urged thereto by a Booddhist priest whose monastery is in the neighbourhood, and is kept in repair by them. The State has made a bridged opening at the western end as an escape to prevent the water from overflowing the road.

The village is connected with Nat-maw on the Salween, about four miles off, by a good road across the rice plains, commenced by Major Broadfoot, which is in repair. This road is much used and has done a great deal to attract population to the neighbourhood. The only public buildings are a Court-house and a Police station. The number of inhabitants of the group of villages was 1,857 in 1868 and 1,958 in 1877.

---

* The intervention of the Booddhist priest and his manual acts, so contrary to pure Bood-dhist practice, mark strongly, both as regards the people and the priesthood, the influence of the customs and habits of the inhabitants of Chittagong.

KHYOUNG-TSOUK.—A village in the Prome district, in 18° 58' 40" N. and 19° 37' 45" E., amongst the hills in the northern portion of the district, on the bank of the Khyoung-tsouk stream, inhabited chiefly by hill garden cultivators.

KHYOUNG-TSOUK.—A river in the Prome district, formed by the junction of two mountain-torrents both rising in the southern slopes of the Padouk spur four or five miles west of the main chain of the Pegu Roma mountains, a subsidiary offshoot from which separates them from each other for the first six or seven miles of their course north-westward. After their junction the river turns south-west and, receiving numerous small and unimportant tributaries on its way down, falls into the south Na-weng near the village of Khyoung-khwa, where the Eng-goon and the Gway meet it, all three discharging their waters by the same mouth. In the short portion of its course which lies in the valley of the south Na-weng the bed is sandy and muddy and the steep banks are lined with elephant grass and bamboos, but higher up the bed is rocky. The hills amongst which it winds are covered with teak and other large forest trees which, when felled, are, in the rains, floated down it to the south Na-weng and to the Irrawaddy. The river is not navigable by boats at any season. At Ka-deng-hnit-tohay, well up amongst the hills, is a " magnificent waterfall which in the dry season appears as an insuper- " able obstruction to the floating down of timber but where, in the height of " the rains, to give the expression of the Burmese foresters of that district, it " is awful to see how one log after the other takes the leap over the rocks " into the abyss below and then quietly floats on in the smooth waters " beneath."*

KING ISLAND.—An island of the Mergui Archipelago forming a portion of the Mergui district of the Tenasserim division, between 12° 19' and 12° 42' N. Lat. and 98° 9' and 98° 21' W. Long. about ten miles from the coast, west of the mouths of the Tenasserim river. Its length from north to south is twenty-six miles and its breadth from east to west ten miles. A high range of hills runs along its western side, leaving on the eastern side a rich alluvial plain twenty miles long and five broad. At the north end there is a fine bay forming an excellent well-sheltered harbour, and on the island at this spot is to be found plenty of good water. The bay is called " French Bay" from having been used by the French ships of war during the wars between England and France, from whence they issued to capture British merchant vessels : the existence of this harbour was then unknown to the British. The island produces the largest timber found in the district, well fitted for masts and spars. It is sparsely inhabited by Burmese and Kareng.

KISSERING.—An island in the Mergui Archipelago attached to the Mergui district of the Tenasserim division, and situated between 11° 32' and 11°47' N. Lat. and 98° 15' and 98° 25' E. Long. off the mouth of the Le-gnya river. It is one of the most fertile and picturesque islands in the group, composed of undulating land of the richest description but now covered with dense forest. During the Siamese rule it was well cultivated, and there was on it a large town of the same name, of which only large heaps of bricks remain to attest that it must have been a place of some size. The town and island

---

* Dr. Brandis' report on the Pegu Forests.

were deserted by the inhabitants when the country was conquered by the Burmese in the time of Aloung-bhoora (*Alompra*).

KO-BENG.—A rising village of the Shwe-tshan-daw circle, Mye-dai township, Thayet district, situated on the Pa-de stream. Ten years ago it was entered in the returns as containing thirteen houses : it now has nearly one hundred.

KO-DOUNG.—A revenue circle in the Angyee township, Rangoon district, separated on the north by the Khanoung and the A-gat creeks from Pyaw-bhway. On the east it is bounded by the Rangoon river, on the south by the Tha-khwot-peng and the A-hparoon rivers, the former separating it from Moot-kywon and the latter from Htan-ma-naing. On the west is the Kaw-hmoo circle from which it is separated by a stream which forms a portion of the Lweng-gyee Eng. The greatest length from east to west is about nine miles and the greatest breadth about eight. In 1876 it had a population of 5,389 souls, or about 103 to the square mile, the greater portion being Kareng and almost the whole agricultural. The soil generally is exceedingly fertile. In 1876 the land revenue was Rs. 46,728 the capitation tax Rs. 7,490 and the gross revenue Rs. 54,868.

KO-GYEE-LOOP.—A small revenue circle in the Prome district to the east of the Zay stream and west of the Tseedaing circle. In 1876 it had a population of 251 souls, a land revenue of Rs. 281, capitation tax Rs. 273 and a gross revenue of Rs. 554.

KO-KAING.—A small village of 377 inhabitants in 1877, north of and a few miles from Rangoon. During the first Burmese war this village was the scene of some severe fighting. The Burman general having erected entrenchments, Major-General Campbell moved out against him on the 15th December 1854 in two columns, the right, under Brigadier-General Cotton, of 540 men from the 13th, 18th and the 34th regiment M. N. I. with 60 of the Governor-General's body guard, the left, under General Campbell himself, 800 strong and composed of detachments of the 38th, 39th, and 41st regiments, and of the 9th 13th 28th and 30th regiments N. I. with 100 men of the body guard. The works were found to consist of two large stockades connected by a central entrenchment ; each wing was about 400 yards long by 200 broad and projected considerably beyond the centre. The right column attacked the centre whilst the left, forming into two divisions, attacked the flanking stockades. In fifteen minutes the whole of the works were in the possession of the assailants. The total number of killed was eighteen, including Lieutenants Darby, Petsy and Jones of the 13th and O'Hanlon of the Bengal Artillery, who died of his wounds, and the wounded to one hundred and fourteen, including seven officers of the 13th.

KOO-BHYOO.—A revenue circle in the Ta-pwon township, in the northern portion of the Henzada district, to the east of the Irrawaddy, to which is now united Goon-gnyeng-dan. The circle contains a good deal of tree forest in which are found Eng (*Dipterocarpus tuberculatus*), Pyeng-ma (*Lagerstrœrnia reginæ*), Pyeng-gado (*Xylia dolabriformis*) and Reng-daik (*Dalbergia cultrata*). In 1876 the united circles had a population of 8,740 souls, and produced a gross revenue of Rs. 16,439, of which Rs. 7,654 were derived from the land, Rs. 8,235 from the capitation tax and the rest from other sources.

KOO-BHYOO.—A revenue circle in the Meng-doon township, Thayet-myo district, having an area of thirty-five square miles, a population in 1876 of 8,345 souls of whom about some 200 are Khyeng and furnishing a revenue in that year of Rs. 5,410, of which Rs. 2,841 were derived from land and Rs. 2,361 from capitation tax. Rather more than eight square miles are cultur-able, and about half are actually cultivated. Eight of the old village tracts are now included within the limits of this circle, of which Koo-bhyoo, Tha-dwon-ngay, Pan-gnyo and Moo were united to it at the annexation and the others have been subsequently added; Doo in 1856, and Oo-yeen-bo and Pazwon-myoung in 1858. The products are rice, sessamum, cotton, plantains, maize, tobacco, chillies, onions, cutch, and thatch grass, and in the Burmese time salt, extracted from a brine spring in Pan-gnyo near the village of Tsan-gyee.

KOOK-KO.—A tidal creek in the Myoug-mya township, navigable by river steamers, and flowing between the Rwe and Pya-ma-law rivers; its western mouth is about three miles below La-bwot-ta.

KOOK-KO.—A revenue circle in the Myeboon township, Kyouk-hpyoo trict, on the shore of Combermere Bay, composed of islands separated by tidal creeks. It has an area of 21 square miles and a population of 2,006 souls. In 1876 the land revenue was Rs. 2,040, the capitation tax Rs. 2,193 and the gross revenue Rs. 4,535.

KOOK-KO.—A village of 600 inhabitants in the revenue circle of the same name in the Mye-boon township, Khyouk-hpyoo district.

KOOK-KO-BENG.—A revenue circle in the Prome district, now formed of several united village tracts, about four miles south-west of Poungday. It has no large villages; the most populous one is Gnyoung-bhyoo-gyee, containing somewhat over three hundred inhabitants.

KOO-LA-DAN.—A river in Arakan which has its sources in the moun-tainous country in the north, somewhere, it is supposed, in the neighbourhood of the Blue Mountain, and with a general N. and S. direction falls into the Bay of Bengal at Akyab, where it is called by Europeans the Arakan river but by the inhabitants of the country Ga-tsha-bha. Before it leaves the hills it is fed by numerous streams, the two largest of which are the Mee from the east and the Pee from the west, and its banks are inhabited by hillmen. It is navigable by vessels of from 300 to 400 tons burden for nearly fifty miles from its mouth, which forms a large harbour with good holding ground, protected from the violence of the S. W. monsoon by the Borongo islands and at its entrance by a rocky islet, called Savage Island, on which stands a light-house erected in 1842 and supplied with more per fect reflecting apparatus in 1871. The entrance is, however, somewhat dan-gerous and difficult and very shallow at low tide, there being then barely 3½ fathoms, necessarily much reduced when a rolling swell sets in.

KOO-LA-DAN.—A township in the north of the Akyab district, adjoin-ing the Hill Tracts and having Mro-houng on the south and east and Oo-rit-toung West on the west. It is divided into eight revenue circles. Except to the south, on the banks of the Koo-la-dan and of its tributary the Pee, the country is hilly and forest-clad. The township contains no large towns and not much cultivation. The head-quarters are on the right bank of the Koo-la-dan river not far from the Maha-moo-nee temple : q. v. The name " Koo-la-dan" is derived from " Koo-la," a western foreigner, and "dan" or "tan" which, when used in this connection, means a locality or quarter, because the captives made by the Arakanese in their raids in Chittagong were settled here : to the present day the tract contains many Musulmans of mixed descent, especially along the right bank of the Koo-la-dan. In 1876 the land revenue was Rs. 47,536, the capitation tax Rs. 18,392 the gross revenue Rs. 68,408 and the population 15,406 souls.

KOO-LA-PAN-ZENG.—A revenue circle in the north of the Ra-thai-doung township, Akyab district, to which has been added Tsaing-dan. In 1874-75 7,199 acres of land were under cultivation and the land revenue realized was Rs. 10,644. The population in 1876-77 numbered 12,648 souls, the capitation tax amounted to Rs. 8,215, the land revenue to Rs. 10,983 and the gross revenue to Rs. 19,806.

KOON-DAN.—A revenue circle in the Hmaw-bhee township, Rangoon district, lying to the west of the low terminal ridge of the Roma mountains, adjoining and north of the town of Rangoon and stretching eastwards to the Poo-zwon-doung river which separates it from the Kyouk-khyoung and Tsit-peng circles of the same township. To the west is the Meng-ga-la-doon circle and to the north Re-tho. The eastern portion of the circle is hilly and unfitted for rice cultivation. Skirting the rice plains on the western side is the Meng-lan or old "Royal road." The circle is traversed by the road from Rangoon towards Prome, running northward ; the principal villages are Pouk-taw with 755 inhabitants in 1876, Kam-bai, where there is a police guard, with 877 inhabitants, Re-goo with 448, and Ta-da-ga-le on the Poo-zwon-doung river with 526. In that year the population of the whole circle was 8,253, the land revenue Rs. 18,117 and the amount of the capitation tax Rs. 7,808.

KOON-DAW.—A revenue circle in the Mye-dai township, Thayet district, within the limits of which are what were, at the preparation of the great register nearly one hundred years ago, the two registered village circles of Kook-ko-hla and Kyet-roon-gyee. It has an area of 30,720 acres of which about 27,000 are unculturable and about 1,900 are cultivated. The principal villages are Goon-daw about a mile and a half inland from the Irrawaddy and Kyet-roon-gyee, on the stream of the same name which unites with other rivulets to form the Retshoon a tributary of the Kye-nee. The principal products are rice, sessamum, cotton, plantains, custard apples and maize. In 1876 the population numbered 2,174 souls, the land revenue was Rs. 1,160, the capitation tax Rs. 2,260 and the gross revenue Rs. 3,503.

KOON-LAY.—A village of seventy houses in the Tham-boo-la circle, Mye-dai township, Thayet district.

KOON-PYENG.—A revenue circle in the Kyouk-khyoung-gale township —now joined to Le-myet-hna—Bassein district, 101 square miles in extent and stretching eastward from the Arakan mountains on the north of the Kwon stream with the Thoung-dan circle on the west and the Kan-nee circle on the south. In the eastern part there is a fair amount of rice cultivation, but towards the west the country is a mass of forest-covered hills gradually rising into the Arakan mountains. The inhabitants of the circle are engaged in agricultural pursuits and in forestry. In 1876 the population was 6,513 souls, the land revenue Rs. 9,737, the capitation tax Rs. 7,812 and the gross revenue Rs. 17,541.

KOON-RO.—A village in the Prome district six miles east of the town of Prome in a large rice tract and within the limits of Ya-thay-myo, or Tha-re-khet-tara, the ruined capital of the ancient Prome kingdom.

KOON-RWA-LENG.—A revenue circle in the Prome district extending along the left bank of the Irrawaddy northwards from the Naweng river and including five of the old village tracts, viz., Koon-rwa-leng, Hpo-goung, Lek-khoop-peng, Mya-rwa, and Nga-pat. In 1876 it had a population of 1,858, the land revenue was Rs. 1,361, the capitation tax Rs. 1,948 and the gross revenue Rs. 4,258.

KOON-TA-LOON.—A revenue circle in the Kan-oung township of the Henzada district westward of Kan-oung, now forming a portion of the Kan-oung Myoma circle, well cultivated towards the north and east.

KOON-TENG-NGAY.—A village in the Prome district inhabited mainly by agriculturists engaged in rice cultivation and situated about two miles west of the village of Loung-gyee.

KOON-TSENG.—A revenue circle of the Prome district about eleven miles east of Prome ; the major portion is under rice cultivation. It is now united to Gaw-ta-maw.

KOOT-THIEN-NA-ROON.—A pagoda in the Shwe-gyeng district at the village of Ayek-thai-ma, about six miles to the north of the town of Bhee-leng. According to the local traditions two brothers, princes, the elder of whom was married, settled in the neighbourhood. The wife of the elder died in giving birth to a daughter and subsequently the elder brother himself died. On his deathbed he gave his brother his deceased wife's ring with an injunction to marry no one whose finger it would not fit. After much search it was found that the ring fitted the orphan niece. She besought her uncle to allow her to build a pagoda before the dreaded marriage took place and so arranged that she was immured in it and escaped the incestuous intercourse at the expense of her life.

KO-TOUNG.—A village in the Peng-ga-daw circle, Mye-dai township, Thayet district, on one of the small feeders of the Khyoung-goung-gyee river. About ten years ago the village, which is now of sixty-five houses, was returned as containing only twelve.

KOUK-GWAI.—A river in the Prome district which rises in the undulating ground north of Wet-htee-gan and, after receiving the waters brought down by the Eng-roon, falls into the Na-weng near Tha-pan-khyo. In the rains small boats can ascend as far as the village of Kam-bhee-la : the banks are moderately steep and the bed sandy ; towards the source they are fringed with tree-forest but from the village of Zee-goon to the Na-weng this stream runs through a small tract of cultivated land.

KOUNG-TSEE.—A revenue circle in the Prome district north-east of Prome, south of the Teng-gyee and Na-weng rivers and occupying the angle formed by the junction of the Kywai river and the Nee-pa-tshe spur of the Pegu Roma mountains. The villages are few in number and, generally, small ; the inhabitants cultivate rice and cotton. The Oot-hpo village tract is now joined to it and in 1876 the land revenue raised in the two was Rs. 576, the capitation tax Rs. 637 and the gross revenue Rs. 1,768. In that year the population numbered 1,280 souls.

KOUNG-TSEE.—A village in the Prome district on the Keng-poon rivulet, which falls into the Teng-gyee near O-htien-goon. It is situated in a patch of rice cultivation in 18° 49' 30" N., and 95° 46' E.

KWE.—A tidal creek in the Nga-poo-taw township, Bassein district, running between the Bassein and the Thek-ngay-thoung mouths of the Nga-won river, varying from 100 to 300 yards in breadth and from two to six fathoms in depth at low water. Near its eastern end a bed of limestone passes under the creek on which there are three fathoms at low tide.

KWE-DAN-SHE.—A village in the Zaing-ga-naing circle, Pegu township, Rangoon district, a few miles below Pegu but on the right bank of the Pegu river. In 1877 it had 582 inhabitants.

KWENG-BOUK-GYEE.—A revenue circle in the Myoung-mya township, Bassein district, having an estimated area of 350 square miles and comprising that portion of the delta of the Irrawaddy lying between the Rwe and the Pya-ma-law rivers which is bounded by the Pan-ma-myit-ta and the Poo-loo natural canals on the north and by the seacoast on the south. The coastline consists of a flat and sandy beach with narrow plains, from $\frac{1}{4}$ to $\frac{1}{2}$ a mile in width and covered with grass jungle, running along its margin. The country as far north as the Kook-ko channel is low and intersected by tidal creeks the banks of which have a deep fringe of heavy tree forest. From the Kook-ko to the northern boundary the country gradually rises, the intricacy of the creeks diminishes, and the plains and habitable spots increase. No hill or stone of any sort has been discovered and the whole circle may be considered as formed of pure alluvial deposit. There are no roads of any sort but excellent water communication. The inhabitants, who in 1876 numbered 2,432, are mainly fishermen and net and trap makers though a few are engaged in cultivation. In that year the land revenue was Rs. 6,648, the capitation tax Rs. 2,855 and the gross revenue, of which about one-quarter was the produce of the fishery and net tax, Rs. 13,380.

KWENG-DA-LA.—A village in the circle of the same name in the Shwe-gyeng township, Shwe-gyeng district, on the Tsit-toung river just below Pooz-won-myoung, with 524 inhabitants in 1877.

KWENG-DA-LA.—A revenue circle in the Shwe-gyeng district occupying both banks of the river just north of the town of Shwe-gyeng and on the west bank stretching down opposite to that town. It has an area of about 80 square miles and a population (in 1876) of 7,793 souls who are principally Burmese. There are several fisheries worked by inhabitants of this circle. At Poo-zwon-myoung pots are largely manufactured for export down the river to the Rangoon district and inland to the hills and elsewhere. In 1876 the land revenue was Rs. 1,853, the capitation tax Rs. 7,082 and the gross revenue Rs. 12,252.

KWENG-GOUK.—A revenue circle in the Oot-hpo township of the Henzada district, having the Bassein district on the south and the Gnyoung-rwa-ngay circle on the north, and extending eastward from the Arakan mountains to the Oot-hpo Myoma circle. To the west the country is hilly and covered with tree forest, where are found Teak (*Tectona grandis*), Eng (*Dipterocarpus tuberculatus*), Pyeng-gado (*Xylia dolabriformis*) and Sha (*Acacia catechu*) ; through these forests roam elephants, bison, tiger and deer. Towards the west the country is open and exceedingly fertile. In 1876 the population numbered 13,731 souls and the gross revenue was Rs. 27,598, of which Rs. 12,353 were from the land revenue and Rs. 12,347 from the capitation tax.

KWENG-HLA.—A revenue circle in the Pa-doung township of the Prome district, to the west of Pyeng-gyee, now joined to the Toung-ngoo circle.

KWENG-HLA.—A revenue circle in the Tha-boung township, Bassein district, lying between the crest of the Arakan hills on the west and the Bassein river on the east, and extending northwards from the Thaboung circle, from which it is separated by the Thien stream, to the Kan-nee circle of the Le-myet-hna township. In the eastern part of the circle there is a good deal of rice cultivation but towards the west the ground rises and the surface of the country is occupied by the well-wooded spurs and eastern slopes of the Arakan Roma. There is a fairly good road through the plains about two miles west of the Bassein river. In 1876 the population numbered 4,564 souls, the land revenue was Rs. 4,339, the capitation tax Rs. 4,795 and the gross revenue Rs. 11,119.

KWENG-LYA.—A village in the Kwon-khyoung circle, Re-gyee township, Bassein district, 12 miles south-west of Nga-thaing-khyoung, on the right bank of the Bassein river, at the southern mouth of the Kwon river, which separates it from the village of Tsha-daw, and a few miles below Nga-pee-tshiep. The inhabitants of the united villages, who are mainly Kareng, are engaged chiefly in agriculture and numbered 1,012 in 1877.

KWON.—A river in the Bassein district which rises in the Arakan hills and falls into the Than-dwe at the shoulder of the bend eastward which that river makes about six miles from its mouth. It is navigable by boats of 30 to 40 feet in length as far as the village of Kwon-khyoung, that is for about two miles, and small boats can ascend two miles further with the flood.

KWON.—A river in the Bassein district which rises in the Arakan mountains and empties itself into the Bassein river between the two adjoining villages of Kweng-lya and Tsha-daw. During the rains it is navigable for boats of fifty or sixty baskets burden as far as Hpan-kha-beng but in the dry weather only as far as the village of Kweng-khyoung and then only at flood tide. About seven miles from its source it is joined by a northern tributary which rises in the Tsheng-ro peak of the Arakan mountains, about 1,400 feet above the sea level. Pyengma (*Lagerstrœmia reginæ*), Pyeng-gado (*Xylia dolabriformis*) and Rengdaik (*Dalbergia cultrata*) are found on its banks, as well as some teak near its source.

KWON.—A river forming the boundary between the Toung-ngoo and the Suwe-gyeng districts on the west of the Tsit-toung river. It rises in the Pegu Roma range and after an easterly course of 60 miles falls into the Tsit-toung about 50 miles south of Toung-ngoo. Owing to the rockiness of of its bed it is not navigable by boats but large quantities of teak and of the produce of the country, of which raw silk forms a large part, are brought down on rafts. About 20 miles from its mouth, near the village of Tsan-gyee, it is for several miles obstructed by rapids with narrow passages between the rocks.

KWON.—A small river in the Henzada district which rises in the Arakan mountains and, flowing eastward through a valley separated from that of the A-loon on the north by a spur of the Roma, falls into that river a few miles above Bhet-rai village. In the rains large boats can ascend far about four miles but no further on account of the rocky nature of the bed and other obstructions, such as trees and bamboos which are then washed down. The banks are steep in some places and flat in others and the bed is sandy, muddy and rocky. Teak is the most important tree growing on its banks.

KWON-DAW.—A revenue circle in the Henzada district, now including Reng-daw and Re-dweng-hla, lying on the southern border of the Myanoung township between Thien-goon on the west and Htan-thoon-beng on the east. The cultivation is carried on chiefly in the centre and towards the south-east of these combined circles the west and north being undulating ground unsuited for rice : about half of Reng-daw is under rice cultivation. In 1876 the population numbered 3,851 souls, the capitation tax produced Rs. 4,250, the land revenue was Rs. 4,879 and the gross revenue was Rs. 9,662.

KWON-GYEE.—A revenue circle in the Gyaing Attaran township of the Amherst district, to which Poon-kaw is now joined. In 1876 the population numbered 868 souls, the land revenue was Rs. 209 and the capitation tax produced Rs. 322.

KWON-HLA.—(*Pronounced Kwan-hla*). A village of the Ka-ma-ke circle in the Amherst district, north-east of and near Ka-ma-ke, in the south of Bhee-loo-gywon. When this township was re-peopled after the annexation a Thoogyee and his followers settled in this village which gave its name to a circle which was united to Ka-ma-ke in 1848. In 1868 the population, principally Talaing, numbered 559 souls and in 1876 705.

KWON-HLA.—(*Pronounced Kwan-hla*). A revenue circle in the Zaya township, Amherst district, divided into two portions by the Htoon-man circle. One portion of it, which is nearly all highland, adjoins the Toung-gnyo range between Htoon-man on the north and the Wa-kha-roo river on the south ; the other, all plain land, is on the bank of the Salween at the mouth of the Wa-kha-roo. The total area of the circle is 14,215 acres. The inhabitants, who in 1868 numbered 732 and in 1876 1,094 souls, are principally Talaing with a few Kareng and Chinese. The principal villages are Kwon-hla and Nee-pa-daw. In the former there were 369 inhabitants in 1868 and under 500 in 1876 and in the latter 363 in 1868 and 790 in 1876. In the latter year the land revenue was Rs. 4,767 (a good many of the inhabitants of the country on the other side of the Wa-kha-roo own and cultivate land here) and the capitation tax produced Rs. 1,027.

KWON-KHYAN-GOON.—A village in the La-wa-dee circle, Angyee township, Rangoon district, which, with the adjacent village of Taw-pa-lwai had, in 1877, 1,233 inhabitants, chiefly Talaing. It does not appear to have increased in size to any considerable extent for in 1858 it contained 200 houses, which represent a population of about 1,000 souls, and in 1868 there were 1,076 inhabitants. It is situated on the Thoon-khwa or Taw-pa-lwai stream, about five miles from its mouth in the To river. The inhabitants are largely occupied in the manufacture of the pots in which brine is boiled down for the extraction of salt. The clay is found in the Taw-gyee near the A-twot lake, or swamp, a few miles north of the village. The pot makers pay no special tax; in the Burmese time each potter's wheel was charged.

KWON-KHYOUNG.—A revenue circle in the Re-gyee township, Bassein district, about 18 square miles in extent. Its largest village is Bhoora-goon. In 1876 the population numbered 2,049 souls, the land revenue was Rs. 1,637, the capitation tax Rs. 2,330 and the gross revenue Rs. 4,754.

KWON-LOUNG.—A village of nearly one hundred and twenty houses on the left bank of the Irrawaddy in the Nga-pyeng circle, Mye-dai township, Thayet district, opposite Kywon-gale island. In the same narrow tract of rice country are the villages of Pyee-beng-hla on the north and Nga-pyeng to the south.

KWON-NEE.—(*Pronounced Kwan-nee*). A village in the Hmaw-won circle, Than-lyeng township, Rangoon district, on a stream of the same name about four miles from its junction with the Ka-ma-ka-root, the united streams falling into the Hmaw-won a little below Kyouk-tan. In 1877 the population numbered 611 souls. A number of Talaing families have been established here ever since the first Anglo Burmese war, attracted to the spot by the fertility of the neighbouring lands and by the convenience of the situation, the stream being broad and navigable by boats of considerable burden as far as the village.

KWON-OON.—A revenue circle in the Thayet township, Thayet district, covering an area of about eight square miles, of which about 600 acres are cultivated at present and some thousand more are culturable; in 1876 the population numbered 5,727 and the gross revenue was Rs. 6,761, of which Rs. 2,313 were derived from the land revenue and Rs. 4,276 from the capitation tax. Formerly this circle formed a portion of Taw-daw-khyoung but was erected into a separate circle in 1855: in 1861 Taw-daw-khyoung was absorbed in Ban-byeng; in 1871 the Re-byoo circle was placed under the Thoogyee of Kwon-oon, who had hereditary rights, as was Mya-tsa-gaing in 1871 on the resignation of the Thoogyee. Still later Ban-byeng with the included Taw-daw-khyoung was added to it. The products are cotton, sessamum, rice, maize and cutch.

KWON-OON.—A village in the Kwon-oon circle, Thayet township, Thayet district, containing about fifty houses, situated on the Pwon stream. Before 1855 it was one of the villages of Taw-daw-khyoung: it was then, together with two other villages, formed into a new circle.

KWON-OON.—A revenue circle in the Tha-ga-ra township of the Toung-ngoo district, east of the Tsit-toung river, near which the country is level but eastwards it is hilly and forest-clad, producing teak and bamboos. In 1876 the land revenue was Rs. 1,257, the capitation tax Rs. 2,274, the gross revenue Rs. 4,181 and the population 3,711.

KWON-RAIK.—(*Pronounced Kwan-raik*). A revenue circle in the Amherst district on the western side of Bhee-loo-gywon and in the central portion of what was the old Daray "Myo" or township, having the sea on the west, the present circle of Daray on the north, Rwa-lwot on the east and Taw-ka-ma on the south. The whole of its surface is an extensive alluvial plain with a total area of 6,452 acres. This is the only circle in the township in which the boundaries fixed by Captain Phayre in 1848 have been changed. When the circle was first established the Kyoon-ka-mee and the Kyoon-tha streams were declared to form the boundary between this circle and Taw-ka-ma but the Kyoon-ka-mee having silted up disputes arose between the two Thoogyee and a portion of what was formerly in Kwon-raik is now included in Taw-ka-ma. The principal village is Kwon-raik, near the stream of the same name : in 1876 it had 978 inhabitants. In 1868 the population was 934, the land revenue Rs. 5,237 and the capitation tax Rs. 905 : in 1876 these had increased to 1,116, Rs. 5,430 and Rs. 1,160 respectively. The principal occupation of the inhabitants is cultivation but a little salt is made and a small revenue is derived from the tax on nets.

KWON-RAIK.—(*Pronounced Kwan-raik*). A village in the circle of the same name in the Amherst district on Bhee-loo-gywon near the little Kwon-raik stream. In 1867 this and the adjoining village of Taw-ka-ma had 904 inhabitants, almost all Talaing with a few Burmans and one or two Chinese, and in 1877 978.

KWON-TAW.—(*Pronounced Kwan-taw*). A revenue circle in the Amherst district in the south of Bhee-loo-gywon, having Ka-la-be on the north, Ka-ma-ke on the east, Taw-ka-ma on the west and the sea on the south. Its surface is an unbroken level of swampy plains, parts of which are occasionally damaged by salt water. In the Burmese time it formed a portion of the Ka-ma-ke circle from which it was separated by Captain Phayre in 1848. It has a total area of 4,891 acres. Of late years the sea has made considerable encroachment and the sites of Kwon-taw and other villages have been swept away since 1848. The land is generally good for rice when not swamped with salt-water and there is little room for any increase in the area so cultivated unless reclamation schemes are undertaken. There is no ground fit for gardens, that is above the usual inundation level. In 1868 the population numbered about 120, the land revenue was Rs. 4,915 and the capitation tax Rs. 127. In 1876 these had increased to 228, Rs. 5,282 and Rs. 230 respectively. The paucity of the population as compared with the land revenue is due to the inhabitants, when their villages were washed away, having removed into neighbouring circles but still working the land.

KWON-THAI.—(*Pronounced Kwan-thai*). A village in the Kharaik-thit circle of the Bhee-loo-gywon township of the Amherst district, on the bank of the Salween at the mouth of the Kharaik-thit stream. The inhabitants numbered 565 in 1867 and 875 in 1877.

KYA-ENG.—A revenue circle in the north of the Kyan-kheng township, Henzada district, south of Akouk-toung, now included in the Tshoon-lai circle.

KYA-ENG.—A revenue circle in the Gyaing Attaran township, Amherst district, occupying the country on both banks of the Za-mee river, just south of the Hpa-thien circle. Hilly and covered with forest the few Kareng who inhabit it do not cultivate largely. In 1876 the population was 1,017, the land revenue Rs. 331 and the capitation tax Rs. 982. The principal village is Kya-eng.

KYA-ENG.—A revenue circle in the north-eastern township of the Tavoy district, about 24 square miles in extent, of which about one-sixth is cultivated. The main products are rice and doorians. In 1876 the inhabitants numbered 2,703, the land revenue was Rs. 4,386, the capitation tax Rs. 2,222 and the gross revenue Rs. 6,827.

KYA-ENG.—A village in the circle of the same name in the Gyaing Attaran township, Amherst district, about four miles east of the bank of the Za-mee, the houses surrounded with orange and other fruit gardens. A small and unimportant little stream of the same name runs through the village which is laid out without any attempt at regularity and with no roads but narrow footpaths through the gardens from house to house. The inhabitants, who are Kareng and are nearly, if not quite, all Christians, numbered 707 in 1877.

KYA-ENG.—A village in the circle of the same name in the Tavoy district which in 1877 had a population of 685 souls.

KYA-GAN.—A revenue circle in the Moung-mya township, Bassein district, with an area of about 111 square miles, on the right bank of the Rwe, north of the La-bwot-ta-loot channel. An outcrop of limestone, rising into small hills, occupies the whole of the northern and central portion of the circle. The inhabitants are principally fishermen and nga-pee makers, though a few are cultivators, and in 1876 numbered 4,833 souls. La-bwot-ta is the principal place. During the fishing season the majority of the inhabitants go south and establish temporary fishing hamlets. In 1876 the land revenue was Rs. 2,762, the capitation tax Rs. 6,365, the other taxes, principally net and trap, Rs. 5,847 and the gross revenue, including the five per cent cess on the land revenue and net tax, Rs. 15,363.

KYA-GAN.—A revenue circle in the Meng-doon township, Thayet district, now joined to Ta-goung-nek.

KYA-GAN.—A village of over one hundred houses in the circle of the same name in the Meng-doon township, Thayet district, close to the northern frontier and about a mile from the 8th boundary pillar, counting westwards from the river.

KYAIK-ATHOOT.—A pagoda in the plains west of the Maulmam hills said to contain a hair of Gaudama and to have been built by King Maha-nee-zee-na. It was restored about thirty-five years ago and is now 135 feet high and 360 feet in circumference at the base.

KYAIK-HPA-NAY.—A pagoda in the extreme north of the town of Maulmain standing on the bank of the Salween river. According to the current tradition it was built by a Talaing—one of the original mythical dynasty which reigned before the foundation of Pegu—to commemorate a victory over the Siamese. It was repaired in 1863 by an inhabitant of Maulmain at his own expense and has now a height of 45 feet.

KYAIK-HPYENG-KOO.—A pagoda in the Martaban township of the Amherst district, founded in 1288 A.D. by King Wa-rie-yoo. The name is supposed to be a corruption of the Talaing "Kyaik-hpyeng-boo" or "Pagoda of the large assembly" from having been built on a spot on which Gaudama had preached to and converted a large assembly of Bhee-loo*.

KYAIK-HTEE-YO.—A peak on the crest of the main dividing range between the Tsit-toung and the Salween just to the east of Tsittoung, between that town and Kyaikhto, which rises to a height of 3,650 feet. The ascent is made in one day from the south-east and in two from Tsit-toung. The pagodas on the top are annually resorted to by crowds of Booddhists, especially Talaing, in February of each year. The view from the summit is exceedingly fine: to the eastward are seen the Martaban mountains, to the south the sea and to the west the great Shwe Hmaw-daw Pagoda of Pegu. The most remarkable features of this hill are the many granitoid boulders scattered about its summit, some of them balanced in the strangest manner on the most prominent rocks. On all the most striking of these boulders small pagodas have been built; of these the two principal are the Kyaik-htee-yo-ga-le (a barbarous word, three-fifths Talaing and two-fifths Burmese) and the Kyaik-htee-yo (whence is derived the name of the hill). This latter, about fifteen feet high, is built on a huge, almost egg-shaped, rounded, granitoid boulder perched on the very summit of a projecting and shelving tabular rock, which itself is separated several feet from the mountain by a rent or chasm, now spanned by a small bamboo footbridge and on the further side drops down perpendicularly into a valley below. On the extreme verge of this sloping rock table, and actually overhanging it by nearly half, is perched this wonderful boulder, thirty feet high and surmounted by the pagoda, reached by a bamboo moveable ladder. The mass appears as if the additional weight of a few pounds, or indeed a strong wind, would send it sliding down from the place it has occupied for unknown centuries crashing into the sloping valley beneath and pious Booddhists believe that it is retained in its position solely by the power of the relic enshrined in the pagoda. This relic is a hair of Gaudama given to a hermit residing on the mountain by the Booddha himself as he was returning from the second heaven of the Nat whither he had gone to preach the law to his mother.

KYAIK-HTO.—A revenue circle in the Tsit-toung sub-division of the Shwe-gyeng district, surrounding the town of Kyaik-hto, about 70 square miles in extent and with a population in 1876 of 7,329 souls. The area under cultivation is small but the fisheries afford a large revenue to the State. In the hills to the north cardamoms are produced to some extent. In 1876 the land revenue was Rs. 708, the capitation tax Rs. 5,623 and the gross revenue Rs. 21,335.

KYAIK-HTO.—A busy, thriving town in the Kyaik-hto Bhee-leng township, Shwe-gyeng district, about half way between Tsit-toung and Bhee-leng, on the Ka-dat river, which is here spanned by a wooden bridge, and on the high road to Maulmain, and lying at the foot of the hills closing in the large plain country which stretches down southward to the coast. It has a population of 2,040 souls. For some years it was the

* Cf. " Bhee-loo-gywon" and note to page 128.

head-quarter station of the Kyaik-hto township and later of the united townships of Kyaik-hto and Bhee-leng. A few years ago the Extra Assistant Commissioner in charge of these two townships was transferred to Bhee-leng, and Kyaik-hto, lying in about the centre, was made the head-quarter station of the Tsit-toung sub-division, the Assistant Commissioner in charge being transferred hither from Tsit-toung. The town consists principally of one long street at right angles to and crossing the Kadat, that portion which lies to the eastward being the largest and most important; here there are cross streets and a few others parallel to the main road. The houses are well and substantially built and the town throughout the year is a centre of trade in cattle, rice in the husk, betelnuts, fish, salt, piece-goods, cotton twist and hardware. The proposed canal to connect the Bhee-leng and Tsit-toung rivers will pass close by Kyaik-hto. At the extreme eastern end, near a group of pagodas and monasteries, is the circuit-house, The town contains a Court-house, a Police Station and a good market. In 1876 the local revenue, in addition to the Imperial taxes, was Rs. 2,443.

KYAIK-KA-LO.—This pagoda, which at present is undergoing repair, is situated about 300 yards west of the Prome road and 1½ miles N. of the village of Tsan-gyee-wa. It stands on the summit of a short spur stretching from the ridge along which runs the high road. There is a small zayat at the junction of the footpath leading to the pagoda and the Prome road. The whole of the ridge is covered with short shrub-growth and long grass.

The footpath leads up to the platform, which is about 60 yards square, entering it by a few steps placed in the centre of the side facing the E. Immediately inside the entrance is a sitting figure of Gaudama Booddha, under a roofed building; behind this is another figure, also of the last Booddha, let into the basement of the "bell," and again on the S. side of the bell there is also another figure similarly let in. From the platform an excellent view is obtained of the undulating ground stretching westwards and southwards, and of the broad expanse of rice-fields eastwards towards the Poo-zwon-doung creek. In the S. E. corner of the platform stands another roofed building containing one large and two small figures of Gaudama.

The basement of the pagoda is octagonal, each side being about 14 yards in length, and is raised some 6½ feet above the level of the platform. On the basement stand 24 small pagodas, some of which are undergoing repair, and from their midst rises the "bell" of the large pagoda, the height of the whole being about 90 feet. On the N. side a portion of the modern brick-facing of the basement has fallen into decay, exposing the large blocks of laterite of which the pagoda is built. A small winding road leads from the S. E. corner of the platform and, skirting the neighbouring monastery grounds, descends into a dell lying between the edge of the platform and the Prome road. In this dell is a small tank, surrounded by a low brick wall, with four small ornamental archways over the steps leading down to the well. The path then winds up the opposite side of the dell and joins the Prome road about 50 yards S. of the point from whence the main path strikes off to the pagoda. There is here an annual festival in the month of Taboung (about March) attended by vast numbers of people.

KYAIK-KA-LWON-BWON.—A pagoda in Martaban supposed to have been founded in the sixth century B.C. by the Bheeloo, who then inhabited the country, to commemorate a miracle performed by Gaudama, who came to preach to and convert them, and to enshrine one of his hairs.

KYAIK-KA-LWON-BWON.—A pagoda standing on a massive laterite base on the hill above the town of Tsit-toung within the old fort walls, supposed to have been built to commemorate an interview between Gaudama and 100 Bheeloo.

KYAIK-KA-MAN-LAI.—A pagoda on Bheeloo island, supposed to have been founded during the reign of a Talaing king named Nan-da-thee-ha-ra-ga.

KYAIK-KA-MAW.—A group of villages in the Than-lyeng township of the Rangoon district, inhabited by Pwo Kareng agriculturists and situated some in the plains and some on the Koondan or undulating ground. There formerly existed here a Talaing city of which no traces remain save a cluster of pagodas on an eminence near which is a conspicuous clump of teak trees.

KYAIK-KA-THA.—A very ancient pagoda in the Shwe-gyeng district between Tsit-toung and Kyaik-hto, about seven miles from the former, built, according to local tradition, by Prince Ka-tha Koom-ma-ra. This Prince, who was the son of one of the minor Queens, was, by order of the Chief Queen, thrown, when an infant, on to the bank of the Tsit-toung river at Kha-ra-tshoo. He was saved and brought to Kyaik-ka-tha where, in after years, he built this pagoda and founded a town, the remains of which are still in existence. Leading up to this pagoda is a curious avenue of other and smaller ones all built, as the Kyaik-ka-tha itself is, of laterite and generally known to the Burmese as " Bhoora-ta-htoung " or the thousand pagodas. Kyaik-ka-tha is the Talaing name.

KYAIK-KA-THA.—A small village of 617 inhabitants in the Tsit-toung sub-division of the Shwe-gyeng district eight miles south-east of Tsit-toung, on the high road, during the rains, from Tsit-toung to Maulmain. Near it is a celebrated pagoda supposed to have been founded by a Prince named Ka-tha Koom-ma-ra who founded a town here, whence the name, Kyaik meaning pagoda in Talaing. The inhabitants live principally by working the neighbouring fisheries.

KYAIK-KAW.—A revenue circle in the Tha-htoon township of the Amherst district, north of Tha-htoon, stretching from the crest of the Martaban hills westward to the Bhee-léng river, with the Dha-noo circle on the north and east (on the other side of the hills) and the Mye-nee-goon circle on the south. The alluvial plains are fertile but are still too much flooded by the spill from the Bhee-leng and by the rain water, which does not flow off rapidly, to be available for much cultivation notwithstanding the protection afforded by the Ka-ma-thaing embankment and the drainage ways which have been cut of late years. These works have done undoubted good for whereas the land revenue in 1868 was Rs. 6,644 it was Rs. 10,618 in 1876. The increase, however, is partly due to the reduction in the rate which was Rs. 2-4 per acre before 1868 and has since been Rs. 1-12, Re. 1, and twelve annas, according to the situation and fertility of the soil.

In 1878 the population, composed mainly of Talaing and Kareng, was 3,336 and the capitation tax Rs. 3,430 ; in 1876 4,969 and Rs. 5,072 respectively. The principal villages are Ka-tha-ba-kareng and Kha-daik ; in 1868 the inhabitants numbered 823 and 350 and in 1876 529 and 539 respectively. The latter of these two was formerly on the bank of the Bhee-leng, but owing to that river having changed its channel it is now some distance inland.

KYAIK-KA-TSHAN.— A pagoda of great sanctity in the Rangoon district, about three miles north-east of the Shwe-dagon pagoda in Rangoon, about 90 feet high and 70 feet in diameter at the base. It was erected, according to Talaing history, about two centuries B. C. by Baw-ga-the-na over one of the relics of Gaudama brought by eight Rahanda. It was partially destroyed in 1733 but was repaired and has been occasionally repaired since. A large assemblage of people takes place at the annual festival in February.

KYAIK-KHA-MEE.—A small circle in the Wa-kha-roo township, Amherst district, of triangular shape, having the Salween and the Wa-kha-roo rivers on one side and the sea on the other and the circle of Hnit-kaing on the east for its base. The total area is 3,996 acres. The principal rice fields are in the alluvial plain near the bank of the Wa-kha-roo, the rest of the circle is upland with a laterite soil and well adapted for gardens. There was formerly a good deal of sugar cultivation but as the land became impoverished the cultivators moved eastwards into other circles. The population is almost entirely congregated in the town of Amherst. It is composed principally of Talaing, with Burmans, Natives of India, Chinese and a few Europeans and Indo-Europeans : in 1868 it numbered 3,085 souls and 3,436 in 1876. In the latter year the land revenue was Rs. 1,852 and the capitation tax Rs. 3,182.

KYAIK-KHA-MEE.—A name sometimes given to the Wa-kha-roo township of the Amherst district. q. v.

KYAIK-KHA-PAN.—A pagoda in Martaban founded in 1199 A.D. by King A-lien-ma.

KYAIK-KOUK.—A handsome pagoda standing on the Than-lyeng Koon-dan, or stretch of low laterite hills which extend from Than-lyeng to Kyouk-tan, just above the village of Ka-gnyeng-goon, four or five miles from Than-lyeng or Syriam, and built almost entirely of large laterite blocks. It is one hundred and thirty one feet in height and twelve hundred feet in circumference at the base. The platform from which it rises is paved with slabs of a reddish stone brought from Upper Burma. The upper part of the structure is ornamented by alternate bands of white yellow and pale greenish-blue metal, which glitter in the sun and to one at a little distance give the pagoda the appearance of being gilded like the Shwe-dagon in Rangoon, the Shwe-Hmaw-daw in Pegu and many others. According to the history of the pagoda, Gaudama, a few years after attaining Booddha-hood, visited Burma and whilst staying on the Martaban hills presented two of his hairs to a resident hermit. In 580 B.C. the hermit came to Than-lyeng and presented the hairs to Ze-ya-the-na the king, who enshrined them in this pagoda which he built for that purpose. Three hundred and fifty years later, in 223 B.C., eight Rahanda or Booddhist monks visited Than-lyeng and presented Baw-ga-the-na, the last independent sovereign, with a bone of Gaudama's forehead and one of his teeth, one of which the pious monarch enshrined in the east side of the pagoda and the other in the Kyaik-ka-tshan pagoda. In 1781 it had partially fallen into ruin and was repaired by King Bho-daw-bhoora, the third son of Aloung-bhoora, who ascended the throne in that year. It has since been considerably embellished by Moung Tha-dwon-oung, an Extra Assistant Commissioner and son of Moung Tsat who headed our Talaing allies in the first Anglo-Burmese war and subsequently escaped with many followers to the Amherst district. The building is now in the charge of a committee of elders of which the present Extra Assistant Commissioner of the township, Moung Bha-gyaw, son of Moung Tha-dwon-oung, is the President.

KYAIK-MA-RAW.—An extensive revenue circle in the Amherst district lying between the Attaran river on the east and the Toung-gnyo chain on the west. It was at first included in the Attaran township, was subsequently transferred to Zaya, and has again of late years been retransferred to Gyaing Attaran. The total area is 28,723 acres. It has a considerable extent of upland but consists chiefly of large plains, intersected by water courses and deeply flooded in the rains when, after a heavy fall, almost the whole circle is covered to a depth of several feet and a small inland sea is formed, across which, when the wind is high, small boats dare not venture. These floods are caused by the volume of water brought down by the Attaran river banking up the streams which flow from the Toung-gnyo chain. The only village of any importance is Kyaik-ma-raw. In 1868 the population, who are principally Talaing, with some Kareng and a few Shan and Chinese, numbered 1,384, the land revenue was Rs. 1,921 and the capitation tax Rs. 1,375. In 1876 these were 2,043, Rs. 3,160 and Rs. 2,087 respectively.

KYAIK-MA-RAW.—A village in the circle of the same name in the Gyaing Attaran township of the Amherst district, about a mile to the west of the Attaran river and not far east of the Toung-gnyo hills. A good road runs from the river bank to the village. In 1877 it had a population of 822 souls.

KYAIK-MA-TAW.—A small pagoda on the hills in the town of Maulmain supposed to contain one of Gaudama's hairs. Of its early history nothing is known.

KYAIK-PA-DAING.—A village in the Pegu circle of the Pegu township, Rangoon district, on the northern bank of the Paing-kywon cutting, which, with the Myit-kyo canal, forms the water-route between the Pegu and the Tsit-toung. It is the head-quarters of the Executive Engineer of the Tsit-toung Embankment and Canal Division. In 1877 it had 877 inhabitants.

KYAIK-PA-NAY.—A pagoda in Maulmain close to the waters' edge on the north point of the land on which the town stands built in the eighth century by the Peguan king Bha-nai-tsiep-tsaw to commemorate a victory over the Shans or Siamese. It was enlarged in 1863 by Moung Shwe Boo and is now 45 feet high.

KYAIK-PA-RAN.—A revenue circle in the Amherst district, occupying a tract of country in the Gyaing Attaran township on the right bank of the Attaran river, and stretching south-east from the Gnyoung-beng-tshiep circle. It is inhabited principally by Talaing. In this circle is found the earth from which the pots for salt boiling are manufactured in Gnyoung-beng-tshiep. In 1876 the population was 2,057, the land revenue Rs. 4,229 and the capitation tax Rs. 1,877.

KYAIK-TAW.—A large village, divided into north and south Kyaik-taw, in the Ien-da-poo-ra circle, Angyee township, Rangoon district, on the bank of the To river, at the mouth of the Doo-reng Kyaik-taw stream, situated in an extensive and fertile plain. In 1877 the united villages had a population of 1,047 souls.

KYAIK-THAN-LAN.—The principal pagoda in the town of Maulmain, occupying a commanding position on the northern spur of the hill over against Martaban, supposed to contain one of Gaudama's hairs. It was founded in 875 A.D. by a hermit named *Tha-gnya* or *Thee-la*. It was subsequently enlarged by Pan-noo-rat, ruler of Maulmain, and again *circa* 1538 A.D. by Wa-rie-yoo king of Martaban. When the country was ceded to the British this pagoda was in ruins but it was repaired in 1831 by Moung Taw-lay, an Extra Assistant Commissioner, with funds collected by public subscription. It measures 152 feet in height and 377 feet in circumference at the base. The name Kyaik-than-lan is supposed to be a corruption of Kyaik-shan-lan or the pagoda of the Shan defeat, and to be so named from the Shan or Siamese having been here defeated by the Peguans or Talaing.

KYAIK-TOUNG-HPO.—A revenue circle, inhabited by Kareng and but little cultivated, lying in the hilly and forest-clad country east of the Dawna range and just south of Mya-pa-daing, in the Houng-tha-raw township of the Amherst district. It contains some valuable teak localities. In 1876 it had a population of 2,349 souls and a land revenue of Rs. 749 whilst the capitation tax produced Rs. 1,126.

KYAI-LET.—A township in the Akyab district, on the right bank of the Koo-la-dan or Ga-tsha-ba river at its mouth, surrounding the town of Akyab. It is an island, generally low and flat, some parts being below high tide.

KYAN.—A revenue circle in the Meng-doon township, Thayet district, amongst the spurs of the Arakan mountains, ninety-one square miles in extent, eighty-three being unculturable mountain waste and about three under cultivation. The population in 1876 numbered 2,284 souls, of whom a fifth were Khyeng. Owing to its situation the patches of hill clearing are numerous. In 1872 Rs. 1,060 were drawn from the circle as land revenue and Rs. 1,460 as capitation tax. In 1876 the figures were Rs. 1,528 and Rs. 1,529 respectively. Six of the old registered villages are included with the limits of the circle but none of them had any Thoogyee in 1853 when Pegu became British territory. The products are rice, sessamum, cotton, maize, tobacco, onions, chillies and cutch.

KYAN-DAW.—A revenue circle in the Shwe-doung township, Prome district, which now includes Rwa-hteng, Thoon-rwa-boung, Shwe-dien-hgnyeng, Kyee-wek, Kyee-daing and Zhe-ma. It is traversed from south to north by the Kyoon stream east of which there is a good deal of rice cultivation. In 1876 there were 816 inhabitants, the land revenue was Rs. 1,800 and the capitation tax Rs. 873.

KYAN-KHENG.—A township occupying the extreme north of the Henzada district, west of the Irrawaddy, adjoining the Prome district on the north and the Myanoung township on the south, and extending westward from the Irrawaddy to the crest of the Arakan Roma mountains which separates it from the Sandoway district of Arakan. The greater portion of the country, especially in the north and west, is hilly and indeed mountainous and covered with dense forest. An embankment extends along the bank of the Irrawaddy southwards from the spur which ends in the Akouk-toung cliff and protects the country inside from inundation on the annual rise of the river. The township is divided into seven revenue circles and in 1876 had a gross population of 31,903 souls and a gross revenue (including the local revenue raised in Kyan-kheng the principal town) of Rs. 73,678, of which Rs. 29,185 were derived from the land, Rs. 32,068 from the capitation tax, Rs. 9,689 from local cesses and rates and Rs. 2,736 from fisheries and other miscellaneous sources.

In 1876 the area under cultivation and the agricultural stock were :—

Area, in acres, under				Stock.								
Rice.	Garden.	Miscellaneous.	Total.	Ponies.	Buffaloes.	Cows, bulls and bullocks.	Goats and sheep.	Pigs.	Carts.	Ploughs.	Oil mills.	Boats.
17,016	1,724	1,526	20,266	108	3,670	7,116	136	718	3,437	2,851	33	325

KYAN-KHENG.—A town in the Henzada district extending for some distance along the right bank of the Irrawaddy about six miles north of Myanoung, with a population in 1874 of 8,744 inhabitants and in 1876 of
It is the head-quarters of an Extra Assistant Commissioner and has a fine market, a police station and a Public Works Department inspection bungalow. It now contains Eng-lat, Rwa-thit and Myo-ma, the last of which was founded by the Talaing *circa* 1250 A.D., and Eng-lat in 1753 by one Moung Khyeng, a Burman who came with a number of followers from the village of Eng-lat in Upper Burma. Rwa-thit was founded in the same year. The inhabitants are principally merchants, cultivators and fishermen. A large trade is done in this town, a great deal of unhusked rice being sent down the river. The local revenue in 1876-77 was Rs. 7,500. Long. 18°19′N. Lat. 95°20′ 10″ E.

KYAN-KHENGMYOMA.—A revenue circle in the Henzada district surrounding and including part of the town of Kyan-kheng, with the Tshoon-lai circle on the north, the Bhet-rai circle on the west, the Rwa-thit circle on the south and the Irrawaddy on the east, and including Pyaw-bhway island, separated from the mainland by a channel of that river. In the south and east the country is under rice with some vegetable gardens but there is not much cultivation in the north, whilst towards the west the country is hilly and forest-clad. In 1867 the land revenue was Rs. 2,584,the capitation tax Rs. 4,965 and the population 4,312. In 1876 these were Rs. 3,577, Rs. 5,012 and 4,972 respectively; adding the sums collected on account of local cesses (including the amount collected in Kyan-kheng town) and fisheries the gross revenue was Rs. 18,458.

KYA-O.—A revenue circle in the Prome district in the southern part of the Pa-doung township. The eastern portion, near the village of Kya-o, contains some rice cultivation but the western consists of forest-covered hills, nowhere perhaps over 100 feet in height; the principal is the Kyouk-tan hill whence a good supply of limestone is obtained and carried to Htoon-bho to be burned. The inhabitants—Burmese and Khyeng—are largely engaged in hill side cultivation and in the manufacture of cutch. In 1876 the population was 892, the land revenue Rs. 1,050, the capitation tax Rs. 1,037 and the gross revenue Rs. 2,117.

KYA-O.—A village in the Pa-doung township of the Prome district, in 18°26′45″ N. and 95°8′20″ E., on the bank of the Kha-wa stream about five miles from its mouth at Htoon-bho. The inhabitants are chiefly cultivators.

KYAT.—See *Toung-gnyo river.*

KYAT.—A river in the Bassein district which has its source in the Arakan mountains and falls in to the Bassein river opposite Le-myet-hna. In the hot weather it is dry. The bed is gravelly to within a short distance of the mouth. In the rains it is connected by several channels with the Tan-daw lake. In a portion of its course it is called the Tha-khwot and lower down the Ta-da.

KYAT.—A revenue circle in the Meng-doon township, Thayet district, on the left bank of the Ma-htoon stream, about twenty-one square miles in extent, of which rather less than five are culturable the remaining sixteen being mountainous and covered with forest. Shut in between the Ma-htoon river on the west and a range of hills on the east, the western spurs of which stretch down to the Ma-htoon, there is but small space for regular cultivation and consequently hill clearings are numerous. The population numbered 1,319 in 1876, almost all of whom were Burmans. The revenue in 1872 amounted to Rs. 1,260, *viz.*, land revenue Rs. 560 and capitation tax Rs. 700, and in 1876 to Rs. 1,631 *viz.*, land revenue 702, capitation tax Rs. 852 and other taxes and rates Rs. 77. The products are rice, cotton, onions, sessamum and plantains.

KYA-THE.—A village of about fifty houses in the Tham-boo-la circle, Mye-dai township, Thayet district.

KYAT-TSENG.—A revenue circle in the Mye-boon township, Kyouk-hpyoo district, between the Le-mro and the Kyat-tseng rivers north of Daingboon, about 20 square miles in extent and with a population of 2,319 souls in 1876. In that year the land revenue was Rs. 3,695, the capitation tax Rs. 2,851, the receipts from the tax on nets and from local cesses &c., Rs. 571 and the gross revenue Rs. 7,117.

KYA-WA.—A village in the Shwe-doung circle, Meng-doon township, Thayet district, containing about seventy houses.

KYA-WENG.—A village in the Rwon East circle, Than-lyeng township, Rangoon district, on the left bank of the Pyeng-ma-gan stream about a mile from its mouth. The inhabitants, who are principally Shan agriculturists, numbered 549 in 1877.

KYAW-KAING.—A small village in the La-moo Lek-wai circle of the northern or Toung-goop township of the Sandoway district, on the right bank of the La-moo and about seven miles from its mouth. In 1877 the inhabitants numbered 473 souls.

KYE-DAING.—A village of sixty houses in the Re-byoo circle, Thayet township, Thayet district, adjoining Khyeng-tsouk (which contains fifty houses), about seven miles north-west of the town of Thayet. Both of these villages are near the centre of a long narrow stretch of rice cultivation extending from Rwa-toung to Oot-shit-goon.

KYEE-GAN-RAI.—A village in the Toung-ma-gyee circle of the Central or Sandoway township of the Sandoway district, on the seacoast three or four miles south of Toung-ma-gyee point. In 1877 the inhabitants numbered 823 souls.

KYEE-GOON.—A village in the Meng-doon Myoma circle, Meng-doon township, Thayet district, close to the right bank of the Ma-htoon river, a short distance south-east of the town of Meng-doon.

KYEE-MA-NO.—A village in the Prome district in 18° 28′ 0″ N. and 95° 37′ 20″ E. a mile and a half north of the Kyat river and not quite three miles east of the lower end of Poung-day, on the eastern edge of the Poung-day rice plain.

KYEE-MA-NO.—A revenue circle in the Prome district to the eastward of Poung-day between the Nwa-dat and the Kyat streams, now joined to Ma-gyee-beng.

KYEE-MYENG-DAING.—A suburb of Rangoon : q. v.

KYEE-THAI.—A large village in the Prome district on the left bank of the Irrawaddy in 18° 37′ 33″ N. and 95° 11′ 30″ E. and, measured along the river bank, about ten miles below Shwe-doung. To the north of this village is the Theng-byoo lake and to the south of it the Eng-bya. In the rains these two unite behind the village and form an extensive tract of fen extending for nearly ten miles north and south and navigable by boats of four hundred bushels burden.

The inhabitants of this village, who in 1877 numbered 743, are engaged in rice cultivation and in fishing but more especially in silk weaving. A good dry-weather road leads due eastward to Shwe-nat-toung, eight miles inland, where an annual pagoda festival is held.

KYEE-THAI.—A revenue circle in the Shwe-doung township, Prome district, on the left bank of the Irrawaddy, between Shwe-doung Myoma and Gnyoung-tsa-re. The villages, of which Kyee-thai, Rwa-tha-goon and Lek-pan-boo are the largest, are mostly on, or close to, the river bank. Rice fields and gardens occupy an extensive area and the rest of the circle, which in general is level, is covered with tree and grass forest. South of Kyee-thai is the

Eng-bya lake which, in the rains, spreads northwards and joins the Theng-byoo, converting the whole of the country behind the village of Kyee-thai and for some miles north and south of it into a vast reedy marsh. In 1876 the population numbered 9,324, the land revenue was Rs. 2,473, the capitation tax Rs. 3,905 and the gross revenue Rs. 6,543.

KYE-MEE.—A village in the Kama township, Thayet district, containing some eighty houses and situated on the bank of the Ma-htoon stream in the Kyouk-tsoung circle. It was formerly the residence of a Thoogyee but in 1862 the last holder of that office was dismissed for bribery and his circle added to Kyouk-tsoung.

KYE-NEE.—A revenue circle in the Henzada district on the western slopes of the Pegu Roma north of the Tsa-doo-thee-ree-goon circle. Rice cultivation is met with near the villages but the remainder of the circle consists of undulating ground and hills increasing in height towards the east, covered with the tree forest in which is found Teak (*Tectona grandis*), Pyenggado (*Xylia dolabriformis*) and Eng (*Dipterocarpus tuberculatus*) ; and where elephants, tigers, bison, hog and deer abound. In 1876 the population numbered 5,725 souls, the land revenue was Rs. 5,277, the capitation tax Rs. 5,608 and the gross revenue Rs. 11,193.

KYE-NEE.—A river in the Thayet district, which rises in the Burmese territories among the lower western slopes of the Pegu Roma and entering the Mye-dai township near the village of Hpoung-teng, about twelve miles east of the Irrawaddy, falls into that river just below the old fort at Mye-dai. Its course within British territory is not more than sixteen miles in a direct line. It brings down a considerable quantity of water during the rains but is useless for navigation and also, owing, it is said, to obstructions in its course in Upper Burma, for floating timber. The bed is gravelly and the banks steep in some places. Useful timber is found on its banks; amongst other trees Eng-gyeng (*Pentacme siamensis*), which furnishes a white, heavy wood extensively used in house-building, and *Acacia catechu* from which the cutch of commerce is extracted. It has several feeders, but none are navigable or of any importance.

KYEK-MA-YA.—A revenue circle in the Ma-ha-tha-man township, Prome district, containing ten village tracts and lying to the east of the Zay stream and just above the Eng-ma swamp. Rice cultivation is extensively carried on in this circle. In 18¯6 the population was 1,572, the land revenue Rs. 2,081, the capitation tax Rs. 1,573 and the gross revenue Rs. 3,674.

KYEK-POUNG.—A river in the Bassein district. Its source is in the Arakan mountains whence it flows for a considerable distance south and then east, joining the Bassein river about five miles below the village of Tsha-daw. Its total length is about twenty-two miles : its breadth at the mouth is forty feet and its depth ten ; the bed is sandy and muddy. The banks are covered with fine timber trees and with bamboos of several kinds. With the flood large boats can ascend for two miles or a little more.

KYEK-RO.—A revenue circle with an area of 26 square miles in the extreme north of Cheduba island, in the Kyouk-hpyoo district, with a population of 3,233 souls in 1876. The principal products are rice and tobacco.

Not far from the coast there are some petroleum wells. In 1876 the land revenue was Rs. 3,139, the capitation tax Rs. 3,385 and the gross revenue Rs. 6,759.

KYEK-ROON.—A village about seven miles inland from the east bank of the Irrawaddy, in the Goon-daw circle of the Mye-dai township, Thayet district, situated on the little Kyek-roon stream, an affluent, from the south, of the Kye-nee river. It contains about one hundred and thirty houses.

KYEK-TAIK.—A revenue circle in the Meng-hla township of the Henzada district, on the northern and southern slopes of the Eng-gyeng-doung spur of the Pegu Roma. To the west the country is low and level and suited for rice cultivation but towards the east it consists of undulating ground and low hills which gradually rise in height till they join the Roma : these hills are clothed with bamboo and tree forest—Teak (*Tectona grandis*), Pyeng-gado (*Xylia dolabriformis*) and Eng (*Dipterocarpus tuberculatus*)—through which roam elephant, bison, tiger, hog and deer. Cutch is manufactured in this circle from the trees found growing in the forests. In 1876 the population was 7,925 souls, the land revenue Rs. 11,824, the capitation tax Rs. 6,470 and the gross revenue Rs. 19,495.

KYEK-TAW-PYOON.—A revenue circle in the Kyouk-hpyoo district, formed of a group of islands north of Kyouk-hpyoo, 13 square miles in extent, partially cultivated, partly with indigo, and with 1,543 inhabitants in 1876, when the land revenue was Rs. 1,247, the capitation tax Rs. 1,757 and the gross revenue Rs. 5,366, Rs. 2,362 having been derived from the net tax and the local cesses. It now includes the Tswon-pan-khyaing circle.

KYEK-TSHOO-DAW.—A small revenue circle in the north-east corner of the Kan-oung township, Henzada district, now united to Kan-oung Myoma.

KYE-REK-DWENG.—A revenue circle in the western township, Tavoy district, 40 square miles in extent, of which about three are cultivated, principally with rice. Salt is made and a fair revenue is derived from the fishery and net tax. In 1876 the population numbered 1,218 souls, the land revenue was Rs. 2,588, the capitation tax Rs. 926 and the gross revenue Rs. 4,400.

KYIEN-TA-LEE.—A village in the southern township of the Sandoway district, formerly the head-quarter station of the township and the residence of the Extra Assistant Commissioner in charge. It is situated about eight miles from the mouth of the Kyien-ta-lee river and is accessible to small sea going vessels. In 1876 it had a mixed population of 389 souls, amongst whom Arakanese predominate. A small body of Police is stationed here.

KYIEN-TA-LEE.—A revenue circle in the southern or Khwa township of the Sandoway district, which now includes Kyien-ta-lee-bya and extends eastwards from the sea coast, north of the Kyien-ta-lee-Re-gyaw circle, to the crest of the Arakan mountains. The principal products are rice and sessamum. The estimated area of the united circles is 390 square miles and in 1876 the population was 2,082, the land revenue Rs. 2,181, the capitation tax Rs. 2,012 and the gross revenue Rs. 6,505. In 1831 a hpoongyee, or Booddhist monk, trading on the superstitious feelings of the people and on the desires and hopes of those who expected that the British Government, having driven out the Burmese, would retire on receiving an indemnity and leave the Arakanese to re-establish their ancient kingdom, pretended that he was a Meng-loung, or the embodiment of a future prince, and raised an insurrection which, for a short time, caused some uneasiness but which was eventually suppressed with far greater promptitude and ease than was at first expected.

KYIEN-TA-LEE.—A river in the Sandoway district which rises in the Arakan hills and, with a general north-west course, falls into the Bay of Bengal in about 17° 58' N. at Bluff Point.

KYIEN-TA-LEE-BYA.—A revenue circle in the Khwa township of the Sandoway district, lying in the mountainous country at the head waters of the Kyien-ta-lee river, having an estimated area of 220 square miles. Its population in 1872 was estimated at 94 souls and the area under cultivation in the same year at 34 acres. It is now joined to Kyien-ta-lee.

KYIEN-TA-LEE-RE-GYAW.—A revenue circle in the southern or Khwa township of the Sandoway district, which extends inland from the sea coast at Bluff Point towards the Arakan mountains. The estimated area is 196 square miles, very little cultivated especially towards the east. In 1876 the population was 1,014, the land revenue Rs. 639, the capitation tax Rs. 804 and the gross revenue Rs. 2,792.

KYOO-DAW-GAN.—A revenue circle in the Prome district west of Poung-day. It is traversed by the high road from Rangoon to the north. It contains no large villages. In 1876 the population was 290, the land revenue Rs. 265 and the capitation tax Rs. 280.

KYOON.— A small stream in the Bassein district which rises in some low laterite hills, south of the village of Le-tshoo, and, flowing in a southerly direction for ten or twelve miles, falls into the Pe-beng. Its mouth is about 100 feet broad. In the rains it is navigable by small boats almost up to its source.

KYOON-BOUK.—A revenue circle in the Shwe-loung township, Thoon-khwa district, having an area of 112 square miles, lying on the right bank of the Irrawaddy. The southern corner is formed into an island by the Hnget-pyaw channel. The country is generally low, flat and covered with grass, and much intersected by creeks on the banks of which are the villages. The inhabitants subsist chiefly by fishing and miscellaneous cultivation, and in 1876 numbered 4,797 souls ; in that year the land revenue was Rs. 5,320, the capitation tax Rs. 5,850 and the revenue derived from all other sources, of which the rent of the fisheries was by far the most prolific, Rs. 10,595.

KYOON-HPA.—A revenue circle in about the centre of the Henzada township of the Henzada district, the larger portion of which is under rice cultivation. On the west is the Ka-baing circle, on the north the Gyoung-kwee, on the east the Lay-dee-kan-hla and on the south the Nat-maw. In 1876 the population numbered 2,821, the land revenue was Rs. 8,780, the capitation tax Rs. 2,992 and the gross revenue Rs. 11,919.

KYOON-KA-NEE.—A revenue circle, occupying about 54 square miles in the northern portion of the Myoung-mya township, Bassein district, and enclosed east and west by the Pya-ma-law and the Kha-louk-thaik channels.

Sugarcane is cultivated on the banks of the Kha-louk-thaik. The inhabitants are Kareng and Burmans and in 1876 numbered 5,954 souls ; in that year the land revenue was Rs. 14,298, a larger amount than that derived from any other circle in the township and from any other circle in the district except Htan-le-beng and Paik-thoung in Thee-kweng, the capitation tax Rs. 6,295 and the gross revenue Rs. 21,410.

KYOON-KA-ZENG.—A revenue circle in the Kyoung-goon township, now joined to Tsam-bay-roon, in the Bassein district, about 120 square miles in extent. The ground is generally low and marshy and unfitted for rice cultivation. The inhabitants of the circle are largely employed in the fisheries. Kyon-ta-nee and the country to the east of it were the scene of the operations carried on in 1853 by the British under Sir J. Cheape and the Bassein Kareng levy under Major (now Lieutenant-General) Fytche against he rebel Myat-htoon. About two miles below Kyoon-ta-nee was Kyoon-ka-zeng, where Myat-htoon established his head-quarters which, on his defeat, was destroyed. In 1876 the population was 3,293, the land revenue Rs. 5,664, the capitation tax Rs. 3,735 and the gross revenue Rs. 18,516, of which the larger portion was derived from the rent of the fisheries.

KYOON-KHA-DAT.—A village in the Hnit-kaing circle of the Wa-kha-roo township of the Amherst district, on the eastern bank of the Wa-kha-roo river near the little Kyoon-kha-dat, one of its tributaries. In 1877 it had 620 inhabitants.

KYOON-KHA-RENG.—A village in the Bassein district, surrounded by rice fields, in the Thee-kweng township, on the Pe-beng river, about five miles above Re-dweng-koon, inhabited chiefly by Talaing and Kareng cultivators.

KYOON-MEE.—A village in the Mye-noo circle, Le-myet-hna township, Bassein district, on the western bank of the Re-nouk stream towards the north-eastern boundary of the district. Close to it is the village of Tsa-re-kweng. In 1877 it had 603 inhabitants.

KYOON-PA-DAW.—A revenue circle in the Shwe-loung township, Thoon-khwa district, about 78 square miles in extent, on the left bank of the Pya-ma-law. The country generally is flat, low and uncultivated though there is some rice cultivation. Shwe-loung, the head-quarter town of the township, is the largest in the circle ; its inhabitants trade much with Bassein and Rangoon and many are employed in fishing. The circle contains a very large number of Kareng villages, situated generally on the banks of the numerous anastomosing streams and channels, the inhabitants of which are mostly gardeners. In 1876 the number of inhabitants was 7,463, the land revenue was Rs. 8,101, the amount of the capitation tax was Rs. 7,038 and the gross revenue was Rs. 17,544.

KYOON-PA-DOOP.—A rich revenue circle in the Shwe-loung township, Thoon-khwa district, about 65 square miles in extent, on the right bank of the Irrawaddy just above the Lan-tha-maing channel. The country is flat, low and much intersected by creeks. The inhabitants, who are engaged in agriculture and fishing, numbered 9,669 in 1876 when the land revenue was Rs. 21,264, the amount of the capitation tax Rs. 9,730 and the gross revenue Rs. 31,983.

KYOON-PA-DOOP.—A tidal creek in the Shwe-loung township, Thoon-khwa district, fourteen miles in length from its mouth in the Tha-rwot-thwot to where it joins the Irrawaddy. It is navigable throughout by river steamers.

KYOON-PA-GOO.—A small stream which divides the Tsit-toung from the Shwe-gyeng sub-division of the Shwe-gyeng district. It rises in the hills east of the Tsit-toung and falls into that river just above Kha-rwai. It is not navigable by large boats.

KYOON-PA-GOO.—A revenue circle in the Tsit-toung township of the Shwe-gyeng district, about 120 square miles in extent, lying on the left bank of the Tsit-toung river with the Kyoon-pa-goo stream on the north, the Poung-loung range on the east and the Tsit-toung circle on the south. It now includes Eng-kwot. It is sparsely inhabited and contains but little cultivated ground. The principal villages are Kha-rwai, near the mouth of the Kyoon-pagoo, and Thien-zayat further south, on the bank of the Tsit-toung. In 1876 the inhabitants, who are mostly Kareng, numbered 3,774, the land revenue was Rs. 1,267, the capitation tax Rs. 1,428 and the gross revenue Rs. 2,758.

KYOON-PYAW.—The head-quarter town of the Tsam-bay-roon township in the Bassein district, on the right bank of the Daga river at the mouth of the Re-gyee, in 17° 17′ N. and 95° 16′ E., with a population in 1876 of 2,490 souls and in 1877 of 2,835. The inhabitants are principally traders and cultivators. Large quantities of the rice grown in the extensive fields in the neighbourhood are sent to Bassein. It contains a Court-house, a Police station and a market. The local revenue in 1876-77 was Rs. 2,655.

KYOON-TA-LEE.—A river which has its source in the Arakan mountains and falls into the Bassein river at Kyoon-ta-lee in 17° 18′ N. and 94° 57′ E. after a south-easterly course of about 18 miles. At its mouth it has a breadth of about ninety feet and a depth of nine, with a sandy and muddy bed. With the flood boats of forty baskets burden can ascend as far as Tsit-ta-ran. On its banks are found bamboos and valuable timber.

KYOON-TA-NEE.—*See Bhaw-dee river.*

KYOON-TA-NEE.—A rich revenue circle in the Donabyoo township of the Thoon-khwa district, adjoining and to the east of the Donabyoo Myoma circle, which now includes A-kyaw and Pyeng-ka-tha. It has gained very largely by the embankments along the Irrawaddy and the land revenue, which in 1867 was about Rs. 1,700, was Rs. 4,458 in 1876, when the population numbered 3,972 souls and the capitation tax was Rs. 3,840. In the same year the gross revenue was Rs. 18,324, very largely derived from the rents of the fisheries and the tax on nets.

KYOON-TOON.—One of the main branches of the Irrawaddy, which takes its origin at a place about ten miles below Gnyoung-doon where another branch, the To, also bifurcates. From this point it follows a S. S. W. course to the sea. During the rains there is a rapid current downwards but at other times it is tidal throughout its length, the rise and fall of the tide at the mouth is, at springs, about seven feet. It is navigable by river steamers or vessels of 300 tons burthen from its northern mouth for about sixty miles, as far as the mouth of the Pee-pa-lwot. For some distance below this, a good deal of its water having found an exit through the Pee-pa-lwot into the Irrawaddy or principal mouth, it is very shallow and fordable at low water, but southwards from the mouth of the Kyoon-ta, which reinforces it with water from the To, the channel is good and it has a depth of not less than four fathoms at low tides. The islands in this river are numerous ; the two principal ones are the Miem-ma-hla, sixteen miles long by three broad, near the mouth, and the smaller Kywon-gnyo-gyee, higher up. Down to the village of Kyaik-pee the banks are generally covered with elephant grass, and from this point southwards with tree-forest. From its commencement to the mouth of the Wa-ra-khaing it is known as the Eng-tai, lower down as the Ma-ran or Kyaik-pee, and towards the coast it is generally called by the inhabitants the Kyoon-toon. By non-residents and Europeans, generally, it is ordinarily called the Dala. During the dry weather boats are daily seen passing down this river conveying plantains, rice, sugar, betel-nut, &c., to the villages on the sea coast ; these return with nga-pee (fish paste), dhanee leaves and poles, the two last for the Rangoon market especially.

KYOON-TOON.—A small river in the Bassein district, about fourteen miles long, of which the last ten are navigable by boats forty feet in length, which falls into the Myoung-mya river at Kwe-lwe village.

KYOON-WON.—A village in the Kyaik-pa-ran circle of the Gyaing Attaran township, Amherst district, on the right bank of the Attaran. In 1877 it had 546 inhabitants.

KYOUK-BHOO.—A revenue circle in the Prome district, in the Padoung township, extending eastwards from the Arakan mountains to within a few miles of the Irrawaddy. The country consists of a succession of spurs and counter-spurs from the main range which are densely covered with tree-forest, among which are found Teak, Pyengado or iron wood, and Sha or cutch. Only in the more level country along the eastern border of the circle does regular rice cultivation occur, and here are situated most of the villages, of which Kyouk-bhoo, Hpo-rwa and Kan-goo are the largest. The Kyouk-bhoo rises in the west of the circle and flows through it eastwards towards the Irrawaddy. The military road from Padoung into Arakan, aross the Toung-goop pass of the Arakan mountains, enters this circle at Gnyoung-khye-douk on the Kyouk-bhoo river from whence westwards it winds amongst and over the hills. At Gnyoung-gyo, on this road, some fourteen miles west of Gnyoung-khye-douk, experiments at forming a sanatarium for the Thayetmyo garrison have been attempted ; one of the great difficulties to be overcome is the scarcity of water during the cold and dry seasons. In 1876 the population numbered 1,826 souls, the land revenue was Rs. 1,005, the capitation tax Rs. 2,185 and the gross revenue Rs. 3,420.

KYOUK-BHOO.—A small village in the revenue circle of the same name in the Padoung township, Prome district.

KYOUK-BHOO —A stream in the Prome district which rises in the Arakan mountains and flows in an easterly direction in a narrow valley between two long spurs for about twenty-five miles when it joins the Tha-nee close to its mouth. On this river, about seven miles in a direct line westwards from the Irrawaddy, is the village of Gnyoung-khye-douk, the first halting-place on the road across the Arakan mountains to Toung-goop in the Sandoway district of the Arakan division. Pemberton, in his report on the eastern frontier of British India published in 1835, states (p. 100) that Lieutenant B. Brown followed the bed of this stream for some distance from the Irrawaddy on his exploration of the Toung-goop pass. Since then a more practicable road has been made. As far as Gnyoung-khye-douk the banks are moderately steep and the bed sandy or gravelly, but from this village to its source the bed is rocky and the banks steep. The hills through which it flows are covered with valuable timber.

KYOUK-GYEE.—A revenue circle in the township of the same name in the Shwe-gyeng district, extending from the Kyouk-gyee river eastwards to the hills, with the Khyoung-bya circle on the north and the Thayet-peng-tat circle on the south, with an area of about 215 square miles and a popu-lation, principally Kareng, of 4,125 souls in 1876. The fishery and net tax produce a large revenue. In 1876 the land revenue was Rs. 2,295, the capitation tax Rs. 2,996 and the gross revenue, including the local funds raised in the large village of Kyouk-gyee, Rs. 9,701.

KYOUK-GYEE.—A village in the circle of the same name in the Shwe-gyeng district, the head-quarters of the Kyouk-gyee township, lying on both banks of the Kyouk-gyee river and on the Shwe-gyeng and Toung-ngoo road 82 miles from the former town, with 1,643 inhabitants in 1877. Although a moderately-sized and busy town, the inhabitants doing a thriving trade, prin-cipally in betel-nut, with the Kareng and others who live in the wilderness of mountains stretching away north and east, with well-built houses and two bridges across the Kyouk-gyee connecting the two quarters, the dense forest which surround it and the high and rocky hills which shut it in, give it a look of solitude and dreariness. Its name is said to be derived from a large and peculiarly shaped stone near it (*Kyouk* "a stone" and *gyee* "big.") In the Burmese time Kyouk-gyee was a fortified town and traces of the old stockade still remain ; in 1809 it was attacked and destroyed by the Zeng-mai Shans. About ten miles to the south is the Hmaw-daw, an unfinished pagoda, held in great reverence by the Burmese, where a festival is held annually in March, and in its neighbourhood is the site of the old city of Kyouk-hmaw ; the surrounding mound and fosse still remain but within is a tangled mass of jungle. The local revenue raised in Kyouk-gyee in 1876-77 was Rs. 1,573.

KYOUK-GYEE.—A river which rises in the north of the Shwe-gyeng district in the hills to the eastward and flows southwards nearly parallel to and near the Tsit-toung into which it falls about eight miles, measured in a direct line above Shwe-gyeng and nearly 20 measured along the tortuous course of the Tsit-toung. About thirty-six miles from its mouth is the town of Kyouk-gyee, lying on both its banks, the two portions connected by bridges ; thus far it is navigable by large boats.

KYOUK-GYEE.—A village in the Ka-myit circle of the Central or Sandoway township of the Sandoway district, lying on both banks of the Ka-myit stream, between eight and nine miles from its mouth and twenty-six miles from Sandoway. In 1877 it had 837 inhabitants. The Thoogyee of the circle resides in this village.

KYOUK-GYEE.—A township in the north of the Shwe-gyeng district, and having Toung-ngoo on the north, the Salween Hill Tracts on the east, the Shwe-gyeng township on the south and west and traversed from north to south by the Tsit-toung river. The eastern portion is highly mountainous and inhabited chiefly by Kareng and contains but little regular rice cultivation, the principal product being betel-nut grown on the hills and brought down to Kyouk-gyee for sale, and teak and other valuable timber. On the extreme west the surface of the country is hilly but between the hills and the river are broad and fertile rice plains. The principal rivers are the Kwon, the Rouk-thwa-wa and the Kyouk-gyee, the first and second flowing westwards respectively to the Tsit-toung and the last southwards, parallel to that river and a short distance east of it, till it turns westward and joins it near Waing village. Except Kyouk-gyee, the head-quarters, it has no village of any importance.

It is divided into seven revenue circles and in 1876 produced a gross revenue, local, Imperial and provincial of Rs. 59,948. In the same year the population numbered 29,519 souls.

KYOUK-HPYOO.—A tidal creek in the Bassein district, Myoung-mya township, which runs from the Peng-le-gale south and west to the Thekngay-thoung, which it joins just below the northern end of the Alay-kywon. It is navigable for some distance by river steamers and at flood tide large boats can pass through its whole length to the Peng-le-gale. A good deal of limestone is quarried from its banks and carried to La-bwot-ta and Ien-may. About six miles from its western mouth a small creek of the same name branches off eastward and joins the Rwe just above the village of Kyouk-maw.

KYOUK-HPYOO.—A revenue circle in the township and district of the same name, occupying the north-western corner of Ramree Island, with an area of 26 square miles and a population in 1876 of 1,620 souls : in that year the land revenue was Rs. 1,972, the amount of the capitation tax Rs. 1,670 and the gross revenue Rs. 3,753. The principal product is sugar.

KYOUK-HPYOO.—A township in the district of the same name, 383 square miles in extent, occupying the northern end of Ramree Island and a group of islands to the north-east nearer the mainland formed by the numerous tidal creeks which intersect the coast. In 1871 the Kwon-khyoung, Ngwe-dweng-too and Kook-ko circles were taken from it and added to others from Akyab and from the An township to form the Mye-boon township. The head-quarters are at Kyouk-hpyoo. The township is now divided into nineteen revenue circles and in 1874-75 produced a land revenue of Rs. 38,745 and Rs. 40,811 as capitation tax. In 1876-77 the corresponding figures were Rs. 39,216 and Rs. 42,976. In that year the population was 39,881 mainly Arakanese and the gross revenue Rs. 133,519. The principal products besides rice are indigo, salt and sugar, for the manufacture of which last 679 mills were at work in 1875-76.

KYOUK-HPYOO.—A town in Arakan, on the northern end of Ramree Island, in 19° 26′ 23″ N. and 94° 33′ 12″ E. the head-quarter station of the Kyouk-hpyoo district, to which it gives its name (*White stone*), said by some to

be derived from the white pebbly beach and by others from a rock with a white pagoda on it the entrance of the harbour : the former derivation appears the most probable and is supported by the best authorities. When Arakan was ceded to the British in 1825, after the first Anglo-Burmese war, a small fishing village occupied the site of the present town. In 1829 the garrison of Sandoway, consisting of one battalion of Native Infantry and a detail of artillery, which formed the greater portion of the troops then stationed in Arakan, was transferred to Kyouk-hpyoo. The chief Civil station was then at Ramree. The Government was strongly urged to transfer the head-quarters of the newly-acquired Province from Akyab to Kyouk-hpyoo but declined to sanction the change. In 1835 Captain Pemberton published a report on the eastern frontier of India and he thus describes Kyouk-phyoo :—
"The Cantonments are built perpendicular to and close upon the seashore,
"which has here a north-western aspect ; the site is a sandy plain bounded
"on the south-west by a low sandstone range and on the east by a small
"creek which separates it from the alluvial ground lying at the base of the
"Na-ga-toung and Oon-khyoung hills. On the east a creek called the Oung-
"choung (*Oon-khyoung*) extends a considerable distance behind the range
"already mentioned, which runs from north-west to south-east. The bunga-
"lows of the officers are only separated from the beach by a narrow strip of
"land a few feet above high water level, and the lines of the sepoys are
"between five and six hundred yards further inland with a southern aspect
"towards the parade ground, which is bounded on the south by a belt of man-
"grove jungle with a small branch of the Oung-choung creek flowing into it.
"The severity of the monsoon is broken by the range of hills bounding the
"Cantonment on the south-west, which varies from 500 to about 2,000 feet in
"height, and it is probably to its protective influence that the station owes
"its comparative salubrity, for in other respects its physical aspect differs but
"little from that observed in other spots of proved unhealthiness. Mangrove
"jungle lines the whole tract extending behind the Cantonment from the
"foot of the hills to the mouth of the Oung-choung creek, and as has already
"been observed, it is intersected in various directions by other inlets which
"are alternately flooded and left dry by the influence of the tide.
"East of the Cantonments and about half a mile distant are the lines
"of the lascars attached to the flotilla of gunboats, which are securely
"moored in a small basin sufficiently capacious to hold them all, and which
"can easily be converted into a very excellent dock. The Oung-choung creek,
"which is about ¾ of a mile further east, is equally well adapted for the
"same purpose on a larger scale, and is more convenient as being much
"nearer the springs from which the few vessels frequenting this port are
"accustomed to obtain their supply of water. It is along the shores of this
"creek, and in the numerous islands on the eastern side of the harbour,
"that the salt of the Province is principally manufactured, which Govern-
"ment formerly received at the rate of seven annas per maund ; the manu-
"facture, however, has never been extensively encouraged, as it has,
"I believe, been found that the inhabitants of the western side of the Bay of
"Bengal contrive to manufacture it at a rate far below that which the Mugs
"considered a fair equivalent for their labour."*

* Report on the Eastern Frontier by Captain R. Boileau Pemberton, 44th N.I., Calcutta, 1835, pp. 91, 92.

The description given above is still fairly accurate. The Court-house, circuit-house and officers' houses are along the sea beach, but the barracks no longer exist. The town now has besides these a gaol, hospital and charitable dispensary, a school-house and a market.

The harbour extends for many miles along the eastern shore of the island, but the approach is dangerous on account of the numerous sunken rocks; the channel is, however, well buoyed.

In 1833 portions of Akyab, Ramree and Sandoway had been united to form a new district, with the head-quarters at An, and in 1838 on account of the extreme unhealthiness of An the head-quarters were transferred to Kyouk-hpyoo. In 1841 the garrison was strengthened for about seven months by a battalion of Native Infantry and a detachment of European Artillery, but in 1850 the whole force was withdrawn and the town, which had sprung up and had by this time considerably increased in size and in importance, commenced to fall away. In 1852 its decadence received a slight check from a battalion of Native Infantry being quartered in the old cantonments, a step taken by the Government on account of the second Anglo-Burmese war, and from the amalgamation of Ramree and An into the Kyouk-hpyoo district and the consequent abolition of the head-quarters at Ramree. In 1855 the troops were withdrawn and from that time forward the town has continued to languish.

According to the official reports the number of inhabitants in each year since 1866 has been :—

1867	..	..	..	..	..	3,689
1868	..	..	..	..	..	2,720
1869	..	..	..	..	..	2,720
1870	..	..	..	..	..	2,692
1871	..	..	..	..	..	2,667
1872	..	..	..	..	..	2,573
1873	..	..	..	..	..	2,562
1874	..	..	..	..	..	2,637
1875	..	..	..	...	..	2,585
1876	:	..	..	..	..	2,620

The local revenue raised in the town from market stall rents and other sources is small. In 1877-78 it was Rs. 2,974.

KYOUK-HPYOO.—A district in the Arakan division 4,309 square miles in extent, comprising a strip of the mainland from the An pass, across the Arakan Roma mountains, to the Ma-ee river and the large islands of Ramree and Cheduba with numerous others which extend southward along the coast of Sandoway. On the north lies the Akyab district, south Sandoway, east and on the other side of the Arakan Roma Upper Burma and west and south the Bay of Bengal. The mainland in the north and east is highly mountainous and forest-clad and the lower portion divided into a number of islands by a labyrinth of tidal creeks which terminate at the foot of the lower ranges and receive the contributions of numerous small streams. Between the mainland and Ramree is a group of islands separated by deep, narrow, salt-water creeks forming the north-eastern shore of the harbour of Kyouk-phyoo—so named from the town on the northern end of Ramree—which extends for nearly thirty miles along the island in a south-casterly direction and has an average breadth of three miles.

South-west of Ramree Island is Cheduba, or Man-oung as it is called by the Burmese and Arakanese.

North-east and east of Ramree and in Kyouk-hpyoo harbour are numerous rocky islands, as Pagoda Rock, the Terribles, the Brothers, the Sisters, etc., rising abruptly from the sea and with no culturable area, whilst off the southern point of Ramree and the southern point of Cheduba are Amherst or Tsa-goo Island and Re-kywon with several smaller islets.

The principal mountains are the Arakan Roma which separate the district from the territories of the King of Burma and send out numerous spurs and subspurs almost to the sea coast.

Mountains.

Within the limits of this district the range is crossed by two main passes which take their names from the two rivers, the Dha-let and the An. The Dha-let pass, in the extreme north, was partially explored during the first Burmese war by a detachment under Major Burke and was proved to be almost impassable by troops, owing as much to the scarcity of water as to the precipitous nature of the ascents and descents, and it is but little used even by the inhabitants of the country. The An pass, farther south, was traversed by a detachment of Sir Archibald Campbell's army on its return from Yandaboo ; it proceeded from Tsheng-hpyoo-kywon on the bank of the Irrawaddy to the village of An, about 45 miles from the mouth of the river, which can be reached by large boats at spring tides in eleven days. In 1830 Lieutenant Pemberton made the march in nine days, starting from Myeng-boo, a village thirty-eight miles below Tsheng-hpyoo-kywon. Going eastward the road from An for some distance traverses a level country, crossing the An in several places, after which, gradually passing into the hills, it strikes the crest of the mountains at a spot 4,664 feet above the sea and 4,517 feet above the first rising ground, from which it is about eighteen miles distant ; on the east the descent is much sharper falling 3,777 feet in eight miles. From this point the road follows the bed of a river in a narrow and rocky ravine for twenty miles, gradually emerging into level and open ground. From the crest eastwards the country belongs to the kingdom of Upper Burma. On Ramree Island there is one main range of mountains with a general N. N. W. and S. S. E. direction, and with an elevation above the plain varying from 500 to 1,500 feet for the principal extent and not exceeding 3,000 feet at the highest point, with lower spurs branching off from it. The general character of Cheduba is that of a well-wooded, fertile island of moderate height and irregular outline, fifteen-and-a-half miles in length ; a band of level plain, but little raised above the sea, extends round the coast, wider on the east than on the west, whilst within this tract are irregular, low, undulating grounds varying from 50 to 500 feet in height, enclosing several higher and detached hills, the loftiest of which, on the south of the island, is about 1,400 feet high.

There are no rivers of any great importance but numerous small streams drain the larger islands and the Dha-let and the An, on the mainland, are both navigable by large boats as far as the two villages of the same names, the first some twenty-five and the other forty-five miles from the mouth of the stream on which each is situated ; above these they are mere mountain torrents navigable only by the smallest canoes and by rafts.

Rivers.

The most important and valuable timber found growing in this district
is Pyeng-gado (*Xylia dolabriformis*). From the An
Forests. southwards throughout the mainland Pyeng-gado forms
compact masses of forest all along the lower hills and adjoining plains;
north of the An to the Dha-let it occurs in patches and north of the Dha-let
appears to cease altogether. On Ramree Island nearly all the hills produce
Pyeng-gado, but as a general rule of an inferior description; on the south,
however, that which remains—for the finest trees have been cut down—is
good. The area drained by the An is, with the exception of level ground near
the stream, covered with bamboo forests, each some few acres only in extent,
containing Pyeng-gado. The western slopes of the spur which extends
between the An and the Dha-let are covered partly with green and partly
with dry forest, the former occupying the greater portion of the area.
The dry forest is found near the upper part of several small creeks which
run towards the sea and here Pyeng-gado is found, partly good and partly
inferior. The actual area of the Pyeng-gado forest has never been accurately ascertained.

In addition to Pyeng-gado the district produces many other valuable trees.
Ka-gnyeng (*Dipterocarpus alatus*) found all over the district, furnishes
the wood-oil so much used for torches, and here the timber is employed
for the tops of boats, and when used as planking in houses in unexposed
situations, lasts for some twenty years. In Ramree Thit-ya (*Shorea obtusa*)
and elsewhere Bhan-bwai (*Careya arborea*), Pyeng-ma (*Lagerstræmia reginæ*),
Htien (*Nauclea parvifolia*) and Shaw (*Beilschmiedia sp.*) are used for house-
posts, the last being much sought after. Boats are made from the Kook-ko
(*Albizzia lebbek*), flooring planks from several kinds of Tha-bye (*Eugenia*),
canoes from Pyeng-ma (*Lagerstræmia reginæ*); the wood of the Kyek-yo (*Vitex
pubescens*) is used for the teeth of harrows and the powdered bark of Bhwai-
zeng (*Bauhinia malabarica*), mixed with oil, for caulking boats. The estimated area of the forest tracts unsuited for cultivation is about 652 square
miles and of the 1,639 square miles of mountainous country not more
than 320 are fit even for toungya; from these, if a demand arose, much
valuable timber could be supplied which can never be used up by local
consumption, whilst it could easily be worked out and shipped to India at
but little expense. The trees which most deserve attention are Ka-gnyeng
(*Dipterocarpus alatus*), found all over the district, three species of Kook-
ko *viz.*, (*Albizzia, procera, lebbek* and *stipulata*), which are plentiful, Kyan
(*Terminalia alata*) and Bhan-bhwai (*Careya arborea*).

Of the geology of this district little is accurately known. Earlier
observers, as Lieutenant Foley and Commander Halsted,
Geology and min-
eral products. considered the numerous islands to be of volcanic origin,
but Mr. Theobald of the Geological Survey of India con-
siders this view as untenable. Numerous small hillocks exist within four miles
of the town of Kyouk-hpyoo situated on rising ground 200 or 300 feet above the
sea level, conical-shaped and formed of mud of a blackish grey colour. On
the top of each is a small opening filled with water through which there is a
frequent discharge of marsh gas and an occasional issue of flames rising to a
great height and illuminating the surrounding country for many miles. Commander Halsted of H. M. S. *Childers* visited every one of the mud "volcanoes"
of Cheduba a few years after the English had obtained possession of Arakan

and " on none with the strictest search could be found any traces of direct
" fire, or of those peculiar formations produced by that agent. Gas alone
" seems to be the one immediately occasioning those strange exceptions
" to the general character of volcanoes. It is no doubt inflammable gas,
" and the light given by some of them in activity has been so great as
" to enable a book to be read by it at a distance of nine miles....The large
" volcanoes of Cheduba are four in number; they are detached mounds
" rather than cones varying from 100 to 1,000 feet above the level of the sea.
" In all these the water or mud is salt.......The minor volcanic rents seldom
" exhibit any change; the larger ones when in eruption, which generally takes
" place during the rains, either throw forth to a considerable height accom-
" panied with flame, fluid mud which spreads over a certain extent, or the
" surface affected boils with the escapement of gas, being too consistent to be
" thrown up." The largest "volcano" is in about the centre of this island and is
called Toung-nee or Mye-nee-toung, 'red earth hill' (Pagoda hill of the charts);
some years ago there was an irruption, or more properly a conflagration,
of marsh gas here which illuminated the town of Ramree some twenty-five
miles distant, and still later as twelve men, kneeling close to the crater, were
worshipping the dragon supposed to reside in the volcano an irruption occurred
three only escaping and the remainder perishing from their clothes taking
fire.

" There are two other volcanoes of small dimensions, and but little
" elevated above the plains where they are found to exist; they are composed
" of the same soil of mud emitting large bubbles of gas; and besides
" these there are two spots whence water alone is brought up by the gas."
" They are composed of a stiff grey clay with large quantities of
" singular fragments of stone, their sides much cut up by the effects of
" rain, their summits quite bare and from 240 to 250 yards in diameter;
" on these are deposed stiff cones of clay, from a few inches to four feet
" in height, and the same variety of dimensions in diameter. These are
" hard on the outside, but filled half way up with thick well-mixed mud,
" which every now and then exudes from a hole at the sides or summit at
" the bursting of a bubble of gas which occurs every three or four minutes.

Earth-oil wells exist in several places and for some years were farmed
out by the State and a tax on their working is still levied in the Tseen-
khyoon circle near the northern end of Ramree Island, on the east coast
in Than-khyoung and, farther south, in Le-doung; and on Cheduba in
Kyet-ro in the north, Man-oung in the centre and Toung-rwa in the
south. Of these the Le-doung wells are the most important and have been
fully described by Major Plant at one time Deputy Commissioner of the
district. " They are situated at and round the bases of some low hills and
" are of various depths. The deepest well is 32 cubits deep with a mouth
" four feet square and a bottom about one cubit square. The sides of the
" well are boarded up and strongly secured by diagonal cross-beams ingeni-
" ously and firmly fixed into retaining posts at the corners of the wooden
" lining; these cross-beams are in the shape of a cutter's main-boom, the
" after end being let into one post and the jaw end embracing the opposite
" post, and this being hammered down fixes the casing. This system of
" diagonal bars is carried down from top to bottom, with intervals of about
" two feet, and consequently acts as a ladder for going up and down the

" well. At the bottom, where the oil collects, is a receptacle about 4 inches
" deep containing water, on the top of which the oil floats......The drawing
" takes place twice a day, morning and evening : a small boy, descending
" to the bottom, scoops up the oil into an earthen jar to which is attached
" a line ; about half way down another lad sits on the cross bars and
" guides this jar up, and from him in turn a man at the mouth guides the
" jar in its perilous ascent......The young boy from the bottom seemed
" a good deal affected : his face was flushed, his body hot and his eyes
" much inflamed and bleary ; the duration of his visit to the bottom was
" about half an hour, he was 12 years of age and had been going down
" the well twice daily for a long time......New wells are constantly being
" dug and yield a remunerative outturn. The oil when brought up
" appeared like a blue whitish water, when poured into a receiver it gave
" out beautiful brilliant straw-coloured rays and the smell was strong
" and pungent. The oil is sold at five bottles per rupee." It is used for
lighting and in small doses medicinally as an emetic. In Cheduba the oil
is much nearer the surface ; there, at the site of the wells—if wells they
can be called—the earth is turned up to a depth of two feet and a bank of
soil raised round a square of about twenty yards, which during the rains
thus forms a shallow pond, the surface of which is in a constant state
of ebullition from the escape of gas. The petroleum collects on the
surface in three different forms. " A green fluid oil first spreads itself
" over the spot where the gas is bubbling up ; as it extends, its edges
" exhibit a brown curdling substance resembling half congealed dripping,
" and amongst this, as it becomes thicker, is seen gathering in spots a
" dark brown substance of the colour and consistency of molasses." This
latter is used to preserve wood and to saturate paper for umbrellas and is
sometimes burnt but the green fluid is that mostly used to supply lamps.
The curdled substance is used with the dark for the coarser purposes to
which it is applied. In the months of March and April the pond gradually
dries up, when the soil is redug and disturbed as much as possible in
preparation for the ensuing season's work.

Limestone is found in several places on Ramree island and is quarried
for local use, according to the limited demand, in the Kyouk-hpyoo and
Kyouk-pyouk circles on the north-west, Rwa-thit on the north and Nga-
khoop-pyeng on the south-east. The limestone is quarried with iron
crowbars and carried to the bank of the nearest stream to be burned.
A hole in the shape of an inverted cone is dug in the ground on the edge of
the bank and filled with raw limestone and a horizontal opening formed
from the side of the bank for the introduction of the fuel. The fire is kept
burning for thirty-six hours and twelve hours are allowed for cooling. The
lime is then differently treated as it is intended for building purposes or for
chewing with betel ; for the former it is placed in a heap and slaked with
fresh or with salt water but for the latter it is put into small earthen pots,
which are about one-third filled with limestone, and fresh water is added and
the whole left to stand for some days, when the water is poured off and
the lime carefully collected.

Iron exists on Ramree and other islands and was formerly smelted
but its place in the market has been taken by foreign importations. Coal
has been found in three places on Ramree and in one on Cheduba, but is

not worked. Specimens from Kan-daing, twelve miles distant from Ramree by road and five and a quarter by sea and one mile from the Keng river, were sent to the coal and mineral committee which sat in Calcutta in 1841 and were pronounced to be of excellent quality for steam purposes, whilst some sent from Hoon, further south, was declared to be almost equally good. The Hoon field lies within one mile of the river of that name, about eight and a half miles south of Ramree in a direct line, but eighteen miles by the road. The third field is at Tan within two miles of Ramree but is, probably, not worth working. The coal from a spot near the western coast of Cheduba in the Toung-rwa circle was pronounced by Mr. Piddington to be "bituminous though not highly so. Its appearance "and the features of some of the specimens are also in its favour." No attempt has been made to examine these coal-fields carefully and scientifically. A considerable quantity of salt is made in the district, which is more fully alluded to under the head of manufactures.

Out of the 4,309 square miles of the district, no less than 3,740

Agriculture. including the area of the streams and creeks, are returned as absolutely unculturable, and in 1876-77 only 165 were actually under cultivation.

The acreage of the various crops grown during each of the last ten years was :—

Years.*	Rice.	Sugar-cane.	Cotton.	Indigo and other dyes.	Hemp and other fibres.	Tobacco.	Dhanee.	Pán vine.	Vegetables.	Orchards.	Total.
1867-68 ..	75,843	1,682	1	64	46	1,149	2,064	132	2,024	1,214	84,219
1868-69 ..	81,060	1,774	4	88	50	1,195	2,167	133	709	2,757	89,937
1869-70 ..	81,570	1,890	2	66	50	1,128	2,184	138	707	2,775	90,516
1870-71 ..	82,410	2,022	1	66	51	1,258	2,192	136	355	2,859	91,370
1871-72 ..	86,822	1,644	1	65	50	1,289	2,264	179	733	3,046	96,093
1872-73 ..	87,685	1,288	8	2	51	1,359	2,291	202	757	3,094	96,730
1873-74 ..	81,348	1,294	2	74	51	1,365	2,298	217	753	3,714	91,11
1874-75 ..	83,627	1,556	2	87	51	1,454	2,362	209	749	3,171	93,278
1875-76 ..	84,089	1,681	2	73	51	1,504	2,451	198	787	3,231	94,067
1876-77 ..	91,155	1,537	1	71	52	1,514	2,477	186	526	3,236	1,00,759

* The official returns in the Administration Reports do not distinguish land actuall' under rice from land left fallow. The figures on page 304 do not include fallow land.

The area of rice land, which is not very productive the average quantity of grain produced per acre being only 900lbs., extends but slowly, and as long ago as 1850-51 the Commissioner reported that "the better lands appear "to have been already occupied." The acreage of rice land paying revenue and the total crop, calculated at 900lbs. the acre, was :—

				Acres.				Tons.
In	1849-50	..	..	53,848	..	..	..	21,189
,,	1859-60	..	..	65,107	..	..	..	26,159
,,	1869-70	..	..	70,445	..	..	..	28,304
,,	1870-71	..	..	71,076	..	..	..	28,557
,,	1871-72	..	..	80,324	..	..	..	32,273
,,	1872-73	..	..	81,142	..	..	..	32,601
,,	1873-74	..	..	81,348	..	..	..	32,684
,,	1874-75	..	..	83,627	..	..	..	33,573
,,	1875-76	..	..	84,089	..	..	..	33,785
,,	1876-77	..	..	84,942	..	..	..	34,126

the sudden increase in 1871-72 was partly caused by the addition to the district of four circles from Akyab in which there were 8,546 acres of cultivated rice land. The whole of this is not consumed in the district, but there are no means of ascertaining how much of the crop finds its way by the creeks to the Akyab market, to be partially cleaned before being exported from the the country, and south to Sandoway for consumption there; but the exports direct from Kyouk-hpyoo have, though never very large, varied considerably; in 1859-60 there were no shipments, but in 1864-65, 613 tons were sent to the Straits and 863 tons of cleaned and uncleaned rice to Indian ports, and in the following year 1,467 tons: in 1866-67 again there were no direct exports. In 1872-73 the Straits took 135 and India 223 tons, whilst in 1873-74 1,234 tons were shipped and in 1876-77, only 18 cwts.

The tobacco is grown chiefly for home consumption and that produced in Cheduba is considered the best.

Though the area on which indigo is cultivated was, in 1876, only 73 acres, it is far larger than anywhere else in the Province except in Henzada. The ground is ploughed in December or January and the seed hand planted after having been soaked in water for a night and kept damp a day or two longer till it has germinated. In March or April when the plant in good soil is from three to four feet high, in poorer from two to three feet, the leaves are gathered for the purpose of extracting the dye, and a month later, by which time the plant has grown about a foot more, the seeds are collected for next year's sowing. There are two pluckings for each sowing and an acre of land sown with about 32lbs. of seed will produce some 15 cwts. of dye. The expenses of cultivating an acre, including the State demand as land revenue, may be taken at about Rs. 89, and the selling price of the dye in the local markets, which has not much varied of late years, at one and a half annas a pound, or Rs. 10-8 per cwt.: thus the profits on each acre are from Rs. 110 to 120 annually.

The soil is not considered favourable for the cultivation of cotton, and such as is grown is for home consumption : it is almost exclusively sown together with rice in toungya or hill gardens, the rice is sown first and the cotton between the rice seeds : the rice reaches maturity first and is reaped, the cotton crop being collected afterwards. Sessamum also is cultivated in toungya.

The market price (per maund of 80lbs) of the most important products during the last ten years has been :—

Year.	Rice.			Cotton.			Sugar.			Tobacco.			Indigo.			Oil-seeds.			Salt.		
	Rs.	A.	P.	Rs.	A.	P.	Rs.	A.	P.	Rs.	A.	P.	Rs.	A.	P.	Rs.	A.	P.	Rs.	A.	P.
1867-68	2	4	0	6	0	0	Not given.			26	0	0	7	8	0	8	12	0	0	12	0
1868-69	2	8	0	6	0	0	3	8	0	25	0	0	7	0	0	4	0	0	0	8	0
1869-70	2	8	0	6	0	0	Not given.			25	0	0	7	8	0	4	0	0	0	6	0
1870-71	2	8	0	6	0	0	2	4	0	25	0	0	7	8	0	4	0	0	0	10	0
1871-72	1	5	0	6	0	0	3	0	0	25	0	0	7	8	0	Not given.			0	9	0
1872-73	1	4	0	6	0	0	3	0	0	Not given.			7	8	0	3	0	0	0	8	0
1873-74	1	8	0	6	0	0	6	0	0	20	0	0	7	8	0	3	0	0	0	8	0
1874-75	1	8	0	6	0	0	6	0	0	Not given.			7	8	0	3	0	0	0	8	0
1875-76	1	8	0	6	0	0	6	0	0	20	0	0	7	8	0	3	0	0	0	8	0
1876-77	2	0	0	6	0	0	6	0	0	Not given.			7	8	0	3	0	0	0	6	0

Cotton and indigo have remained very steady, as might be expected from the fact that they are produced for local consumption only, and the changes in the price of the other articles has varied but little.

Whilst the area under cultivation is extending slowly and prices are remaining almost stationary the rates of wages are the same as ten years ago :—

	Daily rates.						Price of stock.					
	1867-68.			1876-77.			1867-68.			1876-77.		
	Rs.	A.	P.	Rs.	A.	P.	Rs.	As.	P.	Rs.	As.	P.
Labourers												
Skilled	1	0	0	1	0	0	....			....		
Unskilled	0	8	0	0	8	0	....			....		
Carts (per day) ..	1	0	0	1	0	0	....			....		
Boats (do.) ..	1	0	0	1	0	0	....			....		
Plough bullocks, each	....			....			60	0	0	35	0	0
Goats ,,	....			....			Not given.			12	0	0

The market value of agricultural stock appears to have fallen very considerably. To some extent this may be due to the inaccuracy of the returns, for in a country like Burma the acquisition of accurate statistics cannot be hoped for and all that can be done is to form an approximate estimate. It may also partly be due to a natural increase in the number of beasts without an equivalent increase in the area brought under cultivation, for, as already stated, the best lands were taken up years ago, whilst the nature of the country is much against large exports of cattle.

According to the returns appended to the Annual Administration Reports the stock in each of the last ten years was :—

Year.	Buffaloes.	Cows, bulls and bullocks.	Sheep and goats.	Pigs.	Carts.	Ploughs.	Boats.	Oil and sugar mills.
1867-68	27,808	39,792	944	4,833	555	12,680	4,667	Not given.
1868-69	27,629	41,569	917	4,273	539	13,484	4,648	Do.
1869-70	28,709	44,879	981	4,386	535	13,549	4,785	1,205
1870-71	28,373	46,831	721	3,894	452	13,948	4,449	1,328
1871-72	31,496	47,965	958	3,307	446	15,327	5,155	1,273
1872-73	31,140	48,422	939	4,096	492	15,561	5,252	1,052
1873-74	30,410	49,938	867	3,935	544	14,832	5,282	790
1874-75	28,583	51,024	975	4,290	523	15,716	4,954	921
1875-76	29,076	52,817	620	4,920	498	16,000	5,244	1,012
1876-77	29,127	53,062	980	5,228	480	16,010	5,387	1,058

The land is held chiefly by small proprietors who own from one to five acres, seldom more, and who do not often let their land but work it themselves, rarely employing hired labourers ; when they do they pay about Rs. 6-8 a month if the labourer lives with them, as is sometimes the case, or about Rs. 8 if he does not. The census of 1872 shewed that the agricultural adult male population of this district was 26,082 or 19·49 per cent. of the whole, on whom an average of 5·52 persons were dependant and whose holdings averaged 3·85 acres in extent. When land is let the rent, which is fixed beforehand and generally by parol agreement, is paid in kind, and in the case of rice land is very low, being about ten bushels a season. Tenants very rarely employ hired labour ; their mode and standard of living is very similar to that of their landlords but in solvency, in independance, and general circumstances and character they are, perhaps, slightly below the small proprietors. The size of the holdings shews little or no tendency to increase, and it is exceedingly rare for an owner to emigrate into a town and settle there, leasing his land and living on his rents ; indeed, considering the smallness of the properties and the lowness of rent, it would be impossible for any landowner without other means to live on the rent of his estate.

Manufactures.

The principal articles manufactured in the district, besides the silk and cotton cloths woven in almost every house, are indigo, salt, pots, coarse sugar and sessamum oil.

Salt is made in many places, in the dry season, on the banks of the numerous tidal creeks. The annual produce varies considerably, depending upon the local demand for fish-curing and upon the imports from foreign countries into Akyab and Bassein. The quantity manufactured during each of the seven years ending with 1873-74* was :—

1867-68	..	..	Cwts. 84,214	1871-72	..	..	Cwts. 11,681
1868-69	..	..	„ 102,750	1872-73	..	..	„ 8,057
1869-70	..	..	„ 79,226	1873-74	..	..	„ 13,911
1870-71	..	..	„ 80,679				

* No later information is available.

The method employed for the manufacture of the article is simple and inexpensive. The sea water is raised from the creek by means of a trough working on a pivot near its centre, and poured into a shallow tank about six inches deep and left exposed to the sun for about two days and then run into a second and a day or two later into a third; after remaining there for a day or two boiled rice is thrown into it and if the rice floats the brine is passed into a fourth tank, three or four feet deep, from which it is transferred to pots and the water evaporated by boiling.

The earthen pots are made principally in the Ramree Myoma, Kaing-Khyoung and Than-htoung circles, and are sold on the spot to the saltboilers. In the manufacture, which is carried on near the spot where the earth is found, both men and women are employed; the men dig and carry the earth and the women make the pots; generally a man and his wife work together in this way. The earth, which must be perfectly free from salt, is beaten into dust, sifted, and mixed with sand and fresh water, the proportions depending on the purpose for which the pots are to be used: if for salt boiling two-thirds sand and one-third clay; if for holding water and other domestic purposes equal parts. The pots are shaped with the hand and a small wooden mallet, exposed to the sun for one day and kept in the shade for some days longer until a sufficient number to fill a kiln is ready. The day before the pots are put into the kiln they are washed inside and out with a mixture of red clay (brought from a distance) and water, and the burning lasts one night only. The kiln is made by laying on the ground billets of wood over which is spread a layer of cow-dung, the pots are built upon this and covered with straw. The number of pots in each kiln varies from 800 to 1,000 and it takes a man and a woman one month to make and burn this number. Salt pots are sold at about Rs. 6 the hundred and others at half that rate.

Sessamum oil is made during the hot season and principally on the mainland where the sessamum is grown. The oil is expressed by a simple process in which a large pestle is turned round and round in a mortar by a bullock. The small end of a large log is buried some eight feet in the ground leaving the large end, about two feet in diameter, four feet above the surface; this is hollowed out to a depth of two feet: into the cavity thus formed the larger end of a wooden " pestle", six feet long, is inserted, and to the top of this is attached a bar worked by the bullock which is driven round and round the " mortar" in which this " pestle" works, grinding the sessamum seeds thrown in and kept damp by the addition of hot water. In some cases the oil runs off by a hole in the side of the mortar but more often is collected by the exceedingly primitive method of dipping cloths into the mass and when saturated ringing them out. One mill will turn out about 110 lbs. of oil a day. The oil not required for home consumption finds its way principally to Akyab.

Sugar-cane is grown to a considerable extent on Ramree island and a coarse kind of sugar is extracted in numerous places, during the dry season, but chiefly in the Than-htoung circle The sugar-cane is crushed in a press worked by a bullock or a buffalo and the juice boiled down.

Indigo, as already stated, is more extensively grown here than in any other part of the Province. The dye is extracted during the dry season and solely for home consumption. The leaves and slender twigs are placed in a large vessel, generally a small boat, which is filled with water and are allowed to soak for some twenty-four hours, and slaked lime being then added are stirred with a wooden pole worked by hand. The leaves and twigs are then taken out and thrown away and the water left for a day to settle ; when the sediment has fallen to the bottom the water is drained off and the blue liquid deposit is placed in pots and allowed to stand for three or four days until it has solidified and is fit for sale.

By the census taken in 1872 the population of the district was found

Population. to number 144,177 souls; in 1873-74 it had risen to 145,665 and in 1876-77 to 149,035. When Arakan became a portion of the British dominions Kyouk-hpyoo was found more populated than the mainland, and the large tracts of culturable waste in Akyab attracted many of the inhabitants of this district from which for many years there was a steady tide of emigration northwards. Notwithstanding this the immigration was so large that the number of inhabitants increased from year to year. In 1832 the population numbered 66,172 souls ; ten years later 80,072 ; in 1852 107,785 ; in 1862 122,273, and in 1872 as already stated, 144,177, giving an average of 33·46 per square mile.

The population was composed of :—

Arakanese	..	..	..	119,187
Burmese	..	..	..	10,469
Khyeng	..	..	..	10,322
Mahomedans	..	..	..	3,917
Hindoos	..	..	..	185
Other races	..	..	..	97
		Total	..	144,177

The Arakanese inhabit mainly Cheduba, Ramree and the coast of the main land, the Burmese the valley of the An, and the Khyeng the hill country. The Mahomedans are largely of mixed blood, descendants of the captives made by the kings of Arakan in their incursions into Bengal and of the remnants of the followers of Sha Shuja, the brother of Aurungzeb, who inter-married with Burmese and Arakanese women insisting on their, at least nominal, conversion to the tenets of Islam, to which they had no objection.

The total male and female population according to ages was :—

	Males.	Females.	Total.
Not exceeding one year	3,083	2,781	5,864
Above 1 not exceeding 6 years	10,305	9,995	20,300
,, 6 ,, 12 ,,	11,780	11,479	23,259
,, 12 ,, 20 ,,	12,304	12,575	24,879
,, 20 ,, 30 ,,	12,307	11,865	24,272
,, 30 ,, 40 ,,	9,373	9,229	18,602
,, 40 ,, 50 ,,	7,313	6,647	13,960
,, 50 ,, 60 ,,	3,742	3,393	7,135
Above 60	2,849	3,157	6,006
Total ..	73,056	71,121	144,177

Thus at every period up to 60 except between 12 and 20 the males exceeded the females in number, but above 60 the females exceeded the males, which is exactly the reverse of what occurs in Europe where the females are in excess of the males but are shorter-lived.

The number of each sex classed according to religion was :—

					Males.	Females.	Total.
Booddhists	..	..	..	..	..	65,577	64,125	129,702
Mahomedans	..	..	..	..	..	2,023	1,897	3,920
Hindoos	..	..	..	..	..	156	29	185
Christians	..	..	..	..	..	29	18	47
Others (Khyeng &c.) ..	..	..	..	..	5,271	5,052	10,323

In 1876-77 the total population was :—

Males.			Females.			Grand total.	Number per square mile.
Over twelve.	Under twelve.	Total.	Over twelve.	Under twelve.	Total.		
52,770	22,276	75,046	52,326	21,663	73,989	149,035	34

The district does not contain a single town of 5,000 inhabitants. The largest is Ramree, the head-quarters of the township of the same name, on the eastern coast of the island, some thirteen miles up the Tan, a tidal creek. It contains a Court-house, a market and a Police-station, and in 1877 had a population of 4,028 souls. Kyouk-hpyoo on the northern extremity of the island, the head-quarters of the district, a fishing village in the Burmese time, rose in importance after the British conquest but sank on the withdrawal of the troops, and now contains a population of 2,620 souls. It possesses Court-houses, a gaol, market, Police-station, hospital and charitable dispensary, a State school and a circuit-house. It has an excellent harbour, running for miles up the eastern side of the island, approach to which is dangerous on account of the numerous rocks, but the entrance is well buoyed. Cheduba or Man-oung is on the island of the same name near its north-eastern extremity on the bank of a small stream and is the head-quarters of the township with a Court-house and Police-station. Unlike Ramree and Kyouk-hpyoo the number of its inhabitants, who trade with Sandoway, Bassein and Chittagong, is slowly increasing. In 1870 they numbered 1,198 souls ; in 1871 1,234 ; in 1872 1,283 ; in 1873 1,323 ; and in 1877 1,409. An is a village on the river of the same name forty-five miles from its mouth and accessible by large boats during spring tides. In 1870 it contained a population of 1,593 which in 1877 had increased to 1,634. The inhabitants are largely engaged in trade with Upper Burma on the one hand and with the seacoast on the other. The village is the head-quarter station of a township and contains a Court-house, Police-station and a market. Mye-boon was transferred to this district from Akyab in 1870-71 and is the head-quarters of a township with a Court-house, a Police-

Towns and villages.

station and a market. It is situated on an island in the north on the coast of Hunter's Bay. In 1870 it had a population of 1,231 souls which in 1872 had fallen to 1,189 but by 1877 had increased again to 1,230. Besides these the district contained in 1872, when the census was taken, 723 villages with less than 200 inhabitants, 209 with from 200 to 500, 18 with from 500 to 1,000 and one with from 1,000 to 2,000, making a total of 956 towns and villages. In 1877 the number had increased to 983.

Revenue. The Imperial and provincial revenue since the formation of the province has been :—

Year.		Land.	Capitation.	Customs, including fines, &c.	Excise.	Fisheries.	All other items.	Total.
		Rs.	Rs.	Rs.	Rs.	Rs.	Rs.	Rs.
1855-56	..	105,070	78,258	..	8,388	..	4,505	196,221
1856-57	..	112,149	80,748	..	9,463	..	8,331	210,621
1857-58	..	111,641	84,912	..	14,952	..	5,469	216,974
1858-59	..	114,074	83,025	..	20,865	..	10,176	228,140
1859-60	..	119,671	87,221	..	15,014	..	17,485	239,391
1860-61	..	125,884	90,161	..	15,734	..	43,396	275,175
1861-62	..	127,754	91,076	..	19,617	..	50,980	289,427
1862-63	..	128,600	125,306	..	20,573	..	38,544	313,023
1863-64	..	131,521	127,905	..	3,370	..	24,192	286,988
1864-65	..	131,544	132,246	..	22,039	2,016	37,351	325,196
1865-66	..	127,135	132,246	1,730	24,233	2,669	18,117	306,130
1866-67	..	124,960	128,408	209	2,785	2,702	38,759	286,409
1867-68	..	117,668	124,892	..	2,650	2,440	37,100	284,750
1868-69	..	117,670	126,700	450	26,190	3,050	42,680	316,740
1869-70	..	118,350	128,380	..	28,290	3,330	38,420	316,770
1870-71*	..	137,160	140,570	2,430	29,390	4,660	24,690	338,900
1871-72	..	136,790	142,710	..	31,800	4,340	24,020	339,660
1872-73	..	137,670	144,030	..	31,090	5,170	25,130	343,090
1873-74	..	137,310	146,470	2,653	40,670	5,340	28,647	361,090
1874-75	..	141,449	151,021	722	66,286	5,396	35,523	400,407
1875-76	..	142,130	152,790	1,169	79,047	6,235	35,096	416,267
1876-77	..	142,501	153,629	..	93,158	5,375	39,081	433,744

The revenue derived from the salt tax, imposed upon the pots used at the rate of eight annas each, is very fluctuating. The demand for salt depends to some extent upon the fishing season, a considerable quantity of that produced in the district being used for fish-curing, and upon the importation of foreign salt into Akyab and Kyouk-hpyoo whence it spreads over the country exercising a powerful influence upon the local manufacture and consequently upon the revenue derived therefrom. This tax is a decreasing source of revenue, as the home-made product cannot compete in the market, either in quality or in price, with the imported article.

* The large increase is due to the addition of four circles from Akyab: the land revenue, excluding that levied in this tract, was Rs. 120,510 and the capitation tax Rs. 130,710.

The sudden rise in the amount realized from excise duty in 1868-69 was mainly due to the establishment of two opium farms and one spirit farm* to meet legitimately what was found to be a real demand which hither-to had been illicitly supplied by smuggling.

The gross revenue and the total cost of officers of all kinds during the decennial period ending with 1876-77 were :—

YEAR.					Revenue.	Expenditure.
					Rs.	Rs.
1867-68	..	..	..	..	2,84,750	1,38,440
1868-69	..	..	..	..	3,16,740	1,38,600
1869-70	..	..	..	..	3,16,770	86,310
1870-71	..	..	..	..	3,38,900	82,590
1871-72	..	..	..	..	3,39,660	78,920
1872-73	..	..	..	..	3,43,090	81,570
1873-74	..	..	..	..	3,61,091	82,980
1874-75	..	..	..	..	4,00,407	78,433
1875-76	..	..	..	..	4,17,741	81,864
1876-77	..	..	..	..	4,34,545	82,939

Besides this revenue, a local revenue is derived from port and munici-pal funds, a district fund, a five per cent. cess on the land and fishery revenue, a dispensary fund, and market stall rents. The amount thus col-lected during the last ten years has been :—

YEAR.			Port Fund.	Town fund.	Market fund.	Dispensary fund.	Five per cent. cess.	District fund.	Total.
			Rs.	Rs.	Rs.	Rs.	Rs.	Rs.	Rs.
1867-68	..	..	109	341	3,744	234	7,264	648	12,340
1868-69	..	..	386	548	5,517	515	5,801	1,202	13,969
1869-70	..	..	80	2,130	3,190	460	14,980	780	21,620
1870-71	..	..	70	2,610	2,650	240	6,620	1,950	14,140
1871-72	..	..	140	2,580	2,710	170	6,460	1,870	13,930
1872-73	..	..	490	2,600	3,010	490	3,010	1,350	10,950
1873-74	..	..	340	2,720	2,800	220	9,240	2,070	17,390
1874-75	..	..	577	2,851	2,920	237	7,288	1,415	19,702
1875-76	..	..	467	10,074†	..	..	12,529	1,181	24,251
1876-77	..	..	862	2,974	..	..	6,726	3,955	14,517

In the Burmese time the mainland portion of this district formed part
Administration. of Arakan Proper, whilst Ramree and Cheduba were separate and independent Governorships. After the country was ceded to the British Ramree and Cheduba were formed into the Ramree district and placed under an officer styled Principal Assistant Commissioner, and the greater part of the main land formed another dis-trict similarly ruled called Aeng (An). After this arrangement had lasted nearly thirty years An was joined to Ramree and placed under a Deputy Commissioner with his head-quarters at Kyouk-hpyoo and in 1871-72 the area

* The system of farming the licenses to sell opium and spirits has since been abolished.
† Market fund and Dispensary fund included.

was increased by the addition in the north of four circles from Akyab. During the first few years of British occupation the major portion of the garrison of Arakan was stationed at Sandoway. Subsequently it was removed to Kyouk-hpyoo where the force consisted of a regiment of native infantry which furnished a detachment to Sandoway and the escort of the British resident at Ava, a flotilla of gun-boats and a brigade of guns with about 28 men.

The district is divided into five townships each under an Extra Assistant Commissioner. Cheduba consisting of that island and its dependent, Re-gyee, is about 400 square miles in extent and well cultivated with rice, sugar-cane and tobacco; the head-quarters are at the town of the same name near the north-eastern end of the island. Ramree, the head-quarters of which are in the large town of the same name on the eastern side of Ramree Island, is also well cultivated and thickly populated. Kyouk-hpyoo is also on Ramree Island and north of the Ramree township; here a considerable quantity of salt is manufactured. An is a very extensive but mountainous township on the mainland with regular cultivation in the valley of the An river and numerous toungya on the hills where rice, cotton and sessamum are grown; the inhabitants are Kareng, Burmese and Arakanese. Mye-boon is on the northern shore of Hunter's Bay, divided into numerous islands, inhabited principally by Arakanese and producing rice and tobacco.

The police force, under a Superintendent, whose head-quarters are at Kyouk-hpyoo, and 22 subordinate officers, consists of 345 constables, of whom 25 are river police, and their total cost in 1876, including travelling and horse allowance and contingencies of all kinds was Rs. 74,310. Of this number, however, two officers and 35 men were employed as guards over the gaol, treasury, &c., thus leaving 310 men for police work in the district or one to every 481 of the inhabitants. The major portion of the force is located on the mainland in the An township, traversed by the main road across the Roma mountains into Upper Burma, whilst in the north Khyeng are enlisted to keep the hill men in order.

The gaol is at Kyouk-hpyoo, whither it was removed in 1853-54 from Ramree. It consists of brick barracks, thatched with leaves and with wooden floors, in which were confined during 1876 an average of 95 prisoners; long-term convicts are sent to Akyab, those who remain are principally engaged in stone-breaking, but late in 1873 oil-mills, sufficient to give employment to all prisoners sentenced to hard labour, were purchased and set to work. The gross receipts from prison labour in 1876 were Rs. 3,384.

The hospital and charitable dispensary are also at Kyouk-hpyoo, under the charge of the Civil Medical Officer. The buildings were erected some thirty years ago and are partly of masonry and partly of wood : the walls are of bamboo matting plastered and the roof is thatched with dhanee leaves. The hospital consists of a large central ward, with four corner rooms used as a dispensary, an office and a female ward. The number of patients treated in 1876 was :—

In-patients	..	..	211
Out-patients	..	..	698
		Total ..	810

who suffered principally from fevers of a malarious type and from diseases of the digestive organs and of the skin. The hospital is supported by voluntary subscriptions, the major portion being paid by Europeans, and by the State which provides the establishment. The total income in 1876-77 was Rs. 1,794 and the expenditure Rs. 1,535.

As early as 1837 the State established a school in Kyouk-hpyoo which is now classed as "middle." In 1875-76 it had 48 pupils on the rolls and a daily average attendance of 42, all of them taught through the English language. The receipts were Rs. 3,407 from .Government, Rs. 726 from schooling fees and Rs. 81 from the sale of books, making Rs. 4,214 in all. The total cost of educating each pupil was Rs. 100 of which the State defrayed Rs. 81. In 1874 a cess school was started in Cheduba ; the number of pupils on the rolls in 1875-76 was 57 and the total cost of educating each Rs. 22. In 1867 a school was established and supported in Ramree entirely by native effort, and a grant was subsequently made to it. In 1869 the grant was withdrawn and the school was closed for want of funds, but it was re-opened in 1870 on the grant being renewed. A few years later another school was opened by an Eurasian and in 1872-73 the State grant was transferred to it, on account of its superiority. In 1874 it had an average attendance of 54 pupils who paid a small monthly fee. Both have since been closed.

The knowledge of reading and writing is far more general amongst the Booddhists than amongst any other class except the Christians, but this applies only to the males who alone, or almost alone, have any opportunity of learning in the indigenous schools which are almost entirely monastic. At the census taken in 1872 it was found that of male Booddhists 7·83 per cent. under 12 years, 86·11 between 12 and 20 and 91·02 above 20 were under instruction or could read and write, whilst amongst females of the same religion not one under 20 and only ·81 per cent. above that age were at all educated. Amongst the Mahomedans, on the other hand, 5·25 per cent. of females under 20, 9·45 per cent. of males under 12, 87·50 per cent. of males between 12 and 20, and 88·54 of those exceeding 20 years were under instruction or could read and write. The Hindoos are the worst off of all, for no females and no males under 12 (there were only 21 in the district, however, in 1872) are at all educated and only 66·67 per cent. between 12 and 20 and 70·37 per cent. above 20 could read and write. In 1875 an Inspector visited the district and examined the pupils in 83 indigenous primary schools, not including those which were inspected but not examined owing to the absence of the head Hpoon-gyee or of the proprietors ; of these 75 were monastic and eight lay, educating in all 1,405 pupils. Of this number 1,259 pupils belonged to monastic and 146 (124 boys and 22 girls) to lay schools. Of the 83 schools the report was that " 58 may be " considered to be good schools not failing generally to give useful instruc- " tion, viz., 16 monastic and two lay schools in the Kyouk-hpyoo township, " 25 monastic and four lay in Ramree and Cheduba, eight in An and four " in Mye-boon. "

The local mails are carried by a local establishment under the control of the Deputy Commissioner, the cost of which is defrayed from the five per cent. Cess Fund. One line runs from Kyouk-hpyoo *via* Ramree to Cheduba (89 miles) and back, one from Kyouk-

Communications.

hpyoo *via* Talaing-toung to Ma-ee (45 miles) with a branch from Talaing-toung to Lek-pan (15 miles), one from Kyouk-hpyoo to Mye-boon (60 miles) and one from Kyouk-hpyoo to An (57 miles) with branches thence to O-boon (14 miles) and to Dha-let (24 miles). The steamers of the British India Steam Navigation Company call in once a month on their way from Calcutta to Rangoon (*via* Akyab) and the Strait Settlements and *vice versâ*, and from November to May once a month on their way from Calcutta to Sandoway and back. There are thus monthly mails during the rains, and fortnightly at other seasons. During the rains the mails are sent on from Akyab and *vice versâ* in boats which run through the creeks, avoiding the open sea.

KYOUK-HPYOO.—A village in the Kya-gan circle, Myoung-mya township, Bassein district, on the western or right bank of the Rwe, about thirty-eight miles from its mouth. In 1877 it had 596 inhabitants.

KYOUK-HTA-RAN.—A village in the north-eastern corner of the Nga-khoop-pyeng circle, Ramree township, Kyouk-hpyoo district, so named from a rock in the neighbourhood which resembles a stone wall. The inhabitants, who numbered 1,032 in 1877, are engaged in sea fishing, the fish being sent in large quantities to Akyab.

KYOUK-KA-LAT.—A tidal creek in the southern portion of the Alay-kywon at the mouth of the Bassein river, open to boats of from 60 to 70 feet in length at all seasons. At the eastern mouth, where it joins the Thek-ngay-thoung, there are sandbanks.

KYOUK-KHYOUNG.—A long narrow revenue circle in the Hmaw-bhee township, Rangoon district, east of Rangoon, occupying the angle formed by the junction of the Pegu and Poo-zwon-doung rivers, the former bounding it on the south and the latter on the west. To the north and east is the Tsit-peng circle of the same township separated from Kyouk-khyoung on the extreme west by the little Thien-khyoung stream and elsewhere by an imaginary line. The general aspect of the circle is that of a low, flat alluvial plain, with much rice cultivation and with villages dotted here and there. Of forest there is none and of trees but few. The streams are muddy tidal creeks, almost empty at low tide neaps ; at one time it, with Tsit-peng and Dha-bien (now divided into two circles), formed the Daw-bhoon township. When this was broken up it was joined to Than-lyeng and subsequently was added to Hmaw-bhee. A narrow strip 1,000 feet broad, extending along the bank of the Pegu and Poo-zwon-doung rivers from a pillar 6,000 feet up the Pegu to another 13,000 feet up the Poo-zwon-doung, is now included within the limits of the town of Rangoon.

The principal villages are Thien-khyoung about two miles up the stream of the same name, divided into two portions called Thien-khyoung East and Thien-khyoung West, with 1,272 inhabitants in 1868 and 1,097 in 1877, and Khwe-ma with 377 inhabitants in 1868 and 540 in 1877. In 1868 the land revenue was Rs. 10,956 and the number of inhabitants 3,250.

During the last quinquennial period the area under cultivation and revenue were :—

YEAR.	AREA, IN ACRES.				REVENUE, IN RUPEES.			
	Rice, including fallow.	Garden.	Miscellaneous.	Total.	Land.	Capitation tax.	All other taxes.	Total.
1873-74	7,865	13	..	7,178	15,367	4,255	10	19,632
1874-75	9,137	15	..	9,152	17,424	4,293	13	21,800
1875-76	12,561	19	..	12,580	22,138	3,190	66	25,394
1876-77	12,393	19	..	12,412	21,928	3,330	36	25,294
1877-78	12,578	47	..	12,625	25,177	3,845	38	29,060

and the population and agricultural stock :—

YEAR.	POPULATION.						AGRICULTURAL STOCK.					
	Burmans.	Talaing.	Shan.	Natives of India.	All others.	Total.	Buffaloes.	Cows, bulls and bullocks.	Goats.	Ploughs.	Carts.	Boats.
1873-74	1,905	1,317	152	4	3	3,381	1,222	93	8	424	118	167
1874-75	1,993	1,419	180	8	5	3,605	1,114	141	..	460	52	26
1875-76	1,062	1,465	142	2	4	2,675	1,115	153	..	459	91	30
1876-77	1,101	1,436	128	1	4	2,710	1,165	172	..	448	160	125
1877-78	1,342	1,640	124	6	9	3,121	1,385	210	..	556	168	78

KYOUK-KHYOUNG-GA-LE (also called *Thee-da*).—A river in the Bassein district which rises in the Arakan mountains and falls into the Bassein river at the village of the same name. At the village of Khyoung-khwa it is joined by a large tributary from the north. The main stream is muddy at its mouth and sandy and gravelly towards its source, and in the rains is open for a short distance for large boats. The banks are high and clothed with fine forest trees. About a mile below the Hpoon-tso-gyee halting place are mineral springs and four miles lower down salt springs.

KYOUK-KHYOUNG-GA-LE.—A village of 1,780 souls in the Le-myet-hna township, Bassein district, on a stream of the same name about two miles from its mouth in the Bassein river and about six miles above Nga-thaing-khyoung. It was formerly called "Kyaik-taw-pyee-pa-taw" and was at one time the head-quarters of the Kyouk-khyoung-ga-le township before that was broken up.

KYOUK-KHYOUNG-GYEE.—A revenue circle in the Bassein township of the Bassein district on the right bank of the Irrawaddy, with an area of about 49 square miles and bounded on the west by the Than-dwai river. The general aspect is that of a cultivated plain relieved by strips of forest on the banks of the rivers and by a few gently elevated knolls in the north and west. The inhabitants are chiefly engaged in rice and other cultivation and in 1876-77 numbered 5,992. In that year the land revenue was Rs. 13,265, the amount of the capitation tax Rs. 6,860 and the gross revenue Rs. 26,289.

KYOUK-KHYOUNG-GYEE.—A river in the Bassein district which rises in the eastern slopes of the Arakan mountains and runs for eight or nine miles in a southerly direction, nearly parallel with the main range, to its junction with the Wom-bhai, whence it turns off in an easterly direction to the Bassein river. It is navigable for large, masted boats as far as the village of Tha-boung, a distance of about six miles, and for small boats, with the tide, for four miles further.

KYOUK-KHYOUNG-GYEE.—A large and thriving village, with an agricultural population of 1,248 inhabitants in 1877, in the circle of the same name in the Bassein township, on the right bank of the Bassein river about eight miles above the town of Bassein. Before the Kyouk-khyoung-gyee township was done away with this was the head-quarter station. The Thoogyee of the circle now resides here.

KYOUK-KHYOUNG-MYOUK.—A revenue circle in the Ramree township on the south-western coast of Ramree island, ten square miles in extent, in which coarse sugar is to a great extent made. Its population numbered 2,332 in 1876-77 when the land revenue was Rs. 2,034, the capitation tax Rs. 2,550 and the gross revenue Rs. 4,706.

KYOUK-KHYOUNG-TOUNG.—A revenue circle in the southern portion of Ramree island on the western coast, about 42 square miles in extent, cultivated with sugar-cane and indigo principally. It has an Arakanese population of 3,066 souls and in 1876 produced a gross revenue of Rs. 5,436 of which Rs. 2,060 was from the land, Rs. 3,215 from the capitation tax and Rs. 161 from other sources.

KYOUK-MAI.—A village in the Htan-gouk circle, Kama township, Thayet district, in 19° 0′ 30″ N. and 95° 4′ 9″ E., on the right bank of the Ma-de river, a short distance above the mouth of the Moon-ta. In former years it had a Thoogyee of its own but in 1862 that official resigned and it was joined to Htan-gouk.

KYOUK-MAI.—A village about eight miles west of the town of Kama in the Thayet district, near which are two salt springs which were worked in the Burmese time and yielded about fifty pots of brine daily.

KYOUK-MA-TSHENG.—A river in the Thayet district.—See Mway-ro.

KYOUK-MAW.—A revenue circle in the north-eastern township, Tavoy district, having an area of some 12 square miles of which barely one-sixth is under cultivation. Its main produce is rice. In 1876-77 the population numbered 1,690 souls, the land revenue was Rs. 4,578, the amount of the capitation tax Rs. 1,166 and the gross revenue Rs. 5,973.

KYOUK-MAW.—A village in the Kya-gan circle, Myoung-mya township, Bassein district, on the right bank of the Rwe river, about 36 miles from its mouth, containing in 1877 546 inhabitants, who are engaged principally in fishing, fish-curing and salt-making, a few being cultivators.

KYOUK-NEE-MAW.—A revenue circle in the western township, Tavoy district, about 56 square miles in extent, but with very little cultivation, mainly of rice. In 1876-77 the population numbered 1,870 souls, the land revenue was Rs. 1,705, the capitation tax Rs. 1,526 and the gross revenue Rs. 4,612.

KYOUK-PYOUK.—A revenue circle of the Kyouk-hpyoo district on the western coast of Ramree island near its northern end. It has an area of 25 square miles and a population of 2506 souls. Sugar is made to some extent in this circle. In 1876-77 the land revenue was Rs. 1,885, the amount of the capitation tax Rs. 2,645 and the gross revenue Rs. 4,624.

KYOUK-TAING-PYENG.—A revenue circle in the Than-lyeng township, Rangoon district, having the Than-lyeng circle on the west, the Poo-gan-doung circle on the north, the A-gwon (North) circle on the east and the Rwon (East) and Rwon (West) circles on the south. It was originally a portion of Than-lyeng Myo-ma and the Myo-ooke of Than-lyeng and the ruler of the Rwon Shan, who occupied and gave their name to the Rwon circle, had continual disputes as to the limits of their respective jurisdictions. Prince Tharrawaddy, after he had ascended the throne of Burma as Koonboung Meng, visited Rangoon in 1840 A. D., and took the opportunity of settling the dispute. He fixed the Rwon boundary, which was marked by a stone-pillar on the bank of the Hmaw-won river, and cutting off the eastern part of Than-lyeng he formed it into an independent tract which he named Kyouk-taing-pyeng Taik or "the circle beyond the stone-pillar". This arrangement was not of long duration for on the annexation of Pegu it was found that Kyouk-taing-pyeng had again been joined to Than-lyeng. It thus remained till 1867-68 when it was again made independent of Than-lyeng.

The area under cultivation and the revenue realized during each of the last five years were :—

YEAR.		AREA, IN ACRES.				REVENUE, IN RUPEES.			
		Rice, including fallow.	Garden.	Miscellaneous.	Total.	Land.	Capitation tax.	All other taxes.	Total.
1873-74 ..	..	11,085	163	5	11,253	17,043	5,465	1,875	24,383
1874-75 ..	..	16,117	582	8	16,707	23,630	6,350	1,451	31,431
1875-76 ..	..	17,113	285	13	17,411	23,179	6,212	1,370	30,761
1876-77 ..	..	19,344	308	18	19,669	25,409	6,695	1,362	33,466
1877-78 ..	..	21,896	319	25	22,240	30,454	7,190	770	38,414

During the same period the population and agricultural stock were :—

YEAR.		POPULATION.						AGRICULTURAL STOCK.					
		Burmans.	Talaing.	Shan.	Natives of India.	All others.	Total.	Buffaloes.	Cows, bulls, and bullocks.	Goats.	Carts.	Ploughs.	Boats.
1873-74	..	1,409	951	756	..	87	3,203	685	199	..	148	240	49
1874-75	..	1,620	1,212	505	..	104	3,441	809	284	3	204	433	11
1875-76	..	1,852	2,210	399	3	5	4,469	1,439	205	2	184	746	13
1876-77	..	1,783	1,902	644	11	6	4,346	1,399	378	2	147	630	22
1877-78	..	1,800	2,251	596	13	4	4,664	1,458	314	..	143	635	15

KYOUK-TAN.—A revenue circle of the Kyouk-hpyoo district, on the eastern coast of Cheduba, about 12 square miles in extent and with a population of 2,188 souls in 1876-77, when the land revenue was Rs. 2,661 and the gross revenue Rs. 5,212 of which Rs. 2,348 were derived from the capitation tax. The principal crops cultivated are rice and tobacco.

KYOUK-TAN.—A revenue circle in the Myanoung township of the Henzada district, which now includes Gnyoung-myit-tshwai ; on the south is the Htan-thoon-beng, on the west the Kwon-daw and Pa-daw and on the north the Eng-lat circle of the Kyan-kheng township, whilst the Myanoung Myoma circle separates it from the Irrawaddy on the east. By far the larger portion is under rice cultivation. In 1876 the land revenue was Rs. 13,652, the capitation tax Rs. 5,987, the gross revenue Rs. 21,269 and the population 6,124.

KYOUK-TAN.—A revenue circle in the Zaya township of the Amherst district, immediately south of and adjoining the town of Maulmain, with the Ngan-te circle on the east, the Salween river on the west and the Kaw-kha-nee circle on the south. It has a total area of about 5,000 acres. The eastern portion is upland and the remainder undulating and low. The soil is generally poor and by far the greater portion is better adapted for gardens or orchards than for rice cultivation. The population is very miscellaneous, the majority being Tavoyers, the rest largely natives of India, with many Chinese. In 1868 the population numbered 1,199, the land tax was Rs. 5,631 and the capitation tax Rs. 1,625. In 1876 these were : 1,842, Rs 5,444 and Rs. 2,162 respectively.

KYOUK-TAN.—A village in the Than-lyeng township, Rangoon district, on the right bank of the Hmaw-won, about five miles from its mouth, and at the southern extremity of the Than-lyeng Koondan or range of low hills. It derives its name from the reef of rocks which stretches across the Hmaw-won and renders the navigation difficult if not dangerous : on one of these, near the centre of the stream, is a small white pagoda and adjoining and west of the village on the river bank is a pagoda of considerable antiquity, though of no great size ; it is said to have been built about the same time as the Kyaik-kouk or Syriam pagoda, during the life of Gaudama, who died in 543 B.C., but there is no trustworthy authority for its origin and

Booddhism was unknown in Burma at that time. This village is now the head-quarters of the Syriam division, which consists of the Than-lyong and Angyee townships, and contains a Court-house for the Assistant Commissioner in charge and a police station. The population in 1877 was 407.

KYOUK-TAN.—A village in the circle of the same name in the Zaya township of the Amherst district, on the east bank of the Salween and on the left or southern bank of the little Kyouk-tan, which separates it from Maulmain. It is so called from a reef of rocks (*Kyouk-tan*) near the village. In 1877 it had 568 inhabitants.

KYOUK-TSA-RIT.—A village in the Tsam-pa-na-go circle of the Martaban township, Amherst district, north of Kywai-khyan and, like it, between the Martaban hills on the west and the Salween on the east. In 1867 this village had 257 inhabitants and 526 in 1877.

KYOUK-TSOUNG.—A village of about 90 houses in the Kama township, Thayet district, in the lower portion of the valley of the Ma-htoon stream and on the bank of that river, a few miles above the spot where the Pa-nee joins it from the north. It is the residence of the Thoogyee of the circle of the same name.

KYOUK-TSOUNG.—A revenue circle in the Kama township, Thayet district, lying in the lower portion of the valley of Ma-htoon river, bounded N. E. by the Pa-douk and S. W. by the Pan-deng hills and having an area of 16 square miles. The population in 1872 was found to number 2,429 souls of whom some 300 were Khyeng, and the cultivated area measured 2,877 acres, of which 154 were toungya. The larger portion of the circle occupies, comparatively, plain land to the S. W. of the river, which here takes a large bend to the N. E ; this is well cultivated with rice, 2,092 acres in the circle being planted with that cereal. The taxes in 1872 amounted to Rs. 2,540. This circle has been held hereditarily since 1145 B.E.; in 1861 the Thoogyee of Taw-ma, to the south, died and in 1862 the Thoogyee of Kyee-mee, to the north, was dismissed for bribery and these two were joined to Kyouk-tsoung, and in 1871 Tshan-doon, to the east, was also added. It contains several fairly sized villages : Taw-ma of 113 houses in the southern corner of the plain country on the right bank and near to the Ma-htoon ; Kyouk-tsoung further north and on the river, with 88 houses, Kyee-mee still higher up the valley with 80 houses ; and Ma-gyee, with 54 houses, on the left bank a little below Kyee-mee. In 1876 the population was 2,831, the land revenue Rs. 4,019, the capitation tax Rs. 2,973 and the gross revenue Rs. 7,213.

KYOUK-TSWOT-GYO.—A small unnavigable river in the Thayet district which rises in the slopes of the Pegu Roma and falls into the Irrawaddy just above the large village of Gnyoung-beng-tshiep.

KYOUK-TWENG.—A revenue circle in the north-eastern township of the Tavoy district, very sparsely cultivated and with a small population of Kareng. The main products are sessamum and cardamoms. In 1876 the population was 820, the capitation tax Rs. 473, the land revenue Rs. 265 and the gross revenue Rs. 752.

KYOUNG.—A village in the Rwon (West) circle, Than-lyeng township, Rangoon district, situated on a small feeder of the Pyen-ma-gan stream.

The inhabitants, who are principally Shan agriculturists, numbered 623 in 1877.

KYOUNG-GOON.—A revenue circle, about 32 square miles in extent in the southern portion of the Kyoung-goon township (now joined to Tsam-bay-roon) in the Bassein district, on the left bank of the Meng-ma-naing stream and Daga river, not very extensively cultivated with rice. It is generally low and covered with grass and tree-forest. It contains one large village, Kyoung-goon, on the bank of the Daga. In 1876 the population numbered 5,872 souls, the capitation tax was Rs. 6,435, the land revenue Rs. 11,315 and the gross revenue Rs. 18,435.

KYOUNG-GOON.—Formerly a township in the Bassein district, but now joined to Tsam-bay-roon.

KYOUNG-GOON.—A village in the circle of the same name in the Tsam-bay-roon township of the Bassein district, on the western bank of the Daga river about 45 miles from the junction of the latter with the Nga-won. In 1867 it was the head-quarters of a township of the same name and had 602 inhabitants : in 1876 in had 959 inhabitants. Lat. 17° 5' 30" N. Long. 95° 15' 30" E.

KYOUNG-GOON.—A long, narrow revenue circle in the Hmaw-bhee township, Rangoon district, north of the town of Rangoon, from which it is separated by the Meng-ga-la-doon circle. The eastern boundary is the Rangoon and Prome road, running along the crest of the Pegu Roma mountains and separating it from the Re-tho circle of the Hpoung-leng town-ship, and the western the river Hlaing in the south and the Lien-goon circle in the north, whilst the Hmaw-bhee circle lies on its northern border. It is traversed from south to north by the Irrawaddy Valley (State) Railway, with a station at Hlaw-ga 19 miles from Rangoon. The eastern portion consists of hilly ground covered with tree and shrub-forest and highly intersected by ravines ; towards the south-west and west are rice plains drained by small tidal streams, tributaries of the Hlaing. The soil is poor and, as in all the neighbouring low lands, the water a few feet below the surface is brackish so that the inhabitants have to depend on tanks for their water supply. The majority of the villages, all small and of no importance, are situated on the eastern edge of the plain.

The area under cultivation and the revenue during each of the last five years were :—

YEAR.		AREA, IN ACRES.				REVENUE, IN RUPEES.			
		Rice, including fallow.	Garden.	Miscellaneous.	Total.	Land.	Capitation tax.	All other taxes.	Total.
1873-74	..	7,514	52	..	7,566	13,149	4,780	10	17,939
1874-75	..	7,918	49	..	7,967	13,917	5,205	9	19,131
1875-76	..	9,849	212	..	10,061	17,559	4,755	7	22,321
1876-77	..	9,671	271	216	10,158	16,498	4,843	10	21,351
1877-78	..	9,382	296	198	9,876	16,625	4,493	7	21,125

and the population and agricultural stock :—

YEAR.	POPULATION.						AGRICULTURAL STOCK.					
	Burmans.	Talaing.	Kareng.	Shan.	All others.	Total.	Buffaloes.	Cows, bulls and bullocks.	Goats.	Carts.	Ploughs.	Boats.
1873-74	1,916	246	903	395	..	3,460	1,189	308	2	315	308	1
1874-75	2,207	539	1,048	547	11	4,352	1,148	247	..	284	420	7
1875-76	1,583	505	1,440	557	30	4,115	948	486	21	297	506	9
1876-77	1,765	489	1,139	543	20	3,956	769	355	9	285	422	2
1877-78	1,811	257	966	493	12	3,593	517	140	3	163	268	1

KYOUNG-KWEE.—A revenue circle in the Henzada township of the Henzada district, north-west of Henzada, with good soil and well cultivated with rice. The inhabitants, who are mainly cultivators and fishermen, who work the pond fisheries in the circle, numbered 5,309 in 1876 and in that year the land revenue was Rs. 14,401, the capitation tax Rs. 5,287 and the gross revenue Rs. 20,722.

KYOUNG-TAIK.—A village with a population of 613 souls in 1877, on the Twan-te Taw-gyee in the La-wa-dee circle, Angyee township, Rangoon district, inhabited chiefly by Pwo Kareng.

KYOUNG-TSOO.—A collection of some 70 houses on the south, and forming a part, of the outskirts of the Gywon-doung portion of the town of Kama.

KYWAI-KHYAN.—A village in the Tsam-pa-na-go circle of the Martaban township, Amherst district, between the Martaban hills and the Salween. In 1867 the inhabitants numbered 253 souls and 524 in 1877.

KYWAI-KHYAN.—A village in the Moot-kyee circle, Martaban township, Amherst district, to the west of the Martaban hills, west of Moot-kyee and near the Kha-daing stream. In 1867 the population numbered 868 souls and 1,111 in 1877.

KYWAI-LOO.—A small village in the northern township of the Sandoway district, on the Tan-lwai river, inhabited principally by Burmese, at which is stationed a small police force. It is about nine miles by road from Tsha-pyeng and by river can only be reached by small boats. In 1876 it had 962 inhabitants.

KYWAI-LOO.—A revenue circle in the northern township of the Sandoway district, extending westwards from the Arakan hills, south of the La-moo-lek-ya and Tsha-byeng circles, with the Tan-lwai circle intervening between it and the seacoast. Though of considerable area it is, owing to its mountainous nature, but sparsely cultivated by its small Burmese population, who grow sessamum and tobacco principally. In 1876 the land revenue was Rs. 2,851, the capitation tax Rs. 2,252, the gross revenue Rs. 7,931 and the population 2,333.

KYWAI-LOO-LENG.—A village in the Prome district in 18° 30′ 40″ N. and 95° 34′ 5″ E., about a mile west of the northern end of the town of Poungday, inhabited mainly by rice cultivators.

KYWAI-LOO-LENG.—A revenue circle in the Prome district west of Poungday, well cultivated with rice but containing few villages, of which Kywai-loo-leng-ga-le in the west is the largest. In 1876 the population was 523, the land revenue Rs. 780 and the capitation tax Rs. 490.

KYWAI-RAI.—A revenue circle in the Pa-doung township, Prome district, on the Tha-nee stream, which now includes Re-tha. The largest village is of the same name as the circle and is close to the Tha-nee, in the most cultivated portion of the tract. In 1876 the land revenue was Rs. 1,092, the capitation tax Rs. 1,405, the gross revenue Rs. 2,637 and the population 1,271.

KYWAI-RAI.—A village in the Pa-doung township, Prome district, in 18° 43′ 25″ N. and 95° 4′ 40″ E. on the bank of the Tha-nee river a short distance below the mouth of the Bhoo-ro.

KYWAI-THE.—A small unnavigable stream which rises in the Myit-myeng-doung spur of the Pegu Roma and, flowing south-west, traverses the Gnyoung-beng-tshiep circle of the Thayet district and falls into the Irrawaddy a little above Thayet-taw, after having been joined by the Tsit-tsa-ba and the Mywe-bwe. The bed is sandy and the banks moderately steep and fringed with bamboo and Eng (*Dipterocarpus tuberculatus*).

KYWON.—A small river in the Shwe-doung township, Prome district, which has its source in the Poung-khyot circle near the southern boundary of the district and flows northwards through rice fields to the Irrawaddy at Shwe-gyo-goon village just below the town of Shwe-doung, receiving the drainage of the valley between the Prome or Toung-gyee and the Shwe-nat-toung or Kho-lan ranges. It is not navigable for boats and the banks are steep; sandstone is found in its bed as in those of nearly all its tributaries.

KYWON-BOUK.—A village in the Zien circle of the Central or Sando-way township, Sandoway district, lying on both banks of the little Zien stream, about four miles from its confluence with the Sandoway river which it joins near the village of Tsheng-khoung. In 1877 the inhabitants numbered 910 souls.

KYWON-DAING.—A village on the Pa-de river in the Shwe-ban-daw circle, Mye-dai township, Thayet district. It has not more than fifty or sixty houses.

KYWON-DAING.—A revenue circle in the Prome district on the right bank of the Irrawaddy about five miles above the southern boundary of the district. The largest village is Thoo-le-dan—or Thoo-re-dan—on the bank of the river at the mouth of a stream of the same name, and the other hamlets are almost all on the river's edge. The inhabitants, who are principally rice cultivators and gardeners with a few petty traders and fishermen, numbered 3,168 in 1876, when the land revenue was Rs. 3,737, the capitation tax Rs. 3,387 and the gross revenue Rs. 7,818. The circle now includes Tshan-rwa, Tsit-taing and Lee-bwai.

KYWON-DAW-HLA.—A revenue circle in the Prome district, adjoining and west of the southern part of the town of Poungday. In 1876 the population was 6,882, the land revenue Rs. 3,248, the capitation tax Rs. 6,463 and the gross revenue Rs. 19,658. This circle now includes Hpa-lan-bwai and Tsoung-beng.

KYWON-GA-LE.—A village in the Kama circle, Kama township, Thayet district, containing somewhat over 100 houses.

KYWON-GA-LE.—A large village of nearly 200 houses in 19° 3′ 50″ N. lat. and 95° 13′ 30″ E. long., in the Gnyoung-beng-tshiep circle, Mye-dai township, Thayet district, on a large island a little to the north of Gnyoung-beng-tshiep. In the Burmese time it was not registered as a village and a few years ago it contained only 130 houses.

KYWON-GOON.—A revenue circle in the Prome district lying east of the Myit-ma-kha and south of the Wek-poot. Included in it are the old Kywon-goon, Tsa-ba-gyway and Toung-lwe circles. Kywon-goon, in the north, Toung-lwe, in the north-east, and Mye-nan-the, a little to the south of the river in the west, are the largest villages. Rice is cultivated in the northern portion and in patches in the southern. Close to the little village of Khyoung-bya is the Kya-eng formed by a depression in the land and receiving its water-supply from the drainage of the surrounding country; it is of no importance except as a small fishery.

KYWON-KHYOUNG.—A revenue circle in the Thee-kweng township, Bassein district, with an estimated area of 38 square miles, between the Ta-beng and Le-tshoo circles of the same township. To the west the country is undulating and covered with bamboos and wood-oil trees and the largest portion of the circle is uncultivated, open waste. In the north and in the south there are some rice fields. The inhabitants are agriculturists and fishermen. The circle is well intersected by roads. In 1876 the land revenue was Rs. 8,653, the capitation tax Rs. 4,250, the gross revenue Rs. 14,084 and the population 4,561.

KYWON-MA-NGAY.—A village in the Shwe-loung township, Thoon-khwa district, in 16° 25′ N. and 95° 12′ E. on a creek of the same name at its junction with the Irrawaddy exactly opposite the large village of Kywon-pya-that. The general occupation of the inhabitants, mostly Talaing and numbering some 600 souls, is cutting rattans and the manufacture of salt. After the rains they go down to the seacoast to fish.

KYWON-PYA-THAT.—A revenue circle in the Shwe-loung township of the Thoon-khwa district, lying between two branches of the Irrawaddy which unite at its southern extremity and are joined on its northern by the Tha-rwot creek. To the north are the Kywon-bouk and Kyoon-pa-doot circles. The whole circle is deeply intersected by numerous interlacing creeks dividing it into a group of islands. It is low and swampy and subject to inundations. The most important village is Kywon-pya-that in about the centre of the western border of the circle. In 1876 it had 4,077 inhabitants and produced a gross revenue of Rs. 11,552, of which Rs. 4,088 were derived from the land, Rs. 4,678 from the capitation tax and the rest from the net tax.

KYWON-PYA-THAT.—A village on the bank of a branch of the Irrawaddy on the western borders of the circle of the same name in the Shwe-loung township of the Thoon-khwa district.

KYWON-PYA-THAT.—A large tidal creek in the Thoon-khwa district forming the lower portion of the Pan-ta-naw, which unites on both sides by numerous inosculating creeks with the other streams which traverse the Shwe-loung township, and a short distance from the coast joins the Re-tsoo-daing and falls into the sea as the Irrawaddy.

LA-BWOT-KHYAN-MYOUK.—A revenue circle in the Shwe-loung township of the Thoon-khwa district. On the north are the Kyoon-pa-daw and Kyoon-pa-doop circles of the same township, on the east the Kyoon-toon circle, on the south the La-bwot-khyan Toung circle and on the west the Kweng-bouk-gyee, Kyoon-ta-nee and Pyeng-ma-goon circles. Lying in the south of the delta of the Irrawaddy, between the Pyeng-za-loo and Irrawaddy mouths of that river, the country generally is low, liable to inundation, and highly intersected by tidal creeks fringed with low forest and with dhanee palms (*Nipa Fruticans.*) Towards the north there is some rice cultivation. The circle is inhabited principally by Kareng. In 1876 the population was 4,221, the land revenue Rs. 10,730, the capitation tax Rs. 4,858 and the gross revenue Rs. 5,698.

LA-BWOT-KHYAN-TOUNG.—Or South La-bwot-khyan—is a revenue circle in the Shwe-loung township of the Thoon-khwa district, immediately to the south of La-bwot-khyan-myouk (or north) and, like it, lying between the Pyeng-za-loo and the Irrawaddy. The circle is a net-work of tidal creeks and the inhabitants, who are mainly Burmans, are largely engaged in fishing. In 1876 the population was 4,488, the land revenue Rs. 6,514, the capitation tax Rs. 4,640 and the gross revenue Rs. 20,468, of which nearly half was derived from the tax on fishing nets.

LA-BWOT-KOO-LA.—A revenue circle in the Myoung-mya township, Bassein district, lying in the angle formed by the Rwe and the Moung-mya-houng channels and bounded on the south by the Oon-beng which separates it from the Lai-byouk circle. It is very extensively cultivated and only towards the south is there any waste land. The principal means of communication is by water : there are no regular roads, though carts go from village to village after the crops have been reaped. The inhabitants are mainly engaged in rice cultivation and some in sea and river fishing. La-bwot-koo-la on the bank of the Tha-raw-boon (the head-waters of the Rwe) with 1,800 inhabitants and Da-rai-bouk with 679 inhabitants are the largest villages. In 1876 the population was 5,390, the capitation tax Rs. 5,760, the land revenue Rs. 10,630 and the gross revenue 16,933.

LA-BWOT-KOO-LA.—A large village in the revenue circle of the same name, Myoung-mya township, Bassein district, on the western bank of the Rwe river (in this part of the district called the Tha-raw-boon Re-gyaw) in a well-cultivated rice tract eight miles south-east of Myoung-mya. The inhabitants, who numbered 1,800 in 1877, are engaged principally in petty trading, in fishing and in rice cultivation. Lat. 16° 31' N. Long. 95° 3' 30" E.

LA-BWOT-TA.—A tidal creek in the Myoung-mya township, Bassein district, connecting the Thek-ngay-thoung on the west with the Rwe on the east. It is navigable by river steamers for about three miles inwards from the mouth in the Thek-ngay-thoung and is traversible at all times by boats of from 80 to 90 feet in length without masts.

LA-BWOT-TA.—A large village in the Kya-gan circle, Myoung-mya township, Bassein district, with a population of 1,211 souls in 1877, on the Rwe river at the mouth of the La-bwot-ta stream. The principal occupation of the inhabitants during the dry season is the manufacture of nga-pee, or fish paste, and at this time the greater number go to the mouth of the Rwe river for the sea fishing whilst some go to other villages as Hpo-doot, Ta-man-khyoung, &c., where they form temporary hamlets and make salt. The principal trade of the place is in these two articles, salt and nga-pee. Lat. 16° 8' N. Long. 94° 59' E. A small Police force is quartered in this village.

LA-BWOT-TA-ROOP.—A tidal creek in the Myoung-mya township, Bassein district, running east and west between the Thek-ngay-thoung and Rwe rivers, the latter of which it joins just above La-bwot-ta village. Boats 50 feet in length, but without masts, can pass through it at all times and seasons.

LA-BWOT-TA-ROOP.—A village in the Kya-gan circle, Myoung-mya township, Bassein district, on both banks of the La-bwot-ta-roop stream about two miles from its western entrance and about 20 miles from the sea, the residence of the Thoogyee of the circle. The inhabitants, whose principal occupation is the manufacture of nga-pee or fish paste, numbered 529 in 1877.

LA-GWON-BYENG.—A long and narrow revenue circle in the Hpoung-leng township of the Rangoon district having the Htan-daw-gyee circle on the north, the Zaing-ga-naing circle on the east, the Kha-ra-kywon circle on the south and the Ma-hoo-ra circle on the west. Towards the south the country is slightly undulating with rice cultivation and open, waste plains ; towards the north are low laterite ridges covered with bamboo and tree-forest in which are found Pyeng-gado (*Xylia dolabriformis*), Pyeng-ma (*Lagerstrœmia reginæ*) and Ka-gnyeng (*Dipterocarpus alatus*). The inhabitants during the last three years were :—

			1875.	1876.	1877.
Burmese	..	..	580	848	658
Talaing	..	..	30	..	..
Kareng	..	..	2,309	2,021	2,366
Other races	..	..	21	45	50
	Total	..	2,940	2,905	3,074

The area under cultivation and revenue during the last five years were :—

Year.	AREA, IN ACRES.				REVENUE, IN RUPEES.			
	Rice.	Garden.	Miscellaneous.	Total.	Land.	Capitation tax.	All other items.	Total.
1873-74	3,469	56	..	3,525	5,553	3,085	2,170	10,808
1874-75	4,849	75	..	4,924	7,690	3,538	2,170	13,398
1875-76	5,649	144	17	5,820	8,886	3,645	2,170	14,701
1876-77	5,921	98	154	6,173	9,373	3,803	410	13,586
1877-78	6,594	185	120	6,899	10,718	4,115	1,458	16,291

and the agricultural stock :—

Year.	Buffaloes.	Cows, bulls and bullocks.	Ploughs.	Carts.	Boats.
1873-74	1,200	388	358	275	22
1874-75	1,096	225	331	261	12
1875-76	1,305	516	346	271	..
1876-77	1,309	648	377	250	..
1877-78	1,482	682	408	341	..

LAI-BYOUK.—A revenue circle in the Myoung-mya township, Bassein district, with an area of about 77 square miles, lying between the Rwe and the Thek-ngay-thoung rivers, or rather mouths of the Irrawaddy, and bounded on the north by the Myoung-mya-houng and the Oon-beng channels and on the south by the La-bwot-ta-roop. A range of low lime hills runs parallel to the Bassein river, near its left bank, and crops out at the village of Kyouktan-gyee the inhabitants of which find employment in quarrying and burning the lime. There are no proper cart roads but there are footpaths from village to village. The principal cultivation is in the north of the circle. In 1876 the population was 2,546, the land revenue Rs. 4,513, the capitation tax Rs. 2,932 and the gross revenue Rs. 7,701.

LAI-DAW.—A revenue circle in the Ta-pwon township of the Henzada district. The greater portion of the country is covered with grass jungle, with Sha (*Acacia catechu*) and Tha-bye (*Eugenia sp.*) intermixed. In 1876 the population was 6,104, the land revenue Rs. 5,061, the capitation tax Rs. 5,492 and the gross revenue Rs. 10,854.

LAI-RWA.—A revenue circle in the Prome district to the south-east of Prome lying between the Zay river on the east and the Prome hills on the west, and containing eight of the old village tracts, *viz.*, Lai-rwa, Za-noung-deng, Meng-dat, Bya-haw, Lai-gyee, Tsheng-baik, Kywai-reng and Toung-ya-ngay. In 1876 the land revenue was Rs. 1,521, the capitation tax Rs. 840, the gross revenue Rs. 2,536 and the population 852.

LAI-RWA.—A revenue circle in the Pa-doung township, Prome district, separated from the Rwa-boo-le circle by the Tha-nee stream. It contains two of the old circles, *viz.*, Lai-rwa and Tsoon-gan and is fairly well cultivated with rice. In 1876 the land revenue was Rs. 540, the capitation tax Rs. 495, the gross revenue Rs. 1,085 and the population 374 souls.

LA-MAING.—A small river in the Amherst district formed by the junction of numerous mountain streams which have their sources in the western slopes of the Toung-gnyo range. After a short westerly course it falls into the sea in 15° 28' N. about 20 miles above the mouth of the Re.

LA-MOO.—A small river in the Sandoway district which rises in the western slopes of the Arakan mountains and falls into the sea opposite Ramree Island, south of the mouth of the Ma-ee.

LA-MOO-KHYIE.—A village in the Theng-gan-nek circle, Ramree township, Kyouk-hpyoo district, on the east coast of Ramree Island, about a mile inland and about the same distance north of Theng-gan-nek, with a population in 1877 of 550 souls.

LA-MOO-LEK-YA.—A revenue circle in the northern township of the Sandoway district, extending from the Arakan Roma to the sea, separated from Ma-ee on the north by the La-moo stream and on the south from the Khareng-gyee, Kywai-loo and Tan-lwai circles by the Kywai-raing spur and the Tsha-byeng river. Its estimated area is 150 square miles; the greater portion is mountainous and densely wooded and but a small part is suited for regular cultivation. In 1876 the inhabitants, who are mainly Arakanese, numbered 985, the land revenue was Rs. 848, the capitation tax Rs. 799 and the gross revenue Rs. 2,493. The name is derived from its position on the right (*Anglice* left) bank of the La-moo to distinguish it from the La-moo Lek-wai (*Left La-moo*), once independent but now joined to Ma-ee.

LAMPEE ISLAND.—*See Sullivan's Island.*

LAN-THA-MAING.—A village in the Shwe-loung township, Thoon-khwa district, about 17 miles S. by E. from Shwe-loung as the crow flies. It has a population of about 550 souls.

LA-WA-DEE.—A revenue circle in the Angyee township, Rangoon district, 105 square miles in extent; on the north it adjoins Kaw-hmoo and Ien-da-poora from which it is separated by an imaginary line drawn through the Taw-gyee from the Kyouk-ka-lway stream on the west to the Ta-koo-khyan on the east; on the south it is bounded by the To, and on the east it is separated by the Taw-kha-ran and other streams from the Htan-ma-naing circle. Towards the west the ground undulates to some extent and is covered with tree-forest whilst towards the north and east there is some forest and elsewhere rice land. The whole of the circle is naturally fertile; a considerable portion was reduced almost to a swamp after the first Anglo-Burmese war owing to the silting up of one of the main streams—the Ka-ma-ka-lwon. There was formerly a large village of this name on its banks which was entirely deserted after the war, the inhabitants, who used to keep the bed clear, emigrating to Maulmain, and now, during the dry season, there is not a trace of the watercourse remaining even in places where large boats used to anchor.

The population in 1858-59 and during the last four years was :—

Year.				Burmese.	Talaing.	Kareng.	Shan.	All other races.	Total.
1858-59	..	..	..	146	1,533	2,164	..	..	3,843
1874-75	..	..	..	1,113	2,720	2,145	12	12	6,072
1875-76	..	..	..	1,090	3,019	2,376	13	93	6,591
1876-77	..	..	..	2,084	1,987	2,136	170	98	6,475
1877-78	..	..	..	1,683	3,434	2,253	319	140	7,829

The Kareng and Shan are garden and rice cultivators and the Talaing were formerly nearly all salt or salt-pot makers but many have taken to agriculture as, owing to importation, salt-making has ceased to be as remunerative as formerly. The potteries are at the villages of Kwon-khyangoon, Taw-ba-lwai and Ma-yan. The earth is obtained from the high ground of the "Twan-te Taw-gyee." These pots were sold at Rs. 30 to 40 per hundred in 1868 and in 1877 at from Rs. 75 to Rs. 90 per hundred. The highest price known before the annexation of Pegu is said to have been Rs. 15 per hundred.

The principal villages are Kwon-khyan-goon, Thoon-khwa and Kyoung-daik. The area under cultivation and the revenue during the last five years were :—

	AREA, IN ACRES.				REVENUE, IN RUPEES.			
YEAR.	Rice including fallow.	Garden.	Miscellaneous.	Total.	Land.	Capitation tax.	All others.	Total.
1873-74	7,615	213	..	7,828	16,872	9,893	422	25,187
1874-75	8,501	228	..	8,729	18,782	7,358	353	26,493
1875-76	8,867	319	..	9,186	18,987	7,715	75	26,777
1876-77	9,403	335	8	8,746	19,279	8,040	260	27,580
1877-78	9,712	375	44	10,131	20,992	8,838	161	29,991

and the agricultural stock :—

YEAR.	Buffaloes.	Cows, bulls and bullocks.	Sheep and goats.	Carts	Ploughs.	Boats.
1873-74 .. .. :	2,115	442	..	292	734	114
1874-75	2,022	378	..	309	850	252
1875-76	2,031	380	..	311	821	250
1876-77	2,275	458	..	295	566	96
1877-78	2,224	610	7	252	621	85

LAW-THAW.—A small stream rising in the marshy ground to the east of Prome and bringing thence the surplus waters of the swamps which, fed by the Shwe-lay and other streams from the eastward, are the source of the

Zay, a river which, changing its name more than once as it flows south, reaches the sea as the "Rangoon river." Running almost due west through low ground covered with orchards of cocoanuts, plantains, mangoes and betel palms, it joins the Na-weng immediately behind the town of Prome.

LA-YA.—A large and highly fertile circle in the Tsit-toung township of the Shwe-gyeng district, bounded on the east by the Tsit-toung, on the south by the Tsit-toung, the Kha-ra-tshoo creek, and a small creek which runs for a very short distance between these streams and on the west by the new canal from the Pegu to the Tsit-toung river. On the west and south it adjoins the Rangoon district. A small triangular portion on the north-west, with the apex to the south, was taken from it in 1877 and added to the Ma-yen-za-ya circle of Rangoon. The surface of the country is flat and, except in the north-west and west, well cultivated with rice. In 1876 the population was 3,856, the land revenue Rs. 8,998, the capitation tax Rs. 3,845 and the gross revenue Rs. 20,693. None of the villages are of any importance. The only crop cultivated is rice. This circle contains some valuable and important fisheries.

LAY-DEE.—A village in the Tham-boo-la circle, Mye-dai township, Thayet district, of about 60 houses.

LAY-DEE-KAN-HLA.— A revenue circle in the Henzada township, Henzada district. The general aspect of this circle is that of a large plain cultivated with rice. In 1876 the population was 8,101, the land revenue Rs. 16,386, the capitation tax Rs. 6,155 and the gross revenue Rs. 23,863.

LAY-HLA.—A revenue circle in the Toung-ngoo district on the west bank of the Tsit-toung, north-west of Toung-ngoo, very extensively cultivated, especially with rice. In 1876 the population was 3,991, the land revenue Rs. 4,052, the capitation tax Rs. 3,040 and the gross revenue Rs. 7,934.

LAY-MAY.—Literally "Blacknecks." A small sept of Bghai, numbering about 1,000 souls, so called by the Burmese on account of the black rings which they wear round their necks, and by the rest of the clan known as Brec or Pray. They live in the Toung-ngoo district, north-east of Toung-ngoo, and go about almost naked. They are the Ishmaelites among the Karens; their hand is against every one and everyone's hand is against them; they are savage, treacherous and ignorant and live chiefly by plunder.

LAY-MEE-KHO.—A village in the Prome district in 18° 48′ 50″ N. and 95° 28′ 40″ E. on the bank of the small Shwe-lay stream, twelve miles east of Prome. The inhabitants are principally rice cultivators.

LAY-MEE-KHO.—A revenue circle in the Prome district about 13 miles east of Prome containing a good deal of rice land and including three village tracts, Lay-mee-kho, Re-nek and Keng-tee. In 1876 the population was 682, the land revenue Rs. 1,471 and the capitation tax Rs. 807.

LE-GNYA.—A river in the Mergui district which has its source in about 13° 45′ N. in the main range, here not more than 25 miles from the seacoast, and flows with a tortuous course, but generally north, for some 60 miles, past the village of the same name the head-quarters of a township, when it turns west and falls into Whale's Bay some 30 miles further on.

The coast between its mouth and that of the extreme southern branch of the Tenasserim, further north, is divided into numerous islands by highly anastomosing tidal creeks. This river is navigable by boats some distance above Le-gnya, beyond which for some miles the effect of the tide is felt. The bed is sandy and muddy and its mouth very broad. Some distance up there are eddies and whirlpools which render its navigation by unskilled boatmen dangerous.

LE-GNYA.—A small village in the Mergui district of the Tenasserim division, on the left bank of the Le-gnya river in 11° 29′ N. Lat. and 98° 52′ E. Long. 30 miles from its mouth and 78 miles south-east of Mergui, the head-quarters of the township of the same name. During the Siamese rule it was a large and populous place but it is now a long, straggling village with about 181 inhabitants, all Siamese and all cultivators. The public buildings are the Court-house and a Police-station. The name is Siamese and means an open elevated plain.

LE-GNYA.—A township in the Mergui district, extending from the crest of the main range on the east to the sea on the west, including many of the islands of the Archipelago, and stretching up northward along the coast to the Mergui township, the Tenasserim township extending southward between it and the hills for more than half its length. In the south it adjoins Ma-lee-won. It contains only two circles Le-gnya and Bhoot-pyeng. The head-quarters are at Le-gnya. The greater part of the country is mountainous and covered with forest and the area under cultivation is small. In 1876 the population, composed of Malays, Siamese and Chinese, numbered 3,117, the land revenue was Rs. 2,661 and the gross revenue Rs. 4,685.

LE-GNYA.—A revenue circle in the Mergui district of considerable extent occupying the valley of the Le-gnya river and extending northwards to the Tenasserim. In 1876 the population was 1,269, the land revenue Rs. 1,290 and the capitation tax Rs. 871. The largest village is Bhoot-pyeng, 100 miles S. E. of Mergui with 436 Siamese, Chinese and Malay inhabitants in 1876. The two former are cultivators whilst the Chinese work tin mines in various places at some distance from the village.

LEK-GYEE.—A revenue circle in the Prome district to the eastward of Prome amongst the spurs of the Pegu Roma mountains. Though it contains 13 of the old village tracts, viz., Da-la-mai, Tha-hpan-gaing, Za-rit, Dee-thwai-kyouk, Thayet-kaing-gyo, O-gwai, Ko-ran-dan, Kan-bya, Koung-kyai, Haing-shoo-ma-hla, Koo-la-the-gyee, Shwe-ga-ro-thaing and Lek-gyee and is of some extent yet it is sparsely inhabited and yields but a small revenue from land and capitation tax. Various kinds of excellent timber such as Eng (*Dipterocarpus tuberculatus*) and Pyeng-gado (*Xylia dolabriformis*) are found on the hills with which this circle is intersected. In 1876 the population was 903, the land revenue Rs. 988, the capitation tax Rs. 943 and the gross revenue Rs. 1,981.

LEK-HTEK.—A revenue circle in the Zaya township, Amherst district, which now includes Ka-ma-wek. It extends from the Toung-gnyo range on the east to the Ka-ma-oot circle which separates it from the Salween. It has Kwan-te on the north and Ka-law-thwot on the south. A considerable portion is upland and the rest is plain country but liable to inundation towards the south from the defective drainage ; of late years,· however, much has been done in improving the existing waterways and in excavating others. In 1868 the population of the two circles, then separate and independent, was 2,812, the land revenue was Rs. 6,683 and the capitation tax Rs. 2,925. In 1876 there were 3,166 inhabitants, principally Talaing, the land revenue was Rs. 6,847 and the capitation tax Rs. 3,242. The only village of any importance is Ka-ma-wek which in 1877 had 989 inhabitants.

LEK-KHAIK.—A village in the Kaw-hmoo circle, An-gyee township, Rangoon district, about six miles north of Kwon-khyan-goon, inhabited principally by Talaing a few of whom are rice cultivators but the major portion salt-manufacturers. Near it are the ruins of a large pagoda, one of the most considerable of the 37 great pagodas of An-gyee. In 1877 it had a population of 277 souls.

LEK-KHOOT.—A small river in the Bassein district which rises in the Arakan hills and after a S. E. course of little more than eight miles falls into the Bassein rather more than two miles above the village of Kyouk-khyoung-gyee and about a mile below the mouth of the Da-ga. It is navigable by small boats at all times of the tide for about two miles from its mouth.

LEK-KHOOT.—A creek in the Bassein district which joins the Pe-beng river on the south-east and communicates with the Myo on the north and the Bassein river on the west by the Thai-bhyoo and Zhe creeks respectively. In the rains it is navigable by boats of 500 baskets burden which, however, cannot pass into the Bassein as the Zhe only admits boats during the flood tides and then but as far as the market in the town of Bassein.

LEK-KHOOT-KOON.—A village in the Zhe-pa-thway circle, Angyee township, Rangoon district, about one and half miles east of Ka-gnyeng-goon, pleasantly situated a few hundred yards from the seacoast. The inhabitants—who are principally Talaing and cultivators or agricultural labourers—numbered about 250 in 1858 and 638 in 1877. In the neighbourhood are the three small villages of Ta-ma-ta-kaw, Zhe-pa-thway (which gives its name to the circle) and Kareng-khyoung.

LEK-KHOOT-PENG.—A revenue circle in the Prome district a few miles east of Prome, now joined to Koon-rwa-leng.

LEK-KHOOT-PENG.—A village in the Koon-rwa-leng circle, Ma-ha-tha-man township, Prome district, close to the left bank of the Irrawaddy and some two miles north of the mouth of the Na-weng river, in 18° 50′ 30″ N. and 95° 15′ 55″ E., lying in an open waste plain on the bank of a rivulet which falls into the Irrawaddy and near to a natural swampy reservoir of water. The inhabitants, who numbered 521 in 1877, are mainly gardeners and rice cultivators.

LEK-KHWA-DWE.—A revenue circle, 65 square miles in extent, in the An township, Kyouk-hpyoo district, between the seacoast and the western watershed of the valley of the An. Towards the west it is divided into islands by numerous tidal creeks. In 1876 it had an Arakanese population of 1,531 souls, the land revenue was Rs. 1,743, the capitation tax Rs. 1,291 and the gross revenue Rs. 3,154.

LEK-MYOUNG.—A small but increasing village in the Pyeng-bouk circle, Mye-dai township, Thayet district, in a moderate sized rice plain at the north-western extremity of which is the little village of Kyouk-ma-tsheng with some 20 houses. In 1872 Lek-myoung contained 50 houses.

LEK-PA-DAN.—A revenue circle in the Prome district lying to the north-east of the Tsa-bay-gan circle. Its largest villages are Myoung-dan and Roon-goon, one portion of which latter is inhabited by Kareng. It is almost entirely under rice cultivation, is well populated (1,867 souls in 1876) and yields, comparatively, a large revenue from land and capitation tax *viz.*, Rs. 2,895 and Rs. 1,825 respectively in 1876.

LEK-PA-DAN.—A small but very rich and thickly-populated revenue circle in the Tsan-rwe township of the Henzada district, separated from Toung-bo-hla on the north by the Re-gyee, from Kye-nee on the east by an imaginary line running between the Re-gyee and the Thai-bhyoo and with Shwe-loung lying to the westward. The principal product is rice for which the soil is well suited and the carriage easy. In 1876 the population was 10,874, the land revenue Rs. 14,048, the capitation tax Rs. 8,072 and the gross revenue Rs. 24,745.

LEK-PAN.—A village in the A-gwon (North) circle of the Than-lyeng township, Rangoon district, about five miles up the creek of the same name, with 587 inhabitants in 1877.

LEK-PAN-BHYOO.—A revenue circle in the Prome district, some eight miles S. E. of Prome, containing three of the former village tracts, *viz.*, Lek-pan-bhyoo, Mywai-gyee-dweng and Rwa-thit, and cultivated principally with rice. In 1876 the population was 353, the land revenue Rs. 451 and the capitation tax Rs. 368.

LEK-PAN-BHYOO.—A village in the Shwe-doung township, Prome district, on the bank of the Irrawaddy, between Kyee-thay and Gnyoung-tsa-re and about two miles south of the former. Just to the east of this village is the Eng-bya fen, navigable by fairly sized boats in the rains. A good fair-weather road joins it to Kyee-thay but in the rains the communication is almost entirely by water.

LEK-PAN-BYA.—A village on the eastern bank of the river Koo-la-dan, in the circle of the same name in the Oo-rit-toung (East) township of the Akyab district. In 1877 it contained 590 inhabitants.

LEK-PAN-BYA.—A revenue circle in the Oo-rit-toung (East) township of the Akyab district. In 1876 the population was 1,229, the land revenue Rs. 4,849, the capitation tax Rs. 1,630 and the gross revenue Rs. 6,816.

LEK-PAN-DAING.—A village of from 60 to 70 houses, in 19° 20′ 12″ N. Lat. and 94° 4′ 78″ E. Long., in the Kyan circle of the Meng-doon township, Thayet district, on the Ma-htoon river, in the mountainous country formed by the numerous spurs of the Arakan hills. It was formerly one of the villages of a circle of the same name the Thoogyeeship of which was hereditary but on the annexation of Pegu it was found that the family of the original holder was no longer in possession.

LEK-PAN-DAING.—A revenue circle in the Meng-bra township, Akyab district. In 1876 the inhabitants numbered 1,888, the land revenue was Rs. 4,914, the capitation tax Rs. 1,712 and the gross revenue Rs. 6,872.

LEK-PAN-HLA.—A village containing about 50 houses in the Tsheng-doop circle, Mye-dai township, Thayet district, situated in a rice plain on the right bank of the Thai-bhyoo about seven miles from its mouth in the Bhwot-lay.

LEK-PAN-KHOON.—A village of about 50 houses on one of the numerous feeders of the Pa-de stream in the Shwe-ban-daw circle of the Mye-dai township, Thayet district.

LEK-PAN-TAW.—A revenue circle in the Ma-ha-tha-man township, Prome district, which now includes Ngwe-gyaw and Mo-goung. In 1876 the inhabitants numbered 1,044, the land revenue was Rs. 1,841 and the capitation tax Rs. 1,138.

LEK-PAN-TSHIEP.—A village, containing 80 houses, on the right bank of the Irrawaddy some five miles north of Thayetmyo, in the Re-bhyoo circle, Thayet township, close to a spur which comes down to the river bank.

LEK-PAN-TSOO.—A small village, of only 274 inhabitants in 1877, in the Shwe-kyoung-byeng-lek-ya circle of the Central or Sandoway township of the Sandoway district, on the left bank of the unimportant Myeng rivulet near its mouth in the Sandoway river and about five miles below Sandoway ; it is noted for the limestone found in the neighbourhood which was favourably reported on by Dr. Oldham of the Geological Survey of India.

LEK-RAI-DEK.—A revenue circle in the Pa-doung township, Prome district, which now includes Tha-bye-aing. The south-eastern portion of the circle is well cultivated with rice. In 1876 the population was 1,877, the land revenue Rs. 2,037, the capitation tax Rs. 2,123 and the gross revenue Rs. 5,265.

LEK-WAI-ANOUK.—A small revenue circle in the Sandoway district, a short distance north of Sandoway, extending from the Ko-kweng spur on the east to the Sandoway river on the west, separated from the Zien circle on the north by the Kya-tsheng spur and from the Lek-wai-ashe circle on the south by the Byee stream. It has an area of about 30 square miles of which about three are cultivated and barely two more culturable. In 1828 the gross revenue demand was Rs. 3,500 and the number of houses 224 which represents a population of about 1,100 souls. In 1876 it had an Arakanese population of 1,937 souls. The principal products are rice, tobacco, sugar, indigo, cotton and sessamum. In 1876 the land revenue was Rs. 2,815, the capitation tax Rs. 1,534 and the gross revenue Rs. 4,369.

LEK-WAI-ASHE.—A revenue circle north of Sandoway, about 155 square miles in extent, the larger portion of which is unculturable, extending from the Ko-kweng spur to the Sandoway river immediately south of the Lek-wai-anouk circle and separated on the south from the Khyoung-gyee circle by the An-daw spur. In 1828 the gross revenue was Rs. 2,600 and the population between 800 and 900. Its inhabitants, who are mainly Arakanese, numbered 2,110 souls in 1876 when the land revenue was Rs. 2,175, the capitation tax Rs. 1,650 and the gross revenue Rs. 3,875. Rice, sessamum and tobacco are the principal crops.

LEK-WAI-KYWON.—A small revenue circle, about six square miles in extent, in the north-eastern township of the Tavoy district; about one-third is under cultivation, principally with rice. In 1876 the population was 3,199, the land revenue Rs. 2,335, the capitation tax Rs. 2,414 and the gross revenue Rs. 4,884. The chief occupation of the inhabitants is felling and floating various kinds of timber to Tavoy for building purposes; some grow hemp for fishing nets, some cultivate rice and a few are fishermen.

LEK-WAI-KYWON.—A village in the circle of the same name in the Tavoy district in the neighbourhood of which is the site of an old town called Gnyoung-yan.

LEK-YA-MAING.—A revenue circle in the Mro-houng township, Akyab district. In 1876 the inhabitants numbered 1,643, the land revenue was Rs. 4,140, the capitation tax Rs. 1,965 and the gross revenue Rs. 6,389.

LE-MRO.—A river in the Akyab district, erroneously named Lemroo on the maps; the name signifies four towns—*le* four and *mro* a town. Its sources, which have never been explored, lie in the wilderness of mountains which occupy the whole of the northern part of Arakan, spurs and subsidiary spurs of the Arakan Roma hills. Joined by several large streams before it descends into the plains, it has a general N. and S. direction and falls into Hunter's Bay by numerous mouths all of which are interconnected by a net work of tidal creeks, and by the same means communicates with other rivers north-west and south-east.

LE-MYET-HNA.—A revenue circle of the Ta-pwon township of the Henzada district, east of the Irrawaddy, containing a good deal of rice cultivation. In 1876 the population was 7,328, the land revenue Rs. 11,586, the capitation tax Rs. 6,547 and the gross revenue Rs. 18,858.

LE-MYET-HNA.—A town in the Bassein district, with 3,674 inhabitants in 1877, the head-quarters of the township of the same name on the western bank of the Bassein or Nga-won river in Lat. 17° 35′ N. and Long. 95° 13′ 30″ E. containing a Court-house for the Extra Assistant Commissioner in charge of the township, a Market and a Police-station. A protecting embankment has been raised along the margin of the river but notwithstanding this the town is, in high rises, two or three feet under water. A local revenue of Rs. 7,100 was raised in 1876-77 from the town rates and the market stall rents.

It was to this town that the Governor of Bassein retreated on the approach of Major Sale's detachment during the first Burmese war. Major Sale proceeded up the river from Bassein with a small detachment and found the town, then a place of great extent, abandoned.

LE-MYET-HNA.—A township in the Bassein district. The Arakan mountains, from the source of the Kwon stream northwards to the Mo-htee spur, form the western boundary, the Mo-htee spur to its eastern end, thence for a short distance the Tsan-khyoung and thence an imaginary irregular line to the Bassein river near Tsien-pywon, and on the east bank the Re-lai form the northern boundary. The Re-nouk the eastern, and an imaginary line from the Re-nouk to the Bassein at the village of Bhoot-khyoung, the Bassein itself and the river Kwon from its mouth to its source form the southern boundary. The Arakan mountains, in places 1,900 feet high, send down their well-wooded spurs eastwards, leaving a line of plain country between their lower slopes and the Bassein river which gradually passes into low swampy land. The rivers are short and of little or no importance, being little more than mountain torrents navigable only in the plains. The principal town is Le-myet-hna on the bank of the Bassein river, the head-quarters of the township, which in 1877 had a population of 3,674 souls. Two or three miles to the westward of this town is the great Pan-daw lake, which in the dry weather has only two or three feet of water in it but in the rains is navigable by large boats.

For fiscal and administrative purposes the township is divided into seven circles, *viz* :—Tseng-pywon, Le-myet-hna (North), Le-myet-hna (South), Khyouk-tshay (in the old Le-myet-hna township), Mye-noo (east of the Bassein and formerly in Tha-bye-hla now broken up), Thoung-dan and Kwon-pyeng (formerly in Kyouk-khyoung-ga-le now broken up). The population of the township in 1876 was 40,065, the land revenue Rs. 34,309, the capitation tax Rs. 44,216 and the gross revenue Rs. 94,737.

LE-MYET-HNA (NORTH).—A revenue circle in the township of the same name in the Bassein district about 19 square miles in extent, bounded on the north by the Mo-htee spur of the Arakan mountains and extending from that range in a narrow strip E.S.E. to the Bassein river. In the centre there is a fair amount of cultivation but to the west the country is hilly and covered with tree-forest and to the east low and stretching out into extensive plains. About three miles west of the Bassein river is the large Pan-daw lake which has never less than two or three feet of water in it. In the extreme east of the circle, on the bank of the Bassein river, is the town of Le-myet-hna, the head-quarters of the township. In 1876 the population was 5,990, the land revenue Rs. 2,867, the capitation tax Rs. 6,897 and the gross revenue, including the local revenue of the town of Le-myet-hna, Rs. 17,886.

LE-MYET-HNA (SOUTH).—A revenue circle in the township of the same name in the Bassein district, extending in a narrow strip from the Arakan mountains to the Bassein river, between the Le-myet-hna (North) circle and the Kyat stream, with an area of about 42 square miles. It has but a small amount of rice cultivation. The larger portion of the country consists of low hills rising in height towards the west to the Arakan Romas and covered with tree-forest. It now includes the once independent circle of Ka-gnyeng-daing. In 1876 the population of the united circles was 6,064, the land revenue Rs. 4,975, the capitation tax Rs. 6,475 and the gross revenue Rs. 11,814.

LENG-BHAN.—A hamlet in the Shwe-doung circle, Meng-doon township, Thayet district, which some years ago was entered on the returns as having 84 houses. During the Burmese rule Leng-bhan was a separate Thoogyeeship but it was amalgamated with others on the annexation. It is on the Hlwa stream not far from its junction with the Ma-htoon. To the east of the village is a small salt spring which yielded about ten pots of brine daily.

LENG-LENG-GAN.—A revenue circle in the Prome district to the east of and close to the Zay stream ; it contains three of the old village tracts, *viz.*, Leng-leng-gan, Hmaw-gan and Poung-kwai. In 1876 the population was 1,245, the land revenue Rs. 1,086, the capitation tax Rs. 1,250 and the gross revenue Rs. 2,742.

LENG-RWA.—A village in the Prome district about five miles east of the town of Prome, in 18° 48′ N. and 95° 22′ 20″ E., in the northern portion of a large rice plain and about a mile west of the swamp in which the Zay stream, the head-waters of the Myit-ma-kha river, has its source.

LE-TOUNG.—A revenue circle in the Kyouk-hpyoo district, 22 square miles in extent, occupying the extreme north-western corner of the Ramree township, south of the Ran-bouk stream. It had a population in 1876 of 5,344 souls engaged principally in growing and making indigo and sugar and in fishing. About three miles inland near the banks of the Le-toung stream are some petroleum wells, the produce of which is exported. New wells are continually being dug and yield a remunerative outturn. In 1876 the land revenue was Rs. 3,381, the capitation tax Rs. 6,395 and the gross revenue Rs. 10,087.

LE-TSHOO.—A town, with 1,185 inhabitants in 1876, in the circle of the same name in the Thee-kweng township, Bassein district, on the right bank of the Daga river, between two and three miles below Kan-gyee-doung. The inhabitants are mainly rice cultivators.

LE-TSHOO.—A revenue circle in the Thee-kweng township, Bassein district, with an approximate area of 32 square miles, lying along the left bank of the Da-ga river westwards from the Ta-ta-zeng. It is, generally speaking, flat and covered with grass but in the west it is undulating and hilly and in the centre there is an extensive rice plain. The inhabitants, who are mainly Burmese, are engaged in cultivation and in fishing. The principal town is Kan-gyee in 16° 54′ 30″ N. and 94° 58′ E. on the left bank of the Da-ga river. There is a good cart road from Kan-gyee to Bassein. In 1876 the population of the circle was 5,287, the land revenue Rs. 6,739, the capitation tax Rs. 5,995 and the gross revenue Rs. 13,472.

LIEN-GOON.—A village of 638 inhabitants in 1877, in the circle of the same name, in the Hmaw-bhee township, Rangoon district, at the junction of the Thien and Lien-goon streams. The houses extend along both banks of these two rivers in single rows and radiate in three directions from a picturesque group of pagodas, monasteries and thien. The streams are spanned by well-raised makeshift footbridges consisting of single planks supported upon cross bars between wooden posts, but not nailed or fastened in any way, with ricketty bamboo hand rails. Until May 1878 the village was the head-quarters of the township with a Court-house and a Police-station, but these have been moved eastward to Eng-tsien near the Rangoon and Irrawaddy Valley (State) Railway in the neighbour-hood of Pouk-taw where the railway workshops are situated.*

LIEN-GOON.—A revenue circle in the Hmaw-bhee township, Rangoon district, on the left bank of the Hlaing river. It forms an irregular triangle, with the base to the north, separated from the Hmaw-bhee circle by the Hmaw-bhee stream, now silting up, and with the Kyoung-goon circle on

---

* The site of these workshops is often called Eng-tsien but this is a misnomer as there is at the spot a village called Pouk-taw and Eng-tsien is about a mile off in a N. by W. direction.

the east between it and the undulating ground which, in this latitude, represents the Pegu Roma and separated from it by the Kareng and other streams. The face of the country is one vast plain intersected with but slightly anastomosing creeks and rivers, which are tidal to beyond the limits of the circle, with a fringe of La-moo forest along the bank of the Hlaing, and with extensive dhanee plantations between high and low water mark on the river's bank and on the four islands in the wide " spread " of the Hlaing just above Wa-hta-ya. Elsewhere the plain is almost, if not entirely, treeless, even the villages having little or no shelter from the sun. The streams were formerly fringed with brushwood and trees intermixed which afforded shade for the spawning fish and for the fry. The wants of Rangoon for firewood—and Rangoon is distant only a tide's distance by boat and two hours run by rail—have resulted in the denudation of the circle of all timber except La-moo, which is useless even for firewood, and the fish are steadily abandoning their old haunts whilst the people are dependent for firewood on the drift in the Hlaing, stocks of which are to be seen stacked in every village. The principal produce is rice, but the soil is poor and the return only from 30 to 40 baskets an acre. Notwithstanding the proximity of the railway—which runs a few hundred yards east of the boundary of the circle—and the nearness of the Hlaw-ga station, the rice in the husk is taken to the Rangoon market by boats which, with high tides, come up the Lien-goon, Thien and other streams and are loaded at the threshing floors.

The increasing demand in Rangoon for fruits and vegetables has led to a large increase of late years in garden cultivation but still the area so cultivated is comparatively small.

In the rains boats of 500 baskets burden can traverse this circle through the Thai-bhyoo, Tha-ra-goon, Ro-gyee and Lien-goon streams and, since the silting up of the Hmaw-bhee, this is the route generally preferred for the small trade in piece-goods, twist, crockery, needles, salt, nga-pee, etc., upwards, and rice and other vegetable produce (the latter especially from Hmaw-bhee in the circle of the same name) downwards.

The inhabitants of this and of some of the neighbouring circles lying to the south and south-east get their thatch grass from Dee-bai and other places in Pegu, where it is of very good quality whilst there is none available left here partly in consequence of the extension of the land under rice and partly from a large grant of land having been made just to the eastward and for extracting any produce from this, firewood or grass, the factor of the grantee charges exorbitantly. Thatch now (1878) sells at about one rupee a bundle so that to thatch an ordinary Burmese house it costs about Rs. 22 (400 bundles of thatch grass Rs. 16 and 200 bamboos, brought principally from the Ook-kan forests further north viâ the Ook-kan and Hlaing, Rs. 6) ; this is exclusive of " ties " and labour. Here, as elsewhere in the south of the delta of the Irrawaddy, the water a few feet below the surface is brackish and in consequence no wells are to be found their place being taken by tanks in which the water is always to a certain extent stagnant and unpalatable.

The principal villages are Lien-goon, with 638 inhabitants in 1877, at the junction of the Thien and the Lien-goon ; Ro-gyee to the north of Lien-goon with 339 inhabitants ; and Wa-hta-ya, to the south, on both banks of the Hlaing and, consequently, partly in the Ka-tseng circle of the same township, with 412 inhabitants.

During the last five years the population according to races has been :—

Year.	Burmans.	Talaing.	Kareng.	Natives of India.	Arakanese.	Tavoyers.	Chinese.	Shan.	Total.
1873	2,193	608	1,004	19	..	..	30	329	4,183
1874	2,101	714	993	..	..	..	7	329	4,144
1875	2,901	279	946	1	..	..	10	..	4,137
1876	3,283	..	1,097	1	..	..	8	..	4,389
1877	3,391	..	1,087	2	2	2	9	..	4,493

The sudden falling-off in the number of Shan and of Talaing, accompanied by the sudden increase in the number of Burmans, is probably due to a change in the system of enumerating the races, the more especially as it is synchronous with the appointment of a new Thoogyee, who is the enumerator.

During the same period the area under cultivation and the revenue were :—

Year.	Area, in acres under				Revenue, in Rupees.			
	Rice.	Garden.	Miscellaneous.	Total.	Land.	Capitation tax.	All other items.	Total.
1872-73 ..	7,048	3	..	7,051	12,516	4,780	..	17,296
1873-74 ..	8,349	3	..	8,351	14,675	5,022	25	19,722
1874-75 ..	11,159	37	..	11,196	19,623	5,367	..	24,991
1875-76 ..	10,829	36	5	10,870	16,598	5,217	..	21,815
1876-77 ..	10,906	30	7	10,944	18,288	5,267	..	23,556

and the agricultural stock was :—

Year.	Buffaloes.	Cows, bulls and bullocks.	Ploughs.	Carts.	Boats.
1873	1,762	230	895	64	40
1874	1,270	97	493	221	336
1875	741	47	295	191	295
1876	1,315	48	556	167	66
1877	1,469	50	429	194	92

LIEN-GOON.—A revenue circle in the Bassein township, Bassein district, bounded on the south and west by the Than-dwai river and having an area of about 28 square miles. The central portion is occupied chiefly by brushwood and forest, the rice plains being confined to the northern and eastern tracts. It now includes Mai-za-lee. In 1876 the population was 2,756, the land revenue Rs. 5,287, the capitation tax Rs. 2,795 and the gross revenue Rs. 8,349.

LIEN-THA-MAING.—A tidal creek in the Shwe-loung township, Thoon-khwa district, which leaves the Irrawaddy about opposite to the village of Kywon-diet and joins the Pya-ma-law. This is the route taken by steamers plying between Rangoon and Bassein.

LIEP-HLOOT.—A revenue circle in the Ta-roop-hmaw township, Henzada district, on the left bank of the Myit-ma-kha or Hlaing river, containing a good deal of rice cultivation. In 1876 the population was 1,666, the land revenue Rs. 1,854, the capitation tax Rs. 1,480 and the gross revenue Rs. 3,701.

LIEP-KYWON.—A rocky island, uninhabited and very small, off the coast of the Nga-po-taw township of the Bassein district in 16° 23′ N. about one and a half miles from the shore. Immediately to the north, and at no great distance, are two other similar rocks called Oon-kywon.

LIEP-PYA-GYEE.—A sub-tribe of Bghai Kareng. *See Bghai-ka-tew.*

LIEP-PYA-NGAY.—A sub-tribe of the Bghai family of Kareng, so called by the Burmese. *See Bghai-ka-hta.*

LIEP-THOUNG.—A village in the Pyeng-boo circle, Pa-law township, Mergui district, 45 miles north-west of Mergui, on a rivulet of the same name. The inhabitants, who are all Burmese cultivators, numbered 563 in 1877.

LOUNG-GYEE.—A thickly-populated and well-cultivated revenue circle in the Prome district on the Wai-gyee river, west and north-west of Tha-bye-poung-gyee. In the rains boats of five hundred bushels burden can ascend the Wai-gyee from the Myit-ma-kha nearly as far as Loung-gyee village, the largest in the circle, situated a short distance from the river, on its right bank. In 1876 the population was 2,279, the land revenue Rs. 2,274, the capitation tax Rs. 2,305 and the gross revenue Rs. 4,839.

LOUNG-GYEE.—A village in the Prome district, in 18° 32′ 20″ N. and 95° 32′ 15″ E. on the right bank of the Wai-gyee stream, between nine and ten miles from its junction with the Myit-ma-kha, and four miles above Wek-poot where the road from Rangoon to the frontier crosses the Wai-gyee.

LOUNG-GYO.—A revenue circle in the Southern township of the Sandoway district, with an estimated area of 570 square miles, stretching from the Arakan mountains to the sea, and having the Khwa circle on the south and the Tshat-thwa on the north. It contains hardly any cultivation and the inhabitants, who are principally Arakanese, numbered only 978 in 1876. In that year the land revenue was Rs. 619, the capitation tax Rs. 904 and the gross revenue Rs. 2,251.

LOUNG-GYO.—A village in the circle of the same name in the Sandoway district, on the seacoast about 93 miles from Sandoway. In 1877 it had 711 inhabitants.

LOUNG-KAING.—Formerly a separate revenue circle in the Gyaing Attaran township, Amherst district, extending south-west from the Houngtha-raw ; it is now united to its northern neighbour Mee-ga-loon.

LOUNG-KYEK.—A village in the Pyee-tso-gyee circle, Oo-rit-toung east township, Akyab district, on the western bank of the stream of the same name, with 454 inhabitants in 1877. In 1239 A. D. the then reigning sovereign, A-lan-ma-hpyoo, removed the capital from Khyit on the river Le-mro to Loung-kyek (or Loung-krek as it is called in Arakanese). In 1406 the Burmans invaded the country, drove the king, Meng-tsaw-mwon, into Bengal and captured Loung-kyek. On Meng-tsaw-mwon's return in 1430 he removed the seat of government farther inland to Arakan, or Mro-houng as it is now called.

LOUNG-KYEK.—A revenue circle in the Mro-houng township, Akyab district. In 1876 the inhabitants numbered 8,552, the land revenue was Rs. 4,194, the capitation tax Rs. 1,900 and the gross revenue Rs. 6,251.

LOUNG-LOON.—A revenue circle on the sea-coast in the western township of Tavoy in which are included the Southern Mosco Islands. To the north and east is the Eng-tsouk, and to the south the Khadat-ngay circle. In 1876 the population was 3,868, the land revenue Rs. 5,681, the capitation tax Rs. 2,958 and the gross revenue Rs. 9,543. The inhabitants are pricipally cultivators ; some make torches from the oil of the Ka-gnyeng (*Dipterocarpas alatus*). The women make coarse mats, and leaf mats are extensively manufactured. At the village of Tsit-pye salt is made for export.

LOUNG-LOON.—A group of islands off the coast of the Tavoy district. *See Mosco.*

LOUNG-TSHAING.—A revenue circle in the Ra-thai-doung township, Akyab district. In 1876 the inhabitants numbered 2,625, the land revenue was Rs. 7,183, the capitation tax Rs. 2,918 and the gross revenue 10,543.

LOUNG-ZA-LEE.—A revenue circle in the Prome district on the right bank of the Irrawaddy a short distance inland and south of Pa-doung, now united to Myo-kweng. The inhabitants, some of whom are Khyeng, are principally rice cultivators, gardeners and coolies. The Loung-za-lee streamlet, which is of no importance, rises in the northern portion of this circle and flows through it in a S. S. E. direction towards the Irrawaddy.

LWENG-PYENG.—A revenue circle in the Henzada district, east of the Irrawaddy, between Mo-gnyo and Meng-hla. The southern and eastern portions are under rice cultivation but the rest is covered with tree-forest in which Pyeng-gado (*Xylia dolabriformis*) is found. In 1876 the population was 2,846, the land revenue Rs. 2,915, the capitation tax Rs. 2,897 and the gross revenue Rs. 7,539.

LWON-GAN.—A tidal creek in the Nga-poo-taw township, Bassein district, running through the Alay-kywon in the mouth of the Bassein river and uniting the Bassein and the Pyoon-wa creek. It is navigable by large boats from its mouth to the Alay-boûk-khyoung, that is for about five miles, and from thence to the Pyoon-wa, a distance of about four miles, by boats of 200 bushels burden.

MA-DAI-GANGA.—An island in the Kyouk-hpyoo district lying off the east coast of Ramree. It forms a revenue circle which in 1877 had 803 inhabitants and produced as land revenue Rs. 571, as capitation tax Rs. 943 and as gross revenue Rs. 4,076.

MA-DA-MA.—A creek in the Bassein district. *See Myoung-mya-houng.*

MA-DA-MA.—A river in the Shwe-gyeng district which rises in the hills south-east of Shwe-gyeng and flowing first to the west and then to the north falls into the Shwe-gyeng river at the town of that name. A small mountain stream in the dry weather it suddenly fills in the rains. It is not navigable for any but the smallest boats. In the upper part of .its course its bed is rocky and lower down sandy. Betel-nuts and other hill produce are brought down it on rafts to Shwe-gyeng.

MA-DE.—A river in the Thayet district. It rises in the eastern slopes of the Arakan mountains and running eastwards for about 40 miles falls into the Irrawaddy at the town of Ka-ma, dividing it into two parts the southern of which is called Gywon-doung. Its length in a direct line is not more than 30 miles. The bed of the stream is gravelly and sandy for some distance from its mouth but nearer the source the banks are steep and the bed rocky. In the dry season it is not navigable for boats or rafts but in the rains boats of the largest size can ascend for some miles above Ka-ma, and at this time of the year large quantities of produce are floated down on rafts, as well as a few teak logs which are brought into it from its affluents, the Kyee from the south and the Nga-wek and Moon-ta from the north.

MA-EE.—An extensive revenue circle in the Sandoway district, in the extreme north of the Northern township, extending from the crest of the Arakan Roma to the seacoast opposite Ramree. Separated from the Kyouk-hpyoo district on the north by the Ma-ee river and from the La-moo-lek-ya circle on the south by the La-moo stream it now includes La-moo-lek-wai ; towards the east the country is high, mountainous and covered with dense forest. The approximate area is 590 square miles. The little Wai river runs through the circle from east to west : this stream was formerly the boundary between Ma-ee and La-moo-lek-wai. In 1876-77 the population was 2,508, the land revenue Rs. 2,319, the capitation tax Rs. 2,077 and the gross revenue Rs. 6,695. The principal products are rice, sugar-cane, cotton and sessamum.

MA-EE.—A small village of 526 inhabitants in 1877, principally Arakanese with a few Burmese and some Mahomedans, on the left bank of the Ma-ee river about eight miles from its mouth.

MA-EE.—A small river forming the northern boundary of the Sando-way district, navigable for some distance above Ma-ee ; its source is in the Arakan Roma and it falls into the sea opposite Ramree Island.

MA-GWE.—A revenue circle in the Shwe-lay township of the Prome district, now including Khyeng-tsouk, lying north-east of Prome and extending to the Pegu Roma mountains. The country is generally hilly and covered with Teak (*Tectona grandis*), Eng (*Dipterocarpus tuberculatus*), Sha (*Acacia catechu*) and bamboo forest; the soil is sandy, sometimes mixed with clay and gravel. There are no cart roads. There is a pass from the source of the south Na-weng over the Pegu Roma to the Toung-ngoo district. In 1877 the population of the united circles was 579, the land revenue Rs. 370, the capitation tax Rs. 469 and the gross revenue Rs. 934.

MA-GYEE.—A river in the Tha-boung township, Bassein district, rising in the Arakan mountains and having an almost westerly course to the Bay of Bengal, between the Bhaw-mee and Tsheng-ma revenue circles. Boats of from 500 to 600 baskets burden can ascend as far as the mouth of the Kyouk-ta-loon, five miles from the mouth, where the water is three feet deep; thus far the stream is tidal. There is only one village on its banks and that is at it mouth. The bed is rocky but not gravelly.

MA-GYEE.—A village of some 60 houses in the Kyouk-tsoung circle, Ka-ma township, Thayet district, in the lower middle portion of the valley of the Ma-htoon and lying in the narrow strip of country between that river and the Pa-douk hills on the north-east.

MA-GYEE-BENG.—A revenue circle in the Poungday township, Prome district, which now includes Kyee-ma-no, Goon-myeng-myoung, Keng-mwon-khyoon, Tsa-khan-gyee, Tha-zee, Kan-tha, Kan-tseng-ngay and Nat-ta-leng. In 1876-77 the population was 8,748, the land revenue Rs. 4,255, the capitation tax Rs. 3,722 and the gross revenue Rs. 8,132. It is largely cultivated with rice but the villages are small; the most populous is Kyee-ma-no, three miles east of Poungday, with 626 inhabitants in 1877.

MA-GYEE-BENG-KWENG.—A revenue circle in the Pa-doung township, Prome district, in which is now included Byai-gyee. In 1876-77 the land revenue was Rs. 604, the capitation tax Rs. 767, the gross revenue Rs. 1,566 and the population 734.

MA-GYEE-BOUK.—A village in the Shwe-doung township, Prome district, about eight miles south of Shwe-doung and two miles west of the Shwe-nat-toung hills. It is connected with Kyee-thai and most of the surrounding villages by good dry weather cart roads and, with the neighbouring hamlets, Kan-thoon-tseng and Theng-ban-goon, furnishes the cultivators of the large rice tract which lies near it.

MA-GYEE-DAW.—A large village of 130 houses in 19° 2′ 30″ N. Lat., and 95° 16′ 20″ E. Long., on the right bank of the Irrawaddy, about six miles above the town of Thayet and immediately below and adjoining Mya-tsa-gaing. It is in the Mya-tsa-gaing circle of the Thayet township.

MA-GYEE-GOON.—A village in the Mye-dai circle of the Mye-dai township, Thayet district, containing some 130 houses. About twelve years ago it was returned as having only nine houses which would give a population of about 45 souls.

MA-GYEE-HTOON.—A village in the Pa-doung township, Prome district in 18° 39′ 30″ N. and 95° 7′ 50″ E., about seven miles west of the town of Pa-doung and rather more than a mile north of the Kyouk-bho river. Its inhabitants, who numbered 617 in 1877, are chiefly cultivators gardeners and petty traders.

MA-GYEE-HTOON.—A revenue circle in the Pa-doung township, Prome district. In 1876-77 the population was 1,666, the land revenue Rs. 1,432, the capitation tax Rs. 1,685 and the gross revenue Rs. 3,364.

MA-GYEE-KHYO.—A revenue circle in the Ma-ha-tha-man township of the Prome district, extending from near the Zay stream eastward to the Tsheng-lan spur, about 10 miles in a direct line S. E. of Prome ; three of the old village circles are included in it, *viz.*, Ma-gyee-khyo, Hpoung-gyee-bweng and Myoung-bwa. In this circle is the Nghet-pyaw-daw fen which receives its water from numerous small streams flowing from the high ground to the east, the surplus water running into the Zay ; the banks are flat and the bottom muddy. In 1876 there were 732 inhabitants, the land revenue was Rs. 1,322, the capitation tax Rs. 732 and the gross revenue Rs. 2,054.

MA-GYEE-LEE.—A small revenue circle in the Poungday township, Prome district, in which in 1876-77 there were 162 inhabitants. In that year the land revenue was Rs. 150 and the capitation tax Rs. 208.

MA-HA-HTEE.—An image of Gaudama Booddha in the Loung-kyek circle of the Mro-houng township, Akyab district, placed within a pagoda known as the Kyouk-gnyo or "dusky stone pagoda." The image was formerly called Ma-ha-te and of the reason or time of the change in name nothing is known ; it is, probably, a corruption. According to the pagoda history king Kaw-lee-ya, who reigned in Arakan from 1133 to 1153 A. D. and is described as of great power (the kings of Bengal, Pegu, Pagan, and Siam doing him homage), dreamt that in the bed of the Loung-kyek river was a massive stone from which he was to construct an image of the Booddha. He caused search to be made by divers and such a stone of a dusky hue was found. This was raised with red silk cords and an image carved therefrom. It was highly reverenced and remained in good order till the taking of Mro-houng by the British when the head was knocked off.* About 38.years ago it was repaired by two inhabitants of Akyab. Moung Moung commenced the work and on his death his son Moung Shwe Go completed it.

MA-HA-MOO-NEE.—A pagoda in the Akyab district to the N. N. E. of Mro-houng or old.Arakan, one of great celebrity and still visited at certain seasons by numerous pilgrims. The pagoda formerly enshrined an image of Gaudama Booddha. It is impossible to reconcile the facts given in the pagoda history—for the history of every pagoda of any sanctity is carefully recorded on palm leaves—with the accounts of lay chroniclers or with the known facts of history. Of the death of Gaudama in 543 B. C. there can be now, since the researches of General Cunningham, no doubt and the stories of his visits to Burma, even when divested of the miraculous embellishments of over-religous and under-truthful historians, must be rejected as fabulous. As if to convict themselves the Arakanese chroniclers do not scruple to admit the death of Gaudama in the sixth century before Christ and yet to bring him to their country

---

* In Sir Arthur Phayre's history of Arakan, published in the Journal of the Asiatic Society of Bengal (1844), it is stated that " this temple and image were destroyed during the late war, "the height on which the temple stood being occupied as a position by the Burmese forces." Destroyed they were not, but much damaged.

on the wings of the wind with 500 disciples in his train during the reign of Tsan-da-thoo-rie-ya who ascended the throne in 146 A. D. This king is generally reckoned as the head of a new dynasty, though he succeeded a long line of ancestors, because the religion of Gaudama was introduced during his reign—most probably by missionaries from the eastward or from Ceylon. According to the "sacred" histories the Booddha, at the request of Tsan-da-thoo-rie-ya, consented to the construction of a colossal metal statue of himself on which he breathed seven times saying : " My younger brother, Ma-ha-moo-nee, you remain here to be worshipped "by human beings, Nat and Bramha." A temple was built on the Thee-la-gyee-ree (now called the Kyouk-taw) hill to contain the image, and here it remained—the Arakanese Palladium—till the conquest of Arakan by the Burmese in 1784, when it was carried to Amarapoora by the Toung-goop pass (in the present Sandoway district). There it was placed in a building constructed to contain it, called the Maha-myat-moo-nee, about two miles from the city gates, which became the most popular place of worship—if worship it may be called—in the neighbourhood. The image is in the usual sitting attitude on a "Radza-pal-leng" or throne of the peculiar shape used by the king in the state audience hall. The figure is about 12 feet high, with all the limbs in proportion. The face is polished but all the rest of the figure is thickly encrusted with gold leaf, the accumulation of years and of the offerings of thousands of votaries.*

The Arakanese have a tradition that the image sank whilst being floated on a raft down the The-khyoung and Le-mro, whereupon a glittering ball rose from the water and, ascending, disappeared in the clouds, and that the statue now in Ava was constructed by the officers entrusted with the duty of conveying the original from Arakan who feared to report what had occurred. The desire to possess the Ma-ha-moo-nee image was one of the causes of the war which ended in the subjugation of Arakan by the Burmese. An ancient metal bell belonging to this pagoda was kept for many years in front of the court house at Akyab but it has since been restored.

MA-HA-THA-MAN.—A township in the Prome district adjoining the Thayet district on the north and bounded on the east by the Shwe-lay township, on the south by the Poungday township and on the west by the Shwe-doung township, the Irrawaddy, and the tract comprised within the limits of the town of Prome. Before the annexation of Pegu the present Ma-ha-tha-man township consisted of several independent jurisdictions. North of the Na-weng were Thoo-won-na-bho extending from the Irrawaddy to Kyoon-tshoon, east of Thoo-won-na-bho and O-shit-toung, a small tract lying in the extreme east, whilst south of the Naweng were Meng-ga-la-doon, surrounding Tha-re-khet-ta-ra, Tsa-leng-ga-thoo and Mo-goop in the western half of the southern portion of the present township and Ma-ha-tha-man occupying the south-eastern half and towards the north stretching round westwards almost to the Irrawaddy and thus enclosing Meng-ga-la-doon and its southern neighbour Tsa-leng-ga-thoo. The total area of the township is about 670 square miles. The north and north-east portions consist of low hills covered with Eng and other valuable trees which towards the west gradually pass into undulating ground, with

_____

*Yule's mission to Ava: 1857, p. 166.

patches of rice cultivation here and there, and then into an extensive plain, partly under rice and partly open waste, interspersed with clumps of tree forest, which stretches away southwards till, passing Prome, it skirts the hills which form the boundary between this township and Shwe-doung and, inclining slightly eastward between the Shwe-nat-toung hills and the western slopes of the Pegu Roma, runs into the Poungday township. On the west this plain, below Prome, is confined by low, undulating ground gradually passing into Eng-covered hills of no great altitude, which form the Engdaing or belt of Eng-forest extending southwards for many miles, and on the east by the lower spurs of the Roma forming undulating country finally rising into low hills covered with dense tree and bamboo forest. Down the centre of this plain, drained by the Zay, the headwaters of the Myit-ma-kha, which receives all the water from the hilly country east and west brought down by innumerable streams and which widens out every here and there into swamps, fens and morasses, are extensive and rich rice fields. In the hills to the north-east and north cotton is largely cultivated, chiefly by the Khyeng. The principal trees are Eng (*Dipterocarpus tuberculatus*), Pyeng-gado (*Xylia dolabriformis*), and in the east and north-east Sha (*Accia catechu*) from which large quantities of cutch are manufactured.

In the south-eastern corner of the plain a narrow strip of Shwe-lay, the old Ka-la-thien-ga, runs up north into this township.

There are two separate systems of river drainage, one in the north connected with the Irrawaddy and one in the south connected with the Hlaing or Rangoon river through the Zay and Myit-ma-kha. In the extreme north the North Na-weng enters the township from Shwe-lay near Kyouk-pya-goo and flows in a south-south-westerly direction to join the South Na-weng near the village of Myoma in the midst of extensive rice fields. The South Na-weng, the Gway, the Ien-goon and the Khyoung-tsouk all enter from Shwe-lay and the three last—having united near the village of Khyoung-khwaat once fall into the South Na-weng which flows west-south-west to the Irrawaddy at Prome. The whole drainage of the district north of the South Na-weng and a little south of it is thus collected into this one river and so carried to the great artery of Pegu. The Gway, the Ien-goon and the Khyoung-tsouk are not navigable by boats at any time but large quantities of timber are brought down them in the rains from the forests on their headwaters in Shwe-lay. Small boats can ascend the North Na-weng in the rains for some five miles or so as far as the village of Tha-la-peng-tsee; in this township its bed is sandy and its banks moderately steep. Boats of from 50 to 100 bushels burden can in the rains ascend the South Na-weng to beyond the limits of the township ; the bed is sandy and the banks moderately steep.

A very short distance south of the South Na-weng and a few miles east of Prome are a series of swamps and fens fed by the streams from the east which here find level land and are hemmed in by the hills to the west and rising ground to the north. In one of the most northern of these rises the Zay which flows southward, draining a congeries of these reservoirs as it goes till it falls into the great Eng-ma swamp in the Poungday township. It has been supposed that in the rains some of the surplus waters from these swamps find their way to the Na-weng and *vice versa* so that the Zay forms an outlet for the flood waters of the Na-weng when ponded back by a high rise in the Irrawaddy. This view, however, is combated by Mr. Theobald of the Geological Survey whc has examined the country scientifically.

The great northern ,oad from Rangoon runs through a small portion of this township, just south of Prome, and enters it again when it leaves that town running north-east to the Na-weng, which it crosses at Nat-ta-leng, and then north and north-west, past A-lo-daw-ra, into the Thayet district. Another road connects this with Pouk-khoung, the head-quarters of the Shwe-lay township. Fair weather roads traverse all portions of this township.

The principal manufactures are cutch and tari (toddy) sugar.

There are no large towns nor any considerable villages : the largest are Lek-khoop-peng in the Koon-rwa-leng circle with 521 inhabitants in 1877, A-lo-daw-ra in the circle of same name with 448 inhabitants and Dha-koo in the Ma-toung-da circle with 435 inhabitants. The Extra Assistant Commissioner in charge resides and holds his Court at Hpoom-ma-thien, a small village on the Na-weng a few miles east of Prome. Wek-htee-gan, 14 miles north of Prome, is noteworthy as having been the site of a serious defeat of a British column of Madras sepoys in the first war. Four or five miles east of Prome, marked by the ruins of large pagodas and extensive walls, is the great Tha-re-khet-ta-ra or Ya-thay-myo, once the capital of the flourishing kingdom of Prome, whose sovereign ruled over the whole valley of the Irrawaddy, destroyed by the Kan-ran tribe from Arakan, *circa* 100 A. D., now a cluster of villages hidden in brush-wood and surrounded with rice fields.

On the annexation of Pegu, when the township was formed, it was found that no less than 222 village Thoogyee claimed to be registered. Many of the tracts were amalgamated and all were turned into circles. Advantage has been taken of the death, resignation and dismissal of incumbents still further to diminish the number of those officials, whose collections of revenue were necessarily, owing to the small areas of which they had charge, so small that their salaries, derived from a percentage on such collections, were insufficient to support them and the township is now (1878) divided into 50 revenue circles of unequal area and population.

In 1877 the number of inhabitants was 52,360, the land revenue Rs. 61,866, the capitation tax Rs. 48,895 and the gross revenue Rs. 1,16,043.

MA-HOO-RA.—A river in the Rangoon district which has its source in the Pegu Roma to the east of that of the Poo-zwon-doung, of which it is a tributary joining it near the village of Kyaw-zan. Its total course is about 20 miles and at its mouth it is 50 feet wide and six feet deep. Towards the source its bed is rocky but lower down muddy, its banks are covered with grass, tree forest and bamboos.

MA-HOO-RA.—A long, narrow revenue circle in the Hpoung-long township of the Rangoon district, stretching south along the left bank of the Poo-zwon-doung river from its source, about 26 miles in length by three in breadth. To the south is the Kha-ra-kywon circle, to the east the La-gwon-byeng, Zaing-ga-naing and Htan-daw-gyee circles and to the west the Hpoung-gyee and Kywon-ga-le circles. In the southern portion there is a good deal of rice cultivation but the north is hilly and even mountainous, producing a large quantity of teak and other valuable trees such as Reng daik (*Dalbergia sp.*) used for plough and cart poles, and the wood-oil tree, Ka-gnyeng (*Dipterocarpus tuberculatus*).

The inhabitants and the agricultural stock during the last five years were :—

YEAR.	POPULATION.					AGRICULTURAL STOCK.					
	Burmans.	Kareng.	Natives of India.	All other races.	Total.	Buffaloes.	Cows, bulls and bullocks.	Goats.	Carts.	Ploughs.	Boats.
1873-74	2,429	1,897	1	444	4,774	1,309	298	12	155	610	..
1874-75	2,223	1,464	..	500	4,187	1,191	317	8	240	564	1
1875-76	2,871	1,973	..	665	5,494	1,732	610	8	396	807	20
1876-77	2,215	1,978	8	1,451	5,652	1,671	517	1	335	686	8
1877-78	2,296	2,045	4	1,504	5,850	1,805	703	7	455	849	18

and the area under cultivation and revenue :—

YEAR.	AREA, IN ACRES.				REVENUE, IN RUPEES.			
	Rice.	Garden.	Miscellaneous.	Total.	Land.	Capitation tax.	Other taxes.	Total.
1873-74	6,978	67	..	7,045	12,161	5,422	550	18,133
1874-75	9,071	88	..	9,179	15,804	5,232	566	21,602
1875-76	9,454	89	..	9,543	16,484	5,712	582	22,778
1876-77	9,878	89	62	10,029	17,292	5,907	2,201	25,400
1877-78	10,465	94	65	10,624	1,82,112	6,052	339	74,603

MA-HOO-RA.—A large and irregularly built village lying on both banks of the Poo-zwon-doung river (the portion on the right bank generally known as Hpoung-gyee) about 60 miles from its mouth, partly in the Hpoung-gyee and partly in the Ma-hoo-ra circles of the Hpoung-leng township, Rangoon district, in a small patch of rice cultivation surrounded by tree, shrub and grass forest, one march from Hlay-goo, the head-quarters of the township, and two marches from Htouk-kyan, (where the Pegu and Tcung-ngoo road leaves the Rangoon and Pegu road), whether *via* Kya-eng or *via* Hlay-goo. The inhabitants, who are chiefly cultivators and foresters, numbered 944 in 1877. The houses are mostly substantially built and, like almost all those in this part of the country, are thatched either with the leaves of the Tsa-loo palm (*Licuala peltata, Rox.*) or with the fan-shaped leaves of the Taw-htan (*Livistona speciosa, Kurz.*) laid on single and overlapping each other. In the western, or Hpoung-gyee, quarter is a monastery with a Thien, or idol-house, and two fairly good rest-houses. The land in the neighbourhood is poor and on the west liable to inundation. The Poo-zwon-doung here flows between high and steep arenaceous banks, about

30 yards apart at the top. In the rains it flows with great force and rapidity but in the dry season is little more than a series of shallow, muddy pools. At the upper end of the village it is spanned by a substantial wooden bridge connecting the two quarters. The Police station is on the right bank.

MA-HTOON.—A river in the Thayet district, Pegu division, which, rising near the lofty Myeng-ka-dek peak of the Arakan Roma, flows south-east and, eight miles from its source, whilst it is still in the heart of the mountains, enters British territory and crossing the Meng-doon and Ka-ma townships and flowing past the town of Meng-doon falls into the Irra-waddy just above Ka-ma, about 50 miles in a direct line from the spot where it enters the district. Its course is so winding, however, that the actual distance traversed by it in British Burma is about 150 miles. During the rains its waters rise and fall continually, the quantity contained between its banks mainly depending on the rainfall in the hills. At this season of the year it is navigable by boats of the largest size but owing to the sinuosities of the course and the strength of the current it takes 10 or 12 days to reach Meng-doon from Ka-ma : in the cold and hot seasons small boats only can ascend as far as Meng-doon. Large quantities of the produce of its fertile valley—rice, cotton, cutch, sessamum, etc.—are brought down it on rafts and during the rains logs of Teak and Pyeng-gado (*Xylia dolabriformis*), the produce of the forests on the Arakan range, are floated down singly and rafted at its mouth. Flowing amongst hills almost throughout its course it has many small affluents, the most important being the Moo-the, the Hlwa and the Pa-nee : amongst the smaller ones are the Da-ga and the Ta-ma from the west and south and the Kyoon, the Moo, the Nat-myouk and the Dek-shay from the north. The scenery throughout its course is exceedingly picturesque.

During the dry season the fields on the high banks of parts of this river, the tops of which are sometimes 30 feet above the level of the water, are irrigated by means of a simple but ingeniously contrived self-acting under-shot water wheel which is driven by the current. This machine has been in use here time out of mind and is not found elsewhere in Burma yet no tradition exists as to the period of its introduction or the person by whom it was invented. At the spot where the wheel is to work common jungle wood posts, generally eight in number, are driven into the ground in two lines of four posts each parallel to the course of the river, one line close under the bank and the other some distance out in the stream. A strong bar is securely fastened along the top of each line and on these two bars, at right angles to the course of the river, rests the shaft of the wheel, which thus revolves between the two lines of posts which support it. The whole of the wheel, with the exception of the shaft which is of some hard wood, is constructed of bamboo. Attached to the outer ends of the spokes, in a similar position to that of the floats of the paddle of a steamer, are flaps or paddles of coarse bamboo mat work. Alternately with these floats, on either side of the wheel, are placed the buckets, which are joints of bamboo closed at one end by the natural knot of the wood. These buckets, of which there are thus twice as many as there are floats or flaps, are so arranged that as the wheel turns they dip into the water above the wheel and rise from it below at an angle of about 45°. The current acting on the floats the wheel revolves, dipping each pair of buckets successively; these, passing under water and filling, retain, on rising, from two to four pints each which, on arriving at the top, they discharge into troughs that carry the water into the fields and redescend to bring up a fresh supply. The diameter of the wheel, which is sometimes as much as 18 feet, is regulated by the height of the bank, and the shaft is placed at such a distance above the level of the stream that each float in turn passes completely under and the whole of its surface is acted upon by the current. If it should so happen that the force of the water is not sufficient dams are constructed higher up and after two or three days or less, as may be necessary, the dam is cut and the stored water turned on to the wheel.

MAI-HPYOO.—A revenue circle in the Bhoom-ma-wa-dee township, Toung-ngoo district, on the east bank of the Tsit-toung, south of Kan-nee. In 1877 the population was 8,197, the land revenue Rs. 1,627, the capitation tax Rs. 3,366 and the gross revenue Rs. 7,181. It contains two lakes, the Kywai-kyan and the La-man, the former of which is dry in the hot season.

MAI-KA-LA.—A river in the Amherst district which has its source in the western slopes of the Moo-lai-yit mountain and after a short westerly course falls into the Houng-tha-raw.

MAINGY.—A small island in the Mergui Archipelago, a portion of the Mergui district, in 12° 30′ N. Lat. and 98° 7 E. Long. due west of the centre of King Island from which it is about three miles distant. Its central peak is visible for 11 miles.

MAI-PA-LAI.—A river in the Amherst district which rises in the eastern slopes of the Daw-na mountains and after a S.ʼ S. E. course of about 40 miles falls into the Thoung-yeng a short distance below Mya-wa-dee.

MAI-PA-LAI.—A village in the Mya-wa-dee circle of the Houng-tha-raw township, Amherst district, six miles up a small stream of the same name, a tributary of the Thoung-yeng, where a small Police force is stationed. In 1877 it had 531 inhabitants.

MAI-PA-LAN.—A revenue circle in the Bhoom-ma-wa-dee township, Toung-ngoo district which now includes the Bhoom-ma-wa-dee circle. In 1877 the population was 5,600, the land revenue Rs. 1,303, the capitation tax Rs. 2,438 and the gross revenue Rs. 6,393.

MAI-WAING.—A revenue circle in the Salween Hill Tracts, of considerable extent but mountainous and clothed with dense forest. In 1876 the popluation was 4,372, the land revenue Rs. 1,524 and the capitation tax Rs. 2,083.

MAI-ZA-LEE.—A revenue circle, having an area of about 99 square miles, in the Bassein township, Bassein district, lying in the south-western corner of the township between the Arakan hills on the west, the Than-dwai and Kwon rivers on the south, the Hpek Re-gyan on the east and the Nga-kwa stream on the north. The south-east portion is flat and well cultivated but to the west the circle is hilly, the hills increasing in height towards the great Arakan range; the soil here is sandy. It now includes Lien-goon. The inhabitants, of whom many are Kareng, numbered 2,756 in 1876-77 and are chiefly engaged in agriculture. There are no roads but there are footpaths from village to village. In 1876-77 the land revenue was Rs, 5,287, the capitation tax Rs. 2,795 and the gross revenue Rs. 8,349.

MAI-ZA-LEE.—A village in the Bassein township, Bassein district, on the bank of the Northern Mai-za-lee river, about 18 miles north-west of Bassein. The inhabitants are largely engaged in rice cultivation and in 1877 numbered 621.

MAI-ZA-LEE.—A river in the Bassein district which rises in the Arakan hills and, after a south-easterly course of about 30 miles, unites with the Hlaw-ga-ta at a village of that name. It is merely a mountain torrent with a sandy and gravelly bed and is nearly or quite dry in the hot season. Its banks are high and clothed with dense forest in which, towards the source, some teak is found. These two streams, under the former name, flow south for 10 or 12 miles and fall into the Bassein river at the village of Mai-za-lee in about 17° 28′ 30″ N.

MAI-ZA-LEE.—A river in the Bassein district which rises in the Arakan Roma and, reinforced by the Thai-bhyoo, a spur of the mountains separating their sources, falls into the Bassein or Nga-won. It is navigable at all seasons by boats of from 30 to 40 feet in length for about five miles, or as far as Nat-tseng-kweng village.

MA-LEE-WON.—A sub-division lying in the extreme south of the Province and forming a portion of the Mergui district. It is bounded on the east by the main range which separates the Province from Siam and lower down by the Pak-chan river, on the west by the sea and on the north by the Tenasserim township, and includes many of the islands in the south of the Mergui Archipelago and Victoria Island off the mouth of the Pak-chan, which the Siamese claimed for many years but which they eventually acknowledged to be British territory on the settlement of the boundary between the two countries in 1867-68. The coast line is for the most part fringed with mangrove swamp as are the banks of the rivers and creeks. These swamps are in places but a few yards in depth and in others they extend a mile or more inland. The country in the immediate vicinity of Ma-lee-won consists of undulating plains or low hills covered with grass and dotted with trees sometimes single, sometimes in clumps or in groves and here and there in small forests. Towards the north and south-east rise low ranges of hills, spurs of the main dividing range, covered with dense evergreen virgin forest. This forest extends over the greater part of the sub-division, broken here and there by patches of cultivation, villages or tin mines. In the immediate vicinity of the villages and of the spaces cleared for cultivation the forest is usually very dense and in many places almost impenetrable owing to the thick undergrowth and the numbers of canes of various species, but in the interior it is comparatively open and free from brush-wood and scrub. The inhabitants, who numbered only 5,561 in 1877, are Siamese, Chinese and Malays with a few Burmese. The Siamese confine themselves to cultivation and the Chinese to mining, though some of these latter cultivate a little. The Malays, who are mostly congregated in the village of Ban-ka-tsoon and Pa-law-toon-toon, are chiefly occupied during the rains in growing rice and in the dry weather in roaming among the islands of the Archipelago, collecting dammer, scented wood, etc, and in petty trade with the Selung, the inhabitants of these islands, exchanging rice for pearls, sea slugs, etc. The officer in charge of the sub-division was stationed in Ma-lee-won (there has been none since May 1877) and the Extra Assistant Commissioners in Ka-lan-tsaing, a collection of hamlets rather than a village, a few miles below Kra and in Le-gnya. The area brought under cultivation is exceedingly small and the land revenue in 1877 was only Rs. 3,226.

The chief product of the sub-division is tin, obtained by washing the gravel lying immediately below the alluvial deposits in the valley.

In 1860 the Ma-lee-won township or southern portion of the tract, 340 square miles in extent, was farmed out to a Chinaman for Rs. 600 per annnm ; he was provided with a Police force, the pay of which, Rs. 2,400 per annum, he drew in cash but which he is asserted to have paid in tin, and who was practically supreme, subject to a control which was in truth only nominal and, if all accounts are true, exercising, the power of life and death at his own mere pleasure. About five years ago the lease expired and was not renewed and the present sub-division, consisting of Ma-lee-won and Le-gnya, was formed. An English company got a grant of the tin mines and commenced to work energetically, at first with great success, but the works have been abandoned as the lodes were lost. The gross revenue realized in 1877 was Rs. 6,537 of which Rs. 3,311 were derived from the capitation tax.

MA-LEE-WON.—A village in the sub-division of the same name in the Mergui district, about 20 miles from the mouth of the Pak-chan river, with 315 inhabitants in 1876. The name is Siamese and means " Malay Settlement " and was so named from having been founded by Malays. In the neighbourhood are tin mines which had been worked from a remote period by Chinese. In 1873 an European firm obtained a mining lease from the Government but threw it up in 1877 as unprofitable. The Chinese have resumed work, from 80 to 100 men now being employed, and from their less expensive method of extracting the tin and their willingness to accept smaller profits than Europeans look forward to, it pays them. The public buildings are a good Court-house and a Police guard-house.

MA-MYA.—A river in the Henzada district which has its source in the eastern slopes of the Arakan Roma mountains in the Meng-wa-doung circle. It flows in an easterly direction for the first 20 miles and is then deflected to the south-east towards the village of Ma-toung-da, near which it is again deflected, and most abruptly, towards the north until in falls into the Htoo lake. It is navigable, during the rains only, ʾy small boats. Its upper course is exceedingly rocky. It drains a country containing Teak, Pyeng-gado (*Xylia dolabriformis*) and Htouk-kyan (*Terminalia macrocarpa*) of excellent growth, with Eng (*Dipterocarpus tuberculatus*) lower down. It brings down a considerable quantity of sand and ịs thus gradually filling up the lake.

MA-NIE-PGHA.—A sub-tribe of Kareng, a portion of the Sgaw family, inhabiting the hills in the Toung-ngoo district between the Rouk-thwa-wa and the Myit-ngay streams. They are one of the few septs that have any other domestic animals than fowls and swine ; in common with the Pa-koo they breed a few goats and they cultivate the areca palm, rice and a little cc·.

ton. By some they are considered as a portion of the Pwo family on account of the strong nasal sound peculiar to the dialects of that tribe. The majority have embraced Christianity.

MA-NOO-MA-NAW.—A large, 'trowser-wearing sub-division of the Bghai family of Kareng, living in the Toung-ngoo district of the Tenasserim division, north of the Sgaw and between them and the Kareng-nee.

MAN-OUNG.—An island in the Bay of Bengal forming a township in the Kyouk-hpyoo district, more commonly known as Cheduba, with the head-quarters at the town of Man-oung in the north-western part of the island. It extends from 18° 40' to 18° 56' 30" N. Lat. and from 93° 30' to 93° 47' E. Long. and with its southern dependency Re-kywon, otherwise known as Flat Island, covers an area of about 120 square miles. Its general appearance and character is that of a fertile, well-wooded island of moderate height and irregular shape. A band of level plain, but little raised above the sea and of far greater width on the east than on the west, extends round its coast; within this lie irregular, low, undulating hills varying in height from 50 to 500 feet, enclosing several higher detached mounds with steep, well-wooded sides, the highest of which, near the south of the island, rises nearly to 1,400 feet. In the extreme north-west corner, connected with the main island by a series of detached rocks both above and below water with deep channels between them, is a so-called "volcano" from which flames occasionally issue; these are in reality due to a copious discharge of inflammable gas and not to volcanic action.

The inhabitants, who numbered 21,779 in 1875 and 22,078 in 1877, are chiefly Arakanese and are employed in rice and tobacco cultivation and in fishing. A considerable quantity of rice is sent hence during the season and the township is noted for the good quality of its tobacco. Petroleum is found in several spots on the island. The principal villages are Man-oung, Re-kywon, Toung-bhet, Kha-bhoon-maw, Ka-ma, Ta-htoo, and Tsheng-nat-khyoung. The township is divided into eight revenue circles and in 1875-76 the land revenue amounted to Rs. 22,443 and the capitation tax to Rs. 22,913 : in 1876-77 the land revenue was Rs. 22,485 the capitation tax Rs. 23,171 and the gross revenue Rs. 69,029.

Two derivations are given for the name "Man-oung" which signifies "overcoming of the evil disposition." According to an ancient tradition a governor of the Island appointed by Tsan-da-ra I. king of Arakan, who reigned some 2,000 years B. C., so harried the people that they complained to the sovereign who summoned the governor to appear before him. On the governor refusing to attend the Court the monarch struck the sea with a rod and ordered it to bring his disobedient subject into his presence. The sea obeyed and in a few days the dead body of the rebel was washed ashore near the Royal city. According to another account the name was given to the island because it was the place of transportation for those who were considered to be politically dangerous, who were thus rendered powerless for evil and whose evil disposition was thus overcome. The classical name is Mek-kha-wa-dee. The name Cheduba, by which the island is known to Europeans and to natives of India, is said to be a corruption of Char-dhuba or "four capes" from the capes at the four corners of the island.

MAN-OUNG.—Better known as Cheduba, is a small town in the north-west of Man-oung or Cheduba Island, on the bank of the Oon-khyoung, the head-quarters of the Cheduba township. It contains a Court-house, Market, School and Police-station. In 1873 it had a population of 1,323 souls, in 1875 of 1,384, and in 1877 of 1,409. Locally it is known as Zhe-dan.

MAN-OUNG-MYOMA.—A revenue circle in the Kyouk-hpyoo district lying in the north-eastern part of Cheduba Island, 54 square miles in area, with 5,129 inhabitants in 1875 and 5,393 in 1877. The principal products are rice and tobacco. Towards the west of the circle are some petroleum wells. Included in it is Man-oung the head-quarters of the township. The land revenue in 1875 was Rs. 5,304 and the capitation tax Rs. 5,500, and in 1877 Rs. 5,351 and Rs. 5,795 respectively : in the latter year the gross revenue, including that raised in Man-oung, was Rs. 33,274.

MA-OO-BENG.—A revenue circle in the Thoon-khwa township of the Thoon-khwa district. In 1876-77 the population numbered 4,142, the land revenue was Rs. 6,362, the capitation tax Rs. 4,793 and the gross revenue, including that raised in the town of Ma-oo-beng, Rs. 28,793.

MA-OO-BENG.—The head-quarters of the Thoon-khwa district on the bank of the Re-nouk stream, one of the numerous large creeks through which the waters of the Irrawaddy find their way through the Delta, here half a mile wide. The town is a new one, selected as the head-quarters on the formation of the Thoon-khwa district, and the laying out commenced in April 1875. There are three main roads running north and south, intersected at right angles, and at pretty regular intervals, by 10 main cross roads which run east and west. The land on which the town is built is low, the highest portion, *viz.*, towards the north and east, is barely an inch above the level of the high water mark of the river during the rains. The southern and western portions, where are fisheries, are very low, the natural slope of the ground being gradually towards the west, and are flooded during the rains and swampy in October and November. The town contains Court-houses, a small Gaol, a Police-station, a Charitable dispensary and a Market. In 1877 the population was 1,178, and the local revenue raised, in addition to the Imperial and Provincial revenues, Rs. 4,234.

MA-OO-DAING.—A revenue circle in the Meng-doon township, Thayet district, with an area of about 30 square miles and a population in 1877 of 2,411 souls of whom about 400 are Kareng, and yielding in that year a revenue of Rs. 3,351 of which Rs. 1,569 was derived from the land and Rs. 1,527 from the capitation tax. Cows form nearly one-third of the total number of cattle, 1,622 head. The culturable area measures 3,782 acres but only about 1,800 acres are actually cultivated. In 1860 Kan-lay and Ma-oo-daing were joined to form the present circle. The products are rice, cotton, cutch, sessamum, maize, tobacco, onions, chillies and plantains.

MA-OO-KHOON.—A village in the Prome district inhabited chiefly by rice cultivators and situated on the right bank of the Myit-ma-kha about two and a half miles from its source in the Engma lake.

MA-RA-MAN.—A revenue circle in the Shwe-doung township, Prome district, lying between the Kyee-thai circle and the Shwe-nat-toung or Kho-lan hills. In the north-eastern corner, on the first hill in the Kho-lan range, stands the highly sacred Shwe-nat-toung pagoda at which an annual fair is held in March when crowds of people from all parts of the country assemble in the plain near the village of Ma-ra-man. This circle is now joined to Rwa-goon lying on the eastern side of the Kho-lan hills.

MA-RAN-OO.—A revenue circle in the Than-lweng Hlaing-bhwai township, Amherst district, between the Dawna range and the Thoung-yeng river to the east of the source of the Hlaing-bhwai. It is generally mountainous and covered with forest but is to some extent under cultivation by the Kareng who inhabit it. It is now joined to Hlaing-bhwai.

MA-RO-THOUNG SHA-KHAI.—A revenue circle in the extreme north-eastern portion of the Tsam-bay-roon township, Bassein district, bounded on the north and east by townships of the Henzada district, about 65 square miles in extent. Forest-covered land everywhere preponderates over the cultivated and open. A considerable portion of the country has, however, been rendered fit for rice cultivation by the construction of embankments in Henzada which preserve it from inundation. In the southern part of the circle is the Sha-khai-gyee lake, a fine sheet of water about four miles in length and half a mile in breadth formed by a slight depression in the soil; in the rains it is supplied with water by the Daga river with which it communicates by two small streams. Near this lake is the old Myo-goon fort or stockade. In 1876-77 the population was 3,296, the land revenue Rs. 4,838, the capitation tax Rs. 3,672 and the gross revenue Rs. 9,899.

MARTABAN.—A circle in the Amherst district.—*See Moot-ta-ma.*

MARTABAN.—A township in the Tha-htoon sub-division of the Amherst district, bounded on the west by the sea and on the east by the Bheng-laing and southwards from the mouth of that river by the Salween; on the south the Da-ray-bouk, or northern mouth of the Salween, separates it from Bhee-loo-gywon and on the north it is separated from the Tha-htoon township by the Hpa-baing streamlet, a tributary of the Bheng-laing, the Kyoon-hpa, a tributary of the Tsha or Tha-htoon river, and in the extreme north-west by the Tsha itself. East of the Bheng-laing is the Hpa-gat township of the same sub-division and east of the Salween the Gyaing Than-lweng township. A range of hills starts from the south-eastern corner at Martaban and runs up N. N. W. for about 12 miles when it turns north and gradually rises in altitude to the Zeng-gyaik peak, 3,500 feet above the sea level, whence the height diminishes somewhat rapidly. A little north of the Zeng-gyaik hill a spur is thrown out towards the N. N. W., enclosing with the main range the Dhe-ba-rien valley drained by the Reng-gnyiem which bursts through a gorge in the spur at the village of the same name. The spur gradually sinks and ends near Toung-tsoon a little south of the Kyoon-hpa. To the east of the main line of hills the country is forest-clad and with but little cultivation, comparatively. On the west are extensive and fertile plains intersected by numerous streams and creeks which afford an easy outlet for the large quantities of rice grown in the tract. The principal of these are Bheng-loung and the Reng-gnyiem flowing westward to the sea, and the Da-rien and the Kha-daing flowing southward to the Da-ray-bouk. The extreme western portion is, in parts, liable to damage by the entry of the sea water through the various rivers ; in very high tides, especially if a strong westerly or south-westerly wind is blowing, it overtops the banks and spreads over the country which is lower than the coast line. In the south the coast is protected by the sand and mud-covered drift which increases yearly and forms a strong protecting embankment except where pierced by the mouths of the streams; towards the north there are considerable stretches of mangrove swamp. To seaward are vast sand and mud banks, dry at low water, which render any approach by sea-going vessels impossible.

The principal villages are Martaban in the extreme south-east corner on the bank of the Salween, opposite Maulmain, once the capital of a kingdom and more than once besieged by invading armies and, after the annexation of Pegu, the head-quarters of the township till these were removed to Poung ; now it is a straggling village with 1,673 inhabitants : Wai-pa-tan with 1,368, Kywai-khyan with 1,111, Poung with 1,073, Kha-da with 1,104 and Hpa-lat with 1,068. These, with the exception of Kywai-khyan, are, as are almost all the more important villages, along the western slopes of the Martaban hills.

The township, which with Tha-htoon and Hpa-gat was transferred to the Amherst from the Shwe-gyeng district in 1865, is now divided into nine circles, *viz.*, Toung-tsoon, Reng-gnyiem, Poung, Kha-daing, Da-rien, Moo-kyee and Moot-ta-ma west of the hills, Gaw, in the north, partly in the Dhe-ba-rien valley and partly in the plain country to the westward, and Tsam-pa-na-go occupying the whole of the country between the hills and the Bheng-laing and the Salween, except a very small portion in the extreme south which belongs to Moot-ta-ma.

The population in 1876-77 was 31,097, the land revenue Rs. 1,33,599 and the capitation tax Rs. 30,465.

MARTABAN.—A small town in the Amherst district on the right bank of the Salween, immediately opposite to Maulmain, between the river and the eastern slopes of a range of hills which stretches up N. W. and is here crowned by several white pagodas looking down upon the broad expanse of waters, formed by the junction of the united Gyaing and Attaran with the Salween and the fleet of merchant vessels lying in the river off Maulmain.

The town is said to have been built three years after the foundation of Pegu, or in A. D. 576, by Tha-ma-la the first king and then disappears almost altogether from history. In A. D. 1269, when the Peguan kingdom had been conquered by the Burmese and the king of Burma was supreme in ancient Ra-ma-gnya, a sovereign of Talaing race re-built the city " on a rocky " promontory with the country of the Shan on the east and the sea on the " west," and appointed as governor one A-lien-ma. A-lien-ma soon lost his governorship and Ta-la-bya was appointed in his stead. The whole kingdom, disorganized by the attacks on the capital made by the Tartar hordes of Khublai Khan, was falling to pieces and A-lien-ma returned and killed his successor but was himself put to death by one Wa-rie-yoo (who is claimed by the native historians as a Talaing but was most probably by descent a Shan or northern Siamese) who had travelled south-east to the capital of Siam and had eloped with the king's daughter. Wa-rie-yoo declared himself independent and sent aid to the ruler of Pegu who had done likewise ; the combined forces defeated the Burman army sent against them but the two rebel chieftains quarrelled and Wa-rie-yoo overcame his ally, now become his rival, and declared and maintained himself as king of the ancient Peguan kingdom. After a reign of 19 years Wa-rie-yoo was murdered by the two sons of the dethroned king of Pegu and was succeeded by Khoon-law. In A. D. 1323 the capital was transferred to Pegu by Bee-gnya-ran-da but the royal palace and seat of government appear to have remained for some time at Martaban. During the subsequent wars between the Peguans, the Siamese and the Burmese Martaban was several times besieged and captured and on more than one occasion was the last stronghold of the reigning sovereign. The Portuguese historian Manuel de Faria y Sousa speaks of it as being, in 1540, the " metropolis of a great and flourishing kingdom" which was beseiged for seven months by Ta-beng-shwe-htee, king of Toungngoo (who had already taken Pegu the capital of the kingdom), when the governor was starved into surrendering without conditions and was drowned by his conqueror. The account of the riches of the town given by the Portuguese historian is, most probably, exaggerated. The treasure, he says, " amounted to 100 millions of gold. The third day the army had liberty to " plunder, which lasted four days, and was valued at 12 millions. Next the " city was burned, when perished by fire and sword above 60,000 souls, " besides as many male slaves ; 2,000 temples and 40,000 houses were laid " even with the ground. There were in the town 6,000 pieces of cannon, " 100,000 quintals of pepper, and as much of other spices." After this general destruction the victor returned to Pegu " leaving people to rebuild " the ruined city". Towards the end of the sixteenth century the town was taken by the king of Siam who appointed a governor over it and the surrounding country. Some years later the rulers of Martaban appear to have been almost independent but not strong enough to resist either Philip de Brito y Nicote, who had made himself master of Pegu, or the king of Ava who wrested the kingdom from him. From this time forward it remained the seat of a governor appointed by the monarch, Peguan or Burmese, who happened to rule the country.

During the first Burmese war a force under Lieutenant-Colonel Godwin was despatched against the town from Rangoon. The troops arrived off the place on the 29th November 1824 and after a mutual cannonade landed under a heavy fire and advanced to the attack ; the Burman garrison escaped without waiting for the assault and the British found the stockades deserted. A small detachment was sufficient to hold the position until the termination of the war when Arakan and the country east and south of the Salween were ceded to the British, but the intervening country from the Salween to the Arakan Roma mountains was restored to the Burman government.

On the breaking out of the second Anglo-Burmese war Martaban was one of the first places captured. On the 5th April 1852 the troops landed under the personal supervision of General Godwin, the Commander-in-Chief, and carried the works without the loss of a single man and with only eight wounded. On the 26th May following the Burmese advanced against the small garrison but were driven off with the aid of reinforcements sent across the river from Maulmain, and later, in July, were attacked in a position which they had taken up close by whence they were enabled to cause considerable annoyance and forced to abandon it. Early in the following year a column advanced from Martaban northwards and from that time the Burmese made no further attempt to re-take the town.

For several years it was the head-quarter station of the township and contained a Court-house. On the face of the hill opposite Maulmain is a good Circuit-house and below a substantial wooden wharf. On the bank of the Salween is an ancient pagoda, the Mya-thien-dan (*q.v.*), recently repaired and surmounted by a new gilt htee or umbrella. In 1877 the inhabitants numbered 1,673 souls.

MA-TOUNG-DA.—A revenue circle east of the Irrawaddy in the Mo-gnyo township of the Henzada district with the Mo-gnyo circle on the west, the Myoma and Myo-dweng circles on the north, the Kyek-taik circle of the Meng-hla township on the east and south-east, between it and the Pegu Roma mountains, and the Tshay-hnit and Lweng-byeng circles of the Meng-hla township on the south. The southern portion of the circle is low and subject to inundation during the rains but towards the north there is an extensive rice plain and some forest-covered land. In the west and centre of the circle are extensive Cutch (*Acacia catechu*) forests with some Teak and Htouk-kyan (*Terminalia macrocarpa*); in the east are found Teak and bamboos. In 1876 the population was 5,822, the land revenue Rs. 7,517, the capitation tax Rs. 5,425 and the gross revenue Rs. 16,951.

MA-TOUNG-DA.—A revenue circle in the Kan-oung township of the Henzada district, principally undulating and forest-covered but with some extensive rice cultivation, lying about half way between the Arakan mountains and the Irrawaddy, with the Rwe-doung circle on the north, the Gnyoung-rwa-gyee circle on the east, the Thek-ngay-byeng circle on the south, and the Tsee-beng, Shwe-gyeng and Gnyoung-rwa-ngay circles on the west; within its limits is the Dai-pai lake, about one square mile in extent and four or five feet deep in the dry weather. This circle now includes Tsan-rwa and Rwa-ta-ra. In 1876 the population was 3,046, the land revenue Rs. 3,317, the capitation tax Rs. 2,895 and the gross revenue Rs. 6,436.

MA-TOUNG-DA.—A revenue circle in the Prome district on the right bank of the Na-weng and separated from the Irrawaddy by the Koon-ma-leng circle. It now includes also Nat-ta-leng, Da-koo and Tsheng-daing. In 1876 the population was 1,228, the land revenue Rs. 1,249, the capitation tax Rs. 1,122 and the gross revenue Rs. 2,461.

MAULMAIN.—A town situated on the left bank of the Salween at its junction with Gyaing and the Attaran in 16° 29′ N. Lat. and 97° 38′ E. Long., the head-quarters of the Amherst district and of the Tenasserim division. Immediately to the west is Bhee-loo-gywon, a large island 107 square miles in extent, the waters of the Salween flowing westward into the Gulf of Martaban round the north of the island, between it and Martaban, by the Da-ray-bouk, and southward between it and the mainland on which stands Maulmain. This channel is sometimes called the Amherst and sometimes the Maulmain river but now, generally, "the Salween" *par excellence*. The position of this island thus conduces to the idea that the town lies a considerable distance up a river whereas in truth it is on the seacoast but with a large island lying immediately off it, protecting it from the force of the monsoon but shutting out all sea view. To the northward, on the opposite bank of the Salween, is Martaban, once the capital of a kingdom but now little more than a moderate sized village.

Low hills, forming the northern extremity of the Toung-gnyo range, run north and south through the town dividing it into two distinct and very dissimilar portions which touch each other at the northern base of the hills on the bank of the Gyaing. These are crowned at intervals with pagodas in various stages of preservation and decay, from the dark, brick, grass-covered and tottering relic with its rusty and falling htee to the white and gold restored edifice gleaming in the sunlight, and monasteries richly ornamented with gilding, colour and carved work. On the west are four out of the five "divisions" of the town, which extend northwards between the Salween and the hills, from Mopoon with its steam-mills for husking rice, and timber and ship-building yards, to the Military cantonment on the point formed by the junction of the Gyaing and the Salween opposite Martaban, a distance of six miles. Nowhere is the breadth greater than 1,200 yards. This portion, which throughout slopes to the bank of the Salween more or less abruptly, is intersected by three main roads running north and south; one extends the whole distance, with a single row of houses separating it from the Salween, the second, parallel and to the eastward, runs from the Cantonments for a little over a mile, and the third, still further to the east, at its northern end, on the border of the Cantonment, unites with the second and at its southern, near the northern entrance of Mopoon, with the first. Numerous cross roads running east and west up the slope from the Salween connect these three. In this portion are situated the public buildings, the Military Cantonments, the Merchants offices and warehouses, the principal shops and, especially on the western slopes of the hills, the houses of the European residents. The inhabitants are almost entirely Europeans, Eurasians, natives of India and Chinese. The "fifth division", or Daing-won-kweng, is more compact and lies behind the hills in the valley of the Attaran and, with its northern extremity resting on the Gyaing, stretches nearly to the bank of the former river; on the opposite shore is Gnyoung-beng-tshiep, a large village almost a suburb but not included within the limits of the town lands of which the Attaran forms the eastern boundary. This quarter, named after the notorious Daing-won who encamped here when he was sent down by the Burmese Government in 1808 to quell disturbances which had broken out in the south at Tavoy and Mergui, is inhabited principally by Burmans and Talaing.

Like most towns in the province, the houses, except near the bank of the Salween and in Daing-won-kweng, are surrounded by extensive grounds and are nestled in masses of foliage. The view from the hills in the centre of the town is of great beauty, probably unsurpassed in the whole of Burma. Looking westward the foreground is occupied by an extensive wood of trees of every shade of foliage from the dark olive of the mango to the light green of the pagoda tree varied by the graceful plumes of the bamboo with buildings shewing here and there, beyond lies a magnificent sheet of water studded with green islands amongst which stands out conspicuously the little rocky Goung-tsai-kywon completely occupied by one or two white and glittering pagodas and a monastery sheltered by trees, and in the distance, closing the view, are the forest-clad hills of Bhee-loo-gywon and Martaban. Eastward, at the foot of the hills, is a large and regularly laid out town lying on the edge of a rice plain from which, beyond the Attaran, rise isolated fantastically shaped ridges of limestone, bare in parts and elsewhere with the jagged peaks partially concealed by straggling clumps of vegetation and in the extreme distance the faint blue outline of the frowning Dawna spur. Away to the north are the Zwai-ka-beng rocks, an outcrop of limestone some 13 miles in length, too distant to allow an appreciation of their rugged beauty, whilst to the south rise the dark Toung-waing hills, their sombre colour relieved by the glistening white pagoda and the monasteries on their side. Winding through the plain are the Gyaing and the Attaran, shewing here and there like silver bands amongst the green shades of the hills and gardens and the golden tints of the rice fields.

The principal buildings are Salween House, built by Colonel Bogle as a private residence and now the property of the Municipality; the Hospital, a new and handsome wooden edifice nearly complete and destined to take the place of the inconvenient and small dispensary erected many years ago; the public offices of masonry; two churches of masonry for the Roman (dedicated, the one to S. Patrick built in 1857 to replace one built in 1836 and the other to S. Mark built in 1843) and one of wood for the Anglican branch of the Catholic Church (dedicated to S. Mathew and consecrated in 1834 by Bishop Wilson); a masonry Baptist chapel (built in 1833); a large Gaol; the wooden Barracks occupied by the Regiment of Madras Native Infantry which forms the garrison; and the Customhouse, the Post and Telegraph Offices, and the Master-Attendant's Office, all near the Main Wharf.

When this portion of the province was ceded by the treaty of Yandaboo, at the site of the town was found a spacious, irregular quadrangle surrounded by an earthen mound or rampart, all the rest was a mass of tangled tree and brush-wood forest and long grass, and men still living relate stories of the toil undergone and the difficulties surmounted in clearing it. The Civil Commissioner, Mr. Crawfurd, selected Amherst as the best spot for the capital of the newly acquired territory, but the Military Commander, General Sir Archibald Campbell, chose Maulmain as being better supplied with water and as being, from its position opposite Martaban then occupied by the Burmese, the best site, strategically, for the British garrison which was more required to overawe the Burmese officials across the river, to repel desultory attacks and to defend the left bank of the Salween from marauding parties than to keep order amongst the inhabitants of the ceded country. In a few years the Civil Station was moved up to the Cantonment and Maulmain from a waste gradually grew into a thriving commercial town.

The history of its rise and of its vicissitudes is best learned by studying its trade. Along the banks of the Attaran and in other parts of the Amherst district were rich and valuable Teak forests, whilst to the north, in Siamese territory (*Zengmai*), are vast tracts of country producing magnificent timber for which the only outlet is Maulmain. A large trade in Teak soon sprang up and for many years timber formed the principal and indeed the only article of export.

The amount of timber revenue realized was, in :—

		Rs.				Rs.
1836	..	20,804		1847-48	..	96,484
1839-40	..	21,728		1848-49	..	90,649
1840-41	..	29,245		1849-50	..	63,443
1841-42	..	55,108		1850-51	..	79,466
1842-43	..	58,924		1851-52	..	71,628
1843-44	..	54,182		1852-53	..	84,792
1844-45	..	23,711		1853-54	..	102,372
1845-46	..	61,867		1854-55	..	188,354
1846-47	..	88,869		1855-56	..	206,359

The export, in tons, from that year onwards was :—

1856-57	..	28,779		1867-68	..	62,255
1857-58	..	42,326		1868-69	..	98,333
1858-59	..	69,371		1869-70	..	64,769
1859-60	..	77,620		1870-71	..	53,904
1860-61	..	60,218		1871-72	..	57,000
1861-62	..	97,970		1872-73	..	78,657
1862-63	..	75,568		1873-74	..	86,361
1863-64	..	67,660		1874-75	..	76,639
1864-65	..	114,364		1875-76	..	105,154
1865-66	..	118,976		1876-77	..	78,573
1866-67	..	48,190		1877-78	..	123,242

With the gradual settlement of the country and the increase in the population and consequent increase in agriculture rice came into the market for exportation. In 1850 Europe took 18,058 bags, and the gross value of the exports in 1855-56 was Rs. 627,408. The quantity exported increased very largely, with some fluctuations due to the shipments taking place early or late and the returns being invariably closed on the same date.

The quantity, in tons, exported since 1854-55, and the greater quantity was to the United Kingdom, was :—

Year.		Tons.		Year.		Tons.
1855-56	..	16,170		1866-67	..	26,547
1856-57	..	19,405		1867-68	..	23,376
1857-58	..	24,714		1868-69	..	25,626
1858-59	..	16,163		1869-70	..	23,137
1859-60	..	17,766		1870-71	..	37,572
1860-61	..	11,284		1871-72	..	56,257
1861-62	..	28,615		1872-73	..	51,718
1862-63	..	21,492		1873-74	..	71,949
1863-64	..	16,114		1874-75	..	44,788
1864-65	..	21,567		1875-76	..	77,980
1865-66	..	23,670		1876-77	..	55,657

Cotton is exported mainly to Indian ports. In 1865-66 and in 1866-67 a few experimental exports were made to the United Kingdom but the venture was not a paying one. The quantity, in tons, exported in each year from 1854-55 was :—

Year.		Cwt.		Year.		Cwt.
1855-56	..	1,929		1866-67	..	2,902
1856-57	..	5,194		1867-68	..	2,210
1857-58	..	1,376		1868-69	..	4,365
1858-59	..	2,465		1869-70	..	3,813
1859-60	..	2,348		1870-71	..	2,190
1860-61	..	1,442		1871-72	..	1,238
1861-62	..	1,523		1872-73	..	5,259
1862-63	..	1,685		1873-74	..	2,700
1863-64	..	2,058		1874-75	..	1,768
1864-65	..	4,295		1875-76	..	1,491
1865-66	..	1,575l		1876-77	..	2,059

Besides timber, grain and cotton the principal exports are hides and horns with very small quantities of lead, copper, yellow orpiment and stick lac.

The principal imports are cotton twist and yarn, cotton, woollen and silk piece goods, wines, beer and spirits, sugar and betel nuts, the last fetching a higher price than those grown in the country. A noticeable feature is the absence of salt from the list of imports, more than one ship has arrived with this commodity but there has been no sale for it, the country article holding its own as it does nowhere else in this Province.

The value of the imports and exports, the amount of duty realized and the number and tonnage of the ships visiting the port are given in the following tables:—

Value of Imports and Exports of Merchandize and Treasure.

	1855-56.			1856-57.			1857-58.			1858-59.		
	Rs.	A.	P.	Rs.	A.	P.	Rs.	A.	P.	Rs.	A.	P.
Imports.												
Merchandize	32,60,756	0	0	39,55,148	0	0	39,37,903	0	0	24,16,108	0	0
Treasure	3,22,262	0	0	10,81,600	0	0	14,58,975	0	0	30,89,602	0	0
Total	35,83,018	0	0	50,36,748	0	0	53,96,878	0	0	55,05,710	0	0
Exports.												
Merchandize	41,73,453	0	0	51,03,632	0	0	55,09,534	0	0	55,76,321	0	0
Treasure	2,17,464	0	0	2,17,128	0	0	2,76,675	0	0	1,97,538	0	0
Total	43,90,917	0	0	53,20,760	0	0	57,86,209	0	0	57,73,859	0	0
GRAND TOTAL	79,73,935	0	0	1,03,57,508	0	0	1,11,83,087	0	0	1,12,79,569	0	0
Duty realized on Imports	58,437	0	0	74,853	0	0	62,551	0	0	53,410	0	0
Ditto Exports	15,427	0	0	17,321	0	0	21,100	0	0	19,774	0	0
Total duty	73,864	0	0	92,174	0	0	83,651	0	0	73,184	0	0

Value of Imports and Exports of Merchandize and Treasure—(Continued).

	1859-60.			1860-61.			1861-62.			1862-63.			1863-64.			1864-65.		
	Rs.	A.	P.	Rs.	A.	P.	Rs.	A.	P.	Rs.	A.	P.	Rs,	A.	P.	Rs.	A.	P.
Imports.																		
Merchandize ..	35,10,477	0	0	33,80,714	0	0	37,97,452	0	0	34,23,279	0	0	33,32,070	0	0	41,08,485	0	0
Treasure ..	24,20,118	0	0	19,21,627	0	0	44,39,035	0	0	21,13,068	0	0	15,52,359	0	?	28,21,729	0	0
Total .	59,30,595	0	0	53,02,341	0	0	82,36,487	0	0	55,36,241	0	0	48,84,429	0	0	69,30,214	0	0
Exports.																		
Merchandize ..	48,30,962	0	0	43,36,697	0	0	76,99,667	0	0	60,64,901	0	0	53,22,962	0	0	86,78,470	0	0
Treasure ..	1,35,469	0	0	1,27,019	0	0	1,13,313	0	0	76,348	0	0	96,276	0	0	69,892	0	0
Total ..	49,66,431	0	0	44,63,717	0	0	78,12,980	0	0	61,41,249	0	0	54,19,239	0	0	87,48,362	0	0
GRAND TOTAL ..	1,08,97,026	0	0	97,66,059	0	0	1,60,49,468	0	0	1,16,77,490	0	0	1,03,03,669	0	0	1,56,78,576	0	0
Duty realized on Imports	62,342	0	0	67,693	0	0	54,328	0	0	51,873	0	0	49,135	0	0	56,362	0	0
Ditto Exports	53,057	0	C	32,789	0	0	68,085	0	0	58,671	0	0	45,613	0	0	60,034	0	0
Total duty ..	1,15,393	0	0	10,482	0	0	1,22,413	0	0	1,10,544	0	0	94,748	0	0	1,16,396	0	0

Value of Imports and Exports of Merchandize and Treasure—(continued).

Imports.	1865-66.			1866-67.			1867-68.			1868-69.			1869-70.			1870-71.		
	Rs.	A.	P.	Rs.	A.	P.	Rs.	A.	P.	Rs.	A.	P.	Rs.	A.	P.	Rs.	A.	P.
Merchandize ..	44,40,033	0	0	44,90,146	0	0	46,79,377	0	0	44,93,954	0	0	44,06,681	0	0	41,88,911	0	0
Treasure for Government	59,500	0	0	2,09,000	0	0	1,89,400	0	0	9,03,000	0	0	683,600	0	0	7,46,000	0	0
Ditto private persons	34,52,962	0	0	12,72,792	0	0	14,83,396	0	0	13,63,730	0	0	9,87,474	0	0	12,32,680	0	0
Total ..	79,52,495	0	0	59,71,938	0	0	63,52,173	0	0	67,60,684	0	0	60,77,755	0	0	61,67,391	0	0
Exports.																		
Merchandize ..	94,37,989	0	0	53,85,413	0	0	59,05,145	0	0	82,58,575	0	0	61,28,777	0	0	60,96,613	0	0
Treasure ..	99,378	0	0	3,46,525	0	0	1,38,581	0	0	1,39,557	0	0	278,227	0	0	1,23,727	0	0
Total ..	95,37,367	0	0	56,31,938	0	0	60,43,726	0	0	83,98,132	0	0	64,07,004	0	0	62,20,340	0	0
Grand Total ..	1,74,89,862	0	0	116,03,876	0	0	1,23,95,899	0	0	1,51,58,816	0	0	1,24,84,759	0	0	1,23,87,931	0	0
Duty realized on Imports	56,667	0	0	50,877	0	0	57,052	0	0	50,826	0	0	54,667	0	0	40,663	0	0
Ditto Exports	46,710	0	0	39,730	0	0	62,264	0	0	81,434	0	0	66,326	0	0	1,58,715	0	0
Total duty ..	1,03,377	0	0	90,607	0	0	1,11,369	0	0	1,41,260	0	0	1,20,993	0	0	1,99,378	0	0

Value of Imports and Exports of Merchandize and Treasure—(concluded).

	1871-72.			1872-73.			1873-74.			1874-75.			1875-76.			1876-77.		
Imports.	Rs.	A.	P.	Rs.	A.	P.	Rs.	A.	P.	Rs.	A.	P.	Ro.	A.	P.	Rs.	A	P.
Merchandize ..	42,86,890	0	0	49,25,595	0	0	56,12,878	0	0	61,47,940	0	0	61,61,684	0	0	65,20,371	0	0
Treasure for Government	12,85,000	0	0	19,03,649	0	0	18,98,000	0	0	1,33,500	0	0	1,65,000	0	0	2,65,000	0	0
Ditto private persons	9,17,589	0	0	10,79,793	0	0	28,74,100	0	0	28,26,700	0	0	37,19,714	0	0	31,57,596	0	0
Total ..	64,89,479	0	0	79,09,087	0	0	1,04,84,978	0	0	90,98,140	0	0	1,00,46,398	0	0	99,42,967	0	0
Exports.																		
Merchandize ..	70,72,033	0	0	83,14,212	0	0	1,16,78,826	0	0	87,11,095	0	0	121,02,650	0	0	90,88,046	0	0
Treasure ..	1,35,408	0	0	1,80,440	0	0	2,62,303	0	0	5,55,286	0	0	90,443	0	0	1,25,745	0	0
Total ..	72,07,441	0	0	84,94,652	0	0	1,99,41,129	0	0	92,66,381	0	0	1,21,93,093	0	0	92,13,791	0	0
GRAND TOTAL ..	1,36,46,920	0	0	1,64,63,689	0	0	2,24,26,107	0	0	1,83,64,521	0	0	2,22,39,491	0	0	1,91,56,758	0	0
Duty realized on Imports	38,262	0	0	94,235	0	0	97,816	0	0	99,221	0	0	80,010	0	0	95,910	0	0
Ditto Exports	2,65,580	0	0	2,58,376	0	0	1,89,775	0	0	1,68,525	0	0	3,92,241	0	0	2,59,656	0	0
Total duty ..	3,03,842	0	0	3,52,611	0	0	2,87,591	0	0	2,66,746	0	0	4,72,251	0	0	3,55,566	0	0

Number and Tonnage of Vessels arriving at and leaving Maulmain.

	1855-56.		1856-57.		1857-58.		1858-59.		1859-60.		1860-61.		1861-62.	
	No.	Tonnage.	No.	Tonnage.	No.	Tonnage.	No.	Tonnage.	No.	Tonnage.	No.	Tonnage.	No.	Tonnage.
Departures ..	322	72,645	323	83,678	367	112,837	317	106,882	283	88,705	255	71,644	454	146,032
Arrivals ..	342	81,241	311	83,199	413	143,043	320	117,718	286	90,419	274	83,469	460	163,647
Total ..	664	153,886	634	166,877	780	255,870	637	124,600	569	179,194	529	155,113	914	309,679

Number and Tonnage of Vessels arriving at and leaving Maulmain—(continued).

	1862-63.		1863-64.		1864-65.		1865-66.		1866-67.		1867-78.		1868-69.	
	No.	Tonnage.	No.	Tonnage.	No.	Tonnage.	No.	Tonnage.	No.	Tonnage.	No.	Tonnage.	No.	Tonnage.
Departures ..	448	126,571	470	144,497	54	185,700	592	207,684	439	128,043	479	182,629	592	167,510
Arrivals ..	440	131,788	433	146,809	579	213,091	519	185,331	416	131,977	419	114,649	536	168,329
Total ..	883	258,360	903	391,306	1,120	398,851	1,118	393,015	855	259,020	898	247,278	1,128	335,849

Number and Tonnage of Vessels arriving at and leaving Maulmain—(concluded).

	1869-70.		1870-71.		1871-72.		1872-73.		1873-74.		1874-75.		1875-76.	
	No.	Tonnage.	No.	Tonnage.	No.	Tonnage.	No.	Tonnage.	No.	Tonnage.	No.	Tonnage.	No.	Tonnage.
Departures ..	535	139,201	518	141,520	566	163,066	573	160,295	551	197,372	509	190,758	617	266,242
Arrivals ..	450	144,263	469	144,575	472	162,947	502	171,018	506	201,487	474	189,895	584	2 55,313
Total ..	983	280,464	978	295,095	1,188	293,014	1,075	351,313	1,057	398,859	988	380,653	1,151	521,555

Ship-building commenced as early as 1830 when the *Devil*, a schooner of 51 tons, was built by Mr. Warrick. This was followed by the *Woodlark*, a Barque of 250 tons, built in 1832; the *Young Rover*, Schooner, 157 tons, the *Concordia*, Brig, 75 tons and the *George Swinton*, Schooner 70 tons, in 1833, also by Mr. Warrick, and the *Attaran*, Schooner, 70 tons, constructed in the same year by Messrs. Darwood and Bentley. The number of vessels and gross tonnage built in each year since have been :—

Year.		Number.	Gross tonnage.	Year.		Number.	Gross tonnage.
1834	..	4	815	1856	..	2	1,672
1835	..	2	664	1857	..	4	963
1836	..	7	683	1858	..	5	1,797
1837	..	10	2,852	1859	..	..	..
1838	..	10	3,837	1860	..	..	..
1839	..	9	2,070	1861	..	1	858
1840	..	10	2,844	1862	..	1	395
1841	..	6	1,542	1863	..	1	36
1842	..	8	3,165	1864	..	2	833
1843	..	7	2,297	1865	..	..	..
1844	..	3	833	1866	..	..	..
1845	..	4	1,816	1867	..	..	..
1846	..	5	2,267	1868	..	..	..
1847	..	2	555	1869	..	1	51
1848	..	3	1,280	1870	..	1	73
1849	..	4	2,115	1871	..	..	..
1850	..	1	19	1872	..	..	..
1851	..	5	737	1873	..	2	208
1852	..	7	2,492	1874	..	..	..
1853	..	10	4,527	1875	..	2	222
1854	..	4	1,928*	1876	..	..	..
1855	..	2	1,472	1877	..	1	174

The most important amongst these were the steamer *Tenasserim* of 750 tons built in 1841, the steamer *Malacca* of 1,300 tons built in 1853, the ship *Canning* of 1,022 tons built in 1854, the ship *Copenhagen* of 1,017 tons built in 1855, and the ship *Cospatrick* of 1,418 tons built in 1856, and burnt on a voyage with emigrants from England to Australia.

No earlier statistics of the population are available than those of 1839 when there were 17,022 inhabitants, in 1841 there were, 28,685, in 1848 there were, according to the census taken that year, 36,898, and in 1857 23,683 ; since 1862-63 the number has been :—

Years.		Number.	Years.		Number.
1863-64	..	60,889.	1870-71	..	62,337.
1864-65	..	69,386.	1871-72	..	53,653.
1865-66	..	70,349.	1872-73	..	46,472.
1866-67	..	61,429.	1873-74	..	58,873.
1867-68	..	65,566.	1874-75	..	63,841.
1868-69	..	66,022.	1875-76	..	57,719.
1869-70	..	71,534.	1876-77	..	51,607.

* Exclusive of the barque *City of Dublin* the tonnage of which is not now ascertainable.

Men of almost every nation are to be found : English, French, Germans, Dutch, Belgians, Norwegians, Swedes, Greeks, Danes, Americans, Persians, Chinese, Burmans, Shans, and Hindustanis; the numbers in 1872 and in 1878 were :—

YEAR.	Europeans.	Americans.	Eurasians.	Armenians.	Chinese.	Natives of India.	Burmans.	Talaing.	Kareng.	Shan.	Toungthoo.	Total.
1872	652	14	1,534	9	1,484	18,635	11,115	12,162	180	633	54	46,472
1878	*1,279	...	...	...	2,324	1,562	9,607	16,120	106	1,279	...	54,333

The revenue, derived from the Night-watch tax and other local sources, was employed in paying for the Police, in keeping the roads in order and in carrying out such works as were found necessary from time to time, and was administered by the Magistrate under the control of the Commissioner. In 1874 the town was placed under a Municipality with members partly official and partly non-official nominated by the Local Government, and with the Town Magistrate as President. The system of taxation was changed : the Night-watch tax, levied at a fixed rate, was abolished in 1875-76, and a Municipal tax substituted, and gradually, as has been deemed advisable, further changes have been made in altering the rates and in the imposition of new ones for specific objects, such as providing for watering the roads. The actual sources of income at present are, a Municipal tax, receipts from licenses for the wholesale and for the retail vend of intoxicating liquors, slaughter-house licenses, hack-carriage licenses, hack-cart licenses, passenger-boat licenses, the leasing of ferries, land-rent for lands belonging to the Government but administered by the Municipality, sales of land, certain fines and fees, such as fines for breaches of local and license rules, fines for committing nuisances, gambling fines and escheats, cattle-pound fees and fines, and other miscellaneous sources including an annual assignment from the Land Sale Fund. The charges are for collection of taxes and cesses, Police, general management, pay of vaccinators, a health officer, a conservancy establishment, watering roads, surveys, rewards, construction and repairs of roads and bridges and of pounds. The receipts and charges in 1866-67, and during the last three years have been in rupees :—

	1866-67.	1875-76.	1876-77.	1877-78.
Receipts	59,044†	126,817	145,545	114,162
Charges	82,528	106,589	166,766	107,342

* Includes Eurasians.   † Includes a loan of Rs. 10,000.

At the end of 1867-68 the town was Rs. 19,944 in debt but at the end of 1877-78 had a surplus balance of Rs. 6,920.

There is still much room for the expenditure of funds. The roads, owing to their inclination down the slope towards the Salween, require extensive and expensive annual repairs, and nothing could well be more faulty or dangerous than the conservancy system : a system of long-used cesspits, never cleaned, and intermixed with the wells (in some places they are in almost immediate proximity to each other) from which the inhabitants obtain their drinking-water. The outcry in England regarding cesspools and wells has been great and terribly startling facts have been brought to notice but in no single instance has anything so bad been disclosed there as exists here. The streets are watered and the town is to be lighted with oil lamps, and at the present moment several schemes for obtaining a supply of pure water from a distance are under consideration. But the full, nay running over, cesspits are still in use and are to remain so till there is more unanimity amongst the Municipal Commissioners as to how the night-soil shall be disposed of.

The existing rate of taxation per head of population is Rs. 1-11-7.

MAW-RWA.—A village in the Lamoo-lek-ya circle of the Northern township, Sandoway district, on the La-moo river, about 10 miles from its mouth, with a population of 1,070 souls in 1877. The village is accessible by land and by water.

MAW-TOON.—A village in the Tenasserim circle of the Tenasserim township, Mergui district, 16 miles N. W. of Tenasserim, on the right bank of the Tenasserim river. The inhabitants, who numbered 633 souls in 1877, are all cultivators.

MA-YAN.—A small village in the Angyee township of the Rangoon district, remarkable only as having given its name to a quarter of the town of Maulmain (Ma-yan-goon) to which most of its inhabitants fled after the close of the first Burmese war.

MA-YA-TSEN.—A very extensive revenue circle in the extreme north of the Kyouk-hpyoo township of the Kyouk-hpyoo district, lying on the north-eastern shore of Kyouk-hpyoo harbour and consisting of numerous closely-adjoining islands. It is rather more than 45 square miles in extent and has a population of 2,558 souls. In 1876-77 the land revenue was Rs. 2,380, the capitation tax Rs. 3,148 and the gross revenue Rs. 6,482.

MA-YEN-ZA-YA.—A revenue circle in the Rangoon district extending eastwards from the Pegu Roma to the new Pegu and Tsit-toung canal, having the Shwe-gyeng district on the north and east ; from this it is separated by the Bhaw-nee-ga-le stream from its source to the Pegu and Toung-ngoo road, thence by that road to a little north of the village of Pyeng-boon-gyee, thence by the embankment which stretches across the plains to Myit-kyo on the bank of the Tsit-toung and thence, southwards, by the canal. On the south is the Pegu Myoma circle. On the west the country is hilly and forest-clad but east of the Pegu and Toung-ngoo road it is an extensive grass-covered plain (intersected by numerous streams, all connected with the Pyeng-boon-gyee, the Wom-bhai-eng or the Bhoora-ga-le which rise in the west and carry off the drainage of the Pegu hills) for the most part under water during the rains and forming valuable fisheries but with a few spots sufficiently raised to be cultivated with rice. The principal villages are Pyeng-boon-gyee, with 926 inhabitants in 1877, and Bhoora-ga-le, about eight miles further south on the main road, with 249 inhabitants. The population, the area under cultivation and the revenue during the last five years have been :—

YEAR.	AREA, IN ACRES.					REVENUE, IN RUPEES.			
	Rice.	Fallow.	Garden.	Miscellaneous.	Total.	Land.	Capitation.	All other items.	Total.
1873-74	14,206	65	79	70	14,426	14,168	7,410	16,663	38,241
1874-75	17,755	26	42	97	17,920	17,053	8,000	18,941	43,994
1875-76	18,353	77	59	80	18,569	32,313	7,638	4,679	44,630
1876-77	18,194	146	68	116	18,524	17,303	7,996	16,457	41,750
1877-78	17,236	723	84	111	18,154	16,388	8,270	17,071	41,729

and the agricultural stock :—

YEAR.	Buffaloes.	Cows, bulls, and bullocks.	Sheep and Goats.	Pigs.	Ploughs.	Carts.	Boats.
1873-74	2,406	479		41	543	505	32
1874-75	3,191	586	9	23	773	664	9
1875-76	3,777	762		19	844	703	17
1876-77	3,412	1,125		20	839	737	11
1877-78	1,993	759		10	407	401	16

The circle received its present boundaries in 1877, when a small tract in the north-west was added to and a small tract in the north-east taken from the Shwe-gyeng district. The forest-clad hills on the west afford a comparatively safe and easy retreat for out-laws and on several occasions gangs of robbers have formed and sought shelter here, harboured and assisted by some of the Kareng who occupy the villages between the Pegu river and the Pegu and Toung-ngoo road and by the inhabitants of Pyeng-boon-gyee, Wom-bhai-eng and Bhoora-ga-le on that road. It was in attacking one of these bands to the north-east of Bhoora-ga-le that Lieutenant-Colonel Hamilton, the Inspector-General of Police, was killed in 1874.

MAY-KHA-RE.—A small river in the Bassein district which rises in the Arakan mountains, about 13 miles from Pagoda Point, and after an almost southerly course of about 12 miles, past four or five villages surrounded with rice fields, falls into the Bassein river opposite Haing-gyee or Negrais Island. It is tidal as far as Dee-tsoon-rwa, 10 miles up, to which village boats of 300 bushels burden can ascend.

MA-YOO.—A river in Arakan which rises in the hills near the northe'n boundary of the Akyab district and, flowing with a general N. and S. direction, falls into the Bay of Bengal to the N. W. of Akyab Island between the Naaf and the Koo-la-dan. For 50 miles up it has more the appearance of an arm of the sea than of a river. Its mouth is about three miles broad. The entrance is rendered dangerous for vessels of any but the smallest draft by rocks and shoals : the passage used by native boats is in shore on the northern side.

MEE-GA-LOON.—A revenue circle in the Gyaing Attaran township, Amherst district, lying in the angle formed by the Houng-tha-raw and the Gyaing. To the south, and separated from it by an imaginary line only, is the Doo-tie-ya Kha-reng circle and to the westward, separated from it by low hills, is the Pa-ta-ma Kha-reng circle : it now includes Loung-kaing. Its inhabitants are mainly Talaing and numbered 1,859 in 1876-77 when the land revenue was Rs. 3,522 and the capitation tax Rs. 2,147.

MEE-GA-THAT.—A small river in the Amherst district, a tributary of the Za-mie ; rising in the main range to the eastward it enters British territory in 15° 22' 42" N. and 98° 37' 10" E. Its course is about west.

MEE-GYOUNG.—A village in the Kywon-khyoung circle, Thee-kweng township, Bassein district, in 16° 52' 30" N. and 94° 58' E. in the middle of extensive rice fields. The inhabitants, most of whom are Burmans, are engaged mainly in cultivation.

MEE-GYOUNG-RE.—A revenue circle in the Prome district immediately south of the town of Prome and lying along the left bank of the Irrawaddy, containing principally fruit gardens. Two of the old village tracts are included in this circle, viz., Tsaw-oo-tat and Htee-beng. In 1876 the population numbered 914, the land revenue was Rs. 942, the capitation tax Rs. 1,005 and the gross revenue Rs. 2,481.

MEE-HTA-GYIT.—A small river in the Amherst district which falls into the Za-mie from the westward near the village of Kan-nee. It has a valuable Teak forest on its banks.

MEE-TAN.—A small river in the Amherst district which rises in the western slopes of the Moo-lai-yit mountain and after a short westerly course falls into the Houng-tha-raw a few miles above the mouth of the Mai-ka-la.

MEE-THWE-BOOT.—A village of some 90 houses in the Thai-daw circle, Thayet township, Thayet district, on the right bank of the Irrawaddy at the mouth of the Mee-thwe-boot stream, between Htan-doung and Thayet-myo.

MEE-THWE-BOOT.—A small river in the Thayet district which rises in the eastern slopes of the Arakan mountains and, receiving the waters of numerous mountain rivulets, flows eastward and falls into the Irrawaddy just below the town of Thayet, at the village of Mee-thwe-boot. It is not navigable except during the rains and then only by small boats and for two or three miles.

MEE-ZAN.—A revenue circle in the Amherst district extending along the left bank of the Salween northwards from the Hpa-an stream, with the Shwe-gwon circle on the north and the Htee-loon circle on the east. It now includes Kaw-htaw. In 1876 the population was 1,942, the land revenue Rs. 2,087 and the capitation tax Rs. 2,095.

MENG-BOO.—A small river in the Henzada district, Pegu division, which rises in the slopes of the Shan-ma-toung spur of the Pegu Roma in about 18° 30′ N. Lat. and after a south-westerly course of about 30 miles falls into the Myit-ma-kha near the village of Kyouk-wa. Its banks are sleep and its bed sandy and rocky, but in the rains it is navigable for some distance from its mouth by boats of 150 bushels burden. It taps a country in which are some fine Teak tracts.

MENG-BRA.—A township in the Akyab district divided into 15 revenue circles, lying south of Mro-houng and adjoining the Kyouk-hpyoo district, to which a few years ago several circles from this township were added (See Kyouk-hpyoo district—Administrvtion). On the west is the Oo-rit-toung (East) township and on the east the Arakan Hill Tracts. In the south the soil is good, the cultivation extensive, and the country highly intersected by navigable creeks which serve the purpose of roads ; portions are liable to inundation at high tides. In 1876-77 the population numbered 26,893 souls and the revenue was Rs. 92,775 (Rs. 57,840 from land, Rs. 30,784 from capitation tax and Rs. 4,151 from other sources).

MENG-BYENG.—A village of about 70 houses in the Poo-hto circle, Ka-ma township, Thayet district, on the right bank of the Irrawaddy, between Ka-ma and Poo-hto.

MENG-DAI.—A little village of nearly 20 houses in the Meng-dai township, Thayet district, on the Mee-thwe-boot stream, in which a small police force of nine or ten men is stationed.

MENG-DAI.—A village in the Tham-ba-ya circle, Ka-ma township, Thayet district, containing about 90 houses, lying in the lower portion of the valley of the Ma-htoon and between that river and the Hnget-the spur on the S. W. It was originally an independent circle but in 1862, on the resignation of the then Thoogyee, it was added to O-shit-goon, itself since joined to Tham-ba-ya.

MENG-DAI.—A revenue circle in the Thayet township, Thayet district, in the valley of the Mee-thwe-boot stream, to the west of Thai-daw, of late years joined to Moon-za-lie.

MENG-DAI.—A revenue circle in the Prome district stretching north-east from the bank of the Irrawaddy, about eight miles below Prome, to the Prome hills. The country is generally hilly and covered with forest. In the western corner is the Meng-dai quarter of the large town of Shwe-doung, and in the river just opposite is Meng-dai island which forms a portion of this circle. It now includes Za-loon and in 1876-77 the population was 7,169, the capitation tax Rs. 6,970, the land revenue Rs. 1,934 and the gross revenue Rs. 9,535.

MENG-DAT.—A revenue circle in the Meng-doon township, Thayet district. In the Burmese time it contained eight village tracts and was under a Myo-thoogyee subordinate to the Won of Meng-doon. The frontier line chosen by Lord Dalhousie cut Meng-dat in half ; four of the eight tracts remained to the king of Burma and the four which were annexed were made into one circle under one Thoogyee. In the war of 1825 the

Meng-dat Myo-thoogyee fought well against the English; in the war of 1852 his grandson, who had succeeded him in the Myo-thoogyeeship, followed his example and subsequently, on the annexation of Pegu, declined to take office under the British and retired to Upper Burma. The circle covers an area of 27 square miles, of which only some 4,000 acres are culturable (about 2,200 acres actually cultivated) the remainder being hilly and covered with forest :—Teak, Cutch, Palm, Eng-gyeng (*Pentacme Siamensis*) and bamboos. Such cultivation as there is is largely in hill clearings. The soil generally consists of a light slate-coloured clay (in some parts red) mixed with a good deal of sand and here and there pebbles and gravel occur ; the low sandy ground close to the Pa-nee stream is covered with tobacco and vegetable gardens. The population a few years ago numbered 1,504 souls living in 583 houses in 27 villages ; in 1872 it numbered 3,445 souls (2,111 Burmese and 1,334 Khyeng) living in 831 houses in 36 villages, and in 1876 2,596. The revenue in 1876-77 was Rs. 2,390 (land revenue Rs. 763, capitation tax Rs. 1,569 and other taxes and rates Rs. 58.) The products are rice, sessamum, cotton, maize, tobacco and chillies.

MENG-DOON.—A town in the Thayet district in 18° 20′ 12″ N. Lat. and 94° 4′ 74″ E. Long., the head-quarters of the Meng-doon township. It is a pretty little town situated on high land amongst hills on one of the bends of the Ma-htoon river within a few miles of the Arakan mountains. In the Burmese time a Won was stationed here with jurisdiction over "the seven districts at the foot of the hills" (*See Meng-doon township*). After the annexation it was placed under an Extra Assistant Commissioner of the 3rd class, and now an Extra Assistant Commissioner of the 2nd class holds his court here. It has not increased during British rule and now has a population of about 1,600 souls engaged chiefly in agriculture. For some years after the annexation it was occupied by a military force, detached from Thayet-myo ; this was relieved by a detachment of the Pegu light infantry, recruited amongst the Burmans, which was subsequently withdrawn and replaced by police.

According to the current legend the town was founded *circa* 100 A.D. by Tha-moon-da-rie, a fugitive prince of Prome, and was called Bhoom-ma-wa-dee, the Ma-htoon being called Tha-man-da-na-dee and the Prince's palace in the town Ze-yan-bhoon-tha. After reigning in Bhoom-ma-wa-dee for seven years Tha-moon-da-rie, having appointed his uncle, Ze-ta-koo-ta, as Governor, went north and founded the subsequently flourishing kingdom of Pagan.

MENG-DOON.—A township in the Thayet district between Lat. 19° 5′ and 19° 30′ N. and Long. 94° 30′ and 94° 45′ E.

It contains an area of 708 square miles and is bounded on the north by Upper Burma, on the west by the Arakan mountains, on the east by the township of Thayet and on the south by that of Ka-ma.

Its cultivated area in 1871-72 was :—

				Acres.
Rice land	..	..	..	1,162
Gardens	..	..	..	857
Miscellaneous cultivation	..	..	..	4,356
		Total	..	6,375

There were also 3,638 toungya and 3,585 trees assessed separately for revenue.

The revenue was :—

		Rs.
Land revenue	.. ..	12,842
Capitation tax	.. ..	16,195
	Total Rs...	29,037

The population, by the census of 1872, amounted to 26,165 souls, of whom 20,804 were Burmans and 5,361 Khyeng, living in 5,877 houses in 217 villages.

It contained the following cattle :—

Buffaloes ..	.. ..	2,723
Bulls, bullocks and cows	.. .. ..	27,490
	Total ..	30,213

It contains 45 registered village tracts which are now divided amongst nine Thoogyee.

The area under cultivation, revenue, population and agricultural stock in 1876-77 were :—

AREA, IN ACRES.				REVENUE, IN RUPEES.				STOCK.				
Rice.	Garden.	Miscellaneous.	Total.	Land.	Capitation.	All other rates and taxes.	Total.	Buffaloes.	Cows, bulls and bullocks.	Houses.	Villages.	Population.
10,178	653	3,634	14,485	16,962	17,132	2,064	37,964	3,854	17,535	5,982	210	26,039

The present township of Meng-doon, or Meng-doon *cum* Meng-dat, comprises portions of the Burmese districts of Meng-doon, Taing-da and Meng-dat. Proceeding from the east the frontier line cut Meng-dat in two, leaving about one-third to the Burmans and taking the other two-thirds into British territory. It then cut off a very small portion of the north-east corner of the Meng-doon district which it left to Burma, then included a small bit of the southern part of Taing-da in British territory, and then, cutting through Meng-doon, again left the north-west corner of that township to the Burmans. Our township, therefore, includes nearly the whole of the old Meng-doon township, a very small piece of Taing-da and two-thirds of Meng-dat.

Meng-doon is said to derive its name from an event which occurred at a very early period of Burman history. Two sons of Ma-noo-raza, king of Tha-htoon, rebelled against their father and took refuge with the Pyoo-thek, who then inhabited this part of the country. From this circumstance the place became known afterwards as Meng-poon (Prince's hiding-place) subsequently corrupted to Meng-doon. Meng-dat was the place where these princes collected a force of cavalry, hence it was called Myeng-dat (cavalry camp) subsequently corrupted to Meng-dat.

In later times under the Burmese Government Meng-doon was the residence of a Won, a provincial governor of high rank with full power of life and death, who had jurisdiction over Meng-dat, Taing-da, Myo-thit, Pa-dien, Ma-bhai and Nan-tay as well as Meng-doon*. At the settlement of 1783 A.D., there were two Myo-thoogyee in Meng-doon, one of the north and one of the south ; 20 years later the number was reduced and Moung Htwe-hla, the Myo-thoogyee of the north, was removed and Moung Wa, the Myo-thoogyee of the south, remained in office. His descendant, Moung Kee, was in office at the time of the annexation. He fled to Upper Burma and refused to take service under the English Government although invited to do so by the Commissioner. One of his sons is now the Tsit-kai of Taing-da Toung-tsen in Upper Burma but some of his relatives still reside about Meng-doon. No head-men of circles (Taik Thoogyee) came between the Myo-thoogyee and the village head-men (Rwa-thoogyee) in this township but at the town of Meng-doon there resided a numerous staff of officials round the Won. These were a Tsit-kai (subordinate Judge), Na-khan, Tsa-re-gyee (secretaries), Won-tsa-re (clerks to the Won), a Myo-ook, sometimes called Myo-won, a Htoung-hmoo (Gaoler) and a Khoon (superior Judge).

There were 37 hereditary village Thoogyee in 1783 A.D. but the hereditary system does not appear to have struck root very firmly for at the time of the annexation (1854) the number had been reduced to eight and now there are only four left. Although the annexation of Pegu was proclaimed in December 1852 Meng-doon and Meng-dat were not brought under British administration until March 1854 when the then Commissioner of Pegu (now Sir A. P. Phayre) marched there with a small force, took possession of the township, and personally made all the necessary arrangements for its future administration. One Nga Noung, who had been a Government dacoit† in the Burmese time, was at first made both Myo-ook and Thoogyee of Meng-dat and he was shortly afterwards removed in the same capacity to Meng-doon, but his native habits could not be eradicated and he was soon dismissed for embezzlement, on which he returned to his old avocation of dacoit chief in Upper Burma. The present Extra Assistant Commissioner of Meng-doon, Moung Tshouk, was then appointed in his place.

Meng-dat in the Burmese time was under a Myo-thoogyee who was subordinate to the Won of Meng-doon. He had under him eight village Thoogyee, all appointed hereditarily in 1783 A.D. Four only of these village Thoogyee's jurisdictions are now included in British Burma the other four being beyond the frontier line.

In the war of 1825 the Meng-dat Myo-thoogyee, Moung Shwe-oo, was a man of some note. He served against the British with 500 men from Meng-dat and is said to have gained some success at Pan-wa. His grand-

---

* Called the " seven Districts along the Hill" (Toung-tsen Khoo-hnit Kha-raing).

† Most Burman Governors have among their recognized followers one called the dacoit officer (Dha-mya Bo) who is allowed to commit dacoities, on fitting opportunities, with impunity, a share of the spoil, of course, belonging to the Governor.

son, Moung Kareng, was Myo-thoogyee in the second war. He refused to take office under the British Government and retired to Upper Burma on the annexation of the Province. The hereditary system among the Thoogyee had taken as little root here as in Meng-doon, for all the four village Thoogyeeships included within our boundary were held by strangers at the time of the annexation.

When the second war broke out the Won of Meng-doon, Moung Shwe-gnyo, was invested with authority over Tsa-goo, Tsa-laing, Kya-beng and Lay-gaing, as well as over the seven hill districts of Meng-doon. He collected a force of 10,000 men, but did nothing with it. Some of the force mutinied, there was internal fighting, and the Won died at Ma-bhai.

The following table shews the villages which were registered in 1145 B.E., 1783 A.D. and the names of the circles in which they are at present included :—

Registered villages.						Present circle.
Lek-pa-daing						Kyan,
Keng-bwon-toung						ditto.
Kyan						dttto.
Ta-ma						ditto.
Rwa-tha						ditto.
Ka-tswon-myoung						Koo-byoo,
Moo						ditto.
Pan-gnyo						ditto.
Oo-yeen-boo						ditto.
Tha-dwon-gyee						ditto.
Tha-dwon-ngay						ditto.
Doo						ditto.
Meng-rwa-gaing						Meng-doon.
Kaing-ngay						ditto.
Myoung-gyee						ditto.
Tsa-ga-dai						Ma-oo-daing,
Ma-oo-daing						ditto.
Tseng-deng						ditto.
Aing-ma						ditto.
Pai-myouk						Pai-myouk.
Mvonk-pyeng						ditto.
Tsa-ba-tan						Shwe-doung,
Mai-za-lee						ditto.
Da-lay-pyeng						ditto.
Leng-bhan						ditto.
Toung-myeng						ditto.
Khyoung-bouk						ditto.
Gnyoung-maw						ditto.
Nat-mouk						ditto.
Kyap-ka-baing						Kyap.
Hmaik						ditto.
Ta-goung-nek						Ta-goung-nek.
Thwe-gyouk						ditto.
Kya-gan						ditto.
Rwa-boo-lai						ditto.
Tsheng-tha						ditto.

The four registered villages of Meng-dat have been included ever since the annexation in the one circle of that name.

The annual quota of revenue* assessed upon Meng-doon at the settlement of 1145 B. E., was 50 viss of silver or Rs. 6,500 and on Meng-dat 12 viss or Rs. 1,560. Meng-doon had, besides, to furnish, for the personal service of the king, 20 men who were relieved every six months. In time of war Meng-doon had to furnish 500 musketeers and 500 spearmen. After the first war the assessment of regular revenue remained, nominally, the same but an extra cess, called the "tenth" (Dathama), was levied for four years in order to pay off the fine imposed on the Burmese government at the treaty of Yandaboo. This is said to have amounted in the governorship of Meng-doon (far larger than the present township) to 5,000 viss of silver or Rs. 650,000 per annum, and in Meng-dat to 50 viss.

The fixed assessment had to be remitted in full to the Myo-tsa at Amarapoora. The Won, Myo-thoogyee and other numerous officials are said to have obtained their personal revenue chiefly from the sums extracted from suitors in civil and criminal cases. A lawsuit invariably resulted in the ruin of one of the parties.

The last Myo-tsa of Meng-doon was the present king of Burma and from Meng-doon he derived the title of "Meng-doon Prince" by which he was known before his accession to the throne. On his representing, whilst Myo-tsa of Meng-doon, that the annual tribute of 50 viss of silver was insufficient for him the amount was doubled.

MENG-DOON.—A revenue circle in the Meng-doon township, Thayet district, in which is situated the town of Meng-doon, the headquarters of the township. For some years after the annexation the taxes in the town of Meng-doon were collected by the town goung but in 1862 the Oot-hpo Thoogyee was entrusted with this duty and the town made a portion of his circle. The products are rice, sessamum, cotton, plantains, tobacco, onions, chillies and cutch. In 1876-77 the population was 4,178, the land revenue Rs. 3,296, the capitation tax Rs. 2,788 and the revenue from all other sources, including that levied in the town of Meng-doon, Rs. 2,825.

MENG-GA-LA-DOON.—A revenue circle in the Hmaw-bhee township adjoining and north of the town of Rangoon, extending westwards from the ridge of the hills along which runs the Prome road to the Hlaing; on the east is the Koon-dan circle and on the north the Kyoung-goon. The country on the east and south-east is hilly and forest-clad with numerous winding ravines and both by its physical formation and by its (laterite) soil suited only for orchards and vegetable gardens. For some miles from Rangoon almost every inch of available land is planted with jack, mango and other fruit-bearing trees, whilst the ground between the stems is covered with pine-apple plants the fruit being destined for the Rangoon market. These, owing to the dense shade and possibly to the heavy dews and the poverty of the soil, are watery and tasteless when compared with even the Indian fruit. Towards the west the country sinks and here rice is grown, the tidal streams which carry off the water from the hills to the Hlaing affording an easy means of transport to Rangoon.

* Called here the Kwon-bho-daw. It was assessed in Rwek-nee silver of which one viss may be taken as equivalent to Rs. 153, according to Sir A. Phayre.

The area under cultivation and the revenue during the last five years were :—

YEAR.	AREA, IN ACRES.				REVENUE, IN RUPEES.			
	Rice.	Garden.	Miscellaneous.	Total.	Land.	Capitation tax.	All others.	Total.
1873-74	..	3,935	2,269	24	6,228	15,174	7,113	114	22,401
1874-75	..	4,276	2,619	32	6,927	17,120	6,573	144	23,837
1875-76	..	4,261	2,502	43	6,806	15,769	6,895	165	22,829
1876-77	..	4,093	2,592	45	6,730	14,910	6,593	151	21,654
1877-78	..	4,590	2,607	39	7,236	17,417	6,785	156	24,385

and the population and agricultural stock :—

YEAR.	POPULATION.							AGRICULTURAL STOCK.					
	Burmese.	Talaing.	Shan.	Kareng.	Natives of India.	All others.	Total.	Buffaloes.	Cows, bulls and bullocks.	Goats.	Carts.	Ploughs.	Boats.
1873-74	..	..	..	..	..	..	..	..	221	1,542	13	285	342	48
1874-75	..	3,347	..	2,551	875	22	40	6,835	176	126	10	311	323	31
1875-76	..	3,421	..	2,484	509	..	207	6,621	175	1,369	5	251	265	23
1876-77	..	3,603	..	2,188	595	27	167	6,580	142	1,425	1	216	187	36
1877-78	..	3,010	..	2,583	353	11	6	5,963	141	106	..	141	153	8

The number of Shan is comparatively large. They are congregated almost entirely on the undulating ground in the east and south-east and are nearly all gardeners.

Towards the north-eastern corner is the village of Meng-ga-la-doon, near the site of a once flourishing town, founded circa 750 A.D. by Poon-na-ree-ka, of which no traces even remain. The villages are all small hamlets of no importance.

MENG-GA-LA-GYEE.—A revenue circle in the Naaf township, Akyab district, on the bank of the Naaf estuary, divided into three distinct portions by an intervening grant of land. The population in 1875 numbered 2,234 souls, the cultivated area covered 2,226 acres, the land revenue amounted to Rs. 4,852 and the capitation tax produced Rs. 1,970. In 1876 there were 3,569 inhabitants and the gross revenue was Rs. 9,291 of which Rs. 5,674 were derived from the land, Rs. 3,350 from the capitation tax and the remainder from other sources.

MENG-GYEE.—A township of the Henzada district on the east bank of the Irrawaddy extending eastwards from that river to the Pegu Roma with the Ta-pwon township on the north and the Mo-gnyo township on the south. The principal town is Meng-gyee, at one time the head-quarters of the Tharrawaddy district* which now forms a portion of Henzada. The population of the township in 1876 was 15,770 souls, the land revenue Rs. 4,731, the capitation tax Rs. 14,383 and the gross revenue Rs. 36,539.

MENG-GYEE.—A town in the Henzada district with some 1,700 inhabitants, about two miles inland, eastward of the Irrawaddy and about 11 miles south of the latitude of Myan-oung. For some years after the last war a detachment of Native Infantry was quartered in this town and it was made the head-quarters of an Assistant Commissioner; subsequently the troops were withdrawn and the Assistant Commissioner replaced by an Extra Assistant, who in later years has been relieved by an Assistant Commissioner again. It is an important town from which the produce of the neighbouring country, principally rice and cutch, is exported down the river. It contains a Court-house and a Police-station.

MENG-HLA.—A river in the Henzada district. The north and south Meng-hla rise in the western slopes of the Pegu mountains and unite at Tshay-rwa to form the Meng-hla which flows in a south-westerly direction to the Htoo, a distance of about 30 miles. The forests below Tshay-rwa contain Htouk-kyan (*Terminalia macrocarpa*) and Pyeng-gado (*Xylia dolabriformis*) and those above that village Teak.

MENG-HLA.—A revenue circle in the Henzada district, east of the Irrawaddy, lying to the south and west of Tshay-nhit-rwa. In the centre and towards the east rice cultivation is carried on. In 1876-77 the population numbered 8,412 souls, the land revenue was Rs. 12,614, the capitation tax Rs. 7,470 and the gross revenue Rs. 21,139.

MENG-HLA.—A township in the Henzada district extending eastwards from the Hlaing to the Pegu Roma mountains, having the Mo-gnyo township on the north and the Tsan-rwe township on the south; towards the east the country is hilly and is covered with forest where are found Teak and other valuable timber, whilst towards the south, especially in the Meng-hla circle, there is a good deal of rice cultivation. The township is divided into five revenue circles, viz., Kyek-taik, Tshay-hnit-rwa, Meng-hla, Paik-taw and Lweng-pyeng. In 1876 there were 33,191 inhabitants, the land revenue was Rs. 48,025, the capitation tax Rs. 29,173 and the gross revenue Rs. 112,654.

MENG-MA-NAING.—A creek in the Bassein district : the upper portion of the Myoung-mya.

MENG-NGAY-GOON.—A revenue circle in the Prome district extending from about 13 miles east of Prome to the lower spurs of the Pegu Roma mountains. It contains four village tracts, viz., Meng-ngay-goon, Thai-ma-thouk, Taw-rwa, and Aing-touk. In 1876-77 the population was 829, the land revenue Rs. 1,741, the capitation tax Rs. 835 and the gross revenue Rs. 2,576.

MENG-PYENG.—A revenue circle in the Kyouk-hpyoo district on the east coast of Cheduba, between the mouths of the Oon and the Kyee streams. It has an area of about 20 square miles and a population of 3,789 souls of whom a large number are collected in the two villages of Taw-too and

* Tharrawaddy was again separated from Henzada and formed into an independent district in 1878.

Tsheng-nat-khyoung. In 1876-77 the capitation tax was Rs. 4,140, the land revenue Rs. 4,284 and the gross revenue Rs. 8,721.

MENG-PYENG.—A revenue circle in the Kyouk-hpyoo township, Kyouk-hpyoo district, about the centre of Ramree Island and adjoining the Ramree township ; on the north-east is the Kaing-khyoung circle, on north, separated from it by the Tsan-khyoung, is the Than-htoung circle and on the west and south-west the Tha-loo-doung circle. It is about nine square miles in extent and has a population of 1,267 souls. The principal product is sugar made from the sugar-cane which is extensively grown. In 1876-77 the land revenue was Rs. 1,223, the capitation tax Rs. 1,394 and the gross revenue Rs. 2,690.

MENG-RWA.—A village of 50 houses, which gave its name to a circle in the Meng-doon township, Thayet district, now joined to the Meng-doon circle. It is situated at the angle of a sharp bend of the Ma-htoon about two miles south-east of the town of Meng-doon.

MENG-RWA.—A village in the Prome district forming the south-eastern outskirts of the town of Shwe-doung.

MENG-RWA.—A revenue circle in the Shwe-doung township, Prome district, south and east of Shwe-doung. The western portion of the circle is level and highly cultivated whilst the eastern consists of undulating ground and low hills covered with dense forest in which Teak is found in small quantities mixed with Eng (*Dipterocarpus tuberculatus*) and bamboos. The main road from Rangoon to the north runs through the western portion of the circle. Included within its present limits are the once independent village tracts of Kaw-hla, Rwa-pa-lai, Rwa-hla, Tat-thit, Nat-tseng-gan, Rwa-ma, Toung-loon-gnyo, Ka-thit-taing, Htouk-kyan-daing, Toung-tsoon, Heng-gouk, Tha-bye-hla and Wa-lay. In 1876-77 the circle had 3,039 inhabitants and produced a gross revenue of Rs. 7,115 of which Rs. 3,668 were derived from the land, Rs. 3,320 from the capitation tax and Rs. 125 from miscellaneous sources.

MENG-YAT.—An arm of the sea half a mile wide at its mouth, just north of the Than-htoung circle, which stretches inland for three miles in a south-south-westerly direction from the north-eastern coast of Ramree island. At its lower end it is fed by two short main streams.

MENG-YAT.—A long, narrow revenue circle in the Kyouk-hpyoo district extending north-east from the western coast of Ramree island along the left bank of the Meng-yat to within about a mile of the north-eastern coast. To the north-west is the Kyouk-pyouk circle, to the north the Gnyoung-beng-hla circle, to the west and south-west the Than-htoung circle and to the south the Than-khyoung circle. In its northern portion it is intersected by a net-work of tidal creeks which communicate with the Meng-yat. It is 29 square miles in extent and has a population of 1,695 souls. The principal manufacture is salt. In 1876-77 the land revenue was Rs. 1,746, the capitation tax Rs. 1,703 and the gross revenue Rs. 3,640.

MERGUI.—A town in the Tenasserim division in 12° 26′ N. and 98° 35′ E., the head-quarters of the Mergui district, on an island in the principal mouth of the Tenasserim river which falls into the sea about two miles to the north and about one to the south of the town. The harbour admits vessels of 18 feet draught. The banks near the town are hard gravel but towards the sea mud flats extend for some distance, a mud bank of some considerable length shewing itself at low water. Rising almost from high water mark is a low range of hills, on which stand the Court-houses and the old barracks, and round the base of which, west, north and east, the town is built; to the east is the Gaol. The other buildings are the Treasury and Police-office in the same masonry building as that in which the courts are held, the Circuit-house, of wood, on the northern crest of the hill and the Charitable dispensary somewhat lower down; on the beach is the market, with a masonry causeway to the sea covered at high tides, and a little to the south is a substantial wooden pier stretching out to below low water mark. The population has not increased much of late years, having been 9,873 in 1863-64, 10,200 in 1873-74 and 10,731 in 1876-77; it is composed of mixed races, Talaing, Burmese, Malays, Bengalis, Madrassis, Siamese and many Chinese. In former years it was a penal station to which convicts from Bengal were transported. It has a Government school and a Roman Catholic and an American Baptist Mission.

The town, as it now exists, is of comparatively modern date and owes its existence to the Burmans who, after the subjugation of the surrounding country about the middle of the last century, enlarged the few fishing hamlets which they found here. These were the only remains of the once flourishing city mentioned by old travellers in which many English merchants settled and remained peaceably employed and in high favour with the inhabitants till they were attacked and driven out in 1695 (76 being murdered and only 20 escaping) on the East India Company declaring war with Siam, for which purpose Captain Weldon was despatched to Mergui, then a Siamese town. It is mentioned by Cæsar Frederick, the Venetian traveller who visited Burma in 1569, as " a village called Mergui in whose " harbour there lay every year some ships, with veizina (*Sappan wood*) " nyppa and benjamin." In 1780 the Siamese invaded the country but were defeated before Mergui and forced to retreat and in 1821 it was again attacked by the same people and burned down.

During the first Burmese war an expeditionary force under Lieutenant-Colonel Miles, having captured Tavoy, proceeded to Mergui; a heavy fire was opened from the town which was silenced by the guns of the ships and the troops, landing and wading through the mud banks on the beach, escaladed the stockade from which the enemy fled. The town was found deserted but the people soon returned and shewed themselves perfectly indifferent to the change of authorities. A small garrison of Native Infantry was left and from that time Mergui has been a British town. In 1829 a rebellion broke out in Tavoy and the officers in charge at Mergui, panic struck, escaped with the small garrison to one of the neighbouring islands. Shwe Gya, son of the Governor in the Burmese time, assumed and retained charge of the town until a force was despatched from Tavoy where the out-break had been suppressed.

The inhabitants carry on a good trade with the other ports of British Burma and with the Straits Settlements, the principal articles of export being grain (rice husked and unhusked), timber, dried fish, molasses and tin, and the principal imports cotton piece-goods, silk and tea. The Customs duty which is realized from this trade is very small owing to its being mainly with ports in British India.

The value of exports and imports with the amount of duty realized during each of the last 10 years was :—

Year.	Value of Exports, in Rupees,				Value of Imports, in Rupees,				Total value of Imports and Exports.	Duty realized.
	Indian ports.	Foreign ports, including the Straits.	Ports in British Burma.	Total.	Indian ports.	Foreign ports, including the Straits.	Ports in British Burma.	Total.		
1867-68 ..	1,500	40,833	306,017	348,350	..	48,016	268,478	316,494	664,844	4,988
1868-69 ..	8,450	34,982	323,192	366,624	..	51,170	236,634	287,814	654,438	4,348
1869-70 ..	..	49,689	293,665	343,354	..	61,697	165,918	227,615	570,969	4,530
1870-71 ..	2,450	59,243	305,964	367,659	..	78,688	222,898	301,586	669,245	6,247
1871-72 ..	2,392	71,264	275,086	348,742	..	97,502	200,857	298,359	647,101	6,145
1872-73 ..	2,277	71,680	358,583	432,540	..	55,120	238,999	294,119	726,659	2,909
1873-74 ..	5,095	62,070	395,266	462,431	..	76,324	321,850	389,174	351,605	3,798
1874-75 ..	1,350	69,598	397,999	468,947	..	96,471	296,126	392,597	861,544	4,283
1875-76 ..	5,640	73,322	336,622	415,584	..	85,258	223,415	308,673	724,257	5,858
1876-77 ..	18,332	140,317	331,924	490,573	415	134,930	307,731	443,076	933,649	8,052

The grain and timber exported during the same period was, in tons :—

Year.	Grain.	Timber.	Year.	Grain.	Timber.
1867-68 ..	70	9	1872-73 ..	552	166
1868-69 ..	685	16	1873-74 ..	437	34
1869-70 ..	652	25	1874-75 ..	299	135
1870-71 ..	1061	..	1875-76 ..	418	126
1871-72 ..	906	2	1876-77 ..	1,448	21

MERGUI.—A district in the Tenasserim division occupying the southernmost portion of the Province. On the east it is separated from Siam by the main range, and lower down by the Pak-chan river, to the west is the Bay of Bengal and to the north the district of Tavoy. It extends from 9° 58' to 13° 24' N. and from 90° 15' to 98° 35' E., is 206 miles long, has a mean average breadth of about 40 miles—excluding the Mergui Archipelago—

and contains an area of 7,810 square miles. The surface of the country is chiefly mountainous and, consequently, much intersected by streams of which few are at present of any importance except as drainage-ways, being chiefly unnavigable mountain torrents.

In 1875 Tavoy Island, off the mouth of the Tavoy river, was added to it from the Tavoy district, south of which it lies. It extends from 12° 55′ N. to 13° 13′ N. and is about two miles in breadth and 18 miles in length, of moderate height, stretching N. by W. and S. by E. with a peak in the middle and another small one at its southern end. On the east there is a good and safe harbour called Port Owen, with good water and wood. The island is mainly important as the principal place of resort of the *Colocalia fuciphaga*, the nests of which are largely exported to the Straits and China and the right of collecting them leased out by the State.

The whole face of the country, hill and dale, except where cleared for cultivation, is densely clothed with luxuriant vegetation, and towards the interior and on the more elevated situations upon the coast are forest trees of great beauty and size. The coast line, studded with islands, of which within the limits of the district there are no less than 207, is very irregular and for several miles inland very little raised above the level of the sea, consisting for the most part, and particularly to the southward of the town of Mergui, of low mangrove islands entirely unfit for cultivation; here and there, however, are found small plains of fertile land adapted for rice, and occasionally hills of moderate elevation occur upon which are gardens of areca palms and plantains. Towards the interior, after passing the mangrove limits the ground gradually rises till it becomes mountainous, even to the banks of the rivers, and so continues to the grand natural barrier, the lofty chain which divides the Province from Siam.

Two principal ranges traverse the district from north to south in a nearly N. W. and S. E. direction, running almost parallel to each other for a considerable distance, the river Tenasserim winding between them till it turns south and traverses an opening in the westernmost range. The western range soon rises again and below the latitude of Mergui inclines eastward and joins the other at the Khow Phra hill a little above 11° N. Lat. From about 11° 25′ N. Lat. to the extreme southern limit of the district extends another low range forming the western watershed of the Le-gnya and the Pak-chan and joined to the eastern range between the sources of these two rivers by a cross spur. On the east and south the country is filled with these ranges and their offshoots and subsidiary spurs all covered with thick forest.

Mountains.

The most northern pass across the main range into Siam is by the Tsa-raw but this is so difficult that it is almost impracticable and is only used by Kareng. Seventy-six miles further south is another, called by the Burmese "Maw-doung" and by the Siamese "Khow-maun", the one meaning "Tired hill" the other "Pillow mountain", at the source of the Thien-khwon stream; this is the main line of communication between Mergui and the southern provinces of Siam. On the English side the country is so infested with tigers that the natives never attempt the journey unarmed or in less numbers than three. Apart from this the Thien-khwon is navigable only by the smallest boats during that part of the year when travelling is possible. This route is both bad and long and it is also through a line of country where elephants are not procurable, in addition to which there is a scarcity of drinking water on the Siamese side.

From Maw-doung southwards down to the source of the Kra river Siamese form almost exclusively the occupants of the peninsula; the consequence is that the mountains are traversed by more passes than in the same length of any other portion of the boundary line, real or imagined hindrances being removed by former mutual intercourse and by consanguinity. There are five well-known passes which deserve mention.

The first is up the Thien-khwon to the mouth of the Khalaung-khyan-khow, about a mile below Hpoung-tshiep, the landing-place in the Maw-doung route. Thence up the Khalaung-khyan-khow to its source in the main watershed near Khow-lwon, the 'Royal Mountain'. On the eastern side is the source of the Khalaung-khyak-kra. The descent may be made along it but there is a short cut east into the Khalaung Htap-tsa-kay, the boundary of the district of Koo-ee in Siam.

The remaining four passes have the Nga-won river for a common base, the mountains being crossed by following up its eastern affluents.

The first of these is the Khlaung Hta-hpay, at the mouth of which boats and rafts stop as the Nga-won is not navigable higher up. Opposite the Khlaung Hta-hpay is the Khlaung Hta-da-yeng, a tributary of the Khlaung-khyak-kra. The route leads up it as far as the source whence a branch track runs east through a gorge in the Khow-lwon range into the plains of "Htap-sa-kay."

The second is up the Nga-won to the Khlaung-pa-wa-ay and thence up that stream, descending into the Khlaung Hpa-raun, in the district of Aan-ta-hpan.

The third is higher up the Nga-won by the Khlaung Hpa-leu-an and then down the Khlaung-lau-ay, a tributary of the Hpa-raun river.

The fourth is by the source of the Nga-won, skirting a hill called Khow-poon, on the east side of which is the Khlaung Hta-tsay which flows by the town of Khyoon-hpaun and is sometimes called Khlaung Khyoon-hpaun.

Though elephants are plentiful in this part of Siam they are not used by those who come over into our territory so that these passes are not sufficiently cleared to admit of any other mode of travelling than on foot with coolies.

Amongst the mountain ranges are several plains of varying extent the

Plains.

most productive of which is the great plain on the western side of the district, stretching south from Palaw in 12° 58' to Le-gnya in 11° 28' and extending inland to the western range : next in importance is the upper and middle portion of the valley lying to the eastward of the last between the two principal ranges, 100 miles in length and averaging 10 in breadth, possessing a rich alluvial soil and drained by the Tenasserim river but at present almost entirely covered with forest except in the patches cleared by the Kareng and Siamese. In the south is the valley of the Pak-chan, and stretching for 30 miles along the right bank of that river, is a third plain in which the soil is rich and suited for the production of all kinds of tropical produce. Scattered over the face of the district are numerous other small plain valleys with good soil but overgrown with dense forest, the home of the bison, the rhinoceros and the tiger.

The four principal rivers in the district are the Tenasserim, the Legnya, the Pak-chan and the Pa-louk. The Tenasserim has its sources north of the Mergui district which it traverses from north to south in a narrow valley as far as the town of Tenasserim where, joined by the Little Tenasserim flowing from the south and formed by the junction of the Nga-won and the Thien-khwon and, like the Great Tenasserim, recruited by numerous mountain torrents, it turns suddenly westward and flowing through the chain which had confined it reaches the Bay of Bengal in numerous channels into which its waters are divided on reaching the lowland near the coast. It is navigable for all but very large boats as far as the town of Tenasserim but beyond that boats of even moderate tonnage cannot proceed without difficulty. The influence of the tide is felt only 10 miles beyond Tenasserim. The banks are generally high with perpendicular faces but in some places it flows through low land. The Little Tenasserim traverses a somewhat similar valley.

Rivers.

The Le-gnya rises in the main range in about 13° 45′ N. and has a general northerly course for some 60 miles past Le-gnya when it turns west and falls into the Bay of Bengal. It is navigable by boats as far as the tide can be felt, or for some miles above Le-gnya.

The Pak-chan forms the south-eastern boundary of the province. It rises in the main range, near the root of a spur on the northern side of which is the source of the Le-gnya, and flows in a generally southerly direction for 78 miles to Victoria Point. For the first 15 miles of its course it is a small mountain stream but having received the drainage of the hills on each side it soon develops into a navigable river and at its mouth is two and a half miles broad.

The Pa-louk is a small river in the northern part of the district which rises in the Myeng-mo-lek-khat mountain and flows at first southward and then to the west. At its mouth it is about 700 yards broad but above Pa-louk village there are rapids and falls.

The low-lying land along the seacoast from the Le-gnya northwards to the northern mouth of the Tenasserim is highly intersected by muddy tidal creeks whilst the mountainous tracts in the east, north and south are drained by an infinity of torrents, some flowing directly into the sea and others towards every point of the compass in thickly wooded and dark, narrow ravines till, mingling their waters, they reinforce the main channel. In the dry season these are but brooklets, a tiny stream wandering over the sandy bed amongst massive boulders, but in the rains they become now foaming torrents dashing with violence against the steep banks and over rocky ledges and washing the slippery crags with their spray, now sinking into silent, dark pools buried in dense masses of overhanging foliage of every shade and form.

The district has never been accurately geologically surveyed. In 1855 Dr. Oldham of the Geological Survey of India visited Mergui and examined the coal fields and the following account is taken almost verbatim from his report.

Geology and Mineralogy.

In general geological structure this district appears to be tolerably simple, although the relation of the rocks at first proves very deceptive owing to the numerous dislocations and disturbances to which they have been subjected. Resting upon granite a series of highly metamorphosed rocks occur, exhibiting every variety from perfect gneiss and mica slate to hard silicious slates, occasionally chloritic, and to black earthy but micaceous and glossy slates. Through these numerous veins of granite penetrate and ramify in every direction and of all sizes. These are only seen near to the immediate junction of the granite and the bedded rocks, and where this junction is not absolutely traceable the occurrence of similar veins points conclusively to its close proximity.

Resting upon these there is a great accumulation of beds of a pseudo-porphyritic rock, deriving this aspect from imbedded crystalline fragments of felspar which weather out freely or become whitened on exposure. In its most normal character this is an earthy, but highly indurated, rock, with these small irregular disseminated bits of felspar; but this passes by almost insensible gradations on the one hand into hard earthy slaty masses without the disseminated particles, and on the other into grits, containing much rounded fragments of quartz, quartzite, and of these pseudo-porphyritic rocks themselves. These grits often become very coarse and largely conglomeritic. The intercalation, and occasionally regular succession, of these varied deposits renders the bedding of the series traceable, but the rocks have been subjected to very great disturbances and are found dipping in every direction and at all angles. These rocks form all the higher grounds of the outer ranges (as distinct from the central range of mountains dividing the British territory from Siam) in the southern portion of the district. The general character of the series, also, varies materially in different parts, the greater or lesser prevalence of grits and conglomerates and of hard sandstone beds affecting the general aspect.

With this group of rocks, and resting upon it, appear to be associated a considerable thickness of dark coloured blueish and blueish-black earthy beds, frequently thinly laminated and then presenting an imperfectly developed slaty structure. With these occur some beds of very hard, generally dark grey, quartzose grits. In parts, apparently from a greater amount of local igneous action, these slates become silky in aspect and much crumpled. These must be of considerable thickness although their immediate relation to the rocks occurring close to them is obscure. Taking them in connection with the pseudo-porphyritic rocks and the conglomerate and grits below the total thickness cannot be less than 9,000 feet. To these rocks as being best seen in all their varied character in this district, Dr. Oldham applied the distinguishing name of the "Mergui" series.

These are succeeded upwards by a group of hard sand-stone beds, often in thick and massive layers, with thin earthy partings, often in thin laminæ, finer and more earthy. The prevailing colour is of a reddish tint, or reddish white tint, but some of the beds are of a deep red and others of a yellowish earthy tint. A few of the layers are slightly calcareous, and in the upper portion a few thin and irregular bands of earthy limestone of a blueish tint occur. In some of the softer and more earthy beds are fossils (Corals, Gasteropoda, Brachiopoda, Crustacea, &c.) Over these sandstones another series of grey shaly beds occurs, these are occasionally calcareous and when so yield fossils (Spirifera, Producta, &c.) and also pass occasionally into a soft, black, carbonaceous mass with nodular concretions of hard quartz. Some beds of sandstone, often of a dark colour, are associated with the group. Above these come a series of no great thickness (150 to 200 feet) of fine soft sandstones, thinly bedded, and with grey and pinkish-coloured shaly layers intercalated; and upon these appears to rest the hard and thick limestone of the district, as seen near the Tenasserim river and towards the south. This limestone is the representative of the great limestone which is seen so largely developed near to Maulmain and in the Amherst district generally, but which is, comparatively speaking, sparingly present in the south.

The whole of these form one continuous series, and as some of the most important members of that series are best seen in the immediate vicinity of Maulmain, Dr. Oldham designated the group the "Maulmain" beds.

"These Maulmain beds, and down in the succession I have given to the "top of the Mergui group, appear to me," writes Dr. Oldham, "so far as I "can at present judge, to represent the same geological epoch as the "lower carboniferous group of European geologists. The era of the "'Mergui' rocks themselves is not so clear. In many cases pseudo-por-"phyritic beds have much the aspect of some of those curious and inter-"esting igneous masses which are so common in the Silurian districts of "England, while others of the coarse and hard and often almost corneous "sandstones and conglomerates have all the lithological character of many "of the European Devonian series, but as yet their lithological character "is the only evidence as I could not trace any organic remains which could "give a clue to their geological epoch. ......"

"This limestone is by no means deficient in fossils but is, in general, "so hard and compact that it is entirely impossible to get any of the "imbedded organic remains out. On the weathered surfaces and smooth "water-polished faces of the rock their outlined sections can be traced, "worn down perfectly smooth with the general surface, but any attempt to "break them out inevitably results in the fracture of all. Probably if this "rock were anywhere quarried some of these organic remains could be pro-"cured but, unfortunately, here as elsewhere one of the great difficulties a "geologist has to contend with is the total absence of any openings or quar-"ries into the rocks of the district."

"Upon the denuded surfaces and edges of the rocks hitherto described "are a series of beds of conglomerates, of sandstones, of soft and loosely "coherent shales, and of coal, which stretch at intervals over a very large "portion of the southern part of the Tenasserim division. The conglome-"rates are never very coarse, the pebbles seldom exceeding a few inches in "diameter; the sandstones are fine, gritty, pebbly, clean, white quartzose "sands, or earthy and of a yellowish tint; the shale beds are of a blueish "green or blackish tint, and very regularly disposed in thin and frequently "repeated laminæ. The coal itself is also regularly disposed in thin flaky "laminæ, with minute earthy streaks marking its structure."

"Besides their unconformity with the lower rocks, and with difference "in mineral character which these beds offer, there is a total difference in "their imbedded organic remains. In some of the layers of the soft sand-"stones and shales numerous impressions of dicotyledonous leaves are found "of a very recent aspect, and in the beds of papery shale which accompany "the coal (like much of the papery brown coal of Germany) are numerous "fish scales and bones (but seldom anything like a perfect fish) of fresh

" water character. All these circumstances combined point to a very recent
" geological epoch for the formation of these beds, and I have no hesitation in
" entirely agreeing with the opinion on this point formerly expressed by
" Colonel Tremenheere, that these coals are of the tertiary period of geology...
" ....It is an interesting and curious fact, however, that in this district
" there is a very considerable development of rocks which, from their imbed-
" ded organic remains, are certainly of an age somewhat synchronous with
" that of the great ' carboniferous' formation of geologists, but in which no
" beds of coal occur, while thick masses of vegetable matter have been depo-
" sited, and have subsequently been mineralized into good coal, at a compar-
" atively very recent period. This is only an additional instance of how local
" all such deposits must be when compared with large areas, and of how
" the altered circumstances of each locality must most materially affect the
" nature of the rock formed there at any given time."
        " These coal-bearing deposits, the total thickness of which nowhere
" exceeds 900 to 1,000 feet, are never traceable continuously over any very
" extended area. They are cut off and seem heaped up against the project-
" ing ridges of the higher grounds and appear to be divided by these natural
" barriers into a series of isolated and detached portions. In all cases the
" physical conformation of the country now existing, or a conformation very
" slightly differing from that now existing, appears to have determined the
" extent of these deposits, and looking at the general nature of them and of
" their associations I am led to view them as a series of lacustrian (fresh-
" water) deposits formed in small lake-like expansions along the lines of the
" great drainage valleys of the country, wherein the waters became ponded
" back by natural barriers. These deposits also preserve a certain general
" direction and thus mark the line of a great depression, or general valley,
" between the main dividing ridge which here separates Siam from the British
" territories and the outer ridges which come between them and the sea.
" Through and across the line of this outer ridge the general drainage of the
" country is discharged by a series of gorges or narrow rocky channels through
" which the main rivers pass. The Tenasserim river, east of Mergui town,
" discharges the large body of waters which had accumulated throughout its
" extended north and south course together with the tributary waters of the
" Little Tenasserim and its affluents, through a narrow rocky gorge ; and fur-
" ther south, at the Le-gnya river, the drainage of an immense area is all
" discharged through a narrow rocky gorge. All these gorges have a common
" direction nearly east and west, although the general drainage of the
" country and the course of the main streams is almost invariably north and
" south. It is this feature which gives rise to the remarkable and sudden
" alteration in the direction of these rivers, as may be seen by a reference to
" a map of the province."
        Coal was reported to have been discovered in 13 different locali-
ties, but in five of these it was found that a black carbonaceous rock with
quartz nodules, which crumbles into powder on exposure and soils the
fingers, had been mistaken for it. Two sites—on the Nga-won and the
Pa-wot—were not visited as the occurrence of coal was very doubtful, and if
it did exist their position would render it impossible to work it to advantage. At a locality noticed by Dr. Helfer above the falls of the Little
Tenasserim the seams were found only an inch or two in thickness,

extremely irregular in their occurrence and frequently discontinuous, so as to be practically quite useless.

About 1841 the State worked some coal mines at a spot about three-quarters of a mile west of the bank of the Tenasserim and close to the channel of the Thoo-hte khyoung a small stream which here comes down from the higher ridges to the west. The works were abandoned after a year or two and at the time of Dr. Oldham's visit the pits were full of water.

The coal had been extracted entirely by means of open adits sunk on the dip of the bed and along the bank of the small stream, in the bank of which the coal was exposed. Great expenditure had evidently been incurred here as a good broad road-way had been cut through the forest to the bank of the Tenasserim—this had been levelled by embanking and cutting (in one place a cutting of some hundred yards to the depth of nearly 12 feet,)—and a long and straight channel had been excavated for the waters of the small stream in order to divert them from the workings. Many experimental shafts were also sunk in search of the bed of coal and other beds beneath this one, but they appeared to have been put down without any proper system and were for the most part of great size and consequently very costly.

The section of the coal seen was :—

	Descending.
	Ft. In
1. Surface gravel and clay	4 0
2. Stiff tenacious grey clay, with ferruginous markings and coatings on the fissures, which when cut follow the tool and give to the mass a red and ochery aspect,	6 0
3. Brownish-black earthy shale, with fish scales and traces of vegetable remains. The upper surface and outer or exposed parts of this decompose into a clay very similar to that immediately above. For a few inches next the coal it becomes more black in colour, finer shaly and flaky, and the remains of fish are more abundant.	5 6
4. Rotten coaly matter and coal smut	1 0
5. Coal	

		Ft.	In.
Flaky and bright .. .. .. 9 inches to		2	6
Brown shale		0	1½
Coal		0	4
Greyish-brown shale		0	1
Coal, pyrites abundant, much more so than in the upper bed. This is good firm coal, becoming more earthy and flaky towards bottom		2	0
Blackish-grey flaky shale or soft clay, imperfect impressions of stems occasionally, thickness to		0	2¼
Coal, good solid coal, pyrites on partings, rendering it "brassy" ..		1	0
Blackish soft coal shale, or earthy coal, shining and full of pyrites		0	1
Coal, rich flakes of jet coal of ¼ inch, separated by earthy shales, pyrites abundant		0	10
Black shaly smut, with thin streaks of coal in it		0	2
Alternating and very irregular layers of flaky grey-black vegetable mould and of black jetty coal		0	9
Coaly shale, passing into coal		0	8
Alternating clay and coal in thin streaky laminæ ..		0	6
Grey flaky vegetable mould or clay		0	4
Black shale with coal streaks, some of ½ inch thick ..		0	10
Grey clay, flaky, same as before		0	5
Shale, with thin bright streaks of coal, flaky and laminar ..		1	0
		11 10	11 10

6. Greyish-white clay (under clay), flaky and slightly sandy; small and imperfect remains of plants visible	3 6
7. At bottom is more sandy and much harder; sandstone much the same colour and composition as the bed above, but more sandy ..	0 6

					Ft.	In.
8.	Grey soft flaky clay				0	0
9.	Blackish ditto ditto				0	2
10.	Brownish-grey, sandy, clunch clay				1	3
11.	Clay, blueish-grey, soft and flaky, and very similar to that met before, in part				3	0
12.	Sandstone, reddish white, close-grained and quartzose, with ochery stains, clay, hard, stiff, tenacious towards base, more ferruginous and sandy				5	0
13.	Sandstone, ochery and quartzose, decomposing into a yellowish ochery sand				4	0
					46	0

The beds below this continue to be of a similar character, hard quartzose sandstones for some depth, but no coal has been observed in them. Over all the beds noticed above a thick mass of conglomerate was found in sinking one of the shafts to the dip of the coal.

From the detailed section given above, it will be seen that the actual coal seams amount together to six feet eight inches in thickness, while the intervening partings of shale, &c., only form an aggregate thickness of four and half inches, so that the whole could easily be worked in one bed ; and this was done.

The dip or inclination of all the beds is high, being as much as 28° towards 15° N. of E. There is a distinct joint in the masses heading a little E. of N. at the planes of which underlie 60° to 70° to the W.

Throughout the whole thickness of the coal iron pyrites appear, either imbedded in small lumps or forming their crystalline coatings on the joints, often giving the coal, when freshly broken, a richly glittering metallic appearence. The coal, turned out in good cuboidal masses, was easily wrought, and with little waste. It is difficult to ignite but burns freely, breaking up into small fragments which do not coke, and in large heaps requires care to keep up free ignition. It was found to answer well in the small steam engine used at the mines and also proved equal to ordinary " country " coal in sea-going steamers.

The presence of the iron pyrites mentioned above, to which, whether justly or not, was attributed the fact of some of this coal having spontaneously ignited on one or two occasions, would undoubtedly tend to render it unsafe ; but Dr. Oldham was of opinion that this alone would not have been sufficient to condemn it as this mineral is by no means constantly present and much of the coal is so free from it as to be perfectly safe and useful. The waste at the mine would further be a productive source of alum, if economized in that way.

The rapid dip of the beds and the consequent depth to which all shafts would soon have to be sunk to meet the coal was, and still remains, the most serious objection to the profitable working of this coal. In other respects it is well placed. The distance from the pit's mouth to the Tenasserim river is not more than three-fourths of a mile and for the whole way a level road has been formed on which it was intended to lay a tramway.

At the time of Dr. Oldham's visit (February) the waters of the river were very low, though not at the lowest ; but there was then, and there is, probably, at all times of the year, a very tolerable supply in the small stream passing the coal pits. This could readily be ponded back above the coal and a reservoir formed from which a steady supply could be obtained (the amount of water was quite sufficient for driving a very effective water-wheel), and this, probably, would have been both a much cheaper and more useful process than simply diverting the stream as was done.

The next locality on the Great Tenasserim river in which coal has been found is Hien-lap or Hien-lat. This is the name of a small scattered Burmese village situated on the right bank of the river, about six miles further north than Thoo-hte khyoung. The coal beds crop out at the eastern side of a small mountain stream, about three-fourths of a mile to the west of the bank of the Tenasserim. The country between the river and the coal is at present an unbroken forest but it is tolerably level, and presents no real difficulty to the formation of an excellent road. The difference of level between the river bank and the coal, where it outcrops, is very trifling. The occurrence of coal here was made known to Mr. Chase, Deputy Commissioner at Mergui, by some natives who had seen it in their wanderings in the forest. It was not known at the time of the works being carried on at the old mines, and indeed very probably was not then visible as the stream may since then have cut away the bank and exposed it.

The section immediately at the coal gives the following succession :—

	Ft.	In.
Blackish compact flaky shale or slate, abounding in small fish scales, bones, &c., same as those found at Thoo-hte khyoung	4	0
Ditto, more pitchy-looking, with thin laminæ of bright coal	0	6
Coal smut or dirty earthy coal .. .. .. 6 inches to	0	9
Coal, flaky in structure; the separation into laminæ being well seen on exposed surfaces but scarcely visible on the fresh fracture, the coal breaking as readily across these lines as along them ; very thin divisions of more earthy and flaky character mark some of the layers but do not occur in sufficient thickness or number to prevent the whole bed being removed.		

The coal is here not less than 17 feet 6 inches to 18 feet thick. From top to bottom of this splendid bed there is but little variation in quality, all is of good glossy aspect and conchoidal fracture, coming out in large symmetrical masses, which do not, however, bear exposure for any length of time without breaking down. It burns freely and with a good flame, does not coke, but breaks up and leaves but little ashes.

Throughout the bed a few small lumps of iron pyrites and a few thin coatings on the joints occur but not to any extent and by no means so abundantly as in the coal at Thoo-hte khyoung or at Kan-ma-pyeng (to be described below).

The specific gravity of this coal is 1·28, and by analysis 100 parts were found to contain—

Volatile matter, inclusive of water	.. ..	54·6
Carbon	.. ..	45·4
Ashes	.. ..	6·5

The water was found to be 12·6 per cent.[*]

From this place, under the sanction of Mr. Chase, from 70 to 100 tons of coal had been extracted by a Burman and brought to Mergui, from which it was supplied to the H. C. Steamer *Pluto*, and proved a very effec-

---

[*] This analysis, and those given below, made by Dr. F. F. Macnamara, Chemical Examiner to the Government, are given on his authority.

tive and useful coal, keeping up steam well and easily fired. It is, as might be anticipated, of rather rapid combustion, and would be more adapted for tubular boilers than for those of the ordinary construction.

The coal was extracted simply by cutting back on the face of the outcrop, and in doing so only a thickness of about 13 feet of the coal had been touched, the rest being left as not so easily accessible. The cutting extended for about seven yards in length and had, therefore, not been carried to a depth of more then 12 feet. On Dr. Oldham's arrival this was found filled with water, and it had to be cleared before he could see the coal or its relations.

Under contract, the Burmese who excavated here received Rs. 24 for every ton of coal delivered at Mergui, a rate which, however desirable it may have been to encourage such undertakings at first, was very much too high to be maintained, indeed the same man was most desirous of entering on another contract for the delivery of coal at Mergui at Rs. 16, or a reduction of one-third ; but even this was too high a rate. Seeing, however, that in any case the amount of coal which could be procured in that way, without any machinery or any of the most ordinary mechanical appliances, could only be small, and that every yard thus excavated was only tending to injure the mine, if any systematic workings were contemplated, Dr. Oldham advised that such operations should be stopped, and no more coal was, therefore, extracted.

About three-quarters of a mile north of Hien-lap another small village is situated in the forest on the west bank of the Tenasserim, and within its lands coal has been found, exposed by the cutting back of a small mountain rill. This coal at Kan-ma-pyeng is of very similar character and aspect to the others. Its analysis yielded to Dr. Macnamara the following results :—

Specific gravity						1·33
Volatile matter						54·2
Carbon						45·8
Ashes						3·5

The water included above in the amount of volatile matter was 51·52 per cent.

Iron pyrites is unfortunately very abundant in this bed and would render it an unsafe fuel for many purposes, from the danger of spontaneous combustion. For local purposes, however, it would prove a very useful fuel, the more " brassy" portions being rejected, and for such purposes a large amount of good coal might be here obtained.

It is not well seen, and the section is rather obscure. Covered by blackish shale, with some fish scales, &c., we have a bed or layer of slaty or laminar coal of two feet eight inches in thickness. This rests upon a tough, reddish-brown, flaky clay, with carbonaceous partings of 11 inches ; then a two inch seam of pale clay with carbonized impressions of grassy stems ; then four inches of carbonaceous and bituminous shale ; then one foot five inches of ashy-coloured clay with carbonaceous markings. Under these is the main bed of coal, which here gives a workable thickness of about eight feet, divided by some thin layers of earthy shale but yielding large and symmetrical masses of coal.

This coal is at a slightly less distance from the river than at Hien-lap; the path through the forest, cut nearly straight, is 1,090 yards in length and over very easy and favourable ground. The point where it meets the river is, however, by no means so favourable as a shipping-place as near Hien-lap, where there is deep water and a firm solid bank held up by thick beds of conglomerate which are horizontal and, projecting from the bank, form in the dry season an excellent natural landing-place.

Coal, as stated by Dr. Helfer,* also occurs at a considerable distance north of this and above the great rapids of the Tenasserim. This was visited by Mr. Theobald who found that it is in small nodular strings in the sandstone, not more than an inch in thickness, and by no means continuous. These are, therefore, of no practical value whatever.

Dr. Helfer first discovered and described the locality on the Little Tenasserim river in 1848, and then spoke of the coal in the following terms :— " A vein, five feet thick, 240 feet long, visible on the banks of the river, for- " mation above grey, below black clay slate, the lowest stratum apparently " resting—to judge after the general features of the country—upon blue " limestone ;" and again, " close to this, and a continuation of it, an " immense coal field, of either slaty or conchoidal pitch coal, or English " cannel-coal, highly bituminous, without any concomitant of iron pyrites." He states the seam to be in most places six or more feet thick, and dipping 25°. This locality is 121 miles from Mergui and 80 from the town of Tenasserim.†

It is exceedingly difficult to understand Dr. Helfer's account of this coal, as he always speaks of it as cannel-coal and pitch coal, and yet says, it would rank next to Kilkenny coal, which is well known to be an anthracite, or in fact at the other end of the scale altogether.

The Reports of the Coal Committee in 1846 even went further than Dr. Helfer and spoke of " inexhaustible beds of uniformly good quality" (p. 142.) These glowing descriptions were found, on an inspection of the locality by Dr. Oldham, to be unsupported by facts. There is undoubtedly a bed of what at first might readily be mistaken for coal, of six feet thick, and seen in more places than one ; but of these six feet, there are in reality only a few inches of good coal ; the rest is very earthy bituminous shale, with thin streaky laminæ of coal, barely sufficient to support ignition and sustain combustion ; and even the coal which does occur is irregularly distributed in lenticular nodules or lumps imbedded in the general earthy mass, and having often very much the aspect of being the result of the thorough carbonization of masses of wood imbedded in the general heap of vegetable pulp and leafy mud.

There are two distinct beds, separated by an intervening series of sandstone and shales of about 200 feet in thickness ; of these beds, the upper one is decidedly the best, and from its total thickness (six feet) probably about two feet of tolerable coal could be obtained.

The detailed section of the coal beds and associated layers will shew their character. The lower bed gives :—

---

* Dr. Helfer's Second Report : Calcutta, page 36.   † Second Report, p. 37. et seq.

					Descending.	
					Ft.	In.
Clay and gravel on top ..	..	..	..	..	10 to 12	0
Mould, blackish	..	..	..	..	0	6
Ditto red ..	..	..	..	..	0	4
Coaly smut, earthy and ferruginous	..	..	..	2	0	
Coal, flaky, woody in structure ..	..	..	..	0	4	
Clunch clay, grey, flaky, with fragmentary vegetable impressions, abundant and irregular, thin streaks of bright jetty coal—lower three or four inches much lighter in colour ..	..	..	..	1	0	
Coal, brilliant jetty coal, bright and glistening, in places of one foot thick, but dying out to nothing within a few feet, and then again enlarging to eight or 10 inches, very irregularly streaked with blackish shaly clay ..	..	..	..	1	0	
Grey clunchy clay, with many irregular seams of brilliant jetty coal ..				8	0	

Thus, out of a bed or beds which on the surface looked like a bed of coal of more than four feet thick, there is in reality not more than 18 inches, frequently much less, of good coal, and this not in a continuous deposit but in irregular patches.

At the upper bed the detailed section is—

					Descending.	
					Ft.	In.
Black coaly shale ..	..	..	..	..	2	0
Coal and coaly shale ..	..	..	..	..	1	1
Shales, brownish-black and papery, with fish scales, &c. ..	..	0	7			
Coal, bright and good, but with iron pyrites disseminated	..	0	4			
Shales, blackish, with thin laminæ of bright jetty coal ..	..	1	5			
Coal, fair strong coal, laminæ in structure (pyrites)	..	..	3	0		
Clay, grey flaky clay ..	..	..	..	..	....	

Here it will be seen that there is more than three feet of fair coal, which is, however, though not largely, impregnated with iron pyrites.

The analysis of this coal yielded to Dr. Macnamara the following result :—

Specific gravity	..	..	1·37	Percentage of water .. .. 16.
Volatile matter	..	..	49· 7	Inclusive of water.
Carbon ..	..	..	50· 3	
Ashes ..	..	..	8· 5	

With the exception of the iron pyrites this is a good fuel. It comes out in good lumps and is sufficiently hard. The greater portion also of the coaly shale given in this section might be usefully economized for any local purposes if ever this field should be wrought, but is too poor to repay the cost of transport to any distance.

These beds are favorably placed for working, the amount of the dip or inclination is not more than 18° N. to 20° E., and they are very accessible so far as their position with regard to the stream and the surface is concerned ; but the great distance of the place from any port, the very bad state of the small stream down which the coal would have to be conveyed, and the consequently heavy expense of carriage, will preclude these Tsengkoon coals from being worked so long as other and more easily accessible localities can be found.

" The coal is here exposed in the bank of a small tributary stream which " comes in from the south and which is called by the natives the Phlia-o or " fish stream (Siamese name). It occurs in an irregularly developed bed, " varying from one foot to two feet and even two feet six inches in thickness.

"It is throughout of laminar structure, with a seam of fine jetty coal between
"the layers and very numerous nodular lumps and masses of a resinous,
"ambery-looking mineral imbedded; the mass of the coal on the fresh
"fracture having a very dull lustre and hard pitchy and earthy aspect.
"The whole group of rocks here has even a more modern look than the
"beds with coal in the Tenasserim district. The rocks are softer and less
"indurated, and are more irregular and more like recent clays and sands.
"In ascending order the little section of the coal here exposed is as
"follows :—

	Ft.	In.
Blueish-white, grey, and blackish fine sandy mud, with small black patches or stains, evidently the indistinct remains of plants, (seen).	3	0
This passes insensibly into a dark brownish bed of the same kind, with small angular grains of quartz imbedded, and this by insensible gradations becomes of a blacker colour from the streaks of coaly matter and small fragments of carbonized vegetable remains. This does not form any definite bed but is only the upper part of the previous beds, with these slight alterations in texture and composition.	2	8
Coal, resting on the irregular surface of this muddy bed.	1	6
Mud, clunchy and full of disseminated vegetable remains in fragments of carbonized vegetable matter, forming black layers and patches, varying from an almost imperceptible thickness to ½ an inch. In this bed are imbedded irregular patches of brilliant jet coal, with a bright lustre, and having a semi-columnous texture. One maund of this extracted yielded a basket of fine brilliant blazing coal; on the outer portion of this the woody structure was quite visible.	4	0
Coal, fine bright pitchy coal; in seams varying from ½ of an inch to one inch, imbedded in ferruginous mud.	0	10
Mud, fine, silty, greyish-white, with stems and leaves disseminated through it in every direction, both across and along the layers, but slightly carbonized.	4	6
Black ferruginous bed, with small nodular masses of the same resinous ambery-looking mineral noticed above and very thin seams of coal.	0	6

"Over all these comes a layer of gravel, composed of pebbles of quartz-
"ose, hard sandstone and pure white quartz. In this a few small fragments
"of tin-stone occur. This gravel is here from six inches to two feet six
"inches in thickness, and is covered by the stiff, red pseudo-laterite clay,
"so commonly exposed over the country.
"The beds of coal and associated rocks dip at 35° to 38° E. to 15° to 30° N.
"Such is the section in immediate connexion with the coal. Below
"these beds the series of rocks (similarly ascending) consist of whitish,
"earthy, fine sandstone and indurated mud, slightly calcareous, occasionally
"and locally so much so as to form a muddy limestone. To these succeed
"beds of partially angular conglomerates, with beds of clunchy clay and
"muddy sandstones, dipping as before to E. 30° N. This series is about
"300 feet thick. By "partially angular", I mean conglomerates in which the
"angular character of the broken pebbles imbedded is still retained, although
"the sharp edges are slightly worn off. Over these comes the coal group as
"given above, and above this again we have a series of sandstone beds, soft
"and muddy, of thick, clunchy clays and marks occasionally pebbly, and with
"a few seams of unevenly deposited carbonaceous matter of an inch to two
"inches in thickness, and fine pebbly conglomerates. The whole gives a
"thickness of about 600 feet, and has been subjected to several faultings and
"other disturbances by which the dip and arrangements have been much
"affected.

"From this it will be seen that there is not altogether more than 18
" inches of coal, and this can scarcely be called coal, for it is a hard, black,
" slaty shale, somewhat stone coal-like in aspect. It is however very inter-
" esting from the abundant dissemination through it in irregular little nodular
" lumps of the resinous ambery-like mineral I have noticed above. This
" varies in colour from a blueish bottle-green to a rich yellowish tint,
" like fine amber. In fracture it is quite conchoidal and glassy, burns freely
" and from its abundance adds greatly to the blazing qualities of the mass.

" The coal ignites with some difficulty, but then burns with a good flame
" and strong heat, the lumps become red-hot but do not disintegrate, retain-
" ing all their original form. The ashes are white and abundant. The coal
" comes out of the bed in large and solid masses, and if it occurred in any
" abundance would prove a useful fuel for many purposes.

" Above this main bed, as I have mentioned, and separated by about
" 200 feet of sandstones and clays, there is another thin seam of coaly
" matter ; but it is very irregular and in no place more than a few inches in
" thickness, so that it will be perfectly useless as a source of fuel.

In the valley of the Tenasserim the cliffs past which that river flows
are in several places composed of limestone and on specimens, probably
brought from this locality for they came from the eastward of Tavoy and
no limestone is at present known to exist in that district, Dr. Ure reported
that they had " a specific gravity of 27 and were of perfectly pure semi-
" crystalline carbonate of lime akin to statuary marble, well adapted to act
" as a flux in the melting of iron."

In the valley of the Palouk river there are some thermal springs which
were visited and described by Lieutenant (now General) McLeod. " Hav-
" ing ascended as far as I could in a small canoe, which was dragged over
" rapids, I performed the latter part of the journey by land in consequence
" of the river becoming too shallow and the rapids or falls getting stronger.
" In returning, however, I descended the stream the whole way on a small
" bamboo raft, ... There are two spots where the springs show
" themselves, one immediately on the right bank of the river (here about
" 100 feet wide) with some in the river itself, and the other about two or
" three minutes' walk to the northward inland ; and around the former ones
" a mound of circular stones of various sizes was caked together with
" hardened clay having the appearance of stone. The whole of the mound
" had externally a black appearance, and in some places small circular
" basins had been formed by springs now dry. All the springs then
" discharging were close to the water's edge or in the water : they issue
" from under the rocks through a sandy bottom ; the orifices were very
" small and not above two inches deep. The thermometer being dipped
" in the hottest rose to 196° Fahr. Their height above the sea I estimated
" at about 200 feet."

" The second springs, a little inland, are larger and deeper and are
" situated in a small open space. There were some 40 or 50 bubbling
" up along a line of about 50 feet by 20, the largest being at the northern
" extremity. I took the water from two of the large springs, one about three
" and a half feet deep and two feet in diameter, and the other about half the
" size. In both the thermometer indicated a heat of 194° Fahr. ; the ground
" at the bottom is of a dark, shining colour, here and there resembling the

" colour of brick-dust. Though vapours rise from the springs no disagreeable
" smell pervades the atmosphere. There are other springs in a N. N. W.
" direction from this at a place called Pe. There is nothing in the neigh-
" bourhood, that I know of, indicating volcanic agency."

To this account Dr. Evizard adds ; " A rough examination which I
" made shews these springs to be strongly impregnated with sulphuretted
" hydrogen and to contain also a small proportion of iron and carbonate
" of lime."

Almost all the tributaries of the Tenasserim from the eastward contain
gold, according to Dr. Helfer. Near the old town of Tenasserim, where the Great and Little Tenasserim unite, about one anna's weight is sometimes obtained as the result of one season's washing during the rains by one individual. Copper, in the form of grey copper ore, containing from 40 to 50 parts of the metal in combination with antimony, iron and sulphur have, according to Mr. O'Riley, been obtained from several islands of the archipelago. Dr. Helfer reported an occurrence of zinc on the Mergui islands, but Dr. Oldham of the Geological Survey of India states that all the zinc in the Province is imported. According to Dr. Mason there is a very rich deposit of specular oxide of iron on one of the branches of the Palouk river, whilst the brown oxide is very abundant near Mergui. Three specimens were sent to Dr. Ure who said that from their density they would afford good iron in the smelting furnace and he gave their specific gravity as 3·37—3·18—and 3·32, respectively.

Manganese was found in the Tenasserim by Captain (now General) Tremenheere who wrote—" During my stay at the Tenasserim coal basin a
" piece of manganese ore (black coal) of good quality was brought to me by
" a Kareng who stated that it had been found accidentally in the bank of a
" stream called the Thug-goo (*Tha-goo*) which enters the Great Tenasserim
" 17 miles below the coal site. Subsequently several other pieces of
" the same ore were brought to Mr. T. H. Corbin, Assistant to the Com-
" missioner, from the Therabwen (*Thee-ra-bweng*) river, five miles above the
" Thug-goo and from an intermediate spot ....

" In proceeding down the river I visited these spots and found that at
" each a valuable bed of manganese ore existed close to the surface of the
" country. It was impossible, however, to form any definite opinion as to
" the extent of the beds."

The whole surface of the district from the water's edge to the most
elevated mountain ridge is an almost uninterrupted forest. " All ground left to nature is, without discrimin-
" ation, without exception, covered with timber. There
" are no marshes, no sandy plains, no bare rocks, no such thing as an
" American Savannah, nothing resembling a New Holland pasturage, only
" the pygmean endeavours of man, rescuing the soil for his own purposes,
" with the assistance of fire have divested a small fraction of the area from
" the primitive forest*." No less than 4,734 square miles are unculturable
and 3,003 square miles culturable waste, on almost the whole of which
there is valuable timber which has generally been neglected for the Teak of

---

* Dr. Helfer.

Amherst and Pegu. Theng-gan (*Hopea odorata*) exists in abundance especially on the banks of the Little Tenasserim, and its timber is sawn up and used for building purposes and for boats. It is an excellent durable wood when kept under water as in a boat, or under cover as on land, but is liable to split if exposed dry to the sun. Ka-gnyeng (*Dipterocarpus tuberculatus*) is plentiful and if kept free from wet and white ants planks sawn from it would answer as well as those of Teak; its great value, however, is in the oil or rather balsam which it yields, and which is extracted by cutting a large notch in the trunk a few feet from the ground and occasionally stimulating the secretion by scorching the surface of the scar, which is generally converted into charcoal and gives the oil a dirty black appearance. It is used for making torches and as a wood varnish in unexposed situations. Anan (*Fagræa fragrans*), which here reaches the largest dimensions and grows peculiarly straight and free from internal decay, yields a valuable timber which the terodo worm will not attack and which hardens under water. Eng (*Xylia dolabriformis*) is abundant and the timber is more durable in the ground than Teak. Bhan-bhwai (*Caraya arborea*) like the two preceding trees resists decay but is less abundant, denser in grain, more abounding in knots and of samaller size than Anan, but is much prized by the natives for its useful properties. An inferior kind of sandal wood is produced by the Ka-ra-mai both on the mainland and on the islands of the Archipelago and sapan wood exists in the valley of the Tenasserim. The Jack or Pien-nai (*Artocarpus integrifolia*) yields an excellent yellow dye which does not require any of the metallic bases as a mordant and a tenacious milky juice which flows abundantly from recent wounds and furnishes the best bird-lime whilst the red dye obtained from the roots of the Gnyaw-gyee (*Morinda Citrifolia*) is equal to that furnished by the sapan wood.

Bamboos of several kinds are exceedingly abundant all over the district, the islands excepted, and rattans abound.

The useful vegetable products much resemble those of the neighbouring Tavoy district but there is one which deserves especial notice. At the mouth of the Bhoot-pyeng river are groves of Kha-boung. (*Strychnos nux vomica*) at one time very extensive but now considerably thinned by the wasteful manner in which they are destroyed by the inhabitants. The roots are cut away and extracted for use and the tree, no longer supported, in time falls by its own weight or is felled by the wind and is allowed to rot. The roots are dried, and rubbed into powder on a stone and the powder mixed into a thin paste with water and applied to the affected part in cases of rheumatism, producing in time constitutional effects very similar to those caused ay the internal use of strychnine.

South of Mergui and east of Tenasserim, elephants not many years ago were exceedingly numerous, descending into the plains during the rains and during the dry season retiring into the forest-clad mountains. The numbers have considerably diminished of late years as has the number of Rhinoceroses of which two kinds were known, the single and the double-horned, and possibly a third, *Rhinoceros Indicus*, now found principally on the Islands of the Archipelago. The single-horned species was the most common, the double-horned less so; the horns are still eagerly bought by the Chinese for export. Tigers, leopards and cheeta are plentiful as well as several

Animal productions.

400

kinds of deer and wild hog. Turtle eggs are collected on the sand-banks and *bêche de mer* are brought to Mergui whence they are exported to the Straits Settlements. Edible birds'-nests, built by the *Colocalia fuciphaga* in the rocky caverns and crevices of the islands of the Archipelago, mainly on Tavoy Island, are collected from January to April and exported to the Straits, generally direct by the purchaser from Government of the right to collect. Of honey-bees there are several kinds ; one makes its combs on trees and furnishes a transparent, yellowish, syrupy honey, whilst another selects the limestone rocks and produces an aromatic, reddish-brown honey more liquid than the former. Considerable quantities of dammer are collected from the nests or combs of the dammer-bee and used for caulking the seams of boats.

The climate of Mergui is remarkable for its salubrity. The great heat which its tropical situation would otherwise involve dur-
Climate.
ing the months of March, April and May is moderated by the land and sea breezes which follow each other alternately day and night, the latter usually commencing to blow between the hours of nine and 12 in the morning and continuing till sunset, soon after which the land breeze sets in, but with less regularity, and cools the otherwise sultry and oppressive atmosphere. During the rainy months, from June to October inclusive the sun is often obscured and the temperature is on the whole pleasantly cool. The months of November, December, January and February are the cool months. The variation of temperature thermometrically is not grat. —

Year.	May.			July.			December.			1876.
	Sunrise.	2 P.M.	Sunset.	Sunrise.	2 P.M.	Sunset.	Sunrise.	2 P.M.	Sunset.	Mean of maximum readings, May, 80·30 „ „ minimum „ „ 78·50 Highest reading „ „ 92·00 Lowest „ „ 77·00
1867	72	84	73	74	82	70	63	84	70	Mean of maximum „ July, 80·70
1868	77	87	85	75	80	74	64	84	69	„ „ minimum „ „ 80·20
1869	76	86	82	76	80	76	69	80	71	Highest reading „ „ 90·00
1870	75	85	76	75	80	79	69	82	79	Lowest „ „ 78·00
1871	77	85	74	74	83	74	68	80	70	Mean of maximum „ Dec. 83·30
1872	76	86	82	75	80	76	71	83	80	„ „ minimum „ „ 73·10
1873	78	86	83	75	79	77	71	82	80	Highest „ „ 89·00
1874	81	87	86	83	85	81	81	82	81	Lowest „ „ 66·50
1875	90	—*	90	88	—*	90	88	—*	90	

* Not given in returns.

North-easterly and north-westerly winds prevail during the winter and spring months, for the remainder of the year southerly and westerly winds are the most common ; occasionally during the rainy season violent north-westerly storms of wind and rain occur continuing for days together, and storms of thunder and lightning accompanied by torrents of rain are of frequent occurrence chiefly in the months of April and May and again in October and November. The transitions in the state of the weather are subject to a remarkable regularity in their recurrence ; for example, it frequently commences raining at a certain hour in the day, continuing perhaps for several hours and succeeded by an interval of fine weather and this occurs daily nearly at the same moment for several days when a sudden and complete change may take place and the storm or rain which previously had come on in the evening now begins at noon or at some other period of the 24 hours. It often happens also that storms come on daily for several days but on each occasion an hour earlier or later than on the previous one. The most obvious peculiarity of the atmosphere is its humidity.

YEAR.			RAINFALL, IN INCHES.			
			January to May.	June to September.	October to December.	Total.
1867	..	..	..	26·05	131·92	10·30	168·27
1868	..	..	..	44·40	118·80	15·20	178·40
1869	..	..	..	21·30	130·20	13·50	176·00
1870	..	..	..	32·80	107·50	7·40	147·70
1871	..	..	..	47·30	123·90	16·90	188·10
1872	..	..	..	19·70	100·02	9·12	128·84
1873	..	..	..	13·77	132·93	19·20	165·90
1874	..	..	..	39·73	106·61	18·18	164·52
1875	..	..	..	24·79	129·76	15·96	170·51
1876	..	..	..	44·96	112·05	18·09	175·04
Average	..	..	..	31·48	119·37	13·38	165·22

The most prevalent diseases are fevers—ague, remittent, and simple continued—dyspepsia, bronchitis, ophthalmia, rheumatism and abscesses. The low-lying country and the damp, forest-clad valleys are pregnant with miasmatic effluvia but the fevers are readily amenable to treatment. A curious fact is the general absence of ague-cake or enlarged spleen. Small-pox annually carries off a large percentage of the population comparatively—in 1876 as many as 66. The total deaths and the ratio per 1,000 of population in 1876, with the mean of the previous five years was :—

TOTAL DEATHS.	RATIO PER 1,000 OF POPULATION.						FROM ALL CAUSES.	
	Cholera.	Small-pox.	Fever.	Bowel complaints.	Injuries.	All other causes.	For the year.	Average of five previous years.
283	..	6·63	9·38	4·26	·47	6·06	26·83	19·62

History.

Of the early history of Mergui but little is known. Ralph Fitch and Cæsar Frederic both mention it as a country with an important trade, and in 1687 it was visited by Captain Weldon who had been sent thither to declare war with Siam, which shews that at that period it formed a portion of the Siamese dominions. Tenasserim is said to have been founded by the Siamese in 1373 A.D. Towards the end of the eighteenth century it was wrested from the Siamese by Aloung-bhoora and remained Burmese territory until the first Burmese war. After the Burmese conquest the Siamese generally fled and to replace them Burmese colonists were imported by the conquerors and settled in villages in different parts of the country as far south as Le-gnya, beyond which the country remained disputed territory. The whole country remained in a chronic state of rebellion and war. The Siamese, more numerous than the inhabitants of the Burmese colonies which had been established partly by force and were kept up by dread, made continual incursions, carrying away numerous captives, and the Burmese Governors wreaked their vengeance on their own people who would not or did not fight ; especially was this so in 1808 when the Daing-won, who had been sent south to put down a rebellion which had broken out in Tavoy and Mergui, robbed and murdered wherever he went. After disorder had reigned supreme for some 50 years war broke out between the Government of India and the King of Burma and in 1824 Sir Archibald Campbell, commanding in Pegu, despatched a force which, after taking possession of Tavoy, appeared before Mergui on the 6th October 1824 ; a heavy fire was opened from the batteries of the town but this was speedily silenced and the stockade carried by assault. Early in 1825 a Siamese force landed and ravaged the country about Tenasserim but was driven off and from that time Mergui has remained undisturbed in the possession of the English.

Architectural remains.

Except the walls, or rather the foundations of the walls, of old Tenasserim, founded towards the end of the fourteenth century, and one or two pagodas of no very great antiquity the district possesses no architectural remains of any kind. In Tenasserim there is a pagoda called *Wot-tsheng*, built in

1380 A.D. and thoroughly repaired a few years ago, but of no great sanctity. The *Ze-da-won* pagoda on a hill on the banks of the Tenasserim river is supposed to have been built in 1208 A.D. by King Na-ra-pa-tee-tshee-thoo who visited the coast and is visited every year in the month of October by large numbers of pilgrims. The pagoda on the central hill in Mergui was erected in 1803 A.D. by the then Burman Governor and is not important in any way.

This district is far more important from its mineral than from its agricultural wealth, only 73 square miles of country being under cultivation. Rice is grown in the plains and in toungya amongst the hills and small quantities are exported from the coast towns. The area thus cultivated is slowly but steadily increasing. Sugarcane and tobacco are produced to some extent, sessamum is grown with rice in the toungya and the seeds used locally and exported. Areca palms cover 787 acres, rattans are plentiful and the Dhanee (*Nipa fruticans*) is found in perfection and largely cultivated in the mangrove territory, a good deal of coarse sugar being made from the juice of the stem and the leaves used for thatch in the district and to some extent exported. It is in fruits, however, that Mergui is agriculturally richest : Doorians, Mangosteens, Jack, Papaya, Cocoanuts, Guavas, Mulberries, Cashew, Limes, Oranges, Pine-apples, Melons, Plantains, Ka-na-tso or Rangoon grapes (*Pierardia sapota*) and Shaddock are extensively grown, and amongst vegetables, Yams, sweet and Kareng potatoes, cucumbers, gourds and chillies and many others are produced in abundance.

Agriculture.

The more frequent steam communication with Rangoon and Maulmain is tending to increase the area of garden land as the people find a readier sale for the exportable produce.

The area under the principal crops during each of the last ten years was :—

YEAR.		Rice.	Sugar-cane.	Tobacco.	Cocoa-nuts.	Betel-nuts.	Dhanee palms.	Plantains.	Doorians.	Mixed fruit trees.
1867-68	..	30,286	62	45	107	785	3,055	325	216	2,329
1868-69	..	29,883	133	46	110	751	3,112	373	246	2,557
1869-70	..	31,205	148	43	111	752	3,136	422	244	2,619
1870-71	..	25,243	..	47	..	751	3,179	443	245	2,659
1871-72	..	25,713	176	59	123	756	3,203	497	245	2,726
1872-73	..	28,431	23	28	122	682	3,436	428	227	3,150
1873-74	..	29,389	23	49	120	713	3,550	439	243	2,346
1874-75	..	30,137	42	49	120	713	3,691	472	241	3,382
1875-76	..	30,926	59	48	121	725	3,749	497	236	3,594
1876-77	..	31,879	70	43	114	727	3,796	427	236	3,543

The soil is poorer than in any other part of the Province except in Kyouk-hpyoo and Sandoway, the average outturn of rice being only 1,000 lbs. an acre. The gross produce of this cereal in 1876-77, exclusive of that grown in toungya, was thus about 14,230 tons.

The agricultural stock during the same period was :—

Year.	Buffaloes.	Cows, bulls and bullocks.	Elephants.	Sheep and goats.	Pigs.	Carts.	Ploughs.	Boats.	Oil and sugar mills.
1867-68 ..	16,742	223	5	200	350	23	3,020	2,004	Not given.
1868-69 ..	18,564	259	7	210	816	38	3,000	2,071	..
1869-70 ..	19,637	203	10	182	735	24	3,026	2,110	..
1870-71 ..	22,451	215	10	..	684	23	3,042	1,895	12
1871-72 ..	23,897	269	9	156	514	36	3,063	1,911	..
1872-73 ..	23,732	320	9	187	596	39	3,072	1,944	16
1873-74 ..	24,672	331	10	296	910	53	3,056	2,095	17
1874-75 ..	26,389	350	13	255	1,070	58	3,067	2,192	19
1875-76 ..	27,710	449	16	312	1,249	48	3,060	2,452	16
1876-77 ..	27,835	507	18	397	1,327	61	3,075	2,577	20

and the prices of produce and labour, according to the returns given in the annual Administration Reports, were in Rupees :—

Year.	Rice.	Sugar.	Salt.	Tobacco.	Plough bullocks.	Goats.	Buffaloes.	LABOURERS. Skilled.	Unskilled.	Carts.	Boats.
	Per maund of 80 lbs.				Each.			Daily hire. Per man.		Each.	
1867-68 ..	1 8	8 12	3 2	Not given.	40 0	14 0	40 0	1 0	0 8	2 0	0 8
1868-69 ..	1 8	8 12	3 2		40 0	14 0	40 0	1 0	0 8	2 0	0 8
1869-70 ..	1 8	..	1 4		60 0	5 0	40 0	1 0	0 8	2 0	0 8
1870-71 ..	1 8	8 12	3 2		45 0	14 0	40 0	1 0	0 8	2 0	0 8
1871-72 ..	1 8	8 12	3 2		45 0	6 0	60 0	1 0	0 8	2 0	0 8
1872-73 ..	1 12	8 12	3 2	11 8	45 0	6 0	40 0	1 0	0 8	2 0	0 8
1873-74 ..	1 12	8 12	3 2	11 8	45 0	..	40 0	1 0	0 8	2 8	0 8
1874-75 ..	1 12	8 12	3 2	11 8	45 0	6 0	40 0	1 0	0 8	2 8	0 8
1875-76 ..	1 12	14 0	1 5	22 8	45 0	6 0	40 0	1 0	0 8	2 8	0 8
1876-77 ..	2 4	20 0	1 3	20 0	60 0	6 0	40 0	1 0	0 8	2 8	0 8

As a general rule the land is held and cultivated by the owner, though in some very rare cases it is rented out and the owner lives in a town or village, but even in this case the rent which he receives is by no means sufficient to support him and he pursues some trade or occupation ; in some cases, indeed, owners who are unable to work their own land let it out rent free. Mortgages, almost always usufructuary, are rare ; formerly they were by parol agreement or on a document written after the native manner on parabaik, but of late years stamped paper has been adopted, doubtless because the Courts refuse to receive an unstamped document in evidence.

Labourers as a general rule are paid no monthly wages but at the end of the season receive from 50 to 60 baskets of unhusked rice. The average holding of each cultivator is about 5·70 acres, and the number of persons dependent upon each male agriculturist of 20 years of age and upwards, who in 1872 numbered 18,512, is about 6·31.

From the notices of early travellers who described the country when Population. it was under Siamese rule it seems evident that at one time this district was rich and thickly inhabited but it is extremely doubtful if their accounts do not give too glowing a picture of its wealth. On the conquest of the country by Aloung-bhoora almost all the Siamese retired, except from Bhoot-pyeng and Le-gnya south of Mergui where the Burmans never gained a secure footing. The feelings between the Burmese and Siamese were very much those which for centuries existed between the English and the Scots : the one nation was the natural enemy of the other. After the conquest a system of petty warfare was carried on accompanied by kidnapping, plunder and devastation, whilst even within their own limits the Burman conquerors robbed and murdered and the whole frontier was turned into a waste. The Siamese, on the establishment of the British Government, gradually returned and many have settled down into peaceable cultivators. They are an industrious, hardy race, approaching more to the Malay type in their features, and are as a general rule quiet, orderly and obedient. The Burmese are descendants of those who came with the conquering generals of their race and remained after the British occupation, recruited by occasional immigration ; they are found principally in the towns and villages in the fertile tract bordering the seacoast. The Hindoo population—to some extent derived from convicts transported hither from Bengal in former years, partly from camp-followers who came with the troops and remained when these were withdrawn, partly from immigration—is very small and fluctuates considerably from year to year. The Mahomedans are more numerous and increase steadily. The Burmese, Shan and Kareng form the great bulk of the inhabitants, whilst there are more Malays than in the whole of the rest of the Province altogether and more Chinese than in any other part except the town of Rangoon. More than half the Mahomedans other than Malays and very nearly half the Chinese are in Mergui town. As regards the Mahomedans, however, it is worthy of notice that the Malays are vastly more numerous in the district than in Mergui where in 1873 there were only 25 out of a total of 1,261. The Kareng are spread over the district and avoid the large towns. The Selung, a small tribe inhabiting the islands of the Archipelago are, in a low state of civilization and with few comforts. An American Baptist Missionary, Mr. Brayton, reduced their language to writing, established a school and brought out some school books in Selungese. In former years they lived a wandering life passing from island to island with no other habitation than their boats and were frequently carried off as slaves by the Malays. Their principal occupations are fishing, collecting sandal-wood and catching sea slugs which they sell to traders who visit the islands and to the inhabitants of the coast villages ; wild pigs, which are found on some of the islands, are caught and killed by their numerous dogs and a few possess fowls. Mr Kincaid who visited them some thirty years ago wrote : " They have no God, no temple, no priest, no liturgy, no holy day and no

" prayers. In their domestic habits they are free from all conventional
" rules. They are very poor, too, having no houses, no gardens, no culti-
" vated fields, nor any domestic animals but dogs." Their general state
has decidedly improved since the time when this sad picture of their condition was drawn, and though still behind every other race in the Province
they exhibit less fear of their fellow creatures and are tending towards more
settled habits, notably in no longer living solely on board their boats but
having, in places, houses, as yet, it must be said, of a very rude kind.

On the occupation of the country by the British it was found to be
almost depopulated, the result of the border warfare already alluded to and of
the cruelties of the Burmese, especially of the Daing-won in 1808, and contained only some 10,000 inhabitants. In 1837-38 the number had risen to
17,862 and since, partly from immigration and partly from natural causes,
has continued to increase. The population was :—

26,739 in 1847-48.	46,184 in 1871-72.
31,833 in 1857-58.	47,694 in 1872-73.
41,688 in 1867-68.	48,589 in 1873-74.
42,550 in 1868-69.	49,612 in 1874-75.
43,753 in 1869-70.	50,885 in 1875-76.
44,762 in 1870-71.	51,846 in 1876-77.

The following table shews the inhabitants during the last decennial
period classified according to religion :—

YEAR.			Hindoos.	Mahomedans.	Booddhists, including Kareng.	Christians and others.	Total.
1867	..	..	164	2,050	39,302	172	41,688
1868	..	..	203	2,077	40,119	151	42,550
1869	..	..	109	2,190	41,311	143	43,753
1870	..	..	50	2,196	42,390	126	44,762
1871	..	..	44	2,323	43,678	139	46,184
1872	..	..	168	2,351	45,057	118	47,694
1873	..	..	120	2,462	45,780	227	48,589
1874	..	..	246	2,419	46,714	233	49,612
1875	..	..	332	2,486	47,816	221	50,855
1876	..	..	353	2,533	48,750	210	51,846

In 1873 the nationality was :—

Nationality.				Town of Mergui.	District	Total.
Europeans and Eurasians	..	..	..	35	7	42
Portuguese Christians	..	..	..	150	27	185
Burmese	..	..	..	7,380	20,930	28,310
Chinese	..	..	..	1,091	1,294	2,385
Kareng ..	..	..	..	....	8,328	8,328
Madrassis	..	..	..	23	2	25
Bengalis	..	..	..	95	....	95
Siamese	..	..	..	....	5,033	5,033
Malays	..	..	..	25	1,236	1,261
Mahomedans	..	..	..	1,393	1,069	2,462
Selung	..	..	..	....	463	463*
		Total	..	10,200	38,389	48,589

* Approximate.

Here as everywhere else, except in Tavoy, the males are more numerous than the females and this may fairly be ascribed to the immigration of males from other countries, Siam, China, the Straits and India, who rarely or never bring wives or families with them. The total population in 1872 classed according to age, sex and religion was :—

Age	Total Males	Total Females	Total	Christians Males	Christians Females	Christians Total	Boodhists Males	Boodhists Females	Boodhists Total	Mahomedans Males	Mahomedans Females	Mahomedans Total	Hindoos Males	Hindoos Females	Hindoos Total
Not exceeding 1 year ..	1,095	1,063	2,158	50	35	85	978	959	1,937	67	69	136	..	..	..
Above 1 and under 6 years.	4,194	3,884	8,028	124	121	245	3,727	3,396	7,123	340	316	656	3	1	4
Do. 6 do. 12 do.	4,180	3,572	7,752	115	118	233	3,730	3,176	6,906	335	278	613	..	..	..
Do. 12 do. 20 do.	2,955	3,312	6,267	75	99	174	2,620	2,954	5,574	260	259	519	..	..	..
Do. 20 do. 30 do.	3,966	3,995	7,961	138	95	233	3,535	3,614	7,149	292	284	576	1	2	3
Do. 30 do. 40 do.	3,691	3,108	6,799	96	94	190	3,344	2,789	6,133	248	225	473	3	..	3
Do. 40 do. 50 do.	2,225	1,927	4,152	65	38	103	2,083	1,755	3,768	144	134	278	3	..	3
Do. 50 do. 60 do.	1,030	1,030	2,060	33	32	65	907	924	1,831	89	74	163	1	..	1
Do. 60 do.	1,064	951	2,015	15	16	31	950	855	1,805	98	80	178	1	..	1
Total	24,400	22,792	47,192	711	648	1,359	21,804	20,422	42,226	1,873	1,719	3,592	12	3	15

This district contains only one town with more than 5,000 inhabitants and not one with more than 2,000 and less than 5,000.

Towns and villages.

Mergui, the head-quarters, stands on the west of an island of the same name in 12° 26' N. and 98° 35' E. : originally a small village the present town was founded by the Burmese in 1767 A.D., nine years after they had conquered the country. It is built round the base of a small hill on which are situated the Court-house and Treasury and where were formerly the barracks occupied by the troops, and covers an area of 10 square miles. The population, composed mainly of Chinese, who live on the seaboard, Mahomedans, who occupy the part behind the central hill, and Burmese, who are located in the other parts, is steadily but slowly increasing; in 1867 the inhabitants numbered 9,381, in 1873 10,200, of whom 7,380 were Burmese, 1,091 Chinese, 1,393 Mahomedans, and the remainder Europeans and Eurasians, Hindoos and Malays, and in 1877 10,731. It contains two Court-houses, a Police-office, a School-house, a Circuit-house, a Forest-office and a Hospital and dispensary on the central hill, a Gaol in the village at the back, and three Police-stations situated north, south and west, with a masonry market on the sea beach and a wooden and thatched smaller one in the town; from the former a stone wharf projects into the sea, and further south an old and substantial wooden pier extends to below low watermark. Pa-law is a large village of 1,481 inhabitants in the north of the district on the banks of a small stream of the same name, the head-quarters of a township where an Extra Assistant Commissioner holds his court. It is in the centre of a fertile rice tract and does a fair trade in the export of that cereal. Pa-la is another large village on a stream of the same name, about 12 miles south of Pa-law, with a good rice trade. It was a large place during the Siamese rule but has now a population of only 844 souls. Le-gnya, the head-quarters of the Le-gnya township, is on a river of the same name, about two tides up, in 11° 28' N. It was a place of some importance during the Siamese rule but is now a long, straggling village with a population of 181 souls, principally Siamese and Malays with a few Chinamen who cultivate rice and sugar-cane. A small police force is stationed here. Bhoot-pyeng, on the Bhoot-pyeng river, was a large town when the country belonged to the Siamese but is now a small village inhabited by a few Malays and Siamese who are rice and sugar-cane cultivators. In this village a small body of police is stationed. Tenasserim, which gives its name to the whole division, is at the junction of the Great and Little Tenasserim rivers. It was founded in 1373 A.D. by the Siamese and was surrounded by a mud wall faced with brick, the foundations of which are still visible, which enclosed some four square miles. It was captured by the Burman conqueror, Aloung-bhoora, in 1759 and a few years later the inhabitants were put to the sword by the Burman Governor, Moung Tien-gyaw. All that now remains of this ancient town is a small village with 666 inhabitants surrounded by hills covered with dense forest and inhabited by a mixed race of Siamese and Burmese with a few Chinamen. The Extra Assistant Commissioner in charge of the township holds his Court here and a small police force is quartered in the village. The remaining villages, 196 in number, are small and of no importance; 56 contain less than 200 inhabitants, 130 between 200 and 500 and 10 between 500 and 1,000.

The trade of Mergui seems at one time to have been of some impor-
Trade. tance. Cæsar Frederick, who visited the country in about 1569 A.D., speaking of Tenasserim wrote—" A great " river which cometh out of the kingdom of Siam and where this river " runneth into the sea is a village called Mergui in whose harbour there lay " every year some ships with veizina, nyppa and benjamin". James Lamarter, writing in 1592 A.D., speaks of waiting at Point de Galle for " ships from Tenasserim, a great Bay to the south of Martaban in the " kingdom of Siam" and according to Dr. Mason, it is said in some account of a voyage made in 1609 that " the Guzerat vessels came to Siam in June " and July, touching by way at the Maldive Islands and then at Tenasserim " whence they go over to Siam in 20 days." There is now a flourishing trade with Rangoon, Bassein and the Straits Settlements. The principal articles of export are rice, rattans, torches, dried fish, areca nuts, sessamum seeds, molasses, sea slugs, edible birds-nests and tin. Sea slugs, shark fins and edible birds-nests are exported mainly to Singapore and Penang and rice is sometimes carried to the Nicobar Islands, whence are brought in exchange betel-nuts, tortoise-shell and, formerly, not unfrequently goods which the natives had obtained from the wrecks of vessels. The principal imports are piece-goods, tobacco, cotton, earthenware, tea and sugar. The value of the imports and exports since 1856-57 were :—

YEAR.					Total value of exports.	Total value of imports.
					Rs.	Rs.
1857-58	..	..	..	..	..	145,290	111,250
1858-59	..	..	..	..	..	118,180	123,750
1859-60	..	..	..	..	..	114,630	122,120
1860-61	..	..	..	..	..	212,000	121,380
1861-62	..	..	..	..	..	142,850	143,220
1862-63	..	..	..	..	..	161,830	147,320
1863-64	..	..	..	..	..	170,110	110,980
1864-65	..	..	..	..	..	236,080	213,390
1865-66	..	..	..	..	..	247,320	206,280
1866-67	..	..	..	..	..	321,070	242,510
1867-68	..	..	..	..	..	348,350	316,494
1868-69	..	..	..	..	..	366,620	287,810
1869-70	..	..	..	..	..	343,354	227,615
1870-71	..	..	..	..	..	367,659	301,586
1871-72	..	..	..	..	..	348,742	298,358
1872-73	..	..	..	..	..	119,684	275,631
1873-74	..	..	..	..	..	462,411	387,115
1874-75	..	..	..	..	..	392,596	468,946
1875-76	..	..	..	..	..	308,673	115,584
1876-77	..	..	..	..	..	443,070	490,573

The value of the grain exported during each year from 1855-56 was :—

Year.	Export.	Year.	Export.
	Rs.		Rs.
1856-57	8,560	1867-68	24,189
1857-58	15,100	1868-69	28,500
1858-59	7,380	1869-70	24,829
1859-60	5,850	1870-71	88,560
1860-61	18,770	1871-72	34,940
1861-62	14,610	1872-78	16,397
1862-63	18,000	1873-74	19,710
1863-64	17,790	1874-75	12,953
1864-65	16,970	1875-76	16,468
1865-66	6,120	1876-77	42,005
1866-67	28,900		

Revenue.

During the sixteenth century the Peguan sovereigns received from Mergui an annual revenue of 3,000 viss of silver or Rs. 390,000, 30 elephants and all the customs dues of the port; but when it was first occupied by the British the revenue derived from this district was very small, and in 1853-54, 27 years later, was only Rs. 56,500. During the last 23 years it has been as shewn in the following table :—

Year.	Land revenue.	Capitation tax.	Excise.	Fisheries.	Customs.	All other items.	Total.
	Rs.	Rs.	Rs.	Rs.	Rs.	Rs.	Rs.
1854-55	26,220	9,840	8,860	..	..	12,060	56,980
1855-56	27,810	9,690	12,510	..	1,088	11,440	62,080
1856-67	29,860	9,850	12,600	..	2,230	11,570	65,620
1857-58	28,870	12,240	18,820	..	2,250	12,990	70,170
1858-59	42,940	17,440	18,030	..	1,570	12,990	92,970
1859-60	44,550	17,710	24,970	..	1,720	15,990	104,850
1860-61	46,480	17,380	31,390	..	2,770	17,900	115,920
1861-62	46,670	22,310	32,050	500	3,130	12,550	117,210
1862-63	49,460	21,070	23,840	950	3,420	18,530	117,270
1863-64	48,490	21,210	34,150	900	3,100	15,060	122,910
1864-65	48,540	22,130	34,910	7,330	2,790	13,170	128,870
1865-66	54,670	22,250	23,070	7,440	1,630	11,910	120,970
1866-67	51,400	22,860	86,010	8,380	3,480	13,040	135,170
1867-68	52,140	24,140	24,390	8,870	4,990	11,850	126,380
1868-69	51,690	23,830	29,110	10,360	4,850	13,800	133,140
1869-70	53,500	24,520	29,250	10,050	4,580	12,030	133,880
1870-71	54,500	25,120	25,790	10,080	8,250	13,000	136,740
1871-72	55,040	25,690	29,060	11,180	6,150	10,900	138,020
1872-73	60,280	26,970	29,030	11,020	2,910	13,880	143,090
1878-74	62,120	28,780	40,610	11,050	3,800	15,010	161,370
1874-75	68,576	29,412	41,992	10,449	4,823	17,328	167,580
1875-76	64,959	30,252	52,061	11,298	6,534	17,024	182,128
1876-77	66,599	31,037	50,076	10,530	7,390	56,455	182,087

Customs-offices were first established in 1855-56, and in 1861-62 the turtle banks were first leased out for a term of years, more with the object of preserving them from the gradual destruction which they were surely undergoing from their being opened to the people at large than to raise a revenue. In the last 23 years the revenues have more than trebled, whilst the land revenue and capitation tax have increased by 260 and 215 per cent. : the main increase was due to fisheries and excise.

From these revenues the expenditure for officers of all kinds during the last 10 years and the available balances were :—

YEAR.			Gross Imperial revenue.	Total cost of officials of all kinds.	Balance.
			Rs.	Rs.	Rs.
1867	..	..	..	126,380	98,930	27,450
1868	..	..	..	133,140	56,330	76,810
1869	..	..	..	133,880	87,240	46,640
1870	..	..	..	136,740	78,430	58,310
1871	..	..	..	138,020	49,150	88,870
1872	..	..	..	143,090	71,810	71,280
1873	..	..	..	161,370	79,080	82,290
1874	..	..	..	167,580	75,571	92,009
1875	..	..	..	182,128	69,952	112,176
1876	..	..	..	182,007	75,552	106,535

In addition to this Imperial revenue a local revenue is raised from a town fund, a district fund and the five per cent. cess fund. The amounts thus raised during the last 10 years have been :—

				Rs.					Rs.
1867-68	..	..	..	9,800	1872-73	..	..	..	11,780
1868-69	..	..	..	11,300	1873-74	..	..	..	12,250
1869-70	..	..	..	11,210	1874-75	..	..	..	16,532
1870-71	..	..	..	12,100	1875-76	..	..	..	17,319
1871-72	..	..	..	11,500	1876-77	..	..	..	14,956

The principal manufactures in the district are jaggery, sugar-boiling and tin-smelting. Jaggery is made from the juice of the Neepa palm and the manufacture is carried on from November to the following April. The stems of the full grown trees are gently beaten for 15 or 20 days, the fruit is then cut off and the juice which exudes from the ends of the stocks left attached to the tree drains slowly into bamboos placed to receive it : when a sufficient quantity has been collected it is placed in iron pans and boiled down till sufficiently viscid to harden on cooling. The bamboos are carefully washed after each time they are used to prevent the juice from turning sour. Each manufacturer employs one or more labourers according to the number of trees which he works. Ten trees are calculated to yield about 92 lbs. of jaggery in a season, and the largest amount manufactured by any one party may be taken at about 150 times this quantity or 123 cwt., worth about Rs. 225. Sugar is made principally in Tenasserim, Le-gnya and the villages round Mergui Island, and during the N. E. monsoon, that is from November till April. The canes are crushed under a stone roller and the juice caught in a large tub. When a sufficient quantity has been collected it is strained and boiled down to crystallization in iron pans, and the product, which is then of a red hue, is blanched by being placed in large, wide-mouthed earthen pots covered with hay, kept damp by daily sprinkling, and arranged under a shed ; in a few days the upper portion of the contents of the pot are scraped off and the operation repeated until the whole has been whitened and collected. The native method of extracting tin from the ore is as follows. The ore after being well washed is placed in a cylindrical vessel of clay four feet in circumference and six feet in height together with charcoal. At the bottom and on opposite sides, are two orifices, in one of which is inserted the mouth of a pair of bellows, whilst from the other the ore as it melts runs out into a hole dug in the earth to receive it. From this it is cast into oblong moulds and is exported in the ingot shape thus given to it. The cost of smelting is estimated at about Rs. 1-8 per 100lbs. The average number of men employed by each master worker is 60 and each is paid about Rs. 15 a month and is fed. The average of the yield of each man's labour is calculated at about Rs. 80 a month, but there are other expenses besides wages. The tools have to be supplied and in many cases a channel has to be cut to bring water from a neighbouring stream to the site of the works. In many cases the workers receive no food or wages but supply the "proprietor" with tin ore at about Rs. 13-8 per 100 lbs. which on melting yield 66 lbs. of pure tin. In 1877-78 only 13 out of the 29 mines were actually worked.

The administration of the district is at present entrusted to a Deputy

Administration.   Commissioner whose head-quarters are at Mergui, five Extra Assistant Commissioners and a Superintendent of Police. In former years the subordinate administrative officers were called Goung-gyoop, and the Police were under them : they were nine in number and had charge of Pa-law in the extreme north, Ka-beng adjoining it in the south Ta-gnyet to the south-east stretching down to Mergui Island from which it was divided by the Ka-beng river, Ka-lweng on Mergui Island north of the town of Mergui, to the north of which again and adjoining Ta-gnyet was Pa-goot-toung ; west of the Tenasserim river was Taw Nouk-lay and to the south-east Tenasserim, Pa-re-kywon including King's Island and Madra-ma-kan, the last an island opposite the town of Mergui and about three-quarters of a mile distant from it, Le-gnya extending from the main range westwards to the sea between Tenasserim and Ma-lee-won, and lastly Ma-lee-won occupying the whole country south of Le-gnya. In later years the various subordinate jurisdictions were amalgamated into the existing townships, and in 1860-61 the whole of Ma-lee-won was farmed out to a Chinaman who was supplied with police and who collected for his own benefit all the taxes and worked the tin mines, a system which a year or two ago was discontinued and the township again brought under the supervision of the local officers for administrative purposes. The district is now divided into five townships, Mergui, Pa-law, Tenasserim, Le-gnya and Ma-lee-won. Pa-law extends from the Tavoy district in the north along the coast to Mergui township with a narrow strip stretching still further southwards between Mergui and the western hills and in 1876 contained 14,248 inhabitants scattered in numerous villages. South of Pa-law and north of Le-gnya with Tenasserim in the east is the Mergui township with 16,327 inhabitants exclusive of the 10,731 in the town of Mergui. Eastward of Pa-law and occupying the valleys of the two Tenasserim rivers and thus extending behind Le-gnya and Mergui is Tenasserim, the head-quarters of which are at Old Tenasserim and which in 1873 had a population of only 6,494 souls and in 1876 of 6,516. From the Mergui township southwards to the spur which forms the watershed between the sources of the Le-gnya and the Pak-chan the country, with 2,898 inhabitants in 1873 and 3,117 in 1876, is under the Le-gnya Extra Assistant Commissioner, and from this spur southward is Ma-lee-won with 2,250 inhabitants in 1873 and 2,444 in 1876. Ma-lee-won and Le-gnya are included in the Ma-lee-won sub-division. In the town of Mergui there is also an Extra Assistant Commissioner of superior grade. There are thus seven criminal, civil and revenue courts with no village further from any one of them than 60 miles, whilst the average distance is 32 miles.

The Police, under a Superintendent whose head-quarters are at Mergui, was organized in 1862-63 as a part of the general Police force of the Province and consists of 20 subordinate officers and 178 men, of whom 10 are boatmen and 16 are paid from municipal funds. The principal Police stations besides Mergui and Pa-law, Tenasserim, Le-gnya and Ma-lee-won, the head-quarter stations of Extra Assistant Commissioners, are Pyeng-boo-gyee, Bhan-loung and Bhoot-pyeng. In 1876 the cost of the force was Rs. 47,798 of which Rs. 1,980 were defrayed from local funds. In that year it was found necessary slightly to decrease the strength of the force in order to obtain funds wherewith to increase the pay of the Police employed in Ma-lee-won, as it was impossible to get recruits at the old rates.

The gaol, which consists of thatched wooden buildings surrounded by a masonry wall, lying in the valley behind the hill round which the town of Mergui is built, was erected soon after the British occupation of the country, some, if not all, of the laterite with which the wall is constructed being brought from the old walls of Tenasserim. The average number of prisoners confined here is very small, the largest number during the five years ending with 1876 being 25 (all long-term convicts are sent to Maulmain). and the amount made by gaol manufactures is also small, whilst the average cost of each prisoner, Rs. 151 in 1876, is necessarily large owing to few the confined. The number received, which as regards this gaol may be taken as the number sentenced to imprisonment, and the number discharged, during the last five years were :—

YEAR.	Remaining from previous year.	Received.	Total.	DISCHARGED.			Remaining at end of year.	Average daily number.
				Transferred to other Gaols.	Released, died, &c.	Total.		
1872	14	84	98	10	76	86	12	20
1873	12	78	90	27	54	81	9	13
1874	9	67	76	23	47	70	6	12
1875	6	73	79	18	50	68	11	10
1876	11	81	92	35	48	83	9	10

Postal communication within the limits of the district is carried on by district dâk, that is by an establishment directly under the control of the

Deputy Commissioner, and paid for from the five per cent. cess levied on land revenue and fishery and net tax, by which are carried letters free. The lines are from Mergui to Pyeng-byoo-gyee *via* Pa-law (53 miles) and back, from Mergui to Tenasserim (35 miles) and back, from Mergui to Le-gnya and on to Bhoot-pyeng (144 miles) and back, and from Mergui to Ma-lee-won (195 miles) and back. Postal communication with the outside world is carried on by the steamers of the British India Steam Navigation Company which call in once a week on their way between Calcutta and the other sea-ports of the Province, and Penang and other ports to the east-ward, and by the small coasting steamers of the Maulmain Tug Company, which run down to Mergui from Maulmain twice a month.

The Hospital and Charitable dispensary are situated on the extremity of the Mergui hills and consist of a wooden structure with shingled roof, raised about 10 feet from the ground and divided into five compartments. The central part is divided into two rooms serving as office and dispensary and the remainder is used as hospital wards. The number of persons treated during 1876 was 3,295 of whom 169 were in-patients, and during that year the income was Rs. 6,551 and the expenditure Rs. 6,544; the credit balance at the close of the year was Rs. 656.

The education of the inhabitants of the district had been, until late years, principally cared for by the Booddhist priests and the Roman Catholic and the American Baptist Missionaries, but in 1871 the State established a middle class school in Mergui which was welcomed by the inhabitants and has made some progress, a progress which latterly was somewhat checked by the opening of a Roman Catholic school in the town, by the fear which some of the people had that the institution of the State school was to be changed and English no longer taught, by a Chinaman from Penang opening a school for the Chinese, and by the existence of three or four little English schools in which no fees were charged. The State school appears to be recovering gradually, a new school-house has been built as well as a residence for the head master. In 1873, when it was suffering from the above causes it had an average daily attendance of 32 scholars, who paid a fee varying from eight annas to one Rupee.

The number of pupils on the rolls, all learning through the English language, the average attendance and the receipts and charges during the last five years were :—

| YEAR. | | On Rolls on 31st March. | Average number on Rolls monthly. | Average daily attendance. | RECEIPTS, IN RUPEES. | | | Expenditure, in Rs. | COST, IN RUPEES, OF EDUCATING EACH PUPIL. |
					From Government.	From fees and sale of books.	Total.		
1872-73	..	35	48	36	3,939	505	4,444	4,444	95
1873-74	..	71	39	32	3,800	433	4,233	4,233	109
1874-75	..	74	75	62	5,938	520	6,448	5,978	96
1875-76	..	77	78	66	4,598	536	5,134	5,134	78
1876-77	..	66	68	58	4,886	468	5,354	5,354	92

Besides the Government School in Mergui, there are 16 schools aided by the State and inspected by the State officers, of which little can be said except that the scholars are taught, after a fashion, to read and write Burmese.

MERGUI ARCHIPELAGO.—A large cluster of islands which, commencing in the north with Tavoy Island in about 13° 13' N. Lat., stretches southward beyond the limits of British territory. The majority are mountainous, the height of some being 3,000 feet ; Maingy Island in 12° 32' N. Lat. and 98° 7' E. Long. can be seen for 11 miles, and the southern peak of S. Matthew's Island in 10° 52' N. Lat. and 98° E. Long. for 13 miles. Those amongst them which are not bare rocks are clothed with dense vegetation, though some, *e. g.*, Kissering, were formerly well cultivated. They are but sparsely inhabited, a few Burmese and Kareng having settled on one or two. They are the resort of a peculiar race, the Selung (*q. v.*), who rarely or never leave them to visit the mainland. They have been well described as " a cluster of islands and islets with bays " and coves, headlands and highlands, capes and promontories, high bluffs " and low shores, rocks and sands, fountain streams and cascades, moun- " tain, plain and precipice, unsurpassed for their wild fantastic and " picturesque beauty." The most westerly are composed of granite and porphyry, those nearer the mainland of sandstone, grauwacke and conglomerate. They are, probably, rich in minerals. The principal productions are *bêches de mer*, collected by the Selung who exchange them with Burmese and Malays for rice and spirits, and edible birds-nests. The caoutchouc tree is asserted to grow in great abundance on the Islands and Malays from Singapore to extract the gum. No exact enquiries on this point have, however, been made. A branch of the tree was brought to the Deputy Commissioner in 1868-69 and the gum was made in his presence. The islands are infested by snakes and wild animals—tigers, rhinoceros and deer.

MET-TA.—A village in the Tavoy district at which is stationed a small force of Police, once a flourishing Siamese town, on the Tenasserim river at the spot where it commences its great bend west and south.

MET-TA.—A wild and mountainous revenue circle in the north-eastern township of the Tavoy district, inhabited by Kareng of whom there were 1,066 in 1876 : in that year the land revenue was Rs. 551, the capitation tax Rs. 739 and the gross revenue Rs. 1,317. The cultivated area is very small and the main products are sessamum and cardamoms. It now includes Thayet-ngoot.

MIEM-MA-PYA.—A revenue circle in the Prome district on the banks of the Zay just north of the Pa-sheng circle ; in addition to Miem-ma-pya it now includes Shwe-leng, Rwa-tha-sa and Meng-boo. In 1876 the population was 448, the land revenue Rs. 470 and the capitation tax Rs. 480.

MO-BA-LAI.—A lake in the Henzada district. *See Doora.*

MO-BHAW.—A revenue circle in the Shwe-gyeng district, occupying the country from the Tsit-toung to the eastern hills southward from the Ma-da-ma stream to the Kyoon-pa-goo ; to the north is the Ban circle and to the south the Kyoon-pa-goo circle of the Tsit-toung township : the greater portion of the circle is hilly and forest-clad. With an area of 240 square miles it has a population of 6,672 souls who are mainly Kareng. In 1876 the land revenue was Rs. 2,083, the capitation tax Rs. 3,988 and the gross revenue Rs. 8,228.

MO-BHOON.—The northern portion or suburb of Mye-dai *q. v.*

MO-BYA-MYOUK.—(*North Mo-bya*). A revenue circle in the north-eastern corner of the Thee-kweng township, Bassein district, just south of the Daga and west of the Meng-ma-naing creek : on the west it is separated from the Paik-thoung circle by the Kyoon-la-ngoo creek and on the south from South Mo-bya by an imaginary line. The principal villages are Thoung-gyee on the Da-ga with 512 inhabitants and Ashe-khyoung on the Kyoon-la-ngoo with 646 inhabitants. In 1876 the land revenue was Rs. 10,945, the capitation tax Rs. 5,777, the gross revenue Rs. 19,432 and the population 4,739.

MO-BYA-TOUNG.—(*South Mo-bya*). A revenue circle in the Bassein district immediately to the south of North Mo-bya from which it was separated in the early part of 1875. On the west it is separated from the Paik-thoung circle by the Kyoon-la-ngoo creek, on the east from the Kyoung-goon circle of the Kyoon-pyaw or Tsam-bay-roon township and from the Iem-mai circle by the Meng-ma-naing, and on the south from the Thee-kweng circle by the Pan-ma-wa-dee. It contains no villages of any importance. In 1876 the population numbered 4,816 souls, the land revenue was Rs. 9,819, the capitation tax Rs. 5,682 and the gross revenue Rs. 15,992.

MO-GNYO.—A long narrow township in the Tharrawaddy or eastern portion of the Henzada district stretching E. N. E., from the bank of the Irrawaddy to the Pegu Roma mountains between the Meng-hla and Tsan-rwe townships on the south and the Ta-pwon township on the north. Towards the east the country is hilly and covered· with dense forest; the central and western portions are level and well cultivated, principally with rice. The township is traversed from north to south by the Myit-ma-kha or Hlaing, which communicates with the Irrawaddy by channels traversing the Mo-gnyo and Htien-daw circles and falls into the sea as the Rangoon river. The township is divided into six revenue circles, *viz.*, Mo-gnyo, Htien-daw, Reng-daik-beng, Khoo-nhit-rwa, Myo-dweng and Ma-toung-da. The principal villages are Mo-gnyo, Htien-daw, Myo-dweng and Khoo-nhit-rwa in the circles of the same names. In 1876 the population was 45,792, the land revenue Rs. 50,320, the capitation tax Rs. 41,405 and the gross revenue Rs. 105,952.

MO-GNYO.—A revenue circle in the township of the same name in the Henzada district on the left bank of the Irrawaddy, having the Htien-daw circle on the south, Meng-gyee on the north and the Ma-toung-da circle of the Meng-hla township on the east. The ground is low and subject to inundation. The principal crops cultivated are rice, tobacco and vegetables. In 1876 the population was 7,717, the land revenue Rs. 4,656, the capitation tax Rs. 7,500 and the gross revenue Rs. 17,812. In 1868 the gross revenue was Rs. 11,492 and the population 6,592.

MO-GNYO.—A town in the circle and township of the same name in the Henzada district on the left bank of the Irrawaddy divided into two quarters called the north and south quarters respectively. The site of the original village has been swept away by the waters of the river. It is the head-quarters of the township and contains a Court-house and a Police Station. Lat. 17° 58′ 10″ N., Long. 95° 34′ 30″ E.

MO-GOUNG.—A revenue circle in the Mye-dai township, Thayet district, having an area of about 3,840 acres of which some 1,300 are under regular cultivation and 320, about, under toungya, and 500 culturable and 1,720 unculturable waste. It is situated in the triangle formed by the frontier on the north, the Irrawaddy on the west and the Kye-nee river on the south-east. The population in 1872, including travellers and temporary residents, was 1,663 souls, all Burmans, who owned 1,153 head of cattle. It contains three of the old Burmese village tracts, *viz.*, Mo-goung, Rwa-byeen and Rwa-haing. The largest village is Mo-goung which has 206 houses. In 1859 the villages of Shwe-tha-de, Zoung-ya-kyeng and Hpan-lan-khyoung were transferred to the Mye-dai circle, the hereditary Thoogyee of which represented that they were properly in his jurisdiction. The Thoogyee of Mo-goung is now also in charge of Mouk-teng. The products are rice, sessamum, cotton, plantains, maize, chillies and cutch. The area of rice cultivation is comparatively large, *viz.*, about 1,200 acres, and toungya are numerous considering the geographical position of the circle. In 1876-77 the population was 5,709, the land revenue Rs. 2,550, the capitation tax Rs. 3,065 and the gross revenue Rs. 5,809.

MO-NAT.—A village of 50 houses in the Shwe-doung circle, Meng-doon township, Thayet district, close to the larger village of Tsa-ba-tan.

MOO-DOON.—A long, narrow revenue circle in the Zaya township, Amherst district, extending from the Toung-gnyo spur westward to the Salween, lying between the Kaw-pa-ran circle on the south and the Keng-khyoung circle on the north. The amount of upland is small : the plains are extensive, but suffer from defective drainage ; this has been to some extent improved. The greater part of the garden cultivation consists of dhanee. The principal village is Moo-doon, the head-quarters of the township. The population, land revenue and capitation tax in 1868 were 1,978, Rs. 3,573 and Rs. 2,097 respectively, and in 1867 3,268, Rs. 4,175 and Rs. 3,025.

MOO-DOON.—A village in the circle of the same name in the Zaya township, Amherst district, on the main road to the south, nine miles from Maulmain, the head-quarters of the township, with 2,475 inhabitants, including the 1,226 of Moo-doon South. It contains a Court-house, a Public Works Department Inspection Bungalow and a Police-station. In the neighbourhood are some ornamental pieces of water generally known as " the sacred " lakes. "

MOO-KYEE.—A revenue circle in the Moot-ta-ma or Martaban township of the Tha-htoon sub-division of the Amherst district, lying on the western side of the Martaban hills at the corner where the range changes its direction from north-west and south-east to nearly north and south. On the north this circle adjoins Poung and on the south Kha-daing. The land near the hills is liable to floods from the sudden rushes of water after heavy rains, the rest of the circle is moderately fertile. In one place the land is damaged by the overflow of brine from some hot salt springs. Water carriage for the conveyance of the produce to the Maulmain market and elsewhere is available all the year round at spring tides. In 1868 the population was 1,633, the land revenue Rs. 6,683 and the capitation tax Rs. 1,770. Nine years later, in 1877, these were 4,080, Rs. 16,605 and Rs. 4,182 respectively.

MOON.—A village in the circle of the same name, in the Kyouk-gyee township of the Shwe-gyeng district, not far from the right bank of the Tsit-toung river, about 52 miles above the town of Shwe-gyeng, with 669 inhabitants. According to the Burmese local histories its name, corrupted from Moo, is derived from the fact that a certain quantity of the water of the neighbouring stream was found to be heavier than that of the Rouk-thwa-wa by one *Moo* or two annas. In 1830 it was deserted on account of the oppressions of the Governor of Kyouk-gyee, but under his successor it was repopulated. It contains a Government rest-house and a Police-station; about 16 miles to the eastwards is a hot spring the waters of which have not been analyzed. The inhabitants are employed principally in trading in bamboos, torches, betel-nut and timber.

MOON.—A revenue circle in the north of the Kyouk-gyee township, Shwe-gyeng district, on the left bank of the Tsit-toung river about 290 square miles in area and with a population of 4,603 souls, mainly Burmese. A comparatively large revenue is derived from lake and pond fishery and net tax. The circle contains some very fine Teak and Pyeng-ga-do forests; the land revenue in 1876-77 was Rs. 2,192, the capitation tax Rs. 3,935 and the gross revenue Rs. 7,309.

MOON.—A small river in the northern part of the Shwe-gyeng district which has its source in the hills to the east of the Tsit-toung and after a generally westerly course falls into that river near the village of Moon in about 18° 32′ 35″ N.

MOON-TA.—A small stream in the Thayet district, one of the affluents, from the north, of the Ma-de river. It rises in the Kwon-doung spur of the Arakan range and flowing in a south-easterly direction falls into the Ma-de some miles to the east of the mouth of the Nga-wek. Its bed is sandy and gravelly with rocks near the source; it is not navigable by boats. Teak, Eng (*Dipterocarpus tuberculatus*) and Sha (*Cutch;--Acacia Catechu*) are found on the hills amongst which it flows, and logs of the former are floated down it to the Ma-de and so to the Irrawaddy at Ka-ma.

MOON-TSA-LEE.—A revenue circle in the Thayet district, Thayet township, 18 square miles in extent, of which more than 14 are unculturable, and of the rest a little more than one-half is under cultivation, 374 acres being hill clearings. The population in 1872 was 1,154 souls including 153 Khyeng, and 147 Shan of whom there are very few elsewhere in the district. Considering the number of inhabitants the number of cattle, 586 head, was small. The land revenue in 1872 was Rs. 640, the remainder of the revenue, which aggregated Rs. 1,630, being derived from capitation tax. The present Thoogyee is a descendant of the Taik Thoogyee of Khyoung-yo one of the five Taik into which the then Thayet district was divided in the Burmese time. The products are rice, sessamum, maize, plantains and cutch. In 1876-77 the population was 1,935, the land revenue Rs. 1,019, the capitation tax Rs. 1,945 and the gross revenue Rs. 3,412. It now includes the Meng-dai circle.

MOO-RENG.—A small revenue circle with an area of about six square miles in the southern portion of the Kyouk-hpyoo township, Kyouk-hpyoo district, on the west coast of Ramree, now joined to the Keng circle lying on the south.

MOO-RIT-GA-LE.—A village in the Ka-la-be circle of the Bhee-loo-gywon township, Amherst district, south of the Pan-hpa hills. In 1868 it had 795 inhabitants and in 1877 1,230.

MOOT-HTEE.—A revenue circle in the north-eastern township, Tavoy district, 12 square miles in extent, of which about a quarter are under grain cultivation. In 1876 the population was 2,281, the land revenue Rs. 3,373, the capitation tax Rs. 1,762 and the gross revenue Rs. 5,307.

MOOT-KYWON.—A highly cultivated but not very populous revenue circle in the Angyee township, Rangoon district, occupying the northern portion of the island formed by the sea, the Rangoon river and the Thakhwot-peng creek, or the Bassein creek as it is called in the charts. It formerly included the whole of this island but the southern portion was separated from it and formed into the Zhe-pa-thway circle in 1876. This circle and Zhe-pa-thway contained, previous to the first Burmese war, a very considerable Talaing population, many of whom at the close of the war emigrated to Maulmain.

The area under cultivation and the revenue during each of the last five years were :—

YEAR.	AREA, IN ACRES.				REVENUE, IN RUPEES.			
	Rice including fallow.	Garden.	Miscellaneous.	Total.	Land.	Capitation tax.	All other items.	Total.
1873-74	14,144	4	7	14,155	31,098	38,055	2,110	41,363
1874-75	17,724	6	3	17,733	38,724	8,252	4,027	51,003
1875-76	18,062	5	..	18,067	39,466	9,192	1,828	50,486
1876-77	9,716	1	..	9,717	21,047	4,185	884	22,814
1877-78	10,514	2	..	10,516	23,258	4,470	390	28,118

The population and agricultural stock during the same period were :—

YEAR.	POPULATION.					AGRICULTURAL STOCK.				
	Burmans.	Talaing.	Kareng.	All other races.	Total.	Buffaloes.	Cows, bulls and bullocks.	Carts.	Ploughs.	Boats.
1873-74	2,377	3,431	112	20	5,940	1,516	612	367	514	99
1874-75	2,795	3,832	236	13	6,876	2,022	378	309	850	252
1875-76	3,031	4,253	247	18	7,549	1,599	667	275	889	202
1876-77	1,509	1,632	86	7	3,234	542	82	114	221	77
1877-78	1,289	1,898	121	7	3,315	629	298	238	313	222

The largest village is Tsha-daing-mwot with 702 inhabitants in 1877 on the bank of the Rangoon river. The country is generally low and though not too much inundated for rice cultivation yet it is so for the health of the cattle which as a general rule are not housed and in consequence there is annually a comparatively high mortality, especially amongst the buffaloes which are less hardy than bullocks.

MOOT-TA-MA.—More generally called Martaban in English. A revenue circle in the township of the same name in the Amherst district, surrounding the town of Martaban, on the right bank of the Salween and opposite Maulmain. It is of trangular shape having the Martaban mountains, running north-west and south-east, and the Darai-bouk for its two sides and the Kha-daing khyoung, separating it from the Kha-daing and Moo-kyee circles, for its base. Towards the river the land is good but at the foot of the mountains there is some waste land rendered unculturable by the floods of water which rush down from the hills and which the existing drainage channels cannot carry off. At one time garden culivation was comparatively extensive but the high prices realized of late years and the great and increasing demand in the Maulmain market for rice for export has led to a great increase in the area sown with this cereal, but not at the expense of the gardens as garden land is not suitable for rice. In 1868 the land revenue was Rs. 7,577, the capitation tax Rs. 3,167 and the population 3,178. In 1876-77 these were Rs. 14,539, Rs. 4,512 and 4,755 respectively. The only important village is Martaban

MO-TSAY.—A revenue circle in the Ra-thai-doung township, Akyab district. In 1876-77, the population was 2,360, the land revenue Rs. 5,065 the capitation tax Rs. 2,612 and the gross revenue Rs. 8,030. The principal village is A-wa-zee-gaing with 719 inhabitants in 1877.

MO-TSAY-GYEE.—A revenue circle in the Ra-thai-doung township, Akyab district. In 1876-77 the population was 2,256, the land revenue Rs. 9,007, the capitation tax Rs. 2,740, and the gross revenue Rs. 12,651. The principal village is Toung-rwa, with 663 inhabitants in 1877.

MO-PGHA.—A subtribe of the Pwo branch of Kareng, called by the Burmese *Taw-bya* or "wild bees" from the fact of their bringing honey and bees-wax into the Burmese villages for sale. They live in eight or nine villages in the Toung-ngoo district of the Tenasserim division, between the Kan-nee and Thouk-re-khat streams. *Mo-pgha* is the name given to them from one of their villages by the Missionaries but it is a name by which they do not recognize themselves. Small as the tribe is they have two or three different dialects and thus, though they all distinguish themselves by their word for man, some call themselves *Plaw*, others *Pie-do* and others again *Pie-zaw*. Although their language shews them to belong to the Pwo class they wear the same tunic as the Bghai-ka-teu or Tunic Bghai *viz.*, white with red *perpendicular* stripes. They sacrifice a *black* bullock to the lord of the earth and for one without a single white hair they will, at the sacrificial season, give almost any price. Mr. Cross, of the American Baptist Mission, writes of them : "I know of no tribe or variety of Kareng "whose morality is so strict and stern." Many of the people have embraced Christianity and are earnest in promoting education.

MO-POON.—A quarter of the town of Maulmain in which are numerous steam rice-husking mills and saw mills.

MOSCOS.—A group of islands off the coast of the Tavoy district, "which extend in a chain parallel to the coast from Lat. 14° 28' N. D. to Lat. "13° 47' N., and are distant from it from three to five leagues having a safe "channel inside between them and the coast, with soundings mostly from "10 to 15 fathoms, deepening generally near the islands." These islands are divided into three groups, the Northern, Middle and Southern, called in Burmese Hien-tsai, Moung-ma-gan and Loung-loon respectively. "Be- "tween the southern and middle groups there are safe channels and these "are the largest and highest of these islands; the northern part of the "chain is composed of straggling islands of various sizes, with several rocks "above water".

MO-TSA-GYAN.—A revenue circle in the Ta-pwon township, Henzada district separated from the Ta-pwon and Pouk-taw circles on the north by the little Baing stream, a tributary of the Hpoung which falls into the Myit-ma-kha, and with the Le-myet-hna circle of the same township on the north west. On the south are the Mo-gnyo and the Meng-gyee circles and on the west the Po-tsa-daw circle of Ta-roop-maw. The cultivation is principally in the north and has increased considerably of late years. In 1868 the population was 3,866, the land revenue Rs. 2,466, the capitation tax Rs. 3,703 and the gross revenue Rs. 6,207. In 1876-77 these were 4,676, Rs. 6,580, Rs. 4,610 and Rs. 11,571.

MOUK-TENG.—A village in the Mouk-teng circle of the Mye-dai township, Thayet district, on the Kye-nee river, hardly a mile from the frontier and about 11 miles due east from the Irrawaddy. Except as being a frontier Police-post it is of no importance.

MOUK-TENG.—A circle in the Mye-dai township, Thayet district, in which are included no less than six of the old registered circles. The area is 42,880 acres of which only 2,476 were under cultivation in 1871-72, and of these 1,360 were hill clearings. This paucity of cultivation and large number of toungya is due to the fact that by far the larger portion of the circle is mountainous situated as it is on the spurs of the Pegu Roma. The circle contains three fairly large villages, viz., Mouk-teng, Re-nan-ngay and Re-nan-gyee. The last Thoogyee was dismissed in 1870 and this circle was then placed under the Thoogyee of Mo-goung.

MOUNG-BHEE.—A river in the Bassein district which rises in the Arakan hills and after a southerly course of about 12 miles falls into the Kyouk-khyoung-gyee at the village of Moung-bhee. Spring tides go up as far as Thit-poot, neaps as far as Htsiep-gyee. For about six miles from its mouth the banks are fringed with Gnyoung-lan (*Ficus sp.*) and higher up the Nee-pa-tshe (*Morindus sp.*) is abundant.

MOUNG-DAW.—The head-quarters of the Naaf township of the Akyab district, on the Naaf estuary, near the mouth of the Moung-daw. It contains a Court-house, Government Cess School, Telegraph Office, Market-place and Police-station. A ferry boat plies between this town and the Chittagong district. The population in 1877 numbered 547 souls, principally Chittagonians. It is sometimes called Moung-daw-tat or Moung-daw's military post, from a Burmese general of that name having built a stockade there in 1823-24, during the first Anglo-Burmese war. It was to this officer that was entrusted the conduct of the negotiation when the differences between the Burmese in Arakan and the English in Chittagong first arose. Moung-daw was occupied by the British on the 1st February 1825, and was found to have been abandoned by the Burmans.

MOUNG-DEE.—A tidal creek in the Thee-kweng township, Bassein district, which leaves the Pan-ma-wa-dee at Zee-byoo-khyoung and flowing for 15 miles parallel to it, in a general south-westerly direction, joins the Thek-ngay-thoung mouth of the Irrawaddy. It is navigable at all times by the largest boats.

MOUNG-DEE.—A tidal creek in the Shwe-loung township, Thoon-khwa district, with a general north and south direction, parallel to the Irrawaddy and about two miles to the westward of it. In the rains it joins the Ka-way and Lan-tha-maing creeks. It is 80 feet wide at its southern entrance, and in the dry season is navigable by boats 25 feet in length for about two and a half miles up.

MOUNG-MA-GAN.—An irregularly shaped revenue circle in the western township of the Tavoy district, west of Tavoy, and including the Middle Mosco Islands, extending north and south along the seacoast and reaching eastwards to the Tavoy river; on the north is the north-eastern township and on the south the Ka-myaw-keng circle. It is about 26 square miles in extent and not much cultivated. A small revenue is derived from turtle banks. It now includes Myo-houng. In 1876-77 the population was 3,483, the land revenue Rs. 3,646, the capitation tax Rs. 2,666, and the gross revenue Rs. 6,966.

MOUNG-MA-GAN.—A group of islands off the coast of the Tavoy district. *See Moscos.*

MOUNG-MAI-SHOUNG.—A very large revenue circle in the north-eastern township of the Tavoy district, lying on the left bank of the Tavoy river and extending northwards from the Za-ha stream, which' separates it from the north-eastern township, to the Ka-lien-oung Ka-reng circle. Though of extensive area it contains but little cultivation and few inhabitants, the greater portion being covered with tree and grass forest. In 1876-77 the population was 1863, the land revenue Rs. 4,956, the capitation tax Rs. 1,411 and the gross revenue Rs. 4,884.

MRO-HOUNG.—A township in the Akyab district lying to the east of the Koo-la-dan river, so named (*Mro* a town and *houng* old) from containing old Arakan or Myouk-oo, the capital of the Arakanese kingdom before its conquest by the Burmese towards the close of the last century. On the north and east are forest-clad hills but below and to the west of these the country is rich and fertile and towards the south highly intersected by creeks. A fair weather road extends from Mro-houng, the head-quarters, to Meng-bra a distance of about 20 miles, but communication is everywhere carried on chiefly by creeks. About 20 miles north of Mro-houng is the Ma-ha-moo-nee pagoda, still visited by pilgrims, where was formerly the gigantic metal image of Gaudama carried to Ava by the Burmese after the conquest of the country in 1784, and Ma-ha-htee, a temple hardly less sacred.

The township is divided into 12 revenue circles. The gross revenue in 1876-77 was Rs. 94,386, of which Rs. 47,241, were derived from the land and Rs. 29,757, from the capitation tax, the rest from fisheries, excise and other sources. The population in that year was 24,316 souls.

MRO-HOUNG.—A town in the Akyab district of the Arakan division, the head-quarters of the Mro-houng township, in 20° 44′ N. Lat. and 93° 26′ E. Long. The Arakanese name was Myouk-oo or Monkey's egg (the Burmese name for potato) the origin of which is very obscure. It appears to have been known to the geographer Ptolemy under the name of Triglyphon, which would seem to be derived from the cognizance of the town— once a famous seat of Booddhism—the sacred Booddhist triglyph or trident, the three prongs or upright lines representing Booddha, the law, and the congregation and the uniting line at the bottom their unity. It stands at the head of a branch of the Koo-la-dan river about 50 miles from its mouth, almost at the extreme limit of tidal influence, on a rocky plain surrounded with hills. The principal creek is formed of two branches which unite below the hills and pass through the town. The ruins of the ancient fort are still in existence ; they consist of three square enclosures one within the other, surrounded by masonry walls of very considerable thickness, built of stone and brick set in cement ; the stone, it would appear, having been the material originally employed and the brick used in making such repairs as from time to time became necessary.* In some places the repairs were made with wood but this was, in all probability, during the war of 1824-25. The most extensive and laborious work of all, however, is what may be called the outer line of defence, for wherever openings occur in the hills surrounding the town there were erected mounds of earth faced with masonry, the stones of which are exceedingly large ; some of these connecting mounds were of great height, and the spots where the material was excavated were utilized as dykes for defensive purposes but now resemble large natural ponds. At the main gateways the stone walls were high and thick, but where the hills afforded a natural protection a low wall was run along their summits. These massive works have shared the fate of the town and are in ruins but the platform on which stood the palace still remains, and within the sacred precinct stand the Court-house and Police lines. On the conquest of Arakan by the Burmese in 1784 the town made no resistance but yielded after the defeat of the Arakanese monarch in a general action fought some distance from his capital and became the head-quarters of one of the four districts or provinces into which the country was divided.

In 1824, on the declaration of war with Ava, one of the points on which the kingdom was attacked was Arakan. On the 2nd February 1825 the first British detachment crossed the Naaf from Chittagong and after a tedious march the whole division of British troops acting in Arakan, under General Morrison, and the flotilla, under Commodore Hayes, arrived before the town of Arakan on the 28th March. The place was found to be strongly fortified, the Burmans had followed and taken advantage of the old fortifications already described and had added to them. The first attack was unsuccess-

* Some of the stone is said to have been brought from Borongo Island at the mouth of the Koo-la-dan.

ful, but the entrenchments were eventually carried by storm, not without considerable loss.

The capture of this stronghold led to the immediate retirement of the whole Burman army from Arakan and General Morrison cantoned the the greater portion of his troops in the town. When the rains commenced early in May disease broke out in the cantonments and carried off more victims than in any other portion of the country in which British troops were engaged, indeed it may be said, without exaggeration, that the Arakan army was almost destroyed by it. The excessive mortality was due to the site of the town; this was the opinion held at the time by the medical men and it was confirmed by the healthiness of the troops stationed elsewhere, as at Sandoway, Kyouk-hpyoo and Akyab. Dr. Mason wrote in the second volume of the Transactions of the Medical and Physical Society of Calcutta:—"Its site is such as one would at first sight pronounce to be " prolific of those noxious exhalations, whatever they may be, that are " generally allowed to engender intermittent fever. It lies on the banks of " a muddy river, or rather ramifications of a river, buried among hills at a " distance nearly forty miles from the sea and invested on every side with " jungle and morass. The tide overflows the flat borders of the river to a " considerable extent, its reflux converts these into a noisome swamp, and " in this swamp, strange to say, a great part of Arakan is built." Dr. Stevenson recorded that :—" Of the peculiar unhealthiness of the town of Arakan " the Burmese were aware and studiously avoided it in the rains. The " Mugs, too, were aware of it, for, if I am not misinformed, they often "retire to the seacoast, or to some village at a distance when sick ;" and Dr. Burnard's testimony was that:—" The causes of this sickness were too "obvious to be overlooked; the locality was sufficient to satisfy every medi-"cal observer that troops could not inhabit it with impunity." On reading the accounts of the frightful mortality amongst the troops cantoned at Arakan one cannot but wonder that such a site should have remained for 350 years the capital of a kingdom. General Morrison himself fell a victim, for he was obliged by ill-health to leave Arakan before the conclusion of the war and died on his way home.

Soon after the close of the war the troops were removed and the headquarters of the division placed at Akyab. From this time Mro-houng gradually sank in importance and now contains a small population of 2,086 souls of all ages and sexes. In addition to the Court-house and Police-station it contains a market and a Government school.

MRO-KHYOUNG.—A revenue circle in the extreme south of the large island lying between Ramree and the mainland, bounded on the south by the Nga-ga-bouk creek which separates it from Ma-dai-gan-ga island, a revenue circle in the Ramree township, on the east by the Kywai-khya-bouk which separates it from the An township, on the west by Kyouk-hpyoo harbour and on the north by the Tha-loo-doung and Ka-baing creeks which separate it from the Mye-boon township. In 1876 the inhabitants numbered 1,384, the land revenue was Rs. 993, the capitation tax Rs. 1,828 and the gross revenue Rs. 5,067.

MROO.—A hill tribe in Arakan, belonging to the Toung-tha division, numbering 1,500 souls, consisting of the following 15 clans, each under its own petty chief :—Khan-za-na, La-too, Paw-ma-na, Ta-gyee, Dook-tsa, Moveenet, Lee-kho, Han-ma-na, Ma-hee-na, Wa-lien, Khan-tet, Tisiway-net, Bawsheen, Moeetsana, and Letet, and living on the banks of the Mee-khyoung, Thamie-khyoung, the southern part of the Pee-khyoung and the Roo-khyoung. They once occupied the sources of the Koo-la-dan but have been driven out by the Khamie and have gradually moved south and west, many passing into Chittagong, reducing their number in Arakan from 2,800 souls in 1853 to 1,500. The native history of Arakan refers to the Mroo as already in the country when the Burman race entered it and would seem to imply further that they are of the same stock, though this is indignantly denied at the present day by the Arakanese. They have no written language, but some of their words have been collected by Sir Arthur Phayre (*See* Appendix). They are dark-skinned, powerful men with Aryan features. They have three gods, Too-ra-ee, the father, Tsoon-toon, the nat of the hills and Oo-reng, the nat of the streams. Their knowledge of medicine is of the slightest; in colic they apply a heated sword to their stomach, in a headache they bleed the head, and sores and wounds they smear with a paste of earth from an ant-hill or apply a rice poultice. When travelling the Oo-reng is propitiated before each day's journey by a prayer offered by the headman of the party standing in the stream holding some young shoots of grass one pulled up by each member, the whole of which are afterwards stuck in the bank. On arriving on the top of a hill each individual plucks a bunch of grass which he throws on to the ground and thus propitiates Tsoon-toon. The site of a village is chosen by dreams ; a fish betokens riches, a river a plentiful crop of rice, a snake or a dog evil.

Before marriage intercourse is promiscuous. To obtain a wife a man must pay Rs. 200 or Rs. 300, or serve for three years. "At the marriage there " is a big feast. Everyone attending has a thread tied round his right " wrist ; this is done by the oldest woman of the bride's family. The string " must remain on the wrist till it drops off."*. Concubinage is unknown, and no master can have connexion with his female slave, but anyone else may marry her by paying her fine and making her free. In case of divorce the husband is repaid what he gave for his wife who, besides, forfeits all her property. Widows can, but rarely do, re-marry. On the death of a man with a young family the widow and children are taken charge of by the nearest male relative. If the children grow up during the lifetime of the father and marry and settle the father lives with the youngest son who, on his death, inherits his property. The women wear a short petticoat, and the men a strip of cloth round the loins and between the legs. They bury the dead. A few pay regular tax to the British Government but the majority pay a tribute of one rupee a year for each house, collected by the headmen.

MRO-THIT.—A revenue circle in the extreme north-eastern angle of the Kyouk-hpyoo township, Kyouk-hpyoo district, bounded on the south by the Oon-khyoung which separates it from the Tseen-khyoon circle, on the east and north by the sea and on the west by the Kyouk-hpyoo-houng circle.

* Hill Tracts of Chittagong and the dwellers therein, by Captain Lewin, Calcutta, 1869, p. 93.

In 1876-77 the population was 3,438, the land revenue Rs. 1,507, the capitation tax Rs. 2,708 and the gross revenue, including that raised in the town of Kyouk-hpyoo, Rs. 41,529.

MRO-THIT.—A reven' e circle on the bank of the Naaf estuary in the Naaf township of the Akyab district, with a population in 1875 of 2,507 souls, a land revenue in 1874-75 of Rs. 4,691, and producing in 1875-76 Rs. 2,450 from the capitation tax. Mro-thit-khyoung—now independent—was formerly a part of this circle. In 1876-77 the population was 3,361, the land revenue Rs. 4,982, the capitation tax Rs. 3,361 and the gross revenue Rs. 8,595. The only village of any importance is Do-tanrwa on the Mro-thit-khyoung.

MRO-THIT-KHYOUNG.—A revenue circle in the Akyab district on the bank of the Naaf estuary, originally a portion of Mro-thit, with a population, principally natives of the neighbouring Chittagong district, numbering 4,579 souls in 1875. The land revenue, derived from a cultivated area of 3,046 acres, amounted in 1874-75 to Rs. 4,455 and the capitation tax in 1875-76 to Rs. 4,195. In 1876-77 the population was 11,338, the land revenue Rs. 6,136, the capitation tax Rs. 8,342 and the gross revenue Rs. 17,184. The principal villages are Nga-khoo-ra with 795 inhabitants, Hpyoo-ma-ashe with 719 and We-la-toung with 2,721, all on the Mro-thit stream, a branch of the Naaf, and the last lying on either bank, the two quarters called We-la-toung East and We-la-toung West, respectively. The principal products are rice, wood-oil, mustard-seed and salt, the last for home consumption.

MWAY-RO.—A small and insignificant stream in the Thayet district which rises to the east of the Irrawaddy and falls into that river a little south of the village of Pyeng-bouk. To the east of Kyouk-ma-tsheng village it is called the Kyouk-ma-tsheng stream.

MYAING-GA-LE.—A long and comparatively narrow revenue circle in the Hpa-gat township, Amherst district, between the Bheng-laing river and its feeder the Doon-tha-mie on the west and the Salween on the east : on the north is the Myaing-gyee circle and on the south the Bheng-laing circle of the same township, the boundary in either case being marked by an imaginary line drawn east and west between the Doon-tha-mie and the Salween in the former and the Bheng-laing and the Salween in the latter case. The circle is very poor the country consisting of undulating, forest-clad land, low plains annually inundated, and precipitous limestone rocks. The villages are decreasing in size, for whereas none are returned as having 500 inhabitants in 1877, Myaing-ga-le had 518 and Wai-da-rai 539 in 1868. The area under cultivation is very small and except in the immediate neighbourhood of the villages consists entirely of rice. In 1876-77 the population was 2,553, the land revenue Rs. 1,789 and the capitation tax Rs. 2,925.

MYAING-GYEE.—A revenue circle in the Amherst district occupying the northern portion of the Hpa-gat township and lying between the Salween and the Doon-tha-mie ; to the north are the Salween Hill Tracts and to the south the Myaing-ga-le circle of the same township. The face of the country consists of undulating and hilly ground with low valleys and small swamps with very little cultivation to be found anywhere. Some of the forests are valuable, producing Teak and other useful timber. In 1868 the population was 2,833 scattered through nine villages, almost entirely Kareng with a few Talaing, Toung-thoo and Shan. The Kareng, who are wild and ignorant are toung-ya cultivators, the Talaing live on the bank of the Salween and are principally timber salvers and raftsmen, the Toung-thoo and Shan are cultivators. In 1868 the land revenue was Rs. 849 and the capitation tax Rs. 1,791. In 1876-77 the population was 3,374, the land revenue Rs. 1,090 and the capitation tax Rs. 1,364. The principal villages are Mee-zaing, on the bank of the Salween, which had 567 inhabitants in 1868 and 684 in 1877, and Thai-hpyoo-khyoung which had 361 inhabitants in 1868 and 534 in 1877.

MYAN-OUNG.—A township in the Henzada district between Kyan-kheng and Kan-oung and extending westwards from the Irrawaddy to the Arakan hills. To the westward the country is mountainous and produces some valuable timber but between the foot of the hills and the river it is low and was formerly subject to yearly inundations; the embankments constructed along the Irrawaddy now protect a large tract of fertile country in which rice cultivation is extending. The principal town is Myan-oung, at one time the head-quarters of the district, where an Assistant Commissioner in charge of the sub-division is now stationed. It is divided into six revenue circles, viz., Myanoung-myoma, Tan-thoon-beng, Koon-daw, Thien-goon, Pan-daw and Kyouk-tan. In 1876-77 the population was 40,972, the land revenue Rs. 58,865, the capitation tax Rs. 37,655 and the gross revenue, including the local revenue raised in the town of Myan-oung, Rs. 1,15,900.

MYAN-OUNG.—A town on the right bank of the Irrawaddy, formerly the head-quarters of the Henzada (then called the Myan-oung) district, but now the head-quarters of an Assistant Commissioner, with a population in 1876 of 5,859 souls. It is two miles long by about 200 yards broad and contains Court-houses, a small masonry gaol or lock-up with wooden barracks in which, in 1876, an average of 74 persons were confined, a Public Works Department Inspection-bungalow, Circuit-house, Police-station, Charitable dispensary in which 125 in and 761 out-patients were treated in 1876, a good Market-place, a Telegraph office, Post office and a school.

It was formerly the head-quarters of the Pegu Light Infantry; a local battalion raised after the second Anglo-Burmese war and disbanded in 1861-62 when its place was taken by the newly-formed constabulary.

Founded by the Talaing at the same time as Kyan-kheng in the same district, circa 1250 A.D., it was then called Ko-dwot. It was captured by Aloung-bhoora, the Burman conqueror, in 1754 A.D., who built a fort and changed the name to Myan-oung. During the first Anglo-Burmese war it was not defended by the Burmans in their retreat northward before the British force. In 1876-77 the population, including that of the town of Myan-oung, was 12,919, the land revenue Rs. 6,398, the capitation tax Rs. 10,573 and the gross revenue Rs. 31,746. The local revenue raised in 1876-77 was Rs. 8,324.

MYAN-OUNG-MYOMA.—A revenue circle in the Myan-oung township of the Henzada district lying on the right bank of the Irrawaddy north and south of Myan-oung and now including Toung-byeng. Towards the west the ground is undulating but elsewhere it is well cultivated, principally with rice. In 1876-77 the population was 6,340, and the land revenue Rs. 6,398.

MYA-PA-DAING.—A revenue circle in the Houng-tha-raw township, Amherst district, lying between the Dawna range on the east and the Houng-tha-raw on the west with the Daw-lan circle of the Than-lweng Hlaing-bhwai township on the north separated from it by the Pa-da stream, and the Kaw-ka-riet circle on the south. Like all the other circles in this township it is mountainous and with but little cultivation and inhabited principally by Kareng. In 1876-77 the population was 3,705, the land revenue Rs. 2,711 and the capitation tax Rs. 3,503.

MYA-RWA.—A village on the left bank of the Irrawaddy about two miles above the town of Prome. Its name—Emerald village—is derived from a tradition that when Gaudama was travelling about preaching his religion he came hither and having placed some of his hairs in an emerald box presented to him by a dragon he, by his supernatural power, caused it to lodge in a bamboo clump where it shone like fire and was found by two brothers, Ee-zee-ka and Pa-lee-ka, who carried it to a hill further south and erected over it a pagoda, the Shwe Tshan-daw now standing in the town of Prome.

MYA-THIEN-DAN.—A pagoda at Martaban founded in 1281 A.D. by King Wa-rie-yoo. Mya-thien-dan is a corruption of Mya-thien-deng, a name given to the pagoda by reason of its being supposed to have in it an emerald worth 100,000 ticals (Rs. 2,500,000), sent by the king of Ceylon with an embassy in seven ships which was to bring back certain relics of Gaudama, deposited at a spot marked by eight pillars. With the sanction of King Wa-rie-yoo search was made during 24 days but no relics could be found. The embassy was allowed to carry away the eight pillars and on the spot thus left vacant King Wa-rie-yoo built this pagoda.

MYA-TSA-GAING.—A village in the Thayet township, Thayet district, which gives its name to the circle in which it is situated. It is on the right bank of the Irrawaddy about six miles above the town of Thayet.

MYA-TSA-GAING.—A revenue circle in the Thayet township, Thayet district. This circle was formerly in the jurisdiction of the Mye-dai Myo-thoogyee the last of whom, on the advance of the British in 1853, carried off the Taik Thoogyee and most of the inhabitants. Subsequently the brother of this Thoogyee was appointed to the charge of this circle by the English, but he resigned in 1871 and the circle was then placed under the Thoogyee of Kwon-on. The products are rice, maize and betel-leaf.

MYA-TSIEN-KYWON.—A village in the Prome district on an island in the Irrawaddy, nearly opposite the large village of Kyee-thay, attached to the Padoung township.

MYA-WA-DEE.—A revenue circle in the Houng-tha-raw township, Amherst district, extending northwards from the main dividing range along the Thoung-yeng. A mass of forest-clad hills, some of very great height, and having extensive Teak tracts it is sparsely inhabited by Kareng and with little cultivation. In 1876 the population was 2,090, the land revenue Rs. 616 and the capitation tax Rs. 1,139.

MYA-WA-DEE.—A portion of the Kama township (*q. v.*) of the Thayet district, which, before the annexation of Pegu, formed a separate juris-diction under a Myo-thoogyee.

MYA-WA-DEE-MYO-MA.—A revenue circle in the Kama township, Thayet district, on the bank of the Irrawaddy just south of the mouth of the Ma-de In the Burmese time this was a Myo-thoogyeeship. At the time of the annexation the then Myo-thoogyee, Moung Pe, fled into Upper Burma. The Myo-thoogyee always lived at the large village of Gywon-doung on the bank of the Irrawaddy at the mouth of the Ma-de which separates it from the town of Kama. In 1872 on the Thoogyee being dismissed the circle was placed under the Htouk-ma Thoogyee.

MYA-WA-DEE-MYO-MA.—A village of about 80 houses which gives its name to a revenue circle in the Kama township, Thayet district. It is situated on the bank of the Irrawaddy about half way between Kama and Htouk-ma.

MYAY-NA-THA.—A village in the southern portion of the Prome dis-trict close to the Khyoon-khyoon-gya or Wek-poot stream, and about a mile and a half W. S. W. of Kyoon-goon.

MYE-BOON.—A small town in the Kyouk-hpyoo district, the head-quarters of the township of the same name, situated on the shore of Hunter's Bay on an island formed by some of the numerous inosculating tidal creeks which intersect the whole coast of the mainland north of Kyouk-hpyoo. The inhabitants, who in 1877 numbered 1,230 souls, are largely engaged in sea-fishing, the fish being sold in the local markets and exported to Akyab. It contains a Court-house and a Police-station.

MYE-BOON.—A township in the north-western portion of the Kyouk-hpyoo district adjoining Akyab and formed in 1871 from circles taken from other townships in Kyouk-hpyoo and from Akyab. The north-western por-tion is hilly but the south and south-east is intersected by numerous tidal creeks by means of which much of the communication is carried on. The inhabitants are principally Arakanese. The head-quarters are at Mye-boon on an island formed by the creeks noticed above. The principal villages are Thayet-toung, Kan-thoung-gyee and Pouk-htoo-toung. It is divided into 11 revenue circles, *viz.*, Alay-kywon, Nga-man-rai, Kyat-tseng, Daing-boon, Lek-khoop-pye, Ro, Koon-khyoung, Hnit-moung-gya, Ngwe-tweng-too, Kook-ko and Tsek-kaw. In 1877 the population was 19,607, the land revenue Rs. 31,154, the capitation tax Rs. 20,940 and the gross revenue Rs. 76,570.

MYE-DAI.—A small town or village in the Mye-dai township of the Thayet district, the head-quarters of the Mye-dai Myo-won in the Burmese times. The name is derived from the traditional history of Maha-tham-ba-wa and Tsoola-tham-ba-wa, twin sons of Tha-do Ma-ha-raza, the last king of Tagoung, who were born blind. Their father ordered them to be put to death, but their mother preserved their lives ; when they were about 18 years old Tha-do Ma-ha-raza discovered that his orders had not been obeyed, and the young men were then set afloat on a raft in the Irra-waddy ; on their way down the river they obtained their sight by the aid of a Bhee-loo-ma or ogress. The cure was not instantaneous but very gradual and on arriving opposite the site of the present Mye-dai they first saw the sky and exclaimed "the sky is as a cover (Mo-boon) and the earth is underneath (Mye-dai)". Tradition ascribes the construction of the fort at Mye-dai to Tha-moon-da-rit in 100 A.D., during the interval which elapsed between his exile from Prome and the establishment of his kingdom at Pagan. Thirteen centuries later it was rebuilt by Meng-rai-kyaw-tswa, son of the king of Ava, in his unsuccessful expedition against the Talaings to release his mother and sister who had been taken prisoner by King Ra-za-dhie-rit. Since then it has always been considered by Burmans as a river post of considerable importance. On the cessation of the second Anglo-Burmese war the main frontier force was stationed in Prome with a detachment in the Mye-dai fort, but subsequently the detachment was withdrawn and the whole garrison placed at Thayetmyo on the right bank of the Irrawaddy just opposite to Mye-dai. Just to the south of the fort, on the other side of the Kye-nee-khyoung is the new town of Allanmyo (q. v.) which has supplanted Mye-dai.

Colonel Symes, who visited Mye-dai on his way up the river as envoy from the Governor-General to the King of Burma at the end of the last century, thus describes it:—"It is a place of no great magnitude, but "extremely neat; there are two principal streets, and at the north end of the "present town are to be seen the ruins of a brick fort, which, like all other "forts of masonry in the Burmese Empire, is in a state of dilapidation. "On the south and south-east sides the town is enclosed by a deep ravine, "the banks of which are cut perpendicular, and the remains of an old "brick wall were discoverable, which was probably a defence to the former "suburb. We observed many small temples and convents apart from the "town, situated in groves of mango, tamarind and pipal trees of uncom-"mon stateliness and beauty. North of the town about a mile there is a "good deal of cultivation, chiefly of rice; the fields were well laid down and "fenced. This quarter is beautifully wooded, and diversified with rising "grounds. We observed many cart-roads and pathways leading into the "country in various directions. The soil is composed of clay and sand, "and in some places is very stony, particularly near the river."

MYE-DAI.—A township in the Thayet district between Lat. 19° 29' 3" and 18° 50' 3" N., and Long. 95° 13' 30" and 95° 55' E. occupying the whole of the district east of the Irrawaddy.

It contains an area of 921 square miles and is bounded on the north by Upper Burma, on the west by the Irrawaddy, on the east by the Pegu Roma range and on the south by the district of Prome. Its cultivated area in 1871-72 was:—

							Acres.
Rice land	..	..	..	..	..	..	20,019
Garden land	..	..	..	..	..	..	836
Miscellaneous	..	..	..	..	..	..	8,245
						Total	29,100

There were also 4,484 toungya and 6,056 fruit-trees assessed separately for revenue; the revenue was:—

							Rs.
Land revenue	..	..	..	..	..	..	23,346
Capitation tax	..	..	..	..	..	..	34,868
Fisheries	..	..	..	..	..	..	2,672
						Total	60,886

The population according to the census amounted to 63,061 souls, of whom 56,538 were Burmans, 5,825 Khyeng, 420 Kareng, and 278 of other races.

It contained in 1872 the following cattle :—

Buffaloes	..	..	..	..	..	..	2,195
Bulls, bullocks and cows	..	..	..	..	..	..	27,775
					Total	..	29,970

It contains 92 registered village tracts which are now divided among 13 Thoogyees. The number of separate villages is 305 and the number of houses 12,920.

In the Burmese time the township contained the following independent jurisdictions :—Mye-dai Myo, Pya-lo Taik, Pyeng-bouk Taik, Bhwot-lay Taik, Tsheng-doop Taik, Myo-hla Taik and Gnyoung-beng-tshiep Myo. The whole of the last six districts are included in the present township of Mye-dai. Of the Mye-dai Myo about half is left to Upper Burma and a small piece on the west of the Irrawaddy, a portion of the present Kwon-oon circle was cut ꜰꜰ and joined to Thayet, in 1859, as the Mya-tsa-gaing circle. The frontier line cuts the old Mye-dai Myo on the east of the Irrawaddy nearly in half. On the west of the Irrawaddy it includes only a very small bit of the Anouk-bhet Taik of Mye-dai within the British frontier.

On the annexation of Pegu the present township of Mye-dai was divided into three, the Gnyoung-beng-tshiep, the Nga-taik and the Mye-dai. Gnyoung-beng-tshiep and Nga-taik were amalgamated with Mye-dai in 1861.

In 1145 B.E., the officials appointed to the Mye-dai Myo were :—A Myo-thoogyee, sometimes called a Myo-won, over the whole Myo, with two Tsa-khyee or writers ; a Thoogyee and a Tsa-khyee in the Tha-roung Taik, and the same in the Kaw-tham-bee and Anouk-bhet Taik. The number of registered villages was 64 viz. in Kaw-tham-bee 21, Myoma 23, Tha-young 10 and Anouk-bhet 10 ; of these 48 are now in British and 16 in Upper Burma.

Sometimes Mye-dai was placed under a Myo-won who, generally, had the power of the sword ; at other times it was left to the Myo-thoogyee who was not allowed the power of life and death, which was entrusted in such cases to the Myit-tseen-won, or High Sheriff of the Irrawaddy, whose jurisdiction extended all along the banks of the Irrawaddy from Kyouk-ta-loon to the mouths of the river. Judicial officers called Myo-ook and Myo-gaing were sometimes appointed under the Myo-thoogyee.

From the days of King Bhodaw Bhoora to the first war with the English no fixed contingent of soldiers was provided by the Mye-dai Myo but in time of war all the officials from the Myo-thoogyee to the village Thoogyee were bound to attend on summons, with one follower each, and proceed wherever they were ordered, their expenses whilst on service being a charge upon the inhabitants of the Myo. In the war of 1825-26 Moung Shwe-meng, the Myo-thoogyee of Mye-dai. and Moung Bo, the Thoogyee of Tha-roung and Kaw-tham-bee, obtained a decisive victory cver a British force composed of Madras sepoys at Wek-htee-gan in Prome. The Myo of Mye-dai during this war had to furnish a force of 500 soldiers. After the war there was great competition between the families of Moung

Shwe-meng and Moung Bo for the Myo-thoogyee or Myo-won-ship of Mye-dai. Moung Shwe-meng kept it until he died, but after his death although his son Moung Ta-roop was now and then appointed to the post Moung Bo succeeded eventually in ousting the rival family and maintained his position under the corrupt government of the Pagan Meng until the second English war. Proud of his victory in the first war he remained a devoted servant of the king and though he did not venture again to meet the English in the field he opposed them to the utmost of his power; he withdrew as their forces advanced and carried off with him the whole of the population of his Myo. So thoroughly did he succeed in his scheme for depopulating the country that when the British forces arrived at Mye-dai there was not an inhabitant to be found between the Irrawaddy and the Roma range. For some years after the annexation Moung Bo remained in office just beyond our frontier, but slowly and gradually the involuntary exiles whom he had driven off stole back to their deserted fields and villages.

Gnyoung-beng-tshiep Myo (literally Banyan tree landing-place) is said to have been called Mek-kha-wa-dee and to have been first founded by the Shan king of Ava, Mo-hgnyeng-meng-tara, in 800 B. E. (1438 A. D. about), when that monarch came down to make peace with the king of Pegu who was besieging Prome; above it was founded a town called Rama-wa-dee and below it another called Ze-ya-wa-dee.

Before 1145 B. E. 1783 A. D. Gnyoung-beng-tshiep included the five Taiks of Myo-hla, Tsheng-doop, Bhwot-lay, Pya-lo and Pyeng-bouk, besides those now included within its limits; but in the settlement of that year these were made an independent jurisdiction and named Nga-taik (five taik) Myo. Twelve villages in Gnyoung-beng-tshiep were registered, five in Pya-lo, five in Pyeng-bouk, 10 in Bhwot-lay, 10 in Tsheng-doop and 12 in Myo-hla.

The family of the Myo-thoogyee of Gnyoung-beng-tshiep is the oldest in the Thayet district, its genealogy running back to five generations before the time of Aloung-bhoora (1115 B. E. 1753 A. D.) In the time of Aloung-bhoora the Myo-thoogyee was one Moung Myat, who had the title of Wot-ta-na-ze-ya Bo. The king in his expedition to conquer Pegu confirmed him in the possession of his hereditary office but at the same time appointed three other officials, designated respectively a Tsa-khyee, a Po-tsa, and a Khet-tra, it would seem as checks upon the Myo-thoogyee.

At the settlement of 1145 B. E. the Wot-ta-na-ze-ya Bo's son, who had the title of Ze-ta-wot-ta-na-khan, was Myo-thoogyee. The Tsa-khyee, Po-tsa, and Khet-tra-ships were declared hereditary in the families of the persons who then held them; all four of these officials appear to have had a voice in the management of the Myo. The Myo-thoogyee looked after the land revenue and the others after the fishery tax, the customs dues and the broker-age fees. Civil and criminal cases were decided by a court composed of all four. In 1164 B. E. the offices of Tsa-khyee, Po-tsa, and Khet-tra were abolished, the Myo-thoogyee being left as the sole hereditary official. The last Myo-thoogyee was Moung Riet, who succeeded to the appointment (his father having died on service on the Toung-ngoo side) in 1160 B. E., 1798 A. D. at the early age of four years, and finished his career in action against the English near Rangoon in 1852. His son Moung Tet-hpyo (subse-quently an Extra Assistant Commissioner serving under the British

Government) fled with the defeated army of the Shwe-doung Won from Rangoon and succeeded, before the annexation, to the Myo-thoogyeeship of Gnyoung-beng-tshiep. He abandoned his appointment, however, when the British forces advanced and retired temporarily into private life. He was succeeded by Moung Shwe-gnyo, a creature of the Shwe-doung Won, who had once been appointed Myo-ook (under the Myo-thoogyee) in Gnyoung-beng-tshiep. This man took advantage of his position to commit great oppression and was killed shortly afterwards, in revenge, by the villagers.

The offices of the Taik-ook or Pyee-tso, as they were also called, of Nga-taik were made hereditary in 1145; but on the annexation in 1215 B. E., the families of the original officials had disappeared, except in Pyeng-bouk, and the hereditary Thoo-gyee of that circle was dismissed shortly afterwards.

At the earliest Revenue Settlement of which any record is found in the local annals (about 1181 B. E.) the proportions of fixed revenue payable by each of the divisions contained in the present Mye-dai township were as follows :—

Mye-dai-Myo	..	..	60 Viss of Silver or	Rs.	7,800
Gnyoung-beng-tsheip	..	..	10 Ditto	,,	1,300
Pya-lo	..	..	10 Ditto	,,	1,300
Pyeng-bouk	..	..	10 Ditto	,,	1,300
Bhwot-lay	..	..	15 Ditto	,,	1,950
Tsheng-doop	..	..	15 Ditto	,,	1,950
Myo-hla	..	..	20 Ditto	,,	2,600
	Total ..		140 Ditto	,,	18,200

Gnyoung-beng-tshiep had likewise to provide 58 men for the Tsan-shwe-gai war-boat. The whole of the above revenue had to be paid in, nett, to the Myo-tsa, or person to whom the grant was assigned as the source of his income, and the Myo-tsa's establishment was entitled to demand certain sums in addition to this fixed amount. His secretary took 10 per cent. and his writer and treasurer each five per cent. This raised the total amount which had to be remitted to the capital to 165 viss of silver or Rs. 21,840.

As about half the old Mye-dai Myo is now included in Upper Burma the total amount of revenue paid under Burmese rule by the present township may be set down as 130 viss or Rs. 17,290. Besides this amount the officials had to forward sundry annual " presents " to the Court at Ava, which came out of the pockets of the people. The yearly offerings of the Myo-thoogyee, Thoogyee and Pyee-tso were a silver bowl and some broad cotton cloth. The Tsa-khyee and village Thoogyee sent silver bowls of smaller dimensions and some cotton cloth.

The assessment of the ordinary revenue was effected by dividing the owners of cattle into three classes and fixing a certain rate on each class. The owner of four yokes of cattle belonged to the first class. Those who had less to the second or third class. The rate of payment for the first class was fixed at $2\frac{1}{4}$ ticals or about Rs. 3-4-9, of the second class $1\frac{1}{4}$ ticals or about Rs. 1-10-0, and the third class at $\frac{5}{8}$ of a tical or about Rs. 0-12-9. This was exclusive of various fees and presents. The writer's fees were 1-4th, 1-8th, and 1-16th of a tical for the different classes or about Rs. 0-5-0, Rs. 0-2-6, and Rs. 0-1-3. The collection fees were the same as the writer's and a small payment in kind (rice and cotton) besides. The cultivators of toungya paid ¾ of a tical (Rs. 0-15-0) for the first year's growth, ½ tical (Rs. 0-10-0) for the second year and ¼ of a tical (Rs. 0-5-0) for the third year. Lands dedicated to sacred purposes paid at the rate of 1½ baskets of rice in the husk, ½ basket of cleaned rice and a bamboo mat on each yoke of cattle, as well as four annas writer's fees. In Gnyoung-beng-tshiep land paid 10 per cent. on the produce, with fees in addition. In Mye-dai a tax of 50 ticals per annum (about Rs. 65) was paid by all the fishermen. There was a Khoon-daing-oo, or head fisherman, who assessed this on the others and appropriated any surplus himself. In Gnyoung-beng-tshiep fixed sums were paid on the different kinds of nets; some 5 tickals (about Rs. 6-8-0) and some 2½ tickals (about Rs. 3-4-0). There was a tax on slaves, ¼ tical (about Rs. 0-5-0) being paid for each slave. Customs dues were taken from boats wherever they discharged cargoes at the rate of 2 ticals (about Rs. 2-9-6), 1 tical (about Rs. 1-4-9), or ¼ tical (about Rs. 0-5-0) according to the size of the boat; a duty of ¼ basket of rice in the husk from each cart arriving at a mart and 2½ per cent. on that brought by boat were also taken and appropriated to the remuneration of those who had to provide entertainment and transport for any royal messengers or public guests.

Produce brokers were licensed. They were authorized to take one per cent. on the value of the goods sold from the seller and the same from the buyer.

There was a duty on the sale of cattle, and unclaimed cattle were kept for a year and a half and then sold.

Of the fees received by the officials on the decision of lawsuits, of all fines in criminal cases, of the duty on the sale of cattle, of the proceeds of the sale of unclaimed cattle and of the brokers' fees one half was Imperial revenue and the rest the perquisite of the official concerned.

During the reign of Tharrawaddy (1838—1846) the quotas of fixed revenue were seriously increased, but under his successor, Koon-boung Meng, better known as Prince Pagan Meng (1846—1853), they were raised to sums which were collected with the greatest difficulty. These sums are said to have been:—

						Rs.	
Mye-dai	..	..	..	500	Viss or	Rs.	65,000
Gnyoung-beng-tshiep	..	..	..	100	Ditto	,,	13,000
Pya-lo	..	..	..	25	Ditto	,,	3,250
Pyeng-bouk	..	..	..	25	Ditto	,,	3,250
Bhwot-lay	..	..	..	40	Ditto	,,	5,200
Tsheng-doop	..	..	..	40	Ditto	,,	5,200
Myo-hla	..	..	..	60	Ditto	,,	7,800
		Total	..	790	Ditto	,,	102,700

The object does not appear to have been to increase the revenues of the Myo-tsa, as he got little if any more than formerly and nothing from Gnyoung-beng-tshiep, but to pour money into the coffers of the members of the clique which then ruled in the capital.

There are no means of ascertaining the incidence of taxation per head with any approach to accuracy, but even before Koon-boung Meng's time it could not have been less than Rs. 1-8-0 and in the Pagan Meng's time it must have been at least Rs. 7-0-0. In 1872, 18 years after the annexation of Pegu, it was Rs. 1-0-0, and in 1876, including direct and indirect taxes and local funds, in short everything realized by the State, Rs. 1-6-0.

For administrative purposes the township is divided into 13 circles, viz., Mo-goung, Mye-dai Myo-ma, Rwa-toung, Goon-daw, Tham-bhoo-la, Teng-daw, Shwe-ban-daw, Myo-hla, Bhwot-lay, Tsheng-doop, Pya-lo, Pyoung and Gnyoung-beng-tshiep.

In 1876 the land revenue was Rs. 34,582, the capitation tax Rs. 45,429, the gross revenue Rs. 102,776 and the number of the inhabitants 60,700.

MYE-DAI-MYOMA.—A revenue circle of most irregular shape in the Mye-dai township, Thayet district, extending along the left bank of the Irrawaddy from the Mo-goung to the Rwa-toung circle and having the Mo-goung and Goon-daw circles on the east. Towards the south, on the bank of the Irrawaddy, is the small town of Allan-myo, the inland frontier customs station, at which is stationed an Assistant Commissioner and a Police force. The Thoogyee is not an hereditary village Thoogyee but belongs to a family which claims to have had an hereditary title in the Burmese time to the Taik-ook-ship of Mye-dai. His family were deprived of their position by Moung Bo, the last Myo-thoogyee of Mye-dai before the annexation,* and when that took place the present Thoogyee got his title recognized by the British authorities. Since then he has succeeded in having various villages taken from other circles and added to his on the ground that they formerly belonged to Mye-dai Myo-ma. The products are rice, sessamum, plantains, maize and onions. Including the town of Allan, the population, land revenue, capitation tax and gross revenue in 1871-72 and in 1876-77 were :—

Year.	Population.	REVENUE, IN RUPEES.			
		Land.	Capitation.	All other items.	Total.
1871-72 ..	6,383	765	5,125	1,498	7,388
1876-77 ..	7,802	1,405	6,800	16,212	24,417

MYEK-SHOO.—A village in the Prome district, amongst rice fields, some six miles to the east of the town of Prome.

MYEK-SHOO.—A revenue circle in the Prome district, to the east of the town of Prome and containing six of the old village tracts, viz., Myek-shoo, Za-yat-hla, Htoon-thwa, Tsan-gwai, Rwa-doung, and Wai-loung. In 1876 the population was 1,668, the land revenue Rs. 1,740, the capitation tax Rs. 1,702 and the gross revenue Rs. 3,492.

MYE-NEE-GOON.—A revenue circle in the Tha-htoon township, Amherst district, extending in a W.S.W. direction from the Martaban hills to the sea coast just below the mouth of the Bhee-leng river. On the north it is separated from the Kyaik-kaw circle by the Myaik-ta-hpoon stream, and on the south from the Tha-htoon circle and the Toung-tshoon circle of the Martaban township by the Taik-kha-rai, and below the mouth of this stream by the Tsha or Tha-htoon river. It is traversed from north to south by the Tsha, which here runs parallel to the Martaban hills and about a mile and a half to two miles to the westward of them. Except in the rains this stream, which is always shallow, is dry above Tha-htoon, nearly up to which town it is tidal. The country on the east is covered with tree forest and on the lower slopes of the hills, where most of the villages are collected in a long line, the ground is suited only for gardens and of these there are not many. Further west the land is seriously inundated every year, but towards the extreme west and south the ground rises slighty and cultivation is feasible, and the area brought under the plough has of late years largely increased. The land revenue, capitation tax, and population, principally Kareng and Toungthoo with, however, a large number of Talaing, in 1867-68 and in 1876-77 were :—

		1867-68.			1876-77.
Land revenue	.. Rs.	4,703	..	Rs.	11,168
Capitation tax	.. ,,	1,447	..	,,	2,402
Total	.. ,,	6,150	..	,,	13,570
Population	..	1,587	..		2,567

The principal villages are Mye-nee-goon and Noung-ka-la near the hills and Taik-kha-rai in the south-west.

MYE-NEE-GOON.—A village at the western foot of the Martaban hills in the circle of the same name, Tha-htoon township, Amherst district, close to and north of Tha-htoon, almost joined to it by intervening houses and hamlets. In 1868 it had 486 inhabitants and 606 in 1877.

MYE-NEE-GOON.—A village in the Koo-bhyoo circle, Meng-doon township, Thayet district, rather more than a mile to the E.N.E. of the town of Meng-doon, which has increased from 30 to 60 houses. It is situated between the Tsheng-gyee and the Tsheng-reng streams, two small tributaries of the Ma-htoon river.

MYENG-BA.—A village, or group of adjoining villages, in the Mya-tsa-gaing circle, Thayet township, Thayet district, containing over 100 houses, on the right bank of the Irrawaddy close to and south of the boundary pillar, which is sometimes called the "Myeng-ba pillar." In this village are stationed 20 men of the Frontier police.

MYENG-HOOT.—A revenue circle in the southern portion of the Naaf township of the Akyab district on the seacoast, containing 15,680 acres of land of which in 1874-75 2,902 only were under cultivation producing a land revenue of Rs. 2,558. In 1876-77 the population numbered 5,738 souls, the land revenue was Rs. 2,773, the capitation tax amounted to Rs. 3,529 and the gross revenue to Rs. 6,959.

MYENG-OO.—A village of over 100 houses in the Doo-reng-a-bho circle, Mye-dai township, Thayet district, which has considerably increased since the annexation ; before that it was not registered as a village. It is on the left bank of the Irrawaddy opposite to Kyoon-ga-le island, between the river and the main road from Rangoon to Mye-dai.

MYENG-WA-TOUNG.—An extensive revenue circle in the north-west of the Kan-oung township, Henzada district, stretching eastward from the Arakan Roma mountains. Towards the west it is a mass of hills on which are found valuable trees, as Teak (*Tectona grandis*), Pyeng-ma (*Lagerstræmia Reginæ*), Pyeng-ga-do (*Xylia dolabriformis*), Eng (*Dipterocarpus tuberculatus*) and Htouk-kyan (*Terminalia macrocarpa*) and bamboos. Towards the east it is to some extent under cultivation. Steatite is found near the mouth of the Ma-mya stream. It now includes Thai-bo and Meng-ga-ba. In 1876-77 the population was 4,221, the land revenue Rs. 2,961, the capitation tax Rs. 4,152 and the gross revenue Rs. 7,425.

MYE-NOO.—A revenue circle in the Le-myet-hna township of the Bassein district. On the west it is bounded by the Bassein river and on the north-east it adjoins the Henzada district. There is a fair amount of rice cultivation scattered in patches over the circle, which has an area of about 81 square miles, especially towards the west: to the eastward the ground is low and swampy and covered with tree and grass forest. In the north-west and in the south-west are two lakes and there is another in the eastern portion. In 1876 the population was 7,932, the land revenue Rs. 6,005, the capitation tax Rs. 8,425 and the gross revenue Rs. 16,507.

MYIT-GYEE-POUK.—A village in the Toung-ngoo district, about half a mile north of Toung-ngoo inhabited principally by Burman and Shan gardeners and petty traders.

MYIT-KHYENG.—The Pwo family of Kareng, so called by the Burmese. *See Pwo.*

MYIT-LOUNG.—A small stream in the Prome district, an affluent of the Teng-gyee, itself a tributary of the South Naweng. Rising in a spur of the Pegu Roma it flows in a N.N.W. direction through a comparatively open tract of country till it falls into the Teng-gyee near the village of Myo-doung. Its bed is sandy and muddy and its banks moderately steep.

MYIT-MA-KHA.—The name of a stream which rises in the Prome district, a short distance east of Prome, and flows southward through the Henzada district forming the upper portion of the Hlaing, *q. v.*

MYIT-TA-RA.—A river in the Bassein district which rises in the eastern slopes of the Arakan mountains, about 40 miles north of Pagoda Point, and flowing in a south-south-easterly direction for about 30 miles falls into the Bassein river by two large mouths nearly three miles apart, the southern is called the Ka-naw-kyee, forming an island called Kam-bha-la some seven or eight square miles in extent. Boats of 5,000 bushels burden can enter by either mouth and in windy weather the inner passage round the island is preferred by native boatmen to the open Bassein river, there nearly three miles broad. Boats 20 feet in length can ascend from the bifurcation, where rocks impede the passage and up to a little beyond which the river is tidal, to the foot of the hills. About four miles inland the northern or Myit-ta-ra mouth receives a large portion of the waters brought down from the Arakan hills by the Taw-gyee river.

MYIT-TA-RA.—A revenue circle in the Nga-poo-taw township, Bassein district, with an estimated area of about 160 square miles, extending north from the Bhoora-hla circle, between the Arakan range and the Bassein river as far as mouth of the Myit-ta-ra from whence, northwards, it is confined by that stream on the east, narrowing up to a point in the extreme northern corner. From its southern boundary to the Re-goung-gyee stream and from the bank of the Bassein river inland for four or five miles to the eastern slopes of the Arakan mountains the country consists of numerous cultivated plains intersected with forest, from thence northwards the country is hilly and thickly wooded except on Kam-bha-la, the island in the mouth of the Myit-ta-ra river where, towards the south, there are extensive and highly cultivated plains. The principal river, the rest being merely mountain torrents which but for the tides would be dry in the hot weather, is the Myit-ta-ra. The Re-gyaw has a large mouth just into which but no further river steamers can enter. By the Pa-loung—a feeder of the Myit-ta-ra—a pass leads across the Arakan hills to the village of Nga-root-koung. In 1876 the population was 2,301, the land revenue Rs. 3,868, the capitation tax Rs. 2,625 and the gross revenue Rs. 9,428.

MYO-DWENG.—A revenue circle in the Mo-gnyo township, Henzada district, east of the Irrawaddy, stretching down from the Pegu Roma between the Thayet and the Wek streams on the north (which separate it from the Ta-pwon township) and the Htoo on the south (which separates it from the Meng-hla township) : on the east are the Khoo-hnit-rwa, Mo-gnyo and Ma-toung-da circles of the same township. On the east the country is hilly and forest-clad, producing, amongst other less important trees, Teak, Sha (*Acacia catechu*), from which cutch is extracted, and Nee-pa-tshe (*Morinda sp.*), which furnishes a red dye, and bamboos. In the centre and towards the west the country is level and here there is some rice cultivation. In 1868 the gross revenue was Rs. 5,441 and the number of inhabitants 3,559 ; in 1876-77 the population was 6,244, the land revenue Rs. 4,139, the capitation tax Rs. 5,265 and the gross revenue Rs. 9,705.

MYO-GWENG.—A small revenue circle in the Prome district, on the right bank of the Irrawaddy south of Padoung, just below the Re-weng circle. It is traversed by the little and unimportant Loung-tsa-lee streamlet. The inhabitants are petty traders, rice cultivators, gardeners and coolies. It contains no large villages. To it has been added the once independent circle of Loung-tsa-lee. In 1876 the population was 676, the land revenue Rs. 988, the capitation tax Rs. 635 and the gross revenue Rs. 1,768.

MYO-GYEE.—A revenue circle in the Prome district north of Poungday of which the villages of Myo-gyee and Gnyoung-beng-tha form an extension. It is now united to Tha-hpan-gyo.

MYO-HLA.—A large village in the Toung-ngoo district on the bank of the Tsit-toung in 19° 24' 35" N. and 96° 21' 30" E. about five miles south of the frontier in a direct line and about seven by the river, at which is stationed a Police-force.

MYO-HLA.—A thinly-populated revenue circle in the Toung-ngoo district on the right bank of the Tsit-toung and adjoining the frontier of the Province. Near the Tsit-toung the country is low and level but to the west it is very hilly and covered with dense forest. It now includes the Ma-o circle and in 1876 had 1,976 inhabitants. In that year the land revenue was Rs. 476, the capitation tax Rs. 1,778 and the gross revenue Rs. 2,320.

MYO-HLA.—A revenue circle in the Prome district, to the eastward of the town of Prome, containing well cultivated and fertile rice fields, and comprising 10 of the old village tracts, *viz.*, Myo-hla, Rwa-ma-gyee, Ma-ha-bo, Rwa-ma-ngay, Hpoung-gyee-bweng, Myoung-gyee, Rwa-shay, Pouk-pouk, A-tha-lien and Kheng-mee-goon. In 1876 the population of these united tracts was 2,346, the land revenue Rs. 4,706, the capitation tax Rs. 2,310 and the gross revenue Rs. 7,016.

MYO-HLA.—A revenue circle in the Kama township of the Thayet district, lying on the left bank of the Ma-htoon stream and confined on the N.E. by the Padouk spur of the Arakan mountains. Its exact area is unknown, but it contains about 500 acres of cultivated land of which about 100 are under toungya. The population, composed of Burmans, numbered 553 souls in 1872. The villages are few and small. The circle was formerly held hereditarily but in 1871, when the then holder resigned because his income, derived from a percentage on the taxes paid by the people and amounting to some Rs. 80 a year, was insufficient to support him, it was placed under the Thoogyee of the neighbouring circle of Gnyoung won. The products are rice, sessamum, tobacco, chillies and onions.

MYO-HLA.—A revenue circle in the Mye-dai township, Thayet district, containing many villages, of which the only large one is Khoon-gnyeen-nway, and having an area of eighty-three square miles and a population of 3,162 souls of whom over three thousand are Burmans. The number of cattle in 1872 was 2,441 of which 1,620 were bullocks, and the revenue was Rs. 2,760 *viz.*, Rs. 1,020 from the land and Rs. 174 from the capitation tax. Since 1870 it has included Than-rwa. In 1876 the united circles furnished as land revenue Rs. 2,609, as capitation tax Rs. 2,279 and as gross revenue Rs. 5,125.

In this circle are, amongst others, the villages of Weng-wot, Hmwa, Tsa-mya, Gnyoung-aing, Re-byee and Khoon-gnyeen-nway each of which had a Thoogyee in the Burmese time the descendants of whom still exist.

MYO-HOUNG.—A revenue circle in the western township of the Tavoy district ; such cultivation as there is, is principally rice. In this circle, which is somewhat to the north of Tavoy town and on the opposite side of the river, is found the clay from which are manufactured, in Tavoy, the pots used in salt boiling. It is now joined to Moung-ma-gan.

MYO-HOUNG.—A town in the Akyab district, the head-quarters of the township of the same name. *See Mro-houng.*

MYO-KHYOUNG.—A revenue circle in the Kyouk-hpyoo township, Kyouk-phoo district, north of Ma-dai-gan-ga island, 24 square miles in extent. *See Mro-khyoung.*

MYO-LAI.—A stream in the Poungday township of the Prome district which connects the Wai-gyee or Shwe-lay with the Kyat or Toung-gnyo. Leaving the Wai-gyee at Hmat-taing village it runs southward through the town of Poungday and falls into the Kyat a little below the village of Tha-hpan-goon. Throughout the whole of its course it flows through villages and cultivated ground and is at no season navigable by boats. In the dry season water is obtained for drinking purposes by digging holes in its bed. It is one of the numerous inosculating channels which traverse the lower portion of the Poungday plain connecting the Shwe-lay, the Kyat and the Myit-ma-kha and serving to carry off, though not sufficiently rapidly, the violent rush of water which comes down from the neighbouring Pegu Roma mountains during the rains.

MYO-MA.—A revenue circle in the Prome district at the junction of the North and South Naweng rivers, containing two village tracts, *viz.*, Myo-ma and Tha-zee. In 1876 the population was 1,147, the capitation tax Rs. 803, the land revenue Rs. 961 and the gross revenue Rs. 1,764.

MYO-THIT.—A revenue circle in the Kyouk-hpyoo district. *See Mro-thit.*

MYOUK-BHET-MYO.—A township in the north of the Sandoway district with a population in 1875 of 19,437 souls. The name is more a description than a name signifying as it does "northern township." It occupies the whole of the northern part of the district from the Ma-ee river to the Khwett-toung spur and comprises an area of about 1,454 square miles, by far the greater portion of which is mountainous and forest-clad, divided into 10 revenue circles. The rivers are small and of little or no importance and all have a general E. and W. course. The head-quarters are at Toung-goop on the river of the same name.

In 1875, the area under cultivation was :—

		Acres.
Rice land under cultivation and annual assessment	.. ..	7,280
Ditto, fallow do.	.. ..	235
Ditto, under lease or revenue settlement for more than one year and paying revenue	.. ..	3,799
Toungya at As. 8 per acre ..	.. .. ..	754
Ditto, at As. 4 do. ..	.. .. ..	448
Garden and orchard land under annual assessment	.. ..	796
Ditto ditto ditto lease or revenue settlement for more than one year	.. ..	686
Miscellaneous cultivation subject to annual assessment	.. ..	965
Ditto ditto. under lease for more than one year ..	..	75
	Total ..	15,038

The principal products other than the staple, rice, are :—tobacco, sessamum, cotton, pepper, sugarcane, plantains, cocoanuts, betel-nuts, dhanee, betel-vines, peas, hemp and indigo, which are consumed mainly in the township. The products exported are insignificant in quantity and value, the principal are tobacco and sessamum seed, both going to Kyouk-hpyoo, and vegetable products. Indigo is grown only in very small quantities, and that by Khyeng, and is used by them for dyeing home-spun fabrics. There is a little trade in cattle, such as buffaloes and bullocks, carried on between the inhabitants of this township and those of the Prome and Akyab districts.

Of the forest products iron-wood is exported to the neighbouring district of Kyouk-hpyoo and is cut for local use, but the supply fluctuates according to the demand as it is principally used for house-building purposes.

With the exception of the Imperial road across the Arakan Roma having its termination at Toung-goop there are no made roads in the township. Communication between villages is maintained by boats through the various tidal creeks and streams and by foot tracks over the hills; these latter however, are little used except in the dry season. The people are principally engaged in agricultural pursuits and only when their crops do not require their attention do they follow any other occupation. They catch and cure fish for home consumption and some families manufacture salt; salt boiling is principally carried on in the Padeng circle, and in 1875 furnished as revenue Rs. 686-8. Weaving of cotton cloths is universal and is carried on in every house, but merely to meet home requirements.

The gross Imperial and Provincial revenue derived from the township in 1874-75 was Rs. 43,714, made up as follows:—

				Rs.	A.	P.
Land revenue	..	..	..	21,908	15	8
Capitation tax	..	..	..	16,734	0	0
Salt tax ..	..	..	..	686	8	0
Net tax ..	..	..	..	186	4	0
Turtle banks	..	..	..	10	0	0
Timber duty..	..	..	..	1,158	0	0
Excise revenue	..	..	..	1,065	0	0
Miscellaneous revenue ..	..	..	..	1,965	0	0
		Total	..	43,713	11	8

In 1876 the population was 19,520, the land revenue Rs. 22,530, the capitation tax Rs. 17,016 and the gross revenue Rs. 70,902 of which Rs. 48,446 were Imperial and Provincial credited to the various heads given in the preceding paragraph and the rest to Local Funds.

The principal villages, besides Toung-goop, are Ma-ee, Maw-rwa, Tsha-beng, Tan-lwai, Ta-ra-tha, Nga-mouk-khyoung, and Gyee-pywon.

MYOUK-KYWOT.—A village of about 50 houses in 19° 25′ 20″ N. Lat. and 95° 7′ 40″ E. Long. on the Htan-roon stream, an affluent of the Pwon. It is in the Bhan-byeng circle of the Thayet township, Thayet district. The inhabitants are engaged principally in rice and "hill" cultivation.

MYOUK-PYENG.—A village in the Pay-myouk circle, Meng-doon township, Thayet district, containing some 50 houses. It is situated on the Hlo-wa stream contiguous to the village of Kan-ma-naing which has another 50 or more houses in it, at the mouth of the Ma-gyee-goon rivulet. It was entered in the Burmese returns as a registered village and was joined to Pay-myouk by the British Government in 1864.

MYOUNG-GYEE.—A large revenue circle in the Kyan-kheng township, Henzada district, extending eastwards from the Arakan Roma mountains to the Bhet-rai circle, and separated from the A-loon circle of the same township on the north by the Kwon stream and from the Myan-oung township on the south by the Khoung-loung. Towards the north-east there is a little rice cultivation but elsewhere the circle is a confused mass of hills covered with bamboo and tree forest amongst which are found Teak (*Tectona grandis*), Eng (*Dipterocarpus tuberculatus*), Pyeng-ma (*Lagerstrœmia Reginæ*), Pyeng-ga-do (*Xylia dolabiformis*) and Bhan-bhwai (*Careya arborea*). The only river except the two which form the north and south boundaries is the Tsan-da, which unites with the Khoung-loung. In 1876 the population was 2,353, the land revenue Rs. 2,424, the capitation tax Rs. 2,615 and the gross revenue Rs. 5,186.

442

MYOUNG-MYA.—A revenue circle, 163 square miles in extent, in the township of the same name in the Bassein district, between the Thek-ngay-thoung channel on the west, the Myoung-mya-houng on the south and east and the Myoung-mya or Tshiep-gyee on the north. Except in the extreme north-west corner on the island formed by the Khwe-le, which runs between the Myoung-mya and the Thek-ngay-thoung, the surface of the country is generally undulating, the formation towards the centre tending somewhat to a ridge. The population is principally Kareng with some Burmans and a few Shan and is employed in fishing and in the east and north-west in rice cultivation. In the northern part of the circle, surrounded by hills, is a small lake which retains its water all the year round and from which numerous small streams run between the hills. There are no regular roads, but a foot track or bridle road passes through the centre of the circle, touching at all the interior villages. In 1876-77 the population was 6,534, the land revenue Rs. 8,023, the capitation tax Rs. 6,982 and the gross revenue Rs. 15,717.

MYOUNG-MYA.—A township in the Bassein district between the Thek-ngay-thoung and the Pya-ma-law and Pyeng-tha-loo channels on the west and east respectively and stretching up northwards from the seacoast to the Myoung-mya, which forms its northern boundary from the north-western corner eastwards to the mouth of the Kha-louk-thaik, and with a narrow strip—the Kyoon-ka-nee circle—running up still further north between the Kha-louk-thaik and the Pya-ma-law. It has an area, exclusive of the rivers and creeks, of 931 square miles. Down the centre of the township runs the Rwe channel which separates from the Myoung-mya near the village of that name as the Tha-re-boon, and falls into the sea by two mouths, the eastern called the Da-ray-bhyoo. The south-eastern corner is formed by an island which separates the Pya-ma-law into two mouths, that to the eastward called the Pyeng-tha-loo.

The coast line consists of a flat and sandy beach with narrow plains running along its margin from ¼ to ½ a mile in width covered with grass. From the coast as far north as the Kook-ko channel the country is uninhabited during the rains; at other seasons there are numerous temporary fishing hamlets established by the inhabitants of some of the villages inland. The lower portion the country, especially to the eastward, is low and intersected by numerous tidal creeks with the banks having a deep fringe of heavy forest. From the Kook-ko northwards the country gradually rises, the intricacy of the creeks diminishes and the size of the plains and permanently inhabitable spots increases. In the western and central portion of the township, north of La-bwot-ta, in 16° 18′ N., the country rises into small, well-wooded hills, and here small tracts of rice cultivation appear which, farther north, in the centre of the township, increase considerably in size. In the north-western corner an outcrop of Magnesian limestone rises into low hills which are densely wooded. The extreme northern portion consists of a narrow tract of low ground which stretches up some 15 miles N. N. E. between the Pya-ma-law and the Myoung-mya.

The most important streams, besides the numerous and large anastomosing creeks in the lower portion, are the Myoung-mya-houng and the Rwe, which both leave the Myoung-mya at the town of that name, and the Myoung-mya and the Pya-ma-law. The Myoung-mya-houng connects the Rwe on the east with the Bassein river on the west and is navigable in the dry season by boats of from 25 to 30 feet in length. The Rwe is about 160 yards wide at its northern end and 300 yards wide at its southern, with from 20 to 30 feet of water, and is navigable by river steamers. The Myoung-mya runs from the town of the same name to the Pan-ma-wa-dee and is navigable by large boats, possibly by river steamers. The Pya-ma-law is one of the numerous mouths of the Irrawaddy which it leaves at Shwe-loung in the township of the same name, in the Thoon-kwa district, and reaches the sea by two mouths, the Pya-ma-law and the Pyeng-tha-loo. It is navigable by river steamers throughout its entire length; its mouth, where there is an extensive bar, is four miles wide.

The township is now divided into nine revenue circles, *viz.*, Kweng-bouk-gyee, Ka-wek, La-bwot-koo-la, Lay-byouk, Kya-gan, Myoung-mya, Kyoon-ka-nee, Poo-loo, Pyeng-ma-goon and Theng-gan-kywon. In 1876-77 the population was 34,914, the land revenue Rs. 61,541, the capitation tax Rs. 39,491 and the gross revenue Rs. 117,370.

The principal towns and villages are Myoung-mya with 1,715 inhabitants, the head-quarters, on the Myoung-mya creek; Kyoon-ka-nee, in the circle of the same name on the Kyoon-tsien Re-gyaw near its mouth, with 795 inhabitants; Kha-louk-thaik, W. by N. of Kyoon-ka-nee, with 659 inhabitants; La-bwot-ta in the south of the Kya-gan circle, with 1,211 inhabitants; La-bwot-koola near the junction of the Poo-loo and the Tha-re-boon, with 1,800 inhabitants and Da-ray-bouk, a few miles further south, with 679 inhabitants.

MYOUNG-MYA.—A creek in the Bassein district which runs from the head of the Rwe westwards to the Pan-ma-wa-dee and is formed by the junction of numerous creeks coming in from the west and north-west. It is the northern boundary of the township of the same name separating it from the Thee-kweng township of the same district. Its extreme length is 15 miles. Near its northern end is the town of Myoung-mya. The network of creeks in this part of the country is so great that it might almost be said to leave the Daga near Oot-hpc in about 17° 4′ N. and 95° 16′ E. and to run south under various names *e. g.*, Meng-ma-naing and Kha-louk-thaik, till it turns west a little to the east of Myoung-mya and assumes the name of that town. Just before it reaches Myoung-mya it throws off to the southward the Tha-re-boon (the head-waters of the Rwe). From this point westward it offers no obstacles whatever to its navigation by river steamers of 300 tons burden. Above this, that is along those portions called the Kha-louk-thaik and the Meng-ma-naing, large boats can pass at all seasons with the flood tide.

MYOUNG-MYA.—A town in the Bassein district in 16° 45′ N. and 95° E. the head-quarter station of the township of the same name, situated on the Myoung-mya or Tshiep-gyee river. The inhabitants, who numbered 1,715 souls in 1877, are engaged in cultivation and in fishing and in making salt and nga-pee. It was the scene of the first rising amongst the Kareng in 1853 (*See Bassein District :—History*). Formerly it possessed some handsome wooden monasteries and rest-houses but these, together with the town, were burned down in 1861. In the immediate vicinity a wooden chapel has been erected by a Roman Catholic Missionary who has dwelt here for many years. The Extra Assistant Commissioner in charge of the township holds his court in this town. It contains a Court-house, Police-station and a substantial Market and a large pagoda and image of Gaudama, erected, according to the current tradition, by a "foreign king." It was formerly called Tshiep-gyee, Myoung-mya, being about four miles inland from he present site.

In 1876-77 a local revenue of Rs. 239 was realized from the market stall-rents.

MYOUNG-MYA-HOUNG.—A creek in the Myoung-mya township of the Bassein district, which leaves the Tha-re-boon a few miles from its northern mouth, and flowing in a generally south-west direction falls into the Bassein or Nga-won river by two mouths, the northern called the Po-loung-gyee and the southern the Peng-le-ga-le. It is tidal during the dry season and is navigable by boats of from 25 to 30 feet in length.

MYOUNG-TA-NGA.—A poor and straggling village in the Rangoon district on the banks of the stream of the same name, a small tributary of the Hlaing, at a spot where it makes several short serpentine bends and about two miles to the eastward of that river. To the south-east are the remains of an old fort. It is about two tides from Rangoon by the Hlaing and is accessible by land from the same town *via* Hmaw-bhee. The inhabitants who are principally cultivators, or foresters working in the forests on the slopes of the Pegu Roma mountains to the eastward, numbered 917 in 1877.

MYOUNG-TA-NGA.—A revenue circle in the south-eastern portion of the Hlaing township of the Rangoon district, with an area of about 220 square miles ; bounded on the north by the Ma-ga-ree which separates it from the Ook-kan circle, on the east by the Pegu Roma, on the south by the Myo-khyoung, which separates it from the Hmaw-bhee circle of the Hmaw-bhee township and on the west by the Hlaing river. The eastern part of this circle is covered with dense forest (known as the Hlaing forest) abounding in Teak and other valuable woods, the western part towards the Hlaing river presents culturable plains in the neighbourhood of the villages intersected by tracts of forest. Here the area under rice cultivation is increasing steadily and rapidly although the soil is poor, whilst those portions of the circle which are unsuited for this crop and are beyond the limits of the Government forests, that is, west of the railway and adjoining it on the east, are being taken up for gardens and mainly by the Shans who are coming down in increasing numbers from the Shan states and select for their settlements lands fitted for orchards and gardens. They prefer the immediate neighbourhood of Rangoon as giving them a readier market for their produce, but new-comers find the land there to a very great extent already occupied and settle along the railway line. On the hills silk-worms are bred. A large revenue is derived from the net and fishery tax.

During the last five years the area under cultivation and the revenue were :—

YEAR.	AREA, IN ACRES.				REVENUE, IN RUPEES.			
	Rice.	Garden.	Miscellaneous.	Total.	Land.	Capitation tax.	All other items.	Total.
1873-74	5,616	36	52	5,704	9,115	5,655	1,634	16,404
1874-75	6,640	30	38	6,708	10,737	5,645	1,629	18,011
1875-76	7,481	56	19	7,556	11,924	5,585	1,627	19,136
1876-77	8,324	63	232	8,621	13,401	6,245	1,404	21,050
1877-78	8,976	66	155	9,197	14,051	6,425	1,439	21,915

and the population and agricultural stock :—

YEAR.	POPULATION.						STOCK.				
	Burmans.	Talaing.	Shan.	Kareng.	All others.	Total.	Buffaloes.	Cows, bulls and bullocks.	Carts.	Ploughs.	Boats.
1873-74 ..	2,216	674	149	1,674	11	4,724	1,260	143	178	354	29
1874-75 ..							1,351	261	154	406	6
1875-76 ..	1,704	496	60	1,718	11	3,989	1,353	238	328	471	2
1876-77 ..	2,069	937	46	1,602	9	4,663	1,634	713	259	508	162
1877-78 ..	1,686	829	134	2,231	15	4,895	2,030	1,191	434	584	111

MWAI-YO.—A revenue circle in the Prome district, traversed by the Thit-nee-doon stream to the N. E. of Prome and about seven miles inland from the Irrawaddy. In 1876-77 the population was 336, the land revenue Rs. 457, the capitation tax Rs. 325 and the gross revenue Rs. 872.

NAAF.—An arm of the sea forming a portion of the western boundary of the Akyab district and separating the Province from Chittagong. "Naaf" is the Bengali name customarily used by all but Arakanese and Burmese to whom this estuary is known as the *Anouk-ngay*. It is about 31 miles in length and three miles broad at its mouth and shallows considerably towards the head. Owing to the numerous rocks and shoals, the entrance is dangerous. Ferry boats ply regularly between Moung-daw and the Chittagong side. Off the coast are S. Martin's and Oyster Islands, neither inhabited ; on the former thatch-grass grows abundantly and is brought away by the inhabitants of the mainland.

NAAF.—A township in the Akyab district, with its head-quarters at Moung-daw, lying between the Naaf estuary on the west and the Ma-yoc hills on the east and touching the Bay of Bengal towards the south. The Burmese and Arakanese name is Anouk-ngay or "little west" (country)

The northern portion is but sparsely inhabited and is covered with forest, the central is well cultivated by the Bengali and Mug inhabitants and the southern is a narrow, barren and sandy strip of country, with a few villages, which forms a good grazing ground for cattle. It is divided into 10 revenue circles. In 1877-78 it contained 47,456 inhabitants and produced a gross revenue of Rs. 107,623, of which Rs. 40,285 were derived from the capitation tax and Rs. 59,122 from the land revenue.

NAAF (NORTH).—The northern of the two Naaf circles in the township of the same name in the Akyab district. Within its limits is situated Moung-daw the head-quarters of the township. In 1875 the population numbered 6,704 souls and the capitation tax produced Rs. 6,337. In 1874-75 the area under cultivation was 5,292 acres, and the land revenue amounted to Rs. 11,395. In 1876-77 the population was 7,152, the land revenue Rs. 11,668, the capitation tax Rs. 6,535 and the gross revenue Rs. 21,456.

NAAF (SOUTH).—The southern Naaf circle of the township of the same name in the Akyab district. The area under cultivation in 1874-75 was 2,550 acres and the land revenue amounted to Rs. 5,489. In 1875-76 the population numbered 2,610 souls and the capitation tax produced Rs. 2,576. In 1876-77 the population was 2,530, the land revenue Rs. 5,500, the capitation tax Rs. 2,512, and the gross revenue Rs. 8,395. The largest village is Pa-deng, with 400 inhabitants in 1877.

NA-BHOO.—A small stream in the Amherst district which rises in the western slopes of the Dawna range and after a westerly course of about 20 miles falls into the Hlaing-bhwai a few miles above its junction with the Houng-tha-raw.

NA-GA.—A village in the Le-doung circle, Ramree township, Kyoukhpyoo district, about half a mile inland on the western coast of Ramree Island, two miles south of the Ran-bouk stream. The name is derived from its proximity to a so-called volcano. In 1877-78 it had a population of 555 souls. The inhabitants are principally petty traders in miscellaneous products such as betel-nut, tobacco, &c.

NA-LIEN-TSAN.—A small village in the Ma-lee-won circle of the Mergui district, the head-quarter station of the Ma-lee-won township, on the right bank of the Pak-chan 32 miles above Ma-lee-won. In 1877-78 it had 370 inhabitants, principally Siamese with a few Chinese. The public buildings are a small Court-house and a Police-station.

NAN-DAW.—A small pagoda in the Sandoway district on a hill about half a mile north of the town of Sandoway, and on the left bank of the river of the same name, said to have been built by Meng Bhra in 763 A. D., two years later than the neighbouring "An-daw", to contain a rib of Gaudama. It is resorted to principally by the inhabitants of Sandoway during one of the three feast days in March, June and October ; the other two feast days in each of these months being spent at the An-daw and Tshan-daw pagodas respectively.

NAN-RA-GOON.—A village in the Kywon-baw circle of the Ra-thai-doung township, Akyab district, situated on the north bank of the Kha-moung-doon stream, near its source. In 1877-78 it had 512 inhabitants.

NAN-TSHOO-BENG.—A village of some 100 houses in the Pyen-bouk circle of the Mye-dai township, Thayet district. It is situated on the left bank of the Irrawaddy in a large rice plain just to the north of and almost joined to the village of Pyen-bouk which gives its name to the circle.

NAT-KHYOUNG.—A revenue circle in the Gyaing Attaran township, Amherst district, lying on both banks of the Tsa-mee river, just south of Kya-eng, and extending east and west to the watersheds of the valley of that river. Its hills are covered with forest, and the Kareng who inhabit it are able to cultivate only a very small portion of its surface. In 1877 the population numbered 998, the land revenue was Rs. 295 and the capitation tax Rs. 435.

NAT-MAW.—A village in the Henzada district in 17° 34' 10" N. and 95° 30' 30" E. in the circle of the same name, about four miles south-west of Henzada, on the bank of the Nat-maw stream, the inhabitants of which are principally engaged in the fisheries and in rice cultivation. In 1877 they numbered 2,386.

NAT-MAW.—A revenue circle in the Henzada township of the Henzada district having on the north the Kyoon-hpa circle, on the west the Za-lwon township, on the east the Le-dee-khan-hla and Tha-nwon-tha-naw circles, and on the south the Za-lwon township. It now includes Tha-tsee. In 1877 the population was 5,961, the land revenue Rs. 17,751, the capitation tax Rs. 5,812 and the gross revenue Rs. 24,530.

NAT-MEE.—A small circle in the Ka-ma township, Thayet district. It was held by a hereditary Thoogyee who in 1870 A. D. resigned on account of the insufficiency of his income and the circle was then joined to Toon (q.v.), which is sometimes called Nat-mee Toon. The name is derived from the " spirit fire " seen near the village of Nat-mee, the result of the combustion of hydrogen gas which here escapes from the earth (Vide Thayet district: Geology). The products are rice, tobacco, chillies, onions, sessamum, cotton, maize, cutch and plantains.

NAT-MOUK.—A revenue circle in the Prome district, west of the town of Padoung. The south-eastern portion where most of the villages are found contains a good deal of land under rice cultivation. In 1877-78 the land revenue was Rs. 1,190, the capitation tax Rs. 635, the gross revenue Rs. 1,840 and the population 598.

NAT-POO-DEE.—A revenue circle in the Prome district to the west-ward of and close to Poungday, traversed by the main road which runs from Rangoon through Poungday and Prome to the northern frontier of the Province. Nat-poo-dee, situated on this road, is the largest village. In 1877 the land revenue was Rs. 442, the capitation tax Rs. 527, the gross revenue Rs. 1,032 and the number of inhabitants 486.

NAT-POO-DEE.—A village in the Prome district in 18° 28' 25" N. and 95° 33' 50" E., a mile and a half from Poungday on the high road from Rangoon to the frontier. It is inhabited chiefly by rice cultivators.

NAT-TA-LENG.—A little village in the Prome district about four miles in a direct line E. N. E. of Prome town on the main road from Rangoon to Mye-dai which here crosses the river Na-weng over a timber bridge.

NA-WENG.—A river in the Prome district. There are two streams of this name distinguished as the "North" and the "South" Na-weng.

The North Na-weng rises in the Pegu Roma mountains to the north of the Pa-douk spur and flows down the centre of a mountainous and narrow valley till it reaches the plain country. From its source to the village of Tsheng-won its general direction is north-west, thence it runs west to Lekkhoop-peng and from there S. S. W. till it joins the South Na-weng a mile south of the village of Myo-ma. Whilst amongst the hills its bed is rocky, its banks are steep, and its tributaries are mountain torrents, only one of which, the Tswon, which joins it shortly after it has turned westwards, is more than a few miles long; when it enters the plains the bed becomes sandy and the banks moderately steep. Here its affluents increase in size and in length; they are the Tsa-do-gya, the Thit-poot and the Hlai-kadoung from the north, and the Reng from the south, all similar in character having rocky beds and draining narrow bamboo-covered ravines.

The South Na-weng, also, rises in the Pegu Roma immediately to the south of the Pa-douk spur which forms the watershed between these two rivers till they unite at its south-western extremity. As far as the mouth of the Teng-gyee its course is about W. S. W. winding down a narrow valley over a rocky bed and having only mountain torrents as its tributaries. Here it enters the plains and flowing W. N. W. for a short distance it turns S. W. to pour into the Irrawaddy, at the town of Prome, all the drainage of the country lying between it and the long spur of the Roma mountains which forms the northern boundary of the district on the left bank of the Irrawaddy and the drainage of a small belt of country to the south. Whilst still in the hills it receives near Rat-thit the waters of the Teng-gyee which drains a long and somewhat bell-mouthed valley with a general westerly direction. Soon after it descends into the plains the Khyoung-tsouk brings with it the surplus waters from a rocky valley lying between the two Na-weng rivers and separated from them by subsidiary spurs. Just before uniting itself with the Na-weng the Khyoung-tsouk receives two tributaries, the Gway-khyo and the Enggoon. From the mouth of the Khyoung-tsouk to that of the North Naweng the affluents are few and unimportant. Lower down the Kouk-gway falls into it from the north and the Law-thaw from the south. The Koukgway, sometimes called the Kam-bhee-la, rises in the plains in the undulating ground north of the village of Wek-htee-gan and before joining the South Na-weng receives the Eng-roon which has its source in a spur much further to the north; both have sandy beds and are navigable by small boats for a short distance from their mouths during the rains. The Lawthaw in the rains unites with streams which come down from the eastern mountains and pouring their waters into the marshy ground behind the town of Prome are the real source of the Rangoon river. The Thit-kyee rising in the hills 10 or 15 miles north of the Prome district joins the Na-weng about five miles from its mouth.

In the dry season all these rivers are nearly dry but in the rains they bring down vast volumes of water, the drainage of some 700 square miles of country finding its way out by the one mouth of the Na-weng. None of them are navigable by large boats for any distance but in the rains small boats can ascend a short way up those which flow through the plains and the North and South Na-weng as far as the village of Tha-hla-peng-tsee and the mouth of the Teng-gyee respectively. The Na-weng is now mainly used as a channel for floating from the forests on the Roma mountains the teak and other valuable timber * found there, which is rafted at its mouth, and the bamboos growing on the slopes of the more western spurs.

NGA-BYE-MA.—A village in the Amherst district on the right bank of the Attaran river, the head-quarters of the Gyaing Attaran township. In 1875, it had a small population of 233 souls. It contains a Court-house near the wooden wharf and a Police station.

NGA-HLAING.—A small but fertile revenue circle in the Kama township, Thayet district, two square miles in extent, of which only about 160 acres are unculturable. The cultivated area is sown mainly with rice, and with tobacco, sessamum, chillies and onions. In 1877 the population numbered 1,570 and the revenue was Rs. 3,792 of which Rs. 2,033 was derived from the land, Rs. 1,607 from the capitation tax and the rest from miscellaneous sources. None of the villages are of any importance. It now includes Alat-lay, joined to it in 1858 when the Thoogyee, having been concerned in a cattle-theft case, escaped to Upper Burma.

NGA-HLAING-KHYOON.—A revenue circle in the Thayet district, stretching southwards from the extreme north-west corner along the western boundary of the Thayet township, with an area of about 52 square miles of which rather over 46 are unculturable waste. The larger portion of the cultivation is carried on in toung-ya clearings spread over the hills on which this circle is situated. The population, which is almost entirely Burman, numbered 2,852 souls in 1872 and 3,171 in 1877. In the latter year the land revenue was Rs. 1,467, the capitation-tax Rs. 2,174 and the gross revenue Rs. 3,764. The villages are numerous but none of them are large. In former years Nga-hlaing-khyoon formed a portion of the Toung-bhet circle ; in 1847 A.D., one Moung Toot-gyee came hither from Bhan-goon, then in the Kama jurisdiction, with a large number of followers and in order to encourage him the then Burmese Governor withdrew Nga-hlaing-khyoon from Toung-bhet and formed it into a separate circle over which he placed the immigrant leader as Thoogyee. After the annexation the circle was divided amongst five Thoogyees, viz., those of Hpoung-ga-aing, Meng-rwa, Ka-gnyit-kya, Oon-nai-tai-gyee and Nga-hlaing-khyoon. Four of the Thoogyees, one after the other, gradually disappeared, and all on account of serious charges preferred against them and in 1864 the five circles were joined together again. The products are rice, cotton, sessamum, maize, cutch and petroleum of a thick quality similar to that imported from Re-nan-khyoung in Upper Burma. Wells have been sunk near the village of Pa-douk-beng but the yield at present is insignificant.

NGA-KHO-BYENG.—A revenue circle in the Ramree township of the Kyouk-hpyoo district lying in the extreme southern point of the island, about 14 square miles in extent, cultivated with rice and producing also some indigo ; limestone is found towards the north-east. The inhabitants, who are principally Arakanese, numbered 4,002 in 1877-78, when the land

---

* Eng (Dipterocarpus tuberculatus), Pyeng-ga-do (Xylia dolabriformis), Htouk-kyan (Terminalia macrocarpa), Pyeng-ma (Lagerstræmia reginæ) and Bhan-bhwai (Careya arborea).

revenue was Rs. 3,240, the capitation tax Rs. 4,445 and the gross revenue Rs. 8,803. It now includes the Ran-byai-ngay circle.

NGA-KHWA.—A small river in the Bassein district, which rises in the Arakan hills and falls into the Than-dwe. It is navigable by boats 20 feet in length as far as the village of Ma-oo-goon, a distance of two miles.

NGA-KHWA.—A revenue circle in the Tha-boung township, Bassein district west of Bassein town lying along the Arakan hills and bounded on the east by the Than-dwe river, on the north by the Than-lyek-tswon circle of the same township from which it is separated by the Kyouk-khyoung-gyee stream and on the south by the Mai-za-lee circle of the Bassein township from which it is separated by the Nga-khwa stream. It now includes the Shan-kweng circle. The eastern part is flat and pretty well cultivated but the western is hilly; the hills increasing in height toward the Arakan mountains. Limestone is found close to the main range and near the source of the Wom-bhai streamlet, a tributary of the Kyouk-khyoung-gyee. There are no roads but footpaths from village to village. A large majority of the inhabitants are Kareng. In 1877 the population of the united circles was 2,445, the land revenue Rs. 4,364, the capitation tax Rs. 2,525 and the gross revenue Rs. 7,107.

NGA-MAN-RAI.—A revenue circle in the Mye-boon township, Kyouk-hpyoo district, on the northern shore of Hunter's Bay (which is known to Burmese and Arakanese as Nga-man-rai) with an area of about 15 square miles and extending along the Kyat-tseng creek. In 1877 it had a population of 1,613 souls and the land revenue was Rs. 4,990 the capitation tax Rs. 2,050 and the gross revenue Rs. 7,381.

NGA-MOUK-KHYOUNG.—A large village in the Pa-deng circle of the northern township of Sandoway on Pa-deng Island, with 1,396 inhabitants in 1877-78. A considerable quantity of salt is manufactured in the neighbourhood.

NGA-NEE-BA.—A village in the Prome district in 18° 37′ 20″ N. and 95° 29′ 40″ E., about 18 miles S. S. E. of Prome and 13 N. N. W. of Poung-day, lying in a large and well-populated rice tract; it is inhabited chiefly by agriculturists.

NGAN-KHYOUNG.—A thinly-inhabited revenue circle in the Nga-poo-taw township, Bassein district, occupying the southern portion of the strip of land between the Bay of Bengal and the Arakan mountains and extending north as far as the Hnget-pyaw stream. Its estimated area is about 192 square miles and the whole consists of forest-covered hills stretching down towards the sea by gradual slopes and leaving a narrow sandy beach except near Hmaw-deng or Pagoda Point, Cape Negrais, further north, and a few other spots where they enter the sea abruptly forming a bold and rugged escarpment. In one or two places there are small plains cultivated with rice. From December to February native boats can pass up and down this coast; the favourite harbour is between parallel spurs of rock running out into the sea at Poon-gnyet-gyoung on the southern side of Cape Negrais. It is now united with Nga-roop-koung.

NGAN-TE.—A revenue circle in the Zaya township, Amherst district, formed by the amalgamation of the two small Ngan-te and Mai-roung circles. It has the town of Maulmain on the west, the Attaran on the north and east and the Thee-tha-ro and Kyouk-tan circles on the south. Its total area is 4,124 acres. The greater portion of the surface is stony upland and by no means fertile but still adapted for gardens and orchards to the cultivation of which the close proximity of the circle to the town of Maulmain lends a stimulus. Maulmain can be reached from any part by land or by water in two or three hours.

The population and revenue have been :—

| Years. | Population. | REVENUE, IN RUPEES. | | |
		Land.	Capitation tax.	Total.
1858	735	2,059	1,060	3,119
1875	..	2,680	1,400	4,080
1877	1,228	2,531	1,373	3,904

NGA-OUNG.—A small river in the Bassein district which falls into the Bassein river just above the town of Bassein. Boats of 25 feet in length can, at all seasons, ascend for about two miles as far as the village of Thai-gyee-goon.

NGA-PAW.—A revenue circle in the Prome district to the south of the Daw-lee circle. There is a little rice cultivation in the eastern corner on the bank of the Shwe-lay, near the fairly large village of Nga-paw. In 1877 the land revenue was Rs. 484, the capitation tax Rs. 1,180, the gross revenue Rs. 1,884 and the population 1,098.

NGA-PAW.—A village in the Prome district in 18° 37′ 50″ N. and 95° 42′ 5″ E. on the bank of the Shwe-lay river about six miles due west of the Pan-doung spur of the Pegu Roma mountains.

NGA-PEE-TSHIEP.—A large village in the circle of the same name in the Kan-oung township of the Henzada district on the right bank of the Irrawaddy. In 1877-78 it had 2,019 inhabitants.

NGA-PEE-TSHIEP.—A revenue circle in the Kan-oung township, Henzada district, stretching south-west from the bank of the Irrawaddy opposite or a little below Meng-gyee. The country is low and the area under cultivation is not extensive. This circle is now joined to O-bho.

NGA-POO-TAW.—An island in the Bassein river forming a revenue circle in the township of the same name in the Bassein district. The eastern channel between it and the mainland is called the Pan-ma-wa-dee. It is generally low and flat and much intersected by creeks. A peculiar feature is a low range of hills on the west side parallel to the river on the western slope of which stands the town of Nga-poo-taw the head-quarters of the township. The land revenue in 1877 was Rs. 2,996, the capitation tax Rs. 1,922, the gross revenue Rs. 5,068 and the population 1,670.

NGA-POO-TAW.—A village in the Nga-poo-taw circle, Bassein district, the head-quarters of the township of the same name. This village, on an island about 21 miles below Bassein formed by the junction of the Pan-ma-wa-dee river and its tributary the Thek-nga Re-gyawy with the Bassein river, lies on the western slopes of a low range of hills and extends down to the river bank. Stretching northward is a tract of fertile rice land and the village itself lies buried in fruit trees of various kinds. The inhabitants are handi-craftsmen, cultivators and traders, and in 1877 numbered 896.

NGA-POO-TAW.—A township occupying the extreme south-western portion of the Bassein district and extending northwards on both flanks of the Arakan Roma, between the Bay of Bengal on the west and the Thek-ngay-thoung mouth of the Bassein or Nga-won river on the east, to the Tsheng-ma river on the west of the mountains and to the Than-dwe on the east. The limits have several times been altered. Before the annexation of Pegu the country on the west of the Roma formed a portion of Arakan ; shortly after the annexation it, together with a considerable tract to the north as far as the Kyien-ta-lee, was attached to Bassein and formed into the Kyoung-tha township. Later on the portion north of the Khwa was given back to Sandoway and still later, on the Khyoung-tha township being abolished, the two southern circles, Ngan-khyoung and Nga-roop-koung, were added to Nga-poo-taw. The Ta-kaing circle, east of the hills, which is now in the Bassein, was formerly in this township.

The township is divided into two and very dissimilar tracts by the Arakan Roma. The extreme south-eastern consists of a large island 33 miles long by about seven broad, in the broadest part, lying in the Nga-won, with the Bassein mouth on the west and the Thek-ngay-thoung on the east, intersected by numerous anastomosing tidal creeks, and with a rocky promontory running out seawards and ending at Poorian point. Off the Bassein mouth is Diamond Island ; further out at sea the Phaeton shoal ; and still further the Alguada reef. North of this the surface is alluvial. Towards the north the country is flat and covered with forest whilst in the extreme north lime and various kinds of sand-stone rise to the surface and form small hills from 40 to 100 feet high, excessively steep on the western side. At the village of Thit-poot an outcrop of sandstone stretches across the Thek-ngay-thoung channel. In the Bassein channel between the island first described and the mainland, and nearer to the latter, is another small island, Haing-gyee or Negrais, which is celebrated in Anglo-Burmese history as having been the site of an English factory during the last century. Further up the river is Long Island, a long stretch of forest-covered ground with a low ridge of hills running along its eastern side and an outcrop in the river called the Sesostris rocks with eight feet of water over them. Nga-poo-taw island, still further north, is much intersected by creeks, has a low range of hills on the west, on the western slopes of which stands the town of Nga-poo-taw, the head-quarter station of the township. West of the Bassein the general aspect of the mainland from Hmaw-deng or Pagoda point northwards is hilly, the hills being spurs stretching out from the Arakan Roma, thickly covered with tree and grass forest mixed with bamboos. On the east from the Bhoora-hla to the Re-goung-gyee are numerous cultivated plains intersected with forest extending four or five miles inland. West of the Arakan range, nowhere more than 16 miles from the sea, the whole face of the country is mountainous, the spurs and cross-spurs here extending by gradual slopes to the sandy beach, there, as at Cape Negrais, forming rugged and sea-washed escarpments. In a few places, notably about the village of Nat-maw, are small rice plains but, generally, such cultivation as there is on the hill sides.

The Arakan Roma, stretching up northwards, nowhere in this township attain any great elevation. The principal spurs are inclined to the main range at an angle of about 40° while the cross-spurs are nearly parallel to it. The rivers are mountain torrents of little or no importance.

There are two passes across the Arakan hills, one, not much used, from the village of Rwot-pa, the summit 295 feet above the sea level, and one further north from the source of the Po-loung stream with nearly the same elevation.

The only rivers of any size are the Myit-ta-ra and the Than-dwe, which form a part of the northern boundary of the township. The Myit-tara has two mouths, the southern called the Ka-naw-gyee, Kam-bha island lying between them. Both these mouths will admit boats of from 5,000 to 6,000 bushels burden as far as their bifurcation, and native boatmen prefer this way round the island to the open Bassein river. Large vessels can enter the Than-dwe and pass up some six miles as far as the mouth of the Kwon. It has never less than 20 feet of water at the mouth and just inside there are 40 feet which decrease to 28 at the mouth of the Kwon.

Most of the lime at present used in the Bassein district is procured near Tha-man-de-wa and Kyouk-thien-baw, on the Bassein river a few miles below Nga-poo-taw.

The township is divided into 10 revenue circles, one west of the Roma. The land revenue and capitation tax in 1875 aggregated Rs. 50,793. In 1876-77 the population was 20,037, the land revenue Rs. 29,328. the capitation tax Rs. 22,738 and gross revenue Rs. 80,132.

NGA-PYENG.—A circle in the Mye-dai township, Thayet district. The population are almost entirely Burmans with a very few Khyeng. In 1874-75 the land revenue was Rs. 1,913, and the capitation tax Rs. 2,390. The cattle in the circle numbered, according to the census of 1872, 1,656 head, by far the larger portion being bullocks. The principal product is rice, but sessamum, tobacco, maize and plantains are also grown. It now includes Doo-reng-ga-bho and in 1877 the population was 3,301, the land revenue Rs. 2,467, the capitation tax Rs. 3,327 and the gross revenue Rs. 5,987.

NGA-PYENG.—A village in the Mye-dai township, Thayet district, south of Myeng-oo, lying on the left bank of the Irrawaddy in the southern portion of an extensive tract of rice cultivation.

NGA-ROOT-KOUNG.—A trading village in the Nga-poo-taw township, Bassein district at the mouth of the Nga-root-koung stream, containing 499 inhabitants in 1877. Bassein boats passing up dispose of various bazaar goods to the petty shop-keepers of the place in exchange for nga-pee and boats passing down from Sandoway dispose of tobacco in like manner. Lat. 16° 30' 30" N. Long. 93° 22' E.

NGA-ROOT-KOUNG.—A revenue circle in the Nga-poo-taw township, Bassein district, lying between the Bay of Bengal on the south and west, the Tsheng-ma stream on the north and the Arakan mountains on the east. It now includes Ngan-khyoung in the extreme south. The country comprised within these limits presents a mountainous aspect, spurs and branch-spurs running out from the western slopes of the Arakan mountains all covered with thick forest. Here and there are small plains, especially near the villages of Nat-maw and Nga-root-koung, which are cultivated with rice but elsewhere such cultivation as there is is on the sides of the hills. Along the coast-line stretches of sandy beach alternate with rocks jutting out into the sea. There are numerous insignificant islands off the coast and vessels are unable to approach the shore with safety. The land revenue of the united circles in 1877-78 was Rs. 1,172, the capitation tax Rs. 1,848, the gross revenue Rs. 4,299 and the population 2,114. The name means "Black pepper" but the reason of the circle being so called is very obscure.

NGA-ROOT-KOUNG.—A river in the Bassein district which rises in the western slopes of the Arakan mountains and falls into the sea at the village of the same name. Large boats of 400 or 500 bushels burden can at all times and seasons ascend as far Meng-gya-khyoung, or for about three miles. During the rains this river becomes a rushing mountain torrent.

NGA-THAING-KHYOUNG.—A town of 2,289 inhabitants in 1877, on the eastern bank of the Bassein river; the head-quarters of the Nga-thaing-khyoung division of the Bassein district. The inhabitants are mainly traders and fishermen. Large quantities of rice are grown in the neighbourhood. For a short time after the conclusion of the second Burmese war a detachment of Native Infantry from Bassein garrisoned the town. Rather less than a mile to the eastward is the Myit-khyo lake. The town contains a Court-house, a Police-station, a large and substantially built market, a school, a lock-up and a D. P. W. inspection bungalow. In 1876-77 the local revenue was Rs. 6,452. Lat. 17° 20' 30" N. Long. 95° 8' 30" E.

NGA-WEK.—A small mountain stream in the Thayet district which rises in the Kwon-doung spur of the Arakan hills and, flowing east-south-east, falls into the Ma-de (of which it is the largest feeder from the north) near the village of Bhan-byee. The bed is rocky and sandy and towards its source the banks are steep: it is not navigable by boats. Teak and Eng (*Dipterocarpus tuberculatus*) are found on the hills through which it passes.

NGA-WON.—A river in the Pegu division, more commonly known as the Bassein river: *q.v.*

NGA-ZAING-RAING.—A revenue circle in the Meng-bra township, Akyab district. In 1877-78, the population was 2,557, the land revenue Rs. 6,485, the capitation tax Rs. 2,434 and the gross revenue Rs. 9,321.

NGWE-DOUNG.—A revenue circle in the Ra-thai-doung township of the Akyab district. In 1877-78 the population was 2,040, the land revenue Rs. 4,479, the capitation tax Rs. 1,892 and the gross revenue Rs. 6,630.

NGWE-TWENG-TOO.—A revenue circle on the Mye-boon township, Kyouk-hpyoo district, 36 square miles in extent, divided into numerous islands by the inosculating tidal creeks at the mouth of the river Dha-let. In 1877-78 it had a population of 2,060 souls, including the inhabitants of the village of Thayet-toung who numbered about 600. The land revenue was Rs. 3,868, the capitation tax Rs. 2,475 and the gross revenue Rs. 6,567.

NOUK-MEE.—A village in the Thek-ngay-byeng circle, Oot-hpo township, Henzada district, on the west or right bank of the Irrawaddy. In 1877-78, it had 891 irhabitants.

NOUNG-BO.—A village of about 500 inhabitants in the Moon circle, Kyouk-gyee township, Shwe-gyeng district, about four miles due east from the Tsit-toung on the Shwe-gyeng and Toung-ngoo road rather under 20 miles north of Kyouk-gyee.

NOUNG-KA-LA.—A village in the Mye-nee-goon circle, Tha-htoon township, Amherst district, at the foot of the western slopes of the Marta-ban hills, a short distance north of Mye-nee-goon. In 1877-78 it had 894 inhabitants.

NOUNG-LENG-GYEE.—A revenue circle in the Ra-thai-doung township, Akyab district. In 1877-78 the population was 2,390, the land revenue Rs. 7,193, the capitation tax Rs. 2,770 and the gross revenue Rs. 10,562.

NOUNG-LOON.—A revenue circle in the Gyaing Than-lweng township, Amherst district, east of the Zwai-ka-beng hills; on the north it is separated from the Than-lweng Hlaing-bhwai township by the Hpa-an stream, and on the east and south are the Rwon-gnya and Za-tha-byeng circles respectively. In 1876-77 the population was 2,428, the land revenue Rs. 3,305 and the capitation tax Rs. 2,595.

NOUNG-TA-BWAI.—A village in the Mya-pa-daing circle of the Houng-tha-raw township of the Amherst district, on the bank of the Gyaing about six miles from the mouth of the Nga-poo-pa-ta and about one mile from Mya-pa-daing. In 1877-78 it had 921 inhabitants.

NWA-DAT.—A small stream in the Poungday township, Prome district, which rises to the north of Pan-deng-beng in the Shwe-lay township and flows southwards somewhat parallel to and to the eastward of the Myo-lay, falling into the Kyat at Pouk-taw. Throughout its length it flows through rich rice fields between steep banks and over a muddy bed. In the rains it is navigable by small boats but at all other seasons it is dry.

NWA-MA-RAN.—A village in the Prome district, on the left bank of the Irrawaddy between Prome and Shwe-doung. After the annexation of Pegu it was proposed to place the main frontier force at this village but fever having broken out amongst the troops on their first removal hither from Prome it was, probably somewhat precipitately, determined that Nwa-ma-ran was an unhealthy place and Thayetmyo was selected as the military station.

NWA-MA-RAN.—A revenue circle in the Shwe-doung township, Prome district, on the bank of the Irrawaddy, between Prome and Shwe-doung. Parallel to the river and running down the centre of the circle is a line of low forest-covered hills ; in the south-western portion the country is under rice cultivation. The road from Rangoon to the frontier runs through this circle near the bank of the Irrawaddy. It now includes Kyek-hpyoo-doung, Tshan-dweng, Pyeng-beng-gaing, Tseng-ma-khyat, Bhai-lek, Hpo-thien-dan and Htan-beng-gaing. In 1876-77, the population was 2,187, the land revenue Rs. 3,098, the capitation tax Rs. 2,418 and the gross revenue Rs. 5,868.

O-BHO.—A revenue circle in the Kan-oung township of the Henzada district, which includes Aing-ka-law, Nga-pee-tshiep and Kanoung-gnay, on the bank of the Irrawaddy south of the town of Kan-oung. On the north is the Kan-oung circle, on the west the Rwe-doung and Gnyoung-rwa-gyee circles and on the south the Thai-bhyoo circle, all of the same township. In 1876-77 the population was 5,289, the land revenue Rs. 3,789, the capitation tax Rs. 4,953 and the gross revenue Rs. 10,794. The principal village is Kwon-khyan-goon on the bank of the Irrawaddy with 2,074 inhabitants in 1877.

OO-DIEN.—A revenue circle in the Shwe-doung township, Prome district, which now includes Aing-da-leng-ga, Aing, Kyouk-o, Ko-dweng-zeng, Kyouk-o-gyee, Mee-loung, Tshan-rwa and Wa-lay. It lies just to the south of Meng-rwa on the main road to Rangoon from the northern frontier. Almost the entire circle is under rice cultivation. In 1876-77 the population was 1,396, the land revenue Rs. 2,433, the capitation tax Rs. 1,595 and the gross revenue Rs. 4,058.

OO-DO.—A tidal stream in the Bassein district, a tributary of the Hpet-ra which falls into the Than-dwe near its mouth. Boats of about 200 baskets burden can ascend at all seasons of the year with the flood tide as far as the mouth of the Lien-goon, a distance of about three miles.

OOK-KAN.—A revenue circle in the extreme north of the Hlaing township of the Rangoon district separated from the Thoon-tshay circle of Henzada on the north by the Mee-neng and from the Myoung-ta-nga circle on the south by the Ma-ga-ree and extending from the Pegu Roma on the east to the river Hlaing on the west. It is traversed from south to north by the Irrawaddy Valley (State) Railway and there is a station, called Ook-kan, at Pouk-koon about two miles east of Ook-kan village. On the west the country is hilly and forest clad, producing teak and other valuable trees : the greater portion of the circle here is included in the Ma-ga-ree forest reserve. West of the railway the country is low and cultivated with rice but the soil is poor. The land along the Hlaing is slightly raised above the level further inland and in consequence during the rains a strip on the east is converted into a swamp and is unculturable. The Ook-kan stream runs through about the centre from east to west. A feeder road is being made from the Railway station at Pouk-koon westward to Ook-kan where it turns south and crosses the Ma-ga-ree at Bha-loon. The principal villages, are Ook-kan and Pouk-koon, and in the north-east is Htan-bhoo the site of an ancient town now in ruins.

The population and agricultural stock during the last five years have been :—

YEAR.		POPULATION.					AGRICULTURAL STOCK.					
		Burmans.	Kareng.	Shan.	All other races.	Total.	Buffaloes.	Cows, bulls and bullocks.	Goats.	Carts.	Ploughs.	Boats.
1873-74	..	3,064	2,579	212	101	7,756	1,504	372	..	637	734	19
1874-75	..	2,029	3,837	224	2,124	8,214	2,076	532	..	874	877	13
1875-76	..	2,976	2,944	42	2,093	8,055	1,804	377	..	815	811	4
1876-77	..	2,176	2,477	50	2,004	6,707	1,600	468	..	825	815	..
1877-78	..	2,771	2,599	73	1,666	7,109	1,947	472	9	934	972	..

and the area under cultivation and the revenue :—

YEAR.		AREA, IN ACRES.				REVENUE, IN RUPEES.			
		Rice, including fallow,	Garden.	Miscellaneous.	Total.	Land.	Capitation tax.	All other taxes.	Total.
1873-74 ..	..	7,860	137	190	8,187	13,850	9,244	481	23,575
1874-75 ..	..	8,944	154	39	9,137	15,499	9,320	404	25,223
1875-76 ..	..	9,682	123	173	9,978	16.870	9,689	331	26,890
1876-77 ..	..	10,628	177	237	11,042	18,522	9,760	281	28,563
1877-78 ..	..	11,119	160	49	11,400	19,010	10,162	415	29,587

OOK-KAN.—A river which rises in the Pegu Roma mountains and falls into Hlaing at Pyeng-ma-goon: It is a narrow stream, shallow and unnavigable in the dry weather, but in the rains it rises considerably and for some two months in the year is 25 feet above its dry weather level: it then just tops the high steep, banks between which it flows. Towards the source the bed is rocky but in the plains sandy and hard. At the village of Ook-kan the banks are about 40 feet apart. The water is always sweet but at springs in the dry season the tide ascends for a short distance above the mouth raising the fresh water very perceptibly. In the rains large boats can ascend as far as the village of Ook-kan and at this season teak and other valuable timber is brought down from the forests on the east through which it flows and the logs are collected at various places where they are formed into small rafts of one or two logs each. Towards the end of the rains these are collected in the Hlaing near the mouth and there formed into large rafts and floated down.

OOK-KAN.—A village containing a small Police guard in the circle of the same name, between the Irrawaddy Valley (State) Railway and the Hlaing river, a mile and a half to the west of the former and about five west of the latter. It is now being connected with the Ook-kan railway station, which is at the village of Pouk-koon, and with Bha-loon and other villages to the southward by a feeder road. It is a large straggling village on the right bank of the Ook-kan river, here about 40 feet wide between the banks but nearly dry except in the rains, ensconced in a grove of trees and lying in a rice plain with very similar but much smaller villages in its neighbourhood. It has several roads through it with brick-laid pathways down the centre, mostly old and worn out with gaps which in the rains are muddy pools; here and there these gaps have been filled in. It contains two fairly good zayat or public rest-houses, a monastery and two square-built pagodas, one erected in 1877 to cover the remains of a Booddhist monk. The village is said to have been founded about 300 years ago by a Talaing related by marriage to the royal family of Pegu and to have derived its Talaing name, of which Ook-kan (brick tank) is a translation, from the existence of a brick-walled tank in the neighbourhood. The Talaing were soon supplemented by a small influx of Arakanese, and subsequently by Burmese settlers. All three races are represented, and though all use the Burmese language and have completely adopted Burmese customs, yet some of the Talaing still understand their own tongue. Still later some Kareng settled in the village. It contained 713 inhabitants in 1878.

OO-LE.—The name given to the head-waters of the Thoung-yeng river—*q. v.*

OON-BENG-HLA.—A village in the Re-bhyoo circle, Thayet township, Thayet district, on the Thai-bhyoo stream, about three miles to the west of the Irrawaddy. It contains about 70 houses.

OON-KYWON.—*See Liep-kywon.*

OON-NAI.—A village containing from 50 to 60 houses in the Thit-mee-tsoo revenue circle, Kama township, Thayet district. It lies in the triangular valley enclosed by the Toung-mouk-theng-gan spur on the south, the Htoon-doung on the north-west and the Kyouk-poon on the east, and drained by the Kyouk-pwet stream, a small affluent of the Ma-de.

OO-REE-TOUNG.—A pagoda in the Oo-ree-toung circle of the Oo-ree-toung (west) township, Akyab district, on the Thee-la-pat-pa-da hill. It is said to have been built *circa* 1590 A. D., by king Meng-tha-loung on his return from an expedition against the Khyeng and the Mro. When proceeding on the expedition the king had observed what appeared to be a ball of fire on the hill and was informed by his astrologers that it was the effulgence from the skull of Gaudama when he died in one of his earlier existences as a Brahmin.

OO-REE-TOUNG, EAST.—A small township in the Akyab district lying along the seacoast to the west of Meng-bra. It is in general low and intersected with tidal creeks the water in which, but for artificial embankments, would at high tides inundate much of the surrounding country. It is divided into 22 revenue circles. In 1876-77 the population was 35,651, the land revenue Rs. 102,051, the capitation tax Rs. 43,811 and the gross revenue Rs. 155,071.

OO-REE-TOUNG, WEST.—A township in the Akyab district to the west of the Koo-la-dan township. The southern portion is highly intersected with tidal creeks which unite the Koo-la-dan and the Ma-yoo rivers. The cultivation is principally on the right bank of the Koo-la-dan and on both banks of the To, one of its tributaries, at the mouth of the Taw-bya and amongst the numerous creeks in the south. The northern portion is hilly and forest-clad. The name is derived from a high hill on which was built, by one of the kings of Arakan, a pagoda reached by four flights of steps : all is now in ruins. The township, which is divided into 16 revenue circles, had in 1876-77 a population of 35,291 souls and produced a revenue of Rs. 133,477 ; Rs. 90,468 from the land and Rs. 38,966 from the capitation tax, the rest being from miscellaneous sources.

OO-REE-TOUNG.—A revenue circle in the Oo-ree-toung (west) township of the Akyab district. In 1876-77 the population was 3,912, the land revenue Rs. 8,429, the capitation tax Rs. 4,662 and the gross revenue Rs. 13,803. The principal villages are Tan-kho, with 559 inhabitants, on the western bank of the Naaf, aud Poon-na-kywon, close to the Oo-ree-toung pagoda, with 365 inhabitants.

OO-TEE.—A pagoda in the Shwe-gyeng district, formerly called Hmwe-daw because it contained a hair of Gaudama. It stands about a mile north of Shwe-gyeng town on the bank of the Shwe-gyeng river. It was destroyed by an earthquake in 1858 and was re-built by a Hpoon-gyee named Oo-tee, whence its present name.

OOT-HPO.—A town in the Henzada district on the west bank of the Ka-gnyeng stream, four miles west of the Irrawaddy and 29 miles south of Myanoung, formerly a large city founded in the eighth century and then called Kyaik-eng-ga. It is the head-quarters of the township and contains a Court-house and a Police-station. In 1877 the population was 3,826. Long. 17° 45′ 50″ N. Lat. 95° 21′ 10″ E.

OOT-HPO.—A village in the Kyek-taik circle, Mo-gnyo township, Henzada district, between the Irrawaddy Valley (State) Railway and the Hlaing. In 1877 it had 541 inhabitants.

OOT-HPO.—A township in the Henzada district 463 miles in extent, on the west bank of the Irrawaddy between Henzada on the south and Ka-noung on the north. To the westward the country is mountainous and to the east low and formerly liable to inundation on the annual rise of the Irrawaddy, but now protected by embankments which have rendered it possible to cultivate the soil more extensively. It is divided into six revenue circles. In 1877-78 the land revenue was Rs. 46,253, the capitation tax Rs. 48,467 and the gross revenue Rs. 98,660.
The population and agricultural stock in 1877 was :—

Villages.	Inhabitants.	Ponies.	Buffaloes.	Cows.	Bulls.	Bullocks.	Goats.	Pigs.	Carts, and Sledges.	Ploughs.	Oil Mills.	Boats.
149	37,707	224	3,973	3,153	1,650	5,569	55	766	4.546	2,481	78	469

OOT-HPO.—A narrow tidal creek in the Bassein district uniting the Khat-tee-ya, which it joins near its mouth, and the Bassein river a few miles below the mouth of the Than-dwe. It has an average depth of from 15 to 20 feet and is navigable by large masted boats of 60 feet in length.

OOT-HPO.—A revenue circle in the township of the same name in the Henzada district and lying to the east of the Kweng-gouk and Tsee-beng circles and west of the Thek-ngay-byeng circle. The western portion consists of undulating ground but towards the east rice cultivation is carried on to a considerable extent. In 1876-77 the population was 10,542, the land revenue Rs. 9,259, the capitation tax Rs. 9,390 and the gross revenue Rs. 21,109.

OOT-POON.—A village in the A-hpyouk circle, Za-lwon township, Henzada district, on the left bank of the Irrawaddy about a mile south of A-hpyouk. In 1877 it had 833 inhabitants.

OOT-TOO.—A revenue circle in the south-eastern township of the Tavoy district of about 12 square miles in extent. A small revenue is derived from fishery and net tax. The main products are rice, doorians and betel-nuts. In 1876-77 the population was 3,873, the land revenue Rs. 4,933, the capitation tax Rs. 3,162 and the gross revenue Rs. 8,410. The principal villages are Thayet-khyoung the head-quarters of the township, with 925 inhabitants, Pien-daw with 585 inhabitants and Kyouk-myoung with 536 inhabitants.

OOT-TWENG.—A village in the Knoung-ran circle, Ze-a-wa-dee township, Toung-ngoo district, on the Toung-ngoo and Pegu road, about two miles west of the Tsit-toung and seven south of Toung-ngoo. In 1877 it had 739 inhabitants.

OOT-TWENG-GOON.—A village in the Prome district in 18° 31′ 45″ N. and 95° 33′ 40″ E. about a mile south of the Wai-gyee river and a mile and a half west of the northern end of Poungday, inhabited principally by rice cultivators.

OO-ZEE-NA.—A pagoda, 112 feet high, supposed to contain one of Gaudama's hairs, formerly called Kyaik-pa-htan from the white appearance of the ground on which it stands, on the hills in the town of Maulmain, immediately behind the Court-houses. It was built in the reign of Athaw-ka by a hermit named Ma-naw-zee-na aided by a rich man named Mien-dee. It was repaired some 35 years ago by one Oo-zee-na.

O-SHIT-GOON.—A village of 70 houses in the Re-bhyoo circle, Thayet township, Thayet district, about eight miles north-west of the town of Thayet, near the Tha-bye-tsan stream and at the north-western extremity of a long, narrow strip of rice cultivation in which are the villages of Kye-daing, Khyeng-tsouk and Hman-deng.

O-SHIT-GOON.—A small village near the frontier and about 25 miles east of the Irrawaddy in the Tham-boo-la circle, Mye-dai township, Thayet district.

O-SHIT-GOON.—A revenue circle in the Kama township, Thayet district, lying between the Hnget-kha hills on the south-west and the Ma-htoon river on the north-east with an area of 10 square miles and a

461

population in 1872 of 1,054 souls. This, as has been the case with many other circles, was gradually enlarged by the addition to it of others as the Thoogyee died, resigned or were dismissed, and in 1872, on the resignation of its Thoogyee, it was placed under the Thoogyee of Tham-bha-ra. The largest village, which is in about the centre of the circle, is Meng-dai.

O-SHIT-PENG.—A village in the Pa-doung township, Prome district, in 18° 40′ 10″ N. and 95° 6′ 5″ E. on the military road from Pa-doung over the Toung-goop pass, close to the spot where this road crosses the river Tha-nee.

O-SHIT-PENG.—A small village in the Toung-ngoo district, six miles from the frontier and about three miles east of the Tsit-toung, important only as being one in the chain of frontier Police-stations.

OUK-MA-NIEM.—A revenue circle in the Kama township of the Thayet district occupying the upper portion of the narrow valley between the Pa-douk or Tshay-lan and Tha-o-byit spurs having an approximate area of 15 square miles of which not one complete square mile is under cultivation. Out of the 571 acres which are cultivated no less than 222 are occupied by toungya. In 1872 the population numbered 685 or 1·20 to each acre of cultivation and 756 in 1876. The circle is held hereditarily and now includes besides Ouk-ma-niem, Ka-tswon-myoung, the Thoogyee of which died in 1870, and Ouk-ma-myeng, the Thoogyee of which resigned in 1871. In 1876-77 the land revenue of the three circles was Rs. 443, the capitation tax Rs. 842 and the gross revenue Rs. 1,307.

OUK-PAING-KYWON.—A village of about 800 inhabitants in the Paing-kwon circle of the Amherst district.

OUK-RWA.—A village in the Gnyoung-beng-tha circle, Za-lwon township, Henzada district, on the right bank of the Irrawaddy at the mouth of the Gnyoung-beng-tha creek. In 1877 it had 596 inhabitants.

OUNG-BENG-THA.—A revenue circle in the north-eastern portion of the Taroop-hmaw township, Henzada district, adjoining the Prome district, with some rice cultivation towards the south-east.

OUNG-DAING.—A revenue circle in the Kyai-let township of the Akyab district. In 1876-77 the population was 2,263 the land revenue Rs. 7,848, the capitation tax Rs. 2,620 and the gross revenue Rs. 11,023. It contains no villages of any importance: the principal is Re-khyan-byeng, with 299 inhabitants, on the west bank of the Ma-yoo whence there is a ferry to the eastern bank; it is the residence of the Thoogyee.

OUNG-TSHIEP.—A revenue circle in the Oo-ree-toung (west) township of the Akyab district. In 1876-77 the population was 1,535, the land revenue Rs. 5,871, the capitation tax 2,010 and the gross revenue Rs. 8,237. The principal village is Oung-tshiep, with 378 inhabitants on the north bank of the Ro-khyoung—the residence of the Thoogyee.

OYSTER ISLAND.—A small, rocky and dangerous island off the coast of Arakan between the Naaf and the Ma-yoo about 12 miles from the mainland.

OYSTER REEF.—A dangerous sunken reef off the coast of Arakan in 20° 5′ N. Lat. on which an iron screw-pile light-house has been erected.

PA-AING.—A revenue circle in the Shwe-doung township of the Prome district. In 1877 the. population was 1,845, the land revenue Rs. 2,427, the capitation tax Rs. 2,145 and the gross revenue Rs. 4,672.

PA-AW.—A revenue circle in the south-eastern township of the Tavoy district, now joined to Ka-dwai; the main products are sessamum and cardamoms.

PA-BWOT.—A village of 70 houses in the Toon circle, Kama township, Thayet district, on the Pa-nee stream. It gave its name to a circle, which for some years after the annexation of Pegu remained, as it had been in the Burmese time, an independent Thoogyeeship, but in 1863, the Thoogyee being dismissed for bribery, it was united to Toon.

PA-DA.—A village in the Than-lyeng township of the Rangoon district on the Pa-da stream and on the east of the rising ground which extends from Syriam to Kyouk-tan, near the site of an ancient town. The name is said to be derived from the Pali Pa-da—a footstep—because the old town was built in the form of a footstep, the toes pointing north. The ruins of the old town wall, built of hewn pieces of laterite, is still distinctly traceable and the shape of the town can be made out from a neighbouring pagoda. The remains of the palace and of the elephant enclosure are visible. Within the limits are a pair of very ancient twin pagodas now known as the Taw-ra-kyoung Bhoora. The first ruler of Syriam is said to have married the daughter of the ruler of Pa-da. The town was destroyed by the Burmese during the invasion of A-na-raw-hta in the middle of the eleventh century. The inhabitants who are principally Talaing and Shan agriculturists and traders are few in number.

PA-DAN.—A revenue circle in the Hmaw-bhee township of the Rangoon district, occupying the angle formed by the river Hlaing and the Pan-hlaing creek, which unite to form what is commonly known as the Rangoon river, and north of their junction. The aspect of the country is that of a vast plain extensively cultivated · and intersected by numerous tidal creeks, occasionally fringed with low brushwood. Although the soil is probably the most fertile in the whole township yet the average produce is not, on an average, more than 40 bushels to an acre. It does not contain a single village with 500 inhabitants.

The area under cultivation and the revenue during each of the last five years were :—

YEAR.	AREA, IN ACRES.			REVENUE, IN RUPEES.			
	Rice.	Garden.	Total.	Land.	Capitation tax.	All other taxes.	Total.
1873-74	7,153	102	7,255	16,826	4,350	352	21,528
1874-75	7,617	145	7,762	17,984	4,427	344	22,755
1875-76	9,296	159	9,455	21,811	4,560	109	26,480
1876-77	10,565	204	10,769	23,870	4,325	77	28,272
1877-78	10,611	206	10,817	24,930	4,283	86	29,299

The population and agricultural stock for the same period were :—

YEAR.	POPULATION.						AGRICULTURAL STOCK.						
	Burmans.	Talaing.	Kareng.	Shans.	All others.	Total.	Buffaloes.	Cows, bulls and bullocks.	Goats and sheep.	Pigs.	Carts.	Ploughs.	Boats.
1873-74 ..	..	..	..	..	...	..	541	339	1	103	83	438	188
1874-75 ..	1,858	1,494	·493	..	10	3,855	633	421	..	114	94	499	168
1875-76 ..	1,807	1,783	369	..	15	3,974	639	443	..	124	107	513	193
1876-77 ..	1,496	1,815	326	..	21	3,650	663	424	4	198	86	466	197
1877-78 ..	1,252	1,800	44	429	..	3,525	634	376	5	202	100	420	156

PA-DAW.—A revenue circle in the Mro-houng township, Akyab district. In 1877 the population was 1,220, the land revenue Rs. 2,783, the capitation tax Rs. 1,489 and the gross revenue Rs. 4,411.

PA-DE.—A stream which rises in the western slopes of the Pegu Roma and has a westerly course for some distance before it is called the Bhwot-lay :—*q.v.* Many small tributaries join it before it leaves the mountains, and down these large quantities of teak timber are brought during the rains. In the dry weather the water is only a few inches deep and sometimes flows underneath sandbanks. In some places dams of sand are constructed for irrigation purposes and these retain the water in pools several feet deep and some hundreds of yards in length.

PA-DENG.—A revenue circle in the northern township of Sandoway. The principal products are rice and sessamum. In 1838 it contained 580 inhabitants and produced a gross revenue of Rs. 750. In 1877 the population was 2,804, the land revenue Rs. 3,190, the capitation tax Rs. 2,390 and the gross revenue Rs. 6,546.

PA-DOUK-BENG.—A small village of 50 houses in the Nga-hlaing-khyoon circle, Thayet township, Thayet district, about nine miles west, by the present road, from Thayetmyo. It is mainly important as being near the spot at which one or two earth-oil wells have been sunk from which a thick and viscid oil is obtained but in no very large quantities.

PA-DOUK-GOON.—A village in the Toung-ngoo district, occupied by a small Police-force, about a mile and a half east of the Tsit-toung, two and a half miles south of the frontier and a mile N. N. E. of Wa-roon-lai, on a road leading south from Upper Burma.

PA-DOUNG.—A township in the Prome district occupying the whole of the right bank of the Irrawaddy from Thayet on the north to Henzada on the south and stretching westward to the crest of the Arakan mountains, with an area of 1,188 square miles. Along the bank of the river for about a mile inland the ground is level and mostly under rice cultivation ; west of this the ground undulates and then cultivation appears in toungya and on the banks of the small rivers. This undulating ground soon passes into hills and the whole country to the Arakan mountains is a succession of densely-wooded spurs and counterspurs intersected by small streams and mountain torrents. The western boundary of the township and of the district, in the extreme south, is formed by the Kyouk-piet-tha stream which rises in the angle formed by two ridges of hills branching out from a long spur of the Arakan mountains, running close and almost parallel to each other, one in this district and one in Henzada, abutting on the Irrawaddy like a colossal pair of knees and called the Pa-doung and the Kyan-kheng Akouk-toung respectively. The cliffs of the latter rise abruptly from the water and, their scarped faces hollowed out into numerous small caves in which recline images of Gaudama, form a marked feature on the Irrawaddy. It was here that Major Gardner was killed during the second Burmese war.

Growing in these tracts are found Eng (*Dipterocarpus tuberculatus*), Pyeng-ga-do (*Xylia dolabriformis,*) Htouk-kyan (*Terminalia macrocarpa*), Sha (*Acacia catechu*) and Teak (*Tectona grandis*), besides bamboos which are very plentiful. Teak-producing localities are scarcer than they are farther north, but there are some valuable tracts on the side spurs of the Arakan hills, especially near the sources of the Tha-nee, Bhoo-ro, Kyouk-bhoo and Thoo-le-dan streams which, under the Burmese rule and during the first years of the occupation of Pegu by the British, yielded very considerable supplies of planks and of squared logs. That these tracts have been worked extensively is apparent from the large number of full-sized stumps found standing in the forests. In 1858 it was estimated by the Forest Department that the area of the teak-producing localities here was 40 square miles. Owing to the large number of cutch trees (*Acacia catechu*) and to the demand for cutch a brisk manufacture of this article has sprung up.

The principal rivers, all of which except the last rise in the Arakan Roma mountains and are fed by numerous mountain torrents, are the Tha-nee and its two tributaries the Bhoo-ro and the Kyouk-bhoo, the two Thoo-le-dan and the Kha-wa. The Tha-nee has a south-easterly course and flows past several large villages in a somewhat narrow but, in its lower portion, fairly well cultivated valley ; the banks are steep and the bed rocky towards the source, but in the rains boats of 80 bushels burden can ascend as far as the village of Zayat-hla. Near Kaing-gyee it is joined by the Bhoo-ro, and near Bhoo-rwa, a few miles from its mouth, by the Kyouk-bhoo. The Bhoo-ro has an easterly course of about 35 miles ; in the rains boats of 100 bushels burden can ascend as far Kaing-gyee about a mile from its mouth ; the banks are steep and the bed sandy and rocky. The Kyouk-bhoo has an easterly course ; in the rains boats can ascend as far as Gnyoung-khye-douk on the Toung-goop road, up to which the banks are moderately steep and the bed sandy and gravelly, after this to its source the banks are very steep and the bed rocky. Teak and other valuable timber and bamboos are found on the banks of both these streams. The two Thoo-le-dan rivers unite at Ma-toung and fall into the Irrawaddy at the village of Thoo-le-dan. In the rains large boats can ascend as far as Hlay-goo where the united streams leave the hills and enter the plain country which fringes the bank of the Irrawaddy, and small boats for some distance further. The banks up to Hlay-goo are moderately steep and the bed is sandy but beyond this to its source the bed is rocky and the banks are very steep. Teak, Pyeng-ga-do, Htouk-kyan and Sha are met with in the hilly country which these rivers drain and large quantities of bamboos are cut on their banks and rafted and floated down stream for sale at the large villages on the Irrawaddy. The Kha-wa rises in the hills which form the southern boundary of the district and send their spurs northwards and falls into the Irrawaddy at the large village of Htoon-bho, or Toung-ngoo as it is sometimes called. During the height of the rains boats of 150 bushels burden can ascend for four or five miles as high as Tha-bye-hla; from its mouth to this village the banks are somewhat low but above they are steep.

The mineral productions of the township consist of earth-oil and lime-stone. The first, the existence of which was only lately discovered, is found in the north near the village of Toung-bo-gyee, in the bed of a small stream. "At the time of my visit in November 1871," writes Mr. Theobald of the Geological Survey of India, "four shafts had been sunk............ one of "which had been buried by a slip, and two of the others had not struck any "petroleum. The second shaft, however, which is the only one which needs "attention, had been very successful and had yielded some two and a half "viss" (9·125lbs.) "of oil daily at a depth of 35 cubits, till it became filled "with water in the rains when the supply ceased," owing to the pressure of the high column of water on the mouths of the oil-containing cracks and fissures. The limestone which, according to Mr. Theobald, "is procurable in any quantity" is found in the Kyouktan hill, about six miles from Htoon-bho at the mouth of the Kyouk-piet-tha stream in the extreme south-eastern part of the township and is brought to Htoon-bho to be burnt. The way in which the limestone is quarried is thus described by Mr. Theobald in the Memoirs of the Geological Survey of India, Vol. X., Pt. 2, p. 156 :—" The mode of extraction is, however, unsystematic and wasteful "to a degree. The outcrop of the rock is just dug into, and if the rock is "rather slabby, it is simply broken up and extracted in conveniently sized "lumps. No order or regularity is observed in opening a pit, hence a great "waste of labour with, it may be presumed, enhanced cost. If the outcrop "is more massive in character, a large fire is kindled on the bare surface of "the rock, by which the stone is rendered more brittle and easier to break "up and extract. The only tools used are a few light hammers, a crowbar "or so, and a number of wedges both of wood and of iron." In the southern portion of the township, on the banks of the Ma-toung stream, a tributary of the south Thoo-le-dan, about four miles from its mouth, are some salt springs, of no present economic value owing to the importation of foreign salt.

The township, which in the Burmese time was an independent jurisdiction, was, according to the registers prepared after the annexation, divided into 302 village tracts under Thoogyee. These were formed into revenue circles, several being amalgamated together, and this process of amalgamation has gone on as the Thoogyee died, resigned or were dismissed till the number of circles has been reduced to 24. The area under cultivation necessarily varies every year but may be taken roughly as 45 square miles of which 25,000 acres are sown with rice, and the remainder produce miscellaneous crops, such as fruit, chillies, onions, sessamum, tobacco and cotton, which are sold in the villages on the river bank ; cotton cloths, piece-goods and nga-pee being brought up in exchange ; cutch for export is largely manufactured as also a peculiar kind of matting. The principal road is called the Prome and Toung-goop road and runs from just opposite Prome along the bank of the river through Pa-doung and for some miles further southwards when it turns west and passes over the Toung-goop pass into Arakan : it is used principally in the dry season by parties of traders. Besides this there are everywhere, near the river, fair-weather cart roads, but in the hills only tracks for men or unladen cattle and elephants. The principal town is Pa-doung, on the bank of the river, a long, straggling collection of villages hemmed in by rice swamps, with a small population of 2,897 souls. It is here that the Assistant Commissioner who has charge of the division (Pa-doung and Shwe-doung townships) holds his Court. There is also a Police-station and a small bazaar. In 1877 the population was 85,269, the land revenue Rs. 37,917, the capitation tax Rs. 39,832 and the gross revenue Rs. 86,677.

PA-DOUNG.—A sub-division of the Prome district formed in 1875 and consisting of the Pa-doung township on the right and the Shwe-doung township on the left bank of the Irrawaddy. The head-quarters are at Pa-doung.

PA-DOUNG.—A sub-tribe of Pwo Kareng, so called by the Kareng-nee ; a sub-branch of the Bghai family.—*See Taroo.*

PA-DOUNG.—A town in the Prome district on the right bank of the Irrawaddy about 15 miles below Prome, the head-quarters of the Pa-doung sub-division, with a population in 1874 of 2,812 souls and of 2,897 in 1877-78. It consists of one long street, a portion of the military road from opposite Prome across the Arakan Roma to Arakan, with a single row of houses on each side, intersected by cross streets going down to the river on the east and on the west towards the rice plains which shut in the town in that direction. It has a Court-house, Police-station, a small market and a school; and includes the Won-lo and Roon-tshiep quarters. For some years a Telegraph office was kept up, mainly for departmental purposes such as keeping the line clear and repairing it, but the establishment was withdrawn a few years ago. It is the head-quarters of the Pa-doung township and an Extra Assistant Commissioner used to reside here. This continued for some time after the Pa-doung and Shwe-doung townships had been formed into a sub-division and placed under an Assistant Commissioner with his head-quarters at Pa-doung. A ferry boat passes daily between this town and Prome.

Pa-doung is occasionally mentioned in Burman history. About the end of the first century of the Christian era Tha-peng-gnyoo, the last king of old Prome, fled thither after the destruction of his capital, Tha-re-khettra, by the Kan-ran tribe. Many centuries later, in 1784 A.D., the Burman army destined for the conquest of Arakan assembled there, and a large part of it advanced thence over the Toung-goop pass towards the capital of the doomed kingdom. In both the first and the second Anglo-Burmese wars it was the scene of some fighting.

PA-DWON-PIET.—A village with 707 inhabitants in 1877 in the A-hpyouk circle of the Za-lwon township of the Henzada district on the east bank of the Irrawaddy about half a mile south of Oot-hpo. It is said to have been originally called " Tee-toot-maw" or, " the point where owls (the horned owl, *Strix Leschenaultii* of Temminck) catch fish."

PA-GAING.—A village in the Kaw-lee-ya circle of the Shwe-gyeng district, about 25 miles in a straight line S. S. W. of Shwe-gyeng and about two miles north of the embankment running between the Pegu and Toungngoo road and the Tsit-toung at Myit-kyo which forms the boundary between the Shwe-gyeng and the Rangoon districts. It lies in the centre of a tract abounding in fisheries. Immense quantities of fish are captured and prepared for export: in the dry weather Shan assemble in large numbers and buy the fish either dried or salted; these they carry away securely packed in panniers slung across the backs of bullocks: a few carts also come down from Upper Burma and return laden with fish. In the rainy season the village is almost submerged; sometimes so much so that the people have to abandon their houses. In 1877 the population numbered 825.

PA-GOOT-TOUNG.—A revenue circle in the Mergui district, on Mergui island, east of Mergui. In 1877 the population was 2,526, the land revenue Rs. 13,437, the capitation tax Rs. 1,659 and the gross revenue Rs. 15,096.

PAI-BENG.—A creek in the Bassein district which unites the Da-ga and the Bassein rivers. Its upper or northern portion is called Thayet. Large boats can ascend it at all seasons for about 18 miles as far as the village of Re-dweng-goon. Above this for another 18 miles, to Wa-doo, boats of 50 baskets burden without masts can go. During the dry weather the tide is felt as far as Pai-beng village, about 80 miles from the Bassein mouth, and the water is then brackish; in the rains it is sweet.

PAI-BENG.—A revenue circle in the Thee-kweng township, Bassein district, having an approximate area of 56 square miles lying north of the Moung-dee and east of the Ta-ta-zeng stream. The surface of the country is, generally speaking, flat, and the circle is fairly well cultivated, especially in its northern portion. A belt of somewhat heavy forest forms the northwestern boundary of the circle. The inhabitants are chiefly Kareng. The most important village is Re-dweng-goon in 16° 37' N. and 94° 43' E. as far as which large boats can ascend the river from Bassein. A few fair weather cart roads are to be found across the cultivated plains. In 1877 the population was 4,673, the land revenue Rs. 13,471, the capitation tax Rs. 4,752 and the gross revenue Rs. 19,194.

PAI-BENG-GOON.—A revenue circle in the Prome district a few miles east of the town of Prome containing fertile rice fields. In 1877 the population was 334, the land revenue was Rs. 729, the capitation tax Rs. 420 and the gross revenue Rs. 1,212.

PAI-BENG-YENG.—A revenue circle in the Mro-houng township, Akyab district. In 1877 the population was 2,099, the land revenue Rs. 4,047, the capitation tax Rs. 2,697 and the gross revenue Rs. 20,201. The principal village is Myoung-bwai-zhe.

PAI-GOO.—A revenue circle in the township of the same name in the Rangoon district, extending eastward from the Pegu river to the Pegu and Tsit-toung canal and including within its limits the once important town of Pegu, the former capital of the Talaing kingdom. On the north is the Ma-yen-za-ya circle, on the south the Paing-kyoon circle and on the east the La-ya circle of the Shwe-gyeng district. The western portion of the circle is well cultivated, but the east is a vast open plain submerged during the rains. It contains few valuable timber trees but bamboos in abundance.

The area under cultivation and the revenue during each of the last five years were :—

YEAR.	AREA, IN ACRES.				REVENUE, IN RUPEES.			
	Rice, including fallow.	Garden.	Miscellaneous.	Total.	Land.	Capitation tax.	All other taxes.	Total.
1873-74 ..	18,581	203	74	18,858	36,483	14,160	5,571	56,214
1874-75 ..	15,842	119	119	16,074	31,727	14,170	5,100	50,997
1875-76 ..	16,442	213	55	16,710	32,566	13,507	229	46,302
1876-77 ..	17,213	211	63	17,487	34,259	13,557	4,855	52,671
1877-78 ..	18,251	219	63	18,533	36,432	14,005	3,250	53,687

and the population and agricultural stock :—

YEAR.	POPULATION.						AGRICULTURAL STOCK.						
	Burmans.	Talaing.	Kareng.	Shan.	All others.	Total.	Buffaloes.	Cows, bulls and bullocks.	Goats and sheep.	Pigs.	Carts.	Ploughs.	Boats.
1873-74 ..	..	..	..	..	..	..	4,213	1,037	55	92	909	3,003	164
1874-75 ..	..	..	..	..	..	..	4,123	999	42	106	895	998	174
1875-76 ..	1,352	10,493	776	433	255	13,309	3,315	1,824	87	208	971	1,348	100
1876-77 ..	1,212	9,989	1,151	391	139	12,743	1,913	960	..	69	639	608	113
1877-78 ..	1,480	10,431	993	775	171	13,847	3,181	872	8	2	730	729	153

PAIK-THOUNG.—A revenue circle in the Thee-kweng township, Bassein district, stretching south from the Da-ga river into the angle formed by the junction of the Pan-ma-wa-dee and the Ta-ta-zeng. It comprises an estimated area of 91 square miles of level ground, intersected with small and insignificant creeks the banks of which are invariably covered with a fringe of forest of various degrees of depth, dividing the country into numerous detached plains. The principal rice lands are in the north of the circle. The most important village is Hlee-tshiep in 16° 57' N. and 95° 2' 30" E. on the right bank of the Ta-ta-zeng, about a mile from its junction with the Da-ga; the inhabitants are principally rice cultivators. In 1877 the population was 7,427, the land revenue Rs. 24,774, the capitation tax Rs. 6,680 and the gross revenue Rs. 32,999.

PAI-MYOUK.—A circle in the Meng-doon township, Thayet district, 164 miles in extent 155 being unculturable mountainous forest waste, and rather less than four under cultivation, more than one of which consists of hill clearings. The population in 1877 was 2,708 souls, of whom about one quarter were Khyeng. Up to 1864, Myouk-peng, now in this circle, formed a separate Thoogyeeship. The products are rice, sessamum, cotton, maize, tobacco, onions, chillies and cutch. In 1877 the land revenue was Rs. 1,676, the capitation tax Rs. 1,858 and the gross revenue Rs. 3,618.

PAI-MYOUK.—A river in the Thayet district which rises in the Arakan Roma and falls into the Hlwa river from the south. It is not at any time navigable for boats, but teak and other valuable timber is met with on its banks; its bed is sandy and muddy.

PAING-KWON.—A revenue circle in the Than-lweng Hlaing-bhwai township, Amherst district, occupying the tract of country between the Dawna hills on the east, the Hlaing-bhwai and Da-gyaing on the west, and the Daw-lan circle on the south. Its inhabitants are mainly Kareng and numbered 2,432 in 1877, when the land revenue was Rs. 1,063 and the capitation tax Rs. 2,294.

PAING-KYOON.—A village in the Reng-e circle of the Henzada district on the east bank of the Paing-kyoon stream, about a mile east of the Irrawaddy, with 707 inhabitants in 1877.

PAING-KYOON.—A revenue circle in the Pegu township of the Rangoon district, extending eastwards, immediately to the south of the Pegu circle and north of the Gnyoung-beng, from the Pegu river to the Tsit-toung. The eastern portion is annually inundated and rendered unfit for cultivation.

The area under cultivation and the revenue realized during each of the last four years were :—

YEAR.	AREA, IN ACRES.				REVENUE, IN RUPEES.			
	Rice.	Garden.	Miscel-laneous.	Total.	Land.	Capita-tion tax.	Other taxes.	Total.
1874-75 ..	12,475	21	39	12,533	22,728	..	25	22,753
1875-76 ..	13,330	16	37	13,383	24,167	5,320	25,083	54,570
1876-77 ..	14,008	16	37	14,061	25,301	5,637	196	31,134
1877-78 ..	15,985	20	33	16,038	29,015	5,918	121	35,054

and the population and agricultural stock during the last three years :—

YEAR.	POPULATION.					AGRICULTURAL STOCK.				
	Burmans.	Talaing.	Kareng.	All other races.	Total.	Buffaloes.	Cows, bulls and bul-locks.	Carts.	Ploughs.	Boats.
1875-76 ..	488	3,207	168	57	3,920	1,330	181	150	420	10
1876-77 ..	321	4,231	156	..	4,708	1,911	170	280	765	12
1877-78 ..	407	4,555	151	..	5,113	2,190	258	332	831	13

PAING-KYOON.—A creek which unites the Pegu and the Tsit-toung rivers. Formerly very tortuous and about 33 miles long it has been generally deepened and various cuttings made in it so that its length has been reduced to 18 miles. Till the new canal to Myit-kyo was opened it formed a portion of the main water route from Rangoon to Toung-ngoo.

In 1867, during the rains, a small river steamer succeeded with some difficulty in passing through it.

PAING-KYOON-WA.—A small village of 528 inhabitants in 1878, in the circle of the same name, Pegu township, Rangoon district, at the mouth of the Paing-kyoon creek.

PAK-CHAN.—A river in the Mergui district which forms the eastern boundary in the extreme south. The sources lie in the angle formed by the main watershed of the peninsula and a lofty range of hills which divides the drainage of the Ma-lee-won and Le-gnya townships and terminates at the mouth of the Pak-chan in Victoria Point. Its main source lies in this range or spur 1·32 miles distant from its junction with the main watershed, in Lat. 10° 48′ 14″ North, Long. 98° 55′ 40″ East. For the first 15 miles of its course it is an ordinary mountain stream with a bed choked up by masses of disintegrated rocks. Lower down several affluents, discharging a great lateral drainage, unite and form what is called by the Siamese "Khlaung Pak-chan." The width of the river after it has received the combined contents of these streams is about 100 feet and it is navigable up to this point by small boats from July to December. By March the bed is dry down to the vicinity of Kra, excepting in hollows and reservoirs formed by natural obstructions. From the source to Kra, a distance of 30 miles, the general direction of the river is south-west without any appreciable deflection. The next few miles down to the mouth of the May-nam-naw-ey are very tortuous, after which the river runs direct to Victoria Point.

The tidal influence extends in the dry months, i. e. from February to April, as far as "Khow-ka-ta," 10 miles above Kra, at which village the rise and fall at the springs are eight feet. At this time of the year the bed of the river at Kra is almost dry at low water. The banks are cultivated as far as Na-lee-khyan, three and a half miles down, below which point the joint operations of a flood tide and the swollen river cause a general and heavy inundation of the adjacent land. This takes place even in the dry weather and produces a delta-like vegetation of mangrove trees and neepa palms.

At Kra the Pak-chan is 250 feet broad; it is the same six miles lower down, when it receives the contents of the May-nam-naw-ey and enlarges to 350 feet; thence it gradually increases in width towards its mouth, where it is as much as two and a half miles from shore to shore.

Fourteen miles above the mouth the Ma-lee-won and the Khya-oon (or La-oon) rivers fall into it. The former drains the hills to the west; the latter, a fine broad stream, pours in the concentrated drainage of the mountainous region to the south known as Re-noung. Thus far the Pak-chan is navigable, the soundings marked in the published charts being six and seven fathoms. Above this confluence, at high water, it still looks a noble stream two miles broad; but as the tide runs out long flats and sandbanks make their appearance leaving at last an insignificant channel 30 yards wide and three feet deep. Besides these sandbanks there is an obstruction to navigation in a ridge of rocks just below the confluence of the May-nam-naw-ey. As the tide falls the ridge appears on either side leaving a contracted waterway. Through this confined passage the Pak-chan and May-nam-naw-ey force their way with frightful velocity : above this the river takes sudden bends which add to the dangers of the descent. Slack water at high tide is the only safe time for shooting this channel; at any other time it is a very ugly business.

Colonel Fytche in the rainy season of 1864 succeeded in reaching Kra in H. M's Steamer *Nemesis* to meet the Siamese Chiefs and settle our southern boundary, but even then the undertaking must have been hazardous.

The total length of the Pak-chan from its source to its mouth at Victoria Point is 78 miles. The territory on the right or west and north-west bank is called Ma-lee-won and belongs to the British.

On the left or south-east bank are the Siamese Provinces of Kra and Re-noung which are considered valuable for their lead and tin mines. Ma-lee-won on our side is the favourite site of mining operations. Being in the midst of mountains there is no culturable space and the inhabitants depend upon the produce of the lands near Na-lee-khyan and Kra for the means of sustenance. The inundation of the level lands in other parts of the Pak-chan's course below Na-lee-khyan, which is synchronous with the rising tide, prevents their cultivation.

At Kra there is a peculiarity in the river's course which deserves mention. Immediately opposite the village an island has been formed. The main stream had once an eye-shaped bend ; this has been changed probably by excessive floods, the water having worked a channel through the narrow neck of the eye, and permitted in time the passage of the main stream. The island thus formed is acknowledged to be British territory.*

PA-KOO.—A sub-tribe of the Sgaw Kareng family inhabiting the Toung-ngoo and Shwe-gyeng districts of the Tenasserim division. Their dialect is closely allied to that of the Pwo but wants the final consonant. Their tunic is white without stripes and has a narrow band of embroidery at the bottom, the patterns differing for each village. They have suffered considerably from the inroads of the Red Kareng whose forays were rendered the easier in that no one Pa-koo village would help any other. Like the rest of the race they are fond of keeping in their houses stones which they hold to possess miraculous power; the peculiarity of the Pa-koo in this respect is that their stones are supposed to cause the death of any enemy whose foot print is struck with it. About 2,000 have embraced Christianity.

PA-KWON.—A creek formed by the junction, to north of the latitude of Donabyoo, of several others of small size and of no importance : after a south-easterly course it falls into the Bhaw-lay a little above the village of Bhaw-lay where it is 300 feet broad and 20 feet deep. From its mouth upwards for about 10 miles, or as far as the village of Pa-kwon, it is navigable by boats of the largest class.

PA-LA.—A revenue circle in the Pa-law township of the Mergui district on the seacoast south of Pa-law. In 1877 the population was 2,846, the land revenue Rs. 3,231, the capitation tax Rs. 1,761 and the gross revenue 4,996.

---

* Report on the Settlement of the boundary between the Kingdom of Siam and the Tenasserim division of the Province of British Burma, by Lieutenant A. H. Bagge, R.E., 1868.

PA-LA.—A village in the Mergui district of the Tenasserim division, situated on a small stream of the same name, 12 miles from its mouth and 34 miles north of Mergui, in 12° 50' North Lat. and 98° 31' East Long. The inhabitants, who are principally cultivators and fishermen, carry on a small trade in rice, fish and nga-pee. During the Siamese rule it was a place of some importance. In 1877 it had 877 inhabitants.

PA-LAW.—A revenue circle in the Pa-law township, Mergui district, on the seacoast, in the north adjoining Pa-law. In 1877 the population was 3,513, the land revenue was Rs. 7,472, the capitation tax Rs. 1,989 and the gross revenue Rs. 9,461.

PA-LAW-KHYOUNG.—A small Kareng village of 519 inhabitants in 1877, on both banks of the river Pa-law, above the village of that name. The houses are, as is very common amongst Kareng who have settled in the plains in Tenasserim, scattered singly and in groups amongst ill-kept orchards, without any pretence to neatness or order.

PA-LOUK.—A river in the Mergui district which rises in the south-eastern slopes of the Myeng-mo-let-khat mountain on the borders of Tavoy and flows towards the south-west, receiving numerous small mountain streams and falling into the sea in about 13o 8' North, and 98o 36' East. Its mouth is about 700 yards wide but it narrows considerably towards the village of Pa-louk; above this occurs a succession of rapids and falls. The hills on the banks are by no means high until close to the source but are covered with thick forest and high trees. In several spots in the valley of this river there are thermal springs strongly impregnated with sulphuretted hydrogen and containing a small quantity of iron and of carbonate of lime. The hottest raised the thermometer to 196° Fahr. (*Vide Mergui district.*)

PA-LOUNG.—A village in the Bhwai-da circle, Mro-houng township, Akyab district, on the eastern bank of the river Koo-la-dan. In 1877 it had 584 inhabitants.

PAN-BENG-GOON.—A village of about 80 houses in the Koo-bhyoo circle, Meng-doon township, Thayet district.

PAN-DAW.—A town in the Re-gyee township of the Bassein district, on the southern bank of the Re-gyee, a small tributary of the Bassein river, about five miles south of Nga-thaing-khyoung. It is the head-quarters of the united townships of Re-gyee, Bho-daw and Mye-noo, where the Extra Assistant Commissioner resides and holds his court, and is surrounded by very extensive rice plains, the produce of which is exported to Bassein. It contains a Police-station, Court-house, and a market. The population in 1877 was 3,982. It was here that the Talaing army made its last stand against the Burman king Aloung-bhoora (*Alompra*). The town, which stands in 17° 19' 30" North and 95° 10' East, has gradually risen, since the annexation of Pegu, by the gradual increase and final junction of the two neighbouring villages of Re-gyee and Pan-daw and is sometimes called Re-gyee Pan-daw. In 1876-77 the local revenue was Rs. 3,804.

PAN-DAW.—A revenue circle in the south-eastern township of the Tavoy district. In 1877 the population was 2,075, the land revenue Rs. 5,445, the capitation tax Rs. 1,638 and the gross revenue Rs. 7,481. The principal products are doorian, betel-nut and rice.

473

PAN-DAW.—A village in the Tavoy district, in the circle of the same name, on the bank of the river Tavoy. On the river bank about a mile from Pan-daw is a Custom-house, and a warehouse and jetty built by a private individual.

PAN-DAW.—A creek in the Bassein district.—*See Re-gyee.*

PAN-DAW.—A lake in the Bassein district in the Le-myet-hna township, about three miles west of Le-myet-hna, communicating with the Bassein or Nga-won river. In the dry weather it has only two or three feet of water but in the rains it is navigable by boats. The bed is muddy and the banks are covered with forest.

PAN-DAW.—A revenue circle in the Myanoung township of the Henzada district, north of Kwon-daw and east of Thien-goon, which now includes Pek-ma-khan. The western portion is undulating, the rest is well cultivated with rice. In 1877 the population was 6,914, the land revenue Rs. 11,465, the capitation tax Rs. 6,192 and the gross revenue Rs. 18,840.

PAN-DAW-PYENG.—A large revenue circle amongst the islands between Kyouk-hpyoo and the mainland, in the Kyouk-hpyoo township of the Kyouk-hpyoo district, about 40 square miles in extent. In 1875 it had a population of 1,920 souls and produced a revenue of Rs. 3,490, of which Rs. 1,383 was derived from the land. In 1877 the population was 1,966, the land revenue Rs. 1,745, the capitation tax Rs. 2,192 and the gross revenue Rs. 4,901. The principal village is Koo-do-tshiep.

PAN-DENG.—A small village of 764 inhabitants in 1877, on the banks of the river Ka-gnyeng, in the Oot-hpo circle, Oot-hpo township, Henzada district.

PAN-DENG-ENG.—A village of 1,884 inhabitants in the Moung-ma-gan circle of the western township of Tavoy.

PA-NEE.—A river in the Thayet district. It rises to the east of the source of the Moo, in the hills north of British territory, and crossing the frontier near the village of Khwe-douk enters the Meng-dat portion of the Meng-doon township. After a southerly course of about 30 miles from Khwe-douk, during the latter portion of which it runs through the Kama township, it falls into the Ma-htoon a few miles from its mouth at Thamba-ya. It is navigable, during the rains, for boats of 100 baskets burden as far as the village of Meng-dat but it is little used on account of the force of the current and its rapid rises and falls. It has numerous small tributaries but none of any importance.

PA-NGA.—A large and compact circle in the Wa-kha-roo township of the Amherst district, between the Toung-gnyo hills on the east, the sea on the west, the Hnit-kaing circle on the north and the Ka-roop-pee circle on the south. Its total area is 49,471 acres. The eastern half is high, undulating land covered with forest similar in most respects to the upland of the Hnit-kaing circle. The western portion also is undulating but the valleys are wider and are traversed by tidal streams. The present circle now includes Tset-tsai which was joined to it from Hnit-kaing, *circa* 1865. Tset-tsai is not an old territorial division and did not exist under the Burman Government. Some migratory Kareng having located themselves here after Tenasserim passed to the British they were allowed to pay tax through their own Tsaw-kai or headman and Tset-tsai thus acquired a place in the revenue books as a distinct circle. The Kareng having wandered away, it was joined to Hnit-kaing and then, as above stated, to Pa-nga. The soil, generally, is not favourable for rice cultivation and very little is grown. The kweng are small; some situated in narrow valleys are unproductive and liable to floods and others are damaged by salt water. There are many salt manufactories; some belong to the people of the circle and others to inhabitants of other circles who reside here during the salt-making season only. The cutting of fuel for these manufactories furnishes a means of livelihood for many of the residents who are not themselves salt-makers. In 1868 the population was 577, the land revenue Rs. 2,232 and the capitation tax Rs. 775. In 1877 these were 757, Rs. 1,704 and Rs. 757 respectively.

PA-NGA.—A small village in the circle of the same name in the Wa-kha-roo township of the Amherst district, on the northern bank of the Pa-nga stream. In 1868 it had 577 inhabitants, all Talaing, and in 1877 it had 552.

PAN-HLAING.—A village in the Rangoon district on the Pan-hlaing creek at the mouth of the Khat-tee-ya, which flows between it and the town of the same name : q. v. (in appendix).

PAN-HLAING.—A village of 906 inhabitants in 1878, in the Pai-goo circle of the Pegu township, Rangoon district.

PAN-HLAING.—A creek in the Rangoon and Thon-khwa districts which runs from the Irrawaddy at Gnyoung-doon to the Hlaing just above Rangoon. In the dry weather there are numerous shoals between the villages of Khat-tee-ya and Mai-za-lee which render the navigation almost impossible for boats drawing even only two or three feet of water and similar obstructions occur a little below Gnyoung-doon. Large boats going up from Rangoon to Gnyoung-doon, as large numbers do at all seasons of the year, are compelled to follow a somewhat circuitous course : on arriving at Khat-tee-ya they pass up the Pan-daing creek to Pan-daing and thence by a small creek back to the Pan-hlaing above the shoals. In the rains large boats can pass through the whole length. The banks are steep and muddy and covered with grass, trees and plantain gardens.

PAN-HLAING.—A revenue circle in the Angyee township of the Rangoon district, between the Pan-hlaing creek on the north, the Khat-tee-ya Re-gyaw on the west, the Twan-te or Moo-la-man on the south and the Ta-ma-ta-kaw and Meng-hpoon on the east. This circle, which was transferred to Thoon-khwa on the formation of that district and was re-transferred in the latter half of 1875, is a large plain, swampy towards the south. The principal villages are Rwa-thit, with 887 inhabitants, and Zee-bhyoo-goon with 761.

The population and agricultural stock during the last five years have been :—

YEAR.	POPULATION.						AGRICULTURAL STOCK.					
	Burmans.	Talaing.	Kareng.	Shan.	All others.	Total.	Buffaloes.	Cows, bulls and bullocks.	Pigs.	Carts.	Ploughs.	Boats.
1873-74 ..	4,175	702	2,714	..	20	7,611	795	58	..	282	286	598
1874-75 ..	3,696	602	2,314	..	23	6,635	642	78	..	232	293	182
1875-76 ..	3,668	604	2,311	..	11	6,594	585	50	45	196	243	154
1876-77 ..	2,406	3,210	3,073	82	78	8,849	1,250	219	756	82	632	59
1877-78 ..	2,667	3,872	3,514	163	53	10,269	1,460	257	820	160	755	476

and the area under cultivation and the revenue :—

YEAR.	AREA, IN ACRES.				REVENUE, IN RUPEES.			
	Rice.	Garden.	Miscel-laneous.	Total.	Land.	Capita-tion tax.	All other taxes.	Total.
1873-74	6,725	1,061	21	7,807	15,752	9,625	15,187	40,565
1874-75	9,701	502	173	10,376	21,078	8,970	14,816	44,864
1875-76	8,830	754	122	9,706	19,663	9,182	15,863	44,708
1876-77	10,870	1,715	124	12,709	22.931	9,982	14,854	47,767
1877-78	10,180	1,383	137	11,700	22,153	10,887	16,709	49,749

PAN-MA-MYIT-TA.—A tidal creek in the Bassein district, connecting the Pya-ma-law and the Rwe, the former of which it strikes near the village of Ran-ma-naing. It is navigable by river steamers at all times and is the route generally followed by small vessels plying between Rangoon and Bassein.

PAN-MA-WA-DEE.—A creek in the Bassein district. Under the name of the Thee-kweng it leaves the Meng-ma-naing near the village of Htan-ta-beng, in about 16° 50′ N. and 95° 13′ E., and for some 14 miles runs towards the west and then turns south-west. Fifteen miles lower down the Moung-dee separates from it, and flows westward to fall into the Thek-ngay ; 18 miles lower it is again joined from the eastward by the Meng-ma-naing, here called the Myoung-mya or the Tshiep-gyee river, and two miles further by the Thek-ngay from the north ; ten miles below this spot it unites with the Bassein and with that river and the Thek-ngay forms Nga-poo-taw island. River steamers can ascend at all seasons with little diffi-culty as far as the village of Thee-kweng, a distance of 48 miles, where it is about 200 feet broad, and large boats can pass through it into the Meng-ma-naing. At the mouth of the Moung-dee there is an extensive sandbank, but with a clear channel with plenty of water round it. The depth of water at its mouth where it joins the Bassein river is 10 fathoms at low water springs.

PAN-MA-WA-DEE.— A village in the Paik-thoung circle of the Bassein district, in a rice plain south of the Kyoon-la-ngoo, a tributary of the Pan-ma-wa-dee. In 1877-78 it had 680 inhabitants.

PAN-TA-BWOT.—A tidal creek in the Thoon-khwa district with a southern course from the Thoon-khwa, which it leaves just above the village of the same name, to the Bno-doop, which it joins at Kyaik-lat, by which it communicates with the To ; it has a uniform breadth of about 200 yards, and is navigable by the largest boats at all seasons. The banks are steep and covered with grass and tree forest.

PAN-TAING.—A tidal creek in the Thoon-khwa district, about 10 miles long, which unites the Khat-tee-ya and the Bhaw-lay, navigable by boats of 300 baskets burden at all times and seasons ; during the rains it is navigable by river steamers. In some places the banks are steep and are everywhere covered with grass and tree forest ; the bed is muddy.

PAN-TA-NAW.—A township in the Thoon-khwa district north of Shwe-loung having the Henzada district on its north-east and the Rangoon district on its south-east, with an area of about 238 square miles. The greater part is covered with forest and a considerable portion is subject to inundation during the rains. It is divided into five revenue circles. In 1877 the population was 34,971, the capitation tax Rs. 36,181, the land revenue Rs. 28,141 and the gross revenue Rs. 1,64,825.

PAN-TA-NAW.—A revenue circle about 23 square miles in extent in the township of the same name, in the Thoon-kwa district on the left bank of the Irrawaddy between that river and the Re-baw-re-le which here has a large inverted S shaped bend. The country is inundated during the rains but there are parts, especially two plains in the centre and north-west, which are under rice cultivation. The inhabitants are traders, fishermen and agriculturists. In the northern part of the circle, on the bank of the Irrawaddy, is the large town of Pan-ta-naw, the head-quarter station of the township. In 1877 the population was 8,002, the land revenue Rs. 3,580, the capitation tax Rs. 7,655 and the gross revenue Rs. 12,430.

PAN-TA-NAW.—A town in the township of the same name in the Thoon-khwa district on the bank of the Irrawaddy in 16° 58′ N. and 95° 33′ E. with a population of 5,824 souls, the head-quarters of an Extra Assistant Commissioner. It supports its own Police and has a good market. It is about 10 miles south of Gnyoung-doon where the Upper Irrawaddy trade separates into two branches, the one continuing to Rangoon and the other coming to Pan-ta-naw on its way to Bassein. A considerable number of boats call in here and a large business is done ; nga-pee and dried and salted fish being brought from the seacoast and piece-goods and hardware from Bassein and sold for export up the Irawaddy. Some of the inhabitants find employment in fishing.

PAN-TAW.—A revenue circle in the northern township of the Sando-way district extending inland from the seacoast ; it is now joined to Khoo.

PANT-BGHAI.—A sub-division of the Bghai family of Kareng, so called by the English because they wear trowsers. *See Bghai-ka-hta.*

PAN-TSA-NWE.—A revenue circle in the Oo-ree-toung (west) township of the Akyab district. In 1877 the population was 1,351, the land revenue Rs. 3,115, the capitation tax Rs. 1,515 and the gross revenue Rs. 4,950.

PAN-TSHWAI.—A village in the Tsa-doo-thee-rie-koon circle of the Tsan-rwe township of the Henzada district on the north bank of the Thoon-tshay stream. In 1877 it had 636 inhabitants.

PA-PWON.—A revenue circle in the Salween Hill Tracts. In 1877 the population was 4,487, the land revenue Rs. 1,243 and the capitation Rs. 1,825.

PA-PWON.—A village on the banks of the Rwon-za-leng river 95 miles from its mouth in about 18° 6′ N. immediately surrounded by the hills in the midst of which it lies, with a population of 735 souls in 1877. It is the head-quarters of the lately formed Salween district which up to a few years ago formed the Rwon-za-leng sub-division of the Shwe-gyeng district. It extends for some distance along the left bank at the mouth of the little Ta-ra-law mountain stream and there are a few houses on the right bank. It was first established many years ago by some trading Shan from Zeng-mai and its present population is mainly Shan. A strong Police force is quartered in a stockade close to the village. It contains a good Court-house and a temporary hospital and dispensary.

PA-REE-KYWON.—An island in the Mergui Archipelago opposite Mergui.

PA-SHENG.—A revenue circle in the Ma-ha-tha-man township of the Prome district on the Zay stream a short distance above the Engma swamp. Six of the old village tracts are comprised within its limits. In 1877 the population was 1,815, the land revenue Rs. 1,332, the capitation tax Rs. 1,322 and the gross revenue Rs. 2,724.

PA-SHENG.—A village in the Prome district 12 miles south-east of Prome and four miles above the northern end of the Engma lake, on the bank of the Zay stream in 18° 41′ 50″ N. and 95° 26′ 20″ E., inhabited principally by rice cultivators.

PA-SHENG.—A river in the Henzada district which, under the name of the Tshan-da, rises in the Arakan mountains and after an easterly course of about 40 miles falls into the Irrawaddy a little to the north of the latitude of its source, a short distance below Kyan-kheng. Its principal tributaries are the Pa-daw and the A-loon; before receiving either of these it is reinforced by the Khoung-loung, a small mountain torrent which has its source in the Arakan mountains a little to the south of that of the main stream. In the rains boats can ascend for nearly 29 miles to Kyouk-pa-tsat, about a mile above the mouth of the Khoung-loung, but no further on account of the rocks and boulders and the trees and bamboos brought down from the hills. At this season the current here is very strong. The banks are in some places flat and in others steep, the bed muddy, sandy and rocky. The area drained by this river and its tributaries is about 100 square miles. Teak is found widely dispersed over the plains along the lower part of these streams, often alternating with Eng *(Dipterocarpus tuberculatus)*.

PA-TA.—A small river in the Amherst district which forms the boundary between the Houng-tha-raw township on the south and the Than-lweng Hlaing-bhwai township on the north. Its source is in the Dawna spur and after a south-westerly course of some 15 miles its falls into the Hlaing-bhwai river in 17° 42′ N. and 98° 1′ E. four miles above its junction with the Houng-tha-raw.

PA-TA-DA.—A small pagoda in Maulmain near the Kyaik-than-lan supposed to contain one of Gaudama's hairs. Of its early history nothing is known except that it was erected by a rich man named Gaw-ien-da.

PA-TA-MA KHA-RENG.—A revenue circle in the Gyaing Attaran township, Amherst district, on the left bank of the Gyaing east of Kaw-bhien, thinly cultivated and sparsely inhabited by Kareng. In 1877 the population was 888, the land revenue Rs. 227 and the capitation tax Rs. 500.

PA-TEK-MYOUNG.—A revenue circle in the Prome district, stretching up northwards from the Shwe-lay along the right bank of the Pa-tek-myoung rivulet. There is but little cultivation principally rice and cotton, and the villages are few and small. It is now joined Thayet-myoung.

PA-THWAY.—A revenue circle in the Pan-ta-naw township, Thoon-khwa district, about 61 square miles in extent, on the right bank of the Irrawaddy below the mouth of the Bhaw-dee stream. The inhabitants are largely engaged in fishing. In 1877 the population was 8,275, the land revenue Rs. 11,655 the capitation tax Rs. 8,250 and the gross revenue Rs. 30,770.

PA-WOT.—A large revenue circle in the Mergui district occupying the valley of the Tenasserim from the northern end of the district south-wards to Bhan-law. In 1877 the population was 669, the land revenue Rs. 122, the capitation tax Rs. 296 and the gross revenue Rs. 418.

PIE-LA-KHAT.—A village in the Zhe-pa-thway circle, Angyee town-ship, Rangoon district, two miles from the sea coast and four miles west by south from Elephant Point, on a stream of the same name which falls into the Rangoon river about four miles above its mouth. In 1858 the village contained about 40 families of Shan and Burmans most of whom were salt-manufacturers. In 1877 the number of inhabitants had increased to 647.

PEE-PA-LWOT.—A creek in the Thoon-khwa district which flows between the Kyoon-toon and the Re-tsoo-daing rivers carrying into the latter the larger portion of the water of the former which it itself has received mainly from the Irrawaddy river higher up. It is large enough to admit of navigation by river steamers, but they could not pass beyond it into the Kyoon-toon which is, in this portion of its course, exceedingly shallow. The banks are in some places steep and in others sloping and are covered with grass and tree forest. Nearly all the villages on its banks are inhabited by Kareng.

PEGU.—The north-eastern township of the Rangoon district, bounded on the north and east by the Shwe-gyong district of the Tenasserim divi-sion, on the south by the Than-lyeng (Syriam) township and on the west by the Hpoung-leng township. A few years ago the north-eastern circle, Kaw-lee-ya, was transferred to Shwe-gyeng. Within the limits of this township are comprised the old Burman jurisdictions of Pegu on the north-east, Zaing-ga-naing on the north-west, and Zwai-boon on the south. The north-western portion is mountainous and forest-clad : the upper part of the valley of the Pegu river has the character of a table-land with an elevation of some 1,500 feet, with a hilly surface intersected by deep ravines ; towards the south the hills gradually sink into undulating ground and soon pass into level tracts partially cultivated with rice. The country in the north of the valley on both banks of the river is covered with dense evergreen forest, or with forest in which evergreen trees are mixed with Pyeng-ga-do and others which shed their leaves, such as Pyeng-ma and Ka-gnyeng.

The principal river is the Pegu which has its source amongst the spurs of the Pegu Roma in the extreme north and flowing at first towards the S.S.E., gradually bends round and leaves the township in a S.S.W. direction. Whilst still in the hills it is recruited by a number of small mountain torrents and in the plains it receives several small rivers of no great importance. It is navigable as far as Pegu by river steamers in the rains and by large boats at all seasons with the flood. The central portion of the township is traversed by the Paing-kyoon, an artificially widened and deepened creek, or rather series of creeks, which communicates on the east with the Tsit-toung river at Kha-ra-tsoo village and, till the new canal was opened in 1878, formed, during flood tides and in the rains, the usual channel of communication between Rangoon and the towns on the Tsit-toung. A good road runs from Pegu to Rangoon and another is being constructed from Pegu to Toung-ngoo to replace the old "Royal road", now little more than a cart-track, made by the Peguan King Ta-beng-shwe-tee in the middle of the sixteenth century. Besides these there are everywhere good fair-weather tracks from village to village except amongst the northern hills. The construction of a Railway from Rangoon to Toung-ngoo is under consideration.

The principal town is Pegu, on the banks of the Pegu river, where an Assistant Commissioner and an Extra Assistant Commissioner are stationed, containing Court-houses, a bazaar and Police-stations.

Gnyoung-waing and Ka-ma-nat are the principal villages.

Scattered over the face of the country are numerous pagodas of greater or less sanctity and in various stages of decay.

The township is divided into six revenue circles and in 1877-78 produced a gross revenue of Rs. 271,169, of which Rs. 169,850 were derived from the land, Rs. 59,142 from the capitation tax and the rest from miscellaneous sources. In that year the population was 49,655.

PEGU.—A town in the Rangoon district situated on both banks of the river of the same name, 20 miles west of the Tsit-toung, containing (in 1878) a population of 4,337 souls ; the head-quarters of a township and of a sub-division, with Court-houses, Police-stations, a Market, a Post-office and a Government school.

The existing town occupies the space between the river and the ruins of the walls of the ancient town, founded in 573 A. D. by emigrants from Tha-btoon headed by the two princes Tha-ma-la and Wie-ma-la, once the capital of the Talaing kingdom, the sovereigns of which at some periods reigned over the whole valleys of the Tsit-toung and of the Irrawaddy as far as and including Toung-ngoo and Prome, conquered Ava and the seacoast as far as the Pak-chan, and successfully invaded Siam and Arakan. Across the river and connected with the Pegu quarter by a substantial wooden bridge over which runs the Rangoon and Toung-ngoo road is Zaing-ga-naing. Inside the old walls is the great Shwe-hmaw-daw pagoda, an object of greater veneration to the Talaing than even the Shwe Dagon at Rangoon. It is well laid out with broad streets crossing each other, generally at right angles, well raised and metalled, the metal consisting of brick from the old wall. A few houses are within the old wall. The market is on the bank of the river a little above the bridge. The Court-houses are on the top of the wall, which here has been levelled, behind, that is east of the town. The construction of a lock-up and a dispensary near the Court-houses, and the transfer to that neighbourhood of the Police-station of the Provincial Police are now under consideration. The Municipal Police-station is in the town as is the school. The old ditch communicated with the river both above and below the present town, but the openings have been closed, and the stagnant water is at some seasons most offensive. The houses are built of wood and bamboos and are thatched or tiled. The town has more than once been burned down.

Pegu is described by European travellers in the 16th century as of great size, strength and magnificence. Cæsar Frederick, who was here in the latter portion of the sixteenth century, according to the account given in Purchas wrote :—" By the help of God we came safe to Pegu, which are " two cities, the old and the new. In the old citie are the Merchant strangers " and Merchants of the Countrie, for there are the greatest doings and the " greatest trade. This citie is not very great, but it hath very great suburbs. " Their houses be made with canes and covered with leaves or with straw ; " but the Merchants have all one House or Magazon which house they call " Godon, which is made of bricks, and there they put all their goods of " any value to save them from the often mischances which happen to " houses made of such stuffe. In the new citie is the Palace of the King " and his abiding place with all his barons and nobles and other gentle- " men ; and in the time that I was there they finished the building of the " new citie. It is a great citie, very plaine and flat, and foursquare, walled " round about and with ditches that compass the walls round about with " water, in which ditches are many Crocodiles. It hath no Drawbridges " yet it hath 20 gates, five for every square: on the walls there are many " places made for Centinels to watch, made of wood and covered or gilt " with gold. The streets thereof are the fairest that I have seen, they are " as straight as a line from one gate to another, and standing at one gate " you may discover the other ; and they are as broad as that ten or twelve " men may ride abreast in them. And those streets that be thwart are " faire and large; the streets both on the one side and on the other are " planted at the doores of the houses with nut trees of India, which make " a very commodious shadow ; the houses be made of wood and covered " with a kind of tiles in forme of cups very necessary for their use. The " King's Palace is in the middle of the Citie made in forme of a walled " castle, with ditches full of water round about it. The lodgings within

" are made of wood, all over gilded, with fine pinnacles and very costlie
" worke covered with plates of gold ; truly it may be a king's house.
" Within the gate there is a fine large courte, from the one side to the other
" wherein are made places for the strongest and stoutest elephants."

When Aloung-bhoora overran and conquered Pegu in the middle of
the eighteenth century he used every effort and took every means to
destroy all traces of Talaing nationality. He destroyed every house in
the town and dispersed the inhabitants. His great grandson Bho-daw
Bhoora who succeeded in 1781 pursued a different policy and in his time
the seat of the local government was for sometime transferred from
Rangoon to Pegu. Symes who visited it in 1795, thus describes it *
" The extent of ancient Pegue may still be accurately traced by the ruins
" of the ditch and wall that surrounded it; from these it appears to have
" been a quadrangle each side measuring nearly a mile and a half ; in
" places the ditch has been choked up by rubbish that has been cast into
" it, and the falling of its own banks ; sufficient, however, still remains to
" show that it was once no contemptible defence ; the breadth I judged to be
" about sixty yards, and the depth ten or twelve feet, in some parts of it
" there is water, but in no considerable quantity. I was informed that when
" the ditch was in repair, the water seldom in the hottest seasons sunk
" below the depth of four feet. An injudicious fausse-bray thirty feet wide
" did not add to the security of this fortress."

" The fragments of the wall likewise evince that this was a work of
" magnitude and labour; it is not easy to ascertain what was its exact
" height, but we conjectured it at least thirty feet, and in breadth at the
" base, not less than forty. It is composed of brick badly cemented with
" clay mortar. Small equidistant bastions, about 300 yards asunder are
" still discoverable ; there had been a parapet of masonry, but the whole is
" in a state so ruinous, and so covered with weeds and briars, as to leave
" very imperfect vestiges of its former strength."

" In the centre of each face of the fort there is a gateway about thirty
" feet wide ; these gateways were the principal entrances. The passage
" over the ditch is over a causeway raised on a mound of earth that serves
" as a bridge, and was formerly defended by an entrenchment, of which there
" are now no traces." After describing how ineffectual seemed to have been
the endeavours to repopulate Pegu Colonel Symes continues :—" Pegu in its
" renovated and contracted state seems to have been built on the plan of
" the former city, and occupies about one half of its area. It is fenced round
" by a stockade from ten to twelve feet high, on the north and east sides
" its borders are the old wall. † The plane of the town is not yet filled with
" houses, but a number of new ones are building. There is one main
" street running east and west, crossed at right angles by two smaller
" streets not yet finished. At each extremity of the principal street there
" is a gate in the stockade, which is shut early in the evening ; after that
" hour entrance during the night is confined to a wicket. * * * *There
" are two inferior gates on the north and south sides of the stockade."

" The streets of Pegu are spacious. * * * *The new town is well
" paved with brick, which the ruins of the old plentifully supply ; on each
" side of the way there is a drain to carry off the water."

* Embassy to Ava, p. 182 et seq.   † It thus included the Shwa-hmaw-daw pagoda.

After the capture of Rangoon during the first Burmese war the Burman Commander-in-Chief retired to this town and, his forces becoming thinned by desertion, the inhabitants rose against him and handed the place over to the British who garrisoned it with a small force. During the second war it was more stubbornly defended. Early in June 1852 the defences were carried by a force under Major Cotton and Commander Tarleton, R. N., the granaries destroyed and the guns carried away. Without assistance, however, the inhabitants, at whose request the expedition had been sent, were unable to hold the town for a week, and the Burmese reoccupied the pagoda platform and threw up strong defences along the river. In November of the same year a force under Brigadier McNeill was sent from Rangoon to retake the town, which it did after some considerable fighting and with some loss. The main portion of the troops were withdrawn, and a garrison left of 200 men of the Madras Fusiliers, 200 of the 5th Regiment M. N. I., some European Artillery and a detail of Madras Sappers, the whole being placed under the command of Major Hill of the Fusiliers. Hardly had Brigadier McNeill retired when the Burmese attacked the garrison but were driven off. The attacks continued and in the beginning of December the enemy appeared in force and Major Hill with difficulty held the position. A small body of troops was despatched from Rangoon, but this was driven back and forced to retire without communicating with the besieged. General Godwin, the Commander-in-Chief, then moved up the Pegu river in person with 1,200 men, upon which, after some skirmishing, the Burmese retired but as they remained in the neighbourhood the force moved out against them and finally defeated them driving them out of a strong position in the plains where they had thrown up extensive entrenchments.

A local revenue is raised from the rent of the market stalls and from a rate on the land ; in 1877-78 this amounted to Rs. 14,382-12-4.

PEGU.—A river in the Rangoon district which rises in the eastern slopes of the Pegu Roma mountains and flowing at first S.S.E. past the town of Pegu and then S.S.W. falls into the Rangoon or Hlaing river at Rangoon after a total course of about 180 miles. At its mouth it is about one mile broad and deep enough to allow large vessels to ascend for a short distance, where they lie off the mouth of the Poo-zwon-doung to take in cargoes of rice cleaned in the steam mills on the banks of that river. At neaps the tide is felt as high as Pegu and during springs a bore ascends nearly as far. During the rains it is navigable for river steamers as far as Pegu but in the dry season and at neap tides only small boats can ascend to that town. For the first few miles of its course, before it leaves the mountains in which it has its sources, its bed is exceedingly rocky. It taps a country in which is found much teak and other valuable timber and bamboos, and lower down it flows through a considerable area of fertile rice land. As far as the mouth of the new canal, a short distance below Pegu, it forms the main route from Rangoon to the towns on the Tsit-toung.

PEGU.—A revenue circle in the Rangoon district, more properly called *Pai-goo, q.v.*

PEK-LEK.—A small village of 666 inhabitants in 1878 in the Kyouk-taing-pyeng circle, Thanlyeng township, Rangoon district.

PENG-GA-DAW.—A revenue circle in the Mye-dai township, Thayet district containing three of the old registered villages and now joined to Teng-daw. The products are rice, sessamum, cotton, cutch and silk. Near Ta-roop-beng are some salt springs which were worked in the Burmese time.

PENG-GA-DAW.—A revenue circle in the Prome district north of Poungday of which the village of Peng-ga-daw forms an extension. In 1877 the population was 762, the land revenue was Rs. 721, the capitation tax was Rs. 760 and the gross revenue was Rs. 1,481.

PENG-LE-GA-LE.—A creek in the Bassein district, tidal in the dry season, which leaves the Rwe a little south of its northern mouth in the Myoung-mya river and runs, generally, S.W., but with many sinuosities, to the Bassein river which it enters opposite the northern end of Long Island. It communicates with its parent stream, the Rwe, by numerous anastomosing creeks. River steamers could ascend it as far as the village of Htoon-bho. At low tide springs it has, according to Captain Ward's chart, three and a half fathoms of water at its mouth.

PENG-THEE-LA.—A small river in the Toung-ngoo district which rises in the Than-toung mountain of the Poung-loung range and after a westerly course of 20 miles falls into the Tsit-toung. During the rains boats of about 24 feet length can ascend for some four miles.

PHAETON.—A small shoal off the mouth of the Bassein river, on which H.M.S. *Phaeton* struck on the 16th of February 1810, and was, in consequence, obliged to go to Calcutta to repair. It bears S. W. by S. from Diamond Island, distant four miles, and N. by E., distant three and a half miles, from the Alguada reef, having nine fathoms of water close to and two fathoms upon it.

PIE-DO.—A clan of Pwo Kareng.—*See Mo-pgha.*

PIEN-NAI-KHYOUNG.—A revenue circle to which is now joined Mye-ngoo, in the Oo-ree-toung (east) township, Akyab district. In 1877 the population of the united circles was 4,510, the land revenue Rs. 5,020, the capitation tax Rs. 5,427 and the gross revenue Rs. 11,808.

PIEN-NAI-KWENG.—A village in the Kama township, Thayet district; near it is a salt spring capable of yielding 30 pots of brine a day.

PIET-TSWAY.—A village in the Kha-noung-to circle, Angyee township, Rangoon district, on the Kha-noung-to stream, about five miles from its mouth in the Rangoon river. In 1878 it had 796 inhabitants.

PIE-ZAW.—A clan of Pwo Kareng.—*See Mo-pgha.*

PLAW.—A clan of Pwo Kareng, so called by some of themselves.—*See Mo-pgha.*

POON-KAW.—A revenue circle in the Gyaing Attaran township, Amherst district, which has been added to Kwon-gyee.

POO-GAN-DOUNG.—A village in the circle of the same name in the Than-lyeng township of the Rangoon district on the banks of the Poo-gan-doung stream about five miles from its mouth in the Pegu river. In 1868 it had 757 inhabitants and 997 in 1877.

POO-GAN-DOUNG.—A revenue circle in the Than-lyeng township of the Rangoon district extending from the Pegu river eastward to the A-gwon (north) circle from which it is separated by the Lek-pan-zeng creek. On the south are the Than-lyeng and Kyouk-taing-pyeng circles both separated from it by the Bhaw stream. On the north are the two Hpa-goo circles. A considerable area is under rice cultivation especially in the neighbourhood of the Pegu river. With the exception of a fringe of tree forest on the west and a small patch on the south this circle is an extensive plain, the western portion of which is under rice cultivation. A considerable revenue is derived from the fishery and net tax.

The area under cultivation and the revenue during the last five years were :—

YEAR.			AREA, IN ACRES.			REVENUE, IN RUPEES.			
			Rice.	Garden.	Total.	Land.	Capitation tax.	All other taxes.	Total.
1873-74	..	..	20,757	9	20,766	44,540	9,795	9,762	64,097
1874-75	..	..	24,462	10	24,472	52,162	9,688	8,618	70,468
1875-76	..	..	26,260	11	26,271	53,746	10,008	77	63,831
1876-77	..	..	27,323	25	27,348	55,372	10,028	8,048	73,448
1877-78	..	..	27,934	17	27,951	57,942	10,495	7,254	75,691

and the population and agricultural stock :—

YEAR.		POPULATION.						AGRICULTURAL STOCK.						
		Burmans.	Talaing.	Kareng.	Shan.	All others.	Total.	Buffaloes.	Cows, bulls, and bullocks.	Goats and Sheep.	Pigs.	Carts.	Ploughs.	Boats.
1873-74	..	..	..	..	..	..	..	3,643	536	..	262	565	1,523	378
1874-75	..	2,799	5,830	375	138	60	9,184	3,636	501	8	321	561	1,517	301
1875-76	..	2,804	5,953	424	216	125	9,522	3,581	493	4	377	466	1,468	248
1876-77	..	2,643	5,976	881	394	121	9,970	3,768	476	22	216	498	1,482	376
1877-78	..	1,668	7,690	690	118	91	10,257	3,900	528	24	241	506	1,497	330

POO-HTO.—A revenue circle in the Kama township, Thayet district, on the bank of the Irrawaddy to the north of the town of Kama, 48 square miles in extent, of which about 41 are hilly and unculturable and covered with forest, and from four to five actually under cultivation, principally with rice. The population in 1872 numbered nearly 3,000 souls, and the amount paid as tax aggregated Rs. 5,000. The circle was formerly divided amongst five Thoogyee. About 1861 the Thoogyee of Pien-tha-leng was murdered by dacoits and his son who succeeded him resigned a few months afterwards. In 1868 the Thoogyee of Kan-nee died, and his son also resigned a month or two subsequently. In the same year the Thoogyee of Khyeng-tsouk and of Pya-re also resigned. As each of these resignations took place the Poo-hto circle was enlarged. The population in 1877 was 2,645, the land revenue Rs. 2,107, the capitation tax Rs. 3,020 and the gross revenue Rs. 5,709.

POO-HTO.—A village, with 514 inhabitants, in the circle of the same name in the Kama township, Thayet district, close to the right bank of the Irrawaddy, in 19° 6′ 10″ N. Lat. and 95° 14′ 50″ E. Long. Near the village is a salt spring which used to yield about 15 pots of brine a day.

PA-LAW.—A large village in the Mergui district of the Tenasserim division in 12° 58′ N. Lat and 98° 32′ E. Long on the left bank of the Pa-law stream, about 10 miles from its mouth in the sea and 40 miles north of Mergui. It is the head-quarters of a township. It stands in the centre of a large rice-producing country and has a very fair trade, exporting rice, husked and unhusked. It is situated on high and well-drained ground and as it enjoys the advantage of the sea breeze the climate is healthy. During the Siamese rule it was considerably larger : in 1877 it had a population of 1,481 souls of mixed races, Burmese and Kareng with a few Chinese.

POO-LOO.—A tidal creek in the Bassein district which leaves the Myoung-mya river at the village of Poo-loo in about 16° 35′ 30″ N. six miles above and eastward of the town of Myoung-mya and runs south and then west for four miles to the Rwe. It is navigable for river steamers at all times and is traversed by those plying between Rangoon and Bassein ; the banks are densely wooded.

POO-LOO-PYENG-MA-GOON.—Two revenue circles in the Myoung-mya township, Bassein district, now joined together and 28 square miles in extent lying between the Pya-ma-law and the Rwe channels north of the Pan-ma-myit-ta. Such cultivation as exists is principally in the north or Poo-loo portion. The southern part of Pyeng-ma-goon is subject to inundation; of roads there are none but only footpaths from village to village ; water communication is good. A large number of the inhabitants are Kareng. In 1877 the population was 4,285, the land revenue Rs. 9,059, the capitation tax Rs. 5,060 and the gross revenue Rs. 14,564.

POON-NA.—A village of between 80 and 90 houses in the Poon-na circle, Kama township, Thayet district, in 19° 13′ 35″ N. Lat. and 90° 4′ 15″ E. Long. The name of the village originally was Kan-gyee, this was changed to Poon-na in 1786 A. D. A small Police force is quartered in this village.

POON-NA.—A revenue circle in the Kama township, Thayet district, three square miles in extent, half being unculturable and about 600 acres actually under cultivation, almost entirely with rice. The 513 inhabitants are all Burmans. In 1872 the taxes were Rs. 39 on account of land and Rs. 53 on account of capitation tax. The circle was formerly called Kan-gyee, the name being changed to Poon-na in 1786. The products are rice and sessamum. In 1877 the land revenue was Rs. 447, the capitation tax Rs. 565 and the gross revenue Rs. 1,034.

POON-NA.—A village in the Tsheng-paik circle, Oo-ree-toung (east) township, Akyab district, on the south bank of the little Poon-na. In 1877 it had 517 inhabitants.

POON-NA-RIEP.—A large village in the Mo-gnyo circle of the township of the same name in the Henzada district between the Irrawaddy and the Irrawaddy Valley (State) Railway and about three miles west of the latter. The name is said to be a corruption of Poon-na-roop or "image of "a Poon-na" (a Brahmin) but inasmuch as "roop" for an image is a common word, it is difficult to understand why it should have been corrupted into " riep." In 1877 it had 3,351 inhabitants.

POON-NA-TSOO.—A small village, of 550 inhabitants in 1878, in the Pai-goo circle, Pegu township, Rangoon district.

POO-ZWON-DOUNG.—The most easterly suberrb of Rangoon. q. v.

POO-ZWON-DOUNG.—A river in the Rangoon district which has its source in the Pegu Roma mountains in about 17° 8′ N. and falls into the Pegu river at its junction with the Hlaing just below Rangoon, after a southerly course of about 53 miles. It is about 440 yards wide at its mouth and was deep enough to allow of the entry of large ships but is now silting up from the vast quantities of rice husk discharged into it from the mills on its banks. From its source for about 20 miles, above which boats cannot pass in the dry season, its water is sweet. Towards the source its bed is rocky and towards its mouth the banks are steep and muddy. The upper part of its valley produces valuable timber and the lower large crops of rice.

POO-ZWON-MYOUNG.—A village in the Kweng-da-la circle of the Shwe-gyeng district, on the right bank of the Tsit-toung river, some 15 miles above Shwe-gyeng by the river, with a population in 1877 of 1,035 souls. A large number of earthen pots are made here for export.

PO-TSA-DAW.—A revenue circle on the left bank of the Irrawaddy, opposite to Kan-oung, in the Taroop-hmaw township, Henzada district, with but little rice cultivation, miscellaneous products occupying the larger part of the cultivated area. In 1877 the population was 2,732, the land revenue Rs. 1,483, the capitation tax Rs. 2,462 and the gross revenue Rs. 7,094.

POUK-AING.—A revenue circle in the Myedai township, Thayet district, situated in the plains on the left bank of the Irrawaddy, and joined to Bhwot-lay in 1870. The chief products are maize, rice and tobacco.

POUK-BENG.—A small village of 511 inhabitants in 1878 in the Hpa-goo (west) circle of the Than-lyeng township, Rangoon district.

POUK-KHOUNG.—A small village on the stream of the same name in the Prome district about 24 miles N. E. of Prome with which it is connected by a good road, where the Extra Assistant Commissioner in charge of the Shwe-lay township resides and holds his Court : a small Police force is stationed here. In 1877 it had only 254 inhabitants.

POUK-KHOUNG.—A river in the Prome district which rises in the Talaing-hmyaw spur of the Pegu Roma mountains and flows towards the north-west through a narrow valley, nowhere five miles broad, for about 12 miles to the South Naweng which it reaches a short distance from the village of Ma-mya. About four miles from its mouth it passes the village of Pouk-khoung, the head-quarter station of an Extra Assistant Commissioner. The bed is generally sandy and the banks are in some places steep.

POUK-KHOUNG.—A revenue circle in the Prome district to the eastward of Prome amongst the lower slopes of the Pegu Roma spurs ; patches of rice cultivation are found here and there near the villages. In 1877 the population was 2,106, the land revenue Rs. 1,240, the capitation tax Rs. 1,323 and the gross revenue Rs. 3,588.

POUK-NWAY-KHYOON.—A village in the Shwe-doung township, Prome district, four miles S.E. of Kyee-thay, about the same distance due east of the Irrawaddy and eight miles north of Gnyoung-tsa-re: a good fair-weather cart road runs between these three villages.

POUK-OO-GA.—A village on the Re-ngay stream in the Toon circle, Kama township, Thayet district, which contains about 60 houses. During the Burmese time a Thoogyee with hereditary rights was appointed to the circle named after this village and after the annexation it remained separate until 1859 A. D. when the then Thoogyee was dismissed for bribery and the circle subsequently added to Toon.

POUK-TAING.—A small river in the Tavoy district which rises amongst the northern slopes of the Nwa-hla-bo hill and flowing north-west and then west falls into the Tavoy river about five miles below Tavoy.

POUK-TAING.—A revenue circle in the south-west corner of the north-east township, Tavoy district, somewhat south of the town of Tavoy, having an area of about 185 square miles of which about one-fifth is cultivated. Its principal produce is rice. In 1877 the population was 1,540, the land revenue Rs. 3,012, the capitation tax Rs. 1,174 and the gross revenue Rs. 4,337.

POUK-TAN.—A village in Ka-tseng circle, Hmaw-bhee township, the Rangoon district, about a mile up a small creek which falls into the Hlaing, in the centre of a good deal of rice land; the inhabitants are principally engaged in cultivation and in trading. In 1878 the population numbered 718 souls. Lat. 16° 56' N. Long. 96° 7' E.

POUK-TAW.—A revenue circle in the Toung-ngoo district, adjoining Da-gnya-wa-dee. In the south-west there are some low hills but elsewhere it is level and fairly cultivated. Toddy palms (*Borassus*) grow in abundance. In 1877 the population was 4,020, the land revenue Rs. 4,055, the capitation tax Rs. 3,714 and the gross revenue Rs. 8,082.

POUK-TAW.—A village of 60 houses about two miles from the northern frontier and rather more in a south-westerly direction from the second boundary pillar westwards from the Irrawaddy, on the Lek-ma-she-doung. It is in the Kwon-oon circle, Thayet township, Thayet district. It was formerly in the Tan-taw Kyoung circle which in 1861 was joined to Bhan-byeng and this was subsequently added to Toon.

POUK-TAW.—A village in the Koon-dan circle, Hmaw-bhee township, Rangoon district, about three miles N. N. E. of Rangoon and one and a half west of the river Poo-zwon-doung, situated in a fertile rice-producing tract. In 1878 it had 703 inhabitants.

POUK-TAW.—A revenue circle in the northern portion of the Prome district on the North Na-weng river. It now includes Kyoo-wot and Thamba-ra-goon. In 1877 the population was 2,298, the land revenue was Rs. 943, the capitation tax Rs. 1,749 and the gross revenue Rs. 3,127.

POUK-TAW.—A revenue circle in the Ta-pwon township of Henzada district, very largely cultivated with rice. In 1877 the population was 4,625, the land revenue Rs. 4,967, the capitation tax Rs. 4,145 and the gross revenue Rs. 9,377.

POUK-TAW.—A revenue circle in the Meng-hla township of the Henzada district, east of the Irrawaddy and south of Lweng-pyeng. The centre and south-eastern portions are well cultivated, the rest is covered with grass and tree forest in which is found Pyeng-gado (*Xylia dolabriformis.*) In 1877 the population was 7,657, the land revenue Rs. 12,800, the capitation tax Rs. 6,467 and the gross revenue Rs. 20,330.

POUK-TOO-TOUNG.—A village of 1,191 inhabitants in the Tsekkhaw circle, Mye-boon township, Kyouk-hpyoo district.

POUNG.—A village in this circle of the same name, Martaban township, Amherst district, at the foot of the western slopes of the Zeng-gyaik hills. It has a population of 1073 souls.

POUNG.—A very thickly-populated and highly-cultivated revenue circle in the south-western portion of the Martaban township, Amherst district, lying on the west of the Martaban hills, south of Gaw and north of Kha-daing and Moo-kyee with the estuary of the Bhee-leng on the west. The lands in the western portion are very fertile, but in the eastern, along the foot of the mountains, the soil is poor, the fields are liable to damage from sudden rushes of water and the crops suffer from violent squalls of wind, most of the land hereabouts is therefore reserved for pasture. The circle is traversed by several creeks leading out to sea but laden boats never venture out. In the rains water-carriage is available throughout the circle. In 1868 the population was 4,528, the land revenue Rs. 12,712 and the capitation tax Rs. 4,845. In 1877 these were 5,459, Rs. 14,094 and Rs. 5,797 respectively. Some salt is made in this circle. The principal villages are Poung, Kha-da, Ta-koo-wee, Hpa-lat and Zeng-gyaik.

POUNG-DAY.—A township in the south of the Prome district bordering Henzada (Tharrawaddy) and adjoining the Shwe-doung township on the west, the Shwe-lay township on the east and the Ma-ha-tha-man township on the north, including both Poung-day and Eng-ma, formerly independent jurisdictions. West of the Myit-ma-kha, which traverses the township from north to south leaving a narrow strip between it and the Eng-daing, the country is undulating and covered with forest, but to the eastward it is one vast plain highly cultivated with rice, with the long, straggling town of Poung-day in about the centre, with good fair-weather cart roads traversing it in every direction and two main roads constructed by the Public Works Department, one the great high road from Rangoon to the northern frontier, and the other the high road to Ta-pwon which leaves the northern road at Poung-day and seven miles further south passed over the Kan-tha by a wooden bridge and enters the Henzada district. The Kan-tha or Toung-gnyo has silted up very considerably and in consequence the waters have spread and two new channels have been formed, one on each side of the bridge which has thus been cut off from the banks and is being pulled down as useless. The principal stream is the Myit-ma-kha, the head-waters of the Hlaing, which carries off nearly the whole drainage of the country, receiving the Shwe-lay or Wai-gyee or Wek-poot and the Kyat or Kan-tha or Toung-gnyo from the east, and numerous small streams which flow down from the neighbouring rising ground on the west.

Not far from Eng-ma is the Eng-ma lake, an extensive marsh about 10 miles long and four miles broad in the rains; this is a large sheet of water 12 feet deep. The Myit-ma-kha enters it in the north, as the Zay, and leaves it again in the south.

There are few trees of any value to be found east of the Myit-ma-kha, but near Eng-ma is the " Royal Forest," of small extent but consisting entirely of teak of very fine growth. West of the Myit-ma-kha, Eng is found along the undulating ground in considerable quantities.

The principal town is Poung-day where an Assistant Commissioner in charge of the sub-division is stationed.

The township is divided into 35 revenue circles. In 1877 the population was 33,750, the land revenue Rs. 28,814, the capitation tax Rs. 33,419 and the gross revenue Rs. 83,598.

POUNG-DAY.—A long, straggling town in the Prome district in about 18° 27' N. and 93° 34' 49" E. on the main road from Rangoon northward, 33 miles south of Prome, and by the Irrawaddy Valley (State) Railway about 32 miles from Prome, traversed by the Myo-lay, a small creek dry or almost dry in the hot season, at which an Assistant Commissioner is stationed. It has a Charitable dispensary, a covered market-place, a Court-house, Police-station, a Lock-up, a Public Works Department inspection bungalow, a Government school and a Railway Station, and in 1878 had a population of 5,390 souls.

POUNG-KHYOOP.—A revenue circle occupying the southern portion of the Shwe-doung township, Prome district, east of the Kho-lan hills. The centre is under rice cultivation but the eastern and western portions consist of forest-covered hills and undulating ground. The Kyoon stream, which drains the valley between the Shwe-nat-toung or Kho-lan hills on the west and the Prome or Toung-gyee hills on the east, has its source in this circle. In 1877 the population was 594, the land revenue Rs. 563, the capitation tax Rs. 618 and the gross revenue Rs. 1,181.

POUNG-TA-LEE.—A revenue circle in the Ma-ha-tha-man township of the Prome district, lying to the east of Prome. In 1877 the population was 301, the land revenue Rs. 761, the capitation tax Rs. 335 and the gross revenue Rs. 1,096.

PRA-KA-RA.—A clan of the Bghai Kareng family.—See Kareng-nee.

PRA-KA-YOUNG.—A clan of the Pwo Kareng family; so called by themselves.—See Gai-kho.

PROME.—A town in the valley of the Irrawaddy on the left bank of that river in 18° 47' 53" N. and 95° 18' 18" E., the head-quarters of the Prome district. Extending northward from the foot of the Prome hills to the bank of the Na-weng, with a suburb on the other side of that stream, and eastwards for some distance up the Na-weng valley it is divided into several municipal divisions,—Na-weng on the north, Rwa-bhai on the east, Tsheng-tsoo on the south, and Shwe-koo and Tshan-daw in the centre forming, as it were, the heart of the town. The ground on the river bank is high and slopes downwards towards the east and the ditch, excavated in the Burman time, formerly closed the town in on that side and communicated with the Na-weng on the north and, passing through Tsheng-tsoo, with the Irrawaddy on the south and was spanned by several wooden bridges. During the dry weather this ditch was a swamp and a fertile cause of fevers and gave to the town the reputation of being exceedingly unhealthy. It is being filled in, partly with earth brought from the southern hills and partly by that obtained from excavating tanks. On the bank of the river on the high ground opposite the centre of the town are the Police office, the Government school, the Court-houses, with a nicely laid out garden and a fountain in front of them, the small public gardens, the Anglican church in course of erection, and the Telegraph office occupying the small space left between the river and the Strand road. From this road, which extends from one end of the town to the other, from Tsheng-tsoo to the Na-weng, numerous well laid out streets run eastwards and are intersected at right angles by others. Behind and rather north of Tsheng-tsoo and detached from the low hills which shut in the town on the south is the great Shwe Tshan-daw pagoda, shining out conspicuously from amongst the dark foliage of the shrubs and trees which cover the slopes of the hill on which it stands. North of the high laterite ground on which are the Court-houses and under the high bank a sandbank stretches up to the mouth of the Na-weng, under water in the rains but in the dry weather covered with brokers' huts. At this season a fleet of merchant boats is moored along it of which numbers are laden with nga-pee or fish paste, a product of the seacoast tracts, its unpleasant odour pervading the Na-weng quarter of the town. Here, on the high bank a little inland and on the inner side of the Strand, are the markets, consisting of four distinct buildings; one, the largest and newest, occupying the site of the old gaol, which was pulled down when the lock-up was constructed, with the meat-market immediately north of it; to the south, separated from the principal market by a road-way, is the old one, built about 15 years ago to replace one much farther east near the old ditch, and between this old one and the river is the fish market. Farther south, overlooking the river and separated from it by the Strand are the Charitable dispensary and the Lock-hospital, wooden buildings well raised from the ground. In an open space facing and thrown back from the river, a little south of the Court-houses, are two tanks, one east of or behind the other with the travellers' bungalow on the road-way between them. The Railway station, at present the terminus of the Irrawaddy Valley (State) Railway, is just behind these tanks, separated from them by High street, with the engine-sheds a little to the south-west on the southern side of another main street which forms a portion of the Rangoon and Mye-dai road. North of this street and between it and the tanks was the lock-up, built when the old gaol was pulled down, and now being demolished to make way for buildings for the railway. The Baptist Chapel is near the market and a new wooden Roman Catholic Church is under construction in the Tsheng-tsoo quarter. Almost the whole of the town was destroyed by fire in 1862 and the Deputy Commissioner, Colonel D. Brown, seized the opportunity and laid out the streets very much as they are now.

Prome is mentioned in ancient histories as the capital of a great kingdom before the commencement of the Christian era, but the town spoken of was Tha-re-khettra, some miles inland, the remains of which still exist. From the destruction of Tha-re-khettra, about the end of the first century, Prome for many years belonged, sometimes to Ava, sometimes to Pegu, and was sometimes independent, an independence which its rulers never retained for any lengthened period, and after the conquest of Pegu by Aloung-bhoora it remained a Burman town until Pegu was annexed by the British in 1853.

In 1825, during the first war, when Sir Archibald Campbell was advancing northward on the Burmese capital, endeavours were made to induce him to halt before reaching Prome, but he declined to enter into any negotiations until he had arrived at the town. Upon the first appearance of the force before the place, it was partly burned and abandoned by the Burmese troops although strongly fortified and was deserted by the inhabitants. The Commander-in-Chief here entered into winter-quarters and finding by practical experience that the town was liable to inundation from the overflow of the Irrawaddy, placed his troops on the high ground to the southward. Various detachments were sent out to Shwe-doung and towards Toung-ngoo, and after the rains were over the column advanced on Ava. After the signature of the treaty of Yandaboo in 1826 the British evacuated this district with the rest of the valley of the Irrawaddy. During the second Burmese war, in 1852, the town was attacked by the flotilla under Commander Tarleton ; the Burmese Commander fled and Prome was occupied but almost immediately abandoned as there were no troops to hold it. Three months later, in October of that year, the advance from Rangoon took place. The flotilla with the troops on board arrived off Prome on the morning of the 9th October and each ship was cannonaded from a projecting point on the hills south of the town as it passed up, but with very little effect. A portion of the troops were disembarked that evening and after a short fight occupied the northern portion of the town. Next morning the remainder of the force was landed and the whole advanced on the Burmese position on the hills to the south and east held by some 4,000 men, who retreated on to the main army stationed at Ra-thay-myo, some five or six miles to the eastward. On the 15th October Bandoola, the Burman Commander surrendered, and from that time the garrison were mainly employed in expeditions against the enemy, who had collected on the right bank of the river in what is now the Pa-doung township of the district and in the southern portion of the Henzada district, and gradually drove them out. The country was considerably disturbed, the inhabitants were in doubt as to whether the country would be restored to the Burmese or not, and rumours of another war were rife. Gradually the country settled down and a regular Civil Government was established. The British garrison in Prome at first occupied the hills south of the town, but were subsequently transferred to Nwa-ma-ran, four or five miles south near Shwe-doung. In 1854 they were transferred to Tha-yet-myo which was nearer to the frontier and was supposed to be healthier.

The number of inhabitants, according to Symes, was over 30,000 in 1793, but this would seem to be far too high an estimate. There is no information at present available as to the number of inhabitants until 1864, when it was stated to be 22,243, since then the population has been returned as :—

1864	..	..	..	22,243	1871	..	..	..	24,632
1865	..	..	..	21,807	1872	..	..	..	31,157
1866	..	..	..	22,739	1873	..	..	..	25,631
1867	..	..	..	23,420	1874	..	..	..	25,959
1868	..	..	..	25,095	1875	..	..	..	25,390
1869	..	..	..	24,616	1876	..	..	..	25,684
1870	..	..	..	23,915	1877	..	..	..	26,826

The figures for 1872 are those of the special census taken that year and include all wayfarers and casual inhabitants but it is difficult to believe that there were over 4,000 of these, and that the town has progressed so very slowly in population.

The local receipts and charges in 1867-68 and in 1877-78 were Rs. 49,016 and Rs. 23,599, and Rs. 96,380 and Rs. 79,842 respectively.

On the 12th November 1874 a Municipal Committee was appointed consisting of 16 members and a president and the administration of the local funds raised in the town was entrusted to this body ; since then great improvements have been made ; tanks have been dug, swamps filled in, the town lighted with kerosine oil lamps, and public gardens have been laid out. The amount spent on public works from the formation of the Municipality till the close of the year 1877-78 has been Rs. 92,820 out of a gross revenue of Rs. 352,800 including a loan of Rs. 7,260. Next to public works the principal item of charge is for Police.

PROME.—A district in the Pegu division occupying the whole breadth of the valley of the Irrawaddy between the Thayet district on the north and the Henzada and Tharrawaddy† districts on the south. The western boundary, Arakan lying beyond, follows the crest of the Arakan mountains from the root of the Bhee-la spur southward to that of the Ta-goung spur, a distance of about 52 miles. The southern boundary runs eastward for 20 miles along the Ta-goung spur to the source of the Kyouk-piet-tha and thence north-east for seven miles along the bed of that stream to the Irrawaddy. On the left bank of the great river the line is much more irregular. Leaving the bank of the Irrawaddy near the village of Thayet-ta-beng and following no natural features it runs N. E. for five miles, and then, turning S. E., strikes the Prome hills five miles further on ; following the crest of these southwards it turns E. and crossing the Myit-ma-kha, abuts on the Kyat in 95° 30′ ; thence it follows that stream for some distance when it turns north and then north-east and follows the crest of the Pan-doung spur to its root in the Pegu Roma, leaving a strip of Henzada (Tharrawaddy) between the southern portion of Prome and the mountains. The total length of the southern boundary on both banks of the river is 98 miles ; the distance measured in a direct line is about 70 miles. The western boundary line runs northward along the crest of the Pegu Roma mountains from the Thoon-mye-tsaing hill to the point where the Pa-teng-

† Tharrawaddy was separated from Henzada and made into an independent district whilst this work was passing through the press and after the account of Henzada was printed.

kyouk-poon spur leaves the main chain, a distance of 28 miles. The northern limit of the district follows the Pa-teng-kyouk-poon spur of the Pegu Roma and runs in a general W. S. W. direction to the Za-lwon khyoung, a distance of 54 miles : at first it runs about W., then turns alternately S. and W. till its last bend southwards brings it to the banks of the Za-lwon and from this point to the Irrawaddy, a distance of six miles, it follows the course of that rivulet. On the right bank of the Irrawaddy it starts westward from the mouth of the Ya-tha-ya stream and going along its bed for three miles to its source it then follows the crest of the Bhee-la spur for 33 miles more to the Arakan mountains : the total length of the northern boundary line from range to range is 96 miles. The total area comprised within these limits is 2,887 square miles.

The district originally extended northwards as far as the frontier of the Province but in April 1870 the present Thayet district was, on political, fiscal and administrative grounds, separated from it and formed into an independent jurisdiction, and the northern boundary as described above was fixed on as the line of demarcation between the two.

The Irrawaddy flows through the district from north to south dividing it into two portions differing considerably in area, in *Physical Geography.* appearance and in fertility. On the west the Arakan mountains, running nearly parallel to the river, throw off numerous thickly-wooded spurs which stretch far eastward and divide the country into small valleys, drained by short, unimportant and almost unnavigable affluents of the great river, in which but little regular cultivation can be carried on. On the left bank the face of the country, though somewhat the same in the north, is very dissimilar in the centre and south. To the north and north-east of the latitude of the town of Prome the forest-covered spurs of the Pegu Roma, reaching down riverwards, form valleys and ravines in which rush torrents whose waters, as they travel south-west towards the more level country, are gradually collected into three or four larger streams which eventually, a few miles from Prome, unite into one, the Na-weng. The southern and south-western portions of this tract are more level and gradually, south of the Na-weng, pass into large and well-cultivated plains lying between the Pegu Roma and the Irrawaddy and intersected here and there by low ranges of hills having a general north and south direction. Immediately to the south and south-east of Prome are rising grounds of no great elevation which form the northern end of a line of hills extending to the south beyond the limits of the district; between this ridge and the Irrawaddy, which here takes a large bend round westward, lies the Shwe-doung plain, the larger Poung-day plain being on the eastern side of these, the Prome hills. Starting from Shwe-nattoung, some 12 or 14 miles south of Prome, the Kho-lan, another low and independent chain runs south and, like the Prome hills, extends for some distance into the Henzada (Tharrawaddy) district, thus dividing the Shwe-doung plain down the centre. In the head of the tract, round the northern extremity of the Kho-lan ridge, and stretching down the two vales on each side of it, are fertile and extensive rice fields. The remaining portion of the district, bounded on the north by the hilly country which ends some little distance north of the Na-weng river, on the west by the Prome hills, on the east by a broad belt of forest-covered spurs sent down from the

Pegu Roma, is one large, flat plain, the richest and most populous part, watered by numerous streams which, hemmed in from the Irrawaddy by the Prome and Kho-lan hills, send their waters to the Myit-ma-kha, the head of the Hlaing or Rangoon river and thus seawards in a line parallel to, and to the east of, the main river. Fringing the northern bank of the South Na-weng and then, after narrowing considerably behind Prome, extending south along the Zay stream as far as the Eng-ma swamp, where it rapidly widens out eastward so as almost to cover the whole country between the two lines of hills, is the finest rice tract in the district.

Across the Pegu Roma there are, in this district, one or two roads, but these can be used only by men or elephants. A footpath leads from the source of the North Na-weng over the hills to the source of the Myouk-mwe; another from the source of the South Na-weng to the Hpa-loung; and further south there is one from near the source of the Shwe-lay to the Kareng hamlets on the Za-ma-yee, the head-waters of the Pegu river. Over the Arakan mountains a road leads from Pa-doung via Gnyoung-khye-douk to Toung-goop in the Sandoway district in Arakan. It was by this route that the main body of the Burmese army in 1783 A. D. advanced from Prome to the final conquest of the kingdom of Arakan, and that the enormous statue of Gaudama and the large cannon captured in the Arakanese capital were conveyed as trophies to Ava. In 1826, however, Lieutenant B. Browne of the Artillery reported the pass as altogether impracticable for troops or for laden cattle. This officer started from Pa-doung on the 23rd March and reached Toung-goop on the 2nd April, having made eleven marches. The first six, over numerous inferior heights, brought the party to the foot of the mountains which were found to be very precipitous and difficult of ascent. A barometrical observation made at the top of the pass gave the elevation as about 4,000 feet above the level of the last stream crossed. Both on the eastern and the western sides the supply of water was found to be most precarious and scanty. After the annexation of Pegu the then Governor-General, Lord Dalhousie, directed the construction of a good military road across this pass, which was soon reported to be so far complete that a horseman could ride along the whole length of it at any pace. The work was continued year by year and the path widened and gradually metalled but, owing mainly to the increased facilities of communication on the Irrawaddy river, the road has been somewhat neglected and in 1868-69 was reported as "not being a road at all except for pack bullocks". On this road is Gnyoung-gyo where an endeavour has been made to form a sanatarium for the Thayet-myo garrison.

In the first of the four tracts alluded to above, viz., Pa-doung, there are

Rivers. few rivers of any importance most of the streams being short mountain torrents which reach the Irrawaddy before they have time and distance to gather strength and volume. The northern half is drained by the Tha-nee system consisting of three larger and innumerable smaller rivers. The southern half, with the exception of a small area on the south-east, by the Tha-le-dan system, so named from its two main channels; and the triangular space confined between the Irrawaddy stream on the east, the Akouk-toung spur on the south and the Kyaw-kan-lan spur on the north-west, by the Kha-wa.

The Tha-nee rises in the extreme north-west angle and flows E. S. E. for about 25 miles, in a valley south of the spur forming the northern boundary, when, rounding the end of the spur which bounds the valley on the south, it turns southward and 20 miles further on, having received the waters of the Bhoo-ro and the Kyouk-bhoo, joins the Irrawaddy at Pai-gyee. In the rains small boats can ascend as far as Za-yat-hla, a short distance above the mouth of the Bhoo-ro. The Bhoo-ro rises in the Arakan mountains to the south of the source of the Tha-nee and flows south-east for 35 miles in a valley parallel to the valley of that river and separated from it by a long spur, when it falls into the Tha-nee near the village of Gnyoung-beng-tha. Its bed is rocky and its banks are steep and, except during the rains, it is not navigable by boats. The Kyouk-bhoo rises considerably south of the source of the Bhoo-ro and has an easterly course to the Tha-nee which it joins a few miles from the bank of the Irrawaddy. It is navigable during the rains but only by small boats. South of the Kyouk-bhoo is a long spur which reaches down to the river bank, forming the southern limit of the northern system and the rains which fall on the western and south-western hills are carried to the Irrawaddy by the Tha-le-dan streams which rise in the Arakan mountains and unite near the village of Ma-toung, 17 miles from the village of Tha-le-dan where their united waters reach the main river. The southern branch is not navigable by boats but the northern or main branch can be used during the rains by large boats as far as the village of Hlay-goo ; thus far the banks are moderately steep and the bed is sandy. Down these streams are brought large quantities of teak timber. The south-east corner is cut off from the rest by a spur which runs north-east from the Doo-gyo hill on the southern confines of the district to the Irrawaddy and is drained by the Kha-wa which has a short north-easterly course to the village of Htoon-bho ; in the height of the rains boats can ascend for a few miles.

The second tract, the mountainous country east of the Irrawaddy and north and north-east of the town of Prome, is drained by the Na-weng system of rivers of which the most important are the South Na-weng falling into the Irrawaddy at Prome and its tributaries the North Na-weng, the Khyoung-tsouk and the Teng-gyee.

The North Na-weng rises in the Pegu Roma. It first takes a north-westerly course to near the village of Aing-won where it turns west and then flows past Lek-khoop-peng, then running S. S. W. through a large forest-covered but comparatively flat tract of country it joins the South Na-weng. From the mouth for some distance upwards the banks are moderately steep and the bed is sandy, but its character soon changes and the bed becomes rocky and the banks very steep. To the south-west of the source of the North Na-weng and at the junction of the Tsa-ra and Pa-douk spurs is that of the Khyoung-tsouk ; this river, after flowing in a north-westerly direction for some distance, turns S. W. and, uniting with the Gway-khyo, joins the South Na-weng near the village of Khyoung-khwa. It is not navigable by boats but teak timber which is found at its source is floated down it in the rains. The bed is sandy and muddy and the banks are steep. The South Na-weng rises in the main range of the Pegu Roma and flows in a south-westerly direction till it leaves the hilly country when it joins the Teng-gyee and turns west, gradually curving to the S. W., till it reaches the Irrawaddy. In the lower portion of its course the bed is sandy but in the higher portion rocky. The Teng-gyee also rises in the Pegu Roma mountains and taking first a north-westerly and then a westerly course it falls into the South Na-weng just as this stream is entering the flatter country which intervenes between the Irrawaddy and the spurs of the mountains. Though all these rivers are to a certain extent navigable by boats yet they are at present mainly important as the routes by which the valuable timber found covering the hills in which they rise and amongst which they wind is floated down to the Irrawaddy to be rafted at the mouth of the Na-weng.

The Shwe-doung township, between the Irrawaddy and the Prome, hills, has no large rivers; the only one which need be mentioned is the Kyoon which drains the valley between the Prome and the Kho-lan hills and, running through rice fields almost throughout its whole length, falls into the Irrawaddy near the village of Shwe-gyo-goon, just below the town of Shwe-doung.

The surplus water of the extensive plain country lying between the Pegu Roma and the Prome hills south of the latitude of Prome is collected in numerous streams which form, what may for convenience be called the Myit-ma-kha system. The Zay, rising close to the southern wall of Ra-thay-myo or Tha-re-khettra, the capital of the ancient kingdom of Prome and carrying with it the drainage of the country on either bank, flows southward by the foot of the Prome hills between flat banks and over a muddy bottom, here and there widening out into a morass, and fringed with rice fields, till it reaches the northern end of the Eng-ma swamp. To the west, owing to the proximity of the Prome hills, the streams are mere rivulets, but to the eastward there are three sub-systems of drain-age. The Shwe-lay rises in the northern corner of the valley bounded on the south by the Tsheng-lan spur and flowing in a north-westerly direction falls into the Mwai-gyo swamp, one of those formed by the Zay. The Da-thway-kyouk has its source in the southern slopes of the Tsheng-lan spur and flows south-west till it reaches the Zay as the Thit-nee-daw, a few miles above the Eng-ma lake. The Tha-dwot rises in the Nee-pa-tshe spur, a little to the south of the Da-thway-kyouk from which it is separated by a subsidiary offshoot of the main chain, and running S. S. W. falls into the Too which unites the Zay with the Shwe-lay or Wai-gyee. On leaving the Eng-ma swamp the Zay assumes the name of Myit-ma-kha which it retains in this district and for some distance beyond, eventually becom-ing the Hlaing and from Rangoon to the sea the "Rangoon river". Run-ning up north-east between the Nee-pa-tshe and the Pan-doung spur, which here forms the boundary of the district, is a valley down which flows the Shwe-lay. This river rises in the lower slopes of the main range of the Pegu Roma as the Shwe-lay, a designation which it retains till it enters the champaign country; here it is called the Wai-gyee until it nears the village of Wek-poot, a name it assumes and retains until it receives that of Khyoon-khyoon-gya which it carries with it to its junction with the Myit-ma-kha. From its mouth to the village of Tha-bye-poung-gyee it is navigable during the rains by moderate sized boats but west of the Poung-day plains it is choked by sand and rubbish. The Kyat rises in the Henzada (Tharrawaddy) dis-trict, where it is known as the Toung-gnyo, and in the latter portion of its course forms the boundary between Prome and Henzada (Tharra-waddy). The Poungday plains, lying between these two streams, the Wai-gyee and the Kyat, on the north and south and the Myit-ma-kha on the west, are intersected by numerous anastomosing channels, nearly or quite dry in the dry season and filled in the rains. Considerable damage is often done by the debris brought down from the forests on the mountain slopes gradually collecting in the two main drainers of this part of the country, the Wai-gyee and the Kyat, and choking either or both. The rush of water is forced either over or through the banks of the dammed-up stream and spreads over the rice fields into some other course which the following year in its turn gets choked and, overflowing, sends another year's rains to wash away the now dried and decayed refuse which had originally barred the passage in the old channel or to cut a new one in the soft soil of the plain. Owing to the obstructions thus caused to the floating out from the Shwe-lay forests of the teak timber felled therein the Forest department in 1860 cleared out a canal to join the Shwe-lay and the Myit-ma-kha and to avoid a spot in which, west of Poung-day, the former was rendered useless for timber floating purposes by having silted up. Two other streams were left untouched as it was feared that some parts of the country relying partly on the inundations for their rice crops might be laid dry and that others lower down might be flooded.

Of lakes properly so called the district has but two, the Eng-ma and the Shwe-doung Myo-ma. The Dee-doot swamp on the east bank of the Irrawaddy is a depression in the plains receiving its yearly supply of water from the overflow of the Irrawaddy; in the rains it is seven feet deep but in the hot season it is dry. The Nga-pyaw-daw, Peng-lay-dien and Ngwe-gyaw are little else than morasses formed by the overflow of the Zay over its low and sedgy banks; they have some nine feet of water in them during the rains but are almost dry at all other seasons. The Shwe-doung Myo-ma or Theng-bhoo lake is on the east bank of and close to the Irrawaddy opposite to the town of Padoung, and is two miles long and one mile wide in its broadest part. In the dry season it has seven feet of water and in the rains, when the Irrawaddy aids the rainfall in filling it, fifteen; at this period it spreads out and, joining a line of morasses (dry except during this portion of the year) which stretches behind the large village of Kyee-thay, it unites with the Eng-pya in the south. This is of much the same character; it is two and a half miles long and three-quarters of a mile wide and communicates with the Irrawaddy in the rains. The Eng-ma lake is an extensive marsh lying to the east of the Prome line of hills, about 10 miles long and four broad in its widest part: during the rains it is a large sheet of water and about 12 feet deep; in the dry weather it is almost without water and is covered with reeds and long grass. The Zay enters it at its northern and the Myit-ma-kha, the head-waters of the Hlaing or Rangoon river, leaves it at its southern end.

The forest tracts in Prome may be divided into three great groups: one on the west of the Irrawaddy, one in the north-east of the district on the hills drained by the Na-weng, and ore in the south-east on the hills drained by the Shwe-lay. The country drained by the Tha-nee and the Tha-le-dan, though possessing fewer teak localities than the more northern part of the Province, has some which are exceedingly valuable. The spur dividing the two systems of drainage alluded to above is covered with fine large teak trees, and the teak at the sources of the Kyouk-bhoo, the most southern of the main feeders of the Tha-nee, is of fine growth in the small valleys and on the lower slopes of the hills but on the brow of the ridges it is low-branched and crooked. It is certain that under the Burmese rule and during the first years of British occupation this part of the country yielded very considerable supplies of planks and of squared logs. Kyan-kheng and Myan-oung, both in the Henzada district, are the places to which the timber was generally taken. The numerous large Burmese boats, for the building of which Kyan-kheng is noted, were, it is asserted, mostly constructed with timber from these forests. The fact that these tracts were once worked extensively is apparent from the large number of full-sized stumps counted in 1857—59, viz. 240 in a square mile in the north and 560 in the same area in the south. About 40 square miles is the area of the teak localities on this bank of the Irrawaddy in this district and 200 the number of first class trees per square mile.

The two tracts on the east of the Irrawaddy are of the same character and differ mainly in the extent to which they have been worked. Between the Pegu Roma mountains and the river are large stretches of country, generally running north and south at the foot of the hills, covered with Eng (*Dipterocarpus*) forest, in which the principal trees are, besides Eng from which the name is taken, Thit-ya (*Shorea obtusa*), Eng-gyeng (*Pentacme Siamensis*) and Thit-tsee (*Melanorrhœa usitatissima*). Below these are the lower mixed forests and above them the more important dry or upper mixed forests, in which are found Teak (*Tectona grandis*) and other valuable timber. Teak occurs all over the eastern hills in more or less abundance, and the average annual yield since the three-year permit system was introduced in 1862 has been about 10,000 logs.[*] The north-eastern tracts on the Na-weng and its feeders, in some of which there are rocky obstructions, have been far more freely worked than those to the south; so much so indeed that it is necessary to proceed one or two marches into the hills to reach really valuable teak localities, a fact which is accounted for by the vicinity of the town of Prome and by the facility with which, in the rains, timber can be brought down the Na-weng which in the lower part of its course is perfectly clear.

The Shwe-lay forests have been much better preserved owing to the river of that name being blocked up with sand and rubbish in the plains to the west of Poung-day. Since the occupation of the country by the British and the formation of a separate forest department which can control the working of the forests and prevent them from being exhausted, a canal has been constructed to avoid the obstruction and thus to open up these tracts which are probably some of the richest in Pegu, the area covered with teak being estimated at 95 square miles, and the average number of first class teak trees per square mile (in 1857—59) at 2,000. Some parts are still richer, one forest near the village of Gyo-beng-aing, first noticed by the then Assistant Commissioner of Tharrawaddy, Captain (now Colonel) David Brown, having an extent of six square miles and containing, in 1857, 21,202 first class trees or 3,533 per square mile. A disadvantage in these Shwe-lay forests is the want of water in the dry season.

---

[*] This system has been abandoned and the forests of the province are worked by the Forest Department.

There is some teak in the plains also, the most remarkable locality being near Eng-ma where the "Royal forest" consists almost exclusively of that species of timber and the trees are as straight and tall as the finest teak on the hills of the Pegu Roma range.

In addition to teak many other valuable species are found in the various forests, as Eng (*Dipterocarpus tuberculatus*), durable when not exposed to the damp and much used for house posts; Thit-ya (*Shorea obtusa*), white heavy and durable and used in house-building; Eng-gyeng (*Pentacme Siamensis*), also white and heavy and used for the same purpose; and higher up amongst the Teak, Pyeng-gado (*Xylia dolabriformis*), more durable even than teak but extremely hard to work; Htouk-kyan (*Terminalia macrocarpa*), used in house-building; Kook-ko (*Albizzia Lebbek*), black and heavy, used for cart-wheels and oil presses; Pa-douk (*Pterocarpus Indicus*), red and heavy, used for cart-wheels; Reng-daik (*Dalbergia sp.*), heavy, with a red heart used for plough and cart-poles; and Sha (*Acacia catechu*), used for the manufacture of cutch, and the inner wood, being extremely hard and durable, for house-posts, handles, &c. In Pa-douk and Kook-ko the eastern forests and in Sha both eastern and western are extremely rich. It has been estimated that as many as 2,000 trees of the first kind, 1,100 of the second, and no less than 130,000 of the third were felled annually until Pa-douk and Sha were reserved.

The principal pagodas in the district are the Shwe Tshan-daw in the town of Prome and the Shwe-nat-daw some 14 miles south of Prome, standing on the northern point of the line of hills which traverses the Shwe-doung township.

Pagodas.

The Shwe Tshan-daw, on a hill half a mile from the left bank of the Irrawaddy, rises from a nearly square platform to a height of about 80 feet and covers an area of 11,025 square feet. It is surrounded by 83 small gilded temples called "Ze-dee-yan" each containing an image of Gaudama. These, which unite at their bases, form a continuous wall round the pagoda, leaving a narrow passage between it and them. There are four approaches to the platform on which the pagoda stands each consisting of flights of about 100 brick steps, facing N.,S.,E. and W: the northern and western are covered in with elaborately carved and ornamented roofs supported on massive teak-wood posts, some partly gilded and partly painted vermilion. The platform into which the summit of the hill has been levelled is paved with stone slabs, and all round its outer edge is a series of carved wooden houses facing inwards, interspersed with smaller pagodas, containing figures of Gaudama and of Rahan, some in a standing, and others in a sitting or lying position. Between these and the main pagoda are numerous Tan-khwon-daing or posts surmounted by the "Ka-ra-wiet" or sacred bird * with long streamers dependent from their summits and 13 large bells, now partly gilt, hanging, with their rims just off the ground, on two cross bars supported on strong posts; these the

---

* In form something between a goose and a cock. It is often erroneously supposed to be a hanza or goose. This latter is the national bird of Pegu, and however willing Talaing might be to ornament their sacred flagstaffs with an image of their national emblem yet Burmans would not follow the custom whereas the Tan-khwon-daing at Bha-maw and far north are surmounted by a precisely similar figure. The Ka-ra-wiet is the carrying bird of Vishnu, "which has been brought into Burmese mythology with other prominent objects of the Hindu "pantheon."

worshippers strike with the butt end of deer's antlers lying in readiness near them.

When Gaudama was travelling about preaching his religion he arrived near the present town of Prome and landed on an island called Zeng-gyan where he was accosted by a Naga or dragon who begged for three of the preacher's hairs that he might enshrine them in a pagoda. The sage refused, saying that the glory of building a pagoda on that spot to contain his relics was reserved to Ee-zee-ka and Pa-lee-ka, two brothers then at Tha-htoon near the present town of Maulmain. The dragon thereupon presented Gaudama with an emerald box praying that at least he might be allowed to contribute the receptacle in which the sacred hairs would be placed. Accepting the box Gaudama placed in it three of the hairs of his head and by his supernatural power caused it to lodge amongst the branches of a tree on the bank where it shone like fire. Here it was found by the brothers who finally, after much discussion and search for a suitable place, guided by the prophecy that the capital of a flourishing kingdom should be founded close by, selected the hill on which the Shwe Tshan-daw stands and depositing the emerald box on seven ingots of gold erected over it a pagoda seven feet high. Seven days later, after they had returned to their own country, the pagoda sank into the earth and disappeared. Many years later king Dwot-ta-boung earnestly desired that the relics might be restored and in answer to his wish the pagoda reappeared and the king repaired it. Successive kings and governors added to and embellished it but it was not until comparatively of late years that it assumed its present proportions. In 1753 A.D. Aloung-bhoora had it regilt. In 1841 A.D. king Koon-boung Meng, better known as prince Tharrawaddy, had it thoroughly repaired and regilt and surmounted it with a new htee or crown of iron, gilt and studded with jewels, the diameter of the base of which was ten feet. In 1842 A.D. the carved roofs over the northern and western approaches were put up by Moung Toot-gyee, the governor. In 1858 A.D. it was again put in repair at an estimated cost of Rs. 76,800 raised by public subscription by an influential inhabitant of Prome named Moung Tha-shwe, and a few years ago it was regilt at a cost of Rs. 25,000 also raised by public subscription by Moung Shwe An. The annual festival, when the pagoda is visited by thousands of pious Booddhists, is held in Taboung, corresponding to March.

The Shwe-nat-daw pagoda some 14 miles south of the town of Prome is built on the high ground, forming the northern end of the chain of low hills which traverse the Shwe-doung township from north to south: immediately below it is a small plain where assemble annually, during the early portion of the year, vast crowds of people, sometimes as many as 20,000, from all quarters who come for the eight days' festival but nominally to worship at the pagoda. Living for the time in temporary sheds or huts and occupying their time in buying and selling, in looking on at wrestling matches and theatrical representations conducted, as they always are in Burma, in the open air and in other amusements, the scene represents a fair in which the serious business is religious worship. The pagoda profusely gilt and of great height is a conspicuous object for some distance and completely dwarfs the line of small pagodas stretching southward on the crest of the ridge. The palm-leaf history relates that the Shwe-nat-daw was originally built by Tsan-da-de-wee, half-sister and wife of Dwot-ta-boung, the founder of the Prome kingdom who reigned from 443 B.C. to 372 B.C. On one of her journeys the queen came to Nat-toung and was told that it was so called because the hill (*toung*) was surmounted by the image of the tutelary Nat of the neighbour-hood. The queen obtained from her husband two of the six relics of Gaudama which he had miraculously received and from the Rahanda 14 more and enclosing them in a golden box she buried them on the summit of the hill and built over them a pagoda 22½ feet high. King Dwot-ta-boung granted to the pagoda and set apart from secular uses for ever the whole space round it on which its shadow fell between sunrise and sunset and directed that a grand festival should be held there annually on the full moon of Ta-boung (March). Centuries later Thee-ha-thoo, son of Taroop-pye-meng, who established his capital at Prome, repaired the structure and raised its height to 66 feet. About the middle of the sixteenth century Ta-beng-shwe-htee, king of Toung-ngoo, who had conquered Prome, added to the pagoda and increased its height. Since then it has been more than once repaired and regilt.

The early history of the once flourishing kingdom of Prome, like that of the other states which now form portions of British Burma, is veiled in obscurity. Records purporting to be exact exist but, confessedly written long after the occurrences which they profess to relate, fact and fable are interwoven into such an intricate web that it is impossible to disentangle the true from the false. The task of discriminating between authentic statements and the embellishments added by historians more patriotic than truthful is rendered still more difficult, if not indeed, as regards the early periods, impossible, by the great dis-crepancies found in records dealing with the same periods but compiled by chroniclers of different nationalities.

It is most probable that the area of distribution of Gaudama's relics after his death in 543 B.C. marks the limits of his 45 years' wanderings, yet all Burman histories declare that he visited and preached in Burma. The Prome histories commence by asserting that during his peregrinations he arrived at a mountain a little to the N. W. of the present town and whilst looking thence to the south-east over " a great ocean " he observed a piece of cowdung floating with the current, and at the same time a bamboo rat appeared before and adored him. The sage smiled and in answer to a ques-tion of his companion Ananda, prophesied thus : " This rat at my feet " shall be born again as Dwot-ta-boung and in the 101st year of my religion " he shall found, at the spot where that piece of cowdung now is the large " town of Tha-re-khettra, and in his reign shall my religion spread far and " wide. This shall be preceded by five great signs ; there shall be a terrific " earthquake ; this great ocean shall be suddenly dried up ; this mountain " shall be broken and for a part of it shall be a lake ; a new river shall " appear ; and a new mountain shall be raised up." Thus not only does Gaudama prophesy the five miraculous events and the foundation of the town, but he foresees the establishment of an era dating from his death, and by it fixes the time for the fulfilment of his prophecy.* Having thus connected Prome with the great founder of his religion the chronicler

---

* The era of religion was fixed by Ajatasatta or Ayatathat, king of Magadha, in 543 B.C., after the burning of Gaudama's body and the distribution of his remains.

relates a story intended to prove that Dwot-ta-boung was of royal lineage. In 505 B.C. during the reign of Tha-do, 17th king of Ta-goung, a town many miles up the valley of the Irrawaddy, news was brought to the capital that a monstrous wild boar was devastating the country to the southward. The queen's brother, who had been declared heir-apparent, was charged to deliver the land from this scourge and started in pursuit. The boar first fled north-east passing through a narrow passage between two rocks now called *Wek-weng* or "boar's entrance," and then turning south-west and making for a large forest on the right bank of the Irrawaddy he crossed that river a few miles below the present town of Re-nan-khyoung. So enormous was the animal that he not only forded the river without swimming, but did so without wetting more than his feet, whence the name given to the large village at that spot, *Wek-ma-tswot* or "boar not wet." The Prince pursued him hotly and at length overtook and killed him on an island in the river a short distance to the north of the present British frontier, now known as *Wek-hto-kywon* or "boar stabbed island." The Prince having performed the duty upon which he had been sent, instead of returning to Ta-goung determined on leaving the world. "The distance which I have travelled," the chronicler makes him say, " and the number of years that I have been "absent, are very great; if I return to Ta-goung and tell the king of the "death of the boar he may not believe me; I might indeed take the carcase "as evidence of the truth of my story, but even then the presents and "honours with which I should be loaded would still be perishable and endure "during this transitory life only. No! I am already advanced in years; I will "not return to Ta-goung, but will remain here in the woods and becoming a "hermit will strive after Nirwana and lay up treasures for hereafter." Descending the Irrawaddy he selected as the site for his hermitage a spot five or six miles east of the present town of Prome and soon became a Rahanda perfect in the six kinds of wisdom.* Although so holy and so utterly devoid of passion a daughter was born to him two years later. The historian is put to great straits to reconcile this with the holiness and continence of the hermit, and can only find an escape from his dilemma by resorting to the miraculous. Not far from his retreat was a pool to which the recluse went daily for the purposes of nature; a doe which drank of the waters gave birth to a human infant and the hermit, hearing its cries, proceeded to the spot; the startled deer bounded into the forest leaving the child, a girl, of which the hermit constituted himself the guardian. At his prayer milk flowed from his fore and middle fingers and he was thus enabled to bring up the infant given to him. Matters went well till his daughter, whom he had named Bhe-da-rie, was about 17 years old when the holy man, feeling that it was not right for a woman, even his own daughter, to live in the hermitage with him, devised a plan for keeping her away all day. Making a small hole in a gourd, he gave it to Bhe-da-rie and directed her to go to the river daily and fill it to replenish the water-pot standing in his cell. The hole was so small that Bhe-da-rie was kept away at the river bank during the whole of each day.

---

* The six kinds of wisdom which are the attributes of a 'Rahanda' or mortal fit to pass into Nirwana without further transmigrations are (1) the faculty of seeing like a Nat, (2) the faculty of hearing like a Nat, (3) creative power, (4) knowledge of others' thoughts, (5) freedom from passion and (6) knowledge of one's own past existences.

During the hermit's absence from Ta-goung two sons had been born to his sister and brother-in-law but both blind. The king, Tha-do, directed that they should be destroyed but their mother concealed them. Some years later Tha-do, discovering the fraud, repeated his order and the two lads, who had now reached man's estate, were placed with some food on a bamboo raft and cast loose on the Irrawaddy. Passing near the bank at Tsit-kaing a Bhee-loo-ma, or ogress, dropped on to the raft from the over-hanging branch of a Tsit tree and floated down the river with them. Day by day she robbed them of their food as they sat down to eat. One day just as the Bhee-loo-ma was dipping her hand into the dish Ma-ha-tham-ba-wa, the elder of the two brothers, seized her and was about to stab her when she promised to cure their blindness if they would spare her. To this they agreed and she commenced to administer medicines, the raft still floating down the river. As the journey continued the cure progressed ; opposite the pres-ent town of Tsa-leng or "beginning of light" they first saw faint glim-merings ; lower down, just below the present British frontier, they first saw clearly and cried out "*Mo-boon-mye-dai*," that is "the sky is as a cover "and the earth is underneath it" ; the place is called Mye-dai to this day. Continuing on their way they soon arrived at the spot where Bhe-da-rie was endeavouring to fill her gourd. Ma-ha-tham-ba-wa taking it from her enlarged the hole with his dagger and the gourd then rapidly filling she carried it to her father and related what had happened. The old man sent for the two princes, Ma-ha-tham-ba-wa and Tsoo-la-tham-ba-wa, and finding that they were his nephews gave Bhe-da-rie to wife to the elder. This was in the year 60 of the era of religion or 464 B.C. On the night of the mar-riage Gaudama's prediction was partially fulfilled : there was a terrific earth-quake, the sea was dried up, the waters forming a lake near the foot of the hill on which the Booddha had stood, a new river—now called the Na-weng—appeared, and a new mountain rose up perpendicularly in a plain.

Three tribes wandering from the east now arrive at Prome and quarrel as to the possession of the site for a settlement. The Kan-ran and Thek, being beaten, move further westward into Arakan, and the Proo or Pyoo remain and elect a woman as chief. In some histories an account is given of this queen obtaining from the aborigines a grant of as much land as could be enclosed within an ox-hide and, like Dido, cutting the hide into strips. The Pyoo were soon engaged in disputes with their neighbours and at last had to beg for the assistance of Ma-ha-tham-ba-wa and of his brother Tsoo-la-tham-ba-wa, the former of whom married the Pyoo sovereign. After reigning for six years Ma-ha-tham-ba-wa died leaving two children, an infant son by Bhe-da-rie and a daughter by the Pyoo queen : he was succeeded by his brother Tsoo-la-tham-ba-wa who married Bhe-da-rie and after a reign of 35 years was followed by his nephew and step-son Dwot-ta-boung. Dwot-ta-boung married his half-sister Tsan-da-de-wee, daughter of Ma-ha-tham-ba-wa and the Pyoo queen and, all the five events predicted by Gaudama having taken place, shortly afterwards founded the city of Tha-re-khettra or Ra-thay-myo on the spot where his grand-father the hermit lived and his mother, his wife and himself were born. The date of the foundation of this city can be fixed with some certainty, for some of the histories of Prome—all of which agree in giving 101 of the Booddhist religious era as the date—state that it was in the first year after the first great Booddhist council ; and this, it is known from perfectly independent testimony, took place *circa* 443 B.C. Tsoo-la-tham-ba-wa must, therefore, have succeeded his brother in 478 B.C., and Ma-ha-tham-ba-wa have become head of the Pyoo tribe in 484 B.C.

Tha-re-khettra was situated five or six miles east of the present town of Prome and was, according to the annalists, surrounded by a wall 40 miles in length with 32 large and 23 small gates and filled with splendid buildings including three royal palaces with handsome gilt spires. About the beginning of the second century of the Christian era the town was abandoned and fell into ruins, but the remains of massive walls constructed with well burnt bricks 18 inches long by nine wide and four and a half thick, the embankments and the pagodas attest that where now are some seven or eight villages, standing in rice fields and swamps intersected here and there by patches and strips of brushwood, was once a large city, the capital of a flourishing and powerful kingdom.

The next date which can be fixed with any approach to correctness is the accession of a king in the twelfth, or according to some historians, in the twentieth year of whose reign was held the second great Booddhist council. This was called together by Asoka in the twenty-second year of his reign, counting from his accession and in the eighteenth counting from his coronation, and assembled under the guidance of the Arahat Mogaliputra in 241 B.C.

The Burmese annals are by no means trustworthy and it is not till *circa* 90 B.C.* that any statements by historians of other countries can be made available as checks on the Prome historians. About that year the sacred Booddhist scriptures were reduced into writing in Ceylon and this fact, which is noticed in the Burmese palm-leaf chronicles, is stated there to have taken place in the seventeenth year of a king named Te-pa. This sovereign, who was originally a poor student for the priesthood and was adopted by his childless predecessor, must thus have ascended the throne *circa* 107 B.C. He is stated to have been the eleventh sovereign since the foundation of the capital, but this would give over 40 years as the average length of the reign of his predecessors except that of Dwot-ta-boung, who, it is asserted, reigned for 70 years.

The Te-pa dynasty occupied the throne of Tha-re-khettra for 202 years or until 95 A.D., when the monarchy was broken up by civil war and an invasion by the Kan-ran tribe from Arakan. The last king was Thoopa-gnya. His nephew Tha-moon-da-riet fled first to Toung-gnyo S.E. of Prome ; he then crossed the Irrawaddy to Pa-doung but being still harassed by the Kan-ran he went northwards to Meng-doon. He finally recrossed the Irrawaddy and founded the city of Lower Pagan in 108 A.D. In establishing his new kingdom he was greatly assisted by a scion of the old Ta-goung race of kings named Pyoo-meng-tee, or Pyoo-tsaw-tee who married his daughter and afterwards succeeded him.

From about the middle of the 14th to the beginning of the 16th century the greater part of the dominions which had been included in the Pagan kingdom was parcelled out amongst a crowd of adventurers from the Shan states. In about 1365 a descendant of the old Ta-goung dynasty succeeded in re-establishing the Burman monarchy but it lasted only a few years.

---

* Dr. Mason says 93 or 94 B.C. Sir J. Emerson Tennant in his work on Ceylon, 3rd Edition, page 376, says in 89 B.C.

In 1404 Raza-dhie-rit, king of the Talaing kingdom on the south, the capital of which was at Pegu, invaded Burma and passing by Prome and Mye-dai ravaged the country near the capital which was then at Ava. Towards the close of the 15th century the power of the rulers at Ava was so decreased that the monarchy may be said to have ceased to exist. Their dominions were divided amongst a number of independent Burmanised Shan Tsaw-bwa, of whom one was at Toung-ngoo. Thither flocked many Burmans and Booddhist monks, and the rulers and people of Toung-ngoo became more thoroughly Burman than the rest of Burma.

In 1530 A.D. there ascended the throne of Toung-ngoo a monarch who is known in history as Meng-tara-shwe-htee, or Ta-beng-shwe-htee. Four years afterwards he commenced his aggressive career by marching on Pegu. In two campaigns the power of the Talaing king was broken and he fled to Prome. Having subdued the whole of the Talaing country, Ta-beng-shwe-htee removed his capital from Toung-ngoo to Pegu. An alliance was formed against him by the kings of Ava, Prome and Arakan but their forces were cleverly taken in detail by Ta-beng-shwe-htee and his renowned general Bhooreng-noung and utterly defeated in the neighbourhood of Prome, which surrendered in June 1542 A.D. In the later years of his life Ta-beng-shwe-htee is said to have fallen into bad habits from associating with a dissipated Portuguese adventurer. He was murdered in May 1550 A.D., after a glorious reign of only 20 years, in which time he had raised himself from being merely Tsaw-bwa of Toung-ngoo to be lord paramount of Pegu, Tenasserim and Upper Burma as far as Pagan and the kings of Burma and Siam paying him tribute. He was succeeded by the general to whom much of his military success was due, Bhooreng-noung, who in consequence of his having taken six white elephants from the king of Siam, assumed the title of Tsheng-hpyoo-mya-sheng.* It was not without fighting, however, that he obtained possession of the throne. No sooner was Ta-beng-shwe-htee dead, than the rulers of Prome and Toung-gnoo, though they were Bhooreng-noung's own brothers, declared themselves independent and the old royal Talaing family again set up its claim to the throne of Pegu. Bhooreng-noung speedily reduced his refractory brothers to subjection. Commencing with Toung-ngoo he went across from thence to Mye-dai and Ma-lwon, and there obtaining a fleet of boats went down by water to Prome. Having subdued Prome he went northwards and had nearly reached Ava when he was re-called by the intelligence that the Peguans were about to attack Toung-ngoo. This attempt he easily frustrated. He now called a family gathering and distributed the provinces of the empire among his brothers, making them tributary princes of Martaban, Prome and Toung-ngoo.

The great king, Tsheng-byoo-mya-sheng, died 1581 A.D., and his vast empire shortly afterwards fell to pieces. The seat of government was removed after his death to Toung-ngoo, and one of his younger sons, Gnyoung-ranmeng-tara, established his capital at Ava.

The second dynasty of Ava kings which was thus established lasted for about a century and a half, and was ultimately terminated by an invasion from Pegu. The Talaing were driven to revolt by the misgovernment of the officers sent down from Ava. They established their independence and the second king, Byee-gnya-da-la, invaded the Burman territory, captured

---

* Lord of many white elephants.

Ava, and carried off the king a prisoner to Pegu. The whole of Upper Burma was reduced, with the exception of one village, Moot-tsho-bho, some miles to the north of Ava. The headman of this village was one Moung-oung-ze-ya. He refused to surrender to the Talaing conquerors and was repeatedly attacked but invariably unsuccessfully. The fame of his patriotism and ability soon spread and a great crowd of Burmans, who chafed under the domination of the Talaing, gathered round him and acknowledged him as their leader. With their assistance he drove the Talaing out of Ava and the whole of Upper Burma. He then assumed the title of Aloung-meng-tara-gyee, or Aloung-bhoora (corrupted by Europeans into Alompra) and became the founder of the third and present dynasty of Ava kings (1753 A.D.). His native village he dignified with the name of Ra-ta-na-thien-ga-koon-boung. In 1758 he conquered Pegu, and carried away captive to Ava Bya-hmaing-tee-raza, the last of the Talaing kings.

From this period till the annexation of Pegu by Lord Dalhousie at the close of the second Burmese war Prome remained a province of the Burman kingdom.

The district, although adjoining the once famous kingdom of Pegu contains only five Talaing. On the first annexation of the province the present Thayet district, as already stated, formed a portion of Prome and was not separated from it till 1870; up to that year the statistics of population of the two districts are mixed up together. In 1855 the population of what is now Prome numbered 79,226 souls and 171,773 in 1860, in other words it had more than doubled, owing to the gradual quieting down of the country, the return of families to their homes and to immigration from Upper Burma, the tide of which had already set in. When the census was taken in 1872 the number of inhabitants was found to be 274,872, but this included travellers and temporary residents and of these, considering that the Irrawaddy forms the main artery of communication, there must have been very many. Though but little confidence can be reposed in the returns of the Thoogyee yet it is impossible to suppose that they were so seriously out as this would seem to shew them, and this the more especially as having themselves been the enumerators they would not, with the census figures before them, have, in the following year, suddenly brought down the population, as they did, from 274,872 to 266,067 had they not some reasonable explanation to offer. The various races were :—

Population.

Burmese	..	..	..	256,864
Khyeng	..	..	..	10,796
Kareng	..	..	..	2,382
Shan	..	..	..	1,297
Kathay	..	..	..	1,814
Hindoos	..	..	..	285
Mahomedans	..	..	..	1,082
Chinese and persons of mixed Chinese descent	..	..		259
Other races including Europeans, Eurasians, Malays, &c.			..	53
			Total ..	274,872

Except amongst the Khyeng, Kareng and Kathay travellers were probably included under every head but to what extent it is impossible to say.

The population in 1877 was—

Burmans	..	..	..	264,043
Talaing	..	..	..	5
Shan	..	..	..	1,748
Khyeng	..	..	..	9,760
Chinese	..	..	..	229
Kathay	..	..	..	1,080
Kareng	..	..	..	2,895
Natives of India	..	..	..	2,099
All others	..	..	..	319

Total .. 282,178

The Khyeng, a portion of the mountain race which extends far north into Upper Burma and westward into Arakan, are found generally in the country to the west of the Irrawaddy, though there are some villages on the east. When living near the Burmese the men adopt the Burmese costume much more readily than the women whose tattooed faces unmistakeably betray their origin.* In the jungle villages the men are rarely tattooed and wear as little clothing as possible. If those near the plains are questioned they will probably reply that they are Booddhists but their Buddhism is only an outward crust; they follow the example of their Burman neighbours and on the annual pagoda festivals go with the multitude and conform somewhat to the Burman customs. As a race they are naturally cruel to strangers but staunch friends to each other, and a Khyeng dacoit is the embodiment of craft and malice; at the same time more dreaded by the Burmans than any other for his savage cruelties and disliked by the police for his ability, aided by the connivance of his friends, to avoid capture. The Shan are settlers from the north-east of Ava, a patient, hard-working people, who are excellent gardeners; occasionally, however, they take to robbery but rarely in armed gangs. The Kathays, Hindoos by religion, are Manipuris who have resided in Prome for many years, brought thither as Burman captives. They occupy a distinct quarter of the town between the river and the great Shwe Tshan-daw pagoda and are principally engaged in weaving silk poo-tsho and hta-mien, worn by the Burmese and Talaing men and women throughout the Province. Owing to the improvements which are being carried out in Prome many have gone south to Shwe-doung, Kyee-thay and other villages on the east bank of the Irrawaddy. They are found nowhere else in British Burma except in Rangoon where there are only 31 of them. The Hindoos, Mahomedans and Chinese are immigrants who come merely to make money and who are engaged, the first largely in cattle dealing and the other two races in trade, settling in the various towns and larger villages.

The total agricultural population was returned as (and this is probably nearly accurate) 73,505, of whom 38,340 were males above 20 years of age, and the average holding was shewn as 4·42 acres. The number of persons dependent upon agriculture was about 73,505, but it is not possible to attain absolute accuracy on this point as large numbers are agriculturists or fishermen as the season serves, and more still have, under the charge of some person of their families, small retail shops in which articles of almost every sort and kind are offered for sale. That the number of agriculturists is not

---

* This custom of tattooing the face in close lines so as to render it of an almost uniform blue colour is dying out—*vide sub tit " Khyena".*

more than 26·74 per cent. in such an agricultural country is due to the large trading towns, Prome with 31,157, Shwe-doung with 12,654 and Poung-day with 5,630 inhabitants ; deducting these the percentage of agriculturists to the whole population was 68·71.

The total male and female population according to ages was :—

	Males.	Females.	Total.
Not exceeding one year	6,448	6,184	12,632
Above 1 year and not exceeding 6 years ..	22,295	23,422	45,717
,, 6 do. do. 12 ,, ..	21,326	20,302	41,628
,, 12 do. do. 20 ,, ..	18,076	17,152	35,228
,, 20 do. do. 30 ,, ..	22,145	22,339	44,484
,, 30 do. do. 40 ,, ..	20,708	19,344	40,052
,, 40 do. do. 50 ,, ..	13,615	12,422	26,037
,, 50 do. do. 60 ,, ..	7,164	7,648	14,812
,, 60	6,770	7,512	14,282
Total ..	138,547	136,325	274,872

Taking the two sexes between the ages of 20 and 40, which may be assumed to include the vast majority of immigrants, the males exceeded the females by 2,094, and whilst there were more female children between one year and six years old there are more boys born than girls.

According to the official returns the number of inhabitants have been in :—

YEAR.	Males.		Females.		Total.
	Under 12.	Over 12.	Under 12.	Over 12.	
1871	52,669	75,379	50,793	72,614	251,455
1872	47,168	82,120	46,914	80,955	257,157
1873	50,069	86,397	49,928	88,478	274,872
1874	47,307	86,844	46,967	84,949	266,067
1875	45,924	89,367	45,530	87,190	268,011
1876	46,258	89,185	45,547	86,870	267,860

Thus according to the annual returns the males exceed the females both under and over twelve.

The largest product of the district is rice and this is cultivated mainly in the splendid tract of champaign country which stretches
Agriculture. southwards from about the town of Prome and extends from the western slopes of the Pegu Roma to the Irrawaddy, forming the Poung-day and Shwe-doung townships, and is intersected by two narrow ranges of low hills; there is some rice land further north and on the west bank of the Irrawaddy but here the cultivation is mainly garden and toungya. The grain is soft and is unsuited for a long sea voyage and is usually consumed in the district and other parts of the province or is exported northwards to Mandalay. Owing to the opening of the Railway, however, a considerable quantity will now no doubt be brought south to supply the China and Straits markets. Tobacco is grown on the banks of the Irrawaddy after the river has fallen : the area shews no tendency to increase. Cotton is sown on the hill sides and is used for local consump-

tion and is partially cleaned in Prome and sent down to Rangoon for export, sometimes mixed with the shorter-stapled kind from Upper Burma which is brought to Prome to be cleaned. Near Prome and on the hills opposite are numerous fruit gardens, the custard apple predominating ; no less than 593 acres are planted with this tree in the whole district, and 10,231 acres with mixed fruit trees, cocoanut, palm and betel-nut trees numbering some 142,000. The toungya system of cultivation, called *jhoom* in Chittagong, is extensively adopted, the estimated area so worked in 1876-77 being about 9,291 acres ; in no other district except Shwe-gyeng in Tenasserim is it so large and nowhere in such a high proportion to the whole area. This system, which is justifiably objected to as wasteful, is carried on on the hill sides by the Kareng, Yabaing and the poorer Burmans who cannot afford to purchase cattle for ploughing in the plains. This system is not peculiar to Burma; it was or is general in Assam, in the hills of Central India and in Mysore where it is called *coomree*. A portion of the forest is cleared, varying in extent according to the number of the family engaged in the cultivation. The timber is felled in the early part of the dry season and left to dry; just before the rains it is fired and the logs and brushwood reduced to ashes. The ground being thus cleared and the soil enriched all that is necessary is to await the first fall of rain and then to sow the rice, oil-seed or cotton, the first and last often sown together, in which case the rice which ripens about October is then cleared away and the cotton allowed to hold the ground till it ripens its capsules in March. After this the toungya becomes waste. One peculiar kind of injury caused by toungya is the over-luxuriant growth of the dense forest that in most cases immediately occupies the soil, fertilized by the large amount of ashes and not yet exhausted by the single harvest it has yielded. In some respects the toungya system may have its advantages. In this district, especially on the dry hills near the Na-weng, the burning of the trees and shrubs for toungya cultivation does not create a mass of low dense forest as in the other parts of the province ; on the contrary the fertilizing effect of the ashes has the opposite effect for an unusual number of young trees are found on deserted toungya among which there is generally a due proportion of teak.

The area under each principal crop in each year, since Thayet was formed into a separate district, has been, in acres :—

Year.	Rice.	Oil seeds.	Sugarcane.	Tobacco.	Vegetables.	Fruit trees.	Total.	Remarks.
1870-71 ..	150,793	569	24	2,036	29,158		182,580	There were also 1,894 acres under cotton.
1871-72 ..	152,032	533	24	2,266	16,676		..	Cotton 1,775.
1872-73 ..	152,540	1,340	55	2,270	2,667	11,020	169,892	Cotton 1,529.
1873-74 ,.	153,330	1,755	52	2,144	2,437	7,186	166,904	Cotton 18,28.
1874-75 ..	150,951	10	56	1,677	2,923	11,270	166,887	
1875-76 ..	154,296	40	71	1,749	2,959	10,725	169,840	
1876-77 ..	152,450	1,340	55	2,270	2,767	11,020	169,992	Cotton 15,29.
1877-78 ..	151,920	19	94	2,154	3,747	12,155	170,089	

Since 1870-71 inclusive, the agricultural stock, according to the returns given in the Annual Administration Reports, has been :—

YEAR.		Buffaloes.	Cows, Bulls and Bullocks.	Ponies.	Pigs.	Sheep and goats.	Elephants.	Carts.	Ploughs.	Boats.
1870-71	..	17,417	82,948	774	10,379	605	27	28,723	37,737	1,213
1871-72	..	19,702	82,816	681	10,300	679	24	26,256	29,445	1,200
1872-73	..	20,314	85,222	545	10,586	819	22	28,592	31,490	1,313
1873-74	..	18,584	84,917	495	9,875	776	25	28,627	31,451	1,349
1874-75	..	20,085	87,504	481	9,411	609	20	29,888	32,035	1,358
1875-76	..	21,851	90,123	501	9,280	707	21	29,785	32,084	1,362
1876-77	..	20,314	85,222	545	10,585	819	22	28,592	31,490	1,313
1877-78	..	25,606	98,871	523	10,774	855	8	31,599	33,485	1,185

The average quantity of land held by each cultivator is seven acres, generally in one plot, but in some cases intersected by other properties. In Pa-doung the land is a good deal encumbered, owing probably to its having been more thickly inhabited in former years and to many of the inhabitants having crossed the river to Shwe-doung and mortgaged their land to obtain funds for trading, but as a general rule the proprietors every where live close to the land which they own.

One of the most important manufactures of this district is silk, the following account of which is taken from a paper by Colonel Horace Browne, then Deputy Commissioner of Prome, published in September 1870 :—Neither the worm nor the mulberry are indigenous to the province, but were, most probably, imported from China by the valley of the Irrawaddy and not across the hills from India. That this very lucrative manufacture is not more generally spread over the country has been attributed to the fact that it involves taking the life of the chrysalis, an act of impiety looked upon with horror by every rigid Booddhist ; in fact, the silk growers are nearly all Yabaing, a race of the same stock as the Burmese by whom, however, they are looked down upon, and those who breed silk worms live in villages by themselves holding little social intercourse with their neighbours. The fact that the mulberry tree does not grow well on alluvial soil has, it may be presumed, something to do with the limited number of silk growers.

Manufactures.

The Burmese mulberry, which has not been identified by any competent botanist but which has been pronounced not to be the *Morus Indica*, is a thin lanky shrub throwing out several vertical shoots from near the ground and growing to a height of eight or ten feet. It will not flower and is therefore propagated by cuttings. After about three years a plantation ceases to bear good and succulent leaves and is then abandoned or the plants are uprooted. The shrub is grown principally on the sides of hills but a small quantity is planted in alluvial soil by the margins of mountain streams, though the silk produced in such localities is inferior to that obtained where the mulberry is grown on high land. The Burmese name for the tree is *po-tsa-beng*, or " silk worms' food tree". Should the mulberry leaves fail the larvæ are fed on the leaves of the *Broussonetia papy-*

rifera (*Ma-hlaing-beng*, the tree from the bark of which is made the coarse Burmese paper called *parabaik*). The leaves of these two trees are the only ones used as food for the silk worm and the silk produced by worms fed on the leaves of the latter is, comparatively, worthless. The silk is of a very rough and inferior description, admirably adapted for the manufacture of the strong coarse silks so universally worn by the natives of the country, and sells at about five or six rupees a pound in the local market. In 1855 its value in the English market was estimated by the Calcutta Chamber of Commerce at about half of this price. The price of the raw silk when brought to the markets on the river's bank varies from Rs. 4-8-0 to Rs. 7 per lb., the average price being about Rs. 5-12-0 per lb.

The method pursued is rude and careless in the extreme. All the processes are carried on in the ordinary bamboo dwelling-houses of the country which are smoke-begrimed and dirty. The larvæ and cocoons share the accommodation with the family of the house-owner, and live and thrive in close proximity to the place where the culinary and other domestic operations of the household are carried on. The plant of a Burmese silk filature is simple and inexpensive, consisting simply of (*a*) a set of flat trays with slightly raised edges, made of strips of bamboos plaited, from two to four feet in diameter; (*b*) some neatly made circlets of palm leaves three or four inches in diameter; (*c*) some strips of coarse cotton cloth; (*d*) a common cooking pot; (*e*) a small bamboo reel; and (*f*) a two-pronged fork. As soon as the females are impregnated the males are thrown away and the females are placed within the palm-leaf circlets on a sheet of coarse cotton cloth two or three feet square, to which the eggs adhere and which thus becomes covered with circular cartoons of eggs. These when sold fetch about two annas each. When the moths have laid all their eggs, which takes them about a day to do, they are thrown away and the pieces of cloth are wrapped up and left to themselves. About the eighth day the eggs are hatched, the cloths are then opened and the larvæ are swept by a feather on to a tray. The produce of one circular cartoon will, when the worms are full grown, more than fill a large tray two or three feet in diameter. About 12 hours after they are hatched the worms are fed with finely chopped pieces of the tenderest mulberry leaves, and are so fed for the first four or five days, when they shed their skins. After this change they require plenty of strong leaves and, beyond being supplied with food, they receive little or no care. No attention is paid to cleanliness, the frass and remnants of leaves being left in the tray; the larvæ bear very rough handling, being scraped up and tossed about in handfuls when they are moved. Their only enemy is the ichneumon fly, and when such a fly has deposited its eggs in the body of a larva, which soon gives sign of what has occurred, the worm is thrown away. To protect the larvæ the trays are generally kept covered. The larvæ after 30 days, during which they moult four times, are ready to spin their cocoons. The "ripe" ones are picked out by the hand and thrown in heaps on to a small tray in which they are conveyed to the cocooning tray. This is three or four feet in diameter and within it is a large ribbon of plaited bamboo a couple of inches wide, wound round and round in a spiral with its edge on the tray. The larvæ are taken up in handfuls and scattered over the tray with as little care as if they were so many grains of corn. They attach their cocoons, which are completed in 24 hours, to the spiral. The cocoons are torn off the plaited bamboo ribbon and thrown into baskets and two or three days later are placed in a common pot to simmer in water over a slow fire. Above the pot are placed a pair of cross sticks from which a bamboo reel is suspended and beside the pot is a wooden cylinder turning on a pivot. Some filaments of silk are caught and drawn out of the pot, run over the bamboo reel and fastened to the cylinder. The reeler (generally a woman) with an iron fork in one hand and the handle of the cylinder in the other, keeps catching up the filaments in the pot with the fork and reeling them on to the cylinder. The thread produced is coarse and dirty, and is mixed with bits of pupæ and other refuse, all of which go with the silk on to the cylinder. When the silk is exhausted from the pot the larvæ are taken out and fried in oil for the dinner of the household.

The cocoons left to produce the imaginæ are ready in about eight days. As the moths emerge they are put in large covered trays for a day that the males may fecundate the females, when the males are thrown away and the process is again gone through. The cocoons from which the moths emerge are not thrown away, but from them a coarser silk is spun which fetches one-third of the price of that obtained from the undamaged cocoons. The length of the different stages is :—

				Days.
Eggs	..	..	..	..	8—in cold weather 11.
Larvæ	..	..	..	..	30
Cocoon	..	..	..	..	8
Imago	..	..	..	..	1
				47—or in cold weather 50.

The silk growers are quite ready to adopt any measures, whether the introduction of new breeds of silk worms or the improvement of their machinery, which may be expected to be profitable.

The weaving of silk, of which a large quantity is exported, is principally carried on in Prome and Shwe-doung, but not by any means in those towns only : a loom usually forms part of every Burman's household furniture and is worked by the female members of the family. The best cloths are woven from imported Chinese silk, which is more expensive than the native grown, the first costing Rs. 36 and the second Rs. 22 for a viss (3·65 lbs.). The weavers usually buy the silk raw, wind the threads off clear, twist them by means of a wheel and make the resulting thread up into hanks they then boil it in soap and water and dye it of the desired colour, after which they reel it off again : these operations, for a viss or 3·65 lbs. of silk, take fifteen, ten, two, one, five, and one day respectively, and 21 days more are employed in weaving it into a saleable fabric. This quantity of silk would weave into five men's waist cloths for ordinary wear which would sell at about Rs. 13 a piece. A hta-mien or woman's dress is prepared and woven in the same way, but different persons weave the centre part and the lower portion. One viss of silk will produce 30 centres, each about four feet six inches in length, woven each in one day, and selling for about Rs. 2-4-0. Of the bottoms six feet can be woven in one day, and these cost about Rs. 1-12-0 each. The Kathay in Prome and the inhabitants of some of the villages in the district, especially Kyee-thay, are noted for their silk piece-goods, sometimes as many as 24 shuttles being required for the pattern being worked.

In the town of Prome, and there only in this district, are made large and highly ornamented boxes used for keeping Burmese palm-leaf books, in monasteries especially. The box is made of teak and when planed and the carpentering finished it is covered with a mixture of wood-oil and sifted teak saw dust which is allowed to dry ; the uneven parts are then smoothed down and the box is covered with a preparation composed of finely sifted burnt rice-husk, wood-oil and rice water. When this is dry it is rubbed down with a smooth stone and cocoanut husk and water, and is again rubbed with wood-oil. It is again fined down and put in the sun, and when quite dry receives another coat of wood-oil after which it is put away in the shade ; it is again washed, exposed to the sun, smeared with wood-oil and put away to dry. It is now ready for decoration. Figures and flowers are drawn upon it profusely in wood-oil, and a kind of gold size ; it is then washed in the sun with boiled wood-oil and rubbed with cotton wool, after which gold leaf is evenly applied all over it and gently washed with water when it comes away from all the unfigured parts.

A coarse kind of brown sugar is made in the Shwe-doung and Maha-tha-man townships from the juice of the palm tree. The *tari* drawn in the morning is at once boiled to prevent fermentation and is then collected in large pots and boiled again, with continual stirring, till it gets thick when it is allowed to cool till it can be rolled into lumps with the hands or spread upon boards to dry. The price varies from Rs. 20 to Rs. 22-8-0 per 100 viss (365 lbs.) The pots, both for drawing off *tari* from the tree, which cost about Rs. two the 100, and for boiling the sugar, which cost about Rs. 10 the 100, are made in the dry season in Prome and Shwe-doung ; when a good workman will realize a profit of about Rs. 100. In 1877 there were 500 sugar-boilers.

Cutch is manufactured in large quantities in the more wooded townships of Shwe-lay, Maha-tha-man and Pa-doung throughout the greater portion of the year : in the hot weather the work ceases. Three men generally work together, selecting a spot where water is easily obtainable and *Acacia catechu* trees abound. One man is employed in cutting down the trees and in driving the buffaloes that drag them close to the furnace, another in taking off the outside wood and in cutting the heart into chips, and the third in attending to the fires and boiling the chips down. The chips are put into pots holding about 10 viss, or four and a half gallons, each and these are filled up with water and the whole boiled for about 12 hours. When the water is boiled down to one-half of its original quantity the chips are taken out and the liquor is poured into large iron pans and again boiled and stirred till it attains the consistency of syrup ; the pans are then taken off the fire and the stirring continued till they are cool when the contents are spread on leaves in a wooden frame and left for the night ; in the morning the mass is dry, caked and ready to be cut up into pieces for the market. The chips are boiled down twice but there is not much cutch extracted by the second boiling. The daily outturn varies from 36 to 55 lbs. The price varies considerably ; in 1868 it was about Rs. 5-12-0 for a maund of 80 pounds, in 1870 about Rs. 4-8-0, in 1873 about Rs. 2-5-6 and in 1876-77 Rs. 2-5-0 when it was selling at Rs. 9-13-0 in the Rangoon market. It is purchased for export and chiefly by Chinamen who send out brokers to the forests; a very small quantity is consumed locally. It is calculated that three men working steadily for eight months can make about 3,650 lbs. expending for pots, food and buffaloes, Rs. 265. The pots are made chiefly at Meng-boo in Upper Burma and are brought down for sale. This manufacture gave occupation to 2,040 persons in 1877-78 and the number of cauldrons in each manufactory averages from three to four. Owing to the wasteful manner in which the forests were worked, the *Acacia catechu* was yearly getting scarcer. This has been checked, no tree can be felled without permission and a fee of Rs. 5 is charged for each cauldron used. The number of cauldrons in 1876-77 was 2,443 and 2,282 in 1877-78.

The actual amount of revenue obtained from this district during the

Revenue.

Burmese time can never be known as no amount was fixed but each official was almost entitled to extract as much as he could for himself over and above the quota which was due to the State and to the Myo-tsa or the person to whom the revenues had been allotted. These were fixed and were generally levied according to the settlement made by king Bhodaw Bhoora in 1783 and revised in 1801. The larger portion of this Imperial revenue, as it may be called, was raised by a rate on each family, fixed generally by the chief local authority but the assessment on each house was left to the Thoogyee. Certain royal lands near Prome were held by a class of persons called Lamaing on payment of a rent of half the produce, which was stored in the royal granaries at Prome, and they were exempted from all other taxation, a kind of tenure which existed nowhere else in the province. The amount remitted to the capital prior to the second Burmese war was Rs. 167,960.

The gross revenue realized during each of the first 10 years after the annexation, when Thayet and a small portion of Henzada (Tharrawaddy) were included, was, in rupees :—

YEAR.			Land Revenue.	Capitation tax.	Fisheries.	Excise.	All other items of Imperial revenue.*	Total.
1855-56	..	..	177,155	144,231	4,692	29,347	28,209	
1856-57	..	..	201,282	175,897	4,972	20,200	23,905	
1857-58	..	..	279,448	198,089	6,630	20,460	24,852	
1858-59	..	..	213,652	206,842	7,084	15,910	27,207	
1859-60	..	..	251,465	219,590	7,764	21,845	63,459	
1860-61	..	..	260,575	228,840	8,415	19,350	65,052	
1861-62	..	..	257,075	278,571	8,766	17,350	54,371	
1862-63	..	..	265,815	276,824	8,819	17,900	47,092	
1863-64	..	..	262,243	288,187	7,761	22,550	63,836	
1864-65	..	..	270,364	302,970	4,107	24,400	57,197	

* Customs are omitted.

The revenue arranged under the same heads during 1869-70, the year before the division of the district, and during each year subsequently was, in rupees :—

Year.			Land Revenue.	Capitation tax.	Fisheries.	Excise.	All other items of Imperial revenue.	Total.
1869-70	..	..	284,574	340,069	9,429	72,038	96,345	803,280
1870-71	..	..	229,061	248,988	7,973	14,072	67,618	567,712
1871-72	..	..	228,139	252,028	8,677	11,428	57,905	558,177
1872-73	..	..	227,028	255,946	11,811	40,997	47,021	582,803
1873-74	..	..	227,652	258,826	11,902	55,412	46,088	599,880
1874-75	..	..	225,072	261,632	14,575	61,729	45,423	608,432
1875-76	..	..	227,491	262,364	12,029	69,137	50,388	621,409
1876-77	..	..	231,290	267,573	12,405	74,567	60,618	646,353

The gross revenues and the expenditure on officers of all kinds together with the balances available during the last seven years were, in rupees :—

					Gross Revenue.	Cost of officers of all kinds.	Balance.
1871-72	..	..	..	..	558,177	125,424	422,753
1872-73	..	..	..	..	582,800	119,091	462,712
1873-74	..	..	..	..	599,883	131,626	467,254
1874-75	..	..	..	..	608,432	159,181	449,251
1875-76	..	..	..	..	621,409	147,703	473,706
1876-77	..	..	..	..	646,353	235,790	410,563
1877-78	..	..	..	..	685,747	159,137	426,610

The local revenues are derived from town funds raised in towns by a rate on the houses, from the rent of market-stalls, cattle-pound fees and fines, cattle-market fees, &c. and the five per cent. cess fund, an addition of five per cent. to the demand for land and fishery revenue, the proceeds of which are devoted in fixed proportions to the support of the village police, the rural post, education and local roads. There is also the municipal fund raised in Prome and administered by the Municipality which is treated of elsewhere. The amounts thus raised during the three years ending with 1877-78, excluding the local revenue of Prome, were :—

| 1875-76 | .. | Rs. 75,421 | | 1876-77 | .. | Rs. 88,360 |
| | | 1877-78 | .. | Rs. 63,231. | | |

The principal towns are :—

Prome, the head-quarters of the district, which is situated in 18° 47' 53" N.

Towns. and 95° 18' 18" E. on the left bank of the Irrawaddy at the mouth of the Na-weng on the great north road from Rangoon. It is now the terminus of the Irrawaddy Valley (State) Railway.

To the south and south-east it is closed in by low pagoda-topped hills, on one of which stands the conspicuous gilded Shwe Tshan-daw. It is the third largest town in the province, having a population which from 21,000 souls in 1863 had risen to 25,631 in 1873 and to 26,826 in 1877. In 1862 it was burned down and was re-laid out in straight and broad streets by the then Deputy Commissioner, Major (now Colonel) David Brown. It contains Court-houses, two Schools—one for boys and one for girls,—a Hospital and Dispensary, a Lock-hospital, a Telegraph office, and two good and well supplied bazaars besides fish and meat markets, a Travellers' bungalow, Circuit-house, a Baptist chapel and two churches—one for the Anglicans, in course of construction, the other for the Roman Catholics finished. Its principal manufactures are silk cloths, large gilt boxes for holding palm-leaf books, and lacquer ware.

Shwe-doung, in 18° 42' N". and 95° 17' 30" E. is on the left bank of the Irrawaddy at the mouth of the little Koo-la stream, eight miles below Prome, on the north road from Rangoon. It has grown up since the occupation of Pegu by the British from the junction of the two villages of Meng-day to the north and Pyouk-tshiep, or more properly Myouk-tshiep, to the south, lying one on each side of the Koo-la; the old town of Shwe-doung, which has dwindled to a mere village, is some miles further south. In 1866 it had a population of 8,700 souls, which in 1873 had increased to 12,654, and in 1877 to 13,588. It is well laid out with roads and has a flourishing bazaar and a Court-house where the Extra Assistant Commissioner in charge of the township of the same name holds his court. The inhabitants are merchants, rice cultivators, weavers and coolies. A large trade is done in rice produced in the fertile tract lying to the south and east of the town. The local revenue in 1877-78 was Rs. 24,989.

Pa-doung, in 18° 41' N". and 95° 13' 20" E., the head-quarters of the township of the same name and of the sub-division, is on the right bank of the Irrawaddy about 15 miles below Prome on the road across the Toung-goop pass into Arakan. It is somewhat celebrated in Burmese history as having been the place of refuge of Tha-moon-da-riet, king of Prome, at the end of the first century of the Christian era, when the Prome kingdom was destroyed by internal dissensions and by the Kan-ran tribe from Arakan and, many centuries later in 1784 A. D., the place of assembly of the Burman army which conquered Arakan and annexed it to the Burman empire. In both the Anglo-Burman wars there was some fighting here. It is a long narrow town, hemmed in by rice fields on one side and by the Irrawaddy on the other, with one main street running through it along the river bank, a portion of the Toung-goop road. It has never been a large place : in 1868 it had a population of 2,866 souls—Burmese, Shan, Khyeng, Chinese, and natives of Madras and Bengal—and in 1877 of 2,897. It has a bazaar fairly well supplied with the produce of the township, such as rice, chillies, onions, tobacco, sessamum, stick-lac, cutch and a kind of matting. A small local revenue of Rs. 2,994 was raised in 1877-78.

Poung-day, in 18° 27' 9" N. and 95° 34' 49" E., the head-quarters of the Poung-day sub-division of the district, is situated in extensive rice plains, between the Wai-gyee and Kyat rivers on the north and south, 33 miles south-east of Prome, on the main road from Rangoon to the north where the old road from Ta-pwon in the Henzada district joins it, and on the Railway.

It has a good bazaar and a Court-house in which the Assistant Commissioner holds his Court; there are also a Public Works Department inspection bungalow, a Dispensary, a small Lock-up and a Railway station. In 1868 it had a population of 5,549 souls, in 1873 of 5,630 and in 1878 of 5,390. In 1877-78 the local revenue was Rs. 13,238.

Ta-beng-ta-ga, not far from Poung-day, *Peng-ga-daw*, which almost forms a portion of Poung-day, *Toung-loon-myo*, which almost forms a portion of Shwe-doung, and *Kyee-thay* and *Gnyoung-tsa-re* on the right bank of the Irrawaddy, the last near the southern confines of the district, are large and flourishing villages.

The climate of Prome to some extent resembles that of other districts in Burma but it is much drier. The seasons succeed each other with equal regularity. The returns of the nine years ending with 1875 give the rainfall and temperature as :—

Climate.

Year.	RAINFALL, IN INCHES.				AVERAGE TEMPERATURE IN THE SHADE.								
					May.			July.			December.		
	January to May.	June to September.	October to December.	Total.	Sunrise.	2 P.M.	Sunset.	Sunrise.	2 P.M.	Sunset.	Sunrise.	2 P.M.	Sunset.
1867..	8·53	20·27	6·33	35·13	82	92	90	77	86	83	63	80	78
1868..	5·80	35·90	5·20	48·50	80	92	89	77	84	81	65	80	80
1869..	4·40	23·50	5·90	34·00	70	102	99	72	90	82	68	86	80
1870..	9·94	32·73	3·54	46·21	78	88	83	76	88	82	64	80	77
1871..	13·55	38·14	11·42	63·11	78	86	82	76	82	80	64	80	77
1872..	6·11	33·75	6·76	46·62	{94 {80	10 A.M. 4 P.M.	.. ..	85 72	10 A.M. 4 P.M.	.. ..	84 65	10 A.M. 4 P.M.	.. ..
1873..	5·41	35·00	7·57	47·98	{81 {97	10 A.M. 4 P.M.	.. ..	76 81	10 A.M. 4 P.M.	.. ..	82 69	10 A.M. 4 P.M.	.. ..
1874..	4·46	23.41	5·96	33·83	80	94	88	77	86	81	65	84	77
1875..	8·75	30·76	6·19	45·70	79	92	81	77	81	80	63	78	75

For the next two years the returns give :—

Year.	RAINFALL, IN INCHES.				THERMOMETRICAL RANGE.											
					May.				July.				December.			
	January to May.	June to September.	October to December.	Total.	Mean of maximum readings.	Mean of minimum readings.	Highest reading.	Lowest reading.	Mean of maximum readings.	Mean of minimum readings.	Highest reading.	Lowest reading.	Mean of maximum readings.	Mean of minimum readings.	Highest reading.	Lowest reading.
1876 ...	5·90	37·16	5·35	48·41	89·20	82·70	100	75	84·40	76·20	87	73	82·10	62·40	83	60
1877 ...	3·89	41·77	7·80	53·46	101·74	80·31	106	76	85·22	76·12	89	74	82·8	65·6	87	63

In the Burmese time the district was divided into small independent
Administration. tracts, the officers in charge even when not of high
rank communicating directly with the Court at Ava,
administered by Won, Myo-thoogyee, or Tsit-ke, under whom were Taik
Thoogyee, Rwa or Village Thoogyee and Kyedangyee. The Taik Thoogyeeships were generally hereditary offices and on the annexation the incumbents
were, as far as possible, left undisturbed; where they had joined their fortunes with the Burmans or had been killed relatives were, as a rule, appointed
by the British, and in some cases false claimants of hereditary title to appointments which never had been hereditary appeared and were registered.
Under the Thoogyee, each of whom had two peons, were appointed
goungs over, on an average, every hundred families, receiving a salary of
Rs. 10 a month and aiding the Thoogyee in revenue and police duties,
forming in fact a village constabulary as well as being subordinate revenue
officials. In the Burmese time they were appointed by no fixed rule
but at the caprice of the Thoogyee. The district was divided into
tracts called townships, each under a Myo-ook or Extra Assistant Commissioner, entrusted with moderate Fiscal, Judicial, and Police powers. It was
in time found absolutely necessary to reduce the number of Thoogyee and
this was effected by the amalgamation of circles as occasion occurred. At
first the incumbents, whether really hereditary or not, held strongly to their
appointments but as work increased and prices rose many resigned and
others were dismissed for embezzlement and even for dacoity and other
similar offences, and adjoining tracts were joined: the "circle" now
approaches more nearly to the old Taik, a designation erroneously given by
the English to each village tract, no distinction being drawn between the
Rwa-thoogyee or headman of a tract and the Taik-thoogyee or headman of
a circle. The number of Thoogyee has thus been reduced to 140. The
separate jurisdictions also were amalgamated and formed into townships:
Pa-doung on the west bank of the Irrawaddy remaining as the Pa-doung
township, at first under an Extra Assistant Commissioner but now under
the immediate charge of the officer in charge of the sub-division. On
the east bank in the north and east Thoo-won-a-bho, Kyoon-htoon, O-
shit-toung, Ra-thay, Tsa-leng-ga-thoo, Meng-ga-la-doon, Ma-ha-tha-
man and Mo-goop have been formed into the Ma-ha-tha-man township, with the head-quarters at Hpoom-ma-thien, a few miles east of
Prome, and containing 50 circles in 1877. Farther east and north-east,
occupying the whole of the slopes of the Pegu Roma in this district, Myo-
doung, Ka-la-thien-ga, Shwe-lay and Rwa-bien, form the Shwe-lay township
divided into 14 revenue circles, with the head-quarters at Pouk-khoung east
of Prome on the Pouk-khoung stream. Eng-ma and Poung-day have been
united into the Poung-day sub-division under an Assistant Commissioner and
an Extra Assistant Commissioner, with its head-quarters at Poung-day and
containing 35 revenue circles, the richest and most fertile part of the country
except, possibly, Shwe-doung which is on the bank of the Irrawaddy occupying the country in one of its great bends with its head-quarters at Shwe-
doung and contains 17 circles.

The prominent statistics of each township in 1877-78 were :—

Name.	Area, in square miles.	Population.	CHIEF TOWN.		Villages.
			Name.	Population.	
Prome	3	26,826	....	..	..
Ma-ha-tha-man ..	565⅔	54,285	Hpoom-ma-thien ..	..	407
Shwe-lay	722⅔	23,776	Ponk-khoung ..	..	232
Poung-day	328⅔	82,000	Poung-day ..	5,390	486
Shwe-doung ..	80	52,127	Shwe-doung ..	13,588	277
Pa-doung	1,188	43,164	Pa-doung ..	2,897	252

In April 1870, Thayet, up to that time a sub-division of Prome, was separated from it and formed into an independent jurisdiction.

Over the whole is a Deputy Commissioner with three Assistants, two stationed in Prome and one in Poung-day, and five Extra Assistants, one in the town of Prome. In 1862-63 the existing regular Police was organized, and in 1877 consisted of a Superintendent with 35 subordinate officers and 343 men paid from Provincial revenues, and seven officers and 76 men paid from local revenues, besides a small extra force entertained annually for eight days during the fairs at the Shwe Tshan-daw and at the Shwe-nat-toung and Nga-myek-hna, in the Shwe-doung and Pa-doung townships respectively. Of this force 24 men and three subordinate officers were employed as guards over the treasury and the lock-up or gaol, and 83 were on duty in towns, leaving 316 men for general district work. The total strength of all grades of the Provincial Police gives about one man to every seven square miles and for every 603 souls, excluding those in towns where there are Municipal or town Police. The whole cost in 1877 was Rs. 96,811 of which Rs. 67,334 were paid from the Provincial revenues.

The education of the district was for some years solely in the hands of the Booddhist monks and of a few native laymen who established small village schools, and was confined to reading and writing, even simple Arithmetic not being taught ; and not only was this all that the monks even professed to teach, but girls were left almost entirely uneducated, *almost*, for there were some lay schools in which a few girls, though very few, managed to pick up a little knowledge of reading and writing. Almost immediately after the annexation of Pegu the American Baptist Missionaries opened village schools and a Normal School in Prome, and in 1866 the State established a middle class school in the same town. In 1871 a girls' school was opened by the Society for the Propagation of the Gospel, and in 1873 the State started lower class schools in Shwe-doung and Poung-day. The education given in the State school in Prome is in English and Burmese, in Arithmetic, Geography and History. In 1876-77 it had an average daily attendance of 108 pupils, Burmese, Chinese, Eurasians, Mahomedans and Hindoos. The fees paid by the scholars are not high, varying from eight annas to a rupee a month, and these in 1876-77 produced Rs. 1,312, the remaining cost of the school, Rs. 4,459, being defrayed by the State. The girls' school is under the Rangoon Ladies Association and receives a grant-in-aid from the State, and at the end of 1876-77 it had 103 pupils on the rolls, of whom nine were studying English. Its cost, Rs. 2,453, was defrayed partly by subscriptions, donations, fees, fines, &c., (Rs. 478), partly by the State grant of Rs. 2,486.* An American Baptist school for girls which formerly existed was closed in 1876. The object of the town schools, which are supported from local funds, as first started was to teach the usual branches of a middle class education entirely through the medium of the vernacular language. At Shwe-doung the town school at first attracted but few pupils, and at Poung-day the inhabitants, before the school was opened, had asked for one where English might be taught, a request which they repeated after the opening of the vernacular school. Arrangements were accordingly made for reorganizing these two schools and they are now Anglo-Vernacular. The number of pupils, and receipts and expenditure during 1876-77 were :—

Town.	Pupils.				Receipts, in rupees.			Expenditure, in rupees.
	On the rolls at end of year.	Average monthly attendance.	Learning English	Learning Burmese	Fees, fines, &c.	From the State.	Total.	
Shwe-doung ..	22	27	19	3	175	1,235	1,410	1,410
Poung-day ..	55	50	36	19	367	975	1,342	1,342

In pursuance of the scheme for utilizing the monasteries as far as possible in giving a sounder education to the people than that which these institutions had hitherto imparted a deputy Inspector was appointed in 1873-74 to inspect those monasteries in the Thayet and Prome districts the head monk of which would allow his pupils to be examined and to receive the prizes which the State offered to successful scholars. The deputy Inspector's attention was not confined to monasteries but lay village schools were admitted to share in the advantages offered if the proprietors chose, and to such as wished it and were thought worthy, the State appointed salaried teachers and the school became liable to regular inspection, the deputy Inspector acting merely as examiner in the other cases. The results of the examination in this district in 1877-78 were :—

Successful Schools ..	Monastic	..	..	..	85
	Lay	..	..	..	29
Number of scholars attending.	Monasteries ; boys		..	..	2,722
	Lay-schools { boys		..	..	798
	{ girls		..	..	344
Number of prize-winners.	Monastic Schools ; boys		..	..	219
	Lay-schools { boys		..	..	145
	{ girls		..	..	84

* This includes a building grant of Rs. 2,000.

The gaol was first constructed in 1856 and in that year contained an average of 215 prisoners. It consisted of a substantial masonry wall with wooden and mat buildings in the interior. It thus continued for 10 years, prisoners sentenced to more than two years' imprisonment being sent to Rangoon. In 1866-67, when the gaols of the province were classified and the Gaol Department, under an Inspector-General appointed in 1864, began to take shape, the Prome gaol was reduced to a lock-up and the construction of a new gaol at Thayetmyo commenced, the prisoners from Prome being transferred thither on its completion in 1868-69. In 1869-70 the lock-up was completed. It consisted of wooden buildings raised 10 feet from the ground on masonry and surrounded by a brick wall. In 1873-74 it had, including those remaining from 1872-73, 1,226 prisoners of all classes, of whom 813 were acquitted or released on payment of fine, expiry of sentence, &c., two escaped, one was executed, and 825 were transferred to other gaols (prisoners sentenced to more than two months' imprisonment but not more than two years were sent to Thayetmyo, and prisoners sentenced to more than two years to Rangoon). In so small a lock-up it is difficult to carry out any system of intramural labour which shall be at once punitive and remunerative : the prisoners do not remain long enough to learn any trade and it is impossible to employ each one at his own, even supposing that it is of a nature to be rendered effective as a punishment. The labour on which the prisoners were chiefly employed in 1877 was cotton-ginning, rice-husking, soorkee-pounding, that is pounding bricks into dust to be mixed with lime and sand to form mortar for building purposes, and gardening. The average earning of each prisoner employed in hard labour was rather over Rs. 13-11-6 and the nett earnings, after deducting the cost of raw material, was a little over Rs. 11-11-6 thus reducing the cost of the lock-up to the State to Rs. 6,110-5-0 or rather more than Rs. 94 for each prisoner during the year. In 1878 the site was taken over by the Railway department, the prisoners were removed to Thayetmyo and the lock-up pulled down. No prison now exists in Prome.

The telegraph lines in the district are those which run from Rangoon to Thayet and from Prome to Toung-goop in Arakan. The first follows the main road and passes through Poung-day and Shwe-doung to Prome, where the office is situated, and thence northward towards Thayetmyo. It consists of a single wire supported on wooden posts. The other crosses the bottom of the Irrawaddy, a distance of 1,375, yards at the southern end of Prome town, and then follows the right bank of the Irrawaddy through Pa-doung and across the Roma mountains. This also consists of a single line supported on wooden posts. In 1877-78 the number of messages was :—

Sent	..	..	..	..	..	3,484
Transit	..	..	..	..	..	54,006
Received	..	..	..	..	..	3,172

The large number of messages which passed through Prome is due to the fact that all messages to and from the south from and to Thayetmyo and Upper Burma as well as messages from the whole of the province east of the Irrawaddy, including Rangoon, to Calcutta and Europe and *vice versâ* pass through this office.

The principal road in the district is the great northern road from Rangoon to Mye-dai. Entering near Poung-day it strikes the Irrawaddy near Shwe-doung and follows the bank of the river to Prome; thence it proceeds west and crossing the Na-weng at Nat-ta-leng turns north. Shortly after leaving Poung-day it crosses the Wek-poot stream by an iron bridge of 90 feet span, finished in 1871-72 at a total cost of Rs. 35,000, and at Nat-ta-leng the Na-weng is crossed by a bridge consisting of three spans of 60 and three of 22 feet on massive teak piles which was completed in 1873-74 at a cost of Rs. 10,890. The whole distance is now open for cart traffic at all seasons of the year, and is much used south of Prome by the numerous waggons which bring the rice of the fertile Poung-day plains to the river bank at Shwe-doung for export. From Poung-day a road ran southward to Ta-pwon in the Henzada district, crossing the Kan-tha stream by a bridge of two spans of 60 feet and two of 12 feet on wooden piles, completed in 1874-75 at a cost of some Rs. 7,000 and built to replace one carried away a few years earlier by the timber and refuse brought down from the forests during a heavy flood. The river has now silted up in the centre and flows round both ends of the bridge, cutting it off from either shore and it is, therefore, being pulled down. Soon after the annexation of Pegu a military road was constructed across the Arakan hills : it ran along the river bank from opposite Prome to Pa-doung and then turned westwards to the hills, but it is not in good repair. A good road runs from Prome to Pouk-khoung, the head-quarters of the Shwe-lay township. The Irrawaddy Valley (State) Railway traverses this district; the stations are at Poung-day, Tsheng-myee-tshwai, Hmaw-za and Prome. Besides the main roads there are numerous cart tracks in the plains leading from village to village, all traversible by carts with ease during the dry weather. The mails are carried from Rangoon by the railway daily and thence to Thayetmyo by the steamers of the Irrawaddy Flotilla Company which arrive from Rangoon once a week.

PWAI-THA.—A revenue circle in the Taroop-maw township of the Henzada district which now includes the neighbouring circles of Reng-she and Eng-daing-poo : it lies to the east of the great Eng-daing or Eng forest which extends north into the Prome district. Towards the west the ground is undulating and covered with Eng (*Dipterocarpus tuberculatus*). In 1877 the population was 2,510, the land revenue Rs. 1,588, the capitation tax Rs. 2,315 and the gross revenue Rs. 4,628.

PWE-DOO.—A Police post in the Koo-byoo circle, Meng-doon township, Thayet district, at which are stationed about 20 men : near the post is a small village of some dozen houses.

PWO.—One of the three great families of Kareng, so called by another great branch, the Sgaw, and by the English. They designate themselves by the word *Sho*, and the Burmese name for them is *Myit-khyeng*, that is river Khyeng, or *Talaing Kareng*. They are found throughout the Tenasserim division from Mergui to a little above Tsit-toung living in distinct clusters of villages and in Bassein, Thoon-khwa and Rangoon, where they have to a great extent adopted the manners, dress and religion of the Burmans and Talaing. Though the Sgaw, are less muscular than the Pwo, with whom they had a bitter feud, yet they succeeded, by numerous forays before the cession of Tenasserim to the British, in diminishing their numbers in the Mergui district by about one-half and were preparing for another raid when the English took possession of the country.

The sub-divisions are Mop-gha, Ta-roo, Shoung, Ha-shwie and Gai-kho, all of whom wear trowsers except the Mop-gha; these wear tunics, the distinguishing mark of which is a *broad* band of embroidery at the bottom, that of the Pa-koo Sgaw having a narrow band. Those living in the south invariably build their houses so as to face the east; in other respects they differ but little from the rest of their race.

PWON.—A little river in the Thayet district, which rises on the west of the Myeng-ba range, in the Thee-ro-pya-gyee hill, a few miles north of the frontier and enters the Thayet township near the frontier village of Thayet-myeng about nine miles west of the Irrawaddy and flows into that river about a mile and a half north of Thayet-myo. The banks are steep and the bed gravelly and very rocky. Boats of 500 baskets burden can ascend as far as the village of Re-bwek but the river is little used on account of the strength of the current and its sudden rises and falls. In the dry weather it contains only a tiny stream of water often running underneath sandbanks. It has some affluents, such as the Zee-hpyoo and the Tsway-daw but none of them are more than mountain streams.

PWON-GYEE.—A village of some 50 houses in the Nga-hlaing-kyoon circle, Thayet township, Thayet district, on the Pwon stream, near the somewhat smaller village of Meng-rwa. There is a small patch of rice cultivation near these two villages.

PWOT-TSOO.—A village of 862 inhabitants in 1877 in the Pouk-taw circle of the Ta-pwon township of the Henzada district. Its name is said to have been derived from the fact of its having been the residence of many locally-noted turners.

PYA-KYWON.—A revenue circle in the Oo ree-toung (East) township Akyab district. In 1877 the population was 1,266, the land revenue Rs. 5,450, the capitation tax Rs. 1,685 and the gross revenue Rs. 7,417.

PYA-LO.—A large and increasing village in 19° 8' N. Lat. and 95° 16' E. Long., in the circle of the same name in the Mye-dai township, Thayet district, containing 1,286 inhabitants. It is on the main road from Rangoon to Mye-dai and on the left bank of the Irrawaddy, opposite to the Poo-hto hill, at the narrowest portion of the river in this district. Pya-lo has for many years been of some importance. Symes, who visited it at the end of the last century, calls it a town.

PYA-LO.—A circle in the Mye-dai township, Thayet district, on the bank of the Irrawaddy, having an area of 16 square miles of which about 900 acres are under cultivation, mainly with rice. The population in 1872 numbered 1,498 souls, almost all Burmans, who owned 634 head of cattle and paid Rs. 2,200 as taxes of which Rs. 1,460 were on account of capitation tax and the rest on account of land revenue. The Thoogyee of this circle is also in charge of Pyeng-bouk and Ta-zan, making up the area over which he has a revenue supervision to 50 square miles. In 1877 the population of the three was 3,754, the land revenue Rs. 2,447, the capitation tax Rs. 3,782 and the gross revenue Rs. 6,449.

PYA-MA-LAW.—One of the many mouths of the Irrawaddy. At the town of Shwe-loung, in 16° 44' 30" N. and 95° 23' 30" E., it leaves the Pan-ta-naw river, which continues to the sea and with the Eng-tay and other anastomosing creeks debourhes at the Irrawaddy mouth, and runs for about six miles to the N. N. E. Here it curves round W. and S. S. W. and after a course of 90 miles falls into the sea in about 15° 50' N. and 94° 48' E., having, 15 miles above, sent off a large branch eastward to the sea called the Pyeng-tha-loo. Throughout its course it is connected with the Irrawaddy and the Rwe mouths by numerous large and inosculating creeks. It is navigable throughout its whole length by river steamers. At its mouth which is four miles wide, is an extensive bar. The Pyeng-tha-loo at its mouth is about two miles wide and five and a half fathoms deep.

PYA-POON.—A township in the Thoon-khwa district, lying between Bassein on the west, the Bay of Bengal on the south, Thoon-khwa on the north and the Rangoon district on the east. It includes Pya-poon on the south and Eng-tay on the north, formerly independent jurisdic-tions. The whole of the country is low and especially towards the south intersected by numerous inosculating tidal creeks. The plains are in places covered with tree and scrub forest and subject to inundation but elsewhere are well cultivated with rice and other products.

The principal village is Pya-poon, on the creek of that name, where the Extra Assistant Commissioner in charge resides and holds his court.

It is divided into eight revenue circles. In 1877 the population was 44,207, the land revenue Rs. 145,585, the capitation tax Rs. 52,513 and the gross revenue Rs. 263,227.

PYA-POON.—A creek in the Thoon-khwa district forming one of the numerous mouths of the Irrawaddy. It branches off southwards from the To or China Bakir near Kwon-ta and has here, at low water, a depth of three or four feet, but elsewhere it has not less than 12 feet. It is tidal throughout, but the water is sweet throughout the year as low as Pya-poon village. The banks are somewhat steep and muddy and are fringed with forest.

PYA-POON.—A revenue circle in the north-western portion of the town-ship of the same name in the Thoon-khwa district. The northern and western portion of the country is covered with tree and cane forest while the eastern consists of a large plain : the land along the banks of the streams is low and subject to inundation during the rains. A considerable revenue is derived from the fishery and net tax. In 1877 the population was 7,220, the land revenue Rs. 10,087, the capitation tax Rs. 8,135 and the gross revenue Rs. 28,885.

PYA-POON.—A village in the Thoon-khwa district on the Pya-poon mouth of the Irrawaddy with a population of between 1,500 and 2,000 souls, who are mainly engaged in cultivation and in sea-fishing, many resorting during the season to fishing villages on the coast. Lat. 16° 16' N. Long. 95° 40' E.

PYAW-BHWAY.—A large village in the Rangoon district on both banks of the tidal Ka-ma-oung creek about four and a half miles due west of the Rangoon river. The creek is spanned by several high and good wooden bridges broad enough for carts but impassable by all except foot travellers by reason of their steepness and of the central portion being raised above the two ends and approached by a step. This highly inconvenient construction is to allow of the passage of boats which come up in numbers as almost all the rice grown in the fertile Pyaw-bhway and Ko-doung circles is exported by this route. There are, comparatively, but few houses on the north or left bank and these are occupied by Talaing ; on the south or right bank, where the inhabitants are Burmans with a very few Chinese and Mahomedans, the houses are in several rows with roads between them and cross roads running at right angles. There are several pagodas and small zayats. As the water a few feet below the surface is brackish there are no wells, but the inhabitants supply themselves from tanks of which there are three, lined with masonry. In 1878 the population was 3,766. The inhabitants are cultivators and rice cleaners, a very large quantity being husked in the village and sent as cleaned rice to the Rangoon market and in consequence there is a vast quantity of husk which is spread upon the roads. Amongst the rice cleaners the men make about Rs. 25 a month and the women and girls from eight to twelve annas a day. Lat. 16° 40′ N. Long. 96° 13′ E.

PYAW-BHWAY.—A revenue circle towards the north-east of the Angyee township of the Rangoon district. It is bounded on the north-east by the Rangoon river, on the south by the Kha-noung stream and the A-gat-ro separating it from the Ko-doung circle, on the west by the Gnyoung-lien stream separating it from Kaw-hmoo, and on the north by the Ka-ma-oung separating it from Ma-hlaing. Its greatest breadth is about seven miles and its greatest length the same. The population is a very mixed one, Kareng and Talaing predominating. To the north and east there is some tree forest but the rest of the circle is open waste or under rice for which its soil is well suited.

The population and agricultural stock during the last five years were :—

YEAR.	POPULATION.						AGRICULTURAL STOCK.						
	Burmans.	Talaing.	Kareng.	Shan.	All others.	Total.	Buffaloes.	Cows, bulls and bullocks.	Goats and sheep.	Pigs.	Carts.	Ploughs.	Boats.
1873-74 ..	..	..	..	..	..	..	726	960	..	..	338	..	405
1874-75 ..	1,427	3,763	1,158	81	56	6,485	855	1,233	..	..	470	696	534
1875-76 ..	2,965	3,083	1,354	22	100	7,528	643	1,275	23	228	409	710	267
1876-77 ..	4,606	1,590	1,422	..	101	7,719	691	1,266	3	226	385	727	272
1877-78 ..	5,123	1,084	1,658	37	88	7,990	781	1,249	4	346	419	1,155	653

and the area under cultivation and the revenue :—

YEAR.	AREA, IN ACRES.			REVENUE, IN RUPEES.			
	Rice.	Garden.	Total.	Land.	Capitation tax.	All other taxes.	Total.
1873-74 ..	12,411	8	12,419	27,706	8,592	1,223	37,521
1874-75 ..	14,448	8	14,455	32,073	7,965	1,218	41,256
1875-76 ..	14,787	8	14,795	31,576	8,980	2,085	42,641
1876-77 ..	16,340	8	16,348	34,297	9,525	1,202	45,024
1877-78 ..	16,429	8	16,437	34,810	9,912	28	44,750

PYAW-BHWAY-KYWON.—An island in the Irrawaddy included in the Kyan-kheng circle of the township of the same name in the Henzada district, on which is a village of the same name with 809 inhabitants in 1877.

PYEE-KHYA.—A revenue circle in the north of the Mergui district, adjoining Tavoy and separated from the sea by the Pyeng-bhoo circle. In 1877 the population was 1,435, the land revenue Rs. 512, the capitation tax Rs. 1,092 and the gross revenue Rs. 1,514.

PYEE-KYWON.—A revenue circle in the Mergui township of the Mergui district. In 1877 the population was 1,431, the land revenue Rs. 2,476, the capitation tax Rs. 906 and the gross revenue Rs. 3,382.

PYEE-TSO-GYEE.—A revenue circle in the Oo-ree-toung (East) township of the Akyab district. In 1877 the land revenue was Rs. 5,846, the capitation tax Rs. 2,282, the gross revenue Rs. 8,244 and the population 1,814.

PYENG-BENG-HLA.—A village in the Nga-pyeng circle, Mye-dai township, Thayet district, situated at the northern extremity of a large patch of rice cultivation which stretches northwards along the left bank of the Irrawaddy from near the village of Nga-pyeng.

PYENG-BHOO.—A revenue circle on the seacoast in the extreme north of the Mergui district adjoining Tavoy and lying on both banks of the Pa-louk stream. In 1877 the population was 3,583, the land revenue Rs. 2,672, the capitation tax Rs. 2,047 and the gross revenue Rs. 4,719.

PYENG-BHYOO.—A revenue circle in the Naaf township of the Akyab district. In 1877 the population was 1,728, the land revenue Rs. 3,850, the capitation tax Rs. 1,595 and the gross revenue Rs. 5,664.

PYENG-BHYOO-MAW.—A small revenue circle containing about 200 acres, well to the east of Kyouk-hpyoo town. In 1875 it had a population of 244 souls and produced a revenue of Rs. 529 of which Rs. 236 were derived from the land. In 1877 the population was 247, the land revenue Rs. 236, the capitation tax Rs. 303 and the gross revenue Rs. 710.

PYENG-BOON-GYEE.—A village in the Ma-yen-za-ya circle, Pegu township, Rangoon district, on both banks of the little stream of the same name where it is crossed by the main road. The inhabitants, who numbered 912 in 1878, are Talaing and are principally engaged in rice cultivation and in fishing. Lat. 17° 4' N., Long. 96° 39' E.

PYENG-BOUK.—A village in 19° 9' N. Lat. and 95° 16' 15" E. Long. in the Pya-lo circle, Mye-dai township, Thayet district. It is situated on the bank of the Irrawaddy, nearly at the northern end of a rice plain, in the southern portion of which is the large village of Pya-lo.

PYENG-BOUK.—A revenue circle in the Mye-dai township, Thayet district on the bank of the Irrawaddy. In 1871, on the resignation of the Thoogyee, this circle was placed under the Thoogyee of Pya-lo. The products are rice, sessamum, tobacco and plantains.

PYENG-DA-RAY.—A revenue circle in the Pya-poon township of the Thoon-khwa district on the seacoast, extending from the Pya-poon river west-wards to the Da-la. A very large number of the inhabitants are employed as fishermen and a very large revenue, far exceeding that produced from the land and by the capitation tax, is derived from the fishery and net tax. In 1877 the population was 3,579, the land revenue was Rs. 5,508, the capitation tax Rs. 5,110 and the gross revenue Rs. 31,528.

PYENG-DOUNG.—A village in the Shwe-ban-daw circle, Mye-dai township, Thayet district, containing about 66 houses.

PYENG-DOUNG-GOON.—A small village on the Mee-thwe-boot stream in the Nga-hlaing-khyoon circle, Thayet township, Thayet district, in which are stationed about 20 of the Frontier Police; it does not contain more than 20 or 30 houses.

PYENG-GYEE.—A revenue circle in the Prome district, on the right bank of the Irrawaddy along the lower portion of the little Kha-wa stream. The inhabitants are chiefly rice cultivators, but in Pyeng-gyee, a village on the bank of the Irrawaddy, there are some petty traders. In 1877 the population was 979, the land revenue Rs. 1,996, the capitation tax Rs. 1,088 and the gross revenue Rs. 3,239.

PYENG-GYEE.—An island in the Tavoy river, called Crab Island in the charts, about 24 miles below Tavoy.

PYENG-GYEE.—A large village in the Pa-doung township of the Prome district in 18° 30' 50" N. and 95° 9' 40" E. on the right bank of the Irrawaddy just above Htoon-bho, divided into two distinct portions called Pyeng-gyee and Pyeng-gyee Myouk-bhek. It is inhabited by cultivators and petty merchants who supply the villages in the interior with the goods brought up and down the Irrawaddy by the trading boats.

PYENG-KA-THA.—A village in the Henzada district in 17° 18' 40" N. and 95° 33' 40" E. In the neighbourhood of the village is a large clump of mango trees near which the British force encamped when in pursuit of the rebel chief Myat Htoon in 1852-53.

PYENG-KHA-RAING.—A village in the revenue circle of the same name in the Nga-poo-taw township, Bassein district, on the Kha-louk-thaik creek near the mouth of the Bassein river, in 15° 57' N. and 94° 28' E. Near this village are some large rice plains. The inhabitants are cultivators, salt-makers, traders, handicraftsmen and fishermen, the last of whom leave Pyeng-kha-raing in the fishing season to form temporary fishing hamlets

528

such as Kan-tshiep and Zee-thoung. Some of the best varieties of nga-pee manufactured in the Bassein district are made here. It contains a Police-station.

PYENG-KHA-RAING.—A revenue circle in the Nga-poo-taw township, Bassein district, having an area of about 40 square miles, occupying the extreme southern end of the cluster of contiguous islands which lie in the mouth of the Bassein river; it forms a rocky promontory running out into the sea in a southerly direction; the northern portion of it is covered with alluvial deposit but in the south the limestone rises abruptly to the surface. The rocky cliffs at Poorian Point have a perpendicular height of nearly 40 feet. On the western side of this circle there are some large rice plains but the remainder is thickly covered with forest. The inhabitants, Talaing and Burmans, are principally engaged in cultivation, in fishing, and in salt and nga-pee-making. The principal village is Pyeng-kha-raing. In 1877 the population was 1,426, the land revenue Rs. 1,469, the capitation tax Rs. 1,552 and the gross revenue Rs. 5,352.

PYENG-KHYA-TSHIEP.—A large village in the Toung-loon circle, Kyoon-pyaw or Tsam-bay-roon township, Bassein district, on the western bank of the Re-gyee, a tributary of the Da-ga. The inhabitants, who are engaged principally in cultivation, numbered 590 in 1877. A considerable quantity of rice and of timber is exported.

PYENG-KHYOUNG.—A revenue circle in the Oo-ree-toung (east) township, Akyab district. In 1877 the land revenue was Rs. 2,569, the capitation tax Rs. 1,330, the gross revenue Rs. 4,048 and the population 1,126.

PYENG-MA-AING.—A revenue circle in the Ma-ha-tha-man township of the Prome district to the eastward of Prome. In 1877 the population was 463, the land revenue was Rs. 687, the capitation tax Rs. 470 and the gross revenue Rs. 1,224. It now includes Ran-daing.

PYENG-MA-BENG-HLA.—A village in the Tha-bye-hla circle of the Kyoon-pyaw or Tsam-bay-roon township, Bassein district, on high land between the Da-ga and the Re-nouk stream. In 1877 it had 817 inhabitants.

PYENG-MA-BENG-HLA.—A revenue circle in the Re-gyee township, Bassein district, between the Bassein river on the west and the Ta-zeng-hla on the east. The country, which covers an area of some 33 square miles, is flat and open. The inhabitants are engaged to a considerable extent in fishing and some in cultivation. In 1877 the population was 2,365, the land revenue Rs. 4,298, the capitation tax Rs. 2,402 and the gross revenue Rs. 10,523.

PYENG-MA-GAN.—A village in the Rwon (East) circle of the Than-lyeng township, Rangoon district, in 16° 40′ 30″ N. and 96° 30′ E. on the stream of the same name, about five miles from its mouth, inhabited chiefly by Shan cultivators. The entire population numbered 1,249 in 1878.

PYENG-MA-NA.—A revenue circle in the Prome district occupying the hilly country in the south-west portion of the Pa-doung township and extending from the Arakan mountains eastward nearly to the Irrawaddy. The hills are densely wooded ; Teak (*Tectona grandis*), Pyeng-ga-do (*Xylia dolabriformis*), Htouk-kyan (*Terminalia macrocarpa*) and Sha (*Acacia catechu*) are found in tolerable abundance. In the more level portion to the eastward there is some rice cultivation and it is here that the larger villages, as Zee-goon and Pyeng-ma-na, are found. Nearer the Arakan mountains the cultivation is carried on entirely on the toungya system. The Tha-le-dan stream runs through this circle from east to west, the North and South Tha-le-dan rivers joining at the village Ma-toung ; on the latter, about five miles in a direct line E. S. E. from Ma-toung, are some salt springs. The inhabitants of the circle, Burmese and Khyeng, are engaged principally in cultivation and in boiling down cutch, and in 1877 numbered 3,806 souls. In that year the land revenue was Rs. 2,493, the capitation tax Rs. 1,345 and the gross revenue Rs. 7,036.

PYENG-MA-NA.—A village in the Pa-doung township, Prome district, in 18° 32' 40" N. and 95° 6' 15" E. on the Tha-le-dan river about five miles from its mouth ; the inhabitants are chiefly cultivators.

PYENG-THA-LOO.—The eastern mouth of the Pya-ma-law river, from which it bifurcates 15 miles from the sea. Its entrance is about two miles wide and five and a half fathoms deep.

PYENG-TSENG.—A semi-circular piece of water in the Henzada district, north of the Htoo lake, having a length of about five miles and a breadth of about 200 yards. It is bounded on the north, south and west by high ground the drainage from which supplies it with water.

PYE-YA.—A family of Kareng; so called by themselves, by the Sgaw called Bghai, q. v.

PYOO-GOON.—A village in the Prome district, about 10 miles east of Prome in 18° 48' 50" N. and 95° 28" E. inhabited principally by rice cultivators.

PYOON-WA.—A tidal creek in the Alay-kywon at the entrance to the Bassein river. It leaves the Thek-ngay-thoung mouth at Ouk-kywon-rwa, where it is 300 yards wide, and turns up north joining the Thek-ngay-thoung again near the north end of the island 13 miles higher up at Pyoon-wa-rwa where it is only 50 yards broad. Its total length is about 16 miles ; it has a depth of not less than 25 feet at either end so that large boats pass up and down.

PYOUNG-GYEE.—A small village of about 50 houses in the Kyan circle, Meng-doon township, Thayet district. It lies amongst the spurs of the Arakan mountains on the Pyoung rivulet, a small tributary of the Ma-htoon, and about two miles south of Lek-pan-daing on that river. In former years it was under the Thoogyee of Pyoung who was appointed by the Burmese Government with hereditary rights, but the family had disappeared at the time of the annexation of Pegu in 1853.

Q.—For all words which might commence with QU.—e.g. QUENG-HLA.—See KW.

RA-BA-TENG.—A revenue circle in the Kyouk-hpyoo district, towards the north-west of the Ramree township, now included in the Kan-gaw circle.

RA-HAING.—A revenue circle on the coast of the Kyien-ta-lee township, Sandoway district. a little to the north of the mouth of the Khwa,

49 square miles in extent with hardly any cultivation. It is now joined to Khwa-lek-wai.

RA-KHAING-RO.—A village in the Ka-tseng circle of the Hmaw-bhee township, Rangoon district, about three miles west of the Hlaing river, in the middle of a large but not very fertile tract of rice land. The inhabitants, who are principally Talaing and Kareng, are engaged in agriculture and in 1877 numbered 611.

RAI-DAING.—A revenue circle in the Prome district, Shwe-doung township, now joined to Sheng-ngay.

RAI-HLA.—A revenue circle in the Kyouk-gyee township, Shwe-gyeng district, in its northern portion lying on both banks and its southern on the right bank only of the Tsit-toung river or large village of Kyouk-gyee, south of the latitude of the town. It has an area of about 220 square miles and contains a good many lakes and ponds leased out as fisheries. In 1876-77 the population was 5,512, the land revenue Rs. 8,444, the capitation tax Rs. 4,940 and the gross revenue Rs. 14,628.

RAI-KYWON.—A revenue circle of the Kyouk-hpyoo district, about five square miles in area, consisting of a group of islands off the south coast of Cheduba and taking its name from the largest, marked in the charts as "Flat island", in the centre of which is a so-called volcanic hill about 200 feet high. The circle has a small population of 834 souls and produces rice and tobacco. In 1876-77 the land revenue was Rs. 1,161, the capitation tax Rs. 830 and the gross revenue Rs. 2,049.

RAI-LAING.—A revenue circle in the Tavoy district. It extends northward along the right bank of the Tavoy river from the Mro-houng frontier of the Moung-ma-gan circle, from which it is separated by the Kywai-gya, to the Re-ngay—both tributaries of the Tavoy river—which divides it in the north from the Za-dee circle : on the west it is bounded by the hills forming the western watershed of the valley of the Tavoy. In 1876-77 the population was 2,770, the land revenue Rs. 2,445, the capitation tax Rs. 2,129 and gross revenue Rs. 4,704.

RAMREE.—A township in the Kyouk-hpyoo district, about 437 square miles in extent, occupying the southern portion of the island of the same name, more properly called Ran-byai (the classical name is Rama-wad-dee), south of the Kyouk-hpyoo township. The principal products are rice, indigo and sugar ; for the extraction of the last 252 mills were at work in 1874 ; limestone is found in various places on the western and northern coasts and petroleum on the eastern. The head-quarters are at Ramree, towards the east coast. The principal villages are Kyouk-hta-ran with 1,032 inhabitants, Ran-thek with 586 inhabitants, Tsit-pya with 534 inhabitants, Tha-byee-kywon with 649 inhabitants, and Na-ga with 555 inhabitants.

It is now divided into 18 revenue circles, viz., Nga-kho-byeng, Theng-ga-nek, Hoon-toung-bhek, Hoon-myouk-bhek, Kha-moung-khyoung, Kyouk-khyoung (south), Kyouk-khyoung (north), Le-doung, Kan-daing, Ran-bouk, Kan-gaw, Alay-khyoung, Ran-byai Myoma (east), Ran-byai Myo-ma (south), Ran-thek, Theng-bha-kaing, Zee-kywon and Tsa-goo. In 1876-77 the population, composed mainly of Arakanese, was 46,838, the land revenue Rs. 39,149, the capitation tax Rs. 50,806 and the gross revenue Rs. 235,402.

RAMREE.—A small town near the eastern coast of the island of the same name, about 13 miles up the Tan, a tidal river which is not very broad but can be ascended thus far by good sized boats. The town stands on the eastern side of a circular amphitheatre formed by numerous low ranges of partially wooded hills separated by small intervening hollows and ravines. During the existence of the Arakan kingdom it was the seat of the Governor of the island and was then, and is still, called by the Arakanese Tan-myo. After the conquest of the country by the Burmese it was retained as the head-quarters of the Governor but was known to the conquerors as Yan-byai-myo or in other words the principal town of the Yan-byai governorship : this has been corrupted by Europeans into Ramree ; the Arakanese would call it Ram-brai or Ram-bree and the English have but dropped the *b*.

It is difficult to ascertain, with any approach to accuracy, the period when the town was in its most flourishing condition but it was probably in about 1805 A. D., when its inhabitants carried on an extensive trade with Bengal, Bassein and Tavoy.. A few years later it suffered much from the rebellion of Khyeng-bran and from the retaliatory measures of the Burmese. Khyeng-bran appears to have had many adherents in the town and after his defeat large numbers of the inhabitants were killed or forced to fly the country. During the first Anglo-Burmese war the place was occupied without resistance by the troops under General Macbean, the Burmese having evacuated the strong and judiciously-constructed defences before the arrival of the British force. One of these defences was an unusually strong stockade ; within this all civil and military business had been carried on, whence the quarter in which it was situated, one of the five of the town, was, and is still, called Tat-dweng.

On the conquest of Arakan by the British Ramree was made the head-quarters of the district of the same name, and so remained until 1852 when, in consequence of An and Ramree being joined together, Kyouk-hpyoo, till then the head-quarters of An, became the head-quarters of the new district.

In 1853 the population was estimated at about 9,000 souls, of whom nearly two-thirds were Arakanese. On the removal of the head-quarters to Kyouk-hpyoo Ramree sank to the position of the chief station of a township only and since then has considerably decreased in importance. In 1870 it had 4,000 inhabitants, in 1873 3,939, in 1875-76 3,826 and in 1876-77 4,028 who carry on a coasting trade with Chittagong, Sandoway and Bassein. The public buildings are a Court-house, Police-station and an old and a new market-place.

In 1867 a school was opened and supported for some time by native effort ; subsequently a State grant was made to it and when this was withdrawn, in 1869, the school was closed but was re-opened in 1870 on the grant being renewed. In 1872-73 a rival school was started. The grant was transferred to this but in a few years both schools were closed.

RAN-BOUK.—A river in Ramree island which falls into the sea on the south-western coast.

RAN-BOUK.—A revenue circle in the Kyouk-hpyoo district, on the southern bank of the stream of the same name near the centre of the

Ramree township. On the west is the Ran-daing circle and on the east the Ran-thek and Ran-byai Myoma circles. In 1876-77 the land revenue was Rs. 3,969, the capitation tax Rs. 3,471, the gross revenue Rs. 7,696 and the population 3,513 souls. It contains no villages of any importance.

RAN-BYAI MYOMA (East).—A revenue circle in the Kyouk-hpyoo district on the eastei shore of Ramree island north of the mouth of the Tan river, and between it and the Daw-ra-ta and the Rit. On the north is the Ran-thek circle, on the west the once independent Ran-byai Myoma (West) and on the south, on the other side of the Tan, Ran-byai Myoma (South) which now includes Ran-byai Myoma (West). In 1876-77 the population was 2,466, the land revenue Rs. 1,961, the capitation tax Rs. 2,820 and the gross revenue Rs. 5,916.

RAN-BYAI MYOMA (South).—A revenue circle in the Kyouk-hpyoo district, on the eastern coast of Ramree island, and to the west and south of the Ran-byai Myoma (East) circle. To the westward is the Ran-bouk circle and to the southward the Theng-bha-kaing. It now includes Ran-byai Myoma (West). In 1876-77 the population was 4,961, the land revenue Rs. 1,445, the capitation tax Rs. 5,711 and the gross revenue, including that of the town of Ramree, Rs. 35,613.

RAN-BYAI MYOMA (West).—A revenue circle in the Kyouk-hpyoo district, west of Ran-byai Myoma (East) with an area of about 11 square miles, now joined to the Ran-byai Myoma (South) circle.

RAN-BYAI NGAY.—A revenue circle on the south-western shore of Ramree island just north of Nga-kho-byeng to which it is now joined.

RANGOON.—The name usually given to the lower portion of the Hlaing river, q. v.

RANGOON.—A district in the Pegu division occupying the sea board from the mouth of the Tsit-toung westward to that mouth of the great Irrawaddy river which is generally known as the China Bakir but is more correctly called the To, and extending inland up the valleys of the Irrawaddy and the Tsit-toung rivers to the Henzada and Tharrawaddy districts on the west of the Pegu Roma and to the Shwe-gyeng district of Tenasserim on the east. To the west lies Thoon-khwa and to the east Shwe-gyeng. The northern boundary on the north-west leaves the Pegu Roma near the source of the Mee-neng and following that stream westwards to its mouth in the Hlaing turns southward to the mouth of the Re-nat-eng-khyoung ; here turning west it follows that rivulet to the Re-nat-eng and round the northern border of that fen and then on westward along an imaginary line to the Alap-tsheng-eng ; here it inclines south-east to a Ma-oo tree (*Sarcocephalus cadamba*) in about the latitude of Bhiet-naw on the Hlaing ; inclining again south-south-east it strikes the Pa-khwon and following this in a generally southerly direction to its mouth in the Bhaw-lay it runs with that creek southwards to the Pan-taing and along that to Khat-tee-ya on the Pan-hlairg : thence it follows the Khat-tee-ya Re-gyaw to its mouth in the To and hugs the left bank of that river to its mouth except at a spot a few miles below Kyaik-taw where it includes Re-bhoo Island. On the east of the Pegu Roma the line follows the Bhaw-nee-ga-le from its source to the Pegu and Toung-ngoo road : thence that road southwards to the Pyeng-boon-gyee (or Pa-gaing) embankment and along that embankment eastwards to the Pegu and Tsit-toung canal. Here it turns south and follows the canal to its entrance into the Kha-ra-tshoo creek where it turns east again and follows the creek to within a very short distance of the Tsit-toung when it strikes off south-eastwards and follows a small creek running between the Kha-ra-tshoo and the Tsit-toung so as to exclude that portion of the hamlet of Kha-ra-tshoo which lies south of the creek of the same name. Below this the Tsit-toung forms the eastern boundary whilst the sea forms the southern boundary everywhere. The area included within these limits is 5,646 square miles. On the first formation of the district, after the annexation, it included also Bhaw-nee, a strip of country lying along the eastern slopes of the Pegu Roma from the Bhaw-nee-ga-le stream to the Toung-ngoo district, the Kaw-lee-ya circle in the north-eastern corner of Pegu, the Thoon-tshay circle, in the extreme north between the Pegu Roma on the east and the Hlaing on the west, and the whole tract west of its present western border as far as that branch of the Irrawaddy which, in its southward course, is known as the Irrawaddy, the Eng-tay, the Re-tsoo-daing the Pe-mwot and the Irrawaddy again at the mouth, as far north as the latitude of Donabyoo. Bhaw-nee was transferred to Toung-ngoo in 1864, and from Toung-ngoo to Shwe-gyeng in 1866 ; Kaw-lee-ya was transferred to Shwe-gyeng in 1872-73, Thoon-tshay to Henzada in 1873-74, and the western tract to Thoon-khwa on the formation of that district in 1875. In 1876 the present western boundary was definitely fixed whereby a further small tract was added to Thoon-khwa and in 1877 the present northern and north-eastern boundary east of the Roma was laid down and a small tract north of the Pa-gaing embankment was added to Shwe-gyeng and a small tract south of it to Rangoon.

The general aspect of the district is that of a vast plain extending along the seacoast and, slowly rising, stretching north for some 25 miles when, in about the centre, it is met and, as it were, checked by the lower slopes of the Pegu Roma and, struggling up amongst these mountains in the valleys of the Poo-zwon-doung and the Pegu, it folds round them east and west and rolls on forming portions of the valleys of the Tsit-toung and of the Hlaing. South of the Pegu and in the greater part of the valley of the Hlaing or Rangoon, for some distance above the latitude of the town of the same name, the country is everywhere highly intersected by tidal creeks ; the water a few feet below the surface is brackish and undrinkable and wells are useless but further north are streams tidal for some distance and fresh higher up.

The only mountains in the district are the Pegu Roma which enter
Mountains. in the extreme north, where they attain an estimated height of 2,000 feet, the highest elevation of the range, and a few miles lower down fork out into two main branches with several subsidiary spurs. The western branch (which has a general S. S. W. direction) and its off-shoots divide the valleys of the Hlaing and Poo-zwon-doung rivers and, after rising once more in the irregularly shaped limestone hill called Toung-gnyo, a little to the south of the 17th parallel, terminate as a hilly range some 30 miles north of Rangoon. The range is continued as an elevated ridge past that town, where it appears in the laterite hills round the great pagoda and, beyond the Pegu river, in the

Syriam Koon-dan, finally disappearing beneath the alluvial plains of the delta, being last seen in the rocks which crop up in the Hmaw-won stream. The southern portion of this ridge lying between the Pegu river and the Hmaw-won runs in a direction nearly parallel to and. about three miles east of the Rangoon river and, nowhere more than five miles broad, is locally known as the Than-lyeng (Syriam) Koon-dan or " rising ground". The eastern branch continues from the point of bifurcation towards the S. S. E. and, intersected by the Pegu valley, sinks near the town of Pegu and finally disappears south of the Pegu river, where it is represented by an undulating wooded tract of no great extent. The sides of the main range are, as a rule, steep and the valleys sharply excavated, but the upper portion of the Pegu valley has more the character of a tableland with a hilly surface intersected by deep ravines.

From Twan-te southwards to the Tha-khwot-peng or Bassein creek is a tract of high undulating ground some 18 or 20 miles in length covered with forest and locally known as the Twan-te Taw-gyee or " great forest " or as the Twan-te Koon-dan or " rising ground ", on fine days clearly distinguishable from Rangoon.

The principal river is the Hlaing which rises near Prome as the
Rivers.   Zay and entering this district in about 17° 30′ flows
S. S. E., at first through high sandy banks, past Rangoon, falling into the sea in about 16° 30′ as the Rangoon river. It is navigable by the largest sea-going vessels as for as Rangoon at all seasons and during spring tides ships of considerable burden can ascend for 30 miles further, but just below Rangoon the Hastings shoal stretches across the river and bars the approach of ships of heavy draught except at springs. During the north-west monsoon river steamers can ascend to beyond the northern boundary of the district and boats of from 200 to 300 baskets burden can navigate the upper portion at all seasons. The tide is felt beyond the northern boundary and the water is brackish and undrinkable as high as the village of Kywai-koo about 20 miles below Hlaing. From the east it receives the waters of the Ook-kan, the Ma-ga-ree, the Hmaw-bhee, the Lien-goon and numerous small streams which bring down the drainage of the western slopes of the Pegu Roma, and at Rangoon it is joined by the united waters of the Pegu and Poo-zwon-doung rivers which drain the eastern and southern flanks of those mountains and their numerous spurs in this district, whilst on the west it is joined to the Irrawaddy by the Bhaw-lay, the Pan-hlaing and the Tha-khwot-peng and many other smaller tidal creeks. The Ook-kan, which joins the Hlaing at Htan-bhoo-wa, is not navigable during the dry weather but boats of 600 baskets burden can ascend in the rains as far as the village of Ook-kan, a distance of about six miles : below this the banks are flat and sandy but at its source rocky ; it drains a valley containing much valuable timber of different kinds, as Teak, Pyeng-ga-do (*Xylia dolabriformis*) and Pyeng-ma (*Lagerstrœmia reginœ*.) The Hmaw-bhee is a small perennial stream with shelving banks which are topped during the rains and is navigable only by small boats. It is now silting up below Hmaw-bhee, its waters finding their way out through the Lien-goon.

The Poo-zwon-doung rises in the eastern slopes of the southern spurs of the Pegu Roma and falls into the Pegu river at its mouth at the town of Rangoon after a south-easterly course of some 53 miles through a valley at first narrow but suddenly widening out eastwards. At its mouth it is 440 yards broad and large ships could formerly ascend for a short distance to the numerous rice-cleaning mills erected in the Poo-zwon-doung quarter of Rangoon and on the opposite bank. It is now silting up owing to the vast quantities of rice husk discharged from the mills. Small boats can, during the rains, go to within 20 miles of its source where the water is sweet and the banks and bed rocky. For some 30 miles below Ma-hoo-ra or Hpoung-gyee it is, in the dry weather, but a series of muddy pools. The valley through which this river flows is rich in valuable timber in the north and in the south is well cultivated with rice.

The Pegu river rises in the eastern slopes of the Pegu Roma and falls into the Rangoon or Hlaing river at Rangoon. For some distance from its source it traverses a narrow rocky valley and is fed by numerous mountain torrents but below the old town of Pegu it enters a flat and fertile country well cultivated with rice. During the rains it is navigable by river steamers and by the largest boats as far as Pegu but during the cold and hot seasons large boats can ascend that distance during spring tides only. At all seasons sea-going vessels can pass up for a few miles. The tide is felt as far as A-waing some miles above Pegu and during the springs a bore passes up beyond the mouth of the Paing-kyoon creek. This creek with others which unite with it was some years ago deepened and widened so as to admit of boat communication between the Pegu and the Tsit-toung rivers. The eastern mouth was at Kha-ra-tshoo and it was found that it was too much within the influence of the Tsit-toung bore and the creeks themselves were gradually silting up. In consequence a new locked canal has been made which leaves the old channel some miles west of Kha-ra-tshoo and joins the Tsit-toung at Myit-kyo considerably higher up about 16 miles above Tsit-toung. This canal, as already stated, forms a portion of the eastern boundary of the district.

West of the Hlaing the whole country is divided and sub-divided by tidal creeks, many navigable by large boats, which unite the Hlaing and the numerous mouths of the Irrawaddy. The Bhaw-lay leaves the Hlaing at Hle-tshiep and curving round west and then south and flowing between steep and sandy banks and navigable at all seasons by boats of from 300 to 400 baskets burden and during the rains by river steamers, it re-unites with it some 20 miles lower down just above Htan-ta-beng. It is joined in the north by the Pa-kwon which is navigable for some distance by the largest class of boats, and communicates with the Irrawaddy by several small streams : towards the south the Pan-taing unites it with the Pan-hlaing : it is navigable throughout at all times and seasons by boats of 300 baskets burden and during the rains by river steamers. A few miles above Rangoon the Hlaing is joined by the Pan-hlaing which leaves the Irrawaddy at Gnyoung-doon ; during the dry season this creek is impassable except by small boats but in the rains is the usual route of river steamers proceeding to the Irrawaddy from Rangoon. South of Rangoon the principal creek is the Tha-khwot-peng or Bassein which runs between the Rangoon river and the To or China Bakir and is navigable at all seasons, river steamers using it during the dry weather when the Pan-hlaing is closed.

The whole of the valleys stretching round the base of the Pegu Roma
Geology. from and inclusive of the delta of the Irrawaddy to the
Tsit-toung is composed of the homogeneous and some-
what arenaceous older alluvium slightly more sandy towards the east than
in the west, resting on a considerable deposit of sand or gravel. " Along
"the skirts of the Pegu Roma a broad belt of sandy deposits occur,
" lateritic in places" which " acquire great importance in the south, where the
" Pegu Roma sinks down and the Miocene strata composing it becomes
" shrouded from view beneath this detrital talus. For some 35 miles north
" of Rangoon these detrital beds almost conceal the older deposits which
"' only here and there betray their existence beneath them as in the Can-
" tonment gardens in Rangoon, and where the Syriam range finally dis-
"appears on the banks of the Hmaw-won channel". Laterite occurs in
various places as in the elevated ridge of ground whereon the ancient city
of Syriam stood, below Rangoon ; and an incoherent form of this rock
is now in process of formation out of the older or red alluvial clay. In
this district "no very trustworthy proofs occur of the existence at
" present of the undisturbed beds of the fossil wood group, but its former
" extension, even as far south as Rangoon, is proved by the occasional
" occurrence of partly rolled pieces * * * in the gravelly detritus
" which to the south covers up the undisturbed beds of the group, and in a
" measure replaces them along the outer hills "*. " The Roma mountains
" are composed, as far as is known, wholly of beds of later Tertiary age, with
" no intrusive rock of any kind, of laterite slate clay and bituminous often
" dark argillaceous sandstone which last in the higher ridges is hardened
" and indurated, but in lower places is soft and friable, varying in colour
" from bluish to yellowish grey "†.

The forests include tracts of all classes. On the seacoast and on
Forests. the banks of the tidal streams in the south is the
" Mangrove" forest which is the principal source of
the supply of fuel and of light poles for building purposes for the
Rangoon market and where, amongst other trees, are found growing the
Kam-ba-la (*Sonneratia apetala*) which yields a strong, hard wood of coarse
grain and of a red colour used in Calcutta (it is found in the delta of the
Ganges) for boxes for packing beer and wine and the Ka-na-tso (*Heritiera
minor*) furnishing an exceedingly tough and light wood, according to
Dr. Wallich unrivalled for elasticity, hardness and durability. Higher
up on the banks of the Irrawaddy and of the Hlaing rivers is " Lower mixed"
forest where are large quantities of Pyeng-ma (*Lagerstrœmia reginæ*) furnishing a red wood which, though soft, is durable under water, and is used for the
fittings of boats, sometimes for the hulls of canoes, for house-posts, planking, beams, scantling for roofs, carts, and a variety of other purposes, and
Ka-gnyeng (*Dipterocarpus alatus*). Considerable areas of Eng (*Dipterocarpus
tuberculatus*) occur on the high ground east of the Hlaing river towards the
north, and narrower belts towards the south, whence, especially in the
valley of the Ook-kan a considerable number of ogs are extracted and sent
annually to Rangoon. " Dry" or " Upper mixed" forest covers all the
high ground and higher hills except towards the source of the Pegu

---

* Mr. Theobald's report in the Memoirs of the Geological Survey of India, Vol. X., Part 2.
† Dr. McClelland in Records of the Government of India, Vol IX.

river where evergreen forest is met with. Here Thit-ka (*Cedreela toona*) and Pyeng-ka-do (*Xylia dolabriformis*) abound, the former much used of late years for cabinet purposes and the heartwood of the latter lasting as long as teak, but very heavy, a cubic foot weighing from 60 to 66 lbs. The most important tree in this class of forest is Teak (*Tectona grandis*) and the richest localities are on the western feeders of the Pegu river ; the Poo-zwon-doung river in the upper portion of its course flows between hills covered with excellent Teak, and west of the Pegu Roma the Ook-kan and other tributaries of the Hlaing drain valleys containing a good deal of this valuable timber. Much of the forest in the upper part of the Pegu valley is dense "Evergreen" or evergreen mixed with Pyeng-ka-do (*Xylia dolabriformis*) and other trees which shed their leaves. There are two Teak "Reserves" neither of great extent, one on the western slopes of the Roma in the valley of the Ma-ga-ree and one on the right bank of the Pegu not far from its source. There is also a Teak plantation near Kyek-hpyoo-gan on the Prome road.

The local accounts and the Telugu and Tamil traditions seem to shew History. that probably some thousand years B. C. the inhabitants of Talingana visited and colonized the coast of Burma, finding there a Moon population, a branch of the Kolarian tribes of India whose name still remains in the designation by which the Peguans call themselves, whilst "Talingana", the country of the colonists, appears in the word Talaing by which they are known to surrounding nations and through them to Europeans. The palm-leaf histories allude to a city called Aramana on the site of the present Rangoon and assert that during the life time of Gaudama, that is before 543 B. C., the Shwe Dagon pagoda in Rangoon was founded by two brothers Poo (*dove*) and Ta-paw (*plenty*), sons of the king of Ook-ka-la-ba, west of Rangoon and near the modern Twan-te, who had visited India and had met and conversed with Gaudama from whom they had received several of his hairs, but the first notice of the country which can be considered as historical is given in the Sinhalese Mahawanso which speaks of the mission of Sono and Uttaro sent by the third Booddhist Council (held in 241 B. C.) to Savarna-bhoo-mee to spread the Booddhist faith in its purity. It seems clear that the delta of the Irrawaddy was not exempt from the almost "religious war" which prevailed between the followers of the Brahmanic and Booddhistic faiths, the victory eventually passing to the one body in India and to the other in Burma. Here the differences lasted for several hundreds of years until about the end of the eighth century, the Booddhists being recruited in the meanwhile by the arrival of their co-religionists expelled from India. One of the results of these religious differences was the foundation of the city of Pegu in 573 A. D., by Tha-ma-la and Wee-ma-la, sons of the king of Tha-htoon by a mother of Naga descent, who were excluded from the throne of their father. They brought with them 170 families from Tha-htoon and were joined by 330 families from the neighbourhood of the new city. Tha-ma-la was anointed king and would seem to have extended his dominions considerably to the eastward as he is said to have founded Martaban. He was succeeded by his brother Wee-ma-la who founded Tsit-toung and during whose reign the country was unsuccessfully invaded (in 590 A. D.) by the king of Bij-ja-na-ga-ran (*Vizianagram?*). Thirteen kings followed between this period

538

and 746 A. D., and by this time the kingdom had been extended over the whole country of Rama-gnya from the Arakan mountains on the west to the Salween on the east, including the former capital, Thahtoon, which had much declined in importance. Even at this time the Boodhist religion was not generally accepted in the country and the tenth king of Pegu, Poon-na-ree-ka (Brahmin heart), and more especially his son and successor Tek-tha, appears to have been at least inclined towards Hindoo traditions. Tek-tha was miraculously converted by Badra-devi, a young girl whom he had condemned to death on account of her faith but who, on his conversion, became his principal queen. With the death of Tek-tha ended the third dynasty of Pegu, for the succession had been more than once disturbed by usurpers. The length of time during which these three dynasties occupied the throne is doubtful, and it is by no means clear when Tek-tha died.* About 1050 A. D., A-naw-ra-hta, the king of Pagan, conquered the country and it remained subject to the Burmans for some two centuries. The gradual disintegration of the Burman kingdom and the capture of the capital by the Tartars and consequent flight of the king,

* Even so learned and patient an investigator as Sir Arthur Phayre is at a loss to account for the hiatus between Tek-tha's death and A-naw-ra-hta's conquest. In his history of Pegu, by far the most trustworthy work on the subject, published in the *Journal of the Bengal Asiatic Society,* he states, after recording Tek-tha's death :—

" A gap now occurs in the narrative of events which the native historians either have not attempted to bridge over, or have noticed with only a few general statements. In a preliminary sketch to the copy of the history which I possess, it is stated that the first 17 kings, extending from the foundation of the city of Han-tha-wati to king Tek-tha, reigned for a period of 500 years. But in the detailed accounts of the reigns of those kings the sum of the years they are stated to have reigned amounts to only 208. The first part of the history then closes as if a great crisis had been endured. A new chapter is opened which simply states that the destinies of Han-tha-wati were accomplished, the line of kings broken ; and the writer then bursts forth in lamentation over the rule of foreign Burmese kings and their hateful governors. Three of these are mentioned and reviled, and the narrative then passes on to events near the close of the 13th century of the Christian era, when Moguls and Turks overthrew the Burmese monarchy, Pagan was captured, and her king a captive. Supposing that the 17 kings represent in some fashion the events of 500 years, then the close of king Tek-tha's reign would be about A. D. 1073. From that time until the capture of the Burmese capital by the Tartars there is a period of about 211 years, of which the Moon chroniclers say nothing, except the loss of their native kings and the rule of three hated foreign governors. This hiatus is not peculiar to the manuscript history which I possess, but may be traced in others. Thus Dr. Mason from the copy which he followed, dates the foundation of Pegu A. D. 573 and the death of Tek-tha A. D. 841 but immediately after this, there is a blank of more than 300 years. * * * * * The cause of these great discrepancies arises from the Talaing historians having sought to conceal the religious revolutions in their country, during the 9th and 10th centuries, and to avoid narrating the conquest of their country by A-naw-ra-hta, king of Pagan, about A. D. 1050, with its continued subjection to Burma for more than 200 years, and it is strange that in the Burmese Maha Razaweng, though the conquest of Tha-htoon is narrated at great length, nothing is said of the occupation of the city of Han-tha-wati. Yet, no doubt, the city was then taken by the Burmese king. Either then it was supposed that the capture of the ancient city of Tha-htoon rendered special mention of Pegu unnecessary, or the chroniclers hesitated to record the first instance of the falsification of the legend which in the cause of religion assigned to Pegu a perpetual succession of kings in the line of Tha-ma-la Ku-ma-ra. The Talaing historians have endeavoured to represent their country as having been uniformly orthodox Booddhist, while the records they present to us shew that there have been frequent alternations of Booddhism and Brahmanism. The names of the two last kings of the native dynasty, Poon-na-reeka and Tek-tha, with the few notices we have regarding them, shew that their reigns represent periods of religious strifes between the two great sects, and an attempted introduction of a form of worship antagonistic to both. Poon-na-reeka, or " brahmin heart," sufficiently indicates the influence during one period ; while the name Tek-tha, or Tishza, identical with that of the brother of Asoka, points to a corrupt Booddhism, and the re-establishment of that worship. This is typified in the pleasing legend of Badra Devi, and Booddhism has been the cherished religion of the people from that time until now."

circa 1250 A. D., to Bassein, whence if necessary he could have embarked for Ceylon with which Bassein carried on a somewhat extensive trade, was taken advantage of by the Talaing who had never ceased to hate their conquerors, and headed by a man of Burmese descent named A-kham-won they rose in rebellion in Pegu, whilst at the same period a Talaing, or according to Sir A. Phayre a Shan, named Wa-rie-yoo killed the Burman governor of Martaban and made himself master of that town and of the surrounding country. A-kham-won was put to death by his brother-in-law, Leng-gya, after he had reigned two years, and Leng-gya himself was almost immediately killed by A-khyam-won, another brother-in-law of A-kham-won, who ascended the throne. The two rebellious leaders in Pegu and Martaban entered into an alliance and married each other's daughters, and on the king of Burma sending an army southwards they united their forces and defeating the Burmans pursued them as far as Pa-doung, a few miles below Prome. The Talaing then retired to Pegu but disputes arose and A-khyam-won, who on ascending the throne had taken the name of Ta-ra-bya, was seized and carried to Martaban where he was subsequently put to death and Wa-rie-yoo declared himself king of the whole country, a proceeding in which the inhabitants acquiesced. In the meanwhile the Tartars had again invaded Burma and possessed themselves of the capital and numerous petty rulers declared themselves independent ; amongst these was the Shan-Burmese governor of Toung-ngoo, generally called in the European accounts of that period the king of the Burmas, a title which he claimed as against the usurping Shan who ruled in the former capital of the empire.

Wa-rie-yoo was killed by the two sons of Ta-ra-bya and was succeeded in 1306 A.D. by his brother who four years later was put to death by his brother-in-law Meng-ba-la, and his nephew, Meng-ba-la's son Zaw-aw, was proclaimed king. This sovereign extended his dominions southward and declaring himself independent of Siam, to which his predecessor had acknowledged his vassalage, took possession of Tavoy and Tenasserim ; these were lost during the reign of his successor Zaw-zit who transferred the capital to Pegu and assumed the name of Bya-gnya-ran-da. Bya-gnya-ran-da advanced against Prome but was repulsed and killed in 1330 and was eventually succeeded by a son of Khoon-law, the brother of Wa-rie-yoo, who reigned 18 years and was followed by his nephew Bya-gnya-oo who took the name of Tsheng-hpyoo-sheng. During the reign of this sovereign the country was disturbed by the continual incursions of the Shan on the north-east but this did not prevent him from sending an embassy to Ceylon whence he obtained a holy relic of Gaudama which was enshrined in a pagoda built on a spot now included within the limits of Maulmain. A few years later a near relation of his own, named Byat-ta-ba, raised a rebellion against him and succeeded in wresting Martaban from the Peguan dominions and Tsheng-hpyoo-sheng made no endeavour to recover it. Tsheng-hpyoo-sheng was succeeded by his son Raza-dhie-rit in 1385 ; he repelled a formidable invasion of the Burmese and in 1388 regained possession of Martaban and the country to the eastward. He then turned his attention to Myoung-mya, the governor of which, himself of royal blood, had invited the Burmese to invade the country as soon as Raza-dhie-rit ascended the throne, and captured that city and Bassein and pursued the rebel governor's son (he himself had already been taken prisoner) into Arakan. Some years later he advanced against the king of Burma who had occupied Koo-dwot, now called Myan-oung, and drove out his troops, and in 1404, taking advantage of a war which had broken out between Arakan and Burma, he advanced against the latter country and laid siege to Ava but was forced to retire: the following year he again moved up the Irrawaddy and laid siege to Prome ; the town was relieved by the king of Burma and the two monarchs, influenced probably by mutual fear, swore perpetual friendship. A short time later a force was sent into Arakan to aid the people of that country against the Burmese, a duty successfully performed, the Burmese being driven out and the son of the Arakan king, who had fled to Bengal, placed on his father's throne. The Burmans then invaded Pegu but were defeated and driven northward beyond the frontier, Raza-dhie-rit returning in triumph to his capital. A little later another invasion took place with no better success, but in 1411 the Burmans made themselves masters of several places in the delta of the Irrawaddy and failing in their attacks on Myoung-mya and Bassein passed into Arakan whither they were followed by the Talaing, who afterwards moved northwards against Prome but were driven back and pursued by the Burmese who occupied Dala, Dagon (Rangoon), Hmaw-bhee and Syriam. After considerable fighting the Burmans retired, but in the meanwhile the Talaing generals had withdrawn from Arakan. The war continued with hardly any intermission and with varying success till 1414 when the Burmans were finally repulsed. Raza-dhie-rit died in 1421 and was succeeded by his son Bya-gnya Dham-ma Raza who almost immediately after he ascended the throne had to put down a rebellion led by his two brothers Bya-gnya Kan and Bya-gnya Ryaeng. A short time afterwards the Burman king invaded Pegu but eventually married the Talaing king's sister, Sheng-tsaw-boo, and returned to Ava. Bya-gnya Dham-ma Raza died in 1424 and was succeeded by Bya-gnya Kan who is known in history as Bya-gnya-ran-kek. Sheng-tsaw-boo was dissatisfied with her position and aided by two Booddhist monks she escaped to her brother's court *circa* 1439, and eventually ascended the throne in 1454, three kings, Bya-gnya-wa-roo, Bya-gnya-keng and Hmaw-daw, the last of whom was put to death as a tyrant after a short reign of only seven months, having successively ruled the country in the meanwhile. Sheng-tsaw-boo married her daughter to one of the monks who had aided her in escaping from Ava and named him Crown Prince, she herself retiring to Dagon. Devoted to religion and greatly beloved by her subjects she died after reigning for seven years, three of which in Dagon, and to the present day an annual festival is held in her honour at Rangoon. Dham-ma Ze-dee, the ex-monk, succeeded her and was renowned for his wisdom, power, and intercourse with foreign countries, and after his death in 1491, he received the funeral of a Chakrawartti Raja or universal monarch. Bya-gnya-ran, his son, reigned for 35 years and was succeeded by Ta-ka-rwot-bee, in whose reign the country was conquered by the king of Toung-ngoo, Ta-beng-shwe-htee.

It was probably during the reign of Raza-dhie-rit that the country was first visited by European travellers. Nicholas Conti was in Pegu, " a very "populous city, the circumference of which is 12 miles", in 1430. Bya-gnya-ran is described by Hieronimo da Santa Stefano and Luigi Vertomannus ;

the former complains of the delay in getting payment for his goods which were of such a sort that only the lord of the city could purchase them, and the latter writes of that king's great magnificence. Vertomannus states that Pegu was a walled town and that the houses were constructed of stone and lime. It was with this sovereign that Antonio Correa made a treaty of peace at Martaban in 1519, and from this time onwards for many years there was much intercourse between European adventurers and soldiers of fortune and the kings of Pegu who sought their aid. It has already been stated that Ta-beng-shwe-htee, king of Toung-ngoo, known in European accounts as king of the Bramas, conquered Pegu. He had succeeded his father in 1530 at the age of 16 and having repelled an invasion of the Peguans he in turn advanced against their capital which he took in 1538 although the defenders were aided by a force of Spaniards under Ferdinand de Morales. He followed the retreating Ta-ka-rwot-bee to Prome and worsted him in an engagement near that town and then he returned to Pegu; Ta-ka-rwot-bee followed him but died in the forests of Eng-ga-boo between the Hlaing and the Irrawaddy. Thus ended the Shan dynasty founded by Wa-rie-yoo. Ta-beng-shwe-htee now captured Martaban and returning to Pegu was crowned king and, to mark his assumption of the sovereignty, he placed a new htee on the Shwe-hmaw-daw pagoda and another on the Shwe Dagon.

Extending his conquests he besieged and took Prome and after repelling an invasion of the Burmese he ascended the Irrawaddy and made himself master of the country as far as lower Pagan; he then invaded Arakan on pretence of placing the brother of the lately deceased ruler on the throne but the Siamese having invaded Pegu he accepted the homage of the nephew of the claimant whom he was supporting and withdrew. In 1549 he defeated the Siamese army and forced the king of Siam to pay tribute. Somewhat later, he gave way to habits of intemperance and became utterly incapable: several rebellions broke out and to suppress one, headed by Tha-meng-htaw, a son of Bya-gnya-ran, Bhooreng Noung, the heir-apparent, proceeded westwards to Da-la: during his absence Ta-beng-shwe-htee was killed in 1550, at the age of 36, by a brother of Tha-meng-tsaw-dwot, the governor of Tsit-toung, the latter proclaiming himself king. Bhoo-reng Noung marched on Toung-ngoo where his brother was governor but he was refused admission whereupon he invested the place and eventually captured it. In the meanwhile Tha-meng-htaw and Tha-meng-tsaw-dwot were disputing the possession of the kingdom; Tha-meng-tsaw-dwot was taken prisoner and beheaded and Tha-meng-htaw was solemnly consecrated and assumed the title of Za-ga-lee Meng. Bhooreng Noung having taken Toung-ngoo crossed the Roma and laid siege to Prome which was surrendered by treachery and in 1551 he returned to Toung-ngoo, advanced against Tha-meng-htaw whom he utterly defeated close to the capital, and in 1554, after subduing the whole country and putting to death Tha-meng-htaw, who had escaped first to Da-la and then to Martaban and had been betrayed into his hands, he declared war with Burma and in March 1555 captured Ava. In all these operations the Portuguese were of great assistance to Bhooreng Noung whose dominions now extended from Tenasserim to Arakan and from the seacoast northward to the Shan States. Not yet content, he attacked and conquered

Siam in 1563-64, and six years later, on a rebellion against him breaking out there, he again invaded that country and capturing the capital gave it up to plunder, returning to Pegu in 1570 after ravaging the country in many directions. In 1580 he sent an expedition in o Arakan, but died suddenly in 1581.

Although his whole reign of 30 years in Pegu was occupied in continual wars of aggression and in quelling rebellions Bhooreng Noung was not simply a great warrior. He enlarged his capital and greatly strengthened its walls of which the outer one was 7,000 yards long on each face, each with five gates and constructed by and named after a tributary king; within he erected a magnificent palace, and in the neighbourhood he founded another town of which the massive remains still exist. He paid great attention to religion and obtained from one of the kings of Ceylon a holy relic of Gaudama which he enshrined in a pagoda, and in return he sent an embassy to the donor who had complained that he alon of the four kings reigning on the Island was orthodox. This relic subsequently disappeared and Sir A. Phayre suggests that the relic chamber was plundered by de Brito. He abolished the annual sacrifices to the Nat and, viewing with displeasure the killing of animals by the numerous foreigners of his dominions, he forcibly converted numbers to Booddhism.

Bhooreng Noung was succeeded by his son Nanda Bhooreng to whom all the tributary kings did homage except the king of Burma. The army was recalled from Arakan and in order to reduce the king of Burma and to punish him for his intrigues with the rulers of Prome and Toung-ngoo, which these latter had disclosed, Nanda Bhooreng advanced up the Irrawaddy in 1584-85 and forced him to escape into China. In the meanwhile the king of Siam rebelled and four expeditions, all equally unsuccessful, were despatched against him, in 1585, 1587, 1590 and in 1593. The failure of these seems to have embittered the feelings of Nanda Bhooreng and to have rendered him wantonly cruel. " The Booddhist monks of " Talaing race excited his hatred. Numbers of them he forced to become " laymen, and then either exiled or killed them, thousands of the Moon people " abandoned their country and fled, while those caught in their flight were " put to death for the attempt. The country of the delta became depopu- " lated." The country fell into complete disorder. The king of Siam invaded the kingdom but retired, when the kings of Toung-ngoo and Zeng-mai rose in rebellion and the Arakanese seized Syriam. In 1599 Pegu was captured and Nanda Bhooreng sent prisoner to Toung-ngoo and the Arakanese retiring Pegu was left without any ruler. In 1600 Philip de Brito, then in the service of the king of Arakan, was sent to hold Syriam. He, however, proved faithless and sided with the Portuguese Viceroy at Goa and, accepted by the Talaing inhabitants, he declared himself master of Pegu of which he took possession in the name of the king of Portugal. He built a fort and church at Syriam and laid out a new city: he defeated a force sent against him by the kings of Toung-ngoo and Arakan, capturing its commander, the son of the latter, and subsequently he drove off another invading army. He entered into treaties with his former enemy, the king of Toung-ngoo, and with the ruler of Martaban, but he irritated the inhabitants by breaking into and plundering the pagodas, and having treacherously attacked the king of Toung-ngoo, taken his city and burned his palace, was himself attacked by the king of Burma in 1612 and captured and impaled, and the Portuguese power in Pegu was thus finally destroyed.

Pegu remained subject to the king of Burma till 1740 A.D., and it was during this period that the English commenced trading with Rangoon. In 1695 application was made for leave to establish a factory at Syriam, and from 1709 to 1743 English traders were settled there. During this interval the Burmese government, owing partly to invasions from the north and partly to internal dissensions, was falling to pieces and in 1740 the Peguans broke out in rebellion. They took Syriam, which they lost the following year but retook in 1743, and the English having refused to aid them against the Burmans they burned down the factories, whereupon Mr. Smart withdrew the establishment. A year or two later they advanced on Burma, took the capital and annexing the country brought the king to Pegu. They did not retain it long. In 1753 Moung-oung-zaya, Myo-thoo-gyee of Moot-tsho-bo, raised the standard of revolt and gaining a few successes was speedily joined by large numbers of his countrymen. He captured Ava and proclaimed himself king under the title of Aloung-bhoora, thus founding the dynasty now reigning. Within four years he had conquered Pegu, Tavoy and Mergui and had advanced into Siam. The English government sided with neither party but unfortunately some of its officers laid themselves open to considerable suspicion and were held by Aloung-bhoora to have aided the Peguans. Various unsuccessful endeavours were made to re-obtain a footing in Syriam and matters remained in a very unsatisfactory state for many years. In 1824 the first Burmese war broke out and a British force entered the river and took Rangoon. The British retained possession of the country till the close of the war and then restored it to the king of Burma. The disputes which arose on matters of trade and the complaints of British merchants and ship masters of the treatment which they received in Rangoon led to the second Burmese war which broke out in 1852, when Rangoon and Pegu were captured after some severe fighting and the lower portions of the valleys of the Irrawaddy and Tsit-toung annexed to the British dominions, and the Peguan kingdom thus passed to the English.

The principal pagodas in the district are the Shwe Dagon, the Bo-ta-htoung and the Tsoo-lai in Rangoon, the Kyaik-kouk at Syriam, the Shwe-hmaw-daw at Pegu, the Tshan-daw at Twan-te, the Kyaik-ka-tshan a few miles to the north-east, and the Kyaik-ka-lo a few miles to the north, of Rangoon.

Archæology.

The Shwe Dagon, the most celebrated object of worship in all the Indo-Chinese countries, was, it is asserted in the palm-leaf records, founded in 588 B.C. or 43 years before the death of Gaudama when that sage was 35 years old, by Poo and Ta-paw sons of the king of Ook-ka-la-ba (Twan-te), who during a visit to India had obtained from the Booddha himself several of his hairs which, with great ceremony, were enshrined under a pagoda 18 cubits in height; but, as observed by Sir Arthur Phayre, "it cannot be "credited that during the life of Gaudama the Talaing people had through "their own means any communication by sea with India, or that Booddhism "was introduced into the delta of the Irrawaddy at so early a period". The first trustworthy statements are those which relate to the repairs and works carried out by queen Sheng-tsaw-boo in the latter half of the fifteenth century. This sovereign raised its height to 292 feet, made terraces on the hill, paved the topmost one with stone, and set apart land and hereditary slaves for the service of the shrine. Mendes Pinto makes no mention of the pagoda but Balbi, the Venetian, who visited Rangoon, or Dagon as it was then called, towards the end of the 16th century gives a full description of it*.

From time to time the building was enlarged and beautified, especially since the conquest of the delta by the Burmans who seem to have endeavoured, for political reasons, to cause it to eclipse the more purely Talaing pagoda in the ancient capital of the kingdom. In 1768 A. D., king Tsheng-hpyoo-sheng replaced the Talaing htee or crown by one of Burmese form and regilt the outside. In 1871 it was regilt with funds derived from public subscriptions, the donations of pilgrims visiting the shrine, and the rents of the fruit trees standing on the platform, and when the regilding was complete a new htee was put on it. This was made in Mandalay of iron, thickly gilded and studded with jewels, at a cost of Rs. 620,000, brought down the river with great ceremony, received and escorted by a specially deputed British Officer, and elevated amidst grand public rejoicings, the feelings of the Burmans no little elated by the knowledge that their ancient ruler was allowed to re-crown this most sacred edifice. The existing building is 320 feet high and 1,130 feet in circumference at the base, rising from a square platform and surrounded by numerous smaller pagodas and images of Gaudama, and is approached by four sets of stairs facing the cardinal points of the compass. The hill on which the pagoda stands has of late years been to some extent fortified by the English government. During the second Burmese war this hill was defended by the Burmese but was carried by assault by the British troops under General Godwin.

The Bo-ta-htoung is a small pagoda of no great sanctity on the bank of the Rangoon river a little below the Master Attendant's wharf. It is said to have been built by 1,000 officers (*Bo-ta-htoung*) by order of the king of Ook-ka-la-ba on the spot where his son's body had been burned.

The Tsoo-lai pagoda stands in the town in what is now Fytche square and is said to have been originally constructed at the same time as the Shwe Dagon.

The Kyaik-kouk pagoda stands out conspicuously on the Syriam hills and is supposed to contain various relics of Gaudama, some placed in it when it is said to have been first constructed in the sixth century before Christ and others added some 350 years later. It was repaired and beautified by Bhodaw Bhoora son of Aloung Bhoora, in 1781, and then measured 133 feet in height and 900 feet in circumference at the base. It is visited every year at the annual festival in March by large numbers of pilgrims.

The Shwe Hmaw-daw in Pegu is the great pagoda of the Talaing. The palm-leaf records assert that it was first built in the sixth century B.C. to enshrine some of Gaudama's hairs brought hither by two brothers named Ma-ha-tha-wa-ka and Tsoo-la-tha-wa-ka, on a spot selected by the Booddha himself, where, by prophetic power, he knew that a town would one day rise. In 1120 it was repaired by king Tha-ma-la, the founder of the first real city. From this time it was continually enlarged and adorned, each succeeding sovereign vieing with his predecessors in his

---

* *See* Shwe Dagon pagoda.

endeavours to improve and beautify it. The last king of Pegu, Bya-gnya-da-la, renewed the htee. After the Burman conquest the kings paid more attention to the Shwe Dagon than to the Shwe Hmaw-daw but this was not entirely neglected, and in 1791 Bhodaw Bhoora repaired and regilded it, repaired the htee, and built 11 small pagodas round it. It stands on high ground some distance from the present town of Pegu, is octagonal at the base, each side measuring 162 feet, and is 324 feet in height. At a few feet above the platform are two broad ledges one above the other on which are rows of small pagodas completely surrounding the main building, the lower ledge supporting 75 and the upper 53. During the second Burmese war it was the scene of much fighting, being occupied by the British troops and more than once attacked by the Burmese.

The Shwe Tshan-daw at Twan-te is an object of greater veneration to the Talaing than even the Shwe Dagon, as it has not been repaired or kept up by the Burmese. It was erected, according to its palm-leaf history, during the sixth century B.C. by the then ruler of the neighbouring city of Kha-beng as a shrine for some hairs of Gaudama given to three Sinhalese pilgrims and some 400 years later four more hairs were added. It was repaired in 1781 and again in 1866.

The Kyaik-ka-tshan pagoda is in the Hmaw-bhee township a few miles north-east of Rangoon. It was built, it is asserted, in 193 B.C. to cover relics of Gaudama and has been several times repaired, the last occasion being in 1848 when a new htee was placed on it. It is 90 feet high and 220 feet in circumference at the base. It is annually resorted to in March by large numbers of Booddhists.

The Kyaik-ka-lo, built of laterite blocks now faced with brick, stands on the summit of a short spur a little to the west of the Rangoon and Prome road, about 14 miles north of Rangoon. The platform is about 60 yards square. The basement of the pagoda is octagonal, each side being 14 yards long. The height to the htee is about 90 feet. The pagoda is sur-rounded by 24 small ones of much later date. It is resorted to annually by crowds of people for two days of the annual festival in March.

In the town of Rangoon there is a Thien-gyee, or building used for the performance of certain rites and ceremonies peculiar to the Booddhist priesthood, said to have been built at the same time as the Kyaik-ka-tshan pagoda and to contain relics of one of the Rahanda who brought over the remains of Gaudama.

In the An-gyee township are the ruins of ancient pagodas of which 37 were built in various places upon the spots where the holy relics which now repose under the Shwe Tshan-daw at Twan-te rested upon their journey from the seacoast to Kha-beng. Twan-te itself was once a considerable town and the lines of its surrounding wall are still traceable whilst the site of the "Nan-goon" or palace is pointed out by the inhabitants. A short distance from Twan-te is Kha-beng-rwa, the site of an ancient city where reigned Tha-mien-htaw-byeen-tsan and his queen Mien-da-de-wee the founders of the Shwe Tshan-daw pagoda at Twan-te. The ruined walls both of the exterior and of the interior cities are still visible, as well as the remains of several ancient pagodas. At Zaing-ga-naing and in its neigh-bourhood are found massive bricks, glazed tiles ornamented with the heads of animals, large stone tables on which is engraved the history of the town and pagodas, and enormous images, the ruins of the buildings erected by Dham-ma-ze-dee. Meng-ga-la-doon, a few miles north of Rangoon, Hmaw-bhee, between the river Hlaing and the Roma mountains, Hlaing a little to the northward on the left bank of the river of the same and Htan-bhoo in the north-east, near the junction of the Dhat. a small mountain torrent, with the Ook-kan, are sites of ancient towns. Meng-ga-la-doon is said to have been founded by Poon-na-ree-ka, who reigned in Pegu from 746 A.D. to 761 A.D., and called Rama-wad-dee. No traces of its walls now remain. The date of the foundation of Hmaw-bhee is uncertain. It was surrounded by masonry walls, a parapet and a ditch ; the bricks in the walls have been used as ballast for the Railway. The date of the foundation of Hlaing is equally uncertain, but is generally placed in the reign of Raza-dhie-rit (1385—1421 A.D.). The ruins of three pagodas and of the walls are still traceable. These latter appear to have been of brick faced with earth, about 15 feet high, and to have enclosed a square, each side about 1,000 yards long and facing one of the cardinal points of the compass, with a gateway in the centre. The bricks are of the usual Burman shape, long, broad and thin, but well burned. The northern wall is now about 300 yards from the river but must at one time have been much further judging from the erosion of the banks now going on ; an extensive tract of rice-fields and a suburb, probably, occupied the intervening space. The interior is now partly cultivated and partly overgrown with shrubs and grass. Htan-bhoo is said to have been founded about the same time by a son of Raza-dhie-rit who subsequently rebelled against his father and was killed near the town at a spot now called La-ha-ma-ngay where a pagoda was erected by his widow ; the crumbling walls are just traceable. Syriam or Than-lyeng was founded many centuries ago and was once the capital of a petty kingdom ; it will be found fully described *sub. tit.* Than-lyeng. In its immediate neighbourhood is Pa-da, *q. v.*

The climate is generally depressing and retards convalescence, but otherwise it is, as far as a sub-tropical climate can be, pleasant and healthy. December and January are cool, bracing months, very little rain falls and sometimes none. The nights and mornings before sunrise are occasionally very cold, and even piercing and chilly during the prevalence of easterly winds which sometimes blow for short intervals at this season. The dews are very heavy and only dry up with the morning sun. In February the weather commences to get hot and before the close of that month and in March and April, the heat is excessive ; until towards the end of April the wind is generally from the south south-west and rising in the morning, continues all day, blowing with considerable strength, until about 8 P. M. when sometimes a gentle south-west breeze sets in, but then often fails, and then the nights are close and suffocating. Towards the end of April a succession of nor-westers with thunder and lightning issue in the rains, which continue till October : occasionally the whole season is, as it were, pushed back ; the rains do not commence till the beginning or even middle of May and last till the middle of November. This season is peculiarly trying ; whilst rain is falling it is cool but as soon as it stops and the sun comes out the atmosphere is hot and damp and the effect exhausting. Sometimes the mornings and evenings are cool, sometimes humid and oppressive. As the rains gradually ecase the intervals of damp heat are longer until, as the middle or end of November approaches, the nights and mornings become cooler and cooler until the pleasant December and January weather comes round again. At the end of the rainy season, as at the commencement, there is usually considerable electrical disturbance. The average rainfall may be saken at about 115·00 inches.

Persons of robust sanguineous constitution suffer most during the hot season from violent congestion of the lungs and liver, etc., with symptomatic fever, whilst those of feeble lymphatic constitution suffer most in the cains and cold season from fevers of a low type, disease of the spleen, dropsical effusion, rheumatism, and bowel and pulmonary complaints.

The soil of most parts of the district except on the hill sides and undulating ground and where the tides wash over the land as in some parts in the south, is exceedingly fertile, and more especially is this so in the north-eastern and central parts of the Angyee township opposite Rangoon, in the southern part of the Hpoung-leng township east of Rangoon and in parts of the Than-lyeng township south of Rangoon and on the other side of the Pegu river. Here the average yield of unhusked rice is as much as 80 or 100 bushels an acre. North of Rangoon the soil is poorer, yielding only from 30 to 40 bushels, whilst the Ma-yen-za-ya circle in the north-east, beyond the town of Pegu, and the country south and south-eastwards is annually covered with so much water that cultivation can only be carried on in a few spots. Here considerable damage has been done by the leasing out of streams as fisheries ; the lessees erected weirs and embankments and, as the streams are tidal, this caused them to silt up and thus to become unable to carry off the rainfall. This has now been changed, no stream fisheries are here leased and a protecting embankment has been thrown across the plain from near Pyeng-boon-gyee on the Pegu and Toung-ngoo road to Myit-kyo on the bank of the Tsit-toung; how far this embankment will fulfiill the object for which it was made is still doubtful. West of the Hlaing river, from the north to a little south of the Pan-hlaing, but more especially in the extreme north that is the tract forming the Aing-ka-loung and Bhaw-lay circles, the country is liable to inundation. The embankments along the west bank of the Irrawaddy and Nga-won, which protect large areas of good land in the Henzada, Thoon-khwa and Bassein districts, force the flood, which formerly spread west and east but principally west, to flow eastward to a far greater extent than formerly. It enters by the numerous creeks which join the Irrawaddy to the Hlaing, whilst that portion which passes down the Pan-hlaing banks up the Hlaing and makes bad worse. In 1876-77 the crops were ruined over no less than 171,000 acres, entailing much suffering on the people, a serious remission of the land revenue and an extensive emigration.

Some centuries ago the country was highly cultivated, but the continual wars with the Siamese on the one hand and the Burmese on the other, the cruel persecutions to which the inhabitants were sometimes subjected, notably by Nanda Bhooreng at the end of the sixteenth century, and the measures adopted by the Burmese conquerors, depopulated the land. The proceedings of Nanda Bhooreng were so cruel that, to use the words of Bernier, he "converted the country into forests and prevented for many "years the tillage of the land," and Sir Arthur Phayre in his history of Pegu says that " the country of the delta became depopulated and an attempt " was made to drive down the people from upper Erawati, to till the " fertile land of Pegu. But famine and plague raged and there was no " help."

The area under cultivation slowly increased, but the exportation of rice having been prohibited some time before the second Anglo-Burmese war, cultivation was, necessarily, checked. The annexation imparted a new vigour to trade, and the area under rice at once commenced to increase. The extent of land under cultivation by the Burmese may be put down at 50,000 acres.

The richest rice land is in the An-gyee township, that is in the tract west of the Rangoon and south of the Pan-hlaing, and in the lower parts of the valley of the Pegu river : in some places the out-turn is 80 baskets an acre or about 80-fold, equal to one ton three cwt. of rice, and in others as much as 112 baskets equal to one ton twelve cwt. of rice. Towards the north the soil is much poorer and in some places even 30 baskets is considered a good yield.

The gardens and orchards are found principally in the neighbourhood of Rangoon and this for two reasons ; the market is close at hand and the soil is less fitted for rice. North and east of the town are large areas covered with mango, jack, ma-yan and other fruit trees in thick orchards, with pine-apples covering the soil beneath the shade. Shan, market gardeners *par excellence*, mordern immigrants from far beyond British territory, have settled and are settling hereabouts in large numbers and are taking up the undulating ground which suits the crops they prefer. Not only is the Rangoon market kept supplied but fruit is sent up north by the railway for sale in the rice-producing country in the northern part of Rangoon and in Tharrawaddy. From Twan-te on the west and its neighbourhood and from Than-lyeng on the south, across the Pegu river, are brought vast numbers of plantains and mangoes grown in the orchards on the "Koondan" or line of low hills running southwards, whilst from an extensive grove a little north of Rangoon and from another at Hmaw-bhee, both the property of the State and leased annually, are brought many cart-loads of ma-yan, a kind of acid plum much sought after. At Twan-te is a small grove of Sapodilla plum trees producing the royal fruit of the Talaing, esteemed by the Peguan monarchs as the doorian is by the kings of Burma. Close to Rangoon are numerous vegetable gardens, the property of Chinese who supply the market with vegetables and who, in the early mornings, may be met trudging out with buckets giving out an odour anything but pleasing to European nostrils and containing the manure with which, taught by the traditions and the pratice of their own country, they so advantageously supplement the producing properties of the sandy and arid soil.

The area (on which revenue was payable) under rice, of gardens and of miscellaneous cultivation, excluding hill gardens, from 1853-54 to 1877-78 was, in acres :—

Year.	Rice.	Garden.	Miscel-laneous.	Total.	Year.	Rice.	Garden.	Miscel-laneous.	Total.
1853-54	68,056	1,193	—	69,249	1866-67	371,108	14,507	3,561	389,176
1854-55	103,678	3,789	—	107,402	1867-68	379,297	15,312	3,456	398,065
1855-56	152,523	5,120	—	157,643	1868-69	386,950	15,667	5,136	407,753
1856-57	209,278	5,716	2,974	217,968	1869-70	397,858	16,167	3,639	417,664
1857-58	237,183	7,773	3,287	248,243	1870-71	443,960	17,158	3,931	465,049
1858-59	227,207	8,081	3,939	392,118	1871-72	472,987	17,879	4,084	494,950
1859-60	228,467	8,522	4,547	241,536	1872-73†	500,663	18,673	4,857	524,193
1860-61	263,425	11,765	4,839	280,029	1873-74‡	577,833	23,131	4,662	605,626
1861-62	281,709	13,832	5,534	301,075	1874-75	673,619	25,227	5,320	704,166
1862-63	287,964	13,594	6,281	307,839	1875-76§	630,433	14,568	2,062	647,063
1863-64	320,091	12,840	4,622	337,553	1876-77	668,131	15,951	3,718	687,800
1864-65*	338,389	12,974	3,481	354,844	1877-78	701,804	16,930	3,088	721,822
1865-66	352,199	13,715	3,900	369,814					

The acreage of principal crops cultivated since 1866-67 was :—

Year.			Rice.	Oil seeds.	Cotton.	Dhanee palms.	Mixed fruit trees.
1868-69	..	..	380,981	99	80	1,645	18,387
1869-70	..	..	393,170	40	Not given	40	30,020
1870-71	..	..	435,306	51	40	32,688	
1871-72	..	..	471,360	134	107	27,040	
1872-73	..	..	498,202	386	118	27	22,998
1873-74	..	..	577,833	427	47	107	23,483
1874-75	..	..	673,619	106	34	169	30,136
1875-76	..	..	631,615	Not given	Not given	313	28,458
1876-77	..	..	669,313	44	1	678	19,208
1877-78	..	..	671,371	—	—	659	19,679

The agricultural stock during the same period was :—

Year.	Buffaloes.	Cows, bulls and bullocks.	Sheep and goats.	Pigs.	Carts.	Ploughs.	Boats.
1868-69	60,369	20,001	2,417	2,635	14,531	25,214	9,128
1869-70	56,348	20,350	986	7,118	14,479	25,300	8,417
1870-71	56,930	25,778	598	5,824	14,918	25,469	8,297
1871-72	77,422	22,338	843	5,713	14,901	29,270	3,655
1872-73	80,263	23,979	684	6,063	14,695	29,436	9,153
1873-74	84,746	26,993	606	4,999	16,777	31,324	10,230
1874-75	84,871	26,930	483	5,276	17,287	33,987	10,055
1875-76	74,297	29,969	646	5,084	15,598	30,843	6,886
1876-77	76,887	29,330	834	7,587	15,803	29,575	6,060
1877-78	83,721	30,623	1,297	7,034	13,281	26,420	5,239

† Bhaw-nee transferred to Toung-ngoo.   ‡ Thoon-tsay transferred to Henzada.
‖ Kaw-lee-va   ..   Shwe-gyeng   § Three thousand five hundred and sixty-nine sq. miles
of country on the west transferred to Thoon-khwa

The average price of almost every article and the ordinary wages rose greatly. These were, in rupees :—

YEAR.	PER MAUND OF 80 LBS.								PER DAY.				
	Rice.	Cotton.	Sugar.	Salt.	Tobacco.	Cutch.	Cocoanut oil.	Fish, per seer.	Skilled.	Unskilled.	Carts.	Buffaloes.	Bullocks.
	Rs. A.	Rs. A.	Rs. A.	Rs. A.	Rs. A.	Rs. A.	Rs. A.	Rs. A.	Rs. A.	Rs. A.	Rs. A.	Rs. A.	Rs. A.
1868-69	3 0	21 0	14 0	1 7	7 3	13 2	17 8†	0 12	1 8	0 12	2 8	1 1†	1 0†
1877-78	4 10	6 11	16 2	1 7	16 1	14 15	24 10	0 7	1 8	2 0	2 0	2 0	1 10

In 1868 a pair of plough bullocks could be bought for Rs. 100 and a pair of buffaloes for the same amount but in 1877-78 the price had risen to nearly Rs. 200 for a good pair of either.

Mortgages of land were formerly uncommon but are yearly increasing in number. The people are wonderfully neglectful of their plough beasts and many of these die from easily-preventible causes; the people themselves—though herein an exception must be made in favour of the women who are thrifty, thoughtful and careful—are a pleasure-loving race, thinking little of the morrow and recklessly squandering their hard-earned gains in gambling or in dances. Exceptions there are, no doubt, who, *en revanche,* are miserly and hoard their wealth, burying it or hiding it in their grain stores or in the thatch of their houses. Added to this is the influence on them of the Booddhist religion which leads them to spend freely in ornamenting pagodas and in building monasteries in order to accumulate merit to carry them to a higher stage in their next transmigration. The peasants are thus divided into two very dissimilar classes—the many spendthrifts and the few hoarders. In Rangoon are collected men of nearly all races, and of many of these, especially the Chetties, the main object in life is to make money ; they are more grasping than the fabled Jew and to them resort the agriculurists for the means of buying cattle to replace those which they have lost by want of care and even to purchase seed grain which they should have stored but have sold, tempted by the prices offered towards the end of the rains and by their lust for the means of satisfying their desire for gambling, for show and for *bon camaraderie.* The result is appearing more and more year by year in the number of suits for redemption of mortgages with which the time of the Civil Courts is taken up; no deeds are produced, or if they are they are doubtful, disputed, or insufficiently stamped and unregistered and consequently inadmissible as evidence. Latterly, as land has become more valuable, these suits have increased in number and one of the most difficult duties of the judges has been, and is, to discover the nature of the transaction.

The largeness of the holdings as compared with that in other parts of the province renders the employment of hired labour more common. Every owner of eight or nine acres and upwards usually hires labourers in proportion to the size of his holding; these are paid by the season, living with the farmer and performing odd jobs about the house besides

* No quotation is given till 1872-73.   † No quotation is given till 1871-72.

purely agricultural labour : with clothing they supply themselves. The engagement includes ploughing, sowing, reaping, threshing, and garnering and the rate of payment is usually 150 baskets of unhusked rice per man, which may represent any sum from Rs. 100 to Rs. 150 or more according to the market price in December or January. In many cases now-a-days natives of India, almost invariably Madrassis, are hired and more especially for reaping, and the system then is different. The coolies are engaged in bodies varying in number from 20 to 100 and they are paid at the rate of from Rs. 50 to Rs. 80 for an area which usually yields 1,000 baskets, except in Pyaw-bhwai and some other circles which are close to Rangoon where the rate is as high as Rs. 100 and even Rs. 150. The hirer has to supply the labourers with rice, oil and tamarinds. They do not thresh out the grain but move from farm to farm taking up fresh contracts as they finish the one upon which they are engaged and as they work hard so as to get as many contracts as they can in the season they get through their work rapidly and are preferred to Burman labourers by many of the farmers. The gains of the labourer are thus pretty sure ; not so those of the farmer.

Buffaloes may be calculated to work for from three to four years when they succumb to the climate and bad treatment ; plough and cart bullocks somewhat longer. Bearing this in mind and taking the average price of these animals and of rice in the husk at the present day the expenditure and receipts of a family of six persons, a father, mother and four children, owning ten acres of good rice land would be, about :—

	Rs.		
A. *Farm*—			
1.—One-third cost of a pair of buffaloes	60		
2.—One-third cost of a plough	2		
3.—One-eighth cost of a cart	4		
4.—Hire of a labourer to plough, reap, and thresh and do odd jobs	150		
5.—Ten bushels of seed grain	10		
		226	0
B. *Food*—			
6.—Rice (2 pyee a day or about one basket of rice in eight days, 45 baskets a year equal to 100 baskets of rice in the husk)	100		
7.—Fifty viss of ngapee	15		
8.—Curry stuff etc.	15		
		130	0
C. *Clothes*—			
9.—Two Petticoats at Rs. 2-8	5 0		
10.—Two Men's waistcloths at Rs. 3-4	6 8		
11.—Two Turbans at Rs..2-8	5 0		
12.—Two Women's jackets at Re. 1-4	2 8		
13.—Two Men's ditto at Re. 1-4	2 8		
14.—For children (say)	15 0		
		36	8
D. *Miscellaneous*—			
15.—Repairing house and thatching	25 0		
16.—Cheroots, betel, household utensils etc.	30 0		
		55	0
E. *Taxes*—			
17.—Land revenue	20 0		
18.—Capitation tax	5 0		
		25	0
	Say Rs. 480.	472	8

The ten acres, if the land is moderately good, will produce about 600 baskets of rice in the husk which, calculated at the same rate, are worth Rs. 600, and the annual gain should thus be about Rs. 120; but in practice it is very much less as money is expended in silk clothes for festivals, in giving dances, in offerings to the Hpoongyee and in many other ways, and it is certain that such a family, as a general rule, puts by nothing and barely makes both ends meet.

The average holding of each agriculturist has always been larger here than elsewhere in the province, that is always since the British occupation for no statistics are available for any antecedent period from which information on this point can be gained with any approach to accuracy. On the annexation it was found that the average holding was of about 10 acres and according to the census reports of 1872 it was found to be 11·47 acres. It is extremely doubtful if these figures are accurate for it has certainly been the case that in some instances the size of the ordinary holding has been arrived at by dividing the total number of acres in a district on which revenue was paid by the number of inhabitants shewn as "agriculturists", a term which includes many who neither own nor rent land but work as labourers. Dividing the area of rice land, including fallow, by the number of persons who paid revenue on such land—and this is the nearest approach possible to correctness—it appears from the latest returns that the average holding is 19 acres and that of holdings of :—

Up to 10 acres there are	14,352
From 10 to 20 acres	10,055
„ 20 to 30 „	5,599
„ 30 to 40 „	2,980
„ 40 to 50 „	1,623
„ 50 to 100 „	2,081
Over 100 „	151

The area of garden land is always smaller and of this, whether held with or without rice land, there were, in 1877-78 :—

Holdings of from 1 to 5 acres	6,109
„ „ 5 to 10 „	822
Above 10 „	146

In making these calculations the grants of land made revenue free for a term of years under the liberal grant rules of 1861 and of 1865 have been thrown out of consideration : of these there were 54 in 1877 representing an area of 66,160 acres. The grantees pay no revenue for a period fixed in each case when the grant was made and regulated according to the nature of the forest on the land at the time and are entitled to demand any rent they please from those whom they can induce to settle; the legality or equity of the terms is a matter for the Civil Courts if disputes arise. At the end of the lease they are entitled to a renewal at the rates in force according to the scale or at any rate agreed upon between them and the Government not exceeding the highest rate paid by non-grantees in the neighbourhood. The rules were found to work so unsatisfactorily and to conduce so little to any real increase to the cultivation or to the prosperity of the country that in 1872 the issue of any new grants was forbidden.

The continual wars between the Burmans, the Peguans and the Siamese together with internal dissensions considerably

Population. depopulated the once flourishing Talaing kingdom of which this district formed a part and, as if these were not sufficient, several Talaing kings did their best to ruin their country, whilst the Burmans, after the conquest by Aloung-bhoora, took measures which largely resulted in a still further decrease amongst the inhabitants. Nanda-bhooreng, who reigned over Pegu and Ava from 1582 to 1599, by his cruelties during the last few years of his reign forced numbers to abandon their country and so depopulated the delta that none were left to cultivate the soil. The Burmese, after the conquest in 1757, set themselves steadily to extirpate the Talaing language and after the first Burmese war drove many thousands into the neighbouring British provinces of Arakan and Tenasserim. In 1855 the number of inhabitants was returned as 137,130, but the Commissioner expressed his opinion that this was far too low an estimate. "From general observation, it is believed" he stated "that "the districts of * * * * and Rangoon contain about three times the "number of people that are shewn. This is also the opinion of the "officers in charge of those districts". Taking the population at the higher figure of 401,390, which is the Commissioner's estimate, the number per square mile would have been in that year rather under 41, and this in an extremely fertile country of which such glowing descriptions were given by the earlier European travellers in the sixteenth century.

The census taken in 1872 shewed the number of inhabitants, exclusive of those in the town of Rangoon as :—

Burmese	..	..	..	292,794
Talaing	..	..	..	4,943
Kareng	..	..	..	27,305
Shan	..	..	..	5,179
Arakanese	..	..	..	107
Hindoos	..	..	..	934
Mahomedans	..	..	..	518
Chinese	..	..	..	537
All others	..	..	..	7
			Total	332,324

The most noticeable point in this statement is the paucity of the Talaing, the former inhabitants. Doubtless this had been to a considerable extent caused by the cruelties of Nanda-bhooreng already alluded to whose enmity seems to have been especially excited by the Talaing Booddhist monks, thousands of whom he forced to turn laymen and killed or expelled, and by the emigration eastward and westward during the later years of the Burmese rule, but it appears exceedingly probable that many shewn in the returns as Burmans are really pure Talaing and still more of mixed Burman and Talaing blood, for as Sir Arthur Phayre noticed 20 years ago, speaking of the inhabitants of Pegu, "scarcely any one "of Talaing descent calls himself anything but a Burman, so completely "has the national spirit been extinguished". The Kareng—and many even of these prefer to be considered Burmese—are not so numerous here as in other parts of the delta of the Irrawaddy. They beiong to Pwo and Sgaw families, two of the three into which the race is divided, and are industrious agriculturists. Their arrival in the plains is no doubt an event of comparatively late date. Numbers of them have been converted to Christianity and the remainder have to some extent adopted Booddhism as their religion. The Shan have come from the north and east at various periods and are found in colonies, one of which near Rangoon is of very recent date. In the Than-lyeng township are villages occupied by descendants of a number of captives brought away from seven villages in the neighbourhood of Zeng-mai by Aloung-bhoora after his invasion of that country some 125 years ago. The captives were settled in the Rwon circle (to which they gave their name) under a headman of their own and remained there for many years, but latterly many have emigrated to other circles, their numbers being recruited by arrivals from another colony near Pegu, and many are found in Twan-te. The newer colonies retain their dress, customs and language, but the older ones have become thoroughly Burmanised and retain but few traces of their distinct nationality. Amongst the Mahomedans are found two classes, new arrivals from India and descendants of former immigrants. In the Than-lyeng township are descendants of the Indian Mussulmans who resided here during the time that the European factories flourished and although they have received a considerable infusion of Burmese blood they still adhere to their distinctive dress and religion but in everything else are completely Burmanised. They intermarry chiefly among themselves. Amongst the Booddhists are found a number of families who state that they are of foreign origin, who bury their dead under tombs and abstain from pork and who are most probably descended from the converts forcibly made by the Peguan king Bhooreng Noung about the middle of the sixteenth century.

The following table shews the distribution of the population in 1872 according to sexes and religion :—

	Christians.	Hindoos.	Mahomedans.	Booddhists.	Total.
Males	3,911	609	317	171,567	176,404
Females	3,527	325	201	151,867	155,920
Total ...	7,438	934	518	323,434	332,324

The Kareng and other Asiatic races, other than Hindoos and Mahomedans, are included amongst the Booddhists except in the cases of converts to Christianity. The Booddhists, therefore, furnish 97·32 per cent. of the whole population ; Henzada, where there are very few Hindoos, and Shwe-gyeng, where there are very few Christians, alone shewing a higher percentage. The disproportion between the males and females is greater than in any other district except Akyab, and then only if Akyab town be included, whilst Rangoon town is excluded here ; the actual percentage is 53·08 males to 46·92 females.

The population according to age was found to be :—

	Males.	Females.	Total.
Not exceeding one year ..	11,020	9,051	20,071
Above 1 year, not above 6 years	26,269	23,674	49,943
„ 6 „ „ „ 12 „	26,532	23,346	49,878
„ 12 „ „ „ 20 „	21,844	19,855	41,699
„ 20 „ „ „ 30 „	26,534	24,008	50,542
„ 30 „ „ „ 40 „	26,921	24,762	51,683
„ 40 „ „ „ 50 „	18,886	15,817	34,703
„ 50 „ „ „ 60 „	10,061	8,349	18,410
Exceeding 60 „	8,337	7,028	15,365

At none of these ages were the females in excess of the males as was found to be the case at certain ages in several districts, and notably all along the Tenasserim coast and up the valleys of the Salween and of the Tsit-toung towards Toung-ngoo. The number of male agriculturists over 20 was 41,180 or rather more than one-third of the number of the whole male population above that age.

The population of the town of Rangoon is of a very different character as is shewn by the following figures which give the number of the various races living there in 1872 :—

Burmans	..	..	..	..	..	56,918
Talaing	..	..	..	..	..	7,451
Kareng	..	..	..	..	..	525
Shan	..	..	..	..	..	1,217
Arakanese	..	..	..	..	..	195
Hindoos	..	..	..	..	..	15,284*
Mahomedans	..	..	..	..	..	9,608
Chinese	..	..	..	..	..	3,181
Europeans, Eurasians, and Americans	..	..	..		2,384†
All others	..	..	..	..	..	1,982
				Total ..	98,745

The whole population, therefore, of the district, including the capital town of the province, was 431,069.

The population of the district from 1854-55 has been :—

Year.		District.	Town.	Year.		District.		Town.
1855	..	175,185		1867	..	280,231	..	71,186
1856	..	178,889		1868	..	285,400	..	72,675
1857	..	201,633		1869	..	264,495	..	96,942
1858	..	195,759	Inclusive of Ran-	1870	..	457,149	..	93,163
1859	..	221,829	goon town.	1871	..	273,078	..	100,000
1860	..	252,507		1872	..	310,035	..	77,777
1861	..	274,742		1873	..	348,236	..	80,096
1862	..	283,714		1874	..	335,169	..	81,244
1863	..	236,121	.. 61,138	1875	..	276,367	..	80,464
1864	..	249,999	.. 63,956	1876	..	281,992	..	83,322
1865	..	246,149	.. 66,577	1877	..	286,505	..	83,322
1866	..	247,523	.. 69,866					

The most important town is *Rangoon* from which the district takes its name and which is the capital of the province, situated on the bank of the Hlaing, or as it is here called the Rangoon, at the mouth of the Pegu river. In the Burmese time little more than a collection of mat huts grouped with little regularity or order it has risen to its present importance since the occupation of the country by the British. In 1878 it contained 91,458 inhabitants. It will be found described under its own name.

Towns.

Pegu, on the river of the same name, in 17° 19′ N. and 96° 34′ 30″ E., once the capital of a sovereign who ruled from Bengal to Cochin China, the kings of Arakan and of Siam, of Ava, Toung-ngoo, and Prome being tributary to him, never recovered its capture by the Burmese under

* Including 1,906 Christians.
† Of whom 1,926 were British, 37 Italians, 81 Germans, 46 Americans, and the rest Austrians, Dutch, French, Norwegians, &c. &c.

Aloung-bhoora, in 1756 A.D., and is now little more than a large village, the head-quarters of a township, with 4,948 inhabitants. It was founded by Tha-ma-la and Wee-ma-la, sons of the then reigning sovereign of Tha-htoon, who brought with them 130 families and were joined by many more from the neighbourhood. The new kingdom gradually rose in importance as Tha-htoon dwindled and Pegu was enlarged and embellished by many of its rulers. More than once attacked and taken, it sometimes sank into a provincial city again to be made the seat of Government. It was described by Cæsar Fredericke, the Venetian, who visited the country early in the latter half of the sixteenth century, as consisting of two separate portions in one of which resided the trading population and in the other the Court and its surroundings, the latter encircled by a square wall with 20 gates, five in each face, and surmounted at intervals by gilded sentry boxes; the streets were straight and broad enough for 10 or 12 men to ride abreast along them; the houses were of wood and tiled, and the palace was in the centre encompassed by wet ditches and handsomely ornamented and gilded. On the opposite bank of the river are the extensive remains of numerous pagodas and other masonry structures, whilst to the eastward is the celebrated Shwe-hmaw-daw pagoda, within the ruined walls of a fort a mile square built by Bhooreng Noung, who amongst other names assumed that of Tsheng-hpyoo-sheng (the Chaumigrem of the Portuguese writers), as a portion of the town described by Cæsar Fredericke. During the second Burmese war Pegu was twice taken by the British and after the second capture was more than once attacked by the Burmese troops and defended with some difficulty. It is the head-quarters of a sub-division and contains Court-houses, Police-stations, a Telegraph office, a Post office, a School and a Market-place. The inhabitants are mainly Booddhists, with a few Hindoos, Mahomedans and Christians.

Twan-te is another village, once an important town, situated at the northern extremity of the Twan-te Taw-gyee, west of Rangoon, on the banks of the Twan-te stream about seven miles from its mouth in the To river. The site of the old boundary wall is still pointed out by the inhabitants. Near it is the ancient Shwe Tshan-daw pagoda much venerated by the Talaing and not far off the site of the old town of Khabeng.

Syriam, or more properly Than-lyeng, on the eastern bank of the Pegu river opposite Rangoon, was the site of the Portuguese and English factories and the scene in 1612 of the capture and impalement by the king of Burma of de Brito who had made himself master of the country in the name of the king of Portugal and had attained such power that he was able to attack and defeat the king of Toung-ngoo and to seize his capital. The remains of the fort and buildings, including those of a church erected by de Brito, are still in existence and a considerable number of the inhabitants are descendants of the Mahomedan settlers of that period. During the wars between the English and the Burmese it was attacked and taken by the British; after they had retired, on the conclusion of the first Burmese war, Moung Tsat, called the "Syriam Raja", declining to submit to the Burmese on their return when the British evacuated Pegu, attempted to re-establish the Talaing monarchy but was defeated and with his followers driven to seek refuge in Tenasserim where they settled in two parties, one on the banks of the Salween and one further south on the seacoast.

Several other towns are mentioned in Burmese and Talaing history, but none are now of any importance, and all have sunk into villages. Of towns and villages there were in 1872 :—

1,080	with	less	than	200		inhabitants	
392	,,	from		200	to	500	inhabitants.
68	,,	,,		500	,,	1,000	,,
8	,,	,,		1,000	,,	2,000	,,
1	,,	,,		2,000	,,	3,000	,,
1	,,	,,		3,000	,,	5,000	,,
1	,,	,,		5,000	,,	10,000	,,
1	(Rangoon) more than					50,000	,,

The principal articles manufactured are salt, pottery, fish-paste (nga-pee), mats, and silk and cotton cloths; all for **Manufactures.** local consumption, except the pottery and nga-pee which are exported, the latter to Upper Burma. The salt is made during the hot weather at various places along the seacoast and in the Syriam and An-gyee townships, partly by solar evaporation and partly by boiling in iron or earthen pots, the iron yielding the greater out-turn. The method adopted when iron pots are used is as follows :—

A site having been selected a patch sometimes an acre in extent is carefully cleared of scrub, the roots being dug out, and left to the next season when any shrubs or grass which may have sprung up are taken out and the whole carefully levelled. Round this is constructed an embankment, and during the spring tides of February the sea water is conveyed into this cistern by a trough communicating with a platform on the bank of some tidal stream. In March the mud left by solar evaporation on the surface of the enclosed space is scraped off and placed in a filter which has previously been constructed and salt water poured on it. This filter consists of a framework some 15 feet long, five feet wide and one and a half feet deep, raised three feet from the ground on small supports, the bottom is made of rough poles about two inches in diameter laid side by side covered by a mat made of a wild creeper over which is put coarse cloth. Under the filter is a slanting framework of palm leaves which conducts the filtered brine into a trough, and thus to a reservoir or pit some six feet deep dug near the furnace, which is about 15 feet long, 12 feet broad, and four or five feet high, where the boiling pots are arranged. As long as a few grains of boiled rice thrown from time to time into the brine will float the filtering process is continued but as soon as they sink it is stopped and the contents of the filter are thrown away. The boiling is continued day and night, the pots being cleared about every twelve hours, when the contents have evaporated to dryness, and replenished with brine from the reservoir. The furnace is protected by a shed which serves also as a dwelling for the workers.

The method employed when earthen pots are used for boiling is different. During the rainy season a large space is cleared, ploughed and made as smooth as possible and arranged in terraces protected by embankments and when the rains are over a tank near the cleared space is excavated about 30 feet long by 22 feet broad and four or five feet deep. Between December and March the necessary materials such as pots, firewood, &c., are collected (the former principally from Kwon-khyan-goon in An-gyee) and a shed built within which is constructed a kiln of the earthern pots built into the shape of a dome. In the meanwhile, in January, water is let into the higher terraces either by baling or, if the site is low enough, by letting it pass through an opening made in the protecting embankment. After remaining for one day in the upper terrace it is passed into the second and two and a half days later into the last. When the water here collected will float a grain or two of boiled rice it is ready for boiling, but the fields have to be filled two or three times before sufficient salt is extracted from the soil to render the brine ready for the furnace. The pots are very strong and thick but often burst under the tremendous heat to which they are exposed. There are usually two boilings in each 24 hours and each boiling gives about two viss or about 7¼ lbs. of salt. As the boiling season lasts for about two months the average outturn from each pot may be taken at 250 viss or about eight cwt. which at current prices would sell at about Rs. 18 or Rs. 19.

The gross quantity made varies year by year and is decreasing owing to the importation of foreign salt which competes favourably with it in the market. For many years the local article held its own for nga-pee making, but even here it is losing ground and mainly because it is dearer. The increasing cost of firewood also has something to do with it.

Pots for salt boiling are made in Kwon-khyan-goon and in the adjoining village of Taw-pa-lwai in the Angyee township. The work of making salt pots begins in January and ends when the rains commence. Usually four men work together—women are never employed—one mixing the earth, one turning the wheel, one fashioning and one finishing. The earth is brought from Mayan-rwa, a little to the northward, where ordinary pots are made, fine sea sand from the mouth of the river To and the firewood from the Twan-te Taw-gyee. To every two parts of earth one part of sand is added and the mass mixed up with water till it is soft enough to work. The fashioning is done entirely by hand and the pot when fashioned is well beaten with a flat slab of wood; when completed they are put to dry, a process which, as they are very thick, takes a long time, and are then placed in a permanent kiln, about 250 at a time, and burned for 24 hours. The kilns are built against the scarped side of a hill and have the draught-hole close to the hill and the entrance at the other end. The roof is somewhat dome-shaped and has much the appearance of a large unkeeled boat turned topsy-turvy. The inside measurements vary. An ordinary sized kiln is about 20 feet long by 12 broad and 10 feet high from the floor to the centre of the roof. Many of the pots, owing to defective workmanship, crack and break in the burning, in some cases as many as 100 out of the 250 in the kiln. A party of four good workmen will turn out from 100 to 125 salt pots in a day. The price varies, according to the season and the demands of the salt-boilers, from Rs. 45 to Rs. 90 per hundred. A 500-basket boat with four men will carry 25 baskets of sand and make the trip to To-wa and back four times a day. The boatmen are paid eight annas a day each and the cost of 100 baskets of sand is thus Rs. 8 ; the man who brings the earth gets Rs. 2-8 per 100 baskets. The mixer gets one rupee a day, the wheel-turner, fashioner and finisher each Rs. 3 per 100 pots. The expenditure and profits during a season would be about :—

	Rs.	A.	P.
One hundred baskets of sand	8	0	0
Two ,, ,, earth	5	0	0
Eight cords of wood	32	0	0
Mixer, 90 days	90	0	0
Fashioner for 1,250 pots..	37	8	0
Wheel-turner ,,	37	8	0
Finisher ,, ,,	37	8	0
Bamboos, &c.	2	8	0
		250 0 0	
Value of 1,250 pots at Rs. 60	750	0	0
Deduct value of 400 pots damaged in burning ..	240	0	0
		510 0 0	

Nett profit   Say Rs. 250

At other periods of the year the potters at Kwon-khyan-goon and Taw-pa-lwai and throughout the year those of Ma-yan-rwa and Thoon-kwa make cooking pots. The same earth is used as for the salt pots but the sand is from De-da-naw and is used in smaller quantities. Usually a man and a woman work together, the man bringing the earth and the sand and mixing the clay and the woman turning the wheel with one hand and fashioning with the other. A couple can turn out from 100 to 150 pots of sizes in a day. From 250 to 300 are put in each kiln and are burned for 12 hours, a quarter of a cord of wood being used. About one-fifth are cracked or broken in the burning. In the cold weather they sell on the spot for from Rs. 6 to Rs. 8 per 100 and in the rains for about Rs. 5 per 100.

The salt-boilers usually come to buy their own pots but the water and cooking pots are bought principally by persons who hawk them about in boats or take them to the markets in Rangoon and other large places. In some cases persons in Kywon-khyan-goon make advances to the potters at the rate of Rs. 3 per 100 and then resell at market rates. An ordinary water pot costs two annas in Rangoon.

At Twan-te are made large water or oil jars glazed outside with a mixture of galena and rice water, some standing four feet high, commonly known as " Pegu jars", which are used throughout Burma.

Nga-pee is made principally in the An-gyee township. It is of two kinds one called *Nga-pee-goung* and the other *Toung-tha-nga-pee* ; Nga-pee-goung again consists of the ordinary Nga-pee-goung such as is made here and of Nga-tha-louk Nga-pee, made from the Nga-tha-louk or Hilsa (*Clupea palasah*). In making the ordinary Nga-pee-goung the fish are scaled,—if large by hand, if small by means of a bamboo with the end made into a kind of stiff brush and worked amongst a mass thrown together, almost alive, into a wooden mortar—cleaned and the heads of the large ones cut off. They are then well rubbed with salt and carefully packed into a bamboo basket and weights placed on the top. Here they are left for a night, the liquid draining away through the basket. Next morning they are taken out, rubbed with salt, and spread out on a mat and the next day they are put away with alternate layers of salt in large jars and left in a cool place. In a month the liquid which has come to the top has evaporated and left a layer of salt and they are ready for sale. Sometimes the supernatant liquid gets full of maggots before completely drying up ; in this case it is taken off and more salt added. It is a great object both to the makers and to the cooks to keep the fish whole. They are eaten roasted, fried or in curries. In making Toung-tha Nga-pee, which must not be confounded with Bhala-khyan *vel* Tsien-tsa (because it can be eaten uncooked) *vel* Nga-pee-hgnyeng (Arakan) *vel* Gwai (Tavoy and Mergui), the fish are scaled and in large fish the head is removed and the body cut up. They are soaked in brine for a night, taken out and exposed to the sun on a mat till they begin to turn putrid and then brayed in a mortar with salt and packed away in any receptacle and kept for two or three months by which time the paste is fit for sale. This is made into a kind of sauce with other ingredients and is used as a condiment.

In An-gyee are made large coarse mats for the Rangoon market used largely for placing at the bottom of ships holds ; whilst in the Hlaing township a much finer kind is made for which there is a ready sale in the Rangoon market for local use and for export to other parts of the province.

Silkworms are to some extent reared in the Hlaing township, and the process of rearing the worms, collecting and boiling the cocoons and winding the silk is the same as in Prome, Thayet and elsewhere. Silk and cotton cloths are made in almost every house, partly for sale and partly for the use of the household.

The exact amount of the revenue realised in the district before the annexation is not discoverable as no records are obtain-

Revenue.

able to shew the amount raised for their own use by the local officials who received no regular salary but were paid by judicial fees and fines and by whatever they could squeeze from the people over and above the sum fixed by the State as that which was to be remitted annually to the capital either for the Government or for the Myotsa, that is the prince or official to whom the district had been allotted for maintenance. The local revenues may, however, be taken at about two-thirds of the Imperial, if these terms may be used to distinguish the State from the local official demand. The amount of the State demand, which was generally collected according to the settlement made by order of the king Bhodaw-bhoora in 1783 and revised in 1801 just prior to the annexation was :—

					Rs.
1.—House family tax, Burmans and Kareng	..	..	..	..	164,370
2.—Yoke of oxen, or rice land tax	..	..	..	..	73,190
3.—Fisheries	..	..	..	..	103,570
4.—Salt	..	..	..	..	53,820
5.—Transit duties	..	..	..	..	24,440
6.—Timber and forest dues..	..	..	..	..	2,710
7.—Ferries	..	..	..	..	200
8.—Brokers' licenses and miscellaneous..	..	..	..	5,070
9.—Customs	..	..	..	..	260,000
			Total	..	687,370

The amounts were fixed in viss (3·65lbs.) of Rwek-nee silver each of which may be taken as the equivalent of Rs. 130 and the sums given above are calculated accordingly. Adding two-thirds of this for the local revenues the whole sum paid by the population, which, as already shewn was then exceedingly sparse though doubtless more numerous than during the first year or perhaps first two years after the annexation, was Rs. 11,45,600, rather less than the amount realized by the British Government in 1856-57, and rather less than the revenues of the whole of Pegu including Toung-ngoo (which has since been transferred to Tenasserim) in 1853-54.

The British Government adopted, to a certain extent, the Burmese system, if system it can be called, which was not oppressive and suited the people, making such modifications as our experience in Arakan and Tenasserim shewed to be advantageous. The capitation and land taxes were retained but levied according to fixed rates and no longer assessed on each family by the village officer according to his estimate of its means. The fisheries were rented out and the tax on the manufacture of salt was continued in a modified form. Ferries, judicial fines and fees, sea customs, port dues, &c. furnished a share of the gross revenue whilst an excise on spirits and drugs was introduced and transit and broker dues abolished.

There are no details of the collections before 1855-56 now available, but the nett amounts in 1853-54 and in 1854-55 were Rs. 545,093 and Rs. 829,934 respectively. The collections in 1855-56 and in 1877-78 were :—

					1855-56.	1877-78.
					Rs.	Rs.
Land revenue	..	..	..	..	306,960	1,366,391
Capitation tax	..	..	.	..	168,950	350,047
Salt tax	..	..	..	..	32,550	7,076
Fishery tax	..	..	..	..	140,670	104,906
Forest produce	..	..	..	..	Nil.	515
Excise	..	..	..	..	72,680	526,884
Sea customs	..	..	..	..	157,370	2,917,743
Timber revenue	..	..	..	..	50,730	Nil.
Judicial fines and fees, and Law stamps	..		..	..	14,560	31,418
Postage and Telegraph stamps		..	..	..	7,310	1,343,677
Miscellaneous (savings, sale of unclaimed property, &c.)			..	..	8,620	248,450
				Total	960,400	6,897,107

During this period stamps in judicial proceedings and for law papers were rendered obligatory and the telegraph was established. The system upon which the inland fishery tax was first collected was by leasing out lakes and ponds to the highest bidder at auction : this was subsequently changed to annual leases granted by the district officer to inhabitants of neighbouring villages at a rent fixed by himself ; and a year or two ago a modified auction system was substituted at which only *bonâ fide* fishermen living near the fishery can bid, and the lease is for five years instead of for one only as formerly.

The gross revenues of the district, excluding sea customs, but including the Imperial revenue raised in the town of Rangoon, during the 10 years ending with 1877-78, have been :—

Year.	Revenue.	Year.	Revenue.	Year.	Revenue.	Year.	Revenue.	Year.	Revenue.
	Rs.		Rs.		Rs.		Rs.		Rs.
1868-69	2,414,204	1870-71	2,452,037	1872-73	2,671,814	1874-75	3,229,384	1876-77	2,364,559
1869-70	2,350,700	1871-72	2,437,703	1873-74	2,967,255	1875-76	2,281,517*	1877-78	3,107,822

* In this year the Thoon-khwa district was formed and the revenue administration of the town of Rangoon was placed under the Magistrate.

From these figures is excluded a local revenue derived from ferries, lease of stalls in market-places, a town fund raised on the land in Pegu, an addition of five per cent. to the Imperial land and fishery taxes, cattle market fees, &c. The amounts so raised during the ten years ending with 1877-78 were :—

Year.	Revenue.	Year.	Revenue.	Year.	Revenue.	Year.	Revenue.	Year.	Revenue.
	Rs.		Rs.		Rs.		Rs.		Rs.
1868-69	52,241	1870-71	74,118	1872-73	91,476	1874-75	108,255	1876-77	106,886
1869-70	45,568	1871-72	68,502	1873-74	110,379	1875-76	82,991	1877-78	124,696

This does not include the local revenue raised in the town of Rangoon.

Under the Burmese Government this district consisted of several townships each under an officer exercising considerable powers, and the whole was controlled by a Governor who had the power of life and death and communicated direct with the Government at Ava. The townships, of which there were 14 exclusive of Rangoon, were Pegu, Zwai-bhoon, Zaing-ga-naing, Daw-bhoon, A-kha-rien, Hpoung-leng, Hlaing, Eng-ga-bhoo, Hmaw-bhee, Twan-te, Thoon-khwa, An-gyee, Eng-tay and Pya-poon. When the head of the township held his office hereditarily he was called a Myo-thoogyee but when appointed by the State a Myo-ook, and when holding the appointment in virtue of being commander of a royal war-boat a Pai-neng (steersman). The exercise of power by these various officers was very capricious. The subordinate officers in the interior, generally, were in league with robbers whom they entertained, nominally as a kind of Police. After the capture of the lower portion of the delta of the Irrawaddy the country fell a prey to anarchy and it was more than a year before peace was restored. This district suffered less than its neighbours to the west and north, Bassein, Henzada and Tharrawaddy, but still hardly any grain was sown during the rains of the first year. The local jurisdictions were to a great extent retained, a Deputy Commissioner placed in charge of the district and a Myo-ook appointed to each township with moderate judicial, fiscal and Police powers, with Thoogyee in charge of circles and Goung under them, not as formerly at the caprice of the Thoogyee but each in charge of several villages and appointed by the Government. Each Myo-ook was allowed two peons only and every endeavour was made, with gradual but complete success, to check the entertainment by these officials of bands of bravos. The Thoogyee, who were primarily revenue officers but who also were held responsible for the general state of their circles, were paid by a percentage on their revenue collections, whilst the Goung, who were primarily Police officers but were to assist the Thoogyee generally in the collection of the revenue, were paid Rs. 10 a month ; these constituted the village constabulary and, with the Thoogyee, the detective Police. Below the Goung again were appointed Kye-dan-gyee in charge of village tracts whose duties were to assist both Goung and Thoogyee in their duties. In Rangoon Goung were appointed to the several wards or quarters. One of the most important changes made was in the suppression of heads of trades. "There were Ook (heads) over the Kareng of each township, over "the fishermen and over the brokers, over palm juice drawers and "silver-assayers, over the ploughmen of the royal lands, and the cultivators "of the royal gardens. They, alone, took primary cognizance of crimes "and offences amongst those under their charge" and at first it was "found "a matter of no small difficulty to make Thoogyee and others understand "that they had jurisdiction over all residents in the territories under their "charge without reference to this mere personal jurisdiction". With four exceptions little or no change has been made in the general principles of the administration of the district, these exceptions are :—the formation in 1861-62 of a regular Police placed under officers of its own but except in matters of interior economy and discipline subordinate to the district officer; a few years later the formation of an independent prison department; later still the formation of an education department; and a few years ago the almost entire separation of the town from the district. Circles have been amalgamated and placed under one Thoogyee instead of two or three, others have been split into two, townships have been added together and placed under one Myo-ook or Extra Assistant Commissioner and several townships have been joined into a sub-division placed under the immediate control of an Assistant Commissioner or of an Extra Assistant of superior grade, and the limits of the district itself have been varied by handing over outlying tracts to neighbouring jurisdictions—Bhaw-nee in the extreme north on the eastern slopes of the Pegu Roma mountains to Toung-ngoo in 1864 (since joined to Shwe-gyeng), the Kaw-lee-ya circle between the Pegu mountains and the Tsit-toung river to Shwe-gyeng in 1872-73, a narrow strip west of those mountains which formed the Thoon-tshay circle to Henzada during the following year, and lastly the addition of an extensive tract in the extreme west to another in the extreme east of Bassein to form the Thoon-khwa district.

Rangoon is now divided into three sub-divisions each containing two townships, viz. :—

Sub-divisions.	Head-quarters.	Townships.	Head-quarters.	Old townships.	Number of circles.
Hmaw-bhee ..	Hmaw-bhee* ..	Hlaing ..	Taw-la-tai ..	Hlaing ..	4
		Hmaw-bhee	Eng-tsien† ..	Hmaw-bhee and part of Eng-ga-bhoo and of Daw-bhoon.	11
Than-lyeng or Syriam.	Kyouk-tan ..	An-gyee ..	Twan-te ..	An-gyee ..	14
		Than-lyeng	Than-lyeng ..	Than-lyeng and part of Zwai-bhoon.	10
Pegu ..	Pegu ..	Pegu ..	Pegu ..	Pegu and part of Zwai-bhoon and of Zaing-ga-naing	6
		Hpoung-leng	Hlay-goo ..	Hpoung-leng, A-kha-rien, and part of Zaing-ga-naing and of Daw-bhoon	8
				Total ..	53

* Shortly to be removed to Eng-tsien.   † Shortly to be removed to Hmaw-bhee.

In each township there is a court presided over by the Extra Assistant Commissioner in charge who has moderate civil and criminal powers, and in each sub-division a similar court presided over by the Assistant or Extra Assistant in charge with higher powers. The Deputy Commissioner as district judge hears all civil appeals, and on the original side entertains suits of over Rs. 3,000 in value, an appeal and in some cases a second appeal lying from him to the Commissioner of the division. As district magistrate he hears all appeals in criminal cases except those preferred from magistrates of the first class, and officers in charge of sub-divisions usually are of this rank, which lie direct to the sessions judge and himself tries persons accused of the more serious offences except murder and those in which seven years rigorous imprisonment or transportation would be an insufficient punishment : these are committed to the Commissioner sitting as a Court of Session, usually by the magistrate of the sub-division. There are thus 10 courts presided over by officers exercising both civil and criminal as well as revenue powers. No village is more than 44 miles from any court and the average distance is 26 miles. The number of civil suits and appeals instituted and their gross value during 1876 and 1877, the only two complete years since the Thoon-khwa district was formed, were :—

ORIGINAL SUITS.				APPEALS INSTITUTED.	
1876.		1877.		1876.	1877.
Instituted.	Value.	Instituted.	Value.	Instituted.	Instituted.
1,714	Rs. 201,446	1,738	Rs. 263,117	52	85

The number of persons tried and the number of witnesses examined during the same years was :—

1876.		1877.		APPEALS.	
Persons tried.	Witnesses.	Persons tried.	Witnesses.	1876.	1877.
3,846	7,546	3,676	7,531	20	23

For several years after the annexation the more serious crimes, such as murder, gang-robbery, technically called dacoity, and ordinary robbery were far from uncommon. Gradually the district has settled down but gang-robberies are still not altogether unknown. These are sometimes, but rarely, committed by villagers, sometimes by gangs made up partly of inhabitants of the district and partly of upcountry Burmans organized and led by trained dacoits who come down from Upper Burma with this object and return when the rains set in, and sometimes by Kareng-nee who have settled down; the depredations of these latter are confined, generally, to the country about Pegu : the numerous bad characters to be found in the Kyee-myeng-daing and Poo-zwon-doung quarters of Rangoon lend their aid in swelling the number especially in the immediate neighbourhood of Rangoon ; they are not recognized by the persons attacked and they get back before the police have received any information and it is almost impossible to find out who the robbers were.

The number of offences committed varies considerably and it would almost seem as if waves of crime passed over the district at intervals of several years. The two last 1876 and 1877 were bad years and afford no criterion ; indeed there have never been so many dacoities since 1872 as in 1877. The numbers of the more serious offences were :—

Year.	Murder by robbers.	Murder, simple.	Murder, attempts.	Culpable homicide.	Causing grievous hurt.	Causing hurt by dangerous weapons.	Dacoity.	Robbery.	Cattle-theft.	Ordinary theft.	Housebreaking.
1876 ..	2	11	2	7	7	39	1	14	156	978	144
1877 ..	1	12	3	3	12	38	11	28	116	930	124

The police force consists of one Superintendent, one Assistant Superintendent, 45 subordinate officers and 503 policemen. One subordinate officer and eight constables are employed in Pegu and are paid from the local funds of that town : 50 constables are water police ; and four officers and 61 men form the Gaol guard. The total cost of this force during 1877 was Rs. 1,23,049 of which Rs. 1,620 were defrayed from local funds. The great majority of the men are Burmans or Talaing, whilst natives of India are enlisted more to act as guards over the gaol and for other cognate duties.

The district has no special gaol. Prisoners convicted by the magistrates are confined in the Rangoon Central Prison which, at present, is situated in the town of Rangoon.

Schools were opened many years ago by the Missionaries both Roman Catholic and Baptist, but it was not until the Burman government had been displaced that there was any real toleration and schools were for long to be found in Rangoon only, the education of the rural classes being left in the hands of the Booddhist monks. In 1867 there were 54 village missionary schools aided by the Government but principally for Kareng. In 1873 a cess school, that is one the expenses of which are defrayed from the five per cent. cess on the land revenue, fishery rents and fish-net tax, was established in Pegu and has been very favourably reported on. It was in this district that attempts were first made to utilize the existing monastic schools, to raise the teaching given in them, and gradually to bring them under inspection by Government officers. The progress made has not been extraordinarily rapid.

Communication is principally carried on by water, boats passing backwards and forwards along the Hlaing, the Pan-hlaing, Tha-khwot-peng, Poo-zwon-doung and Pegu and the many tidal creeks which exist everywhere except in the north central portion of the district. Advantage was taken some years ago of the Paing-kyoon creek and this and others uniting with it were deepened and widened so that boats could pass through to the Tsit-toung. This improved channel, however, gradually silted up and at its eastern end it was found to be too much exposed to the bore which sweeps up the Tsit-toung and in consequence a new canal has been made running from the old channel, not far from Kha-ra-tshoo, to Myit-kyo on the Tsit-toung, with a lock at its eastern end and another at the Pegu or western end of the old channel. The principal roads are one from Rangoon towards Prome, which from a little north of Hmaw-bhee has been taken up by the Rangoon and Irrawaddy Valley (State) Railway; the Rangoon and Toung-ngoo road which leaves the Prome road at Htouk-kyan $21\frac{1}{4}$ miles from Rangoon and runs eastward across the Hpoung-leng plain to Pegu, crossing the Pegu river by a wooden bridge, and on northwards along the eastern foot of the Pegu Roma. Up to and within the limits of Pegu it is bridged and metalled but beyond the earthwork only has been finished. Another road leads from Dala on the right bank of the Hlaing westward to Twan-te, and a third from Than-lyeng on the left bank of the Pegu to Kyouk-tan, the head-quarters of the Syriam sub-division. Feeder roads are either under construction or are about to be commenced from the Ook-kan station on the Railway, which is at the village of Pouk-koon, westward to Ook-kan, round south through Bha-loon to Myoung-ta-nga and thence to Hmaw-bhee; from Hmaw-bhee eastward to the Railway station and on to the Prome road; and from the Hlaw-ga station eastwards to near Htouk-kyan. The Rangoon and Irrawaddy Valley (State) Railway, after it enters this district from Rangoon, runs nearly due north for $60\frac{1}{2}$ miles to the Mee-neng river, with stations at Tha-maing (about to be removed to Pouk-taw near Engtsien) Hlaw-ga, Hmaw-bhee, Taikgyee and Ook-kan (at the village of Pouk-koon). The line is single and the guage 3·2809 feet.

The mails are carried daily by the Railway from Rangoon northward, and once a week by mail-cart from Rangoon past Htouk-kyan to Pegu. These lines are under the Imperial post-office. In addition there are lines under the Deputy Commissioner and paid for from the cess, from Rangoon to Kyouk-tan and back three times a week, from Rangoon to Twan-te and on to the Thoon-khwa district every day, and from Rangoon to Taw-la-tai, the head-quarters of the Hlaing township, on the Hlaing river at the mouth of the Bhaw-lay, twice a week.

Cattle-markets are held three times a week at Pegu, Htouk-kyan, Kambai, Gnyoung-beng, Bo-khyoop, Htan-ma-naing, Tha-maing and Hmaw-bhee. As in England sales elsewhere are not illegal but every endeavour is made to get sellers to bring their cattle to the markets as the official in charge issues to the buyer a ticket describing the cattle and giving other details and the Police are thus aided in tracing stolen beasts. A small fee

567

is charged. The number of cattle sold and the fees realized during the last three years were :—

	1876.		1877.		1878.	
	Number of cattle sold.	Fees realized.	Number of cattle sold.	Fees realized.	Number of cattle sold.	Fees realized.
		Rs.		Rs.		Rs.
Pegu	5,155	1,631	7,020	2,249	11,890	3,723
Htouk-kyan	4,556	1,402	5,095	1,522	5,412	1,575
Kam-bai	2,594	906	3,078	1,036	5,102	1,687
Gnyoung-beng	4,047	1,397	3,050	1,022	4,105	1,251
Bo-khyoop	20	6	2,593	891	1,656	539
Htan-ma-naing*	75	25	695	243	—	—
Tha-maing ..	—	—	965	301	1,654	504
Hmaw-bhee	—	—	—	—	71	19

RANGOON.—The capital of the Province, 21 miles from the sea, lying on the left bank of the Hlaing river at its junction with the Pegu and the Poo-zwon-doung with a small suburb on the right bank. According to the Talaing traditions the first village established on the site of the present Rangoon was founded circa 585 B.C. by two brothers, Poo and Ta-paw, who had received some of Gaudama's hairs from the Booddha himself and, acting on his instructions, buried them on the summit of a slight laterite elevation and erected over them the Shwe Dagon pagoda. Poon-na-ree-ka, who reigned in Pegu from 746 to 761 A.D., is said to have built or re-established the town which he called Aramana. At some indefinite period it regained its name of Dagon and is thus mentioned in the Talaing histories which relate how king Zaw-zit visited it, circa 685 A.D.; how it was occupied by the Burmese in 1413; how Bya-gnya-keng, the son of Raza-dhie-rit, was appointed its governor by his father, and how Sheng-tsaw-boo, the daughter of Raza-dhie-rit, built herself a palace there in 1460.†

The town gradually sank into a collection of huts near the pagoda and drops out of history. Dala, now a small and unimportant suburb on the opposite bank of the Hlaing, and Syriam, on the opposite bank of the Pegu river, are over and over again noticed as places of importance but of Dagon little or nothing is recorded. Gaspar Balbi came to Pegu in 1579-80 and, apud Purchas, wrote of Dagon "After we were landed we began to goe " on the right hand in a large street about 50 paces broad, in which we " saw wooden houses gilded and adorned with delicate gardens after their " custom wherein their Talapoins, which are their Friers, dwell and look " to the Pagod or Varella of Dogon. The left side is furnished with portals " and shops * * * and by this street they go to the Varella for a good " mile straight forward, either under paint houses or in the open street " which is free to walk in".

---

* This market was transferred to Tha-maing in 1877.

†" Her name is held in high honour among the people to this day and a national festival to " her memory is celebrated once a year at Rangoon."—The History of Pegu, by Sir A. P. Phayre, Journal of the Bengal Asiatic Society, 1873, p. 122.

The English, Portuguese, Dutch and French had factories at Than-lyeng—better known under the Europeanised form Syriam—on the other side of the Pegu river and the governor of Dagon was the principal intermediary through whom the officers in charge of the factories communicated with the Talaing Court at Pegu. The dislike of the Talaing to western foreigners getting a footing in the country and the quarrels between the European "factors", each striving to oust the rest for the benefit of his own government, led the sovereign of Pegu to increase the authority and power of the governor of Dagon until at last that officer rose to the first rank and was second to none in the kingdom. The accounts of the Portuguese and English officials in charge of the factories as they were called, or commercial and state agencies as they might perhaps more correctly be designated, are full of the doings of the governor of Dagon and of their own endeavours to outwit each other and get into his good graces so as to obtain privileges which should nominally give them generally greater facilities for trade but which in reality would be of advantage in strengthening their hands in the continual struggle to drive out their European competitors and secure a monopoly. In the wars which took place between the kings of Pegu and of Burma Dagon often changed hands and when at last, in 1763 the Burman Aloung-bhoora, drove out the Talaing garrison of Ava, then the Burman capital, and eventually conquered the Talaing kingdom he came down to Dagon, repaired, and thus to a certain extent to Peguan feelings desecrated, the great Shwe Dagon pagoda, almost re-founded the town and re-named it Ran-koon* or Rangoon, the name it has ever since borne, and made it the seat of the Viceroyalty which he established. It remained, however, little more than a collection of bamboo huts on a marshy flat, but little above the level of low tides, intersected by narrow and irregular streets. It was the scene of repeated struggles for supremacy between the defeated Peguans and their conquerors the Burmans and up to 1790 continual attempts were made by the former to wrest Rangoon from the latter. The last great revolt was in 1789 or in the beginning of 1790 ; the Burman governor was murdered and the town for a time fell into the hands of the insurgents. Meng-tara-gyee, or Bho-daw Bhoora, was then on the throne of Burma and, it is said with his sanction, the rebellion was crushed with the most savage and brutal atrocities and no similar rising was ever again attempted.

The English having succeeded in obtaining leave to establish a factory in Rangoon surrounded it by a brick wall and hoisted the British colours over it. In 1794 differences arose in Arakan and Chittagong between the East India Company and the Burmese Government and Colonel Symes was sent on an embassy to Ava, one of the results of his mission being that Captain Cox was appointed British Resident in Rangoon. He was re-called in the early part of 1798 and no one was sent to replace him.

Symes thus described Rangoon as he saw it :—" It stretches along the " bank of the river about a mile and is not more than a third of a mile in " breadth. The city or miou (*myo*) is a square, surrounded by a high " stockade, and on the north side it is further strengthened by an indifferent " fosse, across which a wooden bridge is thrown : in this face there are

---

* " The end of the war" from *Ran* war and *Koon* (euphonic causa *Goon*) to be finished, exhausted.

" two gates, in each of the others only one. Wooden stages are erected in
" several places within the stockade, for musqueteers to stand on in case
" of an attack. On the south side, towards the river which is about twenty
" or thirty yards from the palisade, there are a number of huts and three
" wharves, with cranes for landing goods. A battery of twelve cannon, six
" and nine pounders, raised on the bank, commands the river, but the
" guns and carriages are in such a wretched condition that they could do
" but little execution. Close to the wooden wharf are two commodious
" wooden houses, used by the merchants as an exchange, where they usually
" meet in the cool of the morning and evening to converse and transact
" business. The streets of the town are narrow, and much inferior to those
" of Pegu, but clean, and well paved : there are numerous channels to
" carry off the rain, over which strong planks are placed, to prevent an
" interruption to intercourse. The houses are raised on posts from the
" ground ; the smaller supported by bamboos, the larger by strong timbers.
" All the officers of Government, the most opulent merchants, and persons
" of consideration, live within the fort ; shipwrights, and people of inferior
" rank, inhabit the suburbs ; and one entire street, called Tuckally (*Tat-*
" *ga-le*), is exclusively assigned to common prostitutes, who are not per-
" mitted to dwell within the precincts of the fortification."

" Swine are suffered to roam about the town at large : these animals,
" which are with reason held unclean, do not belong to any particular
" owners ; they are servants of the public, common scavengers ; they go
" under the houses and devour the filth. The Burmans are also fond of
" dogs, numbers of which infest the streets ; the breed is small and
" extremely noisy."*

The next published accounts of the town are those given by Snodgrass,
Wilson and others who wrote histories of the first Anglo-Burmese war. It
was then found to extend " about nine hundred yards along the bank of
" the river and to be about six or seven hundred yards wide in its broadest
" part : at either extremity extend unprotected suburbs, but the centre, or
" the town itself, is defended by an enclosure of palisades 10 or 12 feet
" high†, strengthened internally by embankments of earth, and protected
" externally on one side by the river, and on the other three sides by a
" shallow creek or ditch communicating with the river, and expanding at
" the western end into a morass crossed by a bridge. The palisade
" encloses the whole of the town of Rangoon in the shape of an irregular
" parallelogram, having one gate in each of three faces, and two in that of
" the north ; at the river gate is a wharf, denominated the King's wharf."‡
The appearance of the town had a very different effect on Major Snodgrass
from that which it had on Colonel Symes :—

" We had been so much accustomed", says the former, " to hear
" Rangoon spoken of as a place of great trade and commercial importance,
" that we could not fail to feel disappointed at its mean and poor appear-
" ance. We had talked of its custom-house, its dockyards, and its harbour,
" until our imaginations led us to anticipate, if not splendour, at least some

---

* Symes : *Embassy to the Kingdom of Ava* : London, 1800, pp. 205, 206.
† From 16 to 18 feet according to Major Snodgrass, Military Secretary to Sir Archibald Camp-
bell.—*Narrative of the Burmese War* : London, 1827, p. 12.
‡ *Narrative of the Burmese War* by Horace Hayman Wilson : London, 1852, pp. 67, 68.

" visible sign of a flourishing commercial city : but, however humble our
" expectations might have been, they must still have fallen short of the
" miserable and desolate picture which the place presented when first
" occupied by the British troops. The town, if a vast assemblage of wooden
" huts may be dignified with that name, is surrounded by a wooden
" stockade, from 16 to 18 feet in height, which effectually shuts out all view
" of the fine river which runs past it, and gives it a confined and insalubrious
" appearance. There are a few brick houses, chiefly belonging to Euro-
" peans, within the stockade, upon which a heavy tax is levied ; and they
" are only permitted to be built by special authority from the Government,
" which is but seldom granted. *   *   *   *   The custom-house, the prin-
" cipal building in the place, seemed fast tottering into ruins. One solitary
" hull upon the stocks marked the dockyard, and a few coasting vessels
" and country canoes were the only craft found in this great commercial
" mart of India beyond the Ganges".
      *   *   *   *   " The houses in Rangoon and Ava, generally, are built
" of wood, or bamboo ; those of the former material usually belong to the
" officers of Government or the wealthier description of inhabitants : the
" floors are raised some feet above the ground, which would contribute
" much to their dryness, healthiness and comfort, were not the space
" beneath almost invariably a receptacle for dirt and stagnant water, from
" which, during the heat of the day, pestilential vapours constantly ascend
" to the annoyance of every one except a Burmhan."
      " Herds of meagre swine, the disgusting scavengers of the town, infest
" the streets by day ; and at night they are relieved by packs of hungry
" dogs, which effectually deprive the stranger of his sleep by their incessant
" howling, and midnight quarrels."
      This gloomy picture may, perhaps, be partly explained by the fact
that the town was then without inhabitants, for according to Wilson it was
found to be entirely deserted. Very little if any change had taken place
since Colonel Symes visit in 1800. The stockade surrounding the town
proper was found as he found it, the huts or houses as he found them, and
the scavengers were still the dogs and the pigs which wandered over the
streets and under the houses.
      Another account of the town is given in the 27th volume of the Medi-
cal Reports, presented to Parliament in 1842 :—" Except a few houses erected
" by Europeans, the town consists of four rows of reed huts running at
" right-angles to each other, surrounded by a stockade from 10 to 12 feet
" in height and protected by a ditch on the northern side : the river face is
" not more than 600 or 700 yards in length and the whole circuit of the
" stockade scarcely exceeds a mile. The site being level and in the
" immediate vicinity of the river is always damp, and during the wet
" season, which comprises most part of the year, it is little better than a
" mixture of mud and marsh, above which the houses are raised on posts.
      *   *   *   *   " About two miles to the north of the town a small conical
" hill starts somewhat abruptly from the plain, the summit of which is
" formed into a succession of extensive terraces rising over each other and
" surmounted by one of the principal religious edifices of the empire, a
" pagoda 350 feet in height. Connecting this hill with the town is a gradual
" slope along which are two excellent roads proceeding from each extremity of

" the northern face of the stockade to the pagoda and lined with substantial
" teak houses belonging to the priesthood. The ground on either side is
" described as swampy, but it is difficult to find any in the neighbourhood
" which is not so : there are also several large tanks along the road over-
" grown with rushes and weeds and full of mud and stagnant water. To-
" wards the south, as far as the mouth of the river, rice-flats extend on every
" side intersected here and there by low bushes ; but on the north a dense
" jungle reaches almost to the very verge of the pagoda, and, with the excep-
" tion of occasional patches and open plains, forms the only prospect in that
" direction."

The British held Rangoon till the 9th December 1827 when, the second
instalment of the war indemnity having been paid, the troops evacuated
the town in accordance with the terms of the treaty of Yandaboo.

Still later in about 1840, it was thus described. " To a stranger its
" appearance was uninviting and suggestive of meanness and poverty and
" quite dispelled the interest excited by the narratives of travellers and the
" description of scenes and events with which its name had become asso-
" ciated. It was a dull, miserable place and during the rains resembled
" nothing but a vast neglected swamp.

" The principal portion of the town lay within the stockade but the larger
" and more populous part was the suburb called Tat-ga-le on its west face.
" The main street led from the custom-house through nearly the middle of
" the stockade." This was built in the form of an irregular square with its
southern face running for some 1,200 yards parallel to, and from 400 to 500
yards from, the river. The northern face was of similar length, the eastern
face was 605 yards long and the western 210 yards. In the north face there
were two gates and one sallyport, in the south, facing the river, three gates
and three sallyports, in the east two gates, and in the west one gate and
one sallyport.

The town, such as it was, was close to the river bank and in 1841,
when king Koon-boung-meng, better known as prince Tharrawaddy, visited
Rangoon he directed that the town and stockade should be removed about
a mile and a quarter inland to the site of Ook-ka-la-bha and be called by
that name. The ground plan of the new foundation was nearly square with
sides about three quarters of a mile long having the Shwe Dagon pagoda
hill as a citadel on the north-east. The "royal order" was to a certain extent
obeyed ; the principal buildings and government offices were olaced in the
new town and were there when the British force landed and captured
Rangoon in April 1852. It was surrounded by an earthen embankment
16 feet high and eight broad at the top with a ditch running along each
side of the square. Between the new town and the river the ground was
generally low and swampy and under water during spring tides, yet it had
not been entirely deserted. On war between the English and the Burmese
being declared for the second time in 1852 the force despatched against
Rangoon found it far better defended than. in 1824. The troops landed
on the 12th April and succeeded, after severe fighting, in carrying the
stockade at the point of the bayonet and on the 14th the pagoda was
captured by an assault on the east face, the enemy escaping by the northern and western faces. From this time the town has remained in the
possession of the British. Within six months of its capture steps were

taken for laying it out in regular streets, for raising the general level and for keeping out the river. The old stockade was pulled down and the low land raised with earth from the higher ground inland. The work of improvement has continued year by year and the Rangoon of to-day is as unlike the Rangoon of 185.. as modern London is unlike the London of 500 years ago.

The town stands on a promontory formed by two reaches of the Hlaing river on the west and south and the Poo-zwoon-doung on the east. A raised Strand road runs along the southern reach of the former and the space between it and the old ditch is divided into square blocks by broad streets running north and south and crossed at right-angles by others, equally broad, running east and west: each block has narrower streets running through it parallel to each other and lying north and south. The broad streets leading up from the Strand are carried for some distance beyond the canal, which they cross by causeways thus dividing it into a series of tanks, to Commissioner's road and Montgomerie street, the former a continuation westwards of the latter, which for some distance are parallel to the main east and west thoroughfares. Opposite the western end of the old ditch Commissioner's road follows the bend of the river, but at a considerable distance inland, and curves round northward as the lower Kyee-myeng-daing road and runs in that direction to the northern Municipal boundary, enclosing the Kyee-myeng-daing quarter between it and the Hlaing river on the west. Some distance behind Commissioner's road the streets running north and south, here called roads, incline somewhat to the west and are intersected by others, all, or nearly all, planted with trees along each side and enclosing the residences of most of the European and Eurasian inhabitants, each surrounded by a field or garden. Still further north is the Military Cantonment and within its limits, but beyond the houses and barracks, stands the great Shwe Dagon pagoda, the terraced hill from which it rises now fortified. A little to the east of the Shwe Dagon is the "Great Royal Lake", a fine sheet of water with a carriage drive all round it, the land within this drive being called "Dalhousie Park" and open to the public. Immediately north of and opposite the centre of the town is a smaller piece of water called the "Little Royal Lake".

The Rangoon and Irrawaddy Valley (State) Railway, with the terminus in the centre of the town but with an extension eastwards to the goods sheds, follows, generally, the direction of Commissioner's road.

The town is divided into 11 quarters; on the extreme north-west is Kyee-myeng-daing with Aloon next to it: the former, where there is a Railway station, is occupied principally by Burmese but there are two or three rice-husking steam mills. In Aloon, at the bend of the Hlaing, is the government timber depôt. The main portion of the town, or Rangoon proper, consisting of Lam-ma-daw, Taroop-dan (so called from its being largely inhabited by Chinese), and four other quarters, distinguished as N. E. town, N. W. town, S. E. town, and S. W. town, contains the public buildings, the principal merchants' offices and the shops, and is inhabited by persons of all races. Here is the Tsoo-lai pagoda in Fytche square, an open space with a large tank in the centre surrounded by trees and shrubs and with the Roman Catholic Cathedral on its eastern, the Law Courts, for the Recorder, Judicial Commissioner and Small Cause Court Judges, on its southern and the Town Hall on its northern side. On the bank of the river, between it and the Strand, is the Municipal market and a little further east the Sailors' Home. Facing the Strand road and thus looking out on to the river are Holy Trinity Church (Anglican), the office of the Secretaries to the Local Government, the Telegraph Office, the Bank of Bengal, the public offices, the Custom-house, all fine masonry two-storeyed buildings, and several others, equally substantial and almost equally imposing, used as merchants' offices. The Poo-zwon-doung river joins the Hlaing at an acute angle in the extreme east ; the point of junction is called Monkey Point and is crowned by an incompleted battery of which the guns will sweep the approach to the town by river. Stretching along the bank of the Poo-zwon-doung is the Poo-zwon-doung quarter, separated from the central portion of Rangoon by rice fields and in parts by swampy ground covered with mangrove and connected with it by raised and metalled roads. Here are the principal rice-husking steam mills. Stretching along the bank of the Hlaing between Poo-zwon-doung and Rangoon is the Bo-ta-htoung quarter and here, on the edge of the river, are numerous steam saw mills. The principal public buildings besides those already mentioned are the Lunatic Asylum between the Cantonment and the town ; the Gaol immediately to the south of the Asylum ; the Hospital and Charitable Dispensary, east of the Agri-Horticultural Society's Gardens where is the Phayre Museum, and, separated from the latter by Commissioner's road, the High School. Near the Railway station is the Lock-hospital. On the right bank of the Hlaing is the Da-la quarter, a narrow tract extending along the margin of the river, in which are the private dockyards and docks.

Immediately north of the Railway, which runs behind the High School, Gaol, and Lunatic Asylum, is the Military parade ground, with an iron Anglican Church on its northern border. The Military Cantonment extends behind this in a line running east and west, and on the east over-laps it and reaches down southwards for some distance.

The Gaol was constructed soon after the annexation of Pegu and con-sisted of raised wooden barracks surrounded by a high wall. Considerable additions have gradually been made and it now includes extensive work-shops. Owing to its being the principal central prison of the Province the number of convicts confined has very considerably increased and arrange-ments are now being made for the construction of a new central prison a few miles from Rangoon and for the conversion of the present buildings into a district Gaol. The daily average number of prisoners confined in 1862 was 945 and during each of the last seven years was :—

Year.				Convicts.	Under trial.	Civil and excise.	Total.
1871	..	..	..	1,926	73		1,999
1872	..	..	..	1,937	52		1,989
1873	..	..	..	2,212	58		2,270
1874	..	..	..	2,156	39	12	2,207
1875	..	..	..	2,091	26	16	2,133
1876	..	..	..	2,104	24	16	2,144
1877	..	..	..	1,752	24	59	1,835

For a long time the principal labour on which the convicts were employed was in breaking stones and in making roads and filling up swamps. This was gradually stopped and except those employed in the Gaol garden all convicts now work inside the walls. Various branches of manufacture have been introduced, such as weaving, carpentering, iron smith's work, cabinet-making, basket-making, corn-grinding, etc. The gross cost, nett cash earnings of the convicts and nett cost of the Gaol were Rs. 21,188, Rs. 9,447 and Rs. 11,741 respectively in 1862, and during each of the last seven years have been, in rupees :—

Year.				Gross cost.	Cash earnings.	Nett cost.	Nett annual cost per head.		
				Rs.	Rs.	Rs.	Rs.	A.	P.
1871	..	..	..	101,919	23,857	78,062	39	0	9
1872	..	..	..	113,329	73,371	39,958	20	1	5
1873	..	..	..	128,938	125,579	3,358	10	7	7
1874	..	..	..	274,325	136,294	138,031	64	0	4
1875	..	..	..	404,051	185,997	218,054	99	12	0
1876	..	..	..	266,000	189,430	75,570	34	10	7
1877	..	..	..	297,728	201,473	96,255	52	0	0

The Lunatic Asylum was finally completed in 1872. It consists of two portions, one surrounded by a high wall within which are the worksheds and the chambers for separate confinement, and the other with a low wall round it enclosing the flower garden in front and kitchen garden behind, both cultivated by the patients, the overseer's quarters, the Hospital, the necessary out-offices and several small cottages in which the less dangerous patients reside. The gardens are a source of healthy occupation to many of the inmates, whilst basket, rope, and mat-making and oil-pressing employ others. The number of patients has been :—

1872	..	..	151	1875	..	..	192
1873	..	..	172	1876	..	..	204
1874	..	..	188	1877	..	..	220

To the east of the Gaol, but not immediately adjoining it, and lying between Commissioner's road and the parade ground are a Roman Catholic convent and girls' school ; and the new High School, a fine wooden building, this was completed in December 1875 at a cost of Rs. 164,750. In 1869 the Calcutta University consented to an University Entrance Examination being held in Rangoon. The plan was not found to succeed and in view of the present exigencies of the Province a local and lower standard was established and the scheme of examinations for the University abandoned. In 1873 a site was bought and the erection of the existing buildings was commenced. The school was opened on the 2nd March 1874 in the building intended for the residence of the Principal and at the end of the month there were 129 pupils of whom 28 boarded with the Principal. In 1874-75 drawing and law classes were established and a Madrassah department for the education of the children of the numerous Mahomedans in Rangoon was opened ; the law class, however, was soon given up. During the same year a preparatory school was started. It was in this year that some of the pupils succeeded in passing into the higher department. Very soon after the school was started the Professor of Pali, the learned Dr. Mason, died and instruction in that language was carried on by three Burmese masters until 1879 when a master came out from England. In December 1876 two students in the lately-opened Higher department, out of the three who appeared, passed the matriculation examination of the Calcutta University with credit.

The principal statistics of this school are given in the following table :—

Department.	Year.	PUPILS ON THE ROLL AT END OF YEAR.								Average daily attendance.
		Burmese.	Kareng.	Chinese.	Bengalis.	Madrassis.	Europeans & Eurasians.	Jews.	Others.	
Preparatory	1874	..	details	not	given :	total	190	..	..	112
,,	1875	.. 86	—	48	21	18	8	5	—	167
,,	1876	.. 93	1	52	20	31	11	1	—	176
,,	1877	.. 110	1	48	46		4	2		178
Lower	1874	..	details	not	given :	total	107	..	..	75
,,	1875	.. 81	—	18	10	12	8	2	—	92
,,	1876	.. 84	—	23	9	23	12	3	1	111
,,	1877	.. 60	—	23	18		7	3		112
Middle	1874	..	details	not	given :	total	80	..	..	59
,,	1875	.. 62	2	15	2	3	13	1	1	70
,,	1876	.. 60	—	15	2	4	11	2	1	80
,,	1877	.. 65	2	14	16		10	1		74
Higher	1876	.. 6	—	—	—	1	6	—	—	7
,,	1877	.. 4	—	—	1		4	—	—	12

The other schools of the "High" class in Rangoon are S. John's College and the Diocesan School. The former was established by the Society for the Propagation of the Gospel in 1864. The existing building was built in 1869—71 on a site a little to the west of where the Lunatic Asylum now stands ; until then the school had been carried on in a house close by rented by the Society. The school is under the entire control of the Missionaries but as it receives an annual grant-in-aid from the State it is inspected by the Director of Public Instruction. On the 31st March 1878, it had 560 pupils on the rolls of whom 356 were Burmese. The Diocesan School was founded by Bishop Cotton in 1864 and is carried on in a masonry building north of the Hospital and Dispensary. It is supported by a government grant and by subscriptions, schooling-fees, fines, and the sale of books. On the 31st March 1878 there were 52 pupils on the rolls all of whom were Europeans or Eurasians. The only Middle Class school is S. Paul's Institution, founded in 1860 by the Right Reverend the Lord Bishop of Ramatha, Vicar Apostolic (then of Ava and) of Pegu. It is situated close to the Tsoo-lai pagoda. On the 31st March 1878 it had 385 pupils on its rolls of whom 109 were Burmans. The girls' schools are S. John's Convent and Orphanage under the Roman Catholic Bishop, founded in 1862 ; the Diocesan school for girls founded at the same time as the Diocesan boys' school ; another aided school, started in 1869 ; and the Eurasian Home, founded in 1875. All these receive grants-in-aid. The vernacular girls' schools are the Government school founded in 1873 ; S. Mary's school, S.P.G., founded in 1866 ; a girls' school in Kyee-myeng-daing, belonging to the American Baptist Mission ; and a school in Poo-zwon-doung supported by the Rangoon Ladies' Association. There are also several schools of the American Baptist Mission, notably a Theological College for Kareng, which receive no aid from the State.

The Hospital was opened in 1854 in a wooden building situated on the site of the present one. In 1872 the existing fine and airy wooden edifice and all necessary out-offices were completed at a cost of, in round numbers, Rs. 98,000 : in 1873 quarters for the resident Medical Officer were finished at a cost of Rs. 4,820, and in 1874 a separate building for patients suffering from contagious diseases and an operating theatre were put up at a cost of Rs. 10,470.

The total number of patients treated during each of the last 10 years has been :—

Year.		PATIENTS.			Year.		PATIENTS.		
		In-door.	Out-door.	Total.			In-door.	Out-door.	Total.
1868	..	{Details not available}		9,966	1873	..	1,620	8,128	9,718
1869	..			13,485	1874	..	2,154	11,493	13,647
1870	..	1,001	16,383	17,384	1875	..	2,319	12,890	15,209
1871	..	1,218	16,368	17,586	1876	..	2,349	12,620	14,969
1872	..	1,363	12,280	13,643	1877	..	2,510	13,419	15,929

The number of out-patients has fluctuated considerably and this might be expected as it must to a great extent depend upon the general health of the town during the year. On the other hand the number of in-patients has steadily increased. The hospital is supported partly by the State, which provides the medicines and pays the salaries of the Medical officers, partly by voluntary subscriptions and donations, partly by a grant from the Municipality and partly from the fees paid by masters of merchant ships who may send any of their crew to the Hospital for treatment. The establishment is not so well supported as it deserves to be, especially by the Asiatic portion of the community. The subscriptions, donations and amounts received from paying patients were, in rupees :—

Year.	VOLUNTARY SUBSCRIPTIONS.		VOLUNTARY DONATIONS.		RECEIVED FROM PAYING PATIENTS.		TOTAL.	
	European.	Asiatic.	European.	Asiatic.	European.	Asiatic.	European.	Asiatic.
	Rs.	Rs.	Rs.	Rs.	Rs.	Rs.	Rs.	Rs.
1873	2,836	99	353	223	3,080	183	6,279	505
1875	5,378	1,828	1,208	—	1,759	609	8,345	2,437
1877	5,136	1,010	400	—	1,801	200	7,337	1,210

The Lock-hospital is on the west of the old canal not far from the Railway-station. It consists of wooden barracks surrounded by a masonry wall and was completed, at a cost of Rs. 12,000, in 1870-71 and first occupied in 1871-72.

After the close of the second Anglo-Burmese war the garrison of Rangoon was very slowly reduced in strength till 1862 when considerable changes were made. In 1878 it consisted of two batteries of artillery, one battalion of European and one battalion of Native Infantry, with a detail of Sappers, all belonging or attached to the Madras Army and quartered in the Cantonment which extends east and west behind the town near the Shwe Dagon pagoda, the Europeans being on the extreme east, the Artillery in the centre and the Native Infantry on the west. On the northern edge of the parade ground is the (Anglican) Cantonment Church, an iron building erected in 1857, and somewhat further to the east, on Pagoda road, the Roman Catholic Cantonment Church, a masonry building.

The judicial work of the town was at first entrusted to the Magistrate and the Deputy Commissioner of Rangoon. A few years later a Judicial Deputy Commissioner was appointed and the Deputy Commissioner relieved of judicial work arising within the town. Still a few years later a Recorder was appointed and the Judicial Deputy Commissioner's appointment abolished. As work increased various changes had to be made and the judicial staff now consists of a town Magistrate and two Assistant Magistrates, one of whom sits in Kyee-myeng-daing, two Small Cause Court Judges and a Recorder who has civil and criminal powers and supervises all the other Courts. In certain cases, such as confirming sentences of death, the Recorder and the Judicial Commissioner of the province, who otherwise has no jurisdiction in Rangoon, sit together as the "Special Court".

The Police are enlisted under the general Police Act and are under the control of officers appointed by the State but they are paid by the

Municipality. The number employed in 1877 was 28 officers and 216 men who cost in all Rs. 62,628. The proportion of Police was five to every square mile and one to every 341 persons. By far the larger number of cases with which the Police have to deal is composed of minor offences against the person and offences against Municipal bye-laws, the Excise Act, the Police Act and other special Acts.

The revenues of the town are now raised and managed by a Municipal Committee, first appointed on the 31st July 1874, consisting of a President (the Town Magistrate) and 32 members, some *ex-officio*, some officials, and some non-officials. Vacancies are filled up by the Chief Commissioner on the nomination of the President, and the number of members does not always remain the same; at the close of 1877-78 there were only 20. The gross revenue administered by this body in 1877-78 was Rs. 735,826 and the gross expenditure Rs. 708,379.

Since the appointment of this Committee vast improvements have been made. Fine markets have been built, Poo-zwon-doung and Bo-ta-htoung have been supplied with good water brought from the "Great Royal Lakes", the streets have been kept in good order and clean and are watered regularly except during the rains, conservancy has been attended to, the streets have been lighted with kerosine lamps and a scheme is now under consideration for supplying the whole of Rangoon with pure water from a reservoir to be made near Ko-kaing.

The Strand bank, that is the strip between the Strand road and the river, is managed by a Committee which regulates the anchoring of boats and the leasing of the wharves, of which there are six on the north bank, of which the most important are those opposite Godwin street, Latter street, Tsoo-lai Pagoda street and Phayre street.

The formation of a Port Trust Committee which will have charge of the port and port funds is now under consideration.

Through changes of government, laws neglected or ill administered, insurrections, wars, and a dirt-and-marsh-poisoned atmosphere the number of houses and of inhabitants in Rangoon rose and fell year by year until the country passed under British rule. In 1795 there were 5,000 houses registered and allowing five persons to each house (the Burmese government assumed 10) the population would have numbered 25,000 souls. In 1812 there were only 1,500 registered houses, which would give a population of 7,500. In 1826 a census was taken and it was found that there were 1,570 houses and 8,666 inhabitants, or at the rate of 11 persons to every two houses. If this rate was constant the population would have been 27,500 in 1795 and 8,250 in 1812. One of the effects of the first Anglo-Burmese war was to give an impetus to trade and as a natural result the town increased, and more rapidly than was to be expected. In 1852 the number of inhabitants was estimated as being about the same as in 1795.

Long previous to 1795 Rangoon was the asylum of insolvent debtors and of foreigners of desperate fortunes. Fugitives from almost every country in the East were to be met with and not a few Europeans, and apart from such adventurers the town presented a motley assemblage such as few others could produce. Burmans, Taking, Englishmen, Frenchmen, Portugese, Armenians, Persians, Parsis Moguls, Madrassis and Bengalis mingled together and were engaged in various branches of trade and commerce, but the principal merchants were Parsis, Armenians and Moguls who engrossed the greater part of the trade of the town, and the Government frequently selected individuals from amongst them to fill positions of trust relating to trade and transactions with foreigners. In 1810 an Englishman named Rogers was Akouk-won — commonly called Shahbunder in old reports and books — or Collector of Sea Customs. Though the class of inhabitants has much changed, European merchants and their assistants having taken the place of the needy adventurers of no strong moral principles of those days, and rich and influential Asiatics having succeeded to those who took as much delight and as much pains in keeping out European, and especially English, enterprise as in making money, yet the town, frequented as it is by large numbers of ships, contains no small number of European loafers and natives of Bengal and Madras of the lowest character who are too often thought to afford a fair example of the inhabitants of the countries whence they have come and which they have certainly left to their country's good. But especially has the Chinese element very largely increased. The Shan are principally immigrants who have arrived since the annexation of Pegu.

In 1872 a census was taken but this included travellers and the shipping in port. Including these it was found that the races represented were most diverse and that the town was still the resort of men from almost every quarter of the globe.

The returns give the following :—

Europeans and Eurasians ..	3,789	Shan	1,217
Africans	31	Arakanese	195
Australians	4	Kathays	31
Americans	43	Armenians	187
Hindoos	15,261	Malays	127
Moguls	416	Arabs	29
Pathans	19	Afghans	2
Sooratees	315	Jews	85
Burmese	56,918	Parsis	18
Talaing	7,451	Siamese	53
Kareng	525	Chinese	3,181

The annual returns shew the number of houses and the population in each year from 1863 onwards to have been :—

Year.	Houses.	Population.	Year.	Houses. Masonry.	Houses. All other kinds.	Houses. Total.	Population.
1863 ..	Information not available.	61,138	1871 ..	Information not available.			100,000
1864 ..		63,256	1872 ..				77,777
1865 ..		66,577	1873 ..				80,096
1866 ..		69,866	1874 ..				81,244
1867 ..		71,186	1875 ..	596	12,247	12,843	80,491
1868 ..		72,675	1876 ..	670	12,536	13,206	83,222
1869 ..		96,942	1877 ..	728	13,148	13,868	91,458
1870 ..		93,163	1878 ..	921	12,168	13,389	110,700

European factories, or as we should call them now commercial agencies,
Trade. were established in and in the neighbourhood of Rangoon in about the middle of the seventeenth century ; but these, owing to the constant wars, carried on but little trade and indeed soon ceased to exist and it was not until towards the end of the eighteenth century, after the final conquest of Pegu by the Burmans, that there was any extensive development of mercantile transactions.

Soon afterwards the town began to acquire importance and its trade was gradually extended to Penang on the south-east and on the west to Calcutta, Madras, and Ceylon, and eventually to the Mauritius ; but it was with Calcutta that the largest business was done, owing to the great demand in that market for teak timber and the facility with which it supplied the Burmese with British and Indian piece-goods. No direct trade was ever carried on between Burma or Pegu and any European country.

The nature of the land on the banks of the river, the accessibility of the town from the sea, the great rise and fall of the tide, the then existing low rate of wages and the, as it then seemed, inexhaustible supply of teak timber afforded Rangoon great advantages for ship-building. The first rudiments of the art appear to have been received from the French. No information, unless it is locked up in the archives in Fort St. George, is in existence regarding vessels constructed here before 1786, when the workmen were described as being as expert as any in the east and the designs of the vessels they constructed excellent. In that year the *Gimpara*, of 680 tons, and the *Agnes*—there is no record of her tonnage—were launched. The following table is compiled from the only records which I have been able to obtain :—

Year.	Number of vessels.	Aggregate tonnage.	Largest vessel.		Smallest vessel.	
			Name.	Tonnage.	Name.	Tonnage.
1786	2	?	?	?	?	?
1790	1	400	Charles	400	——	—
1795	1	777	Mysore	777	——	—
1800	1	400	Mary	400	——	—
1801	7	3,096	Adamant ..	1,000	Malcolm	90
1802	11	3,412	Marquess Wellesley	1,050	Regina	80
1803	8	2,177	Change	407	Diana	50
1804	8	1,993	Edinburgh }each Perseveranza }	500	Lizard .. .. George }each	70 140
1805	7	2,705	Sha-Hpari ..	1,000	Nancy }	
1806	8	1,032	Commerce ..	362	Strathspey ..	320
1807	9	1,613	Helen	300	Steady	60
1808	7	1,395	Peelumcanza ..	550	Matilda	60
1809	1	41	Alligator	40	——	—
1810	4	1,192	Mentor	500	Juno	40
1811	1	620	Shwe-doung ..	620	——	—
1812	1	248	Argo	248	——	—
1813	4	1,034	Dula	520	Maria	210
1814	8	1,835	Mustapha ..	450	Juno	60
1815	4	1,213	Four Sisters ..	670	Maria	60
1816	3	1,159	Cordelia	430	Ahmoody ..	350
1817	4	2,039	Britannia ..	750	Governor Petrie..	240
1818	3	1,545	Isabella	575	Sha Khoosroo ..	400
1819	3	981	Fatel Mani ..	337	Industry	250
1820	1	800	Perthshire ..	800	——	—
1821	1	177	Fatel Mani ..	177	——	—

The list is clearly incomplete as in 1795 Colonel Symes saw on the stocks several vessels of from 800 to 1,000 tons burden and several others in a state of forwardness, whilst according to the list only one was built in 1795 and there is a blank after that till 1800.

For some time before the commencement of hostilities it was clear to most people in Rangoon that there was every chance of war and ship-building was checked ; when war actually broke out it ceased entirely but recommenced soon after the signing of the treaty of Yandaboo and continued till war was again declared in 1852. During the intervening period 24 vessels, measuring in all 5,625 tons, were constructed. The largest was the *Mariam* of 500 tons. The most important was the *Ra-ta-na-ycen-mwon*, the King's ship which was seized by Commodore Lambert just before the actual rupture between the two governments took place.

It has already been stated that the principal trade of Rangoon was with Calcutta. The number of vessels that sailed from the latter port for the former was, in :—

1801 .. 11 ..	2,120 tons.		1812 .. 8 ..	2,030 tons.
1802 .. 8 ..	1,870 „		1813 .. 7 ..	2,940 „
1803 .. 7 ..	2,761 „		1814 .. 18 ..	3,071 „
1804 .. 2 ..	310 „		1815 .. 12 ..	1,665 „
1805 .. 3 ..	375 „		1816 .. 5 ..	990 „
1806 .. 6 ..	1,062 „		1817 .. 10 ..	3,674 „
1807 .. 5 ..	990 „		1818 .. 3 ..	1,130 „
1808 .. 9 ..	2,237 „		1819 .. 3 ..	1,069 „
1809 .. 6 ..	625 „		*1820 .. 14 ..	6,874 „
1810 .. 7 ..	1,645 „		*1821 .. 15 ..	8,263 „
1811 .. 3 ..	975 „			

During the same period the import shipping from Rangoon was :—

1801 .. 15 ..	6,420 tons.		1812 .. 10 ..	2,665 tons.
1802 .. 22 ..	8,327 „		1813 .. 15 ..	3,571 „
1803 .. 20 ..	7,156 „		1814 .. 28 ..	7,368 „
1804 .. 15 ..	4,008 „		1815 .. 18 ..	3,470 „
1805 .. 18 ..	6,220 „		1816 .. 22 ..	5,702 „
1806 .. 13 ..	4,061 „		1817 .. 26 ..	8,404 „
1807 .. 17 ..	3,655 „		1818 .. 13 ..	5,317 „
1808 .. 23 ..	5,870 „		1819 .. 5 ..	2,167 „
1809 .. 11 ..	3,575 „		1820 .. 10 ..	4,972 „
1810 .. 9 ..	1,780 „		1821 .. 18 ..	8,058 „
1811 .. 12 ..	3,865 „			

These tables do not include the coasting vessels, but the trade carried on by them was very trifling. They were :—

From Rangoon.			To Rangoon.		
Year.	Vessels.	Tons.	Year.	Vessels.	Tons.
1803	1	37	1810	2	125
1805	1	74	1811	2	278
1811	1	104	1812	3	666
1812	2	244	1813	1	204
1813	1	104	1814	3	174
1814	1	74	1815	4	299
1816	1	74	1816	2	148
1817	1	74	1817	2	148
1821	1	222	1819	1	26
—	—	—	1820	1	70
—	—	—	1821	2	159

* Cleared out generally in ballast, in order to bring teak.

The total number of vessels that cleared out annually from Rangoon to all ports for many years prior to 1811 was from 18 to 25 ; from 1811 to 1817, 36 ; from 1817 to 1822, 46 ; and from 1822 to 1825, 56. In 1822 it was calculated that the utmost amount of tonnage likely to find employment annually between Calcutta and Rangoon was 5,400 tons. In the three years 1820-21, 1821-22, and 1822-23, 22 vessels aggregating 9,404 tons entered the port of Calcutta from Rangoon and five vessels aggregating 630 tons the port of Madras.

The Burmese system of government was not one likely to foster trade. The officials either have no salaries at all but are paid by dues which they themselves assess or receive a small pay with the right to dues besides : the will to levy dues is not wanting. The government also required its Viceroy to remit the proceeds of certain duties to the capital and his qualifications were judged of mainly by the amount which he sent up. The port charges varied at different times and under different officers but they were always very high and in addition every possible pretence was used for imposing extra dues. Up to 1813 the dues and presents for the principal officials, claimed from all masters without distinction, were :—

King's agent	.. .. ..	115 ticals,	equal to Rs.	149	
Imperial Government	..	650 ,,	,, ,,	845	
Nakhandaw	.. .. ..	80 ,,	,, ,,	104	
Petty writers	.. .. ..	75 ,,	,, ,,	97	
Chantry ..	.. .. ..	10 ,,	,, ,,	13	
Doorkeeper	.. .. ..	10 ,,	,, ,,	13	
Anchorage dues ..	.. ..	30 ,,	,, ,,	39	
					1,260

On clearing :—

Money charge in lieu of payment in kind	.. ..	35 ticals,	equal to Rs.	65	
Pilotage ..	.. .. ..	300 ,,	,, ,,	390	
Pilot's boat	.. .. ..	25 ,,	,, ,,	32	
					487
					1,747

In that year the Viceroy of Pegu informed the Indian Government that the king of Burma, having become convinced that with such heavy charges to pay merchants could make no profit and that, therefore, if they were continued trade could not be developed, had directed that modifications should be made and some small changes were effected. In 1820 the demands for a ship of 420 tons were :—

Government demand	.. ..	740 ticals,	equal to Rs.	962
Anchorage dues and pilotage inwards	.. .. ..	400 ,,	,, ,,	520
Manifest charge (new)	.. ..	25 ,,	,, ,,	32
Clearance pass ..	.. ..	45 ,,	,, ,,	58
King's messenger to report arrival	45 ,,	,, ,,	58
Pilotage outwards and pilot's boat ..	.. .. ..	187·50 ,,	,, ,,	240
Miscellaneous fees	.. ..	20 ,,	,, ,,	26
Nakhandaw	.. .. ..	50 ,,	,, ,,	65
Total	..	1,512·50		1,961

A new ship built in the river was exempt from charges on her first voyage.

Commanders on landing had to go first to the Custom-house to be searched, then to the Port-officer, then to the place for delivery of the manifest of all cargo, fire-arms, ammunition, and indeed of every article in the ship, for anything that might be omitted was liable to confiscation, then to the Governor, and then to the Re-won. Whenever anyone landed he had to go to the Custom-house to be searched. Up to a few years before the Anglo-Burmese war of 1824-25 all square-rigged vessels were obliged to unship their rudders and land their arms, guns and ammunition; ultimately they were relieved from the necessity of unshipping their rudders on paying 32 ticals (Rs. 41) to the local authorities.

At this period the duty charged on all imports was 12 per cent., on all exports except timber 5 per cent. and on timber 1 per cent. In the early part of the century the export duties were levied from the importer from the interior but later on from the exporter himself. Ships stores paid half duty.

The following is a statement of the commerce with the British settlements in India from 1802 to 1806 :—

Imports.

Year.				Merchandise.	Treasure.	Total.
				Rs.	Rs.	Rs.
1802	..	..	..	..	340,210	111,923	452,133
1803	..	..	..	..	143,523	83,114	226,637
1804	..	..	..	..	163,012	39,643	202,655
1805	..	..	..	..	225,65!	19,579	245,232
1806	..	..	..	..	222,187	———	222,187

Exports.

Year.				Merchandise.	Treasure.	Total.
				Rs.	Rs.	Rs.
1802	..	..	..	..	479,880	9,878	489,758
1803	..	..	..	..	777,357	16,590	793,947
1804	..	..	..	..	458,941	1,684	460,625
1805	..	..	..	..	595,738	57,870	653,608
1806	..	..	..	..	471,070	———	471,070

The exportation of rice and of the precious metals was absolutely prohibited, and it was by adroit smuggling that the latter was carried away. The total imports, it will be seen, exceeded the total exports by Rs. 1,856,638.

The value of the imported articles in 1805 was :—

	Rs.			Rs.
Tin	.. 1,400	Canvas ..	..	1,534
Wine	.. 1,400	Sundries	..	8,332
Woollens ..	.. 5,176	*Imports re-exported.*		
Piece goods ..	126,202	Broad cloth	..	17,196
Opium	.. 15,110	Iron and nails	..	6,528
Grain	.. 2,000	Wines and liquors	..	2,637
Rum	.. 2,336	Velvets ..	..	8,314
Tin and plated ware	.. 4,625	Sundries ..	..	9,395
China ware ..	.. 3,085	Treasure ..	..	19,579
Ironmongery ..	.. 2,148	Total ..		245,232

The articles of export during the same year were:—

					Rs.
Timber	..	..	..	..	461,153
Pepper	..	..	..	..	18,809
Orpiment	..	..	..	..	38,788
Coir and coir cables	..	..	..	..	12,678
Ponies	..	..	..	..	30,867
Cardamoms	..	..	..	..	1,232
Stick-lac	..	..	..	..	657
Wax ..	..	..	..	..	3,249
Sundries	..	..	..	..	28,305
Treasure	..	..	..	..	57,874
			Total	..	653,602

From six years later the returns of the trade between Rangoon and Calcutta shew:—

Imports into Rangoon.

Year.	Merchandise.	Treasure.	Total.	Year.	Merchandise.	Treasure.	Total.
1813-14	414,921	—	414,921	1817-18	116,837	—	116,837
1814-15	560,434	—	560,434	1818-19	123,234	—	123,234
1815-16	469,038	—	469,038	1819-20	49,785	3,375	53,160
1816-17	155,357	—	155,357	1820-21	95,443	—	95,443

Exports from Rangoon.

				Merchandise.	Treasure.	Total.
1813-14	..	..	..	470,952	48,939	519,891
1814-15	..	..	..	423,655	263,531	687,186
1815-16	..	..	..	393,362	178,295	571,657
1816-17	..	..	..	331,873	413,362	745,235
1817-18	..	..	..	398,315	178,000	576,315
1818-19	..	..	..	219,023	——	219,023
1819-20	..	..	..	178,124	60,557	238,681
1820-21	..	..	..	220,994	23,555	244,548

During these years the principal imports from Calcutta were:—

Piece goods	..	..	..	pieces	..	337,431
Raw silk	..	..	..	maunds	..	413
Cotton	..	..	..	,,	..	1,045
Indigo	..	..	..	,,	..	15
Saltpeter	..	..	..	,,	..	86
Sugar	..	..	..	,,	..	3,720
Rice	..	..	..	bags	..	17,845
Pepper	..	..	..	maunds	..	4
Opium	..	..	..	chests	..	25

On the close of the first war Arakan and Tenasserim were ceded to the British. Owing to the production of rice in Arakan and the cessation of all vexatious restrictions on trade Akyab rose to be a large town whilst, unchecked by a high range of mountains or by the acts of the local authorities, the trade of Pegu found an outlet in Maulmain and, speedily increasing, raised that town to a large trading port, a position it to a great extent lost when, after the second Burmese war, Pegu became British territory.

From 1826 to 1852 the average annual number of arrivals and departures was :—

English vessels from 100 to 1,000 tons	20
Chulia vessels from 200 to 600 tons	25
Coasting schooners trading westward .. .. ·	60
Kattoos and junks	20
Total ..	125

A royal present of one piece of cambric, one piece of Palampur, and one Pulicat handkerchief was made by the master of each ship arriving. The port charges were reduced and were levied according to the tonnage of the ship, varying from Rs. 10 to Rs. 500; these went into the coffers of the local government: the anchorage-dues were assigned to one of the queens. The pilotage fees were Rs. 10 per foot of draft but vessels were not obliged to take pilots. Customs dues on imports were levied in kind at the rate of 10 per cent. for the king and two per cent. for the Customs officials. On a vessel arriving from a foreign port the cargo was landed at the Custom-house and the cases opened in the presence of the owners or consignees ; 12 per cent. was taken by the local authorities and the remainder stamped, to shew that duty had been paid, and handed over by the Customs officers. The annual average number of pieces thus collected was 4,500 and the value thereof Rs. 182,000. They consisted chiefly of book-muslins, handkerchiefs of European and of Pulicat manufacture, long-cloth, grey shirtings, broad-cloths, net, manilla mats, etc. Some articles were usually sold and 12 per cent. of the proceeds taken, the balance being made over : these were cocoanuts, betel-nuts, ginger, nutmegs, raisins, ghee, tobacco and a few others. The amount remitted annually to the capital on account of customs dues was about Rs. 211,000.

When Pegu passed to the English trade began to improve and has proceeded with vast strides. Not only was the whole customs system changed and restrictions on importation and exportation removed but the country in the interior was gradually developed and Rangoon has now become the third port in India. Cotton piece-goods, salt and various other articles have poured in whilst rice has more than taken the place of timber, and cutch, hides and horns, and petroleum have added to the export trade.

The value of the export and import trade, excluding treasure, has been, in rupees, in :—

Year.	Imports.	Exports.	Total.
1858-59	12,743,744	8,566,817	21,310,561
1868-69	23,464,602	19,540,551	43,005,153
1877-78	37,777,242	44,143,015	81,920,257

The following tables show the gross exports and imports (excluding treasure) during each of the last five years :—

Gross Exports.

Articles.		1873-74. Quantity.	1873-74. Value.	1874-75. Quantity.	1874-75. Value.	1875-76. Quantity.	1875-76. Value.	1876-77. Quantity.	1876-77. Value.	1877-78. Quantity.	1877-78. Value.
			Rs.		Rs.		Rs.		Rs.		Rs.
Caoutchouc (raw)	cwt.	724	92,229	2,053	125,943	2,249	199,158	4,075	321,712	2,449	160,392
Cotton (raw)	,,	33,070	601,377	45,294	791,828	111,793	2,115,501	117,613	2,096,919	116,369	2,242,391
Drugs and Medicines	Value	...	133,777	...	103,139	...	50,560	...	17,718	...	15,265
Fruits and Vegetables	,,	...	105,439	...	87,222	...	99,219	...	76,394	...	67,669
Grain and Pulse—											
Gram	cwt.	65,908	197,735	55,455	200,491	30,068	239,244	98,380	79,237	53,174	210,789
Rice in the husk (Paddy)	,,	171,108	242,200	185,548	226,900	241,945	396,164	673,627	1,265,774	1,271,360	3,048,547
Rice not in the husk	,,	9,506,084	22,329,088	7,035,697	17,459,819	7,777,966	15,453,363	7,369,081	17,963,086	7,856,139	27,134,843
Wheat	,,	10,943	42,047	0,368	27,227	23,334	56,316	13,328	36,009	14,785	74,956
Pulse	,,	...	...	2,490	4,513	2,389	11,402	34,376	116,305	311,044	1,136,447
Other sorts	,,	21,873	43,757	22,232	54,464	14,908	98,508	9,580	16,482	270	840
Gums and Resins—											
Cutch and Gambier	cwt.	180,394	1,258,362	200,616	1,492,075	173,305	1,561,392	285,794	2,606,146	192,378	1,682,412
Hides (raw)	No.	440,210	1,162,257	284,383	630,020	288,984	718,578	297,369	617,983	246,210	579,756
Horns	cwt.	3,070	46,061	1,039	15,690	2,717	33,939	2,187	41,493	3,133	57,891
Ivory (Unmanufactured)	lbs.	28,446	71,809	4,480	15,585	2,967	25,205	5,390	27,453	13,066	66,836
Jewelry (precious stones, &c),	Value	6,400		4,480	26,500		7,500		31,000		6,960
Lac (all kinds)	cwt.	22,000	709,825	15,108	412,828	9,521	303,979	8,803	151,141	5,692	81,108
Metals—											
Copper	cwt.	56	3,981	187	7,745	477	21,858	1,139	50,111	242	12,806
Lead	,,	496	4,909	373	3,636	391	4,692	2,341	24,925	1,276	28,589
Tin	Grlls.	8,531	100,475	2,177	84,423	1,250	58,135	5,409	49,094	118	3,972
Oils (mineral)	lbs.	673,353	373,244	613,593	278,661	244,551	125,527	458,596	426,346	303,718	248,811
Spices	lbs.	1,431,312	111,505	1,964,652	193,740	1,041,702	192,691	1,824,583	206,019	1,682,568	205,003
Stone (jade)	cwt.	2,495	502,330	5,153	801,369	2,341	418,300	4,077	651,533	3,566	639,601
Tobacco	lbs.	208,039	123,629	153,782	68,649	1,026,646	155,087	1,343,976	231,586	597,433	128,438
Wood—											
Teak	Cub. Tons.	30,396	2,948,403	38,655	2,935,593	65,190	3,253,736	99,147	2,856,495	37,826	2,696,145
Other timber	Tons.	...		...		147	5,830	461	35,390	981	25,110
All other Articles	Value	...	4,229,967	...	5,883,914	...	7,112,792	...	3,914,052	...	3,567,367
Total Merchandise	...	...	34,566,468	...	31,059,554	...	38,550,761	...	33,916,465	...	44,148,015

Gross Imports.

Articles.		1873-74. Quantity.	1873-74. Value.	1874-75. Quantity.	1874-75. Value.	1875-76. Quantity.	1875-76. Value.	1876-77. Quantity.	1876-77. Value.	1877-78. Quantity.	1877-78. Value.
			Rs.		Rs.		Rs.		Rs.		Rs.
Apparel	Value.		505,624		601,099		473,122		606,174		653,673
Candles of all sorts	lbs.	622,748	172,863	634,840	174,777	474,279	174,760	701,624	232,199	330,031	108,982
Canes and rattans	cwt.	20,478	143,046	11,104	77,732	15,369	110,439	11,253	79,295	11,293	83,636
Coals	Tons.	23,387	437,707	29,291	503,788	33,575	440,460	43,231	501,551	59,700	945,996
Cotton twist and yarn	lbs.	3,470,226	3,450,914	4,296,893	4,319,542	2,904,015	2,770,533	4,447,468	3,939,524	4,834,778	4,002,961
Do. piece-goods	Yds.	29,904,062	5,081,903	24,207,653	5,826,943	31,406,733	4,134,066	40,801,359	7,491,665	28,933,125	5,196,906
Dyeing and colouring materials	Value.		201,010		163,340		70,307		56,383		193,050
Earthenware and porcelain	"		307,083		451,494		226,538		457,915		417,372
Glass and glassware	"		78,470		104,172		103,178		122,831		304,214
Jute manufactures, gunny bags	No.	6,544,715	2,614,590	6,584,955	2,794,195	3,934,455	1,051,836	3,549,603	1,206,753	6,216,141	1,723,111
Leather and manufactures,	Value.		111,619		171,790		138,616		146,309		132,808
Liquors:—											
Ale Beer and Porter	Galls.	169,671	361,540	210,732	475,810	83,086	190,908	118,098	290,169	157,501	375,711
Spirits	"	88,215	551,982	99,209	558,898	110,915	617,755	90,413	646,387	104,837	691,531
Wines and Liqueurs	"	89,422	236,164	31,893	222,631	31,402	229,245	26,209	220,020	24,946	219,972
Other sorts	"	4,010	25,333	2,297	17,706	8	185			57	173
Machinery and mill-work	Value.		963,786		964,230		970,393		697,940		970,478
Metals:—											
Brass	Cwt.	2,500	104,925	2,626	107,321	1,200	98,714	2,031	110,898	1,892	123,541
Copper	"	1,105	60,125	866	51,451	4,056	209,897	6,755	320,752	5,162	256,929
Iron	"	70,913	554,318	112,343	592,966	51,179	404,188	113,251	887,328	78,915	663,215
Steel	"	1,494	18,774	5,502	54,778	2,116	23,129	6,416	75,500	1,481	13,964
Tin	"	2,054	98,371	2,229	60,977	1,631	60,608	1,270	76,127	1,177	32,089
Zinc or spelter	"	870	18,774	4,626	27,367	619	15,777	1,353	23,579	2,050	29,747
Oils	Galls.	484,206	714,877	551,870	709,935	721,935	751,660	600,293	907,731	505,522	923,020
Provisions	Value.		694,969		896,102		1,072,652		1,091,365		1,425,134
Salt	Tons.	21,287	421,450	25,623	909,048	82,051	664,513	22,733	453,532	34,275	783,781
Seeds	Cwt.	30,324	262,548	11,475	94,149	23,516	195,715	35,584	283,420	20,127	192,175
Silk raw	lbs.	212,741	916,635	254,835	982,928	176,008	796,494	188,366	632,204	225,501	929,014
Silk piece-goods	Yds.	3,136,766	4,133,711	4,357,724	4,221,357	3,876,013	3,993,673	9,758,604	3,843,443	5,503,059	5,091,375
Spices (betelnut)	lbs.	18,871,259	2,196,445	13,594,731	1,634,367	13,863,948	1,315,960	15,253,100	1,630,625	13,287,995	1,892,444
Sugar	Cwt.	37,485	384,782	30,103	445,744	33,586	425,828	36,598	510,827	46,740	678,340
Tobacco	lbs.	8,939,181	1,604,664	6,246,619	977,709	13,214,612	1,116,335	15,465,947	2,350,912	9,980,226	1,561,857
Umbrellas	No.	120,056	378,076		172,706	143,279	68,632	304,497	138,525	454,900	205,603
Wool manufactures, piece-goods	Yds.	943,319	1,375,713	1,239,084	1,258,685	668,624	1,256,926	880,481	1,732,479	590,507	1,309,956
All other articles	Value.		3,781,508		4,369,965		4,092,300		4,537,660		4,930,426
Total Merchandise			32,609,450		35,554,742		28,265,971		30,621,664		37,777,242

Some of these articles merely pass through the country; candles, cotton-twist, cotton piece-goods, earthen-ware and porcelain, glass and glass-ware, &c., find their v ay directly into Upper Burma whilst caoutchouc, raw cotton, gums and resin s, hides, horns, ivory, lac, mineral oils, spices, tobacco and wood are partly, and jade is entirely, drawn from that country.

The duty levied necessarily depends upon the tariff. During the last five years the import and export duty and the tonnage of vessels entering and clearing out was :—

YEAR.	CUSTOMS DUTIES, IN RUPEES.			GROSS TONNAGE OF VESSELS.		
	Import.	Export.	Total.	Entering.	Clearing out.	Total.
1873-74	843,283	1,896,385	2,739,668	525,470	500,359	1,025,829
1874-75	1,027,830	1,606,520	2,634,350	565,015	493,817	1,058,832
1875-76	939,545	1,909,125	2,848,670	565,954	542,452	1,108,406
1876-77	979,239	1,829,860	2,809,099	477,546	506,549	984,095
1877-78	1,108,269	1,809,465	2,917,734	559,051	540,904	1,099,955

The price of unhusked rice in the Rangoon market in 1819 was about one rupee for 10 baskets. In 1855-56 it was three times, and that of husked rice double, what it was just before. the annexation, but prices had been rising for some years. The following table shews, in Rupees, the average price of one hundred baskets (bushels) of unhusked rice, of cargo rice (partially husked), and of husked rice during the export seasons of each year from 1848 to 1856, and is taken from the Administration Report for 1855-56 :—

YEAR.	Unhusked rice.	Cargo rice.	Husked rice.	Remarks.
1848-49	8	22	31¼	
1849-50	12	28	60	
1850-51	15	35	75	
1851-52	18	40	75	During six months the price of rice rose in consequence of the scarcity then existing to from Rs. 350 to Rs. 400 per 100 baskets.
1852-53	35	65	100*	
1853-54	40	65	100	
1854-55	45	70	128½	
1855-56	53	95	132	

Since then the increase in the supply, great as it has been, has not kept pace with the increase in the demand, and prices have more than doubled:

The rice season commences in about January and ends in May, though purchases are made all the year round. The prices of rice in the husk at the mills in Rangoon during the last seven years have been, per 100 baskets, in rupees:—

Year.	January.	April.	July.	October.
1872	55	54	64	64
1873	60	61	60	65
1874	83	98	90	81
1875	50	58	57	67
1876	55	69	82	100
1877	72	88	135	200
1878	93	130	124	125

Each firm has its one or more brokers and several buyers, the former as a rule residing on the mill premises. At the beginning of the season the firm advances money to the buyer and takes a mortgage on his boat as security, the broker also standing security. The buyer then goes into the country and buys up grain from the cultivators as cheaply as he can and brings it down to the mill where he sells it to the mill-owner at current rates, receiving cash payment. Towards the end of the season the advances are gradually called in by the short payment system, that is that the seller is paid for a portion of the cargo, the rest being taken as against the advance. Many of the cultivators, however, bring down the grain themselves and the brokers and their men go out into the Pegu and Rangoon rivers in small boats and buy up the cargoes which are delivered at the mills on the banks of the Poo-zwon-doung. The brokers are paid by a percentage on every basket delivered whether bought by themselves or by those for whom they have stood security. The rice in the husk is measured at the wharves as it is discharged and is then stored in the mill. There it is winnowed, carried to the top storey, passed between two revolving stones just sufficiently apart to grind off the outer husk, re-winnowed, a blast carrying away the loosened husk, and shot into bags, all by steam machinery. Perfectly cleaned rice will not stand the long sea voyage to England and the grain as it is sent out has still on it an inner pellicle and is mixed with about 20 per cent. of unhusked rice and is technically known as " cargo rice" Owing to the shortening of the distance and time in transit caused by the opening of the Suez Canal and the employment of steamers cleaned rice is gradually taking the place of cargo rice and this although it necessitates change in the plant of the mills which is now, at all events, somewhat expensive, however much it may have been cheapened by new inventions.

As competition is keen and as each firm has only a limited extent of the bank of the river on which to discharge a practice has sprung up of taking delivery in cargo boats in the Pegu river : these, being the property of the firm, can be kept loaded until there is room for them to come alongside the wharves, and an additional inducement is thus offered to the sellers as they do not lose a tide as they may if they sell to firms not using cargo boats and have to wait for room to discharge. This has led to steam-launches being employed to tow out the unladen and to tow back the laden cargo boats and, probably before long, small light-draught steamers will be used to go up the Pegu river and meet the rice boats coming down. No doubt this will interfere with the "buyers against advances" but it is very doubtful if, for many years yet, middlemen will altogether disappear and the peasants and farmers gain sufficient capital and learn enough political economy to cease crying out against "regrating".

RAN-KHYOUNG.—A revenue circle in the Mro-houng township, Akyab district. In 1876-77 the population was 2,531, the land revenue Rs. 4,189, the capitation tax Rs. 2,663 and the gross revenue Rs. 7,097.

RAN-KYWON.—A revenue circle in the Oo-ree-toung (west) township, of the Akyab district. In 1876-77 the population was 1,642, the land revenue Rs. 6,279, the capitation tax Rs. 2,106 and the gross revenue Rs. 8,762.

RAN-THEK.—A revenue circle in the Ramree township of the Kyouk-hpyoo district lying north and north-east of Ramree. It is about 37 square miles in extent with a population of 1,631 souls in 1876-77 when the land revenue was Rs. 1,272, the capitation tax Rs. 1,755 and the gross revenue Rs. 3,249. The principal villages are Ran-thek and Tsit-pya. Limestone is found towards the north.

RAN-THEK.—A village in the circle of the same name, Ramree township, Kyouk-hpyoo district, on the eastern coast of Ramree island, about three miles inland in a direct line, on a tributary of the Ran-thek stream, with a population in 1877 of 586 souls. Limestone is found in the neighbourhood and is burned here and exported to Akyab and other places.

RAN-THEK.—A tidal stream in Ramree island which falls into the sea on the eastern coast.

RAN-WA.—A revenue circle in the Mro-houng township, Akyab district. In 1876-77 the population was 2,020, the land revenue was Rs. 7,080 the capitation tax Rs. 2,464 and the gross revenue Rs. 9,898.

RA-THAI.—A revenue circle in the Prome district a few miles east of Prome, containing nine of the old village tracts. This circle, now a cluster of villages, occupies the site of the once famous capital of the old Prome kingdom which was destroyed in the first century A.D. In 1876-77 the land revenue was Rs. 3,677, the capitation tax Rs. 3,325, the gross revenue Rs. 7,395 and the population 3,117.

RA-THAI-DOUNG.—A revenue circle in the township of the same name in the Akyab district. In 1876-77 the land revenue was Rs. 3,865, the capitation tax Rs. 2,145, the gross revenue Rs. 6,315 and the population 1,699. The principal village, Ra-thai-doung, is the head-quarters of the township.

RA-THAI-DOUNG.—A village in the Akyab district on the left bank of the Ma-yoo river about 18 miles from its mouth, the head-quarters of the township of the same name, containing a court-house for the Extra Assistant Commissioner and a Police station, and with a population of 639 souls in 1877. The name Ra-thai-doung or "hermit hill" is derived from a neighbouring hill on which, in ancient times, there lived a celebrated and miracle-working hermit.

RA-THAI-DOUNG.—A township in the Akyab district, bounded on the north by Chittagong and the Koo-la-dan hills, on the east by the Oo-ree-toung (west) township, on the west by the Ma-yoo range of hills and on the south by the Kwe-dai creek which divides it from Akyab. The cultivated area is mainly on the banks of the Ma-yoo river which traverses the township in a general N. and S. direction. The head-quarters are at Ka-thai-doung. In 1876 the population numbered 55,189, the land revenue was Rs. 119,213, the capitation tax Rs. 53,948 and the gross revenue Rs. 181,121. It is divided into 21 revenue circles. The only tea plantation in the province is in the northern part of this township on the right bank of the Ma-yoo river.

RA-THAI-MYO —The ruins of the ancient capital of the Prome kingdom, known also as Tha-re-khettra, about eight miles west of Prome on the main road northward to Mye-dai. The ruins of massive pagodas and the remains of an extensive embankment strengthened with brickwork remain to mark the site which is now overgrown with shrubs except where the inhabitants of the cluster of villages within the ancient limits have cleared the ground for rice cultivation.

RAT-THA.—A village in the Pa-doung township, Prome district, in 18° 42′ 0″ N. and 95° 5′ 10″ E. on the bank of the Tha-nee river, between seven and eight miles from its mouth and nine miles due west of Pa-doung.

RAT-THA.—A revenue circle in the Pa-doung township, Prome district, on the left bank of the Tha-nee, north of the Kaing-rwa circle which now forms a portion of Rwa-boo-lai. The south-western portion of the circle near the Tha-nee, in which is the village of Rat-tha, contains some tracts of rice cultivation. It is now joined to Kwai-rai.

RAT-THA.—A revenue circle in the Prome district close to, and to the westward of, Poungday. In 1876 the land revenue was Rs. 307, the capitation tax Rs. 373, the gross revenue Rs. 680 and the population 357.

RAT-THIT.—A revenue circle in the Shwe-lay township, Prome district, lying amongst the spurs of the Pegu Roma · mountains north-east of Prome, traversed by the South Na-weng and its tributaries the Khyoung-tsouk and the Teng-gyee. The south-western corner, south of the Teng-gyee and the Na-weng, is pretty level and the soil is fairly well suited for the cultivation of rice ; in the north the country is extremely hilly and is covered with dense forest in which Teak (*Tectona grandis*) Pyeng-ga-do (*Xylia dolabriformis*), Sha (*Acacia catechu*) and other valuable trees abound. In 1876-77 the land revenue was Rs. 1,871, the capitation tax Rs. 2,586, the gross revenue Rs. 7,442 and the population 4,329. It now includes 14 of the old village tracts.

RE.—A revenue circle on the seacoast in the southern portion of the Amherst district in the Re La-maing township. In 1876-77 the population was 2,829, the capitation tax Rs. 3,303 and the land revenue Rs. 3,329. The only place of any importance is Re.

RE.—A town in the circle of the same name in the Re La-maing township of the Amherst district on the northern or right bank of the Re river not far from its mouth. It is the head-quarter station of the township and contains a court-house, a market and a circuit-house. In 1876-77 it had 2,694 inhabitants. During the first Anglo-Burmese war it was occupied without resistance by a small British force despatched from Martaban after the capture of that place. A very small revenue is derived from the market stall rents which, in 1876-77 amounted only to Rs. 270.

RE.—A river which has its source not far from that of the Attaran, at the head of the valley formed by the Toung-gnyo and the Ma-hlwai hills, and falls into the sea in the extreme south of the Amherst district of Tenasserim in 15° 5' N. It receives the greater number of its tributaries from the east and north, few from the south; its course is comparatively short and it is only navigable within the influence of the tide. Its mouth being exposed to the ocean affords no shelter and is difficult of approach owing to rocks and reefs about four miles from the shore.

RE-BAW.—A tidal creek in the Alay-kywon at the entrance to the Bassein river, varying from 100 to 300 feet in width and navigable by large boats.

RE-BAW-KYWON.—A small revenue circle in the Thayet township, Thayet district, on a sand bank in the Irrawaddy river which is nearly submerged during the rains. The crops cultivated are tobacco and vegetables. In 1876-77 the population numbered 148 souls, the capitation tax was Rs. 45, the land revenue Rs. 172 and the gross revenue Rs. 219.

RE-BAW-RE-LE.—A creek in the Thoon-khwa district which leaves the Kyoon-toon or Da-la at the village of Kywai-doon and reaches the Irrawaddy near Ma-gyee-goon. It has a very tortuous course, its length being about 28 miles whilst the distance apart of its two mouths in a direct line is only eight or nine miles. About the middle of its course, near the village of Kyee-khyoung, it approaches from the eastward to within half a mile of the Irrawaddy to curve round eastward again for nearly six miles before it turns south towards the Da-la. In the rains it has five feet of water and is open for boats of 100 baskets burden but in the dry season it is only one or two feet deep. At its junction with the Irrawaddy there is a bar which stops navigation.

RE-BHOO.—A village in the Kha-zaing circle of the Than-lweng Hlaing-bhwai township, Amherst district, to the eastward of the Gyaing, and not far from the source of the Pa-da. In 1876 it had 594 inhabitants.

RE-BHOO-WA.—A village in the Wa-kha-mai circle, Pya-poon township, Thoon-khwa district on the bank of the To, about one mile from the mouth of the Hpo-douk.

RE-BOUK.—A village on the west bank of the Irrawaddy, in the Kya-eng circle, Kyan-kheng township, Henzada district. In 1877 it had 590 inhabitants.

RE-BWEK.—A village of about 50 houses, on the Pwon stream, in the Kwon-oon circle, Thayet township, Thayet district, close to the Taw-law-khyoung and Taw-mhwon, in a small patch of rice cultivation. Near it is the Andaw or Tshwai-daw pagoda, said to have been erected over a holy tooth relic obtained from Ceylon by King Nara-pa-dee-tsee-thoo *circa* 1167 A.D. and deposited by that monarch in this spot in obedience to supernatural signs and portents.

RE-DWENG-GOON.—A village in the Thee-kweng township, Bassein district, in 16° 37′ N. and 94° 43′ E. on the Pai-beng stream. It is surrounded by rice land and the inhabitants are principally cultivators. Large boats of 300 bushels burden can ascend the river as far as this at all seasons, if not carrying yards, and consequently large numbers come up in the rice season to fetch rice for sale to the millers in Bassein.

RE-E.—A small revenue circle in the Mergui township, Mergui district, consisting entirely, of islands of the Archipelago, with no cultivation and only 332 inhabitants in 1876-77, when the revenue, derived solely from the capitation tax, was Rs. 182.

REEF ISLAND.—A small island in the mouth of the Tavoy river, called Kaw-ka-lee in Burmese.

RE-GYAW.—A village in the Kyien-ta-lee circle of the southern township of Sandoway, on the left bank of the Kyien-ta-lee river, 63 miles south of Sandoway. In 1877-78 it had 845 inhabitants.

RE-GYAW.—A village in the Oot-hpo circle, Oot-hpo township, Henzada district, on the banks of the Ka-gnyeng stream. In 1877 it had 563 inhabitants.

RE-GYAW.—A village in the Toung-tsoon circle, Martaban township, Tha-htoon sub-division, Amherst district, lying near the foot of the western slopes of the Dhe-ba-rien spur of the Martaban hills. In 1867 the inhabitants numbered 294 and 632 in 1877.

RE-GYAW.—A revenue circle in the Oot-hpo township, Henzada district, on the right bank of the Irrawaddy below Thek-ngay-byeng, containing some rice cultivation the area of which is increasing owing to the protection from inundation afforded by artificial embankments on the right bank of the Irrawaddy. In 1876-77 the land revenue was Rs. 2,166, the capitation tax Rs. 3,342, the gross revenue Rs. 6,218 and the population 3,583. It contains no villages of any importance.

RE-GYEE.—Two adjoining revenue circles, but under one Thoogyee, in the township of the same name, Bassein district, having an area of about 17 square miles and forming a vast rice plain with here and there low swampy patches and in the north a little open forest. The largest town is Re-gyee Pan-daw in 17° 19′ 30″ N. and 95° 10′ E., the head-quarters of the Extra Assistant Commissioner in charge of the township. There is a good cart-road from Nga-thaing-khyoung to Re-gyee Pan-daw and generally there are fair-weather roads throughout the circle. In 1876-77 there were 7,752 inhabitants, the capitation tax was Rs. 8,462, the land revenue Rs. 1,116 and the gross revenue Rs. 24,342. The principal towns and villages are Pan-daw and Theng-gan-toung.

RE-GYEE.—A revenue circle in the Toung-ngoo district, in the north of the Toung-ngoo Myoma township and west of the Tsit-toung, and separated from that river by the Bhan-oung circle. Towards the north-west the ground is undulating and here is found Eng (*Dipterocarpus tuberculatus*) whilst towards the south there is some rice cultivation; the rest of the circle is covered with tree and grass forest. In 1876-77 the population was 2,158, the capitation tax Rs. 1,526, the land revenue Rs. 1,432 and the gross revenue Rs. 3,060. It contains no villages of any importance.

RE-GYEE.—A creek in the Bassein district, which falls into the Nga-won or Bassein river close to Nga-thaing-khyoung, and in the rains extends eastwards and joins the Da-ga river near Kyoon-pyaw. At this season it is about 15 feet deep and open throughout for large boats ; on its banks, about five miles in a direct line from Nga-thaing-khyoung, is the town of Pan-daw. It is sometimes called the Pan-daw.

RE-HPYOO.—A village of 50 houses, on the Pwon stream not far from its junction with the Irrawaddy, which gives its name to a circle in the Thayet township, Thayet district.

RE-HPYOO.—A revenue circle in the Thayet township, Thayet district, with an area of about 20 square miles, of which about three are actually cultivated and some three more are culturable waste. The inhabitants numbered 2,591 in 1876-77 when the land revenue was Rs. 663, the capitation tax Rs. 2,595 and the gross revenue Rs. 3,342. Oon-beng-hla was added to the circle in 1855 and Khyeng-tsouk in 1860. The products are rice, sessamum, cotton and plantains.

RE-KENG.—A revenue circle in the Meng-gyee township, Henzada (Tharrawaddy) district. In 1876-77 the population was 15,770, the capitation tax Rs. 14,382, the land revenue Rs. 4,730 and the gross revenue Rs. 36,339. The principal towns and villages are Re-keng Meng-gyee (the head-quarters of an Assistant Commissioner), Myit-tha and Tham-bha-ya-goon.

RE-KENG.—A town in the circle of the same name in the Meng-gyee township, of the Henzada (Tharrawaddy) district, on the east bank of the Irrawaddy. It contains a market, a police-station and a dispensary. In 1877 it had 2,997 inhabitants. A small local revenue is derived from the market stall-rents and expended on general improvements : in 1876-77 this amounted to Rs. 2,719.

RE-LA-MAING.—A township in the Amherst district extending along the coast, south of the Wa-kha-roo township, and, in the south, stretching inland up the valley of the Re river to its sources; on the south it is bounded by the high spur which separates the Amherst from the Tavoy district. This township contains some fertile land, especially near La-maing and in the valley of the Re, and soon after the British occupation grain was exported thence to Maulmain for the use of the numerous immigrants who arrived in great numbers from the delta of the Irrawaddy. The Re is the largest river ; it receives most of its tributaries from the north and east and but few from the south ; it is navigable only within the influence of the tides. About four and a half miles off the coast, extending northwards from a little above the latitude of the mouth of the La-maing river, is Ka-le-gouk Island, and the coast is fringed with rocks and small islets. It is divided into eight revenue circles. The population in 1876-77 was 11,788, the land revenue was Rs. 19,965 and the capitation tax Rs. 13,173. The principal villages are Re (the head-quarters), Han-gan, A-tseen, Doo-ra, Ke-la-tha, Ka-maw-ka neng, Kaw-dwot, Taing-ka-maw and Toung-boon.

RE-LE.—A small village in the Myee-noo circle, Le-myet-hna township, Bassein district, on the eastern bank of the Bassein river near the northern boundary of the district. In 1877 it had 526 inhabitants.

RE-MA-NOUK.—A revenue circle in the Pa-doung township, Prome district, touching the Thayet district in the north and lying just to the west of Tha-bye-aing. There are small patches of regular cultivation in the south but almost the whole face of the country is covered with forest. Earth-oil has been found not far from the village of Toung-ho-gyee (q. v.) In 1876-77 there were 958 inhabitants, the capitation tax was Rs. 980, the land revenue was Rs. 2,301 and the gross revenue Rs. 3,326.

PE-MYEK.—A revenue circle in the Shwe-doung township of the Prome district east of the Zay stream and about 12 miles S. E. of Prome, measured in a direct line. Included in it are four village tracts. In 1876-77 there were 1,304 inhabitants, the capitation tax was Rs. 1,405, the land revenue was Rs. 1,899 and the gross revenue was Rs. 3,354.

RE-MYIT.—A revenue circle in the Ma-ha-tha-man township of the Prome district. In 1876-77 the population numbered 299, the capitation tax was Rs. 305, the land revenue was Rs. 367 and the gross revenue was Rs. 672.

RENG-DAIK-GOON.—A village in the Doo-ra circle, Henzada township, Henzada district, on the bank of the Doo-ra lake, about four miles west of the Irrawaddy, near some Reng-daik trees (*Dalbergia sp.*), whence the name. In 1877 it had 902 inhabitants.

RENG-DAIK-KWENG.—A revenue circle in the Poungday township of the Prome district, about six miles east of the Engma swamp : it is principally under rice cultivation. In 1876-77 there were 304 inhabitants. the capitation tax was Rs. 325 and the land revenue Rs. 486.

RENG-DAIK-TAN.—A village in the Prome district, in 18° 35′ 10″ N. and 95° 32′ 55″ E., about half a mile N. E. of the village of Loung-gyee, on the right bank of the Wai-gyee river. It is inhabited principally by rice growers.

RENG-E.—A revenue circle in the Za-lwon township of the Henzada district. which now includes A-twot and Paing-kyoon. In 1876-77 the land revenue was Rs. 3,573, the capitation tax Rs. 3,845, the gross revenue Rs. 16,601 and the population 4,126. The principal village is Paing-kyoon, lying in that portion which formerly constituted the Paing-kyoon circle.

RENG-E.—A small village in the Za-lwon Myoma circle, Za-lwon township, Henzada district, about two miles from the east bank of the Irrawaddy and on the banks of a small lake of the same name. To the eastward of the lake is a pagoda to which the people resort in boats at the full moon of Taw-tha-leng, that is in August.

RENG-GNYIEM.—A village in the circle of the same name in the Martaban township of the Amherst district, on the western side of a gorge in the spur of the Martaban hills which encloses the Dhe-ba-rien valley on on the west. Through this gorge flows the Reng-gnyiem stream on its way to the Tsha or Tha-htoon river, joining this latter at its mouth ; at the village the Reng-gyniem is spanned by a wooden bridge, built some years ago by the then Assistant Commissioner of the sub-division, Mr. J. C. Davis. At the eastern end of Reng-gnyiem the Martaban and Shwe-gyeng road, now being made, will cross the stream close to, almost in, the gorge.

In 1868 Reng-gnyiem had 241 inhabitants and 557 in 1877. The group of houses on the southern bank of the stream, being in another circle, is considered as a separate village though it adjoins, and is nearly one-third of the size of, Reng-gnyiem proper.

RENG-GNYIEM.—A revenue circle in the Martaban township of the Tha-htoon sub-division of the Amherst district, having Toung-tsoon on the north, the Martaban hills on the east, Poung on the south, and the sea on the west. Up to 1876 it extended as far north as the Tha-htoon township, separated from it by the Tsha or Tha-htòòn river. In that year the northern portion was taken from it and formed into the Toung-tsoon circle. The only large village is Reng-gnyiem. In 1876-77 the population was 2,245, the capitation tax Rs. 3,325 and the land revenue Rs. 18,211.

RENG-MA-GOON.—A revenue circle in the Ma-ha-tha-man township of the Prome district. In 1876-77 the population numbered 441, the capitation tax was Rs. 420, the land revenue was Rs. 518 and the gross revenue Rs. 938.

RENG-OON.—A revenue circle in the Tsit-toung sub-division of the Shwe-gyeng district, on the Bhee-leng river, occupying the northern portion of the Bhee-leng township. In 1876-77 the population was 6,499, the capitation tax was Rs. 3,069, the land revenue was Rs. 1,560 and the gross revenue Rs. 5,202. Kareng predominate amongst the inhabitants, and the produce is chiefly rice, betel-nut and sessamum.

RENG-OON.—A village in the Tsit-toung sub-division of the Shwe-gyeng district, on the right bank of the Bhee-leng river, 13 miles above Bhee-leng, with 790 inhabitants in 1877.

RENG-SHE.—A village in the Htan-beng-gyo circle, Re-gyee township, Bassein district, on the western bank of the Nga-won or Bassein river, four miles below Nga-thaing-khyoung. In 1877 it had 995 inhabitants.

RE-NWE.—A small stream in the Shwe-gyeng district which rises in the Pegu Roma and falls into the Tsit-toung. In the plains its bed is shallow and the channel sometimes gets choked by a fallen tree and the rubbish accumulated behind it.

RE-THO.—A revenue circle in the Hpoung-leng township of the Rangoon district, with a population of 8,359 souls, mainly Burmans, in 1876-77. Almost the whole of the circle, except a small tract on the west, is under rice cultivation. In 1876-77 the capitation tax was Rs. 9,138, the land revenue Rs. 34,127 and the gross revenue Rs. 43,265. The principal villages are Tsheng-bhoon and Bha-la-ta-da-gyee.

RE-TSOO-DAING.—A tidal creek in the Thoon-khwa district which flows southward from the Eng-tay and forms one of the network of creeks which intersect that portion of the delta of the Irrawaddy. After the Pee-pa-lwot joins it it is called the Pai-mwot and a little lower down it receives the waters of the Kywon-pya-thut (more correctly the Kywon-bhoora-thad) and thenceforward assumes the name of the great river. In about 17° N. it sends off to the southward a large branch which, under the name of the To or China Bakir, reaches the sea 20 miles W. S. W. of the Hlaing or Rangoon river.

RE-WENG.—A village in the Pa-doung township of the Prome district, about two miles below the town of Pa-doung and one mile inland from the right bank of the Irrawaddy.

RE-WENG.—A revenue circle in the Prome district, on the right bank of the Irrawaddy, just below Pa-doung. The road across the Arakan hills by the Toung-goop pass runs along the river bank through this circle. The inhabitants are mainly cultivators and fishermen. Near the village of Tsee-tha, on the river bank, is the Dee-doot eng or fishery, a depression in the plains, dry in the hot season, receiving its supply of water from the over flow of the Irrawaddy in the rains when it is seven feet deep. In 1876-77 there were 1,913 inhabitants, the capitation tax was Rs. 1,968, the land revenue was Rs. 1,197 and the gross revenue Rs. 4,380.

RO.—A large revenue circle in the Kyouk-hpyoo district, 81 square miles in extent, lying amongst the mountains in the north-east of the Myeboon township and inhabited to the north-east principally by Khyeng. It has but little cultivation. In 1876-77 the inhabitants numbered 1,655, the capitation tax was Rs. 1,350, the land revenue was Rs. 1,103 and the gross revenue Rs. 2,631.

RO-KYWON.—A revenue circle in the Oo-ree-toung (west) township, Akyab district, which includes Ro-ngoo. In 1876-77 the population numbered 2,244, the capitation tax was Rs. 2,635, the land revenue was Rs. 7,849 and the gross revenue Rs. 10,739.

ROO.—A small village on the river Dha-let, in the Dha-let circle, An township, Kyouk-hpyoo district. It is said to have been the capital of a kingdom but was most probably the village of some hill chief somewhat stronger than his neighbours. Local traditions state that the name is derived from the fact of a princess of Sandoway, who had fled hither, becoming mad (aroo). In 1877 it had only 288 inhabitants. It contains a Telegraph station and the signallers and other. Telegraph officials, whose principal, if not only, duty is to keep the line in repair, have made good flower and kitchen gardens.

ROON-GOON.—A village in the Prome district in 18° 34' 20" N. and 95° 29 20" E., about three miles east of the Engma lake, inhabited chiefly by rice cultivators. A short distance to the south is another smaller village of the same name inhabited by Kareng.

ROON-TSHIEP.—A village in the Pa-doung township, Prome district, in 18° 42' 45" N. and 95° 15' 25" E., on the right bank of the Irrawaddy just above and adjoining the town of Pa-doung.

ROON-TSHIEP.—A revenue circle in the Prome district on the right bank of the Irrawaddy to the immediate north of the town of Pa-doung, containing a comparatively large area under rice cultivation. The inhabitants are principally cultivators but in the villages on the river bank there are some traders and fishermen. In 1876-77 the population was 2,052, the land revenue Rs. 3,328, the capitation tax Rs. 2,082 and the gross revenue Rs. 5,745. It now includes Kya-khat.

RO-TA-ROOP.—A village in the circle of the same name in the Oo-reetoung (west) township of the Akyab district on the banks of the Ro. In 1877 it had 659 inhabitants.

RO-TA-ROOP.—A revenue circle in the Oo-ree-toung (west) township, Akyab district. In 1876-77 the population numbered 3,900, the capitation tax was Rs. 2,727, the land revenue was Rs. 2,842 and the gross revenue Rs. 5,838. The largest village is Ro-ta-roop. The principal products are rice, bamboos and cotton.

ROUK-THWA.—A stream which rises in the Poung-loung range in the Toung-ngoo district and after a south-westerly course of about 30 miles falls into the Tsit-toung river about six miles north of the village of Moon (Shwe gyeng district). Several large tributaries join it in the plains. During the last few miles it forms the boundary between the Toung-ngoo and Shwe-gyeng districts. In the rains it is navigable for boats 30 feet long as far as the village of Eng-bhek but during the dry season as far as the village of Rouk-thwa-wa only. From its mouth to Eng-bhek its bed is sandy, thence to its source rocky. It is an outlet for a considerable quantity of areca nuts and for a little teak. Isolated groups of low hills with rounded outlines, and more continuous elevated ground divide the different branches of the stream. Some of these hills are covered with Eng (*Dipterocarpus*) forest others with bamboos. Associated with teak are, amongst other trees Pyeng-ma-hpyoo (*Lagerstrœmia calyculata*) and five specimens of Padouk (*Pterocarpus indicus*).

ROUK-THWA-WA.—A village on the Rouk-thwa stream about five miles from its mouth, lying partly in the Toung-ngoo and partly in the Shwe-gyeng district. During the dry season it can be reached from the Tsit-toung by boats of about 30 feet in length. A small Police force is stationed in this village.

RWA-BOO.—A village in the Prome district in 18° 52′ 0″ N. and 95° 42′ 50″ E. on the bank of the Teng-gyee river about six miles above its junction with the South Na-weng. The inhabitants are engaged principally in agriculture though a few work in the neighbouring teak forests.

RWA-BOO.—A revenue circle in the Shwe-lay township of the Prome district on the Teng-gyee stream just above its junction with the South Na-weng. It is inhabited mainly by petty traders and toung-ya and rice cultivators. In 1876-77 there were 1,053 inhabitants the capitation tax was Rs. 485, the land revenue was Rs. 597 and the gross revenue Rs. 1,367.

RWA-BOO-LAI.—A revenue circle in the Pa-doung township, Prome district, which now includes its western and northern neighbours the Bhoo-bhek and the Kaing-rwa circles. It lies on both banks of the Tha-nee river near its mouth. The inhabitants are principally engaged in cultivating the rice fields which lie in the eastern part of the circle near the Tha-nee. The largest village is O-shit beng on the right bank of the Tha-nee and on the military road from Pa-doung to Toung-goop in Arakan. In 1876-77 the population was 1,131, the land revenue Rs. 1,445, the capitation tax Rs. 1,318 and the gross revenue Rs. 2,826.

RWA-BWA.—A small village of 50 houses on the Tsa-dweng streamlet in the Meng-dat circle, Meng-doon township, Thayet district.

RWA-GOON.—A village in the Shwe-doung township, Prome district, about three miles to the S. S. E. of Kyee-thay, with which it is connected by a good fair-weather road, and the same distance east of the Irrawaddy. In 1877 it had 589 inhabitants.

RWA-GOON.—A revenue circle in the Shwe-doung township, Prome district, west of the great north road from Rangoon and of the Re-myit circle. Almost the whole of its area is under rice cultivation. In 1876-77 the population was 2,108, the captation tax Rs. 2,360, the land revenue Rs. 3,446 and the gross revenue Rs. 5,846.

RWA-HAING.—A small village in the Mye-dai township of the Thayet district, on the left bank of the Irrawaddy, close to the frontier and containing some 50 houses.

RWA-LWOT.—A revenue circle on Bhee-loo-gywon in the Amherst district, having the Bhee-loo-gywon hills on the east, Ka-ma-mo on the north, Kwon-raik on the west, and Weng-tsien on the south. It now again includes the once independent Ka-law which was cut off from it by Captain Phayre in 1848. It is one of the most unproductive circles in the island much of the land being seriously damaged by salt-water. The principal villages are Rwa-lwot, Hnie-moot, Ka-law and Kaw-dwot. In 1876-77 the population was 3,658, the capitation tax Rs. 4,135 and the land revenue Rs. 4,047.

RWA-LWOT.—A village in the circle of the same name in the Bhee-loo-gywon township of Amherst, on the north bank of the Rwa-lwot creek. In 1867 it had 1,135 inhabitants and 1,201 in 1877.

RWA-MA.—A revenue circle in the Shwe-lay township of the Prome district. In 1876-77 there were 1,174 inhabitants, the capitation tax was Rs. 813, the land revenue was Rs. 679 and the gross revenue was Rs. 1,622.

RWA-THA-RA.—A small revenue circle in the Ma-ha-tha-man township of the Prome district a few miles east of Prome. In 1876-77 the population numbered 340, the capitation tax was Rs. 297 and the land revenue was Rs. 308.

RWA-THEK-NGAY.—A revenue circle in the Kyai-let township of the Akyab district. In 1876-77 the population numbered 1,309, the capitation tax was Rs. 1,480, the land revenue was Rs. 3,472 and the gross revenue Rs. 5,262.

RWA-THIT.—A revenue circle in the Ma-ha-tha-man township of the Prome district about 11 miles east of Prome, containing seven village tracts. In 1876-77 the population numbered 1,552, the capitation tax was Rs. 1,405, and the land revenue Rs. 1,857.

RWA-THIT.—A revenue circle in the Kyan-kheng township of the Henzada district, which now includes Eng-lat. In 1876-77 the population was 11,595, the capitation tax Rs. 11,082, the land revenue Rs. 7,523 and the gross revenue Rs. 19,519. The principal villages are Eng-lat, Rwa-thit and Kwe-ma.

RWA-THIT.—A village in the Thee-kweng circle, Thee-kweng township, Bassein district, on the eastern bank of the Kha-louk-thaik stream, about 26 miles east of Bassein. In 1877 it had 658 inhabitants.

RWA-THIT.—A village in the Mo-gnyo Myo-ma Reng-daik-beng circle of the Henzada (Tharrawaddy) district about three miles west of the Irrawaddy Valley (State) Railway, founded in 1860. In 1877 it had 755 inhabitants.

RWA-THIT.—A town in the circle of the same name in the Kyan-kheng township of the Henzada district on the left bank of the Irrawaddy; the head-quarters of the township. It contains a market, a court-house for the Extra Assistant Commissioner, a Police-station and a Public Works Department inspection bungalow. In 1877 it had 3,671 inhabitants.

RWA-THIT.—A large village in the Gnyoung-kwee circle, Henzada township, Henzada district, in 17° 37′ 40″ N. and 95° 26′ 40″ E., near the Da-ga river and six miles north of Henzada, lying in a large tract of rice country in the cultivation of which the inhabitants are mainly occupied. In 1877 it had 2,038 inhabitants.

RWA-THIT.—A village in the Ta-gay circle, Gnyoung-doon township, Thoon-khwa district, on the bank of the Irrawaddy six miles north of Gnyoung-doon. In 1878 it had 755 inhabitants.

RWA-THIT.—A village in the Bhaw-dee circle, Pantanaw township, Thoon-khwa district, on the river Pantanaw and opposite the town of that name. In 1878 it had 917 inhabitants.

RWA-TOUNG.—A revenue circle in the Shwe-lay township of the Prome district. In 1876-77 there were 1,882 inhabitants, the capitation tax was Rs. 1,209, the land revenue was Rs. 1,174 and the gross revenue was Rs. 2,698.

RWA-TOUNG.—A revenue circle in the Mye-dai township, Thayet district, situated on the left bank of the Irrawaddy a little below Mye-dai, in which are contained the two old Burman village circles of Ta-bo and Zien-gyee. In 1876-77 the number of inhabitants was 3,321, the capitation tax was Rs. 4,313, the land revenue was Rs. 693 and the gross revenue Rs. 7,828. The products are rice, sessamum, plantains and maize.

RWA-TOUNG.—A town of the Thayet district situated in 19° 19′ 20″ N. Lat. and 95° 18′ 45″ E. Long. on the left bank of the Irrawaddy just opposite to the Thayetmyo cantonment, with a population of 3,631 souls in 1872 and of 2,643 in 1878 many of whom are engaged in cotton cleaning. An Extra Assistant Commissioner has his court, and a small body of Police are stationed, here. It contains a market and a school-house. It is now a suburb of Allan-myo and its local revenues are incorporated with those of that town.

RWE:—One of the mouths of the Irrawaddy. This creek or river is formed by the junction of a branch of the Myoung-mya called the Poo-loo and of the Tsaga-mya in about 16° 33′ N. and 95° 8′ E., and lower down is joined to the Pya-ma-law and the Bassein river, itself a mouth of the Irrawaddy, by numerous highly anastomosing creeks. Its course is S.S.W. and its length about 60 miles. It is navigable by river steamers at all seasons.

RWE-DOUNG.—A revenue circle in the Kan-oung township of the Henzada district. In 1876-77 the population was 5,802, the capitation tax Rs. 4,840, the land revenue Rs. 1,968 and the gross revenue Rs. 8,574. It now includes Kweng-tha. The only village of any importance is Too-kyan-goon about 14 miles west of the Irrawaddy.

RWEK-GNYO-TOUNG.—A revenue circle in the Naaf township of the Akyab district, on the bank of the Naaf. In 1876-77 the population, composed mainly of natives of India, numbered 3,925, the capitation tax was Rs. 3,949, the land revenue was Rs. 7,292 and the gross revenue Rs. 11,685.

RWON (East).—A revenue circle in the Than-lyeng township of the Rangoon district, lying between the A-gwon (north) circle on the east, the Hmaw-won flowing between them, the A-gwon (south) circle on the south, the Rwon (west) circle on the west and the Kyouk-taing-pyeng circle on the north. Rwon (east) and Rwon (west) formerly formed one circle and at one time included a portion of Kyouk-taing-pyeng. Owing to disputes between the chief of the Rwon Shan, who occupied Rwon, and the governor of Syriam the Burman government made Kyouk-taing-pyeng (q.v.) independent of both. These Shan are the descendants of captives brought away by Aloung-bhoora from seven villages in the Rwon country (that is the tract lying on both banks of the Salween south of the Pa, the western of which is now called the Salween Hill Tracts division, but was long known as the Rwon-za-leng, the eastern portion still belonging to Zeng-mai) who were settled here under their own "Bo" or headman. They have become thoroughly Burmanised and the Shan language is understood only by a few of the older people; the greater number of them are agriculturists. At the north-eastern end of the circle the inhabitants are Talaing. In 1876-77 the population was 5,723, the capitation tax Rs. 6,683, the land revenue Rs. 32,867 and the gross revenue Rs. 39,550. The principal villages are Ee-tha-ya, Meng-rwa, Kya-weng and Pyeng-ma-gan.

RWON (West).—A revenue circle in the Than-lyeng township, Rangoon district, having the Than-lyeng, Kyouk-taing-pyeng and Rwon (east) (q.v.) circles on the north, the Pegu river on the west, the Hmaw-won circle on the south and the A-gwon (south) and Rwon (east) circles on the east. The principal villages are Kyoung-rwa, Kyoon-gan, Kyaik-ka-maw and Kyouk-tan, the head-quarters of the sub-division. In 1876-77 the population was 4,275, the capitation tax Rs. 6,298, the land revenue Rs. 32,075 and the gross revenue Rs. 39,095. A small quantity of salt is made in this circle.

RWON-GNYA.—A revenue circle in about the centre of the Than-lweng Hlaing-bhwai township of the Amherst district. In 1876-77 the population was 2,310, the capitation tax Rs. 2,437 and the land revenue Rs. 2,319. It now includes Kha-zaing. The principal villages are Kha-zaing and Re-bhoo.

RWON-ZA-LENG.—A river in the Tenasserim division which has its sources in the north of the mountainous country forming the Salween Hill Tracts district and flows nearly south through a narrow, rocky valley to the Salween which it joins at Kaw-ka-rit. With a rapid current and a rocky bed it is, even in the dry weather, navigable only with difficulty and when swollen by the rains and boiling in furious eddies or dashing against the rocks which impede its course it is not navigable even by rafts. It derives its name from the fact of its running through a country once inhabited by Rwon Shan which was overrun and annexed by Aloung-bhoora in the latter half of the 18th century many of the inhabitants being brought away captive and settled in a tract south-east of Syriam subsequently known as the Rwon circle.

RWOT-PA.—A small river which rises in 16° 6′ N. Lat. on the western slopes of the Arakan Roma range and after a westerly course of about 10 miles falls into the sea in 16° 11′ N. Lat. The village of Rwot-pa is situated on its right bank about a mile from the coast and large boats can ascend thus far with the flood tide. During the dry season it has no other water than that which it receives from the sea.

SAINT MARTIN'S ISLAND.—An island off the coast of Arakan near the entrance of the Naaf estuary, four or five miles from the shore, formed of two portions united by a dry ledge of rocks. It is low and lined on the west by a reef. Midway between the island and the mainland there are extensive reefs with breakers. It is uninhabited and is visited by the people of the coast who bring away considerable quantities of thatch grass.

SAINT MATTHEW'S ISLAND.—An island in the Mergui Archipelago, lying between 9′ 50′ and 10° 4′ N. Lat. and 98° and 98° 10′ E. Long. It is the most southern of the islands belonging to the British. It forms a portion of the Mergui district. Its highest peak, in the south of the island, in 9° 52′ N. Lat. and 98° E. Long., is visible for 13 leagues.

SALWEEN.—A river in the Tenasserim division with a general north and south course, which falls into the sea by two mouths, one to the westward of Maulmain and one to the south at Amherst. Between these two mouths lies Bhee-loo-gywon or Ogre island. The sources of this river, which have never been explored, are far north in the Himalayas or in the mountains which form their extension eastward. After traversing Yunnan and the Shan and Kareng-nee States to the south of that province of China it enters British territory at the extreme north-eastern corner of the province, and for some distance, as far as the mouth of the Thoung-yeng forms the eastern boundary of British Burma. In this part of its course it is a broad swift stream, navigable by boats and flowing between high, densely-wooded mountains. Towards the south these mountains approach closer and closer till near the mouth of the Thoung-yeng, one of its tributaries which forms the east and the northern and north-eastern boundary of the Amherst district and of the province, the breadth of the stream contracts so much that in some places the bed does not occupy more than 30 yards. Ten miles lower are the great rapids, formed by a bar of rocks stretching completely across the river and impassable even by canoes in the dry season. In the rains when the river is swollen by the mass of water brought down from the vast tract of country which it and its tributaries drain the rush of the water is so strong and the violence of its efforts to pass the rocky ledge is so great that even massive logs of timber are dashed to pieces. Ten miles further south are other but less formidable rapids impassable in the rains. Below this are numerous islands and shoals covered during the floods, when the water rises 30 feet. A few miles further south, after it has received the waters of the Rwon-za-leng from the westward, the hills on the eastern bank recede and those on the western diminish considerably in altitude and the river traverses a more open and level country with characteristic limestone rocks on both banks at intervals rising suddenly out of the plain into serrated lofty ridges. At Maulmain the Salween receives from the eastward the united waters of the Gyaing, formed by the junction of the Hlaing-bhwai and the Houng-tha-raw, and of the Attaran which joins the Gyaing at its mouth ; here the river splits into two branches. The northern flowing between Bhee-loo-gywon and the old town of Martaban, now not navigable by reason of sand banks, was some centuries ago the principal entrance. The southern branch flows past Maulmain and falls into the sea at Amherst by a mouth seven miles wide. By this channel vessels of the largest size can reach Maulmain but the navigation is rendered difficult by the shifting of the sands.

Vast quantities of teak timber from British and foreign forests are annually floated down the Salween and shipped in Maulmain for export. These are dragged into the forest streams by elephants and washed in the rains into the Salween by which they are carried down in whirling masses till checked by a rope stretched across at Kyo-dan some 50 miles from Maulmain. Large numbers of salvors assemble here in the season and raft as many logs as they can which are claimed by the owners—they are marked in the forests—who pay salvage.

SALWEEN HILL TRACTS.—A district in the Tenasserim division. extending from the northern frontier southwards to Kaw-ka-rit on the Salween and occupying the whole of the country between the Salween on the east and the Poung-loung mountains on the west. On the south its boundary is formed by a line drawn eastwards from the Poung-loung range to the mouth of the Mai-gya, a small tributary of the Bhee-leng, and from the Bhee-leng river to the Doon-tha-mie, the course of which it follows for some distance till, turning eastwards, it crosses a low range of hills to the source of the Mai-ga-la which it follows to its mouth in the Rwon-za-leng, and thence to the Salween is marked by that river. On the north is Kareng-nee, on the east Zeng-mai, on the south Amherst and Shwe-gyeng and on the west Shwe-gyeng and Toung-ngoo. The area comprised within its limits is estimated at 4,646 square miles. From the annexation of Pegu until 1872 it formed a sub-division of the Shwe-gyeng district (formerly called the Martaban province and later the Martaban district) under an Assistant Commissioner but in that year was separated from it and constituted an independent jurisdiction. The whole country is a wilderness of mountains ; even the valley of the Rwon-za-leng, the principal river after the Salween, is more a long winding gorge than a valley. The direction of the whole line of mountains, of which there are three principal ranges, is generally N. N. W. and S. S. E., but the innumerable congeries of spurs thrown off by the main systems have no general direction but appear to be thrown up in eccentric masses perfectly bewildering. The slopes are so steep and the sides are so densely wooded that the passage by laden animals is in many places an impossibility, and that of travellers on foot difficult and fatiguing in the extreme. It is through these hills that Shan caravans come down annually to Rangoon and Maulmain and except the routes used by them there are no roads over which laden bullocks can pass, baggage and goods being carried on men's backs ; in many places unladen elephants can only just make the ascents. The country is drained by three principal rivers, the Salween, the Rwon-za-leng and the Bhee-leng, fed by a multitude of mountain torrents pouring down the narrow ravines and boiling over rocks and boulders on their impetuous way to the larger rivers, which seem to partake of the character of their turbulent tributaries, and lash themselves into foam over masses of rock or in very wantonness roll about the pebbles of their beds or whirl in wild eddies as if rejoicing in their might and beauty before the beetling crags and densely-wooded slopes whose feet are bathed by their waters, whilst gigantic forest trees of every hue and glistening with gorgeous flowers bend their branches to protect the cool waters from the burning sun until they emerge into the low country when, deprived of their companions the rocks and wooded hills, they sink into muddy streams with no trace left of their former state but the rapidity of their currents as they glide along swiftly and silently, seeming anxious only to hide their sullied waters in the sea. The Rwon-za-leng which rises in the extreme north is navigable with some difficulty during the dry season as far as Pa-pwon, the head-quarters, but in the rains the rapidity and strength of its current renders the ascent impossible and the descent exceedingly dangerous. Except by small boats and rafts the Bhee-leng is not navigable at all within the limits of this district. The navigation of the Salween is impeded by rapids impassable by boats.

The cultivation is almost entirely in hill-gardens except near Pa-pwon, and in the betel gardens which are permanent.

The crops cultivated during each year since 1871 and the number of Toung-ya and the agricultural stock have been :-

Year.	Rice.	Betel nuts.	Mixed fruit trees.	Toung-ya.	Buffaloes.	Cows, bulls and bullocks.	Elephants.	Carts.	Ploughs.	Boats.
1872	—	1,253	9	10,636	899	34	129	—	—	—
1873	—	1,264	18	11,720	1,486	84	145	3	—	8
1874	—	1,345	15	11,978	1,964	112	174	—	—	2
1875	134	1,411	18	12,078	1,882	267	189	1	—	4
1876	193	1,477	17	12,670	1,868	327	200	1	—	24
1877	280	1,462	6	12,526	2,269	333	215	—	—	—

The inhabitants are almost entirely Kareng, but a few Shan have settled in the neighbourhood of Pa-pwon. The eastern portion of the country was formerly inhabited by Rwon Shan, whence the name Rwon-za-leng : the larger number of these were brought away by Aloung-bhoora and settled in what is now the Syriam township of Rangoon. In 1872 the number of inhabitants was 25,953 and in 1877 26,649.

This district is now placed under an Assistant Commissioner who is stationed at Pa-pwon, a village on the Rwon-za-leng at Administration. the mouth of the little Ta-ra-law stream, under whom is an Extra Assistant Commissioner and six Thoogyees of circles,—Pa-pwon, Kaw-loo-do, Kaw-ka-rit, Kha-daing-tee, Mai-waing and Weng-hpyaing. For some years after the country became British territory it was in a very disturbed state. A Kareng, who styled himself "Meng-loung" or the incarnation of a prince, collected around him the loose characters and evil-disposed persons of the neighbouring countries, Shan and Kareng, and taking advantage of a prediction current amongst the Kareng that a prince of their race was to arise who should drive out the foreigners and establish a new dynasty in Pegu, he persuaded some 1,500 men to join him, reduced this tract to complete subjection, and subsequently descended into the plains and took several villages, the inhabitants escaping into Shwe-gyeng. On the approach of a force of Europeans, sepoys, and police, the party retreated hastily into the hills, and being still pursued Meng-loung escaped into Zeng-mai. On the return of the troops to Shwe-gyeng and Tsit-toung he reappeared on the scene of his former operations and resumed his system of annoyance and aggression on the villages, descending into the plains and even attacking Kyouk-gyee from which he was repulsed with considerable loss by a detachment of the 8th Regiment M.N.I. under Lieutenant Childs. It was impossible for bodies of regular troops to operate with any effect amongst the mountains of this wild country, and a special force was raised consisting of two companies of 100 men each. It was intended that this levy should be composed of Kareng, but it was found impossible to make soldiers of them and Shan and Toungthoo were to a great extent enlisted instead; added to these were two thirds of a company of Native Infantry and a few European Artillerymen, the whole under the immediate orders of the Assistant Commissioner. This force was divided into four bodies, each placed under an European officer, and by these parties acting under the general control of the Deputy Commissioner, Major Berdmore, aided by a diversion made in the south by the Deputy Commissioner of Amherst, Major Briggs, the whole of the disturbed tracts were speedily cleared of the marauders who infested them. Meng-loung was so hard pressed that he and his immediate followers escaped into Kareng-nee and have never since given any trouble.

In 1867 disturbances recommenced; a chief named Deepa attacked and plundered our villages and threatened Pa-pwon and from that time forward dacoities continued. This district forms the base of operations of the Maulmain foresters, that is of those who have purchased the right to extract timber from the vast teak tracts across the Salween : these men yearly come up with large sums in cash which they require for the payment of their workmen, or to pay their dues to the various chiefs, and in consequence the whole of the neighbouring country beyond our borders has become the resort of men of various classes, many of whom acknowledge no settled authority, who collect in bodies under some leader more daring or more capable than themselves and, with Zeng-mai and Kareng-nee as refuges, fall upon the foresters and attack our villages. In order to remedy this state of affairs the Tract was separated from Shwe-gyeng in 1872 and placed under an officer styled " Superintendent, " who is immediately under the Commissioner of Tenasserim, and the police force was considerable strengthened. The Superintendent of the Tract is ex-officio Superintendent of Police, and in 1877 had under him a force consisting of an European Inspector, 16 subordinate officers and 227 men of whom 12 are river police. The force is quartered at Kaw-loo-do, an old post, in the north, and at Kyouk-gnyat and Dha-kweng on the Salween, with a strong reserve at Pa-pwon. No less than 158 of the men are Kareng who are gradually taking to Police work but will not serve for long; as soon as they make enough money to marry they withdraw—without permission if there is any delay in answering their request to be allowed to retire—but they carry away better habits of discipline and a greater readiness to unite in resisting an attack.

The revenue is raised almost entirely from the land and from the capitation tax ; excise on spirits and drugs yielding very little, and judicial receipts, such as fines and forfeitures, sales of unclaimed property and judicial stamps, a little more.

The latest returns available are those for 1876-77, and according to these the receipts were from—

					Rs.	
Land	..	..	..	..	9,615	
Capitation tax	..	..	..	..	10,768	
				Rs.		
Excise	..	..	..	..	805	
Fines and forfeitures	..	..	..	2,418		
Unclaimed property sold	..	..	17			
Savings from pay	..	..	..	69		
Law stamps	..	..	..	1,078		
Miscellaneous	..	..	..	144		
					4,531	
				Total ..	24,914	

SANDOWAY.—A district in the south of the Arakan division, 3,667 square miles in extent, more correctly called *Than-dwai*. On the north it is bounded by the Ma-ee river, which separates it from Kyouk-hpyoo, on the west by the Bay of Bengal, on the south by the Khwa, on the other bank of which is the Bassein district of the Pegu division, and on the east by the Arakan mountains, Bassein, Henzada, Prome, and Thayet occupying the country to the eastward. Its extreme length is 136 miles and its breadth in the north 48 and in the south 24 miles. After the cession of Arakan and Tenasserim by the treaty of Yandaboo, signed in 1826 A.D., the boundaries of the district were :—N. the Dha-let river and the road from Dha-let to Ava ; W. and S. the Ramree channel and the Bay of Bengal ; E., down to the sea, the Arakan Roma range the water parting between the rivers flowing east and west. Some years later the northern part, above the Ma-ee, was separated from it and formed into a separate district, and after the second Burmese war, which resulted in the annexation of Pegu, the southern portion as far north as the Kyien-ta-lee was joined to Bassein, but in 1864 the tract between the Kyien-ta-lee and the Khwa was restored.

The face of the country is mountainous, the Arakan Roma sending out numerous spurs which reach down to the coast and these again throwing out a countless number of side-spurs running on the whole parallel to the Roma, the whole drained by numerous small streams. Not more than one-eighteenth of the surface can be called plain and except here, where rice cultivation is carried on, and on the sides of the hills where clearings are made for *toungya*, the country is thickly covered with forest. From the mouth of the Sandoway river northwards the coast is indented by numerous navigable and inosculating tidal creeks which receive the contributions of many small streams ; by means of these communication can be kept up without the necessity of going out to sea. Southward it presents a rugged and rocky barrier to the ocean with few available places of refuge. The rivers draining the country are but mountain torrents to within a few miles of the coast.

The main range of the Arakan Roma Mountains has in the north a

Mountains.   S. E. by S. direction, but as it proceeds southwards it gradually curves towards the west and at the sources of the Khwa runs nearly due north and south with a slight inclination westwards.   In the north some of its peaks attain an elevation little short of 5,000 feet, but the height gradually diminishes to 3,200 feet at Shouk-beng where the Toung-góop road crosses the range, rising again to 3,600 feet in 18° 21′ 26″ N. and to 4,000 feet a few miles further south.   From this point the range rapidly sinks and at the sources of the Khwa is about 890 feet high.   It is crossed by several passes more or less frequented, which, with one exception (Toung-goop), consist simply of a narrow line of footpath cut through dense forest rarely more than from six to eight feet wide and so much overgrown at the end of every monsoon as to render a good deal of clearance necessary before they can again be used even by foot passengers.   The scarcity of water and the consequent necessity of selecting the halting places with special reference to its supply render the stages of very unequal length.   The most southern of these passes is that which leads from Khwa to Le-myet-hna in the Bassein district : the hills are of no great height, the supply of water is comparatively abundant and the route is practicable for every description of carriage except carts.   North of this are some others, not extensively used, and in the extreme north the Toung-goop pass, the road across which proceeds from the village of that name to Pa-doung on the Irrawaddy in the Prome district.   This route was traversed after the first Burmese war by Lieutenant Browne who pronounced it impracticable for troops or laden cattle although it was the one followed by the main body of the Burman army on the invasion of Arakan in 1784 A.D., and the one by which the enormous image taken at Ma-ha-moo-nee was carried to Ava.   After the second Burmese war a road was made across the pass and rapidly pushed on and in 1854 was " traversible by a horseman at full galop " throughout its length: Since then the road was considerably widened and rendered fit for the passage of troops of all arms, but has been to a great extent abandoned, only a small sum annually being spent on its repair and in keeping the bridges in order.   This route is the one mainly used by traders from Pegu and the telegraph line to Calcutta is carried along it.

The principal rivers are the Ma-ee, the Tan-lwai, the Toung-goop, the

Rivers.   Sandoway, the Kyien-ta-lee and the Khwa, all of which rise in the western slopes of the Arakan Roma Mountains.   The first, which forms the northern boundary of the district, falls into the arm of the sea which separates Ramree Island from the main land, and the second into the same arm some 64 miles farther south : neither are of any great importance.   The Toung-goop falls into the Bay of Bengal by several mouths between about 18° 44′ and 18° 50′ : it is navigable for only a very short distance inland and is rarely resorted to except by country boats in their trafficking voyages along the coast.   The Sandoway river flows past the town of that name and then turning west falls into the sea some 15 miles farther on at Tseng-goung in 18° 32′ N.   The influence of the tide is felt a short distance beyond Sandoway and the river is navigable by the largest class of boats as far as that town.   The roadstead at its mouth, however, is exposed and dangerous and a heavy swell immediately follows any increase of wind from the south-west. The Kyien-ta-lee is a small stream of no importance which reaches the sea at "Bluff-point" in about 17° 59'. The Khwa at first flows south then west and finally turning N., and running for some miles almost parallel to the coast inclines westward again and falls into the Bay in about 17° 36' N. Lat. Its mouth forms a good anchorage for steamers or other vessels having from nine to 10 feet draught only, but the entrance is rendered intricate and difficult by rocks and a bar of sand.

The "newer alluvium" of the Memoirs of the Geological Survey of
Geology.*   India is represented in this district mainly by blown sand, littoral concrete, and mangrove swamp. The "blown sand" or dunes occur most frequently south of the Kyien-ta-lee river, but are occasionally met with farther north, whilst all along the coast "a deposit of somewhat similar origin, only coarser and distinctly accumu- "lated under water, is commonly met with along the course of many of the "less sheltered tidal creeks....it is in fact merely the calcareous sand com- "posed of comminuted shells and corals of living species, consolidated into "a more or less compact calcareous sandstone or ragstone.....It is a deposit "of a very porous character and often yields a supply of sweet water, being "free from organic or other impurities, except perhaps in some places a "little salt.....The elevation of these littoral concretes, and in places corals, "above the present tide limits points to a moderate elevation of the whole "country in a recent period, which there are no grounds for supposing to "have yet ceased. Where the above littoral concrete does not form the "banks of the tidal streams of the Arakan coast, its place is taken by the "fœtid mud, or sand and mud of the mangrove swamps. In low lying "spots within the tideway, whether mud or sand predominates, the deposit "is equally offensive, the whole area being marked by a peculiar flora and "by the abundance of the strange crab, *Thalassina scorpionoides.* Geologi- "cally considered, however, the deposit is insignificant, being extremely "superficial, and rarely covering any great extent of country beyond the "immediate vicinity of the tidal creek   *   *   *

"All along the coast at various spots remnants of the older alluvium can "be detected near the hills, in some places almost buried beneath recent "*debris* swept down by torrents from the adjacent hill sides," their arrange- ment and their proximity to the hills pointing "to their being relics of a "now nearly denuded belt of clays of littoral origin." For all rocks older than the Nummulitic but younger than the Triassic met with in the Province the term "Negrais" has been adopted from their extensive development near the Cape of that name in the Bassein district. Here they occupy the major portion of the country between the Khwa and the spur forming the southern watershed of the Kyien-ta-lee, north of which, except along the upper slopes of the Pegu Roma, is a cretaceous group which has been called the "Ma-ee". "The difference in their mineral character is very great. In some places "massive and flaggy sandstones occur quite unaltered and dipping at mode- "rate angles, whilst in places sections are exposed of highly altered shales "and sandstones; and in some spots the sandstone is seen altered into a "chertzy rock seamed with silica and evidently subjected to an alteration

---

* From "Report on the Geology of Pegu" by W. Theobald, in Vol. X., pt. 2 of the memoirs of the Geological Survey of India.

"of an intense kind   *   *   *   *   The massive
"beds at the base of this group are everywhere most conspicuous
"and of a peculiar greenish hue very characteristic of this rock" which
"is a very fine-grained argillaceous sandstone, rather compact, but
"where exposed to the action of the sea its surface usually presents a
"honeycombed or cancellated appearance.... Subordinate to the thick-
"bedded greenish or cancellated sandstone occurs in an irregular and in
"places almost stringy bed of conglomerate, a prominent feature connected
"with which is its great irregularity and capricious mode of occurrence."

South of the Kyien-ta-lee and on both banks near its mouth are small
outcrops of limestone, the exact position of which as regards the Nummulitic
group has not been ascertained, and about a mile S.S.E. from the village of
Kyien-ta-lee there is, in a cave, a "huge mass of hard compact sandstone."

Of the Cretaceous rocks Mr. Theobald writes:—"The occurrence of rocks
"of Cretaceous age on the eastern side of the Bay of Bengal was first
"established in 1872 by the discovery near Mai-i (*Ma-ee*), in the northern
"part of the Sandoway district, of a single specimen of *Ammonites inflatus*
"Sow. The specimen was found in the bed of a small stream and had
"evidently weathered out of the shales in which the bed of the stream lay,
"but curiously enough, it was unaccompanied by any other fossil whatever,
"though I devoted a day to the careful examination of the spot. The
"specimen was not perfect but of its identity with the Cenomanien *A.*
"*inflatus* Sow, Dr. Stoliczka, to whom I submitted the specimen, had
"not the slightest doubt. The Sandoway district, which stretches from
"Mai-i (*Ma-ee*) to Gwah (*Khwa*), a distance of 124 miles, belongs to
"the province of Arakan, and on this account no less than from the wild,
"uninhabited, and inaccessible character of the greater portion of it, has
"received only a very cursory examination, sufficient to give a general idea
"of its geological structure and relation to the adjoining districts of Pegu.
". . . . It will suffice to say that the Cretaceous rocks extend down from
"the Kyouk-hpew (*Kyouk-hpyoo*) district in latitude 29° 30', certainly as
"far as Kyeantalee (*Kyien-ta-lee*) on the coast, a distance of 94 miles in a
"straight line. Throughout this long tract of country I am aware of no
"fossils having been met met with, save the abovementioned specimen of
"*A. inflatus* Sow., but the occurrence here and there, at intervals, of some
"peculiar beds, seen associated near Mai-i (*Ma-ee*) with the beds from which
"*A. inflatus* was derived, renders the extension of the group thus far as
"certain as it can be in default of any fossils whatever.

"How far the group extends south of Kyeantalee (*Kyien-ta-lee*) is
"uncertain, as a much greater amount of alteration and disturbance is
"found in the rocks along the coast south of Kyeantalee (*Kyien-ta-lee*) than
"north of it; all, therefore, that can be affirmed is, that it is very possible
"that some of the altered rocks and outcrops of limestone met with be-
"tween Kyeantalee (*Kyien-ta-lee*) and Cape Negrais may be of Cretaceous
"age rather than Nummulitic to which group the balance of evidence
"would perhaps tend to refer the bulk of the hill rocks of the southern
"portion of the Arakan range; but in default of precise evidence in the
"form of organic remains these rocks of doubtful age must remain classed
"as I have already classed them, in a provisional group (Negrais) inter-
"mediate in position between the Cretaceous beds and the Tertiaries.

"One bed which I regard as belonging to the group which contains
"A. inflatus is a limestone of a light cream colour, in places exhibiting a
"somewhat speckled or flea-bitten aspect, from the dissemination through
"it of sublenticular crystalline particles, some of which may possibly be of
"foraminiferous origin. The rock is argillaceous, very homogeneous in
"grain, occasionally seamed with calcite, and breaks with a subconchoidal
"fracture. I think it probable that there are more beds than one of this
"character, as in one place a thin bed of it was seen intercalated with the
"shales of this group, whilst at other spots where the rock was much more
"largely developed its relation to any other beds was not so perceptible.
"The first spot where this rock occurs, commencing in the north of the
"Sandoway district, is four miles S.S.W. of Mai-i (Ma-ee), where it consti-
"tutes a small hill not 200 yards in circumference, on the edge of some
"paddy-land bordering a tidal creek. It is here quarried and burnt for
"local use, but a brisk demand for lime would soon make serious inroads
"on the amount of rock here exposed. About 12 miles S. S. E. of this a
"much larger development of what I take to be the same bed occurs at
"some distance up a small stream not laid down on the map, but which may
"be termed the Kama stream, from the name of the village situated on
"its banks. The spot being somewhat out of the way and unapproachable
"for elephants was not visited by me ; but from samples of the rock it is,
"I consider, identical with that at Mai-i (Ma-ee). It is too inaccessible to
"be of any present practical value, especially as the same rock occurs more
"favourably situated elsewhere.
"The next spot where this limestone occurs largely is a few miles
"south-west of Ki-ben-ziaht (Kyee-beng-tshiep), a village on the Tan-loay
"(Tan-lwai) stream, not quite half way from Mai-i (Ma-ee) to the mouth of
"the Sandoway river. It here occurs in considerable quantity in undula-
"ting ground, but its relation to any other beds is not seen. Thus far I
"think there is little doubt that these outcrops are all portions of one and
"the same bed, re-appearing at intervals and probably discoverable at
"more spots than my hasty examination enabled me to detect, but whether
"or no the same bed is identical with some outcrops of rock of very similar
"mineral aspect farther south is not equally clear. For instance, close to
"Tonghoop (Toung-goop), a small outcrop of limestone is seen which may
"belong to this bed and about three miles north of it some limestone,
"which probably is the same ; it is seen in the bed of the stream up which
"the road winds ; and again farther south another outcrop occurs five
"miles north-west of Sandoway. Between Sandoway and Kyeantalee
"(Kyien-ta-lee) limestone occurs at several spots, but usually more or less
"sub-crystalline in character and not so argillaceous as the Kama rock.
"At Sanday (Tsan-tay), four miles above Kyeantalee (Kyien-ta-lee), on the
"opposite side of the river, occurs an argillaceous limestone which may
"belong to this group * *   Besides the above limestone there is another
"peculiar kind of rock which may be used to trace the extent of the Creta-
"ceous group, to which it would seem to belong, to the south. This
"peculiar rock, which is first met with about two and a half miles north-
"east of Kyeantalee (Kyien-ta-lee), is a greyish, rather earthy sandstone,
"which in places exhibits a pisolitic structure from the dissemination
"through it of small globular concretions of carbonate of lime and iron

" (with a trace of magnesia according to an analysis by Mr. Mallet) which
" rarely exceed the size of a small pea. These concretions, which must be
" considered as of contemporary age with the rock and the result of segre-
" gative or crystalline action previous to its consolidation, are sparingly
" distributed through it, and very irregularly likewise, much of the rock
" being quite devoid of them. On decomposing, these concretions leave
" holes containing a little powdery oxide of iron, and impart to the earthy
" sandstone the aspect of an amygdaloidal trap; indeed, the deception is so
" perfect that it requires a careful examination of the bed to realise that it
" is a simple sedimentary and not a volcanic rock. At several spots
" between Kyeantalee (*Kyien-ta-lee*) and Mai-i (*Ma-ee*) this very remarkable
" rock occurs, and though seen but at intervals may, from its very marked
" and peculiar character, be taken as conclusive of the extension over the
" above country of the Cretaceous beds, of which, I believe, it is a member.
" East of Mai-i (*Ma-ee*) the beds of this group attain a great thickness,
" though some of them may belong to older members of the Secondary
" series. The prevailing dip is E. N. E., and the rocks are mainly hard,
" massive sandstones, with some dark shales interspersed. In these shales,
" in some places, flat concretions of limestone occur, both blue and pale-
" gray, rarely more than six inches across and from one to two inches in
" thickness. In none of these beds have I noticed any fossils, though I
" somewhat carefully examined some of these calciferous shales above
" Lyndi (*Leng-dee*), on the Mai-i (*Ma-ee*), where they seemed to promise to
" yield some sort of organism, but without success."

The " Axials " of Triassic age " constitute the core or axis of the Ara-
" kan range towards the frontier," their western boundary coinciding most
probably with the valley of the Ga-moon a feeder of the Ma-ee. South of
the parallel of the frontier of Pegu serpentine nowhere occurs in this district, but "it must be largely developed in some parts of the valley of the
" Mai-i (*Ma-ee*) river to judge by the quantity of pebbles of this rock seen in
" the bed of the river about Lyndi " (*Leng-dee*). Soapstone is a common
accompaniment of serpentine and is " the result of chemical segregation in
" veins which traverse the altered sedimentary rocks of both Axial and
" Negrais groups". Of its occurrence in Sandoway Mr. Theobald writes :—
" There is no place, however, within the limits of Pegu where the mode of
" occurrence of this steatite is so well seen as in the adjoining district of
" Sandoway ; and, as from the greater number and thickness of the veins
" here, the spot may be regarded as a focus of the peculiar action which
" has produced these veins, I shall briefly describe it, in place of any of the
" less noteworthy spots where the mineral occurs to the south, since, save
" in the greater thickness and number of the veins, the description of one
" locality will, in all essential respects, stand for all. The precise position
" of the spot I shall now describe is three miles north-west from Sandoway,
" or nearly midway between Kau (*Gaw*) and the Andau (*Andaw*) pagoda,
" being rather nearer, if anything, to Kau (*Gaw*). I am not sure if the
" rocks around Sandoway should be referred to the Cretaceous group or to
" the Eocene, as what little limestone there is in the neighbourhood does
" not contain fossils, and there is little or no evidence at present to support
" an opinion one way or the other. In the near vicinity of the spot a good
" deal of coarse conglomerate is scattered about, and some queer looking

" septarian masses of compact marl derived from the waste of some shales
" which have once included them. On reaching the low hill which seems
" to be the focus for these veins of quartz and steatite quantities of the
" vein-stuff are seen scattered over the face of the hill, the *debris* evidently
" of veins traversing the rocks at this spot. Most of the veins are of the
" usual small dimensions, but some veins here are far larger than any
" noticed elsewhere, being nearly a foot thick, whereas elsewhere they are
" rarely seen more than a few inches. These veins are composed of the
" ordinary union of steatite and white fibrous quartz, having more or less
" of a chatoyant lustre. The steatite is of the ordinary gray or green colour,
" hard and compact in the thicker parts of a vein but passing into the
" finer variety usually selected for writing purposes. The surface of the
" finer portions of the steatite is smooth and burnished, and the mineral
" exhibits a tendency to develope curved ends, resembling cloves of garlic
" or similar bulbs ; and this is not the result of pressure, but of an appro-
" priate segregative process during the formation of the mineral * * * *
  " A specimen of steatite analysed by Mr. Tween gave the following
" result :—

Water				2·4
Silica				63·11
Oxides of iron and alumina				3·41
Magnesia				30·47
Alkali				a trace.
				99·39

Limestone, intermixed with the tertiary clays and sands of the lower
lands, is abundant and very pure, yielding on assay,—

Carbonate of lime (with some traces of iron, alumina and magnesia				93·6
Insoluble clay				6·4
				100·0

The absence of silica renders it unfit for hydraulic purposes, but its softness and friability make it a valuable adjunct in the preparation of artificial
cements.

Almost the whole face of the country is covered with forest, which may
Forests. be divided into three main classes exclusive of that which
covers the Roma mountains, *viz.* : " Mangrove," on the low
ground within tidal limits ; " Dry," on slightly hilly ground from the plains
up to from 500 to 800 feet above the level of the sea ; and " Green," beginning at or near the plains and covering by far the greater part of the country
up to the Roma. Above the mangrove forest, interspersed amongst the rice
plains, are Pyeng-ma (*Lagerstræmia reginæ*), Ka-gnyeng (*Dipterocarpus alata*),
and some others, but none of these, however, as a rule, appear in large numbers. As soon as the ground rises dry forest appears with great regularity
and forms a belt along the lower part of the hill ranges. The most important
and characteristic trees here are Pyeng-kado (*Xylia dolabriformis*), Pyeng-ma
(*Lagerstræmia reginæ*), Tseng-bwon (*Dillenia pentagyna*) and Myouk-khyaw
(*Homalium tomentosum*), which are the most numerous, and north of Kyien-
ta-lee always appear together : south of this Tseng-bwon has not been observed. In addition to these there are many others of different economic

value and some which more properly belong to the evergreen forest higher up. Ka-gnyeng in most instances here appears singly but in some places in distinct groups forming pure Ka-gnyeng forests. Bamboos are exceedingly scarce. The dense evergreen forest consists of a great variety of trees of which the most important are Eng (*Dipterocarpus tuberculatus*), Toung Thayet (*Mangifera sylvatica*), Theng-gan (*Hopea odorata*) and Ka-gnyoung (*Dipterocarpus turbinatus*), but many others exist the timber of which might be usefully employed. From an economic point of view the three most important trees are Pyeng-kado (*Xylia dolabriformis*) the wood of which, though difficult to work from its hardness, is exceedingly durable and is used in house-building and for railway sleepers ; Eng (*Dipterocarpus tuberculatus*) most plentiful in the northern township, which furnishes a useful timber of some durability if not exposed to the weather and from which is extracted a thick resin (dammer) usually applied to the seams of boats and to render wicker-buckets water-tight ; and Ka-gnyeng (*D. alata*), plentiful in the south, an immense tree from which is extracted an inflammable oil much used for making torches ; the wood is of no great value, but is said to furnish the best charcoal for gunpowder.

The climate generally differs but little from that of the rest of Arakan, or indeed from that of what has been called the " littoral zone " of the Province. The three seasons into which the year is divided follow each other with regularity but with occasional variations in the times of their commencement and in their duration. During the " cold " season from November to February the dews are exceedingly heavy and the evenings and nights cold and chilly, the terrestrial radiation thermometer not infrequently recording only 38° and the winds blowing usually at first from the N.W. and N.E., gradually veering round to E. and W. From February to May dense fogs rise during the evenings and mornings, and the wind comes from the W. Towards the middle of May storms of thunder and lightning with squally weather and S.E. and S.W. winds usher in the "rainy" season, which ends about October with still more violent atmospheric disturbances and strong winds blowing from the S. and S.W., gradually becoming variable till, towards the end of October, they settle and the cold weather again appears.

The rainfall during each of the last 10 years has been :—

YEAR.	January to May.	June to September.	October to January.	Total.
1868	16·40	222·30	14·45	253·15
1869	4·40	178·55	8·55	191·50
1870	33·00	172·85	12·08	217·93
1871	28·44	192·52	12·43	236·99
1872	22·30	167·60	6·60	106·60
1873	22·80	212·50	15·80	251·10
1874	12·58	130·02	10·19	152·79
1875	14·16	201·63	14·64	230·43
1876	14·70	155·86	13·92	184·48
1877	2·54	231·15	17·22	250·91

The mean of the maximum readings in May, July and December in 1877 was, 87° 81° and 79° respectively : the mean of the minimum during the same months 79° 78° and 76° respectively. The highest reading was 90° and the lowest 74°.

The district on the whole is healthy and the town of Sandoway is one of the healthiest if not the healthiest station in Arakan. Its site is more elevated and freer from malarious swamps and noisesome jungle than any other in that division. Cases of ague occur at all seasons and during the cold weather, when the wind is from the N.E. and N.W., fever assumes an epidemic form, largely due to want of care and caution, and if not early checked is apt to pass into the remittent type. Cholera and smallpox occasionally appear but always, it may be said, as importations. Vaccination has made but slight progress : the villages are small and not easily accessible, the population is sparse and fully employed during the winter months in agricultural and other pursuits and the inhabitants of the country are but little inclined to incur considerable trouble and fatigue to obtain the advantages of a prophylactic to which they have, from want of experience of its beneficent effects and from its, to them, novelty an apathetic and indeed sometimes a positive dislike.

According to the palm-leaf histories there reigned in Baranathi (Benares), at a time when the duration of a man's life was ninety millions of years, a descendant of the first Booddh of the present period who had sixteen sons to the eldest of whom, Thamoo-tee-de-wa, he allotted the country now forming this district, and for whom the Nat or spirits built a city near the present Sandoway which was called Dwa-ra-wad-dee. Some kings of this race are represented as Booddhists and some as Hindoos. Many ages later Tsek-kya-wad-dee—the embryo Booddh Gaudama—was king of Baranathi ; and to his son Kan-myeng he gave all the country inhabited by the Burman, Shan, and Malay races. Kan-myeng came to Dwa-ra-wad-dee, dispossessed the descendant of Thamoo-tee-de-wa, a connection of whose he married, and was succeeded by kings of his own line who reigned for a period represented by a unit followed by one hundred and forty cyphers. During the reign of the last of these, named Na-rien-da, the country was attacked by the grandsons of a king who ruled in Mo-goung, the history of whose birth and preservation from death neeo not here be related. "Arriving by sea at the "mouth of the Than-dwai river, they are foiled in their attempts to find the "city, which by some is said to have had the power of soaring above the "earth, out of reach of danger, and by others this is said to have been an "illusion produced by its guardian Bhee-loo-ma. By the advice of a "Rathai, or hermit, the brothers propitiate the guardian Bhee-loo-ma, and "she then withdraws her protection ; the ten brothers now bind the city "to the earth with an iron chain, from which circumstance the present "name Than-dwai (iron bound) is deduced. The city then falls into the "hands of the invaders. The brothers divide their conquest into ten "shares, but make Than-dwai their chief capital. After some time the "eight younger brothers are slain in a conflict with the people of the "country, who appear to have risen against them, and the two elder with "their sister are obliged to fly." The capital is subsequently established to the north and from this time Sandoway appears only as a province of the

Arakan kingdom ravaged alternately by the Burmese and by the Talaing until the conquest of the country by the Burmans in 1784 A.D. It was then formed into a governorship and its Won, or as he is sometimes called its Raja, appeared as one of the commanders of the Burman army which invaded Bengal at the commencement of the first Burmese war. After the capture of Arakan by the British a detachment under General Macbean was sent southwards and ascended the river which had been staked in various places and stockaded, but there was no appearance of the enemy who had withdrawn from all their positions in Arakan upon hearing of the downfall of the capital. The country was ceded to the British by the treaty of Yandaboo and on the withdrawal of General Morrison's army one regiment of Native infantry was left at Sandoway, furnishing detachments to Ramree and Akyab, and portions of the Arakan local battalion were stationed in the town and at various places in the interior. A few years later the military head-quarters were transferred to Kyouk-hpyoo and subsequently the small detachment of two companies was withdrawn. Since then the district has been in charge of the civil officers only.

There is little, as far as our present information extends, worthy of the notice of the Archæologist. Here, as elsewhere in the province but perhaps to a somewhat less extent, the date of the erection of such sacred edifices as are to be found has probably been somewhat thrown back, and stories of the enshrining of relics of the last Booddh have been invented to suit the views of pious religionists, more anxious for the glorification of Gaudama and of their country through him than to record only the truth.

Archæology.

On the hills close to Sandoway are three small whitewashed pagodas ; the An-daw, Nan-daw and Tshan-daw. The An-daw is on the right or northern bank of the river about a mile distant. It is said to have been erected in 761 A.D., by King Meng-tsek-khyoop to cover a tooth of Gaudama, whence the name An-daw. It has been repeatedly repaired. The present building, which is of brick, is 242 feet in circumference and 63 feet high. It is surrounded by a walled enclosure and is approached by a pathway up the hill, the summit of which is 234 feet above the plain. The Nan-daw is on a hill about half a mile north of the town, 480 feet above the level of the plain. It is built of brick, is 38 feet high and is surrounded by a brick wall two feet high and pierced by two gateways. It is approached by an ordinary pathway up the side of the hill without steps. It is said to have been erected in 763 A.D., by Meng-bra to cover a rib of Gaudama. The Tshan-daw is also on the left bank of the river about half a mile south of Sandoway. It is built of brick and is surrounded by a low wall with two entrances. The pagoda itself is 170 feet in circumference at the base and 85 feet high. It is said to have been built in 784 A.D., by Meng-gnyo-kheng to cover a hair of Gaudama brought from Ceylon. The approach from the plain is by a rough path on which are found traces of steps.

Three times a year, in March, April and October, the people of Sandoway and of the neighbouring villages resort to these pagodas, spending one day at each pagoda on each occasion.

Two inscribed stones have been found, one near the village of Byee-wa, on the right bank of the Sandoway river a few miles below the town, and the other in the Northern township. Both are in Sanscrit of the eighth century and one contains the first couplet of the Booddhist text from "Yedharma" down to "Maha Sramana". Silver coins struck by ancient kings of Arakan are occasionally to be met with hung as charms or ornaments round the necks of children, many with the dates and names of the kings in Burmese characters on either side, but some have unintelligible Persian or Nagari characters on the obverse. Occasionally also are found specimens of a smaller coin with impressions of the same primitive character and workmanship; these may be assigned to a very early dynasty of Arakan kings who reigned from about 800 to about 950 A.D. On the obverse, under the king's title is a caparisoned bull couchant and on the reverse the sun, crescent moon and trident. The coin is of the size of a fourpenny-bit. Celts or stone implements of the smooth age are abundant, some of great size, and are fashioned from different kinds of stone.

Out of the 3,667 square miles in the district about 135 are culturable and of this about 72 are actually under cultivation. According to the official returns the area under crops during the last ten years has been, in acres :—

Agriculture.

Year.		Rice.	Oil-seeds.	Sugar-cane.	Cotton.	Indigo.	Fibres.	Vegetables.	Dhanee.	Other trees.	Tobacco.
1868-69	..	28,920	729	411	505	5	27	421	—	577	1,531
1869-70	..	29,135	806	185	547	2	71	466	—	130	1,559
1870-71	..	25,269	799	143	517	2	67	231	—	133	1,601
1871-72	..	25,730	776	87	490	1	70	538	—	109	1,705
1872-73	..	26,116	813	71	492	75	64	581	—	95	1,762
1873-74	..	27,680	838	141	477	20	68	737	1,680	687	1,762
1874-75	..	27,914	941	398	468	2	65	556	—	4,020	1,789
1875-76	..	28,679	998	508	437	3	44	519	1,795	1,385	1,820
1876-77	..	32,326	926	367	443	1	49	624	1,842	1,434	1,914
1877-78	..	34,468	924	264	522	1	48	629	1,862	1,428	1,876

The main crops are rice, sessamum, tobacco, cotton, pepper, sugarcane, dhanee palms, and towards the south yams. Land suited for rice there is but little, and it is not very fairly productive, yielding on an average 940 lbs. an acre. Other crops are more paying and rice is no longer exported from the district. The average rent for rice land is lower than that suited for any other crop. Sessamum and cotton are grown mainly with rice on the hill sides in the hill gardens or toung-ya. Tobacco is largely grown and the cultivation is extending. The plant is said by the natives to have been introduced via China and Burma and not through India, but there is no corroborative evidence on this point, nor is tobacco mentioned anterior to the commencement of the seventeenth century. In this district the plant grows to from four to five and a half feet in height; the leaves nearest to the root are from 18 to 20 inches in length, and from eight to ten in breadth, and

decrease gradually in size upwards. The roots are long and fibrous, and
the stem about two and a half inches in diameter. The chief and best
portions are grown " on old ' Chur ' land, and on the alluvial soil deposited
" during the S.W. monsoon by the numerous mountain streams of the
" Roma range, which run their short course to the sea. These streams
" begin to subside early in October and immediately the soil has become
" sufficiently dry, it is most thoroughly worked up by repeated ploughings
" and harrowings, and every weed carefully extracted."

" The young plants are drawn when about three inches high, and planted
" out from two to three feet asunder in the beginning of November, and
" come to maturity, according to the nature of the soil, towards the end of
" February and all March. When the plants attain the height of 18 inches
" only ten leaves are allowed to remain on each plant, all the extra ones as
" also the tops, and all sprouts and suckers being carefully plucked off, so as
" to throw all the nourishment into the remaining leaves ; this plucking con-
" tinues as new sprouts appear until the final cutting of the crop. The
" plants from their early growth to this stage require constant attention as
" they are very liable to be destroyed by a small worm and by a large
" description of cricket."

" The leaves are considered fit for gathering when their edges commence
" to turn yellow and the surface gets mottled with brownish specks. The
" leaves are picked singly and as fast as they are cut are carried into sheds
" and strung up to dry for seven days, when they are laid out in the sun and
" open air for three days and nights, and then hung up in the sheds again for
" 24 hours. They are then taken down and sorted into three kinds, accord-
" ing to their length, and strung upon thin pieces of bamboo, 30 leaves on
" each slip ; ten of these slips are then bound together and constitute one bo
" or bundle. These bundles are then packed one upon the other and kept
" pressed down and in about a month from this time are sufficiently dry for
" sale." *

The Cuba plant was introduced into the district by Captain (now Sir,
A. P.) Phayre and Captain (now Lieutenant-General) Fytche and thrives
very well, but is not much appreciated by the inhabitants who consider it
inferior in flavour to the earlier introduced plant.

Madder is grown near the Khwa and the cultivation is very profitable ;
the produce is exported to Bassein.

As an almost universal rule the land in the plains is held and worked
by small proprietors holding direct from the State, the holdings averaging
five acres lying altogether and not intersected by other properties. On the
whole the land is not often mortgaged but occasionally when a small sum is
required by a proprietor he will borrow it at enormous interest giving his
land as security and repaying in the course of a season ; if a large sum is
required the land is generally made over to the mortgagee for several years
on the payment of a lump sum on which no other interest is charged, the
mortgagor being entitled to redeem whenever he can on repayment of the
principal. Labourers are never paid by the month but when employed for
the ploughing, or transplanting and reaping seasons receive in the first case
two rupees an acre and their food for the job, and in the second a bushel of

* Report on the Tobacco of the Sandoway district by Captain Fytche.

grain for the day. When land is leased out the rent is almost invariably paid in kind and averages one-third of the yield.

In the hills the cultivators move from place to place each season and cannot be said to own land at all but must be considered as yearly tenants of the State who choose their own land and pay a fixed yearly rent in the shape of a tax which does not vary whatever may be the size of the plot which they cultivate. It is noticeable that in this district these clearings are made mostly by the Khyeng and Burmans; Arakanese do not like this method. Many of the Khyeng cultivate rice-land in the plains.

The quantity of agricultural stock during the last 10 years, according to the published official returns was :—

Year.	Buffaloes.	Cows, bulls and bullocks.	Sheep and goats.	Pigs.	Carts.	Ploughs.	Boats.	Oil and sugar mills.
1868-69 ..	18,753	6,025	917	4,273	787	5,356	1,382	No return.
1869-70 ..	26,730		820	5,050	1,015	5,546	1,573	108
1870-71 ..	28,736		530	2,475	359	5,745	1,427	138
1871-72 ..	23,211	7,273	not given	2,412	874	5,709	1,470	96
1872-73 ..	23,080	6,820	3,220	2,823	867	8,961	1,431	105
1873-74 ..	23,036	7,329	325	2,992	1,388	10,851	1,463	113
1874-75 ..	23,066	7,179	359	2,752	881	10,913	1,395	161
1875-76 ..	24,304	7,016	625	2,861	785	10,548	1,307	170
1876-77 ..	24,709	6,941	329	2,349	716	10,874	1,563	160
1877-78 ..	24,112	7,875	367	2,213	1,028	11,844	1,328	103

and the average prices of cattle and of the most important articles of produce and consumption were, in rupees :—

Year.	Per Maund of 80 lbs.					Fish per seer of lbs.	Plough bullocks each.	Oxen each.	Buffaloes each.
	Rice.	Cotton.	Sugar.	Salt.	Tobacco.				
1868-69 ..	1 14 0	6 0 0	6 0 0	0 12 0	11 0 0	0 4 0	42 0 0	not given	50 0 0
1869-70 ..	2 0 0	9 0 0	8 0 0	0 12 0	11 0 0	0 4 0	30 0 0	20 0 0	50 0 0
1870-71 ..	1 4 0	6 0 0	3 0 0	0 15 4	12 0 0	0 4 0	22 0 0	16 0 0	35 0 0
1871-72 ..	1 4 0	6 12 0	4 0 0	0 15 6	12 0 0	0 4 0	22 0 0	16 0 0	35 0 0
1872-73 ..	1 7 0	6 0 0	6 0 0	1 4 6	12 0 0	0 4 0	25 0 0	16 0 0	45 0 0
1873-74 ..	1 10 0	6 0 0	6 0 0	0 12 5	15 0 0	0 4 0	25 0 0	16 0 0	40 0 0
1874-75 ..	1 12 0	6 0 0	6 7 8	1 3 4	18 0 0	0 5 0	40 0 0	20 0 0	45 0 0
1875-76 ..	1 15 2	8 0 0	4 8 11	1 11 9	18 0 0	0 5 0	40 0 0	20 0 0	45 0 0
1876-77 ..	1 13 0	6 0 0	4 7 0	1 4 0	18 0 0	0 5 0	35 0 0	20 0 0	45 0 0
1877-78 ..	2 7 11	6 0 8	9 13 5	1 2 0	18 0 0	0 5 0	35 0 0	—	45 0 0

Mountainous and forest-clad, with but a small area culturable, the
Population. district has always,' that is always since the British
occupation, been sparsely inhabited and there is no
evidence of its ever having had a numerous population, but the increase has,
on the whole, been proportionately larger than in other parts of Arakan.
In 1828 the number of inhabitants was 19,588 and in 1832, 19,289 ; in 1842
it had risen to 27,660 or 43·40 per cent., and ten years later to 42,886, or
55·0 per cent. The following year, after the annexation of Pegu, it fell to
86,595 as many persons returned to that country whence they had emigrated
during the Burmese time and the whole tract southward from the Kyien-
ta-lee river was joined to Bassein. Ten years later it had fallen still lower
to 32;481. Since then it has increased, partly owing to the restoration of
the country between the Khwa and the Kyien-ta-lee, partly to the return of
people from Pegu who had been unable to obtain their ancestral lands or
who were disenchanted with their old homes and partly to natural causes,
and in 1872 was 51,312.

The numbers of the various nationalities and races was found, at the
census taken in 1872, to be :—

Europeans, Eurasians and Indo-Portuguese			..	16
Chinese	..	..	..	9
Hindoos	..	..	..	86
Mahomedans	..	.:	..	2,021
Burmans	..	..	..	19,188
Arakanese	..	..	..	28,339
Shan	..	..	..	24
Kareng	..	..	..	171
Khyeng	..	..	..	4,731
Other races	..	..	..	10
		Total	..	54,725

This, however, includes 3,413 travellers, wanderers and sojourners.

The Europeans and Eurasians are all officials. The Hindoos are
mainly convicts transported from Hindustan many years ago when Sandoway
was a convict station.

The Mahomedans are of two classes the Mye-doo, who ascribe their
origin to members of a colony from near Ava who originally came as soldiers
with the invading Burman army and who, some 65 or more years ago, were
joined by many of their co-religionists who left Burma during a famine,
and the Kaman, who claim to have come originally from Dehli and to be
descended from the followers of the unfortunate Sha Shuja who was put
to death by the king of Arakan with whom he had sought refuge from his
brother Aurungzeb. Neither of these classes differ much from their Booddhist neighbours except in religion, in the customs which that religion
enjoins, and in education of which they have less.

The Burmans are descended from colonists imported by the Burman
government after the conquest of Arakan and immigrants who have come
in from the adjoining valley of the Irrawaddy. The few Shan and Kareng
have found their way across the Roma since the British occupation and the
Khyeng have long been in the north and east and of late years have spread
into the plains.

Classified according to age and sex the population was :—

		Not above one year.	1 to 6.	6 to 12.	12 to 20.	20 to 30.	30 to 40.	40 to 50.	50 to 60.	Above 60.
Hindoos	Males ..	—	—	—	—	9	25	28	12	12
	Females ..	—	—	—	—	—	—	—	—	—
Mahomedans	Males ..	45	180	160	175	200	135	101	58	64
	Females ..	76	281	179	149	134	71	47˙	34	32
Booddhists	Males ..	1,836	3,410	4,153	3,743	3,621	3,186	2,076	1,103	1,078
	Females ..	1,224	4,518	3,741	3,462	3,510	3,054	1,965	983	897
Christians	Males ..	—	1	1	4	5	1	2	—	—
	Females ..	—	1	—	1	—	1	—	—	—
Others	Males ..	163	435	395	451	392	345	230	125	95
	Females ..	128	405	368	309	383	315	217	101	84
Total	Males ..	2,044	4,026	4,709	4,373	4,227	3,692	2,437	1,298	1,249
	Females ..	1,428	5,205	4,288	3,921	4,027	3,441	2,229	1,118	1,013

The number of females was considerably larger than that of the males amongst the Mahomedans up to 12 years of age and amongst the Booddhists from one to six years, which would seem to shew that amongst the latter the mortality amongst male is considerably greater than amongst female infants, whilst amongst the former the deaths of the two sexes do not vary so much until about the age of puberty, from which time forwards the males are increasingly in excess, doubling the females after 60. There are no means of ascertaining the proportions at various ages between the Arakanese and the Burmans.

The census included what may be called the "floating population". The annual returns for the succeeding years give the inhabitants as :—

Year.			Under twelve.		Over twelve.		Total.		Total.
			Males.	Females.	Males.	Females.	Males.	Females.	
1873 ..	..	..	9,856	9,655	16,667	15,817	26,523	25,472	52,005
1874 ..	..	..	10,249	9,769	17,156	16,401	27,405	26,170	53,575
1875 ..	..	..	10,256	9,754	17,463	16,317	27,719	26,171	53,790
1876 ..	..	..	9,983	9,514	17,755	16,779	27,738	26,293	54,031
1877 ..	..	..	10,686	9,893	18,570	17,633	29,256	27,526	56,782

There are no towns in the district with a larger population than 2,000
souls and by far the larger number of villages have less
Towns. than 200 inhabitants, 62, only, having from 200 to 500
and four from 500 to 1,000. These are nearly all situated in the less hilly
country between the sea coast and the slopes of the Arakan Roma mountains,
many on the coast and many others on the banks of rivers.
The only places of any importance are Sandoway, Toung-goop, Khwa
and Kyien-ta-lee. The foundation of Sandoway is placed in the prehis-
torical period and is attributed to a son of the king of Benares, miraculously
aided. After the conquest of Arakan by the Burmans it was the seat of
governors the last of whom was one of the commanders of the army which
invaded Bengal during the first Burmese war. The town was occupied by
the British forces under General Macbean and was found to have been
abandoned by the Burmese troops. It was then made the head-quarter
station of a district and for some years a military garrison was stationed
in it. It is situated in 18° 25' N. and 84° 30' E. on the left bank of the
Sandoway river about fifteen miles from its mouth in a nearly circular and
well-cultivated plain, open on the east and west, where are the openings
through which the Sandoway flows from the Roma mountains to the sea.
In 1834, it consisted of about 500 houses with 2,000 inhabitants, the
barracks of the two companies of regular troops forming the garrison, being
the right bank of the river to the north. In 1877 it had 1,617 inhabitants,
and had a Treasury, Court-house, Hospital, Market-place, Gaol and Police-
stations, with good roads in it and in its immediate neighbourhood.

Toung-goop is a somewhat smaller town with a population of 1,551
souls in 1877, on the river of the same name, the head-quarter station of the
northern township where, in addition to the Court and offices of the Extra
Assistant Commissioner in charge, there are a Police post and a Telegraph
office communicating with Pa-doung on the Irrawaddy on the east and with
Roo in Kyouk-hpyoo on the west and thence with Calcutta. The military
road across the Arakan Roma terminates at this town.

Khwa is a village on the right bank of the river of the same name at
its mouth and contains a population of 1,029 souls, without including those
of the three adjoining hamlets of Ta-man-rwa, Alay-rwa and Khyeng-tso-rwa.
In 1874 the Extra Assistant Commissioner in charge of the township was
transferred hither from Kyien-ta-lee. It has a small trade with Bassein
and Rangoon to the south and Sandoway to the north; piece-goods, Pegu
jars, crockery and salt being imported.

Kyien-ta-lee is a small village at the mouth of the Kyien-ta-lee river
formerly the head-quarters of the southern township, and accessible to small
coasting craft. Besides these there are 425 villages, nearly all containing
less than 200 inhabitants. .

The trade consists chiefly in the export to Akyab, Kyouk-hpyoo and
Trade and manu- Bassein of rice, tobacco, sessamum, plantains, betel leaf,
factures. salt (made partly by solar evaporation and partly by
boiling), salt-fish, fish paste, dhanee leaves for thatching, and boats, the planks of which are sewn together with rattan binders,
and in the import of piece-goods, twist, betel-nuts, tobacco of an inferior
quality, crockery and hardware and various articles for domestic use
Across the Arakan mountains come from Prome silk and silk cloths and

622

a few minor articles of light weight which can be carried by men. The most important manufacture is thatch from the leaves of the Neepa palm which is in great demand in Akyab and Kyouk-hpyoo as well as locally. Cotton cloths and silk dresses, the latter of which are in good repute, are woven by the women in almost every house. The silk used is obtained from the southern township where silk-worms are bred and from the upper parts of the valley of the Irrawaddy.

During the Burmese rule the only regular revenue was derived from

Revenue.   transit duties and a tax on the land. Five baskets of grain in the husk were taken for each pair of buffaloes used together with half a basket claimed by the keeper of the royal granary for "wastage," but there was no fixed rate and the governors often exacted considerably more. Each basket held 40lbs. In addition to this the various local officials exacted their dues and these in all amounted to nearly 50 per cent. more. In 1828, Captain White, the officer in charge, calculated that every head of a family paid Rs. 17-8-0 a year to the Government, whilst the cost of living for a family of four persons was only Rs. 42 a year :—

			Maunds.	Seers.	Cost Rs.
Rice	..	..	25	16	15
Tobacco	..	..	—	20	4
Salt	..	..	—	33	1
Clothes	..	..	—	—	15
Nga-pee	..	..	—	33	2
Oil	..	..	—	2½	1
House	..	..	—	—	3
Fowls	..	..	—	—	1
					42

In 1831 the total assessment was Rs. 48,530, or about two rupees eight annas a head on the population; 20 years later, in 1851, the amount had risen to Rs. 83,620. Still 20 years later in 1871, when other taxes had been imposed and the population and cultivated area had considerably increased, the gross revenue including Local Funds was Rs. 117,440. The details during the last ten years were, in rupees :—

Year.	Land revenue.	Capitation tax.	Salt tax.	Fishery and net tax.	Excise.	All other items.	Total.	Costs of officials of all kinds.	Nett receipts.
1868-69	48,235	40,519	1,352	1,218	10,562	14,495	115,874	75,925	34,695
1869-70	49,383	41,105	685	1.468	12,565	14,077	119,125	81,174	33,492
1870-71	49,898	42,396	963	1,529	13,145	11,797	119,868	84,228	31,216
1871-72	50,539	42,948	932	1,507	13,439	12,476	121,566	43,230	73,975
1872-73	51,233	43,867	1,002	1,413	15,607	14,627	127,749	72,641	50,487
1873-74	52,736	43,703	1,000	1,222	14,721	14,786	128,168	72,641	50,985
1874-75	53,754	45,276	823	1,301	12,912	19,192	133,258	74,282	51,164
1875-76	54,665	45,731	1,124	1,225	13,622	15,452	131,819	83,448	43,290
1876-77	55,817	45,629	1,331	1,412	16,817	19,513	140,419	100,648	33,743
1877-78	56,845	47,443	635	1,153	19,319	18,835	144,230	—	—

The small local revenue is raised mainly from the municipal tax in Sandoway and from the additional five per cent. on the land and fishery revenue and is devoted to local purposes, such as village police and roads, district post, and education of the simplest kind. This has but little varied: in 1867-68 it amounted to Rs. 4,620 and in 1872-73 to precisely the same amount and in 1877-78, to Rs. 5,800.

The actual incidence of taxation of all kinds, Imperial and Local, direct and indirect in 1868-69, was Rs. 2-8-2 and in 1877-78 Rs. 2-8-8.

Before the first Anglo-Burmese war the government was administered Administration. after the usual Burmese fashion; over the whole was a Won-douk or a Won and under him were Tsit-ke, Myo-ook, Na-khan-daw, Tsa-re-daw-gyee, Taik Thoogyee and Goung; the last appointed by the Thoogyee. When Arakan passed to the English the officers appointed to administer the country appear to have been at a loss to understand the old system and the land tenure. The Taik Thoogyee, who were merely officials, were treated as Zamindars and in the early records are spoken of as "owning" the circles of which they were in charge and the circles as being their "estates". They were, at first, required to pay in a fixed amount of revenue and were left to assess the landowners and tax payers with little if any interference on the European officer's part. Those who did not live in Sandoway were required to have an agent there with whom the officer in charge transacted business. The Thoogyee generally, as far as was ascertained, had a scale by which they regulated the demand, and this it would appear from the records at Sandoway was :—

1.—Married people, well off, with families, bond-servants, farm cattle, &c., Rs. 17.
2.—Married people not so well off, Rs. 15.
3.—Married people depending upon their own labour, married people who were old and could not work, and newly married people with means, Rs. 9.
4.—Married people too old to work and newly married people with little or no substance, Rs. 3-8.

Hpoon-gyee, the maimed and infirm, government servants, the incurably diseased and bachelors were exempt.

Gradually, as the country came to be more understood, the system changed; the Thoogyee fell back into their proper position and the revenue demand from each person was fixed.

For some time after the British occupation the country was in a very disturbed state and robberies and dacoities were numerous. In Febeuary 1829 Nga Tsa-oo, the Thoogyee of Alay-gyo, raised a rebellion; this was speedily suppressed and Tsa-oo's nephew appointed in his place. A few months later Tsa-oo called upon his nephew to resign and on his refusing attacked and captured his village, and remained in possession till 1830 when he was driven across the Roma into Kanoung. In 1831 a Hpoon-gyee of Kyien-ta-lee gave out that he was a "Meng-loung", or embryo king, and caused considerable trouble before the force he raised against the British could be dispersed.

One of the earliest endeavours of the English was to make roads and Captain White reported in 1831 that there was a good road from An to Negrais. No trace of this now remains.

The general administration of the district is now carried on by a Deputy Commissioner who has extensive judicial powers and is the chief revenue authority under the Commissioner of the division. In charge of the three townships are Extra Assistant Commissioners, who are subordinate Judicial Officers and who also supervise the Thoogyee or Kywon or Taik-ook who are in charge of the revenue circles and who, though primarily revenue collectors, aid in the general administration by sending in various returns on matters not purely police or judicial and are expected to aid the police with their influence and local knowledge. Subordinate to the Thoogyee are Kye-dan-gyee or headmen of villages. The village police is composed of Goung appointed one to several villages. The regular police is under a Superintendent, himself subordinate in all matters not purely departmental to the Deputy Commissioner, and in 1877 consisted of 208 men and 17 subordinate officers, which gives about one man to each 18 square miles of country and to every 267 inhabitants. These are paid entirely from the provincial revenues and in 1877 cost Rs. 37,778. In the town of Sandoway, which in former years was a place of transportation for convicts from India, there is now a second class district gaol composed of brickwork buildings with leaf roofs and wooden floors raised four feet from the ground. The number of prisoners is never very large : the greatest average number of all classes in any of the last five years was in 1873, when there were 79, and the smallest in 1875 when there were 37. The total cost of the gaol during the last year was Rs. 17,322 of which Rs. 1,735 were recouped from the value of the prisoners' labour.

The hospital and civil dispensary in charge of the Civil Surgeon are in Sandoway and are in a new building, completed in 1873, built of wood with mat walls and raised four feet from the ground with two male and one female ward, bathrooms, surgery and an office. During 1876 85 in- and 1,873 out-patients were treated, principally for fevers, bowel complaints diseases of the respiratory organs, abcesses, and wounds and injuries. In 1873 the number of out-patients was only 107, in 1874 192, and in 1875 539. The revenue including the amount repayed by the State is small and but little if at all exceeds the expenditure. In 1876 the receipts were Rs. 1,523 and the payments Rs. 1,507. The science of medicine is unknown to the people and the practice is empirical and according to rules extracted from ancient books, varied occasionally by exorcisms of a violent kind. Beyond; perhaps, the rude setting of a broken bone, surgery is not practised. Vaccination is carried on only by the Civil Surgeon and his subordinates, but inoculation is extensively used.

As regards education, little has been done except by the Booddhist monks. With rare exceptions every male Booddhist is sent to a monastery and taught to read and write but in the agricultural parts of the district the services of the boys are required in the fields and the attendance at school is very irregular, and the small learning gained is lost in after life. In towns reading and writing, and in some cases the rudimentary rules of arithmetic, are more fully taught both in the monasteries and in private schools, but the census of 1872 shewed that only 7·45 per cent. of the males under 12, 13·33 of those between 12 and 20, and 33·22 per cent. of those above 20 could read and write or were being taught whilst there was not a single girl or woman who acknowledged to this small amount of instruction. The Mahomedans were still more backward, 7·53 per cent. of, those under 12, not one between 12 and 20, and 11·11 over 20 of the males, and not a single female could read or write or was under instruction : except in towns there are no schools to which they can be sent and the parents prefer that their children should remain uneducated to sending them to the Booddhistic schools. In towns they are better taught and in some cases learn not only sufficient Arabic to enable them to read the Koran but also Hindustani. A middle class school was opened in 1876 and had 44 pupils on the rolls at the end of the year.

SANDOWAY.—The head-quarter town of the district of the same name, on the Sandoway river, about 15 miles from its mouth but only four and a half from the seacoast in a direct line east and west, lying in a basin about 12 miles long by one broad well cultivated with rice and surrounded by hills the only outlets being those through which the river flows. The larger portion of the town, well laid out with good roads crossing each other at right angles, is mainly on the left bank of the river, whilst on the right bank there is a long, straggling suburb, buried in trees and having more the appearance of an independent village. It contains Court-houses, a Police-station, Market, Gaol, Hospital and Dispensary and a Circuit-house, all, except the wall round the gaol, constructed of bamboos or wood and thatched.

It is a very ancient town often mentioned in Arakanese history and is said to have been at one time the capital of a kingdom, more probably of a petty chieftainship. Its original name was Dwa-ra-wad-dee ; according to a current legend this was changed to Than-dwai, the name by which it is now known to the Burmese and Arakanese (Sandoway being an English corruption), from its having been miraculously fastened to the earth by iron chains (from *than* " iron " and *twai*, euphoniæ causa *dwai* " to suspend ").

After the capture of the town of Arakan in 1824 a force was sent southwards to attack Ramree and Sandoway. General Macbean arrived off the mouth of the Sandoway river on the 28th of April and reached the town on the 30th ; stakes had been placed across the stream in several places and stockades had been erected, but these had been abandoned and Sandoway was occupied without resistance. For a few years after the cessation of the war Sandoway was the head-quarters of the troops garrisoning Arakan. Subsequently the head-quarters were transferred to Kyouk-hpyoo, and two companies of Native Infantry detached to Sandoway. Eventually this force was withdrawn and was replaced by a detachment of the Arakan Local battalion, and still later, when this was disbanded, the garrison was withdrawn altogether.

When the British first occupied Sandoway the number of inhabitants was found to be 4,500. During each of the last ten years it has been :—

1868-69	..	.. 1,506	1873-74	..	.. 1,613
1869-70	..	.. 1,523	1874-75	..	.. 1,669
1870-71	..	.. 1,523	1875-76	..	.. 1,505
1871-72	..	.. 1,508	1876-77	..	.. 1,436
1872-73	..	.. 1,548	1877-78	..	.. 1,617

It has a small coasting trade with Kyouk-hpyoo, Khwa and other towns in rice, tobacco, chillies, peas, madder and sessamum and an overland trade in silk and other piece-goods with Prome and Bassein by passes over the Arakan Roma mountains valued at about Rs. 20,000 a year. Owing to the numerous creeks which intersect the coast boats can go as far northward as Akyab, and even beyond, without going out into the open sea.

In the neighbourhood are three pagodas called Andaw, Nandaw and Tshandaw, to which the inhabitants resort three times a year, spending one day on each occasion at each pagoda. In former years steamers were able to ascend as far as Keng-maw, seven miles below Sandoway whence there was a good road to the town. Lat. 18° 25' N. Long. 94° 30' E.

SANDOWAY.—A river in the district of the same name in the Arakan division, which has its source in the Arakan hills and, flowing W.N.W., falls into the sea in about 18° 31' N. About 15 miles up is the town of Sandoway and large boats can ascend thus far, but of late years even small sea-going vessels have to remain at the mouth, inside of which the anchorage is from five to six fathoms, and large vessels have to anchor in the roads. In former years steamers used to ascend as far as Keng-maw, a village some seven miles below Sandoway. The tide is felt for a short distance above Sandoway.

About 50 miles from the mouth there is a thermal sulphuretted hydrogen spring in the bed of the river, the water of which attains a heat of 110° Fahr.

SANDOWAY MYOMA.—A township in the district of the same name, occupying the centre of the district, whence it is sometimes called the Central township, bounded on the east by Arakan Roma, on the west by the Bay of Bengal, on the north by the Northern or Toung-goop township, from which it is separated by the Khwek-loung spur and the river Hoon-bouk, and on the south by the Re-tsan spur and the river Mee-khyoung-rai. It is divided into 14 revenue circles of which the two southern, Toung-ma-gyee and Ka-myit, were joined to it from the southern or Khwa township in 1875. The principal town is Sandoway and the principal river the Sandoway.

In 1875, the cultivated area was :—

	Acres.
Rice land under cultivation and annual assessment	6,894
,, fallow ,, ,, ...	538
,, under lease or revenue settlement for more than one year and paying revenue	2,537
Toungya at eight annas per acre	548
,, ,, four ,, ,, ...	807
Garden and orchard land under annual assessment	1,062
,, ,, ,, lease or revenue settlement for more than one year	12
Miscellaneous cultivation subject to annual assessment	2,208
,, ,, under lease for more than one year	6
Total ..	14,612

The principal products other than rice are tobacco, sessamum, cotton, pepper, sugar-cane, cocoanuts, dhanee, betel-nuts, pan-vines, peas, hemp, and miscellaneous garden produce.

The principal articles exported are tobacco, sessamum oil and seeds, and pan leaves, mainly to the Kyouk-hpyoo and Akyab districts ; the former takes for the making of fishing nets all the hemp that is procurable.

There is also a small trade in cattle, carried on principally by traders from the Bassein district.

The import trade of the township is small and insignificant : the principal articles imported are goods of European manufacture, such as cotton and woollen piece-goods and cotton twist from Akyab, and silk piece-goods from Prome and Bassein, and from the last named district earth-oil and lacquered-ware. Besides these a small quantity of miscellaneous goods of trifling value is imported, chiefly from Akyab.

Iron wood is much used for building purposes but very little, if any, is exported from the township.

In and near the town of Sandoway there are one or two roads but these are only partially metalled : one, running in a westerly direction from Sandoway to the sea, four and a half miles in length, is open for traffic throughout its entire length ; another, following the course of the river northwards for about five miles, is almost if not quite useless owing to the want of bridges. Beyond a radius of five miles from Sandoway communication is carried on chiefly by foot tracks and along the beds of mountain torrents which can only be used in the dry weather. Communication with the northern township is kept up by boats through the various creeks and streams throughout the year and during the N.E. monsoon communication with the south is possible by boats but this route is effectually barred during the prevalence of the S.W. monsoon.

The majority of the people confine their attention to husbandry, whilst only a few may be called traders and they at the best are mere pedlers. The people on the seaboard employ some of their time in fishing, in the preparation of their national condiment ngapee and in the manufacture of salt.

Of skilled labour there is a little and but few persons follow as their sole means of livelihood the occupation of carpenter, blacksmith, umbrella-maker or other employments requiring skill. Of really skilled labour there is literally none.

Weaving is carried on in most families principally to supply home wants, the female members occupying much of their time at the looms.

SANDOWAY MYOMA.—A revenue circle in the central township of the Sandoway district, bounded on the north by the river Sandoway and on the south by the Poung-khyoung spur, with the Shwe-gyoung-pyeng-lek-ya circle on the west and the Khyoung-gyee circle on the east. It now includes Nan-khyoung. The principal products are rice, cotton, tobacco, betel leaves, sugar and indigo. In 1876-77 the population was 2,809, the land revenue Rs. 1,118, the capitation tax Rs. 1,908 and the gross revenue, including that raised in the town of Sandoway, Rs. 25,880.

SAVAGE ISLAND.—A rocky islet in the mouth of the Koo-la-dan river at the entrance to the Akyab harbour, on which stands a masonry lighthouse erected in 1842. A new lantern and light apparatus was supplied in 1870-71.

SELUNG.—A small, quiet and inoffensive race of doubtful origin inhabiting the islands of the Mergui Archipelago. Most probably they were driven out of Malayana by the Malays, of whom they have an hereditary dread, when that race came up from Sumatra. In physical appearance they are between Malays and Burmans. Their language seems to contain words of almost every neighbouring race and in one case, *Maysha*, "man", a word very greatly resembling the Kakhyeng *Masha* which has the same meaning.

They have no fixed abode, living in their boats roaming from island to island in search of sea slugs, fish, shell fish, sapan wood, turtles, shells, pearls and bees' wax which, together with a peculiar kind of mat made by the women during the rains, they exchange with Chinese and Malay visitors for rice, salt, and cloths, and to a great extent for arrack and opium. Occasionally some of them bring their wares to the villages on the seacoast. During the heavy rains as many as 200 will sometimes be found encamped in huts built on poles cut from the forests, walled and roofed with mats which can be rolled up and stowed away in their boats. They rarely remain in the same place for more than a week. They live almost entirely on rice and fish, and occasionally a few hogs are caught and killed by their numerous dogs. When their stock of rice is exhausted they live on a wild root which grows in abundance in the Archipelago and which, " after much maceration in water parts with its poisonous "matter and becomes safe and edible". Formerly they paid a tax to Government of three rupees per boat annually but this was discontinued by Mr. Blundell when Commissioner of Tenasserim and has, happily, never been re-imposed. Their boats are dug-outs with the sides heightened by long pithy stems of a kind of palm impaled upon bamboo spikes fastened into the upper edge; the sail is of palm leaves stitched together and the ropes are of twisted rattan. The bee-hunting season lasts about a month and each " hunt " is preceded by a kind of religious ceremony in which a spirit man having lighted a wax candle chants before it an incantation to the spirits, at the same time drinking freely of spirits which he calls the " honey-water". According to one observer, they have no god, no priest, no liturgy, no holy day and no prayers, but they certainly have a word in their language for God, viz., Too-da, and according to Dr. Stevens they have a traditional belief in a Creator who is the greatest and best of beings.

SGAW.—The most numerous and the most peaceful of the Kareng tribes, consisting of the Sgaw, Ma-nie-pgha, Pa-koo and We-wa clans and inhabiting that portion of British territory lying between 12° and 19° N. Lat. They are found to the east of Zeng-mai and a few have passed westwards into Arakan. By the Burmese they are called *Myit-tho* and by the Pwo *Shan*. Though comparatively a quiet race they have a long-standing and deadly feud with the Pwo whom they have partially exterminated in the Mergui district and against whom they were preparing a raid when Tenasserim was ceded to the British. Their distinguishing dress is a white tunic or smock frock with several parallel narrow bars of red round the bottom.

In their religion and in most of their customs they resemble the other Kareng (*q.v.*), but they have some peculiarities. About January the southern Sgaw have an annual festival for making offerings to the god of the earth and his followers, the spirits of those who are denied admittance into Hades and who execute the punishments awarded by their master to those who swear or use foul language. One curious portion of their belief is that if they swear in their own country they can escape by making propitiatory offerings to the god of the earth, but should they blaspheme in a far-off country they will be killed before dark. To the spirits of their ancestors who have done good in this life, and who watch over births, marriages and children generally, they offer a fowl with a prayer of which the following is a specimen.

"Mothers and Fathers, Theklu, I will offer you a great cock with a "spur fit to stick a rice mortar upon. Take away sickness, take away "disease, take away laziness, take away inefficiency, take away sleepiness, "take away drowsiness, take away inability to obtain, take away inability "to make a living, take away unsuccessfulness, take away want of success, "take away debasedness, take away wretchedness, take away the whole".

Like all the other tribes they believe that every individual has his La, which they call Ka-la, and which is endowed with immortality, receiving after the death of the body the reward due to the individual's actions during life, and which cannot leave the earth until the funeral ceremonies have been completed. When a body is burnt, for they do not bury their dead, a bone is taken from the pile, and one end of a slender bamboo is attached to it. At the other end of the bamboo is a fine thread to which tufts of cotton and pieces of charcoal are fastened alternately, and at the loose end of this thread is a metal ancle- or wrist-ring which is so suspended as to hang just over a brass pot containing a boiled egg, the weight of the ring causing the bamboo to bend down. The whole is in the centre of a large shed round which is hung up the property of the deceased and two torches are placed one at the head and one at the feet, a procession singing dirges going round and round the whole. Then the relatives of the dead approach in succession and touch the brass cup : when the one dearest to the deceased does so the La twists and snaps the string (a feat not difficult for one of the relations to perform with so slender a bamboo and so fine a string) and causes the ring to strike the basin, the bone is then buried and the La is free.

SHA-BOUNG.—A village in the Zee-beng-hla circle of the Prome district about a mile and a half east of the Shwe-lay stream, in 18° 37′ 0″ N. and 95° 43′ 0″ E. on the little Sha-boung rivulet. In former days it gave its name to a registered village tract under an independent Thoogyee.

SHA-KHAI.—A revenue circle in the Tsam-bay-roon (or Kyoon-pyaw) township, Bassein district. In 1876-77 the population was 3,296, the land revenue Rs. 4,838, the capitation tax Rs. 3,672 and the gross revenue Rs. 9,889. During this year the boundary between Bassein and Thoon-khwa was rearranged ; three quarters of Sha-khai were included in the latter district and the remaining quarter was added to the Thoung-daik circle of Bassein.

SHA-KHAI-GYEE.—A lake in the Bassein district communicating with the Da-ga river. It is a fine sheet of water four miles in length and somewhat more than half a mile in breadth, formed by a slight depression. The bed is somewhat muddy and in the dry season there are not more than eight to ten feet of water in the deepest part which is at the southern end, whilst at the northern, where the banks are shelving, there are not more than two or three.

SHANDOO.—A tribe found on the hills and streams in the mass of mountains intervening between the valley of the Irrawaddy in Upper Burma and the plains of Arakan of whom but very few are within the limits of' British authority. Very little is known of them. In the *Journal of the Bengal Asiatic Society* for 1852 Captain Tickell published some notes of this tribe—who call themselves ' Heuma'—the result of an interview with a chief and his follower who ventured as far as Akyab. The country which they inhabit would appear to lie between 22° and 23° N. and 93° and 94° E. ; they are divided into several clans, which according to Captain Tickell's informant, the chief of the Bookees, extend N.E., in the following order :— Bookee, Tha-bhaw, La-lyang, Toon-boo, Roon-hpe, Yang-leng, Hoo-the, Mow-too, Tan-t'lang and Hekka, but of the distance between them nothing could be learned. Their houses are made of timber by the more opulent and of bamboos by the poorer classes, thatched with grass and well raised from the ground. They are rich in poultry and pigs and cultivate such crops as can be raised on the hill sides, such as maize, rice, plantains, yams, cotton, linseed, ect. Elephants are generally shot with large heavy arrows set in trap bows of great size pointing inwards and connected by the same line that pulls the trigger so that the animal passing through or touching the line with his foot receives an arrow in each side ; the people are unacquainted with any poison for their arrow heads. Elephants' teeth form one of their principal objects of barter. The weapons are small bows and arrows (just being superseded by muskets), short spears and shields made of buffalo hide ornamented with brass plates and tufts of buffalo hair dyed scarlet. They are polygamous the number of their wives depending mainly upon their means of paying for them, they may marry two sisters at once : daughters are entirely excluded from succession. Widows are left to the charity of the eldest son who inherits all the property unless he be married before his father's death in which case he gets nothing. They bury their dead, digging a hole in the ground to the depth of a man's height which they pave with stones and line with boards and in this the. corpse, after having been kept for some days in the house, is placed in a supine posture, with the head to the east, together with the weapons used during life : the hole is then covered with sticks, planks and earth and over all a large stone. They regard the sun and the moon as deities and sacrifice pigs and cattle to them at the commencement of the rains. They have no divisions of the year except by seasons.

SHAN-DWOT.—A revenue circle in the Mergui district adjoining the Tenasserim township on the east and shut off from the seacoast by the Pa-law and Pa-la circles on the west. In 1876-77 the population was 1,397, the land revenue Rs. 611, the capitation tax Rs. 928 and the gross revenue Rs. 1,539. The principal village is Pa-law-khyoung-rwa.

SHAN-GAN.—A village in the Ko-doung circle, Angyee township, Rangoon district, with 536 inhabitants in 1877.

SHAN-KWENG.—A revenue circle in the western portion of the Tha-boung township, Bassein district, having an area of about 40 square miles. With the exception of some rice cultivation on the eastern side this circle presents a mass of thickly-wooded hills, spurs and off-shoots from the Arakan range across which there is a pass about 400 feet above the sea level from the village of Tha-boung to Khyoung-thai. The inhabitants are mainly Kareng engaged in agriculture in fields in the plains and in toungya on the hill sides. It now includes Nga-khwa.

The population and revenue during each of the last five years was :—

YEAR.	POPULATION.			REVENUE.		
	Burmans.	Kareng.	Total.	Land.	Capitation tax.	Total.
1874	1,028	1,612	2,640	3,801	2,372	6,173
1875	859	18,021	2,661	4,508	2,390	6,798
1876	1,791	1,684	2,775	4,704	2,482	7,186
1877	1,177	1,268	2,445	4,360	2,525	6,889
1878	1,163	1,233	2,402	4,661	2,570	7,231

and the area under cultivation and the agricultural stock :—

YEAR.	LAND.				AGRICULTURAL STOCK.						
	Under rice, including fallow.	Garden.	Miscellaneous.	Total.	Buffaloes.	Cows bulls and bullocks.	Goats and sheep.	Pigs.	Carts.	Ploughs.	Boats.
1874 ..	2,384	307	56	2,747	963	779	57	561	129	274	120
1875 ..	2,790	341	14	2,145	1,680	730	14	179	169	214	128
1876 ..	2,985	360	16	3,361	1,708	873	7	103	150	449	112
1877 ..	2,722	358	50	3,030	1,147	281	39	180	36	166	35
1878 ..	2,929	356	82	3,367	1,267	321	61	101	41	128	22

SHAN-RWA.—A village in the Pai-kwon circle, Koo-la-dan township, Akyab district, on the western bank of the Koo-la-dan. In 1876 it contained 508 inhabitants.

SHAN-TSOO-GYEE.—A village in the Twan-te circle, An-gyee township, Rangoon district, with 523 inhabitants in 1877.

SHA-PYAN.—A small stream in the Thayet district which rises in the Myit-myeng-doung spur of the Pegu Roma and, flowing in a generally southward direction, falls into the Bhwot-lay river. It is not navigable by boats at any time ; the banks are flat and the bed sandy.

SHA-TAW.—A village in the Myanoung circle of the Myanoung township, Henzada district, on the west bank of the Irrawaddy, with 598 inhabitants in 1877.

SHA-TSEE-BHO.—A village in the Pouk-taw circle, Mo-gnyo township, Henzada (Tharrawaddy) district, about a mile west of the Rangoon and Irrawaddy Valley (State) Railway, with 616 inhabitants in 1877.

SHAW-DOUNG.—A revenue circle in the Kama township, Thayet district, three square miles in extent, of which rather more than one is un-culturable and rather more than another actually cultivated. The inhabitants, of whom a few are Khyeng, numbered 541 in 1876-77 ; the land revenue was Rs. 736, the capitation tax Rs. 700 and the gross revenue Rs. 1,493. The circle now includes Shaw-doung and Rwa-ma, the Thoogyee of the latter having resigned in 1859. The products are rice, sessamum, chillies, onions, tobacco, plantains and maize.

SHENG-BENG-NAN-KAING.—A pagoda in Martaban, supposed to contain one of Gaudama's hairs and to have been erected in the sixth century B.C. by a converted Bhee-loo or ogre. It was repaired in 1807 by the then governor.

SHENG-BHOORENG-KYOUK-TSOUK.—About 20 miles west of Toung-ngoo are two small pagodas thus named which are said to have been erected by order of Asoka in 225 B.C. The name means "built of "stone by the queen". The existing buildings are undoubtedly modern and probably enclose smaller pagodas founded when Toung-ngoo was an inde-pendent kingdom; that is in the fifteenth century, or perhaps earlier, in the twelfth century, when Nara-pad-dee-tsee-thoo visited this portion of his dominions.

SHENG-DHA-WAI.—A highly venerated pagoda in the Tavoy dis-trict, north-east of the village of Moung-mai-shoung, 77 feet high and 301 feet in circumference at the base. It is supposed to enclose a relic of Gau-dama which, released by its possessor, the miraculously-born Theng-gan Meng, alighted at the spot where the pagoda now stands and was received by the people in a golden basket.

SHENG-BENG-THA-ROUNG.—A village in the Htan-le-beng circle, Za-lwon township, Henzada district, on the east bank of the Niek-ban stream, with 714 inhabitants in 1876-77. Close to it is a modern pagoda of the same name.

SHENG-NGAY.—A revenue circle in the Shwe-doung township, Prome district, just to the north of the Shwe-nat-toung or Kho-lan hills. It now includes five village tracts. In 1876-77 the population was 2,142, the land revenue Rs. 4,468 and the capitation tax Rs. 2,322. It contains no villages of any importance.

SHENG-MAW.—A pagoda on Tavoy point, founded in 1204 A.D. by Nara-pad-dee-tsee-thoo, king of Burma, when he visited this part of his territories It is nine feet high and 24 feet in circumference at the base, and is highly reverenced as being supposed to contain a tooth of Gau-dama.

SHENG-MOOT-TEE.—The most famous pagoda in the Tavoy dis-trict, to the south of the village of the same name. It is 58 feet high and 308 feet in circumference at the base. It is said to have been built to enshrine an image that, with a stone and a banyan-tree—both of which are shewn near the pagoda—was miraculously floated from India to the spot where the sacred edifice now stands. An annual festival is held near this pagoda, the people coming on gaily decorated bamboo-rafts with music and dancing.

SHENG-TOUNG-BOON.—A pagoda in the south-eastern township of the Tavoy district, supposed to have been founded in 781 A.D. It is 40 feet high, 100 feet in circumference at the base, and octangular in shape.

SHO.—The Pwo family of Kareng : so called by themselves. *See Pwo.*

SHOUNG.—A small sub-tribe of the Pwo family of Kareng now found near the northern extremity of the Toung-ngoo district of the Tenasserim division but having a tradition that they have been driven northwards from near Tha-htoon. During the Burmese rule a number of their villages were exempted from taxation on condition of a watch being kept up against incursions by the Red Kareng. They wear trowsers like the Gai-kho but not so handsomely embroidered. They number about 700 souls, living in about 20 villages.

SHOUNG-GYO-GOON.—A revenue circle in the Shwe-doung township, Prome district. In 1876-77 the population was 3,799, the land revenue Rs. 3,008, the capitation tax Rs. 4,143 and the gross revenue Rs. 7,571.

SHWE AN-DAW.—A pagoda near the village of Re-bwek, a few miles north of the town of Thayet. This pagoda dates from the time of Na-ra-pad-dee-tsee-thoo, king of Burma (about 1167 A.D.), who is noted for his piety, his communications with Ceylon and his frequent journeys through his dominions. He is said to have received from Ceylon a holy tooth relic of Gaudama and, while escorting it to his capital, he was warned by signs and portents to deposit it at the spot where this pagoda now stands.

SHWE BAN-DAW.—A revenue circle in the Mye-dai township, Thayet district. In 1876-77 the population was 4,761, the land revenue Rs. 3,174, the capitation tax Rs. 2,051 and the gross revenue Rs. 5,431. The principal products are rice, cotton, sessamum, maize and cutch.

SHWE BAN-DAW.—A village in the Prome district, close to and to the south of, Shwe-doung from which it is separated by Doo-reng-ga-bho, the two forming an extension of that town along the bank of the Irrawaddy.

SHWE BHOORA-BAW.—A pagoda in the Kama township of the Thayet district, which was built during the reign of Nara-pad-dee-tsee-thoo (*circa* 1170 A.D.) on the spot where the remains of an old pagoda were discovered.

SHWE DAGON.—The great pagoda of Rangoon and the most venerated object of worship in all the Indo-Chinese countries. At the annual festival in March crowds of pilgrims flock to it from all parts of the country, from the Shan states in the north, from the Kareng-nee states in the north-east and from far above Mo-goung on the Irrawaddy. So great is its renown that the king of Siam not long ago had a fine Zayat, or resting-place for pilgrims, built near it. It stands upon a mound partly natural partly artificial in the angle formed by the junction of the Rangoon or Hlaing and Pegu rivers, about two miles north of the former and three miles east of the latter. The hill on which it is erected has been cut into two rectangular terraces one above the other, each side facing one of the cardinal points of the compass. The upper terrace, which has been carefully levelled and paved, is 166 feet from the level of the ground, and is 900 feet long by 685 feet wide. The ascent to this platform was by four flights of brick steps—one opposite the centre of each face—but the western has been closed by the fortifications lately built. The southern approach is covered with handsomely-carved wooden roofs supported on massive smooth teak and masonry pillars and has at the foot two immense griffins, one on each side. From the centre of the platform the profusely-gilt solid brick pagoda springing from an octagonal base with a perimeter of 1,355 feet, rises with a gradually diminishing spheroidal outline to a height of 321 feet and, supporting a gilt-iron network "umbrella" in the shape of a cone 26 feet high and surrounded with bells

"Shoots upward like a pyramid of fire."

The space round the pagoda is left clear for worshippers but all round the edge of the platform are numerous idol-houses facing inwards, containing images of Gaudama in the usual sitting position, and of the same Booddha in a previous existence receiving from Dipengara, one of his predecessors, the prophetical annunciation that he too should, after the lapse of four Theng-khye,* and the existence and destruction of 100,000 worlds, attain to Booddhahood. Between these idol-houses and the main building are numerous bells, small pagodas, Ta-khwon-daing or sacred posts each surmounted by the figure of a Karawaik (Garuda, the carrying-bird of Vishnu) and bearing a long streamer : the bells are struck by worshippers with the deers' antlers whicn are left lying near them. On the east the space is more choked up with buildings than on the other sides and here stand a small pagoda, an exact representation and the exact size of the old htee or "umbrella" on the summit since replaced by one made in Mandalay, and, covered by a roof, an enormous bell, 7ft. 7½in. in diameter at the mouth, under which a man can stand upright with ease. This bell bears an inscription in Burmese in twelve lines, the latter portion, as translated by Mr. G. Hough, running—" For this meritorious gift, replete with "the virtue of beneficence, may he " (Bho-daw Bhoora, the king who presented the bell) " be conducted to Niek-ban, and obtain the destined " blessing of men,. Nat and Bramha, by means of divine perfection. May " he obtain in his transmigrations the reigning state only among men and " Nat. May he have a pleasant voice, a voice heard at whatever place " desired, like the voice of Kan-tha-meng, Poon-noo-ka, and A-la-ma-ka " when he speaks to terrify, and like Karawaik, king of birds, when he " speaks on the subjects about which Nat and Brahma delight to hear. " Whatever may be his desire or the thought of his heart merely let that " desire be fulfilled. Let him not in the least meet with that towards which " he has no mental disposition and for which he has no desire. When Aree-" madeya shall be revealed let him have the revelation that he may be-" come We-tha-dee Nat, supreme of the three rational existences. In " every state of existence let him continually and truly possess the excel-" lence of wisdom and according to his desire in practices pertaining to " this world and to the divine state so let it be accomplished. Thus, in " order to cause the voice of homage during the period of 500 years to be " heard at the monument of the divine hair in the city of Rangoon, let the " reward of the great merit of giving the great bell, called Maha Ganda, " be unto the royal queen mother, the royal father proprietor of life, lord " of the white elephant, the royal grand father, Aloung-meng, the royal

---

* A Theng-khye is a number consisting of a unit followed by 140 cyphers.

" uncle, the royal aunt queen, the royal sons, the royal daughters, the
" royal relatives, the royal concubines, the noblemen, the military officers
" and teachers. Let the Nat who guard the religious dispensation 5,000
" years, the Nat who guard the royal city, palace and umbrella, the Nat
" who all around guard the empire, the provinces and villages, the Nat
" who guard the monuments of the divine hair around the hill Tampa-
" koot-ta together with the Nat governing Bomma and Akatha and all
" rational beings throughout the universe utter praises and accept the
" supplications."
The legend of the first building of this pagoda dates from a very early
period in the history of the Talaing race. Before the birth of Gaudama a
king reigned over the Talaing in the delta of the Irrawaddy, having his
capital at Ook-ka-la-bha, on the site of the modern Twan-te, 16 miles west
of Rangoon. Near that city lived a pious merchant named Tha-ka-lai who,
on account of his meritorious actions in a previous existence and of his
present worthiness, received a title and high distinction from the king of
the country. This merchant had two sons named Poo or *dove* and Ta-paw
or *plenty*. The two young men, having heard that a famine existed in the
western countries, determined to convey thither a shipload of rice. They
sailed for the west and in due time cast anchor on the coast of the country ;
this, probably, was the shore at the mouth of the Ganges. Landing they
proceeded inland towards the town of Bandawa (Pandooa in the district of
Hugli ?), and having hired 500 carts they returned to their vessel, loaded
them with the rice which they had brought, and returned towards the
city. On their road they were met by a Nat who in a former existence
had been their mother who asked them where they were going to trade
and on their replying that they were going to the city of Bandawa she demanded, "Desire ye gold and silver merchandize, or rather desire ye
"treasure ?" Their answer was " Heavenly treasure." Acting on the advice of the Nat, and guided by her, they travelled for two days and at last
reached the place where Gaudama was sitting under the Yazayatana or
Leng-lwon tree at Gaya near Patna, during the seventh period of seven day's
meditation which immediately preceded his becoming perfect*.

---

* The authority for this statement is Colonel Burney in Asiatic Researches, vol. 20,1836,
p. 187 ; and this would fix the date at 588 B.C. (which is exactly the date given in the legend).
It is not easy to see how Patna could be reached from the coast in three days by a train of
loaded carts. According to Colonel Burney the seven periods of rest were *after* Gaudama had
become perfected and were as follows :—
1. Under the shade of the Peepul tree upon a golden throne which had miraculously risen
from the earth.
2. On a rising ground a short distance from the tree, on which Gaudama stood for seven
days looking at the throne " without winking or blinking".
3. At another spot near the tree, where Gaudama walked backwards and forwards in the
air for seven days.
4. In a golden house which appeared miraculously.
5. Under another Peepul tree.
6. Near the lake of Monzalienda in which dwelt a Naga or dragon, amongst the folds of
whose body Gaudama sat for seven days.
7. Under the Yazayatana tree.
According to Cunningham (Bhilsa Topes, p. 24) the seven weeks were passed *before* Gaudama was perfected, and a few days afterwards Gaudama left Gaya for Benares. There is a
further discrepancy inasmuch as Cunningham states that the seven weeks were passed in four
periods ; four weeks under the Bhodi tree, one under the Peepul, one under the Mahalindo,
and one under the Rajayatana. It will be observed that in the text Gandama gives the two
young men some hairs of his head ; he must, therefore, have been perfected at that time.

The young men in reply to Gaudama stated that they came from a far and an unknown country and Gaudama informed them that his predecessors had left behind in Pegu a bathing garment, a water-dipper, and a staff, hidden in the Thien- ɓoot-tara mount under a wood-oil tree. He then, rubbing his hand over his head, gave to each of them four of the hairs which attached themselves to his fingers ; he re-named them Ta-poo-sa and Hpa-lee-ka, and charged them to deposit these hairs with the other relics.

The two brothers, placing the hairs in a golden casket, rejoined their ship and set out on their return to their own country. On their way they put in at a place called Ezali or Zetta, the king of which insisted upon having two of the hairs. Proceeding onwards they anchored off Cape Negrais, the Naga or Dragon of which lies in wait to sink the ships of those unbelieving voyagers who pay him no respect ; he also demanded two of the hairs which were reluctantly yielded. In seven days more the brothers reached Ook-ka-la-bha and, to their astonishment, found that the four hairs which had been taken from them had, by the miraculous power of Gaudama, been restored and that all the eight were in the casket in which they were originally placed. The king and all the court proceeded to the place where the ship was and received the relics with due honour. In obedience to the instructions of Gaudama search was made for Mount Thien-goot-ta-ra but no one could say where it was till at length the guardian of the earth appeared and pointed out the spot. When the tree on it, under which the relics of the former Booddha were deposited, was felled it " as the three divisions of the mount were not equal it remained " poised horizontally on its centre on the highest peak ; its top touched " not the ground and its root touched not the ground. Therefore the place " was called in the Moon language ' Dagon.' " A relic chamber was prepared underground, and the sacred relics were deposited therein with much ceremony by the king and his officers. With the relics were placed gold, silver and precious stones, and a golden model of the ship, with images of the two brothers holding the helm, which floated miraculously on a mimic sea, and over the relic-chamber was built a small pagoda 27 feet high. The date given in the legend for the erection of this pagoda is B. C. 588. A town soon sprang up near the pagoda and existed for 32 generations until the fall of the dynasty of the sovereigns of Ook-ka-la-bha, when both town and pagoda fell into ruins. Nothing was done to restore the pagoda till 1446 A.D. during the reign of the Peguan king Ba-gnya-raw. The work was continued by his successors until in 1501, when the throne of Pegu was occupied by a female sovereign named Sheng-tsaw-boo, land was allotted and hereditary servitors were set apart for the service of the shrine. At this time the additions and restorations had raised the height of the pagoda to 129 feet. Still further additions were made by the succeeding sovereigns, especially by the Burmese after their conquest of Pegu, the policy of the kings of that race being to increase the splendour of the Shwe Dagon at Rangoon so that it might surpass the Shwe-hmaw-daw at Pegu the ancient building which the Talaing had for so many years reverenced and which was associated with the recollections of their national independence. Owing to these continual additions the pagoda at last, in 1768 reached its present height of 321 feet from the platform on which it stands. In 1774 it was re-gilt by Tsheng-hpyoo-sheng, king of Burma, the amount of gold used being equal to the weight of the king, that is 12st. 3lbs.: the value of the gold was thus about Rs. 94,080. It was again gilt in 1834, and once more before the conquest of Pegu by the British.

A few years ago it was again re-gilt from top to bottom partly by public subscriptions, the amount being raised year by year from the pilgrims who visited the shrine at the great festival, and partly by the rent derived from leasing out the palm trees on the slopes and terraces of the mound on which it stands. This work was completed in 1871 and, with the sanction of the British Government, the king of Burma sent down with great state and ceremony a new Htee of iron covered with solid gold-plating and inlaid with numbers of jewels, 13½ feet in diameter at the base, 47 feet in height, weighing 1¼ tons, and valued at Rs. 620,000. The time selected for the work was the annual festival in November. " From the " 25th October until the 26th November the people were gathering to " Rangoon from all parts of the country and flocking to the pagoda in " crowds. Meantime the arrangements were being made for bringing " down the old Htee of 1774 and carrying up the new one of nearly a " century later. The great difficulty in the coronation was to carry the " different pieces of the Htee up the outside of the great solid cone of the " pagoda proper. This was accomplished by covering the cone with a " basket-work of bamboos, and then constructing a roadway of six strong " ropes which ran in an inclined plane from a point on the platform to a " point on the upper part of the cone. A carriage ran up this roadway on " pullies and brought up each portion of the Htee in succession, which was " then elevated to the summit by a crane."

" The labour and expense of these proceedings were entirely gratuit- " ous. Hundreds of wooden poles, besides 50,000 bamboos and 70 cart- " loads of canes, were used in the construction of the scaffolding. The " labour was distributed amongst different bodies of workmen and artizans, " each having its own head-man and performing its allotted portion with- " out pay or emolument beyond the religious merit which was supposed " to attach to the fulfilment of the task, whilst every working-man was " duly supplied with provisions at the expense of other pious contributors. " For the work of dragging the ropes which drew up the different pieces of " the Htee there were always thousands of volunteers, young and old, who " were only too anxious to lend a hand."[*]

The hill on which the pagoda stands has been fortified by the British so as to serve as a refuge in case of need.

The whole of the early history of this pagoda must be rejected as untrustworthy and the first accounts in which any confidence can be placed are those which relate to the occurrences during the reign of the queen Shengtsaw-boo so late as the beginning of the sixteenth century, though it may be accepted as a fact that a pagoda existed on this spot from much earlier times.

The name is derived from the Talaing word " Takoon," which signifies " a tree or log lying athwart," alluding to the position assigned in the tradition to the tree after it was cut down, and which has been corrupted

[*] Administration report, 1871-72.

into Dagon or Dagun.in Burmese. The word "Shwe" or golden is a
Burmese translation of the original Talaing word prefixed to Takoon. It is
now used generally as a term indicative of excellence.

During the first Burmese war in 1825-26 the strong position where
the pagoda stands was abandoned by the Burmese on the fall of the town
of Rangoon (then situated on the bank of the river some distance to the
south) and, being occupied by the British under Sir Archibald Campbell
from the middle of May to the end of the war, was several times unsuccessfully attacked by the Burmese.

During the second Burmese war in 1852 the position of the town was
found to be entirely changed. A new town had been formed about a mile
and a quarter from the river to the south of the pagoda, which had been
very cleverly worked into the defences to which it formed a sort of citadel.
The Burmese had settled that the British would attack from the south
and had made every preparation for receiving them, having armed the defences with nearly 100 pieces of cannon and jingals and collected a garrison of 10,000 men. The British troops, however, moved to the east front,
turning the Burmese position and passing their stockaded town. After
some hours firing from the heavy guns it was discovered, at about 11 A.M.,
that the east entrance, on which the artillery was playing, was clear and
an assault was ordered. The troops advanced steadily over the intervening 800 yards under the fire of the walls crowded with the enemy. When
the storming party reached the steps a tremendous rush was made and a
deafening cheer announced that the great Shwe Dagon pagoda was a
second time in the hands of the British.[*]

SHWE DAGON.—A pagoda in Martaban, so called because it was
founded at the same time as the great Shwe Dagon pagoda of Rangoon.

SHWE-DAW.—A village in the Prome district in 18° 32' 10" N. and
95° 30' 0" E. on the little Khyoung-gan rivulet about four miles due east
of the southern end of the Eng-ma swamp, and three miles due north of
Rwa-thit on the main road from Rangoon to the northern frontier of the
province. Its inhabitants are chiefly occupied in rice cultivation.

SHWE-DOUNG.—A town in the Prome district, the head-quarters of
the township of the same name, on the right bank of the Irrawaddy, about
eight miles below Prome, on the main road from Rangoon to the north, in
18° 42' N. and 95° 17' 30" E., separated into two parts—the Meng-dai and
Hpyouk-tshiep quarters—by the Koola-khyoung, which is traversed by a
long wooden bridge, and further up, where it is much narrower, by a
masonry structure carrying the main road already alluded to. This town
has risen to its present importance since the occupation of Pegu by the
English; the old town of Shwe-doung or Shwe-doung Myoma, mentioned
in old records and travels, being now a village only, some miles farther
south on the same bank of the Irrawaddy opposite to Padoung. In 1863-

---

* The following extraordinary and incredible statement appears in Sonnerat, "Voyages
"aux Indes Orientales et en Chine" published in 1782:—"Ce dernier (the Shwe Dagon) est
"singulièrement construit; il se termine en cone, et n'a ni portes ni fenêtres: c'est par une
"ouverture pratiqué au sommet, sur lequel on voit la couronne d'or qu'y fit placer Alompra,
"que les Princes, les Seigneurs, et le peuple jettent les richesses immenses qu'ils apportent en
"offrandes. Ce trésor doit être un des plus riches de la terre, si toutefois les Burmans n'ont
"pas trouvé le moyen de-la piller par quelque souterrain."

64 it had not even 5,000 inhabitants, in 1873-74 it had 12,518 and in 1877-78 13,588. On the bank of the Irrawaddy and accessible by large boats, though owing to sandbanks and islands not by steamers, it is the port almost of the Poungday and Eng-ma rice plains, the produce of which has to pass this town on its way to Prome, except that portion which finds its way to Rangoon by the railway, or by dry weather roads northwards behind th Prome hills, and the small portion which finds an outlet southwards during the rains by the Myit-ma-kha and creeks communicating with the Irrawaddy many miles lower down. The Hpyouk-tshiep quarter on the south suffered formerly from the overflow of the Irrawaddy and of the Koola-khyoung the waters of which were forced back into its broad mouth by the rise in the main river, but this has been to a great extent remedied by embankments of no great height but sufficient for the purpose of protecting the lower land within them. It has a good covered Market-place, a Police-station, and a Court-house, and is well laid out with streets generally at right angles. It contains numerous pagodas, monasteries, and zayats or public rest-houses.

SHWE-DOUNG.—A township in the Prome district, bounded by the Irrawaddy on the west, the Henzada (Tharrawaddy) district on the south, the Ma-ha-tha-man and Poungday townships on the east, and the Ma-ha-tha-man township on the north, having an area of about 200 square miles. The eastern boundary is formed by the low Toung-gyee hills which extend from near Prome into the Henzada (Tharrawaddy) district, and are covered with Eng (*dipterocarpus tuberculatus*), forming the Engdaing or Eng-country. From Prome a low chain stretches southward nearly to Shwe-doung, and from Shwe-nat-toung four miles south of that town another low forest-covered ridge extends to the Henzada (Tharrawaddy) district dividing the township into two long plains uniting round the northern end of the Shwe-nat-toung or Kho-lan hills. In the south-west a large corner is cut off by the Doon-ka-la channel, which is choked up with sand just above Gnyoung-tsa-re in the dry weather, but in the rains completely separates into an island the country between it and the Irrawaddy. There are no rivers of any size, the largest being the Kyoon, which drains the plain between the Toung-gyee and Kho-lan hills, and flowing northwards through rice-fields falls into the Irrawaddy at the village of Shwe-gyo-goon near Shwe-doung. The main cultivation is carried on in the centre of the two plains and round Shwe-doung, but garden and miscellaneous cultivation exists to a considerable extent along the bank of the Irrawaddy, where tobacco and vegetables are grown, and inland some sessamum is produced. In the north-east, below Shwe-doung, many palm-trees are grown, and from these are drawn large quantities of tari.

Near Shwe-doung Myoma the principal town in the Burmese time, on the bank of the Irrawaddy, some five miles south of the present town of Shwe-doung, is the Theng-bhyoo lake which in the dry season is about two miles long and one mile wide in its broadest part, and seven (in the rains 15) feet deep. The banks are low and covered with elephant-grass and the bed is muddy but the water clear. This lake receives its supply from the Irrawaddy, as well as from the rains, and in the rainy season extends south wards to the Eng-bya. This is another morass two miles south of Kyee-thai two and a half miles long and three-quarters of a mile wide. At this period of the year boats can ascend the Doon-ka-la channel from Gnyoung-tsa and from thence enter the Eng-bya and go up close to Shwe-doung Myoma.

The principal road in the township is the great northern road from Rangoon, which enters it through the Eng-daing and strikes the Irrawaddy at Shwe-doung, whence it proceeds northwards along the bank to Prome. In addition to this the whole township is intersected with fair-weather cart-roads. The head-quarter town is Shwe-doung, on the bank of the Irrawaddy about eight miles below Prome, which has arisen since the annexation of Pegu by the gradual enlargement of the two villages of Meng-dai and Hpyouk-tshiep, one on each side of the little Koola streamlet at its mouth. It now contains a population of 13,588 souls—merchants, rice cultivators, weavers, fishermen and coolies. It is well laid out with roads and has a good and well-supplied market. The other large places are Doo-reng-ga-bho and Toung-loon-gnyo, which form the southern and eastern out-skirts of Shwe-doung; Kyee-thai, on the river bank, noted for its silk-weaving, and Gnyoung-tsa-re, still larger, further down.

Close to the village of Ma-ra-man, in 18° 37' 30" N. and 95° 17' 0" E., on the northern end of the Kho-lan spur is the celebrated and conspicuous Shwe-nat-toung pagoda, in the plain at the foot of which some 20,000 people assemble annually for seven days in March to worship and hold a fair. Behind the Shwe-nat-toung are six other small pagodas stretching in a line southwards.

On the annexation of Pegu it was found that Shwe-doung was divided into 99 village tracts, each with its own Thoogyee. These tracts have gradually been amalgamated as the Thoogyee died, resigned, or were dis-missed for bad conduct, and there are now only 17 revenue circles under separate Thoogyee. In 1876-77 the population was 25,901, the land reve-nue Rs. 27,438 and the capitation tax Rs. 28,350.

SHWE-DOUNG.—A revenue circle in the Meng-doon township, Thayet district, with an area of 82 square miles, 85 per cent. of which is uncul-turable waste; of the culturable area about 5,000 acres are actually under cultivation, and of these many are hill clearings. In 1872 it had 4,040 in-habitants, of whom a comparatively very large number, viz., 1,196 were Khyeng. Included in the present circle are eight village tracts, the here-ditary Thoogyee of which had disappeared before the annexation. The products are rice, sessamum, cotton, maize, tobacco, chillies, onions, cutch and silk. Upwards of 100 acres are mulberry cultivation, but no silk is reeled; the cocoons are all sold. East of Leng-bhan village is a salt-well which was worked in the Burmese time. In 1876-77 the population was 4,394, the land revenue Rs. 2,967, and the capitation tax Rs. 2,915.

SHWE-DOUNG MYOMA.—A revenue circle in the Shwe-doung town-ship, Prome district, to the north of and adjoining Kyee-thai, and occupy-ing the corner formed by the bend which the Irrawaddy takes a few miles south of Prome. Rice cultivation is not much carried on except in the south-west. The villages are principally on the bank of the Irrawaddy, the largest being Khyoung-toung, close to Kyee-thai at the southern end of the Theng-bhyoo lake. Shwe-doung Myoma, the old Shwe-doung, the town or village which is always thus called in Burmese history, the present town of Shwe-doung having grown up since the annexation and being known by the names of its two quarters, which then were separate villages, Hpyouk-tshiep and Meng-dai, is at the northern end of the same lake and is now but a small village. The population in 1876-77 was 3,332, the land revenue Rs. 1,501, the capitation tax Rs. 3,877 and the gross revenue Rs. 6,066.

SHWE-DOUNG-OO.—A pagoda in the old stockade on high ground to the north of the town of Shwe-gyeng, built in 1809. At one time it was much resorted to by the inhabitants but it has been abandoned since the stockade has been converted into a fort, a powder magazine erected near it, and a guard of sepoys placed close to it.

SHWE-GNYOUNG-BENG.—A revenue circle in the Tha-boung town-ship, Bassein district, about 45 square miles in extent and lying between the Shwe-gnyoung-beng and the Da-ga rivers. In the west there is some rice cultivation but the rest of the circle consists of large waste plains with undulating ground towards the north; the inhabitants are largely engaged in fishing. In 1876-77 the population was 2,426, the land revenue Rs. 1,594, the capitation tax Rs. 2,080 and the gross revenue Rs. 8,570.

SHWE-GNYOUNG-BENG.—A river in the Bassein district, which falls into the Bassein river near the village of the same name in 17° 1′ 0″ N. and 94° 55′ 0″ E., and communicates by several creeks with the Da-ga further eastward. The banks are firm, and in its lower portion the stream is from 100 to 150 feet wide. It is not navigable by large boats for any distance except in the rains, and in the dry season small boats even cannot ascend beyond Tsit-peng-gyee.

SHWE-GOON.—A revenue circle in the Than-lweng Hlaing-bhwai township, Amherst district, on the left bank of the Salween north of Mee-zan. It is inhabited mainly by Kareng, by whom it is to some extent cul-tivated. It contains a tract of teak forest on the bank of the river. In 1876-77 the population numbered 1,994 souls.

SHWE-GYENG.—A revenue circle in the Kanoung township of the Henzada district, on the right bank of the Irrawaddy, thinly cultivated, principally with garden and miscellaneous produce. The principal village is Shwe-gyeng.

The population and revenue during each of the last five years were :—

YEAR.	POPULATION.				REVENUE, IN RUPEES.			
	Burmans.	Kareng.	Others.	Total.	Land.	Capitation tax.	All other items.	Total.
1874	2,217	76	961	3,254	2,063	3,045	666	5,774
1875	2,072	85	1,133	3,290	2,016	3,117	659	5,892
1876	2,183	93	1,140	3,416	921	3,297	528	4,746
1877	2,270	91	1,220	3,581	2,167	3,342	492	6,001
1878	2,520	79	1,042	3,641	2,669	3,402	473	6,844

During the same period the area under cultivation and the agricultural stock were :—

YEAR.	LAND, IN ACRES.				Stock.						
	Rice.	Garden.	Miscellaneous.	Total.	Buffaloes.	Cows, bulls, and bullocks.	Goats and sheep.	Pigs.	Carts.	Ploughs.	Boats.
1874 ..	44	17	505	566	190	72	—	40	84	40	2
1875 ..	96	19	313	428	190	72	—	—	82	39	6
1876 ..	149	34	122	305	260	152	—	—	144	39	9
1877 ..	242	31	158	431	270	100	—	—	152	40	9
1878 ..	294	29	279	602	218	114	15	40	113	40	15

SHWE-GYENG.—A village in the circle of the same name in the Kanoung township, Henzada district, on the west bank of the Irrawaddy, with 650 inhabitants in 1877.

SHWE-GYENG.—A river in the Shwe-gyeng district, which rises in the high mountains north-east of Shwe-gyeng and falls into the Tsit-toung at that town. Above Shwe-gyeng where it receives the Ma-da-ma from the south and where its channel suddenly deepens it is not navigable by any but the smallest boats. Its bed is sandy for some distance up and rocky above.

SHWE-GYENG.—The head-quarter station of the Shwe-gyeng district, in .17° 54′ 40″ N. and 96° 51′ 15″ E., on the left bank of the Tsit-toung river at the mouth of the Shwe-gyeng, with 7,528 inhabitants in 1878. Extending across the angle formed by the junction of the two rivers is a low line of laterite hills on which are the barracks of the small garrison, detached from Toung-ngoo, and a few houses, the remnants of the much larger cantonment which was established here after the close of the second Burmese war. Where these abut on the Tsit-toung river, north of the town, is the old fort and stockade from which the Burmese escaped without waiting for the attack of the English on the advance of the British column from Martaban to Toung-ngoo in 1853. The main portion of the town, which is laid out in straight streets generally at right-angles, lies in the low land between these hills and the rivers, and during the rains is to a great extent flooded. On the right bank of the Tsit-toung there is a small suburb. The inhabitants are principally engaged in trading. The town contains the usual offices of a Deputy Commissioner, a police-office, post-office, hospital and dispensary, school, telegraph-office, and forest-office, a considerable quantity of teak being brought down the Tsit-toung and landed on the river bank for examination and for the receipt of passes from the Forest officer in charge. It is a town of no very ancient date which has gradually increased from a small village, the increase being aided in 1829 by a large influx of the inhabitants of Kyouk-gyee, further north, who had been burned out.

SHWE-GYENG.—A township in the centre of the district of the same name, lying on both sides of the Tsit-toung river : on the west it includes

Bhaw-nee, transferred some years ago from Toung-ngoo, and thus stretches up along the Pegu Roma almost to the extreme north-west corner of the district. Its northern boundary, west of the Tsit-toung, is formed by the Re-nwe and Kyoo rivers, and to the east by a line drawn from the mouth of the Kyouk-gyee to the Shwe-gyeng river and thence by that stream to its source. On the east it is bounded by the crest of the Poungloung range from the source of the Shwe-gyeng to the Kyaik-htee-ro hill; on the south by the Kyoon-pa-goo east of the Tsit-toung and on the west by the Pyeng-boon-gyee or Pa-gaing embankment and the Bhaw-nee-ga-le (thus including Kaw-lee-ya, a circle lately added to it from Rangoon), and on the west by the Pegu mountains. To the north is the Kyouk-gyee township and the Toung-ngoo district, to the east the Salween Hill Tracts district, to the south the Tsit-toung township and the Rangoon district and to the west the Henzada (Tharrawaddy) and Prome districts. The eastern and western borders are highly mountainous and covered with dense forest but between the lower slopes of the hills and the river, more especially west of the Tsit-toung, are tracts of fertile rice land. The principal rivers are the Kyoo and the Da-la-nwon on the east and the Shwe-gyeng on the west, but there are other streams of more or less importance, the majority of them navigable for some distance during the rains. The western portion is traversed by numerous fair-weather cart roads; the main road from Pegu to Toung-ngoo, now being made, and the projected Tsit-toung Valley (State) Railway will run through this township. On the east the main road from Toung-ngoo to Tsit-toung runs along the bank of the river. The town of Shwe-gyeng lies within the township but is not under the jurisdiction of the Extra Assistant Commissioner in charge, who was formerly stationed close to that town on the opposite bank of the Shwe-gyeng but now resides and holds his court at Thayet-tha-mien—more correctly Thoo-rai-tha-mee—a long straggling village on the right bank of the Tsit-toung river. The other principal villages are Poo-zwon-myoung, on the banks of the Tsit-toung, where there is a considerable manufacture of earthen pots, and Gnyoung-le-beng, somewhat inland in the centre of a large tract of rice cultivation. In 1876-77 the population was 49,198, the land revenue was Rs. 25,820, the capitation tax Rs. 38,794 and the gross revenue Rs. 1,47,253.

SHWE-GYENG.—A district in the Tenasserim division, 5,565 square miles in extent, lying in the valley of the Tsit-toung south of Toung-ngoo from which it is separated east of the Tsit-toung by the Rouk-thwa river, and on the west by the Kwon. Its western boundary, which extends from the source of the Kwon to that of the Bhaw-nee-ga-le, is formed by the Pegu Roma mountains as far south as the Kha-la and thence by the eastern of the two spurs into which the main range here separates : west of the main range are the Henzada (Tharrawaddy) and Prome districts, and west of the spur is the Rangoon district. On the right bank of the Tsit-toung it is separated from the Rangoon district by the Bhaw-nee-ga-le as far as the Pegu and Toung-ngoo road, thence by that road to the Pyeng-boon-gyee or Pa-gaing embankment and thence by this embankment to Myit-kyo on the Tsit-toung : here the boundary turns southward and follows the canal to the Kha-ra-tshoo, when, turning eastward, it follows that creek nearly to its mouth winding southward so as to include the village of Kha-ra-tshoo situated in a small triangular patch between the Tsit-toung and the creek. On the east from the source of the Rouk-thwa to the Kyaik-htee-yo the crest of the Poungloung range separates it from the Salween Hill Tracts. From Kyaik-htee-yo the boundary line turns eastward, still dividing the district from the Salween Hill Tracts, and after striking the river Bhee-leng follows it southwards to its mouth. The southern boundary in this part extends along the Kyoon-iek eastward to its mouth in the Kyouk-tsa-rit, here it turns north-east and crossing the Doon-tha-mie and the hills strikes the Salween at Kyouk-tsa-rit. East and south, below the Salween Hill Tracts, the district which adjoins it is Amherst.

The boundaries have more than once been altered. After the second Burmese war it included the Salween and the Tha-htoon sub-division of the Amherst district but did not include Bhaw-nee, and was then called the Martaban province; after the formation of the Chief Commissionership it was called the Martaban district. In 1864-65, Martaban was joined to Amherst and the district was called Shwe-gyeng; a short time later Bhaw-nee, which had originally belonged to Rangoon, was added to it from Toung-ngoo: in 1872 the Rwon-za-leng sub-division was formed into an independent jurisdiction and called the Salween Hill Tracts, and in 1873 the Kaw-lee-ya circle in the south-west was added to it from Rangoon and the village of Leng-bweng from Toung-ngoo. In 1877 the boundary between Shwe-gyeng and Rangoon was changed whereby small tracts were exchanged.

In the north the aspect of the country is highly mountainous, both the eastern and the western range sending down numerous spurs which, on the east, approach to within a few miles of the Tsit-toung. Both ranges diminish in height towards the south and the Pegu Roma recede farther from the river leaving a wide extent of good land. Below Kyaik-hto, a town at the foot of the southern slopes of the Poungloung range, the whole country consists of low lands which comprise extensive plains and scrub forest stretching away as far as the eye can reach with an almost unrelieved sombre appearance and mostly covered with almost impenetrable elephant grass except where rice is grown on some spots suited to its cultivation. Here and there a pagoda, or a group of houses with hardly a tree near them except perhaps a few tall palms, mark the village of some fishermen or salt-boilers who gain a precarious livelihood from the salt-impregnated soil or the muddy waters of the numerous tidal creeks. At high tides the whole of the coast for miles inland is inundated, and so rapidly does the sea advance over the flats that little or no chance is offered to the fisherman or turtle-seeker should he have neglected the warning sound of the advancing waters. During the dry season the upper portion of these plains is easily traversible by carts but during the rains they become one vast sheet of water, with the tops of the tall elephant grass shewing above and almost concealing the pagodas and villages by which alone the boatman can guide his course.

The principal mountains are the Pegu Roma on the west and the
Mountains.   Poungloung on the east both extending from north to south but the latter nearer to the Tsit-toung river. Both are densely wooded, with steep ascents and descents, drained by numerous small streams which, as a general rule, flow all the year round, and inhabited by Kareng and Yabaing. There are several passes over the Pegu Roma but they are mere tracks winding up ravines and along the crests

of spurs. Across the Poungloung range there are three principal routes : the northern is up the valley of the Baw-ga-ta and across the Thayet-peng-keng-dat hill to Kaw-loo-do, the northern police-post in the Salween Hill Tracts ; the central passes up the valleys of the Moot-ta-ma and the Mai-dai and debouches at Pa-pwon ; the southern lies in the valley of the Moot-ta-ma almost to the source of that river and then crosses the high Thwot-ta-bat hill and strikes Hpa-wa-ta on the Bhee-leng river. This range, which at the Tsek-le hill opposite Shwe-gyeng attains a height of about 4,000 feet, terminates above Keng-rwa in the Ke-la-tha hill, crowned by a' conspicuous pagoda said to have been founded many years ago at the same time as the Kyaik-htee-yo on a hill of the same range above Tsit-toung.

The Tsit-toung, above Shwe-gyeng sometimes called the Toung-ngoo river and sometimes the Poungloung, rises in the Burmese territories and enters this district at its northern boundary ; after an exceedingly tortuous course it takes a large S-shaped bend just below Tsit-toung and some miles to the south falls into the Gulf of Martaban by a funnel-shaped mouth seven or eight miles wide up which the spring tides rush with great violence forming a bore and rendering navigation exceedingly dangerous. It is navigable throughout its length in this district by large boats and steam-launches. At the mouth of the river at springs the bore rises to the height of 20 feet. At low water as far as the eye can see the country near the mouth is a succession of low mud flats ; the first appearance of the setting flood is marked in the far distance seaward by the tide-wave which rolls up through the channel leading to the mouth of the river with a low rumbling sound which gradually becomes more and more audible forewarning all who may be in its way and giving timely notice of its advance. On nearing the mouth it throws off small bores into the narrow channels that lead to the different creeks the main body passing up the Tsit-toung with a curling crest which even at Kha-ra-tshoo is, during the springs, some 12 feet high, and is broken only by the serpentine curve of the river a little higher up. In the dry season it sweeps up the river as far as Waing, between Tsit-toung and Shwe-gyeng, but in the rains does not go beyond Weng-ba-daw some seven miles below Tsit-toung. Behind it comes the main body of the tide which breaks over the flats and in a few moments inundates the whole coast for miles. Following the rolling crest of the bore in the river is the "boiling", or as the Burmese call it the "rising", sand in which many a boat is lost after it has withstood the shock of the bore passing. It is simply a chop-sea of heavy sand and water which sometimes acts with such effect upon a boat as to render it a wreck in a few minutes. The banks of the river gradually increase in height but, composed of loose and sandy alluvium, they crumble away very considerably under the influence of the bore and of the rapid current during the rains : except in the neighbourhood of villages where patches of rice or garden cultivation exist they are almost uniformly covered with dense grass. Its affluents are small, generally rocky, and comparatively insignificant streams which serve only as drainage-ways, as means of communication between the villages on their banks, or as outlets for timber and other forest produce. The Kwon, the northern boundary of the district rises in the Pegu Roma and after an E.S.E. course of some 60 miles falls into the Tsit-toung near A-nan-baw about 50 miles below

Toung-ngoo. Its course before it has left the mountains is obstructed by rocks but teak and raw silk are brought down and distributed through the Tsit-toung. The Re-nwe has its source in the Pegu Roma and after a south-easterly course of about 90 miles falls into the Tsit-toung about six miles north of Shwe-gyeng. The banks are steep and rocky near the source and flat near the mouth : in the rains small boats can ascend as far as the village of Waing-gyee. The Bhaing-da, Tsha-re, Kaw-lee-ya, and Bhaw-nee are all streams whose waters are added to those of the Tsit-toung from the westward. A little above the village of Myit-kyo the Da-la-nwon comes in from the west : it is formed by the junction of several small streams and is easily navigable for some distance beyond Thoon-khwa whence, until the Pyeng-boon-gyee embankment was made, boats could easily proceed during the rains to the Pegu river and thus avoid the dangerous bore.

The eastern affluents are the Rouk-thwa in the north which is navigable for a few miles only from its mouth, but serves as an outlet for a considerable quantity of areca nut grown on the hills and for a small quantity of teak ; the Moon ; and the Kyouk-gyee, which rises in the north-eastern part of the district and, fed by the Pa-da and numerous mountain torrents from the Poungloung range, falls into the Tsit-toung about 12 miles above Shwe-gyeng after a southerly course almost parallel to that river and at no great distance from it ; its principal tributary is the Baw-ga-ta. The Shwe-gyeng, which is not navigable except by rafts and very small boats, rises in the Poungloung range, north of Shwe-gyeng and falls into the Tsit-toung at that town after receiving near its mouth the waters of the Moot-ta-ma which has its source in the mountains south-east of Shwe-gyeng near the Thwot-ta-bat hill. South of this the streams are too small to be of any importance except to carry off the rainfall : the two principal are the Kyoon-pa-goo and the Kha-wa, the latter joining the main river at Tsit-toung. Some six or seven miles below Tsit-toung, at the village of Weng-ba-daw, is a small creek almost dry in the dry season but which in the rains communicates with the swollen streams and flooded plains to the eastward and is then the only route to Kyaik-hto and Bhee-leng and thence to Maulmain.

The Bhee-leng or Doon-won river rises in the wilderness of mountains forming the Salween district, and has a generally southerly course to the Gulf of Martaban. Whilst winding amongst the hills it is a rocky, pebbly, mountain torrent rushing over enormous boulders and bathing the feet of forest-clad steeps but as soon as it emerges into the plains it deepens rapidly and soon becomes thick and muddy. The entrance from the sea is difficult and dangerous and the villages on its banks are generally small. For a short portion of its course it forms the highway during the rains between the Tsit-toung and Maulmain. During springs a bore rushes up this river inundating the country round for miles and in the dry season extends as far up as Shwe-hle a few miles below Bhee-leng but during the rains is soon checked by the strong current and mass of water which then comes down from the hills. In the south the banks are low gradually rising towards the north, where at first elephant grass and then tree forest take the place of the mangrove which grows on its banks near the coast. Its affluents are few and insignificant but during the rains it communicates on the east with the Doon-tha-mee, and in the west with the Tsit-toung and the intervening rivers.

The vast plain south of Kyaik-hto, lying between the Tsit-toung and the Bhee-leng, is drained by two principal streams which, in the rains, are interconnected, the whole country becoming a sheet of water. The Ka-dat flows through Kyaik-hto, where it is spanned by a wooden bridge, and continuing towards the S.S.E. falls into the mouth of the Tsit-toung river or the head of the Gulf of Martaban. The Thai-bhyoo, a somewhat larger stream, rises rather farther to the north on the eastern side of the southern end of the Poungloung range and, after a somewhat more tortuous course trending more to the westward, reaches the Gulf about seven miles below the mouth of the Ka-dat. There are bores in both these streams and at flood tides the whole of the lower country through which they flow is flooded.

There are five small lakes in the district four of which *viz.*, Htoon-daw, Tsa-weng, Mwai-dweng, and Mee-khyoung-goung, are in the Moon circle of the Kyouk-gyee township, and the fifth, the Nga-thwai-zoot, is south of Bhee-leng. The Htoon-daw and the Mwai-dweng are both picturesque sheets of water and the former is of some extent and winds round through thick forest encircling a small piece of high land in its centre.

Lakes.

The district has never been accurately geologically surveyed. The Poungloung range on the east "consists of two distinct "groups of rocks an older and metomorphic one, and a "younger one of carboniferous age." * Whether true granite occurs otherwise than in the shape of dykes or not within the limits of this district is a point not yet fully determined. "It may indeed be "doubted" writes Mr. Theobald "if any granite save in the form of veins "occurs in the Poungloung range, or within the British frontier line; though "the schistose rock, of which the Poungloung consist, displays a great ten- "dency to massive structure lithologically resembling granite but neither "intrusive nor in any way dissociated from the more bedded members of the "group :†" and again "I fully admit that lithologically this Kyouk-gyee and "Kyiktyo (*Kyaik-htee-yo*) rock is a perfect granite, but from the identity of "it with a similar granitic rock, which is undoubtedly a member of the schis- "tose group of crystalline rocks, I am led to suspect a similar relationship "for it." ‡

Geology and mineralogy.

North of Kyouk-gyee the gneissose (*Triassic*) rocks of which the Poungloung range is composed extend westwards as far as the Kyouk-gyee river only but towards the south they border the Tsit-toung.

The Pegu Roma on the west and most of the ground intervening between them and the Tsit-toung consists "of a very important series of "beds between the Eocene or Nummulitic group on the one hand, and the "fossil wood group (*post pliocene to pliocene*) on the other......From what we "know of the Yoma its age may be roughly fixed as upper tertiary, covering "probably the whole of the geological epochs named miocene and pliocene."∥

* Theobald : " Geology of Pegu " in *Memoirs of the Geological Survey of India*, Volume X., part 2, page 35.

† Theobald : " Geology of Pegu " in *Memoirs of the Geological Survey of India*, Volume X., part 2, page 13.

‡ Theobald : " Geology of Pegu " in *Memoirs of the Geological Survey of India*, Volume X., part 2, page 140.

∥ Theobald : " Geology of Pegu " in *Memoirs of the Geological Survey of India*, Volume X., part 2, page 80.

The whole of the level and alluvial plains are occupied by an arenaceous and very homogeneous deposit, which most probably had an estuary origin, with patches of coarse sands and gravels along the edge of the lower slopes of the Pegu Roma. West of the Tsit-toung "laterite is generally wanting, " and its occurrence exceptional.........Crossing the Sittang (*Tsit-toung*) " river, good typical laterite undistinguishable from the Midnapore rock, is "found in great force, forming a continuous belt of high ground almost " scarped as regards the abruptness of its margin towards the Sittang " (*Tsit-toung*) and forming a plateau of variable breadth thence to the foot of " the hills, and which covers ground not as yet explored. This is the lateritic " belt which.........may be roughly estimated to rise abruptly from 50 to 60 " feet above the alluvium of the Sittang (*Tsit-toung*) valley. The now " deserted military station of Sittang (*Tsit-toung*) was situated on a steep bluff " of this rock overlooking the river; and a little below this the deposit " sweeps away back from the river, and runs with a slightly sinuous and " somewhat indented outline to Kyeikto (*Kyaik-hto*) and thence to Martaban. " From Sittang (*Tsit-toung*) the deposit runs with a very straight boundary, " modified only by the denuding action of streams which traverse it, as high " as Kyouk-kyee, a distance of 60 miles; beyond which it is continued in a " less regular manner for some 25 miles more.

" I have described this laterite as a basal member of the older alluvium " of the province; but perhaps it would be more correct to describe it as a " shore or marginal deposit of the basin wherein the wide-spread alluvial clay " accumulated, and as the equivalent, so to say, of that rock. At the time " of its accumulation, the waters of the Gulf of Martaban stretched up what " now forms the Irawadi, Sittang (*Tsit-toung*) and Salwin (*Salween*) valleys; " and the drainage from the then peninsular-like land, now constituting the " Arakan, Pegu and Poungloung ranges, contributed towards the formation " along the coast-line of the sandy talus or bank, which now intervenes " between the level plains and the hill country. The Pegu range, consisting " wholly of soft sand and shales, rather deficient in iron, has contributed to " that sandy detritus which fringes the plains of the Sittang (*Tsit-toung*) " valley to the westward, and wherein pebbles and gravel are scarce, and " laterite as a rule wanting. East of the Sittang (*Tsit-toung*), however, the " Poungloung hill ranges composed of metamorphic and altered rocks, " many of them rich in iron, have contributed not only a coarser pebbly " detritus, but the precise elements, silicious, argillaceous and ferruginous, " requisite for the production of typical laterite; and the above described " laterite bank is simply the littoral accumulation of debris brought down " under ordinary conditions of denudation, and identical in its age and mode " of accumulation with the loose sandy deposits on the opposite side of the " valley. The accumulation and transportation of the coarse materials " forming this laterite bank naturally would be more suddenly arrested than " in the case of fine deposits; hence the abrupt scarped outline of the " laterite is, in my opinion, to a great extent an original feature of deposi- " tion, only to a very partial extent modified by subsequent denudation; and " it is probable that this laterite bank at no period extended much " beyond the general line of its present boundary, no outliers, or other " indications of its former extension, being anywhere seen west of the Sittang " (*Tsit-toung*).

"Some 13 miles north of Shuay-gheen (*Shwe-gyeng*) on the line of
"telegraph road is a small bat-cave in the laterite, which has the appearance
"of having originated naturally, probably through the removal, by ordinary
"drainage, of some loose and incoherent portion of the lateritic stratum
"wherein the cave occurs. It is entered from the top by a natural opening,
"and there is also a 'swallow hole' in the roof which may or may not be
"of artificial origin; the cave, however, appears never to have been
"tenanted by any animals save bats, and possesses no features of interest
"whatever."*

The district is, it is supposed, rich in minerals but until it has been
carefully surveyed and the spots at which these occur examined scientifically
no positive statements on this subject can be made. Gold is certainly
found in most of the affluents of the Shwe-gyeng (*Gold washing*) river and
has been more than once worked but the quantity obtained is so small as
not to repay the labour. This river and the mountains at its source have
been examined by Mr. Theobald of the Geological Survey and by a practical
miner and the reports of both point generally to the same conclusions.
Mr. Theobald stated that "the section of the auriferous beds corresponds
"very closely with that given by Sir R. Murchison, in his 'Siluria,' of the
"Russian gold deposits.........From the occurrence of coarse grains in the
"Shuay-gheen (*Shwe-gyeng*) gravels I should infer the occurrence of the metal
"*in situ* in some of the rocks towards the sources of the streams falling into
"the Sittang (*Tsit-toung*) especially the Matuma (*Moot-ta-ma*)......From the
"marked scarcity of quartz pebbles at the gold washings I am inclined to
"believe that quartz is not the matrix or not the sole matrix certainly of the
"Shuay-gheen (*Shwe-gyeng*) gold." He adds that the full amount which an
industrious worker could calculate on making daily would be about five annas.
Subsequently a party of Chinamen started work, but found the result so un-
remunerative that they gave it up. Still later Mr. James Abernethy, aided
by the State, made a further and equally unsuccessful attempt to obtain a remunerative quantity of the precious metal. He condemned the sources of
the Shwe-gyeng as being "steep and rocky and having a hard smooth
"ledge upon which gold is seldom found in great quantities to pay." He
further examined the sources of the Baw-ga-ta with much the same result.

Copper exists in the Kyouk-gyee township and the pits in the neighbourhood attest the fact that it has been at one time worked. Galena is
also found in the same township, as is iron; this latter was worked during
the Burmese time by some Shan and the ore sold at about seven rupees
a hundredweight. Lead and tin are both found in spots north of Shwe-
gyeng but have never been worked. Coal, it is said, exists in Kyouk-gyee
but the site has never been scientifically examined.

The teak forests west of the Tsit-toung are situated mostly in the
plains and consist of isolated patches of limited extent,

Forests.

but containing some timber of great value, situated
generally on the banks of the Re-nwe, Bhaing-da and Kaw-lee-ya rivers,
and further north on the Kwon. East of the Tsit-toung groups of teak trees
are found scattered all along the road from Kyouk-gyee down to Tsit-toung,
but the stems are irregular and the trees seldom tall. Further inland,

* Theobald: "Geology of Pegu" in *Memoirs of the Geological Survey of India*, Volume X.,
part 2, page 57 *et seq.*

higher up the valleys of most of the eastern affluents of the Tsit-toung, considerable quantities of teak are to be found but only a small proportion of the full-sized trees are of regular shape, except in the valleys of the Moon and the Pa-da, a tributary of the Kyouk-gyee. Teak here forms excellent forests on level ground along the banks of the main stream and a good proportion of teak trees is found on the lower hills immediately skirting the valley. Some of the forests are on deep and rich alluvial soil, others on higher, slightly undulating, ground densely covered with a species of *Pollinia* which is characteristic of a peculiar class of teak localities,—a soft grass with long narrow blades, often from six to eight feet high, so that when penetrating a forest covered with it during the rains, you are deeply immersed in it. Yet it offers no serious impediment to progress through a forest, as elephant grass decidedly does; which, however, is not found in teak localities. The teak grass is not very favourable to the springing up of seedlings.

The most valuable trees other than teak are Pyeng-ka-do (*Xylia dolabriformis*), Pyeng-ma (*Lagerstrœmia reginæ*) and Thit-tsee (*Melanorrhœa usitatissima*) yielding a black varnish.

Except in the hills, the climate is generally healthy. From the middle of October to the middle of May it is dry, but heavy

Climate.

dews at night and fogs in the morning prevail during January and February. The day heat is excessive from March till May, but a refreshing breeze generally sets in at from 6 to 7 P. M. The nights and mornings are cool throughout the year. During the dry season the air in almost every part, except towards the coast, is loaded with smoke and particles of burnt matter from jungles being on fire on all sides. Towards the end of May the rains are ushered in by violent thunderstorms and gales of wind, and at their termination the same phenomena in a milder form are experienced.

The principal diseases from which the inhabitants suffer are fevers and bowel-complaints, to which in 1877 no less than 123 and 64 respectively of the 220 deaths were attributed, whilst one was due to cholera and none to small-pox.

The rain-fall and average state of the thermometer during the seven years ending with 1875-76, were:—

	RAINFALL, IN INCHES.				AVERAGE TEMPERATURE IN THE SHADE.								
					May.			July.			December.		
YEAR.	January to May.	June to September.	October to December.	Total.	Sunrise.	2 P.M.	Sunset.	Sunrise.	2 P.M.	Sunset.	Sunrise.	2 P.M.	Sunset.
1869..	14·45	160·20	8·45	183·10	70	96	82	78	88	81	67	83	78
1870..	39·10	129·10	15·60	183·80	78	87	82	76	85	77	58	84	74
1871..	35·50	164·80	16·60	216·90	70	90	74	73	93	77	48	90	50
1872..	22·50	103·60	11·90	138·00	70	96	75	71	84	77	60	85	79
1873..	5·00	109·00	13·90	127·90	76	102	79	79	90	86	69	88	77
1874..	15·10	108·50	8·80	132·40	74	100	77	76	88	82	66	86	78
1875..	19·10	140·10	6·20	165·40	75	99	78	76	88	84	81	88	79

In 1876 and 1877 the rain-fall and the average temperature in the shade were :—

YEAR.	RAINFALL, IN INCHES.				AVERAGE TEMPERATURE IN THE SHADE.												
					May.				July.				December.			
	January to May.	June to September.	October to December.	Total.	Mean of maximum readings.	Mean of minimum readings.	Highest reading.	Lowest reading.	Mean of maximum readings.	Mean of minimum readings.	Highest reading.	Lowest reading.	Mean of maximum readings.	Mean of minimum readings.	Highest reading.	Lowest reading.
1876 ...	17·60	122·10	7·20	146·90	87	78	90	75	87	79	87	75	80	59	83	55
1877 ...	4·80	140·39	11·80	156·99	101·79	109	—	76	86	76	92	74	90	63	91	55

Only 175 square miles of the district are cultivated, but the cultivated area is gradually extending and there are some 3,611 square miles of culturable waste waiting to be taken up. The most fertile portions are on the right bank of the Tsit-toung river towards the south. The principal crop is rice of which 25 different kinds are grown. These with the time of sowing and of reaping, and the outturn of husked grain, are :—

Agriculture.

Name.	When sown.	When reaped.	Outturn of un-husked rice in bushels, per acre.	REMARKS.
Kyouk-gyee	May or June.	January or February.	50 or 60	Generally cultivated.
Nga-tsien	June ..	November or December.	60	Raised principally on the west bank of the Tsit-toung for exportation to Europe, for which purpose it fetches a higher price than other kinds.
Tsa-ba-hpyoo Mee-doon ..	Do. ..	Do. ..	60	Softer grained than the above, and largely cultivated.
Tsa-ba-nek	Do. ..	Close of November.	50	A good and palatable grain, cultivated by many.
Tsa-ba-nek Toung-byaw ..	Do. ..	Do. ..	45	Very similar to above, and cultivated by many.
Toung-byaw .. .	End of June or beginning of July.	January ..	50	Good, cultivated by many, and of higher value than Kouk-gyee in the market.
Ra-haing	June ..	October ..	40 to 45	Has a long but small grain. Not much cultivated, except in case of scarcity, owing to the early ripening, and the consequent difficulty in reaping it.

Name.	When sown.	When reaped.	Outturn of un-husked rice in bushels, per acre.	REMARKS.
Shan-ga-le	Do. ..	November.	35	Rarely or never cultivated for sale, but for home consumption.
Kouk-nhien	July ..	December.	35	Used principally for making cakes.
Nga-khyiek	June ..	October ..	30	Ditto.
Ka-ka-poon	Do. ..	November,	35	Ditto.
E-dee-ma·tat ..	Do. ..	October ..	55	Only cultivated when there is a scarcity.
Kwek-twa	September,	January ..	30	For consumption boiled, and for cakes.
Koon-wa	August ..	October ..	35	Ditto.
Pan-gnyo-gyee ..	Do. ..	Do. ..	40	Ditto ; large grained.
Koon-nee-gyee ..	Do. ..	Do. ..	40	Rough-grained, and but little cultivated.
Nga-sheng-thwa. ..	July ..	Do. ..	45 to 50	When cultivated, the grain is principally used for making cakes.
Kouk-gyee	June ..	October and November.	50	Cultivated in *toungya* by Kareng.
Boo-hpoo-ga-le ..	Do. ..	September,	50	Not much cultivated on account of its early ripening.
Mee-doon	Do. ..	January and February.	50	Grain hard and palatable.
Kouk-yeng	Do. ..	October ..	40	A tough grain, large and short.
Po-wo	Do. ..	September.	40 to 45	Similar to Kouk-nhien.
Poo-pa-rien	Do. ..	Do. ..	40	A scented grain.
Boo-kee	Do. ..	October ..	40	A spotted grain.
Kyo-tseng	Do. ..	September.	40	

Betel-nuts are very largely cultivated on the hill sides near running streams, the water being diverted into the palm-groves by artificial channels. Cotton is to some extent grown in the *toungya*, and to a very .small extent tobacco is cultivated; whilst there is a larger extent of sugar-cane cultivation here than anywhere else, except in Kyouk-hpyoo. Vegetables are abundant and of *toungya* there are more than in any other part of the province. The land generally is not fertile and in the case of no crop is the average outturn per acre large, whilst in some cases, as in that of tobacco and oil-seeds, it is very small.

The area under the principal crops during each of the last seven years was, in acres :—

YEAR.		Rice.	Oil-seeds.	Sugar-cane.	Cotton.	Tobacco.	Vegetables.	Betel-nuts.	Mixed fruit trees.
1871-72	..	50,773	1	Not given	223	11	1,481	4,611	2,106
1872-73	..	56,687	6	702	242	12	991	3,511	2,124
1873-74	..	59,697	9	497	217	4	1,226	3,483	2,099
1874-75	..	63,106	23	1,036	22	16	1,015	3,872	2,201
1875-76	..	60,764	4	438	28	6	900	3,845	2,082
1876-77	..	62,886	12	662	99	4	1,344	3,707	2,047
1877-78	...	67,640	128	1,020	136	9	1,496	3,738	3,619

Rice is the only crop the cultivation of which has really and steadily increased. The chief rice-producing tracts are in the Kaw-lee-ya, Kweng-da-la, Gnyoung-le-beng, Re-hla, Kyouk-gyee and Gamoon-aing circles of which the last is, perhaps, the most important.

The agricultural stock during the same period was :—

YEAR.		Buffaloes.	Cows, bulls and bullocks.	Sheep and goats.	Pigs.	Carts.	Ploughs.	Boats.
1871-72	..	23,652	8,345	350	2,000	4,699	6,108	1,457
1872-73	..	25,113	8,225	350	2,000	4,761	6,395	1,557
1873-74	..	27,502	9,184	400	2,200	4,959	6,740	1,559
1874-75	..	27,950	10,197	450	2,300	5,295	7,219	1,634
1875-76	..	26,911	11,311	398	2,367	5,381	7.040	1,460
1876-77	..	29,076	11,779	416	2,408	5,849	7,336	1,323
1877-78	..	29,203	11,705	398	2,564	5,890	7,364	1,331

And the prices of the more important articles and beasts :—

YEAR.			PER MAUND OF 80 lbs.						Fish per seer.			EACH.					
			Rice.			Salt.						Buffaloes.			Plough bullocks.		
			Rs.	A.	P.	Rs.	A.	P.	Rs.	A.	P.	Rs.	B.	P.	Rs.	A.	P.
1871-72	..	..	2	0	1	1	8	1	0	2	1	60	0	0	60	0	0
1872-73	..	..	1	7	0	3	2	0	0	2	0	60	0	0	60	0	0
1873-74	..	..	2	0	0	1	8	0	0	2	3	70	0	0	60	0	0
1874-75	..	..	2	8	0	2	2	0	0	2	3	70	0	0	60	0	0
1875-76	..	..	2	8	0	2	2	0	0	2	3	70	0	0	60	0	0
1876-77	..	..	2	8	0	2	2	0	0	2	0	70	0	0	60	0	0
1877-78	..	..	2	8	0	2	2	0	0	3	0	70	0	0	60	0	0

The total agricultural population was found by the census taken in 1872 to be about 20·80 per cent. of the whole and the male agriculturists of 20 years of age and upwards 20,209. The average size of each holding is between three and four acres. As a general rule land is held by small proprietors and is very rarely rented out, never for a long term of years. Rice lands are seldom if ever mortgaged, but garden and orchard lands are. Occasionally but not often labourers are hired for rice cultivation and are always paid in kind.

Population. The census in 1872 shewed the number of inhabitants to be 129,485, or 23·26 persons to the square mile, composed of the following races :—

Europeans, Eurasians, and Americans	68
Chinese	157
Hindoos	291
Mahomedans	421
Burmans	41,562
Talaing	33,926
Kareng	43,475
Shan	3,189
Talaing	1,475
Toungthoo	4,887
Other races	34
Total	**129,485**

The most numerous were the Kareng, who are scattered over the hills more especially to the east of the Tsit-toung and belong to two of the great families, Sgaw and Pwo, of whom many are Christians, converted by the American Baptist missionaries. They differ in nothing from their neighbours to the eastward in the Salween Hill Tract. The Talaing are most numerous in the south in the plain country, at one time it would seem thickly populated by them when the Peguan kingdom arose on the decadence of that of Tha-htoon and extended its power from the Irrawaddy to the Salween. The Burmans are found principally in the level country northwards from Tsit-toung. The Toung-ngoo kingdom, the limits of which seem never to have been very accurately defined southwards, extended probably, considerably below the limits of the present Toung-ngoo district, and was thoroughly Burman, so much so that at one period the sovereign was known as the king of the " Burmas " when a Shan family had usurped the throne of the kingdom of Ava. The Yabaing, a retiring race, are found chiefly on the eastern slopes of the Pegu Roma in Bhaw-nee, and are largely engaged in the rearing of silk-worms which is their *specialité*). The Hindoos, Mahomedans and Chinese are all immigrants since the British occupation, as are large numbers of the Shan of whom a whole colony came in some years ago and was placed at Weng-ka-neng in the fork formed by the junction of the Moot-ta-ma and Shwe-gyeng rivers.

The numbers of each sex and age were :—

	Males.	Females.	Total.
Not exceeding one year	4,702	4,359	9,061
Above one, but not above six years	12,257	11,631	23,888
,, 6 ,, ,, 12 ,, ...	11,723	9,951	21,674
,, 12 ,, ,, 20 ,, ...	8,354	9,010	17,364
,, 20 ,, ,, 30 ,, ...	9,627	10,363	19,990
,, 30 ,, ,, 40 ,, ...	10,312	7,594	17,906
,, 40 ,, ,, 50 ,, ...	5,509	3,897	9,406
,, 50 ,, ,, 60 ,, ...	2,448	2,478	4,926
Above 60 ,, ,, ...	3,011	2,259	5,270
Total ..	67,943	61,542	129,485

The most remarkable fact which these figures disclose is the at first gradual and then sudden diminution of the males between one and 20 years of age, a diminution so large that between 12 and 30 the females exceed them in number; whereas between 30 and 40 there is a considerable decrease amongst the females against an increase amongst the males. In 1878 the number of the inhabitants had increased to 139,432.

The principal town in the district, and the only one with more than 5,000 inhabitants, is Shwe-gyeng founded during the last century before the conquest of the country by Aloung-bhoora. Until the British occupation it was never of much importance. It is situated at the junction of the Shwe-gyeng with the Tsit-toung and extends for some miles along the bank of the latter, shut in behind by low laterite hills. which run across the angle from river to river. On these hills at one extremity is situated the old Burman stockade, with the magazine constructed by the English close to the Shwe-doung-oo pagoda, and at the other the houses of the European residents, whilst extending along them are the wooden barracks of the small military garrison detached from Toung-ngoo. The town itself is low and subject to inundation on the rise of the Tsit-toung. It contains a court-house, market-place, post-office, telegraph-office, forest-office, police-office and police-stations, a hospital and dispensary, a school and a small lock-up. The population in 1878 numbered 7,528 souls.

Towns.

The next town in size and importance is Kyaik-hto at the foot of the Poungloung range on the banks of the Ka-dat, a wooden bridge traversed by the high road from Maulmain to Toung-ngoo spanning the river and connecting the principal part of the town on the left bank with the small suburb on the right. It was founded many centuries ago, and is inhabited chiefly by Talaing. The name is derived from two Talaing words signifying "royal boundary" and according to the palm leaf histories was given to the town because the Ka-dat stream was fixed upon by the Tha-ma-la and Wee-ma-la as one of the boundaries between the three provinces into which they divided the Talaing dominions. Tha-ma-la and Wee-ma-la were the two princes, sons of the king of Tha-htoon, who founded Pegu, and more

probably the Ka-dat was at one time the boundary between the rising
kingdom of Pegu and the decaying kingdom of Tha-htoon.   In 1856 it was
attacked by one Nga Thee-la, a Shan, a resident of the neighbouring village
of Keng-rwa, who had been a Thoogyee and had escaped when under trial
for embezzlement, subsequently murdering the Goung-gyoop in charge of the
township and declaring himself in rebellion against the British Government.
He was shot whilst storming the court-house by a sepoy of the small military
detachment of the 13th M. N. I. then in garrison here.   For some years
it was the head-quarter station of the Bhee-leng Kyaik-hto township, and
during the last few years has been the head-quarters of the Tsit-toung
sub-division, the Assistant Commissioner in charge having being transferred hither from Tsit-toung.   It contains a court-house, market-place
and police-station.

Bhee-leng with a population of 2,074 souls, on the right bank of the
Bhee-leng river, was formerly a small village but in 1824, when Oozana, the
governor of Martaban, retired before the British he settled here with a
number of Talaing followers and built a large stockade.   After six years
he was murdered by his A-khwon-won, or principal revenue official, and was
succeeded by one Moung Bo, to whom was allotted a smaller territory than
that ruled by his predecessor.   During the second Burmese war the place
was surrendered to the English and occupied without resistance.   The
town has twice been burned down and has once been attacked by a band
of dacoits.   For some years an Extra Assistant Commissioner was stationed
here, until the Bhee-leng and Kyaik-hto townships were united.   A few
years ago, on Kyaik-hto being made the head-quarters of the sub-division,
the Kyaik-hto Extra Assistant Commissioner was transferred hither.   The
town contains a court-house, circuit-house, police-station and a market-
place.   The inhabitants are principally traders.   A few miles to the north
is the ancient Koot-thien-na-roon pagoda.

Tsit-toung is a small town on the left bank of the Tsit-toung, at the
mouth of the Kha-wa streamlet, confined on the east and south by high
ground, that to the south rising abruptly from the main river.   The town
is supposed to have been founded by Wee-ma-la about 588 A.D.   Little or
no mention is made of it in history till the middle of the sixteenth century
when the reigning king of Pegu, who had sunk almost into imbecility, was
murdered by the governor's brother.   This governor was himself a scion of
the royal family and immediately proclaimed himself king and took possession of Pegu but was shortly afterwards attacked and put to death.   Whether
he was shot in action or was captured and beheaded by Bhoo-reng Noung
is not clear.   During the first Burmese war it was well defended and on the
first attack the British were driven back with the loss of several officers,
amongst them Colonel Conry commanding the force.   During the second
war the Burman governor, Moung Goung, surrendered the town without
firing a shot.   Until a few years ago it was the head-quarters of the sub-
division.   It contains a court-house, market-place and police-station.   On
the high ground above the town to the south is the Kyaik Ka-lwon-bwon
pagoda, constructed of blocks of laterite.   The base is about 50 feet from
the ground and hexagonal, each side about 60 feet in length with three
small terraces : from the centre of this base, which is ascended by a flight
of steps in the masonry on the western side, rises the pagoda some 70 feet

high. On this hill was constructed a regular fort with parapet and ditch, the former built of laterite, and this was for some years garrisoned by a small British force.

Weng-ba-daw is a large village on the left bank of the Tsit-toung about seven miles below Tsit-toung and lying on both banks of the Weng-ba-daw creek across which is a wooden bridge. It is the chief halting-place for boats proceeding up the river. During the rains trade with the country to the eastward and with Maulmain is carried on by boats all of which pass along the Weng-ba-daw creek through the village, which then has a very busy appearance. The inhabitants are Talaing and Burmans who gain their livelihood by trading, rice cultivation and salt manufacturing. A considerable number of salt boiling pots are made in the neighbourhood with clay brought in boats from higher up the river.

Kyouk-gyee; the head-quarters of the township of that name, is on the Kyouk-gyee river, at the foot of the Poungloung mountains, about 34 miles above Shwe-gyeng and only six miles in a direct line inland from the Tsit-toung. It stands on either side of the stream, the two quarters being connected by two bridges. In 1809 it was attacked and destroyed by the Zeng-mai Shan, and for some years subsequently the governorship was disputed. During the second Burmese war the town, though stockaded, was not defended, Moung Bhwa, the governor of Martaban who had fled hither, making his escape with several officials most of whom, however were taken prisoners next day : Moung Bhwa, riding in a cart and commonly dressed, was not recognized and escaped in the crowd. In 1856 it was attacked by Meng Loung, a Kareng who was in rebellion in the Rwon-za-leng, but he was driven off with considerable loss by the small garrison of the 8th Regiment M. N. I. under Lieutenant Childs. The chief trade is in betel-nuts which are brought down from the neighbouring hills by the Kareng cultivators.

Moon is a small village on the stream of the same name north of Kyouk-gyee, founded in 1801 by Burman settlers from Kyoung-bya. In 1830 it was deserted owing to the cruelties of the then governor of Kyouk-gyee within whose jurisdiction it was situated but was repopulated on his dismissal a short time later. It contains a travellers' bungalow.

Thoo-rai-tha-mee more commonly called Thayet-tha-mien is a long and somewhat straggling village on the right bank of the Tsit-toung river, the head-quarters of the Shwe-gyeng township, containing a court-house and a police-station.

Poo-zoon-myoung, founded in 1814, is a straggling but thriving and prettily situated village lying amongst groves of mango and jack trees on the right bank of the Tsit-toung river about nine miles above Shwe-gyeng. The inhabitants are partly Talaing and partly Burmans who for the most part gain their livelihood by the manufacture of earthen jars from a clay found in the neighbourhood and by trading : most of the rice grown in the two great rice-producing circles in the district is carted hither and shipped for transport by the Tsit-toung. The village has once been entirely destroyed by fire.

Gnyoung-le-beng is a large village, some six miles west of Poo-zwon-myoung, in the centre of a large plain highly cultivated with rice. The inhabitants are principally Talaing and Burman cultivators. It contains a police-station. During the disorders consequent on the second Burmese war and the disorganization of the country on the advance by the British troops it was attacked and destroyed by the Thoogyee of a neighbouring village who carried off a considerable quantity of property.

Keng-rwa is a small village between Kyaik-hto and Bhee-leng in the plain at the foot of the southern slopes of the Poungloung range at which a small police force is stationed. It was the scene of an outbreak in 1856 headed by one Nga Thee-la, a Shan inhabitant of the village, who was shot in an attack on the court-house in Kyaik-hto, upon which the rebellion collapsed.

Out of the 512 towns and villages in the district in 1872 no less than 318 had less than 200 inhabitants and 126 had from 200 to 500 whilst 30 had from 500 to 1,000 the remainder having more than 1,000 but not one had 10,000. The number has now risen to 564.

The revenue raised in this district during each of the last 23 years is given in the subjoined table. There was a progressive increase from 1855-56 to 1863-64, the demand having nearly doubled, whilst the demand from excise had reached its maximum in 1860-61 and was rapidly falling. At the end of 1865-66 the whole of the Martaban sub-division was transferred to the Amherst district and in consequence the demand was lower than it had ever been since 1855-56. Since then it has made great strides, and in 1877-78 nearly equalled that in 1863-64.

Revenue.

YEAR.	LAND REVENUE.					Capitation.	Fisheries.	Excise.	All other items.	Total.
	Rice.	Garden.	Miscellaneous.	Toungys.	Total.					
	Rs.	Rs.	Rs.	Rs.	Rs.	Rs.	Rs.	Rs.	Rs.	Rs.
1855-56	62,463	9,078	1,820	22,599	95,960	79,597	25,217	19,063	11,285	231,122
1856-57	88,700	7,617	1,713	21,078	119,808	82,267	34,247	22,493	20,475	278,790
1857-58	92,497	7,168	1,276	19,585	120,526	79,514	46,465	27,042	18,457	292,004
1858-59	104,091	10,711	2,015	20,785	137,542	86,139	47,403	37,901	25,228	334,205
1859-60	115,945	12,174	3,273	25,695	167,087	82,697	59,460	43,044	22,480	364,768
1860-61	133,380	12,763	3,597	21,992	171,732	84,319	66,095	60,600	34,588	417,384
1861-62	132,559	13,112	5,902	27,223	178,196	104,843	84,139	20,846	32,175	420,199
1862-63	124,316	13,144	5,929	26,374	169,763	110,114	76,607	20,311	32,096	408,891
1863-64	127,952	13,213	4,235	20,552	165,952	122,055	67,645	15,009	26,475	397,136
1864-65	85,863	7,789	3,260	10,122	107,034	121,110	60,359	3,180	35,744	327,377
1865-66	102,801	8,417	3,618	10,518	124,634	126,898	59,846	9,229	34,093	349,440
1866-67	32,716	6,750	1,403	10,913	51,782	118,762	58,094	6,849	12,473	247,960
1867-68	34,317	5,855	1,264	11,283	52,719	91,651	60,327	3,650	31,624	239,971
1868-69	32,597	5,822	1,427	10,846	50,692	92,337	62,879	3,440	31,324	240,672
1869-70	33,958	5,905	1,273	11,241	52,377	93,814	64,577	4,122	37,744	252,634
1870-71	36,935	6,412	1,173	11,510	56,030	98,806	63,967	3,316	56,390	273,518
1871-72	61,372	10,999	1,764	7,091	81,226	94,351	64,509	3,799	86,530	330,475
1872-73	69,198	11,049	2,015	7,260	89,522	97,409	69,170	19,894	59,781	335,676
1873-74	79,548	11,044	1,998	7,339	99,929	103,708	81,050	12,221	34,506	331,414
1874-75	85,533	12,071	2,642	7,143	107,389	104,096	78,458	14,232	46,740	350,915
1875-76	82,101	11,784	1,633	6,083	101,601	106,568	77,870	23,711	35,065	344,815
1876-77	84,631	11,471	2,502	6,422	105,026	107,305	75,744	27,291	35,951	351,317
1877-78	91,762	11,242	3,465	6,648	113,117	109,104	105,786	21,311	35,535	384,853

The local taxes derived from municipal and town funds raised in towns, the district fund raised from ferries and other sources outside the limits of towns, and a cess of five per cent. on the land and fishery taxes, in 1868-69 amounted to Rs. 24,080 and in 1877-78 to Rs. 40,851. The total amount, therefore, of taxes of all kinds paid by the people in those years was Rs. 264,752 and Rs. 425,704 respectively.

The only manufactures in the district are pot-making, salt-boiling and silk-spinning. The pots are made at Poo-zwon-myoung, a *Manufactures.* village a few miles above Shwe-gyeng, where clay is procured on the spot; at Kweng-da-la, a short distance lower down; at Tshiep-gyee, in the Kyouk-gyee township; and at Weng-ba-daw, in the Tsit-toung township. At Poo-zwon-myoung the pots are made for export to Rangoon and Maulmain and the intermediate towns and to the Kareng villages on the hills, but at the other places for local consumption. The manufacture lasts throughout the dry season, that is from November to the following May. The clay is put in a pit with water and allowed to remain for one night: next morning the water is drained off and the clay removed to a shallow pit and mixed with the feet with carefully sifted river sand and when well mixed is turned on a wheel into pots of various sizes and shapes. The kilns contain 1,000 pots amongst which are about 200 of the largest kind. The pots when ready are sold the largest size for five rupees and the others for one rupee eight annas the hundred. The annual produce of one man's labour is estimated at 1,000 unburned pots a month, or 7,000 in the season. The manufacture has been in existence for some 25 years.

The pots made at Weng-ba-daw are solely for the salt-boilers. The clay is brought in boats from Poo-zwon-myoung and is paid for by barter at the rate of one boat load of salt for three boat loads of clay delivered, the pot-makers exchanging the pots with the salt-boilers for salt delivered at the rate of 365 lbs. of salt for each 100 pots sold. The process is much the same as that employed at Poo-zwon-myoung and elsewhere except that the sand is not so carefully sifted; the pots are fashioned entirely by hand not even a wheel being used, and each kiln contains about 100 pots only. The whole process, which is carried on only in the salt-working season, that is, in January and February, lasts about 20 days. The yearly outturn averages about 15,000 pots, but this varies according to the requirements of the salt-boilers.

In the Bhaw-nee and Anan-baw circles at the foot and on the lower slopes of the Pegu Roma silk-worms are bred by the Yabaing and the whole system is the same as that followed by the same class in the Thayet and Prome districts. The annual produce is about 9,000 lbs. the value of which on the spot is about Rs. 4,500. The quantity exported, principally to Prome and Shwe-doung where, on account of the number of skilled weavers, there is the best market for it, is estimated at two-thirds of the total produce or some 6,000 lbs.

For administrative purposes the district is divided into four townships *Administration.* in charge of which are 3rd grade Extra Assistant Commissioners or Myo-ook exercising revenue and judicial powers, generally responsible for the administration and bound to supervise those of the 28 Thoogyee whose circles are within the limits of their townships. Two of these townships *viz.*, Tsit-toung and Bhee-leng, form the Tsit-toung sub-division, the other two, Kyouk-gyee and Shwe-gyeng, are directly under the Deputy Commissioner. In the town of Shwe-gyeng there is also an Extra Assistant Commissioner of the 2nd grade or Tsit-kai. For the first year or two after the annexation of the country there were considerable disturbances : whilst Meng Loung was in rebellion in the Rwon-za-leng a Shan named Nga Thee-la, of considerable daring, great influence among his people, and formerly a Thoogyee, succeeded in effecting his escape whilst under trial for embezzlement from the State, and gathering together a few of his own race planned an attack having for its object the murder of the Goung-gyoop or officer in charge of the township by whose instrumentality and zeal his offence had been brought to light. He accomplished his object under circumstances of the most cold-blooded cruelty, and then openly proclaimed himself a rebel and a partisan of Meng Loung. He at length attacked Kyaik-hto where a small detachment of the 13th M. N. I. under a subadar was stationed, but was shot during the attack and his followers were dispersed. A strong police force was now entertained consisting of one subadar, three jemadars, eight havildars, nine naiks and 124 privates for land and interior duty, and a river force of one Superintendent and two Assistant Superintendents, three syrangs, 11 tindals, and 111 privates with a carpenter and a caulker*. Besides these there was a village police composed of Goung over several villages, and the Thoogyee of circles and Kye-dan-gyee of villages aided in detective and preventive police duties and were generally supervised by the Myo-ook, or Goung-gyoop as they were then called, in charge of townships, each of whom also had two peons. This village police still to a certain extent exists and though not under the direct control of the Superintendent aids him and his men by affording information, pursuing gangs of dacoits when they appear and in similar ways. The Goung are appointed by the Deputy Commissioner but are employed mainly on police work in conjunction with and to some extent under the Superintendent ; the Thoogyee and Kye-dan-gyee are revenue officials who are also generally responsible for the peace and quiet of their tracts, as are the Extra Assistant Commissioners in charge of townships.

The existing force, which forms a portion of the general police force of the province under the Inspector-General in Rangoon in all matters of interior economy but under the general control of the Deputy Commissioner, is under a District Superintendent, and the strength in 1877 was one Superintendent, 30 subordinate officers and 332 men, exclusive of one subordinate officer and 16 men paid by the town of Shwe-gyeng but forming a portion of the regular police force giving one man to every 15 square miles and to every 358 of the inhabitants : of these one officer and 22 men were employed as guards over the treasury and lock-up and as escorts to prisoners and 30 officers and 310 men on regular police duty. The total cost was Rs. 76,536.

The small lock-up, situated east of the town in a valley between the military barracks and the court-house, consists of brick-work wards with wooden floors raised three feet from the ground with tiled roofs, surrounded

---

* The "Interior Police" enumerated above were for the Shwe-gyeng district as it at present exists excluding Bhaw-nee and Kaw-lee-ya, but the statistics of the river Police do not distinguish between those employed here and in the Martaban sub-division now joined to Amherst as Tha-htoon.

by a brick wall. The average number of prisoners confined is small as those sentenced to any but short terms are transferred elsewhere : in 1873 the number was 57 of all classes convicted, under trial, and civil prisoners, and 79 in 1877. The labour on which the prisoners are employed besides ordinary gaol service is in working oil and rice-cleaning mills and in the gaol garden from which the vegetables are supplied.

The hospital and dispensary under the Civil Surgeon has been in existence for a long time. A new building was commenced in 1876. The number of sick treated during 1877 was 6,914 of whom 343 were in-patients. It has a small income, derived partly from Government and partly from voluntary subscriptions. In 1877 this was Rs. 3,089.

In 1871 a district middle class school was established by the State which at the end of 1876 had an average monthly number of 58 pupils on the rolls, all studying Burmese; the annual cost of educating each was Rs. 110, of which the State paid Rs. 100. The American Baptist missionaries have also a boys' and girls' school for Kareng, but with these exceptions the education of the people is entirely in the hands of the Booddhist monks and of a few laymen who have started village schools where the girls receive such knowledge of reading and writing as they possess. In many cases, doubtless, those taught in the monasteries to some extent lose in after-life the little knowledge which they gained, but the census figures may be accepted as shewing fairly enough the extent to which the power of reading and writing only is spread.

		PERCENTAGE OF THOSE ABLE TO READ AND WRITE OR UNDER INSTRUCTION UPON THE WHOLE OTHER POPULATION OF THE SAME SEX AND AGE.		
		Not above 12.	12—20.	Above 20.
Hindoos	Males	24·32	60·00	24·60
	Females	4;17	42·86	6·25
Mahomedans..	Males	58·46	57·89	24·68
	Females	4·65	20·00	7·32
Booddhists	Males	9·34	45·01	26·26
	Females	0·13	0·82	0·34
Christians, including Kareng converts	Males	17·80	44·44	22·15
	Females	7·96	20·00	6·40
Others	Males	——	5·71	1·75
	Females	——	——	——
Total	Males	9.50	44·91	26·13
	Females	0.17	0·97	0·38

During the dry season communication from village to village is, except in the case of those bordering the Tsit-toung and Bhee-leng rivers, carried on by carts. Of made roads there are only 16 miles, but the nature of the country presents no difficulty to cart-travelling in the plains, and along the left bank of the Tsit-toung river a fairly good road extends from the northern end of the district to Tsit-toung where it turns eastward and becoming only a cart crack it follows, and keeps as close as possible to, the southern end of the Pounglong range, and passes through Kyaik-hto and Keng-rwa to Bhee-leng. On the right bank of the river a road was made from Pegu to Toung-ngoo by King Tabeng Shwe-htee, who reigned over the Talaing kingdom from 1540 to 1550, having been king of Toung-gnoo from 1530 to 1540, and wells were dug and rest-houses and gardens made at intervals along it for the use of travellers. Of the rest-houses and gardens nothing now remains, but the road, called the Menglan, is still in existence, and though not traversible during the rains it can be used during the dry weather. During the rains travelling is almost everywhere done in boats, and at this season the road from Tsit-toung to Bhee-leng and towards Maulmain is impassable, the whole plain being a vast expanse of reedy water. The journey to Maulmain from the Tsit-toung is then made by boat *viâ* Weng-ba-daw on the west and the Shwe-lay canal on the east which communicates with the Bhee-leng river ·at the village of that name; a few miles lower down the Kyoon-iep creek leaves the Bhee-leng and joins the Kyouk-tsa-rit, which falls into the Bheng-laing, at the extreme south-eastern corner of the district.

To facilitate communication with Rangoon, a canal has been made from Myit-kyo on the Tsit-toung to the Kha-ra-tshoo creek and thence to the Paing-kyoon creek and thus into the Pegu river.

SHWE-HLE.—A revenue circle on the left bank of the Tsit-toung river and south of Tsit-toung town, with an area of about 75 square miles. A good deal of salt is made towards the coast. In 1876-77 the population was 3,067, the land revenue Rs. 5,001, the capitation tax Rs. 9,285 and the gross revenue Rs. 13,113.

SHWE-HPOUNG-DAW-OO (Prow of the royal barge).—A pagoda in the Kama township of the Thayet district which was built during the time of king Aloung-tsee-thoo, circa 1085, at the spot where the royal barge was once moored.

SHWE-HMAW-DAW.—A pagoda in the old fortified town of Pegu in the Rangoon district of the Pegu division. The present name, Shwe-hmaw-daw, is a Burmese corruption of the Talaing Hpoot-daw which in Burmese is Bhoora-byan, flying or winged bhoora or pagoda. It is a pyramidal solid brick building rising to a height of 324 feet from an octagonal base each side of which is 162 feet in length. It stands upon two terraces, one above the other; the larger and lower, about 10 feet from the level of the ground, being an exact parallelogram each of the sides of which is 1,390 feet long; the upper and smaller terrace, of the same shape as the lower, is about 20 feet higher and has a perimeter of 2,736 feet; both are ascended by uncovered flights of stone steps. The base of the pagoda is surrounded by two tiers of smaller ones, the lower of which, six feet from the terrace, contains 75, each 27 feet high and 40 feet in circumference at the base; the upper tier contains 53.

The account of the foundation of the Shwe-hmaw-daw, as given in its sacred record, forms no exception to the general rule that the historians of Burma endeavour to connect every spot and every sacred building with a visit of Gaudama, though there can be no doubt that he never came so far east as Chin-India. According to this chronicle Gaudama, whilst staying on the Mat-koo-la hill near the sources of the Rwon-za-leng river, was visited by two brothers Ma-ha-tha-la and Tsoo-la-tha-la of Zoung-doo, a place on the Pegu river about 20 miles above the present town of Pegu. To them he gave two hairs of his head and, foreseeing that in after years the capital of a powerful kingdom would be founded at Han-tha-wad-dee, he directed the two brothers to enshrine the hairs on the Thoo-da-tha-na Myeng-thee-la hill a short distance west of the Han-tha-wad-dee hill, informing them that in the 1116th year of his religion Tha-ma-la and Wee-ma-la would there establish the Han-tha-wad-dee kingdom. " The two brothers " Ma-ha-tha-la and Tsoo-la-tha-la then took ship and conveyed the sacred " relics enclosed in a casket provided for that purpose by the Thagya " king of their native town, where they were received with great rejoicing. " After holding high festival for seven months and seven days, they proceeded " to obey the instructions they had received, by enshrining the relics on tho " Thoo-da-tha-na hill. Guided by the miraculous power of the Nat and " Bram-ha they speedily arrived at the spot, and then they prayed that an " omen might be given if that indeed was the very place. In answer to " their prayers the great earth shook. This not only supplied the desired " information, but called down a host of Nat and Bram-ha from the upper " regions to take part in the enshrinement of the relics. By them the " shrine was thus prepared. At the bottom of a pit, 10 cubits square, was " laid a slab of pearly white marble, set with diamonds. A similar slab, " set with emeralds, was prepared to cover the mouth of the pit. In the " centre of the bottom slab the Thagya king placed a golden cradle, round " which were ranged images of the chief disciples of Gaudama, each holding " a golden bouquet. These disciples were Tha-ree-pot-tra, Maw-ga-lan, " Thee-ree, Maha Maya, Thee-ree Thoo-daw-dana, Ya-thaw-da-ra, Khe-ma, " Oo-pa-won, Ra-hoo-la and A-nan-da. The sacred relics were then con- " ducted with great pomp from Zoung-doo to the hill, the distance, two " yoozanas (24 miles), being traversed in 14 days. The casket containing " the hairs was then placed on the cradle, and high festival was held " around the shrine. Besides the images of the chief disciples those of the " following persons also were placed in the shrine : Ma-ha-tha-la and Tsoo- " la-tha-la, the disciples A-noo-roo-dha, Ma-ha Ka-tha-pa, Oo-roo-we-la " Ka-tha-pa, Oo-pa-lie-pa-gnya, Isaweggie, the king of the Bram-ha, and his " four wives. Countless offerings were then made, the Thagya king giving " ten billions of gold, each of his four queens forty thousand of silver, " Pien-ta-ka (father of Ma-ha-tha-la and Tsoo-la-tha-la) one thousand of " gold, Ma-ha-tha-la and Tsoo-la-tha-la one thousand and eighty of silver, " and so on. The Thagya king then placed certain Nat to guard the shrine, " and a structure of stone and brick, 50 cubits high and 250 cubits in circum- " ference, was erected over it." A number of people were dedicated to the service of the pagoda by the king of Zoung-doo and 1,050 feet of land to the east, 1,050 to the north, 1,050 to the west and 525 to the south were given to the shrine.

The chronicle at once jumps to the time of A-thaw-ka and the third Booddhist council and relates that the pagodas throughout the country having fallen into decay and the religion of Gaudama having become neglected king Dham-ma-thaw-ka of Patalipoot endeavoured to re-establish both in their pristine splendour and amongst other meritorious works repaired the Shwe-hmaw-daw, the Shwe Dagon and five other pagodas close to Pegu. Ninety men were assigned as pagoda slaves to the first and the land given by king Tha-moon-da-ra-ya of Zoung-doo when the pagoda was first built was again measured and re-granted, having been, it. is to be presumed, taken by carnally-minded persons when the true religion " faded" The chronicle then skips 900 years and brings us to what may be called the historical period. In the year 1116 of Gaudama's era A.D. 573, Tha-ma-la and Wee-ma-la founded the city and kingdom of Han-tha-wad-dee, of which Tha-ma-la was the first sovereign. He found the Shwe-hmaw-daw still in existence and he repaired it, added four cubits to its height, put a new htee on it and dedicated 25 families to its service. His successor, his brother Wee-ma-la, added five cubits, making it 59 cubits high, regilt it, gave it a new htee and dedicated five more families to its service. His nephew Ka-tha-koom-ma-ra, who succeeded him on the throne, raised the height of the pagoda to 64 cubits. The next addition was made in 619 A.D. by A-rien-da-koom-ma, who, as the htee was inclining to the north, directed his chief noble Thoo-ra-thee-dee to repair the structure. This was done and the height increased to 73 cubits, and 47 more families were dedicated to its perpetual service. During his son's reign the htee and the upper portion of the building having been much damaged by a storm, it was repaired, raised to 76 cubits, and presented with a new jewelled htee. Some 17 years later king Gien-da-ra-za added five cubits, making it 81 cubits high, and dedicated three more families to it. Successive sovereigns repaired, added to and regilt the edifice until in the reign of Tha-maing-daw-rwot-ka-lie, probably a descendant of the Martaban race of kings, it attained its present height of 324 feet. The two most noteworthy statements in the chronicle are that A-noo-ma-ra-za, the twelfth king of the original dynasty, in about 1209 A.D. obtained from Thee-ree-dham-ma-thaw-ka, the king of Tha-htoon, a holy tooth relic which he enshrined in the pagoda and that king Dham-ma-ze-dee, who came to the throne in 1502, received from the king of Ceylon a present of 100,000 paving stones, 50,000 of which were used in paving the court or upper terrace. Towards the end of the 18th century the Burman king Bhodaw Bhoora came down to Pegu and the building was again thoroughly repaired but no addition was made to its height. The htee or umbrella, which was 39½ feet high and 46 feet in circumference, was re-gilt at the same time.

During the second Burmese war of 1852-53 the platform was the scene of some sharp fighting. In June 1852 the town was taken by the British but as no troops could be spared it was abandoned and was re-occupied by the Burmese. In November of the same year it was again attacked and taken, but not without some loss, and a small garrison of 400 infantry, two guns, and a detachment of artillery and sappers and miners left in charge. The Burmese commenced their attacks within two days of the withdrawal of the rest of the force and from the 5th to the 14th December closely invested the pagoda, the difficulty of the defence being increased by the necessity of protecting some thousand Talaing women and children who, whilst their male relations were obliged to fight against us in the enemy's ranks, came in to us for protection from their rulers, the Burmese. The first attempt made to relieve Pegu failed, and it was only when a strong force under General Godwin, the Commander-in-Chief, approached from

Rangoon that the Burmese retired towards Shwe-gyeng. Rebellion broke out in Upper Burma on the 17th December and most of the Burmese troops were re-called to the capital, and from that time the garrison remained unmolested until withdrawn after the annexation.

SHWE-HMAW-DAW.—A revenue circle in the Re La-maing township, Amherst district, on the head-waters of the Meng-hla, a tributary from the north-east of the river Re. Mountainous and covered with forest it is but thinly populated by Kareng and sparsely cultivated. Man-oung is now joined to it. In 1876-77 the population was 343, the land revenue Rs. 90 and the capitation tax Rs. 370.

SHWE-KHAROO-TOUK (Shining shell).—A pagoda on the hills above Kama in the Kama township of the Thayet district, said to have been built by Thoo-pa-gnya-na-ga-ra-tshien-na, a fugitive sovereign of Prome

SHWE-KHYOUNG-BYENG-LEK-YA.—A revenue circle on the left bank of the Sandoway river below Sandoway. The larger portion of its culturable area is under cultivation. Rice and tobacco are the principal products. In 1876-77 the population, composed mainly of Arakanese, was 1,369, the land revenue Rs. 2,338, the capitation tax Rs. 1,132 and the gross revenue Rs. 5,908.

SHWE-KOO.—A pagoda in Martaban built in 1785 by Moung Pa-thee, the governor, by order of Bhodaw Bhoora, then reigning in Burma, who, having been born on a Monday, ordered that pagodas to be called ' golden caverns ' (Shwe-koo), the sign of the day, should be erected in various parts of his dominions.

SHWE-KOO.—A pagoda in the town of Tavoy, 50 feet high and 147 feet in circumference at the base, built by order of Bhodaw Bhoora, king of Burma, who reigned from 1781 to 1819.

SHWE-KYWON.—A small island about two square miles in extent forming a revenue circle in the Western township of the Tavoy district, with more than two-thirds under cultivation. The principal products are rice and the dhanee palm. In 1876-77 the population was 398, the land revenue Rs. 4,784, the capitation tax Rs. 340 and the gross revenue Rs. 5,362.

SHWE-LAY.—A township in the Prome district extending along the western slopes of the Pegu Roma from the Henzada (Tharrawaddy) district and the Poungday township northwards to the Thayet district, having the Ma-ha-tha-man township to the west. It includes the old Shwe-lay, Rwa-bien and Myo-doung townships. The whole of the country is exceedingly hilly except in the south-west, and is covered with valuable timber amongst which teak holds a prominent place. There is but little rice cultivation even in the low country, but cotton and the mulberry plant are grown on the hills. The principal streams are the North and South Na-weng and the Teng-gyee, a tributary of the latter and in the south the Shwe-lay, called further westward the Wai-gyee and the Wek-peot. These streams are not navigable in this township but they and their feeders drain a country of great richness in timber which has been considerably worked. The principal trees found are *Acacia catechu, Odina wodier, Pentaptera, Spondia acuminata, Nauclea parviflora, Xylia dolabriformis, Tectona grandis, Careya arborea, Terminalia macrocarpa, Shorea robusta* and several others of which *Hopea odorata* and *Pterocarpus indicus* only need be noticed.

The township contains 14 revenue circles but no large villages. The Extra Assistant Commissioner resides and holds his court at Pouk-khoung, a small village on the little stream of that name, a tributary of the South Na-weng. In 1876-77 the population was 21,963, the land revenue Rs. 10,465, the capitation tax Rs. 15,997 and the gross revenue Rs. 33,482.

SHWE-LAY.—A river in the Prome district, Pegu division. Rising in the western slopes of the Ko-dek spur of the Pegu Roma some five miles from the main range and flowing in a south-westerly direction it drains the valley lying between the Nee-pa-tshe and Pan-doung spurs in the Shwe-lay township and, traversing the centre of the great plain country which lies between the Roma mountains on the east and the Prome hills on the west, falls into the Myit-ma-kha a little to the north of the village of Keng-than. From its source to about the village of Pouk-taw, it is called the Shwe-lay. Its affluents here are of no great importance being merely mountain torrents rushing down from teak-covered hills. From Pouk-taw onwards it is called the Wai-gyee till it nears the village of Wek-poot (where it is crossed by an iron bridge carrying the main road from Rangoon to the frontier) the name of which it assumes and retains till it falls into the Myit-ma-kha as the Khyoon-khyoon-gya. During the rains boats of 500 bushels burden can ascend the river as far as Tha-bye-poung-gyee, some miles above Wek-poot. In the plains north-west of Poung-day its course is choked with sand and rubbish brought down from the forests: above this obstruction it is 100 feet wide and 20 feet deep. Below, it no longer runs in one channel, but by numerous anastomosing streams is connected with the Myit-ma-kha and with the Kyat (or Toung-gnoo) on the south. The main channel near Wek-poot is only 40 feet wide and three feet deep in the dry season. Tapping a rich teak country several more or less successful endeavours have been made to facilitate the removal of the felled logs to the Irrawaddy and, to avoid the great obstruction in the Poung-day plains, a natural channel was improved by the Forest Department in 1860. But as each year the rains in the hills suddenly fill the river and send it rushing down swollen by the torrents which join it with the forest debris which during the dry weather has rolled into their beds down the steep hill-sides between which they dash, new obstructions are formed and the foaming water, checked and dammed up by the accumulated sand and decayed timber which it has itself brought down, in a few hours bursts the banks and finds its way onward generally in old channels, but sometimes in new ones which it cuts in the soft soil of the plain over which it spreads.

SHWE-LOUNG.—A township in the Thoon-khwa district, extending northwards from the seacoast for nearly 100 miles between the Pya-ma-law and the Irrawaddy, the former separating it from the Bassein district. In the north the country forms a large plain covered with scrub forest; south of Shwe-loung there is some rice cultivation but the lower part of the township consists of low uncultivated land cut up into islands by numerous anastomosing tidal creeks thickly fringed with Ka-na-tso (Indian Soondree, *Heritiera minor*) and Lamoo (*Sonneratia acida*), and in many parts producing nothing but mangrove (*Bruguiera rheedii*). In the south these creeks are dotted here and there with temporary fishing villages consisting of a few huts only the inhabitants of which, when the season is over, retire north to the permanent villages situated on higher land, such as Wai-gyee Zayat, Shwe-loung, Taw-ka-noo, Wa-khay-ma and Lan-tha-maing. The approximate area of the township, exclusive of the rivers and creeks is 1,124 square miles. It is divided into six revenue circles. In 1876-77 the population was 34,715, the land revenue Rs. 58,017, the capitation tax Rs. 36,802 and the gross revenue Rs. 120,900.

SHWE-LOUNG.—A village in the circle of the same name in the Tsan-rwe township of the Henzada (Tharawaddy) district on the west bank of the Myit-ma-kha. In 1877 it had 920 inhabitants.

SHWE-LOUNG.—A town in the Thoon-khwa district in 16° 44' 30" N. and 95° 23' 30" E. on the bank of the Irrawaddy at the spot where the Pya-ma-law channel branches off N. N. W., the head-quarters of the township of the same name, the Extra Assistant Commissioner in charge of which resides and holds his court here. The inhabitants are largely engaged in trade with Rangoon and Bassein and many are occupied in the fisheries. A strong police force is quartered in the town.

SHWE-LOUNG.— A revenue circle in the north-west portion of the Tsan-rwe township of the Henzada (Tharrawaddy) district, east of the Irrawaddy, lying on both banks of the Myit-ma-kha or Hlaing river, and containing but little cultivation. In .1876-77 the population was 4,266, the land revenue Rs. 1,022, the capitation tax Rs. 4,177 and the gross revenue Rs. 10,250.

SHWE-LOUNG.—A small revenue circle in the Prome district, a short distance below Pa-doung, close to to the bank of the Irrawaddy. In 1876-77 the population was 166, the land revenue Rs. 131, the capitation tax Rs. 182 and the gross revenue Rs. 488.

SHWE-MO-BOON.—A pagoda at Mye-dai said to have been erected by Ma-ha-tham-ba-wa and Tso-la-tham-ba-wa, the founders of the old Prome kingdom.

SHWE-MOOT-TAW.—A pagoda near the town of Ka-ma in the Ka-ma township of the Thayet district, standing out conspicuously amongst the group which crowns the hills surrounding that town. The legend regarding it is the same as that connected with the pagoda of the same name near Thayetmyo. It is one of those of which there are no less than ten in the Thayet district alone whose name is derived from the tradition that they, erected by the order of Asoka, had all to be completed when the moon was emerging from an eclipse; hence the designation which means "the release of the moon from an eclipse"

SHWE-MOOT-TAW.—A pagoda just below the town of Thayetmyo in the Thayet township of the Thayet district. The legend regarding its erection in the same as that of the Shwe-moot-taw at Ka-ma mentioned above.

SHWE-MYA-OO-SHOUNG. (Emerald hair-knot).—A small pagoda in the Meng-doon township of the Thayet district, which was built so lately as 1833 by a governor of Meng-doon.

SHWE-MYA-THIEN-DAN (Emerald worth a hundred thousand).—A small pagoda in the Mye-dai township of the Thayet district, so called from the tradition that King Nara-pad-dee-tsee-thoo, *circa* 1167, found an emerald of that value in a neighbouring creek which he deposited in the pagoda.

SHWE-MYENG-DENG.—A pagoda in the Ka-ma township of the Thayet district, forming one of the group on the hills surrounding Ka-ma. Its name, which means " conspicuous", is derived from its position. It is said to date from the time of Thoo-pa-gnya-na-ga-ra-tshien-na (*circa* 100 A.D.) a fugitive king of Prome who, during his flight northwards, remained some time at Ka-ma. As subsequently it was found that the desires of many who visited this shrine were answered, it received the second name of Shwe-tsoo-toung-byce or "prayers fulfilled"

SHWE-MYENG-DENG.—A revenue circle in the northern portion of the Bassein township in the district of the same name, with an area of about 21 square miles, extending along the left bank of the Bassein river from Bassein to the Da-ga. The country here assumes an undulating form ; along the bank of the Bassein river it is suitable for rice cultivation but in the centre the undulation is more marked and the ground is thickly wooded : to the east the land is low and open but not well fitted for cultivation. The inhabitants are principally cultivators, fishermen, boatmen and coolies. There is a good cart road from Shwe-myeng-deng to Bassein and to other parts of the circle. In 1876-77 the population was 8,224 the land-revenue Rs. 3,176, the capitation tax Rs. 3,200 and the gross revenue Rs. 6,539.

SHWE-MYO-DOON.—A pagoda in Mye-dai said to have been erected by Ma-ha-tham-ba-wa and Tsoo-la-tham-ba-wa, the founders of the old Prome kingdom.

SHWE-NAN-PAING (Possessor of a palace).—A pagoda on the hills near Ka-ma on the right bank of the Irrawaddy in the Ka-ma township of the Thayet district, said to have been built by Thoo-pa-gnya-na-ga-ra-tshien-na when a fugitive from Prome in the hope that the meritorious work would assist him in regaining possession of his throne.

SHWE-NAT-TOUNG.—A pagoda in the Prome district, about 16 miles south of the town of Prome. It is supposed to have been built during the reign of Dwot-ta-boung, the founder of Prome, by queen Tsan-da-de-wee. According to the tradition in one of her journeys she came to the Nat-toung hill and was informed by the people that on it was placed the image of their tutelary Nat, whence it derived its name of Nat-toung or hill of the Nat. Queen Tsan-da-de-wee determined on building a pagoda on this hill and obtaining from her husband two of the six relics of Gaudama which he had miraculously received and from some Rahanda one hundred and forty more she enclosed them in a gold box set with jewels ; this she placed in a silver box, and the silver box in another golden one. These boxes with their contents she enshrined in the pagoda, 22½ feet high, which she built on Nat-toung. On the completion of the work king Dwot-ta-boung consecrated the whole space round it on which its shadow fell between sunrise and sunset and directed that a grand festival should be held there annually on the full moon of the month of Taboung (about March). When

Thee-ha-thoo, son of Taroop-pye-meng king of Pagan, became king of Prome he repaired the pagoda and raised its height to 66 feet. About the middle of the sixteenth century, Ta-beng-shwe-htee, king of Toun-ngoo, who had conquered Prome, added to the pagoda and increased its height. Many years later it was again repaired by public subscriptions collected by a Hpoongyee of the village of Kyeethai named La-ba-ra-wa. The building, profusely gilt and shining in the sun, stands out conspicuously on the first hill of a low range overhanging the Shwe-nat-toung plain, and has in a line behind it the Nga-tsoo, Pan-bhyoo, Hpo-lay, Hpo-myat, Hpo-tha-bho and Theng-gan pagodas.

The annual festival is still kept up, and in the month of Taboung some twenty thousand people assemble, living for eight days in temporary sheds erected in the plain, occupying their time in worshipping at the pagoda, in buying and selling, and in attending theatrical representations and wrestling matches.

SHWE-THEK-LWOT.—A pagoda in the town of Thayet in the Thayet district. The name being interpreted signifies "Golden life preserved". It was erected by Meng-gyee-tswa-tsaw-kai, the second king of the Ava dynasty, about 1373 A. D. as a thank-offering for the preservation of his life when he, as a child, was taken captive in Thayetmyo by the king of Arakan. This pagoda is still kept in good repair and is remarkable for being one of the most southern hollow pagodas : in Upper Burma erections of this kind are numerous but in the lower country the great majority of the pagodas are of the solid bell-shaped pattern.

SHWE-TSEE-GOON.—A pagoda close to Ka-ma in the Ka-ma township of the Thayet district, said to have been built *circa* 100 A. D. by the Prome sovereign Thoo-pa-gnya-na-ga-ra-tshien-na during his flight northwards.

SHWE-TSHAN-DAW.—A pagoda near Twan-te in the Rangoon distirict of the Pegu division, more venerated by the Talaing than even the great Shwe Dagon of Rangoon. According to its sacred history it was erected in 577 B. C. by Thamien-htaw-byeen-ran, the then king of Kha-beng, now a small village near Twan-te, and his wife Mien-da-de-wee as a shrine for three of Gaudama's hairs given by him to three holy pilgrims from Ceylon, named Thoo-ma-na-hte, Tiek-kha-byeen-gnya and Tha-ga-ra-byeen-gnya on the occasion of their visiting him whilst he was tarrying in the Zeng-gyaik hills. The sage directed them to deposit these hairs on the Me-roo-da hill, as this was the spot on which he had twice closed his previous existence,—once when an elephant and once when a Thameng (a kind of deer). After some difficulty this hill, which is that on which the pagoda now stands, was found and his commands obeyed. Subsequently, in 538 B.C., four more holy hairs were enshrined in the pagoda by king Thamien-htaw-byeen-gnya-kan-de and a hermit named Gyee-ree-ren-ga who had brought them from Tha-htoon where they were in the possession of king Thee-ree-dham-ma-thaw-ka (not to be confounded with the great Athawka of Patali-pot), in obedience to the command of Gaudama given to his favorite disciple Ananda before his attainment of Niekban.

Near the Shwe-tshan-daw is a grove of Thwot-ta-bat trees (*Sapodillc, plum*) seven in number, the only one existing in Pegu. The trees were c t down, it is said by orders of the Talaing rulers, when the Burmans conquered their country because the produce was a royal fruit to be eaten by none but the monarch and the present trees are the shoots of the old stumps.

SHWE-TSHAN-DAW.—The large pagoda in the town of Prome. It is situated about half a mile from the bank of the river and gives its name to a quarter of the town. The hill on which it stands is called Thoo-dat-tha-na and is 138 high. The pagoda, which is gilt all over, is nearly square at the base. The gilt iron net-work htee or conical top is at its base ten feet in diameter. The pagoda itself is solid without any cavity and is now about 180 feet high, and covers an area of 11,025 square feet. It is surrounded by 83 small gilt niches called Ze-dee-yan, each containing an image of Gaudama. These, which unite at their bases, form a continuous wall round the pagoda leaving a narrow passage between it and them, the entrance to which, through a low narrow doorway with a wooden door, is on the east side. There are four approaches to the platform on which the pagoda stands, consisting of flights of about 100 brick steps, one facing each cardinal point of the compass. Two of them only, the northern and the western, are covered with an elaborately carved roof supported on massive teak posts partly gilt and partly painted vermillion.

The platform itself is neatly paved with slabs of stone and all round its outer edge is a continuous series of carved wooden houses containing, in some cases standing in some recumbent, figures of Gaudama, and between these and the pagoda are Ta-khwon-daing or sacred posts surmounted by a Karawaik and with a streamer floating from a point just below the figure of the bird. Besides these there are some 12 or 13 bells, hanging to massive wooden cross-bars supported on posts five or six feet high, which are struck with deers' antlers by those who come to worship. The largest of these bells measures about ten feet in circumference.

The pagoda is supposed to have been first erected by two brothers, Ee-zee-ka and Pa-lee-ka. According to the tradition Gaudama, when travelling, arrived near Prome, and whilst walking about on an island named Zeng-yan was accosted by a naga or dragon who begged for some sacred hairs that he might enshrine them in a pagoda. This request Gaudama refused saying that the glory of building a pagoda to contain his relics must be reserved for two brothers, Ee-zee-ka and Pa-lee-ka, who had gone on a trading expedition to Thoo-woon-na-bhoo-mee (Tha-htoon). The Naga then presented to Gaudama an emerald box praying that, as he might not receive the sacred hairs, he might at least contribute the receptacle in which they would be placed. Accepting the box Gaudama placed in it the relics and by his supernatural power caused it to rise to the height of two palmyra trees and then shoot like lightning to the bank and lodge in a clump of bamboos where it shone like fire. Shortly afterwards Ee-zee-ka and Pa-lee-ka arrived and anchoring at the spot went ashore and discoverd the relics. There is now a small village at this spot about 15 miles from Prome called Mya-rwa or "Emerald village" The relics were brought on board and after some discussion it was determined that three pagodas should be built, one on the spot where the emerald box was found, and which was named Mya-bhoora or Emerald pagoda, and two on the bank exactly opposite the bows and the stern of the vessel, which were called Oo-bhoora or "Ship's stem pagoda" and I'ai-bhoora or "Ship's stern pagoda" respectively. In none of these were the relics enshrined but search was made for a holier place. Having heard of Gaudama's prediction that at the site of the present Prome the capital of a powerful kingdom would be founded they proceeded thither. On their arrival they halted to consider where the best site would be and the spot where they so halted was called Tsway-nway-yat or " Place of discussion " now corrupted into Tsa-re-yat. Here their sailors, immediately after the discussion, built a pagoda which they called Tsway-nway bhoora, or " Discussion pagoda". Such a pagoda, small and gilt and so named, is still in existence. This discussion had no result and the brothers and their crew wandered about seeking a suitable place. One of the crew, a foreigner named Tha-kyit (Sarkies?) wearied and faint, called out, "A-tshoon-hpyat-ba", or "let us come to a decision "; hence the present name " Tha-kyit-htsoon" given to a portion of the town of Prome. At last the hill on which the Shwe-tshan-daw stands was fixed upon and this for the somewhat incomprehensible reason that, on walking over it, the soil adhered to their feet. If the whole tradition was not manifestly fabulous, it might be supposed that here and here alone they found the soil on a rising ground soft enough to enable them to dig the foundations without excessive labour. Having excavated the soil for the foundations they laid therein seven bricks of gold and on these placed the emerald box and over the whole raised a pagoda seven feet high and then returned to their own country. Seven days after they left the pagoda sank into the earth and disappeared. Owing to the prayers of king Dwot-taboung, the founder of ancient Prome, the pagoda re-appeared, and the king repaired it. The Burmese records give no further account of the pagoda but from oral tradition it appears that various kings and governors have gradually added to it until at last it has attained its present dimensions. In 1753 Aloung-bhoora coated it with gold. The pagoda having been damaged by an earthquake, king Tharrawaddy, on his way to Rangoon in 1841, had it thoroughly repaired and re-gilt and put on it a new htee studded with jewels. The roofs over the northern and western approaches were put up by the governor, Moung Toot-gyee, in 1842. Since then it was again damaged by an earthquake and in 1858. was repaired by an influential inhabitant of Prome, Moung Tha Shwe, at a cost of Rs. 76,800 raised by public subscription. It has lately been re-gilt at an estimated cost of about Rs. 25,000 raised by public subscription by one Moung Shwe An. The annual festival is held on the full moon of Taboung, corresponding to March.

SHWE-TSOO-TOUNG-BYEE.—A pagoda in the Ka-ma township of the Thayet district.—See Shwe-myeng-deng.

SHWE-TSOO-TOUNG-BYEE (Prayer fulfilled).—A small pagoda in the Meng-doon township of the Thayet district, said to have been built about 108 A. D. by the uncle of Tha-moo-da-rit, the founder of Lower Pagan.

SHWE-TSWAY-DAW.—A pagoda in the Thayet district.—See Shwe An-daw.

SULLIVAN'S ISLAND.—An island of the Mergui archipelago attached to the Mergui district of the Tenasserim division, about eight miles off the coast and lying between 10 40 and 11 N. Lat. and 97 58' and 98°

E. Long. Its extreme length is 17 miles and its greatest breadth, at its northern end, about six miles. Its highest peak is to the south, almost due west of Boyce's point on the main land, in 10° 41' N. Lat. It is the favourite resting-place of the Selung (*q.v.*) a tribe inhabiting the archipelago.

SYRIAM.—More correctly called Than-lyeng, a sub-division of the Rangoon district composed of the Than-lyeng township south of the Pegu river and east of the Hlaing or Rangoon river and the An-gyee township occupying the whole of the lower portion of the district west of the Hlaing from the Pan-hlaing to the sea. The head-quarters are at Kyouk-tan on the Hmaw-won in the Syriam township.

SYRIAM.—A township in the sub-division of the same name, bounded on the west by the Rangoon river, on the north by the Pegu river, on the east by the Pegu township and on the south by the Bay of Bengal. It is divided into ten revenue circles and in 1877 had a population of 56,141 souls. In that year the land revenue was Rs. 354,995, the capitation tax Rs. 67,698 and the gross revenue Rs. 442,113. The head-quarters are at Syriam.

SYRIAM.—More correctly called Than-lyeng. A town in the Rangoon district of the Pegu division situated in 16° 45' 30" N. Lat. and 96° 19' E. Long: the head-quarter station of a township of the same name. It is on the left bank of the Pegu river about three miles from its mouth, on the northern extremity of the Than-lyeng Koon-dan. The present town, with its adjacent hamlets or suburbs of Ka-thit-taw-rwa, Kan-tsoung-rwa and Kareng-zoo, contains a population of 1,733 souls of Talaing, Burman, Kareng, Mussulman and Shan race. The Ka-thit-taw suburb is inhabited entirely by Mussulmans, descendants of the Indian Mahomedans who resided here when the Portuguese factory flourished. Although they have received a considerable infusion of Burmese and Talaing blood yet they still adhere to their distinctive dress, customs and religion, but in language and everything else are thoroughly Burmanised: they now intermarry chiefly among themselves, and are, consequently, decidedly inferior to the Burmese in physique and appearance. They have two small wooden mosques in the village and behind the town, and they point out the ruins of a considerable masonry building which was, they say, the "Eetya" (Eedgarh) of their ancestors. They are now chiefly engaged in agriculture and form the major portion of the cultivating population of the place. The Kan-tsoung suburb is on the opposite or western side of the town and is inhabited by Shan who are engaged chiefly in garden cultivation. The Kareng-zoo suburb, also called Koon-dan-rwa, is about a mile and a half behind the town and occupied by Talaing and Kareng engaged in rice and garden cultivation.

The town of Than-lyeng, better known to Europeans by the name of Syriam, lies partly within and partly without the old city walls, portions of which, substantially built of earth and laterite, are still standing. According to the Burmese tradition it was founded in 587 B.C. by Ze-ya-the-na, who named it Pa-da, about 50 years later changed to Than-lyeng after Than-lyeng who dethroned A-rien-da-ra-za, son of Ze-ya-the-na, and married his daughter. Little or nothing is known of the town from that time until the commencement of the 17th century. Towards the close of the previous century the king of Arakan, taking advantage of the quarrels between the kings of Toung-ngoo, Ava, and Pegu, and the destruction of the monarchy of the last by the first, took possession of Pegu aided by the Portuguese under Philip de Brito y. Nicote, to whom, in reward for their services, he gave the town of Than-lyeng, which they repaired and fortified. In a short time, however, the king of Arakan found reason to regret his liberality and formed an alliance with the king of Toung-ngoo for the purpose of driving out the Portuguese, but the attack on the town failed and the enterprize was abandoned. Some years later, in 1613, Than-lyeng was besieged and taken by the king of Ava, Nicote impaled alive and all the Portuguese whose lives were spared sent as slaves to the capital, where some traces of them exist to this day in a race of people with light coloured hair and eyes.

In 1631 the Dutch were allowed to establish a factory at Than-lyeng which they retained till 1677.* The date of the establishment of the English factory is not known. In 1698, however, it was re-established and Mr. Bowyear placed in charge of it by the Government of Madras. In 1740 the Peguans expelled the Burmese and captured Than-lyeng without, however, injuring or molesting the English and other foreigners residing there. In 1743 the Burmese retook the town, but held it for three days only, when the Talaings returned, drove out the Burmese, and having strong and not altogether unwarranted suspicions of duplicity on the part of Mr. Smart, then in charge of the factory, burnt it to the ground, and this together with the unsettled state of affairs induced Mr. Smart to retire from the country with the whole establishment. Nothing now remains of these once flourishing Portuguese, Dutch and English factories but substantial ruins of the old church, some tombs of masonry and the foundations of a few masonry houses. The tombs all shew signs of having been dug into : this was done before the occupation of Pegu by the British, by order of the Myo-ook or Burmese petty governor in the expectation of finding treasure. The ruins of the church stand on an elevated ridge just outside the old town walls and give evidence of the great strength and solidity with which it must originally have been built. It was erected in 1749-50 by Monseigneur Nerini, the second Vicar Apostolic of Ava and Pegu and a member of the Barnabite mission which laboured in this country during the last century. The following account of its erection is taken from the life of one of these missionaries, Monseigneur G. M. Percoto, missionary to the kingdoms of Ava and Pegu and Bishop of Massulis :—
" He," Dom Nerini, " was received with favour by the king of Pegu to whom
" he made himself useful by his skill in astronomy, foretelling eclipses and
" so forth, and he ultimately received permission to erect a church of
" masonry at Syriam. The funds for building the church were found by a
" good Armenian merchant, and the building was designed by Father
" Nerini. So well did he succeed that the church when finished was the
" admiration not only of the country but even of the foreigners who came
" to the place. In plan it consisted of a single nave ornamented with

---

* According to Valentyn ; but Dalrymple states that both English and Dutch were expelled some years earlier.

" arches and columns both inside and out.   Its dimensions were as follows :
" length 81, breadth 31 and height 40 French feet.   It was intended
" to have had a domed roof, but the arrival of the Coromandel workmen
" who were sent for to construct it was prevented by the war which arose,
" and the roof was, therefore, completed in another style.   The whole
" building was a marvel to the Peguans, but what they more especially
" admired was a spiral staircase going up inside the tower.   The following
" inscription was placed inside the church :—.

"D. O. M.
" Ad. fidem. Propagandum.
" Clerici. Regularis. Sancti. Paulli.
" Nicolaus. de Aguilar. Nationi. Armenus.
" Margarita. Conjux.
" Ædificabant.
" Anno Domini CIƆIƆCCL."

No trace of this inscription now remains : the roof and west wall have
fallen in. as well as other parts of the building, but the place where the
spiral staircase was with the marks of the steps, the north and south walls
and the eastern end, are still standing.   Father Luigi Galli, in his history of
Christianity in Burma, tells us that—

" Hardly was the labour of constructing the church ended when Father
" Nerini took in hand the building of a roomy house as a parochial
" residence for the bishop and the missionaries shortly expected from
" Italy, as well as a dwelling-place for a number of Talaing children given
" by their parents to the mission.   The dwelling thus constructed had,
" when finished, two halls, eight rooms, and two verandahs.   For symmetry
" there was a wing, the rooms in the lower floor of which were used as
" store-houses, one for a kitchen and another for a bath-room excepted.
" Above was the dormitory and the school-house, which had at the time
" 40 pupils on the rolls.   By the side of the church, and within the spacious
" mission grant, another dwelling was erected for abandoned infants who
" were placed under the charge of matronly dames to be brought up in
" piety, religion and industry.   These various structures gave the place
" an aspect of a little village, but were not, however, constructed without
" cost as about 5,000 Roman scudi had to be expended in the erections.
" The major part of this sum was received from a wealthy and well dis-
" posed Armenian merchant named Nicolas de Aguilar, principally in
" whose honour the marble tablet (alluded to above) was erected."

The mission was established in 1722, and remained unmolested till
the war between the Peguans and the Burmese which resulted in the
destruction of the factories and the temporary supremacy of the Talaing
kingdom, when Monsignor Galizia was killed, but Father Nerini, as we
have seen, was spared and taken into favour by the Peguan king and was
eventually, in 1754, raised to the apostolic vicariate and made Bishop of
Orienza.   The flourishing days of the mission after this were of but short
duration.   In 1756 the bishop was murdered by the Burman sovereign
Aloung-bhoora, then besieging Than-lyeng, because he suspected him of
having sent for a French ship which entered the river with the intention

of assisting the Peguans. From that time till 1760 the mission remained destitute, and was then re-established in Rangoon, Than-lyeng or Syriam being abandoned.

The Myo-ook during the first war in 1824-25 was Moung Tsat whose sister was married to king Bhadoon-meng, fourth son of Aloung-bhoora ; after the capture of Rangoon by the British troops he collected a considerable force and commenced fortifying the town and erecting works to command the entrance to the river. On the 4th August 1824 a force of about 600 men drawn from H. M's. 41st Regiment, the Madras European Infantry Regiment and the 12th M. N. I., under Brigadier Smelt, was sent to dislodge him. The Burmese force was found posted within the walls of the old Portuguese factory, the defences of which had been strengthened with palisades. The storming party was received by a sharp fire, but the enemy evacuated the place before the escalade, and were pursued by a detachment under Colonel Kelly. The British did not retain possession of the town, and this was occupied in December by a portion of the grand Burmese army which had been investing Rangoon. On the commander-in-chief determining to commence his onward march to Prome he detached a force under Colonel Elrington which, on the 11th February 1825, drove out the enemy and re-occupied Than-lyeng. After the conclusion of the war the Talaing, finding that we did not intend retaining possession of the valleys of the Irrawaddy and Tsit-toung and impelled by their long-standing hatred of their Burmese conquerors and by a natural fear that, having deserted to the British on every possible occasion and rendered them every assistance, their former masters would, on their return, notwithstanding the sixth article of the treaty of peace signed at Yandaboo, harrass and injure them to the utmost extent of their power, determined on taking advantage of the weakened state of the Burman empire and on attempting to regain possession of their ancient . kingdom. The leader of the movement was Moung Tsat, the Myo-ook of Than-lyeng, who assumed the title of king. The Talaing were joined by the Kareng and for some time it was doubtful whether the Burmese would be able to suppress the rebellion. They made two or three endeavours to obtain the assistance of the English which Mr. Crawford, then on his way down from Ava, steadily declined to afford. One word from the English, they said, would induce Moung Tsat to give up the enterprize and retire into British territory. Indeed before Mr. Crawford left Rangoon for the capital and when the British troops were still in Rangoon the Burmese local authorities, who clearly foresaw the rising which afterwards took place and knew that Moung Tsat would be the leader, had asked that the English Commissioners should seize him and his friends and followers and hand them over to their tender mercies. The Talaing, on the other hand, asked for no assistance but begged that the British would not interfere but would " stand upright and move neither to the right-hand nor to the left." After some fighting in and round Rangoon, a force arrived from Ava and the Peguans retreated to Than-lyeng, and in 1827 the leaders including Moung Tsat escaped to Tenasserim.

During the second Burmese war the Myo-ook of Than-lyeng repaired the fortifications of his town and prepared to resist the English, but changed his mind and escaped without firing a shot.

TA-BENG-TA-GA.—A village in the Doung-boon circle, Poung-day township, Prome district, a few miles east of the Tha-goon station on the Rangoon and Irrawaddy Valley (State) Railway with 715 inhabitants in 1877 During the rule of the Burmese government a strong stockade existed in the neighbourhood.

TA-DA.—*See Toung-gnyo river.*

TA-DA.—A village in the A-goon (South) circle, Than-lyeng township, Rangoon district with 889 inhabitants in 1878-79.

TA-DA-GA-LE.—A village in the Koon-dan circle, Hmaw-bhee township, Rangoon district, with 555 inhabitants in 1878-79.

TA-GAY.—A revenue circle in the Gnyoung-doon township of the Thoon-khwa district, 103 square miles in extent, containing about 6,600 acres under cultivation and with large fisheries. In 1876-77 the population was 7,611, the land revenue Rs. 13,161, the capitation tax Rs. 7,473 and the gross revenue Rs. 27,429. In 1877-78 the land revenue was Rs. 13,140, the capitation tax Rs. 8,260, the fishery revenue Rs. 13,343 and the population 8,246.

TA-GNYEK.—A revenue circle in the Mergui district east of Mergui and lying in the west of the valley of the Tenasserim. In 1876-77 the population was 2,689, the land revenue Rs. 7,473, the capitation tax Rs. 1,585 and the gross revenue Rs. 9,058.

TA-GNYEK KARENG.—A revenue circle in the Mergui district extending southwards from Shan-dwot to the east of Mergui island. In 1876-77 the population was 1,474, the land revenue Rs. 1,193, the capitation tax Rs. 954 and the gross revenue Rs. 2,147.

TA-GOUNG-NEK.—A revenue circle in the Meng-doon township, Thayet district, about 132 square miles in extent, by far the larger portion of which, over 122 square miles, are wild hilly forest land quite unculturable. The actually cultivated portion covers an extent of some 1,400 acres, leaving about 5,000 acres of culturable land waiting for cultivators. The population is, as regards the whole area, very sparse, numbering 2,804 souls in 1876-77, or not 22 to the square mile. The products are rice, sessamum, chillies, cotton, cutch and silk. In 1876-77 the land revenue was Rs. 1,620, the capitation tax Rs. 1,703 and the gross revenue Rs. 3,439.

TAIK-KOO-LA.—A revenue circle in the Tsit-toung sub-division of the Shwe-gyeng district, extending south-westwards from near Kyaik-hto to the mouth of the Tsit-toung river. It has an area of about 144 square miles, of which the northern portion only is cultivated. The soil is very fertile. A good deal of salt is made in this circle. In 1876-77 the population was 3,920, the land revenue Rs. 3,861, the capitation tax Rs. 3,582 and the gross revenue Rs. 10,293. The principal village is Taing-kaw.

TAING-GYO.—A revenue circle in the Khwa or Southern township of the Sandoway district stretching from the coast to the Arakan hills with an estimated area of 169 square miles, very slightly cultivated, and a population in 1876-77 of 1,041 souls. In 1876-77 the land revenue was Rs. 759, the capitation tax Rs. 950 and the gross revenue Rs. 2,503.

TAING-KA-MAW.—A revenue circle in the Re La-maing township of the Amherst district which now includes Toung-boon. The principal villages are Taing-ka-maw and Toung-boon. In 1876-77 the population was 1,573, the land revenue Rs. 1,727 and the capitation tax Rs. 1,573.

TAING-KA-MAW.—A village in the circle of the same name in the Re La-maing township of the Amherst district on the seacoast to the south of Kaw-dwot. In 1877 it had 859 inhabitants.

TAING-KAW.—A village in the Taik-koola circle of the Tsit-toung sub-division of the Shwe-gyeng district in the plains, 10 miles south-west of Kyaik-hto. In 1877 it had 1,475 inhabitants.

TA-KAING.—A revenue circle in the Bassein township, Bassein district, between the Hpet-rai-gyaw and the Bassein river having an approximate area of 20 square miles. The country generally is one vast plain which is pretty extensively cultivated with rice. It is much inter- sected by creeks and its western boundary, the Hpet-rai-gyaw, is a short passage to Bassein for boats of 200 bushels burden and under. The principal village is Kyek-poung about two miles east of the Bassein river. In 1876-77 the population was 1,897, the land revenue Rs. 5,161, the capitation tax Rs. 1,835 and the gross revenue Rs. 7,257.

TA-KHWON-DAING.—A revenue circle in the Gyaing Attaran town- ship of the Amherst district occupying the hilly and forest-covered country on both banks of the Weng-raw river for a considerable distance from its source. It has but little cultivation. The inhabitants are chiefly Kareng and in 1876-77 numbered 2,486. In that year the land revenue was Rs. 1,228 and the capitation tax Rs. 2,690.

TA-KHWON-DAING.—A tidal creek in the Shwe-loung township, Thoon-khwa district, joining the Da-nwon and the Re-tsoo-daing. Its bed and banks are muddy. Its least depth is nine feet and it is, therefore, navigable by river steamers.

TA-KOO-WEE.—A village in the Poung circle of the Martaban town- ship, Rangoon district, with 652 inhabitants in 1877-78.

TA-LAING-GOON.—A revenue circle in the north-eastern angle of the Prome district, traversed throughout its whole length by the North Na-weng. The country consists generally of undulating and hilly ground covered with dense forest in which Teak (*Tectona grandis*) and Pyeng-ga-do (*Xylia dolabriformis*) abound. The sides of the hills are cleared for cotton cultiva- tion, and tobacco, sessamum and vegetables are grown on the banks of the Na-weng. There are no cart roads. A footpath leads from the source of the Na-weng across the Roma to the Toung-ngoo district. In 1876-77 the population was 2,465, the land revenue Rs. 522, the capitation tax Rs. 1,522 and the gross revenue Rs. 2,769.

TA-LAING-TAI.—A village in the Thoo-te circle, Central township, Sandoway district on the bank of the Zee-goon near the mouth of the Thoo-te. In 1877 it had 853 inhabitants.

TA-LENG-TSHIEP.—A village in the Sandoway circle, Central town- ship, Sandoway district, on the left bank of the Sandoway river one and a half miles above Sandoway. In 1877 it had 530 inhabitants.

TA-MAN-KHYOUNG.—A village of 566 inhabitants in 1877 in the Kan-nee circle, Nga-poo-taw township, Bassein district, on the right bank of the Than-dwe near its junction with the Bassein river. Near it is some rice land. The inhabitants are principally traders, tradesmen, cultivators and fishermen. The little trade that it does is mainly in rice and salted and pressed fish.

TA-MOOT-KYOON.—A revenue circle in the Mergui district extending from the Little Tenasserim eastwards to the main range forming the boundary between Siam and British Burma. In 1876-77 the population was 1,472, the land revenue Rs. 1,203, the capitation tax Rs. 1,095 and the gross revenue Rs. 2,298.

TA-MYA.—A village in the Kan-goo circle, Donabyoo township, Thoon-khwa district, about a mile inland from the Irrawaddy and four miles north-west of Donabyoo. In 1878 it had 523 inhabitants.

TAN.—A river in Ramree island which falls into the sea on the eastern coast. About 13 miles up is the town of Ramree, the ascent by boats taking from three to four hours. The river for about six miles up is lined with dense mangrove swamp which gradually gives place to drier ground until the town is reached. The anchorage is about half a mile from the mouth of the creek,

TA-NEE.—A village in the Thoon-khwa circle of the township and district of the same name eight miles south of Ma-oo-beng and opposite Thoon-khwa (q.v.). In 1878 it had 1,279 inhabitants.

TA-NENG-THA-REE.—A revenue circle in the Tenasserim township of the Mergui district on the left bank of the Tenasserim river. In 1876-77 the population was 2,378, the land revenue Rs. 3,860, the capitation tax Rs. 1,440 and the gross revenue Rs. 5,300. The principal villages are Tenasserim, the head-quarters of the township, and Maw-toon 16 miles to the north-west.

TAN-KHO.—A village in the Oo-ree-toung circle of the Oo-ree-toung (West) township, Akyab district, on the western bank of the Koo-la-dan and south of the Oo-ree-toung pagoda. The name is said to be a corruption of Htan-kho, but this appears to be exceedingly doubtful. In 1877 it had 559 inhabitants.

TAN-LWAI.—A village of 962 inhabitants in 1876-77, nearly all Arakanese, on the Tan-lwai river about a mile from its mouth, in the Northern township of the Sandoway district.

TAN-LWAI.—A river in the Sandoway district, which it traverses from east to west, having its source in the Arakan hills and falling into the sea about 64 miles south of the Ma-ee.

TAN-LWAI.—A small revenue circle in the northern township of the Sandoway district, extending inland from the Kyaing-kywon grant which lies between it and the seacoast, both being just south of the Tsha-byeng circle. The small population, mainly composed of Arakanese, cultivate four-fifths of the culturable area which is about one-half of the whole circle; rice is the principal product. In 1876-77 the inhabitants numbered

1,810, the land revenue was Rs. 3,246, the capitation tax Rs. 1,562 and the gross revenue Rs. 4,808. The principal village is Tan-lwai.

TA-PWON.—A town in the Henzada (Tharrawaddy) district east of the Irrawaddy and about four miles east of the Myit-ma-kha, in 18° 46′ 22″ N. and 95° 49′ 7″ E. with a population of 1,800 souls. in 1876-77 who are principally rice cultivators, traders and fishermen. From this town a good road led northwards to ·Poung-day in the ·Prome district across the Kan-tha or Toung-gnyo stream over a substantial wooden bridge: the Kan-tha has silted up in the centre and 'the water flowed round the ends the bridge cutting it off from the banks: it has in consequence been pulled. down. The town contains a court-house for the Extra Assistant Commissioner, a police-station and an inspection bungalow.

TA-PWON.—A stream which rises in the plains of the Lai-daw circle and flows past Ta-pwon to the Myit-ma-kha. The banks are flat and muddy. During the rains it is navigable·by large boats from its mouth to Ta-pwon, and for smaller boats for some distance higher up, but like most of the streams in this part of the country it is silting up.

TA-PWON.—The northern township of the Henzada (Tharrawaddy) district east of the Irrawaddy, extending from the Pegu Roma westwards to the Irrawaddy and adjoining Prome on the north. The hilly country produces some valuable timber amongst which are considerable quantities of teak. It now includes Ta-roop-maw and is divided into 14 circles and covers an area of 678 square miles. The land revenue in 1877-78 was Rs. 60,221, the capitation tax Rs. 71,231 and the gross revenue Rs. 158,835, including Rs. 7,502 local funds. In 1877 the population was 78,232.

TA-PWON MYO-MA.—A revenue circle in the Ta-pwon township of the Henzada (Tharrawaddy) district; in the south it is subject to inundation but in the north is well cultivated with rice. In 1876-77 the population was 9,374, the land revenue Rs. 6,149, the capitation tax Rs. 8,082 and the gross revenue Rs. 18,840. It now includes Tha-bye-hla and Oung-beng-tha. The principal towns and villages are Ta-pwon, Gyo-le-beng, Thit-ta-ra, Mye-noo, Oung-beng-tha, Htan-ta-beng and Tha-bye-hla.

TA-RA-BHA.—A village in the Kywai-loo circle, Northern township, Sandoway district, lying on both banks of the Tan-lwai stream about four miles from its mouth. In 1877 it had 707 inhabitants.

TA-RA-NA.—A village in the circle of the same name in 'the Gyaing Than-lweng township of the Amherst district on the left bank of the Gyaing below Sandoway Dham-ma-tha. In 1877 it had 1,617 inhabitants.

TA-RA-NA.—A revenue circle in the Gyaing Than-lweng township of the Amherst district on the left bank of the Gyaing. It contains a good deal of rice land under cultivation and is inhabited chiefly by Talaing. In 1876-77 the population was 3,114, the land revenue Rs. 7,385 and the capitation tax Rs. 2,945. The principal villages are Ta-ra-na, Kaw-that and Dham-ma-tha.

TA-RAW-TAW.—A village in the Lek-wai (East) circle, Central township, Sandoway district, on the right bank of the Sandoway river a little below Sandoway. In 1877 it had 650 inhabitants.

TA-REE-KA-LWON.—A revenue circle in the Gyaing Attaran township, Amherst district, occupying an extended stretch of mountainous country on the left bank of the Houng-tha-raw. It is sparsely inhabited by Kareng and very thinly cultivated ; the major portion of its surface is covered by forest. In 1876-77 the population was 506, the land revenue was Rs. 271 and the capitation tax was Rs. 562.

TA-REE-KA-LWON.—A village in the circle of the same name in the Amherst district on the west bank of the Houng-tha-raw not far from the mouth of the Ta-ree-ka-hoon stream. In 1877 it had 672 inhabitants.

TA-ROO.—A sub-tribe of the Pwo family of Kareng residing in the extreme north-east of the province, called by themselves Koo-hta, by the Burmese Bhee-loo " Ogres", and by the Kareng-nee Pa-doung. A portion of the clan shave the whole head except two tufts of hair, one over each temple. They are considered to be a peaceable sept but yet are notorious for their blood feuds amongst themselves and for the slavery which exists. amongst them : they number about 16,000 souls but it is probable that most of these live beyond the British frontier though the native official stationed among the Gai-kho says not. The women wear short togas, and in addition to the brass coils round the neck and below the knee, which distinguish some of their neighbours, they have similar coils above the knee. The men wear trowsers.

TA-ROOP-HMYAW.—A village in the Ta-roop-maw circle, Ta-pwon township, Henzada (Tharrawaddy) district, about a mile east of the Irrawaddy. In 1877 it had 786 inhabitants.

TA-ROOP-HPYOO.—A revenue circle in the Padoung township of the Prome district. In 1876-77 the population was 1,615, the land revenue Rs. 975, the capitation tax Rs. 1,825 and the gross revenue Rs. 2,930.

TA-ROOP-MAW-MYO-MA.—A revenue circle in the Ta-pwon township, Henzada (Tharrawaddy) district, now including Tweng-byai on the left bank of the Irrawaddy, and adjoining the Prome district, with but little cultivation : towards the east the country is undulating and covered with Eng (*Dipterocarpus tuberculatus*) forest. In 1876-77 the population was 6,080, the land revenue was 3,230, the capitation tax Rs. 5,410 and the gross revenue Rs. 9,520. The principal village is Ta-roop-hmyaw.

TA-ROOP-TAW.—A village in the Twan-te circle, Angyee township, Rangoon district, on the lower ground to the north of the Twan-te Taw-gyee, about two miles N.E. from Twan-te. In 1877 it contained a population of 820 souls, Talaing, Kareng and Shan, most of whom are garden cultivators.

TA-THEE.—A village in the Dha-bhien circle, Hpoung-leng township, Rangoon district, with 772 inhabitants in 1878-79.

TAVOY.—A river in the Tenasserim division. The various streams which unite to form this river have their sources in the southern slopes of the Ma-hlwai spur and in the western slopes of the main range in the extreme north of the Tavoy district. Much obstructed by rocks and rapids it has a southerly course, through a narrow valley nowhere more than from ten to 12 miles across, of about 120 miles, and, receiving the waters of numerous small mountain streams, flows past the town of Tavoy, below which it widens rapidly and falls into the sea in about 13° 32' N. having attained a breadth of several miles. It is navigable throughout the year for boats and small craft for about 70 miles from its mouth, but owing to numerous shoals and low islands, the latter cultivated with rice, dhanee palms and other garden produce, not only is the navigation exceedingly intricate but vessels drawing more than seven feet of water cannot proceed above Goodridge plains 30 miles below Tavoy and about 15 miles up. The tide is felt some way above Tavoy.

TAVOY.—The head-quarter town of the district of the same name in the Tenasserim division on the Tavoy river about 30 miles from its mouth with 13,133 inhabitants in 1863-64, 14,506 in 1867-68 and 14,795 in 1877-78.

The town being situated in the valley of the river its position in regard to the surrounding country is low and the north-west and south portion is flooded at high tide and swampy during the rains ; the central portion is about 12 feet above high water level. It is laid out in straight streets and the houses are for the most part built of timber or bamboos and thatched with dhanee leaves. To the east and west are ranges of hills running nearly north and south. The surrounding land is under rice cultivation and during the season is rendered swampy by the small embankments raised to retain the rain water on the fields. It contains court-houses, police-stations, a custom-house, post-office, hospital and dispensary, market, school and a small and new gaol, besides numerous pagodas, monasteries and zayats or rest-houses. The trade is small and of but little importance, and is carried on chiefly with other ports in the province and with the Straits Settlements. The principal exports are rice, dhanee leaves, jaggery, earthen pots, wood oil, timber and fruits, and the principal imports are piece-goods, long cloth, turkey red, silk and cotton velvets, iron, crockery, tobacco and dried vegetables such as onions and chillies. In 1877-78 it had a gross municipal income of Rs. 10,499.

The town was founded in 1751 though the country is noticed much earlier and the ruins of some nine cities exist in various parts of the district, notably at Old Tavoy or Myo-houng a few miles to the north. In 1752 the ruler of the country made overtures to the British to establish a factory in or near his new capital. During the first Burmese war the garrison rose against the commander on the appearance of the British at the mouth of the river and handed the place over to the English, together with the person of the second in command and his family whom they had taken prisoners. For several years a detachment from Maulmain was quartered in the town which was gradually weakened and finally withdrawn. According to one tradition the name is a corruption of a Siamese word meaning " a landing-place for rattans," according to another it was so named because it was celebrated for its armourers, people coming from a long distance to buy swords (*dha* a sword and *way* to buy), according to a third because a miraculous sword was once bought here, and according to a fourth it is a Burmese corruption of the Talaing word *Hta-way*, sitting crossed-legged after the manner of tailors, and the town was thus called because Gaudama was so found by the inhabitants on his visit to the place. The last two traditions are the most incredible of the four, if any credit at all is due to any, which is highly improbable. Lat. 14° 5′ N.; Long 98° 10′ E.

TAVOY.—A district in the Tenasserim division extending along the eastern side of the Bay of Bengal from 13° 15′ to 15° 11′ N., bounded on the north by Amherst, from which it is separated by a range of hills south of the Re river, on the south by Mergui and on the east by the high chain of mountains which forms the boundary between British India and Siam. Its extreme length is about 150 miles, its breadth at the widest part is about 50 miles, and its area 7,200 square miles. Its general aspect is that of a long seacoast tract, hilly and densely wooded, enclosed by mountains on three sides and open on the west towards the sea.

The mouth of the Tavoy river affords excellent anchorage for ships and vessels can anchor along the coast at all times during the north-east monsoon, and during the south-west monsoon do often take secure refuge under the lee of the islands which shelter the coast. There are also one or two coves, as at Kyek-hlwot and Hmaw-rit, in which vessels might find safe anchorage during the south-west monsoon, with three fathoms at low water. Hien-tsai basin, towards the north, is a fine harbour with deep water but its mouth is obstructed by a bar.

The principal islands along the coast are the Moscos. These extend in a chain from 13° 47′ to 14° 28′ N. and are distant from nine to 13 miles from the main land with a safe channel inside. Between the southern and middle groups, which are the largest and highest, there are safe channels; the northern group is composed of straggling islands with several rocks above water.

There are three mountain ranges, *viz.*, the main chain on the Mountains. extreme east, the Nwa-hla-bo in the centre, and a third intervening between the Nwa-hla-bo and the seacoast. The main chain, with a general N.N.W. and S.S.E. direction, rises here occasionally to a height of 5,000 feet, and throwing off numerous densely-wooded spurs offers an almost impassible barrier across which, into Siam, there are but three routes and of these the southern or Mai-bhoora is impracticable for elephants. The northern is by the Htan-doung at the source of the May-nam-naw-ey in Lat. 14° 26′ 53″, N. Long. 98° 32′ E. a Siamese river, from Tavoy, to Kan-boo-ree *via* Met-ta. The southern route is by the Amya pass, 60 miles lower down, which derives its name from a village on the Tenasserim river. By this route the time occupied in travelling from Tavoy to Bangkok would be as follows:—

From Tavoy to Met-ta, by elephants	..	..	2 days.
From Met-ta to Amya, down to the Tenasserim river		..	3 „
From Amya to Ban Wangmeuk, through the Amya Pass, by Kareng coolies	..	..	2 „
From Wangmeuk to Kan-boo-ree by boat down the Tai-pa-ket	..	..	1 „
From Kan-boo-ree to May-khlaung, down the May-khlaung river	..	..	2 „
From May-khlaung to Bangkok by boat, through Maha-chai and Hta-cheen	..	..	2 „
	Total ..		12 days.

There are two objections to this route; the first is the descent of the Tenasserim from Met-ta to Amya through the dangerous rapids and falls so common to it ; the second is that Amya cannot be reached by elephants from the Tavoy side. Baggage has to be carried across the hills by Kareng coolies and if the baggage is too heavy the northern route by Htan-doung must be taken. By it the time occupied would be :—

From Tavoy to Met-ta, by elephants	..	..	2 days.
From Met-ta to Htan-doung by elephants up the Kha-miet stream	..	..	..	2 ,,
From Htan-doung to Deuyeik by elephants following the May-nam-naw-ey	..	..	..	3½ ,,
From Deuyeik to Wangmeuk by elephants	..	..	4 ,,
From Wangmeuk to Bangkok by boats	..	..	5 ,,
		Total ..	16½ days.

The western approach to the Htan-doung pass is very steep.

Thirty-eight miles south of the Amya pass there is another route across the watershed into Siam through the Mai-bhoora pass. The western ascent is up the Mai-bhoora river, an affluent of the Tenasserim. The distance is short but the journey is a long one owing to the irregular rocky condition of the river bed. The descent to the east is down the Mai-bhoora-khyee to Ban Wangmeuk on the Tai-hpa-kek. From Tai-hpa-ngay on the Mai-bhoora-khyee there is a short cut eastward into the Rat-boo-ree and Phayt-cha-boo-ree district of Siam. This pass is a very difficult one and is only used by Kareng.

Bounding the Tenasserim valley on the west and forming the watershed between the Tavoy and Tenasserim rivers is another range thrown off by the main chain in about 14° 42' N. and extending down through the district into Mergui to the great westward bend of the Tenasserim river. The highest point in this range is Nwa-la-bo, a hill about 21 miles N.N.E. of Tavoy. The ascent of this mountain has been several times made and the late Colonel Stevenson thus describes one that he effected some 20 years ago.

" We reached the foot of the range in three marches from Tavoy town
" and computed the distance to be about 21 miles. The path mostly running
" through thick jungle is tolerably good throughout but crosses water in a
" great many places. The ascent was thence accomplished in two stages
" the first occupying two hours and a quarter and following the direct path, the
" very steep and rocky across the ridge to the valley of the Tenasserim, the
" second running up along the ridge in a general southerly direction to the
" summit of the cone. It occupied upwards of six hours.

" The first portion of this ascent (the second stage) was not very steep
" but the forest was very dense ; in some places the jungle of thorny bamboo
" was impervious and delayed us many minutes, once a quarter of an hour,
" while we cut a passage through out a great portion of the path was a very
" clearly defined track of wild animals. As we neared the cone the mountain
" narrowed into a mere spur with precipitous walls clothed with dense jungle—
" the path here was often not more than a yard in width. The cone itself,
" which is the apex of three spurs, rises sharply from the ridge ; we climbed
" about 500 feet—the ascent was extremely arduous. We found its summit
" to be a table of not more than 40 feet in length by less than half that in
" breadth, entirely clothed with stunted trees and dwarf bamboo jungle. On
" the north-east the wall of the ridge is a precipice of 2,000 or even 2,500 feet.

" At 3-30 (it was in January) the thermometer was 65° in the shade ; at
" 6. P. M. 59°; at 10-10 it fell to 57°; at 6 A. M. and until sunrise a few
" minutes afterwards 56°, which was the lowest observed. At 8 A. M., it
" reached only 64° in the r in when shining brightly, nearly corresponding
" with the temperature at 3-30 shade of previous day. .The view on both
" days was much obscured by haze but the boundary range between Tavoy
" and Siam was very clearly visible. The range of view is most extensive
" and panoramic : no mountain approaching it in height appeared within a
" circle of probably 35 miles ; at that distance the peak of one was visible,
" nearly due south, which we supposed to be higher.

" It was very obvious that no table-land was to be found on this ridge
" or the spurs from it of more than a few square feet : 2,000 or even 1,500
" feet below it a small superficies on the sides of the mountain would pro-
" bably be met with here and there.

" As there was not a boiling-point thermometer or mountain barometer
" in Tavoy the height was subsequently taken by the theodolite, but the
" greatest difficulty occurred in obtaining a sufficient base-line ; that selected
" was measured in no less than three lengths ; two of them across water
" could be ascertained only by triangulation. Upon a base-line fixed by
" such a complicated method and measuring hardly a tenth of the distance
" of the object and thereby affording only very acute angles for the measure-
" ment little reliance can be placed. The result obtained made the height
" a little more than 4,500 feet."

The third range, which is of no great height, leaves the Ma-hlwai
spur, the northern boundary of the district, and, forming the western
water-shed of the Tavoy river, extends southward to Tavoy point.

The district contains but little plain country except that in the lower
course of the Tavoy river, and the hills, where not cleared in patches for
temporary cultivation, are covered with dense forest.

The chief rivers are the Tenasserim and the Tavoy. The former is'
Rivers.   remarkable for its two sources, the one rising in the
                               north and flowing south to the Kareng village of Met-ta
where it is joined by the latter which takes it source about 80 miles due
south of the source of the first and flows north ; after uniting they flow
due eastward and then turn south and shortly enter the Mergui district.
For the greater part of its course this river is dangerous to navigate on
account of its rapids.

The Tavoy river has its source in the Ma-hlwai spur and, flowing
southward through a narrow valley and fed by numerous mountain torrents,
falls into the sea at Tavoy point about 40 miles below the town of Tavoy.
From its source nearly to Gnyoung-doon-lai it is not navigable for boats
of any kind ; from this spot as far south as Rwon-lai, about 32 miles above
Tavoy at which place the rapids cease and the tides are felt, it is navigable
by boats drawing not more than three or four feet. Three miles above
the town the character of the river alters and below Goodridge plains it
flows through an alluvial plain and is spread in a wide channel studded
with islands. Hereabouts there are numerous tidal creeks much used by
the inhabitants. This river, which at its mouth is more properly an
estuary being about 15 miles wide, is navigable for vessels of any burden
and its main channel is pretty free from shoals as far as Than-lyeng-tshiep,

or Goodridge plains, on the west bank, about 20 miles from Nghek-thaik or Cap island, a rock at the mouth with a deep channel between it and the land. Ships can find safe anchorage at all times within Cap island and Sheng-maw point. Fresh water is at almost all seasons obtainable along the west shore as far as the most northern rocky islet, Kathay-ma-kywon, inside of which is a fine spring of water known as "English well", called by the natives Eng-ga-nee dweng. At the springs it is safe as far Tavoy for vessels drawing not more than eight feet of water but those drawing seven can scarcely hope to get up at neap tides as the shoals, which are constantly changing their position, nearly fill the channel.

The district has never been carefully examined by a geologist. The mountain ranges appear to be granite. The intervening valleys have occasional patches of clay slate, more or less altered by igneous action, with here and there dykes of claystone and freestone trap. The hills along the seacoast consist almost entirely of granite ; on the east side of them there is abundance of micaceous iron ore and clay ironstone, a good deal of the former being magnetic : nearly opposite the town, on the west bank of the river, is an elevated ironstone ridge, the higher part of the rock being magnetic. The low hills east of the town of Tavoy and those at Sheng-dha-wai above and at Pan-daw and Ka-nek-tha-ree below are all formed of alluvium composed chiefly of gravel with small boulders of sandstone, conglomerate and quartz. This is again covered with soil of the same material decayed and oxidized. The plains are composed of a stiff clay occasionally highly ferruginous. The banks and bed of the Tavoy river are generally clayey but occasionally a rocky stratum of laterite is seen, and the first hilly undulations to the eastward are composed of laterite, clay and sandstone. It is certain that this district formerly yielded tin and lead and there is reason to believe that the tribute to the government of Ava was mainly paid in these metals, but since the British occupation lead has not been worked and tin is collected in but small quantities by washing. Gold is found at the head-waters of many streams, but not in great quantity and it is also proved to exist, though never worked, in the alluvium of Tavoy town. Iron was formerly extracted in the neighbourhood of Tavoy but the work has long ceased to be remunerative. There is a small hill of magnetic iron ore about three miles N.W. of Tavoy, and Dr. Ure, to whom specimens were sent many years ago, reported very favourably of them, observing that the purest specimen contained more than 66 per cent. of the pure metal and that they were perfectly free from litanium. He said "they are all rich enough and "pure enough for making the best quality of bar iron and steel". Copper has been reported to exist in two or three localities at the mouth of the Toung-byouk river.

The mineral springs are of two kinds, sulphurous and saline ; the first, near the forks of the Tenasserim, and the others east and south of Tavoy. Of the former Dr. Mason, writes "All the stones in the springs "are of a bright brass colour produced apparently by the deposition of the "sulphur*". Dr. Helfer considered that they "belonged to the class of "sulphurous mineral waters, tinged slightly with chalybeate, like the water "of Brighton".† Dr. Mason adds "their heat above the atmosphere is not

Geology. (marginal label)

---

* Mason's Burma, 1st Edition, pp. 17, 18. † Dr. Helfer's second Report. 18??

"great. Mr. Bennett at a recent visit found the thermometer to rise in the "hottest spring to 119°. They rise from the slate rocks like the warm "springs of a considerable part of Germany."
The following description of the saline springs is taken in full from Dr. Mason's work. "On the margin of the granite range east of Tavoy "either near the junction of the slate and granite or in the granite itself "is a series of the hottest springs in the province. I have visited four or "five in a line of 50 or 60 miles and found them uniformly of a saline "character. Around one, nearly east of Tavoy, the stones are covered "with an efflorescence resembling Epsom or Glauber salt. Mr. Bennett "found the thermometer in this spring to rise to 144°.......The hottest "springs are at Pai......and according to Phillips they are hotter than "any on record out of volcanic regions, with the qestionable exception of "three springs in China which 'probably exceeded the temperature of the "'air from 70° to 120° degrees'. The principal spring at Pai, for there are "several, is in a httle sandy basin in the midst of granite rocks on the "margin of a cold-water stream where it bubbles up from three or four "vents; on immersing the thermometer into one the mercury rose to "198°,—within 14 degrees of the boiling point. Its location is rather pecu- "liar, not being in a valley like the others I have seen but on the side of a "hill more than a 1,000 feet above the level of the sea and surrounded "by large masses of coarse-grained granite rock, which seem to have been "detached from the summit above".*

Except in the valleys the whole surface of the country is covered with
Forests and vegeta-   dense forest, cleared here and there by the Kareng for
ble products.   toungya, which has never been scientifically surveyed
and examined. Beyond a few straggling trees in the north the existence of teak (*Tectona grandis*) is unknown, but other useful timber abounds. The principal timber trees are :—Theng-gan (*Hopea odorata*) which sometimes grows to a height of 250 feet and furnishes a strong light-brown timber used extensively in the construction of boats and canoes and to some extent for building purposes : a cubic foot weighs 64lbs. Pyeng-gado (*Xylia dolabriformis*), found principally near the forks of the Tenasserim though not uncommon in other parts ; the sap-wood is attacked by white ants and decays easily but the heart-wood is more durable than teak but extremely hard and heavy. Anan (*Fagræa fragrans*), a somewhat common tree which the teredo worm will not attack and which is said to harden by submersion and would be valuable for bridges, piles and other sub-aqueous purposes ; at Tavoy it is used principally for the posts of Booddhist edifices. Pyeng-ma (*Lagerstrœmia reginæ*), valuable in ship- and boat-building as it lasts well under water, used for house posts (for which however it is not well suited as the portion buried in the ground decays) planks, beams, roof-scantling and numerous other purposes. Eng-gyeng (*Hopea suava*), yielding a hard and tough but heavy wood used in boat-building and for planks. Khye (*Syndesmis tavoyana*), a handsome red wood used for furniture which when steeped in ferruginous mud turns to a pure ebony black. Padouk (*Pterocarpus indicus*), the wood resembles mahogany but is heavier, red and coarse-grained, that of the root being

---

* Mason's Burma, 1st Edition p. 18.

closer grained, darker and beautifully variegated; it is much prized and is extensively used in gun-carriages in India. Ka-gnyeng (*Dipterocarpus alata*) the wood of which is not much valued but from which a useful wood-oil is extracted. The medicinal and useful plants are very numerous. " The hills that " bound the valley of the Tavoy river " writes the late Dr. Mason " on both " sides, from their bases to their summits, abound with a tree which pro- " duces a bright gamboge. It is Roxburgh's *Garcinia pictoria*, which he " knew produced a gamboge, which he said, was liable to fade......I coloured " a piece of paper, one band with this gamboge and another with the " gamboge of commerce and subsequently exposed both to the weather " equally for more than twelve months, but without being able to discover " that one faded any more than the other.....It is used by the native doctors " in medicine but not extensively." One of the most inveterate· weeds which springs up in every clearing is a species of *Blumea* which by a very simple process yields good camphor. The late Mr. O'Reilly sent to Calcutta some specimens of that which he had prepared with.more care than is usually taken by the natives and it was reported as " in its refined form in all respects identical with Chinese camphor.* The Padouk produces a gum pronounced by Dr. Morton to be, in its medical virtues, identical with the kino of the druggists. From the *Butea frondosa* exudes a gum declared to be the "gummi rubrum astringens " of the old druggists and according to Mason " M. Guibourt of Paris, " to whom some of it had been sent, states his opinion in his work on drugs " that it is the original ' kino which " ' had entirely disappeared from commerce and was once so much valued " ' as to be sold for nearly a guinea a pound.' " The eastern mountains produce an inferior kind of cinnamon. The *Cassia alata* is much cultivated by the natives for its medicinal properties in diseases of the skin for which the native doctors employ it extensively. The *Terminalia bellerica* produces the Myrobolans which Burmese hold to be medicinal and which when dried is sold in the drug shops. A fungus is found growing at the roots of bamboos· much used as an anthelmintic. The Kareng sow the castor oil plant the seeds of which they use as a mordant. One species of croton is now cultivated for its medicinal virtues and another, also used as a cathartic, grows wild. Among the mangrove swamps the " Sea cocoanut " as it is called by the Burmese (*Carapa obovata*) is common; its fruit is employed as an astringent, especially in cholera. Sarsaparilla (*Smilax ovalifolia*) exists and is used as in Europe. The cashew, which is plentiful, exudes " a fine white transparent gum, like gum arabic, and not " inferior to it in virtue or quality." " The leaves of a very common weed " belonging to the genus *Polanisia* when bruised are said to act as a " sinapism. The dried twisted fruit of a species of *Helicteres* is seen among " the native drugs in the bazaar and is used by Burmese doctors. The " root of a species of *Desmodium* is valued for its medicinal properties. " The Kareng make an infusion of the leaves of a species of *Paratropia*, " which they use for many internal diseases." The seeds of the *Entada scandens* are used as a febrifuge. Wood-oil is said by Dr. O'Shaughnessy to have the same medical properties as copaiba.

---

* Voigt *apud* Mason, p. 486.

There are several sources of vegetable oils. The Ka-gnyeng (*Diptero-carpus alata*) is found in almost all situations. When fully grown oil is extracted from it by scooping out a hollow in the stem, in this a fire is lighted and thereafter the oil collected daily. Each tree will yield on an average 20lbs. a year for five or six years. It is, properly speaking, a balsam which by distillation yields a volatile oil, a resin being left behind : Dr. Helfer says that " laid upon paintings it covers them with a fine trans- " parent coating not liable to turn yellow, and dries quickly.....it is more " transparent than copal or mastic, without smell or taste, shining, brittle, " melts easily, burns with a perfume similar to frankincense, dissolves entirely " in ether, turpentine and substantial oils."† It dissolves caoutchouc making a water-proofing solution and is found to answer as a substitute for fish-oil in curing leather. It is used as a house varnish in places which are not exposed to the weather and largely in the·manufacture of torches. The oil of ben tree is abundant; a species of *Cerbera* from which the Burmese extract a lamp oil is found on the banks.of tidal creeks and a large timber tree, a species of *Bassia* from which the natives extract an edible oil, is indigenous. Dr. Helfer states that the *Melanorrhœa usitatissima*, the Thit-tse, of the Burmese; " is, in the latitude of Tavoy, at home " on the eastern mountains. It affords an excellent black varnish, much used to lacquer wooden and bamboo boxes, the extraction of which from the tree requires caution on account of its vesicant properties. It is used in gilding, the surface of the article being first smeared with this varnish and the gold leaf immediately applied.

" The bark of the *Careya* and of half a dozen different species of " mangrove, the fruit of the sea cocoanut, and the peel of a species of ebony " all abound in tannic acid." The dye-producing plants are numerous. The shoe flower, the juice of the cashew tree, the fruit of the *Melastoma*, the fruit of the *Diospyros mollis*, the fruit of the *Cherbulia terminalia* mixed with an iron clay and the juice of the *Jatropha curcas* give black : the *Ruellia indigofera* gives blue : the sawdust of the jack (*Artocarpus integrifolia*), boiled with alum as a mordant, is used as a yellow dye, and with wild indigo for a green,but the colour is not durable. Towards the east in the valley of the Tenasserim is found the Sapan (*Cæsalpinia sapan*), giving an excellent red dye ; this, owing to the facilities of communication, is taken down to Mergui in the Mergui district. The Kareng most usually prepare their red dyes from the roots of the *Morinda*.

A species of Hibiscus from which ropes are made abounds on the tidal shores, rivers and creeks and the *Sida acuta*, S. *stipulata* and *Urena lobata* all affording a good fibre are abundant.

The animals and animal products differ but little from those of the Malay Peninsula generally. Elephants are found in the northern portion and are said to visit the sea annu-ally but are rarely caught. Two if not three species of rhinoceros are known to exist, and are hunted solely for their horns which are bought by weight by the Chinese for exportation. The tapir though rarely seen is, according to the late Colonel Burney, known to exist, and the orang-outang is reported to be found on the Lek-khat-toung mountain on the seaboard. According to the late Dr. Morton, wild oxen, two species of tiger,

Animal kingdom.

† Dr. Helfer's second report 1839, p. 23.

species of tiger, several species of leopard, the sambur, daray, barking, and mouse deer, the Malay bear, the ant-eater, five or six sorts of monkeys, porcupine, wild hog, several of the civet tribe, and three species of squirrel all exist here. Amongst birds, the horn-bill, the flesh of which is prized by the mountaineers, the Burmese peacock, the silver and black peacock, pheasant; jungle fowl, pelican, wild duck, whistling and cotton teal, curlew, snipe, plover, quail, imperial and green pigeons and doves are all found, as well as king-fishers, snake birds, love birds, orioles, bulbuls, minas (four species) tailor birds, owls and many others. Fish in great variety abound on the coast and in the rivers and are taken all the year round for home consumption and for exportation. The whale is rarely seen but skates and sharks pursue their prey along shore. The pomfret, sole, mullet, mango fish, mackerel, barbel, herring, a species of *thryssa*, sardines and carp abound besides numerous other kinds. The coasts and estuaries are thronged with shell fish, oysters, mussels, cockles, crabs, etc. In the rivers crocodiles are numerous. Lizards of several kinds exist and many species of snakes, but comparatively few are venomous. The sandy beaches of the coast and of the Islands are frequented by turtles and the eggs are eagerly sought for : the right of collecting them is sold by the government.

The cool season commences at the close of the rains in October and
Climate.   continues until the middle of February when the hot weather prevails until the rains which usually begin in the middle of May and continue till the middle of October. The weather during much of the cool season is pleasant and enjoyable, the thermometer scarcely ever reaching 90° in the shade and occasionally in the early mornings falling as low as 56° For a month after the close of the rains the atmosphere is peculiarly fresh and clear. The prevailing winds during this season are easterly, and are often of very considerable force. During the months of December, January and February dense fogs prevail in the mornings till about nine o'clock and it is at this season that the greatest thermometric range is observed, occasionally as much as 30° in one day. Towards the middle of February the weather rapidly becomes warmer but the sea breeze along the coast relieves the intense heat. In April there are occasional squalls of wind and rain from the south-east and about the middle of May the wind veers round to the S.W., there are usually violent thunderstorms, and the S.W. monsoon sets in. After this there is rarely any electric disturbance till October when the rainy season ends in much the same way as it began.

The rainfall and average temperature are given in the following table :—

Year.	RAINFALL, IN INCHES.				AVERAGE TEMPERATURE IN THE SHADE.								
	January to May.	June to September.	October to December.	Total.	May.			July.			December.		
					Sunrise.	2 p. m.	Sunset.	Sunrise.	2 p. m.	Sunset.	Sunrise.	2 p. m.	Sunset.
1867 ..	27·85	160·15	2·75	190·75	Not given.								
1868 ..	11·10	175·30	7·30	193·70	72	90	81	70	86	85	60	90	87
1869 ..	13·10	157·85	19·60	190·55	77	88	86	75	80	79	65	88	83
1870 ..	22·80	156·50	6·30	185·60	76	83	81	75	79	79	65	85	84
1871 ..	39·80	175·00	14·10	229·30	76	83	80	75	80	78	64	82	76
1872 ..	24·30	132·80	6·40	163·50	76	84	81	75	80	78	66	84	78
1873 ..	9·30	184·67	11·57	205·54	78	88	86	75	78	77	67	83	81
1874 ..	51·32	144·52	17·50	213·34	76	82	81	75	80	79	69	83	82
1875 ..	22·30	194·70	1·13	228·30	76	83	81	75	80	80	67	82	79
1876 ..	41·12	165·15	15·25	221·32	—	—	—	—	—	—	—	—	—
1877 ..	23·40	17·75	10·30	21·12	—	—	—	—	—	—	—	—	—

Year.	Average temperature in the shade.											
	May.				July.				December.			
	Mean of maximum.	Mean of minimum.	Highest.	Lowest.	Mean of maximum.	Mean of minimum.	Highest.	Lowest.	Mean of maximum.	Mean of minimum.	Highest.	Lowest.
1876 ..	81·60	76·40	89·20	72·70	78·05	73·00	84·40	71·50	84·80	64·40	88·00	55·50
1877 ..	91·8	75·5	98·	72·	82·	73·8	86·	72·	88·9	72·4	90·	65·

History.   The country having at different periods formed a portion of the dominions of the kings of Siam, of Pegu and of Ava its history is involved in much obscurity. The first settlers were probably Siamese but at a very early date a colony of Arakanese was established who have made their mark on the language. The earliest written accounts of the country state that the Burman king Na-ra-pad-dee-tsee-thoo, who came hither more as a preacher of religion than as a conqueror, founded Kyek-hlwot in Khwe-doung bay not far from the mouth of the Tavoy river in 1200 A.D., the first city ever built in this district. He also built the pagoda on Tavoy point which is the oldest of which there are any records, and was, probably, the first to place Booddhism on a permanent base in this region. Anxious to connect the foundations of their religion with the great Athawka the Booddhist writers assert that in 315 B.C. this king ordered the construction of a pagoda in what is now Tavoy town. Many years later the country was subject to the king of Siam and still later to the soverigns of Pegu, from whom it passed to the kings of Burma, but it was continually suffering from invasions from Siam. About 1752 the ruler of Tavoy set himself up for an independent prince and made overtures to the British government, which had made many endeavours to obtain settlements east of Hindustan, but the terms proposed were. too exorbitant from a pecuniary point of view, and in 1757 Ensign Lister proposed to Aloung-bhoora, then king of Burma, a treaty one of the terms of which was a pledge on the part of the English not to assist the king of Tavoy.*

Soon after this Tavoy again became a province of Siam but in 1759 it surrendered to Aloung-bhoora the great Burman conqueror. In 1760 a British mission was despatched to Pegu to obtain amongst other things, remuneration for the loss of a ship belonging to Captain Whitehill which had been forcibly taken by the Burmese and employed against the king of Tavoy. From this time until the treaty of Yandaboo the country was torn by rebellions and by incursions by the Siamese : in 1791 one Myat Poo rebelled against the Burmans but being worsted escaped with many of the inhabitants across the eastern mountains, and in 1824 Meng Kyaik followed his example. In the first Anglo-Burmese war in 1824 an expedition was despatched against this part of the Burmese Empire. It consisted of details of the 89th Regiment and 7th M. N. I. under the command of Lieut-Colonel Miles. The detachment arrived at Tavoy on the 8th September and took possession of the town, aided by some of the officers of the Burmese garrison who seized the governor and his family and made them over to the British. For some time nothing occurred to disturb our possession but in 1829 a revolt broke out, headed by Moung Da, the former governor, which was at once put down and since then the district has remained without disturbance a portion of the British Empire in India. For some years a detachment of troops was stationed in the town of Tavoy but this was subsequently withdrawn and the district is now guarded solely by police.

None of the pagodas are of any great size nor are any objects of great
Pagodas.   veneration to Burmans and Talaing generally but several are of ancient date and are the resorts of numerous pilgrims from the district at certain seasons when crowds assemble to prostrate themselves before the holy relics which these buildings are

---

* Bayfield in Pemberton. In some accounts it is stated that there was an agreemeut that aid should be given against the king of Tavoy, but from the general conduct of the Burmese it it is more probable that the account in the text is the most correct.

thought to contain, to repeat sentences in honour of Gaudama, for a Booddhist cannot, in strictness, be said to pray, and to dance and sing and amuse themselves as at a fair. The most famous is thé Sheng Moot tee a few miles south of Tavoy, which contains an image and near which are a stone and a banyan tree, all three supposed to have been miraculously floated together across the ocean from India : it is 58 feet high and 300 feet in circumference at the base. On Tavoy point at the mouth of the Tavoy river on the right bank is the Sheng-maw, only nine feet high, founded in 1204 A.D. and said to contain a tooth of Gaudama. North of Tavoy is the Sheng-dha-way 77 feet high of very early date, built on the spot on which a holy relic of Gaudama alighted after flying through the air when released by its possessor. In addition to these there are ten pagodas in the town and suburbs of Tavoy and 19 in the district, all of more or less sanctity and some supposed to be of great age, each of which has its history in which there is more fiction than truth.

The area under cultivation is barely more than one-seventieth of the whole area of the district, yet there are 3,550 square miles of uncultivated culturable waste waiting for population. The absence of roads and other means of communication, the few attractions to immigrants, for equally good if not better soil is found in the more accessible Amherst district to the north, whilst the valley of the Irrawaddy affords a more convenient as well as more fertile site for agricultural settlers, who come mainly from Upper Burma, render it almost certain that it is to its mineralogical and forest resources that Tavoy must trust for its development. Relieved from oppression by its cession to England in 1824, the cultivated area soon increased though the increase was slow : in 1855-56 the area of land under cultivation, other than toungya, was 37,360 acres, or rather over 53 square miles : in 1864-65 it had risen to 46,782, acres or rather over 72 square miles.

The area under each kind of crop during each of the last ten years has been in acres :—

Year.		Rice.	Sugar-cane.	Cotton.	Fibres.	Tobacco.	Vegetables.	Betel-nut.	Dhanee.	Pan-vine.	Mixed fruit trees.
1868	..	42,700	36	—	—	—	276	*	3,105	193	6,811
1869	..	42,001	67	—	—	—	343	*	3,093	193	4,544
1870	..	41,376	75	—	—	—	261	1,575	3,114	194	5,842
1871	..	42,821	52	—	—	—	208	1,567	3,123	223	6,005
1872	..	43,999	36	—	—	—	250	1,831	3,134	221	6,267
1873	..	44,694	28	—	380	4	211	1,841	3,313	177	7,643
1874	..	46,607	39	—	335	6	222	1,787	3,374	180	6,833
1875	..	46,775	68	..	340	8	155	1,797	3,416	176	8,040
1876	..	47,074	92	10	300	4	229	1,800	3,528	176	7,702
1877	..	48,067	87	3	315	5	172	1,805	3,573	169	8,885

* Included in mixed fruit trees.

These figures do not include hill-garden cultivation of which there were from 8,000 to 9,000 acres every year. The soil is by no means rich and the average out-turn of rice is about 1,270 lbs. to an acre.

The banks of the river within the range of the tides when they are low enough to be overflowed are generally cultivated with the Dhanee or Nipa palm, a most valuable product. "Its leaves afford materials for thatching "houses, the extracted juice is drank or converted into molasses, its flower "is made into a preserve, its fruit is eaten, and its roots bind together the "soil on which it grows, whilst its dry branches serve for the fuel with which "its juice is boiled down into sugar." The betel-nut tree is extensively cultivated for local consumption. If the soil in which the seed is planted is suited to it it generally grows to a height of about three feet during the first year and about half of that during each of the succeeding years till it has reached its full growth. In its seventh year it commences bearing, and continues for about 30 years when it is cut down. The fruit is gathered at the end of the rains, when it is husked and soaked for some three days ; it then becomes of a reddish colour.

In fruits and fruit trees the district is particularly rich, doorians, mangoes, tamarinds, jack, mangosteen, lichi, guavas, pawpaw, pine-apples, plantains, pierardia, custard-apples, oranges, sweet limes, shad-dock, citron, pomegranates, melons, cashew-nuts, and other kinds are found in abundance.

The agricultural stock during the last decennial period is shewn to have been :—

Year.	Buffaloes.	Cows, bulls and bullocks.	Sheep and goats.	Pigs.	Carts.	Ploughs.	Boats.
1868 ..	23,924	2,700	303	1,115	296	3,835	1,333
1869 ..	25,700	3,170	416	1,076	330	2,791	1,515
1870 ..	27,040	3,362	408	910	350	2,709	1,596
1871 ..	27,024	3,909	585	702	354	2,957	1,653
1872 ..	28,742	4,637	436	639	380	3,171	1,711
1873 ..	27,238	4,680	382	876	375	3,315	1,702
1874 ..	28,456	5,076	477	962	408	3,345	1,737
1875 ..	27,831	4,833	522	712	452	3,561	1,847
1876 ..	25,369	6,160	687	1,015	451	3,419	1,874
1877 ..	26,603	6,637	549	1,042	502	3,910	1,944

Cows, bulls and bullocks have more than and goats have nearly doubled, and the number of carts and boats has largely increased, but the number of buffaloes and of ploughs has remained almost stationary. This might be expected from the small increase in land under rice and the small size of the holdings. A pair of buffaloes and a plough are necessary for the culti-vation of a holding of two acres and are sufficient for the cultivation of a holding of ten acres. As the increase in land under rice is to a considerable extent due to the gradually increasing size of the farms as adjacent waste land is brought under the plough, and as on an average separate properties cover an area of a few acres only, the increase in ploughs and plough-beasts does not keep pace with the increase in tillage, whilst the increase in boats, carts and draught-beasts does.

The average prices of produce and labour are given in the annual Administration Reports as, in rupees:—

YEAR.	PER MAUND OF 80 lbs.				EACH.		DAILY HIRE.				
							PER MAN.		EACH.		
							Labourers.				
	Rice.	Sugar.	Salt.	Fish.	Plough bullocks.	Buffaloes.	Skilled.	Unskilled.	Cart.	Boat.	
	Rs. A.	Rs. A.	Rs. A.	Rs. A.	Rs. A.	Rs. A.	Rs. A.	Rs. A.	Rs. A.	A. P.	
1868	2 0	2 0	0 12	10 0	40 0	40 0	1 4	0 6	1 8	6 0	
1869	2 0	2 0	0 8	10 0	50 0	40 0	1 4	0 6	1 8	7 0	
1870	2 0	2 0	0 8	10 0	45 0	40 0	1 4	0 6	1 8	6 0	
1871	2 0	2 0	0 9	10 0	45 0	40 0	1 4	0 8	2 0	6 0	
1872	2 0	2 0	0 10	12 8	45 0	40 0	1 4	0 8	1 8	7 0	
1873	2 6	2 0	1 0	12 .8	45 0	40 0	1 4	0 8	1 8	7 0	
1874	2 8	4 0	1 4	12 8	45 0	30 0	1 4	0 8	1 8	7 0	
1875	2 4	4 0	1 4	12 8	45 0	30 0	1 4	0 8	1 8	8 0	
1876	2 4	4 0	1 0	12 8	45 0	30 0	1 4	0 8	1 8	7 0	
1877	2 10	4 0	1 4	12 8	45 0	30 0	1 4	0 8	1 8	7 0	

Though there has been a gradual rise in the price of all articles of food yet the prices of draught and plough cattle and the rate of wages and the cart and boat-hire have remained very much the same. In the Amherst district, which lies to the north of and adjoins Tavoy, the hire of a boat is more than four times as high; this is probably due to the fact that in Amherst the passenger traffic is comparatively large and the boatmen are Chittagonians, whereas in Tavoy people do not travel nearly so much and when they do go about it is in their own boats; in short there is little or no demand for boat service. Buffaloes are extraordinarily cheap and curiously more so than in the more mountainous Mergui district on the south and of less value than bullocks, whereas in parts of the rich delta of the Irrawaddy they are twice the price of plough or draught bullocks.

As a general rule the land is worked by the proprietor but sometimes by tenants. Mortgages are not common: in some cases, mostly in order to obtain money wherewith to pay off debts, an usufructuary mortgage is entered into and in this case the mortgagee holds the land for a fixed period receiving no other return for his money; in others, and this is so especially where the owner embarks in trade, the land is mortgaged as security for the money lent and passes to the mortgagee at the expiration of a fixed period if principal and interest are not paid. Sometimes the mortgagee handing over the money enters into possession and so remains until the principal is repaid. In the first and last cases the mortgagee usually pays the land revenue. There are but few landholders who employ labourers; when they do the wages are generally paid in grain, the value of which amounts to about Rs. 7 a month, and in addition the labourers are fed and housed; the hiring lasts for two months at the commencement and for three at the close of the season. Tenancies are usually created by parol agreement, though in some instances written agreements are prepared: as a general rule the tenant holds the land from year to year paying the land revenue and a rent in kind, the rent varying but the average being the equivalent of about Rs. 2 an acre. Tenants are of the same class and as well off as proprietors, and the land that is let out is the most productive, for poor land is not readily taken and if worked at all must be worked by the owner. The land is gradually tending to accummulate into larger properties but very slowly and mainly owing to the falling in of mortgages, for it is landholders and not urban money-lenders who here advance funds to needy cultivators. Few permanent residents in town own lands which they rent out and never visit, but it is by no means uncommon for working landholders to live in town between working season and working season. In some the average holdings are tending slowly to increase from five acres, the present area, by the mortgage of land to neighbouring landholders and not by residents in towns investing their savings in land and deriving their income from the rent, which is to low to repay them.

A densely-wooded and mountainous country, difficult of access to foreigners and offering few attractions to immigrants, suffering for some centuries from almost continual wars, rebellions and marauding incursions, this district has never been thickly inhabited. It is doubtful who were the first settled, but tradition points to a colony of Arakanese near Tavoy and is supported by some dialectic peculiarities in the language of the present inhabitants who, except in the hills where a few Kareng have patches of cultivation, are almost exclusively native Burmans and Talaing. From the annual official returns it appears that in 1855-56 the population numbered 52,867, souls, who in 1864-65 had increased to 62,427, and in 1872, when a regular census was carefully taken, to 71,827 occupying 12,849 houses in 227 villages, which gives three villages to each 1,000 square miles and not quite ten souls per square mile. From the nature of the country by far the larger portion of the inhabitants are collected in the valley of the Tavoy river, where almost the whole of the arable land is found. The Kareng numbered 5,748, the Talaing 3,797 only and the Burmese 59,361. The Chinese though not so numerous as in the slightly larger, more accessible and to them more attractive, district of Mergui to the south, numbered 1,554, and the remainder of the population was made up of about 400 Hindoos, about 700 Mahomedans and a few Shan, Indo-Portuguese and others. Of agriculturists (that is those engaged in the cultivation of the soil, herdsmen, dealers in cattle and other cognate occupations) there were 31,218, of whom 29,926 or 41·66 per cent. of the whole population, a larger proportion than in any other district of the province except Thayet, were tillers of the ground, and of these only 11,659 were males over 20 years of age, so that the average area of the farms may be taken as 5·48 acres. The number employed in mechanical arts such as bricklayers, carpenters, lime-burners, blacksmiths, jewellers, makers and sellers of pottery, turners, carvers and gilders, weavers, millers, &c. and the number of dealers in vegetable and animal food and in drinks and stimulants, was 19,867 ; of merchants, traders, petty shop-keepers, &c., that is those engaged in trade and commerce, there were only 1,952, whilst of women having no special occupation, persons having no ostensible trade or occupation from which they derive an income, children, &c., there were 16,919. Government servants, professional persons and persons in

Population.

service make up the remainder. The children not over six years of age were 15,434 in number (of whom 7,191 were males and 7,243 females) or 21·49 per cent. of the whole population. Exclusive of Tavoy only three villages contained over 1,000 inhabitants, 27 from 500 to 1,000, 75 from 200 to 500, and 121 less than 200. One noticeable feature is that the women exceed the men in number, and this is the only district in the province in which this was found to be the case.

The annual returns shew the population as having been in :—

YEAR.	ADULTS.		CHILDREN UNDER TWELVE.		TOTAL.		Grand Total.	Number per square mile.
	Males.	Females.	Males.	Females.	Males.	Females.		
1868	16,835	19,511	16,950	15,453	33,785	34,964	68,749	9·54
1869	17,399	20,467	16,969	14,949	34,368	95,416	69,784	9·69
1870	18,190	21,009	16,581	14,719	34,771	35,728	70,499	9·79
1871	18,499	21,226	16,885	14,884	35,384	36,110	71,494	9·92
1872 ·.. ..	18,966	22,023	16,793	14,674	35,759	36,697	72,456	10·06
1873	19,244	22,677	17,201	14,817	36,445	37,494	73,939	10·26
1874	19,677	23,012	17,485	15,305	37,162	38,317	75,479	10·48
1875	20,195	23,401	17,672	15,618	37,867	39,019	76,886	10·67
1876	20,623	24,038	17,853	15,352	38,476	39,390	77,866	10·81
1877	21,624	24,504	18,058	15,536	39,682	40,040	79,722	10·98

The fact that there are more adult females than males and more juvenile males than females, and this steadily year by year, is remarkable.

The only town in the district is Tavoy situated on the left bank of the river of the same name, about 35 miles from its mouth and about seven or eight miles in a direct line, from the seacoast from which it is separated by a range of hills. Its site is low, but slopes gently towards the river ; the central and higher portion is about 12 feet above high-water mark but the north, south and west portions are flooded at high-water and swampy during the rains. On the west it is flanked by the river but on the other three sides the valley is open, unencumbered with jungle vegetation and extensively cultivated with rice. In the neighbourhood are no large bodies of water or swampy lands but the level character of the valley, the heavy rainfall, and the embanking in of the water for rice cultivation render the surrounding country to some extent marshy. The town is well laid out, with three principal streets running north and south, intersected at right angles at pretty regular intervals by four main cross streets. West of Victoria road the houses are generally arranged in rows with but little space between the gable-ends ; in the rest of the town they are principally built in separate enclosures and are shaded with fruit and other trees. In the centre is a large open square unoccupied by houses where formerly was the fort within which were the barracks for the troops—a detachment from Maulmain gradually decreased in strength and finally withdrawn—and the various public buildings. The walls of the fort were of brick and it was partly surrounded by a deep trench and with an entrance in each face. The houses, with few exceptions, are constructed of wood or of bamboos and are raised on posts and thatched with dhanee leave .

Towns,

The present town was founded in 1751 and some years later it was enlarged. There were continual wars between the Peguans and the Siamese and subsequently between the Burmese and the Siamese in all of which the town suffered. During the first Burmese war it was surrendered to the British by the second in command, who made the governor and his family prisoners and handed them over to the English. Five years after the cession of the country by the treaty of Yandaboo a rebellion broke out which was speedily suppressed, and the walls were subsequently, and partly consequently, levelled.

The population in 1873 was 14,575 souls, of whom 6,823 were males and 7,752 females. It was composed of 69 Christians, 762 natives of India, 12,490 Burmese and Talaing and 1,254 others, principally Chinese. In 1877 it was 14,795. Its municipal revenue in the latter year was Rs. 11,458 It contains court-houses, a police-office and police-stations, post-office, hospital and dispensary, bazaars and a gaol.

The police employed in the town, exclusive of the guards over the lock-up and treasury, consisted, in 1877, of two subordinate officers and 16 men.

Besides Tavoy there were, in 1877, 308 villages, the largest of which did not contain 3,000 inhabitants.

With its only port not easy of access, with a small and poor population,
Trade. with but sorry means of communication in the interior and above all producing little for export, the sea-borne trade of the district has never been large and is almost entirely confined to Siam and the Straits; and of in-land trade there is none. The principal imports are piece-goods and other cotton manufactures, raw silk, tea, and such articles as are naturally required by the mixed population of a small town, as crockery, glass-ware, cocoanuts, wines and liqueurs, steel, provisions and oilman's stores, &c., and all in small quantities.

698

The total value of the imports and exports, the duty realized and the tonnage of vessels which entered and cleared during each of the last ten years was:—

	Vessels Cleared Tonnage	Vessels Cleared Number	Vessels Entered Tonnage	Vessels Entered Number	Duty Total Rs.	Duty Exports Rs.	Duty Imports Rs.	Value Total Total Rs.	Value Total Treasure Rs.	Value Total Merchandize Rs.	Value Exports Total Rs.	Value Exports Treasure Rs.	Value Exports Merchandize Rs.	Value Imports Total Rs.	Value Imports Treasure Rs.	Value Imports Merchandize Rs.
1868	—	—	—	—	21,602	18,630	2,972	697,499	—	—	366,981	—	—	330,518	—	—
1869	—	—	—	—	20,942	19,038	1,904	718,658	—	—	413,434	—	—	305,224	—	—
1870	—	—	—	—	20,081	18,104	1,977	664,262	—	—	304,262	—	—	360,160	—	—
1871	12,981	405	11,737	285	19,711	18,000	1,711	809,262	—	—	390,692	—	—	418,570	—	—
1872	16,082	430	14,921	337	25,430	23,526	1,904	1,015,327	356,062	659,245	537,543	100,200	437,343	477,784	255,882	221,902
1873	18,592	425	16,609	298	27,541	25,893	1,648	980,520	365,857	616,703	475,209	126,005	349,204	507,351	239,852	207,499
1874	18,612	304	18,760	284	22,967	21,447	1,520	1,011,235	394,882	616,353	465,170	141,450	323,720	544,065	253,432	292,633
1875	31,660	428	29,039	343	16,537	14,551	1,986	816,501	188,766	627,825	348,564	36,476	312,388	467,727	162,290	315,497
1876	31,128	467	30,966	411	19,992	18,396	1,596	810,847	184,768	626,079	305,936	37,783	268,153	504,911	146,985	357,926
1877	34,583	485	32,538	371	31,314	29,373	1,941	1,029,105	312,708	716,397	497,986	50,170	447,816	531,179	262,598	268,581

Besides this small trade with foreign ports there is a still smaller coasting trade with Maulmain and Rangoon ; dhanee leaves and jaggery, earthen pots and water bottles, doorians and other fruits are carried along the coast, whilst English silk and cotton handkerchiefs, chintzes, silk and cotton velvets and piece-goods come from Maulmain, and tamarinds, chillies, onions, peas, gram and tobacco come from Rangoon. The vessels employed in the coasting trade are principally junks and kattoos owned by Burmans and Chinese of whom some reside in Tavoy.

The two principal manufactures are salt and earthen pots. The salt is made from seawater, partly by evaporation and partly by boiling, and is consumed entirely in the district.
Manufactures.
The pots are made in and near Tavoy town, partly for local use and partly for export along the coast. The clay is brought from near Mro-houng, the site of an ancient city the ruined walls of which still exist, about nine miles up the river. On the spot it sells for 12 annas and at Tavoy for Rs. 2-8 a boat-load of 3,650 lbs. which mixed with about one-third part of sand will make about 200 pots. These take about 15 days to complete and sell at an average of Rs. 18 the 100.

The Imperial revenue raised in the district in 1853-54, the first year for which returns are available, was Rs. 99,170, ten years later it was Rs. 167,590, in 1873-74 Rs. 215,450 and in 1877-78 Rs. 227,367.
Revenue.

The Imperial and Provincial revenues divided out into their main heads and the incidence of taxation per head of population were, during each of the last ten years :—

Year	Land revenue.	Capitation tax.	Salt tax.	Fishery revenue.	Revenue from forest produce.	Excise on spirits and drugs.	Customs.	Miscellaneous.	Total.	Population.	Incidence per head of population.
	Rs.	Rs.	Rs.	Rs.	Rs.	Rs.	Rs.	Rs.	Rs.	Rs.	Rs.
1868-69	91,394	44,843	2,744	6,819	3,900	11,267	22,251	—	193,894	71,185	2 11 5
1869-70	91,879	46,380	2,744	6,515	3,900	15,311	21,286	10,676	198,501	69,784	2 13 6
1870-71	91,878	48,159	2,326	6,052	3,900	7,820	20,445	12,206	192,222	70,499	2 9 10
1871-72	88,243	49,381	1,770	5,895	10,400	13,645	19,711	11,642	198,560	71,494	2 12 5
1872-73	90,226	50,723	2,877	6,042	10,400	12,454	25,430	9,453	207,605	72,456	2 13 10
1873-74	91,591	51,900	2,392	6,261	10,400	16,095	27,542	9,257	215,448	73,939	2 14 10
1874-75	94,383	53,065	2,579	6,850	9,100	16,508	22,968	12,031	217,479	75,479	2 14 1
1875-76	94,782	54,745	2,903	6,955	9,100	18,889	16,537	11,174	210,085	76,886	2 11 8
1876-77	96,191	55,997	2,415	7,137	9,100	18,511	19,991	12,140	221,482	77,866	2 13 7
1877-78	98,006	57,026	2,253	7,355	2,650	14,800	30,920	14,287	227,367	79,122	2 13 11

The gross receipts and the cost of officials of all kinds during the same period were, in rupees :—

YEAR.					Gross receipts.	Cost of officials.
1868-69	..	..	..	..	193,894	62,473
1869-70	..	..	..	..	198,501	60,622
1870-71	..	..	..	..	192,152	91,878
1871-72	..	..	..	..	198,560	61,407
1872-73	..	..	..	..	207,610	56,446
1873-74	..	..	..	..	215,448	61,571
1874-75	..	..	..	..	217,479	64,317
1875-76	..	..	..	..	210,085	68,387
1876-77	..	..	..	..	221,482	73,177
1877-78	..	..	..	..	227,367	77,691

Besides the Imperial and Provincial revenue a so-called local revenue is raised from various sources, such as the renting out of market-stalls, subscriptions and donations to the hospital and dispensary, an assessment levied on land in some of the towns, pound fines and fees, cattle-market fees, ferry fees, and a cess of five per cent. on the land revenue and fishery and net tax. The amount so levied has been, during each of the last ten years, in rupees :—

YEAR.			Port Fund.	Town and Municipal Funds.	District Fund.	Dispensary Fund.	Cess Fund.	TOTAL.
			Rs.	Rs.	Rs.	Rs.	Rs.	Rs.
1868	..	..	—	10,331	257	198	4,612	15,398
1869	..	..	—	10,177	236	} Included in Town and Municipal Funds. {	4,766	15,179
1870	..	..	—	8,878	305		4,784	13,967
1871	..	..	—	9,695	341		4,623	14,659
1872	..	..	—	9,638	323		4,729	14,690
1873	..	..	428	9,296	409		4,808	14,941
1874	..	..	689	9,533	369		4,977	15,558
1875	..	..	1,057	—	10,016	219	5,902	17,194
1876	..	..	960	—	10,213	311	5,080	16,564
1877	..	..	959	10,226	694	273	5,179	17,331

The district was formerly administered by a Deputy Commissioner and six Goung-gyoop in charge of " districts " together with a Tsit-ke or native Judge for the town, Thoogyee of circles and Goungs of clusters of villages. This system in its general features still

Administration.

remains in force*, the main changes being that the " districts " of the goung-gyoop have been amalgamated into three townships,—the north-east, occupying the whole of that portion of the valley of the Tenasserim which lies within the limits of this district ; the south-east, extending from the south along the left bank of the Tavoy river nearly to Tavoy town and stretching eastward to the Nwa-la-bo range which separates the valley of the Tavoy from that of the Tenasserim ; and the west, comprising the whole country between the seacoast and the Tavoy river.† In charge of each is an Extra Assistant Commissioner.

Up to 1861-62 the Police force consisted of the Thoogyee, goung, kye-dan-gyee and two peons which were allowed to each Goung-gyoop, whilst in the town of Tavoy there were five Goung (one for each quarter), six jemadars and 43 peons, whose salary amounted to Rs. 7,800 a year and who on emergency did duty on the river and were sometimes detached into

---

* In addition to his other duties the Deputy Commissioner is now *ex-officio* Collector of Customs.

† Whilst the *Gazetteer* was going through the press the three townships have been made into four (General department notification No. 89, dated 29th March 1878), but no change is made in the text as the account of many circles had been printed and they had been described according to their position in the old townships.

The boundaries of the new townships are thus given in the notification :—

The Central township is bounded on the north by the Za-ha stream, by a straight line from the source of the Za-ha stream to the source of the Tha-bhyo stream, by the Tha-bhyo stream, by the Khwe-tsay stream and by a straight line from the source of the Khwe-tsay stream to the nearest point of the Eastern hills ; on the west by the Tavoy river ; on the south by the Htan-beng-ahoung stream, by a strait line from the source of that stream to the source of the Hien-da stream, by the Hien-da stream, by a straight line from the mouth of the Hien-da stream to the mouth of the Nga Pook Ta-ye stream, by the Nga Pook Ta-ye stream and by a straight line from the source of the Nga Pook Ta-ye stream to the nearest point of the Eastern hills ; and on the east by the Eastern hills.

The South-east township is bounded on the north by the southern boundary of the Central township ; on the west by the Tavoy river and the sea ; on the south by the Ee-it stream, by a straight line from the source of the Ee-it stream to the source of the Thayet-ngoot stream, by the Thayet-ngoot stream, and by a straight line from the mouth of the Thayet-ngoot stream to the nearest point of the Eastern hills ; on the east by the Eastern hills.

The Northern township is bounded on the north by the Kyouk-ta-yan stream and the Ma-lwai range of hills ; on the west by the sea ; on the south by the Nga-byiet-nee stream, by a straight line from the source of that stream to the source of the Kwai-gya stream, by the Kwai-gya stream and by the northern boundary of the Central township ; on the east by the Eastern range of hills.

The Western township is bounded on the north by the southern boundary of the Northern township to the west side of the Tavoy river ; on the west by the sea ; on the south by the sea ; on the east by the Tavoy river.

To this township also belong the Northern, Middle, and Southern Moscos, Corn Island, Cap Island and Reef Island.

Old Townships		Circles.		New Townships.
West	..	.. Za-dee ..	..⎫	
North-east	..	.. Ka-laing-oung	..⎪	
Ditto	..	.. Kha-moung-thway	..⎬Northern.	
Ditto	..	.. Moung-mai-shoung	..⎪	
West	..	.. Ra-laing ..	..⎭	
Town	..	.. Two town circles	..⎫	
North-east	..	.. Za-ha ..	..⎪	
Ditto	..	.. Lek-wai-kywon	..⎪	
Ditto	..	.. Za-lwon ..	..⎬Central.	
Ditto	..	.. Kyouk-niaw	..⎪	
Ditto	..	.. Pouk-taing	..⎪	
Ditto	..	.. Met-ta (North)	..⎭	

the interior of the district, or province as it was then called, whilst the
goung also collected the "Municipal", or as then denominated the "Night-
watch", tax. On the formation of the new Police the whole system was
changed. The Extra Assistant Commissioners and Thoogyee no longer
performed any regular Police duties; the goung remained as rural Police,
and the town Police force was swept away, the goung of quarters only
being retained. The new body which formed a portion of a general Police
force for the whole province was placed under a Superintendent generally
subordinate to the Deputy Commissioner, and was entrusted with the
detection and prevention of crime and the arrest of offenders together with
the duty of furnishing guards for the treasury, lock-up, &c., escorts for
prisoners and the protection of the town. The body thus employed in
1877 was one Superintendent, 20 subordinate officers and 178 men, of
whom 10 were river police. Of this number three officers and 27 men were
employed as guards over buildings and as escorts for prisoners and two
officers and 16 men (paid from the Municipal Funds) in the town, leaving
16 officers and 195 men for ordinary police work, that is one man to every
53 square miles and every 580 inhabitants and one officer to every eight
men. The cost of the force in that year was Rs. 49,628.

The census taken in 1872 shewed that this district was by no means
backward in education, that is to say in the spread of a knowledge of
reading and writing, for which it is indebted to the Booddhist monks and
to the American Baptist Missionaries who have so long laboured here. Of
the population 20·55 per cent. of those under 12 years of age, 46·23 of
between 12 and 20, and 41·54 of those above 20 could read and write or
were under instruction, whilst of the females of those ages 1·62, 5·23 and
1·45 per cent. could do so.

In 1868 a school was opened in Tavoy to which the State gave a grant-
in-aid, and in 1875 this was converted into a State district school. In

Old Townships.	Circles.	New Townships.
North-east ..	.. Moot-htee ..	
Ditto ..	.. Kya-eng	
South-east ..	.. Gnyoung-tsen ..	
Ditto ..	.. Thayet-hnit-khwa ..	
Ditto ..	.. Oot-too	
Ditto ..	.. Pan-daw	
Ditto ..	.. Tshee-daw ..	South.
Ditto ..	.. Ra-gnay ..	
Ditto ..	.. Ka-gnyoon-kywon ..	
North-east ..	.. Met-ta (South) ..	
Ditto ..	.. Kyouk-dweng ..	
South-east ..	.. Ka-zee	
Ditto ..	.. Toung-byouk ..	
Ditto ..	.. Ka-dwai	
West ..	.. Moung-ma-gan ..	
Ditto ..	.. Ka-myaw-keng ..	
Ditto ..	.. Eng-won ..	
Ditto ..	.. Eng-zouk ..	
Ditto ..	.. Shwe-kywon ..	West.
Ditto ..	.. Loung-loon ..	
Ditto ..	.. Khadat-ngay ..	
Ditto ..	.. Khadat-gyee ..	
Ditto ..	.. Kyat-yek-dweng ..	
Ditto ..	.. Kyouk-nee-maw ..	

1876-77 it had 69 pupils on the rolls with an average daily attendance of 61. The charges during the year were Rs. 4,628 and the cost of educating each pupil Rs. 75-14-0. There is also a Kareng Mixed Normal school aided by the State by a grant of Rs. 448-8-0. In 1876-77 it had 20 pupils on the rolls.

The hospital and dispensary in Tavoy is a wooden building with a shingled roof, raised nine feet from the ground on posts and well ventilated. In 1877, 3,616 patients, of whom 126 were in-patients, were treated, principally for fevers, rheumatic affections, ophthalmia, respiratory affections and diseases of the digestive system. The income, exclusive of the State grant and the grant from the Municipal Fund, was Rs. 273.

The prison was originally called a gaol when the town was a place of transportation for convicts from Hindustan. On the penal settlement on the Andaman Islands being established no more Indian convicts were sent here and the gaol was, soon afterwards, reduced to a district lock-up. In 1873-74 a new prison was completed and the Civil Medical Officer placed in executive charge and it was raised to the status of a gaol. In 1877 170 convicts, 48 under-trial prisoners and 17 debtors were confined, whilst the total daily average was 56. Every one of the female prisoners was married. The total cost was Rs. 6,404 or Rs. 108-8-0 per head, considerably less than in any one of the three preceding years. The gross receipts from gaol labour with the value of the plant and articles in store were Rs. 6,358, but as the expenditure was Rs. 5,064 the nett gain was only Rs. 1,294.

TAVOY ISLAND.—An island off the coast of Tenasserim somewhat to the south of the mouth of the river Tavoy. In 1875 it was transferred from the Tavoy to the Mergui district. It extends from 12° 55' N. to 13° 13' N. and is about two miles in breadth and about 18 in length, extending N. by W. and S. by E., of middling height, with a peak in the centre and another at the southern end. On the east there is a good and safe harbour with good water and wood, called Port Owen. The caves in the hills are largely tenanted by the edible-nest-building swallow (*Colocalia fuciphaga*) and the right to take the nests is leased out by the State. The birds build in the dark cavernous limestone recesses of the rocks and their nests are of two kinds, light and dark, the latter being the most prized the former having the birds' feathers mixed with the viscous substance, issuing from the crop and beak, of which the nests are made. The nests are gathered by means of a long bamboo pôle with an iron fork at one extremity and a lighted torch at both, the one to shew the nest and the other to shew the barefooted collector where he may securely tread. They are much prized by the Chinese who boil them down into a nutritious soup and nearly all those collected are exported to the Straits and to China.

TAW-BYA.—A sub-tribe of Pwo Kareng. *See Mo-pgha.*

TAW-DAN.—A revenue circle in the Meng-bra township, Akyab district. In 1876-77 the population was 3,368, the land revenue Rs. 3,545, the capitation tax Rs. 2,341 and the gross revenue Rs. 6,103.

TAW-DAW-KYOUNG.—A small village in the Bhan-byeng circle, Thayet township, Thayet district, containing about 50 houses. Formerly a Thoogyee was appointed to the circle which contained this and five other villages of which Pouk-taw was the largest but he was dismissed in 1861 and his circle united to Bhan-byeng. The inhabitants are mainly employed in rice and hill garden cultivation.

TAW-GAN.—A revenue circle in the Oo-ree-toung (west) township of the Akyab district. In 1876-77 the population was 2,118, the land revenue Rs. 6,687, the capitation tax Rs. 2,830 and the gross revenue Rs. 9,819. The principal village is Ma-yen-peng-reng.

TAW-GYEE.—A river in the Bassein district which has its source in the Arakan mountains and after a tortuous course of some 30 miles, the first part of which is in a general S.E. direction and the last almost due south, falls into the Myit-ta-ra river near its mouth, having, nine miles above, sent off some of its waters due eastward to the Bassein river through the Re-gyaw-gyee, by which also it receives the flood tide.

TAW-HAING.—A revenue circle in the Shwe-doung township, Prome district, lying between the Kyee-thay and Gnyoung-tsa-re circles on the west and south and the Shwe-nat-toung or Kho-lan hills on the east, of which the eastern portion is under rice cultivation the western portion being hilly and covered with forest. The largest village is Tha-khwot-koon in the south, but Ma-gyee-bouk and Kan-thoon-thseng in the north are populous places. The inhabitants are principally rice cultivators, gardeners and tari drawers. In 1876-77 the population was 1,934, the land revenue Rs. 2,165, the capitation tax Rs. 2,110 and the gross revenue Rs. 4,297.

TAW-HMWON.—A village on the Pwon stream in the Kwon-oon circle, Thayet township, Thayet district, containing 50 houses. It is close to Re-bwek in the same circle and to Taw-daw-kyoung in the Bhan-byeng circle, the inhabitants of all of which are mostly cultivators.

TAW-KA-MA.—A revenue circle in the Amherst district occupying the southernmost portion of the old township of Daray. It is a long, narrow strip of flat alluvial plain, 6,276 acres in extent much of which is still covered with mangrove jungle, lying between the sea on the west and the Tsai-ba-la creek on the east, having the Kwon-raik circle on the north and the sea on the south. It now includes some land at its northern end which, when the circles were first formed by Captain Phayre, was assigned to Kwon-raik. The soil generally is fertile but some is damaged by the entrance of seawater. In 1868 the population was 472, the land revenue Rs. 7,155 and the capitation tax Rs. 545. In 1877 these were 659, Rs. 9,045 and Rs. 695 respectively.

TAW-KHA-RAN.—A Talaing village in the Taw-koo circle, An-gyee township, Rangoon district, pleasantly situated amongst clumps of bamboos and groves of fruit trees, about four miles west of Taw-koo. Here also are the ruins of one of the 37 great pagodas of An-gyee. The inhabitants, who are principally cultivators and salt-boilers, numbered 1,092 in 1878.

TAW-KOO.—A revenue circle in the An-gyee township of the Rangoon district, carved out of La-wa-dee and Htan-ma-naing some years ago. In 1876-77 the population was 2,440, the land revenue was Rs. 21,101, the capitation tax Rs. 3,928 and the gross revenue Rs. 25,049. The principal villages are Taw-koo and Taw-kha-ran.

TAW-KOO.—A large Talaing village in the Taw-koo circle, An-gyee township, Rangoon district, on a stream of the same name, about five miles from its mouth, built upon a ridge of high sandy ground which has evidently at one time been the seabeach. The houses are shaded by groves of fine fruit trees amongst which Palmyra palms abound. There are numerous monasteries and zayat, or public rest-houses, and the ruins of a large and ancient pagoda, one of the 37 great pagodas of An-gyee erected over the spot where the holy relic which now reposes under the Shwe Tshan-daw at Twan-te rested upon its journey from the seacoast to Kha-beng (near Twan-te). In 1878 it had 1,341 inhabitants.

TAW-LA-TAI.—A village in the circle of the same name, the head-quarters of the Hlaing township on the right bank of the Hlaing at the mouth of the Bhaw-lay. It contains a court-house, forest-office and police station. It consists of three adjoining villages of which Taw-la-tai, the westernmost, had 562 inhabitants in 1878-79.

TAW-LEE.—A revenue circle in the Prome district on the right bank of the Shwe-lay between the Nga-paw and Pa-dek-myoung circles. There is a little rice cultivation along the banks of the Taw-lee stream, a tributary of the Shwe-lay, especially near its mouth where is the village of Taw-lee, but the largest village is Pyan-khyee-tek up amongst the hills in the north. The inhabitants are engaged chiefly in cultivating cotton and garden produce. In 1876-77 the population was 1,045, the land revenue Rs. 612, the capitation tax Rs. 1,383 and the gross revenue Rs. 2,045.

TAW-MA.—A large village in the Kama township, Thayet district, with 649 inhabitants, lying in 19° 8′ 20″ N. and 95° 5′ 20″ E., in the lower portion of the valley of the Ma-htoon and between that river and the Pan-deng hills to the S.W., close to the former. Until 1861 it was the residence of a Thoogyee but in that year it was joined to Kyouk-tsoung.

TAW-NOUK-LAY.—A revenue circle in the Mergui district at the mouth of the Tenasserim river south of Mergui. In 1876-77 the population was 2,233, the land revenue was Rs. 8,422, the capitation tax Rs. 1,384 and the gross revenue Rs. 9,806.

TAW-POO-LWAI.—A village in the La-wa-dee circle, An-gyee township, Rangoon district, with 510 inhabitants in 1877.

TAW-TA-NEE.—A revenue circle in the Pya-poon township of the Thoon-khwa district on the seacoast between the Pya-poon and To (or China Bakeer) rivers. The inhabitants are largely engaged in fishing.

TAW-TA-NO.—A village in the Kywon-pa-douk circle, Shwe-loung township, Thoon-khwa district on the Wa-khay-ma stream and opposite the village of Wa-khay-ma (q.v.) with 575 inhabitants in 1878.

TAW-TOO.—A village lying on the eastern border of the Meng-byeng circle of the Kyouk-hpyoo district, south of the town of Cheduba. A considerable quantity of rice is grown in the neighbourhood. In 1877 it had 613 inhabitants.

TAY-GYEE-GOON.—A village in the Koon-daw circle, Myanoung township, Henzada district, about 16 miles west of the Irrawaddy. In 1878 it had 523 inhabitants.

TAY-GOON.—A village in the Shwe-doung township, Prome district, just to the south of the town of Shwe-doung of which it forms almost a suburb, there being only a few rice fields between the two.

TAY-GOON.—A revenue circle in the Re-gyee township, Bassein district, occupying the angle formed by the junction of the Shwe-gnyoung-beng stream with the Bassein river, with an area of about 48 square miles. It may be described as a large open plain for the most part waste but with tracts of rice cultivation in the centre and west ; near the Bassein river the country is undulating and the soil gravelly. The inhabitants are Burmese, mainly, and are very largely engaged in fishing as an occupation. The largest village is Ma-gyee-goon in 17° 3′ 30″ N. and 94°58′ E. on the Ta-bhoo stream, a tributary of the Bassein river and the northern boundary of the circle, in one of the large patches of rice cultivation. There are a few dry-weather cart roads and many good footpaths to the villages.

TA-ZAN.—A revenue circle in the Mye-dai township, Thayet district, 17 square miles in extent, of which only 238 acres are cultivated, and of these 166 are on the hills and spurs of the Pegu Roma. The population is small and is spread about in small hamlets the largest containing about 40 houses. The Thoogyee died in 1871 and this circle was placed under the Thoogyee of Pya-lo. The products are rice, maize, sessamum and plantains.

TEK-PYOUK.—A revenue circle in the Toung-ngoo district to the west of the Tsit-toung river, well cultivated towards the east but hilly towards the west. The principal trees are Pyeng-gado (Xylia dolabiformis), Pyeng-ma (Lagerstrœmia reginæ) and Tsit (Albizzia alata). It is traversed by the main road from Toung-ngoo to Pegu. In 1877 the population was 3,809, the land revenue was Rs. 3,288, the capitation tax Rs. 2,868 and the gross revenue Rs. 6,320.

TENASSERIM.—A river in the Mergui district formed by the junction at the town of Tenasserim of two streams known by the same name and distinguished as the "Great" and the "Little". The Bhan rises in the northern slopes of the hills which divide Mergui from Tavoy and flows northward for 68 miles in a narrow valley bounded on the west by the Nwa-la-bo and on the east by the Myeng-mo-lek-khat mountains ; rounding the northern slopes of the latter it bends eastward and at Met-ta joins another river, which has its sources in the extreme north of the Tavoy district. The two, now known as the Great Tenasserim, continue southwards for 230 miles between the Myeng-mo-lek-khat and the great range which marks the boundary between British and Siamese territory. Here it turns to the west and 40 miles further on receives the waters of the Little Tenasserim, the two continuing to the sea as the Tenasserim.

There are several outlets to this river : the two principal ones are separated from each other by Mergui island and the southernmost of all falls into Auckland bay about 25 miles south of Mergui the intermediate space being divided into numerous islands by anastomosing creeks. Large boats can ascend as far as Tenasserim, but above this point canoes and even rafts can barely pass. Above Tenasserim the larger river flows " through an alluvial " valley, varying in breadth from five to 20 miles, having a level or slightly " undulating surface but covered with dense jungle, except where Kareng or

" Siamese have made small clearings. The banks are generally high and
" nearly perpendicular ; in some parts, however, the course of the river is
" through low lands, and there are many islands in its bed giving the scenery a
" picturesque character. The channel is in some places so narrowed as to
" occassion rapids which are passed with difficulty at certain periods."* The
tide is felt ten miles above Tenasserim.

The Little Tenasserim is formed by the junction, about 32 miles above
Tenasserim, of the Thien-khwon and the Nga-won. The Thien-khwon has
its source in the main range in about 11° 38′ N. and flows through a highly
mountainous country in a general W.N.W. direction, with one large bend
to the S.W., for about 50 miles to near Tsa-khai village. The Nga-won
rises in an angle formed by the main range and a spur running out from
the Khow Phra hill towards the N.N.W. in about 11° 14′ N. and runs northward for about 50 miles in a much straighter course than the Thien-khwon
but through a very similar country. From the junction of these two
streams the Little Tenasserim runs N.N.W. for some 40 odd miles to the
Great Tenasserim, on reaching which it has attained a breadth of 118 yards.
Both of these streams are fed by numerous mountain torrents of no great
importance pouring down between the ravines formed in the wilderness of
forest-covered hills through which they flow.

TENASSERIM.—A town in the Mergui district of the Tenasserim
division in 18° 8′ N. and 98° 55′ E. : the head-quarters of a township of the
same name. It is built on a neck of land on the left bank at the confluence
of the Great and Little Tenasserim 33 miles from the mouth of the river
and 40 south-east of the town of Mergui on a rock of old red sandstone
and upon the sides and along the lower slopes of an irregular hill about 200
feet high : the surrounding country is a mass of small hills covered with
dense forest.

Once a large and important city it has, owing to conquest by the
Burmese and since then until 1835 to the repeated attacks of the Siamese,
dwindled to a village of 666 (in 1877) inhabitants of mixed Burmese and
Siamese race and of Booddhist religion. Beyond a few pagodas it contains
no brick or masonry buildings of any kind.

Being surrounded by hills it is often enveloped in the mornings in a
dense fog when the thermometer falls to 72°. At midday, when the mists
have been dispersed by the sun the thermometer marks from 90° to 100°,
and these great changes make the climate unhealthy.

It was founded by the Siamese in the year 1373 A.D., and a stone
pillar, now extant, was, tradition asserts, erected as a memorial of its
foundation. The pillar bears no inscription of any kind but a Burmese
legend relates that a woman was buried alive under it as an offering to
the gods for the future success of the town. It was surrounded by a mud
wall faced with brick, the foundations of which are still visible, built in the
form of an octagon and enclosing an area of about four square miles. The
walls long remained in a dilapidated condition and were eventually pulled
down by Captain (now General) McLeod and the bricks used in building a
gaol at Mergui. The accounts given by old travellers of the wealth,
population and trade of this town are hardly credible for, owing to the
nature of the surrounding country, the suburbs can have been but small

* Pharoah's *Gazetteer of Southern India.*

and no very large population could be congregated in an area of four square miles. There are no magnificent pagodas nor any signs of its ancient greatness, and a few miles below the town a reef of rocks runs right across the river over which a moderately-sized ship's cutter can hardly pass in April and at no season could a vessel drawing more than six feet cross it. It is, however, recorded by a very competent authority* that in 1825 the Bombay cruiser *Thetis* sailed up as far as Tenasserim. In 1759 it was taken by the Burmese conqueror Aloung-bhoora, and some years later the inhabitants were put to the sword by the Burmese governor, the Daing-won. From that time till the occupation of the country by the British it remained, owing to the continual inroads of the Siamese, a petty village, a state from which even now it has not recovered.

TENASSERIM.—A township in the Mergui district extending south-wards in a comparatively narrow strip between the great eastern range of mountains and the Pa-law township, and lower down the Le-gnya township, on the west to the sources of the Little Tenasserim. The head-quarters are at Tenasserim at the junction of the Little and the Great Tenasserim. Mountainous and forest-clad there is but little cultivated land and the population, mainly Kareng, is sparse. In 1877 the land revenue was Rs. 6,710, the capitation tax Rs. 4,178 and the gross revenue Rs. 10,888 : in the same year the number of inhabitants was 6,516. It contains only four revenue circles.

TENASSERIM.—A circle in the extreme west of the township of the same name in the Mergui district, lying round about the village of Tenasserim. In 1877 the population was 2,378, the land revenue Rs. 3,860, the capitation tax Rs. 1,440 and the gross revenue Rs. 5,300.

TENG-DAW.—A revenue circle in the Mye-dai township, Thayet district, with an area of 134 square miles. The revenue derived from this tract of country in 1872 was Rs. 3,450 of which Rs. 1,530 were from land and Rs. 1,920 from capitation tax : the population in the same year was 4,159 souls of whom about two-thirds were Burmans. The number of buffaloes was comparatively large—1,566 out of the 2,414 head of cattle in the circle. In 1871 the Peng-ga-daw circle was placed under the Thoogyee of Teng-daw. The products are sessamum, cotton, cutch and silk : about 40 toungya are planted with mulberry trees and the annual yield of silk is estimated at about 500 lbs. In 1877 the land revenue was Rs. 2,209, the capitation tax Rs. 2,918, the gross revenue Rs. 5,237 and the population 5,853.

TENG-GYEE.—A river in the Prome district which rises in the Pegu Roma mountains, in the acute angle formed by the Neepa-tshe spur with the main range which it leaves at the Thoon-myeng-tsaing peak, and after flowing for some distance in a north-westerly direction between the main range on the east and the spur on the south-west receiving the waters of numerous mountain torrents turns west and joins the South Na-weng near the village of Rat-thit. Its two largest affluents are the Bhan-boung and the Myit-loung, both of which rise in the hills to the south and after traversing a comparatively open tract of country past numerous small villages join it close together three or four miles from its mouth not far from the village

---

* General McLeod to whose account of the Tenasserim division I am deeply indebted.

of Myo-doung. To this village small boats can ascend the Teng-gyee in the rainy season. The banks of the stream are steep and the bed rocky. On its banks are found valuable forest trees ; Teak, Pyeng-gado (*Xylia dolabriformis* or *Iron wood*, more durable even than teak), and Cutch (*Acacia catechu*). The distance from the source to the mouth in a direct line is about 23 or 24 miles, but the actual length is much greater owing to its winding amongst the mountains.

THA-BOUNG.—A township in the Bassein district extending across the Arakan mountains to the seacoast on the west. To the south is the Nga-poo-taw township of the same district, separated from it by the Kwon-khyoung and the Than-dwai on the east of the hills and by the Tsheng-ma stream on the west, and east of the Nga-won, on the other side of the Da-ga or Rwe, is the Thee-kweng township. The strip between the Nga-won river and the Roma is separated from the Re-gyee township by the Bho-daw stream, whilst that on the other side of the mountains stretches up north-ward to the Khwa which divides Bassein from Sandoway. The whole of the centre and the greater part of the western portion is mountainous, forest-clad and uncultivated. The richest circles are Kweng-hla and Keng-lat. In 1861 it was carved out of several other townships. The head-quarters are at Tha-boung on the Nga-won. It is divided into 14 revenue circles.

The population and revenue during each of the last five years have been :—

Year.	Population.	Revenue, in Rs.
1874	29,838	86,225
1875	27,631	95,125
1876	31,388	94,375
1877	29,832	86,039
1878	29,391	78,327

THA-BOUNG.—A revenue circle in the township of the same name in the Bassein district separated from Tsit-ta-ran on the north-east by the Ka-gnyeng-khyoung, from Zee-bhyoo-kweng on the south-west by the Thien or O-bho stream and from Bhaw-mee on the north-west by the crest of the Arakan Roma. On the south-east the circle is bounded by the Nga-won river. The country on the north-west is mountainous and forest-clad and such regular cultivation as exists is found near the Nga-won and near the villages.

The population and revenue during each of the last five years were :—

YEAR.	POPULATION.				REVENUE, IN RUPEES.			
	Burmans.	Kareng.	All others.	Total.	Land.	Capitation tax.	All other items.	Total.
1874	1,609	796	—	2,405	3,505	2,612	135	6,252
1875	1,555	804	—	2,359	3,675	2,712	180	6,567
1876	1,616	733	17	2,366	3,654	2,622	180	6,456
1877	1,673	733	18	2,424	3,727	2,557	180	6,465
1878	1,614	769	21	2,404	2,788	2,460	180	5,482

and the area under cultivation and the agricultural stock :—

YEAR.	AREA, IN ACRES.				AGRICULTURAL STOCK.						
	Under rice, including fallow.	Garden.	Miscellaneous.	Total.	Buffaloes.	Cows, bulls and bullocks.	Sheep and goats.	Pigs.	Carts.	Ploughs.	Boats.
1874	2,004	12	6	2,022	1,327	303	29	186	136	275	63
1875	2,137	18	13	2,168	1,245	265	4	127	113	320	49
1876	2,139	20	13	2,172	1,226	218	4	118	129	299	43
1877	2,156	23	4	2,183	1,728	396	16	368	80	192	91
1878	1,683	21	20	1,724	1,582	270	6	242	294	190	92

THA-BOUNG.—A village in the circle and township of the same name, of which it is the head-quarter station, in the Bassein district on the right bank of the Bassein river about 30 miles above Bassein and at the mouth of the Ka-gnyeng-khyoung. It is a poor and untidy village, with a police-station and a court-house on the river bank. In 1877 it had 604 inhabitants. To the west of the village and separated from it by rice-fields is a small swampy lake.

THA-BOUNG.—The northernmost circle in the Donabyoo township of the Thoon-khwa district. In 1877-78 the cultivated area was 1,055 acres, the population 1,689 and the capitation tax Rs. 1,435.

THA-BYAI-KYWON.—A village in the Mee-khyoung-dek circle, Ramree township, Kyouk-hpyoo district, south-east of the Ran-bouk stream. The inhabitants who are principally rice cultivators numbered 649 souls in 1877.

THA-BYE-GAN.—A village in the Poo-gan-doung circle, Than-lyeng township, Rangoon district, with 740 inhabitants in 1878-79.

THA-BYE-GOON.—A village in the Poo-gan-doung circle, Angyee township, Rangoon district, with 665 inhabitants in 1878-79.

THA-BYE-GYEE-TSOO.—A revenue circle in the Prome district to the east of Poung-day. In 1877 the population was 322, the land revenue Rs. 307 and the capitation tax Rs. 431.

THA-BYE-HLA.—A large village in the circle of the same name in the Kyoon-pyaw township, Bassein district, on the western bank of the river Da-ga and 13 miles east of Nga-thaing-khyoung. In 1877 it had 2,304 inhabitants. It was formerly the head-quarters of the Extra Assistant Commissioner in charge of the Mye-noo township which was broken up in 1861.

THA-BYE-HLA.—A village in the Oung-beng-tha circle, Ta-pwon township, Henzada (Tharrawaddy) district, lying a short distance to the west of the road from Poung-day to Ta-pwon. In 1877 it had 501 inhabitants.

THA-BYE-HLA.—A revenue circle in the Prome district, about a mile north of the Wai-gyee river and six east of the Eng-ma swamp. In 1877 the population was 303, the land revenue Rs. 323 and the capitation tax Rs. 345.

THA-BYE-HLA.—A revenue circle in the Mye-noo township, now joined to Re-gyee in the Bassein district, with an area of about 90 square miles, on the right bank of the Da-ga river. There is a fair amount of rice cultivation scattered about the circle in patches near the villages but in many parts the land is low and swampy. The inhabitants are extensively engaged in fishing. None of the villages are large or of much importance. There is a fair cart road skirting the Da-ga to the east.

The population and revenue during each of the last five years were :—

YEAR.	POPULATION.			REVENUE, IN RUPEES.			
	Burmans.	Kareng.	Total.	Land.	Capitation tax.	All other items.	Total.
1874	3,641	2,263	5,904	4,502	6,627	3,725	14,854
1875	4,182	2,462	6,644	7,411	6,930	3,450	17,791
1876	4,396	2,691	7,087	7,746	7,245	3,360	18,351
1877	4,593	2,821	7,414	7,877	7,505	3,370	18,752
1878	5,005	3,095	8,100	8,216	7,577	3,065	18,858

The area under cultivation and the agricultural stock during the same period were :—

YEAR.	AREA, IN ACRES.				AGRICULTURAL STOCK.						
	Rice.	Garden.	Miscellaneous.	Total.	Buffaloes.	Cows, bulls and bullocks.	Sheep and goats.	Pigs.	Carts.	Ploughs.	Boats.
1874 ..	3,542	313	6	3,861	1,013	711	8	137	246	269	22
1875 ..	4,854	1,073	19	5,946	1,275	1,514	14	215	265	443	64
1876 ..	5,096	1,096	9	6,201	1,862	2,493	219	576	333	923	253
1877 ..	5,253	1,136	13	6,402	1,960	3,921	363	741	529	994	321
1878 ..	5,407	1,263	9	6,679	1,880	9,546	664	1,082	584	3,065	196

The principal villages are Pyeng-ma-beng-hla, Thoung-rwa and Tha-bye-hla.

THA-BYE-KA.—A village in the Weng-kywon circle, Oo-reet-toung (east) township, Akyab district, on the eastern bank of the Khyan-koon-dan stream with 552 inhabitants in 1877.

THA-BYE-KHYOUNG.—A village in the Ta-gay circle of the Gnyoung-doon township, Thoon-khwa district, on the Irrawaddy about eight miles north of Gnyoung-doon. In 1878 it had 679 inhabitants.

THA-BYENG-TSOUNG.—A revenue circle in the Kama township, Thayet district, six square miles in extent. Of the 1,000 culturable acres about 500 are actually under cultivation and in 1872 furnished a revenue of Rs. 360, the capitation tax furnishing Rs. 490 more. The population was a little under 500 souls. In 1870 the hereditary Thoogyee resigned on account of insufficiency of income and this circle was then placed under the Nat-mee Thoogyee and in the same year the two combined circles were joined to Toon. The products are rice, tobacco, chillies, onions, sessamum, plantains and maize.

THA-BYE-POUNG-GYEE.—A revenue circle in the Poung-day township, Prome district, stretching up northwards from Wek-poot past Thit-tshien-goon. The northern part is under rice. Reng-daik-tan and Rwa-hla are the most populous villages. The northern portion, Reng-daik-tan, was formerly an independent village tract. In 1877 the population was 2,783, the land revenue Rs. 2,347, the capitation tax Rs. 2,695 and the gross revenue Rs. 5,117.

THA-BYE-ROON.—A village in the Myo-dweng circle of the Henzada (Tharrawaddy) district, about two miles east of the R. and I. V. (State) Railway. In 1877 it had 555 inhabitants.

THA-BYOO.—A revenue circle in the Donabyoo township of the Thoon-khwa district, 70 square miles in extent. In 1877-78 the area under cultivation was 6,750 acres, the population was 5,728, the land revenue Rs. 11,916, the capitation tax Rs. 6,043 and the gross revenue Rs. 20,474.

THA-BYOO.—A village on the left bank of the river Pegu in the Gnyoung-beng circle of the Pegu township, Rangoon district, about eight miles below Ka-wa. In 1878 it had a population of 797 souls, who were chiefly Talaing.

THA-BYOO-KYWON.—A small village in the Kywon-ga-le circle, Hpoung-leng township, Rangoon district. In 1878 it had 519 inhabitants.

THA-DWOT.—A small stream in the Prome district which rises in the Neepa-tshe spur of the Pegu Roma and, flowing south-west, falls into the Too, one of the numerous anastomosing channels which unite the Zay above and the Myit-ma-kha below the Eng-ma lake, with the Wai-gyee or Shwe-lay (*q.v.*). Its banks are moderately steep and its bed sandy and gravelly. On its banks, especially amongst the hills, are found Bhan-bhwai (*Careya arborea*), Pyeng-ga-do (*Xylia dolabriformis*), Eng-gyeng (*Hopea suava*), Eng (*Dipterocarpus tuberculatus*) and Sha (*Acacia catechu*).

THA-GA-RA.—The northern township of the Toung-ngoo district extending from the frontier southwards on both banks of the Tsit-toung to the Toung-ngoo township on the west, and the Bhoom-ma-wad-dee township on the east, and stretching from the Pegu Roma mountains eastward to the western borders of the Toung-ngoo hill tracts sub-division which commences at the western slopes of the Poung-loung range. On the west the country is hilly, intersected by the numerous spurs thrown off by the boundary range and clothed with dense tree and bamboo forest, where are found Teak, Pyeng-ma, Sha, Thit-tsee and Eng besides other trees of economical value. On the east the country consists of a narrow strip of level plain, partly cultivated with rice and elsewhere covered with tree and grass forest, intersected by numerous fair-weather cart tracks. On the west bank a fairly good road runs from the south towards the frontier. None of the villages are large or of great importance. For the protection of the country a chain of police-posts extends from east to west a few miles below the frontier line.

The inhabitants numbered 13,018 in 1878, and during the same year the land revenue was Rs. 3,457, the capitation tax Rs. 9,503 and the gross revenue Rs. 14,092. The township is divided into six revenue circles. The head-quarters are at Pie-too in the Kai-leng circle, to the west of the Tsit-toung.

THA-GA-RA.—A revenue circle in the Toung-ngoo district, on the left bank of the Tsit-toung south of Myo-hla. The country is generally level and some rice cultivation is carried on near the river bank. In 1878 the population was 738, the land revenue Rs. 96, the capitation tax Rs. 546 and the gross revenue Rs. 736.

THA-HPAN-KHYO.—A revenue circle in the Poung-day township, Prome district, between the town of Poung-day and the river Kyat. It contains only one large village, which is an extension of Poung-day itself. In 1878 the population was 2,413, the land revenue Rs. 2,401, the capitation tax Rs. 2,348 and the gross revenue Rs. 5,074.

THA-HPAN-KHYO.—A revenue circle in the Prome district about six miles east of the head of the Engma swamp. In 1878 the population was 3,430, the land revenue Rs. 2,757, the capitation tax Rs. 3,782 and the gross revenue Rs. 6,568.

THA-HPAN-KHYO.—A large village in the circle of the same name, Poung-day township, Prome district, two miles north-east of Poung-day. In 1878 it had 2,133 inhabitants.

THA-HTOON.—A township lying in the north-western corner of the Tha-htoon sub-division of the Amherst district. On the north, beyond the Kyoon-iek creek, is the Shwe-gyeng district ; on the east, beyond the Kyouk-tsa-rit and Bheng-laing rivers, the Hpagat township ; on the south and separated by the Gaw and the lower portion of the Tsha or Tha-htoon river is the Martaban township ; and on the west, beyond the Bhee-leng river, lies the Shwe-gyeng district. Stretching up northwards, near the eastern border of the township, is a range of hills, a continuation of the Martaban mountains, which rises from the gap through which the river Gaw flows, and attaining its greatest altitude near Tha-htoon gradually sinks and disappears, near the Kyoon-iek, in the Ka-ma-thaing hill. East of this line of hills there is a narrow strip of forest-clad and but slightly-cultivated country, closed in on the east by the Kyouk-tsa-rit and lower down by the Bheng-laing formed by the junction of the Kyouk-tsa-rit with the Doon-tha-mie. Stretching away westward to the Bhee-leng are extensive plains, partially under rice but liable to inundation and, therefore, to a great extent unculturable. This inundation is partly due to the spill of the Bhee-leng directly over its banks and formerly indirectly through the Kyoon-iek which

runs from the Bhee-leng to the Kyouk-tsa-rit. When the Bhee-leng enters
in flood the Kyouk-tsa-rit almost certainly does so also and its waters bank
up those coming in through the Kyoon-iek and thus the northern portion of
the Tha-htoon plain became flooded and as all the outlets are into the Bhee-
leng the water could not escape. Some of it, if the rise was high, found its
way over the low rising ground which divides the plain into a northern or
Thien-tshiep portion and a southern or Tha-htoon portion and, added to the
rainfall, flooded that also, as the mouths of the Tha-htoon and other rivers
have been gradually choked by the silt brought up by the tide. An embankment has been thrown across the northern extremity of the plain from the
Ka-ma-thaing hill to the high bank of the Bhee-leng at Doon-won and this
now affords some protection, but other embankments are wanted and the
outlet channels require improving. At present, except in some spots, if the
rice is planted before the rains in the hopes of its having grown sufficiently
before the floods to overtop them the grain is destroyed by field-mice; if
later the plants are submerged and killed.

Running almost parallel to the hills and at no great distance from
them on their western side is the Tha-htoon river, which after passing
Tha-htoon turns westward and flows past Kaw-than towards the sea.
Between this river and the hills are the most important villages,
Mye-nee-goon and Thien-tshiep which with smaller intermediate ones form
a long and almost continuous line. The township is divided into five
revenue circles and in 1877 produced a gross revenue of Rs. 54,106, of
which Rs. 33,213 were derived from the land and Rs. 28,093 from the capitation tax. In that year the population numbered 21,955 souls.

THA-HTOON.—A revenue circle in the township of the same name in
the Amherst district, in which is Tha-htoon, the head-quarter station of the
township and of the sub-division. In 1877 the population was 3,650, the
land revenue Rs. 5,964 and the capitation tax Rs. 7,527.

THA-HTOON.—A town, with 3,126 inhabitants in 1877, in the Amherst
district, the head-quarters of the township and of the sub-division of the
same name, situated on the eastern edge of the Tha-htoon plain on the
lower slopes of the line of hills which form the western watershed of the
rivers Kyouk-tsa-rit and Bheng-laing and facing the extensive Dhe-ba-rien
valley.

The town now is small and of but little importance but it is one of
the earliest mentioned in Talaing history. Some centuries before Christ
it was the capital of an independent kingdom, inhabited it would seem by
people of an Indian stock from Talingana a name which remains in
" Talaing " the designation amongst the Burmese of the Peguans, called by
themselves "Moon." In the native histories the foundation of the city
is stated to have taken place in the 17th century B.C., but the first account
on which any reliance can be placed is that which relates to the arrival of
Thawna and Oot-tara, missionaries sent to Suvarna-bhoom-mie by the great
Booddhist council held in 241 B.C., who landed at Tha-htoon when it was
a seaport town, a position taken from it by the gradual upheaval of the
coast. Some centuries later a religious envoy was sent hence to Ceylon to
learn more perfectly the doctrines of the Booddha and to procure copies of
the Pee-ta-gat or Booddhist scriptures. After this the town gradually

decreased in wealth and in importance and its place was taken by Pegu, founded in the sixth century A.D. by Tha-ma-la and Wee-ma-la, sons of the king of Tha-htoon, who had been driven out of their father's kingdom. "The city appears to have been laid out on the general plan of ancient "Indian cities, a plan which has been followed in the modern capital of "Burma. The ground plan of the outèr rampart is a square or oblong "within which is an open space of about 153 feet, and then a second but "lower wall, or rampart, and moat. The east and west inner walls are "each 7,700 feet long, while those on the north and south are about "4,000 feet each, enclosing a space of about 700 acres. The angles, how- "ever, are not exact right angles. In the centre of the city is the fortified "royal citadel, measuring from north to south 1,080 feet, and from east "to west 1,150 feet. This was for the defence of the palace, the "'throne-room' being, as is now the case at the Burmese capital, nearly "the centre point of the city. There are two gates or spaces for entrance "in the northern and southern faces of the rampart, but it is impossible "to say how many on the eastern or western. Of the citadel no remains "exist save those of a small pagoda at one corner, the shape of which is "not discernible. The walls are of earth and in some places much "worn away, but some places appear to have been faced with rough "stones."

At about the end of the 10th century, A-naw-ra-hta, king of Burma, overran and annexed Pegu and though no mention is made of the siege and capture of Pegu, the capital, the taking of Tha-htoon is described at length in the Burmese histories. After this Tha-htoon ceased to be of any importance.

"The chief remains of pagodas are situated between the site of the "citadel and the south wall. At present, the largest is a modern one, of "the usual form, built over an old one; near it are three square ones. The "principal of these lies on the eastern side of the great pagoda and though "fast falling into decay still exhibits signs of having once been a beautiful "and eleborate structure. It is built entirely (as are almost all pagodas "in that part of the country which was inhabited by the Talaing) of hewn "laterite. The lower base is 104 feet square and 18 feet high; the second "storey 70 feet square and 16½ feet high; above this is another storey, 48 "feet square and 12 feet high, upon which, again, there is a round pagoda, "the whole structure being about 85 feet in height, but as the two last "parts, viz., the third storey and bell, have been re-built it is impossible to "say what was the original height. I believe that the three square storeys "were in all about 45 feet but, judging from another unrepaired pagoda, "I am of opinion that the bell was more squat than the present, and more "in the shape of a round stupa or topee. The whole face of the pagoda has "been carved in patterns, but the most remarkable part is the second "storey to which access is given by four flights of steps, one in the centre "of each face. About half way up the face are recesses about four inches "deep and two feet three and a half inches by two feet three inches. Into "these are let red clay entablatures on which various figures are depicted "in relief. Few now remain, and they are much multilated: the scenes and "costumes depicted however are very curious. A few I have copied roughly "and will endeavour to describe :—

" (1.)—Four hideous and bearded individuals, riding closely packed
" on the back of an elephant, are pelted with stones by two youths on foot
" behind with their waistcloths tucked up. One of the figures on the elephant
" has his hair done in a knot on the forehead, like a Shan or Kareng; but the
" youths behind have a large knot at the back,—a fashion not now known
" anywhere in Burma or eastwards (though usual in Orissa, I believe)."

" (2).—Represents an equestrian figure with royal head-dress on the
" left, whilst on the right is a standing figure with a royal dress to whom
" an attendant appears to be talking. The ground-work of the piece is a
" series of wavy lines."

" (3).—A small side-piece represents a prince kneeling and offering a
" kind of candelabra."

" (4).—A prince or governor sitting under umbrellas with a man
" kneeling on the left and talking to him with a smile on his countenance.
" In front of the kneeling figure is something which looks like a small box.
" The head of the prince has been knocked off, but I am inclined to think
" from the dress that it is only a governor. Below is a pony tied to a post
" and an attendant kneeling. Both kneeling figures have their hair done
" in a large knot at the side and the upper figure has a sort of halo round
" his head ; but otherwise the clothing is a simple waistcloth, but tucked
" up,—an unusual thing when in the presence of a great man."

" (5).—Is much mutilated and all that can be discerned is a woman
" kneeling before a standing prince whilst in front is a man on a four-wheeled
" cart drawn by a pony."

" (6).—In the upper part are a man and woman, well dressed, riding on
" a four-wheeled cart drawn by ponies. The shape of the cart is curious.
" Below is a potter's shop, shewing a man turning the wheel whilst one
" forms the pot and another, behind, kneads a lump of clay. Pots stand
" on the shelves. All the figures have enormous knots of hair at the back
" of the head."

" (7).—A princess seated amongst her women, whilst one of them has
" got hold of the end of a rope round the neck of a man below the floor.
" The women all wear the Burmese petticoat. What this represents I
" cannot conceive, unless it is connected with a curious custom of the Talaing.
" In every house there is a room where the girls sleep and in the floor of
" this there is a hole. When young men go courting they come under the
" house and, putting their hands through the hole, wake up the young lady
" inside. She, by a certain sign or feel of the hand, immediately knows if
" it is the right man ; should another man come for whom she does not
" care, woe betide him."

" (8).—A king seated on his throne with an attendant standing on each
" side, with the usual hair knot and short tucked-up waist-cloth."

" (9).—A king seated on a throne with persons kneeling before him. In
" the background a man is undergoing punishment with the elbow*."

" (10.)—This is broken in two but the upper compartment shews a man
" in a garden or forest holding an enormous serpent, half of which has been
" broken off ; below, a prince is seated on the ground, whilst three princesses

---

* The person to be punished is made to kneel down and bend forward and is struck on the
back between the shoulders and somewhat lower by the elbow of the punisher : the pain
caused is great.

" kneel on his left, one behind the other. All have a head-dress of " Nagas "
" heads, but the cloths are of the Burmese or Talaing style. I note that
" Dr. Hunter observed a figure similar to that in the upper compartment in
" one of the Orissan rock-cut temples and was unable to conjecture the
" meaning of it.

" (11).—On the left, is a king seated on his throne, whilst an attendant,
" kneeling, announces the arrival of a queen, who appears on the right,
" carried aloft in a seat on the shoulders of four men. Her head-dress is very
" grand and her countenance grave. Behind appear umbrellas, fans and
" fly-flappers.

" (12).—A prince standing on the back of a man who is stretched on the
" ground. A figure in front has hold of a man's hair with one hand whilst
" the other holds a sword. Behind are two kneeling women and around are
" elephants, buffaloes, pigs and other animals. Bas-reliefs of a very similar
" nature are depicted opposite page 164 of Colonel Yule's *Mission to Ava* as
" set round platforms in a monastery at Amarapoora, but these were cut in
" sandstone."

" There can be no doubt that this is one of the most remarkable pagodas
" in Burma ; but I very much fear that the date of its building cannot now be
" decided, except by opening it, unless some information can be got from the
" Talaing who once lived on the spot but who emigrated in a body to Siam
" in the time of Aloung-bhoora (Alompra). The shape of it is said by
" Sinhalese priests who have visited it to be identical with that of the
" Sinhalese pagodas or *dagopas*. Are we, then, to assign it to Booddhaga-
" sha's era ? If so, it must be about 1,380 years old. Another curious
" question also arises,—how is it that the Talaing and Burmese have rejected
" this shape of pagoda, if it be the orthodox one, and at what date did they
" reject it ? It may be that there were two forms brought from Ceylon and
" that the present one suited their eye (which abhors a straight line) better
" than the square."

" Near this pagoda are some large stones covered with writing but so
" worn as to be unreadable : the letters, however, appear to be Talaing. On
" the eastern side of the pagoda is a fine deep tank, about 200 feet square, at
" the bottom of which it is said there is a great bell.

" Near the centre of the west side of the town, and outside of the inner
" wall, is a tank about 150 feet square ; and at the north-east angle, between
" the outer and inner walls, is also another large tank. There are also a
" good many remains of old pagodas, almost all of the square shape, but
" very dilapidated and shewing signs of having been opened by Toungthoo
" and others in their search for hidden treasure. To the east of the pagoda
" tank is an acre or two of ground thickly covered with remains of small
" pagodas, three or four feet high, composed of laterite rings growing
" gradually smaller, and surmounted by a block in the shape of the large bud
" at the end of a plantain bunch. It is not known what these pagodas are
" as they are not seen elsewhere near large pagodas or in numbers. Some
" have been opened and found to contain a deposit of bits of charcoal and
" broken pots. It may have been the custom to erect them over the ashes
" of relatives, or they may have been erected by the victorious army of
" Anaw-ra-hta." *

---

* Notes by Mr. St. John, formerly Assistant Commissioner of Tha-htoon.

THAI-DAW.—A revenue circle in the south-eastern corner of the Thayet township, Thayet district, on the right bank of the Irrawaddy. Out of the 11 square miles contained in the circle no less than eight are unculturable, and of the remaining three rather over one is actually under cultivation, part of it by hill clearings. In 1872 the population numbered 1,886 and in 1877 1,695 souls, of whom a large number live in the village of Htoon-doung on the bank of the river near a hill from which limestone is quarried. Exclusive of lime, the products are rice, plantains and custard-apples. The revenue derived from this circle in 1872 aggregated Rs. 1,920, *viz.*, Rs. 410 from land, Rs. 100 from fisheries and Rs. 1,410 from capitation tax. In 1877 the land revenue was Rs. 446, the capitation tax Rs. 1,788 and the gross revenue Rs. 2,406.

THAI-GAN.—A revenue circle in the Ra-thai-doung township of the Akyab district. In 1877 the population was 6,564, the land revenue Rs. 15,942, the capitation tax Rs. 5,750 and the gross revenue Rs. 22,508.

THAI-GOON.—An inland village in the Dai-da-rai circle, Pya-poon township, Thoon-khwa district, about four miles from the To and south of Dai-da-rai. In 1878 it had 601 inhabitants.

THAI-GOON.—A village of only 346 inhabitants in 1878 in the Tha-hpan-khyo circle, Poung-day township, Prome district, west of Poung-day and close to the left bank of the Shwe-lay or Wek-poot stream and on the Rangoon and Irrawaddy Valley (State) Railway, where the Extra Assistant Commissioner in charge of the township now resides and hold his Court, having been transferred thither from Poung-day shortly after an Assistant Commissioner was stationed in that town. It contains a court-house, police-station, market and railway-station.

THAI-HPYOO.—A small village in the Zhe-khyoung circle, Bassein township, Bassein district on the west bank of the Pai-beng river and about four miles east of Bassein. In 1878 it had 505 inhabitants.

THAI-HPYOO.—A river in the Henzada (Tharawaddy) district which has its source in the Pegu Roma and after a south and west course of about 24 miles falls into the Myit-ma-kha or Hlaing at Bhee-leng.

THAI-HPYOO.—A river in the Shwe-gyeng district, which rises in the hills north of Bhee-leng and flows for some distance parallel to the Bhee-leng river. When in about the latitude of Bhee-leng it turns westward and, flowing through the low country and during the rains united with the numerous creeks in that tract and navigable there by large boats, it falls into the Tsit-toung at its mouth a little south of the Ka-dat.

THAI-HPYOO-KHYOUNG.—A village in the Myaing-gyee circle of the Hpa-gat township, Amherst district with 534 inhabitants in 1877.

THAI-KHYOUNG.—A revenue circle in the south-eastern township of the Tavoy district, sparsely inhabited by Kareng and with very little cultivated area, in which is grown mainly sessamum and betel-nut trees. It is now joined to Toung-byouk.

THA-KHWOT-KOON.—A village in the Taw-haing circle of the Shwe-doung township, Prome district, in 18° 34′ 5″ N. and 95° 15′ 50″ E. between the Irrawaddy and the Shwe-nat-toung hills, about eight miles east of the former and a mile and a half from the crest of the latter and eight miles S.E. of Kyee-thay, with which as with most of the surrounding villages it is connected by good dry-weather cart roads. In 1878 it had 540 inhabitants.

THA-KHWOT-PENG.—A tidal creek in the Rangoon district, in English generally called the Bassein creek. It forms a channel between the Rangoon and the China Bakeer or To rivers, the entrance on the side of the former being about 10 miles from its mouth. From thence it follows a S.S.W. course and debouches upon the To about two and a half miles from the sea. The direct distance between its mouths is 19 miles but its length is 25. During the rainy season this creek has a steady current downwards, and its water is sweet but muddy : at other periods of the year it is affected by the tide from the Rangoon river and from the To which meet near the mouth of the Htan-ma-naing, about seven miles from the Rangoon river. During the springs in the dry season two small bores are formed, that from the To being the larger. Throughout the creek there is a depth of about two fathoms at low water, but the entrance from the Rangoon river is obstructed by shoals and the river steamers have to wait for about half flood before they can enter. During the dry season this creek is the only practicable route between Rangoon and the Irrawaddy for steamers and large boats. The banks are steep, muddy and covered with low forest.

THAI-KYAI.—A revenue circle in the Prome district between the North and South Na-weng rivers near their junction. In 1878 the population was 591, the land revenue Rs. 291, the capitation tax Rs. 450 and the gross revenue Rs. 751.

THA-LAY.—A revenue circle in the Oo-reet-toung (east) township of the Akyab district. In 1876-77 the population was 1,282, the capitation tax Rs. 1,407, the land revenue Rs. 4,656 and the gross revenue Rs. 6,311.

THA-LE-DAN.—A river in the Pa-doung township, Prome district, which falls into the Irrawaddy at the village of Tha-le-dan, from which it takes its name, and is formed by the junction, at the village of Ma-toung situated amongst the hills, of two streams, the North and the South Tha-le-dan.

The North Tha-le-dan rises in the Arakan mountains at the foot of the spur along which passes the Toung-goop road into Arakan, and just below the Tha-bye halting-place. Winding amongst the hills and receiving the waters of many mountain torrents it reaches, four or five miles from the Irrawaddy, a comparatively level and cultivated tract where it turns eastward. It is navigable for boats during the rains for a short distance. It traverses a country rich in teak and other forest timber, of which large quantities are every rainy season floated down to the Irrawaddy. The area of the country drained by this river and its tributaries is about 210 square miles. The South Tha-le-dan, which is never navigable by boats, rises in the Arakan hills considerably to the south of the source of the North Tha-le-dan and flows in a north-easterly direction to that river. The hills amongst which it wanders are covered with Teak (*Tectona grandis*), Pyeng-gado (*Xyla dolabriformis*) and Htouk-kyan (*Terminalia macrocarpa*) and the timber is floated down it to Ma-toung and thence by the North Tha-le-dan to the Irrawaddy.

THA-LE-DAN.—A village in the Pa-doung township Prome district, in 18° 33′ 10″ N. and 95° 8′ 30″ E. on the right bank of the Irrawaddy at the mouth of the Tha-le-dan river. The inhabitants are mainly cultivators, and traders who supply the boatmen and raftsmen on the river and the inhabitants of the inland villages.

THA-LOO-DOUNG.—A revenue circle in the Kyouk-hpyoo district, near the centre of Ramree island, with an area of 15 square miles and a population in 1875 of 3,315 souls, principally Arakanese. The land revenue in that year amounted to Rs. 4,122 and the capitation tax Rs. 3,717. The principal manufactures are indigo, pots for salt-boiling and sugar : 23 sugar mills were at work in 1875. In 1877 the population was 3,261, the land revenue Rs. 4,097, the capitation tax Rs. 3,625 and the gross revenue Rs. 7,927.

THA-LOON-DOUNG.—A revenue circle in the Oo-reet-toung (east) township of the Akyab district. In 1876-77 the population was 928, the capitation tax Rs. 1,125, the land revenue Rs. 3,729 and the gross revenue Rs. 5,079.

THA-LOUNG-BYENG.—A revenue circle in the Meng-wa township of the Akyab district. In 1876-77 the population was 2,519, the capitation tax Rs. 3,144, the land revenue Rs. 3,721 and the gross revenue Rs. 7,077.

THA-MAING.—A large village in the Rangoon district about one and a half miles to the east of the Hlaing river in 17° 1′ 20″ N. and 96° 27′ E. on the Rangoon and Irrawaddy Valley (State) Railway, near an extensive rice plain in cultivating which and in petty trading the inhabitants are chiefly engaged. In 1878 it had a population of 891 souls.

THA-MAING.—A village in the Ka-baing circle, Henzada township of the Henzada district, about 12 miles west of Henzada which had 664 inhabitants in 1877.

THA-MAN-DE-WA.—A revenue circle in the Nga-poo-taw township, Bassein district, extending northwards from the Myit-tara river between the Arakan hills and the Bassein. The general aspect of this circle is undulating and hilly, consisting of low hills reaching back to the Arakan Roma and rising in height to the north and west and covered with bamboos and tree forest. The south-eastern parts includes Long island, a long stretch of jungly ground with a low line of hills along its eastern side parallel to the shore. This island divides the Bassein river into two channels, the eastern of which only is navigable by large vessels, and in this are some formidable rocks called the *Sesostris* rocks, which have eight feet of water over them. The Myit-tara is the only river of any importance. The circle contains no large villages ; the inhabitants are mainly cultivators and fishermen. Near the two villages of Tha-man-de-wa in 16° 25′ N. and 94° 45′ and Kyouk-theng-bhaw, a short distance above it, is found a considerable quantity of limestone which is worked by the neighbouring inhabitants. At Kyouk-theng-bhaw the quantity is considerable but near Tha-man-dewa " the quantity is inexhaustible, the quality good, and the " access easy."*

---

* Mr. Blanford of the Geological Survey of India.

The population and revenue during each of the last five years were:—

YEAR.	POPULATION.			REVENUE, IN RUPEES.			
	Burmans.	Kareng.	Total.	Land.	Capitation tax.	All other items.	Total.
1874	906	1,678	2,584	4,057	2,895	684	7,636
1875	973	1,746	2,719	4,686	3,000	1,200	8,886
1876	1,011	1,801	2,812	5,417	3,087	1,260	9,764
1877	1,089	1,834	2,923	5,432	3,127	570	9,129
1878	992	1,877	2,869	6,059	3,077	1,314	10,450

The area under cultivation and the agricultural stock during the same period were:—

YEAR.	AREA, IN ACRES.				AGRICULTURAL STOCK.							
	Rice.	Garden.	Miscellaneous.	Total.	Buffaloes.	Cows, bulls and bullocks.	Sheep and goats.	Pigs.	Carts.	Ploughs.	Boats.
1874 ..	2,759	7	1	2,764	1,764	50	10	1,158	167	442	70
1875 ..	3,085	12	20	3,117	1,816	57	4	1,272	235	470	129
1876 ..	3,564	14	6	3,584	1,311	57	5	1,576	238	476	126
1877 ..	3,474	14	5	3,493	1,611	204	—	944	209	359	94
1878 ..	3,942	16	23	3,981	1,417	44	—	1,044	178	856	195

THAM-BAN-DENG.—A revenue circle in the Prome district on the right bank of the Irrawaddy a short distance below Pa-doung and including several islands in the river, on one of which, Mya-tsien-kywon, is the largest village in the circle, named after the island. The inhabitants of the circle are petty traders, cultivators and fishermen and in 1877 numbered 1,952 souls. In that year the land revenue was Rs. 1,915, the capitation tax Rs. 1,893 and the gross revenue Rs. 4,219.

THAM-BHA-RA.—A revenue circle in the Ka-ma township, Thayet district, in the valley of the Ma-htoon river, with an area of 13 square miles, of which about 1,600 acres are cultivated, a population of 2,690 souls, principally Burmans, and a gross revenue of Rs. 3,360 in 1872. Its largest village is Tham-bha-ra on the banks of the Ma-htoon, containing 567 inhabitants. Until 1858 Re-nan-tha, which now forms a portion of Tham-bha-ra, was under a separate Thoogyee on whose death in that year the two circles were amalgamated. In 1872 O-shit-goon (q. v.) was placed under the Thoogyee of this circle. In 1877 the land revenue was Rs. 3,567, the capitation tax Rs. 2,915, the gross revenue Rs. 6,744 and the population 2,690.

THAM-BHA-RA.—A village in the circle of the same name in the Thayet district on the banks of the Ma-htoon with 567 inhabitants in 1878, principally cultivators and wood-cutters.

THAM-BHA-YA-DAING.—A village in the Re-gyaw circle, Henzada township, Henzada district, on the west or right bank of the Irrawaddy a few miles above Henzada and four miles east of Oot-hpo. The majority of the inhabitants, of whom there were 1,275 in 1878, are petty traders or gardeners who cultivate cotton, sessamum, tobacco and vegetables.

THAM-BHA-YA-KHOON.—A village in the Re-gyee circle of the Henzada (Tharrawaddy) district, about two miles east of the Irrawaddy. In 1877 it had 617 inhabitants.

THAM-BHOO-LA.—A revenue circle in the Mye-dai township, Thayet district, composed of some 17 or more registered circles. The area is about 200 square miles of which some ten are cultivated and of these only about 30,000 acres are under regular cultivation, the rest being toungya. The revenue in 1872 amounted to Rs. 7,630, of which Rs. 3,170 were derived from the land and Rs. 4,460 from capitation tax. The inhabitants in the same year numbered 11,275 souls of whom 1,888 were Khyeng, and the cattle in the circle were shewn in the census returns as 5,279 head, of which 4,621 were bullocks. There are a considerable number of villages. Nwa-hta was formerly a separate circle, the last Thoogyee of which, before the annexation of Pegu, sold his birthright for a pony to the Thoogyee of Tham-bhoo-la who was transported for life in 1866. Hpoung-ro and Gnyoung-bhoo-khek, which constituted the Hpoung-ro circle, were joined to Tham-bhoo-la in the same year on the death of the then Thoogyee. Before 1853 Tham-bhoo-la was the head-quarters of the Kaw-tham-bee Taik Thoogyeeship, an independent jurisdiction under the Myo-thoogyee or Myo-won of Mye-dai.

The products are rice, sessamum, excellent cotton, plantains, maize and cutch. In 1877 the population was 11,034, the capitation tax Rs. 5,763, the land revenue Rs. 5,205 and the gross revenue Rs. 11,800.

THAM-BHOO-LA.—A small village in the circle of the same name in the Mye-dai township, Thayet district, on the Pa-de stream, between and close to Rwa-thit and Thayet-tsoo, the three together containing about 150 houses. A force of the Frontier Police is stationed here. In the Burmese time it was the head-quarters of the Kaw-tham-bee Taik Thoo-gyee, the last of whom built a very fine monastery, subsequently used by the British as a barrack, which is now rapidly falling into decay. This Thoogyee, Moung Poon Oung, escaped to Upper Burma on the annexation, carrying off many of the inhabitants, and was made Thoogyee of that portion of his old circle which is north of the frontier line. For some years after the annexation a detachment of troops from Thayetmyo was stationed here, this was subsequently relieved by a detachment of the Pegu Light Infantry, a local battalion. The military were finally withdrawn in 1861 since when Tham-bhoo-la has been a police-post.

THA-MEE-HLA.—A revenue circle in the Oo-reet-toung (west) township of the Akyab district. In 1876-77 the population was 4,053, the capitation tax Rs. 3,260, the land revenue Rs. 4,091 and the gross revenue Rs. 7,610.

THA-MEE-HLA-BYENG.—A revenue circle in the Ra-thai-doung township, Akyab district. In 1877 the population was 3,012, the capitation tax Rs. 3,384, the land revenue Rs. 7,066 and the gross revenue Rs. 10,933.

THA-MEE-HLA-KYWON.—*See Diamond Island.*

THA-NAT-PENG.—A village in the Pegu circle, Pegu township, Rangoon district, on the Pegu and Tsit-toung canal. In 1878 it had 691 inhabitants.

THA-NAT-PENG.—A village in the Paing-kywon circle, Pegu township, Rangoon district, with 601 inhabitants in 1878-79.

THAN-DWAI.—A river in the Bassein district formed by the junction of the Kyek-too-rwe Re-gyaw and the Ta-la-khwa and Kyek-too-rwe rivers. The Kyek-too-rwe Re-gyaw leaves the Kyouk-khoung-gyee river about five miles from its mouth and flows southwards. After a winding course of about eight miles it is joined by the Ta-la-khwa from the westward, and three miles further on by the Kyek-too-rwe from the same direction. For 14 miles more, receiving the waters of the Nga-khwa and Mai-za-lee from the west and communicating by creeks with the Hpek-rai on the east, it continues to flow southwards, when it bends sharply to the east and, joined by the Kwon at the elbow of the curve and by the Hpek-rai itself a little further on, falls into the Bassein river just opposite the northern end of Nga-poo-taw island. Large vessels can enter the mouth of this stream, and ascend as far as the Kwon, a distance of about six miles ; the largest native boats can go up about 14 miles further as far as the mouth of the Ta-khwon, one of the channels by which it communicates with the Hpek-rai ; above this point only small boats can pass with the flood tide, and these, owing to the overhanging foliage cannot use masts. Across the mouth is a bar with 20 feet of water inside of which the depth of the stream increases to 40 feet, gradually decreasing to 28 at the mouth of the Kwon.

THA-NEE.—A river in the Prome district, flowing through the Pa-doung township on the western bank of the Irrawaddy. It rises in the eastern slopes of the Arakan mountains in the extreme north-western angle of the district and after running in an easterly direction in a narrow valley between two spurs for some 20 miles it turns south-south-east, rounding the foot of the southern spur which confined it, and falls into the Irrawaddy near the village of Pai-gyee, after receiving the waters of many tributaries, the two largest of which are the Bhoo-ro and the Kyouk-bhoo. The latter portion of its course is through cultivated plains. Its banks are steep and the bed towards the source is rocky. In the rainy season boats of 80 bushels burden can ascend for about 20 miles as far as the village of Zayat-hla. Teak and other valuable timber is met with on its banks and during the rains is brought down into the Irrawaddy to be rafted.

THAN-HTIEP.—A tidal creek in the Thoon-khwa district ; a branch of the To or China Bakeer which, with the Doon-ran (a similar branch) forms the large island known by as Hmaw-bhee Island. The northern mouth of this creek is marked by several islands of which that called Htwon-paw is the largest, comprising an area of four or five square miles. From the southern extremity of this island to the sea (a distance of about nine miles)

724

the Than-htiep runs in a direction nearly due south. It is tidal throughout and at ebb tide in the month of February the water is sweet at about seven miles from the sea and at that time even near the mouth it is merely brackish. The banks are somewhat steep and muddy and are everywhere covered with dense forest.

THAN-HTOUNG.—A revenue circle in the Kyouk-hpyoo district on the north-eastern coast of Ramree island and on the south bank of the Meng-yat, with an area of 38 square miles and a population of 2,677 souls in 1877. Sugar-cane is largely grown and the principal manufactures are sugar—53 sugar mills were at work in 1875,—salt and earthen pots for salt-boiling. The land revenue in 1877 was Rs. 2,741 the capitation tax Rs. 3,077 and the gross revenue Rs. 6,635.

THAN-KHYOUNG.—A revenue circle in the Kyouk-hpyoo district on the south-west coast of Ramree island, 22 square miles in extent, cultivated largely with sugar-cane, for crushing which 235 mills were at work in 1875. In 1877 the population numbered 3,040 souls, the land revenue was Rs. 3,032, the capitation tax Rs. 3,060 and the gross revenue Rs. 6,264. Petroleum is found near the coast towards the north-west.

THAN-LYENG.—A town in the Rangoon district. *See Syriam.*

THAN-LYENG.—A Sub-division of the Rangoon district. *See Syriam.*

THAN-LYENG.—A township in the Rangoon district lying between the seacoast and the Pegu river and bounded on the west by the Rangoon river and on the east by the Pegu township ; it is divided into ten revenue circles. The head-quarters are at Syriam.

THAN-LYENG-MYOMA.—A revenue circle in the Than-lyeng township of the Rangoon district opposite the town of Rangoon. In 1877 the population was 4,484, the capitation tax was Rs. 5,065, the land revenue Rs. 16,378 and the gross revenue Rs. 21,780.

THAN-LYET-TSWON.—The northern circle of the Tha-boung township, Bassein district, having an area of about 61 square miles, with patches of rice cultivation towards the south-east but for the most part uncultivated and hilly. The inhabitants are mainly Burmans who live by cultivation and by making and trading in a red dye extracted from the roots of the Neepa-htse (*Morinda citrifolia*) and ropes from the fibres of the Shaw tree. In 1877 the population was 2,051, the capitation tax was Rs. 2,395, the land revenue Rs. 3,731 and the gross revenue Rs. 6,328.

THA-NWON-THA-NAW.—A village in the circle of the same name in the Henzada township, Henzada district, on the banks of the Nat-hmaw stream. In 1877 it had 1,152 inhabitants.

THA-NWON-THA-NAW.—A revenue circle in the southern part of the Henzada township of the Henzada district lying to the west of Doo-ra, nearly the whole of which is under rice cultivation.

The population and revenue during each of the last five years were :—

YEAR.	POPULATION.				REVENUE, IN RUPEES.		
	Burmans.	Kareng.	Others.	Total.	Land.	Capitation tax.	Total.
1874	1,032	423	6	1,461	4,240	1,367	5,607
1875	1,137	391	6	1,534	4,557	1,525	6,082
1876	1,347	436	6	1,789	4,616	1,607	6,223
1877	1,370	449	6	1,825	4,020	1,540	5,560
1878	1,333	655	6	2,038	4,635	1,722	6,357

and the area under cultivation and the agricultural stock :—

YEAR.	AREA, IN ACRES.				STOCK.						
	Rice.	Garden.	Miscellaneous.	Total.	Buffaloes.	Cows, bulls, and bullocks.	Goats.	Pigs.	Carts.	Ploughs.	Boats.
1874	2,382	30	2	2,414	251	366	10	130	233	114	5
1875	2,505	16	—	2,521	255	268	10	190	193	99	16
1876	2,505	25	—	2,530	327	413	—	104	209	115	5
1877	2,505	25	—	2,530	337	435	—	110	239	124	6
1878	2,505	31	—	2,536	366	507	—	120	282	103	7

THA-RAING.—A revenue circle in the Donabyoo township of the Thoon-khwa district east of the Irrawaddy extensively cultivated on the north and west, but with forest land towards the east and south. It has some small lakes, dry during the hot weather, important only as fisheries. In 1877 the population was 8,782, the land revenue Rs. 18,755, the capitation tax Rs. 8,635 and the gross revenue Rs. 28,507.

THA-RA-WAW.—A village in the Tha-ra-waw-toung-let circle of the Tsan-rwe township, Henzada (Tharrawaddy) district, on the east or left bank of the Irrawaddy. In 1877 it had 584 inhabitants.

THA-RA-WAW-TOUNG-LET.—A revenue circle in the Henzada (Tharrawaddy) district on the left bank of the Irrawaddy low and subject to periodical inundations, except near the bank of the river where the principal cultivation is found. In 1877 the population was 8,122, the land revenue Rs. 8,311, the capitation tax Rs. 7,525 and the gross revenue Rs. 21,440. The circle contains many swamps and small lakes which are leased out as fisheries and produce a large revenue to the State.

THA-RAW-BOON.—A tidal creek in the Bassein district joining the Myoung-mya and Rwe. It leaves the former about a mile east of the town of the same name and runs due south for about 12 miles, joining the Rwe about a mile above Da-rai-bouk. At low tide it has little or no water in it.

THA-RE-KOON-BOUNG.—A revenue circle in the Naaf township of the Akyab district on the seacoast at the mouth of the Naaf estuary, containing 4,880 acres of land, of which 2,939 were under cultivation in 1874-75, producing a land revenue of Rs. 5,759. In 1875-76 the population numbered 2,948 souls, and the capitation tax amounted to Rs. 2,820. In 1877 the population was 4,111, the land revenue was Rs. 6,389, the capitation tax Rs. 3,868 and the gross revenue Rs. 10,717.

THA-RET-KHYOUNG.—A village the Tha-ret-preng circle of the Ra-thai-doung township, Akyab district, on the eastern bank of the stream of the same name. In 1877 it had 798 inhabitants.

THA-RET-KHYOUNG.—A small river in the Henzada (Tharrawaddy) district of the Pegu division, which rises in the Pegu Roma and uniting with the Baw-beng forms the Wek-khyoung, a tributary of the Meng-boo which itself falls into the Myit-ma-kha or Hlaing. The banks are steep and the bed rocky and it is not navigable for boats but it taps a large teak tract in which other valuable timber is found.

THA-RET-KYWON.—A revenue circle in the Oo-reet-toung (east) township of the Akyab district. In 1876-77 the population was 1,716, the capitation tax Rs. 2,140, the land revenue Rs. 6,015 and the gross revenue Rs. 8,508.

THA-RET-PRENG.—A revenue circle in the Ra-thai-doung township of the Akyab district. In 1876-77 the population was 1,698, the capitation tax Rs. 1,880, the land revenue Rs. 3,197 and the gross revenue Rs. 5,331.

THARRAWADDY.—A new district formed in 1878 out of all that portion of Henzada lying to the east of the Irrawaddy except the A-hpyouk and Paing-kywon circles which are still included in the Za-lwon township of Henzada. The head-quarters are at Thoon-tshay on the stream of the same name where it is crossed by the Rangoon and Irrawaddy Valley (State) Railway. The statistics of this new district are included in those of Henzada, q. v.

THA-RWOT-MYAIK.—A tidal creek in the Shwe-loung township, Thoon-khwa district, joining the Irrawaddy and the Dala or Kyoon-toon rivers the former of which it leaves at about 12 miles north of the village of Kywon-pya-that. Its length is about five miles and it is broad and deep enough for steamers.

THA-RWOT-THWOT.—A tidal creek in the Shwe-loung township, Thoon-khwa district, about six miles long, connecting the Pya-ma-law and the Kywon-pa-doot. It is navigable at all seasons by river steamers.

THA-TSEE.—A village in the Pyeng-da-raw circle, Pya-poon township, Thoon-khwa district, on the Pya-poon river and about a mile from Pya-poon. In 1878 it had 540 inhabitants.

THA-TSEE.—A revenue circle in the southern part of the Henzada township, Henzada district, lying to the west of Tha-nwon-tha-naw, formerly subject to periodical inundations, but now rendered culturable by the construction of embankments.

The population and revenue during each of the last five years were :—

YEAR.	POPULATION.			REVENUE, IN RUPEES.		
	Burmans.	Kareng.	Total.	Land.	Capitation tax.	Total.
1874	2,656	—	2,656	8,139	3,227	11,366
1875	2,037	1,198	3,235	4,556	1,525	6,081
1876	3,184	486	3,670	11,234	3,427	14,661
1877	2,567	1,343	3,910	11,281	3,375	14,656
1878	2,915	1,384	4,302	11,368	3,607	14,975

and the area under cultivation and the agricultural stock :—

YEAR.	AREA, IN ACRES.				STOCK.						
	Rice.	Garden.	Miscellaneous.	Total.	Buffaloes.	Cows, bulls, and bullocks.	Goats.	Pigs.	Carts.	Ploughs.	Boats.
1874	4,740	22	24	4,786	787	556	8	227	459	219	10
1875	6,353	68	4	6,425	797	632	—	52	488	313	—
1876	6,392	67	5	6,464	857	1,107	6	132	692	383	—
1877	6,405	67	9	6,481	887	1,329	6	182	811	393	—
1878	6,427	66	8	6,501	921	1,430	6	192	853	395	—

THAY.—A small stream in the Thayet district, unnavigable for boats, which rises in the Myit-myeng-deng spur and flows southward into the Bhwot-lay a little to the east of the mouth of the Sha-pyan. The bed is sandy and the banks moderately high and covered with Eng (*Dipterocarpus tuberculatus*) and other timber.

THA-YA-GOON.—A village in the Hpek-rai circle, Kyan-kheng township, Henzada district, about six miles west of the Irrawaddy. In 1877 it had 648 inhabitants.

THAY-BHYOO-GYEE.—A small and unnavigable stream on the west bank of the Irrawaddy which rises in the Khyee-pa spur and falls into the Pa-nee, itself a tributary of the Ma-htoon. Its banks are moderately steep and its bed sandy, muddy and gravelly. Teak, Cutch and Eng (*Dipterocarpus tuberculatus*) are found on its banks.

THAYET.—The name of the upper portion of the Pai-beng creek in the Bassein district.

THAYET.—A revenue circle in the Thayet township, Thayet district, two square miles in extent of which about 400 acres are under cultivation and 100 more are culturable. Including the town and cantonment of Thayetmyo, which are in this circle, the population numbered in 1872

15,142 souls, of whom 10,804 were Burmans, the remainder being principally Europeans (the troops and officers) and natives of India (the native troops and the camp-followers with a few settlers). The imperial revenue is derived largely from capitation tax which in 1872 produced Rs. 8,410 when the land revenue was Rs. 210 and the fishery and net tax Rs. 300. In the Burmese time there was no village or taik thoogyee as the town was the residence of the myo-thoogyee or governor of Thayet. The products are rice, sessamum, maize and tobacco.

The population in 1876 exclusive of the troops and camp-followers, was 10,427, the land revenue Rs. 778, the capitation tax Rs. 7,835 and the gross revenue Rs. 26,859.

THAYET.—The northern district of the Pegu division. On the east is the Toung-ngoo district, now a portion of the Tenasserim division, on the south the Prome district and on the west the Sandoway district of the Arakan division. Lying immediately to the south of the independent kingdom of Burma the district touches the frontier line of the province, demarcated in 1853 after the annexation of the delta of the Irrawaddy by Lord Dalhousie. The Governor-General directed that the British frontier should run as nearly as possible due east and west from a point on the left bank of the Irrawaddy six statute miles north of the flag-staff at Mye-dai, where the British had their most northern or advanced post. This point was found to be in 19° 29′ 3″. A pillar was erected bearing inscriptions in Burmese and English characters, the latter as follows :—

" This pillar marks the northern boundary of the British province of
" Pegu, laid down by the officers of the Deputy Quartermaster-General's
" staff of the force in Pegu and examined and confirmed in person by the
" Marquess of Dalhousie, K. T., Governor-General of India, on the 28th
" December 1853. The boundary line runs due east from this point,
" crossing the Ken-nyee river at Ledoogwai, over the Yoma range of hills
" at Tattay, and down to the village of Mai-haw on the Sittang river
" from whence it proceeds due east to the summit of the Poung-loung
" range of mountains. Latitude of boundary 19° 29′ 3″." Due west, on the right bank, a similar masonry pillar was erected the inscriptions on which were nearly identical with those on the eastern. The English, after the words " 28th December 1853," runs thus :—" The boundary line runs
" due west from this point, crosses the Letmashedoung, Podotoung,
" Pandengtoung, and Tengdouk range of hills, on each of which pillars
" has (sic) being erected. The line cuts the Kyeedoung peak and proceeds
" from thence due west till it joins the water-shed of the Arakan mountains.
" Latitude of the boundary 19° 29′ 3″."

On the extreme west the country was found to be impassable and no boundary marks exist west of that at Kyee-doung, nine miles from the water-shed of the Arakan range. Between this point, which is a little south of 19° 30′, and the right bank of the Irrawaddy ten other pillars of dry stones were built up at distances varying from three to six miles. On the east 13 similar pillars were placed on a line trending slightly southwards, at intervals of from about two to rather m re than ten miles, the last in this district being at Tat-tai on the summit of the Pegu Roma mountains ; beyond that point the frontier line was continued across the head of what was subsequently called the Toung-ngoo district. The extreme length of the northern boundary of the Thayet district from the Arakan to the Roma mountains is about 93 miles. The western limit follows the crest of the Arakan hills southwards to the root of the Bhee-la spur. The southern boundary follows, generally, water-sheds which in the Burmese time were the boundaries of jurisdictions. Its length from the Arakan mountains along the crest of the spur which receives in succession the names of the Bhee-la, the Wek-khyan and the Toung-myouk-thenggan as far as the source of the Ra-tha-ya stream and thence along the course of that rivulet to its mouth in the Irrawaddy at the village of Zee-aing is 36 miles. To the eastward it extends from the mouth of the Za-lwon (three miles higher up) along the bed of that stream to the Roonbhyoo-goon spur and then following the crest of the Pa-teng-kyouk-poon, sometimes northwards and sometimes eastwards, in a general E. N. E. direction, it strikes the Pegu Roma mountains at a spot 58 miles from the Irrawaddy measured along the line. Measured in a direct line the distance from the root of the Bhee-la spur of the Arakan mountains on the west to that of the Pa-teng-kyouk-poon spur of the Pegu Roma on the east is 74 miles, the actual length of the boundary line being, as shewn above, 94 miles. The Pegu Roma from the root of the Pa-teng-kyouk-poon spur northwards to the frontier forms the eastern limit of the district. The total area according to the Topographical survey conducted by Captains Fitzroy and Edgcome is 2,396 square miles.

The general appearance and the physical and climatic characteristics
Physical aspect. of this district are widely different from those of any other portion of Pegu except, perhaps, some of the adjacent portions of Prome. Here there are no wide open plains or virgin tracts of level land waiting for the plough such as may be seen lower down the valley of the Irrawaddy ; the face of the country, where it does not rise into mountains, is everywhere broken by low ridges of hills, many of them so gravelly and destitute of fruitful soil as to be useless for cultivation. In the narrow valleys between these hills the rice cultivator reaps a precarious harvest and with much greater trouble and expense than has to be undergone to obtain an almost certain return by the cultivators further south. From the Irrawaddy, which traverses the centre of the district, to the boundary chains east and west the ground rises by a succession of hills, each range being generally higher than the one next to it on the side of the river, though in some cases the ridges near the river bank are higher than some of those more inland. This is especially the case in the southern portion near Ka-ma on the right bank where the spurs which run down to the river overtop those behind them. Higher up on the left bank near the village of Pya-lo, the Tsa-ga-doung is conspicuous, still further north, on the opposite side below Thayetmyo, is the Htoondoung rising to 600 feet and at the frontier is the still higher range of the Myeng-ba hills.

The Arakan mountains are a portion of the great Himalayan spur
Mountains. which stretches down to Pagoda point. In that part which separates Thayet from the country lying to the west the ridge does not rise to a greater height than from 4,000 to 5,000 feet, its most elevated points being Kyee-doung on the northern frontier line Nat-oo-doung and Shwe-doung-moung-hnit-ma, a double peak. The summit

is generally a sharp ridge from which start numerous spurs at right angles to the water-shed but at Kyee-doung there are two main ridges of nearly equal height and nearly parallel to each other. The furious storms which sweep along the higher slopes and swirl round the crest keep them bare of large trees and forest growth but from a few hundred feet below the summit as far as the base the sides of the hills are covered with bamboos and fine trees. Major Allan's surveying party, when laying down the frontier line in 1853, ascended the Kyee-doung peak and in his report that officer remarks that:—" The Arakan hills when visited, presented the usual " appearance of all tropical hills—the scenery picturesque, consisting of " grassy slopes edged by deep woods, and watered by fine though slender " streams, the climate temperate. In the month of May, at noon, the " thermometer stood at 84° in the shade."

There are four passes across this range into the Sandoway district which, however, are passable only by persons on foot and that during the dry season and which are but seldom used. The most southern leads from the village of Kaing-gyee-myoung in the Tsee circle of the Ka-ma township up the ravine of the Ma-de stream to the village of Mai-za-lee in Arakan. The distance may be roughly estimated at from 30 to 40 miles, travellers generally sleeping three nights on the road, on which are twelve halting-places at which water can be obtained. During the last Burmese war and for some years subsequently this route was much used, many of the inhabitants of Ka-ma taking refuge in Arakan from the cruelties of the Burmese officials during the war, and for some time after the annexation fleeing from the state of anarchy which inevitably followed until the British officials had crushed the bands of marauders who were left behind by the flying Burmese generals. As the country became more settled most of those who had gone away returned and since then the road is scarcely ever used except by bad characters who consider that a temporary seclusion in the remote forests of Arakan would be of advantage to them. The route by the next pass northwards starts from the village of Rwa-thit on the Hlwa stream in the Pai-myouk circle of the Meng-doon township and debouches on the other side at the village and police-post of Meng-dai on the La-moo stream : the distance is about 30 miles. The third and fourth are close together and are known by the same name—Ma-ee. One leaving the village of Reng-rwa in the Kyan circle of the Meng-doon township leads to the village of Leng-dee on the Ma-ee river in Sandoway, traversing a distance of between 30 and 40 miles in which there are 25 halting-places where water can be obtained ; the other, called the upper Ma-ee pass, is the shorter of the two and leads from the village of Kaing-gyee in the Ta-goung-nek circle of the Meng-doon township to the village of Leng-dee in Sandoway ; this is more frequented than the other three and yet not more than 20 people pass over it during the year.

The Eastern Roma mountains which separate this district from Toung-ngoo are an isolated chain which forms the water-shed between the Irrawaddy and Tsit-toung rivers. Commencing in Upper Burma the range runs southwards and after reaching a height of some 2,000 or 3,000 feet is lost in the plains of the delta near Rangoon. That portion of it which forms the eastern boundary of Thayet nowhere exceeds a height of 2,000 feet above the sea, and for the most part is several hundred feet lower. The main range and the principal spurs are tolerably level along their summits but they rise occasionally into isolated high hills, the sides of which are so steep that the summits are almost inaccessible. They are entirely covered by dense forest in which bamboos of the larger kinds from 70 to 80 feet in height and five inches or more in diameter predominate. Water is found in almost all the small valleys and ravines at all times of the year and the pools abound with a black-looking fish which the Burmans call Nga-yan (*Ophiocephalus sp.*). During the dry season there is a striking dissimilarity between the eastern and the western slopes. On the latter the trees are mostly leafless, the undergrowth is parched and the soil is arid and at this season therefore the wild animals generally pass over to the eastern slopes which remain green and shady. These mountains are traversible at almost all points during the dry season by foot passengers, unladen cattle and elephants, and the paths are used by dealers in cattle and silk. The route which is generally followed starts from the village of Thek-ngay-byeng in the Peng-ga-daw circle of the Mye-dai township and leads to the frontier police-post at Bhoora-goon on the Toung-ngoo side, a distance of from 20 to 30 miles. A road leading by a more southern route from Thayetmyo to Toung-ngoo has been projected and surveyed and the road partly made. This starts from the village of Gnyoung-beng-kyeng near the south-eastern corner of the Mye-dai township and passing along the top of the spur which forms the water-shed between the Pa-de stream and its affluent the Alay and then along the main ridge of the Roma for a short distance to the root of the spur which forms the water-shed between the Tshwa and Kyek-sha rivers in the Toung-ngoo district it follows that and strikes the village of Tsee-let-to about six miles from Toung-ngoo and 61½ from Gnyoung-beng-kyeng.

The Irrawaddy traverses the district from north to south cutting it into two slightly unequal portions of which the larger is on the right bank; entering at the frontier of the province it leaves this district to enter Prome just above the Hpo-oo hill within sight of the town of Prome, having traversed a distance of 43 miles as the crow flies. Within these limits its greatest breadth between the permanent or rainy weather banks is about three miles and its narrowest, between Pya-lo on the left and the Poo-hto hill. some 16 miles below Thayetmyo on the right bank, is not more than a mile. Its banks are everywhere high, in some places hills rising steeply from the water's edge, and nowhere is there any overspill during the rains inundating large tracts of country as is the case lower down in its course. The dry-weather channel varies during the course of years but the variations generally are slow. In 1855 when the military station of Thayetmyo was formed the river at all seasons ran immediately under its site, now, in 1879, during the dry weather there is between the high bank on which the station is situated and the water's edge a sandbank half a mile or more wide. Other instances of the changes in its course may be found in the only two islands of any size which occur in the district, Re-baw opposite the town of Thayetmyo and Gnyoung-beng-tshiep between the village of that name and Ka-ma. In the dry season on the river falling the former is connected with the left bank, the latter with right. Eighty years ago the river when full flowed on the other sides of those islands. The navigable channel varies

Rivers.

considerably owing to the shiftings of the sands yet there are but few places, even when the river is at its lowest in January, February and March, in which a fathom of water cannot be found. The worst spot is near the mouth of the Bhwot-lay where sometimes only four or five feet of water are found for a few days in the year.

The drainage from the two boundary water-sheds finds its way to the Irrawaddy by three main streams on the west and by two on the east : the Pwon, the Ma-htoon and the Ma-de on the one hand and the Kye-nee and the Bhwot-lay on the other. The Pwon is an insignificant stream which rises in Upper Burma to the westward of the Myeng-ba hill and entering British territory near the village of Myeng-byeng joins the Irrawaddy after a course of a few miles just above the town of Thayet. With a strong current and sudden rises and falls in the rains in the dry weather it falls to a tiny stream running often beneath banks of sand. The Ma-htoon or Meng-doon rises north of British territory between two lofty peaks of the Arakan mountains and flowing in a south-easterly direction traverses the frontier line before it descends from the higher range, and falls into the Irrawaddy just above Ka-ma about 50 miles in a direct line from the point where it crosses the northern frontier : owing to its numerous sinuosities however it has in that distance flowed over a course of some 150 miles. During the dry season small boats can always ascend as high as Meng-doon 12 miles south of the frontier and throughout the rains boats of the largest size can generally navigate it : the amount of water contained between its banks being dependent upon the rainfall in the hills its rises and falls are sudden and rapid and the current is so strong that in the rains it takes 10 or 12 days to ascend from its mouth to Meng-doon. Large quantities of the produce of its fertile valley are brought down to the Irrawaddy on bamboo rafts and logs of teak timber are floated down it singly and rafted in the Irrawaddy. It has three main affluents, the Moo, the Hlwa and the Pa-nee. The Moo rises in Upper Burma and passing to the north of Meng-doon joins the Ma-htoon close to that town : it flows all the year round and brings down a considerable volume of water during the rains. The Pa-nee is a large stream which also rises in Upper Burma and entering British territory near the village of Khwe-douk has thence a direct course of about 30 miles till it joins the Ma-htoon a few miles above its mouth at the village of Tham-bha-ra. It is navigable for boats during the rains but is little used owing to the rapidity of its current and to its sudden rises and falls. The Hlwa is a mountain stream which rises near the Shwe-doung peak and flows in a due easterly direction into the Ma-htoon : during the dry season it is a trickling brook. The Ma-de flows from almost the summit of the Arakan range nearly due west of Ka-ma and joins the Irrawaddy at that town after a nearly direct course of 30 miles. It is navigable for large boats for some distance above Ka-ma but during the wet season only ; during the dry season it is not navigable at all even for rafts which during the rains bring down large quantities of produce. It has numerous affluents the most important of which are the Nga-wek and the Moon-ta down which teak timber is floated during the rains. Of the two eastern affluents of the Irrawaddy in this district the Kye-nee rises in the Roma range in Upper Burma and after running for some distance nearly due west it trends to the south and falls into the Irrawaddy just below the site of the old fort at Mye-dai, after a course within the district of about 16 miles in a direct line. It brings down a considerable volume of water but is not navigable nor is timber floated down it on account, it is said, of obstructions in its course in Upper Burma. The Bhwot-lay is so called from the village at its mouth, but higher up in its course it is known as the Pa-de. During the dry weather it is only a few inches deep and in some places flows under sandbanks. In the rains it brings down a large volume of water but is unnavigable for boats owing to its sudden rises and falls and to the rapidity of its current, but at this season a considerable quantity of timber is floated down it and its affluents, the larger of which are the Khyoung-goung-gyee, the Rangoon and the Thaing-bhyoo. In many places after the fall consequent on the cessation of the rains dams of sand are every year skilfully constructed to retain the water in pools several feet deep and some hundred yards in length, the water being used for irrigation. Near its mouth it is spanned by a substantial wooden bridge 450 feet in length across which runs the Rangoon and Mye-dai road.

" The district of Thayet, comprising that portion of the Irrawaddy
Geology*. " valley between the frontier in 19° 30′ and the parallel
" of Ka-ma (or thereabouts) is very simple in its geological
" structure, though it may be said to furnish an epitome (geological) of the
" province inasmuch as an exhaustive description of it would leave little
" to be added to complete the description of the main geological features
" of Pegu.

" On the east and west the district is bounded respectively by the Pegu
" and Arakan ranges, the rocks composing the latter being the older of the
" two geologically; whilst much of the intervening ground is occupied by
" rocks of more recent age than either.

" I will briefly, therefore, describe the rocks from west to east, or in
" their ascending order, geologically speaking ; but for any detailed account
" of them, the Records of the Geological Survey may be consulted (No. 4 for
" 1869; No. 1 for 1870 ; and No. 2 for 1871), and the maps of the province
" now preparing for publication in the office of the Geological Survey†.

" The Arakan range at the frontier (including the subordinate ranges
" outside the central axis, one of which, the Kyee-doung, or eastern Arakan
" range as it is called in one map, is of scarcely inferior proportions)
" consists of a group of argillaceous and silicious beds of very varied
" mineral character, in places displaying a very high degree of metamor-
" phism, but as a rule presenting a merely sub-schistose appearance or
" even beyond induration little appearance of direct metamorphism what-
" ever. The typical schistose groups of the bed are in fact of very local
" development and are mainly confined to the vicinity of serpentine and
" to the argillaceous portion of the group constituting the main axis of
" the range. These sub-schistose beds are somewhat soft and traversed
" by occasional thin seams of quartz, and as far as known are infossiliferous,
" though under more favorable circumstances for examination it is very
" probable that organic remains may be detected in them, as in such forest
" clad-mountains as these all effective search for such is next to impossible.

* Furnished to the Deputy Commissioner, Thayet district, by W. Theobald, of the Geological Survey of India (Ed).
† Since published (Ed.)

734

"East of the main range the Kyee-doung range presents very similar
"features, but leaving this and crossing the range between Pa-thee (a
"village three miles from the frontier on a feeder of the Ma-htoon) and
"Kondeinzu (*Koon-daing-tsoo*) (Kong-deng-keng on map) a group of silicious
"beds comes in much traversed by small veins of calcite, many of the
"beds being hard and coarse silicious grits, very harsh, and often covered
"on their weathered surface with a ferruginous glaze which imparts a
"peculiar appearance to them.

"In the vicinity of Kondeinzu (*Koon-daing-tsoo*) an enormous thickness
"of beds of very varied character comes in, both sandstone and shells
"regularly intercalated with one another, and varying from a foot to one
"inch in thickness—prevailing colour blueish or grey. The coarser beds
"are white speckled, which white speckled beds may be said to distinguish
"the upper axials, as the whole group has been termed. This portion of
"the group contains a little limestone, though it is only hereabouts met
"with in loose blocks, and was not noted *in situ.* Further to the south, in
"the bed of the Hlwa stream, a fine section of these beds is seen, display-
"ing a thickness of nearly 4,000 feet; but beyond an indeterminate cardita
"and a few other fossils in indifferent preservation no clue to the precise
"age of the beds has been obtained—a single specimen of halobia indicat-
"ing a jurassic age was found in limestone more to the south, probably
"from a bed corresponding somewhat to the horizon of the "cardita" bed
"in the Hlwa section (*vide* Geological Records, No. 2 of 1871). This group of
"axials does not extend much beyond 50 miles from the frontier, south of
"which the Arakan range consists wholly of beds more or less altered and
"indurated of nummulitic age. In my paper in the Records *loc. cit.* on the
"'axials of western Prome,' the upper axials are shewn to rest on a series
"of shaly beds, which, at the time, I considered identical with the altered
"shales met with to the south, and which are well displayed in the cuttings
"on the Prome and Toung-goop road. Subsequent investigation, however,
"has enabled me to correct this view; and the axial group really terminates
"north of the Toung-goop road; and thence to Cape Negrais the range
"consists of newer rocks. Considerable difficulty, however, attaches to
"the precise demarcation of the limits of two groups of rocks of not very
"dissimilar mineral character, and very deficient in fossils, in a country
"which may not inaplty be described as of the wildest and most impene-
"trable character.

"The dip of the beds of this group is usually high, and though there
"is great disturbance among them and local irregularity the general strike
"of the beds is pretty uniform and coincident with the prevailing strike of
"the range, that is, S.S.E.—N.N.W. The average breadth of this group is
"12 miles, or a trifle less, measured at right angles from the dividing crest
"of the range. How far these beds extend to the westwards has not yet
"been ascertained, but probably to the same extent as to the eastward.

"To the eastward of these 'axials,' comes in a bed of rocks, shales,
"sandstones and limestone, of eocene age, varying in breadth from 16
"miles at the frontier where narrowest, to over 50 miles in the parallel of
"Akouktoung† where they extend uninterruptedly from the river to the

---

* In the Prome district (Ed.).
† Akouk-toung is situated in the south of the Prome district (Ed.).

" Arakan coast. The thickness of this nummulitic group is very consider-
" able, not falling far short of 4,000 feet, though it is not easy to form an
" exact estimate from the absence of any well-marked divisions in so large
" a group which would facilitate one so doing. The group comprises shales
" and sandstone at the base in regular beds ; the shales largely predomin-
" ating in this portion of the group.

" 'The shales are blue or grey, and as a rule singularly devoid of
" organic remains, though a few fish scales are found with them,
" and a few small nummulites are here and there met with. Above
" these shales occur thick-bedded massive argillaceous sandstones well
" exhibited near the village of Hlwa, on the Ma-htoon stream below Meng-
" doon. Above these a thick series of sandstones and arenaceous shales,
" in many of which ill-preserved fossils occur, come in, which are fairly
" displayed on the road between Meng-doon and Eng-byee to the E.N.E.
" One of the highest beds of the group is a limestone profusely charged in
" places with nummulites, and occasionally containing corals and shells
" among which pecteus are commonest. A good section of these higher
" beds of the nummulitic group occurs in the Tha-boo-la stream north of
" the village, which need not be given *in extenso*, as it presents no
" particular features of interest.

" This portion of the nummulitic group is mainly interesting from
" being that wherein the Thayetmyo coal is situated. This coal has been
" already reported on by Dr. Oldham, and it will suffice, therefore, to say
" that it occupies much the same position in Pegu that the Salt Range coals
" do in the Punjab, both being deposits of carbonaceous matter, more or
" less irregular and capricious in their development, and forming subordi-
" nate beds on the group of shales which normally seem to underlie the
" widely-spread nummulitic limestone. The nummulitic limestone is well
" developed on the flank of the range running a little west of Hpoung-aing,
" a frontier village 21 miles from Thayetmyo. The limestone here extends
" for nearly seven miles. West of this much nummulitic limestone crops
" out forming the surface of much of the country, and a second line of the
" same rock occurs, commencing from a point six miles W.S.W. from
" Hpoung-aing and running with occasional interruptions for nearly 12
" miles, when it dies out a little to the east of Tha-boo-la. Beneath this
" several arenaceous and shaly beds occur in places so profusely charged
" with nummulites as to approximate in character to a limestone, and
" which seem to pass into such a rock, but these beds are less common in
" the Thayetmyo district than further south and need not be here dwelt
" upon.

" These nummulitic rocks are confined to the west bank of the
" Irrawaddy, *i.e.* within the limits of the province of Pegu. 'The Limestone
" hill ' as it is called, below Thayetmyo consists of an isolated mass of
" nummulitic strata, brought up by faults through the newer strata which
" constitute the whole surrounding country ; and, as was first pointed out
" by Dr. Oldham, though so close to the river no nummulitic rocks
" are exposed in its banks, which consist of the newer group. A few
" salt-springs rise within the area of the nummulitic group, but they
" are comparatively rare, and at the present day of no practical import-
" ance.

"Leaving the area occupied by the nummulites in an easterly
"direction, the whole country as far as, and inclusive of, the Pegu range
"itself, consists of a new group of rocks of presumedly miocene age, save
"a somewhat irregular area near the river, occupied by a still newer group
"which will presently be described.

"This vast group embraces beds of the most diverse mineral character,
"except limestone, which is of extremely rare occurrence, and very local and
"circumscribed. The sandstones vary from an incoherent rock to one
"hard and compact, and many of the beds contain numerous fossils which
"have not as yet been specifically identified, save in a few instances. The
"general aspect of the fauna is, however, undoubtedly miocene ; but this
"question may be passed over at present, as far as details are concerned.

"The shales of this group are generally blue and clunchy, those
"towards the base being devoid of fossils, whilst some of the higher beds
"abound in the most delicately preserved organisms, foraminifera and a
"variety of shells, both univalve and bivalve, with an occasional fragment
"of a pteropod or crab. This clay occurs in the river bank close to Kama
"though here it is often concealed from view by the deposit of river silt
"thrown down by the subsiding waters of the river, and also east of Allan-
"myo not far from the village of Kyouk-khyoung-ga-le. Traces of this bed,
"or of one very similar to it, are exposed nearly opposite to Prome, the
"fine gorge above which place lies between rocks of this group, and
"another bed, remarkably rich in fossils, occurs exactly opposite the circuit-
"house, but which need not be further considered here.

"In several spots near Thayetmyo the sandstones contain fossils, but
"not as a rule well preserved and often merely in the shape of ferruginous
"casts. Occasionally, however, the sandstone matrix is extremely hard
"and the fossils well preserved ; but from the character of the rock great
"difficulty is experienced in extricating the shells, save in a fragmentary
"condition. Close to the Lime hill on the river bank a hard sandstone
"occurs, profusely charged with a curious orbitolite, or species of fora-
"minifera, which when alive must have resembled nothing more than a
"small and rather thin pancake, though, from the compactness of the
"rock, nothing save fragmentary portions of a specimen can be obtained.

"In the gorge above Prome a thickness of these beds of upwards of
"2,000 feet is displayed on the west bank of the river, and the entire
"thickness of the group cannot safely be estimated at less than 4,000 feet.

"Several salt-springs rise through the beds of this group, the principal
"of which are at Tsan-gyee near the frontier on the west bank, and Re-tsan
"and Le-myoung on the east bank of the river, 13 miles N.E. of Kama.

"A hot spring occurs near the mouth of the Bhwot-lay stream four
"miles from the 'Lime hill' but as it occurs in the bed of the river it is
"frequently covered over by sand.

"Nine and a half miles N.N.W. by N. from Kama is situated the spot
"where the curious manifestation known as the 'Spirit Fire' takes place.
"Beyond a few stones in the jungle displaying traces of fire there is no
"peculiarity about the spot; and the fire is simply the result of the
"ignition of hydrogen gas which here escapes from the earth. Hydrogen gas
"is a common accompaniment of the brine springs throughout the province,
"giving rise at Tsan-gyee and elsewhere to the furious ebullition the brine

" pools often display ; and in all such cases the gas may easily be ignited
" by applying a light to the surface of the pool at any point the gas may
" be issuing from.

" Where the gas rises in jungle and gets stored up in subterranean
" cracks a more or less uninterrupted supply is secured which, once ignited
" either by man or accidentally by the progress of a jungle fire, gives rise
" to such a simple, but to the superstitious natives, portentous phenomenon
" as the ' Spirit Fire'.   At the time of my visit the fire was extinct, but it is
" doubtless capable of revival periodically.

" On the important question of petroleum a few words will here suffice.
" At some two or three spots only on the west bank of the Irrawaddy is
" this mineral known to occur within the province of Pegu.

" One of these, from which oil of a very similar character to the
" Re-nan-khyoung oil of Upper Burma has been within the last few years
" extracted, is situated near the village of Pa-douk-beng seven miles N.N.W.
" from Thayetmyo.   The oil is obtained from a well sunk through the soft
" miocene sands and shales which constitute the surface of the country in
" the neighbourhood.   In all cases, however, the source of the oil, in my
" opinion, lies deeper and must be referred to some of the carbonaceous
" beds associated with the nummulitic limestone ; by the exposure of which
" beds to a process of subterraneous distillation at a considerable depth
" the mineral oil has been produced."

Petroleum is also obtained at Bhan-byeng about nine miles (by the
present road) west from the town of Thayetmyo ; of the oil obtained here
Mr. Theobald remarks elsewhere :—" The beds in which the oil occurs are
" blue shales, with some few intercalated beds of hard, rather calcareous
" sandstone, and contain numerous fossils, costrea, tellina, arca, solen,
" pecten (two species), cytherea (?) conus, cyproa, tunitella, crabs' claws, a
" small barnacle, one or two branching corals, and teeth of two species of
" the shark family, characteristic of the great miocene formation of the
" district, the distance from the nearest point of the nummulitic formation
" being four miles.   The beds are on about the same geological horizon as
" those wherein the"......" wells near Padouk-beng were sunk, and the
" entire intervening country seems to consist of the same beds dipping in
" different directions at unusually low angles."

" The geological position of the oil here is undoubtedly curious, as on
" the presumption that it originates in the under-lying nummulitic group
" a thickness of beds, speaking in round numbers, of some 2,000 feet and
" probably more must intervene between the source of the oil and the beds
" wherein it here finds its way to the surface.   It is not my opinion that
" the entire intervening thickness of beds is necessarily saturated with oil
" but rather that it rises through these strata along certain lines of fracture
" and permeability (such as a crushed anticlinal would afford) till meeting
" with such porous beds as the more arenaceous of these clays are which
" here form the surface of the country, it becomes diffused among them in
" an irregular fashion.   The soft shales and arenaceous beds dip all over
" this country at low angles as a rule, and from their yielding character
" give us indications of the condition or arrangement of the rocks far
" beneath them ; but the above suppositions of mine, of the oil rising from
" a great depth to the surface along certain lines of disturbance, is in

" accordance with what may be presumed to be the condition of the lower
" strata, and the result of these deeply-seated forces and movements whose
" maximum effect we see in the elevation of the Arakan hills to the west."
    " With the above diagnosis of the conditions under which the oil is
" here met with it is obvious that no trustworthy opinion can be formed
" beforehand of the success that would attend the sinking of a deep shaft,
" but that it all depends on the shaft being so sunk as to intercept the
" path (so to speak) along which the oil, here seen diffused through the
" strata, rises from below ; in which case it is probable a fair amount of
" oil might be won."
    That any very large supply of earth-oil would be obtained even by
more extensive working and by sinking deeper wells seems doubtful, for the
same geological authority, Mr. Theobald, has recorded :—" Presuming then
" that the American oil is produced by the same process of subterraneous
" distillation of carbonaceous beds as our Indian oil is supposed to be we
" have at once an adequate reason for the difference in production of the
" trickling wells of Ava, which yield their supplies drop by drop, as it were,
" compared with the rush of oil frequently met with in America, and some-
" times possessing the force of an Artesian spring ; for the coal fields of
" America almost as much exceed in their development the coal fields of
" Great Britain as those of Great Britain do the puny deposits of the
" nummulitic age wherein our Indian oils originate. I especially name
" the newer coals as I am unacquanited with any reason for supposing
" that any Indian Petroleum is derived from our more useful and workable
" coals of Palæozoic age."
    Both at Padouk-beng and at Bhan-byeng the oil labours under the
disadvantage of having to undergo several miles of extensive land carriage
before it can be brought to the place of shipment on the river bank.   The
oil at Padouk-beng is thick and viscid like that which is obtained at
Re-nan-khyoung in Upper Burma, whilst that at Bhan-byeng is a pure
lubricating fluid of considerable value in Europe.
    " Above the group last described comes a small number of beds of no
" great thickness, but at present of rather circumscribed area, but which
" are interesting as being the source whence the large quantity of fossil-
" wood, so common in the form of rolled fragments in the gravels about
" Thayetmyo has been derived.   An account of these beds is contained in
" the Records of the Geological Survey, No. 4 for 1869.
    " The principal divisions of this group are an upper sand here and
" there gravelly and conglomeratic, and in places characterized by a pro-
" fusion of concretions of the hydrated peroxide of iron ; and a lower series
" of thin-bedded fine silty clay, with occasional strings of a coarse sand and a
" few small pebbles.   Both groups were formerly far more extensive than
" at present but denudation has reduced these to an area of about 700
" square miles ; a sixth of which may be occupied by the upper sand—the
" bed in which the fossil-wood of the district occurs in the shape of silicised
" trunks of trees, mineralized in situ and in places associated with fossil
" bones of mammalia, reptiles and cartilaginous fish teeth.   These bones
" doubtless belong to the same fauna as that which has yielded the inter-
" esting fossils brought by Crawford from Ava, a list of which is contained
" in the catalogue of fossils in the Museum of the Asiatic Society of Bengal,

"by the late Hugh Falconer M.D. As a rule, however, the bones found
"in the Thayet district are far less perfectly mineralized than those
"brought from Ava; and in some spots where they are not uncommon so
"friable that few or none remain perfect or are able to withstand the action
"of the elements when no longer protected by the matrix of rock in which
"they occur—occasionally however a few small bones may be be found
"perfectly mineralized and indestructible by ordinary atmospheric action
"—a good section of these sandy beds may be seen three miles east of
"Shwe-ban-daw or 15 miles east of Allanmyo and also between O-mouk
"and Le-ma, 19 miles E.S.E. from Thayetmyo.

"The fossil-wood in this group in not confined to the sand at the top
"as some pieces are found somewhat rarely dispersed throughout, both in
"the passage beds which intervene between the topmost divisions and the
"miocene beds below, and also in the upper sand, though not as far as
"is known in the fine clays beneath the sand; but it is in this upper sand,
"apparently in the uppermost portion of it, that the fossil-wood abounds
"most, occurring in the form of trunks of trees silicified *in situ*, some of
"which cannot have been less than 50 or 60 feet in length at the time they
"were encased in the sand. Perfectly as these logs have in many instances
"been silicified, the structure has to a great extent been obliterated by
"decay prior to their mineralization, and all that can be said of such
"specimens as I had examined microscopically at home is that the trees
"are exogenous and not conifers.

"These trunks are nowhere bored by teredo or other molluscs, and
"this, taken in connection with their condition and surrounding, helps to
"point out the condition under which these sands were accumulated. The
"presence of mammalian remains alike points in the same direction, and
"supports the conclusion that, after a period during which marine con-
"ditions prevailed, as indicated by the fossils at the base of the group, a
"deposition of silty and ultimately sandy beds took place in fresh water,
"wherein the remains of animals were swept by rivers and the huge trunks
"of trees floated about till water-logged and partially decayed, and which
"on sinking became then and there permeated and mineralized by silica
"held in solution by springs emptying into a great lake or system of lakes.
"To treat, however, on this more or less theoretical point is foreign to
"my present purpose; and I will close the account of these beds by an
"extract from the Records, Part 4 for 1869, on the manufacture of iron
"formerly carried on in sundry spots within the area of these fossil-wood
"gravels:—
    "Next to the presence of silicified wood a remarkable development of
"concretionary peroxide of iron seems to characterize the sand I am
"describing. The ore occurs occasionally as a thin band up to perhaps a
"thickness of three inches, breaking up or jointing into rhomboidal
"concretionary masses of different sizes and shapes. More usually the
"ore occurs in the form of variously-shaped concretions from one to four
"inches in length, though occasionally even larger. These concretions
"are found both in the sand and the conglomerate to which last, when
"numerously developed, they impart a peculiar varnished look which might
"sometimes be almost styled (but for the technicality of the term) viscous
"or slaggy.

"The more usual shape of these concretions is flattish oval or
"amygdaloidal, but they occur spherical, cuboidal, cylindrical with both
"flat and hemispherical ends, discoidal and in any intermediate forms, but
"always symmetrically proportioned, and the result of a segregative action
"or process in the clayey and ferruginous components of the bed when in a
"plastic condition.

"Of whatever shape, however, their structure is extremely uniform,
"consisting of an external crust of concentric layers of brown hematite
"surrounding a kernel of pure white or yellowish clay, lying loose and
"shrunken in the interior.

"Externally, these nodular concretions are roughened from the adhesion
"of the sand enveloping them; but this rough crust scales off readily, leaving
"their surface perfectly smooth. Internally they often present a blistered
"appearance from the mammilary crystallization of zenionite which lines
'them becoming, on exposure to the atmosphere and rain, lustrous and
'burnished. When the bed has been of too harsh a character to permit
'the regular segregation of the ore, it is found lining sinuous cavities in
the coarse matrix having flat approximated walls, evidently caused by
shrinkage, which gives such portions a very peculiar aspect and one
which simulates a viscous condition. In some places even a botryoidal
structure is induced when the rock is less coarse.

"Under the Burmese rule this ore was extensively smelted..............
Remains of furnaces exist which were merely rectangular kilns cut in the
firm alluvial clay of some steep bank which gave easy access at top for
replenishing ore and fuel, and below for withdrawing the products. Such
furnaces are numerous about Shwe-ban-daw, Kywon-ga-le, and Re-baw
together with slag heaps sometimes of no inconsiderable dimensions.
Throughout the area of these upper sands however, slag may be found
scattered about, as the iron-workers shifted their scene of operations
from spot to spot, wherever charcoal and ore were for the time most
plentiful.*

"The works must in many cases have been conducted in the dry
season only, as the hearths of some furnaces still standing open into the
beds of streams, which during the rains would certainly have found an
entrance to them. The blowing apparatus was probably the effective
vertical cylinder bellows, formed of large bamboos, still in use in the
district by blacksmiths; but the oldest inhabitants could give me no
particulars of the manufacture.　　＊　　　＊　　　＊　　　＊

"West of the Irrawaddy a belt of these sands stretches from Kyee-
'doung, five miles N.N.W., from Thayetmyo in a slightly curved direction,
'to a point on the Ma-htoon stream three miles north of Kama, but the
'group is here much broken up by denudation, the upper bed being often
"absent and the logs of silicified wood derived from it lying scattered about
"and more or less rolled in the surface detritus and gravel overspreading
"the country.

"No volcanic rocks occur in the Thayet district, except serpentine
"which constitutes the Byee-doung hill, on the Ma-htoon stream, six miles

* Symes speaks in his "Account of an embassy to the kingdom of Ava" published in 1800,
page 242, of having passed between Gnyoung-beng-tshiep and Mye-dai "Samban famed for its
"iron manufactury."

"from the frontier, and stretches for nearly six miles in length in a
"N.N.E. direction.

"About a mile east of Tham-bha-ya-beng, and again about the same
"distance east of Thayet-tsan at spots lying respectively 23 and 25 miles
"E.S.E., about, from Thayetmyo two small patches occur of a rock having
"a most deceptive resemblance to a trap or greenstone. From the rock
"decaying at the surface into a deep black mould the hill, on the summit
"of which in either case the rock occurs, is known to the Burmese by the
"name of Mye-nek-toung (Black earth hill). A third locality occurs some
"five miles to the S.E. of these two and here the bedded character of the
"rock is distinctly seen which is not the case in the other localities. The
"rock is in fact a local ash-bed or trap-ash, arranged under water but
"possessing the constitution of a greenstone whence the close resemblance
"to that rock of the compacter portions of the bed present. The bed no
"doubt is the result of some display of volcanic activity in the immediate
"neighbourhood during the accumulation of the miocene beds with which
"the ash-bed is associated, and connected doubtless with the same display
"of volcanic action as that to which the extinct crater of Poop-pa-doung in
"Upper Burma is due; and probably when the intermediate country is
"better known, other spots may be discovered tending to unite the volcanic
"manifestations at these distant spots."

Brine-springs are found in many localities in the district but chiefly on
the west bank of the Irrawaddy. Most of them were worked and small
quantities of salt obtained from them under the Burman government by
evaporation and boiling, but this is an occupation which since the annexation
of Pegu has been entirely abandoned as unprofitable. On the east of the
river there were two sets of wells from each of which about 50 pots of
strong brine were obtained daily: one of 17 wells of considerable depth at
the village of Bwet-gyee about a mile from the bank of the Irrawaddy and
the other of four wells on the banks of the Tsha-dweng-khyoung (salt-well
creek) about two miles from the village of Taroop-beng. On the west there
were six:—near the village of Tsan-gyee yielding daily 14 pots; near
Leng-gan yielding about ten pots; near Poo-hto on the bank of the river
yielding 15 pots; near Tha-hpan-gyo, about six miles from Ka-ma, yielding
30 pots, near Pien-nai-kweng also yielding 30 pots; and near Kyouk-mai,
eight miles west of Ka-ma, yielding about 50 pots.

Extensive lime quarries exists in the Htoon doung range (Lime hill) a few
miles south of Thayetmyo. The stone is taken to the villages of Htoon-doung
and Pie-tha-lien on the river bank and there burnt. The average annual
production may be set down at about 900 tons. The lime, which is of superior quality, is sold at the spot at from Rs. 8 to Rs. 13 per 100 baskets.

Six-sevenths of the district is covered with forest, most of it low and
Forests. scrubby. Bamboos abound but the more useful forest
trees are scarce except in the higher ranges of hills.
Teak is found nearly all over the district, but even the best is very inferior
and not to be compared with that which grows in the valleys of the rivers
Tsit-toung and Salween. Near the Irrawaddy the teak trees are invariably
short and crooked, but whether this is due to the soil and to climatic
influences or to the want of forest conservancy in the Burmese time
cannot be positively asserted. The best teak is on the eastern range of hills.

The following is a list of the useful trees which are commonly found in the district, compiled from Dr. Brandis' list of woods :—

Botanical name.	Native name.	Weight per cubic foot in lbs.	Economic uses.
Tectona grandis (teak) ..	Kywon ..	40 to 51	Monopolized by Government, used extensively in ship-building, for houses, beams, furniture of every description, and in the Indian Arsenals and Gun-carriage manufactories.
Dipterocarpus tuberculatus.	Eng ..	55	Very common and much used in house-building. When not exposed to damp it is very durable.
Acacia catechu (cutch) ..	Sha ..	56	Very common. Immense quantities are annually consumed in the manufacture of cutch : used also for house posts, handles &c., the heart-wood being exceedingly hard and durable.
Xylia dolabriformis (Iron wood).	Pyeng-ga-do ..	60 to 66	Common : more durable even than teak but extremely hard to work and too heavy to float.
Odina wodier ..	Nabai ..	65	Used for oil-presses, sheaths of swords, &c. Might be a valuable furniture wood.
Terminalia macrocarpa ..	Htouk-kyan ..	58	A large tree, very common : used in house-building, but not very durable.
Blackwellia tomentosa ..	Myouk-khyaw .. (Monkey's slipping tree so called from its smooth stem).	56	Common : wood tough, colour light-yellow, not very durable ; used for teeth of harrows.
Vitex leucoxylon ..	Htouk-sha ..	42	Common : used for cart-wheels.
Tamarindus indica ..	Magyee ..	..	Fruit tree : wood little used.
Diospyros burmanica ..	Tay-beng ..	..	Abundant. Black heavy wood used for knife-handles and sheathes.
Hopea odorata ..	Theng-gan ..	64	Very scarce. Dark heavy wood ; excellent for boats.
Artocarpus claplasha ..	Toung-pien-nai ..	39	Ditto Ditto.
Nageia latifolia ..	Thit-meng ..	50	White and light ; close-grained.
Anogeissus acuminata ..	Roon-beng ..	50 to 57	Brown and heavy : used for pestles and mortars.
Pongamia glabra ..	Theng-weng ..	60	Black heavy wood : used for ploughs and harrows.

Botanical name.	Native name.	Weight per cubic foot in lbs.	Economic uses.
Albizzia lebbek ..	Koot-ko ..	48	Black and heavy: used for cart-wheels and oil-presses.
Pterocarpus indicus ..	Padouk ..	60	Not plentiful. Red and heavy: used for cart-wheels.
Ulmus integrifolia ..	Myouk-tshiep ..	..	White and heavy: used by carvers for images.
Pentacme siamensis ..	Eng-gyeng ··	55	White and heavy: used extensively for building.
Shorea obtusa ..	Thit-ya ..	57	White and heavy: durable, used for building.
Bombax malabaricum ..	Lek-pan ..	28	Light white wood, easily worked but easily destructible: used for coffins.
Nauclea cordifolia ..	Hnaw-beng ..	..	Yellow and light ; used for flooring and rafters.
Albizzia lucida ..	Than-that ..	..	Black and heavy: used for cart-wheels, pestles, &c.
Chikrassia tabularis ..	Reng-ma ..	24	Yellow and heavy : used for axles.
Vitex alata ..	Kyet-ro ..	45	Yellow and heavy: strong and lasting, used for house-posts, tool-handles, &c.
Pancovia rubiginosa ..	Tshiet-khyee ..	66	White and heavy, grain mottled: used for house-posts.
Holarrhena codaga ..	Let-htoop-thien.	..	White and light: used for soles of shoes.
Streblus aspera ..	Oop-hnai ..	..	White and light : used chopped up and mixed with tobacco root for smoking.
Schleichera trijuga ..	Gyo ..	70	White and heavy: used for anchors, pestles, mortars, &c.
Dalbergia cultrata ..	Reng-daik ..	64	Heavy wood with red heart : used for plough and cart-poles.
Careya arborea ..	Bhan-bhwai ..	55	Red wood: used for carts, house-posts, &c.
Heterophragma adeno-phylla.	Hpet-than ..	48	White and heavy: used for house-posts.
Berrya amonilla ..	Hpet-won ..	62	Reddish and heavy: used for cart-axles and for poles of ploughs and carts.

Here as elsewhere in the province the felling within the limits of the government forests of teak, thit-ka and thit-kha-do is forbidden, padouk (*Pterocarpus indicus*) can only be felled by persons who obtain a trade-permit, that is permission to cut timber for sale on payment of duty, and 11 other kinds by persons who have trade-permits, or free-permits to cut for their own use in a forest not more than three miles from their houses. For many years these government forests extended between the Pegu Roma and a line drawn southwards from Mye-dai through the junction of the Bhwot-lay and the Pa-de from the frontier southward throughout the district on the left bank of the Irrawaddy but in 1876 the whole of the country west of the Irrawaddy was declared to be government forest land.

But little wild large game is found in the central portion of the district, due partly to the annual destruction by jungle fires of all grass and underwood, and partly to the indiscriminate

Animal kingdom.

shooting persevered in by the natives in season and out of season. A stray tiger, a few leopards, wild cats and barking deer which are found almost all over the district, constitute the few natives of the plains, except that the Htameng or brow-antlered rusa, a splendid stag, is occasionally met with in the comparatively open plains and rolling hills on the south-west of the Mye-dai township. In the uninhabited mountain ranges to the east and west are elephants, rhinoceros, tigers, black bear, leopards, sambur deer hog deer, barking deer and wild hog. Deaths from the bites of wild beasts seldom occur. Occasionally a tiger is known to attack the small parties of men who venture far into the Arakan hills in search of forest products, and occasionally leopards kill and devour a bullock or a buffalo in the lowlands.

Pea-fowl are scarce but silver pheasants are found in large numbers, especially in the mountains. Jungle-fowl and painted-partridge, handsome birds which perch on trees and have a shrill crow, are found all over the district. From September to December snipe in small numbers may be found in the rice swamps, but wild duck and teal find no resting-place except in the Irrawaddy where, during the cold weather, they may sometimes be seen in large flocks.

"The avifauna of Burma is in general intermediate to that of India "and the Malay peninsula, modified a good deal by local circumstances. "Thayetmyo and the whole valley of the Irrawaddy above Poungday, where "the annual rainfall is normally below 60 inches, has an avifauna more "Indo-Chinese than the delta, and in many cases presents affinities to the "birds of the dry plains of Upper India. Many of the birds of the Thayet-"myo district, have their range southwards abruptly limited and do not "occur below the Prome district, nor are they replaced by slightly modified "species. The common partridge (*F. Sinensis*) and the crested pied "cuckoo (*O. Jacobinus*), both common birds in Thayetmyo, may be quoted "as instances."

Except in the Irrawaddy there are hardly any fish in the district. The most plentiful kinds are the *Hilsa* or sable fish (*Nga-tha-louk*); the *Nga khyeng*, a kind of carp; *Nga thaing*, another kind of carp; various species of cat fish and the mullet. The *Nga-rwe*—one of the kinds of cat fish —grows to an enormous size, some weighing as much as 365 lbs. are credibly reported to be sometimes caught near Ka-ma, but never appear in the market. The most profitable fisheries are those in lagoons amongst sandbanks in the river, worked only during the dry seasons by means of dams, nets and other implements. For such fisheries a yearly rent is charged. For the privilege of fishing in the river the fishermen take out a license, the cost of which varies with the net used.

Poisonous snakes are not uncommon but owing probably to the houses being built on piles deaths from snake-bite are by no means frequent. The poisonous snakes as far as is at present known are the Naja tripudians— of which all six varieties described by Sir J. Fayrer are found and are called by the Burmans *Mwe-houk,`Ngan-wa, Ngan-poot, Ngan-gya, Ngan-tsoung* and *Ngan-byouk*—Ophiophagus elaps (*Leng-wa*), Hamadryas (*Ngan-tsoung*), Bungarus fasciatus (*Ngan-than-khwe-tswot*), Callophis (*Mwe-kyeng-koung*), Bungarus cœruleus (*Ngan-daw-she*), Daboia (*Mwe-bwe*), Echis carinata (*Mwe-bwe-a-tsit*), Platurus fischeri (*Tsheng-byit-mwe*).

Thayet lies on the southern edge of that middle Irrawaddy zone
the chief characteristic of which is its extreme dryness
when compared with the delta on the south or the valley
of the upper portion of the river on the north. The climate here approximates generally to that of Upper Burma and is as different from the climate of the seaboard districts, as that of the Upper Provinces of India is from the climate of Lower Bengal. The rain-fall is about one-fourth of what it is in many places on the coast.

Climate.

The following table shews the rain-fall during each of the last 15 years :—

Year	January	February	March	April	May	June	July	August	September	October	November	December	Total
1878	—	—	—	·09	5·36	8·28	9·35	4·99	5·01	8·16	1·75	—	35·99
1877	—	—	—	·40	3·88	12·52	9·01	20·13	4·25	9·56	1·90	—	62·55
1876	—	—	—	—	3·27	4·14	6·72	6·59	5·51	4·76	3·94	—	34·93
1875	—	—	—	5·10	5·02	11·17	13·60	7·30	5·66	4·00	·28	—	53·32
1874	—	—	·10	·79	8·23	6·08	6·13	10·81	7·55	12·22	·56	—	52·47
1873	—	—	—	·20	5·16	8·8	8·60	6·00	5·88	6·77	3·14	—	43·52
1872	—	—	—	·10	7·23	11·40	6·15	7·89	3·19	3·33	—	—	39·29
1871	—	—	—	·29	8·46	7·70	9·03	10·71	12·00	6·80	—	—	54·85
1870	—	·3	—	·5	12·30	6·98	7·89	5·72	6·18	2·60	—	—	40·59
1869	—	—	—	2·20	4·20	6·70	5·85	5·85	2·60	6·30	—	—	33·20
1868	—	—	·97	·10	6·60	7·82	9·17	11·42	6·07	7·06	2·05	—	50·75
1867	—	—	—	·25	9·75	5·52	7·50	8·35	9·32	2·12	2·57	1·10	45·48
1866	—	—	—	—	3·00	13·52	7·17	8·07	10·00	6·25	7·55	—	51·78
1865	—	—	—	·30	7·17	9·45	9·52	6·47	—	5·30	4·57	—	51·78
1864	—	—	—	—	·90	13·90	10·90	5·80	4·10	6·40	—	—	42·00
1863	—	—	—	—	5·15	8·55	9·22	6·00	9·00	6·97	3·37	—	42·36

Thayet is but rarely mentioned in the Burmese annals. In the
early dawning (semi-mythical period) of Burmese history
History. the country of which Thayet forms a part appears to
have been inhabited by the Pyoo, one of the three tribes from whose
fusion the present Burman race has sprung, the other two being the Kanran
or Kanyan and the Thek. Sometimes the Pyoo and Thek are spoken of
as one tribe. In after years, when Indian missionaries had converted the
people to Booddhism and when each and every part of Indo-China received a
classical Pali name, taken generally from the names of countries mentioned
in the sacred books, the lower portion of the Thayet district belonged, it
would appear, to Tharekhettra (Prome) whilst the upper portion belonged
to Thoonaparanta (Tsa-goo, Tsa-leng) on the right or west bank of the
Irrawaddy and to Tam-pa-dee-pa (Pagan, Ava) on the left or east bank.
The dominons of the first Burman monarchy, the capital of which was at
Ta-goung, never extended so far south as Thayet but when the Prome
dynasty was founded by king Dwot-ta-boung, circa 444 B.C., this district
formed a portion of his territories.

On the destruction of the Prome dynasty, about the end of the first
century of the Christian era, Tha-moon-da-riet, the fugitive Prome ruler,
escaped to, and remained a few years at, Meng-doon, where he built a city
on the site of the present town, and ruled for seven years. He then
appointed his uncle as governor and going north founded a kingdom at
Pagan. Here he was succeeded by a scion of the old Ta-goung race and
the kingdom flourished for more than 1,100 years. During that period
this district formed an integral portion of that monarchy. The last
king of Tha-moon-da-riet's dynasty appointed his son Meng-sheng-tsaw as
governor of Thayetmyo. His father Kyaw-tswa Meng was dethroned by
three Shan brothers one of whom established himself at Peng-ya. This
king's son founded a kingdom at Tsa-gaing and both monarchies existed
contemporaneously for about 60 years, when another Shan chieftain conquered them both and carried away their ruling sovereigns. A descendant
of the old Ta-goung dynasty, named Tha-do-meng-bya, seized the opportunity and succeeded, in 1365, in re-establishing the Burman monarchy,
fixing his capital at Ava. During this period the ruler of Thayetmyo,
who had been left undisturbed, was practically independent, as was the
ruler of Prome, one of the family of Thee-ha-thoo, son of Taroop-pye-meng
and brother of Meng-sheng-tsaw, who asserted, and for sometime maintained, his independence. At this period the Prome territories extended
almost up to Thayetmyo, the Nga-hlaing-deng creek on the east bank of
the Irrawaddy nearly opposite to the town of Thayetmyo having been
their northern limit. In the reign of the second king of Ava, Meng-gyee-
tswa, Thayetmyo, which was the king's birth-place, was a favoured portion
of his dominions. After his reign it is very seldom that mention is
made in Burmese history of any places in Thayetmyo, with the exception
of Mye-dai which is represented as being a strong fort, so strong that
hostile forces passing up and down the Irrawaddy generally left it in their
rear without attempting to besiege it. In course of years it was parcelled
out amongst various governors and so remained until the annexation of
Pegu by the British, when it was formed into a sub-division of the Prome
district.

The ordinary amount of Revenue raised in the district under the
Revenue. Burmese government for remission to the capital was
about Rs. 50,000 : the largest amount of which there is
any record, which was raised just before the annexation of Pegu, was
Rs. 102,340. This was exclusive of the demands made on the people to
meet the want of the local officials, as none of the revenue came back to
them in the shape of salaries.

It was raised in different ways in different provinces : in Myo-dai the
owners of cattle were divided into three classes according to the number of
beasts they possessed and a rate fixed on each class, fishermen were taxed,
and landing, market, and brokerage fees were levied. In Thayetmyo the tax
was sometimes levied on cattle-owners, sometimes at so much per house,
sometimes on land, and was paid in kind and in lead, and at one time during
the reign of Koon-boung-meng, better known as Prince Tharrawaddy, the
revenue was altogether remitted and Thayetmyo was required to furnish,
equip and pay 500 soldiers. In Ka-ma the gross demand for each circle
was fixed by the Myo-thoogyee and for the people of each village by the Taik-
thoogyee; this quota the Rwa-thoogyee levied as best he could.

The imperial revenue demand in each year since Thayet formed an
independent district has been, in rupees :—

YEAR.	Land.	Capitation tax.	Excise.	Nets and fisheries.	All other items.	Total.
1870-71	69,945	89,787	58,298	4,077	40,380	269,899
1871-72	67,530	97,320	54,102	4,426	40,624	271,976
1872-73	64,671	102,501	32,959	3,373	29,706	241,931
1873-74	85,623	105,736	32,631	3,507	36,710	270,645
1874-75	88,772	109,118	34,985	3,219	46,005	290,575
1875-76	96,038	111,171	39,772	3,056	52,336	310,213
1876-77	89,619	113,231	43,185	3,333	56,825	314,058
1877-78	100,763	123,343	43,563	3,598	48,655	318,122

The detail of the figures in the column headed " All other items "
was :—

YEAR.	Fines, forfeitures, &c.	Unclaimed property sold.	Postage and Telegraph stamps.	Stamps in Civil Suits, on law papers, &c.	Miscellaneous.	Total.
1870-71	14,138	460	7,272	16,492	2,018 *	40,380
1871-72	19,214	762	6,808	11,982	1,858 †	40,624
1872-73	10,690	263	7,540	11,199	14	29,706
1873-74	11,886	501	8,851	15,102	370	36,710
1874-75	16,605	342	10,130	18,887	41	46,005
1875-76	17,750	501	11,235	21,903	947	52,336
1876-77	13,370	251	23,582	17,899	1,723	56,825
1877-78	11,161	24	16,676	16,860	1,834	46,855

* Includes Rs. 1,511 Income tax and Rs. 49 Forest produce.
† Includes Rs 116 Income tax

In addition to this imperial revenue a so-called local revenue is raised from a tax on land covered by buildings in certain towns, from market-stall rents, a cess on the land and fishery revenue, and other sources. This during the same period was :—

	Rs.			Rs.
1870-71	 23,011	1874-75	..	.. 42,820
1871-72	 28,310	1875-76	..	.. 44,134
1872-73	 38,725	1876-77	..	.. 53,775
1873-74	 40,295	1877-78	..	.. 55,179

The taxation per head of population was :—

YEAR.	Population.	TAXATION PER HEAD.		YEAR.	Population.	TAXATION PER HEAD.	
		Imperial:	Total.			Imperial.	Total.
		Rs. A. P.	Rs. A. P.			Rs. A. P.	Rs. A. P.
1870-71 ..	126,121	2 2 2	2 5 0	1874-75..	143,321	2 0 5	2 5 1
1871-72 ..	132,604	2 0 9	2 4 4	1875-76..	146,518	2 1 10	2 6 8
1872-73 ..	140,470	1 11 6	1 15 11	1876-77..	147,228	2 3 2	2 7 11
1873-74 ..	142,533	1 14 4	2 2 10	1877-78..	148,234	2 2 4	2 8 3

The actual collections never can agree with the demand, partly owing to remissions which have to be made, partly to some portion of the demand for one year being collected in the next and partly to defaulters.

The actual collections of imperial revenue and the cost of the civil officials of all kinds was, in rupees :—

YEAR.	Cost of officials of all kinds.	Gross revenue.	YEAR.	Cost of officials of all kinds.	Gross revenue.
1870-71	66,709	269,899	1874-75	75,187	290,575
1871-72	84,904	271,976	1875-76	79,385	310,213
1872-73	124,818	241,934	1876-77	251,723	317,755
1873-74	99,425	270,645	1877-78	84,577	320,482

Under their native government Burmans were accustomed to periodical
Population.   enumerations of the people as this was a necessity of
their fiscal and political system. Under the British government such enumerations are annual. About the month of August in each year the native tax-collector (Taik-thoogyee) of each circle prepares

a population-roll shewing the name, age and occupation of every permanent resident within his circle. As the Thoogyee and the people are accustomed to this yearly process and as the rolls are connected with the collection of the capitation tax, in which the Thoogyee has a personal interest, being paid by a commission on the collections, these rolls are in the main correct.

For rural circles they are probably as accurate as it is possible to make them. In large towns, especially where there is a large floating population, they are not so accurate; but in all probability there is no part of India which possesses such correct annual statistics of population as is furnished by these rolls in British Burma.

In August 1872, in addition to the annual numbering of the people by the Thoogyee, a regular census was taken for the first time. Its results proved the general accuracy of the annual returns. The population of the district, as shewn by the annual returns for the first year after the annexation compared with the same returns for the previous year, proves that though the population of the district may not have increased with such gigantic strides as that of other districts of the province which have greater natural advantages it has still increased in a most remarkable manner under British rule. If the scanty natural resources of the district are taken into consideration the increase is perhaps the most remarkable in the province. The district certainly possesses a larger proportion of population to cultivated or culturable area than any other.

That it should retain such a large population, to whom the richer districts of the delta offer so many more advantages is probably due to its proximity to the frontier line and to its possessing a climate much more like that of Upper Burma than is found in the fertile plains of the south.

In making a comparison between the earlier and the later population returns those for 1854, the first year of our administration, may be rejected as not entirely trustworthy. Those for 1855 may be taken as giving a tolerably accurate estimate of the population for that year.

The increase in each township since then will be seen from the following table :—

Township.	Population according to returns for 1855.	Population according to returns for 1860.	Population according to returns for 1872.	Population by census of 1872.	Remarks.
Mye-dai ..	15,611	20,084	55,114	63,061	The difference of 16,346 souls between the population rolls and the census returns is accounted for by the population of cantonments, the boat population and the floating population of towns not being included in the former.
Thayetmyo ..	6,452	12,899	29,256	35,633	
Meng-doon ..	9,506	14,993	25,540	26,165	
Ka-ma ..	11,363	14,379	30,560	31,957	
Total..	42,482	62,355	140,470	156,816	

The total male and female population according to ages was as follows :—

	Males.	Females.	Total.
Not exceeding one year	3,503	3,504	7,007
Above one, but not above six years	12,638	12,409	25,047
,, 6 ,, ,, 12 ,,	11,039	10,329	21,368
,, 12 ,, ,, 20 ,,	10,439	10,876	21,315
,, 20 ,, ,, 30 ,,	14,893	13,440	28,333
,, 30 ,, ,, 40 ,,	13,129	10,476	23,605
,, 40 ,, ,, 50 ,,	8,118	6,726	14,844
,,. 50 ,, ,, 60 ,,	4,155	4,030	8,185
,, 60	3,408	3,704	7,112
Total ..	81,322	75,494	156,816

The number of each sex classed according to religion was :—

RELIGION.	Males.	Females.
Booddhists	69,992	67,260
Hindus	1,587	442
Christians	1,029	367
Mahomedans	910	264
Others, chiefly spirit worshippers	7,804	7,161
Total ..	81,322	75,494

Out of the total population of 156,816 souls, 107,086 or about two-thirds were found to be dependent solely on agriculture. The number of males above 20 years of age who were so occupied was 29,025.

The numbers belonging to the other principal classes of occupations were :—

Coolies	6,655
Hawkers	4,473
Shopkeepers	3,943
Cutch boilers	1.321
Oil makers	213
Musicians and Actors	198
Brokers	177
Blacksmiths	153

The following tables shew the state of education, according to the census of 1872, among the males and females of the different religious persuasions :—

RELIGION	Total male population not exceeding 12 years.	Total able to read or write, or under instruction.	Total female population under 12 years of age.	Total able to read or write, or under instruction.
Booddhist	23,991	2,773	23,318	121
Hindoo	207	44	169	9
Mahomedan	141	46	114	13
Christian	154	59	127	39
Others	2,687	18	2,514	1
Total ..	27,180	2,940	26,242	183

RELIGION.	Total male population exceeding 12 years.	Total able to read or write, or under instruction.	Total female population above 12 years of age.	Total able to read or write, or under instruction.
Booddhist	46,001	31,538	42,942	803
Hindoo	1,380	595	273	18
Mahomedan	769	162	150	20
Christian	875	743	240	165
Others	5,117	296	5,617	1
Total ..	54,142	33,634	49,252	1,007

Of the total male Burman population above the age of 12 years about two-thirds are able to read and write but among the female Burman population above the same age only one in fifty is able to read and write. This result is due to the admirable system (admirable as far as the male population is concerned) of almost every boy being sent to spend some portion of his early years in a monastery to be instructed by the Hpoongyee or Booddhist monks in religion and in the arts of reading and writing. Girls are excluded from this advantage.

The numbers of different nationalities according to the census were as follows :—

Races.							Number.
Burmans							137,016
Khyeng							14,475
Natives of India							3,458
Europeans							822
Kareng							420
Indo-Burmans							199
Eurasians							170
Shan							166
Chinese							62
Hebrews							8
Arakanese							7
Arabs							6
Talaing							4
Americans							1
Australians							1
Parsees							1
						Total	156,816

The population according to age and sex during each of the last eight years according to the rolls of the Thoogyee was :—

YEAR.		MALES.			FEMALES.			Grand Total.
		Over 12.	Under 12.	Total.	Over 12.	Under 12.	Total.	
1870		37,453	26,873	64,326	36,327	25,468	61,795	126,121
1871		44,567	22,706	67,273	44,933	20,398	65,331	132,604
1872		44,857	26,811	71,668	42,861	25,941	68,802	140,470
1873		45,435	27,180	72,615	49,597	20,321	69,918	142,533
1874		48,487	24,918	73,405	48,364	21,552	69,916	143,321
1875		50,492	24,374	74,866	47,596	24,056	71,652	146,518
1876		49,210	25,982	75,192	49,329	22,707	72,036	147,228
1877		49,290	26,305	75,595	49,611	23,028	72,639	148,234

Notwithstanding the inhospitable character of the soil and notwithstanding that the Upper Burma officials jealously prevent the removal of women and children, cattle, and household implements from their country, this district annually receives a large accession to the number of its inhabitants by immigration across the frontier. Running as the frontier line does over hilly ground covered for the most part with densely-growing forest the Burman officials are but partially successful in their efforts to prevent the depopulation of their frontier districts. There the villages are every year decreasing in number and but that such villages contain a considerable number of men who are "wanted" by the police of British Burma their sites would speedily be nothing but refuges for wild beasts. There being no waste low-lying lands available for rice cultivation the immigrants betake themselves at once to toungya. Some few settle down as cotton cleaners or general coolies in the towns of Thayet and Allan, whilst a few, after a year or two, adopt the wiser course of passing on to the richer districts lower down where their labour is so much more productive. The great bulk of the population is of the pure Burman race, unmixed with Talaing blood as in the delta of the Irrawaddy or with Shan blood as in the upper portion of Burma Proper. Concerning the characteristics and peculiarities of the Burman, much need not be said ; his virtues which are many, and his failings which are not a few, are much the same here as in every other part of his extensive country. He here, as elsewhere, displays much spasmodic energy and general laziness ; much love of feasts and shows ; much disregard of the sacredness of human life and much tenderness for the lives of inferior members of the animal kingdom ; much arrogance and inconsiderateness when placed in high position ; and last, though not least, much general truthfulness, and amongst unsophisticated villagers, the very un-oriental trait of being quite unable to tell a specious falsehood, a trait which is as honourable to himself as it is convenient to those who have the government of his country. His occupations are cultivation on a small scale and petty trading. Actual poverty is almost unknown but riches are never accumulated. If any individual does by a stroke of good luck or by a most unusual exercise of thrift, amass a few thousand rupees he is sure to spend the greater portion of it in the erection of a pagoda or a monastery or some similar work of religious merit.

The Khyeng[*] of whom there are over 14,000 in this district are a variety of the so-called Mongolian family who have never made for themselves a place in history and whose language and traditions may be said to be unknown to any but themselves. They hold themselves to be descended from the two last-born of the goddess Hleeneu who, male and female and coming from the same egg, married. When Hleeneu distributed her gifts among her children no spot was left for her youngest but inhospitable mountain ranges. These she assigned to him and gave him elephants and horses and cattle. By various artifices his elder brother, the Burman, cheated him out of nearly everything and he was at last left with fowls, goats and pigs only. Even his forest-covered hills were to a certain extent taken from him and his race has never had a country of its own but wanders over the mountain ranges.

Agriculture. The principal crops cultivated have been, in acres:—

Year.					Rice.	Oil-seeds.	Cotton.	Tobacco.
1870-71	..	..	..	..	..	49,294	6,999	4,768	4,086
1871-72	..	..	..	..	..	62,713	7,073	5,954	4,383
1872-73	..	..	..	..	..	63,341	7,978	5,214	4,094
1873-74	..	..	..	..	..	57,484	2,916	4,769	4,040
1874-75	..	..	..	..	..	58,049	3,041	4,164	3,439
1875.76	..	..	..	..	..	59,556	7,949	5,331	3,332
1876-77	..	..	..	..	..	61,143	8,182	4,079	3,676
1877-78	..	..	..	..	..	68.844	8,325	3,944	4,387

[*] *See sub. tit. Khyeng.*

Of rice, the staple commodity of British Burma, this district produces but little. It is probably the only one in the province which not only does not export but does not even grow enough for its home consumption. Traffic in grain here is exactly the reverse of what it is elsewhere. In other districts rice flows to the marts on the river bank where it is dearest ; here it is cheapest on the river-bank and dearest at places further removed from the river.

There are five different methods of raising a crop *viz* :—

1st.—On the ordinary rice swamp-land in low-lying plains, where the local fall of rain alone, or that assisted by natural drainage from neighbouring high lands, is sufficient.*

2nd.—On lands which though level are so high that the drainage from them of the local fall of rain is too rapid to allow of rice being raised by such natural supply alone and for the irrigation of which in the rainy season dams or water-courses have to be constructed.†

3rd.—On land near the river-bank which is submerged during the highest rises of the river and cannot therefore be planted until the last high rise of the river has subsided.‡

4th.—In Toungya or Hill clearings.

All the above are wet-weather crops.

5th.—Ma-yeen a hot-weather crop raised by irrigation-works the water being obtained by throwing dams across streams or by water-wheels.

For the wet-weather crops, with the exception of Toungya, ploughing operations are commenced about June or July as soon as the earth has been thoroughly saturated with rain ; small nurseries of rice plants being at the same time raised on plots which are generally on somewhat higher land than the rest so that the amount of water in them can be regulated from time to time. Rice here is never sown broad-cast in the fields but is always planted out.

The ploughing apparatus is merely a harrow with long teeth. The plougher stands on the bar and the harrow is dragged about the water-sodden field till a smooth surface of mud is obtained. In land of the first and second descriptions rice can be planted out as soon as the fields and the young rice plants are ready, and this is generally in July and August. On land of the third description the cultivator must wait until the last high rise of the river has gone down, or he will very likely lose his crop and have to plant a second time. This land is planted generally in September. In November the wet-land rice harvest begins, and the crops are generally all got in by the end of the first week in December.

In Toungya the rice seed, which is of a different kind to wet-land rice, is scattered broat-cast over the side of a hill about May or June and is reaped in October.

The Ma-yeen, or irrigated hot-weather crop, is generally obtained by throwing a dam across a stream in the dry season and leading the water off above the dam by side channels over the fields. In some rare instances two crops are thus obtained from the same ground in one year.

The Ma-yeen rice is planted in January, February and March and is reaped about three months afterwards.

---

* Mogoung Lay—*i.e.* fields which derive their supply from the sky.

† Tshay Lay—from " Tshay " a dam.
‡ Ta-tshay Lay.

A considerable quantity of wet-weather rice land belongs to the second class, *i.e.* it is dependent on dams and irrigation channels for its water supply. Our system of government is probably not so favourable for the construction and maintenance of such works as was the native *régime*. To make them or to keep them in a state of efficiency it is necessary that the whole body of cultivators whose lands are benefited by them should annually give their quota of labour. Under native rule some one of this number was appointed to be headman* and he had summary power to compel by the lash or by fine any refractory villager. Such a communal institution, useful as it is, can, however, hardly be brought into accord with Anglo-Indian law. Among a considerable body of cultivators there generally happen to be some who from idleness, or perhaps from a mere wanton desire to exhibit their newly-acquired independence and to shew that they cannot be made to work as they would be under Burman rule, will refuse to contribute their quota of labour for the general good. Their neighbours do not approve of having to do the work of others as well as their own, and so the dam breaks down or the water channel silts up.

During the dry season some of the lands along the banks of the Ma-htoon khyoung are irrigated by means of a very simple but ingenious contrivance in the shape of a self-acting water-wheel, which raises a continuous supply of water to a height of some 30 feet. It is certainly unique in its way, as far as Burma is concerned, and it is doubtful whether any precisely similar contrivance is used any where else.

The Meng-doon water-wheel.

The banks of the Ma-htoon, where a view can be obtained at once of several of these spider-like machines in ceaseless motion, their shafts humming loudly, and the waters splashing and sparkling all over them, form a singularly interesting spectacle†.

The result of a number of experiments made to ascertain the yield of wet-weather rice crops in this district, is that the highest known yield is 82 baskets or bushels‡ per acre and that the average is only 42 bushels per acre. On lands which are artificially irrigated and cropped in the dry season the yield is somewhat greater, a series of experiments having shewn that it is almost invariably between 59 and 70 baskets per acre, but the grain on such land is somewhat coarser than the wet-weather rice. The weight of a standard basket of unhusked rice in the season that it is reaped is about 45 lbs. The yield of an acre therefore at 42 baskets is 1,890 lbs., or 23 maunds and 2 seers. A basket of good unhusked rice if well cleaned will give 31 lbs. of rice.§

Yield of rice land.

---

* Tshay-daing.
† See *sub. tit.* Ma-htoon.
‡ The standard basket contains 2218· 19 cubic inches.
§ The following was the result of an experiment made in the Gaol to ascertain the actual out-turn in rice husking. A basket of unhusked rice weighing 45 lbs, 10 oz. produced :—

				lbs.	oz.
Clean rice	..	..	..	30	10
Broken rice	..	..	..	2	0
Tour, or rice dust	..	..	..	1	0
Chaff	..	..	..	12	0
		Total	..	45	10

The produce of an acre in rice then amounts to 1,302 lbs., or 15 maunds 36 seers. The value of the grain on the spot varies much according to the locality and the season. Generally speaking unhusked rice is cheapest at the river-bank and dearest in the interior; but an extraordinarily good harvest will do much to equalize prices. The harvest of 1872 was an unusually good one, and unhusked rice sold at Rs. 50 per 100 basket on the river bank, near the frontier; Rs. 40 per 100 baskets lower down the river; and Rs. 60 per 100 baskets at Meng-doon. In 1870, when the harvest was a bad one, it sold for Rs. 75 on the river-bank at Thayetmyo, and went as high as Rs. 120 at Meng-doon. Taking the average produce to be 42 baskets per acre and the average price on the spot Rs. 60 per 100 baskets the average value of the gross produce of an acre will be Rs. 25.

No less than 61 different kinds of rice are known to the cultivators of this district. The following is a list of their Burmese names and the character of each different kind of grain.

Name.	Grain hard or soft.	Remarks.
Nga-hpyoo-ga-le	Hard	a 5 months' rice.
Nga-loo-kwot	do	a 6 Ditto.
Oo-shit	do	a 4 Ditto.
Kwon-tsa	do	a 5 Ditto : grown only in toungya.
Hnan-the	do	a 4 Ditto : Ditto.
Pyo-gyee	do	
Nga-loo	do	
Hle	do	
Hnan-wa	do	
Tsa-ba-hpyoo	do	
Myo-pai-dwe	do	a 2½ months' rice.
Da-gyeng-twe	do	
Le-hnan-pwa	do	
Khwon-nee-peng-to	do	
Neema	do	
Mo-reng	do	a toungya rice.
Kyien-thee	do	Ditto.
Rahaing	do	
Kouk-pyouk	do	Ditto.
Tha-bye-roung	do	Ditto.
Nga-tsan-hpyoo	do	Ditto.
Hle-tshan-nee	do	
Hle-tshan-hpyoo	do	
Kwon-tsa-nee	do	Ditto.
Kwon-tsa-hpyoo	do	Ditto.
Kha-khyeng	do	
Thoon-la-hpyoo	do	
Tshan-nee-ga-le	do	
Nga-kyouk	do	
Kouk-reng-hbyoo	do	
Kouk-reng-thoon-la-hpyoo	do	
Hpyoo-myo	do	
Tshan-gyaw-hpyoo-ga-le	do	
Nga-loo	do	
Kareng-gyaw	Middling	
Nga-kyee	Soft	a 6 months' rice.
Koung-hgnyeng-nga-khyiet	do	a 5 Ditto.
Rwe-toop-reng-koung-hgnyeng	do	a 5 Ditto.
Nga-poot-gyee	do	

Name.			Grain hard or soft.		Remarks.
Kywet-thwa ..	..	..	Soft	..	
Hkaw-mai ..	..	..	do	..	
Toung-kareng	..	..	do	..	a tonngya rice.
Pwe-doop ..	..	..	do	..	Ditto.
Tsit-ta-goung	..	..	do	..	Ditto.
Kyaw-tseng ..	..	..	do	..	
Kya-thoung-pwe	..	..	do	..	
Re-thway ..	..	..	do	..	
Pek-wa-gyee ..	..	..	do	..	
Peng-gwa ..	..	..	do	..	Ditto.
Loo-hpyoo ..	..	..	do	..	Ditto.
Mwe-tsoot-gyee	..	..	do	..	
Tshan-nee ..	..	..	do	..	
Thee-htap ..	..	..	do	..	
Kouk-lignyeng	..	..	do	..	
Poot-wa-kouk-hgnyeng ..		..	do	..	
Khaw-pai-kyouk-lignyeng		..	do	..	
Kya-thoung-bwe	..	..	do	..	
Kyaw-zeng ..	..	..	do	..	
Rwet-lien ..	..	..	do	..	
Mwe-tsoot ..	..	..	do	..	Ditto.
Nga-khyiep ..	.,	..	do	..	

The much and deservedly-abused system of toungya * cultivation finds its stronghold in this district. About January or February the toungya-cutter selects a piece of land on the slope of a hill which is covered, and the more thickly the better, with bamboos or tree jungle. Everything growing upon it is felled with a dha, or heavy chopper, and is left on the ground for a couple of months to be thoroughly dried. About April, or any time before the first fall of rain, this is fired ; great care being required in the meantime to see that it is not accidentally or mischievously set fire to, as in such case the brush-wood only would be burnt, leaving the larger trunks to encumber the ground.

Immediately after the first fall of rain the surface of the toungya is " tickled " with a spud to allow the thick layer of ashes to amalgamate with the soil. The seed is then scattered broad-cast. The usual crops are rice and cotton, or sessamum and cotton, with numerous kinds of vegetables. The toungya has to be carefully weeded during the rainy months. The rice or sessamum is reaped in September or October and the cotton then springs up and is ready for picking from December to April. The average area of a toungya cultivated by one family is about two acres, and the value of the produce varies from Rs. 50 to 100. After the crops are reaped the toungya is abandoned and left to relapse into jungle. The cotton plants, however, generally maintain their vitality for another year and yield a small crop of inferior cotton.

On some of the better lands the growth of jungle is so rapid that toungya can be formed on the same spot every fourth year.† Generally, however, toungya land is worked only every seventh year.

The cotton of Thayet is probably the best that is produced in Indo-China. Before the annexation of Pegu it was in great request among the

---

* Hill clearing from Toung, a Hill—called " Jhoom " in Assam.
† Such lands are generally of a rich red colour, and are called " kwon" lands.

Chinese of Yunan and Western China. The produce of the district was monopolized by Chinese merchants who established factories for cleaning it on the banks of the river; from thence it was exported by boat to Amarapoora and Bha-maw, and from the latter place on the backs of mules to China. Its price then at Amarapoora used to be sometimes as much as two and a half annas a pound. Since the annexation of Pegu the course of the trade has changed and all the cotton of the district goes down the Irrawaddy to Rangoon. The merits of the Thayet cotton appear to be that it is exceedingly strong, its colour is good and its seeds are abundantly enveloped in wool. Its demerits are that it is coarse and rather short and most tenaciously attached to the seed. It is grown entirely in toungya* i.e. in temporary clearings on the sides of hills. It is generally sown together with rice or sessamum. These products are reaped about the close of the rainy season (September and October). The cotton plants then spring up and the cotton is ready for picking about January, February and March. The plants are of two kinds, known to the Burmese as the "large" and the "early cotton."† The early kind is a plant which does not grow more than three or four feet high and its bolls are ripe in December and January. The large kind reaches a height of from six to ten feet and its seed does not ripen until a month or two later. The produce of the two kinds is hardly distinguishable. That which is grown in the Mye-dai township on the east of the Irrawaddy, especially about Tham-boo-hla is much superior to that grown on the west of the Irrawaddy, and is probably the best cotton grown in Burma. The cotton is all carted in its uncleaned state to the marts on the banks of the river. That produced on the east of the Irrawaddy is brought to Allanmyo and Rwa-toung; that produced in the Thayet township is brought to Thayet-myo; while the produce of the Meng-doon and Ka-ma townships finds its way to the town of Ka-ma.

At Allanmyo, Rwa-toung and Ka-ma there are extensive cotton-cleaning factories where all the cotton that is brought to market is cleaned and roughly baled before being exported to Rangoon. At Ka-ma cotton-cleaning is not carried on, the cotton being sent down in its raw state to Prome.

The cotton-cleaning machine which is in universal use in Burma is a simple and not very effective apparatus. It consists of a rough frame-work of four posts, a bamboo pedal, a fly-wheel and two cylinders placed close to one another, the upper one being a thin one of iron and the lower somewhat larger and of wood. The bamboo pedal is attached by a string to the fly-wheel and the wooden cylinder has a handle at the end opposite to the fly-wheel. The operator, standing in front of the apparatus, with one foot works the pedal which communicates a rapid motion to the fly-wheel and thence to the iron cylinder; with one hand he turns the handle of the wooden cylinder and with the other he feeds the machine, inserting small quantities of cotton between the two cylinders which catch it up and whilst the wool passes through between the cylinders the seed, which is too large to pass, is separated from the wool and left behind.

---

* As toungya are not measured the area under cotton cultivation cannot be given with accuracy.
† Wa-gyee and Wa-yeng.

With this apparatus one operator will clean about 12 viss (43 lbs.) of raw cotton in a day, turning out about 4½ viss (16 lbs.) of cleaned cotton.* There are about 4,000 of these machines at work in this district, 3,000 on the east side and 1,000 on the west side of the river. They are in full work only for about half the year, cotton-cleaning in the rains, when the cotton is damp and labour not so plentiful, being but little carried on. A calculation based on the number of machines, the number of days which they work in the year, and the amount which each machine will clean in a day, makes the estimated amount of raw cotton which is cleaned in a year 728,000 viss, or 1,153 tons. Taking the average ratio of cleaned to uncleaned cotton to be 100 to 265, the amount of cleaned cotton turned out in a year will amount to 274,717 viss (435 tons). This is not all the produce of this district only, as small quantities are smuggled across the frontier from Upper Burma.

The average price of raw cotton at the marts on the river bank during the last few years has been Rs. 20 per 100 viss and of cleaned cotton Rs. 60 per 100 viss ; cart-hire from the interior costs about Rs. 5 for every 30 miles, an ordinary cart carrying about 150 viss at a time.

The only oil seed grown in the district is the *Sessamum Indicum* (the Indian *Til*). This is grown both in toungya and on level land ; when grown in toungya it is sown generally with cotton at the commencement of the rainy season, May or June, and is reaped in September or October ; when grown on level land it is sown about September or October and reaped about December and January.

Chillies are extensively cultivated ; sometimes on the slopes of hills, but generally on the alluvial flats in the bed of a stream which are more or less under water during the rains and dry in the dry season only. The Burmans shew great care in their cultivation of this plant. The soil is industriously harrowed and pulverized and kept clear of weeds until the crop is off the ground. The seedlings are planted after the close of the rains and the crop is gathered in March and April. The maximum produce of an acre is about 300 viss (1,095 lbs).

On the cultivation of onions and garlic also an unusual amount of care is bestowed by Burmans. They are grown invariably in the beds of streams during the dry weather.

This is the largest tobacco-growing district in Burma. The plant is grown chiefly on banks in the Irrawaddy which are submerged during the rains and in the beds of the smaller streams. Some foreign varieties have been introduced and are flourishing. Considerable care is shewn in the cultivation of the plant, but the native method of drying the leaf in the sun takes away from the value of the produce. The largest outturn per acre is about 400 viss (1,460 lbs).

One of the products of the district is cutch or *Catechu*, which is extracted from the inner wood of the *Acacia catechu* by cutting it up in small chips, boiling the chips in water, evaporating the solution to the consistency of syrup over a fire, and then exposing it to the air to harden. It is cut up into squares of about nine inches in breadth and length and

---

* The out-turn is more in the case of the Mye-dai cotton. At Thayet-myo 280 viss (9 cwt.) of raw cotton will turn out 100 viss (3 cwt. 21 lbs.) of cleaned cotton, whilst 250 viss (8 cwt. 4 lbs.) of Mye-dai cotton will give 100 viss of cleaned cotton.

three inches in thickness, wrapped up in leaves and carted to the river bank for conveyance to Rangoon. The two districts of Prome and Thayet-myo supply the greater portion of the cutch which is manufactured in British Burma. Previous to the annexation of Pegu the production of this article in Burma appears to have been small, the wants of the local market being soon supplied and the exports being almost nothing. Since the annexation, however, the manufacture both in Upper and British Burma has gone on increasing rapidly. The cutch-making season proper lasts from October to March ; very little is made from July to September and hardly any at all from April to June.

A cutch tree three feet in girth at the base is considered to have arrived at maturity and to be in the best condition for making cutch. It takes a tree from ten to 20 years, according to the nature of the ground to reach this size. Those situated in the valleys near water grow faster than those on more elevated ground. Owing to the vigour with which the manufacture of cutch has been carried on during the last few years the number of trees in available localities is sensibly diminishing. A cutch tree to be useful to a cutch manufacturer must be situated within an easy distance, say three or four miles miles, from water during the dry season. Owing to the growing scarcity of trees in such localities, the cutch manufacturers began felling small under-sized trees, thereby imperilling the supplies of future years and a system of forest conservancy with regard to cutch has been introduced.

Sericulture is carried on in the Teng-daw and Peng-ga-daw circles in the township of Mye-dai; Kyouk-hpyoot in the township of Ka-ma ; Ban-goon in the township of Thayet; and Shwe-doung in the township of Meng-doon. All these, with the exception of Ban-goon, are situated on the lower slopes of the Arakan mountains west of the Irrawaddy, or of the Pegu Roma range east of the Irrawaddy. In Ban-goon the culture is carried on in the alluvial valley of the Pa-nee stream.

The species of the mulberry plant on which the worms are fed has not yet been identified by any competent botanist*. It is a thin lanky shrub throwing out several vertical shoots from near the ground and growing to a height in the most favourable localities of from eight to ten feet. It bears no perceptible fruit and is propagated by cuttings.†

In Mye-dai the plant is sometimes grown in toungya everywhere else it is grown on level land. After about three years it ceases to produce good and succulent leaves and is then abandoned.

When mulberry leaves fail the worms are kept alive with the leaves of the *Broussonetia papyrifera,* an abundant wild plant, but the silk they produce when fed on this is comparatively worthless.

Very little silk is reeled on the west of the Irrawaddy, the eggs being exported to the silk-growing localities on the east, the best silk being

---

* The Honorary Secretary, Rangoon Agriculture Society. and Mr. Scott, Curator to the Botanical Gardens, Calcutta, have pronounced it *not* to be the *Morus Indica,* but have not declared to what species it does belong.

† The Burman name is Po-tsa-beng—literally " worms' food tree." It is not indigenous, *i.e.* it is never found in a wild state. Concerning the period at which, and the country from which, this tree and the silkworm were first introduced into Burma nothing definite can be ascertained from the traditions of the people. It is supposed to have been introduced by the valley of the Irrawaddy from China.

obtained on the east whilst the lands on the west of the river produce the best eggs.

The price of the silk varies from Rs. 15 to Rs. 10 per viss (3·65 lbs)*. The silkworm is a multivoltine, running its cycle of existences in from 47 to 50 days, of which it passes in the egg eight to 11 days, in the worm stage 30 days, in the cocoon eight days, and as a moth one day. Its true specific name is doubtful. It has been called *Bombyx Arakanensis.*

The largest area that can be ploughed by a cultivator with a single pair of buffaloes in this district is estimated to be five acres; a pair of bullocks will plough rather less. The actual average area of the rice cultivator's farm amounts only to 3 acres 10 annas 6 pies. A 200-basket plot is considered to be the ordinary amount which one man and a pair of bullocks will cultivate. The area of this according to king Aloung-tsee-thoo's standard† would be 3 acres 9 annas 6 pies corresponding very nearly with what is now found to be the average size of the cultivators' holdings.

According to the statements of the best informed natives the money value of the expenses of cultivating a 200-basket plot are as follows :—

Size of farms.

Cost of cultivation.

		Rs.	A.	P.
1	Hire of bullocks or value of bullocks' labour ..	15	0	0
2	Five baskets of seed rice at 0-8-0 per basket ..	2	8	0
3	Hire of ploughs or value of cultivator's labour ..	20	0	0
4	His food	15	0	0
5	Hire of 20 women for planting at ¼ basket of rice per woman	5	0	0
6	Feeding the women	1	0	0
7	Hire of 22 reapers at ¼ basket each	5	8	0
8	Feeding the reapers	5	0	0
	Total ..	69	0	0

If the cultivation yields 200 baskets of rice the value of the crop in an ordinary year when rice sells at Rs. 70 per 100 baskets will be Rs. 140. As a rule, however, cultivation is never carried on by hired labour and the only part of the work that is not done entirely by the cultivator and his own family is that of planting and reaping and in this as often as not the cultivators mutually assist one another. If rice has to be paid to the planters and reapers it is not paid until after the crop has been got in and threshed.

---

* Mr. Blechynden observes with regard to the Burmese silk that the thread is much thicker than Bengal silk, being reeled with twice the number of cocoons, and that though there was no market for such silk in India, it would fetch in London from 10 to 11 shillings a pound.

† The " Ta-ya-geng", or " Pay" as it was called in the olden time, is said to have been defined by king Aloung-tsee-thoo 447 B.E. 1058 A.D., and is a square equal to 280 English feet, or acres 1-12-9.

The Burmans have, or had in former days, three recognized cubit measures. The Than-doung, measuring 24 Burmese or 18 English inches ; the Tsheng-daing-toung, measuring 28 Burmese or 21 English inches ; and the Lay-bhwai-toung, measuring 32 Burmese or 24 English inches. Seven Lay-bhwai cubits made one " Ta," twenty Ta made one " Gyo," and a square measuring a " Gyo" on each side was a " Pay" or " Ta-ya-geng."

The agricultural stock during each of the last eight years was :—

Year.	Buffaloes.	Cows, bulls and bullocks.	Sheep and goats.	Pigs.	Carts.	Ploughs.	Boats.	Oil mills.
1870-71	8,354	61,396	304	5,661	15,253	15,781	870	Not given.
1871-72	9,666	67,990	443	6,962	16,502	19,024	1,028	..
1872-73	10,795	73,227	527	7,736	17,789	20,584	1,074	..
1873-74	11,250	75,718	403	9,646	18,431	21,627	809	..
1874-75	11,415	73,865	292	9,726	18,655	22,280	883	557
1875-76	12,388	77,546	417	10,083	19,206	23,766	756	641
1876-77	13,333	82,806	302	9,574	19,547	24,577	903	676
1877-78	15,011	86,843	231	9,609	20,204	25,575	994	634

and the prices of produce and labour for the same period were :—

Year.	Wages per diem.		Carts per day.	Per Maund of 80 lbs.					Each.	
	Skilled.	Unskilled.		Rice.	Linseed.	Cotton.	Salt.	Tobacco.	Plough Bullocks.	Buffaloes.
	Rs. A.	Rs. A.	Rs. A.	Rs. A. P.	Rs. A. P.	Rs. A. P.	Rs. A. P.	Rs. A. P.	Rs. A.	Rs. A.
1870-71	1 8	0 7	1 8	2 4 0	3 8 0	3 2 0	1 15 0	5 11 0	45 0	65 0
1871-72	1 8	0 7	1 8	2 5 4	3 5 4	4 6 1	1 2 6	8 12 3	50 0	60 0
1872-73	1 8	0 7	1 8	2 0 9	5 4 0	4 6 0	0 13 0	5 9 0	40 0	50 0
1873-74	1 8	0 7	1 8	2 3 0	5 4 4	4 6 0	0 13 0	5 9 0	40 0	50 0
1874-75	1 8	0 7	1 8	2 10 0	5 0 0	4 0 0	0 13 0	5 0 0	40 0	50 0
1875-76	1 8	0 8	1 8	2 10 0	5 0 0	5 0 0	0 13 0	6 10 0	45 0	50 0
1876-77	1 8	0 6	1 8	2 10 0	5 0 0	Not given	1 0 0	6 10 0	45 0	50 0
1877-78	1 0	0 8	1 8	3 9 6	5 0 0	3 8 0	1 0 0	6 0 0	45 0	50 0

The buffaloes are increasing in number very rapidly partly by breeding and partly by importation from the southward. They do not thrive so well as in the more humid delta and are employed chiefly in the fields along the bank of the Irrawaddy and its larger affluents. Cows, bulls and bullocks, on the other hand, will endure a far drier climate and though they have greatly increased in number the increase has not been so great as amongst buffaloes. Both buffaloes and bullocks are used mainly for agricultural and draught purposes and the larger increase in the number of the former is, no doubt, due to the larger increase in the cultivation of the lower and moister lands.

The murrains which carry off so many head of agricultural beasts in the seacoast tracts are rare here and when a spreading disease does break out the people themselves establish a system of quarantine. The following diseases are known and distinguished :—Rinderpest (Kyouk-poak-na ; literally small-pox): Malignant sore throat (Kyiet-na) : Pleuro-pneumonia (Thai-gyce-oo-roung ; literally liver-big-bowel-swell) : Foot and

mouth disease (Sha-na-khwa-na ; literally tongue-disease hoof-disease) :
Anthrax fever (Doung-than-na).

In the prices of most articles there has been a complete revolution
during the last 20 years. The usual price of unhusked
rice before the annexation of Pegu was from Rs. 20 to
Rs. 25 per 100 bushels ; latterly it has been from Rs. 50 to Rs. 60 and even
more. Sessamum seed ranged from Rs. 50 to Rs. 125 ; during the last few
years it has fluctuated between Rs. 180 and Rs. 380. Uncleaned cotton
was sold at from Rs. 5 to Rs. 10 per 100 viss (365 lbs.) lately it has ranged
between Rs. 17 and Rs. 28. Cutch sold at from Rs. 3 to Rs. 10 now it
fetches from Rs. 15 to Rs. 24. Chillies cost Rs. 5 now they sell at Rs. 7
in Meng-doon where they are chiefly grown but rise sometimes to Rs. 28 at
the marts on the bank of the Irrawaddy. Onions cost Rs. 5 per 100 viss
in the Burmese time ; now they cost Rs. 8 or Rs. 10 at Meng-doon, but rise
sometimes to Rs. 40 on the bank of the Irrawaddy. Tobacco cost Rs. 10
per 100 viss ; now it ranges between Rs. 20 and Rs. 30. Bullocks sold
for Rs. 10 each ; now for Rs. 50. A male buffalo fetched Rs. 15 ; now
it costs from Rs. 50 to Rs. 60. Thus it is in plough cattle that there has
been the greatest increase and this is undoubtedly due to the increase
in the area under the plough, itself the result of a more settled and
reasonable government.

On the annexation of Pegu a frontier custom-house was established
at Mye-dai and dues were levied on the export and
import of certain articles. The exports on which dues
were levied and the rates of such dues were—rice, an anna a basket (5s.
per ton) ; rice in the husk half that rate ; salt, four annas a maund (14s. 2d.
per ton) ; betel-nut and all preparations of fish, 10 per cent. *ad valorem.*
Dues at the rate of 10 per cent. *ad valorem* were levied on imports of
all kinds with the exception of coin, precious stones, cotton, grain and
pulse and living animals, which were free, and teak timber and spirits
for which special rates were provided by Act XXX. of 1854. Dues were
l vied at these rates until June 1863. In the mean time the trade which
c ssed the frontier had more than doubled. The total value was, in :—

				Imports.	Exports.	Total.
				Rs.	Rs.	Rs.
1855-56	..	..	..	1,494,970	2,157,280	3,652,260
1862-63	..	..	..	3,866,000	4,496,450	8,362,450

This source of revenue was abandoned by the treaty made with the
king of Burma on the 10th November 1862. That treaty provided for
an optional abolition of inland customs on both sides of the frontier and
it likewise granted the boon of freedom from sea-customs duties to goods
landed in Rangoon for transport into Upper Burma. The English government did not wait for the expiry of the year mentioned in Article 7 of

the treaty but on the 23rd June 1863 ceased to collect customs dues upon the frontier. About four years afterwards (May 1867) the Burmese government, though it wou'd not abolish the duties taken on their side of the frontier, made a consider' ble reduction in the rates. The duty on imports was reduced from Rs. 10 to Rs. 5 per cent. *ad valorem* and export duties hitherto levied at Rs. 6 per cent. were reduced to Rs. 5 per cent. *ad valorem*. Later in the same year, October 1867, the Burmese government bound itself by treaty to levy no more than the above reduced rates for a period of 10 years, the British government agreeing not to re-impose the frontier customs duties as long as the Burmese government should collect only the 5 per cent. *ad valorem* duties.

The conclusion of the treaty had a stimulating effect upon the trade passing by the Irrawaddy between British and Upper Burma. Although duties have ceased to be levied on the British side an establishment is still maintained to register the value of goods carried by boats and steamers and the returns shew that the value of the trade so registered was in 1866-67 Rs. 11,174,690, and in the succeeding year more than double that, or Rs. 23,632,910 ; and the total value of the trade during the succeeding years was—

Year.		Rs.	Year.		Rs.
1868-69	..	19,552,870	1873-74	..	23,291,405
1869-70	..	20,223,880	1874-75	..	26,484,135
1870-71	..	22,073,610	1875-76	..	25,949,561
1871-72	..	21,590,990	1876-77	..	27,289,480
1872-73	..	23,434,224	1877-78	..	31,828,251

The principal articles of export are betel-nuts, cotton twist and yarn, crockery-ware, nga-pee or dried and salted fish and fish paste, piece-goods (cotton, woollen and silk), rice husked and unhusked, salt and raw silk ; and of import are cotton (raw), home-made cotton and silk piece-goods, indigo, safflower, cutch, grain, hides, jaggery and molasses, gums and resins, lac, oil-seeds, lacquered-ware, petroleum, ponies, jade, precious stones, pickled tea and wheat.

Towns. The only places in the district which can be dignified with the name of towns are Thayet-myo, Allan-myo, Rwa-toung, Ka-ma and Meng-doon.

Thayet-myo (Lat. 19° 18′ 6″ Long. 95° 16′ 18″) with a population of 10,170 souls, is entirely a creation of British rule and has arisen round the military cantonments. It contained in the Burmese time only 200 or 300 houses. It is situated on high undulating land on the river bank. The site is dry, gravelly and healthy. It has a well-built masonry market which gives a yearly increasing revenue. At the northern end of the town where non-inflammable roofs have been made compulsory all the houses are good and substantial. This town is the head-quarter station of the district. There are three civil and criminal courts, the Deputy Commissioner's, Assistant Commissioner's and that of a Myo-ook (Extra Assistant Commissioner). There is also a Cantonment Magistrate for the Cantonment. The Cantonment of Thayet-myo was founded in 1854, the troops which during the war were garrisoned at Prome having been moved there during that year.

Allan-myo (Lat. 19° 22′ 50″, Long. 95° 17′ 20″) so called after Major Allan*, the Officer of the Madras Quartermaster-General's Department who demarcated the frontier line, is a new town which has taken the place of the old Burman town of Mye-dai. The fort at Mye-dai having been occupied by British troops a native village sprung up just to the south of it on the opposite side of the Kye-nee-khyoung which here enters the Irrawaddy. The situation being a favourable one as an outlet for the produce of a large tract on the east of the river the village rapidly rose into a town. It was at one time in a most crowded and filthy condition but has since been extended and improved. A substantial market has been built. An Assistant Commissioner who is also *ex-officio* Assistant Collector of Customs resides here. In 1878 the number of inhabitants was 6,841.

Rwa-toung (Lat. 19° 19′ 20″ Long. 95° 18′ 45″) on the bank of the Irrawaddy is just opposite to the cantonments of Thayet-myo. It has a population of 8,696 souls of whom many are engaged in cotton-cleaning. A Myo-ook (Extra Assistant Commissioner) has his court here.

Ka-ma or Ka-ma *cum* Gywon-doung is situated on the right bank of the Irrawaddy in Lat. 19° 1′ 0″ Long. 95° 11′ 0″, at the mouth of the Ma-de river ; the town to the south of the stream being Gywon-doung and that to the north, Ka-ma.

It is prettily situated on low hills most of them crowned by a pagoda or a monastery. It has a population of 8,244 souls of whom all are cultivators or petty traders. The town is a short distance below the mouth of the Ma-htoon and all the surplus produce of the valley of that river consisting of tobacco, chillies, onions, cutch and cotton, that does not go straight down to Prome is disposed of here. A Myo-ook (Extra Assistant Commissioner) holds his court here.

Meng-doon (Lat. 18° 20′ 12″ Long. 94° 4′ 78″) is a pretty little town on high land on one of the bends of the Meng-doon or Ma-htoon river within a few miles of the foot of the Arakan mountains. It has not increased under British rule having formerly been the seat of government of a Won with his numerous staff. It contains a population of 4,218 souls, chiefly engaged in agriculture. A Tsit-kai (Extra Assistant Commissioner 2nd class) has his court here.

Administration. Just prior to the annexation the district was administered by the following officials of the higher ranks :—A Won (an official of the third rank)† at Meng-doon ; Myo-thoogyee or provincial governors who are officials of the fourth-class at Thayet-myo, Mye-dai, Ka-ma, and Gnyoung-beng-tshiep, and Taik-thoogyee or heads of circles in the five circles between Mye-dai and Gnyoung-beng-tshiep. All these were independent of each other and subordinate only to their respective "Myo-tsa" or "eaters of districts" that is princes of the blood or court favourites at Amarapoora to whom the revenues of the tract were assigned. During the war of 1852 not one of these leading officials espoused the cause

---

* " A-lan " in Burmese means a " flag " and most Burmans connect the name with the fact of this being the most advanced post at which the British flag was hoisted.

† I have not been able to trace any appointment of a Won-douk or official of the second rank, and Hlwot-daw Meng-gyee or officials of the first rank never rule provinces but remain at the capital as " cabinet ministers."

of the English. During the war of 1825-26 many men who had held high rank in the Burman service joined the winning side on the supposition that what the British had once taken they would keep ; and when Pegu was ultimately evacuated the lot of such of these men as could not get away to the British provinces of Tenasserim and Arakan was a cruel one : both they themselves and their families were generally put to death by the Burman government. Dreading a repetition of such conduct on our part in 1852 all Burmans of high rank steadfastly maintained their allegiance to the national cause and retired as our troops advanced ; dragging with them wherever it was possible, as in some frontier districts, the whole of the population. The only officials of the old *régime* who were available to carry on the administration of the country were the lowest of all, the rwa-thoo-gyee or heads of villages.

The first Commissioner of Pegu, Major (now Sir A. P.) Phayre, was strongly in favour of maintaining all these petty village officials in their former position and allowing their appointments to continue to be held by hereditary succession ; the rule which was thus laid down was sometimes perhaps abused, for any person, however small his abilities and qualifications might be, who could establish the shadow of a claim to an hereditary village thoogyeeship had the appointment conferred upon him and some few who had no valid title to the distinction managed to get themselves and their villages on to the hereditary list.*

Every village which from the information available at the time of annexation was believed to have been a registered village at the settlement of 1783 A.D. was entered in our rolls as a separate fiscal unit. No less than 256 village tracts were so registered and whenever a man put forward hereditary claims to the headship of any of such villages that is to be a *rwa* (village) thoogyee, he received the appointment and received also a step in official rank by being dubbed a "*taik*-thoogyee", or headman of a circle.†

For some years these petty officials clung with considerable tenacity to their appointments, but in process of time as perquisites decreased whilst work increased, when the villagers refused to be squeezed as formerly and the Deputy Commissioner became more exacting in his demands for reports and returns which the Thoogyee was seldom able to prepare himself and for the preparation of which, therefore, he had to pay, these hereditary officials began to find that their position was no longer what it had been. Instead of being autocrats with power to levy taxes as they liked they were nothing but under-paid and hard-worked underlings. Under these circumstances many of them came to the conclusion that their appointments were not worth holding. Advantage has been taken of vacancies to amalgamate these small village tracts and the number of separate Revenue Circles or Thoo-gyeeships in 1870 was 81, and the

---

* At the settlement of 1783 A.D., the lowest division made was the registered village tract which might contain one or more actual villages, and an hereditary village Thoogyee was appointed to each registered village.

† The words taik (administrative circle) and taik-thoogyee (headman of an administrative circle) thus acquired somewhat different meanings to those which they had under Burmese rule. Under the Burmese government the word "taik" meant what its etymology denotes *viz.,* a collection of administrative units, the units being the village tracts, but under English rule the lowest units have been styled "taik". Now however that these units are being amalgamated our "taik" again approaches its original meaning.

number of Thoogyee has since been reduced to 47. After the annexation the officials appointed for the Civil, Criminal and Revenue administration of the district, the head-quarters being then at Prome, were one or more Assistant Commissioners at Thayet-myo, a Collector of Customs at Mye-dai, Myo-ook (now called Extra Assistant Commissioners) at Mye-dai, Thayet-myo, Bhwot-lay, Gnyoung-beng-tshiep, Meng-doon, Meng-dat, Ka-ma and Mya-wad-dee and the Thoogyee of circles who had only revenue and police powers. Subsequently Meng-dat was joined to Meng-doon and in 1861, on the formation of the existing police force, the Myo-ook and Thoogyee were deprived of police powers, and the number of the former reduced, Bhwot-lay and Gnyoung-beng-tshiep being amalgamated with Mye-dai, and Mya-wad-dee with Ka-ma. At the same time the Pegu Light Infantry, a local corps, was broken up and its place taken by the police, bodies of whom relieved its four detachments in this district, at Tham-boo-la and Kadeng-matha on the east and Meng-doon and Re-myit on the west bank of the Irrawaddy.

In 1870 Thayet was separated from Prome and formed into a separate district as it was found that, owing to the increased prosperity of the country and the increased work which year by year is thrown on to the shoulders of the Deputy Commissioner, the Deputy Commissioner of Prome whilst occupied with important administrative duties at and near Prome was unable to pay that attention which was desirable to frontier politics or to keep strict watch over the frontier freebooters who made constant inroads on our territory from Upper Burma. At present the administration of the district is conducted by a Deputy Commissioner at Thayet who is *ex-officio* Collector of Customs; an Assistant Commissioner at Allan-myo who is also Assistant Collector of Customs, an Assistant Commissioner at Thayet, four Extra Assistant Commissioners at Thayet-myo, Rwa-toung, Ka-ma and Meng-doon, and the Thoogyee of circles. Under the Deputy Commissioner is a Superintendent of Police in charge of about 845 men, subordinate officers and constables, stationed at various points in the district, who is aided by an Assistant Superintendent.

THAYET-HNIT-KHWA.—A revenue circle of about 12 square miles in extent south of Gnyoung-tsee, in the south-eastern township of the Tavoy district, sparsely populated and not much cultivated. Rice is the principal produce. In 1877 the population was 983, the land revenue was Rs. 2,552, the capitation tax Rs. 716 and the gross revenue Rs. 3,395.

THAYET-MYO.—A township in the Thayet district between latitude 19° 29′ 3″ and 19° 5′ 0″ north, and longitude 95° 16′ 30″ and 94° 45′ east. It contains an area of 192 square miles and is bounded on the north by Upper Burma, on the west by the township of Meng-doon, on the east by the Irrawaddy and on the south by the township of Ka-ma.

Its cultivated area in 1871-72 was—

				Acres.
Rice land	..	..	..	8,065
Garden land	..	..	..	795
Miscellaneous	..	..	..	1,634
		Total	..	10,494

It contained also 1,506 toungya and 2,160 trees assessed separately. The revenue was—

Land	..	..	..	Rs.	7,747
Capitation tax	..	..		„	23,967
Fisheries	..		..	„	522
			Total	.. Rs.	32,236

The population by the Census of 1872 was 35,633 of whom 30,524 were Burmans, 3,183 natives of India, 821 Europeans, 678 Khyeng, 58 Chinese and 369 of other races.
It contained the following cattle :—

Buffaloes	..	..	..	364
Bulls, bullocks and cows		..	..	14,741
		Total	..	15,105

It has 49 registered village tracts which are now divided among nine Thoogyee. In 1878-79 the population was 19,498 and the gross revenue, Rs. 25,700.

The present township of Thayet-myo corresponds nearly with what was the Myo-thoogyeeship of Thayet-myo in the Burmese time. The frontier line, however, cut off about one-third of the old Myo-thoogyeeship which it left to Upper Burma. This part is known in Upper Burma as the district of Thayet-gyan.* The present township has received additions from Mye-dai and Ka-ma. In 1859 so much of the old Mye-dai Anouk-bhek circle as is below the frontier line, forming our circle of Mya-tsa-gaing, was taken away from Mye-dai and made over to Thayet-myo. In the same year the circle of Bhan-goon which had always belonged to Ka-ma was also joined to Thayet; and in 1871 the circle of Nga-tshaw was taken from Ka-ma and given to Thayet.

During the last century the interior divisions of the township of Thayet-myo have undergone more changes than those of any other part of the district. In the time of king Tsheng-goo-meng (1138 B.E., 1776 A.D.)—the debauched grandson of the great Aloung-bhoora—one Moung To was hereditary Myo-thoogyee of Thayet-myo and the Myo-thoogyeeship was divided into three circles (Taik) under Taik-ook. The three circles and their Taik-ook were—

Toung-bhek circle, under Moung Hpa, containing 33 villages.
Myouk-bhek circle, under Moung Shwe Loo, containg 33 villages.
Myoma circle, under the Myo-thoogyee himself, containing 33 villages.

The Toung-bhek and Myouk-bhek circles were separated by the Pwon-khyoung. The two Taik-ook had before this held their offices hereditarily for two or three generations.

In the oppression which prevailed in Tsheng-goo-meng's time the population decreased and when Bhodaw-bhoora prepared the Doomsday-book in 1145 B.E. (1783 A.D.) there were found to be only 63 inhabited villages. Of these 36 were entered as registered villages in the Doomsday-book, the headmen of these villages, the Myo-thoogyee, one Tsa-khyee and two

---

* Gyan or Kyan, Burmese—Anglice, "left."

Taik-hmoo making the number of hereditary officials up to 40. The Myo-thoogyeeship remained hereditary in the family of Moung To with one interval only up to the time of annexation. Moung To was succeeded by his son Moung Po and Moung Po by his son Moung Thaing. This Moung Thaing was a great favourite of king Tharrawaddy who gave him higher titles and insignia of rank than were given to any other Myo-thoogyee. His father Moung Po with 500 men from Thayet fought under the Ban-doo-la in the war of 1825-26, first in Arakan and then in Pegu, and as his men wasted away he attempted to raise another 500 in Thayet but was unsuccessful as the people had become terrified and deserted their villages to avoid the conscription.

In the Poo-gan Meng's time (1846—53), which was a period of the most flagrant corruption and extortion, the Myo-thoogyee, Moung Thaing, lost the office which had been held by his family for several generations. Every appointment in the kingdom was then openly sold to the highest briber of the junta which exercised all the powers of government.* Two men, Moung Bo and Moung Myat-tha-oo in succession bid higher than Moung Thaing for the Myo-thoogyeeship, and he therefore had to retire for a time, but he was reinstated in 1852 when the breaking out of the war rendered it necessary for the Burmese government to secure the services of men of influence and note. He retired to Upper Burma at the close of the war. His son succeeded him in the Myo-thoogyeeship of so much of Thayet-myo as has been left to Upper Burma.

When king Hpa-gyee-daw was on the throne (1182 B.E., 1820 A.D.) he appointed his brother the Koon-boung Prince, afterwards king Tharrawaddy, to be Myo-tsa of Thayet-myo. When the Koon-boung Prince ascended the throne he made his son, the Pa-khan-meng, Myo-tsa; and on the death of the latter, his son, the Hpo-hla Prince, succeeded him. When the Poo-gan Prince succeeded his father Koon-boung Tha-yet was given to one of his sisters, called the Tsoo-bhoora, afterwards the chief consort of her brother the late king.

In the year 1200 B.E. (1838 A.D.), just after the accession of king Tharrawaddy when his son the Pa-khan-meng was Myo-tsa of Thayet, the hereditary Taik-hmoo were dismissed and the Myo-thoogyeeship was divided into five Taik-thoogyeeships among which the 36 registered villages were distributed as follows :—

Taik-thoogyeeship in 1200, B.E.	Registered villages.				Name of present circle in which village is situated.
Myouk-bhek ..	Ma-toung-da	..	..	..	Bhan-byeng.
	Re-bwek ..	..	..	..	Kwon-oon.
	Pouk-taw ..	..	..	..	Bhan-byeng.
	Kwon-oon ..	..	..	..	Kwon-oon.
	Toop-kaing ..	..	..	..	Bhan-byeng.
	Pa-nga ..	..	..	..	Do.
	Taw-taw-kyoung	..	..	..	Do.

* The members were—
The Alay-nan-ma-daw Queen.
The Kyouk-padoung Meng-gyee, Moung Shwe Kyee.

The Pabai Atweng-won.
The Tsam-pa-na-go- Atweng-won, Moung Po.
The Shwe-doung-won, Moung Hmoon.
The Kyee-won, Moung Bhwa.

Taik-thoogyeeship in 1200, B.E.	Registered villages.	Name of present circle in which village is situated.
Khyoung-ro ..	Meng-dai ..	Meng-dai.
	Le-daing-tseng	Thai-daw.
	Thai-daw ..	Do.
Myit-khyoung ..	Re-bhyoo ..	Re-bhyoo.
	Hman-deng-gyee	Do.
	Nga-law-ka ..	Tsa-aing.
	Tsheng-dai ..	Do.
	Lek-pan-tshiep	Re-bhyoo.
	Khyeng-tsouk	Do.
	O-shit-goon	Do.
	Hmau-deng-ngay	Do.
	Htan-roon ..	do.
	Kyee-daing ..	do.
	Rwa-toung ..	do.
	Oon-ba-la ..	do.
Myoms	Myeng-ba ..	Bhan-byeng.
	Ka-gnyit-kye	do.
	Myouk-kywot	do.
	Thayet-myeng	do.
	Pwon-khyoung	do.
	Ta-zee-gouk	Upper Burma.
	Tsit-tha ..	do.
	Oon-nai-tai-gyee	do.
	Pwon-ngay ..	Nga-hlaing-gyoon.
Toung-bhek	Hpoung-ga-daw	Upper Burma.
	Hpoung-aing	Nga-hlaing-gyoon.
	Meng-rwa ..	do.
	Pwon-gyee ..	do.
	Nga-hlaing-gyoon	do.

When we made our list of registered villages immediately after the annexation several not entitled to that distinction were included. Thus the four quarters of the town of Thayet-myo have each been entered as a registered village. The following villages also which were not in the list of 1200 B.E. appear in the present list :—Kyouk-aing, Re-baw-kywon, Moon-za-lee, Rwa-thit, Pyeen-doung, Tsa-aing and Pe-kha-deng-tee-too-beng. Pwon-khyoung and Oon-nai-tai-gyee which were in the list of 1200 are not in our list.

THAYET-MYO.—The head-quarters station of the Thayet district lying in 19° 18′ 16″ N. Lat. and 95° 16′ 18″ E. Long., on the right bank of the Irrawaddy about 11 miles south of the northern frontier of the province. The town together with the military cantonment, where the frontier force in Pegu is quartered, is situated near the centre of an extensive and gently undulating plain, well raised above the river, the limit of which to the north is defined by a small range of hills opposite Mye-dai and to the south by a second and very similiar range which stretches from the Irrawaddy in a north-westerly direction and which nowhere rises to a greater elevation than 800 feet, its average height being considerably less. The undulating plain is formed entirely of sand and gravel similar to, and a continuation of, that which is seen well-exposed on the banks of the river at this spot. The gravel is composed, principally, of much-rolled and rounded pebbles of quartz, of many varieties of granites, of hard silicious slates and of nodules of ferruginous sands. In it are found numerous, and occasionally very large, masses of silicified wood (chiefly though not exclusively endogenous) and, though rarely, fossilized bones. It occurs in regular layers associated with sand and occasionally with earthy shaly beds. Though for the most part loosely aggregated and but slightly coherent the sands and gravel are sometimes found cemented into hard conglomerates and sandstone by peroxide of iron, forming a dark red ferruginous bed.

In the rainy season when the Irrawaddy, then one and a half miles wide, rolls immediately beneath the cantonment and everything is green and fresh the aspect of the place is pleasant but in the dry season, when every blade of grass is burnt up, the surrounding hills are half obscured by haze and the smoke of the jungle-fires, and the river has retreated to its dry weather channel on the left bank leaving an extensive sandbank the glare from which increases the heat, the place generally wears a parched, dreary and suffocated appearance.

The name ' Thayet-myo ' in its present form signifies " Mango city " but this is said to be a corruption or abbreviation of its original name of That-yet which, according to a legend, is derived from one of its early rulers, who, fearing that if his sons grew to manhood they would rebel against him, killed them as soon as they were born and hence his city obtained the name of That-yet-myo or ' City of slaughter'. At last his favourite queen when enceinte determined that if she gave birth to a son she would preserve its life ; as soon as the child was born she changed it for the daughter of one of her attendants whom she sent away with her own son to Toung-tseen Taing-da (north of Meng-doon) ; here the young prince was brought up as became his birth. When the king of Thayet grew old his enemies attempted to seize his capital and finding himself put to great straits he lamented that he had killed all his sons who might now have aided him. The queen who had preserved her son seized the opportunity and receiving the king's assurance that he would not injure the young man she sent for the prince who assembled a force, routed his father's enemies and restored to him his territories. The place where the young prince halted before entering Thayet-myo is still called Meng-dai or Prince's tent.

Although the existence at Thayet-myo of one of the Shwe-moot-taw pagodas said to have been erected by Asoka, or as he is called in the Burmese histories ' Theeree Dhamma Thawka ', in 520 B.C. is cited as a proof that in those early days it was a town of importance yet it holds really but a low position as regards antiquity amongst other places in the district. Thayet-myo rose to importance only on the downfall of the Pagan monarchy. It was founded about 1306 A.D. by Meng-sheng-tsaw, son of Kyaw-tswa the last king of Pagan, who built in it a fort and a palace and becoming lord of Thayet ruled over as much of the surrounding country as he could bring under his sway, but in nominal subordination to the three Shan brothers who had overthrown his father. In 1333 A.D., the king of Arakan attacked and captured Thayet-myo and carried off to Arakan Meng-tsheng-tsaw, his wife, their three sons and some daughters. Subsequently they were released and went to Pan-ya where one of the Shan brothers was reigning ; one of the daughters, Tsaw-oom-ma, was possessd of extraordinary beauty and became the wife of four successive sovereigns of Pan-ya, the last of whom was Tha-do-meng-bya, the founder of Ava, on whose death in 1367 A.D. her brother Ta-ra-bya-tsaw-kai was elected king and assumed the name of Meng-gyee-tswa-tsaw-kai. He appointed one of his brothers to be governor of Prome and another to be governor of Myeng-tsaing. In 1373 A.D. the king of Arakan who had conquered Thayet-myo died and the inhabitants of that country offered the throne to the now powerful king of Ava who appointed his uncle Tsaw-mwon-gyee to be tributary king. In the midst of his power the king of Ava did not forget Thayet-myo. He built the Shwe-yen-goung pagoda, since carried away by the river, as a thank-offering for the preservation of his life when carried away captive and he founded the Shwe-thek-lwot pagoda which still stands.

In the course of years the town gradually sank in prosperity and size and on the annexation of Pegu by the British in 1853 contained only 200 or 300 houses.

The rapid increase of the town since the annexation is mainly due to the fact that it is the frontier military station. The cantonment, which was founded in 1854, covers one and a half square miles of ground and is situated on slightly undulating ground on the bank of the Irrawaddy just north of the town. During the war which preceded the annexation the main body of troops above Rangoon was stationed at Prome with a detachment at Mye-dai on the left bank of the Irrawaddy opposite to Thayet-myo. It was at first intended that the main frontier force should be placed at Nwa-ma-yan, a pleasant spot a few miles below Prome, but fever having broken out on the first removal of the troops from Prome Nwa-ma-yan was held to be unhealthy and Thayet-myo, to the exclusion of Mye-dai, was selected as the frontier military station, and the frontier brigade in Pegu has been stationed there ever since. There is some difference of opinion as to whether the best selection possible was made. Though a healthy station Thayet-myo is enclosed on the west and south by ranges of hills which impede the circulation of air and shut out the cool south-westerly breezes which blow during the hottest portion of the year, whilst on the other hand the two hills near the old fort of Mye-dai and the new town of Allan-myo on the opposite bank of the river are comparatively cool and salubrious and on these hills has been formed a sanitary camp to which the troops in Thayet-myo are moved on the appearance of epidemic disease in the garrison. From a military point of view also Mye-dai is, it would seem, a better site than Thayet-myo. A distinguished officer in one of his reports remarks—" I am convinced that the whole of " our frontier force is on the wrong side of the river" and " All military men " must concur in opinion that the position of our infantry force is a false " one at Thayet-myo, that it is on the wrong side of the river. Our pro- " posed main line of communication from our base at Rangoon by a trunk " road is on the opposite (or left bank) of the river and no military operations " are possible on the right bank (or Thayet-myo side). In this view I find " myself materially supported by a memorandum by the Major-General " commanding the division. In the 6th paragraph he writes—' A force is " ' thus left alone on the side where it is obviously least likely to be attacked " ' or useful and where, under present circumstances, it is probable that it " ' would, on a sudden outbreak, find itself, at least for a time, forced into " ' inaction. The troops at Thayet-myo are in a position to act with the " ' minimum of advantage to themselves and the maximum of advantage " ' to the enemy. As things now are there are no boats in which troops

" ' could be moved across in case of necessity, there is no cover on the
" ' opposite bank under which they could land, and there is absolutely noth-
" ' ing to prevent the enemy using their best endeavours to oppose a crossing.'
" Furthermore the General points out that ' from the breadth of the
" ' Irrawaddy it is impossible to close its passage, especially at night, by guns
" ' from one side of the river and thus a large force might pass down stream
" ' in boats.' " The same officer adds that in his opinion as a military
engineer " our position at Thayet-myo is unsatisfactory in the that it
" leaves the head of the trunk road unprotected, and that it cannot prevent
" a hostile force from marching down on Prome." Various plans have
been suggested for remedying the existing state of affairs, the two most
important being (a) to keep the main body of troops at Thayet-myo with
a strong detachment at Mye-dai, and (b) to remove the main body to Mye-dai
retaining a strong detachment in Thayet-myo. The objections to the
latter plan seem to be mainly that the government would have to forego
the large sums of money spent at Thayet-myo. in erecting and improving
the fort and in providing the excellent existing accommodation for
troops.

The strength of the military force at this station has varied with years
in a decreasing ratio, and at present consists of a field battery of artillery,
a wing of a European regiment and a native infantry corps, all on the
strength of the army of the Madras presidency. To the north of the
cantonment on the bank of the river is a small fort, containing the arsenal
and commissariat stores, which has lately been improved and strengthened
and rendered capable of containing the women and children of the garrison
and being held by a small force in the event of the troops having to move
out of the cantonment. In its former condition with its great length of
parapet and small guard it would have been of little use against even a
determined Asiatic enemy.

As is always the case in a town in the neighbourhood of a military
cantonment the inhabitants are of numerous races, Europeans, Indo-
Europeans, Hindoos, Chinese, Parsis, Jews, Afghans, Mahomedans of
various races as Moguls, Suratees, etc., Burmans, Shan and Arakanese.

None of the published returns classify the inhabitants according to
races but the total population during the last 15 years is given in the
following table :—

1863	..	..	6,854	1871	..	..	8,379
1864	..	..	7,443	1872	..	..	15,142*
1865	..	..	7,766	1873	..	..	9,918
1866	..	..	8,543	1874	..	..	9,851
1867	..	..	8,906	1875	..	..	9,830
1868	..	..	8,474	1876	..	..	10,427
1869	..	..	8,607	1877	..	..	10,701
1870	..	..	9,053	1878	..	..	10,000

The temperature from May to October is generally equable. From
November to the beginning of March the thermometer ranges between
42° at night and 84° in the hottest part of the day; from March to May

---

* These figures include the floating population and the troops and camp-followers living in
the cantonment.

it sometimes goes up to 111° in the shade; the nights and mornings are nevertheless generally cool and pleasant, the thermometer marking sometimes 66° in the early mornings.

The thermometric range since 1866 is given below:—

Year.	Rainfall, in inches.				Average temperature i' the shade.								
	January to May.	June to September.	October to December.	Total.	May.			July.			December.		
					Sunrise.	2 P. M.	Sunset.	Sunrise.	2 P. M.	Sunset.	Sunrise.	2. P. M.	Sunset.
1867	10·00	30·25	4·80	45·05	Not given.								
1868	7·47	33·75	9·10	50·15	66	91	74	78	87	85	67	81	71
1869	6·40	20·50	6·30	33·20	81	94	91	81	83	81	60	85	76
1870	12·38	26·15	2·60	41·13	78	91	87	77	86	82	68	84	83
1871	8·75	40·02	6·08	54·85	78	89	85	77	85	82	59	81	79
1872	7·23	29·35	3·33	39·91	78	93	91	77	85	83	61	82	81
1873	5·36	28·25	9·81	43·42	79	99	97	76	89	79	60	81	80
1874	9·12	30·57	12·78	52·47	80	98	96	77	88	86	60	81	80
1875	10·81	37·21	5·27	53·29	88	88	87	77	87	86	57	81	79
1876	3·99	26·10	8·70	33·79	—	—	—	—	—	—	—	—	—

Year.	Average temperature in the shade.											
	May.				July.				December.			
	Mean of maximum readings.	Mean of minimum readings.	Highest reading.	Lowest reading.	Mean of maximum readings.	Mean of minimum readings.	Highest reading.	Lowest reading.	Mean of maximum readings.	Mean of minimum readings.	Highest reading.	Lowest reading.
1876	98·40	82·69	105·00	76·03	87·19	78·87	90·00	76·00	83·80	56·77	86·00	52·00
1877	107·00	79·00	111·00	72·00	89·50	77·00	93·00	74·00	84·200	59·00	88·60	54·80

Thayet-myo since its first occupation as a military station has had the reputation of being a very healthy locality for European troops. In one of the earliest reports, written by Dr. Rankine, the following remarks occur:—" The ratio both of admissions and deaths to strength in H. M's. "29th Regiment is moderate if not low, and speaks well for the climate "of the station in relation to European constitutions." Dr. Rankine then proceeds to shew that the death-rate of the regiment was much lower than that of other regiments serving in Bengal and to point out that the sickness and mortality had decreased with each year of residence since its arrival from that Presidency. At this early period the native troops were by no means so fortunate. They suffered severely from fever and bowel-complaints which carried off great numbers and necessitated the invaliding of others, but this appears to have been in great part due to the diet and accommodation for when these were improved the mortality and sickness at once commenced to decrease and the native regiments now enjoy excellent health. At first the climate seemed inimical to European women and children, especially to the latter, whose annual death-rate during the first three years averaged 153 per 1,000, but this also was found to be due to bad diet and accommodation. The station is now one of the healthiest occupied by troops of the Madras presidency. In 1871 the death-rate amongst the European troops was only 11 per 1,000 and amongst the native troops six per 1,000, and in 1872 it fell to 5·6 and 2·8 per 1,000 respectively.

The most common diseases both amongst the troops and the inhabitants are paroxysmal fevers, dysentery, diarrhœa, and rheumatism, acute and chronic. Disease of the liver occurs amongst the European troops but is not so prevalent as in India proper: the native Burmans rarely suffer from this form of disease. Boils and pustular eruptions on the skin are common to Europeans, especially on first arrival, and though never serious are sufficiently troublesome.

Regarding the wells Dr. Sinclair, Chemical Examiner states—" The " whole place is impregnated with sodium chloride, and to such an extent " at some spots as to indicate the existence of beds of it at no great dis- " tance from the surface. This sodium chloride gives rise to the brackish- " ness of the water. Lime and magnesia are especially abundant, both as " sulphates and carbonates. These make the water hard and to some " degree unpalatable. Alum, peroxide of iron and phosphates make up " the remaining mineral constituents."

The town contains a well-built masonry bazaar or market, a district gaol, a circuit-house and court-houses. Besides the Deputy Commissioner, an Assistant Commissioner and an Extra Assistant Commissioner are stationed here. The Deputy Commissioner is *ex-officio* Collector of Customs, the customs establishment being maintained on a small scale mainly to register the value of goods carried by boats and steamers as, consequent on a commercial treaty with the king of Burma, no duties have been levied since the 23rd June 1863.

The Municipal revenue is derived from the rent of market-stalls, assessments on houses and other sources and the amounts actually collected in 1871-72 and in 1878-79 were Rs. 19,390 and Rs. 24,696, respectively, the expenditure during these years being Rs. 8,780 and Rs. 19,367.

The gaol, which is a large substantial building erected in 1869, is built on the radiating system and is surrounded by a strong masonry wall. In former years the district gaol was at Prome, then the head-quarters of what are now the Prome and Thayet districts, but it was thought more advisable to place it near the military force at Thayet-myo, the advantages resulting therefrom being held to outweigh the disadvantages arising from having a large number of prisoners congregated together so much nearer to the frontier. It is the district gaol for both the Thayet and Prome districts for convicts sentenced to not more than two years imprisonment, but on the one hand its proximity to the frontier rendering it an undesirable place of confinement for long-term convicts and on the other the system in force in the province necessitating the massing together in " central gaols " of all criminals sentenced to lengthened periods of confinement, all delinquents to whom more than two years imprisonment has been awarded are transferred to Rangoon. The average daily number of prisoners confined in 1871 was 552 and in 1872 483. In 1878 the Prome Lock-up was abolished and all sentenced prisoners were sent either to this gaol or to Rangoon.

In 1877 the daily average number of each class confined and the total daily average of the whole gaol were :—

	Daily average of each class.		
	Males.	Females.	Total.
Convicts	446	9	455
Prisoners under trial	5	—	5
Debtors and persons imprisoned for breach of the Excise Act ..	5	1	6
Total daily average ..	456	10	466

The cost per head of average strength during 1874 and the three succeeding years was Rs. 53-6-10, Rs. 44-3-6, Rs. 49-6-2 and Rs. 46-15-3 respectively.

This gaol is on the whole healthy. The daily average number of sick in 1877 was only 12 and the ratio of deaths from all causes per cent. of average strength was 5·49. The principal disease is fever, remittent and intermittent.

The prisoners are employed in cotton-cleaning, spinning and weaving, husking rice, pressing oil (sessamum), weaving bamboo mats, making coir and ropes, stone-breaking, carpentry, blacksmiths' work, etc. An ice machine was started in 1878 to supply, on payment, ice to the troops, hospitals and private residents.

Up to April 1870 Thayet-myo was the head-quarters of the Thayet division of the Prome district, with an Assistant Commissioner in charge, subordinate to the Deputy Commissioner of Prome, but from that date it has been the head-quarters of the Deputy Commissioner of the then formed Thayet district.

THAYET-MYOUNG.—A large revenue circle in the Prome district in the extreme south-eastern corner of the Pa-doung township, on the right bank of the Kha-wa stream. The western portion is hilly and covered with forest, the eastern, where most of the villages are found, is cultivated with rice. In 1876 the population numbered 1,796, the land revenue was Rs. 3,744, the capitation tax Rs. 2,448 and the gross revenue Rs. 6,457.

THAYET-MYOUNG.—A revenue circle in the Shwe-lay township of the Prome district, lying amongst the higher western slopes of the Pegu Roma mountains, and extending westwards as far as the Pa-dek-myoung stream. It now includes Bhan-bhwai-goon on the east as well as Thayet-myoung. In the high hills forming its eastern boundary is the source of the Shwe-lay river. Such cultivation as there is is of rice and cotton and is carried on in toungya near the villages. The surface of the country here as in the Thien-goon circle just to the south (q.v.) is covered with forest in which teak abounds. For many years these valuable forests, estimated as covering an area of 70 square here and in the neighbouring circles, were preserved almost intact owing to the Shwe-lay river being blocked up in the plains west of Poung-day which rendered it impossible to bring out logs of timber, but since the annexation of Pegu the government have taken charge of these as reserved teak forests and the channels in the plains having been cleared and improved timber is annually brought out. This tract was described by Dr. Brandis, then Superintendent of Forests in this province, as "probably one of the richest teak forests in "Pegu." A disadvantage is the scarcity of water in the dry season near the best teak localities. In 1876-77 the population numbered 1,478 souls, the land revenue was Rs. 597, the capitation tax was Rs. 1,868 and the gross revenue Rs. 2,830.

THAYET-NGOOT.—A revenue circle in the north-east township of the Tavoy district, with a very small population of Kareng and hardly any cultivation. Sessamum seeds and cardamoms constitute the principal produce. It is now joined to Metta.

THAYET-PENG-TAT.—A revenue circle in the Shwe-gyeng district occupying the south-eastern portion of the Kyouk-gyee township, east of the Tsit-toung river. It has an area of about 200 square miles and a population in 1876 of 1,969 souls who are principally Kareng. The area under cultivation is very small. The land revenue in 1876 was Rs. 624, the capitation tax Rs. 843 and the gross revenue Rs. 1,499.

THAYET-PENG-TSHIEP.—A village in the Kyek-taik circle, Mo-gnyo township, Henzada (Tharrawaddy) district, on the east bank of the Khwe stream with 696 inhabitants in 1878.

THAYET-PYENG.—A narrow revenue circle in the Ra-thai-doung township, Akyab district, extending eastward from the Ma-yoo hills to the west bank of the Ma-yoo river, between the A-gnoo-maw circle on the south and the Kyeng-kywon circle on the north. In 1877 the land revenue was Rs. 8,197, the capitation tax Rs. 1,880, the gross revenue Rs. 5,831 and the population 1,698.

THAYET-THA-MIEN.—The name of a circle and of a village in the Shwe-gyeng district. See Thoo-yai-tha-mee.

THEE-DA.—A river in the Bassein district. See Kyouk-khyoung-ga-le.

THEE-GOON.—A village in the Thayetmyo district. See Tsa-aing.

THEE-KWENG.—A revenue circle in the east central part of the Thee-kweng township of the Bassein district, bounded on the north and west by the Pan-ma-wa-dee, and with Kway-lway on the south and Iem-mai on the east, with an approximate area of 45 square miles.

The population and revenue during each of the last five years were :—

YEAR.	POPULATION.				REVENUE. IN RUPEES.			
	Burmans.	Karens.	All other races.	Total.	Land.	Capitation tax.	All other items.	Total.
1874	1,734	2,977	—	4,711	7,404	4,470	250	12,160
1875	1,806	3,097	50	4,953	10,036	4,800	250	15,086
1876	1,946	3,275	39	5,260	10,508	5,390	250	16,148
1877	2,935	2,916	51	5,902	10,609	5,512	250	16,371
1878	2,892	2,843	42	5,777	13,116	5,432	250	18,798

and the area under cultivation and the agricultural stock during the same period :—

YEAR.	AREA, IN ACRES.				AGRICULTURAL STOCK.						
	Under rice, including fallow.	Garden.	Miscellaneous.	Total.	Buffaloes.	Cows, bulls and bullocks.	Sheep and goats.	Pigs.	Carts.	Ploughs.	Boats.
1874 ..	3,815	17	5	3,837	1,742	758	27	1,895	195	1,102	460
1875 ..	5,176	48	8	5,232	1,912	1,109	20	2,361	253	1,198	578
1876 ..	5,410	54	19	5,483	2,374	1,281	15	2,318	428	999	629
1877 ..	5,476	50	16	5,542	2,643	1,420	15	2,231	480	886	663
1878 ..	6,779	74	11	6,864	3,119	658	13	321	601	1,107	619

THEE-KWENG.—The name of the upper portion of the Pan-ma-wa-dee (*q.v.*)

THEE-KWENG.—A township in the east of the Bassein district, having Kyoon-pyaw on the north, the Thoon-khwa district on the east, Myoung-mya on the south and Bassein on the west. The northern boundary is formed by the Daga river, the eastern by the Meng-ma-naing and Za-lai-taw creeks and the southern by the Myoung-mya. It is divided into two unequal portions by the Pan-ma-wa-dee which traverses it from N.E. to S.W. and unites the Meng-ma-naing and the Myoung-mya streams. The face of the country is generally level with slight undulations here and there. A large part is covered with forest but portions are well cultivated with rice. It is divided into ten revenue circles. The head-quarters are at Kan-gyee-doung on the Daga. In 1876-77 the number of inhabitants was 51,946, the land revenue was Rs. 130,395, the capitation tax Rs. 54,600 and the gross revenue Rs. 196,094.

THEE-KWENG.—A village in the circle and township of the same name on the southern bank of the Pan-ma-wa-dee, 32 miles east of Bassein. In 1878 it had 539 inhabitants.

THEE-THA-RO.—A revenue circle in the Gyaing Attaran township of the Amherst district, lying between the Toung-gnyo hills on the west and the Attaran on the east, with the Mai-roung circle on the north and the Kyaik-ma-raw circle on the south. The Toung-gnyo hills descend more suddenly into the plains on this side than on the west and there is no continuous belt of up-land at their base. The surface of the circle presents a number of small plains many much flooded by the waters of the Attaran and of its affluents from the westward. Here and there are patches of up-land. The soil is naturally poor and is rendered worse by the constant floods. The inhabitants are mainly natives of India, who have settled down here chiefly for the sake of the pasturage, Talaing and Shan, with a sprinkling of Burmans and Chinamen. The Indians come from various parts of India and are industrious but litigious : many of them are transported convicts or their descendants. The principal village is Pien-nai-goon. In 1876-77 the inhabitants numbered 1,725, the land revenue was Rs. 2,366 and the capitation tax Rs. 1,773.

THEK-KAW.—A revenue circle in the Amherst district, in the Bhee-loo-gywon township, on the eastern side of the hills which traverse that island. On the east is the Salween, on the north the Ka-hgnyaw circle and on the south Kha-raik-thit. Bo-nek which is now included was formerly independent but was added to it in 1851 as the commission was too small to support a Thoogyee. The village of Nat-maw also, which appears to have been at one time under a separate Thoogyee more probably for police than for revenue purposes, has been joined to this circle. The total area is 5,298 acres ; the soil is about the most unproductive in Bhee-loo-gywon. In 1876-77 it had 1,811 inhabitants, the land revenue was Rs. 3,864 and the capitation tax Rs. 1,743.

THEK-NGAY.—A creek in the Bassein district flowing between the Bassein and Pan-ma-wa-dee rivers and forming the north-eastern boundary of Nga-poo-taw island. It is about five miles long and is navigable by river steamers which take this route when proceeding to and from Bassein and Rangoon viâ the Myoung-mya.

THEK-NGAY-BYENG.—A revenue circle in the Henzada district on the right bank of the Irrawaddy opposite Htien-daw.

The population and revenue during each of the last five years were :—

YEAR.	POPULATION.				REVENUE, IN RUPEES.			
	Burmese.	Kareng.	Others.	Total.	Land revenue.	Capitation tax.	Other tacs.	Total.
1874	5,998	993	81	7,072	5,081	7,092	5,760	17,933
1875	6,353	931	81	7,365	5,372	7,637	8,588	21,597
1876	6,353	937	189	7,429	3,746	7,725	8,498	19,969
1877	6,605	1,037	104	7,746	5,820	7,900	8,431	22,151
1878	6,804	1,121	192	8,117	5,922	8,220	8,514	22,656

and the area under cultivation and agricultural stock :—

YEAR.	AREA, IN ACRES.				AGRICULTURAL STOCK.						
	Rice land including fallow.	Garden land.	Miscellaneous cultivation.	Total.	Buffaloes.	Bullocks, cow, and bulls.	Goats.	Pigs.	Carts.	Ploughs.	Boats.
1874 ..	1,243	108	2,033	3,384	579	1,147	14	131	352	258	174
1875 ..	1,574	140	1,842	3,556	950	1,212	6	243	531	290	183
1876 ..	1,445	144	981	2,570	970	1,252	5	162	564	302	157
1871 ..	1,551	162	1,883	3,896	980	1,287	—	180	583	310	163
1878 ..	1,711	191	2,329	4,231	1,014	1,378	—	254	614	325	166

THEK-NGAY-BYENG.—A village in the Tha-noon-tha-naw circle of the Henzada township, Henzada district, about 12 miles south-west of Henzada, on the Nat-maw stream. In 1877 it had 881 inhabitants.

THEK-NGAY-THOUNG.—The eastern mouth of the Bassein river, leaving the main channel opposite Long Island.

THEK-NGAY-THOUNG.—A large village with 1,019 inhabitants in 1877, in the Nga-poo-taw township, Bassein district, in 15° 58' 30" N., and 94° 85' E. This village, with its southern neighbour, Oon-khyoung, which in reality forms a part of it, lies on the right bank of the Thek-ngay-thoung river, on a large island which separates the Thek-ngay-thoung from the Bassein, at the mouth of the Gway khyoung which unites these two. The inhabitants are principally fishermen, and salt and nga-pee-makers, with some cultivators and tradesmen, carpenters, blacksmiths, etc. The principal exports are rice, salt, and nga-pee, the two last of which are made here. The strip of plain along the coast at this place affords ground suitable for rice cultivation, and produces an abundance of excellent grass on which the numerous cattle feed. During the fishing season many of the inhabitants go out and form temporary fishing hamlets such as Tha-may-bhyoo above and Thoung-ga-le below.

THENG-BHA-KAING.—A revenue circle in the Kyouk-hpyoo district on the eastern coast of Ramree island, south of Ran-byai-myoma (south), about 14 square miles in area with a population of 1,441 souls. The principal products are salt, indigo and sugar. Twenty-eight sugar-mills were at work in 1875. In 1877 the land revenue was Rs. 1,426, the capitation tax Rs. 1,597 and the gross revenue Rs. 4,256.

THENG-BHAW-GYENG.—A quarter of the town of Bassein on the west bank of the Bassein river.

THENG-BOON-TAN.—A revenue circle in the Oo-ree-toung (west) township, Akyab district, which in 1877-78 had a population of 1,121 souls. In that year the capitation tax was Rs. 1,487, the land revenue Rs. 4,384 and the gross revenue Rs. 6,114.

THENG-BOON-TAN.—A village in the circle of the same-name in the Oo-ree-toung (west) township of the Akyab district, on the southern bank of the Theng-boon-tan stream. In 1877 it had 769 inhabitants.

THENG-GA-NEK.—A revenue circle in the Kyouk-hpyoo district on the south-eastern coast of Ramree island just north of Nga-kho-byeng, with an area of ten square miles cultivated mainly with rice, and an Arakanese population of 1,830 souls. The land revenue in 1877 amounted to Rs. 1,878, the capitation tax to Rs. 1,327 and the gross revenue to Rs. 2,774.

THENG-GA-NEK.—A village with about 672 inhabitants on the east coast of Ramree island in the circle of the same name, about a mile inland and a short distance north of the Hoon stream.

THENG-GAN-KYWON.—A revenue circle in the southern part of the Myoung-mya township, Bassein district, extending between the Thekngay-thoung and Rwe channels from the sea to the La-bwot-ta natural canal. It is flat and level and has a sandy soil and where uninhabited it is covered with a thin and scattered forest. Like all this part of the country it is cut up into small islands by numerous creeks. The inhabitants are mainly engaged in fishing and nga-pee making, a very few finding employment in agriculture.

The population and revenue during each of the last five years were :—

YEAR				Population.	REVENUE, IN RUPEES.			
					Land.	Capitation tax.	All other items.	Total.
1874	..	..	..	626	736	1,022	6,400	8,158
1875	..	..	..	675	1,053	1,100	5,876	8,029
1876	..	..	..	746	781	1,095	1,977	3,853
1877	..	..	..	729	822	1,032	2,946	4,800
1878	..	..	..	603	729	1,047	3,212	4,988

and the area under cultivation and the agricultural stock during the same period :—

YEAR.	AREA, IN ACRES.				AGRICULTURAL STOCK.						
	Under rice, including fallow.	Garden.	Miscellaneous.	Total.	Buffaloes.	Cows, bulls and bullocks.	Sheep and goats.	Pigs.	Carts.	Ploughs.	Boats.
1874	708	—	10	718	194	—	—	—	33	55	19
1875	997	11	24	1,032	274	8	—	64	34	57	43
1876	735	—	20	755	303	22	—	12	38	65	78
1877	753	8	9	770	305	—	—	7	12	30	27
1878	687	6	7	700	356	136	14	61	85	85	86

THENG-GAN-GOON.—A village in the Tsa-doo-thee-ree-goon circle, Tsan-rwe township, Henzada (Tharrawaddy) district, on the north bank of the Thoon-tshay stream, with 506 inhabitants in 1877.

THENG-GAN-TOUNG.—A village in the Re-gyee (south) circle, Re-gyee township, Bassein district, on the southern bank of the Re-gyee stream, a branch of the Da-ga, six miles south-east of Nga-thaing-khyoung. In 1877 it had 1,405 inhabitants.

THENG-KHYOUNG.—A revenue circle in the Kyouk-hpyoo district on the north-east coast of Ramree, west of Ma-dai island, 18 square miles in extent with a population of 2,125 souls. Sugar-cane is grown and a coarse sugar manufactured in this circle and 26 mills were at work in 1875. The land revenue in 1877 was Rs. 3,829, the capitation tax Rs. 2,377 and the gross revenue Rs. 6,442.

THE-PYA.—A clan of the Bghai family of Kareng; so called by the Gaikho. *See Kareng-nee.*

THIEN.—A small river in the Bassein district which rises in the Arakan mountains and after a S.S.E. course of about ten miles falls into the Bassein at the village of Kyoung-kweng. It is 50 feet wide at the mouth and seven feet deep and its bed is sandy and muddy; its banks are covered with fine timber. The water is somewhat brackish. There is a pass across the Arakan hills from the source of this river.

THIEN-GOON.—A revenue circle in the Myanoung township, Henzada district, now including Ko-eng, which extends from the Arakan Roma down the valley of the Pa-daw eastwards to the Kwon-daw and Pa-daw circles, almost to the plain country bordering the Irrawaddy. The whole area consists of undulating ground and of hills which increase in height towards the main range and are covered with dense bamboo and tree forest, containing Teak (*Tectona grandis*), Eng (*Dipterocarpus tuberculatus*), Pyeng-gado (*Xylia dolabriformis*) and Sha (*Acacia catechu*), in which roam elephants, bison, wild cow, tiger, hog and deer. In the vicinity of the villages small patches of rice cultivation are met with.

The population and revenue during each of the last five years were :—

YEAR.		POPULATION.				REVENUE, IN RUPEES.			
		Burmese.	Kareng.	Others.	Total.	Land.	Capitation tax.	Other tax.	Total.
1874	..	1,412	24	298	1,734	1,537	1,935	—	3,472
1875	..	1,557	30	364	1,951	1,792	2,175	—	3,967
1876	..	1,419	29	381	1,820	1,867	2,072	20	3,959
1877	..	1,500	26	392	1,918	1,990	2,060	20	4,070
1878	..	1,529	51	289	1,869	1,846	2,207	22	4,075

and the area under cultivation and the agricultural stock :—

YEAR.	AREA, IN ACRES.				AGRICULTURAL STOCK.				
	Rice land including fallow.	Garden land.	Miscellaneous.	Total.	Buffaloes.	Bullocks, Cows, and Bulls.	Pigs.	Carts.	Ploughs.
1874	1,550	6	3	1,559	481	433	332	191	210
1875	1,691	9	—	1,700	578	642	211	293	278
1876	1,743	14	1	1,758	342	688	152	317	258
1877	1,839	10	2	1,851	735	882	253	389	253
1878	1,872	6	6	1,884	882	932	215	377	302

THIEN-KHYOUNG.—A village in the Kyouk-khyoung circle, Hmaw-bhee township, Rangoon district, in a very extensive tract of rice land about half a mile up a small creek which falls into the Poo-zwon-doung river, divided into two distinct parts or groups of houses some little distance apart. The inhabitants, who numbered 1,798 in 1878, are principally engaged in rice-cultivation and in trading.

THIEN-PA-GA.—A revenue circle in the Meng-bra township, Akyab district. In 1877-78 the population was 1,443, the capitation tax was Rs. 1,887, the land revenue Rs. 2,637 and the gross revenue Rs. 4,656.

THIEN-TOUNG-PYOO-TSOO.—A village in the Koo-la-pan-zeng circle in the Ra-thai-doung township of the Akyab district, on the western bank of the Tseng-deng stream. In 1877 it had 544 inhabitants.

THIT-GNYO-GOON.—A large village in the Shwe-myeng-deng circle, Bassein township, Bassein district, on the left bank of the Bassein river, in 16° 47' 30" N. and 94° 49' E., about a mile above the town of Bassein. A considerable number of large glazed pots are manufactured here for the Rangoon and Bassein markets (the process is described *sub. tit.* Manufactures ; Bassein district). Of late years the manufacture of ornamental pottery-ware has been introduced but the designs are more florid than graceful.

THIT-HPYOO-BENG.—A revenue circle in the Re-gyee township, Bassein district, to the S.E. of Htan-beng-gyo from which it is separated by the Oot-hpo. It has an area of about 21 square miles and is well cultivated with rice, but at spots in the extreme east and west there are low hills. The inhabitants are mainly engaged in agriculture and some are fishermen. There are good fair-weather cart roads.

The population and revenue during each of the last five years were:—

YEAR.	POPULATION.			REVENUE, IN RUPEES.			
	Burmans.	Kareng.	Total.	Land.	Capitation tax.	All other items.	Total.
1874	3,014	329	3,343	7,898	4,052	1,310	13,260
1875	3,095	557	3,652	8,233	4,345	1,310	13,888
1876	3,236	493	3,729	8,410	4,372	2,110	14,892
1877	3,535	270	3,805	9,087	4,755	2,110	15,952
1878	3,570	572	4,142	9,295	4,762	2,114	16,171

and the area under cultivation and agricultural stock :—

YEAR.	AREA, IN ACRES.			AGRICULTURAL STOCK.						
	Under rice, including fallow.	Garden.	Total.	Buffaloes.	Cows, bulls and bullocks.	Sheep and goats.	Pigs.	Carts.	Ploughs.	Boats.
1874	4,841	7	4,848	825	2,088	4	84	380	704	11
1875	5,107	16	5,123	1,218	4,413	—	163	416	927	73
1876	5,179	16	5,195	1,280	2,522	2	148	436	970	18
1877	5,519	32	5,551	1,664	2,533	3	23	469	981	19
1878	5,661	34	5,695	1,067	2,622	6	40	473	1,175	6

THIT-KYEE-DENG.—A river which rises in the Myit-myeng-doung spur and falls into the Na-weng in the Prome district at Htan-goon six or seven miles from its mouth. In the hot season this stream is dry but in the rains small boats can ascend it as far as the village of Lay-rwa. In some places the banks are steep in others low and flat, the bed is muddy. Eng (*Dipterocarpus tuberculatus*) is found near its source but for the last seven miles of its course it flows through the tract of cultivated low land which lies along both banks of the Na-weng from a little east of the junction of the north and the south Na-weng to the Irrawaddy.

THIT-MEE-TSOO.—A small revenue circle in the Prome district about 13 miles east of Prome. In 1877 the population was 174, the land revenue was Rs. 296 and the capitation tax was Rs. 178.

THIT-MEE-TSOO.—A revenue circle in the south-eastern angle of the Ka-ma township, Thayet district, running up northwards between Toung-tsa-gaing and Htouk-ma, two circles under the same Thoogyee. Out of the 15,360 acres which form the tract about 700 only are cultivated and some 600 more culturable. In 1872 the population numbered 1,006 souls and the revenue aggregated Rs. 1,550. In 1877 the population was 1,023, the land revenue was Rs. 817 the capitation tax Rs. 1,070 and the gross revenue Rs. 1,980.

THIT-NA-BHA.—A village in the Le-myet-hna circle of the Ta-pwon township, Henzada (Tharrawaddy) district, lying on both banks of the Mai streamlet. In 1878 it had 1,075 inhabitants.

THIT-NAN-THA.—A small stream in the Toung-ngoo district forming the northern boundary of the Kan-nee circle and the southern of the Kwon-oon circle. It rises in the Thit-poot hills and after a westerly course of about 16 miles falls into the Tsit-toung some distance north of Toung-ngoo at the village of Kareng. In the rains it is navigable for a short distance by boats of from 20 to 25 feet long, its bed is rocky.

THIT-NEE-DAW.—A river in the Prome district, also called Dha-thwai-kyouk (q.v.).

THIT-NEE-DAW.—A revenue circle in the Poung-day township, Prome district. In 1877 the population was 3,197, the land revenue was Rs. 2,515, the capitation tax Rs. 3,192 and the gross revenue Rs. 9,952. It now includes 10 of the old village tracts.

THIT-POOT.—A small stream in the northern portion of the Prome district not navigable by boats which rises in the long spur of the Roma mountains that forms, in that part of the country, the boundary between the Prome and Thayet districts, and, flowing due south down a narrow valley or more properly a long ravine for a little more than six miles, falls into the north Na-weng near the village of Tham-ba-ya-goon.

THIT-TA-RA.—A village in the Ta-pwon circle, Henzada (Tharrawaddy) district, about two miles west of the Rangoon and Irrawaddy valley (State) Railway. In 1878 it had 903 inhabitants.

THIT-TSHIEN-GOON.—A revenue circle in the Prome district east of Tsa-bay-gan, rich in rice cultivation. Its largest village is Shwe-daw. In 1877 the population was 1,913, the land revenue was Rs. 2,559, the capitation tax Rs. 2,133 and the gross revenue Rs. 4,748.

THOO-HTE.—A river in the Sandoway district which has its sources in the Arakan hills, and after a winding course towards the west falls into the sea about 10 miles south of Tree point.

THOO-HTE.—The northern revenue circle in the central, Myoma, or Sandoway township, of the Sandoway district, extending along the banks of the Thoo-hte stream from the Arakan mountains to the sea. Two or three miles across on the coast it spreads out to 24 miles wide amongst the spurs of the Arakan Roma mountains and covers an estimated area of 340 square miles. It has a population of 3,593 souls, mainly Arakanese, who cultivate more than half of the small culturable area. The principal products are rice, tobacco and sessamum. The land revenue in 1875 was Rs. 4,205 and the capitation tax Rs. 2,866. In 1877 these were Rs. 4,481 and Rs. 2,821 respectively and the gross revenue was Rs. 7,322.

THOO-HTE-KWENG.—A village in the Kyouk-taing-pyeng circle, Than-lyeng township, Rangoon district, with 569 inhabitants in 1878.

THOO-NGAY-DAW.—A revenue circle in the Mro-houng township, Akyab district. In 1877-78 the population was 1,059, the land revenue was Rs. 2,941, the capitation tax Rs. 1,400 and the gross revenue Rs. 4,488.

THOON-KHWA.—A village in the La-wa-dee circle, An-gyee township, Rangoon district, with 979 inhabitants in 1878, who are chiefly cultivators and pot-makers. The village is situated at the junction of the Taw-pa-lwai and Ka-ma-ka-lwon streams about one and a half miles southwest of Kwon-khyan-goon. It has only been in existence since the first Anglo-Burmese war but many of the former inhabitants of Taw-ta-nee and of Ka-ma-ka-lwon have, since the annexation of Pegu, returned from Tenasserim, whither they had fled, and established themselves here.

THOON-KHWA.—A village in the Rwon (east) circle of the Rangoon district with a population of about 725 souls, mainly Talaing, on the creek of the same name in 16° 42′ 30″ N. and 95° 49′ E. The inhabitants are principally engaged in trading, fishing and nga-pee-making.

THOON-KHWA.—A revenue circle in the Nga-poo-taw township, Bassein district, occupying the northern end of the island in the mouth of the Bassein river between the Bassein and the Thek-ngay-thoung mouths ; on the south and west it is bounded by the Pywon-wa natural canal. Its area is about 38 square miles of which but little is cultivated. The inhabitants, Talaing with a sprinkling of Kareng, Burmans and Shan, are chiefly engaged in sea-fishing and in making salt. At the northern end of the circle magnesian carbonate of lime and various kinds of sandstone rise abruptly to the surface forming small hills from 50 to 100 feet in height and excessively steep on the western side towards the Bassein river. At the village of Thit-poot an outcrop of green-tinted sandstone stretches across the Thek-ngay-thoung.

The population and revenue during each of the last five years were :—

YEAR.	POPULATION.				REVENUE, IN RUPEES.			
	Burmans.	Kareng.	All others.	Total.	Land.	Capitation tax.	All other items.	Total.
1874	174	75	1,605	1,854	1,978	2,287	6,655	10,920
1875	200	73	1,506	1,779	2,581	2,257	3,054	7,892
1876	172	82	1,529	1,783	2,810	2,270	3,596	8,676
1877	273	82	1,648	2,003	3,410	2,435	2,897	8,742
1878	258	144	1,617	2,019	3,979	2,502	1,576	8,057

and the area under cultivation and the agricultural stock :—

| YEAR. | AREA, IN ACRES. | AGRICULTURAL STOCK. | | | | | | |
	Under rice, including fallow.	Buffaloes.	Cows, bulls and bullocks.	Sheep and goats.	Pigs.	Carts.	Ploughs.	Boats.
1874 ..	1,435	564	—	11	44	84	259	131
1875 ..	1,781	540	13	9	133	175	283	148
1876 ..	1,934	569	11	—	64	39	176	120
1877 ..	2,369	639	15	6	91	54	311	200
1878 ..	2,715	692	27	3	85	59	157	226

THOON-KHWA.—A small stream in the Rangoon district which flows past Thoon-khwa village and taps a tract of rice land. It is navigable for boats of about 300 baskets burden at all times and seasons and is tidal for the last six miles of its course. Its banks are low and muddy and fringed with tree forest.

THOON-KHWA.—A tidal creek in the Alay-kywon at the entrance to the Bassein river, varying from 100 to 300 feet in width and navigable by large boats.

THOON-KHWA.—A township in the district of the same name divided into four revenue circles. The country is generally low and well-cultivated, the principal product is rice. The population in 1877 was 27,318, the land revenue Rs. 55,779, the capitation tax Rs. 32,436 and the gross revenue Rs. 186,038.

THOON-KHWA.—A revenue circle in the district of the same name in the Southern portion of the Thoon-khwa township. Extensive plains for the most part form the larger portion of this circle which towards the south are under rice but on the north from the lowness of the ground and from the extensive ponds and swamps are unsuited for cultivation but afford occupation to fishermen. In 1877 the population was 11,397, the land revenue was Rs. 31,976, the capitation tax Rs. 13,775 and the gross revenue Rs. 68,831.

THOON-KHWA.—A village in the circle of the same name in the Thoon-khwa district on the Ma-oo-beng river about eight miles south of Ma-oo-beng, the head-quarters of the Extra Assistant Commissioner in charge of the Thoon-khwa township. It contains a police-station and a court-house. The inhabitants, who numbered 855 in 1877-78, are mostly fishermen who leave the village during the working season and return during the rains.

THOON-KHWA.—A district of the Pegu division, formed in 1875, lying between Bassein on the west and Rangoon on the east and extending from the Bay of Bengal to Henzada in the north. The whole face of the country is flat and intersected by a net-work of muddy tidal creeks and almost equally muddy rivers all communicating directly or indirectly with the Irrawaddy

which traverses the district from north to south; of these some are almost
dry at low tides, leaving exposed banks of fœtid mud, whilst others are
navigable by river steamers at all seasons of the year, at low tide neaps
s well as at high tide springs, and all are more or less fringed with forest.
Owing to the continuous deposit of silt the country along the margins of
the water-courses is raised and the district is thus divided into a congeries
of basin-like islands.

The principal rivers are the To or China-bakir, the Pya-poon, the
Kyoon-toon or Da-la and the Irrawaddy. The To leaves
Rivers. the Kyoon-toon at Kyoon-ka-yeng and falls into the Bay
of Bengal by three mouths, the To, the Than-htiep and the Doon-ran,
about 70 miles from its origin. At its narrowest part it is about 500 yards
broad and at its widest about a mile; the depth varies from two and a half
to nine fathoms. During the dry season river steamers reach the
Irrawaddy through this channel. The Pya-poon leaves the To near Hpo-
doot and varies in depth from three to 12 feet. The Kyoon-toon leaves the
Irrawaddy about 10 miles below Gnyoung-doon at about the same place as
the To, and flows S.S.W. to the sea. It is navigable by river steamers for
some distance from its source but it then shallows considerably; in it
are many islands. The Irrawaddy enters the district in the extreme north
and throwing off numerous branches it falls into the Bay of Bengal west
of the Kyoon-toon. The creeks are of all sizes, from broad, deep streams
navigable by steamers to narrow passages barely wide enough or deep
enough to allow the passage of a canoe. Almost every-where the banks
are fringed with tree forest.

The whole tract is alluvial and the geology is precisely similar to that
Geology. of the west of Rangoon and the east of Bassein.

The coastline is generally marked by sandy patches or by the fœtid
mud or sand and mud of the mangrove swamps, and with the exception of a
patch of "newer alluvium", that is the deposit thrown down by the
existing Irrawaddy, the whole district consists of " older alluvial clay " of
a very homogeneous nature "differing mainly from the older clay of the
" Gangetic basin by being less rich in lime but otherwise resembling it in
" general appearance and mode of deposition and arrangement." Under
certain conditions of exposure and weathering it assumes an imperfect
lateritic appearance superficially. This older clay rests on a considerable
deposit of sand or gravel "varying much with the locality. At Gnyoung-
" doon, at the top of the tide-way, this bottom bed consists of clean sand with
" a few small quartz pebbles sparingly dispersed here and there through it ;
" and it is the presence of this under-bed of sand which so greatly favours
" the abrasion of the channel of the Gnyoung-doon stream and is the indirect
" cause of the broad shallow just below the junction of that stream with the
" Irrawaddy."

Of forest trees there are few of any real importance at present, but
Reng-daik (*Dalbergia cultrata*), Pyeng-ma (*Lagerstrœmia regina*) and Ka-
gnyeng (*Dipterocarpus lœvis*) are found towards the north. No State
forests or reserves exist anywhere.

The inhabitants are principally Burmans and Kareng and number only
38·97 to the square mile. It is thus the most sparsely populated district in
Pegu, yet it is more largely inhabited than any district out of that division

The following table gives the number of inhabitants in each year since the district was formed, according to the latest available returns.

Year	Houses — Masonry	Houses — Other kinds	Houses — Total	Over 12 years — Males	Over 12 years — Females	Under 12 years — Males	Under 12 years — Females	Total — Males	Total — Females	Grand Total	Number per square mile	Christians	Hindus	Mahomedans	Booddhists
1875	2	38,904	38,906	64,236	57,507	33,589	31,478	97,825	88,985	186,810	34·00	21*	91	245	186,453
1876	5	39,789	39,794	67,906	61,437	37,416	35,275	105,322	96,712	202,034	37·00	11*	78	426	201,519
1877	5	41,662	41,667	71,183	66,949	37,673	35,170	108,856	102,119	210,975	38.97	2,958	54	389	207,574

* The numerous Karong Christians have evidently been including amongst Booddhists.

There has thus been an important increase and one which evidently is seriously affected by the excess of immigration over emigration. As regards arrivals in and departures from a district the returns may be accepted as fairly accurate, and they show a very large difference in favour of the district. There is no doubt that some shewn amongst both classes are not new-comers from or out-goers to other provinces or foreign states but it is certain that there has been an influx of men from Upper Burma, whilst the floods in 1876 induced many to leave the northern portion of Rangoon to settle in Dai-da-rai and other places in Thoon-khwa where land was easily obtainable. It is therefore very doubtful if population will continue to increase at the same rate as has hitherto obtained.

Towns and villages.

The largest town is Gnyoung-doon, with 9,290 inhabitants, on the left bank of the Irrawaddy at the western mouth of the Pan-hlaing creek, here called the Gnyoung-doon. It owes its existence almost to the increased trade brought about by the annexation of Pegu and the removal of the vexatious restrictions imposed by the Burmese. The inhabitants are mainly traders and brokers and it is a general *rendezvous* of boat-owners; those coming downwards bringing grain, tea (pickled), oils, vegetables and silk and those coming from below, salt, nga-pee, piece-goods, crockery and earthenware, &c.

Pan-ta-naw is a much smaller place, east by south of Gnyoung-doon, also on the bank of one of the mouths of the Irrawaddy near the mouth of the Bhaw-dee stream. The inhabitants who numbered 5,824 in 1877-78, are mainly brokers and traders who deal in the large quantity of nga-pee brought up from the lower country and disposed of here for export northwards.

Donabyoo is on the right bank of the Irrawaddy some distance above Gnyoung-doon and contains a population in 1877-78 of 4,099 souls. During the first Anglo-Burmese war it was stockaded and defended, at first successfully, by the Maha Ban-doo-la but was abandoned by the Burmans when he was killed by the bursting of a shell. No attempt to hold it against the English was made in the second war.

Ma-oo-beng, the head-quarters, is little more than a village built on low ground and noteworthy principally on account of the mosquitos which torment the inhabitants. According to the latest published returns the district contains 783 other villages.

Revenue.

The total revenue demand during the first year was Rs. 1,024,306 and in 1877-78, the latest year for which returns have been published, Rs. 1,243,371. The following table shews under what heads there was the largest increase :—

Year.	Land.	Fisheries and Nets.	Salt.	Forest produce.	Capitation tax and land assessment in lieu.	Excise on spirits and drugs	All other items.	Total.
	Rs.	Rs.	Rs.	Rs.	Rs.	Rs.	Rs.	Rs.
1875-76	347,928	327,946	2,131	1,825	209,685	88,241	46,556	1,024,306
1876-77	377,866	325,686	539	1,793	218,570	72,803	50,721	1,047,978
1877-78	403,310	448,666	1,744	1,263	224,908	115,364	48,116	1,243,371

In addition to this Imperial revenue there are Local Funds raised and spent in the district.

The following table shews the gross revenue and the incidence per head of population :—

Year.	Revenue.			Population.	Incidence per head.
	Imperial and Provincial	Local.	Total.		
	Rs.	Rs.	Rs.		Rs. A. P.
1875-76	1,024,306	35,050	1,059,356	186,810	5 10 9
1876-77	1,047,978	77,135	1,125,113	202,034	5 9 1
1877-78	1,243,371	67,713	1,311,084	210,975	6 3 5

The principal crops cultivated were, in acres :—

Year.	Rice.	Sugar-cane.	Dhanee.	Fruit trees.	Vegetables.	Oil seeds.	Total.
1875-76 ..	163,664	—	191	22,391		120	186,370
1876-77 ..	177,405	—	—	25,717		399	203,521
1877-78 ..	189,635	246	183	18,741	8,289	159	217,253

Thus except fruit trees, vegetables and rice, hardly anything is grown. This is the only district entirely free from toungya. The land is not very fertile and much less so than in the neighbouring districts of Bassein, Henzada and Rangoon, and this for every kind of crop grown in all four.

The agricultural stock has naturally increased with the extension of cultivation.

Year.	Buffaloes.	Cows, bulls and bullocks.	Sheep and goats.	Pigs.	Carts.	Ploughs.	Boats.
1875-76	24,875	7,888	435	5,986	6,572	8,331	7,349
1876-77	25,842	8,510	393	6,022	6,772	12,333	8,563
1877-78	28,120	9,425	462	5,125	5,234	14,127	8,147

Nowhere in Pegu are there so few cows, bulls and bullocks as compared with buffaloes.

The district is divided into three sub-divisions, Ma-oo-beng, Pantanaw and Gnyoung-doon and these again into six townships two in each, *viz.*, Thoon-khwa and Pya-poon, Gnyoung-doon and Donabyoo, Pantanaw and Shwe-loung. In addition to the officers in charge of these tracts of country there are a Superintendent of Police and a Civil Medical Officer.

Administration.

During the first Anglo-Burmese war no resistance was offered to the British Army in this district as it exists at present except at Donabyoo. Early in 1825 the troops advanced from Rangoon, the land column under the Commander-in-Chief moving up the valley of the Hlaing and the water column under Brigadier Cotton making its way to the Irrawaddy ; Sir Archibald Campbell's march was unopposed, the Tharawaddy Meng, a brother of the reigning sovereign who some years later ascended the throne after a successful rebellion, retiring as the British advanced. The Bandoo-la, who had commanded Burmese armies in Manipur and in Arakan, threw himself into Donabyoo which he strongly fortified ; the main stockade commanded the river and was protected by two others lower down. General Cotton's force arrived on the 7th March 1825, and having landed advanced in two columns to the attack. The first stockade was carried but the other two were defended with greater obstinacy. Captains Rose and Cannon were killed and the greater number of the troops engaged killed or wounded. General Cotton thereupon withdrew his force and applied to the Commander-in-Chief for reinforcements. Sir Archibald Campbell at once returned to Sa-ra-wa (Tha-ra-waw) and passing his troops across the Irrawaddy, an operation which took five days, established his head-quarters at Henzada. After a two days halt, during which a detachment under Colonel Godwin was sent against the Kyee Won-gyee whose troops escaped before the British came across them, Sir Archibald Campbell moved down the right bank to Donabyoo where he arrived on the 25th March. Batteries were at once erected, the works being greatly impeded by sorties of the enemy, and on the 1st April the enfilading batteries and on the 2nd the breaching batteries opened fire. Very shortly the enemy was observed to be in full retreat and an advance being ordered the stockades with a large quantity of stores and guns were captured. The Maha Ban-doo-la had been killed the day before by the bursting of a shell whilst he was inspecting the works. The united columns then continued their advance without opposition. At Taroop-maw envoys came in asking the British Commander to halt and enter into peace negotiations, but Sir A. Campbell declined to stop the advance. During the second war Donabyoo was undefended but after the occupation of Prome one Nga Myat Htoon, an ex-Thoogyee of a small circle, succeeded in collecting a body of men and openly defied the British, capturing our boats passing up and down the river, ravaging the country, pillaging every village which furnished fuel to the steamers, driving off thousands of people and cattle and rendering all regular government impossible. Captain Hewett I.N., surprised and defeated a large body which had collected in Donabyoo and in the early part of January 1853 this town was again attacked and the enemy driven out, but the British force on moving into the interior was forced to retire. On the news reaching Rangoon in February 1853 a force of which Captain Loch, C.B. R.N., assumed command, consisting of 158 seamen, 62 marines, 300 men of the 67th B.N.I. under Major Minchin, with two three-pounders from E.I.C. steamer Phlegethon, was despatched to operate against Myat Htoon. Landing at Donabyoo the column advanced into the jungles towards the chieftain's stronghold but were taken in flank and driven back, Captain Loch, mortally wounded, being among the first to fall. "Out of 225 "Europeans who advanced to the attack six were left dead on the field and "53 were wounded. The loss of the Bengal Regt. amounted to five men "killed and 18 wounded; in all 82 casualties."* At this period Captain Fytche, who had been appointed to the civil charge of the Bassein district and had arrived from Sandoway in January, almost unaided by the weak military garrison in Bassein but well supported by a small and valuable force of seamen furnished by Captain Rennie from the Zenobia and Nemesis, was occupied in clearing his district of the marauding parties, remnants of the Burmese forces, which still infested it. The result partly of this second repulse of a British force and partly of Captain Fytche's operations in the south was an immediate accession of strength to Myat Htoon. Sir John Cheape who was commanding in Prome now descended the river in person in command of a force composed of 200 men of the Royal Irish under Major Wigston, who had distinguished himself in the operations in the neighbourhood of Prome, 200 men of the King's Own Light Infantry under Captain Irby, a company of the 67th B.N.I. under Captain Hicks, 200 men of the 4th Sikh local regiment under Major Armstrong, 70 sappers, two guns and some rocket-tubes, and landing at Henzada advanced against the enemy but before coming across him made a flank movement to the eastward and striking the Irrawaddy at Za-lwon proceeded down the river to Donabyoo. Here he was joined on the 6th March by reinforcements from Rangoon consisting of 130 men of the Staffordshire Volunteers under Major Holdich, two mortars and some commissariat stores, and on the 7th the force advanced. In the meanwhile Captain Fytche, who had left Bassein with 90 seamen and marines, four guns and 2,000 Burmans and Kareng and was moving on Myat Htoon from the south by three different roads, came across and drove in his outposts on the 3rd, but was subsequently forced to retire. From the 3rd to the 17th but little was done, the force under Captain Fytche being too to weak to attack alone and Sir John Cheape finding greater difficulties in his way than he expected. On the 17th the two forces moved on towards Myat Htoon's position; Captain Fytche encountered little resistance but Sir John Cheape's advance was strongly though ineffectually opposed. Numerous breast-works had been thrown up and the Burmans fought well behind them. The works were at last carried and the enemy dispersed. The British loss during the expedition was severe, 12 officers and 95 men being wounded and two European officers, one Native officer and 18 warrant officers, non-commissioned officers and rank and file being killed. Myat Htoon himself escaped but gave no more trouble and the country gradually settled down.

THOON-TSHAY.—A village of 961 inhabitants in 1878 on the stream of the same name, an affluent of the Hlaing, in the south, and now the head-quarters of the Tharrawaddy district. It contains a court-house and police-stations and is on the Rangoon and Irrawaddy Valley (State) Railway. The American Baptist Mission has a station in the village.

It was occupied by Sir Archibald Campbell without resistance on the 26th February 1825 on his advance towards the north during the first Anglo-Burmese war and the column halted here for two days till it was rejoined by two native battalions which had been left behind at Hlaing lower down the valley. Lat. 17° 36′ 47″ N.; Long. 95° 50′ 59″ E.

THOON-TSHAY.—A revenue circle in the Tharrawaddy district, in the extreme south, about 64 square miles in extent. In the west the ground is low and cultivated with rice but towards the east it is very hilly, the hills being off-shoots from the Pegu Roma and covered with valuable timber. The inhabitants are principally Burmans, of whom many are engaged in the fisheries in the neighbourhood. The circle was transferred from Rangoon some years ago.

The population and revenue during each of the last five years were :—

	POPULATION.				REVENUE, IN RUPEES.			
YEARS.	Burmans.	Kareng.	All other races.	Total.	Land.	Capitation tax.	All other items.	Total.
1874	6,935	1,658	76	8,669	17,437	8,994	5,000	31,431
1875	8,301	1,658	700	10,659	20,551	9,757	4,410	34,718
1876	7,384	2,639	962	10,985	20,920	9,832	5,147	35,899
1877	6,549	2,383	2,331	11,263	21,373	9,788	5,075	36,229
1878	7,930	2,980	1,384	12,294	22,892	10,904	10,695	44,491

and the area under cultivation and the agricultural stock :—

	AREA, IN ACRES.				AGRICULTURAL STOCK.						
YEARS.	Under rice including fallow.	Garden.	Miscellaneous.	Total.	Buffaloes.	Cows, Bulls and Bullocks.	Sheep and Goats.	Pigs.	Carts.	Ploughs.	Boats.
1874	5,528	76	195	5,899	1,145	1,242	41	351	657	843	69
1875	11,789	84	80	11,953	1,266	1,482	6	40	1,046	954	62
1876	12,083	55	63	12,201	1,340	1,479	8	47	1,078	652	64
1877	12,177	57	156	12,390	1,420	1,516	10	64	1,203	705	70
1878	13,219	59	68	13,338	1,428	1,530	12	70	1,220	700	76

THOO-YAI-THA-MEE.—A village on the right bank of the Tsit-toung river about 30 miles below Shwe-gyeng; the head-quarters of the Extra Assistant Commissioner in charge of the Shwe-gyeng township. It contains a substantial and commodious court-house and a police-station, and a pagoda at which a festival is held annually in November in honour of the founder, a princess who, having lost her betrothed, a Siamese prince, lived a life of celibacy and of charity. In 1878 it had 907 inhabitants.

THOO-YAI-THA-MEE.—More commonly called Thayet-tha-mien. A revenue circle in the Shwe-gyeng district extending along the right bank of the Tsit-toung river as far as the Tsit-toung sub-division and containing the large village of Thoo-yai-tha-mee or Thayet-tha-mien, the head-quarters of the township. It has an area of about 200 square miles and a population in 1878 of 6,460 souls, principally Talaing. In 1877 the capitation tax was Rs. 6,235, the land revenue Rs. 2,869 and the gross revenue, the greater portion of which was derived from the fisheries, Rs. 20,084.

THOUK-RE-GAT.—A river in the Toung-ngoo district which rises in 19° 28′ N. Lat. amongst the wilderness of mountains to the east of the Tsit-toung river and after flowing southwards for some miles turns west on leaving the hills about 20 miles east of Toung-ngoo and joins the Tsit-toung five miles south of that town, draining an area of about 1000 square miles. Its former name was Mya-khyoung or "emerald stream" from its greenish colour, but this was changed to Thouk-re-gat, *circa* 1191 A. D., when King Na-ra-pa-dee-tsee-thoo drank of its waters. Its numerous feeders have their sources in the slopes of mountain ranges with an average elevation of 4000, rising in some places to 7000, feet, and keep it so well supplied that it is but little affected by the extreme drought of the hot weather, and its waters are always clear, cool and refreshing. Between its upper course and the Tsit-toung river is enclosed a mountain tract nearly 20 miles wide and rising to an elevation of 4000 feet. From its mouth to the foot of the hills, where it takes its westerly bend and where it receives the waters of the Kyai and Myit-ngan, its bed is of sand mixed with granite boulders, beyond that it is very rocky. On the whole of the hilly country which it drains teak was at one time extensively spread but a vast amount has been destroyed by the hill-clearings of the Kareng; wherever the slopes of the hills are too steep for Toungya cultivation there and there only teak has been preserved. Pyeng-ga-do (*Xylia dolabraformis*) is found in large quantities as well as *Garuga pinnata, Shorea obtusa, Cordia sp.* and *Gmelina arborea.* For commercial purposes, however, the value of these forests is limited on account of the broken slopes of the valleys and the rocky nature of the bed of the main stream and of its tributaries. In the plains and lower hills nearer its mouth teak is found interspersed with Eng (*Dipterocarpus tuberculatus*) and other green forest trees. A good deal of teak and other timber, canes, bamboos and sessamum are brought down this river to the Tsit-toung.

THOUNG-DAN.—A revenue circle in the Kyouk-khyoung-ga-le township, now joined to Le-myet-hna, in the Bassein district, about 100 square miles in extent, comprising the hilly and mountainous country on the east of the Arakan Roma between the Mai-za-lee stream on the north and the Kyouk-khyoung-ga-le on the south. Eastwards, towards the Bassein river which forms the eastern boundary of the circle, are plains fairly well cultivated and passing into low swampy land. The inhabitants are mainly agriculturists, petty traders and fishermen. It contains several large villages—Kyouk-khyoung, Tsan-rwa, Kek-koo-ma-gyee-beng-tsoo and Lek-pan-beng.

The population and revenue during each of the last five years were :—

YEAR.	POPULATION.				REVENUE, IN RUPEES.			
	Burmans.	Kareng.	All other races.	Total.	Land.	Capitation tax.	All other items.	Total.
1874	6,609	1,520	9	8,138	6,034	8,775	2,080	16,889
1875	7,076	482	21	7,579	6,393	8,870	2,080	15,343
1876	7,155	439	22	7,616	6,844	8,662	2,080	17,586
1877	7,071	401	20	7,492	6,840	8,420	2,099	17,359
1878	7,036	377	15	7,428	6,620	7,892	2,080	16,592

and the area under cultivation and the agricultural stock :—

YEAR.	AREA, IN ACRES.				AGRICULTURAL STOCK.						
	Under rice including fallow.	Garden.	Miscellaneous.	Total.	Buffaloes.	Cows, bulls and bullocks.	Sheep and goats.	Pigs.	Carts.	Ploughs.	Boats.
1874	3,492	100	127	3,719	1,515	2,311	15	7	393	386	105
1875	4,025	190	154	4,369	1,551	1,559	27	158	600	546	195
1876	3,955	213	125	4,293	2,019	1,790	50	97	491	497	263
1877	3,969	207	162	4,338	1,680	1,663	49	156	543	964	353
1878	3,965	209	182	4,356	1,751	1,805	74	96	484	942	107

THOUNG-DOO.—A tidal creek in the extreme southern portion of the Shwe-loung township, Bassein district, between the Ka-ka-ran and the Pyeng-tha-loo or eastern mouth of the Pya-ma-law which it meets near its mouth. It is at all times navigable by the largest boats.

THOUNG-GA-LE.—A tidal creek (the western half of which is called Hnget-kywon) in the lower portion of the Nga-poo-taw township, traversing the large island in the mouth of the Bassein river and running between the main and the Thek-ngay-thoung mouths, varying from 80 to 200 feet in width and at low water having a depth of from one and a half to three fathoms. The banks are low and muddy and covered with rank jungle.

THOUNG-GYEE.—A village in the Mo-bya (north) circle of the Thee-kweng township, Bassein district, on the southern bank of the Da-ga river. In 1878 it had 512 inhabitants.

THOUNG-RWA.—A village in the Tha-bye-hla circle, Kyoon-pyaw township, Bassein district, on both banks of the Re-gyee, a branch of the Da-ga, and eight miles south-east of Nga-thaing-khyoung. In 1878 it had 724 inhabitants.

THOUNG-GYENG.—A river in the Amherst district, forming its northern boundary and separating it from territories nominally if not actually belonging to the kingdom of Siam. Its source is in 16° 27' 47" N. and 98° 50' 50" E. and its course to the Salween, a distance of 197 miles, is about N.N.W. Like most rivers that drain mountainous tracts its breadth varies considerably : below the Hmaing-lwon-gyee, a large affluent from the north which unites with it close to its mouth, the breadth is as much as 1000 feet, above it there are places where it does not exceed 100. From Mya-wa-dee, an old and once fortified town, now a village, on the left bank in 16° 42' 15" N. and 98° 32' 30" E. to its mouth there are 47 rapids and falls down which the water rushes with great velocity rendering navigation impossible; besides these rapids there are rocky gorges formed by the meeting of spurs from the opposite ranges. This river is of importance as the outlet for the timber brought down from the rich teak forests which cover the mountains amongst which it and its tributary, the Hmaing-lwon-gyee, flow, but the working of these is a tedious and expensive operation owing to the great distance over which the timber has to be floated before it reaches the Salween and to the obstructions in the course of the river. The dragging of the logs to the banks of the Thoung-gyeng, or of such of its tributaries as admit of floating, is done during the rains and the cool months of the dry season; from this time to the end of the rains the logs are left lying on the banks and are then floated down in batches of some thousands at a time, all loose and singly, and the foresters close the rear with boats, rafts and elephants pushing on the logs that lie behind or extricating those jammed between the rocks. It is an advantage of this stream that although it is of considerable size it is so shallow that soon after the rains elephants can march along its bed without interruption; this shallowness, however, renders it necessary that the logs should not be rafted and should be followed by a working party and prevents greater progress than at the rate of about two miles a day. The time required to float the timber from the upper forests to the Salween is estimated at four months.

THOUNG-TAIK.—A revenue circle in the Kyoung-goon township, now joined to Tsam-bay-roon, in the Bassein district, about 69 square miles in extent, on the east bank of the Da-ga river, which here winds considerably in sudden and sharp curves. The surface of the country is generally flat but is not extensively cultivated. In the western portion of the circle is a lake some three miles long by half a mile broad which in the rains communicates with the Da-ga; in the dry weather it has some five feet of water in it.

The population and revenue during each of the last five years were :—

Year.	Population.				Revenue, in rupees.			
	Burmans.	Karengs.	All other races.	Total.	Land.	Capitation tax.	All other items.	Total.
1874	1,867	1,692	—	3,559	2,542	3,830	410	6,782
1875	2,191	1,944	—	4,135	8,288	4,802	120	13,210
1876	2,494	2,095	2	4,591	6,000	4,912	120	11,032
1877	2,995	2,285	—	5,280	6,245	5,225	120	11,590
1878	3,008	2,536	—	5,544	7,688	5,827	1,211	14,726

and the area under cultivation and the agricultural stock :—

Year.	Area, in acres.				Agricultural stock.						
	Under rice including fallow.	Garden.	Miscellaneous.	Total.	Buffaloes.	Cows, bulls and bullocks.	Sheep and goats.	Pigs.	Carts.	Ploughs.	Boats.
1874	1,213	445	—	1,658	635	427	—	129	84	159	89
1875	3,960	1,207	322	5,489	679	370	4	145	93	237	47
1876	2,983	848	179	4,010	944	809	3	62	142	439	59
1877	2,977	892	276	4,145	1,126	523	10	97	123	515	63
1878	3,288	1,814	—	5,102	1,118	599	11	161	148	529	55

TO.—A tidal creek or mouth of the Irrawaddy known in the charts as the China-bakir. It leaves the Kyoon-toon or Dala river at the village of Kywon-khareng and after running in a south-easterly direction for about 70 miles falls into the gulf of Martaban between the Rangoon and the Than-htiep rivers. It varies in width from 500 yards to one mile, and in depth from two and a half to nine fathoms at low water. The banks from the mouth to Taw-ta-nee are very low and muddy and a great portion of the country it traverses is inundated during the rains; above that village the banks are steep and covered with grass and tree jungle. For about 16 miles from its mouth the water is salt during floods. During the dry weather at spring tides a bore is formed, sometimes over 18 inches in height, which flows up the Tha-khwot-peng or Bassein creek. From the mouth of the Tha-khwot-peng northwards it is navigable throughout but below this, towards the sea, a bar renders it unnavigable. From the Tha-khwot-peng upwards it forms the dry-season route for steamers and large boats from Rangoon to the Irrawaddy.

TO-KHYOUNG-GYEE.—A village in the Rangoon district on the Poo-zwon-doung river about 12 miles from its mouth, surrounded by a very extensive tract of rice land. The inhabitants, who are principally Talaing, are largely engaged in rice cultivation and some are gardeners and others traders. Lat. 16° 15' 30" N. Long. 96° 16' E.

TO-MA-YAN.—A revenue circle in the Pya-poon township, Thoon-khwa district. In 1877 the land revenue was Rs. 28,720, the capitation tax Rs. 5,170, the gross revenue Rs. 89,634 and the population 3,007 souls.

TOUNG-BHEK-KYWON.—A revenue circle in the Meng-bra township, Akyab district. In 1877-78 the population was 1,804, the capitation tax Rs. 2,440, the land revenue Rs. 3,259 and the gross revenue Rs. 5,894.

TOUNG-BHEK-MYO.—The descriptive name of the southern township of the Sandoway district, occupying the whole of the country between the Arakan Roma and the Bay of Bengal from the Tsa-wa river southwards to the Khwa, the boundary of the district. It has an area of 1,290½ square miles and is divided into six revenue circles. The whole surface of the country is exceedingly mountainous and all the rivers that drain it, except the Khwa, have a general east and west direction and are small and unimportant; the Khwa forms a good harbour but the entrance is impracticable for large vessels owing to a bar as its mouth.

In 1875 this township had a cultivated area of 9,831 acres as follows :—

	Acres.
Rice land under cultivation under annual assessment	6,393
Do. do. fallow do. do. do. do.	123
Do. do. under lease or Revenue settlement for more than one year and paying revenue	795
Toungya at 1-8-0 per acre	242
Do. at 1-4-0 do.	750
Garden and orchard land under annual assessment	501
Miscellaneous cultivation subject to annual assessment ..	1,027
Total ..	9,831

The principal products other than rice are tobacco, sessamum, sugar-cane, dhanee, plantains, cotton, pepper, madder, mulberry, pan-vines, cocoanuts and miscellaneous vegetable products.

The exports from the township consist of sessamum oil and seed, silk, madder, cotton, sugar, torches, nga-pee, dried and salt fish, turtle eggs and a few head of cattle.

The imports mainly consist of cotton, wollen and silk piece-goods and twist, dyed and undyed, lacquered ware, and miscellaneous articles of no intrinsic value.

The most important of the forest products in this township is the wood-oil derived from the *Dipterocarpus tuberculatus* and another species of the same genus, *D. alatus*, which is used by the people in the manufacture of torches.

There are no made roads : communication is maintained during the dry weather with Bassein and the northern parts of the coast by means of small country-built boats which coast along within sight of land ; internal communication is maintained along the beds of mountain streams and the little embankments dividing the rice fields, passable enough in the dry weather for foot passengers but exceedingly difficult and dangerous during the monsoon months when these streams become perfect torrents; during this season the township is practically shut out from all communication.

A foot-track leads towards the Bassein district which is traversed by cattle-dealers, pedlers and a considerable number of natives of India who for financial reasons choose this route for reaching Bassein where they seek and obtain employment as coolies during the rice-shipping season.

Communication between the head-quarters of the Extra Assistant Commissioner and the head-quarter station of the district (Sandoway) is kept up by a police patrol weekly, and the few letters, principally Government correspondence, are conveyed by it; the journey takes a week each way.

The people are mainly occupied in tilling the soil, in fishing for the supply of home wants, and in the preparation of nga-pee which they barter and sell in order to meet their other little requirements. Soon after the close of the harvest numbers of families are occupied in the manufacture of torches, wood-oil being obtainable in large quantaties; the manufacture is not confined to adults but is carried on by the entire family. Each adult can make 50 torches per diem and the average market value of them is from Rs. 8 to Rs. 10 per mille whilst the oil usually fetches Rs. 2 per maund of 82 lbs.

In the Sandoway district silk-worm rearing is wholly confined to this township and is principally carried on by people who make hill clearings and grow miscellaneous products such as sugar-cane, cotton, vegetables, &c.; the total area devoted to the cultivation of the mulberry tree as food for the worms in 1875 was a trifle under 10 acres, and the number of persons engaged in this branch of industry in the same year was 94. The silk is reeled and put in skeins and for the most part is used in the manufacture of home-spun fabrics, a small quantity only finding its way to Bassein the major part being disposed of within the district. The average value of the silk obtained is from Rs. 18 to Rs. 22 per viss (lbs. 3·65). The madder is exported to the Bassein district.

Weaving is carried on by the female members of every household, the fabrics woven being simply to meet home wants.

The gross revenue in 1874-75 amounted to Rs. 26,779, and was derived from the following sources :—

					Rs.
Land revenue	..	..	..	..	..	11,483
Capitation tax	..	..	..	..	..	13,372
Salt tax ..	..	..	..	..	..	119
Net tax ..	..	..	..	..	..	20
Turtle-banks	..	..	..	..	..	815
Timber duty	..	..	..	..	..	4
Excise on liquors and drugs	..	..	..	..	220
Miscellaneous	..	..	..	..	756
				Total	26,779

In 1877-78, the two northern circles having in the interval been transferred to the Central township, the land revenue was Rs. 6,994, the capitation tax Rs. 9,046 and the gross revenue Rs. 21,304. The population in that year numbered 9,919.

TOUNG-BHO-GYEE.—A small village in the Pa-doung township, Prome district, about 12 miles west of the Irrawaddy, opposite Prome, on a little streamlet, a tributary of the Bhoo-yo, across which a dam has been thrown and the water stored for the irrigation of the neighbouring rice fields.

About three miles up this streamlet earth-oil has been discovered and wells sunk, one of which in 1872 was fairly successful, though it was then by no means certain whether it would pay to deepen the shaft and continue the working and it has since been abandoned.

TOUNG-BHO-HLA.—A small revenue circle in the Tharrawaddy district north of Lek-pa-dan, the greater part of the rice cultivation of which is towards the west. Cutch is here made from the Sha (*Acacia catechu*) trees found growing in the circle.

The population and revenue during each of the last five years were :—

Year.	Population.				Revenue, in rupees.		
	Burmans.	Kareng.	All other races.	Total.	Land.	Capitation tax.	Total.
1874	..	2,642	1,667	2	4,317	8,447	4,155	12,502
1875	..	2,613	1,851	10	4,474	11,045	4,543	15,588
1876	..	2,676	1,926	77	4,679	10,880	4,650	15,530
1877	..	3,179	2,072	4	5,255	12,441	4,900	17,341
1878	..	3,402	2,054	113	5,569	12,777	5,238	18,015

and the area under cultivation and the agricultural stock :—

Year.	Area, in acres.				Agricultural stock.					
	Under rice including fallow.	Garden.	Miscellaneous.	Total.	Buffaloes.	Cows, bulls and bullocks.	Sheep and goats.	Pigs.	Carts.	Ploughs.
1874	..	4,780	17	5	4,802	1,345	760	10	243	701	730
1875	..	6,214	64	84	6,345	1,425	955	4	177	750	795
1876	..	6,746	42	28	6,816	1,452	1,047	6	198	804	801
1877	..	7,060	40	43	7,143	1,504	1,324	15	271	966	858
1878	..	7,240	38	35	7,313	1,516	1,484	25	265	1,061	860

TOUNG-BHO-HLA.—A village in the Prome district in 18° 31′ 45″ north and 95° 33′ 40″ east on the right bank of Way-gyee river between the villages of Loung-gyee and Way-gyee.

TOUNG-BOON.—A revenue circle in the Re La-maing township, Amherst district, just south of Kaw-dwot, and extending inland from the seacoast; it is now joined to Taing-ka-maw. It has a small population of agriculturists, mainly Talaing.

TOUNG-BOON.—A village in the circle of the same name, Re La-maing township, Amherst district, with a population of 750 souls in 1877-78.

TOUNG-BYOUK.—A river in the Tavoy district formed by the junction of numerous torrents which rise in the range of mountains forming the eastern water-shed of the Tavoy valley, close to and north of the great Myeng-mo-lek-khat hill. It falls into the Tavoy river about 30 miles below Tavoy through a mouth about half a mile wide. A few miles before it disembogues it describes a semi-circle southwards with a radius of about three miles. At high-water it is navigable by boats for a considerable distance.

TOUNG-BYOUK.—A revenue circle in the south-eastern township of the Tavoy district with a few Kareng inhabitants and but little cultivated. The principal products are betel-nuts and sessamum. In 1877-78 the population was 1,397, the capitation tax Rs. 1,181, the land revenue Rs. 683 and the gross revenue Rs. 1,898.

TOUNG-GNYO.—A river in the Tharrawaddy and Prome districts forming in parts of its course the boundary between the two, and there called the Kyat or the Kan-tha. It has its sources in the western slopes of the Pegu Roma between the Poon-doung and the Toung-gnyo spurs : it first takes a southerly and then a south-westerly course and falls into the Myit-ma-kha. In the rains boats can pass up for some distance. The main road from Poung-day to Ta-pwon crosses this river near the village of Tha-hpan-goon and a wooden bridge of two spans of 60 feet and two of 12 feet was completed some years ago at a cost of Rs. 7,920 to replace one swept away by the teak logs and rubbish from the forests tapped by this stream brought down during a heavy flood. The river has now silted up and the water flows round the bridge on both sides thus cutting it off from the banks and rendering it useless. The country about the sources and the upper course contains some of the finest teak tracts in the district.

TOUNG-GNYO.—A revenue circle in the north-eastern corner of the Tharrawaddy district in the Ta-pwon township, on the upper course of the Toung-gnyo river. Almost the whole of the circle consists of undulating ground and hills which increase in height as they reach the Roma and are covered with tree forest amongst which, especially on the Toun-gnyo and its tributaries, is found Teak (*Tectona grandis*). The population and revenue during each of the last five years were :—

YEAR.	POPULATION.				REVENUE, IN RUPEES.		
	Burmans.	Kareng.	All other rules.	Total	Land.	Capitation tax.	Total.
1874	2,478	362	368	3,208	932	2,681	3,615
1875	2,279	446	423	3,148	1,111	2,760	3,871
1876	2,631	538	650	3,819	1,114	2,826	3,940
1877	2,532	502	428	3,462	1,128	2,916	4,044
1878	2,476	381	430	3,287	1,222	3,053	4,275

and the area under cultivation and the agricultural stock :—

Year.	Area, in acres.			Agricultural stock.				
	Under rice including fallow.	Garden.	Total.	Buffaloes.	Cows, bulls, and bullocks.	Pigs.	Carts.	Ploughs.
1874 ..	1,051	9	1,060	714	365	—	303	304
1875 ..	1,463	3	1,466	631	88	10	268	244
1876 ..	1,439	4	1,443	797	179	12	365	387
1877 ..	1,349	4	1,353	1,055	218	48	273	477
1878 ..	1,453	7	1,460	1,038	115	59	265	368

TOUNG-GNYO.—A revenue circle in the Mro-houng township, Akyab district. In 1877-78 the population was 1,295, the capitation tax Rs. 1,642, the land revenue Rs. 4,777 and the gross revenue Rs. 6,683.

TOUNG-GNYO.—A village in the Ta-gnyek circle, about 13 miles south-east of Mergui with 589 inhabitants in 1878, all cultivators.

TOUNG-GOON ZEE-GOON.—A revenue circle in the Ta-pwon township, Tharrawaddy district, the greater portion of which is covered with grass and tree forest amongst which Teak (*Tectona grandis*) and Sha (*Acacia catechu*) are found.

The population and revenue during each of the last five years were :—

Year.	Population.				Revenue, in rupees.		
	Burmans.	Kareng.	All other races.	Total.	Land.	Capitation tax.	Total.
1874	5,724	16	11	5,751	4,014	5,253	9,267
1875	5,755	3	5	5,763	5,873	5,375	11,248
1876	6,512	5	7	6,524	5,987	5,913	11,900
1877	5,040	5	47	7,092	5,971	6,480	12,451
1878	7,402	4	63	7,469	6,000	6,765	12,765

and the area under cultivation and the agricultural stock :—

Year.	Area, in acres.				Agricultural stock.						
	Under rice including fallow.	Garden.	Miscellaneous.	Total.	Buffaloes.	Cows, bulls and bullocks.	Sheep and goats.	Pigs.	Carts.	Ploughs.	Boats.
1874 ..	2,734	30	—	2,764	1,187	1,364	20	8	839	873	12
1875 ..	4,165	42	81	4,288	1,137	1,389	20	—	765	827	15
1876 ..	4,265	44	91	4,400	1,335	1,568	12	8	836	956	16
1877 ..	4,289	32	96	4,417	1,387	1,513	20	30	843	968	16
1878 ..	4,351	24	48	4,423	1,100	1,647	21	31	957	1,064	19

TOUNG-GOOP.—A village on the left bank of the river of the same name, about six miles from its mouth, in the Sandoway district, the head-quarters of the northern township. It contains a court-house, police-station and telegraph office. The main route across the Arakan Roma from Pa-doung debouches at this town. In 1877 the population was 2,219 souls.

TOUNG-GOOP.—A revenue circle in the northern township of the Sandoway district, on the river of the same name. With a large area only a small portion is culturable, about half of which, or between 3,000 and 4,000 acres are cultivated. The inhabitants are mainly Arakanese. Rice and tobacco are the principal products. The population and capitation tax in 1875 and the land revenue in 1874-75 were 4,215, Rs. 3,622 and Rs. 5,216. The name which signifies "bent hill" is derived from a peculiarly curved spur of the Arakan Roma lying within the limits of the circle. In 1877 the population was 4,432, the capitation tax Rs. 3,768 and the land revenue Rs. 5,700.

TOUNG-GOOP.—A river which rises in the Sandoway district in the western slopes of the Arakan hills and flowing past the large village of the same name falls into the open sea a little to the south of the southern end of Ramree. Two large low islands intersect its course and divide its mouth into three channels.

TOUNG-KHYOUNG.—A revenue circle in the Oo-ree-toung (east) township, Akyab district. In 1877-78 the population was 2,433, the capitation tax Rs. 3,095, the land revenue Rs. 8,921 and the gross revenue Rs. 12,595.

TOUNG-LAY.—A revenue circle in the Prome district on the Teng-gyee river. The inhabitants are principally cultivators. There are a few patches of regular rice cultivation principally near the village of Toung-lay in the west; the rest of the circle eastward is extremely hilly and covered with dense forest. In 1877 the population was 1,332, the capitation tax Rs. 614, the land revenue Rs. 391 and the gross revenue Rs. 1,080.

TOUNG-LAY.—A village in the Prome district in 18° 51' 55" N. and 95° 45' 20" E. on the bank of the Teng-gyee river and at the foot of a subsidiary spur of the Pegu Roma mountains.

TOUNG-LOON.—A revenue circle in the Tsam-bay-roon township, now united to Kyoung-goon, in the Bassein district on the right bank of the Da-ga, between that river and the Hmaw-the, with an area of about 28 square miles. It is extensively cultivated with rice except in the south-eastern portion where the ground is somewhat high and undulating and is covered with tree forest. The inhabitants are mainly agriculturists but a small revenue is derived from fisheries. Kyoon-pyaw, the head-quarters of the township, is the largest town and in 1878 had a population of 2,835 souls. Pyeng-khya-tshiep higher up the Da-ga is a large village. There are good fair-weather cart roads throughout the circle, and along the high ground to the south-east the road is passable at all seasons.

The population and revenue during each of the last five years were :—

YEAR.	POPULATION.				REVENUE, IN RUPEES.			
	Burmans.	Kareng.	All other races.	Total.	Land.	Capitation tax.	All other items.	Total.
1874	5,063	907	71	6,041	12,112	8,145	1,081	21,338
1875	5,950	991	81	7,022	13,263	9,285	1,010	23,558
1876	6,551	1,135	83	7,769	12,094	9,222	700	22,016
1877	6,966	1,191	114	8,271	12,960	9,750	700	23,410
1878	7,041	1,064	105	8,210	13,062	9,645	230	22,937

and the area under cultivation and the agricultural stock :—

YEAR.	AREA, IN ACRES.				AGRICULTURAL STOCK.						
	Under rice including fallow.	Garden.	Miscellaneous.	Total.	Buffaloes.	Cows, bulls, and bullocks.	Sheep and goats.	Pigs.	Carts.	Ploughs.	Boats.
1874	7,210	115	—	7,325	1,709	1,808	62	856	345	878	147
1875	7,927	118	—	8,045	1,159	2,558	46	163	452	908	165
1876	7,215	123	—	7,338	1,048	2,127	26	130	500	982	159
1877	7,882	216	—	8,098	1,030	2,124	33	102	412	822	132
1878	8,086	215	—	7,041	1,102	4,160	130	194	549	1,181	141

TOUNG-LOON-GNYO.—A village in the Prome district which adjoins Meng-rwa and forms the eastern outskirts of the town of Shwe-doung.

TOUNG-LOON-TSOO.—A village in the Anouk-bhek circle, Henzada township, Henzada district, on the west bank of the Irrawaddy and about half a mile south of Henzada. In 1877-78 it had 3,081 inhabitants.

TOUNG-MA-GYEE.—A revenue circle on the coast of the Sandoway district, in the south-eastern corner of the central or Sandoway township. It contains a little rice cultivation and has a population of 1,394 souls. In 1877-78 the land revenue was Rs. 1,299 and capitation tax Rs. 1,306.

TOUNG-NGOO.—A township in the Toung-ngoo district on the west bank of the Tsit-toung, stretching inland to the Pegu Roma and having the Tha-ga-ra township on the north and the Ze-ya-wa-dee township on the south. The whole of the west is intersected by the numerous spurs thrown off by the Pegu Roma mountains and is drained by many small torrents, many of which unite to form the Kha-boung, a stream which joins the Tsit-toung a little south of the town of Toung-ngoo. Between the hills and the river are well-cultivated rice plains. About nine miles from the river, in the latitude of Toung-ngoo, on the bank of the Kha-boung where it leaves the hills, is the old town of Toung-ngoo founded in 1279 A. D., by Tha-won-gyee and Tha-won-ngay on the site of a still more ancient city. The level portion of the township is traversed by numerous fair-weather cart tracks and a road is being constructed from Toung-ngoo westwards across the Roma mountains to Thayet-myo. Excluding the town the number of inhabitants in 1877-78 was 16,982 and the gross revenue Rs. 24,475.

TOUNG-NGOO.—The head-quarters of the district of the same name on the right bank of the Tsit-toung river, 170 miles from Rangoon by land and 295 miles by water and about 37 miles in a direct line from the northern frontier. It is regularly laid out and contains a good bazaar, court-houses, gaol, hospital and dispensary, a Roman Catholic chapel, an Anglican church, Baptist schools, and several police-stations. A redoubt completed in 1864 in the form of a square with four salient angles on which are mounted eight guns is situated on the south-east of the town proper and in the Cantonment are the barracks of the garrison, ordinarily consisting of a wing of an European regiment, a regiment of Native Infantry and a battery of Artillery. About a mile and a half north of the town a small stream empties itself into the Tsit-toung and about two miles south the Kha-boung joins that river. On the west, inside the old wall, is a small sheet of water about one and a half miles in length and half a mile in breadth, and surrounding the town is the old fosse 170 feet broad which, during the rains, always contains water. The site of the town is slightly higher than the level of the surrounding country, which is open and cultivated, in some places covered with low jungle and during the rainy season, when the water is retained in the rice fields, becomes an extensive marsh. Large suburbs, chiefly to the east and south, are included within the municipal limits. The first town founded on the present site was Dwa-ya-wa-dee now known as Myo-gyee, a suburb of the existing town, which was built towards the end of the fifteenth century by a usurper named Meng-gyee-gnyo who subsequently, in 1510 A. D., founded Toung-ngoo or, as it was then called, Ke-too-ma-tee. Inside the walls he built a palace, the ruins of which are still in existence, and converted loathsome swamps into four ornamental lakes. During the second Burmese war the town surrendered to the British who took possession without firing a shot. In 1873 the population, exclusive of the military garrison and camp-followers, numbered 10,195 souls, and in 1872 the gross municipal revenue was Rs. 7,190. In 1877-78 the population was 12,414 and the revenue Rs. 59,470. A fairly good road extends from the town northwards towards the frontier, and another southwards to Htan-ta-beng village on the bank of the Tsit-toung.

TOUNG-NGOO.—A district in the extreme north of the Tenasserim division, 6,354 square miles in extent, bounded on the north by Upper Burma from which it is separated by a line of masonry pillars marking the boundary line fixed by Lord Dalhousie when he annexed Pegu after the second Anglo-Burmese war; on the west by a high range of mountains known as "the great water-shed"; on the south by the Shwe-gyeng district, its limits in this direction being marked by the Rouk-thwa-wa and the Kwon streams; and on the west by the Pegu Roma. In 1861 was added to it from Rangoon a tract of mountainous and densely-wooded country called Bhaw-nee, lying along the eastern slopes of the Pegu Roma south of the Kwon river, but some years ago this was joined to Shwe-gyeng.

Traversing the district are three mountain ranges—the Pegu Roma on the west and the Poung-loung and "Great water-shed"
Mountains. or as it is sometimes called the "Nat-toung Range" on the east of the Tsit-toung,—all having a general north and south direction but the Poung-loung range trending eastward to meet the Nat-toung on the south. The Pegu Roma commence to rise above the surrounding country nearly abreast of Re-me-theng in Upper Burma : the general direction of the chain before entering British territory is S. by W. and after that about 5° E. of S. : it attains its greatest height beyond the southern limits of Toung-ngoo but in this district some of its more lofty peaks are 1,200 feet above the sea, and the average elevation is between this and 800 feet. Towards the south the spurs spread out considerably, but further north the hills are lower and the forest with which they are covered is deciduous so that, notwithstanding the steepness of the slopes, some of the tracks across from Toung-ngoo to the valley of the Irrawaddy offer, during the dry season, but few obstacles to the passage of animals. The hills between the great water-shed and the Tsit-toung have an alititude ranging from 2,000 to 3,500 feet, further to the east are higher ranges their tops covered with pine forests and rising from 4,000 to 6,000 feet with a bold outline and exceedingly steep flanks, while still further to the eastward are the Nat-toung mountains looming in all their massive grandeur, with the magnificent Nat-toung, a very triton among minnows, proudly lifting his bare head 8,000 feet above the sea and towering above a succession of lower hills and spurs of every conceivable size and shape which lie between him and his big-brethren to the north. On the eastern side of this main chain is seer the Salween coursing to the S.E. at a distance of only 12 miles, the intervening mountains having much the same character and appearance as those to the westward. The innumerable congeries of spurs abutting from the main systems, and forming the water-courses in the gorges down their flanks, have no general direction but appear to be thrown up in masses perfectly bewildering. The difficulty that these subordinate hills oppose to a passage through the country may be gathered from the fact that though the distance from Toung-ngoo to Nat-toung is not more than 25 or 30 miles it is a six days trip, and from Nat-toung to the Salween, 12 miles off, a four days journey. The general appearance of these hills as seen from Toung-ngoo has been thus described by Dr. Mason. "The "granite mountains of Toung-ngoo on the east exhibit an almost perfectly "crystaline structure. They are not rounded like the mountains of "Scotland nor have they the flat summits of the Cape Table mountains. "They do not rise in mural masses like the hills of Missouri, nor in pointed "peaks like the mountains of Ceylon......Look at a fine specimen of "Derbyshire spur, cover it, in imagination, with a thin moss and then "fancy all the parts uniformly expanded a thousand-fold. The result will "be a Toung-ngoo mountain ridge as seen some eight or 10 miles distant "across a deep valley with a turbulent stream in the gorge. The prisms, "with their sharp edges lying uppermost, often appear as perfect as in "cabinet specimens, while the trees and gigantic bamboos on their sides "are no larger in the vision than the lowest moss.

"On some of the faces of the crystals, when thrown up to the horizon, "may be seen here and there a Kareng village, the long single house

808

"looking like a little box laid on a shelf; while the roads from one
"to another are frequently on the edges of cubes which lift only triangular
"prisms above the surface, the path scarcely wide enough for two to walk
"abreast, with a smooth descent on each side at an angle of 45 degrees.
"The roads down and over these crystals often defy the skill of an elephant
"to follow them and to reach a point not six miles distant is not uncom-
"monly the work of a whole wearisome day."

The whole of the rest of the district lies between the two main ranges
of mountains and forms the upper portion of the valley of the Tsit-toung,
which on the east has an average breadth of not more than five miles
while on the west it stretches a distance of some 20 miles till it reaches
the Roma range or some of its innumerable spurs. Near the frontier the
valley to the west of the river "has an exceedingly rugged appearance,
"and so irregular is the country that cultivation can only be carried on
"on the banks of the various small streams and on the cleared patches on
"the side of the hills."* The country is here wild and difficult but a few
miles below the frontier "the Pegu hills recede giving place to plains in
"the vicinity of the river which gradually widen as Toung-ngoo is
"approached, carrying with them a continuous level strip on the opposite
"bank of four or five miles in width, beyond which the mountains rise
"with great rapidity. To the south of Toung-ngoo the plains increase in
"breadth by the diverging course of the river. A large tract of wild
"country, about 25 miles in width, is thus left on their west"* from which
rise the numerous spurs of the Roma range already alluded to.

The Tsit-toung, the only large river, rises in Burmese territory in the
hills south-east of Ava about 25 miles north of Gnyoung-
rwe in 21° 20' N. and 96° 55' E. and falls into the sea at
the head of the Gulf of Martaban after a total course of 350 miles, of
which about one half are in the Province, but the stream is so tortuous
that the development of the last 175 miles is little short of 300. South
of the frontier line the banks are high and hilly nearly to Toung-ngoo,
below which they are uniformly low on the west' whilst on the east the
hills abut on them in several places. Throughout its course it is, in the
dry season, shallow and full of shoals, but with efficient pilots steamers of
very light draught can ascend as far as Htan-ta-beng whence there is a
good bridged road to Toung-ngoo. In the rains it rises from 18 to 24
feet, and is then navigable for steamers of considerable draught but is at
present unapproachable for such vessels either by its mouth or any other
channel. Three miles below the town of Toung-ngoo the Bhoom-ma-wa-
dee Re-gyaw leaves the parent stream on the east to re-unite with it lower
down, forming a large island some 20 miles in length.

The tributaries of the Tsit-toung, which are important only in as much
as they develop the natural resources which the district possesses and none
of which ever completely dry up, are, on the west, the Tshwa, the Kha-boung,
the Hpyoo and the Kwon, and on the east, the Bheng-byai, Kan-nee, Thouk-
re-gat and Rouk-thwa-wa. Those which descend from the Roma carry with
them such quantities of earthy matter as to form along their winding course
to the Tsit-toung high borders of silt which are so much raised above the
general levels of the adjacent parts of the valley as to be free from inundation.

The Tshwa rises in the Pegu Roma and after an easterly course of 60 miles falls into the Tsit-toung about 24 miles north of the town of Toung-ngoo. In the rains boats of from 30 to 35 feet in length can ascend as far as Ayo-doung, a village situated amongst the spurs of the Roma some distance inland. All along its course are found sandstone and other rocks. A considerable quantity of teak is annually floated down this stream to the Tsit-toung and the inhabitants of the hill villages send down raw silk, the produce of the silk-worms which they breed.

The Kha-boung rises in the Pegu Roma on the northern edge of the Thit-pa-loo spur, from the southern slope of which flows the Hpyoo. After a course of 68 miles it falls into the Tsit-toung two and a half miles south of Toung-ngoo. In the rains boats of 100 baskets burthen can ascend as far as the small village of Tsan-re which lies hidden amongst the hills : towards the source the banks are steep and the bed rocky. It is an outlet for much teak and areca-nuts and for some sessamum seed. Its name is derived from the Kha-boung (*Strychnos nux vomica*) which is plentiful as a large tree in the forests on its banks.

The Hpyoo rises in the Pegu Roma on the southern slope of the Thit-pa-loo spur and falls into the Tsit-toung 28 miles south of Toung-ngoo, near the village of Oot-hpyat, after a south-easterly course of 70 miles : in the rains good-sized boats can ascend as far as Meng-lan, beyond which it is impracticable owing to the rocky nature of its bed ; the banks are steep and the bed rocky and sandy. A small quantity of teak and a considerable quantity of raw silk find their way down this stream. Its name is derived from a colony of Hpyoo, or Pyoo, who settled on its banks, probably coming from Prome of which, according to Burmese history, they were the inhabitants.

The Kwon rises in the Pegu Roma ; it has an easterly course of about 60 miles and falls into the Tsit-toung 50 miles south of Toung-ngoo. Its bed is extremely rocky but a good deal of teak and raw silk are brought down as well as Iron-wood (*Xylia dolabriformis*), Theng-gan (*Hopea odorata*), used for boats, and Thit-ya (*Shorea robusta*) used in the construction of carts, oil-mills and rice-mills.

The Bheng-byai rises in the Poung-loung range and after a south-westerly course reaches the Tsit-toung 30 miles north of Toung-ngoo ; it is not navigable by boats but it renders accessible a considerable quantity of teak.

The Thouk-re-gat rises in the main chain to the eastward and after flowing in a southerly direction for some 35 miles on the east of the Poung-loung hills turns west and passing through this range empties itself into the Tsit-toung some five miles south of Toung-ngoo. Receiving as it does the waters of several perennial streams, fed from inexhaustible reservoirs in the mountains, it is but little affected by the extreme drought of the hot season and its waters are always clear, cool and refreshing. It owes its present name to a tradition of its waters having once been drank by Nara-pa-dee-tsee-thoo, king of Pagan, who is said to have visited Toung-ngoo in 1191 A.D.: its ancient name was Mya-khyoung or " Emerald stream " due to the greenish hue of its waters. Large quantities of Teak (*Tectona grandis*) Theng-gan (*Hopea odorata*) canes, mats, bamboos and sessamum seeds are brought down this river.

The Rouk-thwa-wa rises in the Poung-loung range and falls into the Tsit-toung about six miles north of the village of Moon in the Shwe-gyeng district. It is an outlet for a considerable quantity of areca-nuts and for a little teak and other minor products. The Kan-nee also rises in the Poung-loung range and fa. s into the Tsit-toung about five miles north of Toung-ngoo. A moderate quantity of teak, boats, bamboos and sessamum find their way to Toung-ngoo by this stream.

The soil of the valley of the Tsit-toung is a tenaceous and arenaceous alluvium which towards the frontier is bounded by rising ground composed of the clayey beds and superincumbent sands of the fossil group on which Mr. Theobald, in the records of the Geological Survey of India, Vol. X. part 2, pages 73 *et sequentia*, remarks :—

"There are satisfactory grounds for assuming that the fossil-wood group "originally extended as far south as Rangoon, and that sundry traces of "its presence beneath the gravelly surface accumulations may be detected "along the line of the outer skirts of the Pegu Yomah, after leaving Rangoon "long before the principal remnants of the beds still existing are met with "in Eastern Prome. On the eastern or Martaban side, however, of the "Pegu Yomah, the removal of the fossil-wood sand appears to have been "more complete as I not only failed to find any fragments of fossil-wood. "myself, but ascertained by repeated enquiries that none such were known "to occur to villagers who are perfectly familiar with the silicified wood or "'Engynchouk' from the use which is made of it, as a substitute for flint, "wherever it occurs. On nearing from the south the banks of the Kaboung "Choung (*Kha-boung-khyoung*), which falls into the Sittoung (*Tsit-toung*) "a little below Tonghoo (*Toung-ngoo*) near Lat. 18° 53', I first heard of "fossil-wood, which, I was told, occurred not rarely northwards of the "Kaboung (*Kha-boung*) and I first detected small fragments of fossil-wood "within a few miles of the Kaboung (*Kha-boung*) on its right or southern "bank, where, however, such fragments are scarce and small. Crossing the "Kaboung (*Kha-boung*) at a spot about two miles north-west of Tha-bhet-"kway (*Tha-bhek-khwe*) and 15 miles west of the confluence of the Kaboung "(*Kha-boung*) large masses of fossil-wood are seen scattered over the hill "side, some of which are three or four feet in length, and derived apparently "from a single huge stem broken in pieces by its own weight as the soft "sand in which it was originally entombed was removed in an irregular "manner by atmospheric action. From this place for a distance of 25 "miles northwards fossil-wood is not rare at a variety of spots scattered "in the outer hills ; after which, though the same beds seem to prevail to "the frontier, the fossil-wood is absent. As a rule, the uppermost or fossil-"wood beds are chiefly met with along the outer hills, giving place by degrees "as we proceed west to the underlying beds of the Prome group ; but near "the frontier, in the Magoo Choung just above its junction with the Choung-"ma-nay* (*Khyoung-ma-ngay*) and higher up the stream still nearer the "Yomah, that is, within three or four miles of it, large pieces of fossil-wood

Geology.

---

* " The names Magoo and Choung-ma-nay are not given in the map (Fitzroy's) but the former "nearly corresponds in position with the stream called Hsokay (one probably being an affluent "of the other) whilst the Khyoung-ma ngay is probably identical with the Kyouk ma-hseng of the "map."

" are seen, showing that much of this ground was overspread by the incoher-
" ent fossil-wood beds, though now next to wholly removed by denudation.
" Throughout this area the rocks are not well seen, being masked by
" detritus and overspread with dense tree forest. The dips are rather more
" irregular than is usually the case with the older groups, and from the
" nature of these upper sands, it is far from easy to say whether or not any
" material unconformity exists between them and the often highly inclined
" beds whereon they rest; from analogy I am, however, inclined to think
" that there is little unconformity between them, as on the western side
" of the range these uppermost beds have participated in the movements
" which have affected those beneath them, and to which the general
" disintegration of this incoherent group may be largely due. The area
" in Tonghoo (*Toung-ngoo*) mainly occupied by these beds may be roughly
" estimated as not far short of 700 square miles, of which eighty miles is
" composed of outliers east of the Sittoung (*Tsit-toung*) flanking the Poung-
" loung range.
    " I have already mentioned the great similarity which exists between
" a tract of country composed of the lower or more argillaceous beds of this
" group and an ordinary alluvial plain; and this similarity may be well
" seen between the Kaboung (*Kha-boung*) and the frontier, and were our
" observations to be restricted it would often be impossible to decide to which
" group the beds composing the surface of the country belonged; but in all
" such cases we have only to extend our examination and we sooner or later
" come to the boundary of the alluvium if moving towards the east or, if
" in the opposite direction, we soon find the seeming alluvium or clayey
" champaign country give place insensibly to the low outlying hills of the
" Yomah, composed of the same materials. This may be seen throughout
" the whole country lying north and south of the village of Amot-kyee-kon
" (*A-hmat-gyee-goon*) on the Hswah Choung (*Tshwa Khyoung*) where it de-
" bouches from the hills, and we may here traverse miles of perfectly level
" tree forest seemingly alluvial but which in reality lies within the area of
" the clayey beds of this group, denuded of its uppermost sands. I am
" inclined to think that these clayey beds are rather more developed as
" respects thickness in the Tonghoo (*Toung-ngoo*) district than they are in
" Prome, and are perhaps a trifle coarser and less homogeneous. One of the
" best sections I know of these beds is on the main road running from Ton-
" ghoo to the frontier, between the villages of Nyoung Kyat (*Gnyoung-kyat*)
" and Myohla, where the road descends from the high plateau formed by
" these clays to the alluvial plain of the Sittoung (*Tsit-toung*) one and three
" quarter miles south-west of the latter village. The deposit is here seen
" to consist of a thick bed of sandy clay, devoid of any distinct bedding, and
" with but a few small pebbles dispersed through it. Locally these pebbles
" are commoner, as they may sometimes be seen on the surface weathered
" out of the clay, though their presence is exceptional. It is commoner
" to find a little grouty laterite strewed over the surface and in places the
" clay itself is converted at the surface into tolerably compact laterite quite
" undistinguishable from the laterite pertaining to the newer deposits on
" the opposite side of the Sittoung (*Tsit-toung*) further to the south near
" Shuaygheen (*Shwe-gyeng*). This leads me to notice one of the most
" curious and deceptive instances of change of mineral character in the

" present group that I am acquainted with, though it is of local character
" and dependent on the conditions under which the deposit here origi-
" nated.

" As a matter of fact little or no laterite, certainly nothing like a con-
" tinuous deposit, occurs from north of the village of Paday (*Pa-de*) to the
" frontier, a distance of 28 miles. Towards the frontier the alluvial plain of
" the Sittoung (*Tsit-toung*) is bounded by rising ground, most of it exceedingly
" flat, arid and uninhabited in consequence, composed of the clayey beds and
" superincumbent sands of the fossil-wood group. The sandy beds, however,
" do not extend south of the Pyeng-tha-le Choung (*Pyeng-thee-la*) which
" enters the Sittoung (*Tsit-toung*) 16½ miles below the frontier. South of
" this these sandy beds have been removed by denudation and the alluvium
" is thence bounded by the crystalline and gneissose rocks of the Poung-
" loung range. East of the village of Paday (*Pa-de*), however, a small
" outlier of the group has survived, on the end of which stands the Kannee
" Pagoda overlooking the Sittoung (*Tsit-toung*) and a little further south a
" a more considerable outlier which stretches below Tonghoo (*Touny-ngoo*) to
" close on the banks of the Thouk-yay-gat (*Thouk-re-gat*) river. These two
" outliers are, lithologically considered, typical laterite, distinguishable only
" from the great belt of laterite met with south of Kyouk-kyee by being in
" places charged with huge boulders which greatly reduce the lateritic
" cement wherein they are embedded ; but a close examination of these
" interesting deposits has convinced me that, geologically speaking, they
" are portions of the fossil-wood group and the extreme termination of
" the group to the south on the eastern side of the Sittoung (*Tsit-toung*),
" denudation having entirely swept away the group on that side of the
" river below the junction of the Thouk-yay-gat (*Thouk-re-gat*) in Lat.
" 18° 53 . The lithological constitution of both these outliers is the same
" and to it in part may be due their preservation when the less coherent
" portion of the group was removed by denudation. The bulk of the
" deposit may be described as a sandy clay, differing but little from that
" met with to the north of the Sittoung (*Tsit-toung*) within the area of this
" group ; but an additional feature it here presents is the great number
" of pebbles contained in it which, weathering out, give the appearance
" of the country being composed of gravel beds ; where, however, a section
" is displayed it is seen that the gravel is merely a surface accumulation,
" the result of denudation, which has removed the finer sand and clay
" and left the surface encumbered with the pebbles originally dissem-
" inated through the bulk of the rock. This can be well seen along the line
" of road between Kannee and Kon-meng-eing (*Koon-meng-aing*) and thence
" to Paday. The same may be said of the road south from Kon-meng-eing
" (*Koon-meng-aing*) to Hlay-myoung and thence to the well-known Pagodas
" at Myar-soh-ni-moung, five miles east-south-east of Tonghoo on the north
" bank of the Thouk-yay-gat. North of Hlay-myoung it is not usual to find
" stones in the clay larger than would be ordinarily called pebbles, and which
" in the aggregate might be termed gravel ; but between Hlay-myoung and
" Myar-soh-ni-moung these stones in many spots give place to the coarsest
" shingle with pebbles averaging three or four inches in length, and not
" rarely containing boulders six or eight inches or more long. Where this
" coarser shingle is most abundant the clayey element is proportionately

" diminished and the rock passes into what may be called a mortar bed of
" the coarsest shingle cemented into a compact rock by a sandy ferruginous
" clay or laterite : in fact this laterite, though I have said it belongs to the
" fossil-wood group, is undistinguishable from the laterite of Martaban to
" the South, of a newer date, and the reason is, doubtless, either that both
" are derived from the waste of the same rocks in the Poung-loung hills
" to the eastward, or what may partly be the case, the newer laterite is
" largely composed of detritus produced by the denudation of the lateritious
" beds of the present group.

" The cause of this great difference in lithological character in these
" beds from that anywhere noticed to the westward seems to me sufficiently
" obvious, and lies in the fact that the Poung-loung range of hills formed the
" eastern shore of that Pliocene, and in part probably Post Pliocene, sea,
" wherein the whole fossil-wood group was deposited ; and that these coarse
" outliers are the remants of a zone of similar character which fringed its
" shores wherever they were favourable for its production ; and it is quite
" within the bounds of the probable that the coarse shingle and boulders I
" have described as scattered over the hill slopes in western Prome, especially
" along the Mudday (Ma-de) Choung, may be the debris of a similar local
" deposit, now too much broken up and denuded to be cognisable as such,
" but which originally marked the western shores of the Post Pliocene sea
" and coincided in general terms with the line of the outer hills of the
" Arakan range, which would give a breadth of open sea in the parallel of
" Tonghoo of about 100 miles.

" No fossil-wood, to my knowledge, occurs east of the Sittoung, though
" I am aware that a contrary statement has been made by natives to Major
" Lloyd at Tonghoo ; but after examining the ground for the express purpose
" I am unable to confirm the fact. The fossil-wood where plentiful is com-
" monly used as a flint, and I have noticed in this district a man when
" questioned if he knew of any fossil-wood in the neighbourhood put on a
" blank look of not comprehending what fossil-wood was but when its use
" was explained to him as used for procuring a light at once say ' yes, there
" is plenty of that stone' which on examination has proved to be a silicious
" rock, equally useful no doubt, but totally unlike the article sought. Certain
" it is, I was never able myself either to find or hear of any fossil-wood being
" found east of the Sittoung (Tsit-toung) and none I believe exists there.

" Very little if any of the peculiar nodular oxide of iron which so charac-
" terises the uppermost bed of this group in Eastern Prome, occurs in Ton-
" ghoo, but it would seem to be represented by some irregular tabular masses
" of manganese ore which occur in some of the beds of sandstone forming
" the low range of hills dividing the Yaynay (Re-ne), and Seing Choung
" (Tsaing Khyoung), from the Sittoung. This ore occurs in irregular strati-
" form masses of an inch or two in thickness and in irregular nodules often
" sub-botryoidal in character and of a black colour, and is composed, accord-
" ing to an analysis by Mr. Tween, as follows :—

Loss on heating	..	..	..	4 0
Oxide of manganese	..	..	..	28 0
Iron	..	..	..	8 2
Clay and sand	..	..	..	64 8
				100 0

To the westward this fossil-wood group is bounded by the "Pegu "group" in which the bulk of the Pegu Roma is comprised, of upper tertiary age covering probably the whole of the geological epochs known as Miocene and Pliocene, whilst to the eastward, confining it within much narrower limits on the left bank of the Tsit-toung, are the gneissose rocks of the Poung-loung range, of the age of which nothing is known. Of the so-called granite mountains east of Toung-ngoo, Mr. Theobald, in the work already cited, page 140, observes. "The connexion of a granite or granitoid "rock with a distinctly schistose group of beds may be seen on the road from "Tonghoo to Layto, where the schistose and crystalline characters of the "beds are seen to give place insensibly to the granitoid habit, huge masses "of the latter type of rock being seen weathering out of the softer bed of "the former character. I am not sufficiently familiar with the area of this "granitoid rock to pronounce confidently that none of it is true granite, but "I am greatly inclined to question if any is."

Limestone appears in various places east of the Tsit-toung river, and north-east of Toung-ngoo a light grey marble is quarried for lime.

The Toung-ngoo forests west of the Tsit-toung are situated on the Kwon, Hpyoo, Bhan-loung, Kha-boung, Tshwa, Myo-hla and Doung-hla-gnya rivers. Some of these are confined to the borders of these streams in the lower plains, and some of them extend up into the Roma hills, occupying the narrow ridges and slopes of some of the lower heights.

Forests.

The lower Kwon forests commence on the Kwon about midway between the confluence of that river with the Tsit-toung and the foot of the hills. This part of the valley consists of beds of sand resting on laterite, and where it is not cultivated the low ground free from forest is covered with wild sugar-cane. The forests consist of *Dalbergia, Barringtonia, Acacia, Bombax, &c.* The water-mark on the trunks of the trees shews that the forests are liable to inundation but on slight elevations composed of a sandy soil teak is found; at first the trees are small but on pursuing the course of the stream towards the hills very fine timber is seen growing on its high sandy borders along with other fine timber as *Pentaptera, Xylia* and *Melicocca,* an occasional wood-oil tree, and *Blackwellia* a tall tree with light-coloured smooth bark that is never absent from the teak forests.

At the foot of the hills the Upper Kwon forests commence and are found on low ranges of hills composed of a sandy kind of slate clay; occasionally the laterite of the valley rises a short distance on the foot of the outer hills but soon disappears on their abrupt declivities to the evident improvement of the teak timber. The ordinary soft slaty rock of the hills then appears and above this the ridge is crowned with a narrow belt of teak together with the other trees with which it is usually associated except the wood-oil tree which is confined to the dry alluvial banks of the lower streams.

The only good forests on the Hpyoo are situated near the falls, those below the falls having been very much worked. They are situated on low hills at the base of the Roma range lying close to the bank of the stream about two miles from the village of Meng-lan and extend from thence for the space of three or four miles to the falls : they were here at one time extensive but have been much exhausted. Above the falls where the forests have not been worked there is a large quantity of teak timber. The teak here grows on the same kind of slaty rock covered with the same rich but light sandy soil as in the Kwon forests.

The Bhan-loung takes its rise in some low ground situated between the Hpyoo and the Kwon and on its banks is a small forest situated on alluvial soil similar to that of the lower Kwon. The forest extends from the banks of the Bhan-loung nearly to those of the Hpyoo about three or four miles distant and to within six miles of the Tsit-toung. From its close vicinity to the Tsit-toung and the convenience with which timber may be carried away this forest has been greatly worked.

There are no teak forests on the banks of the Kha-boung after it reaches the plains but about three miles west of Tha-bek-khwe teak trees begin to appear on the summits of the low hills on the north bank of the stream and continue at intervals for four or five miles when occasional teak trees are found on both sides. The most numerous trees composing the forests are *Xylia, Pentaptera* and teak, nearly in the order they are here given ; after these come *Semecarpus, Nauclea, Æglœ,* and *Cedrela toona. Strychnos* is so plentiful in the forests on this stream as a large tree as to give its name to the stream itself, Kha-boung being the Burmese name of *Strychnos nux vomica.* Teak continues to occupy a second or third place in the forests for several days journey up to the source of the stream and at the pass between Toung-ngoo and Prome occasionally appearing on the narrow ridges to the exclusion of most other trees, except *Xylia* and *Pentaptera.* The soil is here the same as that of the higher Kwon and Hpyoo forests, namely a light grey sandy, but rich soil resting upon and passing into slate clay of a sandy structure and friable consistence.

The forests on the Tshwa commence on the north bank at the village of A-hmat-gyee-goon, to the west of which there is a low ridge consisting of a river sediment 30 or 40 feet in thickness resting on laterite and some 50 feet or so at its highest part above the level of the plains. Along this ridge or high bank, which follows the course of the stream and is occasionally intersected by it, some fine teak trees occur in straggling clumps. The forests on the north side of the river follow the borders of its tributaries which drain the low but undulating plains to the foot of the hills about nine miles distant. Throughout this tract teak is found scattered about more or less on the higher ground. The belt of forest occupied at intervals by teak along the main river is on an average half a mile broad, in some places more and in some less. Intervals of two or three miles occur without teak, followed by a succession of small forests or patches where teak is the prevailing tree for a similar space of two or three miles and in this way the forest extends for several days journey along the banks of the stream. In one place small round flat hills of laterite protrude through the soil on which are stunted scraggy trees of *Dipterocarpus alatus, Buchanania, Shorea* and *Rondeletia tinctoria* but no teak, although the latter of large size grows on the light sedimentary soil at their foot. On the south bank of the river a similar chain of small forests are found to that described on the north bank, extending to the banks of the Tsit-toung, a distance of about 12 miles. The trees here associated with teak are *Xylia dolabriformis, Pentaptera glabra, Terminalia chebula, Careya arborea, Strychnos, Hamiltonia, Nauclea cordifolia, &c.*

The forests east of the Tsit-toung are situated in the small branching and winding valleys of the Rouk-thwa-wa, Thouk-re-gat and other streams descending from the Poung-loung mountains and the great water-shed.

The valley of the Rouk-thwa-wa at its exit towards the Tsit-toung forms, for a few miles, broad plains partially cultivated; these plains are open towards the Tsit-toung but enclosed to the east by broad low hills composed of laterite, with forests of *Dipterocarpus alatus* and *Melanorrhœa usitatissima*. The teak forests are situated in the valleys beyond these hills, where the soil is composed of sediment washed down from the hills, and commencing at a distance of eight or ten miles from the Tsit-toung extend eastward along the course of the narrow valleys to a distance of 16 miles from the Tsit-toung, branching off in various directions; they stretch towards the north for about eight miles from the Rouk-thwa-wa. The teak is widely dispersed throughout these valleys, growing along with *Melicocca*, *Careya* and other trees with which it is usually associated; some of the finest Pyeng-ma (*Lagerstrœmia reginœ*) in the province is found in these forests.

The Thouk-re-gat forests are situated in the valley of the Thouk-re-gat, a stream of considerable size rising within the Poung-loung mountains. The teak forests are confined to the valleys lying between the small hills at the foot of the mountains; they commence about six miles south-east of Toung-ngoo and extend from thence along the valleys on both sides of the hills for about six miles. Throughout these valleys teak is found growing in a light dry sandy but rich soil washed down from the neighbouring hills. The higher hills are composed of soft granite, the lower of laterite. The trees found with teak in these forests are *Shorea robusta*, *Melicocca trijuga*, *Walsura piscidia*, *Pentaptera* and *Xylia*. These are all very plentiful and afford excellant timber.

The Kan-nee forests lie in a valley separated from that of the Thouk-re-gat by broad rounded arid hills of laterite with forests of *Dipterocarpus alatus*, *Melanorrhœa* and *Diospyros melanoxylon*. Descending into the Kan-nee valley teak of large growth is found along with *Shorea*, *Xylia*, *Melicocca* and *Pentaptera* of great size, the three last extending to the banks of the Tsit-toung, while the teak and *Shorea* extend up the course of the valley still attended by the other trees already mentioned as well as *Macroclina hookerii*, *Cedrela toona*, *Odina wodier* and *Bassia sp.* The Kan-nee forests commence at about the distance of five or six miles from the Tsit-toung, not far from the village of Kan-nee, and extend to the eastward along the course of the valleys of the river and its branches: the soil is rich alluvium resting on laterite.

The Kareng forests are situated in a valley of the same name about eight miles north of Kan-nee. The two valleys are separated by similar low hills of laterite to those already described, having in addition to the trees already noticed several species of *Gardenia*. The teak forests extend eastward along the valley and are confined to the alluvial soil. The other trees found with teak are *Shorea*, *Pentaptera*, *Melicocca* and *Xylia*, the three last of gigantic growth, extending to the banks of the Tsit-toung.

The Thit-nan-tha forests extend along the course of the valleys of that iver and its tributaries for 10 or 12 miles from the Tsit-toung. The south side of the valley is formed by a low ridge of granite extending from the mountains on the east at the head of the valley to within a few miles of the Tsit-toung; while the northern side is formed of broad undulating hills of laterite which, likewise, ramify through the middle of the valley. The laterite is covered with *Dipterocarpus alatus, Melanorrhœa, Diospyros, Rondeletia* and *Gardenia,* together with *Acacia catechu.* The granite hills do not present much difference from the vegetation of the valley. On them are *Callicarpa arborea, Strychnos,* and *Menispermum.* In the valleys and alluvial flats between the hills and along the course of the streams teak is found together with two species of *Pentaptera, Melicocca, Walsura* and *Shorea* as before. These forests formerly extended right down the delta of the valley but have been cleared away to make room for rice cultivation for a distance of some miles from the Tsit-toung. North of this are two small forests on the Kwe-thay and the Bheng-byai rivers.

For house purposes the trees most commonly used are Eng (*Dipterocarpus tuberculatus*) Pyeng-ma (*Largerstrœmia reginœ*) Pyeng-ga-do (*Xylia-dolabriformis*) and Hlee-tsa (*L. tomentosa*) and for boat-building, Theng-gan (*Hopeaodorata*) Koung-hmoo (*Parashorea Stellata.*) Toung-bien (*Artocarpus echinatus*) and Ka-gnyeng (*Dipterocarpus alata*). Cart-wheels are generally made of Theng-gan and Padouk (*Pterocarpus indicus*).

It is more than doubtful if Toung-ngoo ever was for any length of time an independent kingdom. According to the palm-leaf histories A-thaw-ka (Asoka) in 321 B.C., sent for the chiefs of Toung-ngoo and giving them various relics of Gaudama directed them to transport them to Toung-ngoo and to erect pagodas over them. Accordingly four small pagodas were built, each seven and a half feet high, two eight miles to the east and two 20 miles to the west of the present town, and a report made to A-thaw-ka who signified his approval. From this time till the close of the twelfth century of the Christian era the history of Toung-ngoo is blank : the story of A-thaw-ka, the pagodas and relics evidently have been invented by some historian, more pious than truthful, who desired to connect his country with the earliest spread of Booddhism to Indo-China.

In 1191 Na-ra-pa-dee-tsee-thoo, king of Pagan, whose name appears in Tavoyan, Talaing, Burman and Toung-ngoo histories and who is everywhere described as a religious monarch who did much firmly to establish Booddhism in Burma and the adjacent countries, came down the Irrawaddy and sailing out to sea entered the Tsit-toung and ascended as far as Toung-ngoo in search, it is said, of the pagodas built some 1,500 years before by order of A-thaw-ka. The pagodas were found, but overgrown with trees and brushwood, and were cleaned and repaired and raised to 45 feet in height. Na-ra-pa-dee-tsee-thoo appointed as governor his favourite minister, or according to some his son, Nanda-thoo-ree-ya, to whom he had given his daughter to wife, .and proceeded to Tavoy. At this period therefore Toung-ngoo was subject to Pagan.

Nanda-thoo-ree-ya soon died and was succeeded in the government by his son, Meng-hla-tsaw, who in his turn was succeeded by his son Tha-won-lek-ya who removed the seat of government to a spot on the banks of the Tshwa, a tributary of the Tsit-toung, about 20 miles north of the present Toung-ngoo, and founded a large town which he called Kya-khat-wa-da-ran. The country increased in prosperity until 1256 A.D., when Wa-rie-yoo, the king of Martaban, marched northwards and invaded Toung-ngoo, and having taken Tha-won-lek-ya prisoner sent him to Byoo, a village about 14 miles south of Shwe-gyeng.* Here two sons were born to him, Tha-won-gyee and Tha-won-ngay. Before his death he directed them to go to Ze-ya-wa-ta-na and to build a city on the ruins which they would find near the banks of a large affluent of the Tsit-toung. In 1278, after their father's death, they ascended the Tsit-toung but, mistaking their father's instructions, they went up the Kha-boung instead of the Tshwa and finding some ruins near its source they built a town on the spur of a hill, which they called "Toung-ngoo" from *toung*, a hill, and *ngoo* a projecting spur. This was in 1279 and is most probably the event to which Sangermano alludes when he says that Toung-ngoo was founded by a prince of Pagan in 1252 A.D., Tha-won-gyee and Tha-won-ngay being a noble of the Pagan court. At about the same time that these two princes founded Toung-ngoo a man called Kareng-ba, by some supposed to have been a Kareng by others a Burman so nick-named from his having adopted a Kareng lad, established a settlement on the eastern bank of the Tsit-toung which was called Kareng-myo or Kareng city. The brothers having heard of this and finding that the site which they had selected was too small entered into communication with Kareng-ba, and the three agreed to found a new town which they did in 1299 A.D., and called it Dha-gnya-wa-dee.

Tha-won-gyee was declared king, Tha-won-ngay heir-apparent and Kareng-ba prime minister.

The Pagan kingdom had commenced to fall to pieces in 1250 A.D., and the reigning sovereign had been unable to come to Tha-won-lek-ya's aid when he was attacked by Wa-rie-yoo, and for many years the whole country was in confusion, prince warring with prince, and usurper after usurper being murdered by some false ally or by some other pretender and numerous petty rulers declaring themselves independent. Toung-ngoo thus remained without interference from the north or from the south and Tha-won-gyee was enabled to consolidate his kingdom.

Tha-won-gyee was murdered in 1317 A.D., after a reign of 18 years, by his brother, Tha-won-ngay, at a place on the bank of the Tsit-toung to this day called Noung-byeng-tshiep. Tha-won-ngay, who ascended the throne after murdering his brother, died of fever in 1324 after a reign of seven years, leaving a widow and an infant son. The widow fearing Kareng-ba plotted against him unsuccessfully and was, with her son, put to death, when Kareng-ba declared himself king and appointed one Theng-pan-ka as his prime minister. Kareng-ba died in 1342 A.D., after a reign of 18 years and was succeeded by his son-in-law, Lek-ya-ze-ya-theng-gyaw, whose younger brother Htouk-lek-ya wrested the government from him in 1344 A.D., and was in his turn deposed two years later by Theng-pan-ka who usurped the throne. Notwithstanding the internal disturbances which accompanied these successful murders the Toung-ngoo kingdom had greatly increased in power, many Burmans having fled thither at the successive usurpations which at about the same time took place

---

* Dr. Mason, in his work in Burma (2nd Edit. p. 64) states that it was the first governor's *son* who founded Kya-khat-wa-da-ran and who was taken prisoner by Wa-rie-yoo. The palm-leaf histories from which the account in the text was taken have it *grandson*.

in what is now Upper Burma, and it had been still further strengthened by the advent of numerous Booddhist monks who had escaped from the massacres ordered by the infidel prince Tho-han-bwa in Ava, and Theng-pan-ka sent embassies to the rulers of Pegu, Burma* and Siam. This is evidently the Thien-pa-ka of Dr. Mason, but by that author he is called the third king and is said to have acquired five Shan provinces whereas according to three palm-leaf histories obtained from some learned monks in Toung-ngoo he is represented as the sixth monarch and as having had a peaceful reign of 17 years. He died in 1363 A.D., and was succeeded by his son Pyaw-khyee-gyee, who at the time of his father's death was staying with the king of Pegu. Pyaw-khyee-gyee entered into an alliance with the Talaing king who was at enmity with the rulers of Ava and Prome, the latter of whom like so many other petty princes had declared himself independent, and having thus incurred their displeasure he was invited to Prome and was there treacherously murdered. His son Pyaw-khyee-ngay and his nephew Tsaw-ka-det who had accompanied him escaped and for three months were engaged in wresting the throne of Toung-ngoo from the regent, who on hearing of the king's death had seized it. Pyaw-khyee-ngay was proclaimed king in 1370 A.D., and in 1374 was succeeded by Tsaw-ka-det who, hated by his people, was murdered in 1378 by a Hpoon-gyee who seized the sceptre.

Whilst on his way to pay a visit to the king of Ava his Shan subjects rebelled and seized Toung-ngoo; he returned at once and succeeded in recapturing the royal city when he put all the Shan to death. He was succeeded in 1392 A.D. by his son Tsaw-oo, who after reigning for a year was, on account of his youth the chronicles say but without accounting for the power of interference exercised, deposed by the king of Ava, and one Ta-ra-pya appointed in his stead. Ta-ra-pya was succeeded in 1403 by Goung-gyee whose first act after ascending the throne was to order a general massacre of the Shan. For some time he governed well but becoming childish his people dethroned him in 1406 A.D., and put Theng-kha-ra on the throne. This king died of disease after a reign of four years and was succeeded by his son and namesake Theng-kha-ra II. who was murdered by the Shan in 1411 A. D., the second year of his reign. Tsaw-lwot-peng-ka-ra prince of Pa-doung was the next king, but whether he was elected by the people or owed his elevation to usurpation or to appointment from Ava is uncertain, but Pa-doung being a town on the Irrawaddy below Prome his title would lead to the idea that it was by appointment. Having paid a visit to the king of Ava he felt so annoyed at the want of respect shewn to him at the court of ·that monarch that on his return he declared war and conquered several of the states tributary to Ava. Some years later he made an alliance with the king of Pegu, the great Ra-za-dhie-rit, to whom he gave his daughter in marriage, and in 1417† the two sovereigns attacked Prome. The army of the king of Toung-ngoo consisting of 20,000 infantry, 1,000 cavalry and 200 elephants, under the command of Thamaing Pa-yoon crossed the Roma, whilst that of the king

---

* In the Burman histories the King of Burma is said to have exacted presents from Theng-pa-ka, probably with as much truth as is contained the Burmese account of the close of the first Anglo-Burmese war.

† Mason says in 1428, or one year after the date given in this account as that of his death.

of Pegu, composed of 5,000 men in 700 boats, commanded by Ba-gnya Pa-thien, ascended the Irrawaddy. Prome was taken and with it much booty including the Royal white elephant. Tsaw-lwot-peng-ka-ra died in 1427 A. D. after a reign of 15 years from fever contracted whilst out hunting.

From this time until the reign of Ze-ya-thoora II., in the commencement of the sixteenth century, the interference in the affairs of the kingdom both by the king of Ava and by the king of Pegu was continual, and the kings of Toung-ngoo were little else than governors appointed sometimes by one power sometimes by the other. The Pa-doung-meng was succeeded by his son Oozana but next year the king of Pegu came up the river and having encamped at the mouth of the Kha-boung creek sent for Oozana and put him in confinement and placed upon the throne Tsaw-oo, who had been dethroned in 1393 A.D. by the king of Ava. On returning to his capital the king of Pegu made Oozana ruler over some of his own districts. Some years afterwards the king of Ava sent an expedition against Toung-ngoo and king Tsaw-oo was killed in action. In 1437 Tshara-hpyoo was appointed king by the sovereign of Ava: he died in 1443 A. D. and was succeeded by his son Goung-ngay, who was treacherously murdered by his brother-in-law, Nay-kyaw-deng in 1451 A. D. Nay-kyaw-deng was celebrated for his dissolute habits and was finally killed by one of his followers, whose sister he had dishonoured in his presence. In 1458 A. D. Ze-ya-thoo-ra I., governor of Toung-dweng, was appointed king by the king of Ava without prejudice to his former appointment as governor of a province. Seven years afterwards however he removed him and sent the Mye-dai prince, Ze-ya-theng-gyan, as king. When the king of Burma died Ze-ya-theng-gyan threw off all allegiance to the court of Ava upon which an expedition was sent against him. He sought and obtained assistance from the king of Pegu but in a pitched battle which took place in 1470 A. D. near the mouth of the Kha-boung the allied forces were worsted and the Toung-ngoo king taken prisoner. He was taken to Ava and subsequently pardoned and entrusted with the government of two districts in the Ava dominions. In succession to Ze-ya-theng-gyan Tsee-thoo-kyaw-deng was proclaimed king. He was succeeded by his son Tsee-thoo-ngay in 1481 A. D., who, four years later was killed by Meng-gyee-gnyo who usurped the government and was recognized by the kings of Pegu and Siam. He and his successor, Ta-beng-shwe-htee, raised the kingdom of Toung-ngoo to the highest point it ever reached.

Shortly after ascending the throne he was involved in war with Pegu and after signally defeating the Peguan army which had entered his territories he invaded the enemy's country and gained another brilliant victory: for this service in humiliating his hereditary foe, the king of Ava gave Meng-gyee-gnyo the title of Ze-ya-thoo-ra, by which he is known in history, and sent him all the insignia of royalty. He transferred his capital to the site of the present city of Toung-ngoo where he built a city, employing it is said 107,424 persons in the work, which he called Ke-too-ma-tee or "possessed of the royal standard". The city was finished in 1510 A. D. and he then assumed the title of Maha-thee-ree-ze-ya-thoora, shortly after which Nara-pa-dee, king of Ava, assisted by a Shan Tsaw-bwa, sent an expedition against him which was completely routed, and the

independence of the Toung-ngoo kingdom was secured by the defeat of Nara-pa-dee and the capture of Ava by Shan in 1526 A. D. Ze-ya-thoo-ra died in 1530 A. D. when 72 years old, after a reign of 45 years and was succeeded by his son Meng-ta-ra-shwe-htee or Ta-beng-shwe-htee the greatest of all the Toung-ngoo sovereigns. He invaded Pegu four times, the first three expeditions which he headed failing. The fourth and successful attempt took place in 1538. He overran the whole kingdom and was proclaimed king of Pegu, and appointed a Shan named Meng-ya-theng-ga-thoo as governor of Toung-ngoo. Meng-ya-theng-ga-thoo died in 1548 and was succeeded by Thee-ha-thoo a younger son of Ta-beng-shwe-htee. Ta-beng-shwe-htee was murdered in 1550 and rebellion at once broke out. His eldest son Bhoo-reng-noung retired on Toung-ngoo and being refused admission by Thee-ha-thoo invested the place and eventually captured it, and having succeeded in overcoming his enemies was proclaimed king of Pegu under the title of Tsheng-hpyoo-mya-sheng. Meng-rai-kyaw-teng was appointed governor of Toung-ngoo and on the death of his uncle, Tsheng-hpyoo-mya-sheng, in 1581 the kings of Arakan and of Burma intrigued with him, but he disclosed their plans. In 1599 he attacked the king of Pegu who surrendered and was with the heir-apparent taken to Toung-ngoo. Boves, a jesuit, writing in 1600 thus speaks of the war—
" It is a lamentable thing to see the banks of the rivers set with infinite
" fruit-bearing trees now overwhelmed with the ruins of gilded temples
" and noble edifices; the ways and fields full of skulls and bones of
" wretched Peguans, killed or famished and cast into the rivers in such
" numbers that the multitude of carcases prohibiteth the way and passage
" of any ships : to omit the burnings and massacres committed by this,
" the cruelest tyrant that ever breathed."*

The king of Pegu and the heir-apparent were, as has been said, carried off to Toung-ngoo : shortly afterwards the king of Siam with a view of restoring the king to his throne besieged Toung-ngoo but was obliged to withdraw, when the king of Pegu was put to death, to prevent any fresh-invasion, on the principle that there can be no dispute when the cause is removed.

This prince who had assumed the name of Maha-thee-ha-thoo-ra-dhamma-raza built the golden palace in Toung-ngoo, the ruins of which are still to be seen, repaired and beautified the lakes excavated by Ze-ya-thoo-ra II. and erected the Shwe Tshan-daw pagoda. He died in 1606 A. D. and was succeeded by his son, Nat-sheng-noung-thee-ree-maha-dhamma-raza, the last king of Toung-ngoo. Pegu had been utterly despoiled and as the power of that kingdom sank that of their hereditary rivals and fierce foes, the Burmese, rose. Pegu was in great disorder. Philip de Brito y Nicote had seized the country in the name of the king of Portugal and entered into an alliance with Maha-thee-ha-thoo-ra-dhamma-raza but he quarrelled with Nat-sheng-noung-theeree-maha-dhamma-raza, and captured Toung-ngoo. Pegu was eventually conquered by the king of Burma in 1612 and Toung-ngoo never regained its independence.

Out of a total area of 6,354 square miles only 59 are actually under
Agriculture. cultivation. The major portion of the district is hilly
and the population is sparse, and a good deal of such agriculture as there is is carried on in toungya. Of rice some 30 kinds are

---

* Boves in Purchase, ii, 1748.

grown in the lowlands, some yielding a soft and sweet grain for home consumption, others a harder grain more fitted for export. The Kareng of the hills have distinctive names for more than 40 kinds of all shades from pearly white to jet black.

In the plains the seed is either sown broadcast in the inundated fields, or is sown in nurseries and transplanted in June and is not reaped till December. In the hills the grain is planted in cleared spots in April whilst the ground is still dry and the harvest is gathered in some portions of the district as early as August, in others a month or two later. Tobacco thrives well and cotton flourishes. Wheat has been tried with success and the culture of English potatoes has succeeded almost beyond the expectations formed. Sessamum is grown in the hill clearings and sugarcane in the plains. Mulberry is cultivated both by Kareng and Yabaing but principally east of the Tsit-toung.

The area under the principal crops during each of the last 10 years is given, in acres, in the following table:—

YEAR.	Rice.	Oil-seeds.	Sugar cane.	Cotton.	Mixed fruit trees.	Vegetables.	Tobacco.
1868-69	29,412	57	36	217	1,074	1,709	43
1869-70	33,987	200	102	211	1,186	1,415	49
1870-71	28,933	528	70	174	866	3,368	73
1871-72	29,711	217	72	162	1,120	1,083	89
1872-73	30,450	135	92	227	1,049	1,167	61
1873-74	30,986	221	115	66	1,368	371	86
1874-75	31,015	180	208	22	902	1,168	30
1875-76	31,294	69	227	20	1,195	771	24
1876-77	32,188	70	143	41	1,222	909	44
1877-78.	32,537	220	199	24	834	1,080	7

As might be expected from the physical configuration of the country the area under rice increases very slowly. Before the annexation, as shewn by the small revenue derived from it, it was very small. The fluctuations in the other crops are very great, the most stationary being tobacco. These are usually grown on sandbanks and in the beds of rivers left dry after the rains are over and in places where elephant grass springs up and is annually cleared, as along the borders or the rivers, being allowed to grow again when the crop sown is reaped. Inundations are particularly favourable to it as increasing the richness of the soil by depositing alluvium and by destroying the rice plants on lowland thus driving the owners to this kind of cultivation as a makeshift.

The agricultural stock, according to the returns in the Administration reports was :—

YEAR.			Buffaloes.	Cows bulls and bullocks.	Sheep and goats.	Pigs.	Carts.	Ploughs.	Boats.
1868-69	..	..	7,833	4,763	671	3,315	2,998	5,884	396
1869-70	..	..	8,748	4,936	610	3,110	3,007	6,131	438
1870-71	..	..	8,305	5,383	600	3,200	3,114	6,250	897
1871-72	..	..	8,521	6,182	580	2,253	3,479	6,068	495
1872-73	..	..	8,942	5,555	610	2,285	3,546	6,099	480
1873-74	..	..	9,875	6,318	625	2,396	3,521	6,058	415
1874-75	..	..	9,590	6,384	630	2,350	3,107	6,176	303
1875-76	..	..	9,962	6,153	520	1,136	3,141	6,266	254
1876-77	..	..	10,110	5,768	495	1,120	3,179	6,255	281
1877-78	..	..	11,434	6,477	316	1,283	3,388	6,270	301

Of late the number of plough cattle has increased with greater strides than formerly and this without an equivalent increase in plough land, whereas the number of animals more used for draught and the number of carts and of ploughs especially, has not been so largely added to, and this is perhaps mainly due to an increase in the area of the holdings.

Here as everywhere else in the province prices have risen considerably during the last 30 or 40 years, whilst the wealth of the people and the security of life and property have increased. The rise was rapid just before and immediately after the annexation but has been slow since and by no means uniform. The value of rice has risen by about 25 per cent. whilst the price of cattle has fallen, buffaloes having on an average cost Rs. 60 each in 1868 and Rs. 50 each in 1878 and plough bullocks Rs. 50 and Rs. 45 in those years respectively. The price of fish, the principal article of food after rice, was Rs. 0-8-0 a seer of 40lbs. in 1878 as in 1868.

The amount transmitted from this district to the prince or Court official to whom it had been granted as the source of his revenues was, just before the annexation of Pegu :—

Revenue.

	Rs.
1—House (family) tax paid by Burmans and Kareng ..	26,220
2—Tax on rice land levied according to the number of yokes of oxen required to plough it	810
3—Tax on fisheries	1,220
4—Tax on Betel-nut trees and other palm tree plantations ..	1,680
5—Brokers licenses and amounts obtained from miscellaneous sources	130
Total ..	30,060

The local officials received all fines and fees in judicial proceedings besides what they could exact from the people. On the occupation of the country by the British customs duties were imposed, the brokers tax was swept away, the other taxes were altered and all judicial receipts were credited direct to the state, and in 1855-56 the revenues, including that derived from customs, amounted to Rs. 94,050 or about Rs. 2-11-0 per head of population. In 1863 the customs duties were abolished in accordance with the terms of a commercial treaty concluded with H. M. the King of Burma and at first this considerably affected the revenue but in 1873 the gross receipts under all heads amounted to Rs. 188,360 or slightly more than double the sum realized 18 years earlier and in 1877-78 to Rs. 256,465. The following table shews the increase under each main head :—

	1855-56.	1873-74	1877-78.
	Rs.	Rs.	Rs.
Land	26,310	33,525	34,732
Capitation	25,870	47,291	52,498
Fisheries	4,690	10,859	13,253
Customs	13,940	—	—
Excise	150	53,337	61,574
All other items	23,690	43,345	94,408
Total ..	94,050	188,357	256,465

The amounts under each main head during each of the last 10 years have been, in rupees :—

Year.	Land.	Capitation.	Fishery.	Excise.	All other items.	Total.	Local Funds.	Grand Total.
1868-69 ..	32,337	42,452	7,361	34,861	40,233	157,244	32,525	189,769
1869-70 ..	32,671	44,017	7,741	30,101	37,506	152,036	26,881	178,917
1870-71 ..	31,949	43,901	7,546	34,546	46,852	164,794	30,616	195,410
1871-72 ..	32,263	45,108	7,451	41,483	34,871	181,176	32,725	213,901
1872-73 ..	32,835	46,918	10,733	41,824	43,672	185,982	36,830	222,812
1873-74 ..	33,525	47,291	10,859	53,337	43,345	188,357	37,995	226,352
1874-75 ..	33,191	49,125	10,372	55,815	46,755	195,158	64,961	260,119
1875-76 ..	32,864	47,444	10,395	63,591	44,464	198,758	62,488	261,246
1876-77 ..	34,292	48,030	10,838	59,729	64,945	217,834	66,337	284,171
1877-78 ..	34,732	52,498	13,253	61,574	94,408	256,465	58,004	314,469

The land revenue has remained nearly stationary and this is due to the small increase in the cultivated area. The receipts from the capitation tax have risen with the increase in the population, and the larger amount received on account of the fisheries is to some extent due to a change in the system of leasing them, from issuing licenses at fees fixed by the Deputy Commissioner to selling the licenses by auction. The excise revenue has almost doubled, and this is the result of a larger consumption of opium and spirituous and fermented liquors and· to the increase in the number of shops for the vend of these articles. In 1868-69 there was one opium shop in which 300 seers of opium were sold and one for the sale of spirits. In 1877-78 there was one shop for the sale of opium in which 390 seers were sold (558 seers having been sold in 1875-76 and the sudden decrease being attributed to smuggling) and seven shops for the vend wholesale of spirits of kinds and six for the retail sale of wine and beer. The very large increase in the Local Fund receipts which commenced in 1874-75 and has generally continued is the result of the establishment of a Municipality in Toung-ngoo, which in that year raised a revenue of Rs. 35,470, the revenue of the town in 1873-74 having been Rs. 15,661.

In 1855-56, a year or two after the annexation of Pegu, this district, which had then much the same limits as now, had a population of 34,957 souls of whom 17,255 were males and 17,702 females. In 1873 the number had risen to 82,318 of whom 42,178 were males and 40,140 females. At the census taken in 1872 it was found that the numbers of the Indo-Chinese races were :—

Population.

Burmans			51,213	Talaing			449
Kareng			15,857	Arakanese			2,252
Shan			7,986	Yabaing			3,243
Toung-thoo			300	Khyeng			92

The Yabaing and Shan are more numerous here than in any other part of the province and they alone require a separate notice. The Yabaing are nominally Booddhists and have priests and monasteries of their own but their Booddhism holds but lightly to them and in sickness and trouble they propitiate the Nat or tutelary spirits of the hills, the streams and the forests. They are found almost entirely on the slopes of the Pegu Roma and their principal employment is the cultivation of the mulberry tree and the rearing of silk-worms. As far as is known they speak Burmese with here and there a few peculiarities in their pronunciation of the language and they themselves declare that they belong to the same family whilst their dress and general appearance bears out their assertion. As regards civilization they hold perhaps an intermediate place between the Burmans and the Kareng and are as ignorant as the latter of all useful and mechanical arts and attend to agriculture simply to obtain sufficient food for home consumption. Nothing of their history and traditions is known.

Fifteen or sixteen years ago the Shan numbered only about 250 souls. They all or nearly all speak Burmese and their children learn to read Burmese only ; their numbers are continually being increased by immigration. A number of this race under the Gnyoung-ywe Tsaw-bwa have settled in a suburb of Toung-ngoo.

According to the returns published in the annual Administration Reports, which are derived from the reports and returns of the Thoogyee of circles and may be accepted as fairly accurate, the population during each of the last 10 years has been :—

YEAR.			Men.	Women.	Males.	Females.	Total.	Number per square mile.
					CHILDREN UNDER 12.			
1868-69	..	..	21,586	21,422	17,586	16,356	76,950	9·55
1869-70	..	..	22,187	21,965	17,980	17,125	79,257	10·00*
1870-71	..	..	22,287	21,397	17,981	16,741	78,406	12·18
1871-72	..	..	21,953	21,466	18,001	17,010	78,430	12·34
1872-73	..	..	22,345	21,739	19,011	17,919	81,014	12·70
1873-74	..	..	22,649	21,959	19,529	18,181	82,318	12·95
1874-75	..	..	22,928	23,119	19,512	18,764	84,323	13·27
1875-76	..	..	22,815	21,782	20,079	19,233	83,909	13·20
1876-77	..	..	23,117	22,438	19,798	19,050	84,403	13·27
1877-78	..	..	24,543	23,405	21,127	20,153	89,228	14·04

The principal manufactures are raw silk, saltpetre and gunpowder.

Manufactures. The Yabaing and Kareng cultivate the mulberry extensively and supply the market with raw silk. The saltpetre manufacture is carried on by the Kareng in the north-eastern portion of the district. From various caverns in the hills they dig out earth highly charged with nitrate of lime, due to the decomposition of bats dung (the Kareng name for saltpetre is bla-ay " bat dung"), and to this is added a strong lye made from straw-ashes; the resulting liquor is strained and boiled down till the saltpetre crystallises. The bats dung furnishes the nitrate of lime and the lye the carbonate of potash, which give an insoluble carbonate of lime and the soluble nitrate of potash. The manufacture is carried on once a year only, and each operation seems to exhaust the supply formed in the 30 caves in the Ha-shwie and Pa-doung country where the salt is made; the annual yield may be roughly estimated at lbs. 5,500. The salt is used in the manufacture of gunpowder which is made by most of the wild tribes in the north-eastern portion of the district: the sulphur is obtained from the Shan to the north and north-east of British territory and the charcoal is made on the spot. The exact proportions in which the three ingredients are mixed has not been ascertained nor is it known whether any particular wood is preferred for the charcoal. Some of the north-eastern tribes are said to be able to turn out as good guns as the Shan but this is extremely doubtful.

The only town in the district is Toung-ngoo, on the right bank of the

Towns. Tsit-toung river, some 36 miles from the northern boundary of the province, in 18° 55′ 24″ N. and 96° 31′ 4″ E., and about 170 miles north of the sea in a direct line but 295 miles

* In 1869-70 Bhaw-nee with an area of 1,696 square miles and a very sparse population was transferred to Shwe-gyeng.

by the river, built on a site from 200 to 300 feet above the sea level and but slightly raised above the surrounding country, which is open and cultivated, in some places covered with low jungle where the vegetation consists of long grass and shrubs, and during the rains becomes a vast marsh. The town proper is enclosed by a huge square earthwork fortification faced with brick each of the sides being one and a quarter miles in length, and each in former years pierced with several gate-ways, the position of more than one of which is now visible, the whole being surrounded by a shallow fosse 170 yards broad and always containing water during the rains. Extensive suburbs, chiefly to the south, are included within the municipal limits. The town is regularly laid out and is clean and well kept, the houses are, with few exceptions, built of timber and bamboos with floors raised from two to eight feet from the ground. At the south-east angle of the town a square redoubt, 400 feet square in the interior, on which are mounted eight guns, was constructed in 1864 ; here are the magazine and the civil treasury as well as military stores of all kinds. The ordinary garrison of the town consists of a wing of an European regiment, a Native infantry regiment and a battery of artillery. The principal public buildings are a market-place, a gaol, the barracks for the troops, the court-houses and the hospital and dispensary.

In 1877 the town had a population, exclusive of the garrison and camp-followers, of 13,087 souls, and a Municipal income of Rs. 66,030.

A noticeable feature about this district is the large proportion of villages with less than 200 inhabitants of which at the census there were found to be 589 out of the total of 650, and 13 only with more than 1,000 inhabitants. The number of villages in 1877-78 had risen to 681.

Of these there are but few: about six miles west of Toung-ngoo is
<dl><dt>Archæological remains.</dt></dl>
Dha-gnya-wa-dee founded in 1279 A.D., once a place of considerable import nce the ruins of which are still traceable but it is now represented only by a few hamlets outside the former walls. Some 24 miles N. W. of Toung-ngoo, at Tshwa, are the ruins of another ancient town, the first mentioned in Toung-ngoo history, founded in 1194 by Nan-da-thoo-ree-ya the son-in-law and minister of Nara-pa-dee-tsee-thoo king of Pagan. South of Toung-ngoo and 31 miles from it is Ze-ya-wa-dee, founded in 1550 by Bhoo-reng-noung the heir-apparent to the throne of Pegu to which he succeeded de jure that year but de facto not for some little time later after defeating the rebellious governor of Tsit-toung who had usurped the sovereignty on the murder of Ta-beng-shwe-htee. The ruins of the town and of a fort of considerable size are all that remain to attest its former grandeur.

The trade is entirely free, neither import nor export duties being now
<dl><dt>Trade.</dt></dl>
levied. The exports are principally betel-nuts, nga-pee or fish-paste, dried fish, tobacco, silk, cotton and woollen piece-goods, raw silk and salt ; and the principal imports, timber lacquered-ware, pickled tea, sessamum oil, silk and cotton piece-goods, jaggery and molasses, cutch, stick-lac, chillies, garlic and onions, and cattle and ponies. The bulk of the export trade finds an exit by the Tsit-toung river. An increasing trade is carried on overland with the Shan states whence caravans come every year bringing stick-lac and other articles

and purchasing betel-nut largely. The value of the trade in 1872-73 and in 1877-78 was :—

		Exports.	Imports.	Total.
		Rs.	Rs.	Rs.
1872-73	..	553,770	1,243,650	1,797,420
1877-78	..	571,870	2,600,780	3,172,650

The general principles of the administration of the district have but little changed since the first occupation of the country by the British. Then as now a Deputy Commissioner was in charge with Myo-ook under him in charge of townships, both grades of officers exercising judicial and revenue powers; under the Myo-ook or Extra Assistant Commissioners were Thoogyee of circles, revenue officers who collected the taxes but were at the same time generally responsible for the quiet and good order of their tracts, Goung of groups of villages who were mainly employed in police duties, and Kye-dan-gyee of villages who aided both Goung and Thoogyee. The administrative strength now consists, exclusive of the Thoogyee and other subordinate officials, of six Extra Assistant Commissioners in charge of townships, an Extra Assistant Commissioner for the town of Toung-ngoo and two Assistant Commissioners, the whole subordinate to the Deputy Commissioner. In addition to these there are a Superintendent of Police under the general control of the District Officer, a Civil Surgeon, and Executive Officers of the Public Works and Forest Departments.

For the first year or two after the annexation there were military detachments in various places in the interior but by 1855-56 these had all been withdrawn and the guardianship of the country as well as the prevention and detection of crime and the arrest of offenders was entrusted to the local officials of all grades, and to a body of 80 men and two officers raised specially to guard the frontier.

In 1861 the existing Police force was raised and in 1878 it consisted of 37 subordinate officers and 391 men, and of these 35 officers and 330 men were for general police duty in the district, including that of guarding the whole frontier line and preventing the irruptions of bands of dacoits.

The present gaol was completed in 1870-71 but was occupied by the prisoners for some time previously. It is laid out on the radiating principle with work-shops and cook-rooms &c. in the space between the wards, the whole surrounded by a square wall. The buildings are of brick with iron roofs and earthen floors, the prisoners sleeping on benches two feet from the ground. Attached to the prison is a garden cultivated by convicts from which are obtained all the vegetables consumed in the gaol.

The old hospital and charitable dispensary has been converted into a lock-hospital and a new hospital has been built. In 1877 the number of patients treated was 6,959 of whom 317 were in-patients : the principal diseases were dysentery and diarrhœa, ague, worms, rheumatic and chest affections, syphilis, diseases of the eye, ulcers, scabies and injuries.

The education of the people is largely in the hands of the Booddhist monks, the American Baptist missionaries and the Roman Catholic mission, the State making grants-in-aid either in the form of gross payments or in giving teachers and prizes. The various schools in the town of Toung-ngoo are—The Kareng Young Men's Normal school of the Toung-ngoo Institute, the Kareng female Normal school, the Kareng Colony day school and the D'Oyley Burmese girls' school, all of which were founded and for many years carried on by the late learned Dr. Mason, at one time of the American Baptist mission. There are also a Kareng Normal school of the American Baptist mission, a school for Burmese, Eurasians and Natives of India under the Roman Catholic missionary, an S. P. G. school, a girls school, and a Shan training school, besides the Monastic schools and schools kept by lay Booddhists. In the district the Baptists have some 100 schools in various villages and the Roman Catholics several. There is also a State school of the middle class. Several years ago the missionaries considered that the district, as regards education, would not compare unfavourably with any of its size, but the census taken in 1872 has shewn that as regards the knowledge of reading and writing—and it entered into no deeper details—it compares not unfavourably with every other district large or small. Taking into consideration only the Booddhists, that is Burmans, Kareng, Shan, Yabaing and others of cognate race and excluding all of those races who are Christians, the figures of the census shew that of those able to read and write or under instruction the percentages upon the whole of such population of the same age and sex were :—

MALE.			FEMALE.		
Not exceeding 12 years.	Between 12 and 20 years.	Above 20 years.	Not exceeding 12 years.	Between 12 and 20 years.	Above 20 years.
16·26	91·78	85·61	0·42	0·62	1·66

The rivers form the principal channels of communication during the
Communications. rains and to some extent all the year round, but during the dry season carts can and do traverse the plains from village to village. The "royal road" made by Tabeng-shwe-htee, the Toung-ngoo monarch who conqured Pegu and ascended the throne of that kingdom in 1537 A.D., from Pegu to Toung-ngoo with wells and rest-houses here and there, has fallen into decay and though easily traceable is but a cart track. Two new and important roads are however in course of construction ; one leading from Rangoon to Toung-ngoo, and the other along the frontier across the Pegu Roma hills from Toung-ngoo to Thayet-myo, the frontier station in the valley of the Irrawaddy. From Toung-ngoo a road leads to the village of Htan-ta-beng on the bank of the Tsit-toung

some seven and a half miles lower down, as far as which the river is navigable by steamers of light draught if carefully piloted.

TOUNG-NGOO.—A village in the Prome district. *See Htoon-bho.*

TOUNG-NGOO.—A revenue circle in the Prome district. *See Htoon-bho.*

TOUNG-RENG-KYWON.—A revenue circle in the Mro-houng township Akyab district. In 1877-78 the population was 1,357, the capitation tax Rs. 1,510, the land revenue Rs. 4,660 and the gross revenue Rs. 6,768.

TOUNG-RWA.—A small revenue circle in the Ka-ma township, Thayet district, on the bank of the Irrawaddy to the north of the mouth of the Ma-htoon river, three square miles in extent, of which about two are under cultivation and one is unculturable. The population in 1877-78 was 849, the capitation tax Rs. 978, the land revenue Rs. 1,830 and the gross revenue Rs. 3,062. For some years after the annexation of Pegu the present circle was held by two Thoogyee : in 1783 Kyouk-o had a Thoogyee of its own, but in 1828 he abandoned his tract which was added to Won-lo-gaing. In 1862 the Won-lo-gaing Thoogyee died and his tract was added to Toung-rwa. The products are rice, tobacco, sessamum and plantains.

TOUNG-RWA.—A village with 663 inhabitants in 1878 in the Mo-tsee-gyee circle, Ra-thai-doung township, Akyab district.

TOUNG-RWA.—A revenue circle of the Kyouk-hpyoo district, covering an area of about 31 square miles in the southern portion of Man-oung (Cheduba), with a population of 3,496 souls. Rice and tobacco are the principal crops raised. In the north of the circle there is a hill supposed by some to be volcanic but the eruptions according to Mr. Theobald of the Geological Survey of India are due to marsh gas : to the southward petroleum is found. Land revenue Rs. 3,324, capitation tax Rs. 3,575.

TOUNG-THA.—Hill tribes of Arakan so called by the Burmese but including several distinct tribes as Shandoo, Kyaw, Mroo and Anoo, *q. v.*

TOUNG-TSA-GAING.—A revenue circle in the Ka-ma township, Thayet district, with an area of 10,240 acres (8,000 unculturable), a revenue in 1872 of Rs. 2,160 and a population in the same year of 998 souls. It is situated in the south-eastern portion of the township to the immediate north of the southern boundary of the district and on the right bank of the Ma-de river. It comprises the ancient circles of Toung-tsa-gaing, Gnyan-daw, Nga-mai and Kan-gnyeng-daing. In 1858 the Thoogyee of Toung-tsa-gaing was dismissed and the Thoogyee of Kan-gnyeng-daing got the two circles ; on the death of the Thoogyee of Gnyan-daw that circle was joined to Nga-mai, and in 1866 the Thoogyee of Nga-mai was dismissed and his two circles united to Toung-tsa-gaing and Kan-gnyeng-daw. In 1871 this collection of circles was placed under the Thoogyee of Mya-wa-dee-myo-ma and in 1872 when he was dismissed were, with Mya-wa-dee-myo-ma, placed under the Htouk-ma Thoogyee.

TSA-AING.—A revenue circle in the Thayet township, Thayet district, on the bank of the Irrawaddy to the immediate north of the town of Thayet-myo, having an area of three square miles only with the comparatively large population of 1,716 souls of whom a few are Khyeng and natives of India. One third of the tract is unculturable waste. The products are rice, sessamum, tobacco, chillies, onions, maize and plantains. In 1877-78 the capitation tax was Rs. 1,825, the land revenue Rs. 497 and the gross revenue Rs. 2,373.

TSA-AING.—A large village in 19° 19′ 25″ N. Lat., and 95° 15′ 30″ E. Long., in the circle of that name in the Thayet-myo township, Thayet district, on the right bank of the Irrawaddy at the mouth of the Ka-way stream, just above the Thayet-myo cantonment, with 1,225 inhabitants almost all Burmans; near it is a patch of rice cultivation.

TSA-BA-TA.—A revenue circle in the Oo-ree-toung (west) township of the Akyab district. In 1877-78 the capitation tax was Rs. 2,037, the land revenue Rs. 5,320, the gross revenue Rs. 7,665 and the population 1,685 souls.

TSA-BA-TAN.—A large village of over 100 houses in 19° 8′ 20″ N. Lat., and 94° 53′ 20″ E. Long., in the Shwe-doung circle, in the south of the Meng-doon township, Thayet district, on the Shoo streamlet an affluent from the south of the Hlwa. It was the principal village in an independent Thoogyeeship up to 1861 when it was united to Shwe-doung.

TSA-BAY-GAN.—A revenue circle in the Poung-day township of the Prome district. In 1877 the population was 3,459, the capitation tax Rs. 3,535, the land revenue Rs. 3,715 and the gross revenue Rs. 7,276.

TSA-BAY-YOON.—*See Tsam-bay-roon.*

TSA-BHO-KYWON.—A revenue circle in the Ra-thai-doung township, Akyab district. In 1877-78 the land revenue was Rs. 4,632, the capitation tax Rs. 1,392 the gross revenue Rs. 6,319 and the population 1,254 souls.

TSA-BYENG.—A small unnavigable stream in the Toung-ngoo district which rises in the Pegu Roma range and after an easterly course of 14 miles turns south-east and five miles further on flows into the Loon-ran, a tributary of the Tshwa. There is a pass across the Roma the road to which is up this stream and the Za-diep-hpo spur.

TSA-DAW-GYA.—A stream which rises in the southern slopes of the spur forming the northern boundary of the Prome district on the east, and flowing due south falls into the north Na-weng near the village of Wek-toung. It is not navigable by boats, its bed is rocky and its banks moderately steep and fringed with bamboo. It has a small tributary joining it from the westward which flows through the most open of the valleys formed by the numerous subsidiary spurs which stretch down from the northern hills to the bank of the north Na-weng and the two together drain an area of about 20 square miles.

TSA-DOO-THEE-REE-GOON.—A revenue circle in the Tharrawaddy district adjoining the Rangoon district and stretching westward from the Pegu Roma mountains with a good deal of rice cultivation towards the west.

The population and revenue during each of the last five years were :—

YEAR.	POPULATION.				REVENUE, IN RUPEES.		
	Burmans.	Kareng.	All others.	Total.	Land.	Capitation tax.	Total.
1874	5,548	497	—	6,045	9,675	6,095	15,770
1875	6,259	997	39	7,295	14,713	7,316	22,029
1876	6,392	997	39	7,428	16,286	7,288	23,574
1877	7,491	532	170	8,193	16,186	7,618	23,794
1878	8,200	692	229	9,121	16,477	8,050	24,527

and the area under cultivation and the agricultural stock :—

YEAR.	AREA, IN ACRES.				AGRICULTURAL STOCK.						
	Under rice, including fallow.	Garden.	Miscellaneous.	Total.	Buffaloes.	Cows, bulls and bullocks.	Sheep and goats.	Pigs.	Carts.	Ploughs.	Boats.
1874	5,170	35	23	5,228	990	1,020	9	127	879	665	70
1875	7,982	126	14	8,122	1,148	960	64	365	1,053	738	50
1876	8,825	107	26	8,958	1,228	900	42	184	895	713	45
1877	8,705	138	14	8,857	1,308	1,171	49	340	1,340	730	42
1878	8,949	132	6	9,087	1,569	1,169	60	378	1,514	949	50

TSA-GOO.—An island forming a revenue circle of the Kyouk-hpyoo district, off the south point of Ramree and opposite the mouth of the Toung-goop river, called Ing-goo or Amherst island in the charts. It is about 11·5 square miles in extent and contains a population of 2,631 souls. Land revenue Rs. 2,741, capitation tax Rs. 2,692.

TSAING.—A revenue circle in the Toung-ngoo district, bordering Upper Burma and extending eastwards from the Pegu Roma. The country consists of a mass of low hills covered with forest in which are found teak, Theng-gan (*Hopea odorata,*) Thit-tse (*Melanorrhœa usitatissima*) and bamboos. In 1877-78 the population was 917, the capitation tax Rs. 569, the land revenue Rs. 155 and the gross revenue Rs. 732.

TSAING-PYWON.—A revenue circle in the Le-myet-hna township, Bassein district, about 52 square miles in extent. It is pretty extensively cultivated in the southern portion but towards the west it is hilly and where it extends over the Arakan Roma is mountainous. A pass from the Toung stream leads over the hills at an elevation of about 1,500 feet above the sea. Towards the south-east the ground is low and subject to inundation. The inhabitants are engaged in agriculture and in fishing. In 1877-78 the population was 3,589, the land revenue Rs. 2,834, the capitation tax Rs. 3,967 and the gross revenue Rs. 7,809.

TSAING-PYWON.—A village in the Dham-bhee circle of the Henzada district, about a mile south-east of the Nga-won. In 1878 it had 1,059 inhabitants.

TSA-KHAN-GYEE.—A village in the Kyoon-hpa circle, Henzada township, Henzada district, about 10 miles west of Henzada. In 1877-78 it had 722 inhabitants.

TSA-KHAN-GYEE.—A village in the Prome district in 18° 26′ 45″ N. and 95° 7′ 20″ E. half a mile north of the Kyat river, and about three miles east of the southern end of Poung-day. The inhabitants are chiefly rice cultivators.

TSAM-BAY-ROON.—A township in the Bassein district about 649 miles in extent. From the junction of the Daga and Bassein rivers this township extends in a north-easterly direction as far as the Henzada district. The Daga which in the north forms its north-western boundary flows through it from about Thoung-rwa to Kyoung-goon from whence it forms its southern limit. In the south-east a strip of country stretches along the left bank of the Meng-ma-naing stream, separating the northern parts of the Thee-kweng and Shwe-loung townships. The northern tract or that portion which lies to the east of the Daga constituted formerly a separate township, called Kyoung-goon, the Extra Assistant Commissioner in charge living in the village of the same name. In the south-western corner the country is undulating and to the north-east of this is a tract of rice cultivation. Further north and east the land is in some parts low and swampy in others covered with tree and grass jungle, passing, near the junction of the Daga and Shwe-gnyoung-beng, into good rice land again, succeeded by more marsh and jungle. In the north-east corner a large area has been rendered available for rice by an embankment thrown up along the Nga-won or Bassein river.

The Bassein, the Daga and the Shwe-gnyoung-beng are the largest and most important streams ; a short portion only of the first, however, is connected with this township. The head-quarters of the township are at Kyoon-pyaw in 17° 17′ N. and 95° 16′ E. on the banks of the Daga. It is divided into eight revenue circles and in 1877-78 had 43,820 inhabitants. In that year the land revenue was Rs. 65,147, the capitation tax Rs. 48,393 and the gross revenue Rs. 151,864.

TSAM-BAY-ROON.—A revenue circle in the township of the same name now joined to Kyoung-goon in the Bassein district, having an area of about 55 square miles and lying on the right bank of the Daga river, between that and the Shwe-gnyoung-beng. The country is generally low and swampy and much intersected by creeks and but little rice cultivation is carried on. The inhabitants are mainly employed in fishing from which a large portion of the revenue of the circle is derived. There are good roads across the plains in the dry weather but they are impracticable in the rains.

The population and revenue during each of the last five years were:—

YEAR.	POPULATION.			REVENUE, IN RUPEES.			
	Burmans.	Kareng.	Total.	Land.	Capitation tax.	All other items.	Total.
1874	1,623	1,837	3,460	3,073	3,440	4,360	10,873
1875	1,808	1,810	3,618	4,459	3,685	4,310	12,454
1876	1,871	1.751	3,622	4,578	3,785	2,980	11,343
1877	2,151	1,995	4,146	4,465	4,052	2,693	11,210
1878	1,903	2,147	4,050	6,120	4,152	2,581	12,853

and the area under cultivation and the agricultural stock:—

YEAR.	AREA, IN ACRES.				AGRICULTURAL STOCK.						
	Under rice, including fallow.	Garden.	Miscellaneous.	Total.	Buffaloes.	Cows, bulls and bullocks.	Sheep and goats.	Pigs.	Carts.	Ploughs.	Boats.
1874 ..	2,001	12	20	2,033	1,893	684	2	693	322	425	134
1875 ..	2,852	45	20	2,917	1,904	684	2	693	322	625	141
1876 ..	2,998	34	11	3,043	1,893	684	2	693	322	625	132
1877 ..	2,870	40	21	2,932	1,408	545	4	191	269	621	65
1878 ..	3,957	40	28	4,025	1,334	591	14	293	349	698	306

TSAM-PA-NA-GO.—A circle in the Martaban township, Amherst district, on the right bank of the Salween below the Bheng-laing river. In 1877-78 the population was 4,402, the capitation tax Rs. 4,327 and the land revenue Rs. 3,893.

TSAN-BOO-TSHEE-MEE.—A pagoda at Mergui on the hill in the centre of the town built at the commencement of the present century by the Burman governor.

TSAN-GYEE.—A petty village in the Kyoo-byoo circle, Meng-doon township, Thayet district, to the eastward of Meng-doon, about four miles from the frontier, noteworthy only from the fact that near it is a salt well known as the Pan-gnyo well, from which were formerly extracted about 14 pots of brine daily.

TSAN-KENG.—A village in the Ta-gay circle, Gnyoung-doon township, Thoon-khwa district, on the left bank of the Irrawaddy, a mile below Dona-byoo, with 776 inhabitants in 1878.

TSAN-KHYOUNG.—A village in the Rwa-toung circle of the Mye-dai township, Thayet district, which during the last few years has increased largely. In 1878 it had 679 inhabitants, traders in cutch, sessamum seed and cotton, agriculturists and cattle-dealers.

TSAN-RWA.—A village in the Thoung-dan circle, Le-myet-hna township, Bassein district, on the southern bank of the Mai-za-lee, about seven miles west of Le-myet-hna. In 1878 it had an agricultural population of 744 souls.

TSAN-RWE.—A town of 1,193 inhabitants in the Henzada (Tharra-waddy) district, on the Hlaing river, a short distance above the spot where it enters the Rangoon district, the head-quarters of the Tsan-rwe township. It contains a court-house and a police-station.

TSAN-RWE.—The southern township of the Henzada (Tharrawaddy) district, east of the Irrawaddy, to which some years ago was added the Thoon-tshay circle of the Rangoon district. To the east the country is mountainous and forest-clad producing teak and other valuable timber, but to the west low and liable to inundation. It is traversed from north to south by the Hlaing river which receives the drainage of the Pegu moun-tains and communicates by creeks with the Irrawaddy on the west. The population in 1878 was 62,859 and the land revenue was Rs. 82,761.

TSAT-RO-GYA.—A revenue circle in the Kyai-let township of the Akyab district adjoining Akyab. In 1878 the population was 823, the capitation tax Rs. 1,007, the land revenue Rs. 4,143 and the gross revenue Rs. 5,420.

TSA-WA.—A revenue circle on the coast of the central township of the Sandoway district, south of Sandoway, of considerable size with a population of 2,795 souls, principally Arakanese, and producing a land revenue of Rs. 2,908 in 1874-75 and Rs. 2,392 as capitation tax. Rice is the main product and many of the villages along the coast as far Gaw are partly supplied from this circle. In 1877 the population was 2,990, the capitation tax Rs. 2,408 and the land revenue Rs. 3,078.

TSAW-KAI.—A revenue circle in the Prome district on the south Na-weng just above its junction with the north Na-weng, it contains three of the old village tracts. In 1877 the population was 3,027, the capitation tax Rs. 1,546, the land revenue Rs. 1,840 and the gross revenue Rs. 3,616.

TSAW-KAI.—A village in the Prome district on the south Na-weng river about four miles above the mouth of the north Na-weng, on the extreme north-east edge of a large rice tract which stretches down to Prome.

TSEE-BENG.—A revenue circle in the Henzada district west of the Irrawaddy and north-west of and adjoining the Oot-hpo circle containing a good deal of land under rice cultivation.

The population and revenue during each of the last five years were :—

YEAR.	POPULATION.				REVENUE, IN RUPEES.		
	Burmese.	Kareng.	Others.	Total.	Land.	Capitation tax.	Total.
1874	6,521	627	308	7,456	9,234	7,453	16,687
1875	7,263	152	37	7,452	9,435	7,605	17,040
1876	7,258	377	311	7,946	9,435	7,703	17,138
1877	7,938	379	285	8,062	9,523	7,820	17,343
1878	7,710	431	370	8,511	9,504	7,942	17,446

and the area under cultivation and the agricultural stock :—

YEAR.	AREA, IN ACRES.			AGRICULTURAL STOCK.						
	Under rice, including fallow.	Garden.	Total.	Buffaloes.	Cows, bulls and bullocks.	Goats.	Pigs.	Carts.	Ploughs.	Boats.
1874	5,803	298	6,101	579	3,170	14	131	1,464	832	6
1875	5,926	305	6,231	510	3,195	6	243	1,337	813	14
1876	5,968	308	6,276	456	3,328	1	253	1,434	781	3
1877	5,972	322	6,294	471	3,366	2	269	1,472	812	3
1878	5,972	324	6,296	461	3,632	9	372	1,647	854	—

TSEE-DAING.—A revenue circle in the Prome district stretching eastward from near the Zay stream. In 1877 the population was 291, the capitation tax Rs. 282, the land revenue Rs. 290 and the gross revenue Rs. 598.

TSEE-GOON.—A village in the Kyoung-kwee circle, Henzada township, Henzada district, near the Kyoon-hpa stream, and about four miles north of Henzada. In 1877-78 it had 614 inhabitants.

TSEE-KA.—A village in the Hpan-kha-beng circle, Ta-pwon township, Henzada (Tharrawaddy) district, on the east bank of the Irrawaddy, with 810 inhabitants in 1878.

TSEEN-DOOT.—A village in the circle of the same name in the Oo-ree-toung (east) township, Akyab district on the northern bank of the Tsee-doot creek, about a quarter of a mile from its junction with the Khwe-koo river. In 1878 it had 765 inhabitants.

TSEEN-DOOT.—A revenue circle in the Oo-ree-toung (east) township, Akyab district. In 1877-78 the population was 1,402, the capitation tax was Rs. 1,965, the land revenue Rs. 4,964 and the gross revenue Rs. 7,542.

TSEEN-KHYOON.—A revenue circle of the Kyouk-hpyoo district stretching across the northern end of Ramree island with an area of 24 square miles and a population of 2,569 souls. The principal product is sugar, for the manufacture of which 126 mills were working in 1875. Petroleum is found near the sea on the west. Land revenue Rs. 3,453, capitation tax Rs. 2,782.

TSEE-THA.—A village in the Pa-doung township of the Prome district, in 18° 41′ 20″ N. and 95° 12′ 30″ E., on the right bank of the Irrawaddy just below Pa-doung of which it forms almost one of the suburbs.

TSEK-KAW.—A village in the Tha-byoo circle, Thoon-khwa district, on the right bank of the Pantanaw river nearly opposite the mouth of the Pan-hlaing creek, in 17° 3′ 30″ N. and 95° 41′ 20″ E., with 972 inhabitants in 1878.

TSEK-KHAW.—A revenue circle in the Mye-boon township, Kyouk-hpyoo district, amongst the islands at the mouth of the Dha-let river. It has an area of 42 square miles and a population of 3,162 souls of whom more than two thirds are collected in the villages of Kan-khoung-gyee and Pouk-too-toung. It was formerly comprised within the Meng-bra township of Akyab from which it was transferred in 1871. Land revenue Rs. 3,855, capitation tax Rs. 2,770.

TSEK-LAI-DOUNG.—A revenue circle in the Shwe-gyeng township, Shwe-gyeng district, east of the Tsit-toung river. In 1877-78 the population was 3,207, the capitation tax Rs. 1,158, the land revenue Rs. 2,705 and the gross revenue Rs. 3,998.

TSHA-BYENG.—A small river which rises in the Arakan mountains and traversing the northern portion of the Sandoway district from east to west falls into the strait which separates Ramree island from the main land.

TSHA-BYENG.—A revenue circle in the northern township of the Sandoway district. The inhabitants, who are chiefly Arakanese and numbered 1,048 in 1878, cultivate about one half of the culturable area which is not one fiftieth of the whole circle. In 1878 the capitation tax was Rs. 1,020, the land revenue Rs. 1,127 and the gross revenue Rs. 2,177.

TSHA-BYENG.—A village in the circle of the same name in the Sandoway district on both banks of the little Tsha-byeng stream, about eight and a half miles from its mouth. In 1878 it had 701 inhabitants.

TSHA-DWENG.—A village at the foot of a spur of the Pegu Roma mountains in the Peng-daw circle, Mye-dai township, Thayet district. It is situated on the Tsha-dweng, a small stream which joins the Khyoung-koung-gyee from the north; near the village are four salt wells (hence the name) which were worked in the Burmese time and used to yield some 50 pots of brine daily. After the annexation of Pegu salt-making was gradually given up as it became less and less profitable. The village now contains about 60 houses.

TSHA-GA.—A village in the Tha-raing circle of the Donabyoo township, Thoon-khwa district, six miles north of Donabyoo and on the other bank of the Irrawaddy with 1,335 inhabitants in 1878.

TSHAI-TA-LA.—A revenue circle in the Prome district just east of the town of Prome. In 1877 the population was 335, the capitation tax Rs. 370, the land revenue Rs. 655 and the gross revenue 1,121.

TSHA-MA-LOUK.—A village containing 902 inhabitants on the bank of the Pan-hlaing river in the Thoon-khwa district, in 16° 59 N. and 95° 48 30″ E. with well-made brick-laid streets and containing several old pagodas and some fine monasteries and zayat or public rest-houses. A good deal of nga-pee is made here and a large number of the inhabitants are engaged in the fisheries during the dry season.

TSHA-TAING-MOOT.—A Talaing village in the Moot-kywon circle, An-gyee township, Rangoon district, on a stream of the same name which falls in to the Rangoon river three miles above the village of Moot. At the time of the annexation of Pegu it contained only one or two families of fishermen and the majority of the present inhabitants, who numbered 769 in 1878, have immigrated from Hmaw-won on the opposite side of the Rangoon river.

TSHAN-DAW.—A small pagoda on the hills on the left bank of the Sandoway river about half a mile south of Sandoway, built in 784 A.D. by king Gnyo-kheng to contain a hair of Gaudama. The inhabitants of the town of Sandoway spend one day at this pagoda during March, June and October every year, passing the other two days of the feasts at the An-daw and Nan-daw pagodas.

TSHAN-DAW-SHENG.—A pagoda in the Akyab district on Borongo or Mye-ngoo island. The foundation of the pagoda is attributed to a Naga or dragon. Poo and Ta-paw, two brothers, of Ook-ka-la-bha in Pegu, having visited Hindoostan obtained from Gaudama eight of his hairs which they carried towards their own country. On arriving at the mouth of the Koo-la-dan they were forced by tempestuous weather to anchor and the Naga observing the divine effulgence of the relics assumed a human form and received two of the hairs on condition of quieting the waves, a condition which he loyally performed. The two hairs he buried in the ground raising a mound of sand over them and many years later the existing building was erected over the spot.

TSHAN-DAW-SHENG.—A pagoda in Tavoy 22 feet in height and 63 feet in circumference at the base, supposed to enclose some of the hairs of Gaudama and a pot and bedstead adorned with emeralds sent by the king of Ceylon.

TSHA-POO-GAN.—A small village in the La-wa-dee circle, An-gyee township, Rangoon district, which, with the neighbouring hamlets of Ka-thit-goon and Thit-kya-goon, had a population of 527 souls in 1879, Kareng, Burmans and Talaing. These three villages are situated on the south-east edge of the Twan-te jungle (Taw-gyee). There was formerly a Talaing town here, the lines of the old town wall still existing at a place called Myo-goon on the edge of the forest a little to the north of Tsha-poo-gan.

TSHAT-THWA.—A revenue circle in the Southern township, Sandoway district, extending from the coast to the Arakan mountains south of Taing-gyo, having an estimated area of 121 square miles, with a good deal of cultivation as compared with its size. It has a population of 2,465 souls, mainly Burmese. The principal products of the circle are rice, and sessamum. Land revenue Rs. 1,661, capitation tax Rs. 2,162.

TSHAT-THWA.—A village in the Southern township of the Sandoway district, on the seacoast at the mouth of the Tshat-thwa river, about 16 miles south of the mouth of the Kyien-ta-lee. It has a mixed population of 658 souls, amongst whom Arakanese predominate. A small police force is stationed here. Silk-worms are largely reared in the neighbourhood.

TSHAW-KO.—A clan of the Bghai tribe numbering about 4,500 souls, living in the north-eastern part of the Toung-ngoo district, south-east of the Gai-kho country and separated from the Ha-shwie by the great watershed between the Salween and Tsit-toung rivers. They are the most degraded of all the Kareng tribes with the rest of whom they have little or no intercourse, hardly ever leaving their mountain fortresses except to make raids on their neighbours, on whom, as well as on each other, they often make most cruel and wanton attacks. Cutaneous disorders of the worst kind prevail amongst them, scrofula and goitre are common, but fever and bowel-complaints are their greatest scourge. Their most dangerous weapon is the cross-bow from which they discharge poisoned arrows, the poison being extracted from a tree known only to a few. The men wear close-fitting, short, white breeches ornamented with red and black stripes : the women, a short, dark petticoat, and a loose, brown, fringed jacket. Both sexes, but more especially the women, wear many rude ornaments of lead about the neck, and sometimes from 12lbs. to 15lbs. of brass on the legs. Below the knee round the calf the men wind from 100 to 300 yards of fine cord.

TSHAY-BENG.—A village in the Za-lwon circle, Za-lwon township, Henzada district, about half a mile from Za-lwon. In 1878 it had 605 inhabitants.

TSHAY-HNIT-RWA.—A revenue circle in the Tharrawaddy district, east of Mo-gnyo and extending to the Pegu Roma. To the east is undulating ground passing into forest-clad hills on which are found Teak (*Tectona grandis*), Pyeng-ga-do (*Xylia dolabriformis*), Eng (*Dipterocarpus tuberculatus*), Htouk-kyan (*Terminalia macrocarpa*) and bamboo, and through which roam elephant, bison, tiger, hog and deer.

The population and revenue during each of the last five years were :—

YEAR.			POPULATION.				REVENUE, IN RUPEES.		
			Burmans.	Kareng.	Others.	Total.	Land revenue.	Capitation tax.	Total.
1874	..	..	4,841	408	—	5,249	4,715	4,779	9,494
1875	..	..	4,890	618	1	5,509	7,359	4,987	12,346
1876	..	..	5,369	668	2	6,039	7,774	5,386	13,160
1877	..	..	5,842	506	1	6,349	7,872	5,868	13,740
1878	..	..	6,057	604	10	6,671	8,293	6,175	14,468

and the area under cultivation and the agricultural stock :—

YEAR.	Rice land including fallow.	Garden land.	Miscellaneous cultivation.	Total.	Buffaloes.	Cows, bulls and bullocks.	Goats.	Pigs.	Carts.	Ploughs.	Boats.
	AREA, IN ACRES.				AGRICULTURAL STOCK.						
1874 ..	2,760	25	65	2,850	1,740	525	—	200	811	850	*Nil.*
1875 ..	4,531	29	51	4,611	1,907	577	4	250	1,071	871	
1876 ..	4,798	31	50	4,879	2,105	641	12	260	1,157	966	
1877 ..	4,850	31	59	4,940	2,149	714	4	261	1,216	939	
1878 ..	5,162	29	49	5,240	2,143	824	—	251	1,198	1,052	

TSHEE-AING.—A revenue circle in the Ka-ma township, Thayet district, occupying the extreme north-east angle formed by the Irrawaddy river on the east and the Ya-tha-ya stream on the south ; on the west and north it is shut in by the Pa-gan hills. It has an area of three square miles only, and only 228 acres of cultivation. In 1872 the population numbered 440 souls, and the revenue which it yielded in the same year was Rs. 630. In 1877-78 the population was 457, the capitation tax Rs. 463, the land revenue Rs. 257 and the gross revenue Rs. 759.

TSHEE-BENG-KWENG.—A village in the Hpek-rai circle, Kyankheng township, Henzada district, about two miles north of the Pa-ta-sheng. In 1878 it had 609 inhabitants.

TSHEE-DAW.—A revenue circle in the south-eastern township of the Tavoy district, producing principally rice, sessamum and cardamoms. A small revenue is derived from the fishery and net tax. In 1877-78 the population was 2,308, the capitation tax Rs. 1,792, the land revenue Rs. 2,281 and the gross revenue Rs. 4,279.

TSHEE-GOON.—A large village in the Ta-pwon township of the Tharrawaddy district on the Irrawaddy Valley (State) Railway, with 1,789 inhabitants in 1878.

TSHENG-BAIK.—A revenue circle in the Oo-ree-toung (east) township, Akyab district. In 1877-78 the population was 2,721, the capitation tax Rs. 3,562, the land revenue Rs. 11,206 and the gross revenue Rs. 15,529.

TSHENG-BAIK.—A cluster of villages known as Tsheng-baik north, Tsheng-baik south and Mro-tee-na on the Kan river, in the Oo-ree-toung (east) township of the Akyab district. Tsheng-baik south is the headquarters of the Thoogyee of the Tsheng-baik circle and in 1878 had 629 inhabitants.

TSHENG-DAI.—A revenue circle in the Prome district on the Irrawaddy a few miles north of Pa-doung, well cultivated in the south and hilly in the north, inhabited by cultivators, fishermen and traders, most of the last living in the large village of Tsheng-dai on the river bank and the road from Pa-doung to the village of Pyouk-tshiep opposite Prome. Re-byeng is now included in this circle. In 1877 the population was 3,463, the capitation tax Rs. 3,670, the land revenue Rs. 3,884 and the gross revenue Rs. 8,526.

TSHENG-DAI.—A village in the Pa-doung township, Prome district, in 18° 45′ 50″ N. and 95° 17′ 0″ E. on the right bank of the Irrawaddy a short distance above Pa-doung. The inhabitants are cultivators and petty traders.

TSHENG-DEK-MAW.—A village in the Pien-nai circle of the Oo-ree-toung (east) township of the Akyab district, on the eastern bank of the Tsheng-dek-maw river. On the map of the Akyab district published by the Surveyor-General it is called Changdeimena. In 1878 it had 1,396 inhabitants.

TSHENG-DOOP.—A revenue circle in the Mye-dai township, Thayet district, with an area of 55 square miles. The principal products are rice, sessamum and cotton. In 1877-78 the population was 2,739, the capitation tax Rs. 2,281, the land revenue Rs. 3,417 and the gross revenue Rs. 5,909.

TSHENG-HPYOO-KYWON.—A revenue circle in the Oo-ree-toung (west) township, Akyab district. In 1877-78 the land revenue was Rs. 8,256, the capitation tax Rs. 3,972, the gross revenue Rs. 12,737 and the population 3,554 souls.

TSHENG-KHOUNG.—A village in the Tsheng-khoung circle, Ta-pwon township, Tharrawaddy district, about two miles east of the Irrawaddy, with 1,212 inhabitants in 1878, who are principally engaged in cultivation and fishing, a few being traders.

TSHENG-KHOUNG.—A revenue circle in the Ta-pwon township, Tharrawaddy district. The country is low and towards the west is subject to inundation.

The population and revenue during each of the last five years were :—

YEAR.	POPULATION.				REVENUE, IN RUPEES.			
	Burmans.	Kareng.	Others.	Total.	Land revenue.	Capitation tax.	Other taxes.	Total.
1874 ..	1,412	24	298	1,734	1,537	1,935	—	3,472
1875 ..	1,557	30	364	1,951	1,792	2,175	—	3,976
1876 ..	1,419	29	381	1,820	1,867	2,072	20	3,959
1877 ..	1,500	29	392	1,918	1,990	2,060	20	4,070
1878 ..	1,529	51	289	1,869	1,846	2,207	22	4,075

and the area under cultivation and the agricultural stock :—

YEAR.	AREA, IN ACRES.				AGRICULTURAL STOCK.					
	Rice land including fallow.	Garden land.	Miscellaneous cultivation.	Total.	Buffaloes.	Cows, bulls and bullocks.	Pigs.	Carts.	Ploughs.	Boats.
1874 ..	1,550	6	3	1,559	481	433	332	191	210	
1875 ..	1,691	9	—	1,700	578	642	211	293	278	
1876 ..	1,743	14	1	1,758	342	688	152	317	258	Nil.
1877 ..	1,839	10	2	1,851	735	882	253	339	258	
1878 ..	1,872	6	6	1,884	882	932	215	377	302	

TSHENG-KHOUNG.—A large and tolerably compact village situated at the mouth of the Sandoway river, about 15 miles below Sandoway. The mail steamers usually land the mails here, lying some four miles off in the offing. In 1877 it had 706 inhabitants.

TSHENG-KHOUNG.—A revenue circle in the central township, Sandoway district, at the mouth of the Sandoway river, with a population of Arakanese of 902 souls, and a small extent of cultivation. Land revenue in 1874-75 Rs. 350 capitation tax and Rs. 746. It is now included in Za-dee-byeng.

TSHENG-MA.—A river in the Tha-boung township, Bassein district, which rises in the Arakan mountains and flowing between the Tsheng-ma and Nga-root-koung revenue circles falls into the Bay of Bengal at the village of the same name in 16° 43′ N. and 93° 26′ 30″ E. This stream is tidal for five miles, as far as the mouth of the Kyien-nee, one of its tributaries, and boats of about 80 baskets burden can at high tide get up thus far.

TSHENG-MA.—A revenue circle in the Tha-boung township, Bassein district, with an approximate area of 192 square miles, lying between the Bay of Bengal on the west and the Arakan mountains on the east, south of the Ma-gyee stream. It is almost entirely devoid of cultivation and consists generally of mountainous tracts covered with grass, bamboos and forest. There are hardly any villages and the population is very sparse. The inhabitants are chiefly engaged in boat-building and in fishing. In 1878 the populatation was 1,104, the capitation tax Rs. 1,020, the land revenue Rs. 555 and the gross revenue Rs. 2,161.

TSHENG-MA-NAING.—A village in the Tsheng-khoung circle, Ta-pwon township, Tharrawaddy district, on the east bank of the Irrawaddy with 891 inhabitants in 1878.

TSHENG-MA-O.—A revenue circle of the Prome district just north-north-east of the Kan-bhee-la circle containing four of the old village tracts. In 1877 the population was 645 the capitation tax Rs. 653, the land revenue Rs. 921 and the gross revenue Rs. 1,574.

TSHENG-MA-THE.—A village in the Dham-bhee circle, Henzada district, about two miles south of the Nga-won. In 1878 it had 798 inhabitants.

TSHENG-MYEE-TSHWAI.—A revenue circle in the Prome district lying to the east of the Prome hills, about eight miles south-east of Prome measured in a direct line, and containing three of the old village tracts. In 1877 the population was 926, the capitation tax Rs. 910, the land revenue Rs. 808 and the gross revenue Rs. 1,984.

TSHENG-MYEE-TSHWAI.—A village in the Prome district about eleven miles in a direct line south-east of Prome and about six miles north of the Eng-ma lake. A small force of police is stationed in this village.

TSHENG-NAT-KHYOUNG.—A village in the Meng-byeng circle, on Cheduba island. Rice is extensively grown in the neighbourhood and exported to Akyab. In 1878 it had 763 inhabitants.

TSHENG-RWA-KYOON.—A village in the Tshoon-lai circle, Kyan-kheng township, Henzada district, on the bank of the Irrawaddy with 578 inhabitants in 1877-78.

TSHIEP-GYEE.—A village in the An-gyee township, Rangoon district, with 790 inhabitants in 1878.

TSHIEP-GYEE.—*See Myoung-mya creek.*

TSHIEP-THA.—A village in the Tshoon-lai circle, Kyan-kheng township, Henzada district, on the bank of the Irrawaddy. In 1877-78 it had 893 inhabitants.

TSHIEP-THA.—A village in the circle of the same name in the Thoon-khwa district 18 miles north-west of Ma-oo-beng, with 619 inhabitants in 1878.

TSHIEP-THA.—A revenue circle in the Pya-poon township of the Thoon-khwa district. During the rains the whole circle is inundated to a greater or lesser extent according to the undulations of the ground. After the water has fallen numerous small mudbanks appear and on these rice is sown. Gardening and fishing form the principal occupation of the inhabitants who in 1877 numbered 4,713; in that year the land revenue was Rs. 5,834, the capitation tax Rs. 5,138 and the gross revenue Rs. 14,112.

TSHOON-GOON.—A prettily situated village in the extreme south of the Oot-hpo circle, Henzada district, on the right bank of the Tham-ba-ya-daing at its junction with the Nga-won, with several pagodas and monasteries. Immediately opposite, on the other bank of the Nga-won is Myo-gweng where there is a Public Works Department inspection bungalow. In 1879 it had 174 inhabitants.

TSHOON-LAI.—A revenue circle in the north of the Kyan-kheng township of the Henzada district, principally hilly with a small area under rice cultivation. Some cotton is produced in this circle.

The population and the revenue during each of the last five years were:—

YEAR.	POPULATION.				REVENUE, IN RUPEES.			
	Burmese.	Kareng.	Others.	Total.	Land revenue.	Capitation tax.	Other taxes.	Total.
1874	3,194	208	252	3,654	2,629	3,945	778	7,352
1875	3,415	230	264	3,909	2,594	3,935	768	7,297
1876	3,692	135	83	3,910	2,631	3,908	711	7,250
1877	3,636	147	159	3,942	2,959	3,965	714	7,638
1878	3,586	128	143	3,857	2,571	3,998	939	7,508

and the area under cultivation and the agricultural stock :—

YEAR.	AREA, IN ACRES.				AGRICULTURAL STOCK.					
	Rice land including fallow.	Garden land.	Miscellaneous cultivation.	Total.	Buffaloes.	Cows, bulls and bullocks.	Pigs.	Carts.	Ploughs.	Boats.
1874 ..	1,248	57	392	1,697	689	199	—	93	120	65
1875 ..	1,255	19	380	1,675	657	199	5	175	123	110
1876 ..	1,258	36	401	1,695	700	187	12	365	346	81
1877 ..	1,263	40	579	1,882	816	211	—	419	320	77
1878 ..	1,270	40	358	1,668	909	211	25	446	379	85

TSHOO-RIT-KHYOUNG.—A village in the Lek-ya-maing circle, Mro-houng township, Akyab district, on the western bank of the stream of the same name, with 551 inhabitants in 1878. It is the residence of the Thoogyee of the circle.

TSHWA.—A revenue circle in the Toung-ngoo district, stretching eastwards from the Pegu Roma and occupying the country drained by the Tshwa river and the Loon-ran and its tributaries. The greater portion of the circle is intersected by numerous offshoots from the Pegu Roma mountains producing Teak, Sha (*Acacia catechu*) and other valuable trees, but on the east there is a little rice cultivation. Silk-worms are reared to a considerable extent in this circle. In 1877-78 the population was 2,973 the capitation tax Rs. 2,330, the land revenue Rs. 469 and the gross revenue Rs. 2,823.

TSHWA.—A river in the Toung-ngoo district. It rises in the Pegu Roma mountains and flowing towards the east for about 30 miles in a narrow valley between the Aw-ga-le and the Ouk-khyeng-too spurs, which send down numerous offshoots, and receiving the waters brought down by many mountain torrents it turns up north round the foot of the Aw-ga-le and joined by the Loon-ran inclines north-east and traversing a comparatively plain country falls into the Tsit-toung some 30 miles further on about 24 miles north of Toung-ngoo. In the rains boats of from 30 to 35 feet in length can ascend as far as the village of Ayo-doung some 38 miles from its mouth where the valley narrows considerably and whence their further course is checked by the rocks and boulders in the bed of the stream. The country which it drains produces teak and other valuable timber of which large quantities are brought down annually for the Toung-ngoo market together with raw silk prepared by the inhabitants who breed silk-worms extensively.

TSIEN-DENG.—A revenue circle, in the Oo-ree-toung (west) township, Akyab district. In 1877-78 the land revenue was Rs. 4,467, the capitation tax Rs. 1,644, the gross revenue Rs. 6,334 and the population 1,848 souls.

TSIT-PENG.—A revenue circle in the western portion of the Hmaw-bhee township of the Rangoon district, on the left bank of the Poo-zwon-doung river, containing a large area of fertile and cultivated rice land. In 1878 the population was 4,211, the capitation tax Rs. 4,675, the land revenue Rs. 27,095 and the gross revenue Rs. 31,790.

TSIT-PENG.—A village in the Kyouk-taing-pyeng circle, Than-lyeng township, Pangoon district, with 828 inhabitants in 1879.

TSIT-PENG.—A village in the circle of the same name in the Rangoon district. In 1878 it had 754 inhabitants.

TSIT-PYA.—A village in the Ran-thek circle of the Ramree township Kyouk-hpyoo district, with a population of 534 souls in 1878. Lime is burned in the neighbourhood for export to Akyab.

TSIT-TOUNG.—A town in the Shwe-gyeng district on the left bank of the Tsit-toung river in about 17° 25' N. and 96° 52' E., 50 miles below Shwe-gyeng by the river, lying at the mouth of a small stream on low ground which rises suddenly to the southward, forming a high laterite bluff on which there is an ancient pagoda built on a laterite foundation and where formerly stood the barracks inside the fort now unoccupied, and more gradually to the eastward but on both sides shutting in the town : on the high ground east of the town stands the wooden court-house with a straight road leading up to it from the river bank. Stretching away to the north-east along the stream are extensive plains. This town was for some years after the annexation of the country the head-quarters both of the Tsit-toung township and of the Tsit-toung division, but a few years ago the Assistant Commissioner was transferred to the more central position of Kyaik-hto about 13 miles inland. There is here a bazaar and a police-post but it is not a thriving town nor one likely to make much progress as it is not from its position suited for trade. In 1874 it had a small popula-tion of 1,126 souls and in 1878 only 978. The inhabitants trade with the Kareng and Toungthoo of the neighbouring hills.

TSIT-TOUNG.—A township in the Shwe-gyeng district south of the Shwe-gyeng township, on both banks of the Tsit-toung river, the larger portion being on the east; on the west is Rangoon, and on the east and south-east the Bhee-leng Kyaik-hto township. On the north-east the country is hilly whilst to the south it is low and subject to inundation but on the west exceedingly fertile. The principal town is Tsit-toung founded *circa* 582 A.D., by Tha-ma-la, the first king of Pegu, on the left bank of the Tsit-toung river at the mouth of the Kha-wa stream. A few miles lower down is Weng-ba-daw at the entrance to the Weng-ba-daw creek, which in the rains leads to the flooded plains on the east and thus by various creeks and channels to the Bhee-leng river and on to Maulmain.

TSIT-TOUNG.—This river, which is remarkable for its extraordinary trumpet-shaped mouth, the velocity and dangerous nature of the tidal-wave which sweeps up it, the enormous quantity of silt held in suspension in its waters and its tortuous course, not inaptly likened to the writhings of a wounded snake frequently deviating to every point in the compass within the distance of a few miles, rises in the hills in Upper Burma some 25 miles north-east of Re-me-theng and about 130 above Toung-ngoo, and flows southward through the Toung-ngoo and Shwe-gyeng districts, and in the extreme south between Shwe-gyeng and Rangoon, till it reaches the gulf of Martaban. Between Toung-ngoo and Htan-ta-beng, a village some 10 miles lower down, it widens considerably and is difficult of navigation owing to its winding channel and numerous sandbanks, and in the dry weather is not here navigable by boats drawing more than from two and half to three feet. Below this it narrows and the current is rapid, and from Moon southwards to Shwe-gyeng the main impediments to navigation are the many bends with sharp curves and the strong current. South of Shwe-gyeng, where it receives from the eastward the united waters of the Shwe-gyeng and the Moot-ta-ma streams, the river gradually widens, and the current alone impedes the ascent of large boats. Soon after passing Tsit-toung it takes a large serpentine curve west and south, and then rapidly broadens till on nearing the gulf it is almost impossible to tell where the river ends and the sea begins. With a breadth of seven or eight miles at its mouth it rapidly contracts assuming the shape of a funnel. The great tidal wave of the Indian ocean, joined by the tide coming up from the the south-east along the coast of Tenasserim, rushes with irresistible force into the mouth and with no lateral escape sweeps up the river forming a bore with an angry foaming crest 20 feet high, and at springs still from nine to 12 at Kha-ra-tsoo, which carries everything before it. Following the crest is a heavy chop sea of sand and water, as dangerous almost to boats as the curling wave which precedes it. Broken by the large curve already alluded to the bore is no longer dangerous above Weng-ba-daw. The tide is, in the dry season, felt even as high as Moon, but in the rains owing to the greatly increased volume of water brought down, as far as Shwe-gyeng only. Boats rarely pass below Kha-ra-tsoo at the mouth of the Paing-kywon or Kha-ra-tsoo creek which, until the new canal to Myit-kyo was opened, formed the highway of communication during the rains and in the dry season for some 14 days in each month before, at, and after springs, to the Pegu river and thence to Rangoon. During the rainy season communication with Maulmain, which is at this period entirely by boat, is kept up through the Weng-ba-daw creek, the entrance to which is about seven miles below Tsit-toung. Above Kha-ra-tsoo are some very extensive sandbanks covered by six or seven feet of water at neap floods which, as the tide falls rapidly when the ebb sets in, necessitate great care and attention in the boatmen proceeding up or down. The area drained by this river between the Pegu Roma and the Poung-loung mountains is about 22,000 square miles of which some 7,000 are in British territory, and it has a total course of about 350 miles of which the last 175 are through British Burma ; the development of these 175 is little short of 300. On the west the banks are uniformly low but on the east hills abut on the river in several places. Its principal feeders are : on the west, the Tshwa, the Khyoung-tsouk, the Kha-boung, the Hpyoo and the Kwon; and on the east, the Khwe-thai, the Thit-nan-tha, the Kan-nee, the Thouk-re-gat, the Rouk-thwa-wa the Kyouk-gyee and the Shwe-gyeng and Moot-ta-ma which unite at their mouths.

By the inhabitants of the villages on the banks it is sometimes called the Poung-loung and sometimes the Toung-ngoo river.

TSIT-TOUNG.—A revenue circle in the Shwe-gyeng district lying on the left bank of the Tsit-toung river and on three sides of the town of that name. It has an area of about 240 square miles and a population of 6,242 souls. It contains a large number of valuable fisheries. Large numbers of salt-boiling pots are made in this circle, the clay being brought from above Shwe-gyeng but the manufacture taking place here for convenience in selling. In 1878 the capitation tax was Rs. 5,625 and the land revenue Rs. 4,324.

TSIT-TA-RAN.—A village of 537 inhabitants in the Htouk-ma revenue circle, Ka-ma township, Thayet district. It is situated on the bank of the Irrawaddy at the mouth of the little Thwe-thouk rivulet in 18° 53′ 45″ N. and 95° 13′ 10″ E. In 1868 the Thoogyee died and his village tract was joined to Htouk-ma.

TSOO-LAI.—A slight elevation in the town of Rangoon, now in Fytche Square, on which stands a pagoda erected to commemorate the assembling together there of Ook-ka-la-bha, king of Twan-te, together with the two Talaing, Poo and Tha-paw (bearers of the eight hairs from the head of Gaudama subsequently enshrined under the Shwe Dagon pagoda), and their followers, when in search of the site designated by Gaudama as the final resting-place of the sacred hairs.

TSOUNG-KHWET.—A revenue circle in the Ta-pwon township, Tharrawaddy district, extending westward from the Pegu Roma, for the most part hilly and covered with forest, containing Teak (*Tectona grandis*), Eng (*Dipterocarpus tuberculatus*) and Sha (*Acacia catechu*).

The population and revenue during each of the last five years were:—

YEAR.	POPULATION.				REVENUE, IN RUPEES.		
	Burmese.	Kareng.	Others.	Total.	Land revenue.	Capitation tax.	Total.
1874	2,161	221	69	2,451	629	2,617	3,246
1875	2,566	188	61	2,815	771	2,810	3,581
1876	2,693	163	57	2,913	708	2,855	3,563
1877	2,723	162	60	2,945	695	2,875	3,570
1878	3,045	176	63	3,284	784	3,018	3,802

and the area under cultivation and the agricultural stock :—

| YEAR. | AREA, IN ACRES. | | | | AGRICULTURAL STOCK. | | | | | |
	Rice land including fallow.	Garden land.	Miscellaneous cultivation.	Total.	Buffaloes.	Cows, bulls and bullocks.	Pigs.	Carts.	Ploughs.	Boats.
1874	949	16	—	965	605	501	—	280	304	
1875	1,305	16	—	1,221	798	514	100	318	319	*Nil.*
1876	1,315	16	—	1,331	934	577	151	363	363	
1877	1,321	18	—	1,339	987	646	181	386	379	
1878	1,326	18	—	1 344	978	481	224	511	439	

TSWAY-DAW.—A revenue circle in the Pa-doung township, Prome district, a short distance north-west of Pa-doung, containing a few villages, the largest of which is Tsway-daw, and a small area of rice cultivation. It is now joined to Re-ma-nouk.

TSWON-PAN-KHYAING.—A revenue circle in the Kyouk-hpyoo district, formed by a group of islands north of the town of Kyouk-hpyoo, altogether about eight square miles in extent, with a small population of 445 souls. Land revenue Rs. 451, capitation tax Rs. 475.

TSWON-RAI.—A village in the Meng-bra township, Akyab district, on the Khyan koon-daing river, the head-quarters of the Toung-bhek circle, with 732 inhabitants in 1878.

TUNIC-BGHAI.—A sub-tribe of Bghai Kareng. *See Bghai-ka-tew.*

TWAN-TE.—A creek in the Rangoon district which connects the Moo-la-man with the To river, and flows past Twan-te as far as which it is navigable for the largest boats at all seasons. The banks, which are covered with grass jungle, are somewhat steep and the soil a sandy loam.

TWAN-TE.—A revenue circle in the west of the An-gyee township of the Rangoon district. To the east is an extensive plain with very little cultivation and to the west undulating ground thickly wooded. A large number of pots are made in this circle near the village of Twan-te. In 1879 the population was 5,777, the capitation tax Rs. 8,060, the land revenue Rs. 7,795 and the gross revenue Rs. 18,793.

TWAN-TE.—A town in the Rangoon district with 1870 inhabitants in 1879 in 16° 41′ 30″ N. and 96° 0′ 30″ E., the head-quarters of the An-gyee township, with a court-house and a police-station. It is pleasantly situated at the northern extremity of the 'Twan-te Taw-gyee' or 'great jungle' on the banks of the Twan-te stream about seven miles from its mouth in the To or China Bakir. This stream is connected with the Rangoon river by the Moo-la-man but the passage is very difficult for boats in the dry weather. A few years ago a highway of communication existed between Twan-te and Rangoon in the Ka-ma-oung or Dala creek, which is now entirely blocked up.

Twan-te occupies the site of an old Talaing town the walls of which are still traceable, and the site of a "Nan-daw" or Palace is pointed out by the inhabitants. In its immediate neighbourhood is the Shwe Tshan-daw pagoda, an object of greater veneration to the Talaing than even the Shwe Dagon at Rangoon, as it has never been kept up or improved by the Burmans as the latter has been (*vide Shwe Tshan-daw*).

Close to the town is a grove of seven Thwot-ta-bhat trees (*Achras sapota*) the fruit of which was much valued by the Talaing monarchs. These are said to be merely off-shoots of the old trees which were cut down by order of the Talaing rulers when the Burmese conquered the country. Although the high land behind the town is fertile and admirably adapted for cultivation very little use was made of it till after the annexation of Pegu. Since then a considerable colony of Shan has settled here and these industrious people, living together in Shan-tsoo about a mile south of the town, have made extensive clearings.

Twan-te is celebrated for its large earthenware jars, supplying the Rangoon market and indeed the greater portion of the delta of the Irrawaddy : besides these the chief articles sold in the town are rice, betel-leaf, coarse reed mats, largely used for placing under the cargo in ships holds, dried fish, nga-pee, and a small quantity of sugar-cane and bamboos.

In 1858 a rebellion broke out here, headed by a fisherman, which was speedily suppressed but not until the rebels had made themselves masters of the town and seized the Extra Assistant Commissioner in charge.

WA-BHO.—A revenue circle in the Oo-ree-toung (west) township, Akyab district. In 1877-78 the population was 1,295, the capitation tax Rs. 1,942, the land revenue Rs. 4,860 and the gross revenue Rs. 7,065.

WA-DAW.—A village in the Prome district in $18°\ 38'\ 20''$ N. and $95°\ 19'\ 45''$ E. on the main road from Rangoon to the frontier between three and four miles S.S.E. of Shwe-doung, and between Wa-lay and Re-myek. A departmental rest-house has been built here by the Public Works Department for inspecting officers.

WA-DAW-KWENG.—A village in the Le-myet-hna (north) circle of the Le-myet-hna township, Bassein district, about nine miles west of Le-myet-hna with 572 inhabitants in 1878.

WAI-HPA-DAN.—A village with about 1,360 inhabitants in 1878 in the Darien circle on the southern coast of the Martaban township, Amherst district.

WAI-KA-LEE.—A revenue circle in the Zaya township, Amherst, district, on the bank of the river of the same name, extending to the sea-coast a short distance north of the mouth of the Wa-kha-roo river. Its inhabitants, who are not numerous, are mainly Talaing agriculturists. In 1877-78 the population was 727, the capitation tax Rs. 672 and the gross revenue Rs. 4,057.

WAI-GYEE.—A village in the Kyoon-pa-daw circle, Shwe-loung township, Thoon-khwa district, on the Shwe-loung river about seven miles south of Shwe-loung, with 613 inhabitants in 1878.

WAI-GYEE.—A river in the Prome district. *See Shwe-lay.*

WA-KHA-ROO.—A small village of 620 inhabitants in 1878 near the source of the river of the same name in the Amherst district, once a flourishing town which gave its name to the river. The city walls and a large pagoda of considerable antiquity remain.

WA-KHA-ROO.—A township in the Amherst district, lying between the Toung-gnyo hills on the east and the sea on the west. To the north is the Zaya township, separated from it by the Wa-kha-roo river, and on the south the Re La-maing township, separated from it by the Tha-bye stream. At its northern extremity it has a breadth of 15 miles but lower down of seven miles only. Its extreme length is 28 miles. The chief physical characteristics are extensive tracts of upland covered with tree forest among which are scattered small rice plains of no great fertility. There are extensive tracts damaged by salt water along the coast. Here and there are lofty hills of granite and other igneous formations. The great hindrance to the rapid development of the resources of this township is its isolation and want of means of communication with the rest of the district during a great part of the year. The township is indeed intersected everywhere with large tidal creeks but most of them debouch in the open sea and are, therefore, useless for native craft during the whole of the more or less boisterous weather of the rainy season. A branch of the Maulmain and Re road is now completed and connects Amherst with Maulmain and this has done much for the northern portion of the township but as the distance between the two towns by road is 55 miles whilst the distance by water is only 30 miles which can be traversed in one tide the road is not much used for traffic. The continuation of this road throughout the length of the township and on to Re will be of great advantage. A canal connecting the head-waters of the Wa-kha-roo with the creeks which flow westward into the sea was once dug by the Daing-won, a Burman general of local celebrity, but this has been neglected and has become useless.

At the time of its capture by the British the township was almost depopulated. In the successive rebellions of the Talaing against the Burmans and the constant predatory incursions of the Shan from the south and east the whole population had either voluntarily gone over or had been carried away captives to Siam. Now and then after the British occupation some of the former inhabitants succeeded in eluding the vigilance of the Siamese authorities and returned to their native district but the great majority of the present inhabitants are Talaing who have immigrated from Pegu and their descendants.

The township takes its name from Wa-kha-roo (Wan-kroo in Talaing) near the source of the Wa-kha-roo river now a village but once a town of importance.

WA-KHA-ROO.—A river in the Amherst district which has its source in the western slopes of the Toung-gnyo spur and after a westerly course of some 30 miles, generally through a hilly country, falls into the sea just north of Amherst. For a few miles it is navigable by ships of the largest burthen and its mouth forms a fine and safe harbour. It is the boundary between the Wa-kha-roo and the Zaya townships.

WA-KHA-MAY.—A village in the circle of the same name in the Pya-poon township, Thoon-khwa district, on the river To about six miles north-east of Pya-poon, with a population of 559 souls in 1878. The inhabitants are employed in cultivation and and in cutting rattans which find a ready sale being employed in the manufacture of the cables of dhameng, or large fish traps, used on the coast.

WA-KHA-MAY.—A revenue circle in the Shwe-loung township, Thoon-khwa district. In 1877-78 the population was 5,992, the capitation tax Rs. 7,700, the land revenue Rs. 36,098 and the gross revenue Rs. 53,496.

WA-KHAY-MA.—A village on both banks of the Wa-khay-ma in the Shwe-loung township of the Thoon-khwa district. That portion which lies on the north bank is called Taw-ta-no. The group of houses on the southern bank contained 1,417 inhabitants in 1878 and Taw-ta-no contained 575. It is the largest village in the township and has a considerable trade in rice and other articles.

WA-KHOOT.—A village on the eastern bank of the Pien-nai khyoung in the Eng-ya-khyaing circle, Oo-ree-toung (east) township, Akyab district, with 612 inhabitants in 1877-78.

WA-NEK-KOON.—A village in the Ma-hoo-ra circle, Hpoung-leng township, Rangoon district, on the main road from Rangoon to Pegu, with 576 inhabitants in 1878. There is here a Public Works Department inspection bungalow.

WA-ROON-TSHIEP.—A village in the Ma-hlaing (east) circle of the An-gyee township, Rangoon district, with 515 inhabitants in 1878.

WE-DEE.—A revenue circle in the western township of the Tavoy district, about nine square miles in extent of which under two are cultivated. The principal products are grain and dhanee palms. It is now joined to Eng-tsouk.

WEK.—A river in the Tharrawaddy district formed by the junction of numerous mountain torrents and small streams, the two principal being the Baw-beng and the Thayet, all having their sources in the western slopes of the Pegu mountains towards the south of the Ta-pwon and north of the Meng-gyee townships, which falls into the Meng-boo near the village of Kan-ta-lee.

WEK-HLA-GA-LE.—A village in the Toung-bho-hla circle, Tsan-rwe township, Tharrawaddy district, about eight miles east of the Myit-ma-kha, with 910 inhabitants in 1878.

WEK-HTEE-GAN.—A revenue circle in the Ma-ha-tha-man township, Prome district, north of Prome. In 1877-78 the population was 1,850, the capitation tax Rs. 1,532, the land revenue Rs. 2,015 and the gross revenue Rs. 3,913.

WEK-HTEE-GAN.—A small village in the Prome district on the Kouk-khwai stream, an affluent of the Na-weng, and 12 miles N.E. of Prome as the crow flies, situated on low swampy, sandy ground merging into forest. In the first Burmese war of 1824-25, after the capture of Prome, Sir A. Campbell detached a force of Madras Native infantry to drive the Burmans back from the advanced position which they occupied in this village. The result of this attempt was disastrous, and the troops were repulsed with loss and forced to retire on Prome. In 1878 it had only 190 inhabitants.

WEK-POOT.—A revenue circle in the Prome district, on the Wek-poot or Shwe-lay river. The largest village is Wek-poot on the main road from Poung-day to Prome ; Gyo-beng-hla just north of Wek-poot and Rwa-hla rather more than a mile east of that village are the next in size. In 1877-78 the population was 1,817, the capitation tax Rs. 1,690, the land revenue Rs. 936 and the gross revenue Rs.2,661.

WEK-POOT.—A village in the Prome district in 18° 29′ 10″ N. and 95° 28′ 5″ E. on the Wek-poot or Shwe-lay river. The main road from Rangoon to the northern frontier of the province runs past the village and crosses the river on an iron bridge resting on two masonry abutments without piers.

WEK-POOT.—A river in the Prome district. *See Shwe-lay.*

WENG-BA-DAW.—A creek nearly dry in the dry season which joins the Tsit-toung at Weng-ba-daw and, during the rains, communicates towards the east with the numerous streams in the large plains south of Tsit-toung and Kyaik-hto : at this season it forms a portion of the main route for country boats to Maulmain from the towns on the Tsit-toung river and from Pegu and Rangoon. At Weng-ba-daw it is spanned by a wooden bridge.

WENG-BA-DAW.—A large village of over 1,000 inhabitants on the left bank of the Tsit-toung river about eight miles below Tsit-toung at the mouth of the Weng-ba-daw creek. It is the chief halting-place for boats passing up the ;Tsit-toung. During the rains the Weng-ba-daw creek which runs through the village and is spanned by a bridge near its mouth forms the first portion of the route, then entirely by water, from the Tsit-toung river to Maulmain. The inhabitants, who are partly Burmans and partly Talaing, are engaged in agriculture, in salt manufacture and as brokers, the village doing a thriving trade in grain brought from the extensive plains to the eastward.

WENG-KYOON.—A revenue circle in the Oo-ree-toung (east) township, Abyab district. In 1877-78 the population was 1,492, the capitation tax was Rs. 1,882, the land revenue Rs. 3,667 and the gross revenue Rs. 5,767.

WENG-PYAING.—A revenue circle in the Salween Hill Tracts district. In 1877-78 the population was 3,659, the capitation tax Rs. 1,732 and the land revenue Rs. 1,970.

WENG-RAW.—A river in the Amherst district which rises in the eastern slopes of the Toung-gnyo spur near its bifurcation from the main range and flows northwards to join the Za-mie. This, like nearly all the rivers in this district, is formed by the junction of numerous small mountain torrents none of which can claim to be the parent stream. The upper portion of the valley of this river is hilly but the lower part is a wide plain with slight undulations and with numerous isolated masses of grey limestone rock, often several miles long, rising abruptly to a height of several hundred feet, the ground in the neighbourhood being generally covered with dense evergreen forest.

WENG-TSIEN.—A revenue circle in Bhee-loo-gywon in the Amherst district which now includes Moo-rit-gyee. It extends frm the Tsai-ba-la stream on the west to the hills on the east, with Kha-raik-thit on the south and Rwa-lwot on the north. These two circles originally formed a portion of Kha-raik-thit and were made into separate circles by Captain (now Sir Arthur) Phayre in 1848. The northern and eastern portions are hilly but in the south-west is a flat alluvial plain. In 1868 the land revenue aggregated Rs. 7,150 and the capitation tax Rs. 1,596; in that year the population was 1,557. In 1877-78 these were Rs. 7,651, Rs. 2,100 and 2,151 respectively.

WENG-TSIEN.—A village in the circle of the same name in Bhee-loo-gywon in the Amherst district adjoining Khyoung-tshoon, the head-quarters of the township, of which it really forms a portion. In 1868 it had 593 inhabitants and 698 in 1878.

WE-WA.—A small sept of the Sgaw Kareng tribe inhabiting the country next to the Bghai and so called because their dialect is a mixture of Sgaw and Bghai the word *We-wa* meaning "backwards and forwards". They are in the lowest stage of civilization and till lately not a woman knew how to weave; the consequence is that they obtain their clothes from other clans and have no distinctive dress, some wearing trowsers, some Bghai tunics and some Sgaw or Pwo tunics.

WON-DOUK-KWENG.—A village in the Hpek-rai circle, Kyan-kheng township, Henzada district, west of the A-toon stream, with 652 inhabitants in 1878.

WON-LO.—A revenue circle in the Prome district, on the bank of the Irrawaddy just below the town of Pa-doung of which it forms an outskirt. In 1877-78 the population was 1,788, the capitation tax Rs. 1,795, the land revenue Rs. 457 and the gross revenue Rs. 3,890.

WON-TAY-THAI-GOON.—A village in the Lai-daw circle, Ta-pwon township, Tharrawaddy district, about a mile west of the Rangoon and Irrawaddy Valley (State) Railway with 696 inhabitants in 1877-78.

WOT-TSHENG.—A pagoda at Tenasserim on the bank of the Tenas-serim river in the Mergui district, erected by the Siamese *circa* 1380 A.D.

YANDOON.—*See Gnyoung-doon.*

YANG-LAING.—A sub-tribe of the Bghai family of Kareng, so called by the Shan. *See Kareng-nee.*

ZA-DEE.—A revenue circle in the western township of the Tavoy district, thinly populated and sparsely cultivated. A small revenue is derived from turtle-banks. In 1877-78 the population was 2,239, the capitation tax Rs. 883, the land revenue Rs. 1,326 and the gross revenue Rs. 2,322.

ZA-DEE-BYENG.—A revenue circle in the central township of the Sandoway district, on the left bank of the Sandoway river at its mouth, about nine square miles in extent of which two are culturable. The inhabitants, who numbered 2,375 souls in 1877, are principally Arakanese. Rice is the principal article produced. In 1877-78 the capitation tax was Rs. 1,816, the land revenue Rs. 1,782 and the gross revenue Rs. 3,690. It is now included in Tsheng-goung.

ZA-DEE-BYENG.—A village in the circle of the same name in the central township of the Sandoway district, about five miles from Sandoway, on the left bank of the Sandoway river and the right bank of the little Myeng stream, with 1,404 inhabitants in 1878.

ZA-HA.—A revenue circle in the north-eastern township of the Tavoy district, very thinly inhabited and sparsely cultivated. It has an area of about 24 square miles ; rice is the main product. In 1877-78 the population was 502, the capitation tax Rs. 386, the land revenue Rs. 2,409 and the gross revenue Rs. 2,937.

ZAING-GA-NAING.—A cluster of villages in the Rangoon district on the right bank of the Pegu river opposite the town of Pegu. The population in 1878-79 numbered 1,841 souls—Burmans, Talaing, Shan and Kareng, who are engaged in rice cultivation and in petty trading. Further north is old Zaing-ga-naing founded *circa* 1462 by the then reigning sovereign ; the surrounding country is thickly covered with pagodas and other sacred edifices. A short distance from Zaing-ga-naing was Ra-thaï-myo the remains of which, over-grown with jungle, are still in existence, including enormous bricks and glazed tiles with figures of animals. Lat. 17° 19′ 30″ N. Long. 96° 33′ 50″ E.

ZAING-GA-NAING.—A revenue circle in the Pegu township of the Rangoon district on the right bank of the Pegu river and extending for some distance northwards into the hills formed by the spurs of the Pegu Roma range. Rice is grown in the neighbourhood of the villages and along the bank of the Pegu river, elsewhere the country is hilly and jungly and covered with bamboo and tree forest in which are Pyeng-ma (*Lagerstrœmia reginæ*), Pyeng-ga-do (*Xylia dolabriformis*) and Bhan-bhwai (*Careya arborea*) : hog, deer, sambur, tiger and occasionally wild elephants are met with. In 1877 the population was 8,903, the capitation tax Rs. 11,428, the land revenue Rs. 22,957 and the gross revenue Rs. 35,373.

ZA-LAI-DENG.—A revenue circle in the Ma-ha-tha-man township, Prome district. In 1877 the population was 589, the capitation tax Rs. 642 and the land revenue Rs. 1,383.

ZA-LAI-TAW.—A tidal creek in the extreme south-east corner of the Shwe-loung township, Thoon-khwa district, running from the Irrawaddy to the sea. It is about nine miles long, the upper portion of its course is due west and the lower due south ; with the Irrawaddy and the Bay of Bengal it forms the Za-lai-taw island. Boats going out to sea by the Irrawaddy usually go down this creek.

ZA-LWON.—A revenue circle in the north-eastern township of the Tavoy district. It has an area of about 40 square miles but is thinly populated and sparsely cultivated, mainly with rice. In 1877-78 the population was 1,345, the capitation tax Rs. 966, the land revenue Rs. 2,089 and the gross revenue Rs. 3,159.

ZA-LWON.—A township of the Henzada district south of Henzada, divided into two very unequal portions by the Irrawaddy, the larger lying to the westward of that river. The principal town where the Extra Assistant Commissioner is stationed, is Za-lwon.

ZA-LWON.—A town in the township of the same name in the Henzada district, on the right bank of the Irrawaddy, and lying between the bank of the river and the main embankment. It contains a court-house, police station, and Public Works Department inspection bungalow. The bank is yearly cut away by the river and the town is gradually, and of late rapidly, being carried away so much to that in order to save the materials the bazaar was pulled down in 1879. Close to the town is a celebrated image which was carried off by the British during or after the second Burmese war, and was subsequently returned. The Burmese believe that the British were unable to melt it down and its voyage has added greatly to its sanctity. In 1879 the town had 4,637 inhabitants.

ZA-LWON.—A revenue circle in the Za-lwon township, Henzada district, on the right bank of the Irrawaddy river surrounding the town of Za-lwon. The general aspect is that of a vast plain entirely under rice cultivation.

Year.	POPULATION.			REVENUE, IN RUPEES.			
	Burmans.	Others.	Total.	Land tax.	Capitation tax.	Other taxes.	Total.
1874	4,380	551	4,931	455	4,450	2,019	6,924
1875	3,719	552	4,271	476	4,485	1,212	6,173
1876	4,379	582	4,961	470	4,587	1,137	6,194
1877	3,841	531	4,372	484	4,152	2,544	7,180
1878	4,234	556	4,790	437	4,250	2,697	7,384

and the area under cultivation and the agricultural stock:—

Year.	AREA, IN ACRES.				AGRICULTURAL STOCK.						
	Under rice, including fallow.	Garden land.	Miscellaneous.	Total.	Buffaloes.	Cows, bulls and bullocks.	Goats.	Pigs.	Carts.	Ploughs.	Boats.
1874	199	24	—	223	13	336	19	37	114	23	46
1875	199	35	1	235	10	415	12	77	117	49	31
1876	200	26	2	228	36	471	—	2	183	79	35
1877	204	26	1	231	5	407	49	105	167	65	33
1878	194	24	—	218	8	528	19	84	102	14	82

ZA-MIE.—A small river in the Amherst district which rises in the main range near the pass of the Three Pagodas in 15° 18′ N. and 98° 25′ 29″ E.

and flows for some 80 miles in a general N.N.W. direction to join the Weng-raw and form the Attaran. The last 40 miles of its course are navigable but the strong current renders the ascent difficult and foresters only go further south than the 16th parallel of latitude. It is formed by the junction of several streams, some of which are as much as 40 yards broad but are shallow and fordable.

ZA-NOUNG-DAW.—A revenue circle in the Ma-ha-tha-man township, Prome district. In 1878 the population was 238, the capitation tax Rs. 227 and the land revenue Rs. 422.

ZAY.—A river in the Prome district. *See Hlaing.*

ZA-YA.—A township in the Amherst district lying immediately to the south of the town of Maulmain and stretching along the left bank of the Salween and the coast as far as the Wa-kha-roo river and extending inland to the bank of the Attaran ; to the south is the Wa-kha-roo township, and to the east the Gyaing Attaran. From north to south a range of hills runs down the coastline leaving a fertile and well-cultivated strip of country, nowhere more than 12 miles in breadth, between it and the sea, drained by numerous small streams with a general east and west direction none of which are of any importance.

ZA-YAT-GYEE.—A village in the Tsa-doo-thee-ree-goon circle, Tsanrwe township, Tharawaddy district, on the north bank of the river Thoontshay with 998 inhabitants in 1878.

ZA-YAT-HLA.—A revenue circle in the Pan-ta-naw township, Thoonkhwa district. In 1877 the population was 6,384, the capitation tax Rs. 6,625 and the land revenue Rs. 2,269. This circle is a vast plain covered with tree and grass jungle with some rice cultivation, especially at is northern end.

ZA-YAT-KOON.—A village in the Bhwai-beng-gan circle, Poung-day township, Prome district, north-east of Poung-day with 520 inhabitants in 1878.

ZA-RAI-ZAN.—A revenue circle in the Gyaing Than-lweng township, Amherst district. In 1878 the population was 960, the capitation tax Rs, 1,095 and the land revenue Rs. 4,553.

ZA-RAI-ZAN.—A village in the circle of the same name in the Amherst district on the bank of the Gyaing, with 701 inhabitants in 1877.

ZA-THA-BYENG.—A village in the circle of the same name in the Amherst district on the right bank of the Gyaing, the head-quarters of the Gyaing Than-lweng township. It is well laid out in bricked streets and contains a court-house and a police-station. In 1878 it had 2,160 inhabitants.

ZA-THA-BYENG.—A revenue circle in the Gyaing Than-lweng township, Amherst district, extending northwards from the bank of the Gyaing The principal village is Za-tha-byeng the head-quarters of the township. In 1878 the population was 3,042, the capitation tax Rs. 2,700 and the gross revenue Rs. 4,340.

ZA-THENG.—A revenue circle in the Gyaing Than-lweng township, of the Amherst district. In 1877-78 the population was 791, the capitation tax Rs. 805 and land revenue Rs. 3,778.

ZEE-BENG-HLA.—A revenue circle in the Poung-day township, Prome district, on the left bank of the Shwe-lay at the foot of the Pegu Roma mountains. In 1877 the population was 3,686, the capitation tax was Rs. 3,517 and the land revenue Rs. 2,478.

ZEE-BENG-KWENG.—A village in the Daga circle, Re-gyee township, Bassein district, on the northern bank of the Daga about eight miles from its mouth, with 538 inhabitants in 1878.

ZEE-BENG-TSHIEP.—A village in the Kywon-ga-le circle, Hpoung-leng township, Rangoon district, with 524 inhabitants in 1878.

ZEE-BENG-WA.—A village in the Kywon-ga-le circle, Hpoung-leng township, Rangoon district, with 725 inhabitants in 1878-79.

ZEE-GOON.—A small village in the Tha-raing circle, Donabyoo township, Thoon-khwa district, on the left bank of the Irrawaddy about four miles north of Donabyoo, with 501 inhabitants in 1877.

ZEE-HPYOO-GOON.—A village in the Pan-hlaing circle, An-gyee township, Rangoon district, with 723 inhabitants in 1878.

ZEE-HPYOO-KWENG.—A revenue circle in the Tha-boung township, Bassein district. In 1877 the population was 747, the capitation tax Rs. 937, the land revenue Rs. 2,032 and the gross revenue Rs. 3,072.

ZEE-HPYOO-TSHIEP.—A revenue circle in the Nga-poo-taw township of the Bassein district. The population and revenue during each of the last five years were:—

Year.				POPULATION.			REVENUE, IN RUPEES.			
				Burmans.	All other races.	Total.	Land revenue.	Capitation tax.	All other items.	Total.
1874	..	..	..	666	530	1,196	2,243	1,457	2,319	6,019
1875	..	..	..	646	536	1,182	1,990	1,492	2,242	5,524
1876	..	..	..	542	510	1,052	1,417	1,452	2,515	5,384
1877	..	..	..	883	200	1,083	1,221	1,480	2,132	4,833
1878	..	..	..	901	176	1,077	1,301	1,445	1,763	4,509

and the area under cultivation and the agricultural stock :—

YEAR.	AREA, IN ? RES.				AGRICULTURAL STOCK.						
	Under ri in-cluding fallow.	Garden.	Miscellaneous.	Total.	Buffaloes.	Cows, bulls and bullocks.	Sheep and goats.	Pigs.	Carts.	Ploughs.	Boats.
1874	1,808	1	9	1,818	327	—	—	—	55	102	32
1875	1,587	1	4	1,592	675	10	2	12	104	168	90
1876	1,147	1	7	1,155	518	11	2	45	68	143	73
1877	970	1	9	980	458	11	7	58	63	93	90
1878	2,011	1	1	2,013	434	6	3	13	50	100	72

ZEE-HPYOO-ZAT.—A revenue circle in the Nga-poo-taw township, Bassein district. In 1877 the population was 1,083, the capitation tax Rs. 1,480, the land revenue Rs. 1,221 and the gross revenue Rs. 4,908.

ZEE-THOUNG.—A tidal creek in the Mai-kywon at the entrance to the Bassein river, running southwards from the Kyouk-ka-lat creek to the sea, navigable at all seasons by boats of from 40 to 50 feet in length.

ZEE-YA.—A revenue circle in the Mro-houng township, Akyab district. In 1877-78 the population was 1,986, the capitation tax Rs. 2,997, the land revenue Rs. 3,305 and the gross revenue Rs. 6,492.

ZE-MA-THWAY.—A revenue circle in the south of the Tha-htoon township of the Amherst district. In 1877-78 the population was 2,806 and the land revenue Rs. 4,009.

ZENG-KYAIK.—A pagoda on the Zeng-kyaik hills north-west of Martaban supposed to have been founded in the fourth century B.C. and to contain one of Gaudama's hairs.

ZENG-GYAIK.—A village in the Poung circle, Martaban township, Amherst district, at the foot of the western slopes of the hills of the same name, with 853 inhabitants in 1878. Strictly it is a name given in the returns to a small group of villages so situated not one of which is named Zeng-gyaik.

ZE-TA-WON.—A pagoda in a forest in the Mergui district visited by many pilgrims annually in October, supposed to have been built *circa* 1208 A.D. by Na-ra-pa-dee-tsee-thoo who visited Mergui.

ZE-YA-WA-DEE.—A township in the Toung-ngoo district, divided into four revenue circles, with a population of 22,835 souls in 1877, in which year it produced a gross revenue of Rs. 40,616.

ZE-YA-WA-DEE.—A revenue circle in the township of the same name in the Toung-ngoo district. In 1877 the population was 9,071, the capitation tax Rs. 6,752, the land revenue Rs. 5,660 and the gross revenue Rs. 14,635.

ZHE-GNYOUNG.—A village in the Pegu circle, Pegu township, Rangoon district, with 612 inhabitants in 1878-79.

ZHE-GYEE.—A village in the Pegu circle, Pegu township, Rangoon district, with 686 inhabitants in 1878-79.

ZHE-PA-THWAY.—A revenue circle in the An-gyee township, Rangoon district, on the seacoast, carved out of Moot-kywon a few years ago. In 1878 the population was 4,448, the capitation tax Rs. 5,450, the land revenue Rs. 20,640 and the gross revenue Rs. 27,110.

ZIEN.—A revenue circle in the central township of the Sandoway district extending inland from the mouth of the Sandoway river. It has an estimated area of 70 square miles and had a population, mainly Arakanese, of 1,455 souls in 1877. The cultivated area which is mainly under rice is under three square miles. In 1877-78 the capitation tax was Rs. 1,150, the land revenue Rs. 2,363 and the gross revenue Rs. 2,513.

ZOOT-THOOT.—A revenue circle in the Tsit-toung sub-division of the Shwe-gyeng district, extending northwards from the seacoast along the right bank of the Bhee-leng river. It has an area of about 110 square miles and had a population of 4,573 souls in 1877-78, when the capitation tax was Rs. 4,082 and the land revenue Rs. 11,885.

APPENDIX.

A-DA.—A village in the Doora circle, Henzada township, Henzada district, about three miles west of the Irrawaddy on the banks of a stream of the same name which has its source in the Doora lake, with 1,112 inhabitants in 1879.

A-GYEE-TAW.—A revenue circle in the Ra-thai-doung township, Akyab district. In 1879 the population was 2,759, the land revenue Rs. 7,152 and the gross revenue Rs. 9,908.

A-HTOUNG.—A village in the Thoung-daik circle, Kyoon-pyaw township, on the eastern bank of the Daga, near the north-east of the Bassein district, with a population of 541 souls in 1878.

AIN-DA-POORA.—*See Ien-da-poora.*

A-KYAW.—The population of this village (*vide* p. 30) was 1,002 in 1878.

A-LA-MYO.—A village in the Kan-goo circle, Donabyoo township, Thoon-khwa district, about six miles north of Donabyoo with 506 inhabitants in 1878.

ALAY-KYWON.—A village in the Kyoung-kwee circle, Henzada township, Henzada district, between the Kyoon-toon and Kyoung-kwee streams, about three miles north of Henzada, with 685 inhabitants in 1879.

ALAY-THAN-GYAW.—A revenue circle in the Naaf township of the Akyab district. In 1879 the population was 2,761, the land revenue Rs. 5,087 and the gross revenue Rs. 8,014.

A-LIEN-A-LAY.—A village in the Bhaw-lay circle, Hlaing township, Rangoon (Han-tha-wa-dee) district, on the right bank of the Hlaing, with 532 inhabitants in 1878.

A-MAI-KHENG.—A revenue circle in the Oo-ree-toung (west) township, Akyab district. In 1879 the population was 1,415, the land revenue Rs. 3,406 and the gross revenue Rs. 5,247.

AMBARREE.—A revenue circle in the Kyai-let township, Akyab district. In 1879 the population was 1,654 and the gross revenue Rs. 10,002.

AMHERST.—The town of Maulmain now forms a separate district altogether independent of Amherst.

A-NAN-PYAING.—A village in the Keng-khyoung circle, Zaya township, Amherst district, about seven miles from Maulmain on the west of the Amherst road near the Kyouk-ta-loon hill with 523 inhabitants in 1878.

ANEMAY.—*See Iem-mai.*

A-NGOO-MAW.—A village on the southern bank of the Ma-yoo in the A-ngoo-maw circle, Ra-thai-doung township, Akyab district, with 658 inhabitants in 1878. The Thoogyee of the circle lives here.

A-NGOO-MAW.—A revenue circle in the Ra-thai-doung township of the Akyab district. In 1879 the population was 2,153, the land revenue Rs. 5,674 and the gross revenue Rs. 8,040.

A-PENG-HNIT-TSHAY.—A village in the Tsam-bay-roon circle, Kyoon-pyaw township, Bassein district, on the southern bank of the A-peng-hait-tshay creek, with 503 inhabitants in 1878.

A-POUK-WA.—A village in the Theng-gan-nek circle, Koo-la-dan township, Akyab district, on the right bank of the Koo-la-dan, with 863 inhabitants in 1878.

A-TSEE.—A village in the circle of the same name in the Re La-maing township, Amherst district, with 664 inhabitants in 1878.

BHA-GOON-NA-RWA.—A village situated in the Koo-la-pan-zeng circle, Ra-thai-doung township, Akyab district, at the source of the Ma-yoo river, with 682 inhabitants in 1878. The name is said to be derived from Sanscrit and to mean " dangerous by reason of tigers".

BHAN-BYENG.—A revenue circle in the Ma-ha-tha-man township, Prome district. In 1877 the population was 328, the capitation tax Rs. 337, the land revenue Rs. 467 and the gross revenue Rs. 804.

BHOORA-KHYOUNG.—A village in the La-bwot-khyan (south) circle, Shwe-loung township, Thoon-khwa district, with 803 inhabitants in 1878.

BHOO-RA-MAW.—A village in the Thoo-hte circle of the Central township, Sandoway district, on both banks of the Thoo-hte about ten miles from its mouth, with 1,051 inhabitants in 1877.

BHOORA-MYA.—A revenue circle in the Mro-houng township, Akyab district. In 1879 the population was 1,806, the land revenue Rs. 4,450 and the gross revenue Rs. 6,680.

BHOOT-KHYOUNG.—A village in the circle of the same name in the Re-gyee township, Bassein district, on the left bank of the Nga-won about six miles above Nga-thaing-khyoung, adjoining Doung-gyee. In 1878 it had 522 inhabitants.

BHOOT-KO-YOUNG.—A revenue circle in the Ma-ha-tha-man township, Prome district, which now includes 12 of the old village tracts. In 1877 the population was 1,881, the capitation tax Rs. 1,990, the land revenue Rs. 2,782 and the gross revenue Rs. 4,772.

BO-GA-LE.—A village in the Pya-poon circle, Pya-poon township, Thoon-khwa district, on the Kyoon-toon at the mouth of the Kyaik-pee, with 786 inhabitants in 1878.

BOO-DOUNG.—A revenue circle in the Oo-ree-toung (east) township, Akyab district, with 1,700 inhabitants and a gross revenue of Rs. 8,998 in 1879.

DHAM-BHEE.—A village in the circle of the same name in the Henzada township, Henzada district, on the left bank of the Nga-won about twelve miles from its mouth in the Irrawaddy, and about two miles above the mouth of the Tham-bha-ya-daing, with 858 inhabitants, many of whom are up-country men, in 1879.

DAI-GOON.—A revenue circle in the Bassein district. In 1877 the population was 2,429, the capitation tax Rs. 2,540, the land revenue Rs. 8,863 and the gross revenue Rs. 11,356.

DOUNG-GYEE.—A revenue circle in the Bassein district. In 1877 the population was 4,291, the capitation tax Rs. 4,862, the land revenue Rs. 679 and the gross revenue Rs. 9,204.

DWA-RA-WA-DEE.—A revenue circle in the Toung-ngoo township, Toung-ngoo district. In 1877 the population was 2,911, the capitation tax Rs. 2,756, the land revenue Rs. 534 and the gross revenue Rs. 8,375.

DA-WAY-KHYOUNG.—A village in the Tsit-peng circle, Hmaw-bhee township, Rangoon district, with 572 inhabitants in 1878.

DHA-BIEN.—A village in the Hpoung-leng township, Rangoon district, on both banks of the stream of the same name at its mouth in the Pegu : that portion lying on the left bank is called North Dha-bien and is in the Kha-ra-kywon circle, that lying on the other bank is the larger, and is called South Dha-bien and is in the Dha-bien circle. In 1878 the two had 3,648 inhabitants.

EN-DA-POORA.—*See Ien-da-poora.*

EN-GOON.—A village in the Bhwot-lay circle, Thayet district, with 691 inhabitants, principally rice cultivators, in 1878.

ENG-LAT.—A portion of the town of Kyan-kheng, *q.v.*

ENG-MA-NGAY.—A revenue circle in the Poung-day township, Prome district, which includes five of the old village tracts. In 1877 the population was 3,961, the capitation tax Rs. 4,050, the land revenue Rs. 4,876 and the gross revenue Rs. 14,795.

ENG-TA.—A village in the Tha-raing circle, Donabyoo township, Thoon-khwa district, four miles inland from the Irrawaddy and about eight miles north-east of Donabyoo, with 502 inhabitants in 1878.

ENG-YA-KHYAING.—A revenue circle in the Oo-ree-toung (east) township, Akyab district, with 1,638 inhabitants in 1879, when the capitation tax was Rs. 1,800, the land revenue Rs. 2,705 and the gross revenue, Rs. 4,889.

EN-MAY.—*See Iem-mai.*

GOON-GNYENG-DAN.—A village in the Htan-ta-beng circle, Thee-kweng township, Bassein district, on the eastern bank of the Kyoon-toon, near its source, with 530 inhabitants in 1878.

GNYOUNG-BENG.—A village in the Pegu circle, Pegu township, Rangoon district, with 637 inhabitants in 1878.

GNYOUNG-KHYOUNG.—A village in the circle of the same name in the Donabyoo township, Thoon-khwa district, on the right bank of the Irrawaddy ten miles south of Donabyoo, with 1,699 inhabitants in 1878.

GNYOUNG-NEE.—A village in the Kyouk-taing-pyeng circle, Than-lyeng (Syriam) township, Rangoon district, with 585 inhabitants in 1878.

GYOUNG-WAING.—A village in the Tea-doo-thee-nee-goon circle, Tsan-rwe township, Tharrawaddy district, on the bank of the Thoon-tshay, with 693 inhabitants in 1878.

GNYOUNG-WAING.—A village in the Thee-kweng circle, Thee-kweng township, Bassein district, on the eastern bank of the Pan-ma-wa-dee, and about 15 miles to the east of Bassein. In 1878 it had 865 inhabitants.

GNYOUNG-WAING.—A village in the Pegu circle, Pegu township, Rangoon district, with 1,498 inhabitants in 1878.

GYO-GYA-GAN.—A village in the Mo-tsa circle, Ta-pwon township, Tharrawaddy district, about 16 miles east of the Irrawaddy with inhabitants in 1878.

HAN-THA-WA-DEE.—The district formerly known as Rangoon has (1879) been completely separated from the town and is now thus called, after the old Pegu kingdom which is thus called in Burmese. The head-quarters are about to be transferred from Rangoon to Eng-tsein a few miles to the north of Rangoon on the Rangoon and Irrawaddy Valley (State) Railway.

HLAY-HLA.—A revenue circle in the Toung-ngoo township, Toung-ngoo district. In 1877 the population was 3,991, the capitation tax Rs. 3,040, the land revenue Rs. 4,042 and the gross revenue Rs. 7,934.

HMAW-ZA.—A small village of 399 inhabitants, in 1877, in the Prome district, about four miles east of Prome amongst the ruins of Tha-re-khet-tra, the ancient capital of the Prome kingdom. Near the village is a station on the Irrawaddy Valley (State) Railway.

HNAI-GYO.—A village in the circle of the same name, in the Donabyoo township, Thoon-khwa district, on the Nat-maw stream at its junction with the Kan-ngoo-gyee, with 548 inhabitants in 1878.

HNEE-MOOT.—A village in the Rwa-lwot circle, Bhee-loo-gywon township, Amherst district, on the southern bank of the Rwa-lwot stream, with 542 inhabitants in 1878.

HNEE-PA-DAW.—A village on the Kwon-hla circle, Zaya township, Amherst district, on a stream of the same name, with 590 inhabitants in 1878.

HNGEK-PYAW.—A village in the Kyoon-bouk circle, Pantanaw township, Thoon-khwa district, at the mouth of the Hngek-pyaw, a tributary of the Irrawaddy, with 579 inhabitants in 1878.

HNIT-KAING.—A village in the circle of the same name, in the Wa-kha-roo township, Amherst district, about four miles from Amherst, on the Wa-kha-roo river, with 561 inhabitants in 1878.

HPOON-KYWAI.—A revenue circle in the Mro-houng township, Akyab district, with 1,357 inhabitants in 1879. In that year the land revenue was Rs. 4,512, the capitation tax Rs. 1,737 and the gross revenue Rs. 6,301.

HPWAI-DA.—A revenue circle in the Koo-la-dan township, Akyab district. In 1879 the population was 2,713, the capitation tax Rs. 3,057, the land revenue Rs. 5,161 and the gross revenue Rs. 8,220.

HTAN-BENG-GOON.—A village in the Lweng-byeng circle, Mo-gnyo township, Tharrawaddy district, on the bank of the Myit-ma-kha, with 801 inhabitants in 1878.

HTAN-TA-BENG.—A village in the Doora circle, Henzada township, Henzada district, about four miles west of the Irrawaddy on the bank of the Doora lake, with 1,361 inhabitants in 1879.

HTAN-TAW-GYEE.—A revenue circle in the Pegu township, Rangoon (Han-tha-wa-dee) district. The whole circle is a mass of forest-clad hills with a few patches of rice land in the valleys. Most of the inhabitants are Yabaing and gain their livelihood by cultivating toungya and cutting bamboos. In 1878 the population was 3,844, the capitation tax Rs. 4,248, the land revenue Rs. 3,530 and the gross revenue Rs. 7,778.

HTAN-TAW.—A village in the Kyan-kheng circle, in the township of the same name of the Henzada district, with 810 inhabitants in 1879.

HTIEN-GOON.—A village in the Ma-hlaing (west) circle, An-gyee township, Rangoon district, with 512 inhabitants in 1878.

HTOON-DOUNG.—A revenue circle in the Koo-la-dan township, Akyab district. In 1879 the population was 1,784, the capitation tax Rs. 1,728, the land revenue Rs. 3,724 and the gross revenue, Rs. 5,497.

HTOON-DOUNG.—A village in the Thai-daw circle, Thayetmyo township, Thayet district, a few miles below Thayetmyo, in the immediate neighbourhood of some low hills containing limestone. The inhabitants, who numbered 639 in 1878, are cultivators, wood-cutters, and lime-burners.

IE-THA-YA.—A village in the Rwon (east) now called the Rwon circle, Than-lyeng (Syriam) township, Rangoon district, with 857 inhabitants in 1878.

KA-BAI.—A revenue circle in the Tha-boung township, Bassein district. In 1877 the population was 2,353, the capitation tax Rs. 2,397, the the land revenue Rs. 2,366 and the gross revenue Rs. 9,434.

KA-GNYENG-KHYOUNG.—A village on the southern bank of the stream of the same name in the Mee-hgnyo-toung circle, Ra-thai-doung township, Akyab district, with 622 inhabitants in 1878. The Thoogyee of the circle lives here.

KA-GNYENG-KWENG.—A village in the Tha-nai-tha-bouk circle, Za-lwon township, Henzada district, on the west bank of the Bya-gnya stream, with 582 inhabitants in 1879.

KA-KYA-BEK-PYOO-TSOO.—A village on the right bank of the Ma-yoo in the Koo-la-pan-zeng circle, Ra-thai-doung township, Akyab district, with 540 inhabitants in 1878.

KA-LOUNG.—A village in the circle of the same name in the Pan-ta-naw township, Thoon-khwa district, on the Bhawdee stream at its junction with the Pan-ta-naw river about a mile north of Pan-ta-naw, with 987 inhabitants in 1878.

KA-LWENG.—A village in the circle of the same name in the Mergui district on the Ka-lweng creek, three miles north-east of Mergui, with 891 inhabitants in 1878.

KA-MEE-KYWAI.—A revenue circle in the Meng-bra township, Akyab district. In 1879 the population was 1,581 and the gross revenue Rs. 6,725.

KAN-BYAY.—A revenue circle in the Meng-bra township, Akyab district. In 1879 the population numbered 1,621 and the gross revenue was Rs. 6,443.

KAN-BYENG.—A revenue circle in the Ooo-ree-toung (east) township, Akyab district, with 739 inhabitants and a gross revenue of Rs. 5,221 in 1877.

KAN-HLA.—A village in the Lay-dee-kan-hla circle, Henzada township, Henzada district, west and in the immediate neighbourhood of Henzada, with 946 inhabitants in 1879.

KAN-TOUNG-GYEE.—A village in the Tset-khaw circle, Mre-boon township, Kyouk-hpyoo district, near the mouth of the Dha-let, with a population of 1,116 souls in 1878. A considerable quantity of rice is grown in the neighbourhood for export to Akyab.

KARENG HILL TRACTS.—A division of the Toung-ngoo district. The locality which, in 1876, was formed into this division is that portion of the Toung-ngoo district lying to the eastward of the Tsit-toung river which is inhabited by various tribes of Kareng. On the south it is bounded by the Thouk-re-khat, on the north by the frontier line of the province, on the west by the eastern water-shed of the Tsit-toung and on the east by the crest of the Ga-moon range of mountains which form the boundary of western Kareng-nee or the Red Kareng country : this tract, although within our geographical boundaries, had never until 1876, been brought under regular administrative control ; the tribes who occupy it are Bghai, and Sgaw (Gai-kho) ; some of the former are quiet and industrious and have been largely influenced by the teaching of the missionaries but the Tshaw-kho sept and the Gai-kho are more unsettled.

The immediate cause for the extension of administrative and protective measures was the distress to which the inhabitants had for several years been exposed through the almost annual destruction of their crops by vast hordes of rats which infested the country, eating up everything that came in their way. To relieve the scarcity and ward off famine supplies of grain were provided by the Toung-ngoo district officers and the expediency of placing the tribes under more thorough and distinct control soon became apparent. An Assistant Commissioner was placed in charge with a police force of two European Inspectors, two first class and two second class Sergeants, and 110 men. This force was at first principally engaged in cutting bridle-paths through the tract to open up communication between the different police-stations (of which there are five besides one at Liep-tho the head-quarter station of the division) and in building houses for themselves. The annual cost of the establishment for the administration of this tract, exclusive of the pay of the Assistant Commissioner, is Rs. 28,000.

KA-WAI.—A village in the Kyoon-pa-doot circle, Shwe-loung township, Thoon-khwa district, on a stream of the same name, with 895 inhabitants in 1878.

KA-WEK.—A village in the Eng-za-ya circle, Thoon-khwa township, Thoon-khwa district, on the Ma-oo-beng or To river, 19 miles from Ma-oo-beng, opposite to the mouth of the Twan-te creek of the Rangoon district, with 996 inhabitants in 1878.

KAW-KAT.—A village in the Tha-nai-tha-bouk circle, Za-lwon township, Henzada district, on the left bank of the Kaw-kat stream with 592 inhabitants in 1879. The inhabitants are engaged in agriculture and trade, large numbers of boats coming up from Pan-ta-naw in Thoon-khwa. The construction of a road from this village to Za-lwon is under consideration.

KAY-THA-LA.—A village on the western bank of the Proon-shay stream in the Proon-shay (or Pyoon-shay) circle, Meng-bra township, Akyab district, with 562 inhabitants in 1878.

KHA-MOUNG-KHYOUNG.—A revenue circle in the Oo-ree-toung (east) township, Akyab district. In 1879 the population was 1,806, the land revenue Rs. 2,455 and the gross revenue Rs. 4,809.

KHA-NOUNG-RWA.—A village in the A-gwon (south) [now called the Ta-da] circle of the Than-lyeng (Syriam) township, Rangoon district, with 917 inhabitants in 1878.

KHA-OON-MAW.—A village in the Man-oung circle on Cheduba island in the Kyouk-hpyoo district, north-east of the town of Cheduba, in the neighbourhood of which a good deal of nga-pee is manufactured. In 1878 it had 586 inhabitants.

KHAT-TEE-YA.—A village lying on both banks of the stream of the same name at the mouth of the Khat-tee-ya Re-gyaw, partly in the Rangoon (Han-tha-wa-dee) and partly in the Thoon-khwa district, with 2,166 inhabitants in 1879.

KHOO.—A revenue circle in the northern township of the Sandoway district to which is now added Pan-htaw. In 1877 the population was 2,857, the capitation tax Rs. 2,376, the land revenue Rs. 2,791 and the gross revenue Rs. 5,253.

KHOON-GNYENG-NWAY.—A village in the Than-rwa circle, Thayet-myo township, Thayet district, with 597 inhabitants in 1878, whose principal occupation is cultivating rice and sessamum.

KHOUNG-LOUNG.—A revenue circle in the Meng-bra township, Akyab district. In 1879, the gross revenue was Rs. 8,076 and the population 1,639.

KHWA-TSHOON.—A village in the Thee-gan circle, Ra-thai-doung township, Akyab district, situated at the junction of the Ma-yoo, the Koo-la-pan-zeng and the Tseng-deng-bwa. In 1878 it had 748 inhabitants.

KHWA-TSHOON.—A village in the Kywon-baw circle, Ra-thai-doung township, Akyab district, situated at the junction ef the Ka-moung-doon, Lek-ya-dek and Lek-wai-dek creeks. In 1878 it had 682 inhabitants.

KHWE-DOUK-KHYOUNG.—A revenue circle in the Ra-thai-doung township of the Akyab district. In 1879 the population was 1,622, the land revenue Rs. 4,684 and the gross revenue Rs. 6,418.

KHYA-RA-BENG.—A revenue circle in the Shwe-lay township, Prome district. In 1877 the population was 881, the capitation tax Rs. 1,042, the land revenue Rs, 417 and the gross revenue Rs. 1,459.

KHYIET-TOUNG.—A village on the western bank of the Thai-dan, Kyien circle, Meng-bra township, Akyab district, with 673 inhabitants in 1878.

KHYOUK-RWA.—A village in the circle of the same name in the Oot-hpo township, Henzada district, on the right bank of the Nga-won where it receives the waters of the Nan-ga-thoo and makes its first great bend southwards. The southern part of the village is called Khyouk-rwa and the northern Keng-tat; they were formerly separate but have gradually run into each other. In the Burmese time a small post was kept up in the latter, whence the name. The bank is gradually being eaten away by the river and in 1879 one of the numerous pagodas was pulled down just in time to prevent its falling and carrying away the relic enshrined in it. During high rises in the rains the whole village is under water and the country behind is flooded, the water rushing in with considerable violence and finding its way out into the Nga-won, which curves round some miles lower down as it were to meet it. In 1879 the two villages had 864 inhabitants.

KHYOUNG-BYA.—A village in the Dai-da-rai circle, Pya-poon, township, Thoon-khwa district, two miles south of Dai-da-rai, with 935 inhabitants in 1878.

KHYOUNG-WA.—A village in the circle of the same name in the Kyan-kheng township, Henzada district, about four miles west of the Irrawaddy with 483 inhabitants in 1879.

KHYOUNG-DOUNG.—A revenue circle in the Ra-thai-doung township, Akyab district. In 1879 the population was 2,424, the land revenue Rs. 5,518 and the gross revenue Rs. 8,490.

KHYOUNG-HPEE-LA.—A revenue circle in the Mro-houng township, Akyab district. In 1879 the population was 1,134, the land revenue Rs. 3,470 and the gross revenue Rs. 5,907.

KO-HNIT-RWA.—A village in the circle of the same name in the Mo-gnyo township, Tharrawaddy district, on the Rangoon and Irrawaddy valley (State) Railway and about 16 miles east of the Irrawaddy, with 1,487 inhabitants in 1878.

KOO-LA-BOON.—A revenue circle in the Mro-houng township, Akyab district, with 1,426 inhabitants in 1879. In that year the land revenue was Rs. 4,369 and the gross revenue Rs. 6,255.

KOO-LA-KHYOUNG.—A village in the Tha-ra-waw (north) circle, Tsan-rwe township, Tharrawaddy district a little to the north of Tha-ra-waw, with 1,263 inhabitants in 1878.

KOON-BOUNG-THA-RA-TSHIEP.—A village on the left bank of the Koo-la-dan in the Oot-kywek circle, Mro-houng township, Akyab district, with 860 inhabitants in 1878.

KOON-DAN.—A village in the Gnyoung-khyoung circle, Donabyoo township, Thoon-khwa district, about two miles from the Irrawaddy behind the village of Gnyoung-khyoung, with 724 inhabitants in 1878.

KOUNG-KYAW-HTENG.—A revenue circle in the Mro-houng township, Akyab district. In 1879 the population was 1,489, the capitation tax Rs. 1,782, the land revenue Rs. 5,686 and the gross revenue Rs. 7,471.

KOUNG-RAN.—A revenue circle in the Za-ya-wa-dee township, Toungngoo district. In 1877 the population was 5,935, the capitation tax Rs. 4,938, the land revenue Rs. 4,351 and the gross revenue Rs. 11,578.

KWA-HNEE.—A village in the Hmaw-won circle, Than-lyeng (Syriam) township, Rangoon district, with 623 inhabitants in 1878.

KWAN.—For places, especially in Amherst, the names of which commence with *Kwan See Kwon.*

KWE-MA.—A village in the Rwa-thit circle, Kyan-kheng township, Henzada district, on the left bank of the Pa-ta-sheng, with 720 inhabitants in 1879.

KWE-MA.—A village in the Kyouk-khyoung circle, Hmaw-bhee township, Rangoon district, with 640 inhabitants in 1878.

KWENG-GOUK.—A village in the circle of the same name in the Oot-hpo township, Henzada district, lying on both banks of the Nan-ga-thoo, not far from the lower slopes of the Arakan Roma mountains. It is the head-quarters of the Thoogyee and contains a police-station. In 1879 the inhabitants numbered 1,003 souls.

KWON-KHYAN.—A village in the Lek-pa-dan circle, Tsan-rwe township, Tharrawaddy district, with 515 inhabitants in 1878.

KWON-KHYAN-GOON.—A village in the O-bho circle, Kanoung township, Henzada district, close to the Irrawaddy and on the right bank. It derives its name from the numerous betel gardens in the neighbourhood. In 1879 it had 508 inhabitants.

KWON-TA-MOO.—A village in the Htoon-man circle, Za-ya township, Amherst district, with 527 inhabitants in 1878.

KYA-ENG.—A village in the Hpoung-gyee circle, Hpoung-leng township, Rangoon (Han-tha-wa-dee) district, with 548 inhabitants in 1878.

KYAIK-KHA-NA.—A village in the Kywon-oo circle, Hmaw-bhee township, Rangoon (Han-tha-wa-dee) district, with 711 inhabitants in 1878.

KYAIK-LAT.—A village in the circle of the same name in the Pya-poon township, Thoon-khwa district, at the junction of the Pya-poon, Hpo-douk and Kyaik-lat streams, with 2,649 inhabitants in 1878.

KYAIK-PEE.—A village in the Kyoon-toon circle, Pya-poon township, Thoon-khwa district, on the Kyoon-toon river about 60 miles from the sea, with 520 inhabitants in 1878.

KYAW-SHENG.—A revenue circle in the Oo-ree-toung (east) township, Akyab district, with 1,542 inhabitants and a gross revenue of Rs. 5,821 in 1879.

KYEK-POUNG.—A village in the Ta-kaing circle, Bassein township, Bassein district, on a small creek and about two miles to the west of the Bassein river eight miles below Bassein, with 524 inhabitants in 1878.

KYA-NEE.—A village in the circle of the same name in the Tsan-rwe township, Tharrawaddy district, with 606 inhabitants in 1878.

KYEK-TAIK.—A village in the circle of the same name in the Mo-gnyo township, Tharrawaddy district, on the southern bank of the Khwe stream, with 686 inhabitants in 1878.

KYENG-KYWON.—A revenue circle in the Ra-thai-doung township, Akyab district. In 1879 the population was 1,212, the land revenue Rs. 4,100 and the gross revenue Rs. 6,433.

KYE-NOOP-THEE.—A village on the right bank of the Ma-yoo in the Koo-la-pan-zeng circle, Ra-thai-doung township, Akyab district, with 502 inhabitants in 1878.

KYIEN.—Two revenue circles distinguished as East Kyien and West Kyien now joined together, in the Meng-bra township of the Akyab district. In 1879 the population numbered 4,148 and the gross revenue was Rs. 9,976.

KYIEN-KHWE-MAW.—A village on the stream of the same name about a mile from its mouth, in the Kyien-khwe-maw circle, Oo-ree-toung (east) township, Akyab district, with 763 inhabitants in 1878.

KYIEN-KHWE-MAW.—A revenue circle in the Oo-ree-toung (east) township, Akyab district. In 1879 the population was 2,042, the land revenue Rs. 3,678 and the gross revenue Rs. 6,221.

KYOON-BAW.—A revenue circle in the Ra-thai-doung township, Akyab district. In 1879 the population was 2,805, the land revenue Rs. 7,055 and the gross revenue Rs 10,242.

KYOON-HTA.—A village in the Pya-poon circle of the township of the same name in the Thoon-khwa district at the head of the Kyoon-hta creek, with 533 inhabitants in 1878.

KYOON-HTIEN.—A village in the Pa-doung township, Prome district, south of Pa-doung. In 1877 it had 639 inhabitants.

KYOON-GAN.—A village in the Rwon (west) [now called the Kyouk-tan] circle, Thanlyeng (Syriam) township, Rangoon district, with 549 inhabitants in 1878.

KYOON-KA-DWON.—A village in the Pyeng-da-ray circle, Pya-poon township, Thoon-khwa district, on a stream of the same name about six miles from the sea, with 734 inhabitants in 1878.

KYOON-KA-NEE.—A village in the circle of the same name in the Myoung-mya township, Bassein district, on the southern bank of the Khyoon-tsien creek, with 795 inhabitants in 1878.

KYOON-KHA-RAING.—A village in the Kyoon-pa-daw circle, Shwe-loung township, Thoon-khwa district, south-east of the village of Wai-gyee and about a mile distant from the Wai-gyee river, with 560 inhabitants in 1878.

KYOON-KOO.—A village in the Pya-poon circle of the township of the same name in the Thoon-khwa district, about a mile distant from Pya-poon, with 522 inhabitants in 1878.

KYOON-OO.—A revenue circle in the Hlaing township, Rangoon district, adjoining Thoon-khwa and lying on the northern bank of the Pan-hlaing. The cultivated portion is almost entirely in the south-east, the remainder being covered with grass and tree forest and intersected by a network of creeks the overflow from which swamps the country and renders rice cultivation impossible. The villagers living on the bank of the Pan-hlaing have large plantain gardens whilst those in the interior of the uncultivated portion are generally fishermen. In 1878 the population was 4,286, the capitation tax Rs. 4,388, the land revenue Rs. 12,875 and the gross revenue Rs. 31,536

KYOON-TAING.—A village in the Zayat-hla circle, Pan-ta-naw township, Thoon-khwa district, at the head of the Kyoon-taing creek on the borders of Thoon-khwa and Bassein, with 903 inhabitants in 1878.

KYOON-TA-MA.—A village in the Eng-za-ya circle, Thoon-khwa township, Thoon-khwa district, on the bank of the Irrawaddy six miles south of Gnyoung-doon, with 651 inhabitants in 1878.

KYOON-TSIEN.—A village in the Kyoon-pa-doop circle, Shwe-loung township, Thoon-khwa district, about a mile from Wa-khay-ma, with 537 inhabitants in 1879.

KYOUK-GYEE-TSOO.—A village in the Pegu circle, Pegu township, Rangoon district, with 542 inhabitants in 1878.

KYOUNG-KWEE.—A village in the circle of the same name in the Henzada township of the Henzada district, about two miles west of the Irrawaddy and two miles north of Henzada, on the bank of a small lake of the same name. In 1879 it had 546 inhabitants.

KYOUNG-TAIK.—A village in the Myanoung circle, in the township of the same name in the Henzada district, not far from the right bank of the Irrawaddy, with 579 inhabitants in 1879.

KYOUK-TAW.—A revenue circle in the Koo-la-dan township, Akyab district. In 1879 the population was 1,560, the capitation tax Rs. 1,917, the land revenue Rs. 3,619 and the gross revenue Rs. 5,563.

KYOUK-TAW.—A village on the right bank of the Koo-la-dan in the Kyouk-taw circle, Koo-la-dan township, Akyab district, with 1,080 inhabitants in 1878. It is the head-quarters of the township and contains a court-house, a market and a police-station. A little to the eastward is a hill crowned with a pagoda said to cover the last bone (*os coccygis*) of Gaudama's spine.

KYOUNG-GOON.—A village in the Myo-dweng circle, Mo-gnyo township, Tharrawaddy district, about a mile east of the Rangoon and Irrawaddy Valley (State) Railway close to the Gyo-beng-gouk station, with 646 inhabitants in 1878.

KYOUNG-WAING.—A village in the Ma-hlaing (east) circle, An-gyee township, Rangoon district, with 520 inhabitants in 1878.

KYWAI-DEK.—A revenue circle in the Meng-bra township, Akyab district. In 1879 the population was 1,581, the land revenue Rs. 4,905 and the gross revenue Rs. 6,725.

KYWAI-KYO.—A village on the right bank of the Ma-yoo, in the Ngwe-doung circle, Ra-thai-doung township, Akyab district, with 640 inhabitants in 1878.

KYWON-GA-LE.—A village in the Tsheng-goung circle, Ta-pwon township, Tharrawaddy district, on the east bank of the Irrawaddy, immediately opposite to Myanoung in Henzada, with   inhabitants in 1878. The telegraph line here crosses the Irrawaddy by a submerged cable.

KYWON-GA-LE.—A revenue circle in the Hpoung-leng township, Rangoon (Han-tha-wa-dee) district, with a considerable area under rice. In 1878 the population was 3,987, the capitation tax Rs. 4,873, the land revenue Rs. 14,500 and the gross revenue Rs. 19,373.

KYWON-GOON.—A village in the circle of the same name in the Poung-day township, Prome district, north-west of Poung-day, with 989 inhabitants in 1877.

KYWON-GOON.—A village in the Kyoon-pa-daw circle, Shwe-loung township, Thoon-khwa district, on the Wai-gyee river, with 510 inhabitants in 1878.

LA-HA-DHA-YEK.—A village in the Poo-gan-doung circle, Than-lyeng (Syriam) township, Rangoon district, with 544 inhabitants in 1878.

LA-HA-GYAW.—A village in the Kyoon-hpa circle, Henzada township, Henzada district, on the bank of the La-ha-byeng-kyay marsh, ten miles west of Henzada, with 718 inhabitants in 1879.

LAMAING.—A village in the Gnyoung-beng-tha circle, Za-lwon township, Henzada district, two miles west of the Irrawaddy and a mile north of the Gnyoung-beng-tha, with 715 inhabitants in 1879.

LA-MOO-GYEE.—A village in the Wa-kha-may circle, Pya-poon township, Thoon-khwa district on the Pya-poon about four miles north-east of Pya-poon, with 520 inhabitants in 1878.

LAY-GYEE-KWENG.—A village in the Kyoon-hpa circle, Henzada township, Henzada district, about ten miles west of Henzada, with 663 inhabitants in 1879.

LEK-PA-DAN.—A village in the circle of the same name in the Tsan-rwe township, Tharrawaddy district, about six miles east of the Myit-ma-kha, and on the Rangoon and Irrawaddy Valley (State) Railway, with 568 inhabitants in 1878. There are here a police-station and a Public Works Department Inspection bungalow.

LEK-PAN-GOON.—A village in the Tsa-doo-thee-ree-goon circle, Tsan-rwe township, Tharrawaddy district on the bank of the Thoon-tshay with 629 inhabitants in 1878.

LE-MRO.—A revenue circle in the Mro-houng township, Akyab district. In 1879 the population was 2,683, the land revenue Rs. 2,328 and the gross revenue Rs. 5,633.

LIEN-GOON.—A village in the Tha-nai-tha-bouk circle, Za-lwon township, Henzada district, on the eastern bank of the Tsheng-pyee stream, with 734 inhabitants in 1879.

LIEP-KHYOUNG.—A village in the Dham-bhee circle, Henzada township, Henzada district, on the left bank of the Nga-won about six miles from its mouth in the Irrawaddy and about six miles above Dham-bhee, with 589 inhabitants in 1879.

LWENG-LYENG-RWA.—A village in the circle of the same name in the Mo-gnyo township of the Tharrawaddy district, about a mile south of the Tsheng-tshaing stream, with 1,366 inhabitants in 1878.

MA-HA-THA-MAN.—A revenue circle in the township of the same name in the Prome district to which is now joined Tha-tsee. In 1877 the population was 1,147, the capitation tax Rs. 803, the land revenue Rs. 961 and the gross revenue Rs. 1,764.

MA-HLAING (East).—A revenue circle in the An-gyee township, Rangoon (Han-tha-wa-dee) district. In 1878 the population was 3,165, the capitation tax Rs. 4,333, the land revenue Rs. 19,511 and the gross revenue Rs. 24,375.

MA-HLAING (West).—A revenue circle in the An-gyee township, Rangoon (Han-tha-wa-dee) district. In 1878 the population was 6,475, the the capitation tax Rs. 7,323, the land revenue Rs. 37,158 and the gross revenue Rs. 46,861.

MAI-TSA-LEE.—A village in the Oot-hpo circle, Oot-hpo township, Henzada district, on the bank of the Ka-gnyeng stream, with 488 inhabitants in 1879.

MA-LEK-TO.—A village in the Thoon-khwa circle, Thoon-khwa township, Thoon-khwa district, on the Ma-oo-beng, two miles northeast of Thoon-khwa, with 818 inhabitants in 1878, who are almost all fishermen.

MAULMAIN.—This town now forms a separate district independent altogether of Amherst.

MAW-KHYE.—A village in the Mya-wa-dee circle, Houng-tha-raw township, Amherst district, on the bank of the Thoung-gyeng near Mya-wa-dee, with 803 inhabitants in 1878.

MA-YAN-KHYOUNG.—A village in the Tha-boung circle, Donabyoo township, Thoon-khwa district, on the Irrawaddy about two miles north of Donabyoo, with 585 inhabitants in 1878.

MA-YENG-BENG-RENG-RWA.—A village on the eastern bank of the Kya-ma-thouk stream, in the Taw-gan circle, Oo-ree-toung (west) township, Akyab district, with 586 inhabitants in 1878. The Thoogyee of the circle lives here.

MENG-BRA.—A village in the Kyien circle, Akyab district, the head-quarters of the Meng-bra township with a court-house, a market and a police-station. In 1878 it had 829 inhabitants.

MENG-GAN.—A revenue circle to which is now joined Kyek-kaing-dan, in the Kyai-let township, Akyab district. In 1879 the population of the two was 1,361, the land revenue Rs. 7,007 and the gross revenue Rs. 10,098.

MENG-RWA.—A village in the Poo-gan-doung circle, Than-lyeng (Sriam) township, Rangoon (Han-tha-wa-dee) district, with 546 inhabitants in 1878.

MIET-THA-LENG.—A village in the Thoon-khwa township, Thoon-khwa district, on the Pan-ta-bwot about five miles north of Kyaik-lat, with 1,004 inhabitants in 1878.

MO-GOUNG.—A village in the circle of the same name in the Thayet district, with 903 inhabitants in 1878.

MO-HOOP.—A village in the Gnyoung-doon circle, Gnyoung-doon township, Thoon-khwa district, about two miles south-east of Donabyoo, with 589 inhabitants in 1878.

MO-KHAING-GYEE.—A village in the Pegu circle, Pegu township, Rangoon (Han-tha-wa-dee) district, with 634 inhabitants in 1878.

xiv.

MO-MA-KHA.—A village in the Khat-tee-ya circle, Thoon-khwa township, Thoon-khwa district, about two miles from the bank of the Khat-tee-ya stream, with 540 inhabitants in 1878.

MOO-KYEE.—A villa;e in the circle in the same name in the Martaban township, Amherst district, on the Kha-daing stream, with 530 inhabitants in 1878.

MOO-RIT-GYEE.—A village in the Weng-tsien circle, Bhee-loo-gyoon township, Amherst district, with 660 inhabitants in 1878.

MOOT-TA-LA.—A village in the Pegu circle, Pegu township, Rangoon (Han-tha-wa-dee) district, with 567 inhabitants in 1877.

MOUNG-MA.—A village in the Hpa-goo (west) [now called the Hpa-goo] circle, in the Than-lyeng (Syriam) township, Rangoon district, with 1,529 inhabitants in 1878.

MRO-HOUNG.—A revenue circle in the township of the same name in the Akyab district. In 1879 the population was 4,273, the land revenue Rs. 2,919 and the gross revenue Rs. 9,916.

MROUNG-BWAI-ZAI.—A village on the northern bank of the Mroung-bwai stream in the Pai-beng-reng circle, Mro-houng township, Akyab district, with 852 inhabitants in 1878. The Thoogyee of the circle lives here.

MYAING.—A village in the Tha-nai-tha-bouk circle, Za-lwon township, Henzada district, on the Zwai-ka-raing stream, an affluent of the Nat-maw or Kyoon-hpa river, with 657 inhabitants in 1879. It can be reached at all seasons by boats from Pyeng-ma-goon on the Nat-maw, and a proposition for constructing a road between it and Za-lwon is under consideration.

MYA-PA-DAING.—A village in the circle of the same name in the Houng-tha-raw township, Amherst district, with 666 inhabitants in 1878.

MYEK-RAI-PYOO-TSOO.—A village in the Tha-rai-koon-boung grant, in the Naaf township of the Akyab district, on the Chittagong road, with 874 inhabitants in 1878.

MYENG-TAI.—A village in the Za-lwon circle of the township of the same name in the Henzada district, on the right bank of the Irrawaddy about half a mile north of Za-lwon, with 575 inhabitants in 1879.

MYE-NOO.—A village in the Ta-pwon circle of the township of the same name in the Tharrawaddy district, about two miles north-west of Ta-pwon with   inhabitants in 1879.

MYIT-KYO.—A village in the Myanoung circle of the township of the same name in the Henzada district, on the right bank of the Pa-ta-sheng at its mouth, the river separating it from Kyan-kheng. Every year during the dry season a temporary bridge is thrown across the Pa-ta-sheng which is taken down before the rains or it would be swept away by the large volume of water which then comes down from the hills through this channel. In 1879 it had 1,252 inhabitants.

MYIT-THA-RWA.—A portion of Meng-gyee in the Re-kheng township, Tharrawaddy district, with 1,743 inhabitants in 1878.

MYO-DWENG.—A village in the circle, of the same name in the Mo-gnyo township, Tharrawaddy district, about eight miles east of the Rangoon and Irrawaddy Vally (State) Railway, with 713 inhabitants in 1878. It was once a walled city and the capital of Tharrawaddy.

MYO-KWENG.—A village in the Dham-bhee circle of the Henzada township, Henzada district, on the left bank of the Nga-won, immediately opposite the mouth of the Tham-bha-ya-daing, with 890 inhabitants in 1879. There is here a Public Works Department Inspection bungalow. The telegraph line crosses the Nga-won from this village to Tshoon-goon.

MYOUK-PYENG.—A revenue circle in the Oo-ree-toung (east) township, Akyab district, with 1,775 inhabitants in 1879, when the gross revenue was Rs. 4,307.

MYOUNG-RWA.—A village in the Kyek-taik circle, Mo-gnyo townsip, Tharrawaddy district, on the north bank of the stream of the same name with 519 inhabitants in 1878.

MYO-WENG.—A village in the Pegu circle, Pegu township, Rangoon (Han-tha-wa-dee) district, with 766 inhabitants in 1878.

NAN-DAW-GOON.—A village in the Donabyoo circle, Donabyoo township, Thoon-khwa district, on the bank of the Irrawaddy about two miles below Donabyoo, with 732 inhabitants in 1878.

NGA-KHOO-RA.—A village in the Mro-thit-khyoung circle, Naaf township, Akyab district, on the Mro-thit, a tributary of the Naaf, about one and a half miles from its mouth. In 1878 it had 795 inhabitants.

NGAN-KHYOUNG-PYOO-TSOO.—A village in the Meng-ga-la-gyee circle, Naaf township, Akyab district, on the eastern bank of the Meng-ga-la-gyee creek, three miles from it mouth. In 1878 it had 690 inhabitants.

NGA-PEE-TSHIEP.—A village in the Htan-beng-gyo circle, Re-gyee township, Bassein district, on the left bank of the Nga-won about five miles below Nga-thaing-khyoung. In 1878 it had 569 inhabitants.

NIEK-BAN.—A village in the Paing-kyoon circle, Pegu township, Rangoon district, with 579 inhabitants in 1878.

O-BHO.—A village in the Pegu circle, Pegu township, Rangoon (Han-tha-wa-dee) district, with 574 inhabitants in 1878.

OOK-KYWEK.—A revenue circle in the Koo-la-dan township, Akyab district. In 1879 the population was 3,070, the capitation tax Rs. 3,775, the land revenue Rs. 9,418 and the gross revenue Rs. 13,202.

OON-BENG.—A village in the Pya-poon circle, Pya-poon township, Thoon-khwa district, about four miles north of Pya-poon, with 770 inhabitants in 1878.

OUK-RE-GYAW.—A village in the Ma-hlaing (west) circle, An-gyee township, Rangoon (Han-tha-wa-dee) district, with 504 inhabitants in 1878.

PA-LOUNG-BYENG.—A revenue circle in the Meng-bra township, Akyab district. In 1879 the population was 2,824 and the gross revenue Rs. 6,820.

PIEN-NAI-GOON.—A village in the Thee-tha-ro circle, Gyaing Attaran township, Amherst district, on the left bank of the Attaran, with 657 inhabitants in 1878.

POON-NA-KYWON.—A revenue circle in the Koo-la-dan township, Akyab district. In 1879 the population was 1,735, the land revenue Rs. 3,403, the capitation tax Rs. 1,986 and the gross revenue Rs. 5,403.

POUK-TAING.—A village in the Tshoon-lai circle, Kyan-kheng township, Henzada district, with 626 inhabitants in 1879.

POUK-TAW.—A village in the circle of the same name in the Tapwon township, Tharrawaddy district, about 11 miles east of the Myit-makha, with 595 inhabitants in 1878.

POUNG-DAW-BRENG-PYOO-TSOO.—A large village on the eastern bank of the Ma-yoo in the Koo-la-pan-zeng grant in the Ra-thai-doung township, Akyab district, with 2,784 inhabitants in 1878. The whole grant contains about 9,600 acres and is principally cultivated with tea.

POUNG-DAY.—A revenue circle in the township of the same name in the Prome district. In 1877 the population was 3,961, the capitation tax Rs. 4,050, the land revenue Rs. 2,304 and the gross revenue Rs. 9,537.

PRA-KHYOUNG.—A revenue circle in the Meng-bra township, Akyab district, to which is now joined Hteng-daing. In 1879 the population was 1,535 and the gross revenue Rs. 6,543.

PROO-MA-ASHE.—A village on the southern bank of the Proo-ma stream in the Mro-thit-khyoung circle, Naaf township, Akyab district, with 719 inhabitants in 1878.

PYENG-DA-RAY.—A village in the circle of the same name in the Pya-poon township, Thoon-khwa district, on the seacoast at the mouth of the Kyoon-toon, with 949 inhabitants in 1878.

PYOON-SHAY.—A revenue circle in the Meng-bra township, Akyab district. In 1879 the population numbered 3,117 and the gross revenue was Rs. 10,834.

RA-KHAING-KHYOUNG.—A village in the Ko-doung circle, An-gyee township, Rangoon (Han-tha-wa-dee) district, with 724 inhabitants in 1878.

RA-LA (East).—A revenue circle in the Koo-la-dan township, Akyab district. In 1879 the population was 3,825, the capitation tax Rs. 3,194, the land revenue Rs. 4,162 and the gross revenue Rs. 7,731.

RA-LA (West).—A revenue circle in the Koo-la-dan township, Akyab district to which is now added Koo-la-dan. In 1879 the population was 2,247, the capitation tax Rs. 1,405, the land revenue Rs. 2,159 and the gross revenue Rs. 3,568.

RANGOON.—The town of Rangoon now forms a separate district, and the old Rangoon district is called Han-tha-wa-dee.

RAN-KHYOUNG.—A revenue circle in the Mro-houng township, Akyab district. In 1879 the population was 2,822, the capitation tax Rs. 3,328, the land revenue Rs. 4,499 and the gross revenue Rs. 7,827.